Street by Street

C000138379

ESSEX

Enlarged areas BASILDON, CHELMSFORD, CLACTON-ON-SEA, COLCHESTER, FELIXSTOWE, HARLOW, HARWICH, IPSWICH, SOUTHEND-ON-SEA, SUDBURY

Plus Bishop's Stortford, Braintree, Cheshunt, Enfield, Grays, Haverhill, Hoddesdon, Ilford, Romford, Waltham Abbey, Walthamstow

2nd edition September 2005
© Automobile Association Developments Limited 2005

Original edition printed May 2001

Ordnance Survey® This product includes map data licensed from Ordnance Survey® with the permission of the Controller of Her Majesty's Stationery Office. © Crown copyright 2005. All rights reserved. Licence number 399221.

Published by AA Publishing (a trading name of Automobile Association Developments Limited, whose registered office (from 1st October 2005) will be Fanum House, Basing View, Basingstoke, Hampshire RG21 4EA. Registered number 1878835).

Mapping produced by the Cartography Department of The Automobile Association. (A02543)

A CIP Catalogue record for this book is available from the British Library.

Printed by Oriental Press in Dubai

Ref: ML031z

Key to map pages	ii-iii
Key to map symbols	iv-1
Enlarged map pages	2-21
Main map pages	22-351
Index – towns & villages	352-354
Index – streets	355-413
Index – featured places	413-422
Acknowledgements	423

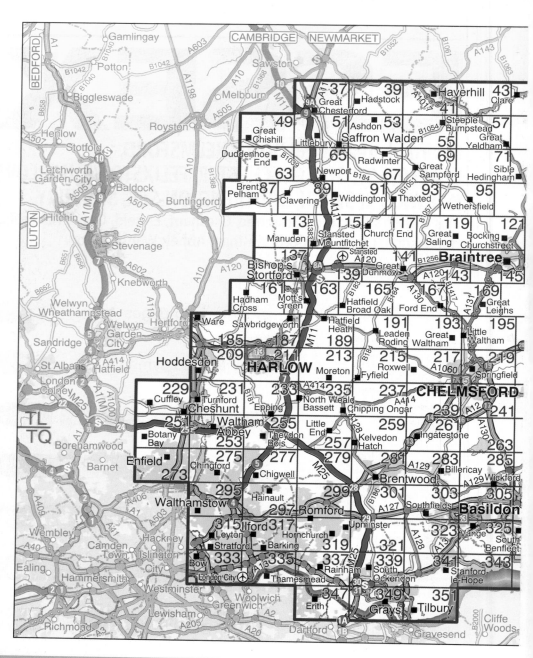

Scale of enlarged map pages 1:10,000   6.3 inches to 1 mile

| 0 | | 1/4 | miles | 1/2 |
| 0 | 1/4 | 1/2 | kilometres | 3/4 | 1 |

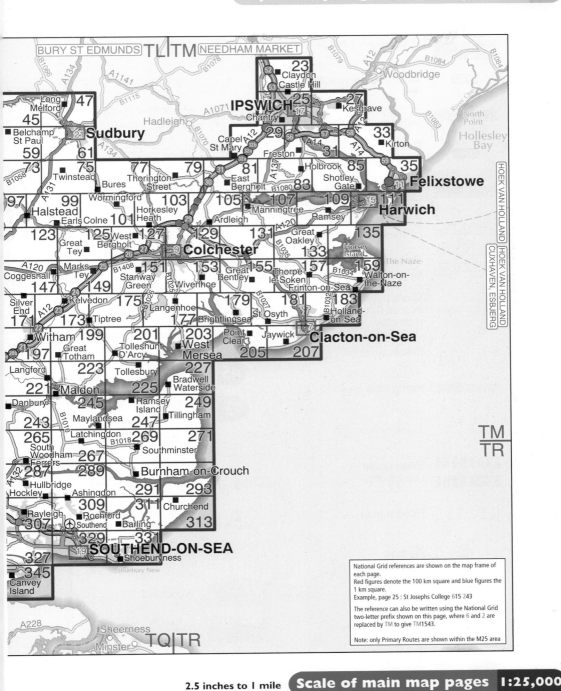

BURY ST EDMUNDS

23 Claydon
Castle Hill

Woodbridge

IPSWICH
25
Chantry
17

27 Kesgrave

North Point

Hollesley Bay

45
Long Melford

47

Belchamp St Paul

Sudbury

Hadleigh

29

Capel St Mary
33 Kirton

31

59
73

61

Twinstead

75

Bures

77 Thorington Street

79

East Bergholt

81

Freston

Holbrook

83 Shotley Gate

85

35

Felixstowe

97

Halstead

99

Wormingford

103 Horkesley Heath

105

Manningtree

107

Ramsey

109

111

Harwich

Earls Colne 101

Ardleigh

123

Great Tey

125 West Bergholt

127

Colchester

129

131

Great Oakley

133

135

Horsey Island

The Naze

Marks Tey

149

151 Stanway Green

153

Great Bentley

155

Thorpe-le-Soken

157

159

Walton-on-the-Naze

Coggeshall

147

Wivenhoe

Frinton-on-Sea

Silver End

171

Kelvedon

175

Langenhoe

179

181

183 Holland-on-Sea

173 Tiptree

177 Brightlingsea

St Osyth

Witham

199

201 Tolleshunt D'Arcy

203 West Mersea

Point Clear

Jaywick

Clacton-on-Sea

197

Great Totham

205

207

Langford

223

Tollesbury

227 Bradwell Waterside

221 Maldon

225

Danbury

245 Ramsey Island

249 Tillingham

243 Maylandsea

247

265 Latchingdon

269

271

South Woodham Ferrers

267

Southminster

287 Hullbridge

289

Burnham-on-Crouch

Hockley

291

293 Churchend

309 Rochford

311

Rayleigh

307 Southend

313

329 Barling

331

Canvey Island

327

345

SOUTHEND-ON-SEA
Shoeburyness

Shoebury Ness

Sheerness
Minster

TM
TR

National Grid references are shown on the map frame of each page.
Red figures denote the 100 km square and blue figures the 1 km square.
Example, page 25 : St Josephs College 615 243

The reference can also be written using the National Grid two-letter prefix shown on this page, where 6 and 2 are replaced by TM to give TM1543.

Note: only Primary Routes are shown within the M25 area

2.5 inches to I mile   **Scale of main map pages 1:25,000**

0   1/2   miles   I   I 1/2

0   1/2   I   kilometres   I 1/2   2

iv

Junction 9	Motorway & junction	Underground station
Services	Motorway service area	Light railway & station
	Primary road single/dual carriageway	Preserved private railway
Services	Primary road service area	LC Level crossing
	A road single/dual carriageway	Tramway
	B road single/dual carriageway	Ferry route
	Other road single/dual carriageway	Airport runway
	Minor/private road, access may be restricted	County, administrative boundary
	One-way street	Mounds
	Pedestrian area	45 Page continuation 1:25,000
	Track or footpath	3 Page continuation to enlarged scale 1:10,000
	Road under construction	River/canal, lake
	Road tunnel	Aqueduct, lock, weir
P	Parking	465 ▲ Winter Hill Peak (with height in metres)
P+	Park & Ride	Beach
	Bus/coach station	Woodland
	Railway & main railway station	Park
	Railway & minor railway station	Cemetery
		Built-up area

	Featured building		Abbey, cathedral or priory
	City wall		Castle
A&E	Hospital with 24-hour A&E department		Historic house or building
PO	Post Office	Wakehurst Place NT	National Trust property
	Public library	M	Museum or art gallery
i	Tourist Information Centre		Roman antiquity
i	Seasonal Tourist Information Centre		Ancient site, battlefield or monument
	Petrol station, 24-hour Major suppliers only		Industrial interest
†	Church/chapel		Garden
	Public toilets		Garden Centre Garden Centre Association Member
	Toilet with disabled facilities		Garden Centre Wyevale Garden Centre
PH	Public house AA recommended		Arboretum
	Restaurant AA inspected		Farm or animal centre
Madeira Hotel	Hotel AA inspected		Zoological or wildlife collection
	Theatre or performing arts centre		Bird collection
	Cinema		Nature reserve
	Golf course		Aquarium
▲	Camping AA inspected	V	Visitor or heritage centre
	Caravan site AA inspected		Country park
	Camping & caravan site AA inspected		Cave
	Theme park		Windmill
			Distillery, brewery or vineyard

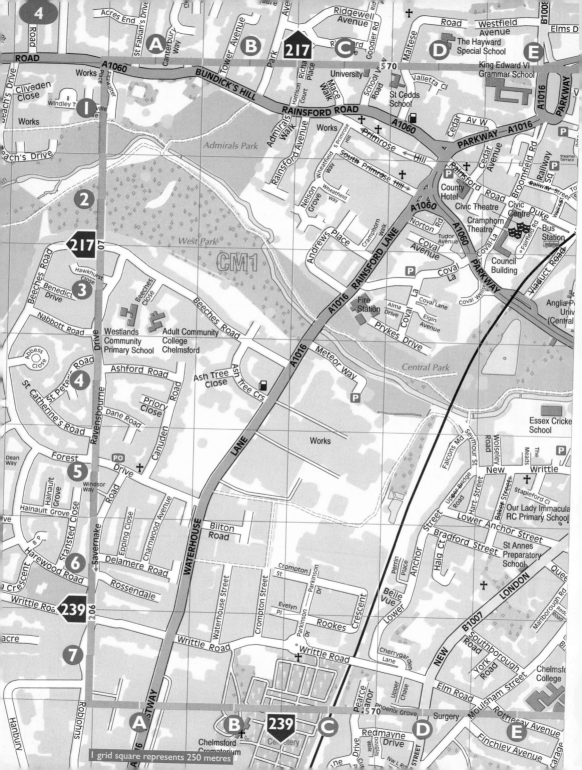

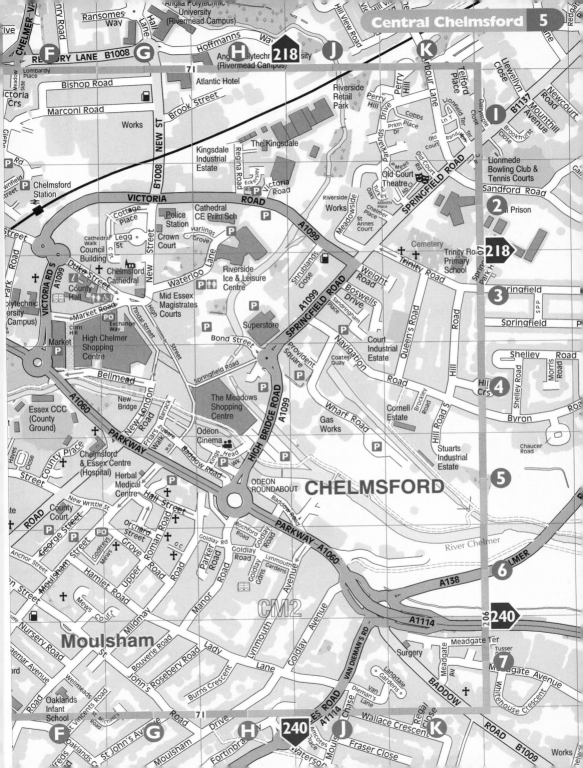

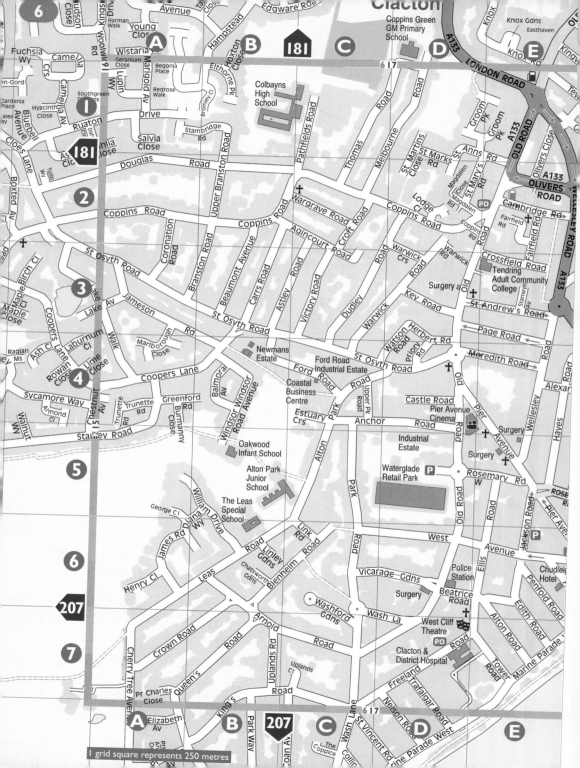

I grid square represents 250 metres

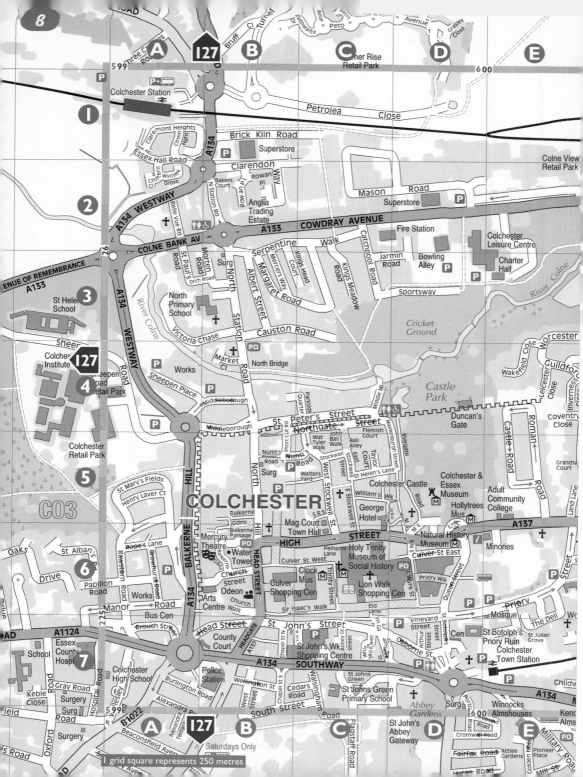

COLCHESTER

1 grid square represents 250 metres

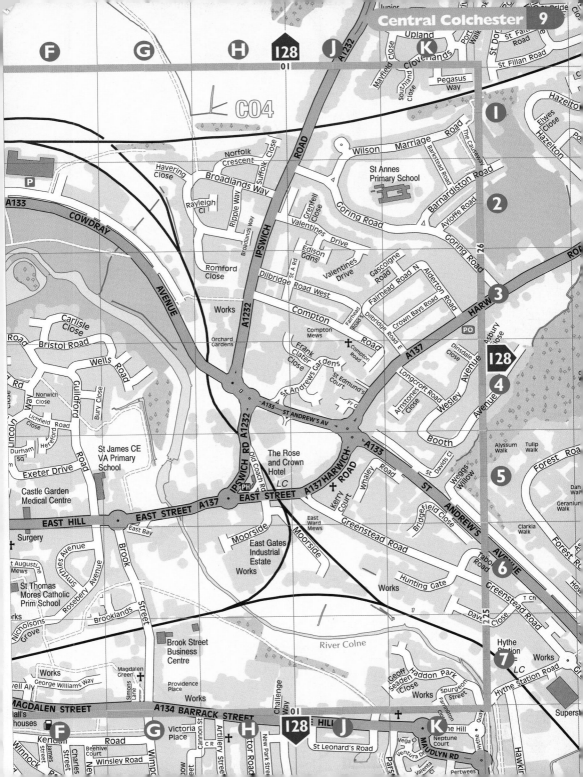

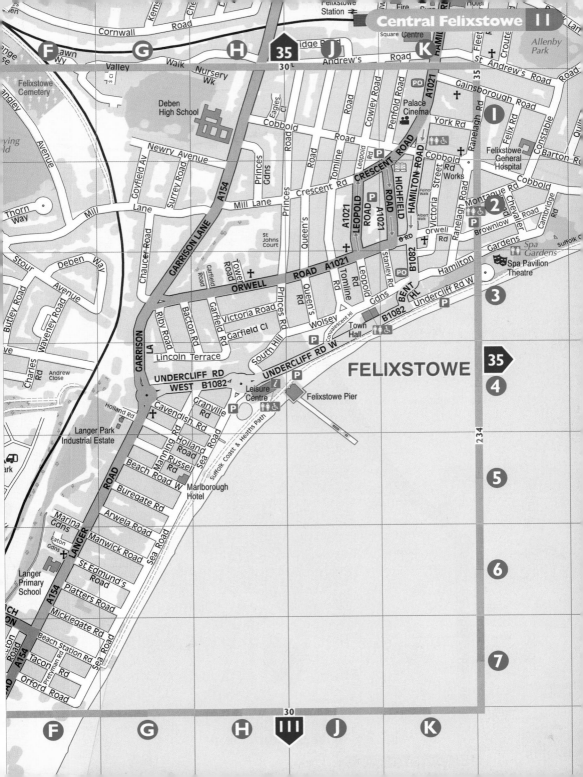

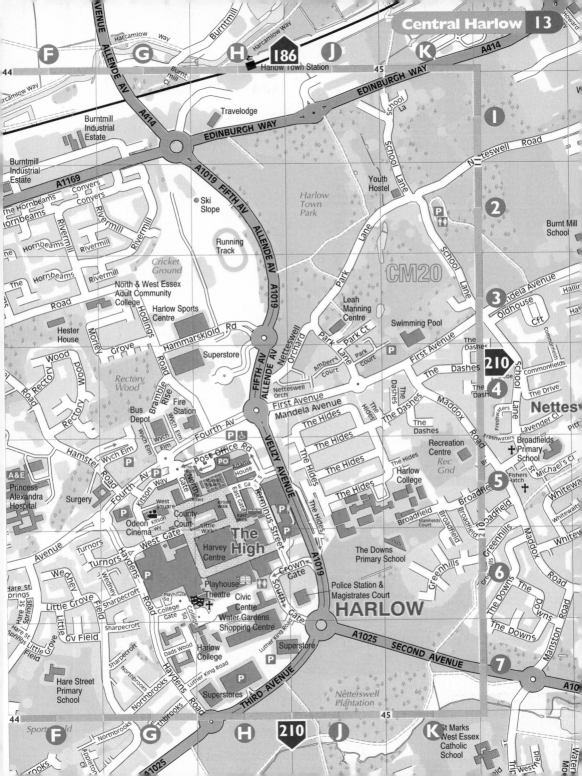

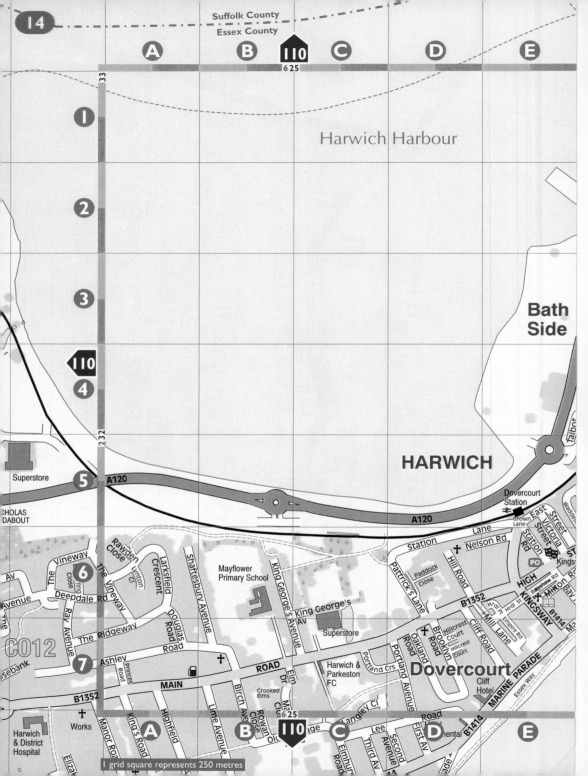

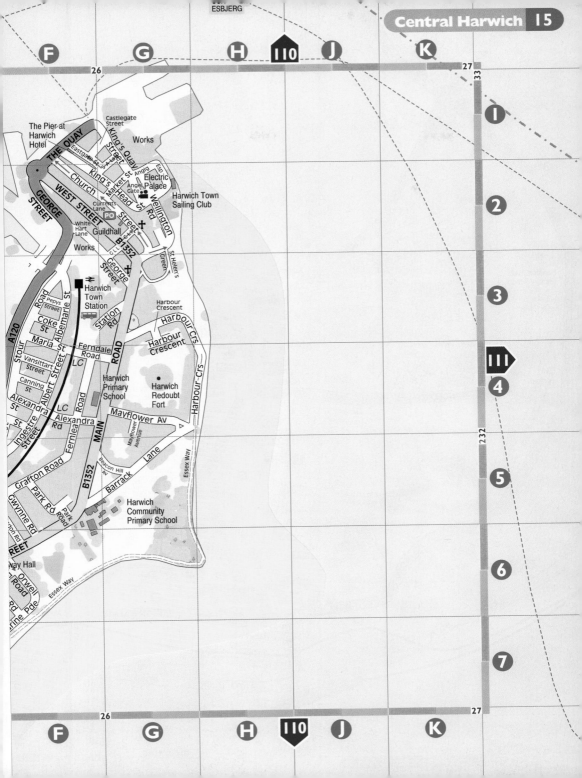

ESBJERG

F G H ▲110 J K

26 27 33

I

Castlegate Street

The Pier at Harwich Hotel

Works

2

King's Quay Street

THE QUAY
Eastgate St

King's Head St
Market St
Angel Gate

Electric Palace

Church St

Harwich Town Sailing Club

Currents Lane

WEST STREET

PO

GEORGE STREET

Wellington Rd

White Hart Lane

Guildhall

Works

St Helen's Green

3

B1352

George Street

Harbour Crescent

Pepys Street

Harwich Town Station

Coke St

Maria St
Albemarle St

Harbour Crs

III

Stout Rd

Vansittart Street

Ferndale Road

Station Rd

Harbour Crescent

4

Canning St

Alexandra St

LC

Main Road

Harwich Primary School

Harwich Redoubt Fort

Harbour Crs

Ingestre St

Albert Street

LC

Alexandra Rd

Mayflower Av

Mayflower Avenue

Fernlea Rd

Beacon Hill Av

2 32

5

Grafton Road

Park Rd

B1352

Barrack Lane

Park Road

Essex Way

Gwynne Rd

Harwich Community Primary School

6

Way Hall

Orwell Road

Essex Way

STREET

arine Pde

7

F G H ▼110 J K

26 27

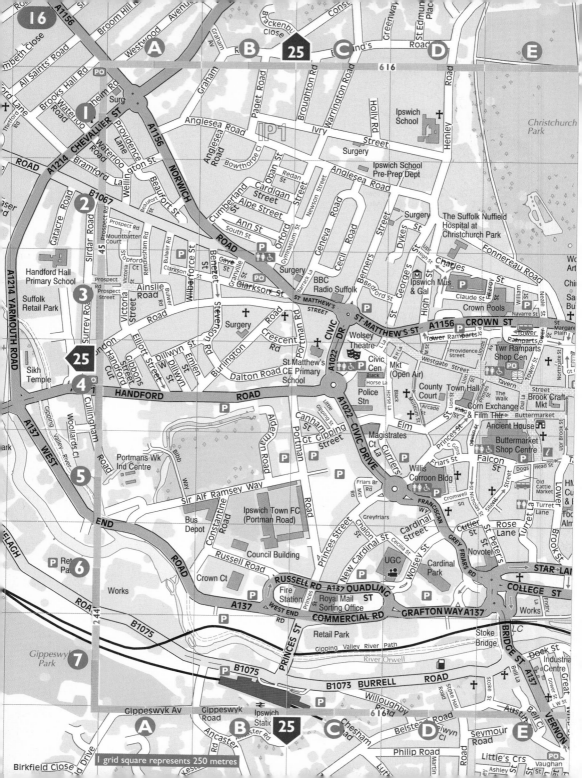

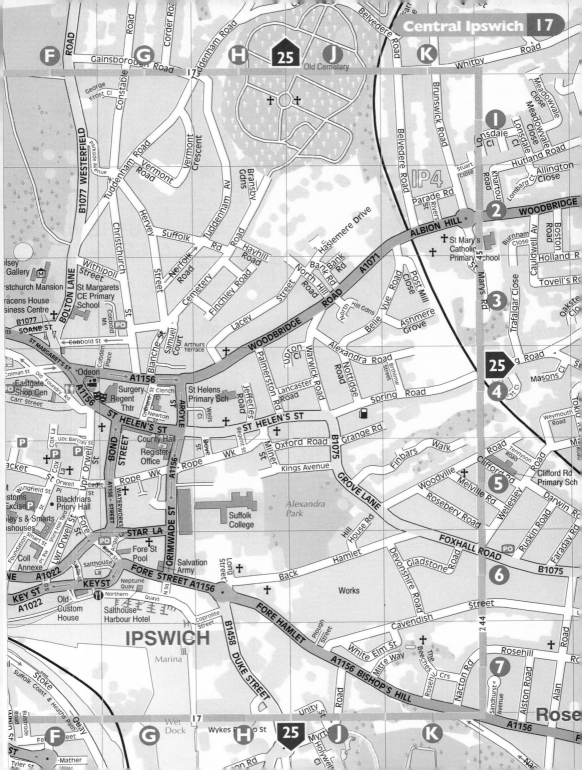

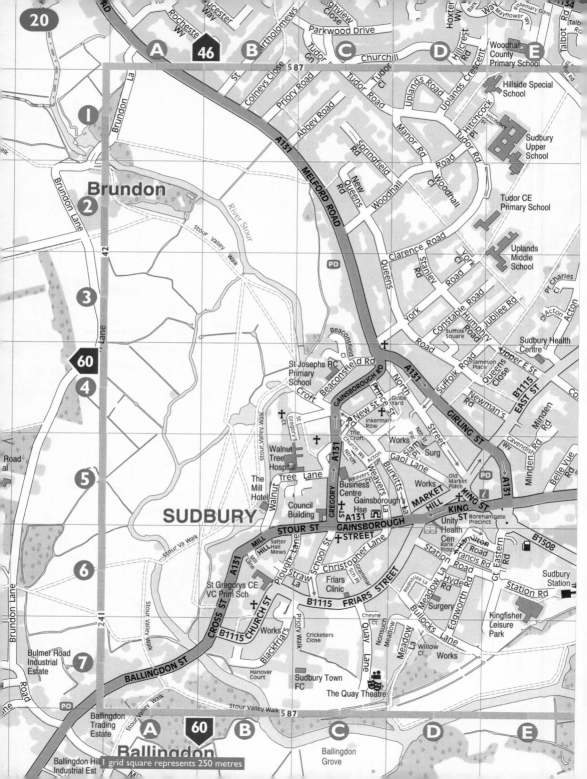

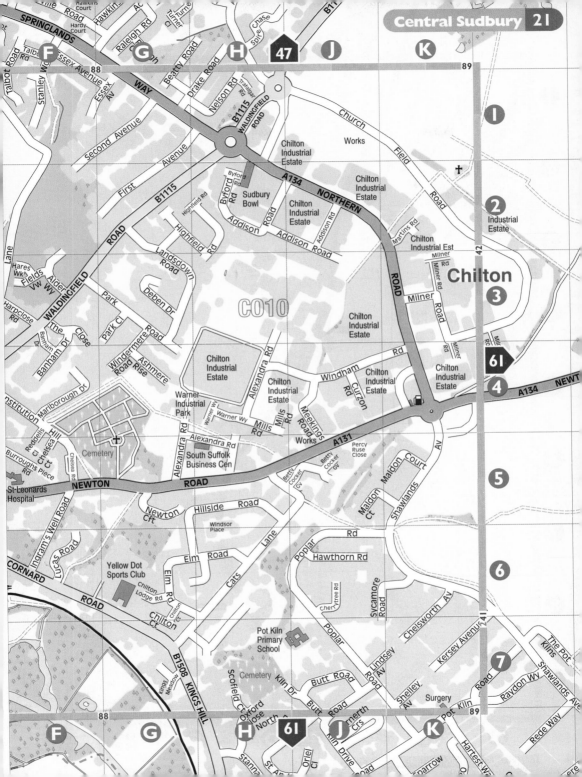

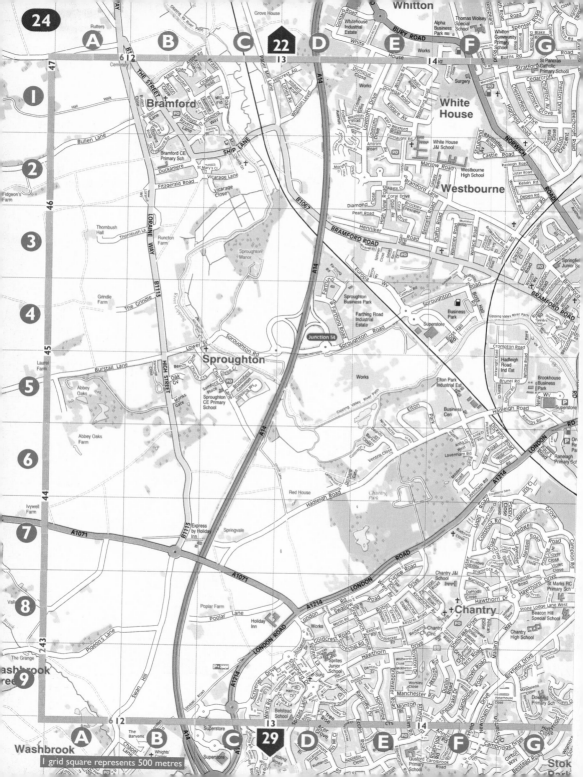

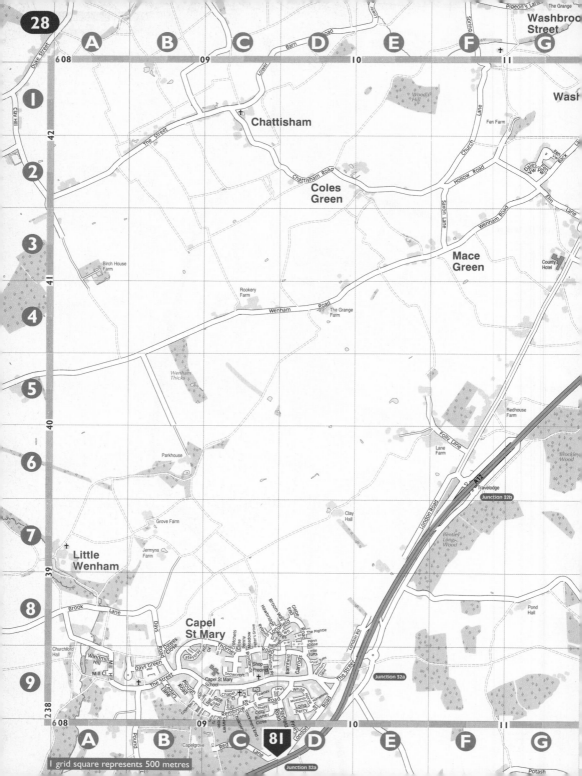

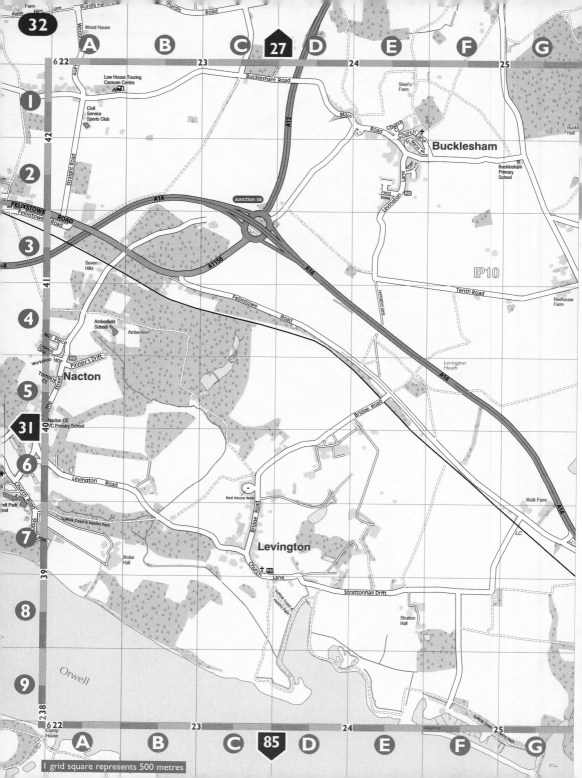

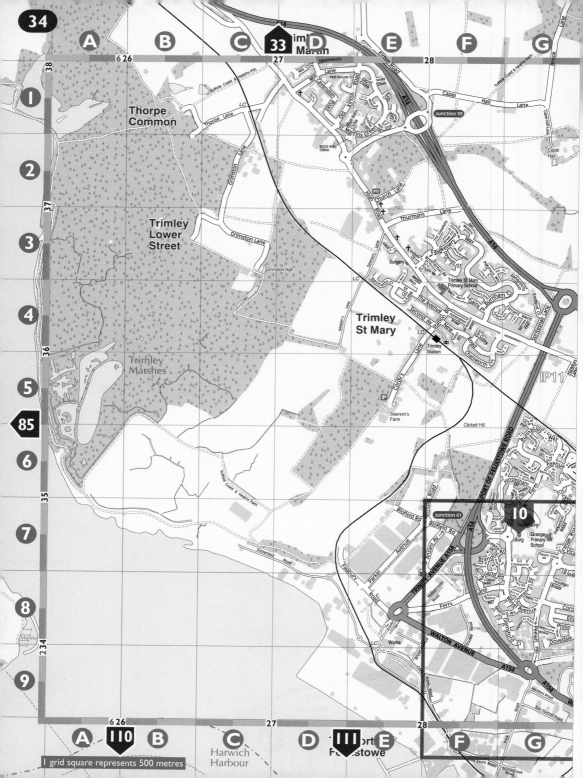

A B C 33 im D E F G
Martin

6 26 27 Junction 59 28

38

Thorpe Common

37

Trimley Lower Street

Grimston Lane

Grimston Hall

36

Trimley Marshes

Trimley St Mary

Trimley Station

85

IP11

35

Junction 61

10

Suffolk Coast & Heaths Path

Oysterbed Road

Marina

234

TRINITY AVENUE A154

WALTON AVENUE

A154

A 6 26 B C D E F G
110

Harwich Harbour 27 rt 28
Felixstowe

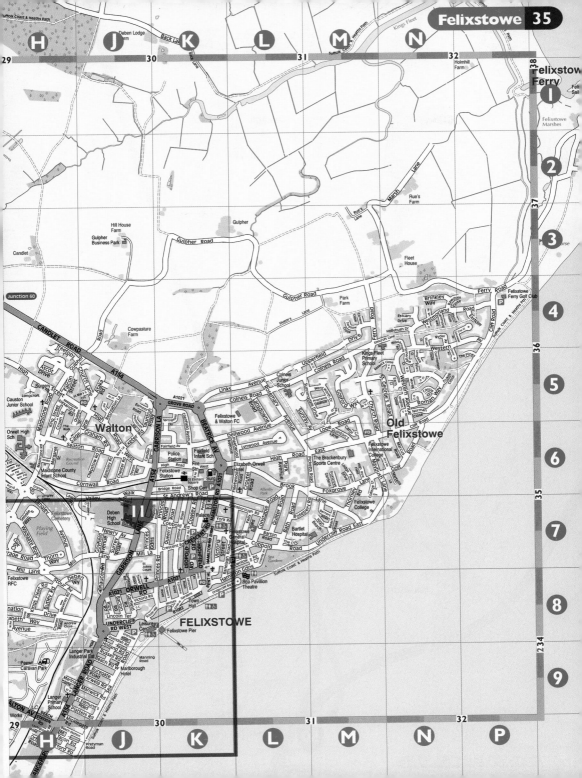

Linton

H J K L M

52 53 54 55 47

Linton Village

I

CAMBR

Abington Park Farm

2

ogical dens

46 HADST

ire County County

3

Icknield Way Path

Park Farm

4

Cambridgeshire County
Essex County

45

Icknield Way Path

5

WALDE

Pen Farm

38

Cow Lane

Crave Hall Farm

Hadstock Common

6

44

Burtonwood Farm

Icknield Way Path

7

Icknield Way Path

Park Farm

8

243 BTL

9

52 53 54 55

H J K L M N P

51

Chesterford Park

Raven Green Farm

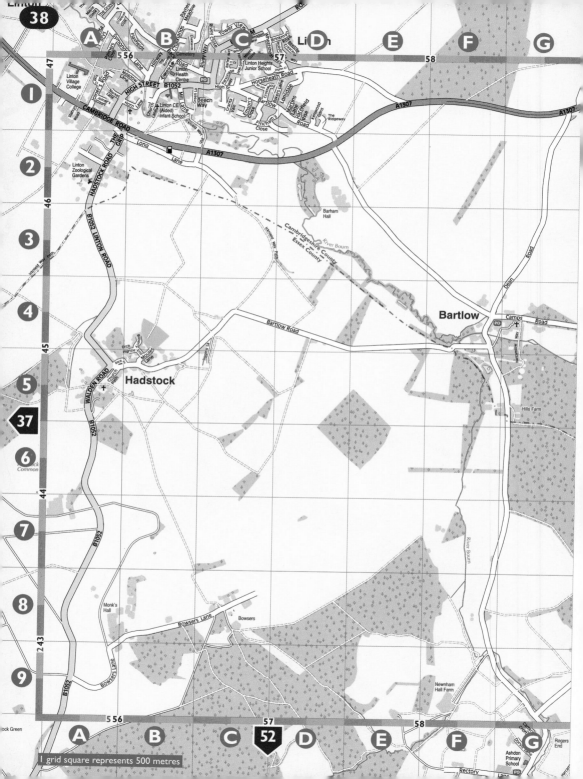

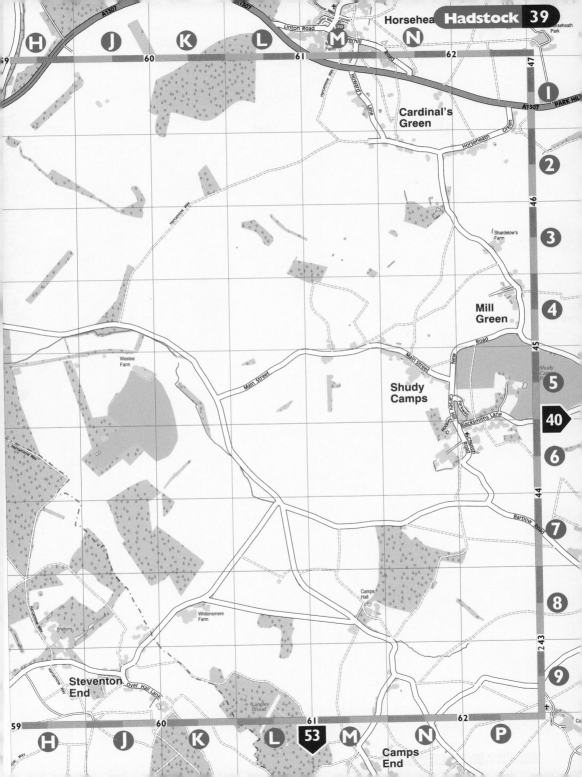

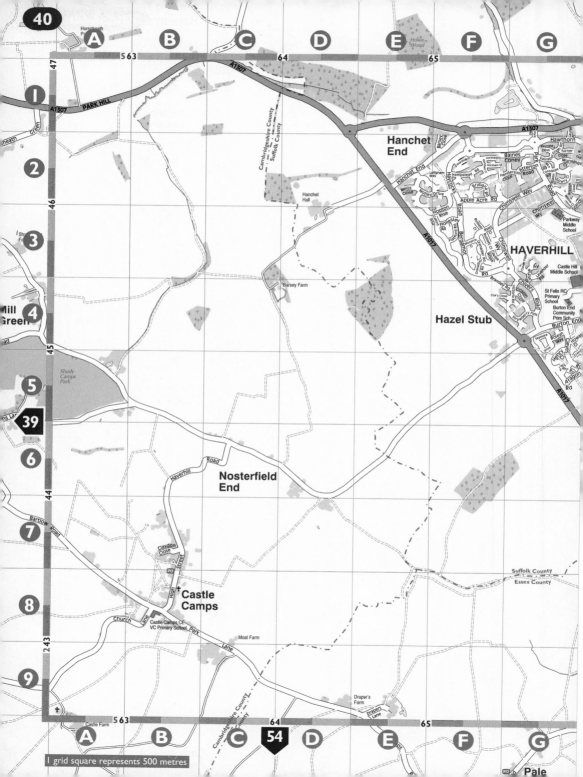

A **B** **C** **D** **E** **F** **G**

47

570 B1061 HAVERHILL ROAD

Risbridge

Brockley Green

Stonebridge Farm

Hundon Road

Kedington

Dash End

71 72 PH

School Crs

King's Meadow

River Stour

Stour Valley Path

Dene Close

King's Hill

Arms Lane

Silver St

Rectory Road

Barton Gv

Sim's Lane

Baythorne Lodge

Crooks Hall

Bank Way

1

2

46

3

4

Calford Green

45

Woodland Green

Oupals Road

5

Stour Valley Path

Cain's Hill

41

Crunch

Rowley

6

WATER LANE

A1017 HILL

44

A1017

Sturmer

Hill Lane

Linnets Lane

Boyton End

Stour Valley Path

7

Roost End

River Stour

Water Hall Farm

8

243

Floriston Hall

Wixoe

CHAPEL

9

Upper House Farm

A1017

New England

Stour Valley

MILL RD A1032

RIDGEWELL ROAD

ASH HILL

A1017

Baythorne End

570 B1054 71 72

A **B** **C** **56** **D** **E** **F** **G**

Ryland

1 grid square represents 500 metres

Parsonage Farm

H J K L M

73 74 75 76 47

Wentford Farm

B1063

Chilton Street

I

Wentford View

2

March Place

De Burgh Place

Clarence Rd

46

Clarence Rd

Leys Farm

Upper Common

3

Police Station

Clare County Primary School

Lords Wood

Cemetery

4

Canham's Farm

Sur

Bench Barn Farm

California Farm

45

NETHERC

Westfields

Clare Rd

Lutus Cl

A1092

5

Stonard's Farm

Sur

A1092

STOKE ROAD

44

Farmer's Farm

River Stour

Mill Farm

6

Suffolk County

Essex County

Ashen Road

Claret Hall

Stour Valley Path

44

243

7

Moor Hall

Stour Valley Path

Hollow Road

Blacksmiths Hill

A1092

Boyton Vineyard

PO

Cemetery

Stours

8

Chapel Street Farm

STREET A1092

THE STREET

Ashen

Church Farm

Lane

Stoke by Clare

Stoke College

Ashen Hill

Doctor's Lane

Ashen House

Hollow Road

9

Suffolk County

Essex County

River Stour

Stour Valley Path

Laund's Farm

Ashen Hall

Ovington Hall

73 74 75 76

Baythorne Park

H J K L

57

Pannel's Ash

M N P

Foxes Road

Ashen Road

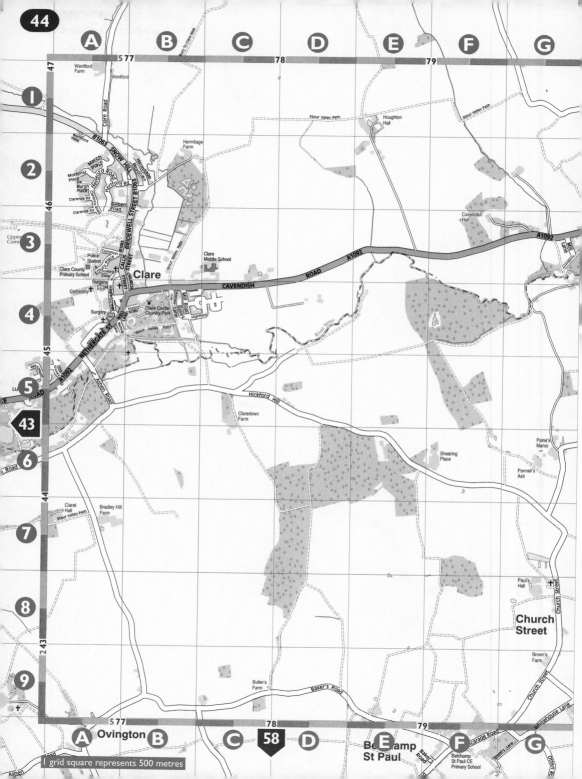

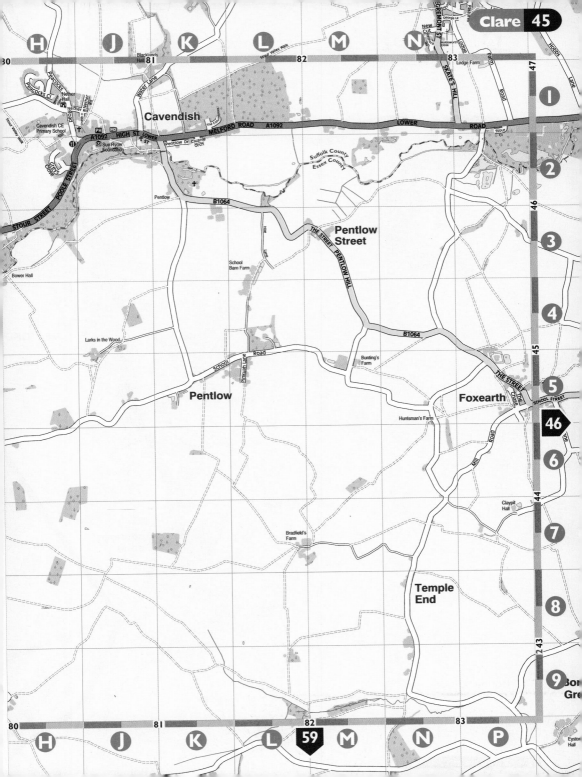

H   J   K   L   M   N

CREMONT ST
George Ln
Chadworth Close
New Cut
Lodge Farm

Blacklands Hall **81**   Stour Valley Walk   **82**   **83**

Lodge Farm
SKATE'S HILL

I

Peacocks Ct
Nether Hall
Nether Rd
Nether Rd
Water Lane

Cavendish CE Primary School
PH
PO
Sue Ryder Foundation

Cavendish
The Common
MELFORD ROAD   A1092   LOWER   ROAD
A1092   HIGH ST   LOWER ST
Pentlow Dr   Cluanie Orch
Stour

2

46

STOUR STREET
POOLE STREET
CRES'S CLOSE
River Stour
Pentlow

Suffolk County
Essex County

45

Pentlow
B1064

Pentlow Street
THE STREET PENTLOW HILL

3

Bower Hall
School Barn Farm
Hoe Lane

4

Larks in the Wood
School Road
Pinkuah Lane

B1064
Bunting's Farm

THE STREET
THE CLOSE
SCHOOL STREET
Foxearth

5

Pentlow
Huntsman's Farm

46

MILL ROAD

6

Claypit Hall

44

Bradfield's Farm

7

Temple End

8

243

9 Bor... Gre...

80   81   82   83

Eysto... Hall

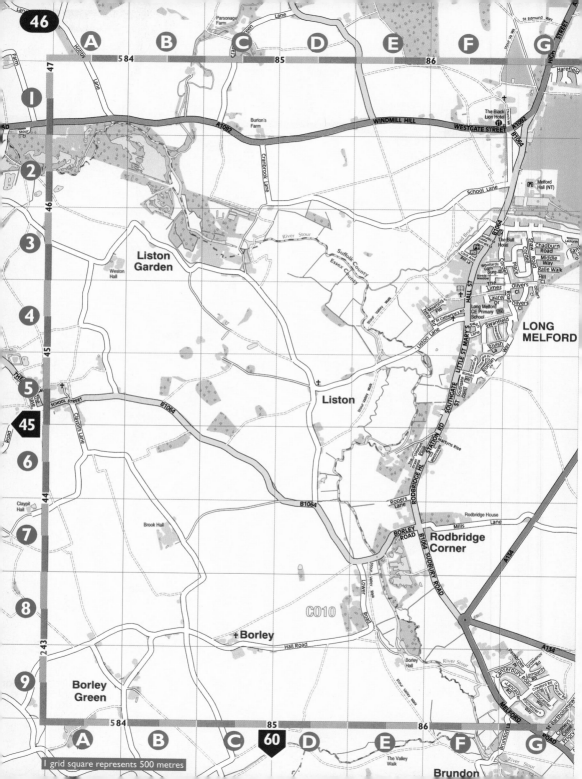

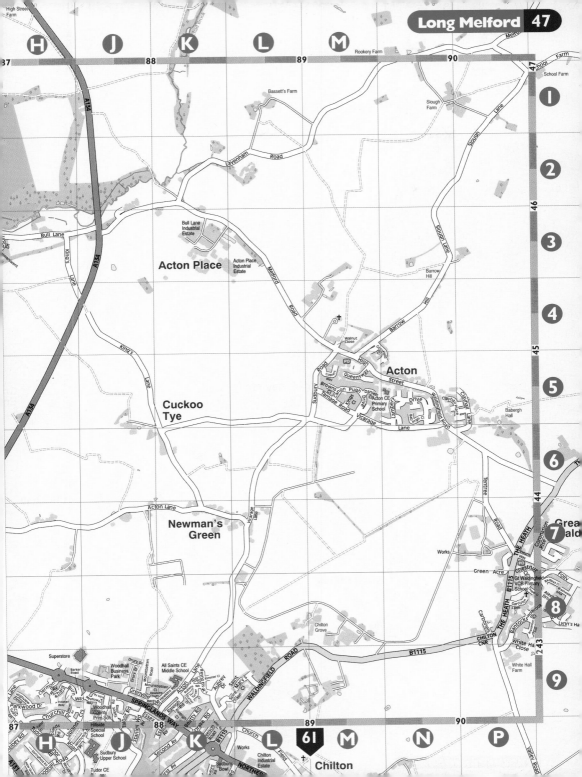

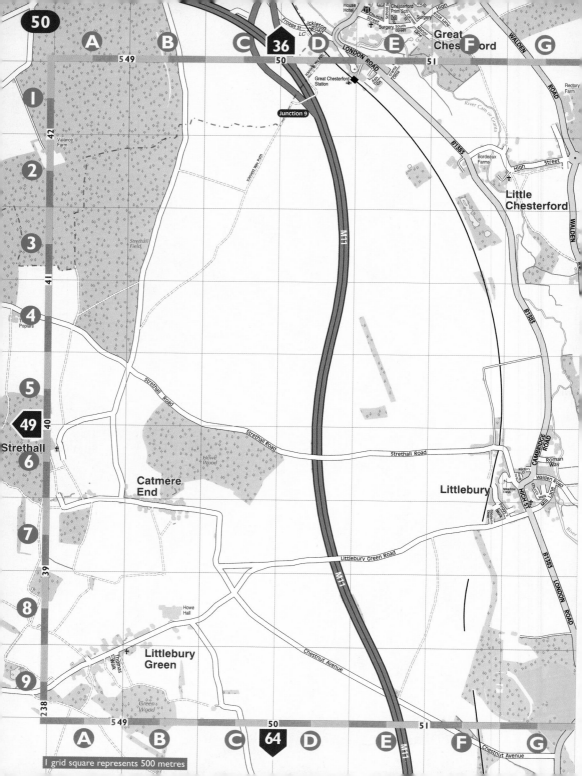

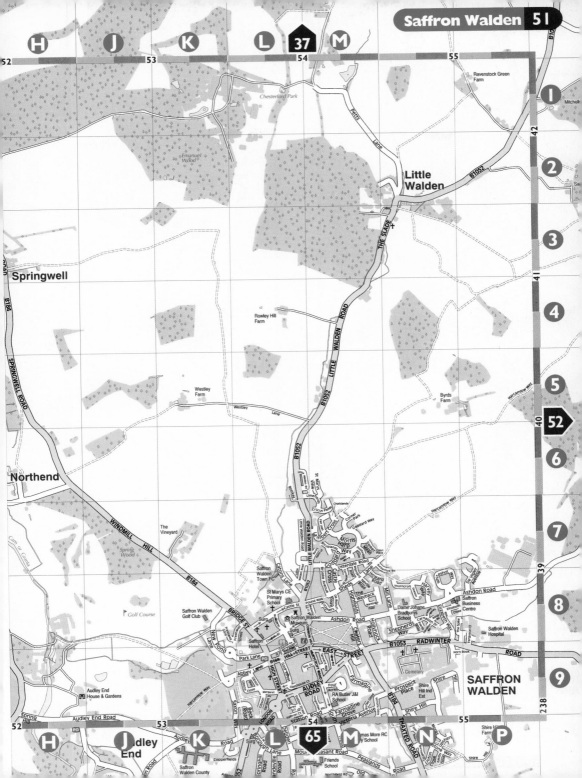

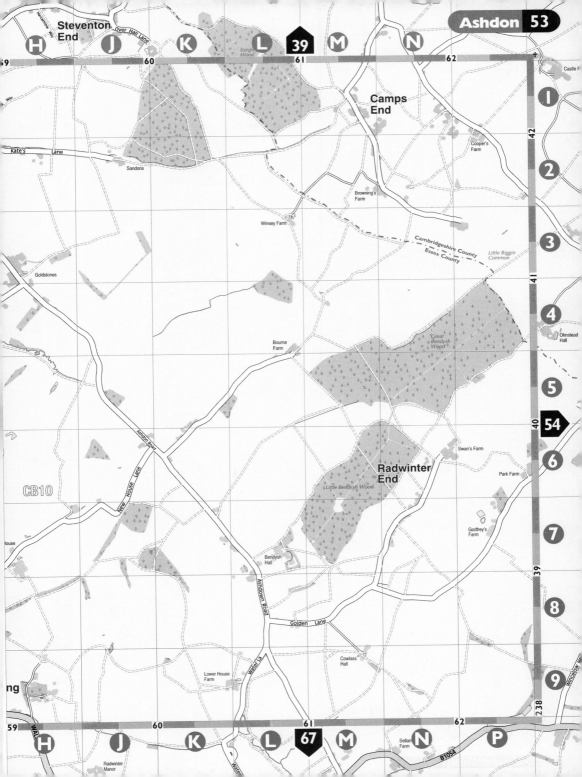

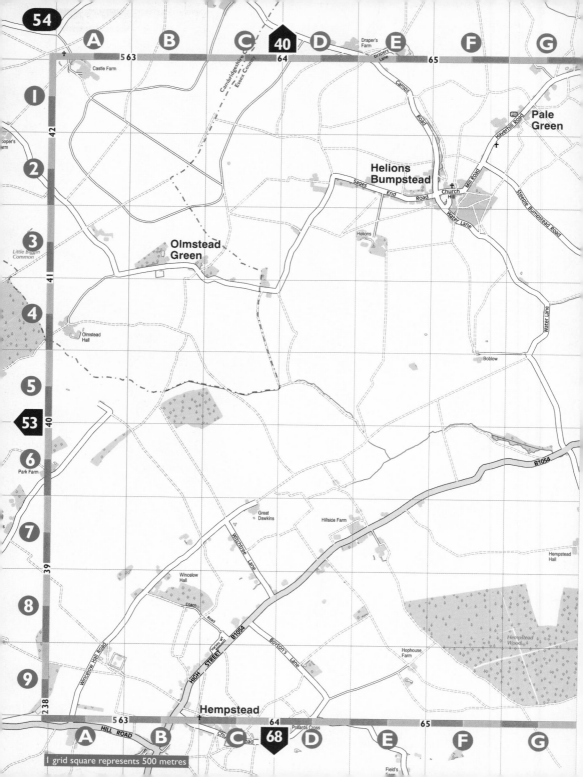

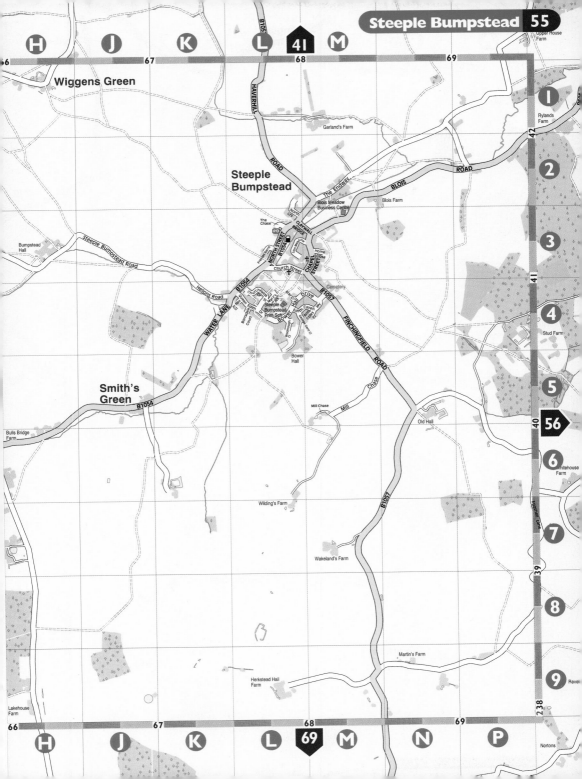

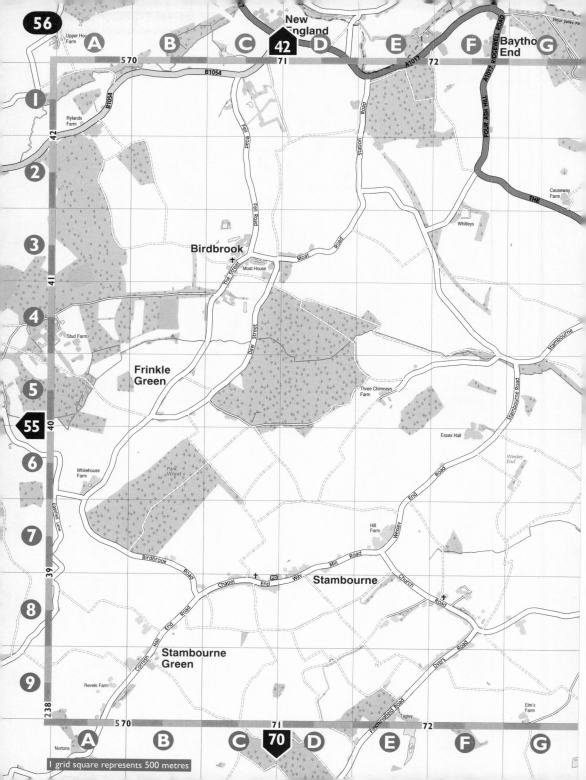

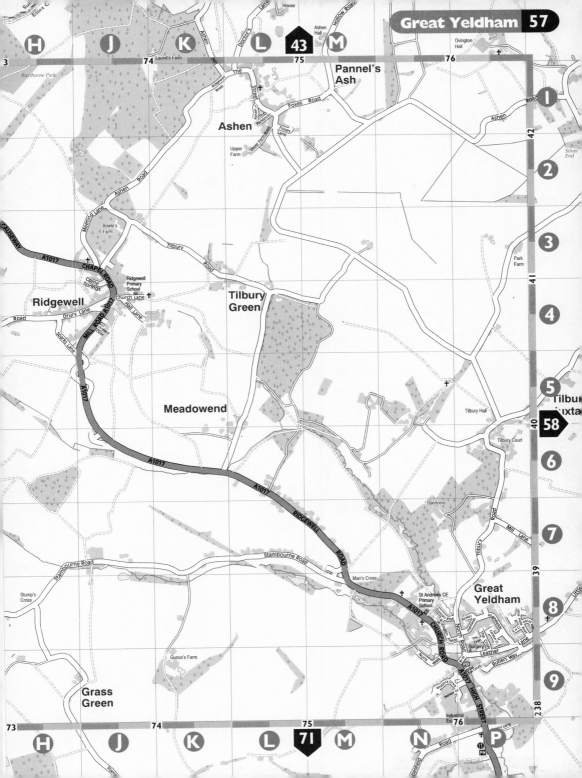

H J K L **43** M

Great Yeldham **57**

I 42
2
3 41
4
5
58 40
6
7 39
8
9 2 38

Ashen Hall
Ovington Hall

3 74 75 76

Baythorne Park

Pannel's Ash

Silver End

Ashen

Laund's Farm

Doctor's Lane
Hollow Road
House

Ashen Hill Road
The Street
Foxes Road
Foxes Lane
Upper Farmhouse

Upper Farm

Park Farm

CAUSEWAY A1017

Meeting Lane

Bowie's Farm

CHAPEL ROAD

Colne Springs

Ridgewell

Ridgewell Primary School

Church Lane
Hall Lane

Tilbury Green

Tilbury Road

Ashen Road

Drury Lane

MILL ROAD A1017

Sparks Lane

A1017

Road

Meadowend

A1017

Tilbury Hall

Tilbur juxta

Tilbury Court

A1017 RIDGEWELL ROAD

Spencers

Tilbury Road
Mill Lane

Stambourne Road

Stambourne Road

Man's Cross

St Andrews CE Primary School

Great Yeldham

Stump's Cross

CHURCH ROAD
North Road

Surgery

Leather

Butlers Way

Gunce's Farm

A1017 HIGH STREET

Grass Green

Industrial Est

Road

PH

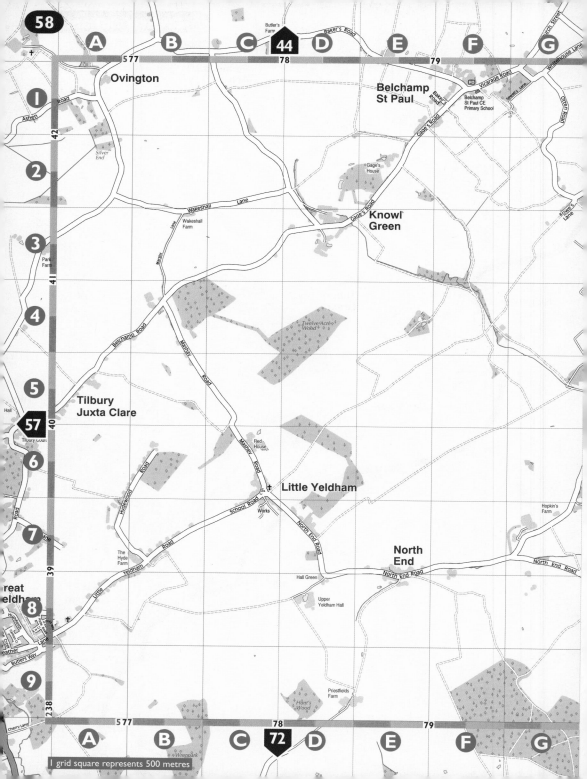

58

A **5 77** B C **44** Baker's Road D E F **79** G

1
Ashen Road
42

Ovington

Butler's Farm

78

Belchamp
St Paul

Whitehouse Lane
Vicarage Road

Belchamp
St Paul CE
Primary School

Sewell's Lane
Otten Road

Baker's Road

2

Silver
End

Gage's
House

Gage's Road

Foxe's
Lane

3
41
Park
Farm

Maplin

Wakeshall Lane

Wakeshall
Farm

Gage's Road

Knowl
Green

4

Belchamp Road

Maplin Road

Twelve Acre
Wood

5

Tilbury
Juxta Clare

Hall

57
40
Tilbury Court

Maplin Road

Red
House

6

Hydewood Road

7
39

Road

The Hyde
Farm

Little Yeldham Road

Little Yeldham

School Road

Works

North End Road

Hopkin's
Farm

North
End

North End Road

North End Road

8

reat
eldham

Butlers Way

Little Yeldham Road

Hall Green

Upper
Yeldham Hall

9
2 38

Cherry Lane

5 77

Priestfields
Farm

Hunt's
Wood

78

A **5 77** B C **72** D E **79** F G

Wrenpark

1 grid square represents 500 metres

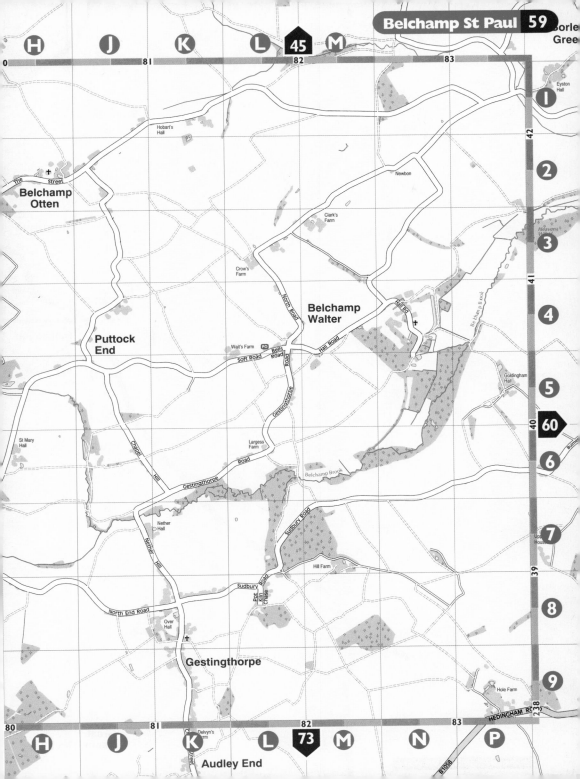

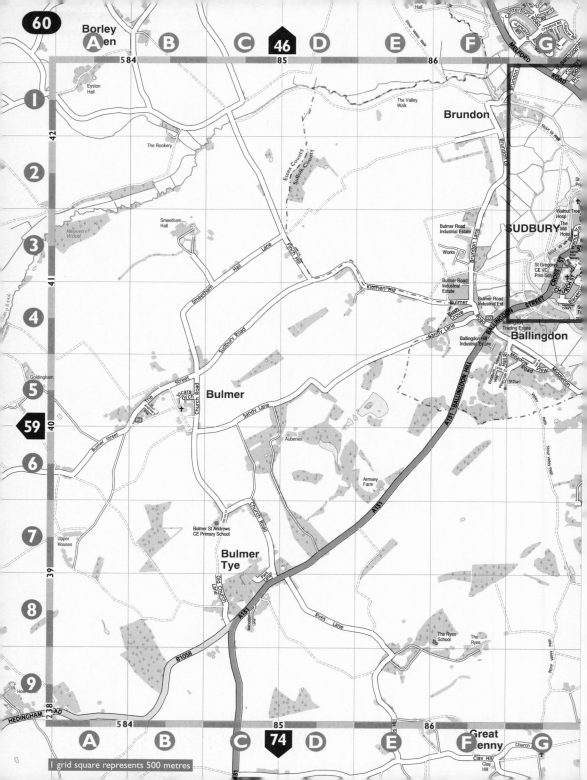

60

Borley
A en

B

C

46

D

E

F

MELFORD

G

5 84

85

86

1

42

Eyston
Hall

The Valley
Walk

River Stour

Brundon

2

41

The Rookery

Essex County
Suffolk County

Stour Valley Walk

SUDBURY

Walnut Tree
Hosp

The
Mill
Hotel

3

Smeetham
Hall

Heaven Wood

Finch Hill

Lane

Kitchen Hill

Bulmer Road
Industrial Estate

Works

Bulmer Road
Industrial
Estate

St Gregorys
CE VC
Prim Sch

CROSS

CHURCH ST

4

Smeetham

Hall Lane

Sudbury Road

Bulmer

Burn
Grove

Sandy Lane

Bulmer Road
Industrial Est

Ballingdon
Trading Estate

Ballingdon Hill
Industrial Estate

BALLINGDON

STREET

Ballingdon

Meadow Road

Middleton

5

Goldingham

The
Street

Church Road

Vicars
Orch

Bulmer

Sandy Lane

Auberies

A131 BALLINGDON HILL

Hall Rd

Stour

59

40

Bulmer Street

6

A131

Armsey
Farm

7

39

Upper
Houses

Church Road

Bulmer St Andrews
CE Primary School

Part Lane

**Bulmer
Tye**

Ryes Lane

The Ryes
School

The Ryes

8

Old Church Lane

A131

B1058

9

Hole Farm

HEDINGHAM

2 38

AD

Clay Hill

Clay
Hill

A

5 84

B

C

74

85

D

E

86

F

**Great
Henny**

Church

G

I grid square represents 500 metres

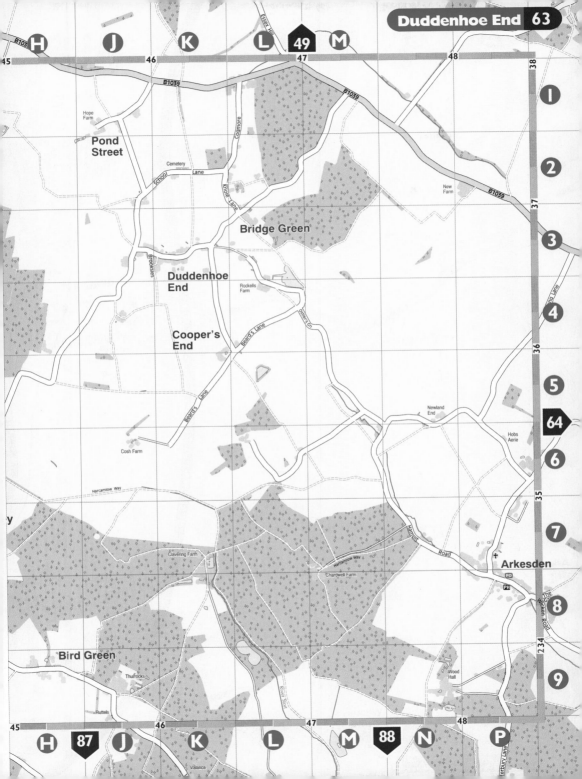

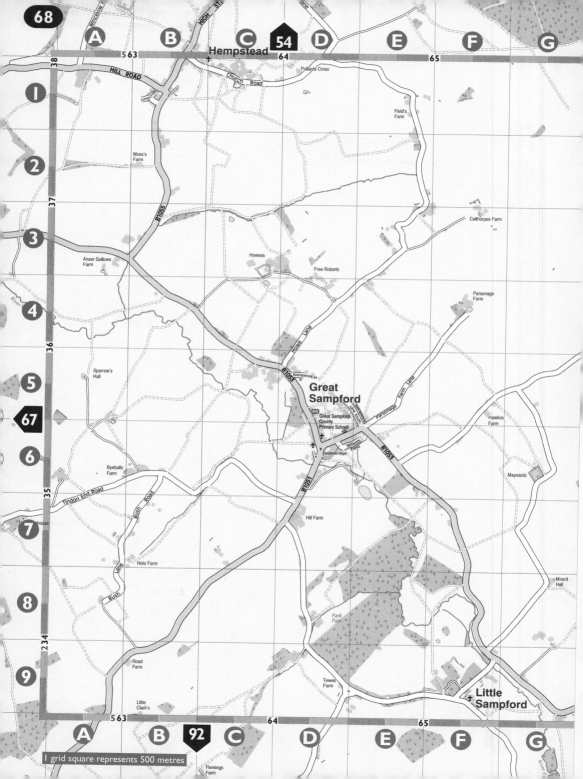

H J K L 55 M

66 67 68 69 38

1

Norfo

Revels Fa

Cornish Hall End Road

2

37

Lopham's
Farm

Spain's End
Farm

Shore Hall

Cemetery

Heard's Lane

**Cornish
Hall End**

Heard's Lane

3

Whitleys

4

36

Tinkers
Green

Old House
Farm

Lowerhouse

Jekyll's
Farm

Cornish
Hall

Jekylls Lane

5

70

Belcumber
Hall

**Little
London**

6

35

Rook
Hall

B1057

Obourne's
Farm

Ho
Str

7

Ye

Howe Farm

8

234

Hawkin's
Hill

Darielay
Farm

Howe
Hall

LITTLE LONDON HILL

9

Mill
End

66 67 68 69

Buck
End

Garland's

Brent

H Grass Green J K L 57 M N

3 74 75 38

Park Lane PO Church Lane St Margarets CE Primary School

Sambourne Road

Berwick Hall

Toppesfield

Toppesfield Hall

The Causeway

Great Yeldham Road

Great Yeldham Road

Cainsford End Rd

Hill

Oliver's Farm

Cust Hall

Hoses

Lane

Barr Hall

Blois Hall

Birdgreen Farm

Tattersall's Farm

Redhouse Farm

Morris Green

Scotneys

Toppesfield Road

Ind Estate 76

Cherry Lane

PH

Works

River Colne

POOLE STREET

37

36

35

234

Bloom's Farm

Kentish Farm

Delvin End

Grave's Hall

Highstreet Green

Carter's Farm

Burnt House Farm

Cuckoo

Cuckoos Farm

School Rd

1
2
3
4
5
6 72
7
8
9

73 74 75 76

H 95 J K L M 96 N P

Deek's Farm Sugar Lane

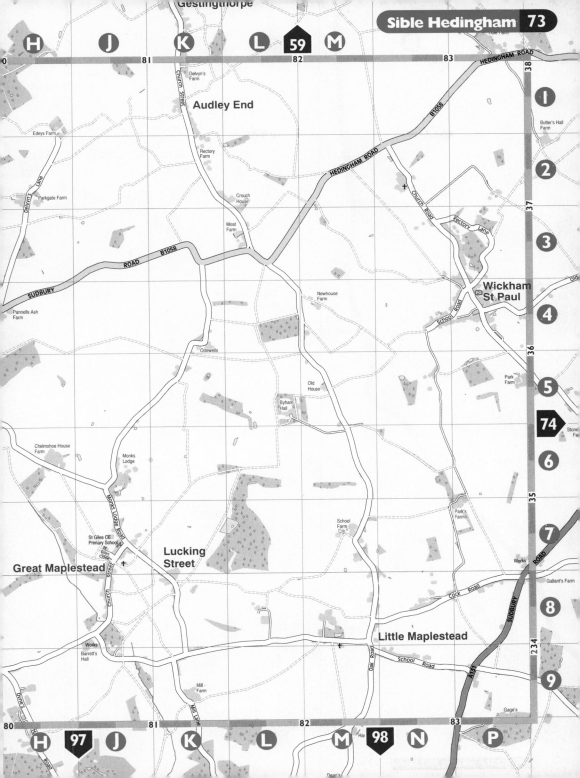

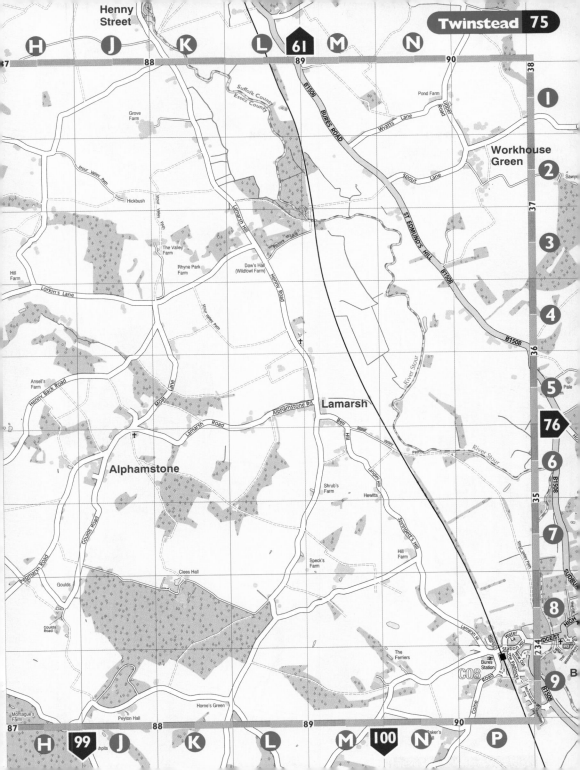

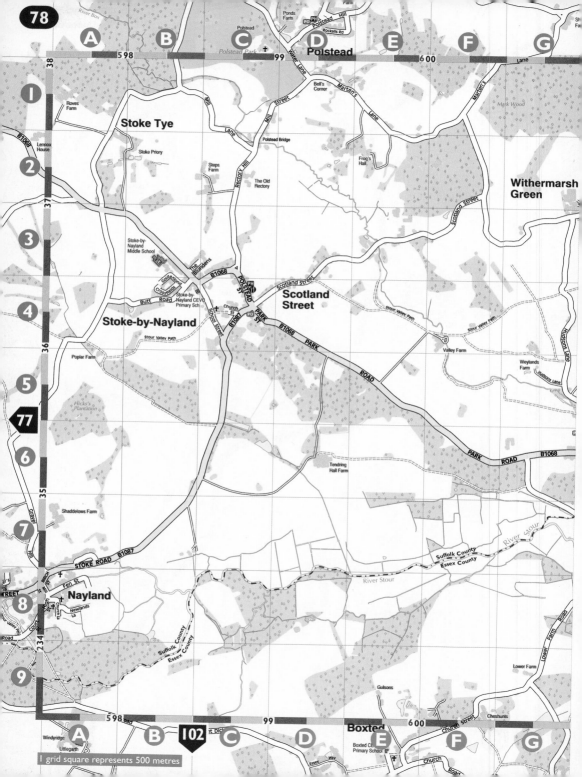

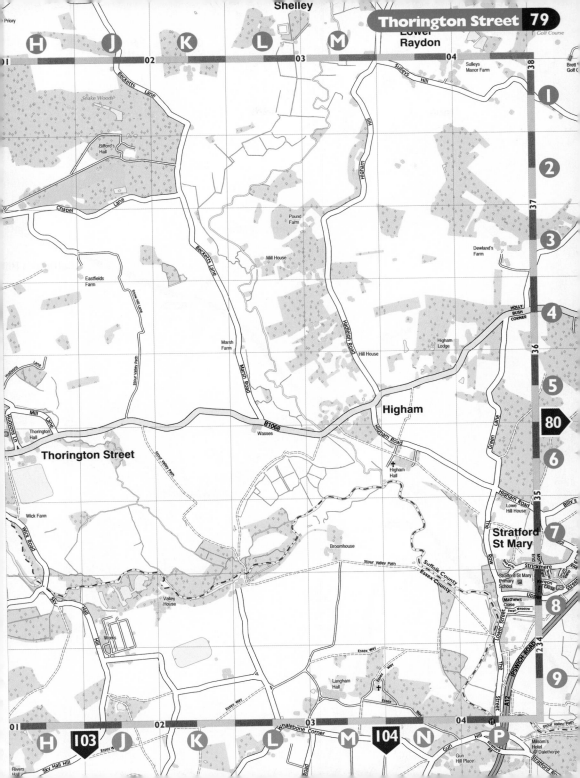

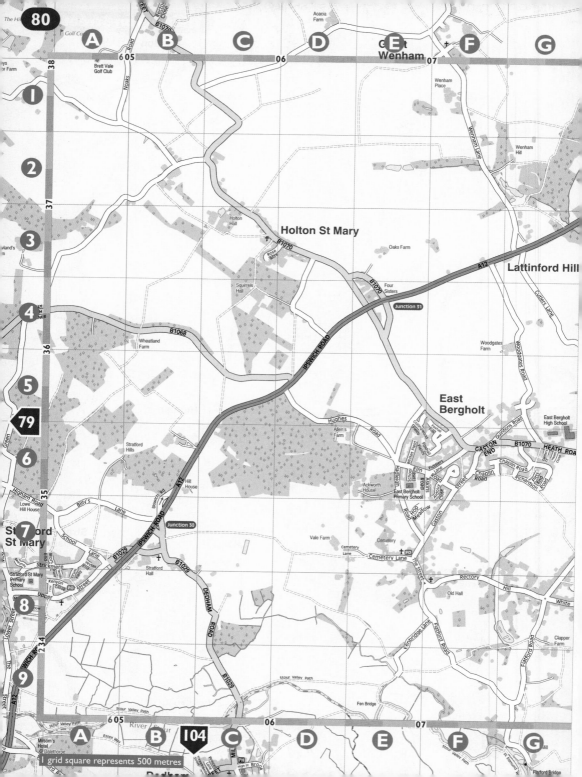

Orwell

H J K L **32** M

2   23   24   25   38

Marina

Suffolk Coast & Heaths Path

I

2

37

River

3

Orwell

4

36

Wade's Lane

Red House Farm

Hill House

5

Charity Farm

34

Church End

Shotley Hall

6

Frogs Alley

Shotley Walk

Boot Drain

Pear Tree Farm

Oldhall Road

35

Warren Lane

B1456

Erwarton Walk

Orwell View Road

Shotley Marshes

7

Shotley

Garden

THE STREET B1456

Surgery

Kingsland

Queensland

Kingsland

Church Lane

Shotley Primary School

Over Hall

B1456

8

Gate Farm Road

Suffolk Coast & Heaths Path

Chilton Rd

Great Harlings

Tudor Cl

Blake Av

Link Rd

Kirkton Cl

Marina

234

Ganges Museum

Lloyd Rd

Kitchener Way

Lower Harlings

Ganges

Shotley Gate

PO

Caledonia

Erwarton Bay

Stourside

Estuary Road

Bristol Hill

Shotley Sailing Club

9

Victoria Dr   King Edward VII Drive

22   23   24   25

H **109** J K L M **110** N P

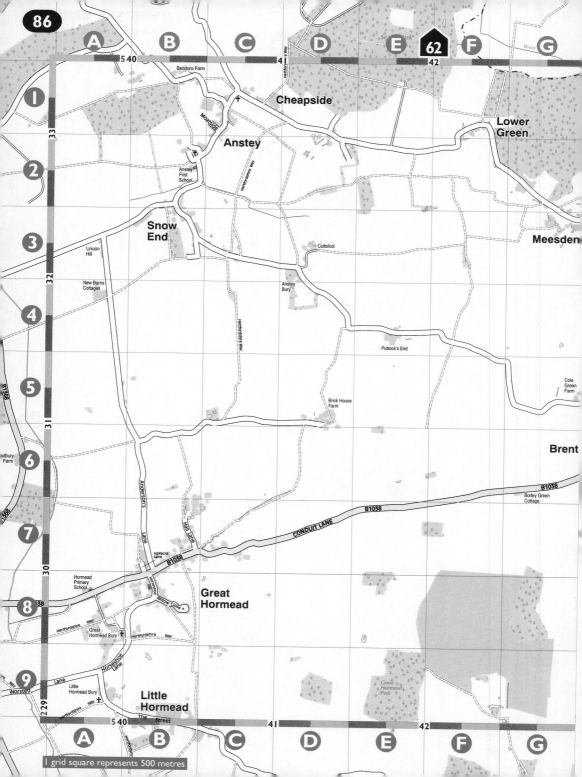

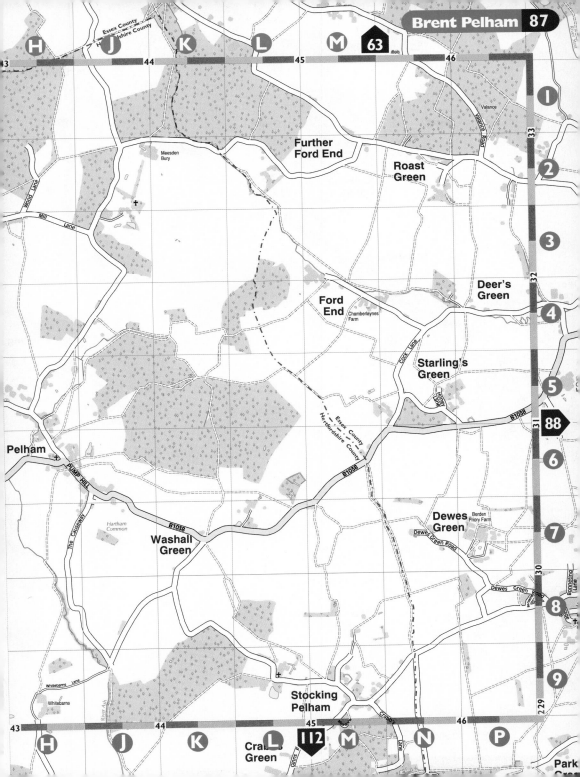

H J K L M **63** ittels

44 45 46

Valance

Wood Lane

Mill Lane

Meesden Bury

Further Ford End

Roast Green

Valance Road

Deer's Green

Ford End

Chamberlaynes Farm

Cock Lane

Starling's Green

Honey Lane

Essex County
Hertfordshire County

88

B1038

Pelham

PUMP HILL

B1038

The Causeway

Hartham Common

Washall Green

B1038

Dewes Green

Berden Priory Farm

Dewer Green Road

Dewes Green Road

Bonnington Lane

Whitebarns Lane

Whitebarns

River Ash

Stocking Pelham

Crabb's
Green

Cramp
Lane

Park
Green

1 2 3 4 5 6 7 8 9

33 32 31 30 229

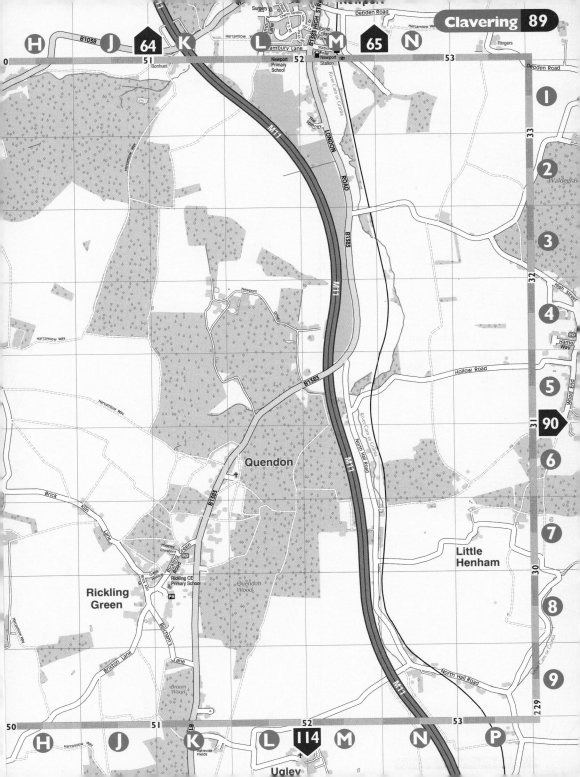

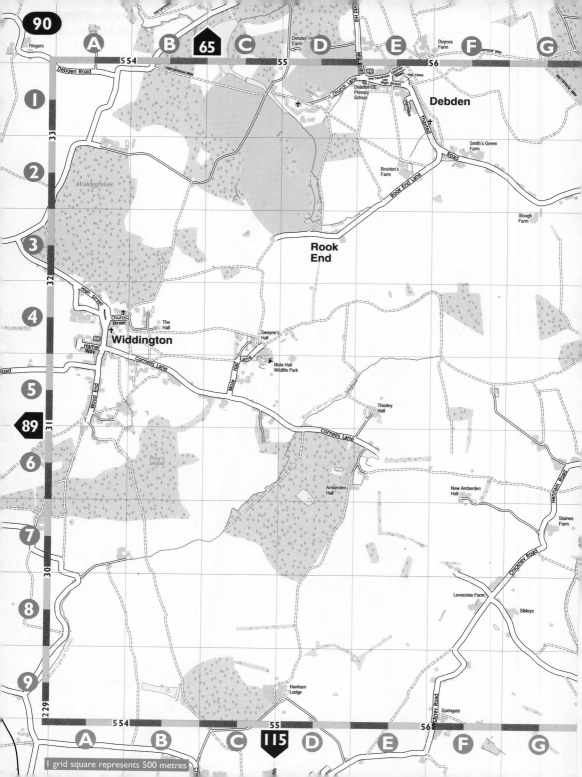

Tewes Farm

Hawkin's Hill

Danielay Farm

H **J** **68** **K** **Little Sampford** **L** **M** **69** **N**

4 65 66 67

Brent Hall

1

B1053 BRENT

33

River Pant

Garland's Farm

Yorr's Lane

Gamber's Hall

2 Fi

Pitley Farm

32

Hill Hall

3 Little Farm

Hawkspur Green

4

Cook's Lane

Beslyns

BEAVER ROAD

The Hydes

Moor Hall

Bridg End North

5

31 BRIDGE END

94

HIGH STREET VINE ST

Mill Cl

6

Black Lane

Bell Lane

High St. Brook Street

Slones

styles

Paul's Farm

Little Bardfield

PO

Dorham Lodge

The Cottage Museum

7

Markswood Farm

B1057

DUNMOW ROAD

30

B1057 ROAD

8

Charity Farm

DUNMOW

9

2 29

The Grove

64 65 66 67

Dui Farm

Green

Farm's Farm

H **J** **K** **L** **118** **M** **N** **P**

H   J   70   K   L   M   71

72   73   74   Morris Green

Wethersfield Airfield

Hall

Sculpin's Farm

Chanute Avenue

Drive   Langley Av.

Lane   Hester Av.

Shaw

Whitehall Farm

Wright's Farm

Mitchell Circle

Scott   Cannon Circle

Avenue

Vandenbury Circle

Fairy Farm

New Barns

Poor Park

Gray's Farm

33

32

Patten's Farm

Gray's Lane

Hill

Hudson's

Brickkiln Green

Lower Green

Willowbrook Lane

Pouches Hall

School Green

Blackmore End

PH

31

96

Hereward W.

High Street

Gardens

Saffron

B1053

Wethersfield CE Primary School

West Dr.

Manor House

Widleybrook Lane

Widewbrook Lane

Golden's Farm

BRAINTREE

ROAD

B1053

Boydell's Farm

Danes Vale Farm

Hyde Farm

Hyde Lane

Shinb

30

Redfants Manor Farm

Valley Farm

Oak Hill

Rotten End

Wethersfield Road

Cliff Crescent

PH

Clifield

Bartlands

Shalford

Water Hall

71   72   73   74

H   J   K   L   120   M   N   P   **Beazley End**

Lane

Iron Bridge Farm

Codham Little Park Dme

1
2
3
4
5
6
7
8
9

229

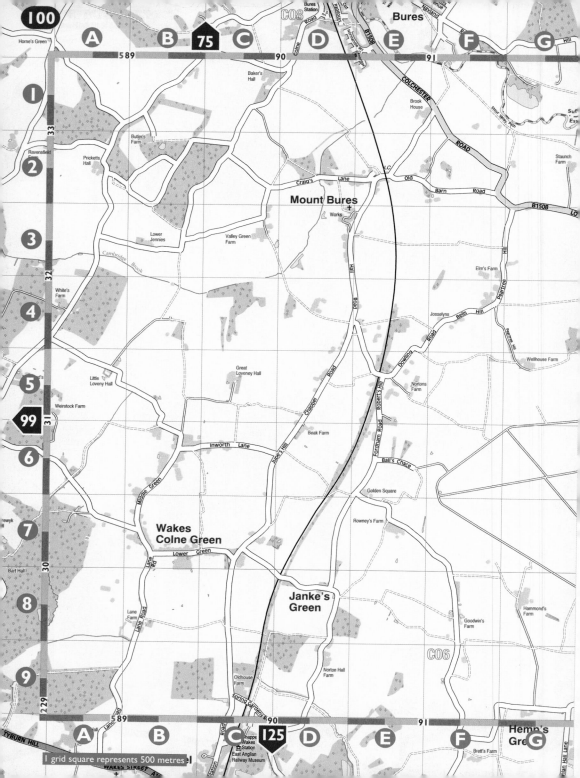

H   J   **76**   K   L   M   **77**

2   93   94   95

H   J   K   L   **126**   M   N   P

92   93   94   95

Wormingford

Fordham

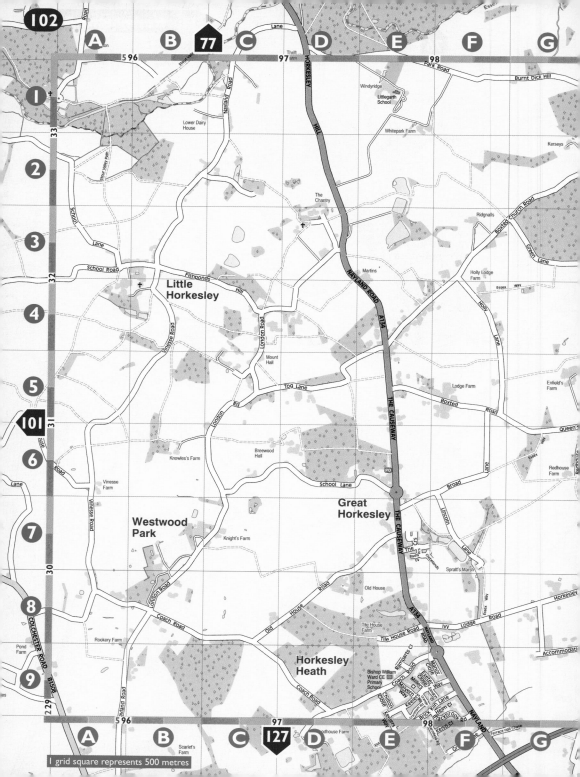

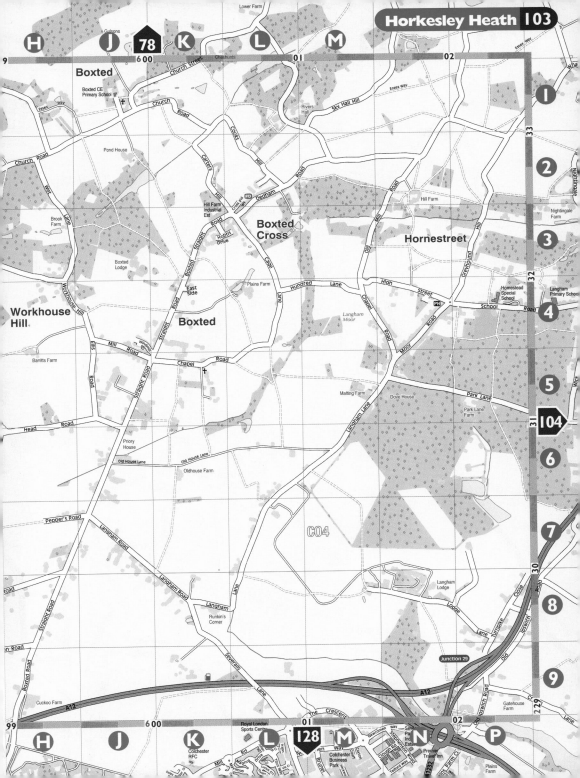

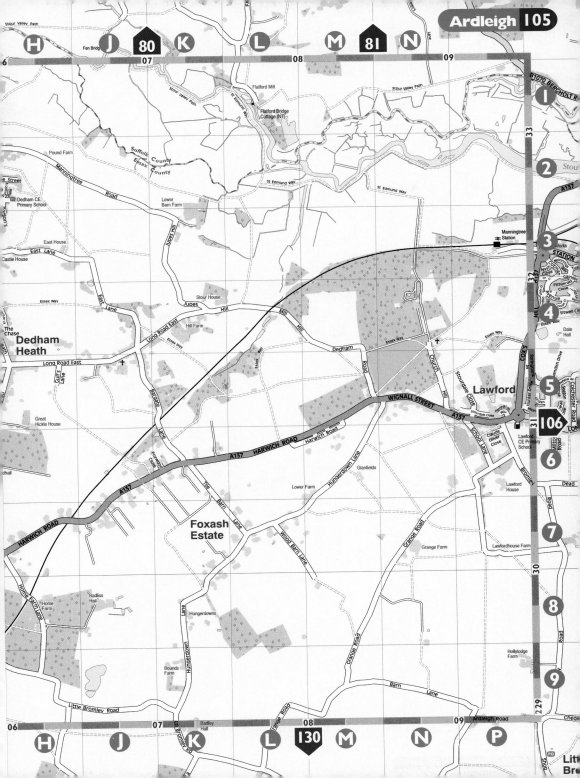

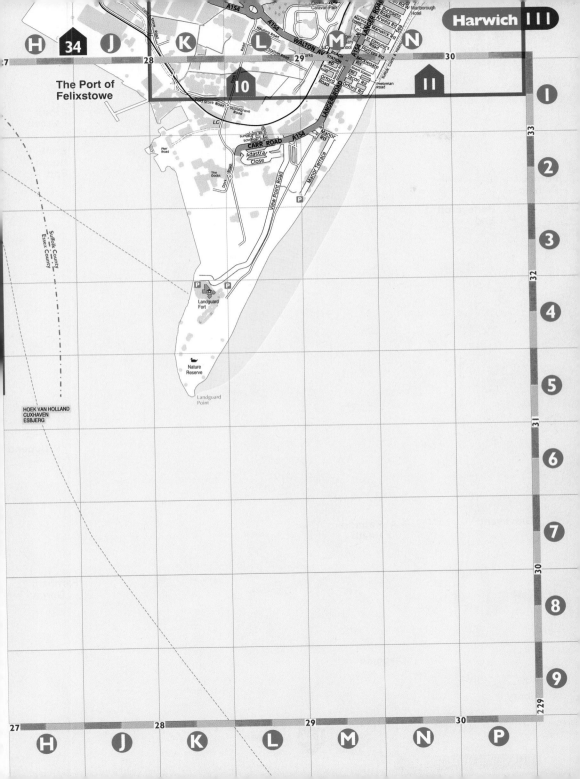

H 34 J K L M N

28 29 30

**The Port of
Felixstowe**

10

II

Hamilton Road
Gold Store Road
Stonegrove Road

LC

Pier Road

CARR ROAD
Adastra Close
The Docks
Dock
Boat
Works

View Point Road

Manor Road
Manor Terrace

Orford Road
Orford Rd

Tacon Road
Pretyman Road

A154

WALTON AV
STATION
BEACH

LANGER ROAD

St Edmund's Rd
Marwick Rd
Burgeate Rd
Arwela Rd
Hattons Rd
Micklegate Rd

Marlborough
Hotel

Suffolk County
Essex County

Landguard
Fort

P P

Nature
Reserve

Landguard
Point

**HOEK VAN HOLLAND
CUXHAVEN
ESBJERG**

1
33
2
32
3
4
5
31
6
7
30
8
9
229

27 28 29 30

H J K L M N P

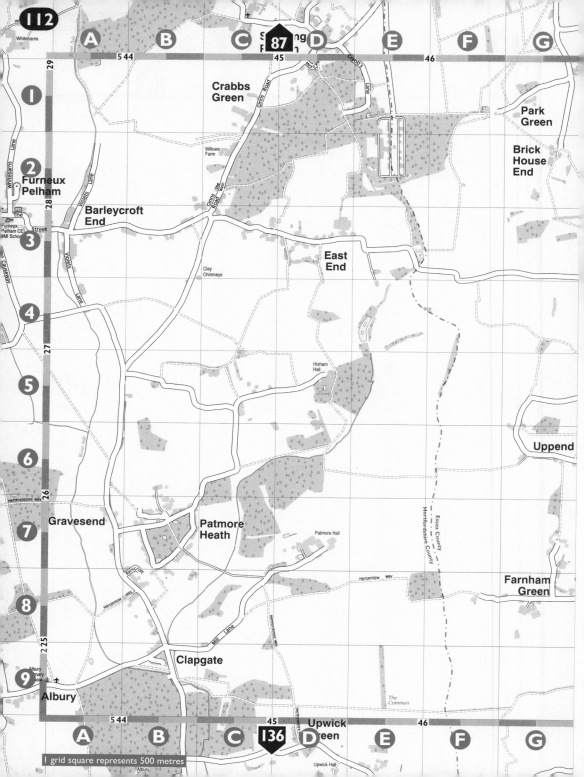

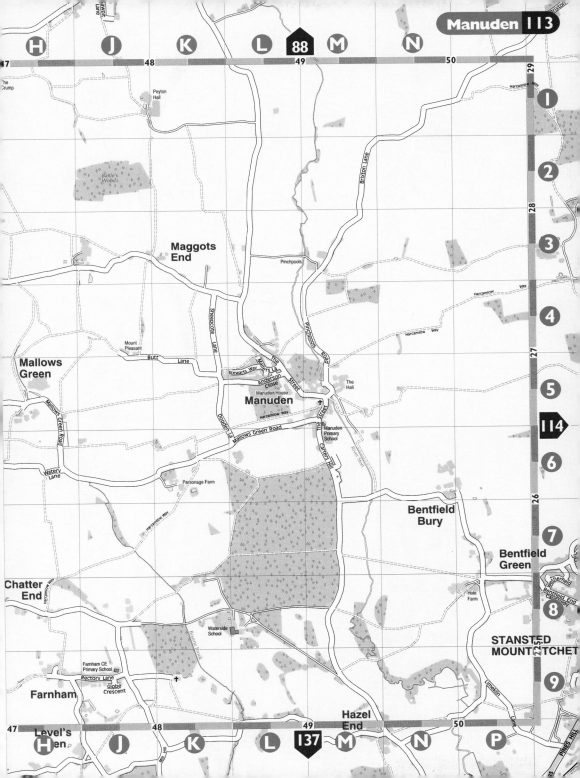

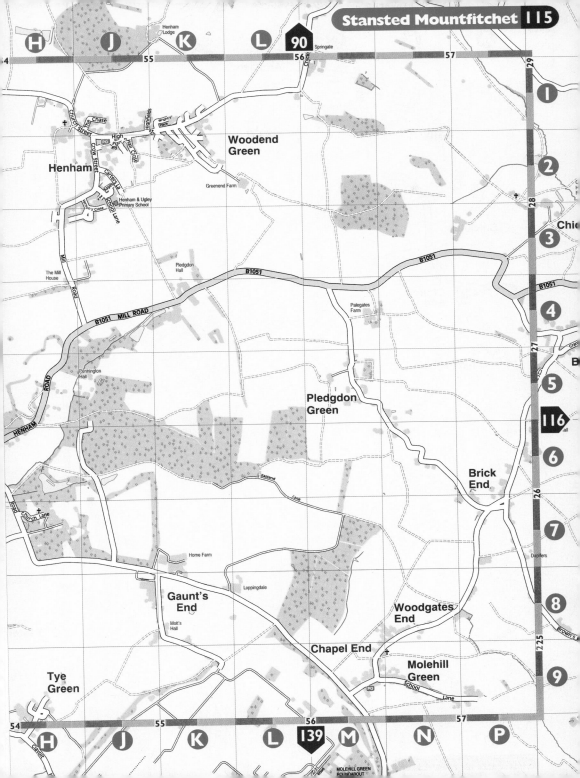

Woodend Green

Henham

Henham Lodge

Springate

Church Street
Chase
High Yard
Hall Close
Highfields
Wright's Piece
Crow Street
Carters La

Henham & Ugley Primary School
School Lane
Gepps La
Priory Close

Greenend Farm

The Mill House

Mill Road

B1051
B1051 MILL ROAD

Pledgdon Hall

Pennington Hall

Palegates Farm

B1051

Pledgdon Green

Brick End

Eastend Lane

Home Farm

Gaunt's End

Loppingdale

Mott's Hall

Woodgates End

Chapel End

Molehill Green

School Lane

Tye Green

Church Lane
Road

Dapifers

Brown's

MOLEHILL GREEN ROUNDABOUT

H J K L 90 Springate
55 56 57

Chickney

29
I
28
2
Chic
3
B1051
4
27
Cran
B
5
116 Hall
6
26
7
8
Brown's
225
9

H J K L 139 M N P
54 55 56 57
Carvall

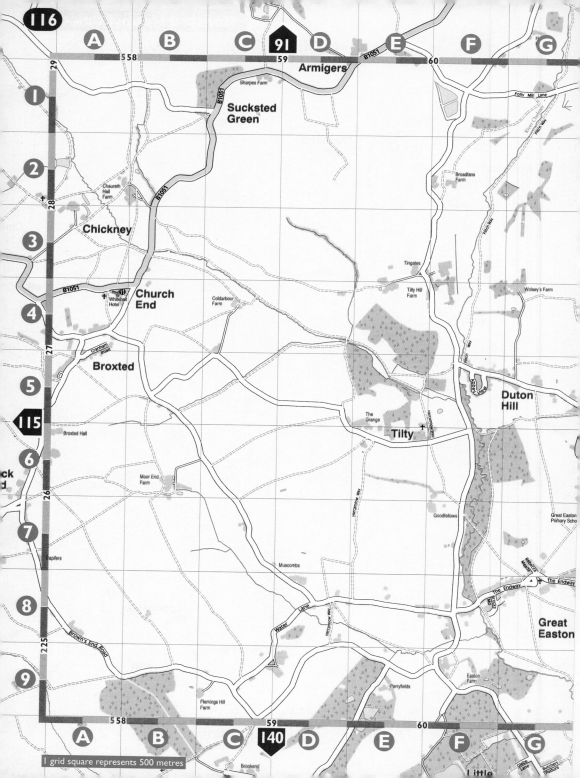

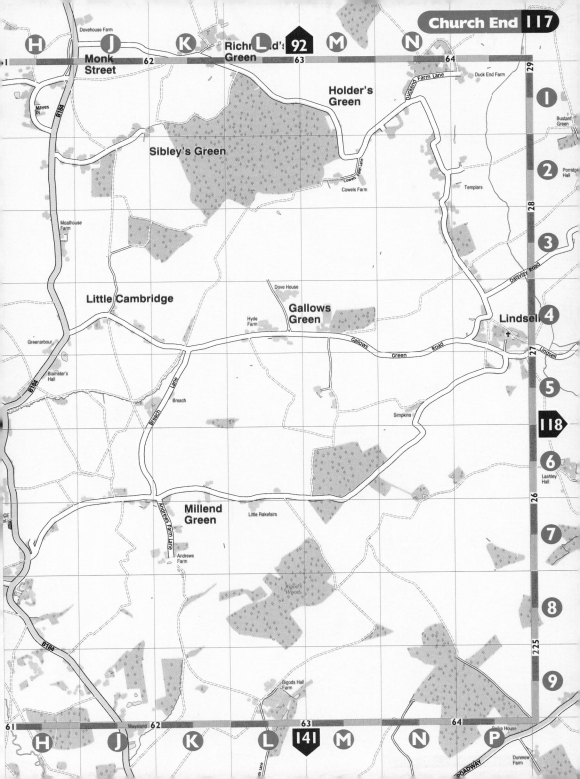

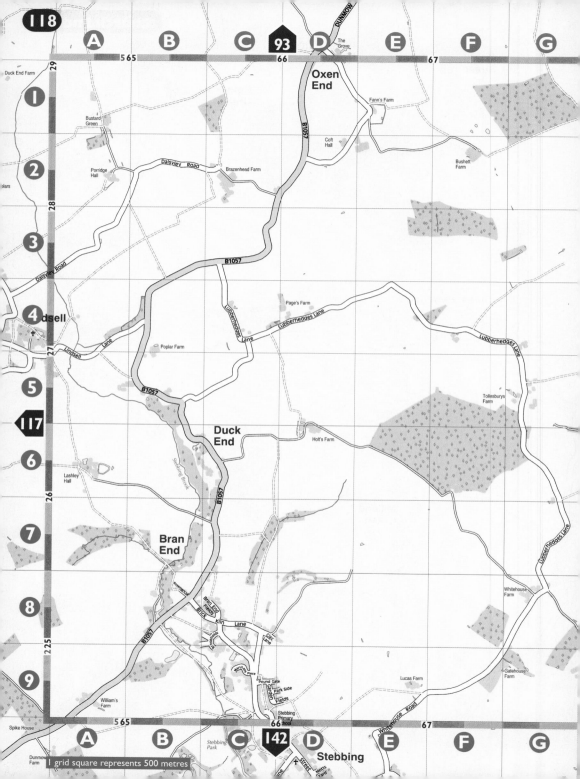

94

H J K L M N

69 70 71

29

1

2

28

3

Park Hall

Great Lodge

Hunt's Farm

Little Lodge

Dynes Farm

Plums Lane

New Green Farm

Elms Farm

Shalfo Green

4

27

Parso

Bar

Long Green Lane

Bardfield Saling

Woolpits

Bardfield Road

Jasper'
n

5

120

6

26

Pudneys Farm

Woolpit's Road

Crow's Green

Great Saling

Piccotts Lane

Piccotts Farm

7

Bett's Farm

Saling Grove

Piccotts Lane

Mount's Farm

8

225

Badcocks Farm

9

Andrewsfield (Saling) Aerodrome

68 69 70 71

Onchor's Farm

Bacons Farm

Old Hall

96

H J K L M

Bocking Churchstreet

High Garrett

Fennes Road

122

145

H J K L M N P

122

A   B   C **97** D   E   F   G

579   80   81

Greenhouse

Park Lane

Limes

Upper Beazley Farm

Road

Grange Close

Greenstead Hall

I

Froyz Hall Farm

Letche's Farm

Bourne Brook

2

Peter Farm

Peterfield's Lane

New Road

Aylett's Farm

Plaistow

Penny Pot

Gladfen Hall

Plaistow Green

3

Rayne Hatch Wood

Green

Road

Highbarn Hall

Ward's Farm

STEAD

ROAD

4

Rayne Hatch Farm

Boultwood's Farm

on's Farm

5

121

Church Farm

6

Keritishes Farm

Brookes's Farm

Longsland Lane

Folly Green

7

Woolmer Green Farm

Madgements Road

Gower's Farm

Nunty's Lane

8

Covenbrook Hall

Back Lane

Woodhouse Farm

Rectory Road

Stisted CE Primary School

Kings Lane

Back Lane

9

Golf Course

Braintree Golf Club

The Street

Garten

Stisted

A   B   C **146** D   E   F   G

579   80   81

Old Road

Campsea Lane

Dog

Road

Pattiswick Hall

29 28 27 26 25

A1017

A131

1 grid square represents 500 metres

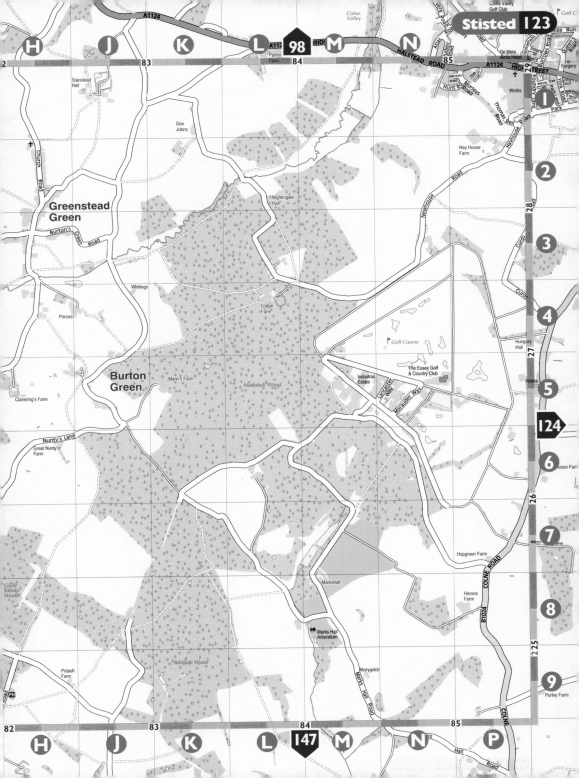

99

A1124

Earls Colne

White Colne

Wakes Colne

TYBURN HILL

COLCHESTER ROAD

123

148

1 grid square represents 500 metres

105

129

154

Little Bromley Road

Bounds Farm

Badley Hall

Grange Road

Ardleigh Road

Chequers Road

Rose Farm

PO

Little Bromley

Norman's Farm

Ardleigh Road

Morrow Lane

Old Shields Farm

Waterhouse Farm

Waterhouse La

Lt Bromley Rd

Burnt Heath Cottages

Burnt Heath

ROAD

Burnt Heath Cottages

Back Road

Mill Lane

Briar Road

Bromley Cross

Tilley's Lane

Little Bromley Hall

Spratts Lane

Church Road

Spratts Lane

B1029

ARDLEIGH ROAD

Carringtons Road

Carringtons Road

Newhouse

Carringtons Road

Carringtons Farm

Little

Bromley Road

Badley Hall Road

Badley Hall

Cotta... Road

Bush Farm

B1029 HALL

ROAD

C07

Moverton Road

Great Bromley

A120

Gt. Bromley St Georges CE Primary School

PO

BROOK STREET

B1029

Mary Lane North

Stone Road

The Chase

Cowey Green

Tenpenny Brook

Hamilton Lodge

PARSONS HILL

Camp Road

Mary Lane North

Church Road

225

Lodge Farm

Cold Hall

Cold Hall Chase

Back Lane West

A120

Fairfield Close

Back Lane East

Chase Road West

Mary Lane South

MeadowClose

A133

Elmstead Market

Church Road

Yard Close

Johnson's Road

Chapel Lane (Glebe)

PO

Market Field School

The Beth Chatto Gardens

The Chase

Bromley Road

Bottles Hill

Mill Farm

Harwich Road

Hare Green

Brundells Road

B1029

Chapel Lane

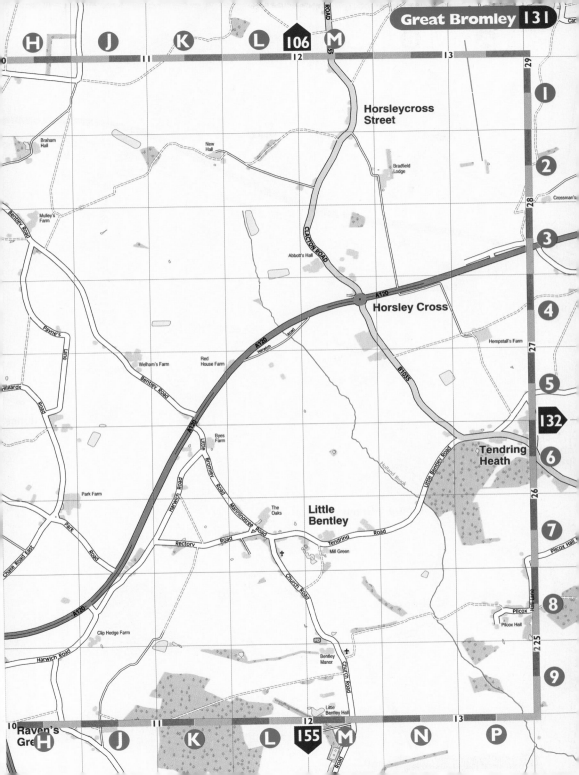

Farm

H J K L 108 M

7 **HARWICH** 18 19 20 29

Bowl Farm

A120

Brickkiln Farm

Southhouse Farm

1

Great
Hall

Oakley Road

Redhouse Farm

Great
Oakley Lodge

Sparrow's
Farm

The Sollis

2

Surgery

28

White House

B1414

3

Oakley Road

Parkers
Farm

Wix Road

Holt Farm

HARWICH RD

Partridge C

**Great
Oakley**

HIGH STREET

Back
Lane

Turn Road

Mosses Farm

4

The Avenue

Great Oakley
CE Primary
School

Sorrells Close

B1414

SCHOOL RD

Pesthouse

Lane

27

Houbridge
Hall

Stones Green Road

Red
Barn
Lane

Wineturn

5

Green

Brooklands

Marden's Farm

BEAUMONT ROAD
CROSS HILL

134

Moze Cross

6

26

Ratcliff's Farm

B1414

Old Moze
Hall

Wix Road

Coys Lane

Potland

New Moze
Hall

7

The
Oak

HARWICH ROAD

Oldhouse Farm

8

225

Beaumont

apel Road

9

Church Lane

B1414

HARWICH ROAD

17 18 19 20

H J K L 157 M N P

Barker's Farm

Beaumont Hall

Beaumont
Quay

Pennyhole
Bay

Stone
Marsh

Nature
Reserve

The
Naze

H J K L 117 M

I
2
3
4
5 B1256
142
6

Maysland
62
63
64

Spike House
Dunmow Farm
THE BROADWAY
Old House
CM6
Park Road
Elmbridge Farm
Lower Hall
Marks Farm
Ravens Farm
Newton Hall
Dunmow Sports Centre
The Parsonage
Helena Romanes School
B184
B1057
Crouches
Churchend
CHURCH END
CHURCH ST
BEAUMONT HILL
CHURCH ST
B1057
The Charters
Church Gdns
St Edmunds Flds
St Edmunds Flds
Miller's Cft
Windmill Cl
Merks Hall
Ford Farm
Riverside
Braintree Road
BRAINTREE ROAD

THE CSWY
NORTH ST
Grev Lane
Berbice Lane
The Poplars
Godfrey Way
Giles's
Gaffrey Way
Elmems
Great Dunmow Prim Sch
Boelmert Crt
Starr Hotel & Restaurant
Counting House Lane
Kings Court
The Maltings
Crayfields
Chequers Lane
Milll Lane
The Great Dunmow Maltings Museum
Braintree Road
Chestnut Gr
Sunbank
Sunfield

Woodside Way
Spruce Av
Newton
Woodlands
Park Drive
Way Dr
Cypress
Jubilee Ct
Stortford Road
High Meadow
High Flds
St Marys Prim Sch
Standrums
Surgery
New Street
Council Buildings
Station Road
Station Yard
Mill Park

GREAT DUNMOW
A120
Minchins
Bedfords
Pharisee Green

Superstore
STORTFORD ROAD
Folly Farm
B1256
Woodview Rd
Springfields
B1256
Fitch Way
Filtch Industrial Est
Ongar Road Trading Est
Ash Grove
Lukin's
B184
ONGAR RD
Normansfield
Lower
Oak End Park
Chelmsford Road Industrial Estate
CHELMSFORD RD
B184
Langleys
Fitch Way
Hoblongs Industrial Estate

Olives or Shingle Hall
B184
ONGAR ROAD
Clapton Hall
Trulons
Clapton Lane
Mountain's Lane
Works
Broadgroves
Works

7
21
8
9

A120
CHELMSFORD RD
Watts Close
Barnston Green

H J K L 166 M N P **Barnston**
61
62
63
64
Pharisee House
Puttocks

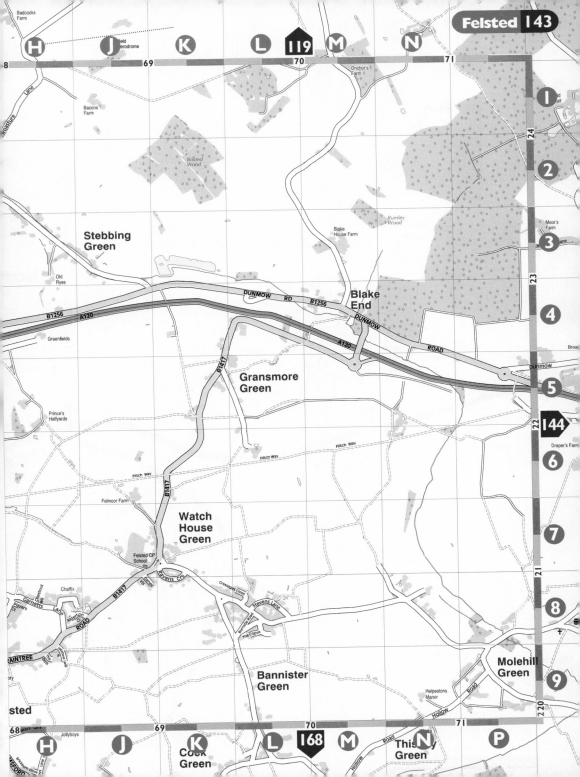

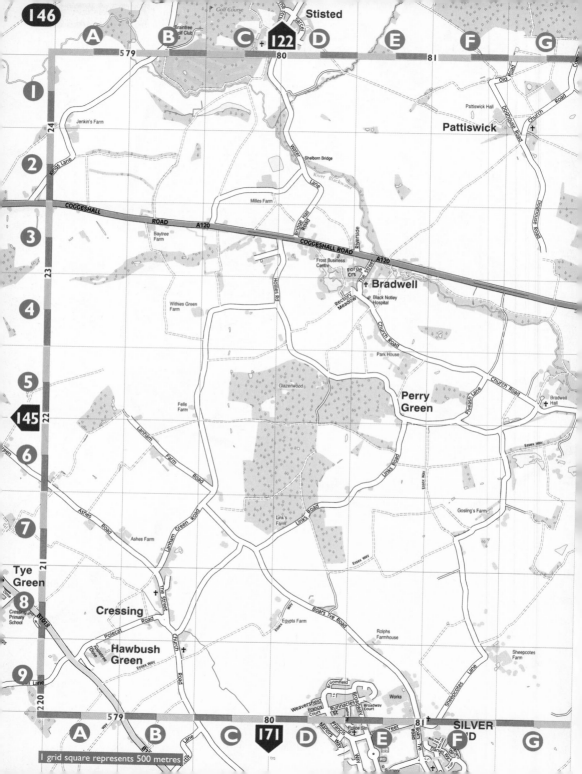

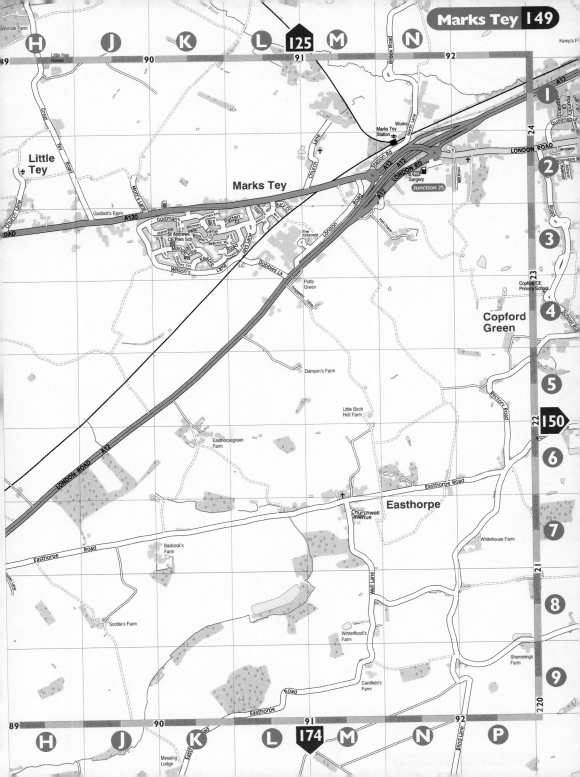

A   B   C   134   D   E   F   G

621   22   23

Horsey
Land

I

24

2

3

23

Kirby Creek

The
Wade

4

Birch
Hall

Marsh
House

Sneating
Hall

WALTON ROAD

Kirby-
le-Soken

WALTON-O

5

B1034

Maltings Lane

Quay Lane

Vista Avenue

Percival
Road

22

157

King's
Farm

THE

STREET

Pyesang
Road

Horsey
Road

Dugmore Avenue

Edith Road

Chartfield
Drive

WALTON ROAD

B1034

6

Shums Hill

Hill
Home

Hamford
CP School

B103

7

THORPE

ROAD

C013

Kirby
Primary
School

Woburn
Avenue

Village Close

Buckfast

FRINTON

N-SEA

Triangle
Shopping
Centre

21

Kirby
Cross

Halstead Road

Holland Rd

ROAD

8

Birch Hoe
Farm

Kirby Cross
Station

B1033

Frinton
Cemetery

Laburnum
Crescent

Sycamore Way

9

220

Addison
Road

Green End
Farm

Hamilton

Laxton
Grove

Green End Lane

B1092

Frinton on
Sea Primary
School

Wilton Wood Road

Frinton Station

LC

Pole
Barn

Greenway

St Philip

Fifth Avenue

The Close

Third Av

Second Av

1 grid square represents 500 metres

24 25 26 27

1
24
2
3
23
4
5
22
6
7
21
8
220
9

The Naze

Walton
Channel

Hedge-end
Island

Walton
Hall

The Twizzle

Marina

Old Hall Lane

Second Avenue
First Av
Third Av
Park
Grove

Naze Lane

Louise Close
Road

Florence Rd
Beatrice Road
Percival Rd
Green Lane

Surf Parade

Hall Lane

The Frinton &
Walton Heritage Museum

Walton &
Frinton
Yacht Club

CO14

N-THE-NAZE

Frinton & Walton
Swimming Pool
Walton
Primary
Sch

Mill Lane

Saville Street
Standley
Rd

East Terrace

PRINCE'S ESP

KIRBY ROAD

Wade

Clays

HIGH STREET

Cemetery
Works

Walton-on-the-
Naze Stn.

The

Parade

Pier Approach

Promenade

Walton Pier

Tendring
Technology
College

WALTON ROAD

Columbine Way
Woodside

Central Avenue

Rainham
Way

Woodberry
Way

Southcliff

Southcliffe
Dve

Eaton Way

Quendon Way
Graces
Way

Cliff Way

Walden

Stanford
Way

Peacehaven
Lane

Waltham Way

Winchester
Road

Eton Road

Oxton

St Mary's Rd

Esplanade

Cedar
Cl

H J K L M N P

24 25 26 27

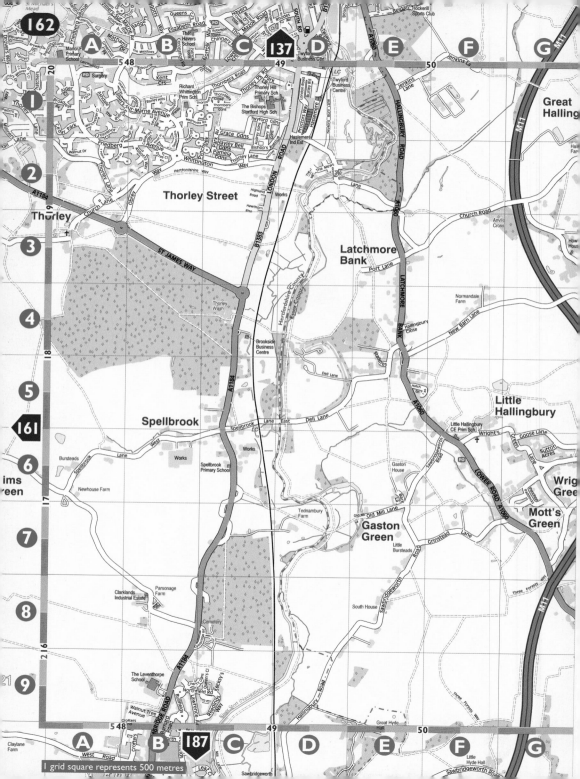

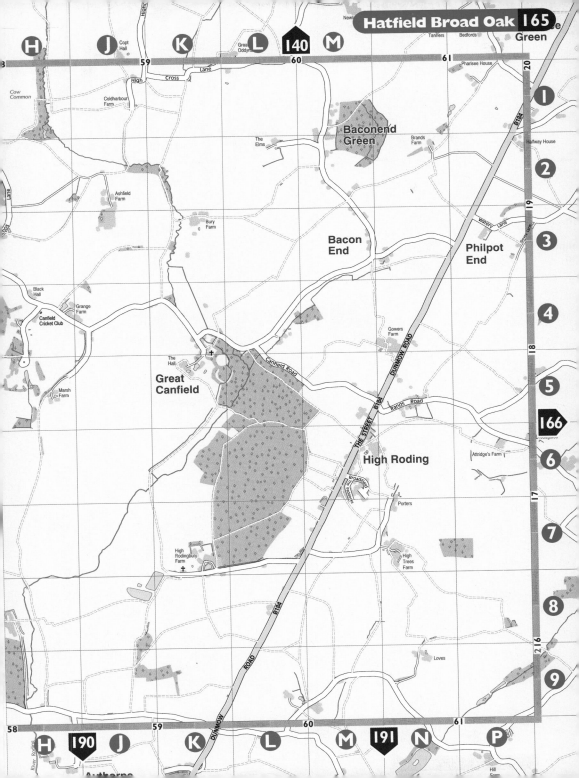

166
harisee Green

141

165

191

Barnston

Wellstye Green

Bishops Green

Garnetts

CHELMSFORD ROAD
A130

Broadgrove

Works

Martels

Sallets Green

Garnetts Wood

Pyes Farm

Quoins

Mudwall

Broadgates

ridge's Farm

County Farm

Poplar

Barnfield

Cromps

Little Leys

Peakins

Maidens

Yewtree

Chimballs

Bushbarns

Greens Farm

Upper Harveys

Trutons

Puttocks

Coopers

Mountains Farm

Roffey

Halfway House

hilpo nd

Egg Lane

Philpot

Waters Lane

Pepies Lane

Mountains Farm Road

Calston Hill Lane

High Easter Road

B184

562

63

64

5 62

63

64

1 grid square represents 500 metres

A B C D E F G

1 2 3 4 5 6 7 8 9

20 19 18 17 2 16

Station Road
PH
Felsted Preparatory School
Felsted
Spinwood PK

H 66 **J** **K** **L** 67 **142** **M** Mill Road 68 **N** **Felsted** 20

Fishes
Fids
Bakers Lane
Jollyboys

B1417 CHELMSFORD ROAD

1

Causeway End

Johnson's Lane South
Johnson's Lane South
Causeway End Road

Coble Green

19

Glandfield's Farm

2

Barnston Lodge

Absol Park

River Chelmer

B1417

3

River Chelmer

Parsonage Lane

Bennett's Lane

North End

Great Broadfields Farm

Brook Hill

18

4

Onslow Green

Black Chapel Lane

Camsix Farm

5

Hall Chase

Coppice Lane

Parkgate

A130

Lawn Hall

King's Farm

Well Chase

Ford End

Wallace Lane

168

Mill Lane

6

17

Church Lane

Sandon Hill

Back Lane

White Notley Road
Barns
Woods Road

Ford End CE Primary School

7

Oldpark Farm

Ringtail Green

A130

8

Blunts

216

Rolphy Green

Pleshey Road

9

Park Lane

Park Farm

Croft

H 65 **192** **J** 66 **K** **L** 67 **M** **193** 68 **N** **P**

1 grid square represents 500 metres

172

A   B   C   147   D   E   F   G

20   583   84   85

Storey's Wood

1

Gate   Road

2   Porter's Farm   Park Farm

Parkgate Farm   Leapingwells   Felix Hall

19

3   Ford Farm   Hollow   Road   Felix Place

LC   Cemetery   Church Street

4   Clark's Farm   Church Hall

Cranes   Crabb's Farm

18   Rivenhall CE Primary School

5   Junction 23   B1024   LONDON ROAD

171   PO   Ashman's Farm

St Mary's Close   Hoo Hall   Hole Farm

6   Rivenhall   Stovern's Hall   LC

17   Oak Road   Brickhouse Farm

7   Golf Course   Dunwards Hall

Henry Dixon Road   A12   River Blackwater

CM8   Foxmead Farm   Braxted Park Golf Club

8   Rivenhall Oaks Golf Club   The Drive   Rivenhall End

16   New Close   Braxted Park Road

Witham Cemetery   Hall Broad Farm   Golf Course

9   Junction 22   Braxted Park House

Walnut Drive   Works   Waterside Business Park

A   583   B   197   C   D   E   F   G

Coler Farm   84   85

1 grid square represents 500 metres

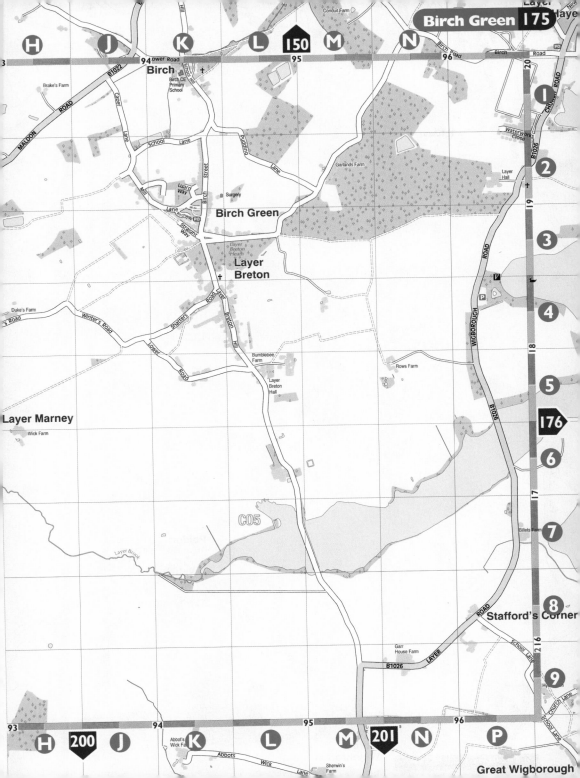

Layer
Haye

H   J   K   L   **150**   M   N

94   Lower Road   95   96   Birch Road   Birch   Road

Birch

B1022

Brake's Farm

Conduit Farm

Birch CE Primary School

MALDON ROAD

Caper Lane

School Lane

Mill Lane

Pudding Lane

Birch Street

Surgery

Luard Way

Birchway PO

Birch Green

Straight Way

Layer Breton

Layer Breton Heath

Garlands Farm

Layer Hall

Waterworks Close

CHURCH ROAD

B1026

1

2

Layer Hall

3

4

WIGBOROUGH ROAD

Layer Marney

Duke's Farm

's Road

Winter's Road

Lower Road

Shatters Road

Layer Breton Hill

Wick Farm

Bumblebee Farm

Layer Breton Hall

Rows Farm

5

176

6

20

19

18

17

B1026

7

Billets Farm

C05

Layer Brook

Garr House Farm

B1026

LAYER ROAD

Stafford's Corner

School Lane

216

8

9

Hy

Church Lane

93   **200**   94   95   96   **201**

H   **200**   J   K   L   M   **201**   N   P

Abbot's Wick Farm

Abbots   Wick   Lane

Sherwin's Farm

Great Wigborough

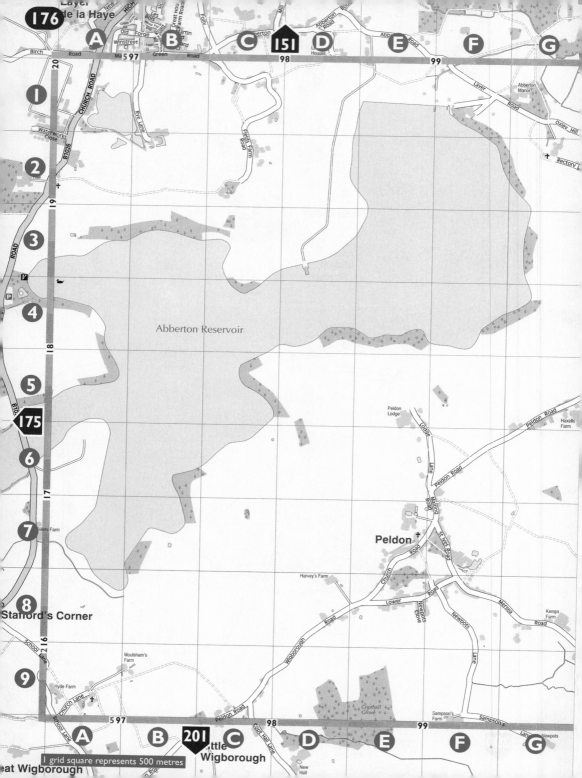

Layer de la Haye

A   B   C   151   D   E   F   G

1

2

3

4

Abberton Reservoir

5

175

6

7

Billets Farm

8

Stanford's Corner

9

Peldon Lodge

Haxells Farm

Peldon

Harvey's Farm

Kemps Farm

Moulsham's Farm

Hyde Farm

Copthall Grove

Sampson's Farm

New Hall

A   B   201   C   D   E   F   G

Little Wigborough

Great Wigborough

1 grid square represents 500 metres

FRINTON-ON-SEA

Holland

Frinton-on-Sea
Lawn Tennis Club

Frinton
Golf Club

Golf Course

Holland Gap

Sandy Point

Chevaux de
frise Point

Holland
Haven

158

H J K L M

21 22 23 24

H J K L M N P

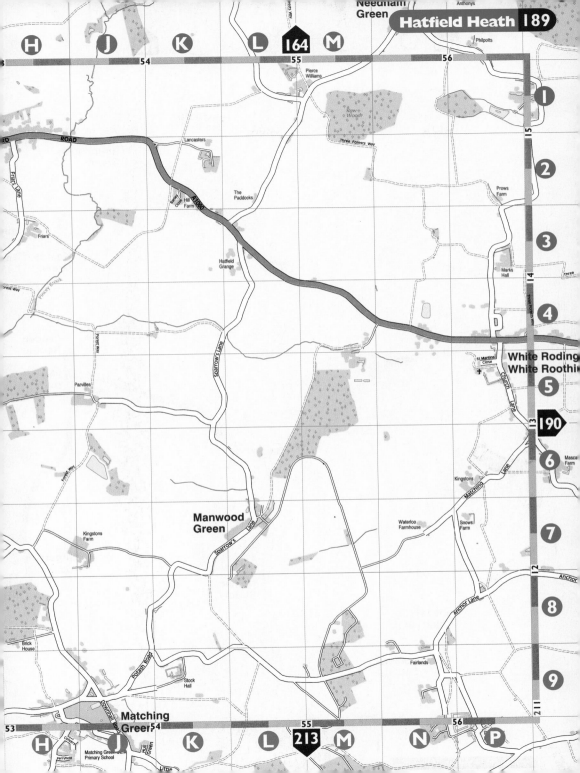

H J K L **166** M

Loves

Greens Farm

61 62 63

I

15

Hopkins

School Lane

Hill Farm

Biggs Close

The Street

2 Stage Cross

The Street

Haydens

The Street

✝ High Easter

Slough Road

3

14

Friar's Grange

River Can

Lower House

Essex Way

4

Lord's Wood

Lowerhouse Farm

Havron's Lane

Elbow

5

Crippings

Kingston

192

13

High Easter Road

Clatterford End

Armor

6

Mott's Green

Amadyes

Essex Way

Tye Green

The Hill

Gurtons Farm

Mill Road

Good Easter

7

12

Garnish Hall

School Road

✝ Souther Cross Road

Short's Farm

Essex Way

8

CHELMSFORD

Farmbridge End Road

The Colletts

ROAD

Marks Hall Lane

Four Wantz

Fouchers

River Can

Ladyland

Fortescues

9

211

Brick House

Blue House Farm

Fountain Road

Farmbridge End

60 61 62 63

A1060

H J K **215** L M N P

Bolding Hatch

SALT'S GREEN

Chalk End

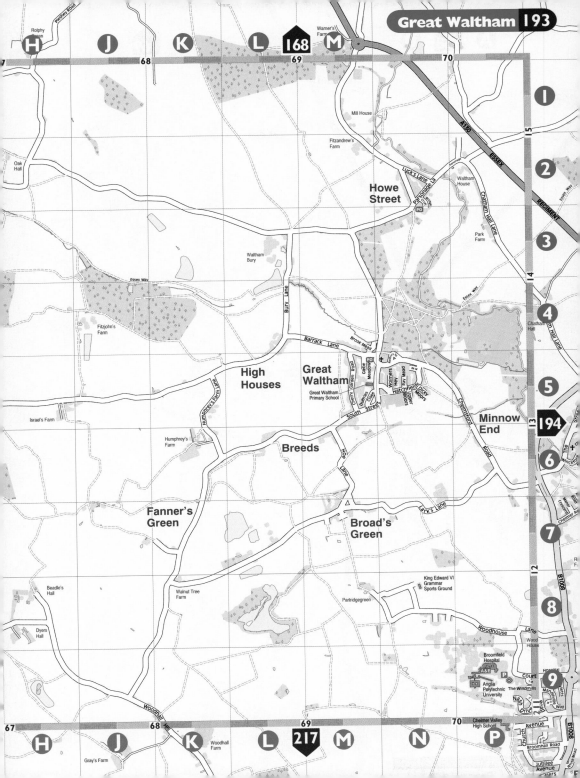

H   J   K   L   176   M

96   97   98

Farm

Hyde Farm

Copthall
Grove

Lower Moulsham's
Farm

Peldon Road

Little
Wigborough

New
Hall

1

Sherwin's
Farm

Great Wigborough

Chestnuts
Farm

Copt Hall Lane

15

Rowse's Farm

Peldon Road

2

D

Maldon Road   Maldon Road

Copt
Hall

Abbotts
Hall

3

14

Abbots Hall Saltings

4

Salcott Creek

Copthall
Saltings

Street

Quinces
Corner

Salcott Channel

5

13   202

Old Hall
Marshes

6

Old Hall
Farm

7

Joyces
Head

Pennyhole Fleet

12

8

Old Hall Lane

Old Hall Creek

Tollesbury
Fleet

9

North Channel

11

95   96   97   225   98

H   J   K   L   M   N   P

Carrington
Farm

Oyster
Business
Centre

Great Cob
Island

Thurstable

South Channel

B1026

A | 176 | B | C | D | E | 177 | F | G

599 | | Sampson's | Sampson's Lane | 600 | | 01 | Strood

1
New Hall

15

2

Ray Island Nature Reserve

Bonner's Saltings

3

14

Sampsons Creek

Strood Channel

Wellhouse Farm

4

Copthall Saltings

Feldy Marshes

COLCHESTER ROAD

B1025

EAST MERSEA ROAD

5

201

13

Little Ditch

Thorn Fleet

Mersea Fleet

WEST MERSEA

Dabchicks Sailing Club

6

7

Pennyhole Fleet

12

Cobmarsh Island

Besom Fleet

Mersea Quarters

8

Quarters Spit

9

211

North Channel

A | B | C | 226 | D | E | F | G

1 grid square represents 500 metres

204

A 178 B C D E 179 F G

East Essex
station Society
seum

1 I

Stone Point

15

Ivy House

North Barn

East Road

Shop Lane

My Lane

Nature
Reserve

Mersea
Stone

Coine
Way

New Way

2

East Road

Broman's
Farm

Broman's Lane

East Road

Fen Farm

P

Cudmore Grove
Country Park

3

14

4

Brightlingsea
Reach

5

203 13

6

7

12

8

9

2 11

6 06 07 08

A B C D E F G

1 grid square represents 500 metres

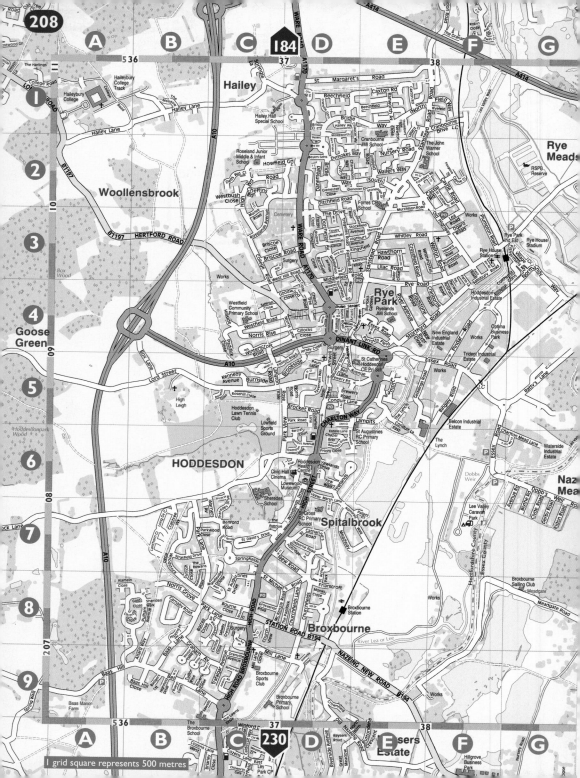

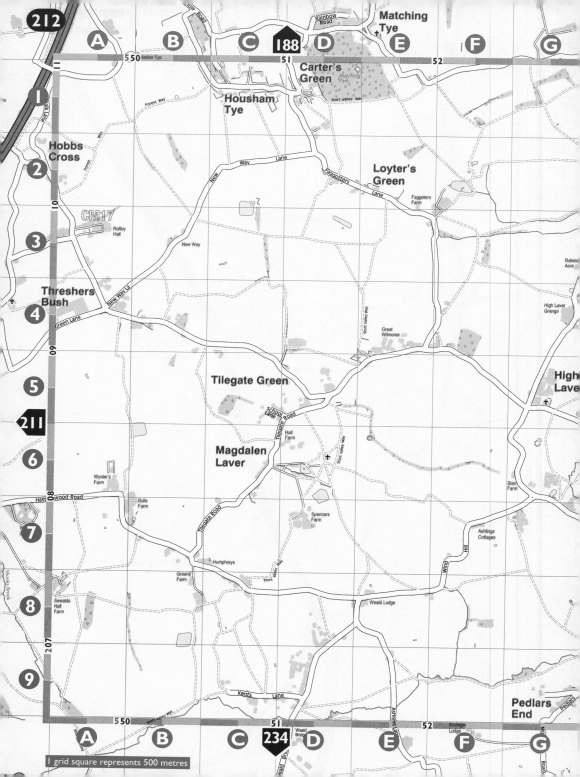

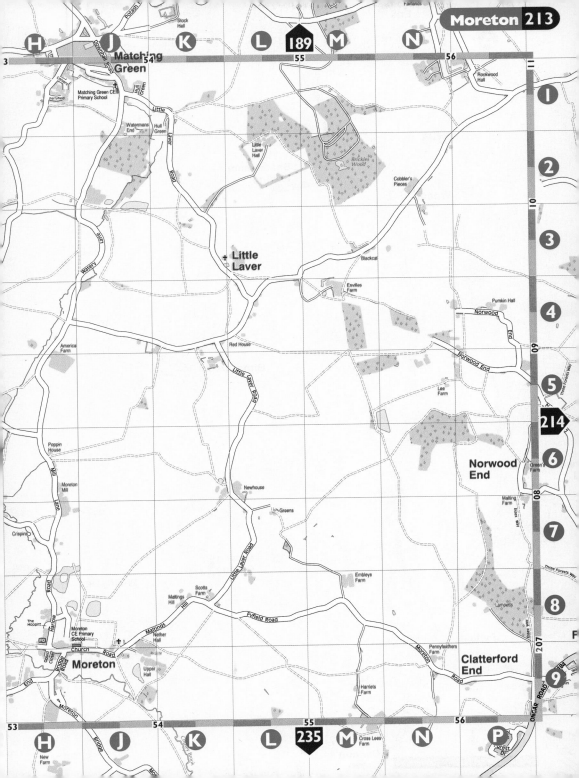

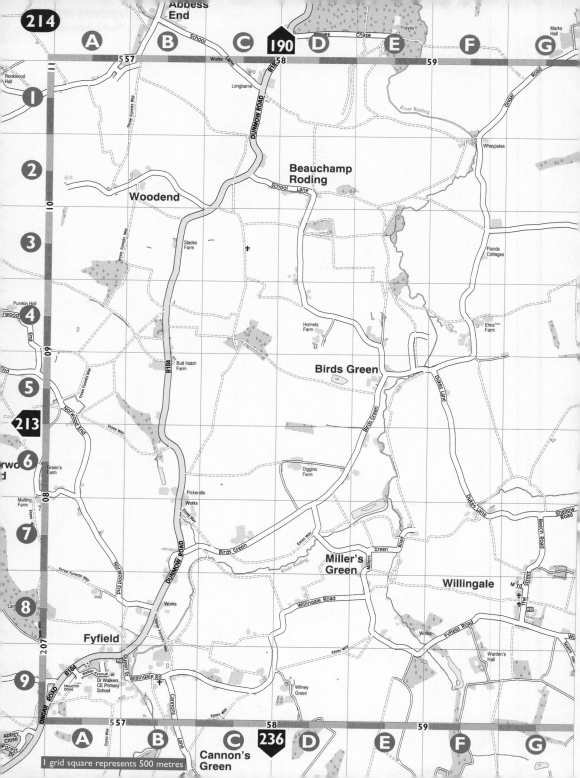

Abbess End

A B C 190 D E F G

557 School Lane Works Lane B184 58 59 Onger Road

Frayes Chase Marks Hall

1 Rookwood Hall Longbarns River Roding Whaypules

2 Woodend School Lane Beauchamp Roding

3 Slades Farm Flands Cottages

Three Forests Way B184 End 10 B184

Pumkin Hall

4 rwood Hornets Farm Elms Farm

5 Butt Hatch Farm Birds Green

Norwood End Essex Way Dukes Lane

6 Norwo d Green's Farm Diggins Farm Birds Green

Pickerells Works

7 Malting Farm Birds Green Green Road Snellow Road Beech Road

8 Lar Works Miller's Green Willingale M Yd Street

Fyfield Willingale Road Warden's Hall

Three Forests Way Norwood End DUNMOW ROAD Works Fyfield Road

9 B184 Houchin Drive Dr Walkers CE Primary School Witney Green Wo

ONGAR ROAD Walker Avenue Willingale Rd Essex Way

Abbey Close Forest Dr 207

A 557 B C 236 D E F G

Cannon's Green

I grid square represents 500 metres

199

H J K L M N

89 90 91

Park Wood Moor's Farm

Whitehorse Farm

Lane

School Road

Beckingham Street

Beckingham Business Park

Long's Farm

Little Renters Farm

M D'Arcy

Tolleshunt

Beckingham Hall

Tolleshunts Farm

I

Church Lane

Little Totham Hall

Church Road

Clarks Farm

Wash Lane

Little Totham Road

Rockleys Farm

2

10

B

3

Lane

Little London Farm

Falcons Hall Farm

Folly Faunts House

CM9

Higham Chase

Higham Farm

Joyce's Chase

4

60

Blind Lane

Wash

Chappel Farm

Maldon Agricultural Museum

Sorrel Cl

Pearl Tree Cl

Head Street

Church Street

Goldhanger

St Peters Cl

St Peter's

Oxford Chase

5

224

Rook Hall

Cobb's Farm

MALDON ROAD B1026

Fish Street

Thistley Cl

6

08

Gardener's Farm

Bound's Farm

7

Vaulty Manor

B1026 **GOLDHANGER** ROAD

Mill Beach

Osea Road

Hilly Pool Point

The Stumble

8

207

Decoy Point

9

River Blackwater

The Chase

Way Point

88 89 90 91

H J K L M N P CM9

CM9

245

Osea Farm

A B C D E F G

592 93 94

Gorwell
Hall

I

MALDON

ROAD

Brook House
Farm

White
House
Farm

B10

2

B1026

Prentice
Hall Farm

Hyde Farm

Joyce's

Chase

3

Paget's

Lane

Hall

Lane

Higham
Farm

Wycke
Farm

Prentice

4

60

Joyce's
Farm

Lauriston
Farm

5

Rolls
Farm

6

08

Gore
Saltings

Goldhanger Creek

Thirstlet Creek

7

8

Stumble

207

9

592 93 94

CM9 A B C D E F G

Osea
Farm

Osea
Island

East Point

1 grid square represents 500 metres

H J K L 201 M N

96 97 98

Tollesbury
Fleet

Old Hall Creek

North Channel

Great Cob
Island

1

South Channel

I

Carrington
Farm

North Road

Mallard Close
Comstat Close
Shamrock Close
Endeavour Close
Valerie Close
Thurstable Close

Thurstable Way

Thurstable
Road

Woodrolfe Creek

Oyster
Business
Centre

P

Woodrolfe
Road

Works

Tollesbury
Sailing Club

Woodrolfe
Park

Tollesbury
Wick Marshes

2

10

EST STREET

St John's
Street

Surgery

Elysian
Gdns

St John's Ct

Kents Farm

New Road

Station Road

The Chase

HIGH ST

Sceptre Cl

EAST STREET

Kents
Grass

Woodrolfe
Road

Orchard
Close

Crescent Rd

Kings
Wk

The Mount

Tollesbury
Primary School

Church Street

Tollesbury

Cemetery

Mell
Road

Mell

Gannet

Woodrolfe Farm
Lane

Bohuns
Hall

Mell Road

Old
Wharf

Wycke Lane

3

Mell Farm

4

09

Decoy
Farm

Mill Creek

5

226

6

Mill
Point

08

7

8

207

River   Blackwater

9

95 96 97 98

H J K L 247 M N P

The
Stone

226

A   B   C   202   D   E   F   G

599   600   01

1   North

Great Cob
Island

South Channel

Shinglehead
Point

2   10

3

River Blackwater

4   09

5   Bradwell
Nuclear Power
Station

225

6   08

Pewet Island

7   Bradwell Quay
Yacht Club

Bradwell Creek   **Bradwell
Waterside**

Works

Down
Hall

Eastend Road   East Hall

8   207   Westwick
Farm   Trusses Road

Woodyards   **East End**   Eastend Road

Brett Dudley Dr.

Hockley Lane Close

WATERSIDE ROAD   High Street   Kingswood Court   Eastend Road

9   St Cedds CE
VA Primary School   Hockley Close

Bradwell-on-Sea   Hockley

Bradwell
Lodge

B1021   Bacons Chase
Maldon Road   Bacons

A   599   B   C   600   248   D   E   F   G

Delameres

1 grid square represents 500 metres

H J K L 203 M

03 04 05

11

1

2

10

3

4

09

5

6

08

7

8

207

9

Sales Point

Tip Head

East Hall Farm

Eastlands

Eastend Road

St Peter's Way

Munkins Farm

St Peter's Way

02 03 04 05

H J K L 249 M N P

Bradwell

St Peter's Way

H J K L **211** M N

I

Rundells

Horseshoes Farm

Canes Farm

Canes Lane

LANE

CANES

Little Weald Hall

North Weald Golf Club

2

Crupsey Brook

Rye Hill Road

Esgors

Vicarage

3

LONDON

HIGH ROAD

Orchard Farm

Upland Road

West Pl

Upper Clapton RFC

Blake Hall

Weald Hall Lane

Weald Hall Lane

Weald Hall

Merlin Way

Church Lane

Rayley Lane

4

Thornwood Common

Carpenters

Kyme Lane

Industrial Estate

Rowley

Duck Lane

North Weald Airfield

The Limes Medical Centre

5

NORTH WEALD BASSETT

Lancaster Road

234

HIGH ROAD

B1393

Woodside

Woodside

ROAD

FOREST

Merlin Way

Blenheim Way

York Road

B181

Hampden Cl

6

Roughtalys

The Lower Forest

Silver Birch Rd

Pike Way

Hawks Cl

Park

Kiln Road

Tempest

North Weald Station

Wintry Park Farm

EPPING

ROAD

Roughtalleys Wood

7

THORNWOOD ROAD

Coopersale

Woodlands

B181

Franning

Barnfield

Woodberry Down

Bergen Ct

The Plain

Winch View

The Limes Medical Centre

Institute

Vicarage

Garnon Mead

Cheyen Close

Birchfield Rd

Institute Rd

Gernon Bushes

Essex Way

M11

8

Works

PO

Works

St Margarets Hospital

PALMERS HILL

Troy's Ct

Granville Rd

Fairfield Road

Works

Coopersale & Theydon Garnon CE Sch

Coopersale Common

9

Barnfield

Council Building

Surgery

Police Station

Epping Ongar Railway

CM16

Theydon Gr

Wedgewood

STREET

EPPING

Stonards

Hill

Hoblions

202

46 47 L **255** M N P

H J K

Gaynes Park

Mount Farm

Coopersale

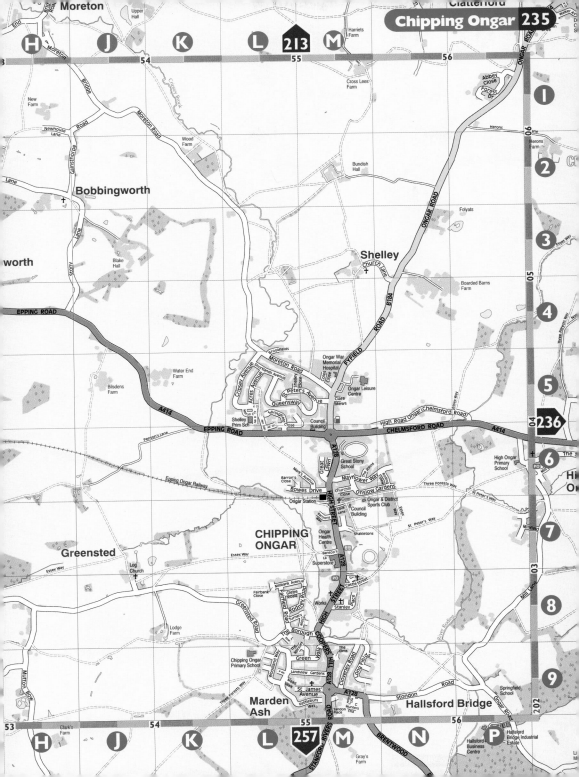

Pigstye Green

Radley Green

Norton Heath

Cooksmill Green

Elkins Green

Grid references across top: H, J, K, L, 223, M, N
Grid references down right side: 1, 2, 3, 4, 5, 246, 6, 7, 8, 9
Grid references across bottom: H, J, K, L, 267, M, N, P

Labels visible on map:

- Point
- Chase
- River Blackwater
- West Point
- CM9
- Osea Farm
- CM9
- Southey Creek
- Mundon Stone Point
- Coopers Creek
- Illney Farm
- New Hall Lane
- Lawling Creek
- Mayland Creek
- Brookmead Farm
- St Peter's Way
- Brick House Farm
- Mundon Creek
- Harlow Sailing Club
- Nipsells Chase
- Marina
- North Drive
- Nipsells Farm
- The Esplanade
- Promenade
- Maylandsea Medical Cen
- St Peter's Way
- Derby Cl
- Orchard Road
- Imperial
- West Avenue
- Surgery
- Bramley Way
- Wembley Avenue
- Katonia Av
- Princes Avenue
- The Drive
- Industrial Estate
- **Maylandsea**
- St Peter's Way
- Lawling Mdl

Grid coordinate numbers: 88, 89, 90, 91, 02, 03, 04, 05, 06

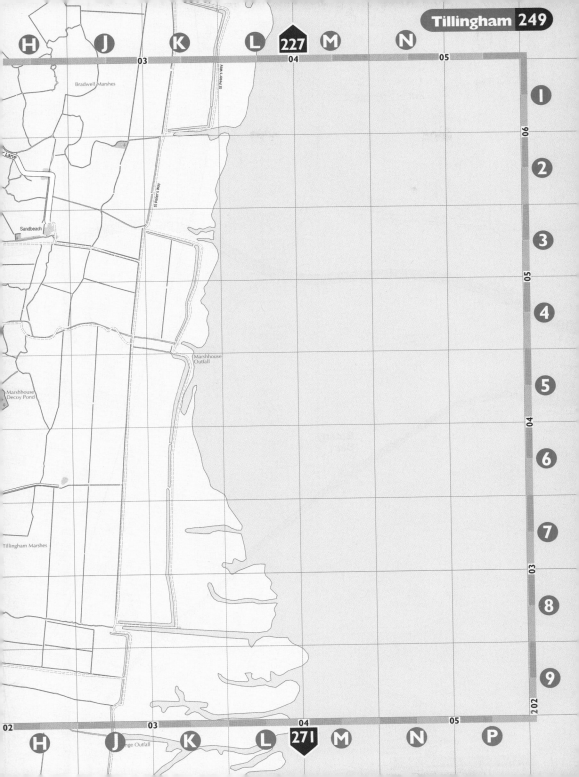

Northaw
250

A B C 228 D E F G

NORTHAW
Park Farm
ROAD WEST B156
5 29
30
31

Colesdale Farm
Colesdale

Kingsmead
South Drive
Theobald
Merchant's Drive
Cuffley Primary School

1

Chain Walk
Burnt Farm
Burntfarm Ride

2

Barvin Park
Woodside Ave
Close
Drive

Cattlegate Farm

M25
The Paddocks

3

Hertfordshire County
Enfield
5 opers Lane Road

Cattlegate Road

Glasgow Stud

Crewsbarn Ride

4

Holly Hill Farm

Crews Hill Station
Crews Hill
Crews Hill Golf Club

Crev

5

th Lodge rm

A1005
THE RIDGEWAY

Beech Avenue
Cypress Avenue
Rosewood Drive
Wrotham Gardens
The Whitewebbs Museum of Transport & Industry

Botany Bay

Lodge Lane
East
Botany Bay Cricket Club

Golf Course
Chain Walk

St Johns CE Primary School
Stravield Road

EN2

6

7

London Loop

A1005
THE RIDGEWAY

London Loop

8

Park Farm
Hadley Road

Royal Chace Hotel
Oak Avenue
High
Oaks

The Kings Oak Private Hospital
Chase Farm Hospital

Sketty Court
P

Cemetery
Conredge
Close

9

London Loop

Ridge Crest

THE RIDGEWAY
Hadley Road

Farorna Walk
Hardy Way
Fairview Road

Lavender Hill
Bramart Way
A1005

Go Holts ta

Hortwhite's

School
Farnan
Audrey Road
Cavell Drive
The Grove

Enfield Hotel
Audley

A1005
Chase Green

London Loop

5 29
30
272
31

A B C 272 D E F G

Middlesex University (Trent Park Campus)

1 grid square represents 500 metres

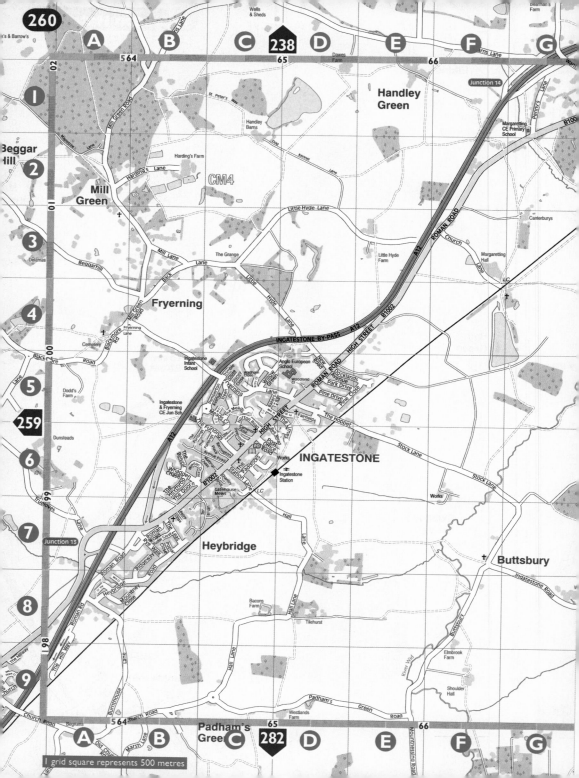

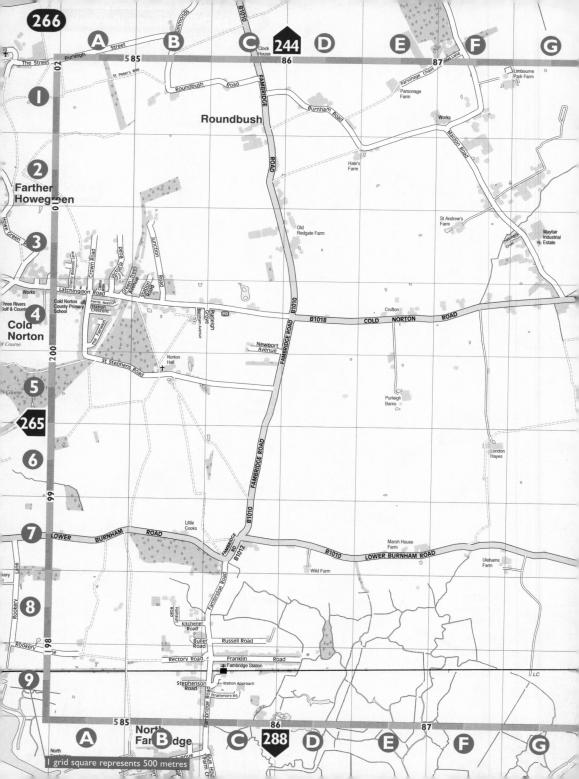

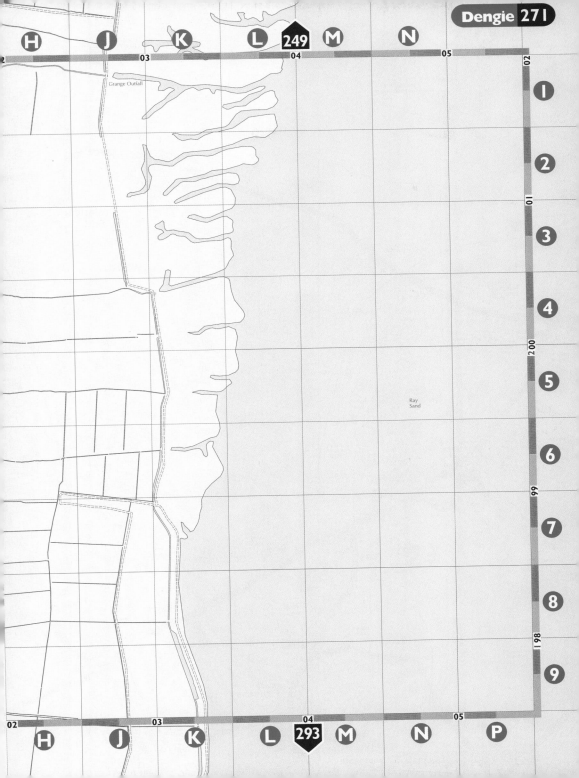

Grange Outfall

Ray
Sand

H J K L **269** M

96 97 98

Stoneyhills

Newman's Farm

Brook Farm

Twizzlefoot Bridge

West Wick

Marsh Road

Marsh Road

Dammer Wick

Glendale School

Primary School

the Leas

Eastern Road

BURNHAM-ON-CROUCH

Burnham on Crouch Primary School

Arcadia Road

Essex Road

Wick Road

Burnham Wick

Orchard Road

Ramblers Way

Argyle Road

HIGH STREET

Royal Burnham Yacht Club

Belvedere Road

Royal Corinthian Yacht Club

Redward

River Crouch

Ringwood Bar

292

Branklfeet

Wallasea Island

H J K L **311** M N P

95 96 97 98

I
2
3
4
5
6
7
8
9

97
96
95
94
93

H J K L **271** M N

03 04 05

I

97

2

3

96

4

Foulness
Point

5

95

6

7

94

8

9

193

Holliwell Point

Great Shell
Corner

East Newlands

Courtsend

The Chase

New
House Farm

Fishermans
Head

02 03 04 05

H J K L **313** M N P

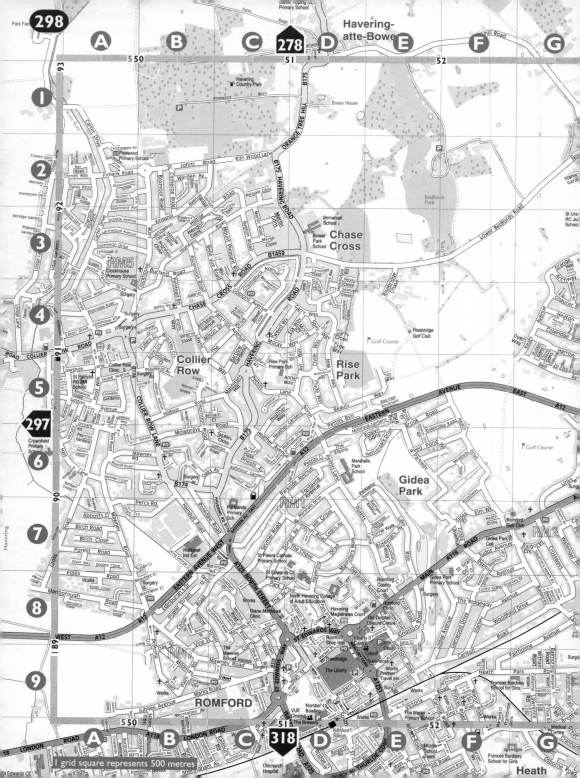

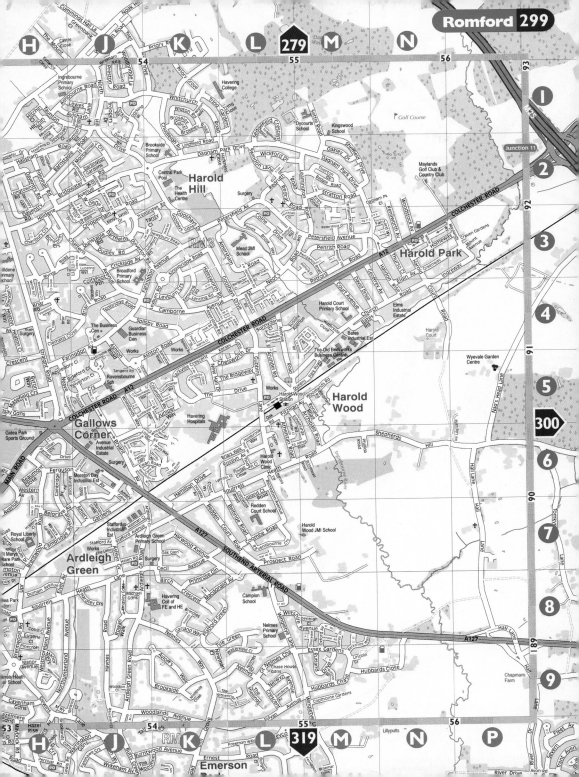

281

321

302

H J K L M N

Ingrave

Herongate

Little Warley

Childerditch

West Hon on

CM13

Thorndon Park

Thorndon Country Park

Thorndon Park Golf Club

BRENTWOOD ROAD

A128

Brentwood Road

SOUTHEND ARTERIAL ROAD   A127

A127

TILBURY ROAD

Common Road

Middle Road

Childerditch Lane

The Avenue

Hartswood Road

Billericay Road

Hartswood Golf Club

Brentwood RFC

Golf Course

Halfway House

Travelodge

Ingrave Johnstone CE Primary School

West Horndon Primary School

Childerditch Industrial Park

Kelrose Swimming Pool Centre

Hatch Farm

Heron Hall

Park House

Cockerhall Farm Industrial Estate

Roses Farm

Magple La

Rectory Chase

Little Warley Lodge

Home Farm Road

60 61 62 63

I 1 2 3 4 5 6 7 8 9

H J K L M N P

H   J   K   L   289   M   N

89   90   91   93

Scott's Hall

1

Apton Hall Farm

Ballards Gore Golf Club

Golf Course

Ballards Gore

Apton Hall Road   Apton Hall Road   Gore Road   Paglesham   Road

Biggins Farm

92

SS4

2

Little Stambridge Hall

Stewards Elm Farm

3

Wheatfields

PO

Cagefield Road

Stewards Elm Farm Lane   4m

Brick House

Great Stambridge

Ragstone Lodge

Hampton Barns

Roach Valley Way   Barton Hall

4

Little Stambridge Road

91

Lingfield Drive

Coombes Grove

Rochford Swimming Pool

Winters

Stambridge Primary School

Great Stambridge Hall

Waldens

River Roach

5

ROCHFORD

Rochford Adult Community College

Stambridge Road

Mill Lane

Broomhills

310

6

Walton

Purdeys Industrial Estate

Works

Rochehall Way

Roach Valley Way

River Roach

90

7

Muck Hall

Purdeys WY

Purdeys Industrial Est

Fleet Hall

8

Sutton Bridge Farm

Crowstone Preparatory School

Butler's Farm

Sutton Road

Shopland Road

Sutton Hall

189

New Hall

9

Stone House Farm

Stonebridge

8   89   90   91

Temple Farm

H   J   K   L   329   M   N   P

SS2

Council Building

Smither's Chase   Smither's Farm

Shopland Hall

Beauchamps   Road

Essex County

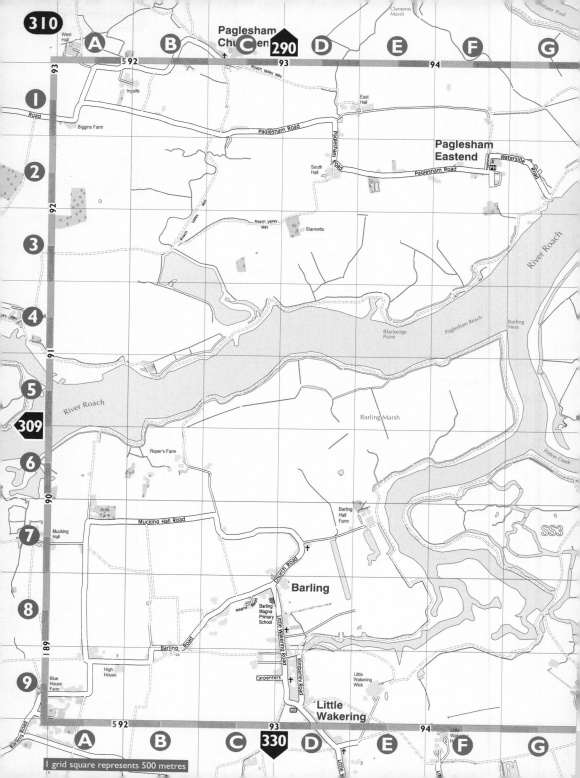

H J K L 291 M N

96 97 98 93

1

2

River Roach Quay Reach 92

Horseshoe Corner

3

Potton Point

4

91

5

312

Potton Island The Middleway Shelford Creek 6

90

7

New England Island

New England Creek 189

Fleet Head

8

Havengore Island

Rushley Island 9

95 96 97 98

H J K L 331 M N P

Oxenham Farm

312

A B C **292** D E F G

Monkton
Barn

†

I

599 600 01

PB

Churchend

93

2

Reach

Foulness Island

Priestwood

92

East Wick

Horseshoe
Corner

Rugwood Farm

3

4

Great
Burwood Farm

91

Rugwood Head

5

311

6

Asplins
Head

90

7

Shefford
Head

8

89

9

A B C D E F G

Head 599 600 01

1 grid square represents 500 metres

Lodge Farm

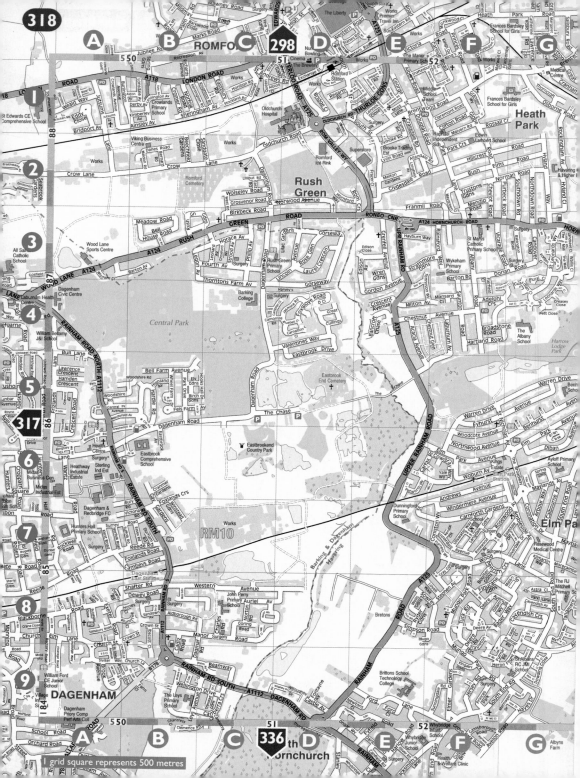

A B C 300 D E F G

I

557 58 59

Junction 29

River Drive

River Dr

Bird Lane

A127

SOUTHEND ARTERIAL ROAD

Folkes Farm

Codham Hall

SOUTHEND

WARLEY ROAD

A127

Great Warley Hall

Church Lane

B186

Fleet Av

Fleet Ct

Drive

Severn

Trent Avenue

Forth Rd

Stour Wy

Pentire

Front Lane

Dee La

Isis Dr

Griffin Av

Lexington Wy

Roseberry Ct

Engayne Primary School

Queens Gdns

Macon Wy

Moor Lane

Rosebery Gdns

Humber Dr

Avon

Chelmer Rd

Marley Av

Kennet

The Leas

Clyde Crescent

Waycross Rd

Brunswick Av

Fairholme Gdns

The Cobbles

Acacia Gdns

Laburnham Gdns

Limerick Gdns

Upminster Trading Park

2 Mase... Russin Av

Spenser...

Tithe Barn Museum

Upminster Golf Club

Esdaile Gdns

The Fairway

Holden

Ingrebourne

Brockmans cl

Surgery

Kings Gardens

Park Av

Kerry Gdns

Kerry Drive

Essex County Havering

Essex County Havering

Franks Farm

WARLEY STREET

3 Claremont Gdns

Avenue

Eversleigh

Gardens

Gardens

Willow Wk

Peterborough Av

Westbury Farm

Puddle Dock

Works

Works

Devncourt Gardens

Upminster Station

UPMINSTER

B187

4 New Pl Gardens

Rectory Gdns

Front Lane

St Albans

Chester Av

Worcester Av

Winchester Av

Canterbury

Lichfield Terrace

Boyd Sch

B187

ST MARY'S LANE

B186

B187

Works

Cedar Gdns

Derham Gardens

Argyle Gardens

Coopers Company & Coburn School

Eaton Road

Westbury Terrace

Ashvale Gdns

James Oglethorpe Primary School

The Chase

Pike Lane

Clay Tye

Clay Tye Farm

5 Gardens

Ashleigh Gdns

319

Drive

Cranham Hall

Broadfields Farm

6 Park

Avenue

Brackenden...

Gaynes School

Hobbs Hole

Cranham Place

White Post Farm

RM14

7 The Q...

Upminster Cemetery

South Essex Crematorium

B1421

Pike Lane

OCKENDON ROAD

B1421

North Ockendon

Church La

Church Lane School

B186

OCKENDON ROAD

Fen Lane

Top Meadow Golf Club

8 Sunnings Lane

Stubbers Lane

Manor Farm

Pea Lane

OCKENDON ROAD

NORTH ROAD

9 Bramble Farm

Sunnings Lane

Dennises Lane

Stubbers (Outdoor Pursuits Centre)

Pea Lane

M25

Dennises La

Havering Thurrock

557 Dennises 58 59

A B C **338** D E F G

85 84 86 87 88

I grid square represents 500 metres

H J K L **301** M N

West Horndon

West Horndon Primary School

Cadogan Avenue

Station Road

PO

Dunmow Gdns

Freshwell Gdns

I

Horndon Industrial Park

Works

West Horndon Station

St Mary's Lane

88 BURY ROAD

2

Brentwood

St Mary's Lane

3

Monks Farm

Old Englands Farm

Field House

Tillingham Hall

87

4

Peartree La

Bury Farm

Dummies Lane

Slose

5

Thurrock Havering

Fen La

86 322

6

Blankets Farm

Hatch Farm

Home Farm

Fen Lane

Corner Farm

Golf Course

Havering Thurrock

Fen Farm

Fen Lane

Mar Dyke

Stone Hall

Horndon Rd

The Elms Farm

7

85

8

9

84

60 61 62 63

H J K L **339** M N P

Rushley
Island

H   J   K   L   311   M

96   97   98

Oxenham
Farm

Bridge Road

Havengore
Head

Samuel's
Corner

Stairs Rd
Stairz Road

Haven
Point

New   Road

Glebe
Close

Beach Court

Broomways

LC   Morrin's
Chase

Wakering
Stairs

Mariners Court

Seaview

Drive

Estuary
Gardens

Goldsworthy
Drive

Victoria Drive

Cupids
Chase

LC   Cherootee Chase

Black
Grounds

Suttons

LC

Butts Rd

Essex County
Southend-on-Sea

Pigs
Bay

88

87

86

85

184

H   J   K   L   M   N   P

96   97   98

H J K L 325 M N

75   76   77

Northwick

Works

Northwick Road

Roscommon Way

CANVEY R 84
St Marks Road
A130
Holland
Vil
Dt

1

St Marks Road
Mulberry Rd

Markets Service Road
Kings Road

Charfleet
Industrial
Estate
Runwood Road
Charfleet Rd

2

Charfleet
Ind Estate

International
Business Park
Business
Centre

Kings Road

Furlmen
Industrial
Park

Ormsby
Road
Clifton
Road

83

Haven Road

3

Holehaven Creek

Lower
Horse

Shellhaven Point

4

82

Oil Refinery

Coryton

Hole
Haven

Shell
Haven

Coryton
Wharves

5

344

6

Thames
Haven

81

Thurrock
Medway Towns

Sea
Reach

River Thames

7

80

Blythe
Sands

8

9

74   75   76   77

H J K L M N P

Canvey Point

Chapman Sands

Castlepoint Museum
Prout Industrial Estate
Silverpoint Marine

Leigh Middle

Leigh Beck

Leigh Beck Primary School

B1014

POINT ROAD

Approach Rd

Canvey Island FC

Marine Parade

Point Road

Bommel Av

Brevland Road

River Thames

337

348

Purfleet

RM19

A1306 ARTERIAL ROAD PURFLEET

Channel Tunnel Rail Link under construction

Purfleet By-Pass

LONDON ROAD PURFLE

Beacon Hill
Industrial Estate
Wingrove
drive
Beacon Hill
Linnet Way
Oakhill Rd

Purfleet
Station

Mill Hotel

Premier
Travel Inn

Purfleet
Primary School

Tank Lane

Water
Surgery Lane

Council
Building

Marine
Court

Milehams
Industrial
Estate

Fanns Farm

Mar Dyke

LONDON ROAD

A1306

TANK HILL ROAD

A1090

River Thames

Crayford Ness

Long Reach

Dartford Marshes

Darent Valley Path

Cherry Tree Road

Landau Way

Darent Industrial Park

Dartford Drive

Nordale Crescent

Ness Road

Burner Road

Works

Joyce Green Lane

Crayford Marshes

Kent County
Bexley

Works

Littlebrook
Business Centre

Stones
Marshes

Camp
Mead

A206 UNIVERSITY WAY

University Way

Joyce Green Lane

McCudden Rd

Cornwall Rd

Grove

Barnwell Rd

Strickland

Cemetery

Wodehouse Road

Chaucer Wy

Hardy Dr

Wordsworth Way

Henderson
Drive

Marsh Street

Marsh Street

A282

Mary Rose Cl

CROSSWAYS BOULEVARD

A206

Masthead
Close

Express on
Holiday Inn

Amen

A282

DA1

Sandpit Road

Swan
Business Park

Millside
Industrial Estate

Burnham
Trading Estate

Temple Hill

Riverside
Industrial
Estate

Priory

Lawson Rd

Holy Trinity
CE Prim Sch

Victoria Industrial
Park

Business
Centre

Welcome Av

Hall Road

Spearman Road

Temwick Drive

Darent Valley Path

Edmunds Rd

Keyes

Shakespeare Rd

Coleridge Rd

Sheridan

Farnol Rd

Wellcrest

Primary
School

Hilltop

Lansbury Av

Kingsley Av

Junction 1a

Cotton

DA1

VICT

A226

Abberton 177 H2
Abbess End 190 B9
Abbess Roding 190 A8
Abbey Field 151 P1
Abridge 277 J3
Acton 47 N5
Acton Place 47 K3
Aimes Green 231 J7
Aingers Green 155 K9
Akenham 22 C6
Aldborough Hatch 296 F8
Aldersbrook 315 M3
Aldham 125 N7
Allen's Green 161 L7
Alphamstone 75 J6
Alresford 153 P6
Althorne 267 P7
Anstey 86 C2
Ardleigh 104 C9
Ardleigh Green 299 H7
Ardleigh Heath 104 F7
Ardley End 188 G3
Arkesden 63 P7
Armigers 116 D1
Ashdon 42 E6
Asheldham 269 N2
Ashen 57 K1
Ashingdon 288 E9
Audley End 65 J1
Audley End 71 J4
Aveley 338 A7
Aythorpe Roding 190 E1
Bacon End 165 M5
Baconend Green 165 M1
Baddow Park 242 C2
Baker Street 340 A6
Ballards Core 309 N1
Ballingdon 60 C4
Balls Green 154 F1
Bamber's Green 140 A3
Bannister Green 143 L9
Bardfield End Green 92 D6
Bardfield Saling 119 H6
Barham 22 F1
Barking 296 C7
Barkingside 296 C7
Barleycroft End 112 A3
Barling 310 D8
Barnehurst 346 C8
Barnes Cray 346 D8
Barnston 166 E1
Barstable 304 C9
Bartholomew Green 144 B7
Bartlow 38 F4
Basildon 2 C4
Bath Side 14 E3
Battlesbridge 286 A6
Baythorne End 42 F9
Beacon End 126 C9
Beacon Hill 198 C6
Beauchamp Roding 177 D2
Beaumont 133 J8
Beazley End 120 F1
Beckton 334 A6
Becontree 317 L7
Bedlar's Green 138 D9
Beggar Hill 259 P2
Belchamp Otten 59 H2
Belchamp St Paul 58 E1
Belchamp Walter 59 M4
Bell Common 254 E2
Belstead 29 L5
Belvedere 346 A3
Bentfield Bury 113 N7
Bentfield Green 113 P7
Bentley 81 P2
Bentley 280 B2
Berden 88 B4
Berechurch 151 P5
Berners Roding 215 H3
Bicknacre 242 C8
Biggin 350 D4
Billericay 283 K5
Birch 175 K1
Birchanger 138 B4
Birch Green 175 K3
Birchhall Corner 104 D6
Birdbrook 56 B5
Bird Green 63 H9
Birds Green 214 D5
Bishops Green 166 D5
Bishop's Stortford 137 H7
Blackheath 152 C6
Blackmore 259 J1
Blackmore End 95 N6
Black Notley 145 L9
Blacksmith's Corner 29 L4
Blackwall 332 C7
Blake End 143 M4
Blasford Hill 194 A9
Bobbingworth 235 J2
Bocking 145 J2
Bocking Churchstreet 121 J7
Bocking's Elm 181 K8
Boreham 219 K3
Borley 46 C8
Borley Green 46 A9
Botany Bay 250 C6
Bournes Green 330 A4
Bovinger 234 E5
Bow 332 D2
Bow Common 332 D5
Bowers Gifford 325 K1
Boxted 103 J1
Boxted 103 K4
Boxted Cross 103 L3
Boyton Cross 216 C4
Boyton End 42 E6
Boyton End 92 C3
Bradfield 107 L8
Bradfield Heath 107 J8
Bradwell 146 E4
Bradwell-on-Sea 226 E9
Bradwell Waterside 226 C7
Braintree 145 J3

Braiswick 127 L5
Bramford 24 B1
Brandy Hole 287 K4
Bran End 118 B7
Brantham 47 N8
Brays Grove 211 H4
Breeds 193 L6
Brent Pelham 86 C6
Brentwood 280 E8
Brewer's End 139 J8
Brick End 115 P6
Brick House End 112 G2
Brickkiln Green 95 M4
Bridge End 93 P5
Bridge Green 63 L3
Brightlingsea 179 J5
Brightwell 27 P8
Brimsdown 274 B1
Broad Green 48 E7
Broad Green 148 D3
Broadley Common 209 N8
Broad's Green 193 M7
Broad Street Green 222 D3
Brock Hill 284 G3
Broke Hall 24 F3
Bromley 332 E3
Bromley Cross 130 B3
Brook Street 300 B1
Broomfield 218 A1
Broxbourne 208 D8
Broxted 116 A5
Brundon 60 F1
Buckhurst Hill 275 M9
Bucklesham 32 F2
Building End 62 D2
Bulls Cross 251 M6
Bulmer 60 C5
Bulmer Tye 60 D7
Bulphan 322 A5
Bumble's Green 221 K3
Bures 76 A9
Bures Green 76 B6
Burnham-on-Crouch 291 J3
Burnt Heath 130 A2
Burnt Mills 305 H5
Burrsville Park 182 B6
Burton End 138 F2
Burton Green 123 J5
Bury Green 136 D7
Bury Green 251 N1
Bush End 164 B1
Bush Hill Park 273 K5
Buttsbury 260 F7
Butt's Green 241 L7
Calford Green 42 A4
California 26 A5
Cambridge Town 330 B8
Campions 187 N7
Camps End 53 M1
Canary Wharf 332 D8
Canewdon 289 L6
Canfield End 140 C7
Canning Town 333 L5
Cannon's Green 236 C1
Canvey Island 344 B3
Capel St Mary 28 B8
Cardinal's Green 39 N1
Carter's Green 212 D1
Castle Camps 40 B8
Castle Green 335 K1
Castle Hedingham 72 D5
Castle Hill 23 H9
Catmere End 50 B6
Cattawade 106 C1
Causeway End 167 N1
Cavendish 45 J1
Chadwell Heath 297 L9
Chadwell St Mary 350 A1
Chafford Hundred 349 H1
Chalk End 215 P1
Chalkwell 328 B6
Chalvedon 304 F9
Chantry 24 F8
Chapel End 115 M9
Chapel Row 264 D4
Chappel 104 H5
Chase Cross 298 C5
Chatham Green 194 C1
Chatter End 112 G8
Chattisham 28 C1
Cheapside 206 A1
Chelmer Village 218 G8
Chelmondiston 84 E2
Chelmsford 5 J5
Cherry Green 91 H8
Cheshunt 229 N9
Chickney 116 A3
Chignall St James 216 C3
Chignal Smealy 192 C9
Chigwell 276 C8
Chigwell Row 277 J8
Childerditch 301 J8
Chilton 21 K3
Chilton Street 43 N1
Chingford 274 C7
Chingford Green 274 F7
Chingford Hatch 295 H1
Chipping Hill 197 H1
Chipping Ongar 235 L7
Chitts Hills 126 C7
Chrishall 48 C7
Church End 52 E3
Church End 85 L4
Church End 116 B1
Church End 120 B2
Church End 136 C4
Church End 141 M3
Churchend 312 D1
Churchgate 229 N8
Churchgate Street 187 N9
Church Langley 211 L3
Church Street 44 C8
Clacton-on-Sea 72 L1
Clapgate 112 B9
Clapton Park 314 C6

Clare 44 B5
Clatterford End 191 L5
Clatterford End 213 P9
Clatterford End 234 C9
Claverhambury 231 L6
Clavering 88 B5
Claydon 22 D5
Clayhall 296 A6
Clay Hill 251 H7
Clifftown 18 D6
Coalhill 285 K1
Cobbs Fenn 96 C1
Cobler's Green 168 A2
Cock Clarks 243 J8
Cock Green 168 D1
Coggeshall 147 M4
Coggeshall Hamlet 147 P6
Colchester 8 A5
Coldharbour 346 F2
Cold Norton 265 P4
Cole End 66 C5
Coles Green 28 D2
Collier Row 298 B5
Colliers Hatch 234 B9
Colne Engaine 99 H7
The Commons 22 A5
Cook's Green 182 C3
Cooksmill Green 238 A1
Coopersale Common 253 L8
Coopersale Street 253 K5
Cooper's End 63 K4
Copdock 29 H5
Copford 150 A2
Copford Green 149 P4
Coppall Green 253 N5
Corbets Tey 319 N7
Cornard Tye 61 P5
Cornish Hall End 69 L4
Corringham 341 P1
Coryton 343 H4
Countess Cross 99 J6
Courtsend 293 J8
Coxtie Green 280 A4
Crabbs Green 112 C1
Cradle End 136 E6
Craig's End 70 D2
Cranbrook 316 B2
Cranham 320 B2
Crawley End 48 G5
Crays Hill 304 C2
Creekmouth 334 F5
Creeksea 290 D5
Cressing 146 A8
Crews Hill 250 C5
Cripple Corner 74 D7
Crockleford Heath 129 K5
Crockleford Hill 129 H6
Cross End 74 F9
Crow Green 280 D2
Crow's Green 119 K7
Cuckoo Tye 47 K5
Cuffley 228 E7
Curling Tye Green 221 K8
Curtismill Green 278 E2
Custom House 333 P7
Cutlers Green 91 H6
Dagenham 318 A9
Danbury 242 A3
Danbury Common 242 B5
Daw's Cross 99 P2
Deal Marsh 326 C1
Debden 91 L1
Debden Green 91 J5
Debden Green 254 D8
Dedham 104 F1
Dedham Heath 105 H4
Deer's Green 87 N1
Delvin End 71 N6
Dengie 270 B1
Dewes Green 87 N7
Doddinghurst 258 E2
Dorking Tye 76 C5
Dovercourt 14 D7
Downham 284 D4
Dry Street 323 N4
Duck End 94 B1
Duck End 118 C6
Duck End 138 B5
Duckend Green 144 B3
Duddenhoe End 63 K3
Dutch Village 344 A1
Duton Hill 116 F5
Earls Colne 99 K3
East Bergholt 80 F5
East End 81 N7
East End 112 D3
East End 209 P2
East End 226 E8
East Gores 148 F2
East Ham 333 P2
East Hanningfield 263 P2
East Horndon 302 A8
Easthorpe 149 N7
East Mersea 203 N3
East Tilbury 351 J2
Eastwick 186 C8
Eastwood 327 P1
Edney Common 238 D5
Eight Ash Green 126 E7
Elder Street 88 D6
Elkins Green 259 J1
Elmdon 49 K6
Elm Park 318 C7
Elmstead 129 P7
Elmstead Heath 155 P4
Elmstead Market 150 A9
Elmstead Row 154 A6
Elsenham 114 E5
Emerson Park 319 K1
Enfield 273 H3
Enfield Highway 273 P1
Enfield Lock 252 C7
Enfield Town 273 J2
Enfield Wash 252 B8
Epping 233 H9

Epping Green 228 C1
Epping Green 232 B3
Epping Upland 232 D7
Erith 346 E3
Erwarton 84 C7
Eversley 304 G8
Fair Cross 316 G7
Fairlop 296 F5
Fairstead 170 C7
Falkenham 32 G2
Fanner's Green 193 J7
Farmbridge End 191 M9
Farnham 113 H9
Farnham Green 112 G8
Farther Howegreen 265 P2
Faulkbourne 171 J6
Feering 173 H2
Felixstowe 11 J4
Felmore 304 F7
Felsted 142 G9
Fiddlers Hamlet 255 K2
Finchingfield 94 B8
Fingringhoe 153 H9
Flack's Green 195 N2
Flamstead End 229 N7
Fobbing 324 C9
Ford End 167 N6
Fordham 125 P1
Fordham Heath 126 C6
Fordstreet 125 P4
Forest Gate 315 K7
Forry's Green 96 D2
Forty Hill 251 L9
Foster Street 211 N4
Four Wantz 191 J9
Foxash Estate 105 K7
Foxearth 45 P5
Fox Hatch 258 C8
Fox Street 129 H5
Frating 154 F3
Frating Green 154 F3
Freezy Water 252 B6
Freston 30 E7
Friday Hill 274 G9
Frinkle Green 56 B5
Frinton-on-Sea 183 L1
Frogs' Green 66 E1
Fryerning 260 B4
Fryerns 3 K1
Fuller's End 114 F7
Fuller Street 169 N9
Fullwell Cross 296 E5
Further Ford End 87 L2
Fyfield 214 A8
Gainsborough 31 H2
Gainsford End 70 F5
Galleyend 240 B7
Galleywood 240 B8
Gallows Corner 299 J5
Gallows Green 117 L4
Gallows Green 126 A6
Gamble's Green 195 L2
Gants Hill 316 A1
Garnetts 166 E5
Gaston Green 162 E7
Gaunt's End 115 K8
Gay Bowers 242 D5
Gestingthorpe 59 K9
Gidea Park 298 E5
Gilston 186 E7
Gilston Park 186 D6
Gilwell Park 274 F2
Globe Town 332 A3
Goff's Oak 229 H7
Goldhanger 223 N4
Good Easter 191 N7
Goodmayes 317 J4
Gooseberry Green 282 F5
Goose Green 132 A4
Goose Green 132 B8
Gore Pit 173 K1
Gosfield 97 H8
Grange Hill 296 E3
Grange Park 272 F4
Gransmore Green 143 L5
Grass Green 57 J9
Grays 349 J5
Great Amwell 184 B7
Great Baddow 240 C5
Great Bardfield 94 B7
Great Bentley 155 J6
Great Berry 323 H2
Great Blakenham 22 A3
Great Braxted 198 D9
Great Bromley 130 D6
Great Burstead 303 K2
Great Canfield 165 K5
Great Chesterford 56 F9
Great Chishill 48 B8
Great Clacton 181 N8
Great Claydons 241 M9
Great Cornard 61 N5
Great Dunmow 141 K7
Great Easton 116 C8
Great Hallingbury 162 G1
Great Henny 74 F1
Great Holland 182 G2
Great Horkesley 102 D7
Great Hormead 86 B4
Great Leighs 169 J7
Great Maplestead 73 H7
Great Notley 144 E8
Great Oakley 133 G5
Great Oxney Green 238 G1
Great Parndon 210 C5
Great Saling 143 H5
Great Sampford 68 D5
Great Stambridge 309 M5
Great Tey 135 H7
Great Totham 198 B8
Great Totham 198 F5
Great Wakering 330 F3
Great Waltham 193 M5

Great Warley 300 D5
Great Wigborough 201 K1
Great Yeldham 57 P8
Greenhithe 348 C9
Greenstead 128 E9
Greenstead Green 123 H2
Greensted 235 H7
Greensted Green 234 G7
Green Street 136 D5
Green Street 259 N5
The Green 170 D1
Green Tye 161 H4
Greenwich 30 D1
Gubbion's Green 169 M5
Hackney Wick 314 D6
Hacton 319 K7
Hadham Cross 160 D3
Hadham Ford 136 A6
Hadleigh 327 H3
Hadstock 38 B5
Hailey 208 C1
Hainault 296 G4
Hale End 294 G3
Hallingbury Street 163 L1
Hallsford Bridge 235 N9
Halls Green 209 M5
Halstead 97 N6
Halstead 97 N6
Hammond Street 229 H5
Hamperden End 91 H6
Hanchet End 40 E2
Handley Green 260 E1
Hardy's Green 150 A8
Hare Green 130 F9
Hare Street 210 C4
Harkstead 84 A7
Harlow 13 J6
Harold Hill 299 K2
Harold Park 299 N3
Harold Wood 299 M5
Hartford End 168 A5
Harwich 14 D5
Hastingwood 211 N7
Hatfield Broad Oak 164 A8
Hatfield Heath 188 C1
Hatfield Peverel 196 E8
Havering-atte-Bower 277 C9
Hawbush Green 146 A9
Hawkin's Hill 69 H9
Hawkspur Green 93 L3
Hawkwell 308 B2
Hay Green 299 P3
Hazeleigh 243 J6
Hazel End 113 M9
Hazel Stub 40 F4
Heath Park 318 G1
The Heath 23 J7
Heckfordbridge 150 E6
Helions Bumpstead 54 E2
Hellman's Cross 164 G3
Hemley 33 P1
Hemp's Green 125 N1
Hempstead 54 C9
Henham 115 H2
Henham 115 H2
Henley 23 K1
Henny Street 61 J9
Herongate 301 P5
Heybridge 222 C5
Heybridge 260 C7
Heybridge Basin 222 E8
Heydon 48 D5
Higham 79 N5
Higham Hill 294 B6
Highams Park 294 E4
High Easter 191 M2
Highfields 173 J6
High Garrett 121 M5
High Houses 193 L5
High Laver 212 C5
High Ongar 236 A6
High Park Corner 153 K8
High Roding 165 M6
Highstreet Green 71 H7
The High 13 H6
High Wych 187 J3
Hill Green 88 D2
Hinxton 36 B5
Hobbs Cross 211 P2
Hobbs Cross 255 L6
Hockerill 137 N8
Hockley 287 M9
Hoddesdon 208 B6
Holbrook 81 K3
Holder's Green 117 M1
Holland-on-Sea 182 F8
Holton St Mary 80 D3
Holyfield 230 F7
Homerton 314 A8
Honey Tye 77 L5
Hook End 258 F5
Hope End Green 139 P9
Hope's Green 325 P4
Horkesley Heath 102 G9
Hornchurch 319 J4
Horndon on the Hill 340 C1
Horne Row 241 H4
Hornestreet 103 N3
Horseman Side 279 K3
Horsleycross Street 131 N4
Housham Tye 212 C1
Howe Green 163 H3
Howe Green 241 H7
Howegreen 265 M1
Howe Street 169 M3
Howe Street 193 M2
Howlett End 91 H3
Hullbridge 287 H5
Hunsdon 185 M3
Hunsdonbury 185 M6
Hurst Green 181 N3
Hutton 281 M5
Hutton Mount 281 L5
Hyde Chase 242 G6

The Hythe ... 152 E2
Ickleton ... 36 B8
Ilford ... 316 C5
Ingatestone ... 260 D6
Ingrave ... 301 M3
Inworth ... 173 L5
Ipswich ... 17 C7
Ivy Chimneys ... 254 F2
Jack's Hatch ... 210 C9
Janke's Green ... 100 D8
Jasper's Green ... 120 A5
Jaywick ... 206 E4
Katherines ... 209 P6
Kedington ... 42 C1
Keelars Tye ... 153 M3
Keeres Green ... 190 G3
Kelvedon ... 173 J4
Kelvedon Hatch ... 258 A7
Kesgrave ... 26 G5
Kettle Green ... 160 B4
Keysers Estate ... 230 E1
Kingsmoor ... 210 D8
King Street ... 236 E7
Kingswood ... 324 A1
Kirby Cross ... 158 C5
Kirby-le-Soken ... 158 D5
Kirton ... 33 M6
Knowl Green ... 58 E5
Laindon ... 303 L8
Lakeside ... 348 D2
Lamarsh ... 75 M5
Lamb Corner ... 104 E4
Lambourne ... 277 L3
Lambourne End ... 277 K6
Langdon Hills ... 323 H2
Langenhoe ... 177 H5
Langford ... 221 N4
Langham ... 104 A4
Langley ... 62 F7
Langley Green ... 148 E6
Langley Lower Green ... 62 G8
Langley Upper Green ... 62 H4
Latchingdon ... 220 H4
Latchmore Bank ... 162 D5
Lattinford Hill ... 80 G3
Latton Bush ... 211 H7
Lawford ... 105 P5
Layer Breton ... 175 L5
Layer de la Haye ... 151 J9
Layer Marney ... 175 H5
Lea Bridge ... 314 A5
Leaden Roding ... 190 G4
Leavenheath ... 47 L4
Lee Chapel ... 82 B7
Lee-over-Sands ... 205 K6
Leigh Beck ... 345 H2
Leigh-on-Sea ... 327 N5
Lessness Heath ... 346 A4
Level's Green ... 117 H1
Levington ... 32 C7
Lexden ... 127 K7
Leyton ... 314 G5
Leytonstone ... 315 J3
Limehouse ... 332 B7
Lindsell ... 117 P4
Linford ... 340 G9
Lippitts Hill ... 275 J1
Liston ... 46 D5
Liston Garden ... 46 E8
Little Baddow ... 220 A7
Little Bardfield ... 93 L6
Little Bentley ... 131 M7
Little Braxted ... 197 M2
Little Bromley ... 130 G1
Little Burstead ... 303 H5
Littlebury ... 50 F6
Littlebury Green ... 50 B9
Little Cambridge ... 117 J4
Little Chesterford ... 50 F2
Little Chishill ... 49 L3
Little Clacton ... 181 N2
Little Cornard ... 61 P7
Little Dunmow ... 142 D7
Little Easton ... 140 F1
Little End ... 257 K4
Little Hadham ... 136 B4
Little Hallingbury ... 162 F5
Little Heath ... 297 K8
Little Henham ... 89 P7
Little Horkesley ... 102 B4
Little Hormead ... 86 B9
Little Ilford ... 316 B7
Little Laver ... 213 L3
Little Leighs ... 169 H7
Little London ... 69 L6
Little London ... 88 C8
Little Maplestead ... 75 M8
Little Mascalls ... 240 F9
Little Oakley ... 109 M9
Little Oxney Green ... 238 E2
Little Parndon ... 62 D9
Little Sampford ... 92 F4
Little Tey ... 149 H2
Little Thurrock ... 349 M2
Little Totham ... 199 H8
Little Wakering ... 310 D9
Little Walden ... 51 N2
Little Waltham ... 194 B6
Little Warley ... 301 J6
Little Wenham ... 28 A7
Little Wigborough ... 201 N1
Little Yeldham ... 58 D8
Littley Green ... 168 C6
Long Gardens ... 74 C4
Long Melford ... 46 G4
Loughton ... 276 A3
Loves Green ... 238 B5
Lower Bobbingworth Green ... 213 M7
Lower Edmonton ... 273 K8
Lower Green ... 86 F1
Lower Green ... 95 N5
Lower Green ... 240 B9
Lower Green ... 241 H5
Lower Holbrook ... 83 P6
Lower Nazeing ... 230 G2

Lower Sheering ... 187 P3
Lower Street ... 83 J8
Low Street ... 350 G4
Loxford ... 316 D7
Loyter's Green ... 212 E2
Lucas End ... 229 J1
Lucking Street ... 75 K7
Mace Green ... 28 F3
Magdalen Laver ... 212 C6
Maggots End ... 113 K3
Maidenhall ... 35 J8
Maldon ... 222 C8
Mallows Green ... 113 H5
Manningtree ... 106 A4
Manor Park ... 315 P6
Manuden ... 113 L5
Manwood Green ... 189 K7
Maple End ... 67 J2
Marden Ash ... 235 L9
Margaret Roding ... 190 F7
Margaretting ... 261 H1
Margaretting Tye ... 261 K2
Mark Hall North ... 187 H9
Mark Hall South ... 211 H1
Marks Gate ... 297 M6
Marks Tey ... 149 L2
Martlesham ... 27 M1
Martlesham Heath ... 27 K2
Mashbury ... 192 D8
Matching ... 188 F8
Matching Green ... 189 J9
Matching Tye ... 188 E9
Mayland ... 211 M5
Maylandsea ... 245 M9
Maypole Green ... 151 N5
Meadowend ... 57 K5
Meesden ... 86 C3
Messing ... 173 H4
Middleton ... 61 H6
Mile End ... 128 B2
Mile End ... 332 B4
Millend Green ... 117 K7
Miller's Green ... 212 A6
Mill Green ... 39 P4
Mill Green ... 260 A2
Mill Hill ... 287 L2
Mill Meads ... 332 G2
Minnow End ... 193 P5
Mistley ... 106 F4
Mistley Heath ... 106 G6
Molehill Green ... 115 N9
Molehill Green ... 145 P9
Monk Street ... 92 C9
Montsale ... 270 E9
Moreton ... 213 H9
Mott's Green ... 162 G7
Moulsham ... 5 F7
Mount Bovers ... 307 N4
Mount Bures ... 100 D2
Mount End ... 255 N2
Mountnessing ... 259 N9
Mowden ... 220 A2
Much Hadham ... 160 D2
Mucking ... 341 L6
Muckingford ... 350 G1
Mundon ... 244 F8
Nacton ... 32 A5
Navestock Heath ... 279 H1
Navestock Side ... 279 P1
Nayland ... 78 A8
Nazeing ... 231 L1
Nazeing Gate ... 231 M4
Nazeing Long Green ... 231 K4
Nazeing Mead ... 208 G6
Needham Green ... 164 B9
Nether Street ... 160 E8
Nether Street ... 190 D8
Nevendon ... 305 H4
Newbury Park ... 316 E1
New England ... 42 D9
Newgate Street ... 228 D3
Newman's End ... 188 E7
Newman's Green ... 47 K7
New Mistley ... 106 F5
Newney Green ... 216 C9
Newport ... 65 H9
New Thundersley ... 306 A8
Nine Ashes ... 236 F8
Noak Bridge ... 303 N6
Noak Hill ... 279 K8
Noak Hill ... 303 N6
North Benfleet ... 305 L7
North End ... 58 C7
North End ... 167 K5
North End ... 168 A6
Northend ... 14 H6
Northend ... 269 J4
North Fambridge ... 288 D7
North Ockendon ... 320 E7
North Shoebury ... 330 E5
North Stifford ... 339 H7
Northumberland Heath ... 346 B6
North Weald Bassett ... 233 M9
North Woolwich ... 333 P9
Norton Heath ... 237 H4
Norton Mandeville ... 236 C4
Norwood End ... 213 P6
Nosterfield End ... 40 C1
Nounsley ... 220 D1
Nuper's Hatch ... 278 D6
Oakwood ... 272 C5
Old Felixstowe ... 35 N6
Old Harlow ... 187 L8
Old Heath ... 152 D5
Old Mead ... 114 G3
Olmstead Green ... 54 B5
Onslow Green ... 167 J4
Orsett ... 340 C5
Orsett Heath ... 340 A4
Osidge ... 272 B8
Ostend ... 271 D5
Ovington ... 58 A1
Oxen End ... 118 D1
Oxley Green ... 199 P3

Padham's Green ... 282 C1
Paglesham Churchend ... 290 C9
Paglesham Eastend ... 310 F2
Pale Green ... 54 G1
Palmers Green ... 272 D9
Panfield ... 120 D8
Pannel's Ash ... 57 M1
Parkeston ... 109 P4
Parkgate ... 167 K5
Park Green ... 112 G1
Parney Heath ... 104 C4
Parsonage Green ... 217 P5
Parson's Heath ... 128 E6
Paslow Wood Common ... 236 E9
Passingford Bridge ... 256 C9
Passmores ... 210 E6
Paternoster Heath ... 199 P1
Patmore Heath ... 112 C7
Pattiswick ... 146 F1
Peartree Green ... 258 G7
Pebmarsh ... 98 G1
Pedlars End ... 212 G9
Peldon ... 176 E7
Pentlow ... 45 K5
Pentlow Street ... 45 M3
Pepper's Green ... 217 J1
Perry Green ... 146 E5
Perry Green ... 160 C5
Pharisee Green ... 141 H9
Philpot End ... 165 P3
Piercing Hill ... 257 J1
Pigstye Green ... 237 J1
Pilgrims Hatch ... 280 E3
Pin Mill ... 31 M9
Pinnacles ... 210 B3
Pipps Hill ... 303 N7
Pitsea ... 324 G1
Plaistow ... 333 J3
Plashet ... 315 N8
Pledgdon Green ... 115 M5
Pleshey ... 192 F2
Point Clear ... 205 J2
Ponders End ... 273 P4
Pond Street ... 63 J2
Poplar ... 332 D7
The Port of Felixstowe ... 35 H1
Potash ... 81 P2
Potter Street ... 211 L5
Powers Hall End ... 196 F1
Presdales ... 184 B5
Priory Heath ... 31 K1
Prittlewell ... 328 F3
Purfleet ... 347 M3
Purleigh ... 243 P9
Puttock End ... 59 J4
Puttock's End ... 164 E1
Queen's Park ... 283 H2
Quendon ... 89 J1
Racecourse ... 25 N9
Radley Green ... 237 M3
Radwinter ... 67 K2
Radwinter End ... 67 J1
Rainham ... 336 C5
Ramsden Bellhouse ... 284 C7
Ramsden Heath ... 284 C4
Ramsey ... 109 J4
Ramsey Island ... 246 G2
Rank's Green ... 169 N5
Raven's Green ... 155 H1
Rawreth ... 284 B9
Rawreth Shot ... 285 P9
Rayleigh ... 306 G4
Rayne ... 144 B4
Reader's Corner ... 240 D5
Redbridge ... 295 M9
Rettendon ... 263 N8
Richmond's Green ... 92 E9
Rickling ... 88 C4
Rickling Green ... 88 E6
The Ridgeway ... 228 A6
Ridgewell ... 57 H4
Ringtail Green ... 167 N8
Rise Park ... 298 D5
Rivenhall ... 172 A6
Rivenhall End ... 172 D7
Roast Green ... 87 N2
Robinhood End ... 70 C4
Rochford ... 309 H5
Rodbridge Corner ... 46 B4
Romford ... 298 B9
Rook End ... 90 D3
Roost End ... 42 B7
Rosedale ... 229 L7
Rose Green ... 76 F1
Rose Green ... 125 K2
Rose Hill ... 25 N7
Rotten End ... 95 M9
Roundbush ... 266 B1
Roundbush Green ... 190 F2
Row Green ... 144 G8
Row Heath ... 181 K2
Rowhedge ... 152 F6
Roxwell ... 216 C5
Roydon ... 209 L2
Roydon Hamlet ... 230 M7
Rudley Green ... 243 M7
Russell Green ... 242 D3
Runwell ... 285 K7
Rush Green ... 206 G1
Rush Green ... 318 D2
Rushley Green ... 72 E5
Rushmere St Andrew ... 26 C5
Rushmere Street ... 26 E2
Rye Meads ... 208 G2
Rye Park ... 208 E4
Sabine's Green ... 279 J1
Saffron Walden ... 51 P9
St Lawrence ... 247 L5
St Margarets ... 208 D1
St Osyth ... 180 E9
St Osyth Heath ... 181 H4
St Vincent's Hamlet ... 279 M7
Salcott-cum-Virley ... 200 F4
Samson's Corner ... 179 K4
Samuel's Corner ... 331 J2

Sandon ... 241 H4
Sawbridgeworth ... 187 J2
School Green ... 95 N5
Scotland Street ... 78 D4
Seawick ... 206 B5
Seven Kings ... 316 F3
Seven Star Green ... 126 C7
Sewards End ... 52 D9
Sewardstone ... 274 F1
Sewardstonebury ... 275 H4
Shalford ... 119 J4
Shalford Green ... 119 P4
Sheering ... 188 C4
Shelley ... 235 M3
Shellow Bowells ... 215 J7
Shenfield ... 281 H6
Shoeburyness ... 330 F8
Shop Corner ... 84 F8
Shotgate ... 305 N1
Shotley ... 85 K8
Shotley Gate ... 85 N8
Shrub End ... 151 L2
Shudy Camps ... 39 N5
Sible Hedingham ... 72 B7
Sibley's Green ... 117 J2
Silver End ... 171 M1
Silvertown ... 333 M9
Skye Green ... 148 D5
Slade Green ... 346 F7
Smith's Green ... 55 J5
Smith's Green ... 139 N7
Smythe's Green ... 174 F3
Snow End ... 86 B3
South Benfleet ... 326 B3
South Bromley ... 332 C6
Southchurch ... 329 M6
South-end ... 160 C7
Southend-on-Sea ... 18 D2
Southey Green ... 96 F3
South Fambridge ... 288 C4
Southfields ... 340 E7
Southfields ... 340 F7
Southgate ... 272 D7
South Green ... 177 P2
South Green ... 283 L9
South Hanningfield ... 263 J9
South Heath ... 180 C2
South Hornchurch ... 336 C1
Southminster ... 268 C6
South Ockendon ... 338 F4
South Stifford ... 348 G5
South Weald ... 280 B8
South Woodford ... 295 K6
South Woodham Ferrers ... 265 J8
Spellbrook ... 162 B5
Spitalbrook ... 208 D7
Springfield ... 218 C5
Springwell ... 51 H3
Sproughton ... 24 C5
Stafford's Corner ... 175 P8
Stagden Cross ... 22 D8
Stambourne ... 58 M6
Stambourne Green ... 87 N5
Stanbrook ... 91 P8
Stanford-le-Hope ... 341 N3
Stansted Abbotts ... 185 H8
Stansted Mountfitchet ... 113 P8
Stanway ... 150 F1
Stanway Green ... 150 G3
Stapleford Abbotts ... 278 C5
Stapleford Tawney ... 256 B6
Starling's Green ... 87 N5
Start Hill ... 138 D7
Stebbing ... 142 C4
Stebbing Green ... 143 J3
Steeple ... 246 D7
Steeple Bumpstead ... 55 L2
Stevenson End ... 39 H9
Stewards ... 210 F8
Steward's Green ... 255 J2
Stickling Green ... 88 C2
Stisted ... 122 D9
Stock ... 261 N6
Stocking Green ... 54 G4
Stocking Pelham ... 87 L9
Stoke ... 25 K7
Stoke by Clare ... 43 K8
Stoke-by-Nayland ... 78 A4
Stoke Park ... 29 P1
Stoke Tye ... 78 A1
Stondon Massey ... 258 D4
Stonebridge ... 309 N9
Stones Green ... 132 G5
Stoneyhills ... 269 H9
Stow Maries ... 265 M5
Stratford ... 332 F9
Stratford Marsh ... 332 E9
Stratford New Town ... 314 F8
Stratford St Mary ... 79 P7
Strethall ... 49 P6
Stroud Green ... 308 C5
Sturmer ... 41 P7
Stutton ... 82 D7
Sucksted Green ... 116 C1
Sumners ... 210 A5
Sunken Marsh ... 326 F4
Sunnymede ... 283 L6
Surrex ... 148 D4
Swallows Cross ... 259 J7
Swan Street ... 75 J9
Takeley ... 139 L6
Takeley Street ... 139 J7
Tarpots ... 325 P1
Tattingstone ... 82 D2
Tattingstone White Horse ... 54 B9
Taverners Green ... 164 D5
Temple End ... 116 B2
Temple Fields ... 187 H8
Temple Hill ... 347 J9
Temple Mills ... 314 E7
Tendring ... 156 C1
Tendring Green ... 132 B7
Tendring Heath ... 131 P6

Terling ... 195 P1
Thamesmead ... 334 G7
Thaxted ... 92 C5
Theydon Bois ... 254 E7
Theydon Garnon ... 255 K6
Theydon Mount ... 255 P6
Thistley Green ... 168 E1
Thorington Street ... 79 H6
Thorley ... 161 P3
Thorley Houses ... 137 P1
Thorley Street ... 162 B2
Thornwood Common ... 233 J4
Thorpe Bay ... 330 A7
Thorpe Common ... 54 B1
Thorpe Green ... 157 J2
Thorpe-le-Soken ... 157 J4
Thorrington ... 154 C9
Threshers Bush ... 211 P4
Thundersley ... 306 B9
Tilbury ... 350 B6
Tilbury Green ... 57 L4
Tilbury Juxta Clare ... 58 A5
Tiley Green ... 212 C5
Tilekiln Green ... 138 C8
Tilkey ... 147 N2
Tillingham ... 258 D8
Tilty ... 116 E6
Tindon End ... 67 N8
Ty's Cross ... 258 F4
Tiptree ... 173 N7
Tiptree Heath ... 225 H2
Tollesbury ... 225 H2
Tolleshunt D'Arcy ... 200 B8
Tolleshunt Knights ... 199 P2
Tolleshunt Major ... 199 M8
Tolmers ... 228 D5
Toot Hill ... 234 E9
Toppesfield ... 71 J2
Totham Hill ... 198 F7
Totham Plains ... 199 J7
Trimley Lower Street ... 34 B5
Trimley St Martin ... 33 L9
Trimley St Mary ... 34 E4
Trims Green ... 161 P6
Turnford ... 230 A4
Twinstead ... 74 F3
Twinstead Green ... 74 D3
Tye Common ... 282 C9
Tye Green ... 67 H6
Tye Green ... 115 H9
Tye Green ... 148 C8
Tye Green ... 191 P6
Tye Green ... 210 E5
Tylers Causeway ... 228 A1
Tyler's Green ... 234 C3
Ugley ... 114 D4
Ugley Green ... 114 D4
Ulting ... 220 F4
Upminster ... 319 P4
Uppend ... 112 G6
Upper Dovercourt ... 109 N5
Upper Street ... 53 H8
Upper Walthamstow ... 294 F8
Upshire ... 253 M2
Upton ... 315 L9
Upton Park ... 333 M1
Upwick Green ... 136 D1
Vange ... 324 D2
Wakes Colne ... 124 G1
Wakes Colne Green ... 100 B3
Wallend ... 334 B1
Waltham Abbey ... 253 H2
Waltham Cross ... 251 P3
Waltham's Cross ... 94 C7
Walthamstow ... 294 C8
Walton ... 35 J6
Walton-on-the-Naze ... 43 J8
Wanstead ... 315 L2
Ware ... 184 C2
Warley ... 300 E2
Warren Heath ... 31 M1
Washall Green ... 86 C1
Watch House Green ... 143 K7
Water End ... 52 G4
Waterhales ... 279 J5
Watton's Green ... 278 G5
Weeley ... 156 C3
Weeley Heath ... 156 C8
Weir ... 306 F7
Wellstye Green ... 166 F3
Welshwood Park ... 128 G6
Wendens Ambo ... 64 B3
Wennington ... 337 K7
West Bergholt ... 127 H4
Westbourne ... 44 F2
Westcliff-on-Sea ... 328 D7
Westerfield ... 25 M8
West Hanningfield ... 262 G5
West Horndon ... 321 M1
Westley Heights ... 323 K4
West Mersea ... 202 G6
West Thurrock ... 348 F4
West Tilbury ... 350 F4
Westwood Park ... 102 B7
Wethersfield ... 94 G5
Wherstead ... 30 B5
Whiteash Green ... 97 J4
White Colne ... 101 J1
White House ... 24 F1
White Notley ... 170 F4
White Roding or
White Roothing ... 189 P5
Whitton ... 24 C9
Wicken Bonhunt ... 64 G9
Wickford ... 284 G8
Wickham Bishops ... 197 N7
Wickham St Paul ... 75 P4
Widdington ... 90 D4
Widford ... 160 D8
Widford ... 259 M4
Wiggens Green ... 55 H1
Willingale ... 214 F9
Willows Green ... 169 H1
Wimbish ... 67 H3

Wimbish Green 67 K6	Wixoe 42 E8	Wood Green 253 M4	Woollensbrook 208 A2	Wormley West End 229 M1
Winchmore Hill 272 C7	Woodend 214 B2	Woodham Ferrers 264 E5	Woolverstone 30 G9	Wrabness 108 C5
Winter Gardens 326 B9	Woodham Green 115 L2	Woodham Mortimer 242 G5	Workhouse Green 75 P2	Wright's Green 162 G6
Witham 197 K3	Woodford 295 L3	Woodham Walter 220 F9	Workhouse Hill 103 H4	Writtle 239 H2
Withermarsh Green 78 G2	Woodford Bridge 296 A4	Woodhill 241 N4	World's End 272 F3	Young's End 169 K1
Witnesham 23 P2	Woodford Green 295 K4	The Woodlands 83 J2	Wormingford 101 J3	
Wivenhoe 153 J5	Woodford Wells 275 L9	Woodside 233 L5	Wormley 230 B5	
Wix 132 F2	Woodgates End 115 N8	Woodside Green 163 J4	Wormleybury 229 N2	

USING THE STREET INDEX

Street names are listed alphabetically. Each street name is followed by its postal town or area locality, the Postcode District, the page number, and the reference to the square in which the name is found.

Standard index entries are shown as follows:

Aalten Av *CVI* SS8 ....**345** J2

Street names and selected addresses not shown on the map due to scale restrictions are shown in the index with an asterisk:

Abbotshade Rd *BERM/RHTH* SE16* **332** A8

GENERAL ABBREVIATIONS

ACC...ACCESS	CTYD...COURTYARD	HLS...HILLS	MWY...MOTORWAY	SE...SOUTH EAST
ALY...ALLEY	CUTT...CUTTINGS	HO...HOUSE	N...NORTH	SER...SERVICE AREA
AP...APPROACH	CV...COVE	HOL...HOLLOW	NE...NORTH EAST	SH...SHORE
AR...ARCADE	CYN...CANYON	HOSP...HOSPITAL	NW...NORTH WEST	SHOP...SHOPPING
ASS...ASSOCIATION	DEPT...DEPARTMENT	HRB...HARBOUR	O/P...OVERPASS	SKWY...SKYWAY
AV...AVENUE	DL...DALE	HTH...HEATH	OFF...OFFICE	SMT...SUMMIT
BCH...BEACH	DM...DAM	HTS...HEIGHTS	ORCH...ORCHARD	SOC...SOCIETY
BLDS...BUILDINGS	DR...DRIVE	HVN...HAVEN	OV...OVAL	SP...SPUR
BND...BEND	DRO...DROVE	HWY...HIGHWAY	PAL...PALACE	SPR...SPRING
BNK...BANK	DRY...DRIVEWAY	IMP...IMPERIAL	PAS...PASSAGE	SQ...SQUARE
BR...BRIDGE	DWGS...DWELLINGS	IN...INLET	PAV...PAVILION	ST...STREET
BRK...BROOK	E...EAST	IND EST...INDUSTRIAL ESTATE	PDE...PARADE	STN...STATION
BTM...BOTTOM	EMB...EMBANKMENT	INF...INFIRMARY	PH...PUBLIC HOUSE	STR...STREAM
BUS...BUSINESS	EMBY...EMBASSY	INFO...INFORMATION	PK...PARK	STRD...STRAND
BVD...BOULEVARD	ESP...ESPLANADE	INT...INTERCHANGE	PKWY...PARKWAY	SW...SOUTH WEST
BY...BYPASS	EST...ESTATE	IS...ISLAND	PL...PLACE	TDG...TRADING
CATH...CATHEDRAL	EX...EXCHANGE	JCT...JUNCTION	PLN...PLAIN	TER...TERRACE
CEM...CEMETERY	EXPY...EXPRESSWAY	JTY...JETTY	PLNS...PLAINS	THWY...THROUGHWAY
CEN...CENTRE	EXT...EXTENSION	KG...KING	PLZ...PLAZA	TNL...TUNNEL
CFT...CROFT	F/O...FLYOVER	KNL...KNOLL	POL...POLICE STATION	TOLL...TOLLWAY
CH...CHURCH	FC...FOOTBALL CLUB	LA...LANE	PR...PRINCE	TPK...TURNPIKE
CHA...CHASE	FK...FORK	LDG...LODGE	PREC...PRECINCT	TR...TRACK
CHYD...CHURCHYARD	FLD...FIELD	LGT...LIGHT	PREP...PREPARATORY	TRL...TRAIL
CIR...CIRCLE	FLDS...FIELDS	LK...LOCK	PRIM...PRIMARY	TWR...TOWER
CIRC...CIRCUS	FLS...FALLS	LKS...LAKES	PROM...PROMENADE	U/P...UNDERPASS
CL...CLOSE	FLS...FLATS	LNDG...LANDING	PRS...PRINCESS	UNI...UNIVERSITY
CLFS...CLIFFS	FM...FARM	LTL...LITTLE	PRT...PORT	UPR...UPPER
CMP...CAMP	FT...FORT	LWR...LOWER	PT...POINT	V...VALE
CNR...CORNER	FWY...FREEWAY	MAG...MAGISTRATE	PTH...PATH	VA...VALLEY
CO...COUNTY	FY...FERRY	MAN...MANSIONS	PZ...PIAZZA	VIAD...VIADUCT
COLL...COLLEGE	GA...GATE	MD...MEAD	QD...QUADRANT	VIL...VILLA
COM...COMMON	GAL...GALLERY	MDW...MEADOWS	QU...QUEEN	VIS...VISTA
COMM...COMMISSION	GDN...GARDEN	MEM...MEMORIAL	QY...QUAY	VLG...VILLAGE
CON...CONVENT	GDNS...GARDENS	MKT...MARKET	RBT...ROUNDABOUT	VLS...VILLAS
COT...COTTAGE	GLD...GLADE	MKTS...MARKETS	RD...ROAD	VW...VIEW
COTS...COTTAGES	GLN...GLEN	ML...MALL	RDG...RIDGE	W...WEST
CP...CAPE	GN...GREEN	MNR...MANOR	REP...REPUBLIC	WD...WOOD
CPS...COPSE	GND...GROUND	MS...MEWS	RES...RESERVOIR	WHF...WHARF
CR...CREEK	GRA...GRANGE	MSN...MISSION	RFC...RUGBY FOOTBALL CLUB	WK...WALK
CREM...CREMATORIUM	GRG...GARAGE	MT...MOUNT	RI...RISE	WKS...WALKS
CRS...CRESCENT	GT...GREAT	MTN...MOUNTAIN	RP...RAMP	WLS...WELLS
CSWY...CAUSEWAY	GTWY...GATEWAY	MTS...MOUNTAINS	RW...ROW	WY...WAY
CT...COURT	GV...GROVE	MUS...MUSEUM	S...SOUTH	YD...YARD
CTRL...CENTRAL	HGR...HIGHER		SCH...SCHOOL	YHA...YOUTH HOSTEL
CTS...COURTS	HL...HILL			

POSTCODE TOWNS AND AREA ABBREVIATIONS

ABR/ST...Abridge/Stapleford Abbotts	CHLM/GWD...Chelmsford/Galleywood	GPK...Gidea Park	MGTR...Manningtree	SLH/COR...Stanford-le-Hope/Corringham
ABYW...Abbey Wood	CHLM/WR...Chelmsford/Writtle	GRAYS...Grays	MHAD...Much Hadham	SOCK/AV...South Ockendon/Aveley
BARK...Barking	CHONG...Chipping Ongar	GRH...Greenhithe	MNPK...Manor Park	SOS...Southend-on-Sea
BARK/HLT...Barkingside/Hainault	CHTY...Chantry	GTDUN...Great Dunmow	NHMKT...Needham Market	SOSN...Southend-on-Sea north
BCAYE...Billericay east	CLAY...Clayhall	GVE...Gravesend east	PEND...Ponders End	SRTFD...Stratford
BCAYW...Billericay west	CLPT...Clapton	GVW...Gravesend west	PIT...Pitsea	STAN...Standon
BCTR...Becontree	COL...Colchester	HADL...Hadleigh	PLMGR...Palmers Green	STHGT/OAK...Southgate/Oakwood
BELV...Belvedere	COLN...Colchester north	HAR...Harwich	PLSTW...Plaistow	STSD...Stansted
BERM/RHTH...Bermondsey/Rotherhithe	COLS...Colchester south	HARH...Harold Hill	POP/IOD...Poplar/Isle of Dogs	SUD...Sudbury
BETH...Bethnal Green	COLW...Colchester west	HCH...Hornchurch	POTB/CUF...Potters Bar/Cuffley	SWCM...Swanscombe
BKHH...Buckhurst Hill	COS...Clacton-on-Sea	HERT/BAY...Hertford/Bayford	PUR...Purfleet	SWFD...South Woodford
BOC...Burnham-on-Crouch	CRW...Collier Row	HLW...Harlow	RAIN...Rainham (Gt Lon)	THMD...Thamesmead
BOW...Bow	CVI...Canvey Island	HLWE...Harlow east	RAYL...Rayleigh	TIL...Tilbury
BROX...Broxbourne	DAGE...Dagenham east	HLWS...Harlow south	RBRTR...Rural Braintree	TOTM...Tottenham
BRTR...Braintree	DAGW...Dagenham west	HLWW/ROY...Harlow west/Roydon	RBRW/HUT...Rural Brentwood/Hutton	UED...Upper Edmonton
BRW...Brentwood	DART...Dartford	HOC/HUL...Hockley/Hullbridge	RBSF...Rural Bishop's Stortford	UPMR...Upminster
BRWN...Brentwood north	EBAR...East Barnet	HOD...Hoddesdon	RCFD...Rochford	VGE...Vange
BSDN...Basildon	ED...Edmonton	HOM...Homerton	RCHLM...Rural Chelmsford	WAB...Waltham Abbey
BSF...Bishop's Stortford	EHAM...East Ham	HOO/HM...Hoo St Werburgh/Higham	RCOLE...Rural Colchester east	WALTH...Walthamstow
BUNT...Buntingford	EMPK...Emerson Park	HSTD...Halstead	RCOLW...Rural Colchester west	WAN...Wanstead
BURES...Bures	EN...Enfield	HVHL...Haverhill	RCOS...Rural Clacton-on-Sea	WAP...Wapping
BXLYHN...Bexleyheath north	ENC/FH...Enfield Chase/Forty Hill	IL...Ilford	REDBR...Redbridge	WARE...Ware
BXLYHS...Bexleyheath south	EPP...Epping	ING...Ingatestone	RIPS/CAP...Rural Ipswich south/Capel St Mary	WCHMH...Winchmore Hill
CAN/RD...Canning Town/Royal Docks	ERITH...Erith	IP...Ipswich	RIPW...Rural Ipswich west	WCHPL...Whitechapel
CBE/LIN...Cambridge east/Linton	ERITHM...Erith Marshes	IPNE...Ipswich northeast	ROM...Romford	WDBR...Woodbridge
CBS...Cambridge south	FBAR/BDGN...Friern Barnet/Bounds Green	IPSE...Ipswich southeast	ROMW/RG...Romford west/Rush Green	WFD...Woodford
CDW/CHF...Chadwell St Mary/Chafford Hundred	FOS...Frinton-on-Sea	KVD/TMI...Kelvedon/Tiptree/Mersea Island	ROY...Royston	WICKE...Wickford east
CHDH...Chadwell Heath	FSTGT...Forest Gate	KESG...Kesgrave	SAFWN...Saffron Walden north	WICKW...Wickford west
CHES/WCR...Cheshunt/Waltham Cross	FX...Felixstowe	KIR/NAC...Kirton/Nacton	SAFWS...Saffron Walden south	WIT...Witham
CHESW...Cheshunt west	GDMY/SEVK...Goodmayes/Seven Kings	LAIN...Laindon	SBF/HAD...South Benfleet/Hadleigh	WOOL/PLUM...Woolwich/Plumstead
CHIG...Chigwell	GNTH/NBYPK...Gants Hill/Newbury Park	LEY...Leyton	SBN/FI...Shoeburyness/Foulness Island	WOS/PRIT...Westcliff-on-Sea/Prittlewell
CHING...Chingford	GNWCH...Greenwich	LOS...Leigh-on-Sea	SBW...Sawbridgeworth	WOTN...Walton-on-the-Naze
		LOU...Loughton		WTHK...West Thurrock
		MAL...Maldon		

A

Aalten Av CVI SS8 ....345 J2
Aaron Hill Rd EHAM E6 ....334 B5
Abbas Wk SUD CO6 ....61 M5
Abberton Rd COLS CO2 ....151 M9
K/T/MI CO5 ....177 K2
Abbess Cl CHLM/WR CM1 ....217 M9
Abbey Cl CHONG CM5 ....235 P1
HOC/HUL SS5 ....286 C6
ROM RM1 ....318 E1
Abbey Ct WAB EN9 ....252 E4
Abbey Crs RCOS CO16 ....157 K5
Abbey Dale Cl HLWE CM17 ......211 K4
Abbey Flds RCHLM CM3 ....263 N2
Abbey Gate Rd COL CO1 ....147 P5
Abbey La RCOLW CO6 147
SAFWN CB10 ....51 L9
SRTFD E15 ....332 C2
Abbey Meadow HSTD CO9 ....72 C7
Abbey Ms WALTH E17 ....316 C9
Abbey Rd BARK IG11 ....282 C7
BCAYW CM12 ....282 C7
CHES/WCR EN8 ....252 B4
EN EN1 ....273 K4
GNTH/NBYPK IG2 ....286 C7
HOC/HUL SS5 ....286 C7
SRTFD E15 ....332 C2
SUD CO10 ....20 C1
Abbey St PLSTW E13 ....333 K4
RCOS CO16 ....157 K5
SAFWN CB10 ....36 B7
Abbey Turning MAL CM9 ....221 N8
Abbey Vw GTDUN CM6 ....116 F5
Abbeyview WAB EN9 ....252 F3
Abbey Wood La RAIN RM13 ......337 J2
Abbotsbury Cl CHTY IP2 ....32 F2
SRTFD E15 ....332 F2
Abbots Cl BRWN CM15 ....281 K7
COS CO15 ....181 P7
MGTR CO11 ....132 F2
RAIN RM13 ....273 M8
Abbots Ct LAIN SS15 ....305 M6
Abbotsford Rd
GDMY/SEVK IG3 ....317 H4
Abbots Gdns RCOS CO16 ....180 F9
Abbotshade Rd
BERM/RHTH SE16 * 332 A8
Abbotshall Av
STHGT/OAK N14 ....272 B9
Abbots La RCOLW CO6 ....126 D8
Abbotsleigh Rd RCHLM CM3 ......286 C1
Abbotsmead MAL CM9 ....222 A6
Abbots Ride BCAYE CM11 ....283 K6
Abbot's Rd COLS CO2 ....152 D5
EHAM E6 ....333 N1
Abbots Wk SBN/FI SS3 ....350 B6
Abbotsweld HLWS CM18 ....210 E6
Abbots Wick La K/T/MI CO5 ......200 F1
Abbotswood SBF/HAD SS7 ....326 F1
Abbotswood CLAY IG5 ....296 A7
Abbott Rd HAR CO12 ....110 A4
POP/IOD E14 ....332 G6
Abbotts Cl CHLM/WR CM1 ....5 K2
LOS SS9 ....327 P1
ROMW/RG RM7 ....298 A7
THMD SE28 ....41 P6
Abbotts Ct HVHL CB9 ....259 P3
Abbotts Crs CHING E4 ....294 C1
ENC/FH EN2 ....272 C1
Abbotts Dr SLH/COR SS17 ....341 M8
WAB EN9 ....253 K4
Abbotts Hall Cha
SLH/COR SS17 ....341 M8
Abbotts Park Rd LEY E10 ....314 F2
Abbotts Pl CHLM/WR CM1 ....5 J2
Abbotts Ri WARE SG12 ....184 G8
Abbotts Rd HVHL CB9 ....41 K4
Abbotts Wy BSF CM23 ....162 B2
WARE SG12 ....184 G8
Abbs Cross Gdns HCH RM12 ....319 H5
Abbs Cross La HCH RM12 ....319 H5
Abdy Rd HAR CO12 ....109 P6
Abell Wy CHLM/GWD CM2 ....97 N3
Abels Rd HAR CO12 ....218 C7
Abenberg Wy
RBRW/HUT CM13 ....281 K8
Abensburg Rd CVI SS8 ....526 C9
Aberavon Rd BOW E3 ....332 B3
Abercorn Cl COLN CO4 ....317 J1
Abercorn Wy WIT CM8 ....197 K2
Abercrombie Dr EN EN1 ....251 M9
Abercrombie Wy
HLWW/ROY CM19 ....210 D5
Aberdeen Rd PEND EN3 ....273 P5
Aberdeen Gdns LOS SS9 ....327 K4
Aberdeen Wy IPNE IP4 ....26 A2
Aberdour Cl K/T/MI CO5 ....177 H5
Aberfeldy St POP/IOD E14 ......332 F6
Aberfovle Cl IPNE IP4 ....26 B2
Abingdon Ct PIT SS13 ....304 F6
Abingdon Rd GDMY/SEVK IG3 ..317 H6
RCOS CO16 ....181 M7
Abraham Ct UPMR RM14 ....319 M4
Abraham Dr WIT CM8 ....171 M1
Abram's La ROY SG8 ....48 F5
Abreys SBF/HAD SS7 ....306 D8
Abridge Cl CHES/WCR EN8 ......252 A5
Abridge Gdns CRW RM5 ....297 P3
Abridge Rd CHIG IG7 ....276 F5
EPP CM16 ....255 H7
Abridge Wy BARK IG11 ....335 J2
Acacia Av COLN CO4 ....128 F7
HCH RM12 ....318 E4
Acacia Cl CHSEW EN7 ....229 K6
IPSE IP3 ....31 L1
Acacia Dr MAL CM9 ....221 P9
SOS SS1 ....329 P6
UPMR RM14 ....319 M6
Acacia Gdns UPMR RM14 ....320 C2
WIT CM8 ....172 A9

Acacia Rd ENC/FH EN2 ....251 J9
PIT SS13 ....305 K7
WALTH E17 ....314 B1
WAN E11 ....315 H4
Accommodation Rd
COLN CO4 ....102 G9
Acer Av RAIN RM13 ....337 J5
Acer Gv RPW IP8 ....29 L1
Achilles Wy BRTR CM7 ....145 L1
Achnacone Dr COLN CO4 ....145 L1
Ackroyd Dr BOW E3 ....332 D5
Acland Av CCOLW CO3 ....127 K8
Acorn Av BRTR CM7 ....144 G4
HSTD CO9 ....97 N7
Acorn Cl CHING E4 ....294 E2
COLN CO4 ....128 E5
ENC/FH EN2 ....263 F9
MAL CO12 ....110 A7
MAL CM9 ....222 A6
RIPW IP8 ....28 D8
Acorn La POTB/CUF EN6 ....228 D8
Acorn Pl VGE SS16 ....323 H1
The Acorns HOC/HUL SS5 ....287 P9
Acorn St WARE SG12 ....185 N5
Acremore St SLH/COR SS11 ....136 C7
Acre Rd DAGE RM10 ....318 A9
Acres Av COLN CM5 ....155 L5
Acres End CHLM/WR CM1 ....217 M7
The Acres SLH/COR SS17 ....341 N2
Acton Cl CHES/WCR EN8 ....252 B1
ED N9 ....273 M8
RIPW IP8 ....24 B1
SUD CO10 ....20 E3
Acton Gdns RIPW IP8 ....22 B9
Acton Gn SUD CO10 ....20 E5
Acton La SUD CO10 ....20 E3
Acton Pl SUD CO10 * 20 C5
Acton Rd RIPW IP8 ....24 B1
Ada Gdns POP/IOD E14 ....332 G6
Adair Rd IP IP1 ....24 E5
Adalia Crs LOS SS9 ....327 L4
Adalia Wy LOS SS9 ....327 L4
Adam Rd CHING E4 ....294 C5
Adams Ct CHTY IP2 ....25 K8
Adams Ct WICKE SS11 ....65 K1
Adamsfield CHESW EN7 ....229 L5
Adams Gld RCFD SS4 ....308 E1
Adams House HLW CM20 ....13 H5
Adamson Rd CAN/RD E16 ....333 K6
Adams Pl KESG IP5 ....27 H4
Adams Rd CAN/RD E16 ....333 K6
Adams Rd SLH/COR SS17 ....341 M4
Adam Wy WICKE SS11 ....285 K3
Adastral Ct IP IP1 ....111 L2
Adderley St POP/IOD E14 ....332 F6
Addington Rd BOW E3 ....332 D5
CAN/RD E16 ....333 H4
FX IP11 ....34 F2
Addis Cl PEND EN3 ....24 A2
Addison Av STHGT/OAK N14 ....272 A5
Addison Gdns GRAYS RM17 ....349M2
Addison Rd BARK/HLT IG6 ......296 F2
POS CO15 ....158 B9
PEND EN3 ....251 P9
SUD CO10 ....21 J2
WALTH E17 ....294 E9
WAN E11 ....315 K1
Addison Wy RIPW IP8 ....22 B4
Adelaide Ct EN EN1 ....251 K8
Adelaide Dr COLS CO2 ....152 B5
SBF/HAD SS7 ....326 A5
Adelaide Rd IL IG1 ....316 C4
IPNE IP4 ....26 C5
LEY E10 ....314 F5
TIL RM18 ....350 A6
Adelaide St HAR CO12 ....110 A3
Adeliza Cl BARK IG11 ....316 D9
Adelphi Crs HCH RM12 ....318 E4
Adelsburg Rd CVI SS8 ....344 F1
Aden Rd IL IG1 ....316 C2
PEND EN3 ....274 B5
Adine Rd PLSTW E13 ....333 K4
Adley St HOM E9 ....314 B7
Admiral Pl BERM/RHTH SE16 ..332 B2
Admirals Cl SWFD E18 ....295 L8
Admirals Wk CHLM/WR CM1 ......4 B1
HOD EN11 ....208 E7
RCOLE CO7 ....153 J6
SBN/FI SS3 ....350 C9
Adnams Wk RAIN RM13 ....318 F7
Adomar Rd BCTR RM8 ....317 L5
Adstock Wy GRAYS RM17 ......349 J2
Advice Av CDW/CHF RM16 ......339 V9
Aetheric Rd BRTR CM7 ....145 H5
Affleck Rd COLN CO4 ....128 F8
Afton Dr SOCK/AV RM15 ....338 E6
Agar Road Ad WOTH CO14 ......159 M6
Agate Cl CAN/RD E16 ....333 N6
IP IP1 ....24 E2
Agate Rd COS CO15 ....6 E6
Agincourt Rd COS CO15 ....6 B2
Agister Rd CHIG IG7 ....297 H2
Agnes Av IL IG1 ....316 A3
LOS SS9 ....327 L4
Agnes Cl EHAM E6 ....334 B7
Agnes Gdns BCTR RM8 ....317 L6
Agnes St POP/IOD E14 ....332 B3
Agricola Pl EN EN1 ....273 L4
Aidan Cl DAGW RM9 ....317 M6
Ailsa Rd WOS/PRIT SSO 328 D6
Ailsa St POP/IOD E14 ....332 F3
Ainger Rd HAR CO12 ....109 P6
Aingers Green Rd RCOLE CO7 ..155 L9
Ainsley Av ROMW/RG RM7 ......318 B1
Ainsley Cl ED N9 ....273 K7
Ainslie Rd IP IP1 ....16 A3
Ainslie Wood Crs CHING E4 ....294 E1
Ainslie Wood Gdns CHING E4 ..294 D2
Ainslie Wood Rd CHING E4 ......294 D2
Aintree Av EHAM E6 ....333 P1

Aintree Crs BARK/HLT IG6 ......296 D6
Aintree Gv UPMR RM14 ....319 L5
Aire Dr SOCK/AV RM15 ....338 E4
Airfield Wy HCH RM12 ....318 D8
Airlie Gdns IL IG1 ....316 C3
Airthrie Rd GDMY/SEVK IG3 ....317 J3
Aisthorpe RIPS/CAP IP9 ....28 B9
Aisne Rd COLS CO2 ....151 N2
Aisthorpe RIPS/CAP IP9 ....28 B9
Aix Cl BRTR CM7 ....145 L1
Akenfield Cl RCHLM CM3 ....287 H1
Alafin Vls MGTR CO11 * 81 N9
Alamein Cl BROX EN10 ....208 A8
Alamein Rd BOC CM0 ....291 H4
CHLM/WR CM1 ....217 N5
COLS CO2 ....151M4
LOS SS9 ....307 P9
Alan Dr RCOS CO16 ....181 N4
Alan Gdns ROMW/RG RM7 ......317 P2
Alan Cv LOS SS9 ....307 P9
Alan Hocken Wy SRTFD E15 ....333 H2
Alan Rd IPSE IP3 ....25 N7
WIT CM8 ....172 A7
Alan Wy COLW CO3 ....151 J2
Alban Sq WDBR IP12 ....27 N1
Albany Cl CHLM/WR CM1 ....217M6
RCOLW CO6 ....127 H5
Albany Ct EPP CM16 ....232 C9
Albany Gdns East COS CO15 ....7 K2
Albany Gdns West COS CO15 ....7 K3
Albany Pde PEND EN5 ....252 A8
Albany Pl PEND EN3 * 252 A8
Albany Park Av PEND EN3 ......280 E5
Albany Rd BRWN CM15 ....280 E5
CHDH RM6 ....317 N1
HCH RM12 ....315 H6
MNPK E12 ....315 N6
PEND EN3 ....252 A7
RAYL SS6 ....307 K6
RCOLW CO6 ....127 J3
TIL RM18 ....350 B6
WALTH E17 ....314 B1
WICKW SS12 ....305 J1
The Albany IPNE IP4 ....25M3
Albany Vw BKHH IG9 ....275 K7
Alba Rd HLWE CM17 ....211 K2
Albatross Cl EHAM E6 ....334 A4

Albemarle Cl IP IP1 ....218 C5
Albemarle Cl HAR CO12 ....15 F3
Alberta Cl KESG IP5 ....27 H4
Alberta Rd BXLYHN DA7 ....346 B6
EN EN1 ....273 L5
Albert Av CHING E4 ....294 D1
Albert Cl CDW/CHF CM16 ......349M1
RAYL SS6 ....307 K7
RCFD SS4 ....288 D9
Albert Crs CHING E4 ....294 D1
Albert Dr LAIN SS15 ....305 K9
Albert Gdns COS CO15 ....7 J3
HLWE CM17 ....211 L4
RCOLW CO6 ....150 A2
WCHPL E1 ....332 A6
Albert Ms POP/IOD E14 * 332 B7
WOS/PRIT SSO * 18 C4
Albert Pl RCOLW CO6 ....150 A2
Albert Rd BCTR RM8 ....275 M8
BKHH IG9 ....291 H4
BOC CM0 ....291 H4
BRTR CM7 ....145 K3
CAN/RD E16 ....333 P8
CHING E4 ....294 F3
IL IG1 ....316 D4
LEY E10 ....314 F5
LOS SS9 ....307 P9
PEND EN3 ....274 A5
RAIN RM13 ....336 F1
RAYL SS6 ....307 K7
RCFD SS4 ....308 D1
RCOS CO16 ....156 C6
ROM RM1 ....319 J2
SBF/HAD SS7 ....326 A4
SBN/FI SS3 ....350 C9
SUD CO10 ....21 H4
SWFD E18 ....295 L8
WALTH E17 ....314 C1
WIT CM8 ....172 B9
Albert Sq SRTFD E15 ....315 H7
Albert St BRW CM14 ....300 F2
COL CO1 ....8 B5
HAR CO12 ....15 F4
Albert Wk FX IP11 ....34 F5
Albion Cl ROMW/RG RM7 ......318 C1
Albion Ct BCAYW CM12 * 283 H7
Albion Gv COLS CO2 ....152 B1
Albion Hl IPNE IP4 ....17 K4
Albion Ms IPNE IP4 ....17 K4
Albion Pk LOU IG10 ....275 N4
Albion Rd SBF/HAD SS7 ....325 P2
SBN/FI SS3 ....350 F3
SOS SS1 ....18 D5
SUD CO10 ....21 H4
SWFD E18 ....295 L7
WALTH E17 ....314 C1
WOS/PRIT SSO 18 B7
Albion Ter K/T/MI CO5 ....155 H7
Albion Ter CHING E4 ....274 E5
Albrighton Crt ENC/FH EN2 ....250 F9
Albuhera Cl ENC/FH EN2 ....250 F9
Albury Grove Rd
CHES/WCR EN8 ....252 C4
Albury Ms MNPK E12 ....315M3
Albury Ride CHES/WCR EN8 ..252 A1
Albury Rd STDN SG11 ....136 B4
Albury Wk CHES/WCR EN8 ....252 C5
Alconbury BXLYHN DA7 ....347 J1
Alconbury Rd RAYL SS6 ....306 D3
Alcotes BSDN SS14 ....129 N3

Aidborough Ct GTDUN CM6 * 92 B6
Aldborough Rd DAGE RM10 ....318 B8
UPMR RM14 ....319 L4
Aldborough Rd North
GDMY/SEVK IG5 ....296 G9
Aldborough Rd South
GDMY/SEVK IG3 ....316 F5
Aldbury Ms ED N9 ....273 J6
Aldeburgh Cl HVHL CB9 ....41 H5
Aldeburgh Gdns COLN CO4 ....128 C3
Aldeburgh Pl WFD IG8 ....295 K1
Aldeburgh Wy
CHLM/WR CM1 ....218 C6
Alden Av SRTFD E15 ....333 J5
Alder Av UPMR RM14 ....319 L6
Alderbury Lea RCHLM CM3 ....242 C9
Aldercar Rd RCOLW CO6 ....162 A1
Alder Cl BSF CM23 ....162 B3
HOD EN11 ....208 E3
LAIN SS15 ....303 L1
Aldercroft Cl IP IP1 ....218 C5
Aldercroft Rd IP IP1 ....218 C5
Alderman Av BARK IG11 ....335 H3
Alderman Howe Ldg
COLN CO4 ....128 C3
Alderman's Hl HOC/HUL SS5 ..287 M2
Alderman Wk SLH/COR SS17 ..323M9
Alderney Gdns WICKE SS11 ....285 H6
Alderney Rd ERITH DA8 ....346 F5
WCHPL E1 ....332 A4
Aldersbrook Av EN EN1 ....273 J4
Aldersbrook La MNPK E12 ......316 A5
Aldersbrook Rd MNPK E12 ......315M4
WAN E11 ....315M4
Aldersey Gdns BARK IG11 ......316 E8
The Alders WCHMH N21 ....187M2
Alderton Cl BRWN CM15 ....276 B5
LOU IG10 ....276 B3
Alderton Crs HDN NW4 ....143 H8
Alderton Hl LOU IG10 ....276 A4
Alderton Ri LOU IG10 ....276 A4
Alderton Rd CDW/CHF RM16 ..340 F6
....9 K3
Alderton Wy LOU IG10 ....276 A4
Alderwood Dr ABR/ST RM4 ....277 P2
Aldham Gdns RAYL SS6 ....306 C4
Aldingham Gdns HCH RM12 ....318 F7
Aldington Cl CHDH RM6 ....317 K2
Aldon Cl HAR CO12 ....218 C7
Aldous Cl RCOLE CO7 ....80 F6
Adria Rd SLH/COR SS17 ....323M9
Aldrich Wy CHING E4 ....294 F3
Aldridge Av PEND EN3 ....252 D8
Aldridge Cl CHLM/GWD CM2 ..218 F7
Aldridge Wk STHGT/OAK N14 ..272 D6
Aldrin Cl SLH/COR SS17 ....341M5
Aldringham Ms FX IP11 ....34 C6
Aldrin Wy LOS SS9 ....308 B9
Aldworth Rd SRTFD E15 ....315 H9
Aldwych Av BARK/HLT IG6 ....296 D6
Aldwych Cl HCH RM12 ....318 F4
Ale Founder Cl COLN CO4 ......128 F9
Alestan Beck Rd CAN/RD E16 ..333 N6
Alethea Farm Pl HSTD CO9 * 57 L1
HSTD CO9 * 57 P7
Alexander La BRWN CM15 ......281 K4
Alexander Ms
CHLM/GWD CM2 ....241 J8
Alexander Rd BRTR CM7 ....145 H2
VGE SS16 ....323 J2
Alexandra Av K/T/MI CO5 ......202 C6
Alexandra Cl CDW/CHF RM16 ..340 C9
Alexandra Ct STHGT/OAK N14 ..272 B4
Alexandra Dr RCOLE CO7 ......153 K3
Alexandra Rd BOC CM0 ....290 C5
CHDH RM6 ....317 L1
....8 A7
EHAM E6 ....334 B3
FX IP11 ....34 H5
HAR CO12 ....72 C8
HSTD CO9 ....79 P2
IPNE IP4 ....17 J3
LEY E10 ....314 F5
LOS SS9 ....307 N4
PEND EN3 ....274 A5
RAIN RM13 ....336 E1
RAYL SS6 ....307 H4
RCFD SS4 ....308 D1
RCOS CO16 ....156 C6
ROM RM1 ....319 J2
SBF/HAD SS7 ....326 A4
SBN/FI SS3 ....350 D9
SUD CO10 ....21 H4
SWFD E18 ....295 L7
WALTH E17 ....314 C1
WIT CM8 ....172 B9
Alexandra St CAN/RD E16 ....333 K5
HAR CO12 ....15 F4
SOS SS1 ....19 G5
Alexandra Ter COLW CO3 ......127 P9
Alexandra Wy
CHES/WCR EN8 ....252 C4
Alexandria Dr RAYL SS6 ....306 D3
Alcotes BSDN SS14 ....129 N3

Alford Rd ERITH DA8 ....346 B3
Alfreda Av HOC/HUL SS5 ......286 C9
Alfred Gdns WICKE SS11 ......285 J7
Alfred Rd BKHH IG9 ....275 N8
BRW CM14 ....280 G8
SOCK/AV RM15 ....337 P8
SRTFD E15 ....315 J7
Alfred's Gdns BARK IG11 ....334 C3
Alfred St BOW E3 ....332 C3
GRAYS RM17 ....349M4
Alfred's Wy (East Ham &
Barking By-Pass) BARK IG11 ..334 F2
Alfred Ter WOTH CO14 ....159 K6
Alfriston Vls WALTH E17 * 294 F8
Alfreg Rd WIT CM8 ....196 G4
Algars Wy RCHLM CM3 ....264 G9
Algers Cl LOU IG10 ....275 H4
Algers Rd LOU IG10 ....275 H4
Alghers Md LOU IG10 ....275 N6
Alibon Gdns DAGE RM10 ......317 P7
Alibon Rd DAGE RM10 ....317 P7
Alice La BOW E3 ....332 C1
Alicia Av WICKE SS11 ....285M9
Alicia Cl WICKE SS11 ....285M9
Alicia Wk WICKE SS11 ....285M9
Alicia Wy WICKE SS11 ....285M9
Alienor Av BRTR CM7 ....94 A7
Alison Cl EHAM E6 ....334 D6
Allandale SBF/HAD SS7 ......326 A5
Allandale Rd EMPK RM11 ....318 E2
PEND EN3 ....252 A6
Allard Cl CHESW EN7 ....229 K3
Allard Wy BROX EN10 ....208 B9
Allberry Gv CHTY IP2 ....24 C5
Allectus Grs GRAYS RM17 ....349 L3
Allenby Dr EMPK RM11 ....319 K3
Allenby Rd CHTY IP2 ....24 C5
Allen Cl RCOLW CO6 ....150 A2
Allende Av HLW CM20 ....352 C2
Allen Rd BOW E3 ....332 C2
RAIN RM13 ....337 H5
Aliens Cl RCHLM CM3 ....219 L3
Aliens Rd BOW E3 ....284 B3
PEND EN3 ....
Allensway SLH/COR SS17 ....341 N2
Allen Wy RCOS CO16 ....205 H1
Allerton Cl RCFD SS4 ....308 D1
Alley Dock LOS SS9 ....327 N6
Alleyndale Rd BCTR RM8 ....317 K4
Alleyway Vw COS CO15 ......206 F4
Alleyn Pl WOS/PRIT SSO 328 D5
Aliey Rd KIR/NAC IP10 ....33M7
Allfields HAR CO12 ....110 A6
Allhallows Rd EHAM E6 ......333 P6
Allianz Ra PLSTW E13 ....333M4
Allington Cl IPNE IP4 ....
Allington Cl BCAYE CM11 * ..283 L9
Allis Ms HLWE CM17 ....211 K2
Allison Cl GRNFL N11 ....283 K3
Allistonway SLH/COR SS17 ..341 N2
Allmains Cl WAB EN9 ....231 L4
Allnutts Rd EPP CM16 ....255 L3
Alloa Rd GDMY/SEVK IG3 ....317 J4
Allonby Gdns WFD IG8 ....332 D5
All Saints Av COLN CO4 ......151 K2
All Saints Cl BRWN CM15 ....258 E6
BSF CM23 ....137 M6
CHIG IG7 ....277 J9
CHLM/WR CM1 ....273 L8
DTCH/LGLY SL3 ....273 L8
All Saints' Rd IP IP1 ....25 H4
Allwood Rd CHESW EN7 ....229 L2
Alma Av CHING E4 ....294 F4
Alma Cl CHING E4 ....294 F4
SBF/HAD SS7 ....327 L4
WICKW SS12 ....304 F1
Alma Ct CHLM/WR CM1 ......4 D5
Alma Dr CHLM/WR CM1 ......4 D5
Alma Rd PEND EN3 ....274 B4
SBF/HAD SS7 ....327 K4
Alma St SRTFD E15 ....315 J6
Alma Ter BOW E3 ....332 C1
Almere SBF/HAD SS7 ....326 A5
Almond Av HOC/HUL SS5 * ..287 H5
WICKW SS12 ....284 G9
Almond Cl CDW/CHF RM16 ..350 B1
COS CO15 ....207 H1
K/T/MI CO5 ....175 P7
RCOLE CO7 ....153 K3
Almond Dr CHTY IP2 ....25 J3
Almonds Av BKHH IG9 ......275 K8
Almond Wk CVI SS8 ....344 C1
Almond Wy COLN CO4 ......128 F7
Almshouse La EN EN1 ....251 G1
Alnwick Cl VGE SS16 ....322 C1
Alnwick Rd CAN/RD E16 ....333M6
Alpe St IP IP1 ....16 B2
Alpha Cl BRTR CM7 ....145 K4
Alpha Ct COL CO1 ....72 C8
Alpha Gv POP/IOD E14 ....332 B7
Alphamstone Rd BURES CO8 ..75 L5
Alpha Pl BSF CM23 ....137 L6
Alpha Rd BOC CM0 ....291 H4
CHING E4 ....294 D9
PEND EN3 ....251 P8
SUD CO10 ....20 D4
SWFD E18 ....295 L7
WALTH E17 ....314 C1
Alpha Ter CBE/LIN CB7 ....40 B8
Alpine Wy EHAM E6 ....334 B5
Alport Av COLS CO2 ....151M2
Alracks LAIN SS15 ....
Alresford Gn WICKW SS12 ..305 K1
Alresford Rd RCOLE CO7 ....153M6
Alsa Gdns CHTY IP2 ....114 F5
Alsa St STSD CM24 ....114 F5
Alston Wy BSF CM23 ....25 N7
Alston Vis MGTR CO11 * 106 C4
Altair Pl LAIN SS15 ....303 N3
Altbarn Cl COLN CO4 ......128 D2
Altbarn Rd COLS CO2 ......152 E1
Altham Gv HLW CM20 ......210 F1
Althorne Ct PIT SS15 ......304 C6

Althorne Gdns SWFD E18 .....295 J8
Althorne Wy DAGE RM10 .....317 P4
  RCFD SS4 .....289 M6
Althorpe Cl HOC/HUL SS5 .....307 N1
Altmore Av EHAM E6 .....316 A9
Alton Dr COLW CO5 .....127 L9
Alton Gdns SOSN SS2 .....328 F1
Alton Hall La RIPS/CAP IP9 .....82 G5
Alton Park La COS CO15 .....206 F3
Alton Park Rd COS CO15 .....6 C5
Alton Rd COS CO15 .....6 E6
Alton St POP/IOD E14 .....332 E5
Aluric Cl CDW/CHF RM16 .....350 C2
Alverstoke Rd HARH RM3 .....299 K4
Alverstone Rd MNPK E12 .....316 B6
Alverton Cl BRTR CM77 .....144 E8
Alverton Wy COLN CO4 .....128 C4
Alveston Sq SWFD E18 * 295 K6
Alvis Av COS CO15 .....206 D6
Alwen Gv SOCK/AV RM15 .....338 E5
Alwyne Av BRWN CM15 .....145 J4
Alyssum Cl CHLM/WR CM1 .....218 E5
Alyssum Wk COLN CO4 .....128 E8
Amanda Cl CHIG IG7 .....296 E3
Amanda Ms ROMW/RG RM7 .....298 B9
Ambassador Gdns EHAM E6 .....334 A3
Amber Av WALTH E17 .....294 B5
Amberley Cl RCOLE CO7 .....153 K5
Amberley Ct BKHH IG9 .....275 M7
  EN EN1 .....273 L6
  LEY E10 .....314 C5
  PLMGR N13 .....272 E8
Amberley Wy ROMW/RG RM7 .....298 A8
Amberry Ct HLW CM20 .....13 J4
Amber St SRTFD E15 * 314 G8
Ambleside EPP CM16 .....255 H1
  WICKE SS11 * 285 N9
Ambleside Av HCH RM12 .....318 G7
Ambleside Cl LEY E10 .....314 E2
Ambleside Ct COS CO15 .....7 J4
Ambleside Crs PEND EN3 .....274 A2
Ambleside Dr SOS SS1 .....19 K4
Ambleside Gdns
  HOC/HUL SS5 .....286 G6
  REDBR IG4 .....295 P8
Ambleside Wk CVI SS8 * 344 C1
Ambridge Rd RCOLW CO6 .....105 P3
Ambrose Av COLW CO3 .....151 J2
Ambrose Cl DART DA1 .....346 E9
Amcotes Pl CHLM/GWD CM2 .....240 B2
Ameland Rd CVI SS8 .....326 D8
Amerells Rd RCOS CO16 .....181 M1
America Hl NHMKT IP6 .....23 P2
America St MAL CM9 .....222 B9
America Vw VGE SS16 .....322 C1
Amersham Cl HARH RM3 .....299 L4
Amersham Rd HARH RM3 .....299 K5
Amersham Wk HARH RM3 .....299 L5
Amery Gdns GPK RM2 .....299 J7
Amesbury Dr CHING E4 .....253 K2
Amesbury Rd DAGW RM9 .....317 L9
  EPP CM16 .....254 C1
Amethyst Rd WAN E11 .....314 C6
Amidas Gdns BCTR RM8 .....317 J6
Amid Rd CVI SS8 .....326 F9
Amity Rd SRTFD E15 .....315 J9
Amos Hl SUD CO10 .....74 E1
Amoss Rd CHLM/GWD CM2 .....240 E2
Ampers End BSDN SS14 .....3 K6
Ampleforth Rd ABYW SE2 .....335 J3
Amwell Cl WKMH N21 * 273 J4
Amwell Ct HOD EN11 .....208 D4
  WAB EN9 * 253 H3
Amwell End WARE SG12 .....184 A4
Amwell Hl WARE SG12 .....184 B6
Amwell La WARE SG12 .....184 D6
Amwell St HOD EN11 .....208 D5
Amy Warne Cl EHAM E6 .....333 P5
Ancaster Rd CHTY IP2 .....25 J7
Anchorage Hl MAL CM9 .....222 B8
The Anchorage SBN/FI SS3 .....330 C2
Anchor Bvd GRH DA9 .....347 P9
Anchor Cl BRAIN CM7 .....335 J3
  CHES/WCR EN8 .....230 A7
Anchor End MGTR CO11 .....106 F4
Anchor Hl RCOLE CO7 .....153 J7
Anchor La CHONG CM5 .....189 N8
  MAL CM9 .....222 B6
  MGTR CO11 .....106 E4
  RCFD SS4 .....289 M7
  RCOLE CO7 .....105 H4
Anchor Reach RCHLM CM5 .....287 H5
Anchor St BSF CM23 .....137 M8
  CHLM/GWD CM2 .....6 C6
Anchor Yd IG IG1 * 173 P9
  K/T/MI CO5 .....173 P9
Anders Fall LOS SS9 .....308 B9
Anderson Cl CHLM/WR CM1 .....217 N6
Anderson Ct BSF CM23 * 113 L5
  WCHMH N21 .....272 E4
Anderson Rd HOM E9 .....314 A8
  WFD IG8 .....295 N7
Andersons SLH/COR SS17 .....341 N3
Anderson's La BUNT SG9 .....86 B6
Anderson Wy BELV DA17 .....336 A9
Andover Av CAN/RD E16 .....316 A5
Andover Cl COS CO15 .....182 B7
Andrea Av CDW/CHF RM16 .....339 J9
  BRTR CM7 .....145 J1
  SLH/COR SS17 .....341 L1
Andrewes Gdns EHAM E6 .....333 P6
Andrews Cl BKHH IG9 .....275 M8
Andrews Farm La
  GTDUN CM6 .....117 K2
Andrews La CHES EN7 .....229 K7
Andrews Pl CHLM/WR CM1 .....218 C3
Andrew St POP/IOD E14 .....332 G6
Andros Cl IPSE IP3 .....30 C3
Andwell Cl ABYW SE2 .....335 J9
Andyk Rd CVI SS8 .....345 H2

Anemone Ct COLN CO4 .....127 M5
Anerley Rd WOS/PRIT SS0 .....18 A3
Angela Cl WDBR IP12 .....27 N1
Angel Cl VGE SS16 .....324 C3
Angel Ga HAR CO12 .....15 G2
Angelgate Esp HAR CO12 .....15 G2
Angelica Dr EHAM E6 .....334 B5
Angel La GTDUN CM6 .....141 L6
  IPNE IP4 .....17 G6
Angel Rd RIPW IP9 .....24 B1
Angel Wy ROM RM1 .....298 D9
Angle Rd WTHK RM20 .....348 G4
Anglesea Dr IP IP1 .....16 B2
  RCOLE CO7 .....153 K6
Anglesey Dr BSF CM23 .....137 H7
Anglesey Dr RAIN RM13 .....336 F4
Anglesey Gdns WICKE SS11 .....305 L2
Anglesey Rd PEND EN3 .....273 N3
Angle Side BRTR CM7 .....145 L4
Anglia Cl COLS CO2 .....151 L5
Anglia Rd WAN E11 .....314 C5
Anglia Wy BRTR CM7 .....145 L4
Anglo Rd BOW E3 .....332 C2
Angus Cl IPNE IP4 .....26 A2
Angus Rd PLSTW E13 .....333 M5
Anita Cl East CHTY IP2 .....24 F6
Anita Cl West CHTY IP2 .....24 F6
Anjou Gn CHLM/WR CM1 .....218 F4
Annabel Cl POP/IOD E14 .....332 E6
Annabel Av CDW/CHF RM16 .....340 E6
Annalee Gdns SOCK/AV RM15 .....338 E5
Annalee Rd SOCK/AV RM15 .....338 E5
Anna Neagle Cl FSTGT E7 .....315 K6
Anne Cl RCOLE CO7 .....179 L7
Anne Heart St WTHK RM20 .....348 G2
Anne St E14 * 10 E4
  PLSTW E13 .....333 K4
Annett Cl WICKW SS12 .....305 M2
Anne Wy BARK/HLT IG6 .....296 D5
Annie Besant Cl BOW E3 * 332 C1
Annis Rd HOM E9 .....314 B8
Ann St IP IP1 .....16 B2
Ann Suckling Rd HVHL CB9 .....41 K1
Ansar Gdns WALTH E17 .....294 B9
Ansgar Rd SAFWS CB11 .....65 M2
Anson Cha SBN/FI SS3 .....330 D6
Anson Cl HAR CO12 .....110 B6
  RCHLM CM5 .....287 H2
  ROMW/RG RM7 .....298 A6
Anson Crs KESG IP5 .....27 N1
Anson Wy BRTR CM7 .....145 M2
Anstead Dr RAIN RM13 .....336 F2
Anstey Cl LOS SS9 .....307 N8
Antelope Av CDW/CHF RM16 .....349 K1
  COLN CO4 .....128 C4
Anthony Av BCAYE CM11 .....305 L1
Anthony Dr SLH/COR SS17 .....341 M1
Antill Rd BOW E3 .....332 B5
Antill Ter WCHPL E1 .....332 A6
Antlers CVI SS8 .....344 C3
Antlers Hl CHING E4 .....274 F4
Antonia Cl HVHL CB9 .....41 P4
Antoniuis Wy COLN CO4 .....128 C1
Anton Rd SOCK/AV RM15 .....338 E4
Antony Cl CVI SS8 .....326 E9
Antrim Rd IP IP1 * 24 E2
  SBN/FI SS3 .....330 C6
Anvil Wy BCAYW CM12 .....283 J3
  CHLM/WR CM1 .....218 D3
Anworth Cl WFD IG8 .....295 L3
Anzani Av FX IP11 .....10 A2
Anzio Crs COLS CO2 .....151 M4
Apeirdoorn SBF/HAD SS7 .....305 N8
Aperfield Rd ERITH DA8 .....346 E4
Apollo Cl EMPK RM11 .....318 C4
Apollo Pl WAN E11 .....315 H5
Apple Acre Rd HVHL CB9 .....41 N4
Appleby Cl CHING E4 .....294 F3
  RIPW IP9 .....29 L1
Appleby Dr HARH RM5 .....299 H2
  VGE SS16 .....322 C1
Appleby Rd CAN/RD E16 .....333 K6
  CHES/WCR EN8 .....229 K5
Appledene Cl RAYL SS6 .....306 G5
Appledore Av SBN/FI SS3 .....330 B5
Appledore Cl HARH RM5 .....299 H5
Appledore Rd PIT SS13 .....305 H9
Appleford's Cl HOD EN11 .....208 C3
Applegarth Dr
  GNTH/NBYPK IG2 .....296 G8
Applegarth Rd THMD SE28 .....335 J8
Apple Ga BRW CM14 .....280 C4
Apple Gv EN EN1 .....273 K2
Apple Rd WAN E11 .....315 H5
Applerow LOS SS9 .....308 A9
Appleton Cl BXLYHN DA7 .....346 A7
Appleton Flds BSF CM23 .....162 B1
Appleton Rd LOU IG10 .....276 C2
  SBF/HAD SS7 .....325 N3
Appleton Wy HCH RM12 .....319 J3
Apple Tree Cl HSTD CO9 .....98 B6
Apple Tree Ct BRTR CM7 .....146 A9
  SOSN SS2 .....329 M3
Apple Tree Crs BRWN CM15 .....258 F9
Apple Tree Rd WICKE SS11 .....285 L8
Apple Wy CHLM/GWD CM2 .....240 E5
Applewood Dr PLSTW E13 .....333 L4
Appleyard Ter PEND EN3 * 251 P7
Appold St ERITH DA8 .....346 E4
Approach Rd BCAYE CM11 .....304 C2
  CVI SS8 .....345 J2
The Approach COS CO15 .....206 F4
  EN EN1 .....273 N1
  RAYL SS6 .....306 F4
  UPMR RM14 .....321 N5
Apsley Cl WBF CM23 .....162 B1

Apton Ct BSF CM23 .....137 L7
Apton Flds BSF CM23 .....137 L8
Apton Hall Rd RCFD SS4 .....309 H1
Apton Rd BSF CM23 .....137 L7
Arabia Cl CHING E4 .....274 F6
Araglen Av SOCK/AV RM15 .....338 E5
Aragon Cl COS CO15 .....206 E4
  ENC/FH EN2 .....250 E8
  LOU IG10 .....275 P5
  SOSN SS2 .....328 F2
Aragon Dr BARK/HLT IG6 .....296 D4
Aragon Rd HVHL CB9 .....40 G5
  RCHLM CM5 .....287 J4
Arakan Cl COLS CO2 .....151 L5
Arandora Crs CHDH RM6 .....317 J2
Arbery Rd BOW E3 .....332 B3
Arbor Rd CHING E4 .....274 C9
Arbour Cl BRW CM14 .....300 G2
Arbour La CHLM/WR CM1 .....218 C7
  WIT CM8 .....197 P2
Arbour Rd PEND EN3 .....274 A3
Arbour Wy COLN CO4 .....128 D4
  HCH RM12 .....318 C7
Arcade Buildings COS CO15 * 7 F5
Arcade Chambers COS CO15 * 7 F5
Arcade Man COS CO15 * 7 F5
Arcade Pl ROM RM1 .....298 D9
Arcade St IP IP1 .....16 D4
The Arcade WALTH E17 * 294 D8
  WICKE SS11 * 285 J8
Arcadian Gdns SBF/HAD SS7 .....326 F2
Arcadia Rd BOC CM0 .....291 H3
  CVI SS8 .....344 G2
Arcadia St POP/IOD E14 .....332 D6
Arcany Rd SOCK/AV RM15 .....338 E4
Archangel Gdns CHTY IP2 .....24 F7
Archangel St
  BERM/RHTH SE16 .....332 A9
Archates Av CDW/CHF RM16 .....349 K1
Archer Av SOSN SS2 .....329 M3
Archer Crs K/T/MI CO5 .....174 B8
Archers EPP CM16 .....210 B8
Archers Cl BARK/HLT IG6 .....283 H8
Archers Ct PEND EN3 .....273 P1
Archers Flds PIT SS13 .....304 C6
Archery Fields COS CO15 .....182 B8
The Arches SAFWN CB10 * 51 L9
Archibald Rd HARH RM3 .....299 M5
Archway HARH RM3 .....298 G3
Archway Rd CHLM/WR CM1 .....218 D4
  THMD SE28 .....335 L6
Arden Crs CHLM/WR CM1 .....319 L9
Arderne Cl HAR CO12 .....110 A6
Ardleigh VGE SS16 .....322 A7
Ardleigh Cl EMPK RM11 .....299 J7
Ardleigh Ct BRWN CM15 .....281 J6
Ardleigh Gdns
  RBRW/HUT CM13 .....281 P5
Ardleigh Green Rd
  EMPK RM11 .....299 J9
Ardleigh Rd RCOLE CO7 .....104 E5
  RCOLE CO7 .....130 A3
  WALTH E17 .....294 C5
Ardleigh Ter WALTH E17 .....294 C5
Ardley Crs RBSF CM22 .....188 G3
Ardley Rd RAYL SS6 .....306 G3
Ardmore La BKHH IG9 .....275 L7
Ardmore Pl BKHH IG9 * 275 L6
Ardmore Rd SOCK/AV RM15 .....338 E4
Ardra Rd ED N9 .....274 A1
Ardwell Av BARK/HLT IG6 .....296 D9
Arethusa Ph GRH DA9 * 348 E9
Argall Av LEY E10 .....314 B2
Argall Wy LEY E10 .....314 A1
Argents La COLW CO3 .....126 E5
Argent St WTHK RM20 .....349 H4
Argent Wy CHESW EN7 .....229 J6
Argus Cl ROMW/RG RM7 .....298 A5
Argyle Gdns UPMR RM14 .....320 A5
Argyle Rd BOC CM0 .....291 J4
  CAN/RD E16 .....333 L2
  IG IG1 .....316 B4
  RCOS CO16 .....183 J3
  SRTFD E15 .....315 H6
  WCHPL E1 .....332 A4
Argyle St IPNE IP4 .....17 G4
Argyll Rd CHLM/GWD CM2 .....218 F6
  GRAYS RM17 .....349 K3
  WOS/PRIT SS0 .....18 A3
Ariel Cl COLN CO4 .....128 F3
Arisdale Av SOCK/AV RM15 .....338 E3
Arjan Wy CVI SS8 .....343 P2
Arkley Crs WALTH E17 .....294 C9
Arkley Rd WALTH E17 .....294 C9
Arkwright Rd CHES/WCR EN8 .....252 B4
Arkwrights HLW CM20 .....11 L4
Arkwrights Rd HLW CM20 .....210 G2
Arlington Crs CHES/WCR EN8 .....252 B4
Arlington Gdns HARH RM5 .....299 K5
  IG IG1 .....316 A2
Arlington Rd SOSN SS2 .....329 M5
  STHGT/OAK N14 .....272 A8
  WFD IG8 .....295 K5
Arlington Wy BCAYW CM12 .....282 G3
Arlow Rd WCHMH N21 .....272 F7
Armada Cl LAHN SS15 .....323 L1
Armadale CVI SS8 .....344 C1
Armadale Wy EHAM E6 .....334 D6
Armagh Rd BOW E3 .....332 C1
  SBN/FI SS3 .....330 C7
Armagh Ter MGTR CO11 * 106 F4
Armfield Rd ENC/FH EN2 .....251 J9
Armidale Wk COLS CO2 .....152 B4
Armiger Wy WIT CM8 .....197 L2
Armitage Rd SOS SS1 .....329 N5
Armonde Cl RCHLM CM5 .....219 K2
Armond Rd WIT CM8 .....197 H1
Armor Rd PUR RM19 .....348 A2

Armourers Cl BSF CM23 .....161 N1
Armoury Rd RCOLW CO6 .....127 J3
Arms La HVHL CB9 .....42 C2
Armstead Wk DAGE RM10 .....317 P9
Armstrong Av WFD IG8 .....295 H3
Armstrong Cl BCTR RM8 .....317 L2
  EHAM E6 .....334 A6
  SLH/COR SS17 .....342 C2
  SLH/COR SS17 .....341 M8
Armstrong Rd SBF/HAD SS7 .....306 A8
Arne Cl SLH/COR SS17 .....341 L2
Arne Ct LAIN SS15 .....303 K7
Arne Ms LAIN SS15 .....303 K7
Arnett Sq CHING E4 .....294 C3
Arneways Av CHDH RM6 .....297 L8
Arnham Av SOCK/AV RM15 .....337 P8
Arnheim Rd RCOLW CO6 .....291 H4
Arnhem Av SOCK/AV RM15 .....337 P8
Arnhem Gv BRTR CM7 .....145 H1
Arnhem Rd CHLM/WR CM1 .....217 M5
Arnold Av SOS SS1 .....329 K7
Arnold Av East PEND EN3 .....252 D8
Arnold Av West PEND EN3 .....252 C8
Arnold Cl IP IP1 .....16 D4
Arnold Dr COLN CO4 .....128 F9
Arnold Pl TIL RM18 .....350 D6
Arnold Rd BOW E3 .....332 D3
  COS CO15 .....6 B7
  DAGW RM9 .....337 J2
  WAB EN9 .....252 F5
Arnolds Av RBRW/HUT CM13 .....281 M4
Arnolds Cl RBRW/HUT CM13 .....281 M4
Arnolds Farm La
  RBRW/HUT CM13 .....281 P2
Arnolds Wy RCFD SS4 .....288 D9
Arnold Vls K/T/MI CO5 .....173 P7
Arnold Wy CHLM/GWD CM2 .....240 B7
Arnott Cl THMD SE28 .....335 K8
Arnstones Cl COLN CO4 .....9 K3
Arragon Rd EHAM E6 * 333 N1
Arran Cl ERITH DA8 .....346 C4
Arran Ct WICKW SS12 .....305 L1
Arran Dr MNPK E12 .....315 N3
Arras Rd COLS CO2 .....151 N2
Arrendene Rd HVHL CB9 .....41 J2
Arrow Rd BOW E3 .....332 E3
  COLN CO4 .....128 B3
Arrowsmith Rd CHIG IG7 .....296 C2
Arsenal Wy CAN/RD E16 .....334 B9
Arterial Av RAIN RM13 .....337 H4
Arterial Rd SBF/HAD SS7 .....306 B7
Arterial Rd North Stifford
  CDW/CHF RM16 .....338 G9
Arterial Rd Purfleet
  PUR RM19 .....347 N2
Arterial Rd West Thurrock
  WTHK RM20 .....348 C1
Artesian Cl ROM RM1 .....318 E1
Arthingworth St SRTFD E15 .....333 H1
Arthur Ct CHLM/WR CM1 .....217 N6
Arthur Rd CHDH RM6 .....317 K2
  ED N9 .....273 L8
  EHAM E6 .....334 A2
  PLMGR N13 .....273 H9
  RCOLE CO7 .....153 K3
  RIPS/CAP IP9 .....72 C9
  SUD CO10 .....61 L5
Arthurs Ter IPNE IP4 .....17 G3
Arthur St CO CO1 .....8 D7
  ERITH DA8 .....346 E5
  GRAYS RM17 .....349 M4
Arthy Cl RCHLM CM5 .....196 D8
Artillery Cl GNTH/NBYPK IG2 .....316 D1
Artillery Dr HAR CO12 .....109 M7
Artillery St COL CO1 .....128 C9
Arun TIL RM18 .....351 K2
Arun Cl CHLM/WR CM1 .....218 B6
Arundel Cl CHES/WCR EN8 .....229 N7
  SRTFD E15 .....315 K6
Arundel Dr SLH/COR SS17 .....341 M8
  WFD IG8 .....295 K4
Arundel Gdns GDMY/SEVK IG3 .....317 H4
  RAYL SS6 .....306 E2
  WCHMH N21 .....272 F7
Arundel Rd DART DA1 .....347 H9
  HARH RM3 .....299 L4
  SBF/HAD SS7 .....305 N8
  WICKE SS11 .....285 H7
Arundel Wy BCAYW CM12 .....283 K2
  IPSE IP3 .....26 B8
Arwela Rd FX IP11 .....11 C5
Arwen Gv RCHLM CM5 .....286 F2
Asbaston Ter IG IG1 * 316 D8
Asbury Cl COLN CO4 .....128 E7
Asbury Dr RCOLW CO6 .....149 L1
Ascension Rd CRW RM5 .....298 B5
Ascham Dr CHING E4 .....294 E4
Ascham End WALTH E17 .....294 B5
Ascot Cl BARK/HLT IG6 .....296 F5
  BSF CM23 .....137 P6
  SBF/HAD SS7 .....306 E8
Ascot Dr FX IP11 .....11 K5
  IPSE IP3 .....26 A8
Ascot Gdns HCH RM12 .....319 K6
  PEND EN3 .....251 P7
Ascot Gv CVI SS8 * 344 D9
Ascot Rd EHAM E6 .....334 A9
Ashanti Cl SBN/FI SS3 .....330 E6
Ashbeam Cl RBRW/HUT CM13 .....300 F3
Ashbocking Rd NHMKT IP6 .....23 J1
Ashbourne Av SWFD E18 .....295 L8
Ashbourne Rd BROX EN10 .....208 D3
  HARH RM3 .....299 H1
Ashbridge Rd WAN E11 .....315 H2
Ashbrook Rd DAGE RM10 .....318 A3
Ash Bungalows BRTR CM7 .....145 H5
Ashburnham Gdns
  UPMR RM14 .....319 N3
Ashburnham Rd BELV DA17 .....336 B2
  SOS SS1 .....18 E3
Ashburton Av
  GDMY/SEVK IG3 .....316 G6
Ashburton Rd CAN/RD E16 .....333 K6
Ashbury Gdns CHDH RM6 .....297 L9
Ashby Cl CDW/CHF RM16 .....340 F6
Ashby Ri BSF CM23 .....137 N5
Ashby Rd WIT CM8 .....197 K5

Ash Cl BRWN CM15 .....280 C4
  COS CO15 .....207 H1
  RCHLM CM5 .....196 D8
  RCOLE CO7 .....179 K6
  ROMW/RG RM7 .....298 A4
Ashcombe Cl COLN CO4 .....308 E4
Ashcombe Cl LOS SS9 .....307 L9
Ashcombe Wy RAYL SS6 .....307 L9
Ashcroft Rd BOW E3 .....332 B3
Ash Dr IP IP1 .....24 G2
Ashdale Gdns COLS CO2 .....162 A1
Ashdale Rd KESG IP5 .....27 L1
Ashdene Cl HOC/HUL SS5 .....287 H6
Ashdon Cl RBRW/HUT CM13 .....281 M1
  SOCK/AV RM15 .....338 E6
  WFD IG8 .....295 L3
Ashdon Rd SAFWN CB10 .....53 J6
  SAFWN CB10 .....51 J6
Ashdon Wy VGE SS16 .....323 K4
Ashdown Cl BRTR CM77 .....144 E6
  SLH/COR SS17 .....323 N9
Ashdown Crs CHES/WCR EN8 .....230 D7
  SBF/HAD SS7 .....327 H2
Ashdown Rd PEND EN3 .....273 P2
  SAFWN CB10 .....53 L8
Ashdown Wk ROMW/RG RM7 .....298 A5
Ashdown Wy COLN CO4 .....128 E8
Ashen Cl SUD CO10 .....158 G6
Ashendene Rd CHESW EN7 .....228 G4
Ashenden Rd CLPT E5 .....314 B7
Ashen Hl SUD CO10 .....43 K9
Ashen La SUD CO10 .....43 K8
Ashen Rd HSTD CO9 .....57 J2
  SUD CO10 .....43 P6
  SUD CO10 .....44 A5
Ashes Cl WOTN CO14 .....158 G6
Ashes Rd BRTR CM77 .....146 A7
Ash Fall WIT CM8 .....197 P8
Ashfield Av COS CO15 .....306 C4
Ashfield Farm Rd MAL CM9 .....220 G3
Ashfield Rd STHGT/OAK N14 .....272 D1
Ashfields LOU IG10 .....276 A1
  PIT SS13 .....305 H8
Ashford Av BRW CM14 .....280 E9
Ashford Cl WALTH E17 .....314 C1
Ashford Crs PEND EN3 .....273 P1
Ashford Rd CHLM/WR CM1 .....4 A4
  EHAM E6 .....316 A8
  SWFD E18 .....295 L6
Ash Gn RCFD SS4 .....289 L7
  SAFWN CB10 .....50 E1
Ash Ground Cl FX IP11 .....54 E1
  MGTR CO11 .....81 N9
Ashgrove Rd GDMY/SEVK IG3 .....316 G3
Ash Groves SBW CM21 .....187 P2
Ashingdale Cl CVI SS8 .....344 F3
Ashingdon Cl LEY E10 .....294 F1
Ashingdon Hts RCFD SS4 .....288 C7
Ashingdon Rd HOC/HUL SS5 .....288 C7
Ashlea Cl HVHL CB9 .....41 L5
Ashlea Rd HVHL CB9 .....41 L5
Ashleigh Cl LVS SS9 .....326 D8
Ashleigh Dr LOS SS9 .....328 A6
Ashleigh Gdns UPMR RM14 .....320 A5
Ashley Av BARK/HLT IG6 .....296 C6
Ashley Cl SLH/COR SS17 .....341 P2
Ashley Gdns CDW/CHF RM16 .....339 M6
  COLW CO3 .....127 M9
Ashley Rd CHES/WCR EN8 .....229 N2
Ashley Rd CHING E4 .....294 D2
  FSTGT E7 .....315 M9
  HAR CO12 .....110 A6
  PEND EN3 .....273 P1
Ashley St IP IP1 .....25 K7
Ashlin Rd SRTFD E15 .....314 G6
Ashlong Gv HSTD CO9 .....97 P5
Ashlyn Gv EMPK RM11 .....299 J7
Ashlyns Pl PIT SS13 .....304 F8
Ashlyns La EPP CM16 .....212 G9
Ashlyns Rd EPP CM16 .....252 C9
  FOS CO13 .....183 M1
Ashmans Mw RCHLM CM14 .....272 B4
Ashmead STHGT/OAK N14 .....272 B4
Ash Meadow MHAD SG10 .....160 E3
Ashmere Gv IPNE IP4 .....17 K3
Ashmere Ri SUD CO10 .....21 G4
Ashmole Pr COS CO15 .....158 G8
Ashmour Gdns ROM RM1 .....298 G2
Ashpole Rd BRTR CM7 .....121 L6
Ash Ride ENC/FH EN2 .....250 F5
Ash Ri HSTD CO9 .....97 P8
  RCOLW CO6 .....77 N8
Ash Rd CVI SS8 .....344 C6
  COS CO15 .....154 A6
  SBF/HAD SS7 .....327 H4
  SRTFD E15 .....315 H7
  WARE SG12 .....184 D1
Ashstead Cl RCOS CO16 .....181 L7
Ashton Cl CHTY IP2 .....24 D9
Ashton Gdns CHDH RM6 .....317 M1
Ashton Pl CHLM/GWD CM2 .....218 F8
Ashton Rd HARH RM3 .....299 J4
  PEND EN3 .....252 B6
  SRTFD E15 .....314 G7
Ashton Sq POP/IOD E14 * 332 F7
Ash Tree Cl CHLM/WR CM1 .....4 A4
Ash Tree Crs CHLM/WR CM1 .....4 A4
Ash Tree Dr LAIN SS15 .....309 L3
Ash Tree Fld HLW CM20 .....12 C3
Ashurst Av SOSN SS2 .....329 N4
Ashurst Cl DART DA1 .....346 E8
  K/T/MI CO5 .....152 C6
Ashurst Dr BARK/HLT IG6 .....296 D9

CHLM/WR CM1 ....218 C4
GNTH/NBYPK IG2 ....316 C1
Ashvale Dr UPMR RM14 ....320 B4
Ashvale Gdns CRW RM5 ....298 C2
UPMR RM14 ....320 B4
Ashville Rd WAN EN11 ....314 C4
Ash Wk SOCK/AV RM15 ....338 C3
SOS SS1 ....19 J5
Ash Wy COLW CO3 ....151 J5
HOC/HUL SS5 ....287 P8
Ashway SLH/COR SS17 ....324 A9
Ashwells Rd BRWN CM5 ....280 C2
Ashwin Av RCOLW CO6 ....150 A2
Ashwood Av RAIN RM13 ....336 C5
Ashwood Rd CHING E4 ....274 C9
Ashworth PI HLWE CM17 ....211 L5
Ashworths CVI SS8 * 326 D8
RCFD SS4 ....308 D1
Askews Farm Rd
GRAYS RM17 ....349 H5
Askew Vis PLMGR N15 * 272 C9
Askins Rd RCOLE CO7 ....80 F6
Askwith Rd RAIN RM13 ....336 C2
Asland Rd SRTFD E15 ....332 C1
Aspen CI CVI SS8 ....344 D1
HVHL CB9 ....41 H2
NHMKT IP6 ....22 A2
Aspen Ct LAIN SS15 ....303 K6
RBRW/HUT CM15 ....281 K9
Aspen Gv UPMR RM14 ....319 M6
The Aspens BSF CM23 ....157 N4
Aspen Wy COLN CO4 ....128 E7
HAR CO12 ....109 J9
PEND EN3 ....252 A5
POP/IOD E14 ....332 F7
RCOLW RM15 ....338 G5
Aspin Ms SAFWN CB10 ....51 M7
Asquith Av SBF/HAD SS7 ....306 F9
Asquith CI BCTR RM8 ....317 K3
Asquith Dr COLN CO4 ....62 C8
Asquith Gdns SBF/HAD SS7 ....306 F8
Assanune Ct RCFD SS4 ....308 E1
Assington St SUD CO10 ....76 F1
Astell Ct FOS CO13 * 183 N1
EA 2 E4
Aster CI BSF CM23 ....137 J8
RCOS CO16 ....181 N1
Aster Ct CHLM/WR CM1 ....218 E5
RCOS CO16 ....181 N1
Aster Rd CHTY IP2 ....24 F7
The Asters CHESW EN7 ....229 J7
Astley GRAYS RM17 ....349 J4
Astley Rd RCOS CO15 ....6 B5
Aston Rd LAIN SS15 ....303 J9
Aston St WCHPL E1 ....332 E6
Astor Av ROMW/RG RM7 ....318 A1
Astra CI HCH RM12 ....318 C8
Ataka Rd FX IP11 ....35 J5
Atcost Rd BARK IG11 ....335 H5
Athelstan Ct HARH RM5 ....299 L5
Athelstan Gv BOW E3 ....332 C2
Athelstan Gdns WICKE SS11 ....285 J7
Athelstan Rd COLW CO3 ....151 M1
HARH RM5 ....299 L5
Athenia CI CHESW EN7 ....228 C8
Atherstone CI CVI SS8 ....344 F5
Atherton Rd CVI SS8 ....344 F5
Atherton End SBW CM21 ....187 M1
Atherton Gdns
CDW/CHF RM16 ....350 D2
Atherton Rd FSTGT E7 ....315 J8
Atherton Ms CHTY IP2 ....24 J8
CLAY IG5 ....295 P6
FSTGT E7 ....315 J7
Athlone C WALTH E17 ....294 C7
Atholde Gdns EN EN1 ....273 K4
GDMY/SEVK IG3 ....317 H2
Atholl Rd CHLM/GWD CM2 ....218 E6
GDMY/SEVK IG3 ....317 H2
Athol PI CHLM/GWD CM2 ....218 E6
Athol Sq POP/IOD E14 ....332 F3
Athos Rd CVI SS8 ....326 F9
Atkinson Rd CAN/RD E16 ....333 M5
Atkins Rd LEY E10 ....314 E1
Atlanta Bvd ROM RM1 ....318 D1
Atlantis CI BARK IG11 ....335 J5
Atlas Ct RCOLW CO6 ....99 H9
Atlas Rd DART DA1 ....347 L8
PLSTW E13 ....333 K2
RCOLW CO6 ....98 C9
Atley Rd BOW E3 ....332 D1
Atridge Cha BCAYW CM12 ....283 H4
Atterton Rd HVHL CB9 ....40 G2
Attlee Ct GRAYS RM17 ....349 K1
Attlee Gdns COL CO15 ....128 C9
Attlee Rd THMD SE28 ....335 J7
Attlee Ter WALTH E17 ....294 E8
Attwoods CI CHLM/GWD CM2 ......218 A4
Aubrey CI CHLM/WR CM1 ....218 A4
Aubrey Dr SUD CO10 ....47 K9
Aubrey Rd WALTH E17 ....294 D8
Aubrietia CI HARH RM5 ....299 K5
Auckland Av RAIN RM13 ....336 E4
Auckland CI CHLM/GWD CM1 ......217 M6
EN EN1 ....251 N7
TIL RM18 ....350 B7
Auckland Rd IL IG1 ....314 E5
LEY E10 ....314 D3
Audeigh PI CHIG IG7 ....296 B5
Audley Cl BRTR CM7 ....144 E7
Audley Cft SWFD E18 ....295 J8
Audley Dr CAN/RD E16 ....335 L8
Audley End Rd SAFWS CB11 ......54 H7
Audley Gdns GDMY/SEVK IG3 ....316 G4
LOU IG10 ....276 E1
WAB EN9 ....252 F4
Audleys CI SOSN SS14 ....328 F1
Audley Wy BSDN SS14 ....159 H8
Audrey Gdns BSF CM23 ....162 C2
Audrey Rd IL IG1 ....314 D5
Audwick CI CHES/WCR EN8 ....230 A7
Augurs La PLSTW E13 ....333 L5

Augustine Ct WAB EN9 ....252 E3
Augustine Wy RCHLM CM5 ....242 C8
Augustus Ct COLN CO4 ....128 C1
HVHL CB9 ....41 H4
Augustus Wy WIT CM8 ....197 H4
Aukingford Gdns CHONG CM5 ....235 L5
Aukingford Gn RCHLM CM5 ....235 L6
Auriel Av DAGE RM10 ....318 C8
Austen CI BRTR CM7 ....145 K6
LOU IG10 ....276 E2
THMD SE28 ....335 J8
TIL RM18 ....350 D7
Austen Dr ING CM4 ....261 J7
Austen Rd HARH RM5 ....261 J7
Austin Av COS CO15 ....206 D6
Austin St CHTY IP2 ....16 E7
Austral Dr EMPK RM11 ....319 J2
Austral Wy RCHLM CM5 ....267 P6
Auton Cft SAFWN CB11 ....65 L2
Autoway COLN CO4 ....128 D3
Autumn CI EN EN1 ....273 N1
RCOS CO16 ....181 M8
Autumn St BOW E3 ....332 D1
Avalon CI ENC/FH EN2 ....272 F1
Avebury Rd WAN E11 ....314 G3
WOS/PRIT SS0 ....18 C1
Aveley By-Pass
SOCK RM15 ....337 P7
Aveley CI ERITH DA8 ....346 E4
SOCK/AV RM15 ....338 A8
Aveley Rd UPMR RM14 ....319 N9
Aveley Wy MAL CM9 ....244 A2
Aveline Rd RCOLE CO7 ....104 E9
Aveling Park Rd WALTH E17 ......294 D6
Avelon Rd CRW RM5 ....298 C5
RAIN RM13 ....336 F1
Avenons Rd PLSTW E13 ....333 K5
Avenue Rd HARH RM5 ....299 L5
BSF CM23 ....157 M8
CHLM/GWD CM2 ....218 E6
EPP CM16 ....254 E6
ERITH DA8 ....346 B5
HARH RM5 ....315 L2
HOD EN11 ....208 G7
ING CM4 ....260 C6
LOS SS9 ....327 P6
SBF/HAD SS7 ....326 B5
STHGT/OAK N14 ....272 B6
WFD IG8 ....295 M5
WIT CM8 ....197 K1
WOS/PRIT SS0 ....18 C4
Avenue Ter WOS/PRIT SS0 * 18 C4
The Avenue BCAYW CM12 ....283 H6
BSF CM7 ....145 J3
CHING E4 ....294 C3
COLW CO3 ....127 M9
COS CO15 ....182 C6
CVI SS8 ....344 E2
FX IP11 ....34 E4
GRH DA9 ....348 E9
GTDUN CM6 ....141 M8
HAR CO12 ....133 L4
HCH RM12 ....319 J4
HOC/HUL SS5 ....286 G5
HOD EN11 ....208 C7
IG9 ....25 K2
LOU IG10 ....275 P5
RBRW/HUT CM15 ....301 H3
RCHLM CM5 ....242 C4
RCHLM CM5 ....288 B1
RCOLE CO7 ....153 J5
RCOLW CO6 ....126 G4
RIPW IP8 ....29 H5
ROM RM1 ....298 C8
SBF/HAD SS7 ....327 H5
SLH/COR SS17 ....324 C9
WAB EN9 ....231 M4
WAN E11 ....315 L1
WIT CM8 ....197 K1
WIT CM8 ....197 K1
Avery Gdns GNTH/NBYPK IG2 ....296 A9
Avey La LOU IG10 ....253 K8
Aviary CI CAN/RD E16 ....333 J5
Aviation Wy SOSN SS2 ....308 D8
Avignon CI COLS CO2 ....152 C2
Avila Cha CHLM/GWD CM2 ....240 A9
Avila Sq WCHPL E1 ....332 A6
Avocet CI FOS CO13 ....158 F8
K/T/MI CO5 ....173 J3
K/T/MI CO5 ....202 C5
Avocet Ct FX IP11 * 11 C5
Avocet La KESG IP5 ....26 C9
Avocet Wy MAL CM9 ....222 D6
Avon CI RCFD SS4 ....308 D2
Avondale CI LOU IG10 ....276 A6
RAYL SS6 ....307 J5
Avondale CI WFD IG8 ....295 L5
Avondale Crs PEND EN3 ....274 B2
REDBR IG4 ....295 N9
Avondale Dr LOS SS9 ....328 A2
LOU IG10 ....276 A5
Avondale Gdns SLH/COR SS17 ..323M9
Avondale Rd CAN/RD E16 ....333 H5
COS CO15 ....25 J9
IPSE IP5 ....272 F8
PLMGR N13 ....272 A4
RAYL SS6 ....326 A3
VGE SS16 ....304 D1
WALTH E17 ....314 D2
Avon Gn SOCK/AV RM15 ....338 E6
Avon Ms CHLM/WR CM1 ....217 L7
Avon Rd CHLM/GWD CM2 ....240 A6
HOC/HUL SS5 ....287 H2
SBW CM21 ....187 M1
Avon Wy COLN CO4 ....128 C8
SBN/FI SS3 ....330 C8

SWFD E18 ....295 K8
Avril Wy CHING E4 ....294 F2
Avro Rd SOSN SS2 ....308 E9
Axe St BARK IG11 ....334 D1
Axon PI IL IG1 ....316 D4
Aylands Rd PEND EN3 ....252 A6
Aylesbeare SBN/FI SS3 ....330 E6
Aylesbury Dr CVI SS8 ....315 J8
VGE SS16 ....182 G7
Aylesbury Rd RCHLM CM5 ....322 C1
Aylets Fld HLWS CM18 ....210 F6
Aylett CI CVI SS8 ....344 F1
Aylett Rd UPMR RM14 ....319 P4
Ayletts CHLM/WR CM1 ....194 A9
Aylev Cft EN EN1 ....273 M4
Aylmer Rd BCTR RM8 ....317 M5
WAN E11 ....315 J2
Ayloffe Rd COLN CO4 ....21 K2
DAGW RM9 ....317 N8
Ayloffs CI EMPK RM11 ....299 K8
Ayloff's Wk EMPK RM11 ....299 K9
Aylsham La HARH RM5 ....299 H1
Aylsham Rd HOD EN11 ....208 A3
Aymer CI SAFWN CB11 ....332 A6
Aynsley Gdns HLWE CM17 ....211 K5
Aynsworth Av BSF CM23 ....137 M4
Ayres CI PLSTW E13 ....333 K3
Ayr Gn ROM RM1 ....298 D5
Ayron Rd SOCK/AV RM15 ....338 E4
Ayr Rd ENE IP4 ....26 A2
Ayr Wy ROM RM1 ....298 D5
Azalea Av WICKW SS12 ....285 H9
Azalea CI IL IG1 ....316 C7
Azalea Ct WFD IG8 * 295 H4
Azalea Ms RCOS CO16 ....344 D5
Azalea Wy RCOS CO16 ....181 J9

B

Baardwyk Av CVI SS8 ....345 H2
Baas HI BROX EN10 ....208 A9
Baas HIll CI BROX EN10 ....208 B9
Baas La BROX EN10 ....208 B9
Babbacombe Gdns
REDBR IG4 ....295 P8
Babergh CI SUD CO10 ....47 N5
Babington Rd BCTR RM8 ....317 K7
HCH RM12 ....318 C3
Back Hamlet IPSE IP5 ....17 H6
Back HI CBE/CBH CB1 ....36 A5
RIPS/CAP IP9 ....83 M5
Back La BRTR CM7 ....123 D9
CDW/CHF RM16 ....338 F8
RCHLM CM5 ....283 M7
RIPS/CAP IP9 ....82 D3
RIPW IP8 ....28 G2
SAFWN CB10 ....50 B9
WAB EN9 ....231 M2
WIT CM8 ....198 A8
Back La East RCOLE CO7 ....130 F9
Back La West RCOLE CO7 ....130 E8
Back Rd CHLM/WR CM1 ....238 C1
KIR/NAC IP10 ....33 M7
MAL CM9 ....200 G8
RCOLE CO7 ....130 A2
Back Waterside La
RCOLE CO7 ....179 L8
Bacon Link CRW RM5 ....298 A3
Bacon Rd NHMKT IP6 ....20 D8
Bacons Cha BOC CM0 ....248 D1
Bacons Dr POTB/CUF EN6 ....228 D7
Bacon's La RCOLW CO6 ....125 H4
Bacton Rd FX IP11 ....11 C5
Badburgham Ct WAB EN9 ....253 J5
Baddeley CI PEND EN3 ....252 A6
Baddow CI DAGE RM10 ....335 P1
WFD IG8 ....295 N3
Baddow Hall Av
CHLM/GWD CM2 ....240 F3
Baddow Hall Crs
CHLM/GWD CM2 ....240 F3
Baddow Place Av
CHLM/GWD CM2 ....240 F4
Baden Powell CI DAGW RM9 ....335 M1
Baden Powell Dr COLW CO5 ....151 H5
Baden Rd IL IG1 ....316 C7
Bader CI IPSE IP5 ....26 B9
Bader Ct KESG IP5 ....27 M4
Bader Wy HCH RM12 ....318 F8
Badger Gv BRTR CM7 ....145 L3
Badger Hall Av SBF/HAD SS7 ....326 D2
Badgers BSF CM23 ....137 K9
Badgers Bank CHTY IP2 ....240 A9
Badgers CI CHLM/GWD CM2 ....240 A9
ENC/FH EN2 ....272 G1
WOS/PRIT SS0 ....18 C5
Badgers Gn RCOLW CO6 ....149 K3
Badgers Gv RCOLW CO6 ....102 E7
Badgers Keep BOC CM0 ....240 A9
Badgers Md CDW/CHF RM16 ....307 H2
HOC/HUL SS5 ....287 K2
The Badgers VGE SS16 ....304 E1
Badgers Wy SBF/HAD SS7 ....326 D2
Badger Hall Rd RCOLE CO7 ......130 E5
Badlis Rd WALTH E17 ....294 D6
Badlow CI ERITH DA8 ....346 D5

Badminton Ms CAN/RD E16 ......333 K8
Badminton Rd BROX EN10 ....208 B8
Badminton Rd COS CO15 ....206 F5
Badshah Av IPSE IP5 ....26 A8
Bag La ING CM4 ....259 P5
Bagleys Spring CHDH RM6 ....297M8
Bagshaw Rd HAR CO12 ....14 E6
Bagshot Rd EN EN1 ....273 L6
Bahram Av KESG IP5 ....27 K4
Bailey CI CHTY IP2 ....24 F5
HVHL CB9 ....41 H1
PUR RM19 ....348 A2
Bailey CI COLW CO3 ....150 F2
Bailey La SUD CO10 ....48 C9
Bailey Rd LOS SS9 ....327 L4
The Bailey RAYL SS6 ....308 F5
Bailie CI RAIN RM13 ....336 C4
Bainbridge Dr K/T/MI CO5 ....174 A9
Bainbridge Rd DAGW RM9 ......317 N6
Baines CI COLW CO3 ....151 J1
Baines Coney HVHL CB9 ....41 M4
LEY E10 ....314 D5
Baird Rd EN EN1 ....273 N2
Bakehouse Ct SAFWN CB10 * 51 L8
Baker Av RCHLM CM5 ....196 D9
Baker Ms MAL CM9 * 222 C9
Baker Rd RIPS/CAP IP9 ....85M9
Bakers Av WALTH E17 ....314 E1
Bakers CI RCHLM CM5 ....264 C9
Baker's Ct BSDN SS14 ....304 F5
COL CO1 ....6 B2
CBE/LIN CB1 ....38 C1
CHLM/GWD CM2 ....262 A2
COLN CO4 ....128 C6
EPP CM16 ....232 G9
GTDUN CM6 ....167 P1
MAL CM9 ....260 C5
RCHLM CM5 ....199 K8
Bakerscroft CHES/WCR EN8 * ..230 A7
Bakers Farm CI WICKE SS11 ....284 F5
Bakers Fld ING CM4 ....261 L7
Baker's La BRTR CM7 ....144 F9
HLWW/ROY CM19 ....209M3
Bakery CI BOC CM0 ....248 B7
Bakery Ms WOS/PRIT SS0 * 18 E5
Balaams La STHGT/OAK N14 ....272 C8
Balaam St PLSTW E13 ....333 K3
Baldocks Rd EPP CM16 ....254 F5
Baldock St BOW E3 ....332 E2
WARE SG12 ....184 A2
Baldry CI RIPW IP8 ....29 L1
Baldwin's HI LOU IG10 ....254 A8
Baldwin's La RCOLW CO6 ....124 D7
Bale CI COLW CO3 ....151 H2
Bale Rd WCHPL E1 ....332 B5
Bales Ter ED N9 * 273 J1
Balfe CI COLW CO3 ....151 H2
Balfour CI WICKW SS12 ....305 K2
Balfour Ms ED N9 ....273M9
Balfour Rd GRAYS RM17 ....349M2
IL IG1 ....316 C4
Balgonie Rd CHING E4 ....274 C7
Balgores Crs GPK RM2 ....298 C7
Balgores La GPK RM2 ....298 C8
Balgores Sq GPK RM2 ....298 C8
Balham Rd ED N9 ....273M8
Balkerne Gdns COL CO1 ....8 B6
Balkerne La COL CO1 ....8 B6
Balkerne Pas COL CO1 ....8 B6
Balladeir Wk POP/IOD E14 ......332 E5
Ball Aly COL CO1 ....8 C5
Ballance Rd HOM E9 ....314 A8
Ballards CI DAGE RM10 ....336 A1
Ballards Rd DAGE RM10 ....336 A1
Ballards Wk LAIN SS15 ....303M8
Ballast Quay Rd RCOLE CO7 ....153 K6
Ballater CI IP IP1 ....22 F8
Ballingdon HI SUD CO10 ....60 F5
Ballingdon St SUD CO10 ....76 D3
Balliol Av CHING E4 ....294 C1
Ball La COLS CO2 ....152 B9
Ball's Chace RCOLW CO6 ......100 E6
Ball's Rd MI RCHLM CM5 ......242 E4
Balmerino Av SBF/HAD SS7 ....332 C2
Balmer Rd BOW E3 ....332 C3
Balmoral Av COS CO15 ....150 G1
SLH/COR SS17 ....341M2
Balmoral CI BCAYE CM11 * 283M7
Balmoral Gdns HOC/HUL SS5 ..307M1
IL IG1 ....316 E4
Balmoral Rd BRWN CM5 ....280 C5
Balmoral Rd BRWN CM5 ....280 C5
FSTGT E7 ....315M6
GPK RM2 ....298 C8
HAR CO12 ....14 E6
LEY E10 ....314 E4
PEND EN3 ....252 A6
WOS/PRIT SS0 ....18 C3

Banister CI RCOS CO16 ....181M8
Bankart La CHLM/GWD CM2 ....218 E7
Bank Buildings CHING E4 * 8 B3
SUD CO10 ....20 D6
Bankfoot GRAYS RM17 ....349 J2
Bank Rd IPNE IP4 ....17 J3
Bankside ENC/FH EN2 ....273 N2
Bankside CI RCHLM CM5 ....265 H8
Bankside Rd IL IG1 ....316 D7
Banks La EPP CM16 ....255M2
Banks St BRTR CM7 ....145 J5
Bann CI SOCK/AV RM15 ....338 E7
Banner CI PUR RM19 ....348 A2
Bannister Dr
RBRW/HUT CM13 ....281M5
Bannister Gn WICKW SS12 ....305 K1
Banson's La CHONG CM5 ......235M7
Bansons Wy CHONG CM5 ......235M7
Banstead Gdns ED N9 ....273 J9
Banters La RCHLM CM5 ....169 K4
Banting Dr WCHMH N21 ......272 E4
Bantocks Rd SUD CO10 ....47 P8
Bantoft Ter IPSE IP5 ....26 B9
Banton CI EN EN1 ....273 N1
Banyard CI KESG IP5 ....27 J4
Banyards EMPK RM11 ....299 J4
Banyardway RCFD SS4 ....308 D3
Barbara CI CHES/WCR EN8 ....156 D8
Barbel CI CHES/WCR EN8 ......252 D4
Barbel Rd COLN CO4 ....128 C6
Barber Ct WCHMH N21 ....273 H4
Barberry CI HARH RM5 ....299 H5
Barbers Rd SRTFD E15 ....332 E2
Barbot CI ED N9 ....273M9
Barbour Gdns COLS CO2 ......155 J4
Barbour Gn WICKW SS12 ....305 J2
Barbrook La K/T/MI CO5 ......174 A7
Barbrook Wy RCHLM CM5 ....264 E4
Barchester St POP/IOD E14 ..332 E5
Barclay CI CHOG EN11 ....208 A6
Barclay CI HOD EN11 ....208 C6
Barclay Dr WFD IG8 ....295 K1
Barclay CI PIT SS13 ....305 K6
PLSTW E13 ....333M4
WALTH E17 ....315 J5
Barclay Wy WTHK RM20 ......348 C3
Bardell CI CHLM/WR CM1 ....217 N5
Bardenville Rd CVI SS8 ....345 H2
Bardfield SW BRW CM14 ......280 F8
Bardfield VGE SS16 ....324 D1
Bardfield Av CHDH RM6 ......297 L7
Bardfield Rd BRTR CM7 ......119 L6
COLS CO2 ....152 B5
GTDUN CM6 ....118 G3
RAYL SS6 ....306 D4
Bardfield Wy FOS CO13 ....158 G8
RAYL SS6 ....306 D4
Bardwells Yd RCHLM CM5 * ..265 P3
Barfield Av K/T/MI CO5 ......201 K8
WAN E11 ....315 J3
Barfields LOU IG10 ....276 B5
Barfields Gdns LOU IG10 ..276 B5
Barfields Pth LOU IG10 ....276 B5
Bargate La RCOLE CO7 ....105 J5
Barge House Rd CAN/RD E16 ..334 C3
Barge Pier Rd SBN/FI SS3 ....330 D9
Barham Ct ROMW/RG RM7 ..298 A6
Barington Ct
RBRW/HUT CM13 ....281M5
Bark Burr Rd CDW/CHF RM16 ..339 J9
Barker CI CHTY IP2 ....24 E6
HVHL CB9 ....106 A4
MGTR CO11 ....47 H9
Barker Rd SUD CO10 ....47 H9
Barking Rd EHAM E6 ....333 H6
POP/IOD E14 ....333 H6
Barkis CI CHLM/WR CM1 ..217 L4
Barkstead Rd COL CO4 ......9 K1
Barkwood CI RAIN RM13 ..336 F1
Barlee CI SAFWS CB11 ......88 B5
Barley CI RBSF CM22 ....323 H5
VGE SS16 ....304 E5
Barleycorn Wy EMPK RM11 ..319 L1
Barley Ct SAFWS CB11 ......51 J9
Barley Fld BRWN CM15 ......258 C7
Barley Hills BSF CM23 ......162 B1
Barley La GDMY/SEVK IG3 ..317 H1
Barleylands Rd LAIN SS15 ..303 N4
Barley Mead RCHLM CM5 ..242 E4
Barley Ponds Rd WARE SG12 ..184 C5
Barley Wy CBE/LIN CB1 ......38 C1
COLW CO3 ....150 G1
Barling Rd SBN/FI SS3 ......329 P2
Barlon Rd MGTR CO11 ....130 E5
Barlow's Reach
CHLM/GWD CM2 ....218 F7
Barlow Wy DAGW RM9 ....336 C6
Barlow Wy South DAGW RM9 ..336 C6
Barnabas Rd HOM E9 ......314 A8
Barnaby Rudge
CHLM/WR CM1 ....217 N4
Barnaby Wy CHIG IG7 ....276 B9
Barnard Acres WAB EN9 ..231 H2
Barnard CI SAFWS CB11 ..64 G8
VGE SS16 ....324 D5
Barnardiston Rd COLN CO4 ..9 J2
Barnardiston Wy WIT CM8 ..197 J1
Barnard Dr BARK/HLT IG6 ..296 D8
Barnardo Dr BARK/HLT IG6 ..296 D8
Barnardo Gdns WCHPL E1 * ..332 A6
Barnardo St WCHPL E1 ......332 B6
Barnard Rd CHLM/GWD CM2 ..240 B8
EN EN1 ....273 N1
LOS SS9 ....327 L4
SBW CM21 ....187M1
Barnards Av CVI SS8 ....344 C1
Barnards Fld GTDUN CM6 ..118 C5
Barnby St SRTFD E15 ......333 H1
Barncombe CI SBF/HAD SS7 ..306 A9
Barncroft STDN SG11 ......112 B8

Barncroft Cl *COLN* CO4 ....128 C4
LOU IG10 ....276 B4
Barncroft Ct *LOU* IG10 ....276 B4
Barncroft Rd *LOU* IG10 ....276 B4
Barnehurst Av *BXLYHN* DA7 ......346 B6
Barnehurst Cl *BXLYHN* DA7 ....346 B6
Barnes Cl *MNPK* E12 ....315 N6
Barnes Rd *IL* IG1 ....316 D7
Barnes St *POP/IOD* E14 ....332 B6
Barnet Park Rd *WALTH* SS11 ......285 L6
Barnett Cl *ERITH* DA8 ....346 E7
Barnfield *EPP* CM16 ....233 H7
FX IP11 ....34 G5
K/T/MI CO5 ....173 J2
MGTR CO11 ....106 C4
RBSF CM22 ....164 B8
RIPS/CAP IP9 ....28 D9
Barnfield Cl *HOD* EN11 ....208 D3
WAB EN9 ....231 J1
Barnfield Ms *CHLM/WR* CM1 ....217 P5
Barnfield Pl *WIT* CM8 ....197 J5
Barnfield Rd *RCOLW* CO6 ....127 M1
Barnfield Way *CHLM/WR* CM1 ....126 F9
Barn Gn *CHLM/WR* CM1 ....218 D3
Barnhall Rd *MAL* CM9 ....200 A2
Barnham Dr *THMD* SE28 ....334 C8
Barnham Pl *KESG* IP5 ....26 E5
Barn Hi *HLWW/ROY* CM19 ....209 L7
Barn La *MGTR* CO11 ....105 N9
Barn Md *BRTR* CM7 ....145 N4
BRWN CM15 ....258 F6
HLWS CM18 ....210 F6
The Barn *GRAYS* RM17 * 349 L2
Barn View Rd *RCOLW* CO6 ....147 P5
Barnwell Dr *HOC/HUL* SS5 ....307 N1
Barnwell Rd *DART* DA1 ....347 L8
The Barnyard *VGE* SS16 ....323 H2
Baron Gdns *BARK/HLT* IG6 ....296 D7
Baronia Cft *COLN* CO4 ....128 D4
Baron Rd *BCTR* RM8 ....317 L3
Barons Ct *FX* IP11 ....35 N5
Baronsdale Cl *IP* IP1 ....25 J2
Baron's La *RCHLM* CM3 ....243 P9
The Barons *BSF* CM23 ....137 J9
Barons Wy *VGE* SS16 ....233 J2
Barrowwood Wy *COLS* CO2 ......151 N4
Barrack La *HAR* CO12 ....15 G5
IP IP1 ....16 C3
Barrack Rd *CHLM/WR* CM1 ....192 C7
Barrack Sq *CHLM/GWD* CM2 .....5 G4
Barracks Rd *SUD* CO10 ....76 G2
Barrack St *COL* CO1 ....128 C9
MGTR CO11 ....107 J8
Barra Gld *WICKW* SS12 ....505 L2
Barrass Ct *PEND* EN5 ....252 D7
Barr Cl *RCOLE* CO7 ....153 K5
Barrel Cl *RCOLE* CO7 ....154 F3
Barrells Down Rd *BSF* CM23 .....137 K5
Barrett La *BSF* CM23 ....137 J3
Barrett Rd *WALTH* E17 ....294 F8
Barrier Point Rd *CAN/RD* E16 ....333 M9
Barrington Cl *BSDN* SS14 ....304 E7
CHLM/GWD CM2 ....240 F4
CLAY IG5 ....296 A5
RCOS CO16 ....181 M3
SBN/FI SS3 ....330 D5
Barrington Gdns *BSDN* SS14 ....304 E7
COS CO15 ....182 D8
Barrington Hi *LOU* IG10 ....276 D2
Barrington Pl *ING* CM4 ....260 C6
Barrington Rd *COLS* CO2 ....152 B1
LOU IG10 ....276 D2
MNPK E12 ....316 B8
Barringtons Cl *RAYL* SS6 ....306 C4
Barron's Ct *CHONG* CM5 ....135 J5
Barrow Cl *WCHMH* N21 ....272 C9
Barrowell Gn *WCHMH* N21 ....272 C8
Barrowfield Cl *ED* N9 ....273 N9
Barrow Hall Farm
SBN/FI SS3 * 330 B1
Barrow Hall Rd *SBN/FI* SS3 ....330 B1
Barrow Hi *SUD* CO10 ....47 N4
Barrow La *CHESW* EN7 ....251 L1
Barrowsand *SOS* SS1 ....330 A8
Barrows Rd
HLWW/ROY CM19 ....210 A3
Barry Cl *CDW/CHF* RM16 ....350 B1
Barryfields *BRTR* CM7 ....95 K9
Barry Rd *EHAM* E6 ....333 P6
Barsey Cl *HVHL* CB9 ....40 F7
Barstable Rd *SLH/COR* SS17 ....341 L3
Bartholomew Cl *SAFWN* CB10 ...96 F9
Bartholomew Dr *HARH* RM5 ......299 J6
Bartholomew St *BSF* CM23 ....137 L8
Bartholomew St *IPNE* IP4 ....17 K4
Bartle Av *EHAM* E6 ....333 P2
Bartlett Cl *POP/IOD* E14 ....332 D6
RCHLM CM5 ....245 N9
Bartletts *RAYL* SS6 ....307 K7
Bartley Dr *SBF/HAD* SS7 ....305 N9
Bartley Rd *SBF/HAD* SS7 ....305 N9
Bartlow End *PIT* SS13 ....304 G7
Bartlow Gdns *CRW* RM5 ....298 C5
CBE/LIN CB1 ....38 C1
CBE/LIN CB1 ....39 P7

Bartlow Side *PIT* SS13 ....304 G7
Barton Av *DAGE* RM10 ....318 B3
Barton Cl *CHIG* IG7 ....276 D8
CHTY IP2 ....24 F9
RCHLM CM3 ....264 G8
Barton Dr *HVHL* CB9 ....42 C1
Barton Gv *HVHL* CB9 ....42 C1
Barton Mdw *BARK/HLT* IG6 ......296 C8
Barton Rd *FX* IP11 ....35 L7
HCH RM12 ....318 F3
Bartram Av *BRTR* CM7 ....145 M3
Bartrip St *HOM* E9 ....314 B8
The Barvens *RIPW* IP8 ....29 J1
Barwell Wy *WIT* CM8 ....197 K2
Barwick Rd *FSTGT* E7 ....315 L6
Baryta Cl *SLH/COR* SS17 ....341 K4
Basbow La *BSF* CM23 ....137 L6
Basedale Rd *DAGW* RM9 ....337 J9
Baseing Cl *EHAM* E6 ....334 B7
Basil Av *EHAM* E6 ....333 P3
Basildon Av *CLAY* IG5 ....296 B5
Basildon Dr *LAIN* SS15 ....303 K8
Basildon Rd *LAIN* SS15 ....303 M7
Basil Ms *HLWS* CM17 ....211 K2
Basin Ap *POP/IOD* E14 ....332 B6
Basin Rd *EHAM* E6 ....222 F7
Baslow Wk *CLPT* E5 ....314 A6
Bassenthwaite Rd
SBF/HAD SS7 ....306 B9
Bassett Gdns *EPP* CM16 ....234 A5
Bassett's La *CHONG* CM5 ....257 L2
MAL CM9 ....220 D7
Bassingbourne Cl *BROX* EN10 ...208 C8
Bassingbourn Rd *STSD* SM24 ....139 J4
Bassingbourn Rbt
RBSF CM22 ....139 J5
Bastable Av *BARK* IG11 ....335 H2
Bata Av *TIL* RM18 ....351 J5
Batavia Rd *CVI* SS8 ....344 A1
Bate-Dudley Dr *BOC* CM0 ....226 E8
Bateman Cl *BARK* IG11 ....316 D8
Bateman Rd *CHING* E4 ....294 D3
RCOLE CO7 ....179 K5
Batemans Rd *RCOS* CO16 ....181 L1
Bates Rd *HARH* RM5 ....299 M4
MAL CM9 ....222 C7
Bate St *POP/IOD* E14 ....332 C7
Bath Rd *ED* N9 ....273 N8
FSTGT E7 ....315 N8
FX IP11 ....35 L7
Bath St *CHTY* IP2 ....25 L8
RCOLE CO7 ....179 L6
Bathurst Rd *IL* IG1 ....316 C5
Baton Ct *PUR* RM19 ....348 A2
Battery La *RIPS/CAP* IP9 ....85 N9
Battery Rd *THMD* SE28 ....334 C9
Battisford Dr *RCOS* CO16 ....181 N5
Battle Rd *ERITH* DA8 ....346 B2
Battlesbrook Rd *COLS* CO2 ....152 E4
Battles La *KESG* IP5 ....27 J4
Battleswick *BSDN* SS14 ....304 D6
Batt's Rd *BOC* CM0 ....246 E9
Baud Cl *STDN* SG11 ....136 D4
Bawdsey Av *ONTH/NBYPK* IG2 ...296 C8
Bawdsey Cl *FX* IP11 ....35 N4
RCOS CO16 ....181 L9
Bawn Cl *BRTR* CM7 ....145 J2
Bawtree Wy *CHLM/WR* CM1 .....145 K1
Baxter Av *SOSN* SS2 ....18 D1
Baxter Rd *CAN/RD* E16 ....333 M6
IL IG1 ....316 C7
Baxters *RCHLM* CM3 ....242 D3
Bayard Av *RCOLE* CO7 ....179 L6
Bay Cl *CVI* SS8 ....344 E3
Bayleys Md *RBRW/HUT* CM13 ...281 M8
Bayley St *HSTD* CO9 ....72 E5
Bayliss Av *THMD* SE28 ....335 J1
Baylis Cl *STHGT/OAK* N14 ....272 D4
Bay Manor La *WTHK* RM20 ......348 C4
Baymans Wd *ERWN* CM15 ....281 H8
Baynard Av *GTDUN* CM6 ....142 D8
Baynards Crs *RCOS* CO13 ....158 F9
Bayne Cl *EHAM* E6 ....334 A6
Baynes Cl *EN* EN1 ....251 M9
Bay Rd *HAR* CO12 ....14 B6
Baythorne St *BOW* E3 ....314 A2
Bay Tree Cl *BRTR* CM7 * 144 C4
CHESW EN7 * 229 L6
Bay Vw *BOC* CM0 ....247 H2
Bay View Crs *HAR* CO12 ....109 M7
Baywood Sq *CHIG* IG7 ....297 J1
Bazely St *POP/IOD* E14 ....332 F7
Bazile Rd *WCHMH* N21 ....272 F5
Beach Ap *RCOS* CO16 * 206 A6
Beach Av *LOS* SS9 ....328 B6
Beach Ct *SBN/FI* SS3 ....531 H5
Beach Crs *COS* CO15 ....206 E6
Beach Rd East *FX* IP11 ....355 M7
Beach Rd West *FX* IP11 ....11 G5
Beach's Dr *CHLM/WR* CM1 ....217 L8
Beach Station Rd *FX* IP11 ....35 L7
Beach Wy *COS* CO15 ....206 E6
Beachway *CVI* SS8 ....344 E3
Beachy Rd *BOC* CM0 ....227 F5
Beachy Rd *BOW* E3 ....314 D9
Beacon Flд *FX* IP11 ....35 H6
Beaconfield Av *EPP* CM16 ....232 G8
Beaconfield Rd *EPP* CM16 ....232 G8
Beaconfield Wy *EPP* CM16 ....232 G8
Beacon Hts *RCOS* CO16 ....205 J2
Beacon Hi *BRW* CM14 ....257 P7
MAL CM9 ....221 P9

PUR RM19 ....347 N3
Beacon Hill Av *HAR* CO12 ....15 F5
Beacon Hill Rd *BRW* CM14 ....257 N7
Beacon Rd *ERITH* DA8 ....346 G5
WARE SG12 ....184 D2
Beaconsfield Av *COLW* CO5 ......127 P9
Beaconsfield Cl *SUD* CO10 ....20 C3
Beaconsfield Rd *CAN/RD* E16 ....333 J4
COS CO15 ....182 E8
ED N9 ....273 M9
IP IP1 ....24 G4
LEY E10 ....314 F5
PEND EN3 ....252 A7
SUD CO10 ....20 C4
WALTH E17 ....314 C1
The Beacons *LOU* IG10 ....254 B8
Beacontree Av *WALTH* E17 ....294 G5
Beacontree Rd *WAN* E11 ....315 J2
Beacon Wy *COLW* CO5 ....126 F9
RCOS CO16 ....205 J2
The Beadles *RBSF* CM22 ....162 E5
Beadle Wy *RCHLM* CM3 ....145 K5
Beadon Dr *BRTR* CM7 ....145 K5
Beads Hall La *BRWN* CM15 ......280 E5
Beale Rd *BOW* E3 ....332 C2
Beale Rd *BOW* E3 ....332 C1
Beam Av *DAGE* RM10 ....336 B2
Beambridge *PIT* SS13 ....304 F9
Beambridge Ms *PIT* SS13 ....304 F9
Beaminster Gdns
BARK/HLT IG6 ....296 C7
Beamish Ct *EPP* CM16 ....234 B4
Beamish Rd *ED* N9 ....273 M7
Beams Wy *BCAYE* CM11 ....283 K9
Beamway *DAGE* RM10 ....318 C9
Bear Cl *ROMW/RG* RM7 ....314 C8
Beanfield Rd *SBW* CM21 ....161 M9
Beansland Gv *CHDH* RM6 ....297 M6
Bear Cl *ROMW/RG* RM7 ....318 A1
Beardmore Pk *KESG* IP5 ....27 N3
Beardow Gv
STHGT/OAK N14 * 272 B5
Beardsfield *PLSTW* E15 ....304 C9
Beard's La *SAFWS* CB11 ....63 K1
Bearing Cl *CHIG* IG7 ....297 H1
Bearing Wy *CHIG* IG7 ....297 H1
Bearsted Dr *PIT* SS13 ....325 H1
Bear St *RCOLW* CO6 ....77 N8
Beaton Cl *BRW* CM14 ....348 E9
Beatrice Av *CVI* SS8 ....344 E1
IPSE IP3 ....35 K5
Beatrice Cl *HOC/HUL* SS5 ....307 N1
IPSE IP3 ....25 P8
PLSTW E13 ....333 K4
Beatrice Rd *COS* CO15 ....6 D6
ED N9 ....273 P6
WALTH E17 ....294 D2
WOTN CO14 ....159 L4
Beatty Rd *BRTR* CM7 ....145M2
Beatty La *BSDN* SS14 ....304 D5
Beatty Rd *RCHLM* CM5 ....287 J2
Beatty Rd *CHES/WCR* EN8 ....252 C4
IPSE IP3 ....26 A9
SUD CO10 ....21 G1
Beattyville Gdns *CLAY* IG5 ....296 B3
Beauchamp Rd *FSTGT* E7 ....315 L9
Beauchamps *BOC* CM0 ....268 C9
Beauchamps Cl
CHLM/WR CM1 ....217 K1
Beauchamps Dr *WICKE* SS11 ....285 M9
Beaufort *EHAM* E6 ....334 E5
Beaufort Cl *CDW/CHF* RM16 .....349 J1
CHING E4 ....294 E5
EPP CM16 ....233 P6
ROMW/RG RM7 ....298 B8
Beaufort Gdns *BRTR* CM7 ....145 K2
IL IG1 ....316 B5
Beaufort Rd *BCAYW* CM12 ....282 C6
CHLM/GWD CM2 ....218 F7
Beaufort St *IP* IP1 ....16 A2
SOSN SS2 ....329 L5
Beaulieu Av *CAN/RD* E16 ....333 L8
Beaulieu Gdns *DAGE* RM10 ......318 A9
Beaulieu Dr *WAB* EN9 ....252 E5
Beaulieu Gdns *WCHMH* N21 .....273 H6
Beauly Wy *ROM* RM1 ....298 D5
Beaumont Av *COS* CO15 ....6 B3
RCOLE CO7 ....179M6
Beaumont Ct *COLN* CO4 ....127 P3
GPK RM2 ....299 H6
WOTN CO14 ....158 G7
Beaumont Ct *HVHL* CB9 ....41 L5
Beaumont Crs *RAIN* RM13 ....318 F8
Beaumont Gdns
RBRW/HUT CM13 ....281M5
Beaumont Gv *WCHPL* E1 ....332 A4
Beaumont Wy *HVHL* CB9 ....41 L5
Beaumont Ms *CHESW* EN7 ....229 J5
Beaumont Pk *CHLM/WR* CM1 ....244 C2
Beaver Cl *COLW* CO5 ....127 H8
Beaver Rd *BARK/HLT* IG6 ....296 F7
Beazley Cl *WARE* SG12 ....184 B2
Beazley End *WICKW* SS12 ....305 K1
Bebington Cl *BCAYW* CM12 ....283 H5
Beccles Cl *WICKE* SS11 ....285 J8
Beccles Dr *BARK* IG11 ....316 G8
Beccles St *POP/IOD* E14 ....332 C6
Beche Rd *COL* CO1 ....152 C1
Beckenham Gdns *ED* N9 ....273 K9
Becker Green Rd *BRTR* CM7 .....145 N4
Becket Av *EHAM* E6 ....334 C5

Becket Cl *RBRW/HUT* CM13 .....300 F3
RCFD SS4 ....308 E2
Becketts Wk *WARE* SG12 * 184 A5
Becket Dr *SLH/COR* SS17 ....341 L1
Becketts *LAIN* SS15 * 303 H9
Beckets Farm Cl *FX* IP11 ....79 J1
Becket Wy *RCHLM* CM5 ....287 H3
Beck Farm Cl *CVI* SS8 ....345 J2
Beckford Rd *MGTR* CO11 ....106 B9
Beckingham Rd *MAL* CM9 ....223 K1
MAL CM9 ....200 B8
Beckingham St *MAL* CM9 ....223 K1
Beckmead Rd *COS* CO15 ....345 J2
SAFWN CB10 ....97 L3
Becontree Av *BCTR* RM8 ....317 J6
Becontree Cl *COS* CO15 ....182 A5
Bective Rd *FSTGT* E7 ....315 K6
Becton Pl *ERITH* DA8 ....346 A4
Bedale Rd *ENC/FH* EN2 ....251 H8
HARH RM5 ....299M2
Beddington Rd
GDMY/SEVK IG3 ....316 G2
Bedells Av *BRTR* CM77 ....145 L9
Bede Rd *CHDH* RM6 ....317 K1
Bedford Cl *BRTR* CM7 ....145 L2
K/T/MI CO5 ....174 A8
RAYL SS6 ....306 G6
Bedfords Hi *CHLM/WR* CM1 .....192 B5
Bedford St *IP* IP1 ....16 G2
Beddoes Av *WICKE* SS11 ....286 B9
Bedwell Rd *RBSF* CM22 ....114 E4
Beecham Ct *LAIN* SS15 ....303 K7
Beech Av *BKHH* IG9 ....275 L8
BRTR CM7 ....145 J1
ENC/FH EN2 ....98 B6
RAYL SS6 ....306 G4
RBRW/HUT CM13 ....281 J9
RCOLE CO7 ....153 J5
UPMR RM14 ....319 N5
Beech Cl *BOC* CM0 ....290 C2
ED N9 ....273 M5
HCH RM12 ....318 G5
LOU IG10 ....276 C2
RBSF CM22 ....329 J5
RIPW IP8 ....24 B5
Beechcombe *SLH/COR* SS17 .....324 D4
Beechcroft Av *BXLYHN* DA7 .....346 C6
TIL RM18 ....351 H2
Beechcroft Cl *CVI* SS8 ....344 B2
IP IP1 ....24 C1
SWFD E18 ....295 L6
Beechdale *WCHMH* N21 ....272 E8
Beeches Cl *CHLM/WR* CM1 * ....A A3
SAFWS CB11 ....65 K2
Beeches Rd *CHLM/WR* CM1 .....217M9
MAL CM9 ....222 A6
WICKE SS11 ....285 J8
The Beeches *BRW* CM14 ....280 E9
CHING E4 ....274 C7
IPSE IP3 ....35 J7
MGTR CO11 ....106 B5
NHMKT IP6 ....22 D4
SAFWS CB11 * 65 H1
TIL RM18 ....350 C7
Beechfield *HOD* EN11 ....208 D1
SBW CM21 ....187 N2
Beechfield Gdns
ROMW/RG RM7 ....318 B2
Beechfield Rd *ERITH* DA8 ....346 D5
WARE SG12 ....184 C2
Beechfield Wk *WAB* EN9 ....252 C5
Beech Gdns *DAGE* RM10 ....318 A9
Beech Gv *BARK/HLT* IG6 ....296 F5
HAR CO12 ....109 L9
HSTD CO9 ....72 C8
HVHL CB9 ....41 H2
IPSE IP3 ....25 N8
KESG IP5 ....26 E4
SOCK/AV RM15 ....337 P9
Beech Hall Crs *CHING* E4 ....294 C4
Beech Hall Rd *CHING* E4 ....294 C4
Beech Hill Gdns *WAB* EN9 ....253 L7
Beechlands *BSF* CM23 ....137 L9
Beech Ms *WARE* SG12 ....184 A5
Beechmont Gdns *SOSN* SS2 .....328 F2
Beech Rd *CHLM/WR* CM1 ....254 G1
HOC/HUL SS5 ....287 H6
KESG IP5 ....26 E4
SBF/HAD SS7 ....326 C4
SUD CO10 ....20 E4
WIT CM8 ....172 A6
Beech St *ROMW/RG* RM7 ....298 B8
Beech Tree Gdns *CHING* E4 ......275 J7
Beech Wk *DART* DA1 ....346 F9
Beech Wy *CBE/LIN* CB1 ....38 E1
Beechwood Cl *CHING* E4 ....294 A3
COLS CO2 ....151 N4
Beechwood Dr *WFD* IG8 ....295 J3
Beechwood Gdns *CLAY* IG5 ......296 A9
RAIN RM13 ....336 C5
Beechwood Ms *ED* N9 ....273 K9
Beechwood Pk *SWFD* E18 ....295 K7
Beechwood Crs *VGE* SS16 ....326 D8
Beedell Av *WICKE* SS11 ....305 L1
WOS/PRIT SS0 ....328 E4
Beehive Cha *BRW* CM15 ....258 G5
Beehive Rd *SUD* CO10 ....59 L4

Beehive St *COL* CO1 * 128 B9
RBSF CM22 ....188 F1
Beehive La *BSDN* SS14 ....3 G4
CHLM/GWD CM2 ....240 A6
REDBR IG4 ....296 A9
Beehive Rd *CHESW* EN7 ....228 G5
Beeleigh Av *SLH/COR* SS17 ......323 K4
Beeleigh Cha *MAL* CM9 ....221 N7
Beeleigh Cl *COLS* CO2 * 152 B5
SOSN SS2 ....329 L5
Beeleigh Cross *BSDN* SS14 ......304 D8
Beeleigh East *BSDN* SS14 ....304 D8
Beeleigh Link
CHLM/GWD CM2 ....218 E9
Beeleigh Rd *MAL* CM9 ....222 A8
Beeleigh West *BSDN* SS14 ....304 C7
Beeston Dr *CHES/WCR* EN8 ......230 A6
Beggarhill *ING* CM4 ....259 N2
Begonia Cl *CHLM/WR* CM1 ....218 E5
Begonia Pl *RCOS* CO16 ....333 P5
Beke Hall Cha North
RAYL SS6 ....306 B3
Beke Hall Cha South
RAYL SS6 ....306 B3
Bekesbourne St
POP/IOD E14 * 332 B6
Bekeswell La
CHLM/GWD CM2 ....239 N7
Belchamp Rd *HSTD* CO9 ....58 A4
Belchamps Rd *WICKE* SS11 ......285 L8
Belchamps Wy *HOC/HUL* SS5 ...307 P2
Belcham's La *SAFWS* CB11 ....89 K8
Belcher Rd *HOD* EN11 ....208 D4
Beldams La *BSF* CM23 ....137 L8
Beldams Gate *RCOS* CO15 ....157 K5
Beldams La *BSF* CM23 ....137 N9
Belfairs Cl *LOS* SS9 ....327 N4
Belfairs Dr *CHDH* RM6 ....317 K2
Belfairs La *LOS* SS9 ....327 N4
Belfairs Park Cl *LOS* SS9 ....327 M1
Belfairs Park La *LOS* SS9 ....327 L1
Belgrave Av *GPK* RM2 ....299 H7
Belgrave Cl *CHLM/GWD* CM2 ....240 C3
IPNE IP4 ....25 H2
LOS SS9 ....307 L8
RAYL SS6 ....306 E3
STHGT/OAK N14 ....272 B4
Belgrave Gdns
STHGT/OAK N14 ....272 C4
Belgrave Rd *BCAYW* CM12 ....283 H4
IL IG1 ....316 B4
LOS SS9 ....307 L9
PLSTW E13 ....333M4
WAN E11 ....315 L2
Belgrave St *WCHPL* E1 ....332 A6
Bellamaine Cl *THMD* SE28 ....334 C9
Beligrove Cl *COLS* CO2 ....158 E8
POP/IOD E14 * 332 D9
Bellamy Rd *CHES/WCR* EN8 .....230 B8
CHING E4 ....294 C5
ENC/FH EN2 * 273 J1
Bell Av *HARH* RM3 ....298 G5
Bell Cl *CHTY* IP2 * 152 E4
COLS CO2 ....193 H4
Bell Common *EPP* CM16 ....254 F2
Bell Ct *RCHLM* CM3 * 263M8
Bellcroft *WIT* CM8 ....197 K1
Belle Staines Pleasaunce
CHING E4 ....274 D8
Belle Vue *CHLM/GWD* CM2 ....4 D6
Bellevue Av *SOS* SS1 ....329 K6
Bellevue Pl *SOS* SS1 ....329 K6
Belle Vue Rd *COL* CO1 ....8 A2
CRW RM5 ....298 F8
IPNE IP4 ....17 J3
RCOLE CO7 ....153 J6
SUD CO10 ....20 E5
WALTH E17 ....294 G6
Bellevue Rd *BCAYW* CM12 ....184 B3
EMPK RM11 ....319 L3
SOSN SS2 ....329 K5
Bell Farm Av *DAGE* RM10 ....318 B5
Bell Farm Gn *BCAYW* CM12 .....283 J4
Bellfield *VGE* SS16 ....324 D3
Bellfield Av *RCOLE* CO7 ....179M6
Bellfield Cl *RCOLE* CO7 ....179M6
Bellfield Gdns *HLWE* CM17 ......211 K4
Bellfield Rd *RCOLE* CO7 ....179M6
Bell Fld *BURES* CO8 ....75M5
Bell Ley *EHAM* E6 * 314 D3
Bell Hill *BURES* CO8 ....75 H5
RCHLM CM5 ....241 P5
Bell Hill Cl *BCAYW* CM12 ....283 J8
Bellhouse Crs *LOS* SS9 ....327 N1
Bellhouse La *BRW* CM14 ....280 B4
LOS SS9 ....327 N2
Bellhouse Rd *LOS* SS9 ....307 N9
Bell House Rd
ROMW/RG RM7 ....318 B3
Bellingham La *RAYL* SS6 ....306 C5
Bellingham Pi *K/T/MI* CO5 ....173 H2
Bell La *BROX* EN10 ....208 D1
BRTR CM7 ....120 D8
BRTR CM7 ....99 P6
CAN/RD E16 ....333 K8
CHTY IP2 ....16 E7
ENC/FH EN2 ....252 B8
EPP CM16 ....96 G5
PEND EN3 ....252 A8
WARE SG12 ....160 C9
Bellmaine Av *SLH/COR* SS17 ....341 N1
Bellmead *CHLM/GWD* CM2 ....5 F4
Bell Md *CBE/LIN* CB1 ....260 C6
SBW CM21 ....187M2
Bell-Reeves Cl *SLH/COR* SS17 ...341 K3
Bell Rd *ENC/FH* EN2 ....251 J9
HAR CO12 ....15 G3
Bells Cha *CHLM/GWD* CM2 ....240 D4
Bells Hi *BSF* CM23 ....137 K7
BURES CO8 ....100 F4
Bells Hill Rd *VGE* SS16 ....324 A4
Bells Rd *SUD* CO10 ....59 L4

Bell St CHLM/GWD CM2 ... 240 E4
SBW CM21 ... 187 M2
Bell Wk WOS/PRIT SS0 ... 328 E2
Bell Whf LOS SS9 * ... 327 P6
Belmer Rd STSD CM24 ... 138 G2
Belmonde Dr CHLM/WR CM1 ... 218 C4
Belmont Av ED N9 ... 273 M7
UPMR RM14 ... 319 L4
WICKW SS12 ... 304 F1
Belmont Cl CHING E4 ... 294 G2
CHLM/WR CM1 ... 218 D4
WFD IG8 ... 295 L1
WICKW SS12 ... 284 G9
Belmont Crs COLN CO4 ... 128 D4
Belmont Hl SAFWS CB11 ... 65 H8
Belmont Park Rd LEY E10 ... 314 E1
Belmont Pl COL CO1 ... 152 D2
Belmont Rd ERITH DA8 ... 346 A5
GRAYS RM17 ... 349 J3
HCH RM12 ... 319 J5
IL IG1 ... 316 D5
RIPW IP8 ... 29 L1
Belsize Av COS CO15 ... 206 C6
Belstead Av CHTY IP2 ... 25 J8
Belstead Rd CHTY IP2 ... 29 P1
Belsteads Farm La
CHLM/WR CM1 ... 218 C1
Belstedes LAIN SS15 ... 303 L9
Beltinge Rd HARH RM3 ... 299 L7
Beltona Gdns CHES/WCR EN8 ... 230 A6
Belton Br LOS SS9 ... 327 N6
Belton Cnr LOS SS9 * ... 327 N6
Belton Gdns LOS SS9 ... 327 M6
Belton Rd WAN E11 ... 315 H6
Belton Wy BOW E3 ... 332 D5
Belton Wy East LOS SS9 ... 327 M6
Belton Wy West LOS SS9 ... 327 L6
Beltwood Rd BELV DA17 ... 346 B2
Belvawney Cl CHLM/WR CM1 ... 217 M5
Belvedere Av CLAY IG5 ... 296 C6
HOC/HUL SS5 ... 307 M1
Belvedere Cl RCHLM CM3 ... 242 C3
Belvedere Pl MAL CM9 ... 244 A2
Belvedere Rd BOC CM0 ... 291 H5
BRW CM14 ... 280 C9
IPNE IP4 ... 25 N3
LEY E10 ... 314 B3
RCHLM CM3 ... 242 C3
THMD SE28 ... 335 L8
The Belvoir ING CM4 ... 260 B6
Bembridge Cl COS CO15 ... 182 A5
Bemerton Gdns FOS CO13 ... 158 D8
Bemsted Rd WALTH E17 ... 294 C7
Benacre Rd IPSE IP3 ... 25 P9
Benbow Dr RCHLM CM3 ... 287 H2
Bencroft CHESW EN7 ... 229 M5
Benderloch CVI SS8 ... 344 B1
Bendish Rd EHAM E6 ... 315 P9
Bendlowes Rd BRTR CM7 ... 94 A7
Benedict Dr CHLM/WR CM1 ... 217 M9
Benedictine Ga
CHES/WCR EN8 ... 230 B6
Benets Rd EMPK RM11 ... 319 M3
Benezet St IP IP1 ... 16 B2
Benfield Wy BRTR CM7 ... 145 L4
Benfleet Park Rd
SBF/HAD SS7 ... 325 N3
Benfleet Rd SBF/HAD SS7 ... 326 D4
Benford Rd HOD EN11 ... 208 C7
Bengal Rd IL IG1 ... 316 C6
Benhall Cl RCOS CO16 ... 181 K9
Benhooks Av BSF CM23 ... 137 K9
Benhurst Av HCH RM12 ... 318 G6
Benjamin Cl EMPK RM11 ... 318 F1
Ben Jonson Rd WCHPL E1 ... 332 B5
Benledi St POP/IOD E14 ... 332 G6
Bennet Ct COLN CO4 ... 128 F9
Bennett Cl BRTR CM7 ... 145 K6
WOTN CO14 ... 159 H6
Bennett Rd CHDH RM6 ... 317 M1
IP IP1 ... 24 E3
PLSTW E13 ... 333 M4
Bennett's Av RCHLM CM3 ... 263 L6
Bennett's Castle La
BCTR RM8 ... 317 K6
Bennett's La GTDUN CM6 ... 167 J3
Bennett Wy RCHLM CM3 ... 196 D8
Benningfield WARE SG12 ... 160 C8
Benningfield Rd WARE SG12 ... 160 C9
Bennington Rd WFD IG8 * ... 295 H4
Bennions Cl HCH RM12 ... 319 J8
Bennison Dr HARH RM3 ... 299 J6
Benn St HOM E9 ... 314 B8
Benrek Cl BARK/HLT IG6 ... 296 D4
Benskins Cl BSF CM23 ... 87 P8
Benskins La ABR/ST RM4 ... 279 J7
Benson Av PLSTW E13 ... 333 M2
Benson Rd GRAYS RM17 ... 349 L4
Bentall Cl HSTD CO9 * ... 98 A8
Bentalls BSDN SS14 ... 303 P7
Bentalls Cl SOSN SS2 ... 329 H2
Bentfield End Cswy
STSD CM24 ... 114 A8
Bentfield Gdns STSD CM24 ... 114 A8
Bentfield Rd STSD CM24 ... 114 A8
Bentham Rd HOM E9 ... 314 A8
THMD SE28 ... 335 J8
Bent Hl FX IP11 ... 11 K3
Ben Tillet Cl BARK IG11 ... 317 H9
CAN/RD E16 * ... 334 A8
Bent La IPNE IP4 ... 26 D3
Bentley Av COS CO15 ... 206 D6
Bentley Cl BSF CM23 ... 137 L9
Bentley Dr GNTH/NBYPK IG2 ... 316 D1
HLWE CM17 ... 211 K4
Bentley La RIPS/CAP IP9 ... 82 E5
RIPW IP8 ... 29 L5
Bentley Ms EN EN1 ... 273 K4
Bentley Rd IP IP1 ... 24 D2
MGTR CO11 ... 131 H3
RCOS CO16 ... 155 P9
WIT CM8 ... 171 M9
The Bentleys SOSN SS2 ... 308 A8
Bentley Wy WFD IG8 ... 275 K9
Benton Cl BRTR CM77 ... 145 P8
WIT CM8 ... 197 K5
Benton Gdns SLH/COR SS17 ... 323 N9
Benton Rd IL IG1 ... 316 E3
Bentons WAB EN9 * ... 231 H1
Bentonwood SBF/HAD SS7 ... 326 F1
Bentry Cl BCTR RM8 ... 317 M4
Bentry Rd BCTR RM8 ... 317 M4
Benvenue Av LOS SS9 ... 308 A8
Benworth St BOW E3 ... 332 C3
Benyon Pth SOCK/AV RM15 ... 338 F2
Berberis Cl VGE SS16 ... 322 G2
Berberis Wk COLN CO4 * ... 128 F8
Berbice La GTDUN CM6 ... 141 K4
Berdens VGE SS16 ... 324 C1
Berechurch Hall Rd COLS CO2 ... 151 M5
Berechurch Rd COLS CO2 ... 151 N5
Berecroft HLWS CM18 ... 210 E8
Beredens La
RBRW/HUT CM13 ... 300 C6
Berens Cl WICKE SS11 ... 285 L7
Beresford Cl SBF/HAD SS7 ... 326 G2
Beresford Ct BCAYW CM12 ... 282 G3
Beresford Dr WFD IG8 ... 295 M1
Beresford Gdns CHDH RM6 ... 297 M9
EN EN1 ... 273 K3
SBF/HAD SS7 ... 326 F2
Beresford Rd CHING E4 ... 275 H7
SOS SS1 ... 19 K6
WALTH E17 ... 294 E5
Bere St WAP E1W ... 332 A7
Bergamot Rd HVHL CB9 ... 40 F3
Berg Av CVI SS8 ... 326 G9
Berger Rd HOM E9 ... 314 A8
Bergholt Av REDBR IG4 ... 295 P9
Bergholt Rd COLN CO4 ... 127 N5
MGTR CO11 ... 106 A1
Beridge Rd HSTD CO9 ... 97 N6
Beriffe Pl RCOLE CO7 * ... 179 L6
Bering Wk CAN/RD E16 ... 333 N6
Berkeley Av CLAY IG5 ... 296 B6
CRW RM5 ... 298 B4
Berkeley Cl IPNE IP4 ... 25 M2
UPMR RM14 ... 319 N4
Berkeley Dr BCAYW CM12 ... 283 H3
EMPK RM11 ... 319 M3
Berkeley Gdns K/T/MI CO5 * ... 152 G7
LOS SS9 ... 327 K5
WCHMH N21 ... 273 J6
Berkeley La CVI SS8 ... 344 D3
Berkeley Rd COS CO15 ... 7 F1
MNPK E12 ... 315 P7
Berkeley Ter TIL RM18 * ... 350 B5
Berkely Dr CHLM/GWD CM2 ... 218 E9
Berkley Av CHES/WCR EN8 ... 252 A4
Berkley Cl COLN CO4 ... 128 D3
Berkley Hl SLH/COR SS17 ... 341 M1
Berkley Pl CHES/WCR EN8 * ... 252 A4
Berkshire Cl LOS SS9 ... 327 M1
Berkshire Rd HOM E9 ... 314 C8
Berkshire Wy EMPK RM11 ... 299 M9
Bermuda Rd KIR/NAC IP10 ... 31 L3
TIL RM18 ... 350 B7
Bernal Cl THMD SE28 ... 335 L7
Bernard Cassidy St
CAN/RD E16 * ... 333 J5
Bernard Cl FOS CO13 ... 158 F8
Bernard Crs IPSE IP3 ... 26 A9
Bernard Gv WAB EN9 ... 252 E3
Bernard Rd ROMW/RG RM7 ... 318 B2
Bernards Cl BARK/HLT IG6 ... 296 D4
Berners End GTDUN CM6 ... 166 F1
Berners Rd FX IP11 ... 35 M7
Berners St IP IP1 ... 16 C3
Berners Wk BSDN SS14 ... 304 C7
Berners Wy BROX EN10 ... 230 C2
Bernice Cl RAIN RM13 ... 337 H4
Bernside BRTR CM7 ... 145 J4
Bernwell Rd CHING E4 ... 275 H9
Berrimans Cl COLN CO4 ... 128 E9
Berrybank Cl CHING E4 ... 274 F8
Berry Cl DAGE RM10 ... 317 P7
HCH RM12 ... 319 H7
IPSE IP3 ... 31 M1
VGE SS16 ... 323 J1
WCHMH N21 ... 272 G7
WICKW SS12 ... 304 C1
Berry Field Cl WALTH E17 ... 294 E8
Berry La VGE SS16 ... 323 J2
Berryman Cl BCTR RM8 ... 317 K5
Berrys Ar RAYL SS6 * ... 306 G5
Berry Ter SUD CO10 * ... 20 C5
Berry V RCHLM CM3 ... 287 H2
Bersham La CDW/CHF RM16 ... 349 J2
Berther Rd EMPK RM11 ... 319 K2
Berthold Ms WAB EN9 ... 252 E3
Berthons Gdns WALTH E17 * ... 294 G9
Bertram Av RCOS CO16 ... 181 N4
Bertram Rd EN EN1 ... 273 M3
Bertrand Wy THMD SE28 ... 335 J7
Bert Wy EN EN1 ... 273 L3
Berwick Av CHLM/WR CM1 ... 217 P3
Berwick Cl CHES/WCR EN8 ... 252 D4
Berwick La CHONG CM5 ... 256 D3
Berwick Pond Cl RAIN RM13 ... 337 J2
Berwick Pond Rd RAIN RM13 ... 337 K2
Berwick Rd CAN/RD E16 ... 333 L6
RAIN RM13 ... 337 J2
Berwood Rd SLH/COR SS17 ... 341 N2
Beryl Av EHAM E6 ... 333 P5
Beryl Rd HAR CO12 ... 109 N7
Beslyns Rd BRTR CM7 ... 93 P5
Bessie Lansbury Cl EHAM E6 ... 334 B6
Betchworth Rd
GDMY/SEVK IG3 ... 316 F4
Bethany St RCOLE CO7 ... 153 J7
Bethell Av CAN/RD E16 ... 333 J4
IL IG1 ... 316 B2
Betjeman Cl BRTR CM7 ... 145 K6
CHESW EN7 ... 229 M7
RAYL SS6 ... 307 J4
Betjeman Ms SOSN SS2 ... 329 H4
Betjeman Wy CHONG CM5 ... 235 L5
Betony Crs BCAYW CM12 ... 282 G3
Betoyne Av CHING E4 ... 295 H1
Betoyne Cl BCAYE CM11 ... 283 L6
Betsham Rd ERITH DA8 ... 346 E5
Betterton Rd RAIN RM13 ... 336 D2
Bettons Pk SRTFD E15 ... 333 H1
Betts Av KESG IP5 ... 27 N4
Betts Green Rd RCOS CO16 ... 156 G9
Bett's La HOC/HUL SS5 ... 307 N1
WAB EN9 ... 209 M9
Betts Rd CAN/RD E16 ... 333 L6
Betty Cocker Gv SUD CO10 ... 21 H5
Betula Ter CHES/WCR EN8 * ... 252 B2
Beulah Rd EPP CM16 ... 233 H8
HCH RM12 ... 319 H5
WALTH E17 ... 294 E9
Beult Rd DART DA1 ... 346 F8
Bevan Av BARK IG11 ... 317 H9
Bevan Wy HCH RM12 ... 319 L6
Beveland Rd CVI SS8 ... 345 K2
Beverley Av CVI SS8 ... 344 C2
K/T/MI CO5 ... 202 G5
Beverley Cl CDW/CHF RM16 * ... 340 E6
EMPK RM11 ... 319 L2
WCHMH N21 ... 273 H7
Beverley Crs WFD IG8 ... 295 L5
Beverley Dr FOS CO13 ... 158 F7
Beverley Gdns CHESW EN7 ... 251 L1
EMPK RM11 ... 319 L2
SOSN SS2 ... 328 F2
Beverley Ri BCAYE CM11 ... 283 K7
Beverley Rd BXLYHN DA7 ... 346 B7
CHING E4 ... 294 G3
COLW CO3 ... 127 N9
DAGW RM9 ... 317 M6
EHAM E6 ... 333 N3
IPNE IP4 ... 25 N3
Beverly Cl BROX EN10 ... 208 B9
Bevin Cl BERM/RHTH SE16 ... 332 B8
Bevington Ms WIT CM8 ... 197 L2
Bewcastle Gdns
ENC/FH EN2 ... 272 D3
Bewick Ct HSTD CO9 ... 72 D7
Bewley Cl CHES/WCR EN8 ... 252 A1
Bexhill Cl COS CO15 ... 207 H4
Bexhill Dr GRAYS RM17 ... 349 H4
Bexley Av HAR CO12 ... 110 A7
Bexley Gdns CHDH RM6 ... 297 J9
ED N9 ... 273 J9
Bexley Rd ERITH DA8 ... 346 B5
Beyers Gdns HOD EN11 ... 208 D2
Beyers Prospect HOD EN11 ... 208 D2
Beyers Ride HOD EN11 ... 208 D2
Bibb Wy IP IP1 ... 16 A5
Bibby Cl SLH/COR SS17 ... 341 P2
Bickenhall SBN/FI SS3 ... 330 C6
Bickerton Point RCHLM CM3 ... 287 J2
Bickley Rd LEY E10 ... 314 E2
Bicknacre Rd RCHLM CM3 ... 241 P9
Bicknoller Rd EN EN1 ... 251 L9
Biddenden Ct PIT SS13 ... 305 H9
Bidder St CAN/RD E16 ... 333 H5
Bideford Cl HARH RM3 ... 299 H5
WOS/PRIT SS0 ... 328 B1
Bideford Gdns EN EN1 ... 273 K6
Bideford Rd PEND EN3 ... 252 C8
Biggerstaff Rd SRTFD E15 ... 332 F1
Biggin La GRAYS RM17 ... 350 C4
Biggs Grove Rd CHESW EN7 ... 229 K6
The Bight RCHLM CM3 ... 287 J3
Bignalls Cft COLN CO4 ... 128 D3
Bignold Rd FSTGT E7 ... 315 K6
Bigods La GTDUN CM6 ... 141 L1
Bijou Cl K/T/MI CO5 ... 174 A7
Bilberry End CBE/LIN CB1 ... 38 B4
Billericay Rd RBRW/HUT CM13 ... 301 P4
Billers Cha CHLM/WR CM1 ... 218 F4
Billet La EMPK RM11 ... 319 J3
SLH/COR SS17 ... 341 M4
Billet Rd CHDH RM6 ... 297 K7
WALTH E17 ... 294 A5
The Billett SLH/COR SS17 * ... 341 N4
Billings Cl DAGW RM9 ... 317 K9
Billy's La RCOLE CO7 ... 80 A7
Bilsdale Cl COLN CO4 ... 128 D3
Bilton Rd CHLM/WR CM1 ... 4 B6
ERITH DA8 ... 346 F5
SBF/HAD SS7 ... 327 H3
Bilton Wy PEND EN3 ... 252 C9
Bincote Rd ENC/FH EN2 ... 272 E2
Bingham Cl SOCK/AV RM15 ... 338 E6
Bingley Rd CAN/RD E16 ... 333 M6
HOD EN11 ... 208 F5
Binley Rd CHLM/GWD CM2 ... 218 D9
Binsey Wk ABYW SE2 ... 335 K9
Birchalls STSD CM24 ... 114 B7
Bircham Rd SOSN SS2 ... 329 H4
Birchanger La BSF CM23 ... 138 A4
Birch Av HAR CO12 ... 14 B7
PLMGR N13 ... 273 H9
RCOLE CO7 ... 155 K6
Birch Cl BKHH IG9 ... 275 N9
BRTR CM7 ... 144 F4
CAN/RD E16 ... 333 H5
COS CO15 ... 207 H1
CVI SS8 ... 344 C2
RAYL SS6 ... 306 F4
RCFD SS4 ... 289 M7
RCOLE CO7 ... 179 K7
ROMW/RG RM7 ... 298 A7
SBF/HAD SS7 ... 305 N8
SOCK/AV RM15 ... 338 G4
Birch Crs EMPK RM11 ... 299 K8
SOCK/AV RM15 ... 338 G3
Birchcroft Rd IP IP1 ... 25 J1
Birchdale HOC/HUL SS5 ... 286 G5
Birchdale Gdns CHDH RM6 ... 317 L2
Birchdale Rd FSTGT E7 ... 315 M7
Birchdene Dr THMD SE28 ... 335 H8
Birch Dr MGTR CO11 ... 81 N8
Birche Cl LOS SS9 ... 327 P2
The Birches EPP CM16 ... 234 A5
FOS CO13 ... 158 F8
RBRW/HUT CM13 ... 281 H9
SBF/HAD SS7 ... 305 P7
STHGT/OAK N14 ... 272 E5
Birches Wk
CHLM/GWD CM2 ... 239 P8
Birch Fall RCOLW CO6 ... 77 N8
Birchfield Rd CHES/WCR EN8 ... 229 N8
Birchfield St POP/IOD E14 ... 332 D7
Birch Gdns DAGE RM10 ... 318 B5
Birch Gn WICKW SS12 ... 285 J9
Birch Gv KESG IP5 ... 27 N5
WAN E11 ... 315 H5
Birchington Cl BXLYHN DA7 ... 346 A6
Birch La ING CM4 ... 261 N6
Birch Ri WIT CM8 ... 197 P6
Birch Rd BOC CM0 ... 248 B6
COLS CO2 ... 150 G9
ROMW/RG RM7 ... 298 A7
Birch St COLS CO2 ... 175 K2
RCOLW CO6 ... 77 P8
Birchway COLS CO2 ... 175 K3
Birchwood BSF CM23 ... 138 A4
SBF/HAD SS7 ... 305 N8
Birch Wood Cl K/T/MI CO5 * ... 202 G6
Birchwood Cl K/T/MI CO5 ... 174 B9
RBRW/HUT CM13 * ... 300 F3
Birchwood Dr KESG IP5 ... 26 D2
LOS SS9 ... 328 B4
Birchwood Rd COLN CO4 ... 104 B4
RCHLM CM3 ... 243 J8
SLH/COR SS17 ... 324 A9
Birchwood Wy K/T/MI CO5 ... 174 C8
Birdbrook Cl DAGE RM10 ... 318 B9
RBRW/HUT CM13 ... 281 L5
Birdbrook Rd HSTD CO9 ... 56 B7
Birdbush Av SAFWS CB11 ... 65 L2
Bird La K/T/MI CO5 ... 174 B9
RBRW/HUT CM13 ... 300 F6
UPMR RM14 ... 300 A9
Birds Cl BCAYE CM11 ... 284 B3
SAFWN CB10 ... 36 A8
Birds Farm Av
ROMW/RG RM7 ... 298 A5
Birdsfield La HOM E9 ... 332 C1
Birds Gn CHONG CM5 ... 214 C7
Birkbeck Rd ENC/FH EN2 ... 251 J9
GNTH/NBYPK IG2 ... 296 E9
RBRW/HUT CM13 ... 281 N5
ROMW/RG RM7 ... 318 C3
Birkdale Av HARH RM3 ... 299 M4
Birkdale Ri RCHLM CM3 ... 196 E8
Birkfield Cl CHTY IP2 ... 25 H7
Birkfield Dr CHTY IP2 ... 24 G9
Birkin Cl K/T/MI CO5 ... 173 N9
Birling Rd ERITH DA8 ... 346 C5
Birs Cl WICKE SS11 ... 285 J7
Biscay SOSN SS2 ... 308 B8
Biscay Cl HVHL CB9 ... 41 M4
Bishop Rd CHLM/WR CM1 ... 5 F1
COLS CO2 ... 151 K3
STHGT/OAK N14 ... 272 A6
Bishops Av BRTR CM7 ... 145 L3
BSF CM23 ... 162 C2
CHDH RM6 ... 317 K1
PLSTW E13 ... 333 L1
Bishops Cl EN EN1 ... 273 N1
FX IP11 ... 35 N5
PIT SS13 ... 304 F5
WALTH E17 ... 294 E8
Bishops Ct CHES/WCR EN8 * ... 229 N9
Bishopscourt Gdns
CHLM/WR CM1 ... 218 D7
Bishops Dr RCOS CO16 ... 206 A6
Bishopsfield HLWS CM18 ... 210 F6
Bishop's Hall Rd BRWN CM15 ... 280 E5
Bishop's Hl IPSE IP3 ... 17 J7
Bishop's La HSTD CO9 ... 74 E6
K/T/MI CO5 ... 173 P6
Bishops Park Wy BSF CM23 ... 136 G8
Bishops Pl WIT CM8 * ... 198 A7
Bishops Rd SLH/COR SS17 ... 341 N2
WICKW SS12 ... 305 J4
Bishopsteignton SBN/FI SS3 ... 330 B6
Bishops Wk BRWN CM15 ... 281 J8
Bisley Cl CHES/WCR EN8 ... 252 A3
RCOS CO16 * ... 181 L7
Bisson Rd SRTFD E15 ... 332 F2
Bistern Av WALTH E17 ... 294 G7
Bittern Cl CHESW EN7 ... 228 G4
CHTY IP2 ... 24 F8
K/T/MI CO5 ... 173 J3
Bixley Dr IPNE IP4 ... 26 D6
Bixley La IPNE IP4 ... 26 E6
Bixley Rd IPSE IP3 ... 26 C8
Blackacre Rd EPP CM16 ... 254 F7
Black Barns FX IP11 ... 34 F4
Blackberry Rd COLW CO3 ... 150 F2
Blackborne Rd DAGE RM10 ... 317 P8
Black Boy La MGTR CO11 ... 108 D4
Blackbrook Rd RCOLW CO6 ... 102 F9
Blackbush Av CHDH RM6 ... 297 L9
Blackbushe BSF CM23 ... 137 P5
Black Bush La
CDW/CHF RM16 ... 340 E1
Blackbush Spring HLW CM20 ... 211 H2
Black Chapel La GTDUN CM6 ... 167 K5
Blackdale CHESW EN7 ... 229 M6
Black Ditch Rd WAB EN9 * ... 252 F6
Black Ditch Wy WAB EN9 ... 252 E6
Blackdown Av KESG IP5 ... 26 E5
Black Fan Cl ENC/FH EN2 ... 251 H9
Blackfriars SUD CO10 ... 20 B7
Blackfriars Ct IPNE IP4 * ... 17 F5
Blackgate Rd SBN/FI SS3 ... 330 F7
Blackheath COLS CO2 ... 152 B6
Black Horse La IP IP1 ... 16 D4
Blackhorse La EPP CM16 ... 234 C4
WALTH E17 ... 294 A7
Blackhorse Rd WALTH E17 ... 294 A7
Blackhouse La SUD CO10 ... 61 L7
Blacklands Cl SAFWS CB11 ... 65 K2
Black La BRTR CM7 ... 93 N6
Blackley La RCHLM CM3 ... 169 J2
Black Lion Ct HLWE CM17 * ... 187 K8
Blacklock CHLM/GWD CM2 ... 218 F8
Blackman Wy WIT CM8 ... 197 K3
Blackmore Av CVI SS8 ... 344 E3
Blackmore Cl HVHL CB9 ... 41 J2
Blackmore Ct WAB EN9 ... 253 K3
Blackmore Md ING CM4 ... 259 J1
Blackmore Rd BKHH IG9 ... 275 P6
BRWN CM15 ... 258 B8
GRAYS RM17 ... 349 M3
ING CM4 ... 258 F3
Blackmores LAIN SS15 ... 302 F9
Blackshots La
CDW/CHF RM16 ... 339 M7
Blacksmith Cl BCAYW CM12 ... 283 J3
CHDH RM6 ... 317 K1
CHLM/WR CM1 ... 218 D3
Blacksmiths Aly ING CM4 ... 259 H1
Blacksmiths Cl BSF CM23 ... 136 G9
Black Smiths Cl WARE SG12 ... 184 D5
Blacksmiths Hl SUD CO10 ... 43 J7
Blacksmiths La CBE/LIN CB1 ... 39 P6
HAR CO12 ... 110 A5
RAIN RM13 ... 336 E1
SUD CO10 ... 60 C8
WIT CM8 ... 197 P7
Blacksmiths Wy SBW CM21 ... 187 J3
Black Swan Ct WARE SG12 * ... 184 A3
Blackthorn Av COLN CO4 ... 128 F7
Blackthorn Cl CHLM/WR CM1 ... 239 H1
IPSE IP3 ... 31 L1
Blackthorn Ct VGE SS16 ... 323 H2
Blackthorne Dr CHING E4 ... 294 G1
Blackthorne Rd CVI SS8 ... 344 F2
Blackthorn Rd
CDW/CHF RM16 ... 339 L8
HAR CO12 ... 110 A6
HOC/HUL SS5 ... 288 A8
IL IG1 ... 316 E7
WIT CM8 ... 171 M9
Blackthorn St BOW E3 ... 332 D4
Blackthorn Wy BRW CM14 ... 300 G2
MAL CM9 ... 199 P2
RCOLW CO6 ... 77 K4
Blacktiles La WDBR IP12 ... 27 M1
Blackwall Br CHLM/WR CM1 ... 216 E6
Blackwall Tunnel Ap
POP/IOD E14 ... 332 F7
Blackwall Tunnel Northern Ap
BOW E3 ... 332 E3
Blackwall Wy POP/IOD E14 ... 332 G7
Blackwater SBF/HAD SS7 ... 326 C2
Blackwater Av COLN CO4 ... 128 F6
Blackwater Cl BOC CM0 ... 291 H3
CHLM/WR CM1 ... 218 B5
MAL CM9 ... 222 F8
RAIN RM13 ... 336 C5
SBN/FI SS3 ... 330 D5
Blackwater Dr K/T/MI CO5 ... 202 D6
Blackwater La WIT CM8 ... 197 L4
Blackwater Wy BRTR CM7 ... 145 K2
Blackwell Cl CLPT E5 ... 314 B6
Blackwell Dr BRTR CM7 ... 144 F2
Blackwood Chine
RCHLM CM3 ... 287 H2
Bladen Dr IPNE IP4 ... 26 E6
Bladon Cl BRTR CM7 ... 121 H8
K/T/MI CO5 ... 174 B8
Bladon Wy HVHL CB9 ... 41 L2
Blagden's La STHGT/OAK N14 ... 272 C8
Blaine Dr FOS CO13 ... 158 F7
Blair Cl BSF CM23 ... 137 H7
IPNE IP4 ... 26 D6
Blair St POP/IOD E14 ... 332 F6
Blake Av BARK IG11 ... 334 F1
RIPS/CAP IP9 ... 85 M8
Blake Cl MGTR CO11 ... 106 A4
RAIN RM13 ... 336 E1
Blake Dr BRTR CM7 ... 145 M2
RCOS CO16 ... 181 N7
Blake Gdns DART DA1 ... 347 L9
Blake Hall Dr WICKE SS11 ... 305 M1
Blake Hall Rd CHONG CM5 ... 234 F5
WAN E11 ... 315 K3
Blake Rd CAN/RD E16 ... 333 J4
IP IP1 ... 22 G9
WIT CM8 ... 171 N8
Blaker Rd SRTFD E15 ... 332 F1
Blakesware Gdns ED N9 ... 273 J6
Blamsters Crs HSTD CO9 ... 97 N8
Blanchard Cl FOS CO13 ... 158 B7
Blanchard Gv PEND EN3 ... 252 D8
Blanchard Ms HARH RM3 ... 299 L4
Blanche St CAN/RD E16 ... 333 J4
IPNE IP4 ... 17 G4
Blandford Cl ROMW/RG RM7 ... 298 A8
Blandford Crs CHING E4 ... 274 F6
Blandford Rd IPSE IP3 ... 26 C8
Blaney Crs EHAM E6 ... 334 C3
Blatches Cha LOS SS9 ... 308 A9
Bledlow Cl THMD SE28 ... 335 K7
Blenheim Av
GNTH/NBYPK IG2 ... 316 B1
Blenheim Cha LOS SS9 ... 327 N3
Blenheim Cl BRTR CM7 ... 121 H8
HOC/HUL SS5 ... 287 P8
HVHL CB9 ... 41 L2
MGTR CO11 ... 81 N8
RCHLM CM3 ... 242 C8
ROMW/RG RM7 ... 298 B8
SBW CM21 ... 187 J4
UPMR RM14 ... 320 B3
WCHMH N21 ... 273 H7
Blenheim Ct BSF CM23 ... 137 H7
WFD IG8 ... 295 L4
WICKE SS11 * ... 305 M2
Blenheim Crs LOS SS9 ... 327 P3
Blenheim Dr COLS CO2 ... 152 B6
Blenheim Gdns RCHLM CM3 ... 245 P9
SOCK/AV RM15 ... 337 N8
Blenheim Ms LOS SS9 ... 327 P3
Blenheim Park Cl LOS SS9 ... 328 A2
Blenheim Rd BRWN CM15 ... 280 D5
COS CO15 ... 6 B6
EHAM E6 ... 333 N3
IP IP1 ... 25 H4
WALTH E17 ... 294 A7
WAN E11 ... 315 H6
Blenheim Wy EPP CM16 ... 233 P6
K/T/MI CO5 ... 174 B8
Blessing Wy BARK IG11 ... 335 K2

Blickling Cl *CHTY* IP2 ....25 J9
Blickling Rd *BRTR* CM77 ....144 F6
Blind La *BCAYW* CM12 ....302 C1
  CHLM/GWD CM2 ....241 K6
  CHLM/GWD CM2 ....262 E4
  K/T/MI CO5 ....174 E2
  MAL CM9 ....200 A3
  MAL CM9 ....223 K4
  MAL CM9 ....244 C8
  RCOLW CO6 ....126 D7
Blindman's La
  CHES/WCR EN8 ....230 A9
Blithbury Rd *DAGW* RM9 ....317 J8
Blockhouse Rd *GRAYS* RM17 ...349M4
Blofield Rd *FX* IP11 ....10 A1
Blois Rd *HVHL* CB9 ....55 N2
Blomville Rd *BCTR* RM8 ....317M4
Blondin St *BOW* E3 ....332 D2
Bloom Cl *FOS* CO15 ....158 G8
Bloomfield Av *FOS* CO15 ....158 F7
Bloomfield Crs
  GNTH/NBYPK IG2 ....316 C1
Bloomfield Rd *CHLM/NEW* EN7 ...229 H4
Bloomfield St *IPNE* IP4 ....26 A5
Blossom Cl *DAGW* RM9 ....335 N1
Blossom La *ENC/FH* EN2 ....251 H9
Blount St *POP/IOD* E14 ....332 B6
Blountswood Rd
  HOC/HUL SS5 ....287 K9
Blower Cl *RAYL* SS6 ....307 J4
Bloxhall Rd *LEY* E10 ....314 C3
Blue Anchor La *TIL* RM18 ....350 F2
Blue Barn Cl *FX* IP11 ....54 B1
Blue Barn La *RIPW* IP9 ....22 A4
Bluebell Av *FSTGT* E7 ....315 N7
  RCOS CO16 ....181 M9
Bluebell Cl *CHTY* IP2 ....24 F7
  ROMW/RG RM7 ....318 C4
  WIT CM8 ....197 H1
Bluebell Dr *CHESW* EN7 ....229 J7
Bluebell Wy *WFD* IG8 ....316 C8
Bluebell Wd *BCAYW* CM12 ....282 E4
Bluebird Cl *WFD* IG8 ....295 K3
Bluebird La *DAGE* RM10 ....317 P9
Bluebird Wy *THMD* SE28 ....334 E9
Bluecoat Rd *WARE* SG12 ....184 A3
Bluegate La *RIPS/CAP* IP9 ....81 K2
Bluehouse Av *RCOS* CO16 ....181 K9
Blue House Farm Cha
  RCHLM CM3 ....288 C1
Bluehouse Rd *CHING* CM4 ....275 H9
Bluehouses *VGE* SS16 ....2 D6
Bluemans *EPP* CM16 ....234 C5
Bluemans End *EPP* CM16 ....234 C5
Blue Mill La *MAL* CM9 ....220 G7
Blue Mills Hl *WIT* CM8 ....197 L5
Blue Rd *K/T/MI* CO5 ....173 P8
Bluestem Rd *IPSE* IP5 ....31 L2
Blunden Cl *BCTR* RM8 ....317 K3
The Blundens *RCOLW* CO6 ....78 B5
Blunts Hall Rd *WIT* CM8 ....196 F5
Blunts Wall Rd *BCAYW* CM12 ....282 F7
Blurton Rd *CLPT* E5 ....314 A6
Blyford Rd *RCOS* CO16 ....181 K9
Blyford Wy *FX* IP11 ....10 B7
Blyth Av *SBN/FI* SS3 ....330 B7
Blyth Cl *CHTY* IP2 ....30 A1
Blythe La *RCOLE* CO7 ....153 J6
Blythe Rd *HOD* EN11 ....208 C7
  SLH/COR SS7 ....303 K7
Blythe Wy *MAL* CM9 ....244 E8
  SBF/HAD SS7 ....305 P6
Blyth Rd *THMD* SE28 ....335 K7
  WALTH E17 ....314 C2
Blyth's Meadow *BRTR* CM7 ....145 J5
Blyth's Av *BRTR* CM77 ....144 C4
Blyth's Whf *POP/IOD* E14 * 332 B7
Blythswood Rd
  GDMY/SEVK IG3 ....317 H13
Blyth Wk *UPMR* RM14 ....320 B2
Blythwood Gdns *STSD* CM24 ....114 A9
Blyton Cl *WICKW* SS12 ....305 J2
Boadicea Wy *COLS* CO2 ....151M2
Bober Av *RCFD* SS4 * 310 F2
Boardman Av *CHING* C4 ....274 E4
Boardwalk Pl *POP/IOD* E14 ....332 F8
Boars Tye Rd *WIT* CM8 ....146 D8
Boat Quay *CAN/RD* E16 ....333M7
Bob Anker Cl *PLSTW* E13 ....333 K3
Bobbits Wy *RCFD* SS4 ....308 G5
Bobbingworth Mll
  CHONG CM5 ....234 F3
Bobbits La *RIPS/CAP* IP9 ....29 N2
Bobbits Wy *RCOLE* CO7 ....153 K6
Bober Ct *COLS* CO2 ....152 C7
Bocking End *BRTR* CM7 ....145 H4
Bockingham Gv *PIT* SS13 ....304 F7
Bocking Pl *BRTR* CM7 * 145 K2
Bocking's Gv *RCOS* CO16 ....181 L8
Bodell Rd *CDW/CHF* RM16 ....339 L9
Bodiam Cl *EN* EN1 ....273 J1
  IPSE IP5 ....26 C7
Bodiam Rd *IPSE* IP5 ....26 C7
Bodley Cl *EPP* CM16 ....232 C9
Bodmin Cl *KESG* IP5 ....26 F5
Bodmin Rd *CHLM/WR* CM1 ....218 C6
Bohemia Cha *LOS* SS9 ....327M7
Bohn Rd *WCHPL* E1 ....332 B5
Bohun Cl *RCHLM* CM3 * 169 J6
Bois Hall Rd *HSTD* CO9 ....98 A6
Boley Dr *COS* CO15 ....7 J1
Boley Rd *COS* CO15 ....251 N9
Boleyn Cl *BCAYW* CM12 ....208 A7
  CDW/CHF RM16 ....316 B6
  LOS SS9 ....307M8
  LOU IG10 ....275 P5
  WALTH E17 ....314 D1
Boleyn Gdns *DAGE* RM10 ....318 B9
  RBRW/HUT CM13 ....281 K9
Boleyn Rd *EHAM* E6 ....333 N2
  FSTGT E7 ....315 K9
Boleyns Av *BRTR* CM77 ....121 J9
Boleyn Wy *BARK/HLT* IG6 ....296 D3

COS CO15 ....206 E4
  HVHL CB9 ....40 C4
  RCHLM CM3 ....219 L2
Boley Rd *RCOLW* CO6 ....99 N9
Bolford St *GTDUN* CM6 ....92 A6
Bolingbroke Cl *RCHLM* CM3 .....169 J6
Boiney Dr *LOS* SS9 ....307 M8
Bolton La *IPNE* IP4 ....17 F3
Bolton Rd *FSTGT* E7 ....315 J4
The Boltons *WFD* IG8 * 295 K1
Bommel Av *CVI* SS8 ....345 K2
Bonchurch Av *LOS* SS9 ....327 N4
Bond St *CHLM/GWD* CM2 ....5 H3
  GRAYS RM17 ....349M4
  IPNE IP4 ....17 G5
  SRTFD E15 ....315 H7
Bonham Cl *COS* CO15 ....182 B8
Bonham Gdns *BCTR* RM8 ....317 L4
Bonham Rd *BCTR* RM8 ....317 L4
Bonington Cha
  RBRW/HUT CM13 ....281 L9
Bonington Rd *HCH* RM12 ....319 J7
Boniham Hl *SBW* CM21 ....187 L3
Bonner Wk *CDW/CHF* RM16 * 349 J1
Bonneting La *BSF* CM23 ....88 A8
Bonney Gv *CHESW* EN7 ....229M9
Bonnington Rd *IPSE* IP5 ....30 F1
Bonnings Cha
  RBRW/HUT CM13 ....281 L9
Bonnygate *BSDN* SS14 ....3 K3
Boone Pl *WIT* CM8 ....197 K2
Boons Cl *RCHLM* CM3 ....219 K3
Boot Drift *RIPS/CAP* IP9 ....85 H4
Bootham Cl *BCAYW* CM12 ....282 C7
Bootham Rd *BCAYW* CM12 ....282 C7
Booth Av *COLN* CO4 ....9 K5
Booth Cl *THMD* SE28 ....335 J8
Booth La *KESG* IP5 ....27 K3
Booth Pl *BOC* CM0 * 291 H3
Borda Cl *CHLM/WR* CM1 ....217 P6
Borden Av *WCHMH* N21 ....273 J5
Border's La *LOU* IG10 ....276 B3
Boreham Av *CAN/RD* E16 ....333 K6
Boreham Cl *WICKE* SS11 ....305 N2
Boreham Rd *BOC* CM0 ....291 J6
Borehamgate Prec *SUD* CO10 ......20 E5
Borehamgate Sq *SUD* CO10 * 20 E5
Borley Rd *SUD* CO10 ....46 E7
Borman Cl *LOS* SS9 ....308 B9
Borough La *SAFWS* CB11 ....65 L1
The Borough *CHONG* CM5 ....255 L8
Borrodale Ct *HVHL* CB9 ....55 L4
Borrell Cl *BROX* EN10 ....208 B8
Borret Av *CVI* SS8 ....344 D1
Borrowdale Av *HARH* RM3 ....299 H5
Borrowdale Cl *REDBR* IG4 ....295 P8
  SBF/HAD SS7 ....306 C9
Borrowdale Rd *SBF/HAD* SS7 .....306 C9
Borthwick Ms *WART* E15 * 315 H6
Borthwick Rd *SRTFD* E15 ....315 H6
Borwick Av *WALTH* E17 ....294 C7
Borwick La *BCAYE* CM11 ....304 D3
Bosanquet Rd *HOD* EN11 ....208 F5
Boscawen Gdns *BRTR* CM7 ....145 L2
Boscombe Av *EMPK* RM11 ....319 L2
  GRAYS RM17 ....349 N2
  LEY E10 ....314 C2
  WICKW SS12 ....284 E8
Boscombe Cl *CLPT* E5 ....314 B7
Boscombe Rd *SOSN* SS2 ....19 J2
Bosgrove *CHING* E4 ....274 F7
Boss Hall Rd *IP* IP1 ....24 F4
Bostock Rd *CHTY* IP2 ....30 C1
Boston Av *RAYL* SS6 ....306 E3
  SOSN SS2 ....18 D1
Boston Rd *EHAM* E6 ....333 P3
  IPNE IP4 ....25 N4
Boswell Av *RCFD* SS4 ....308 E2
Boswells Dr *CHLM/GWD* CM2 ....5 J3
Bosworth Cl *HOC/HUL* SS5 ....308 A3
  WALTH E17 ....294 C5
Bosworth Crs *HARH* RM3 ....299 H5
Bosworth Rd *DAGE* RM10 ....317 P6
Botanical Wy *RCOS* CO16 ....180 D9
Botany Dr *BRTR* CM7 ....145 N5
Botany La *RCOS* CO16 ....156 E9
Botany Ter *PUR* RM19 ....347 N5
Botany Wy *PUR* RM19 ....347 M3
Boteliers *VGE* SS16 ....323M2
Boteley Cl *CHING* E4 ....274 G8
Botha Rd *PLSTW* E13 ....333 L5
Bothwell Cl *CAN/RD* E16 ....333 K5
Botney Hill Rd *BCAYW* CM12 ......302 D3
Bouchers Md *CHLM/WR* CM1 ......218 E4
Boulcott St *WCHPL* E1 ....332M4
Boulderwood Rd
  SBF/HAD SS7 ....325 N1
The Boulevard *RCFD* SS4 ....308 B8
  WFD IG8 ....296 B4
Boulter Gdns *RAIN* RM13 ....318 G6
Boulton Rd *BCTR* RM8 ....317 M4
Boult Rd *LAIN* SS15 ....303 K7
Boultwood Rd *EHAM* E6 ....334 A6
Bounces La *ED* N9 ....275 N8
Bounces Rd *ED* N9 ....275 N8
Boundary Av *WALTH* E17 ....314 C2
Boundary Cl *GDMY/SEVK* IG3 ....316 F6
Boundary Dr
  RBRW/HUT CM13 ....281 P6
Boundary La *PLSTW* E13 ....333 N4
Boundary Rd *BARK* IG11 ....334 E1
  BSF CM23 ....137 M9
  COLN CO4 ....153 H2
  ED N9 ....275 P5
  HVHL CB9 ....41 N6
  LOS SS9 ....307 L7
  PLSTW E13 ....333M2
  ROM SM1 ....318H11
  UPMR RM14 ....319M5
  WALTH E17 ....314 C2
Boundary St *ERITH* DA8 ....346 E5
Bounderby Gv
  CHLM/WR CM1 ....217M5
Bounstead Hl *COLS* CO2 ....151 M9

Bounstead Rd *COLS* CO2 ....151 N7
Bourchier Av *BRTR* CM7 ....145 N1
Bourchier Wy *HSTD* CO9 ....97 N8
Bourne Av *LAIN* SS15 ....303 H7
  STHGT/OAK N14 ....272 D8
Bournebridge Cl
  RBRW/HUT CM13 ....281 P6
Bournebridge Hl *HSTD* CO9 ....122 C1
Bournebridge La *ABR/ST* RM4 ...278 A6
Bourne Cl *BROX* EN10 ....208 C8
  HSTD CO9 ....97 N8
  LAIN SS15 ....303 H7
  WARE SG12 ....184 A2
Bourne End *EMPK* RM11 ....319 M2
Bourne Gdns *CHING* E4 ....294 E1
Bourne Hl *CHTY* IP2 ....30 C2
  PLMGR N13 ....272 E8
Bourne Hill Cl *PLMGR* N13 * 272 E8
Bournemouth Park Rd
  SOSN SS2 ....329 J3
Bournemouth Rd *COS* CO15 ....182 G7
Bourne Rd *COLS* CO2 ....152 B2
  FSTGT E7 ....315 J5
  HVHL CB9 ....41 L3
  RCOLW CO6 ....127 H4
Bournes Gn *SBN/FI* SS3 * 329 P4
Bournes Green Cha
  SBN/FI SS3 ....330 B4
Bourne Ter *STHGT/OAK* N14 .....272 C7
The Bourne *BSF* CM23 ....137 N6
  STHGT/OAK N14 ....272 D7
  WARE SG12 ....184 A2
Bouvel Dr *BOC* CM0 ....268 G9
Bouverie Rd *CHLM/GWD* CM2 ....5 G7
Bouvier Av *PEND* EN3 ....251 P8
Bovey Wy *SOCK/AV* RM15 ....338 E5
Bovingdon Rd *BRTR* CM7 ....120 C5
Bovinger Wy *SOS* SS1 ....329 N5
Bowbank Cl *SBN/FI* SS3 ....329 N5
Bow Bridge Est *BOW* E3 ....332 E3
Bow Common La *BOW* E3 ....332 C4
Bowden Dr *EMPK* RM11 ....319 K5
Bowdens La *RCOLW* CO6 ....101 L1
Bowdon Rd *LEY* E10 ....314 D2
Bowen St *POP/IOD* E14 ....332 E6
Bower Cl *CRW* RM5 ....298 C4
Bower Farm Rd *ABR/ST* RM4 .....278 B9
Bower Gdns *MAL* CM9 ....222 A8
Bower Hall Dr *HVHL* CB9 ....55 L4
Bower Wall La *K/T/MI* CO5 ....205 H5
Bowerl Hl *EPP* CM16 ....255 H2
Bowera La *BSDN* SS14 ....304 D7
Bowerman Rd
  CDW/CHF RM16 ....350 B2
Bowers Cl *WIT* CM8 ....171M2
Bowers Court Dr *PIT* SS13 ....325 L1
Bowers Rd *SBF/HAD* SS7 ....326 A1
Bower St *WCHPL* E1 * 332 A6
Bowes Dr *CHONG* CM5 ....235 L6
Bowes Rd *BCTR* RM8 ....317 K6
  RCOLE CO7 ....153 K5
Bowfell Dr *VGE* SS16 ....323 J2
Bowhay *RBRW/HUT* CM13 ....281 L8
Bowland Av *RIPW* IP9 ....29 L1
Bowland Rd *WFD* IG8 ....295M3
Bowles Gdn *EN* EN1 ....251 N6
Bowley St *POP/IOD* E14 ....332 C7
Bowling Rd *WARE* SG12 ....184 B3
Bow Locks *BOW* E3 ....332 F4
Bowman Av *CAN/RD* E16 ....333 K7
  LOS SS9 ....307 L9
Bowmans Pk *HSTD* CO9 * 72 D5
Bowmont Cl
  RBRW/HUT CM13 ....281 L5
Bown Cl *TIL* RM18 ....350 C7
Bowness Rd *BXLYHN* DA7 ....346 A7
Bowness Wy *HCH* RM12 ....319 H7
Bowood Rd *PEND* EN3 ....274 A1
Bow Rd *BOW* E3 ....332 D3
Bowsers La *SAFWN* CB10 ....88 A8
Bow St *SRTFD* E15 ....315 H7
Bowthorpe Cl *IP* IP1 ....16 B2
Bowyer Cl *EHAM* E6 ....334 A5
Box Cl *LAIN* SS15 * 303 L6
Boxford Cl *RAYL* SS6 ....306 C4
Boxford Ct *FX* IP11 ....10 B2
Boxgrove Rd *ABYW* SE2 ....335 J9
Boxhouse La *RCOLE* CO7 ....104 D3
Box La *BARK* IG11 ....335 K2
  HOD EN11 ....208 B4
Boxley La *RBSF* CM22 ....164 E5
Boxley St *CAN/RD* E16 ....333 L8
Box Mill La *HSTD* CO9 ....97 P5
Boxmoor Rd *CRW* RM5 ....298 B2
Boxoll Rd *DAGW* RM9 ....317 N6
Boxted Church Rd
  RCOLW CO6 ....102 F3
Boxted Cl *BKHH* IG9 ....295 P7
Boxted Rd *COLN* CO4 ....127 N7
  RCOLW CO6 ....102 F5
Boxted Straight Rd
  COLN CO4 ....105 K3
Boyce Gn *SBF/HAD* SS7 ....326 A4
Boyce Hill Cl *LOS* SS9 ....327 L1
Boyce Rd *SBN/FI* SS3 ....330 C6
  SLH/COR SS17 ....341 K2
Boyce View Dr *SBF/HAD* SS7 ......325 N4
Boyce Wy *PLSTW* E13 ....333 K4
Boyd Cl *CVI* SS8 ....137 N6
Boyd Ct *WICKW* SS12 ....305 L2
Boyden Cl *SOSN* SS2 ....329 N4
Boydlands *RIPS/CAP* IP9 ....28 C9
Boyles Ct *COLS* CO2 ....152 C7
Boyne Dr *CHLM/WR* CM1 ....218 C5
Boyne Rd *DAGE* RM10 ....317 P5
Boyton Cl *HVHL* CB9 ....41 K1
  SBF/HAD SS7 ....326 C1
Boyton Rd *IPSE* IP5 ....31 H2
Boytons *LAIN* SS15 ....303 L3
Boytons Acre *SAFWS* CB11 ....65 L1
Boyton's La *SAFWN* CB10 ....54 C8

Brabant Rd *RCHLM* CM3 ....288 B1
Brabazon St *POP/IOD* E14 ....332 E6
Brabner Gdns *BCAYE* CM11 ....284 B4
Brace Cl *CHESW* EN7 ....228 C4
Bracelet Cl *SLH/COR* SS17 ....323 N9
Brace Wk *RCHLM* CM3 ....287 H5
Brackendale Av *KESG* IP5 ....27 K3
Brackenbury Cl *IP* IP1 ....25 J5
Bracken Cl *EHAM* E6 ....334 A5
  LOU IG10 ....276 E8
Brackendale *BCAYE* CM11 ....283 L5
  WCHMH N21 ....272 E8
Brackendale Av *PIT* SS13 ....325 H2
Brackendale Cl *HOC/HUL* SS5 ....287 P9
Brackendale Gdns
  UPMR RM14 ....319 P6
Bracken Dell *RAYL* SS6 ....307 H5
Brackenden Dr
  CHLM/WR CM1 ....218 C4
Bracken Dr *CHIG* IG7 ....296 C3
Brackenhayes Cl *CHTY* IP2 ....25 J8
Bracken Ms *ROMW/RG* RM7 ....317 P1
Brackens Dr *BRW* CM14 ....300 C2
The Brackens *COLN* CO4 ....128 C4
  EN EN1 ....273 H6
The Bracken *CHING* E4 ....274 F6
Bracken Wy *K/T/MI* CO5 ....177 H5
  SBF/HAD SS7 ....306 D8
Brackley Cl *FX* IP11 ....34 G6
Brackley Rd *PIT* SS13 ....304 F6
Brackley Sq *WFD* IG8 ....296 C9
Bracks La *RCOLW* CO6 ....148 E3
Bradbourne Rd *GRAYS* RM17 .....349 L4
Bradbourne Wy *PIT* SS13 ....325 H1
Bradbury Dr *BRTR* CM7 ....144 C3
Bradd Cl *SOCK/AV* RM15 ....338 F5
Braddock Cl *CRW* RM5 ....298 B5
Bradfield Cl *CAN/RD* E16 ....317 H7
Bradfield Rd *CAN/RD* E16 ....333 K3
  MGTR CO11 ....107 N9
Bradford Bury *LOS* SS9 ....307M9
Bradford Rd *IL* IG1 ....316 E5
Bradfords Ct *BRTR* CM7 ....145 K2
Bradford St *BRTR* CM7 ....145 K2
  CHLM/GWD CM2 ....4 D6
Bradgate *POTB/CUF* EN6 ....251 J1
Bradgate Cl *POTB/CUF* EN6 ....228 C7
Brading Av *COS* CO15 ....182 B6
Brading Crs *WAN* E11 ....315 L4
Bradleigh Av *GRAYS* RM17 ....349M4
Bradley Av *SBF/HAD* SS7 ....326 C2
  GTDUN CM6 ....141 K4
  SBF/HAD SS7 ....326 C2
Bradley Common *BSF* CM23 ....137 P5
Bradley Link *SBF/HAD* SS7 ....326 C1
Bradley Ms *WART* E15 ....315 H6
Bradley Rd *PEND* EN3 ....252 B8
  WAB EN9 ....251 L4
Bradley Stone Rd *EHAM* E6 ....334 A6
Bradley St *CHTY* IP2 ....25 J6
Bradley Wy *RCFD* SS4 ....308 F6
Bradshaw Rd *CDW/CHF* RM16 ...339 K8
Bradstock Rd *HOM* E9 ....315 H1
Bradwell La *DAGE* RM10 ....317 P4
Bradwell Cl *HCH* RM12 ....318 G8
  SWFD E18 ....295 J8
Bradwell Gn
  RBRW/HUT CM13 ....281M5
Bradwell Rd *BKHH* IG9 ....275 P7
  BOC CM0 ....246 F7
  BOC CM0 ....247 K4
  BOC CM0 ....248 B5
Brady Av *LOU* IG10 ....276 D1
Bradymead *EHAM* E6 ....334 B6
Braemar Av *BXLYHN* DA7 ....346 B9
  WALTH E17 ....94 A8
Braemar Crs *LOS* SS9 ....327 K4
Braemar Gdns *EMPK* RM11 ....319M1
Braemar Pl *PLSTW* E13 * 333 J4
Braemore Cl *SWF* SS9 * 326 C9
Braeside Crs *BXLYHN* DA7 ....346 B9
Braganza Wy *CHLM/WR* CM1 .....218 E3
Brain Rd *WIT* CM8 ....197 H1
Braintree Av *REDBR* IG4 ....295 P9
Braintree Rd *BRTR* CM7 * 94 A8
  BRTR CM77 ....120 B1
  DAGE RM10 ....317 P5
  GTDUN CM6 ....317 P5
  GTDUN CM6 ....142 C9
  ROM SM1 ....121 P2
  RCHLM CM3 ....169M8
  WIT CM8 ....197 K1
Brain Valley Av *BRTR* CM77 ....145 L8
Braiswick *COLN* CO4 ....127 P5
Braiswick La *COLN* CO4 ....127 M8
Braiswick Av *ROMW/RG* RM7 .....317 P2
  COLN CO4 ....127 P5
Braithwaite Av
  ROMW/RG RM7 ....317 P2
Braithwaite Dr *COLN* CO4 ....127 P5
Braithwaite Rd *PEND* EN3 ....274 C2
Bramall Cl *SRTFD* E15 ....315 J7
Bramble Cl *CHESW* EN7 ....40 C2
  LOS SS9 ....307 L8
Bramble Crs *SBF/HAD* SS7 ....327 K1
Bramble Cft *ERITH* DA8 ....346 B2
Bramble Dr *IPSE* IP5 ....31 L1
Bramble La *GTDUN* CM6 ....142 D5
  UPMR RM14 ....319M5
Bramble Ri *HLW* CM20 ....13 G4
Bramble Rd *CVI* SS8 ....344 F1
  SBF/HAD SS7 ....307 J9
  WIT CM8 ....171M9
The Brambles *BOC* CM0 ....269 J6
  BRTR CM7 * 145 H3
  BSF CM23 ....137 M8
  CHES/WCR EN8 ....252 A1
  CHIG IG7 ....296 C8
  COLW CO3 ....151 J5
  LAIN SS15 ....303 H7
Bramble Tye *LAIN* SS15 ....303 N6
Bramble Wy *RCOLW* CO6 ....77 K4

Bramblewood *RIPW* IP8 ....24 D9
The Bramblings *CHING* E4 ....294 G1
Bramerton Rd *HOC/HUL* SS5 ......307 N1
Bramfield Rd East *RAYL* SS6 ....307 K5
Bramfield Rd West *RAYL* SS6 ......307 K5
Bramford La *IP* IP1 ....25 H4
Bramford Rd *IP* IP1 ....24 D5
  NHMKT IP6 ....22 A3
Bramhall Cl *CHTY* IP2 ....29 M1
Bramley Cl *BRTR* CM7 ....145 K5
  COLW CO5 ....127 L8
  RCOLE CO7 ....154 A6
  STHGT/OAK N14 ....272 A4
  WALTH E17 ....295 M4
  WFD IG8 ....295 M4
Bramley Crs *GNTH/NBYPK* IG2 ...316 B1
Bramley Gdns *LAIN* SS15 ....303 K7
Bramley House Ct
  ENC/FH EN2 * 251 J7
Bramley Pde *STHGT/OAK* N14 ...272 B3
Bramley Pl *CHLM/GWD* CM2 ......240 C5
  DART DA1 ....346 F9
Bramley Rd *HVHL* CB9 ....40 F3
  STHGT/OAK N14 ....272 A4
Bramleys *SLH/COR* SS17 ....341 L2
Bramley Shaw *WAB* EN9 ....253 J3
The Bramleys *RCFD* SS4 ....308 E2
  RCOLW CO6 ....147 P5
Bramley Wy *RCHLM* CM3 ....245 P9
Brampton Cl *CHESW* EN7 ....229M7
  SLH/COR SS17 ....323 P9
  WOS/PRIT SS0 ....328 B2
Brampton Rd *EHAM* E6 ....333 N4
Bramshaw Rd *HOM* E9 ....314 M8
Bramston Ct *BARK/HLT* IG6 ....296 G3
  CHLM/GWD CM2 ....240 E2
Bramston Link *LAIN* SS15 ....302 F8
Bramston Vw *WIT* CM8 * 197 J2
Bramston Wy *LAIN* SS15 ....302 F9
Bramwoods Rd
  CHLM/GWD CM2 ....240 D2
Brancaster Dr *BRTR* CM77 ....144 D4
Brancaster Rd
  GNTH/NBYPK IG2 ....316 F1
Brancepeth Gdns *BKHH* IG9 ....295 K8
Branch Rd *BARK/HLT* IG6 ....297 J2
  POP/IOD E14 ....332 D7
  SBF/HAD SS7 ....327 H4
Brancroft Wy *PEND* EN3 ....252 B9
Brand Ct *BRTR* CM7 ....121 J8
Brand Dr *K/T/MI* CO5 ....177 J2
Brandenburg Rd *CVI* SS8 ....326 C9
Brandesbury Sq *WFD* IG8 ....296 B5
Brandeston Cl *SUD* CO10 ....47 P8
Brandeston La *BCAYW* CM12 ......283 H3
Brandon Cl *BCAYW* CM12 * 283 H3
  CHESW EN7 ....229 K5
Brandon Groves Av
  SOCK/AV RM15 ....338 F3
Brandon Rd *BRTR* CM7 ....144 C4
  FX IP11 ....10 B2
  WALTH E17 ....294 F8
Brandreth Rd *EHAM* E6 ....334 A6
Brands Cl *SUD* CO10 ....61 M5
Brandville Gdns
  BARK/HLT IG6 ....296 C8
Bran End Flds *GTDUN* CM6 ....118 C8
Branfill Rd *UPMR* RM14 ....319 N4
Branksome Av *HOC/HUL* SS5 .....287 P9
  SLH/COR SS17 ....341 L1
  WICKW SS12 ....284 E9
Branksome Cl *SLH/COR* SS17 .....341 K2
Branksome Rd *SOSN* SS2 ....19 J2
Bransby Gdns *IPNE* IP4 ....17 H2
Branscombe Ct *FOS* CO15 ....158 G9
Branscombe Gdns *SOS* SS1 ....330 A6
  WCHMH N21 ....272 F6
Branscombe Sq *SOSN* SS2 ....330 A5
Branscombe Wk *SOS* SS1 ....330 A5
Branston Rd *COS* CO15 ....6 A5
Brantham Hl *MGTR* CO11 ....81M9
Brantwood Av *ERITH* DA8 ....346 B5
Brantwood Gdns
  ENC/FH EN2 ....272 D3
  REDBR IG4 ....295 P9
Brantwood Rd *BXLYHN* DA7 ....346 A7
Brassinghams Crs *K/T/MI* CO5 ...174 B7
Braxted Brd *ERITH* DA8 ....346 D5
Braxted Cl *RCFD* SS4 ....308 D3
Braxted La *WIT* CM8 ....198 D5
Braxted Rd *WIT* CM8 ....198 B6
Braxteds *LAIN* SS15 ....303 H9
Braybrooke *BSDN* SS14 ....3 L1
Braybrooke Gdns *SAFWS* CB11 .....65 L1
Bray Ct *RCOLW* CO6 ....127 J3
Bray Crs *BERM/RHTH* SE16 ....332 E5
Bray End *RCOLW* CO6 ....333 J7
Brayers Ms *ROD* IG4 ....308 F2
Bray Ldg *CHES/WCR* EN8 * 230 B6
Brays La *RCFD* SS4 ....308 F2
Braziers Ct *COLN* CO4 ....127 C3
Braziers Cl *LAIN* SS15 ....303 N6
Braziers Quay *BSF* CM23 ....137M9
Brazier's Wood Rd *IPSE* IP5 ....31 H2
Breach Barns La *WAB* EN9 ....231 K9
Breachfield Rd *COLS* CO2 ....151 M4
Breach La *DAGW* RM9 ....335 P5
  GTDUN CM6 ....117 J5
Breach Rd *WTHK* RM20 ....348 C4
Bread & Cheese La
  BROX EN10 ....229 K4
Break Egg Hl *BCAYE* CM11 ....283 L5
Bream Gdns *EHAM* E6 ....334 B1
Breamore Rd *GDMY/SEVK* IG3 ...316 G4
Breams Fld *VGE* SS16 ....323 K2
Bream St *BOW* E3 ....314 D9
Brecon Cl *CHTY* IP2 ....25 J9
  PIT SS13 ....304 A7
Brecon Rd *PEND* EN3 ....275 P5
Brede Cl *EHAM* E6 ....334 B5
Bredfield Cl *FX* IP11 ....34 G6

Bree Av RCOLW CO6 .....149 K3
Bree Hl RCHLM CM3 .....286 F2
Bremer Ms WALTH E17 .....294 E8
Brempsons BSDN SS14 .....2 E5
Brendans Cl EMPK RM11 .....319 K5
Brendon Cl ERITH DA8 .....346 D6
Brendon Dr KESG IP5 .....26 E5
Brendon Pl CHLM/WR CM1 .....239M1
Brendon Rd BCTR RM8 .....317 N3
Brendon Vls WCHMH N21 * 273 K6
Brendon Wy EN EN1 .....328 B1
  WOS/PRIT SS0 .....328 B1
Brennan Rd TIL RM18 .....350 C7
Brent Av RCHLM CM3 .....264 G8
Brent Cl FOS CO15 .....158 C7
  WIT CM8 .....197 H2
Brent Hall Rd BRTR CM7 .....94 A2
Brenton St POP/IOD E14 .....332 B6
Brent Rd COLN CO4 .....333 K6
Brentwood Rd
  CDW/CHF RM16 .....350 C2
  CHONG CM5 .....235 M9
  COS CO15 .....182 D7
  RBRW/HUT CM13 .....301 L2
  RBRW/HUT CM13 .....322 A3
  ROM RM1 .....318 E1
Bressey Av EN EN1 .....251 M9
Bressey Gv SWFD SE18 .....295 J6
Bressingham Gdns
  RCHLM CM3 .....286 F1
Bretons LAIN SS15 .....2 A5
Brett Cl IP IP3 .....24 F5
Bretten Cl RCOS CO16 .....181 K9
Brett Dr RCHLM CM3 .....265 H9
Brettenham Av WALTH E17 .....294 D5
Brettenham Dr SOS SS1 .....329 M6
Brettenham Rd WALTH E17 .....294 D6
Brett Gdns DAGW RM9 .....317 M9
The Bretts KESG IP5 .....27 K3
Brevet Cl PUR RM19 .....348 A2
Brewers Ct BSF CM23 .....157 H9
Brewery La STSD CM24 .....114 B9
Brewery Rd HOD EN11 .....208 D5
Brewhouse Wk
  BERM/RHTH SE16 .....332 B8
Brewood Rd BCTR RM8 .....317 J8
Brewster Cl CVI SS8 .....344 D2
Brewster Rd LEY E10 .....314 E3
Brian Bishop Cl WOTN CO14 .....159 J4
Brian Cl CHLM/GWD CM2 .....240 A4
  HCH RM12 .....314 D2
Brian Rd CHDH RM6 .....237 K9
Briar Cl BCAYE CM11 .....283 C9
  BKHH IG9 .....275 M8
  CHES/WCR EN8 .....229 P8
  HOC/HUL SS5 .....308 A3
  PLMGR N13 .....273 H9
Briardale Av PUR RM19 *.....110 A5
Briarfields FOS CO13 .....158 D4
Briarhayes CHTY IP2 .....25 J9
Briarhayes Cl CHTY IP2 .....25 J9
Briarleas Gdns UPMR RM14 .....320 B2
Briarley Cl BROX EN10 .....230 C1
Briar Md LAIN SS15 .....303 J8
Briar Rd HARH RM5 .....299 J4
  RCOLE CO7 .....198 C8
Briarsford WIT CM8 * 197 L5
The Briars CHES/WCR EN8 .....252 B1
  HLWS CM18 .....210 F6
Briars Wk HARH RM5 .....299 K6
Briarswood CHESW EN7 .....229 K7
  CHLM/WR CM1 .....
  CVI SS8 .....326 D9
Briar Vw BCAYE CM11 .....283 L9
Briarwood BSDN SS14 .....258 C7
Briarwood Av COS CO15 .....182 F7
Briarwood Cl LOS SS9 .....327 N1
Briarwood Dr LOS SS9 .....327 N1
Briarwood End COLN CO4 .....128 C4
Briary La ED N9 .....273 K9
The Briary WICKW SS12 .....284 C9
Briceway SL/COR SS17 .....341 N2
Brickbarns RCHLM CM3 .....169 J6
Brick Ct GRAYS RM17 * 349 K4
Brickcroft BROX EN10 .....230 B5
Brickenden Ct WAB EN9 .....253 J3
Brickfield La K/T/MI CO5 .....25 L8
  VGE SS16 .....324 C4
Brickfield Rd BOW E3 .....332 E4
  EPP CM16 .....233 J8
  VGE SS16 .....324 C4
Brickfields RCHLM CM5 .....287 H1
Brickfields Wy RCFD SS4 .....309 H6
Brickfield Ter RIPS/CAP IP9 * 85 J5
Brickhouse La K/T/MI CO5 .....202 E5
Brick House La CHLM/GWD CM2 .....
Brick House La MAL CM9 .....199 J4
Brickhouse Rd RCOLW CO6 .....54 D2
Brick Kiln Cl FX IP11 .....
  RCOLW CO6 .....147 P3
Brick Kiln La GTDUN CM6 .....118 B8
  RCOLE CO7 .....154 D9
  RCOLW CO6 .....129 H1
  SAFWS CB11 .....
Brick Kiln Rd CHLM/GWD CM2 .....241 H5
  COL CO1 .....
Brick Kiln Wy BRTR CM7 .....145 N4
Brick La EN EN1 .....273 N1
Brickmakers La COLN CO4 .....128 A5
Brickman's Hi MGTR CO11 .....107 H5
Brickspring La MAL CM9 .....198 E5
Brickstock Furze
  .....281 K7
Brick St COLW CO3 .....126 E6
Brickwall Cl BOC CM0 .....290 C4
Bridewell St SUD CO10 .....44 B3
Bridge Av UPMR RM14 .....319M5
Bridgebrook Cl COLN CO4 .....128 E6
Bridge Cl EN EN1 .....273 N1
  GRH DA9 .....348 A1
  RBRW/HUT CM13 .....281 H9

ROM RM1 .....318 D1
SBN/FI SS3 .....330 D7
Bridgecote La LAIN SS15 .....305 N5
Bridge Ct GRAYS RM17 * 349 L4
Bridge Cft RCHLM CM3 .....195 N2
Bridge End WALTH E17 .....294 F5
Bridge End La BRTR CM77 .....144 F6
Bridgefield Cl COL CO1 .....9 K6
Bridge Foot WARE SG12 * 184 A5
Bridge Ga WCHMH N21 .....273 H6
Bridge Hall Rd BRTR CM77 .....146 D5
Bridge Hl EPP CM16 .....254 G3
  RCOLW CO6 .....101 P3
Bridge House Ct
  WICKW SS12 * 285 H9
Bridge House Quay
  POP/IOD E14 .....332 F8
Bridgeland Rd CAN/RD E16 .....333 K7
Bridgemans Gn RCHLM CM3 .....267 H5
Bridgend Ct RCHLM CM3 .....265 H9
Bridgend Rd EN EN1 .....251 P5
Bridgenhall Rd EN EN1 .....251 L9
Bridge Pde BCAYW CM12 * 282 C5
  WCHMH N21 * 273 H6
Bridge Rd CHONG CM5 .....213 H9
  ED N9 .....273M9
  EHAM E6 .....316 A9
  ERITH DA8 .....346 F6
  FX IP11 .....35 K6
  GRAYS RM17 .....349 L4
  HARH RM5 .....299 H2
  HSTD CO9 .....57 P9
  HSTD CO9 .....97 P6
  IP IP1 .....16 E7
  LAIN SS15 .....305 N1
  SAFWN CB10 .....51 K8
  SBN/FI SS3 .....330 D3
  SRTFD E15 .....332 C1
  WALTH E17 .....314 C2
  WICKE SS11 .....285M9
Bridge St BRTR CM7 .....94 A6
  BRTR CM7 .....94 B2
  BSF CM23 .....157 L7
  BURES CO8 .....76 A9
  CHLM/WR CM1 .....239 J1
  HARH RM5 .....299 J2
  HSTD CO9 .....57 P9
  IP IP1 .....16 E7
  LAIN SS15 .....51 K8
  SAFWN CB10 .....197 J5
  WIT CM8 .....
Bridge Ter MAL CM9 * 222 B6
  SRTFD E15 .....314 C9
  SUD CO10 * 20 E4
Bridge Vw GRH DA9 .....348 E9
Bridgewater Rd SRTFD E15 .....332 F1
Bridgeway BARK IG11 .....316 C9
Bridgewater Dr LOS SS9 .....328 A1
Bridgwater Rd CHTY IP2 * 24 E9
  HARH RM5 .....299 H2
Bridgwater Wk HARH RM5 .....299 J2
Bridle Cl HOD EN11 .....208 D1
  PEND EN3 .....252 C7
The Bridle Pth WFD IG8 .....295 H4
Bridleway BCAYE CM11 .....283 L5
Bridle Wy HOD EN11 .....208 D2
  WARE SG12 .....184 D6
Bridle Wy North HOD EN11 .....208 D1
Bridle Wy South HOD EN11 .....208 D2
The Bridleway COLW CO3 .....126 D6
Bridlington Rd ED N9 .....273 N6
Bridon Cl RCHLM CM3 .....263 N5
Bridport Av ROMW/RG RM7 .....318 A1
Bridport Rd CHLM/WR CM1 .....218 C6
  ROMW/RG RM7 .....145 N1
  WY BRTR CM7 .....273 P7
Brierley Av ED N9 .....273 P7
  K/T/MI CO5 .....203 P7
Brierley Cl EMPK RM11 .....319 H1
Brierley Rd WAN E11 .....314 C6
Brierly La ENC/FH EN2 .....251 H6
Brigadier Hl ENC/FH EN2 .....251 H6
Brigadier Wy SBN/FI SS3 .....330 E8
Bright Cl RCOS CO16 .....181 N7
Brighten Rd RIPT SS0 .....18 C5
Brightlingsea Pl POP/IOD E14 .....332 C7
Brightlingsea Rd RCOLE CO7 * 153 K2
  RCOLE CO7 .....179 J3
Brighton Av SOS SS1 .....329 L5
  WALTH E17 .....294 C9
Brighton Rd COS CO15 .....182 G7
  EHAM E6 .....334 B5
Brights Av RAIN RM13 .....336 G4
Brightside BCAYW CM12 .....282 F4
  FOS CO13 .....158 F7
The Brightside PEND EN3 * 252 A9
Brights Wk KESG IP5 .....32 E6
Brightwell Av WOS/PRIT SS0 .....18 A1
Brightwell Cl FX IP11 .....10 B1
Brigstock Rd BELV DA17 .....346 A2
Brigstock Rd CHLM/WR CM1 .....218 C6
Brimsdown Av LAIN SS15 .....303 J9
  PEND EN3 .....252 B9
Brimstone Ct BRTR CM7 .....145 H6
Brimstone Rd RIPW IP8 .....71 P9
Brindles CVI SS8 .....344 C1
  EMPK RM11 .....299 K8
Brindles Cl RBRW/HUT CM13 .....281M8
  TIL RM18 .....351 H2
Brindley Rd COS CO15 .....182 C5
Brindwood Rd CHING E4 .....274 D9
The Bringey CHLM/GWD CM2 .....240 F4
Brinkley Crs COLN CO4 .....128 E5
Brinkley Grove Rd COLN CO4 .....128 D2
Brinkley La COLN CO4 .....128 D2
Brinkley Wy FX IP11 .....11 J3
Brinkworth Cl HOC/HUL SS5 .....308 A1
Brinkworth Rd CLAY IG5 .....295 P7
Brinkworth Rd HOM IG5 .....314 C8
Brinsmead Rd HARH RM5 .....299 M8
Brion Pl POP/IOD E14 .....332 F5
Brisbane Rd IL IG1 .....316 D2
  IPNE IP4 .....26 C5
  LEY E10 .....314 E4

Brisbane Wy COLS CO2 .....152 B5
Briscoe Cl HOD EN11 .....208 C3
  WAN E11 .....315 J4
Briscoe Rd HOD EN11 .....208 C4
  PIT SS13 .....337 H2
  RAIN RM13 .....337 H2
Brise Cl RAYL SS6 .....306 F2
Bristol Ct WIT CM8 .....197 H4
Bristol Hl RIPS/CAP IP9 .....85 N9
Bristol Hill Pk RIPS/CAP IP9 .....85 N9
Bristol Park Rd WALTH E17 * 294 B8
Bristol Rd COL CO1 .....25 J4
  EHAM E6 .....334 C3
British Est BOW E3 .....332 C3
British Legion Rd CHING E4 .....275 J8
British St BOW E3 .....332 C3
Britric Cl GTDUN CM6 .....142 E8
Brittain Rd BCTR RM8 .....317 M5
Brittany Wy COLS CO2 .....128 F9
Britten Cl COLN CO4 .....323 H1
  VGE SS16 .....323 H1
Britten Crs CHLM/GWD CM2 .....240 E2
Britton Cl RAYL SS6 * 306 G6
Brittons La ING CM4 .....261 N9
Brixham Cl COS CO15 .....207 H4
  RAYL SS6 .....306 C2
Brixham Gdns GDMY/SEVK IG3 .....316 F7
Brixham St CAN/RD E16 .....334 A8
Brixton La BSF CM23 .....113M2
Broad Cl HOC/HUL SS5 .....307 P1
Broadclyst Av LOS SS9 .....327 N1
Broadclyst Cl SOS SS1 .....329 P5
Broadclyst Gdns SOS SS1 .....330 A5
Broadcroft Crs HVHL CB9 .....41 K5
Broadfield Rd RBSF CM22 .....137 L4
  GTDUN CM6 .....165M6
  HLW CM20 .....13 K5
Broadfield Cl MHAD SG10 .....160 E4
  ROM RM1 .....298 E9
Broadfield Rd RBSF CM22 .....139 P7
Broadfields CHESW EN7 .....228 G8
  RCOLE CO7 .....153 K2
  SBW CM21 .....187 J3
Broadfields Av WCHMH N21 .....272 F6
  PEND EN3 .....273 N2
Broadlands Av PEND EN3 * 273 N2
  RAYL SS6 .....306 C4
Broadlands Cl PEND EN3 .....273 N2
Broadlands Rd HOC/HUL SS5 .....308 A1
Broadlands Wy COLN CO4 .....9 H3
  IPNE IP4 .....26 C6
Broad La ROCLW CO6 .....102 F6
Broadlawn LOS SS9 .....327M2
Broadleaf Av BSF CM23 .....161 P1
Bradley Rd
  HLWW/ROY CM19 .....210 A7
Broadmayne BSDN SS14 .....2 D3
Broad Mead BRWN CM15 .....258 C8
  RIPW IP8 .....24 D9
Broadmead Rd COLN CO4 .....128 F6
  WFD IG8 .....295 L4
Broadmere Rd IP IP1 .....24 F5
Broad Oak WFD IG8 .....295 L2
Broadoak Av PEND EN3 .....252 A5
Broadoak Cha MAL CM9 * 198 F6
Broad Oak Cl CHING E4 .....274 G8
Broad Oak La ERITH DA8 .....346 C5
Broadoaks EPP CM16 .....254 G2
Broad Oaks RCOLW CO6 .....77 L1
  WICKW SS12 .....305 K1
Broad Oaks Cl SAFWN CB10 .....66 C7
Broadoaks Crs BRTR CM7 .....145 N2
Broadoak Rd CDW/CHF RM16 .....128 E4
Broad Oak Wy RAYL SS6 .....307 H5
Broad Pde HOC/HUL SS5 .....307 P1
Broad Rd HC HCH RM12 .....318 F4
Broad St DAGE RM10 .....317 P9
  HVHL CB9 .....41 J3
  RBSF CM22 .....164 A7
Broad Street Green Rd
  MAL CM9 .....222 D3
Broadstrood LOU IG10 .....254 B8
  RCOS CO16 .....180 D8
Broadview Av
  CDW/CHF RM16 .....339 N9
Broad Wk HLW CM20 .....13 H5
  HOC/HUL SS5 .....308 A1
  MAL CM9 .....222 F7
  SWFD E18 .....295 K7
Broadwalk SWFD E18 .....295 K7
The Broad Wk North
  RBRW/HUT CM13 .....281 K9
The Broadwalk South
  RBRW/HUT CM13 .....301 K1
Broadwater Gdns
  RIPS/CAP IP9 .....85M9
Broadwater Gn LAIN SS15 .....302 G9
Broad Wy HOC/HUL SS5 .....288 A9

Broadway BARK IG11 .....334 D1
  COS CO15 .....206 F6
  GPK RM2 .....349M6
  GRAYS RM17 .....
  LOS SS9 .....
  PIT SS13 * 324 C1
  RAIN RM13 .....336 F4
  SRTFD E15 .....314 C9
  SUD CO10 * 44 A4
  TIL RM18 .....350 A7
  WIT CM8 .....146 E9
Broadway Av HLWE CM17 .....187 J8
Broadway Cl WFD IG8 .....295 L3
Broadway Ct WIT CM8 .....146 E9
Broadway Pde CHING E4 .....294 F3
The Broadway BCTR RM8 .....317 N4
  ED N9 .....273M9
  GTDUN CM6 .....141 N2
  HLW CM12 .....118 C6
  LOU IG10 .....276 D2
  PIT SS13 * 324 C1
  PLSTW E13 .....333 K2
  SOS SS1 * 19 F5
  VGE SS16 .....
  WICKW SS12 .....285 J8
Broadway West LOS SS9 .....327 N6
Brock Cl K/T/MI CO5 .....174 B7
  WIT CM8 .....197 H4
Brockdish Av BARK IG11 .....316 C7
Brockenhurst Dr SLH/COR SS17 .....341 K5
Brockenhurst Gdns IL IG1 .....316 D7
Brockenhurst Wy
  RCHLM CM3 .....242 C9
Brocket Cl CHIG IG7 .....296 C1
Brocket Rd HOD EN11 .....208 G1
Brockett Rd CDW/CHF RM16 .....350 B1
Brocket Wy CHIG IG7 .....296 F2
Brock Gn SOCK/AV WI5 .....338 E6
Brockham Cl RCOS CO16 .....181 L7
Brockham Dr
  GNTH/NBYPK IG2 .....316 D1
Brocks Hl WICKE SS11 .....284 C3
Brock Hill Dr WICKE SS11 .....284 C5
Brockles Md
  HLWW/ROY CM19 .....210 D7
Brockley Crs CRW RM5 .....298 B4
  IP IP1 .....24 E2
Brockley Rd CHLM/GWD CM2 .....281 K7
Brockley Pl BOW E3 .....332 E4
Brock Rd PLSTW E13 .....333 L5
Brocksford Av RAYL SS6 .....307 J6
Brocks Md GTDUN CM6 .....116 F8
Brocksparkwood
  RBRW/HUT CM13 .....281 L9
Brockton Cl ROM RM1 .....299 H4
Brockway Cl WAN E11 .....315 H4
Brockwell La K/T/MI CO5 .....173 H4
Brodie Rd CHING E4 .....274 F7
  ENC/FH EN2 .....251 H8
  SBN/FI SS3 .....330 E8
Brodie Wk WICKW SS12 .....305 L2
Brodlove La WAP E1W 332 A2
Brograve Cl CHLM/GWD CM2 .....240 C7
Broke Av RIPW IP8 .....24 C1
Broke Hall Gdns IPSE IP5 .....26 C7
Brokesley St BOW E3 .....332 C4
Broman's La K/T/MI CO5 .....204 B2
Bromefield St WAB EN9 .....253 K5
Bromeswell Rd IPNE IP4 .....25M2
Bromfelde Rd BCAYE CM11 .....304 B2
Bromfords Cl WICKW SS12 .....304 C2
Bromfords Dr WICKW SS12 .....304 C2
Bromhall Rd DAGW RM9 .....317 J8
Bromleigh Cl CHES/WCR EN8 .....230 B7
Bromley GRAYS RM17 .....349 J4
Bromley Cl CHTY IP2 .....25 K8
  RCOS CO16 .....6 B1
Bromley Hall Rd POP/IOD E14 .....332 F5
Bromley High St BOW E3 .....332 E5
Bromley La CHES/WCR EN8 .....230 B7
Bromley Rd COLN CO4 .....128 F7
  MGTR CO11 .....105 P6
  RCOLE CO7 .....179 H4
Bromley St WCHPL E1 .....332 A5
Brompton Cl BCAYW CM12 .....283 H5
Brompton Dr ERITH DA8 .....346 C5
Brompton Gdns MAL CM9 .....243 P2
Bronte Cl BRTR CM7 .....145 K6
  ERITH DA8 .....346 A5
  FSTGT E7 .....315 K6
  GNTH/NBYPK IG2 .....296 B9
  TIL RM18 .....350 D7
Bronte Gv CART CO9 .....94 C4
Bronte Ms SOSN SS2 .....329 H4
Bronte Rd WIT CM8 .....171 N8
Bronze Age Wy BELV DA17 .....346 B1
Brook Av DAGE RM10 .....318 A9
Brook Cl BRTR CM7 .....
  K/T/MI CO5 .....199 N1
  MAL CM9 .....198 B9
  MAL CM9 .....220 G9
  RCFD SS4 .....
Brook Crs CHING E4 .....294 D1
Brookdale Av UPMR RM14 .....319M5
Brookdale Cl UPMR RM14 .....294 D7
Brook Dr SLH/COR SS17 .....324 B5
Brooke Av SAFWN CB10 .....51M7
Brooke Gdns BSF CM23 .....137 P7
Brook End SBW CM21 .....187 L2
Brook End Rd
  CHLM/GWD CM2 .....218 G8
Brook End Rd North
  CHLM/GWD CM2 .....218 F7
Brook End Rd South
  CHLM/GWD CM2 .....218 G9
Brooker Cl CLPT E5 .....
Brooker Rd GRAYS RM17 .....349 K3

Brooker Rd WAB EN9 .....252 F4
Brooke Sq MAL CM9 .....223 H8
Brook Farm Cl HSTD CO9 .....72 D6
Brook Farm La RIPS/CAP IP9 .....85 K3
Brookfield EPP CM16 .....233 K4
Brookfield Av WALTH E17 .....294 E8
  RBRW/HUT CM13 .....281 M5
Brookfield Gdns
  CHES/WCR EN8 .....230 A6
Brookfield La CHES/WCR EN8 .....229 N7
Brookfield La East
  CHES/WCR EN8 .....230 A6
Brookfield La West
  CHES/WCR EN8 .....229 P7
Brookfield Pth CHING E4 .....294 G3
Brookfield Rd ED N9 .....273M9
  EHAM E6 .....314 B8
  IP IP1 .....24 G2
Brookfields Cl LOS SS9 .....327 N1
Brook Gdns CHING E4 .....294 E1
Brook Hall Rd K/T/MI CO5 .....153 J8
Brookhampton St
  SAFWN CB10 .....36 B6
Brook Hl GTDUN CM6 .....167 L4
  RCHLM CM5 .....194 A6
Brookhill Wy IPNE IP4 .....26 E7
Brookhouse Gdns CHING E4 .....295 H1
Brookhouse Rd RCOLW CO6 .....124 F7
Brookhurst Cl
  CHLM/GWD CM2 .....218 C8
Brooking Cl BCTR RM8 .....317 K5
Brooking Rd FSTGT E7 .....315 K7
Brookland K/T/MI CO5 .....173 P9
Brooklands COL CO1 * 9 F7
  COS CO15 .....206 D6
  WICKW SS12 .....284 C9
Brooklands Ap ROM RM1 .....298 C8
Brooklands Cl
  ROMW/RG RM7 .....307 P9
Brooklands Ct WCHMH N21 .....273 J4
  EMPK RM11 .....299 H9
Brooklands Gdns ROM RM1 .....298 C8
Brooklands La
  ROMW/RG RM7 .....298 C8
Brooklands Pk LAIN SS15 .....302 G9
Brooklands Ri MGTR CO11 .....81 N9
Brooklands Rd MGTR CO11 .....106 B1
Brooklands Sq CVI SS8 .....344 B3
Brooklands Wk
  CHLM/GWD CM2 .....239 P5
Brook La BRWN CM15 .....258 G2
  CHLM/GWD CM2 .....240 C7
  FX IP11 .....35 L6
  KIR/NAC IP10 .....28 A8
  RIPS/CAP IP9 .....28 A8
Brooklane Fld HLWS CM18 .....211 J6
Brooklyn Av LOU IG10 .....275 P5
Brooklyn Dr RAYL SS6 .....306 G1
Brooklyn Ms HAR CO12 * 14 D7
Brooklyn Rd HAR CO12 .....14 D7
Brookman's Av
  CDW/CHF RM16 .....339M8
Brookmans Cl UPMR RM14 .....320 B2
Brookmans Rd CM4 .....261 L7
Brook Md LAIN SS15 .....305 J8
Brook Meadow
  CHLM/GWD CM2 .....
Brook Meadow HSTD CO9 .....72 C8
Brook Mdw Cl WFD IG8 .....295 H3
Brook Park Cl WCHMH N21 .....272 C5
Brook Ri CHIG IG7 .....276 B8
Brook Rd BKHH IG9 .....295 N5
  BOC CM0 .....248 A5
  BRW CM14 .....280 C9
  CHES/WCR EN8 .....252 C4
  EPP CM16 .....254 G5
  GNTH/NBYPK IG2 .....316 F1
  GPK RM2 .....299 H6
  K/T/MI CO5 .....199 N1
  LOU IG10 .....275 P4
  RAYL SS6 .....306 F7
  RCOLW CO6 .....149 N1
  SBF/HAD SS7 .....325 P5
  SBW CM21 .....187 L3
  STSD CM24 .....114 B9
Brooksbank St HOM E9 .....314 A8
Brooksby Wk HOM E9 .....314 A7
Brooksby's Wk HOM E9 .....314 A7
Brookscroft Rd WALTH E17 .....294 E5
Brooks Hall Rd IP IP1 .....16 A3
Brookside BARK/HLT IG6 .....296 D5
  BCAYE CM11 .....283 K2
  CVI SS8 .....299 N3
  EMPK RM11 .....299 K9
  HLWW/ROY CM19 .....210 A6
  HOC/HUL SS5 .....308 A3
  HOD EN11 .....208 D5
  WAB EN9 .....252 E5
  WCHMH N21 .....272 E5
Brookside Av SBN/FI SS3 .....330 A7
Brookside Cl COLS CO2 .....152 C2
Brookside Crs POTB/CUF EN6 .....228 D6
Brookside Gdns EN EN1 .....251 N7

RCOLE CO7 ....104 G1
RCOLE CO7 ....130 D6
RCOLE CO7 * 153 J6
RCOLW CO6 ....98 F7
Brook Ter HSTD CO9 ....72 D6
Brook V RCOS CO16 ....180 D9
Brook Vw CHLM/GWD CM2 ....241 H4
GTDUN CM6 ....92 B5
Brookview CHTY IP2 ....29 N1
Brook Wy CHIG IG7 ....276 B9
Brookway RAIN RM13 ....336 C5
Broom Cl CHESW EN7 ....229 M6
Broom Crs IPSE IP5 ....30 F1
Broome Gv RCOLE CO7 ....153 J4
Broome Rd SOCK/AV RM15 ....338 A8
Broom Rd BCAYE CM11 ....283 L3
Broomer Pl CHES/WCR EN8 ....229 P8
Broom Farm Rd RBSF CM22 ....114 F5
Broom Fld FX IP11 ....35 H6
Broomfield HLW CM20 ....187 J9
KESG IP5 ....27 L4
SBF/HAD SS7 ....326 G2
WALTH E17 ....314 C2
WIT CM8 ....146 D9
Broomfield Av BROX EN10 ....230 B5
LOS SS9 ....328 A1
LOU IG10 ....276 A5
RAYL SS6 ....306 D4
Broomfield Cl CRW RM5 ....298 C3
Broomfield Common
RIPW IP8 ....24 C5
Broomfield Crs RCOLE CO7 ....153 J4
Broomfield Gn CVI IG8 ....326 C9
Broomfield Ms KESG IP5 ....27 M4
Broomfield Rd CHDH RM6 ....317 L2
CHLM/WR CM1 ....4 E2
PIT SS13 ....304 F9
RBSF CM22 ....188 F1
Broomfields Ct PIT SS13 ....304 F9
Broomfields Ms PIT SS13 ....304 F9
Broomfields Rd PIT SS13 ....304 F9
Broomford St POP/IOD E14 ....332 M6
Broomfords Dr WICKW SS12 ....304 C1
Broomham Cl CHLM/WR CM1 ....218 A1
Broomhall Rd CHLM/WR CM1 ....217 P5
Broomhayes CHTY IP2 ....25 H9
Broomhill RIPS/CAP IP9 * 83 L5
Broom Hill Rd IP IP1 ....25 H5
Broomhill Rd GDMY/SEVK IG3 ....147 H4
WFD IG8 ....295 K3
Broomhills Cha BCAYW CM12 ....305 H2
Broomhills Rd K/T/MI CO5 ....202 C6
Broomstick Hall Rd WAB EN9 ....253 H5
Broom St SUD CO10 ....61 L5
Broom Wy K/T/MI CO5 ....177 J3
RIPS/CAP IP9 ....28 C8
Broomways SBF/FI SS3 ....331 H5
Broomwood Gdns
BRWN CM15 ....280 D5
Broomwood La ING CM4 ....261 P9
Broseley Gdns HARH RM3 ....299 K1
Broseley Rd HARH RM5 ....299 K1
Brotherton Av FX IP11 ....34 E3
Broton Dr HSTD CO9 ....97 P6
Brougham Cl SBN/FI SS3 ....350 F2
Brougham Glades COLW CO3 ....150 C1
Broughton Cl COLS CO2 ....151 M3
Broughton Rd IP IP1 ....16 C1
RCHLM CM3 ....287 H2
SBF/HAD SS7 ....327 J4
Browne Cl BRW CM14 ....280 E7
Brownfield St POP/IOD E14 ....332 F6
Browning Av SOSN SS2 ....329 H4
Browning Cl COLW CO5 ....127 J9
WALTH E17 ....294 F8
Browning Dr WICKW SS12 ....305 H2
Browning Rd BRTR CM7 ....145 K6
DART DA1 ....347 L9
ENC/FH EN2 ....251 J8
IP IP1 ....22 C9
MAL CM9 ....244 B2
MGTR CO11 ....106 B1
MNPK E12 ....316 A8
WAN E11 ....315 J2
Brownings Av CHLM/WR CM1 ....217 P6
Brownlea Gdns
GDMY/SEVK IG3 ....317 N4
Brownlow Bend BSDN SS14 ....3 K5
Brownlow Rd FSTGT E7 ....315 K6
FX IP11 ....35 L7
Brownlows Cl GTDUN CM6 ....190 F5
Browns Av WICKW SS11 ....285 L6
Browns Cl SUD CO10 ....47 M5
Brownsea Dr WICKW SS12 ....305 M2
Browns Gv WICKW SS12 ....151 K2
Brown's End Rd GTDUN CM6 ....158 A4
Browns Gv KESG IP5 ....27 J4
Brown's Rd WALTH E17 ....294 D7
Broxbourne Av WAN E11 ....295 L8
Broxbourne House BOW E3 ....332 E4
Broxbourne Rd FSTGT E7 ....315 K5
Broxburn Dr SOCK/AV RM15 ....338 D7
Broxhill Rd ABR/ST RM4 ....278 F9
Broxted Dr WICKW SS12 ....305 K1
Broxted End WICKW SS12 * 305 K1
Bruce Av HCH RM12 ....319 J4
Bruce Gv CHLM/GWD CM2 ....219 P5
WICKE SS11 ....305 M1
Bruce Rd BOW E3 ....332 E3
CHLM/WR CM1 ....239 J1
GRAYS RM17 ....
Bruces Wharf Rd
GRAYS RM17 ....349 K4
Bruce Wy CHES/WCR EN8 ....252 A3
Bruff Cl COLN CO4 ....127 P5
Bruff Dr WOTN CO14 ....159 H7
Bruges Rd CVI SS8 ....344 F3
Brundells Rd RCOLE CO7 ....154 E1
Brundish IP15 ....324 F1
Brundon La SUD CO10 ....20 A1
Brunel Cl ROM RM1 ....298 D8
TIL RM18 ....550 C7
Brunel Rd BRTR CM7 ....145 K5
CHTY IP2 ....24 F5
COS CO15 ....182 C5
LOS SS9 ....307 M8
SBF/HAD SS7 ....306 A8
WALTH E17 ....314 B1
WFD IG8 ....296 A2
Brunel St CAN/RD E16 ....333 J6
Brunel Wy COLN CO4 ....128 D1
RCHLM CM3 ....286 F1
Brunner Rd WALTH E17 ....294 C9
Brunswick Av UPMR RM14 ....320 B2
Brunswick Gdns
BARK/HLT IG6 ....296 D4
Brunswick House Cut
MGTR CO11 ....106 F5
Brunswick Pl RAYL SS6 ....306 E3
Brunswick Rd IPNE IP4 ....17 K1
LEY E10 ....314 F5
PEND EN3 ....252 D6
SOS SS1 ....329 L6
Brunswick St WALTH E17 ....294 F9
Brunton Pl POP/IOD E14 ....332 B6
Brunwin Rd BRTR CM77 ....144 C4
Brunwins Cl WICKE SS11 ....285 L9
Brushwood Cl POP/IOD E14 ....332 E5
Brussels Cl HAR CO12 ....110 C7
Brussum Rd SUD CO10 ....344 C3
Bruton Av WOS/PRIT SS0 ....328 B1
Bryan Rd BERM/RHTH SE16 ....332 C9
BSF CM23 ....137 L6
Bryanstone Mews COLW CO3 ....151 H1
Bryanstone Rd
Branston Rd TIL RM18 ....350 D7
Bryant Av HARH RM3 ....299 J6
SOS SS1 ....329 M8
Bryant Link CHLM/GWD CM2 ....218 C2
Bryant's La MAL CM9 ....242 G3
Bryant St SRTFD E15 ....314 G9
Brybank Rd HVHL CB9 ....40 F2
Bryce Cl WARE SG12 ....184 A1
Bryce Rd BCTR RM8 ....317 K6
Brydges Rd SRTFD E15 ....314 C7
Brymay Cl BOW E3 ....332 D2
Bryn Farm Cl BSDN SS14 ....3 H6
Bryn-y-Mawr Rd EN EN1 ....273 L5
Bryon Av FX IP11 ....34 E9
Bryony Cl HVHL CB9 ....41 H2
Buchanan Cl SOCK/AV RM15 ....337 P7
WCHMH N21 ....272 E4
Buchanan Gdns WLSDN NW10 ....305 J2
Buchanan Wy RCHLM CM3 ....267 H4
Buckenhoe Rd SAFWN CB10 ....51 M7
Buckeridge Wy BOC CM0 ....226 E8
Buckerills RP13 S 324 F1
Buckfast Av FOS CO15 ....158 E8
Buckfast Cl CHTY IP2 ....25 H9
Buckhatch La RCHLM CM3 ....263 P7
Buck Hl BRTR CM7 ....145 J6
Buckhurst Wy BKHH IG9 ....275 N9
Buckingham Hill Rd
CDW/CHF RM16 ....341 H7
Buckingham Rd
HOC/HUL SS5 ....307 N1
HVHL CB9 ....41 H5
IL IG1 ....316 E4
LAIN SS15 ....303 M7
LEY E10 ....314 E5
SRTFD E15 ....314 B8
SWFD E18 ....295 J5
Buckingham Sq
WICKE SS11 * 305 M2
Buckland SBN/FI SS3 ....330 B5
Buckland Rd LEY E10 ....314 F4
Bucklebury Heath
RCHLM CM3 ....286 C2
Bucklers Cl BROX EN10 ....230 C1
Bucklers Dr BRW CM14 ....300 F2
Bucklesham Rd IPSE IP5 ....26 C9
KIR/NAC IP10 ....33 K4
Buckles La SOCK/AV RM15 ....338 F5
Buckley Cl DART DA1 ....346 E7
SLH/COR SS17 ....323 N9
Buckley's CHLM/GWD CM2 ....240 E3
Buckleys Cl WIT CM8 ....197 P7
Buckley's La RCOLW CO6 ....124 C9
Buckrell Rd CHING E4 ....274 C8
Buck's Horns La RIPW IP8 ....29 K3
Buckters Rents
BERM/RHTH SE16 ....332 B6
Buckwoods Rd BRTR CM7 ....145 J5
Buckwyns Cha BCAYW CM12 ....282 F2
Buckwyns Ct BCAYW CM12 * 282 G4
Buddleia Cl CHTY IP2 ....24 F7
Buddleia Ct RCOLE CO7 ....153 H5
Bude Cl KESG IP5 ....26 F5
WALTH E17 ....294 C9
Budna Rd CVI IG8 ....326 C9
Budoch Dr GDMY/SEVK IG3 ....317 H4
Buffett Wy COLN CO4 ....128 F9
Buglers Ri CHLM/WR CM1 ....239 J2
Bugsbys Wy GNWCH SE10 ....333 H9
Bugsby Wy KESG IP5 ....27 K4
Buick Av COS CO15 ....206 C6
Building End Rd ROY SG8 ....62 G2
Bulbecks Wk RCHLM CM3 ....286 C3
Bulford La BRTR CM7 ....145 M9
Bulford Mill La BRTR CM7 ....145 M9
Bullace Cl COLN CO4 ....128 E4
Bullards Pl BETH E2 ....332 A3
Bullbanks Rd BELV DA17 ....345 M3
Bull Cl CDW/CHF RM16 ....339 J9
VGE SS16 ....324 D1
Bullen Cl RIPW IP8 ....24 B1
Bullen La RIPW IP8 ....24 B1
Buller Rd BARK IG11 ....316 F9

LAIN SS15 ....303 J8
RCHLM CM3 ....266 B8
SBW CM21 ....162 B9
Bullfields SAFWS CB11 ....65 H9
POTB/CUF EN6 ....228 D9
Bullfinch Cl COLN CO4 ....128 C7
HAR CO12 ....109 P7
Bullfinch Dr HSTD CO9 ....98 B7
Bull Hill Rd COS CO15 ....182 A8
Bullivant St POP/IOD E14 ....332 F7
Bull La DAGE RM10 ....318 A5
HOC/HUL SS5 ....307 J5
K/T/MI CO5 ....173 P9
MAL CM9 ....222 A8
RAYL SS6 ....306 G5
SAFWS CB11 ....62 E7
SUD CO10 ....37 P8
Bullocks La SUD CO10 ....20 D6
Bullock Wood Cl COLN CO4 ....128 E3
Bull Rd SRTFD E15 ....333 J2
Bulls Cliff FX IP11 * 11 H4
Bull's Cross EN EN1 ....251 M6
Bulls Cross Ride CHESW EN7 ....251 M4
Bullsmoor Cl CHES/WCR EN8 ....251 P5
Bullsmoor Gdns
CHES/WCR EN8 ....251 N5
Bullsmoor La EN EN1 ....251 M5
Bullsmoor Ride
CHES/WCR EN8 ....251 N5
Bullsmoor Wy
CHES/WCR EN8 ....251 N5
Bullwell Crs CHES/WCR EN8 ....230 B8
Bullwood Ap HOC/HUL SS5 ....307 L2
Bullwood Hall La
HOC/HUL SS5 ....307 K3
Bullwood Rd HOC/HUL SS5 ....307 K3
Bulmer Rd SUD CO10 ....60 F4
Bulmer St SUD CO10 ....60 F4
Bulow Av CVI SS8 ....251 M6
Bulphan By-Pass UPMR RM14 ....322 B4
Bulphan Cl WICKW SS12 ....305 K1
Bulrush Cl BRTR CM7 ....145 L5
Bulstrode Rd CHTY IP2 ....17 F7
Bulwark Rd SBN/FI SS3 ....330 D6
Bulwer Court Rd WAN E11 ....314 C5
Bulwer Rd IP IP1 ....16 A3
WAN E11 ....314 C5
Bumbles Green La WAB EN9 ....231 L4
Bumfords La RCHLM CM3 ....220 D4
Bumpstead Rd HVHL CB9 ....41 L7
Bunces La WFD IG8 ....295 J4
Bundick's Hl CHLM/WR CM1 ....4 A1
Bung Rw WIT CM8 ....198 C5
Bunsen St BOW E3 ....332 B2
Bunters Av SBN/FI SS3 ....330 B8
Buntingbridge Rd
GNTH/NBYPK IG2 ....296 E9
Bunting Cl CHLM/GWD CM2 ....240 A5
ED N9 ....274 A7
Bunting Rd CHTY IP2 ....24 E8
Bunting Ter EHAM E6 ....333 L5
Bunyan Cl IP IP1 ....23 H9
Bunyan Rd BRTR CM7 ....145 H3
WALTH E17 ....294 B7
Burbage Cl CHES/WCR EN8 ....252 B1
Burcham St POP/IOD E14 ....332 G7
Burchell Rd LEY E10 ....314 E5
Burches LAIN SS15 ....303 M6
Burches Rd SBF/HAD SS7 ....306 D6
Burches Ms SBF/HAD SS7 ....306 A6
Burchwall Cl CRW RM5 ....298 A6
Burden Wy WAN E11 ....315 L4
Burdett Av WOS/PRIT SS0 ....18 B5
Burdett Rd POP/IOD E14 ....332 C6
SOS SS1 ....19 K7
Burdetts Rd DAGW RM9 ....335 N1
Buren Av CVI SS8 ....345 H2
Bures Rd RCOLW CO6 ....76 C9
SOS SS0 ....61 C5
Burfield Cl LOS SS9 ....308 A3
Burfield Rd LOS SS9 ....308 A3
Burford La BARK/HLT IG6 ....296 D8
BCTR RM8 ....317 K5
Burford Gdns HOD EN11 ....208 D5
PLMGR N13 ....272 E9
Burford Rd EHAM E6 ....333 P5
SRTFD E15 ....314 C9
Burford St HOD EN11 ....208 D5
Burgage Ct WARE SG12 * 184 A3
Burgate Cl DART DA1 ....346 E8
Burges Cl EMPK RM11 ....319 J1
SOS SS1 ....330 B8
Burges Rd EHAM E6 ....316 B9
SOS SS1 ....329 P8
Burgess Av SLH/COR SS17 ....341 M4
Burgess Fld CHLM/GWD CM2 ....218 E7
Burgess Pl KESG IP5 ....27 N4
Burgess Rd SRTFD E15 ....315 H6
Burgess St POP/IOD E14 ....332 D5
Burghley Av BSF CM23 ....137 H7
Burghley Cl BRTR CM77 ....144 E8
CHTY IP2 ....25 H9
Burghley Ms CDW/CHF RM16 ....
WAN E11 * 295 J5
Burghley Wy CHLM/GWD CM2 ....240 B5
Burghstead Cl BCAYW CM12 ....283 H7
Burgundy Gdns PIT SS13 ....304 G7
Burke Cl IP IP1 ....22 G9
Burke Rd CHLM/WR CM1 ....229 N7
Burke St CAN/RD E16 ....333 J6
Burkitts La SUD CO10 ....20 C5
Burland Rd BRWN CM15 ....280 C2
CRW RM5 ....298 B3
Burleigh Cl BCAYW CM12 ....283 J3
Burleigh Gdns
STHGT/OAK N14 ....272 B7
Burleigh Pde
STHGT/OAK N14 * 272 C7
Burleigh Rd CHES/WCR EN8 * 252 B2

EN EN1 ....273 K3
Burleigh Sq SOS SS1 ....330 A6
Burleigh Wy ENC/FH EN2 ....273 J2
POTB/CUF EN6 ....228 D9
Burlescoombe Cl SOS SS1 ....329 P6
Burlescoombe Rd SOS SS1 ....330 A5
Burlescoombe Rd SOS SS1 ....329 P6
Burley Cl CHING E4 ....294 D2
Burley Hi HLWE CM17 ....211 L4
Burley Rd BSF CM23 ....162 D1
CAN/RD E16 ....333 M6
Burlington Av
ROMW/RG RM7 ....318 A1
Burlington Cl EHAM E6 ....333 P6
Burlington Ct PIT SS13 ....304 G7
Burlington Gdns CHDH RM6 ....317 M2
SBF/HAD SS7 ....307 M5
Burlington Pl WFD IG8 ....275 K9
Burlington Rd COLW CO3 ....8 A7
ENC/FH EN2 ....251 J9
IP IP1 ....16 B4
Burmanny Cl COS CO15 ....181 N7
Burnaby Rd SOS SS1 ....329 K7
Burncroft Av PEND EN3 ....274 A2
Burne Av WICKW SS12 ....304 F1
Burnell Ga CHLM/WR CM1 ....218 F4
Burnells Wy STSD CM24 ....124 D5
Burnel Wk HARH RM3 ....299 J3
Burnell Wk RBRW/HUT CM13 ....300 F5
Burnels Av EHAM E6 ....334 B5
Burnet Cl RIPW IP8 ....29 M2
Burnett Cl HLWW/ROY CM19 ....
Burnett Pk HLWW/ROY CM19 ....210 C8
Burnett Rd ERITH DA8 ....347 J4
LOU IG10 ....276 D2
Burnham Av IP IP1 ....
IPNE IP4 ....34 F4
WOTN CO14 ....159 J6
Burnham Ct COS CO15 ....207 H4
IP IP1 ....16 B4
Burnham Rd BOC CM0 ....269 H7
CHING E4 ....294 C2
CHLM/WR CM1 ....218 C6
DAGW RM9 ....317 J9
LOS SS9 ....327 M5
MAL CM9 ....243 J5
MAL CM9 ....266 D1
RCHLM CM3 ....264 E9
RCHLM CM3 ....268 M4
ROMW/RG RM7 ....298 B7
WICKE SS11 ....286 B5
Burnham Rd Summerhill
RBRW/HUT CM13 ....267 N6
Burnley Rd WTHK RM20 ....348 C6
Burnsall Cl SAFWS CB11 ....65 N1
Burns Av CHDH RM6 ....317 K2
COLW CO3 ....151 J1
PIT SS13 ....324 C1
Burns Cl BCAYE CM11 ....
ERITH DA8 ....346 E6
MAL CM9 ....244 B1
WALTH E17 ....294 F8
Burns Crs CHLM/GWD CM2 ....5 G7
Burnside CVI SS8 ....345 J3
Burnside CVI SS8 ....208 C5
HOD EN11 ....187 L2
SBW CM21 ....332 A3
Burnside Av SBF/HAD SS7 ....218 A6
Burnside Crs CHLM/WR CM1 ....317 K4
Burnside Rd BCTR RM8 ....350 C6
Burns Pl TIL RM18 ....22 F9
Burns Rd IP IP1 ....143 L8
Burnstie Rd GTDUN CM6 ....102 G1
Burnt Dick Hl COLN CO4 ....250 G4
Burntfarm Ride ENC/FH EN2 ....
Burnthouse La
RBRW/HUT CM13 ....260 A9
Burnthouse Rd RCOLW CO6 ....124 D6
Burntmill La HLW CM20 ....186 D9
Burnt Mills Rd PIT SS13 ....304 C6
Burntwood Av EMPK RM11 ....319 J1
RBRW/HUT CM13 ....
Burnway EMPK RM11 ....319 K2
Burrard Rd CAN/RD E16 ....333 K6
Burr Cl HAR CO12 ....109 M7
VGE SS16 ....322 F1
Burrell Rd CHTY IP2 ....16 C7
Burr Hill Cha SOSN SS2 ....328 F3
Burroughs Piece Rd SUD CO10 ....20 C5
Burrow Gn CHIG IG7 ....277 H8
Burrow Rd CHIG IG7 ....297 H2
Burrows Cl RCOS CO16 ....181 N7
Burrows Rd SLH/COR SS17 ....341 K4
Burrs Rd COS CO15 ....182 B9
Burrsville Ms COS CO15 ....182 B8
Burrswood Pl MAL CM9 ....222 E8
Burses Wy RBRW/HUT CM13 ....281 L6
Bursland Rd PEND EN3 ....252 A1
Burslem Av BARK/HLT IG6 ....297 H5
Burstall Cl RCOS CO16 ....180 B2
Burstead Dr BCAYE CM11 ....283 L9
Burstead Gra BCAYE CM11 ....303 L1
Burton Cl HVHL CB9 ....41 H6
SLH/COR SS17 ....323 N9
Burton Dr PEND EN3 ....252 D2
Burton La CHESW EN7 ....229 N7
Burton Pl CHLM/GWD CM2 ....5 G7
Burton Rd LOU IG10 ....276 D3
SWFD E18 ....295 J5
Burtons Ct SRTFD E15 ....314 C9
Burton's Green Rd HSTD CO9 ....123 H5
Burt Rd CAN/RD E16 ....16 C7
Burwash NHMKT IP6 ....23 P2
Burwell Av CVI SS8 ....326 C9

Burwell Rd LEY E10 ....314 B3
Burwood Gdns RAIN RM13 ....336 E5
Bury Cl BERM/RHTH SE16 ....332 A8
COL CO1 ....9 F4
RCOLW CO6 ....149 L3
Bury Farm La BCAYE CM11 ....304 C4
Bury Flds GTDUN CM6 ....142 F9
Bury Green Rd CHESW EN7 ....251 M1
Bury Holme BROX EN10 ....230 C2
Bury La EPP CM16 ....252 E9
RCHLM CM5 ....193 L4
RCHLM CM5 ....286 C8
ROY SG8 ....48 G9
Bury Lodge La STSD CM24 ....138 D3
Bury Rd CHING E4 ....274 C3
DAGE RM10 ....318 B7
EPP CM16 ....253 F1
HLWE CM17 ....187 K8
IP IP1 ....22 E8
Bury St ED N9 ....273 M7
Bury St West ED N9 ....273 K6
Bury Rd RCOS CO16 ....180 D9
Bury Water La SAFWS CB11 ....64 F8
Burywoods COLN CO4 ....127 L5
Bushbarns CHESW EN7 ....229 M8
Bushberry Rd HOM E9 ....314 B8
Bush Av RCOS CO16 ....230 C1
Bush Cl GNTH/NBYPK IG2 ....296 G5
Bushell Wy CO5 ....158 F8
Bush Elms Rd EMPK RM11 ....318 F2
Bushey Av SWFD E18 ....295 J7
Bushey Cl CHING E4 ....274 F9
RCHLM CM5 ....287 H1
RIPS/CAP IP9 ....28 C9
Bushey Cft HLWS CM18 ....210 F5
Bushey Ley BRTR CM7 ....145 N3
Bushey Rd PLSTW S15 ....333 M2
Bushfields LOU IG10 ....276 B4
Bush Gv SUD CO10 ....60 F4
Bushgrove Rd BCTR RM8 ....317 L6
Bush Hall Rd BCAYW CM12 ....283 K3
Bush Hi WCHMH N21 ....273 H6
Bush Hill Pde EN EN1 ....273 J6
Bush Hill Rd WCHMH N21 ....273 J5
Bush La SAFWN CB10 ....68 A8
Bushman Gdns RIPW IP8 ....24 B1
Bush Rd BKHH IG9 ....295 N1
SAFWN CB10 ....68 B7
WAN E11 ....315 J2
Bushway BCTR RM8 ....317 L6
Bushwood WAN E11 ....315 J3
Bushy Md LAIN SS15 ....303 J7
Butcher Rw POP/IOD E14 ....332 A7
SAFWN CB10 ....56 E7
Butchers La RIPS/CAP IP9 ....28 D9
WOTN CO14 ....159 J7
Butchers Pasture
GTDUN CM6 ....140 G1
Bute Rd BARK/HLT IG6 ....296 C9
Butler Cl SAFWS CB11 ....65 M9
Butler Rd BCTR RM8 ....317 J6
HSTD CO9 ....97 N6
Butlers Cl CHLM/WR CM1 ....218 A1
Butlers Dr CHING E4 ....
Butlers Gv VGE SS16 ....323 J3
Butler's La MGTR CO11 ....108 B7
SAFWN CB10 ....52 B3
Butler Smith Gdns KESG IP5 ....27 H4
Butlers Wy HSTD CO9 ....72 P3
Butley Cl PIT SS13 ....29 P2
Butley Rd FX IP11 ....11 F3
Butneys BSDN SS14 ....5 F2
Buttall Cl GRAYS RM17 ....349 N5
Butterbur Cha RCHLM CM3 ....286 F2
Buttercross La EPP CM16 * 253 H9
Buttercup Cl BCAYW CM12 * 283 H4
HARH RM3 ....299 J3
RIPW IP8 ....24 B1
Buttercup Wk WIT CM8 ....171 M9
Buttercup Wy BOC CM0 ....269 H6
Butterfield Rd RCHLM CM3 ....219 K3
Butterfields WALTH E17 ....294 F9
Butterfield Sq EHAM E6 ....36 D6
Butterfly Gdns IPNE IP4 ....26 B6
Butteridges Cl DAGW RM9 ....335 N1
Buttermarket IP IP1 ....16 E4
Buttermere BRTR CM7 ....144 F7
LAIN SS15 ....303 J4
Buttersweet Ri SBW CM21 ....187 M3
Butterworth Gdns WFD IG8 ....295 K3
Butterys SOS SS1 ....329 M6
Buttfield Cl DAGE RM10 ....318 A8
Butt La BSF CM23 ....113 J5
Buttlehide RCHLM CM3 ....222 B9
Buttlys es GTDUN CM6 ....140 G6
Buttondene Crs BROX EN10 ....230 E3
Button Rd CDW/CHF RM16 ....349 J2
Butt Rd COLS CO2 ....151 N1
RCOLW CO6 ....78 B4
Buttsbury Wk WIT CM8 ....140 G6
Buttsbury Rd IL IG1 ....316 D7
Buttsbury Ter ING CM4 ....261 M7
Butt's Green Rd
CHLM/GWD CM2 ....241 L8
EMPK RM11 ....319 L2
Butts La RCHLM CM3 ....242 B3
SLH/COR SS17 ....341 K5
Butts Paddock RCFD SS4 ....289 G3
Butts Rd SLH/COR SS17 ....341 K4
The Butts BROX EN10 ....230 C1
Butts Wy CHLM/GWD CM2 ....239 M7
Buxey Cl WOTN CO14 ....159 K8
Buxhall Crs HOM E9 ....314 C8
Buxton Cl LOS SS9 ....327 K3
Buxton Ct LOS SS9 ....327 K3
WFD IG8 ....295 N1
Buxton Dr WAN E11 ....295 H8
Buxton Rd CDW/CHF RM16 ....339 P9
CHING E4 ....274 D6
COLS CO2 ....152 B3
EHAM E6 ....333 P5
EPP CM16 ....254 F6

ERITH DA8 ...346 C5
GNTH/NBYPK IG2 ...316 F1
RCOLW CO6 ...147 N5
SRTFD E15 ...315 H7
WAB EN9 ...253 K2
WALTH E17 ...294 B8
Buxton Sq LOS SS9 ...327 K3
Buyl Av CVI SS6 ...326 E9
Byculiah Av ENC/FH EN2 ...272 C2
Byculiah Rd ENC/FH EN2 ...272 C2
Byefield Cl BERM/RHTH SE16 ...332 B9
Byelands Cl BERM/RHTH SE16 ...332 A8
Byfield LOS SS9 ...308 A8
Byfield Cl BERM/RHTH SE16 ...332 B9
Byfield Ct RBRW/HUT CM13 * ...281 M1
Byfletts VGE SS16 ...324 E2
Byford Cl SRTFD E15 ...315 H9
Byford Rd RAYL SS6 ...307 H4
SUD CO10 ...21 H2
Bygrove St POP/IOD E14 ...332 E6
Bylam La RIPS/CAP IP9 ...84 B2
Byland Cl CHTY IP2 ...25 H9
WCHMH N21 ...272 E6
Bylands Cl BSF CM23 ...137 J8
Byng Crs RCOS CO16 ...15 K5
Byng Gdns BRTR CM7 ...145 M2
Bynghams HLWW/ROY CM19 ...210 A5
Byng St POP/IOD E14 ...332 D9
Bypass Rd RCOS CO16 ...180 E8
By-Pass Rd SLH/COR SS17 ...341 L4
Byrd Ct LAIN SS15 ...305 K7
Byrd Rd BRWN CM15 ...258 D3
Byrd's Farm La SAFWN CB10 ...51 M7
Byrne Dr SOSN SS2 ...528 F1
Byron Av COLW CO5 ...127 J8
MNPK E12 ...315 P8
SOSN SS2 ...329 J4
SWFD E18 ...295 J7
Byron Cl BRTR CM7 ...145 K6
CVI SS8 ...344 F1
THMD SE28 ...335 K8
Byron Ct ENC/FH EN2 ...272 C1
LAIN SS15 ...303 J8
Byron Dr ERITH DA8 ...346 A5
WIT CM8 ...197 P2
Byron Gdns TIL RM18 ...350 D6
Byron Rd DART DA1 ...347 N9
IP IP1 ...22 F8
LEY E10 ...314 E3
RBRW/HUT CM13 ...281 N6
WALTH E17 ...294 C6
Byron St POP/IOD E14 ...332 F6
Byron Ter ED N9 * ...273 P6
Byron Wy HARH RM3 ...299 H5
Byrony Cl WIT CM8 ...171 L9
Bysouth Cl CLAY IG5 ...21 H2
Bywater Pl BERM/RHTH SE16 ...332 B8
Bywater Rd RCHLM CM3 ...286 F2

C

Cabborns Crs SLH/COR SS17 ...341 L9
Cabinet Wy CHING E4 ...294 C3
LOS SS9 ...307 M9
Cables Cl BELV DA17 ...346 B1
Cabot Sq POP/IOD E14 ...332 D8
Cabot Wy EHAM E6 ...333 N4
Cadenhouse Ms COLW CO5 ...127 H8
Cadges Ct SUD CO10 * ...4 E4
Cadiz Rd DAGE RM10 ...318 B9
Cadmere La CHES/WCR EN8 ...230 B7
Cadmus Rd IP IP1 ...24 E4
Cadogan Av
RBRW/HUT CM13 ...321 N1
Cadogan Cl HOM E9 ...314 C9
Cadogan Rd SWFD E18 ...295 L7
WCHMH N21 ...272 F4
Cadogan Ter HOM E9 ...314 C8
Caernarvon Av EMPK RM11 ...319 M3
HOC/HUL SS5 ...307 N1
Caernarvon Dr CLAY IG5 ...296 B5
Cage End RBSF CM22 ...164 A8
Cage End Cl RBSF CM22 ...164 A8
Cagefield Rd RCFD SS4 ...309 M5
Cage La COLN CO4 ...103 L3
Cairns Av WFD IG8 ...296 A3
Cairns Rd COLS CO2 ...152 B4
Cairo Rd WALTH E17 ...294 D8
Caister Dr PIT SS13 ...304 D9
Caistor Park Rd SRTFD E15 ...333 J1
Caithness Cl IPNE IP4 ...26 A3
Caladonia La WICKW SS12 ...305 K2
Calais Cl CHESW EN8 ...229 J5
Calamint Rd WIT CM8 ...196 C1
Calbourne Av HCH RM12 ...318 C7
Calcott Cl BRW CM14 ...280 E7
Calcutta Rd TIL RM18 ...350 A7
Caldbeck WAB EN9 ...252 G4
Caldecot Av CHESW EN7 ...229 L8
Caldecott Wy CLPT E5 ...314 A5
Caldecot Wy BROX EN10 ...230 C1
Calderon Rd WAN E11 ...314 F6
Caldwell Rd SLH/COR SS17 ...341 J4
Caldy Rd BELV DA17 ...346 A1
Caledonian Cl
GDMY/SEVK IG3 * ...317 J3
Caledonia Rd RIPS/CAP IP9 ...85 N9
Caledon Rd EHAM E6 ...334 A1
Caiford Dr HVHL CB9 ...40 F5
California Cl COLN CO4 ...128 C3
California Rd RAYL SS6 ...318 D4
Calian Gv SOCK/AV RM15 ...338 F7
Callingham Cl POP/IOD E14 ...332 C5
Callis Rd WALTH E17 ...314 C1
Callis St SUD CO10 ...44 A3
Callowood Crt RCHLM CM3 ...243 N9
Calmire Cl HVHL CB9 ...41 J4
Calne Av CLAY IG5 ...296 C5
Calshot Av CDW/CHF RM16 ...339 J9
Calshot Wy ENC/FH EN2 ...272 C2
Calverley Cl BSF CM23 ...162 B2

Calverley Crs DAGE RM10 ...317 P4
Calvert Dr PIT SS13 ...305 H6
Calverton Rd EHAM E6 ...334 B1
Camberley Av EN EN1 ...273 K5
Camberley Rd IPNE IP4 ...26 C4
Camberton Rd BRTR CM7 ...121 H9
Cambeys Rd DAGE RM10 ...318 B7
Camborne Av ENC/FH EN2 ...272 G2
Camborne Rd KESG IP5 ...26 C4
Camborne Wy HARH RM3 ...299 L4
Cambourne Av ED N9 ...274 A6
Cambrai Dr COLS CO2 ...151 N1
Cambria Ct CVI SS8 ...343 P2
MGTR CO11 ...106 C5
Cambrian Av
GNTH/NBYPK IG2 ...296 F9
Cambrian Rd LEY E10 ...314 D2
Cambridge Av RSTFD E15 ...299 H7
HSTD CO9 ...72 D9
Cambridge Cl CHES/WCR EN8 ...229 P8
HVHL CB9 ...41 H2
ING CM4 ...261 L7
VGE SS16 ...322 C1
WALTH E17 ...314 C1
Cambridge Ct SOS SS1 * ...18 E5
Cambridge Dr CHTY IP2 ...29 N1
Cambridge Gdns
CDW/CHF RM16 * ...350 B2
EN EN1 ...273 M1
RCFD SS4 ...308 D2
WCHMH N21 ...273 J6
Cambridge Pde EN EN1 * ...273 M1
Cambridge Pk WAN E11 ...315 K1
Cambridge Park Rd WAN E11 ...315 K2
Cambridge Rd BARK IG11 ...316 D9
CBE/LIN CB1 ...38 A1
CHING E4 ...274 C7
COLW CO5 ...151 M1
CVI SS8 ...344 C2
FOS CO15 ...159 H9
FX IP11 ...35 L7
GDMY/SEVK IG3 ...316 F3
HLW CM20 ...197 P2
KESG IP5 ...26 F5
SAFWS CB11 ...50 C6
SAFWS CB11 ...64 G7
SBW CM21 ...162 B8
STSD CM24 ...114 A8
WAN E11 ...315 K1
WOS/PRIT SS0 ...18 D5
Cambridge Ter ED N9 * ...273 L6
Cambridge Wy BURES CO8 ...76 A9
HVHL CB9 ...41 H2
Cambus Rd CAN/RD E16 ...333 K5
Camden Cl CDW/CHF RM16 ...350 C2
Camdenhurst St
POP/IOD E14 ...332 B6
Camden Rd CDW/CHF RM16 ...350 B2
IPSE IP3 ...26 A7
WALTH E17 ...314 C1
WAN E11 ...315 L1
Camellia Av RCOS CO16 ...181 M9
Camellia Ct CHLM/WR CM1 * ...218 E5
HARH RM3 ...299 K5
Camellia Gns RCOS CO16 ...181 M9
Camelot Cl CHLM/WR CM1 ...217 N6
WOOL/PLUM SE18 ...334 G9
Camelot Gdns PIT SS15 ...305 H7
Camel Rd CAN/RD E16 ...333 N8
Cameron Ct BRTR CM7 ...121 J7
BRW CM14 ...300 F1
ING CM4 ...260 C6
LOS SS9 ...327 M4
SLH/COR SS17 ...323 M8
SUD CO10 * ...46 F5
Cameron Ct WARE SG12 ...184 A2
Cameron Cl CHES/WCR EN8 ...252 A4
Cameron Pl WICKW SS12 ...305 K2
Cameron Rd GDMY/SEVK IG3 ...316 F3
Cam Gn SOCK/AV RM15 ...338 G6
Camoise Ct HSTD CO9 ...71 J2
Camomile Dr WICK SS11 ...285 K8
Camomile Wy COLN CO4 ...127 M5
Camomile Rd ROMW/RG RM7 ...318 C4
Campbell Av BARK/HLT IG6 ...296 D6
Campbell Ct CHLM/GWD CM2 ...239 P7
HLWE CM17 ...211 J4
ROM RM1 ...298 D5
WICKW SS12 ...305 J2
Campbell Dr COLN CO4 ...128 F5
Campbell Rd BOW E3 ...332 D5
EHAM E6 ...333 P1
IPSE IP3 ...31 J1
SRTFD E15 ...315 H6
WALTH E17 ...294 C8
Campden Crs BCTR RM8 ...317 K6
Campden Wy BCTR RM8 ...317 J6
Camperdown Rd CVI SS8 ...326 F9
Camper Ms SOS SS1 * ...329 L8
Campernell Cl RCOLE CO7 ...179 L5
Camper Rd SOS SS1 ...329 L8
Campfield Rd SBN/FI SS3 ...330 D8
Campine Cl CHES/WCR EN8 ...230 A7
Campion Cl EHAM E6 ...334 A1
ROMW/RG RM7 ...318 C4
Campion Gdns WFD IG8 ...295 K2
Campion La RCOLW CO6 ...79 L3
Campion Pl THMD SE28 ...335 J8
Campion Rd CHTY IP2 ...24 G7
COLS CO2 ...152 B1
Campions LOU IG10 ...254 D8
Campions Hl RCOLW CO6 ...77 L8
The Campions SBN/FI SS3 * ...330 B6
STSD CM24 ...114 B4
Campion Wy RCOLW CO6 ...77 K4
WIT CM8 ...197 H1
Cample La SOCK/AV RM15 ...338 F7
Camp Rd RCOLE CO7 ...130 E8
Campsey Rd DAGW RM9 ...317 J9
Camps Rd CBE/LIN CB1 ...38 G4
HVHL CB9 ...41 J4
HVHL CB9 ...54 E1

Campus Rd WALTH E17 ...314 C1
Cam Rd SRTFD E15 ...332 G1
Camulodunum Wy COLS CO2 ...151 M5
Camulus Ct BRTR CM7 ...145 K4
COLS CO2 ...151 K4
Cam Wy WIT CM8 ...196 G2
Camwood Gdns IPSE IP5 ...26 B4
Canada La BROX EN10 ...230 B3
Canada Rd ERITH DA8 ...346 G5
Canada Sqaure POP/IOD E14 ...332 E8
The Canadas BROX EN10 ...230 B3
Canada St BERM/RHTH SE16 ...332 A9
Canal Ct GRH DA9 ...347 P9
Canal Rd WCHPL E1 ...332 B4
Canberra Cl CHLM/WR CM1 ...217 M6
COLS CO2 ...152 B5
DAGE RM10 ...318 C9
HCH RM12 ...319 H6
IPNE IP4 ...26 C5
Canberra Crs DAGE RM10 ...318 C9
Canberra Rd EHAM E6 ...334 A1
Canberra Sq TIL RM18 ...350 B7
Cander Wy SOCK/AV RM15 ...338 E7
Candlelight Ct SRTFD E15 ...315 J8
The Candlemakers SOSN SS2 ...329 H1
Candlet Gv FX IP11 ...35 J6
Candlet Rd FX IP11 ...35 H4
Candover Rd EMPK RM11 ...318 G3
Candy St BOW E3 ...332 C2
Candytuft Rd CHLM/WR CM1 ...218 E5
Cane Hl HARH RM3 ...299 J6
Canes La HLWE CM17 ...233 M1
Canewdon Vw WICKE SS11 ...285 J6
Canewdon Gdns WICKE SS11 ...285 K6
Canewdon Hall Cl RCFD SS4 ...289 L6
WOS/PRIT SS0 ...18 A4
Canewdon View Rd RCFD SS4 ...308 F1
Canfield BSF CM23 ...137 K6
Canfield Rd CTDUN CM6 ...165 L5
RAIN RM13 ...319 H6
WFD IG8 ...295 P4
Canford Av WICKW SS12 ...284 G6
Canford Cl CHLM/GWD CM2 ...240 D3
ENC/FH EN2 ...272 F1
Canhams Rd SUD CO10 ...61 L5
Canham St IP IP1 ...16 C4
Canna Gdns WICKW SS12 ...284 G6
Canney Rd BOC CM0 ...246 C6
Can Hall Rd WAN E11 ...315 J6
Canning Rd SRTFD E15 ...333 H2
WALTH E17 ...294 B8
Canning St HAR CO12 ...115 F4
Cannington Rd DAGW RM9 ...317 K8
Cannon Cir BRTR CM7 ...95 J2
Cannon Dr POP/IOD E14 ...332 D7
Cannon Hl STHGT/OAK N14 ...272 D9
Cannon Hl CHLM/GWD CM2 ...240 B7
Cannon Ms WAB EN9 ...253 K6
Cannon Rd COL CO1 ...128 C9
STHGT/OAK N14 ...272 D9
Cannons Ct BSF CM23 ...137 M6
COLS CO2 ...151 N2
Cannons La CHONG CM5 ...214 B9
RBSF CM22 ...164 A8
Cannons Md BRWN CM15 ...258 D3
STSD CM24 ...114 A8
Cannons Mill La BSF CM23 ...137 M5
Canon Av CHDH RM6 ...297 K9
Canonbury Rd EN EN1 ...251 N3
Canon Cl CHLM CB9 ...41 J2
SLH/COR SS17 ...341 N3
Canonium Ms K/T/MI CO5 ...173 H5
Canon Pugh Dr SUD CO10 ...47 M5
Canons Brook
HLWW/ROY CM19 ...12 C7
Canons Cl RCHLM CM3 ...242 B9
Canons Ga CHES/WCR EN8 ...230 C5
HLW CM20 ...12 C4
Canonsleigh Crs LOS SS9 ...327 P5
Canonsleigh Rd DAGW RM9 ...317 J8
Canopy La HLWE CM17 ...211 K2
Cansey La MGTR CO11 ...107 J9
Canterbury Av CHLM/WR CM1 ...4 A1
DART DA1 ...347 P9
RBRW/HUT CM13 ...300 F3
WTHK RM20 ...348 B6
The Canters SBF/HAD SS7 ...326 E1
Cantley Gdns
GNTH/NBYPK IG2 ...316 D1
Canton St POP/IOD E14 ...332 D6
Cantrell Rd BOW E3 ...332 D4
Canuden Rd CHLM/WR CM1 ...4 A5
Canute Ct RCFD SS4 ...289 H6
Canvey Rd CVI SS8 ...326 A8
LOS SS9 ...327 L5
PIT SS13 ...305 L9
Canvey Wk CHLM/WR CM1 ...218 E5
Canvey Wy SBF/HAD SS7 ...325 M3
Canwick Gv COLS CO2 ...152 A5
Capadocia St SOS SS1 ...329 M8
Cape Cl BARK IG11 ...316 C9
COLW CO5 ...151 J1
Capel Cl BRTR CM7 ...144 C4
CHLM/WR CM1 ...4 A5
Capel Dr FX IP11 ...10 B1
FX IP11 ...34 C1
SLH/COR SS17 ...341 M5
Capel Pk FOS CO15 ...158 F7

Capel Rd BRTR CM77 ...144 C4
COLW CO5 ...151 M1
FSTGT E7 ...315 L6
Capelston LAIN SS15 ...19 F5
Capel Ter SOS SS1 ...175 J1
Caper La COLS CO2 ...175 J1
Capital Pl HLWW/ROY CM19 ...210 B4
Capon Cl BRW CM14 ...280 E7
Capons La EHAM CM5 ...242 D4
Cappell La WARE SG12 ...184 F7
Cap Pillar Ct RCOLE CO7 ...153 J4
Capstan Cl CHDH RM6 ...297 J6
Capstan Ct GRH DA9 ...347 P9
Capstan Pl COLN CO4 ...128 E9
Capstan Ride ENC/FH EN2 ...272 F1
Capstan Sq POP/IOD E14 ...332 F8
Capstan Wy
BERM/RHTH SE16 ...332 B8
Captains Rd K/T/MI CO5 ...202 E6
Captains Wood Rd MAL CM9 ...222 B1
Capulet Ms CAN/RD E16 ...333 K8
Capworth St LEY E10 ...314 E2
Caracalla Wy COLN CO4 ...128 B1
Caradon Ct WAN E11 ...315 H5
The Caravan Site
SOCK/AV RM15 ...348 A1
Caravel Ct CDW/CHF RM16 ...349 J1
Caraway Cl PLSTW E13 ...333 L5
Carbis Cl CHING E4 ...274 G7
Carbis Rd POP/IOD E14 ...332 C6
Carbonels SUD CO10 ...47 P8
Carbone Cl POTB/CUF EN6 ...282 C1
Carbury Cl HCH RM12 ...319 H8
Cardew Drift KESG IP5 ...27 J5
Cardiff Av CHTY IP2 ...30 B1
Cardiff Rd PEND EN3 ...273 J1
Cardigan Gdns
GDMY/SEVK IG3 ...317 H4
Cardigan Rd BOW E3 ...332 C2
Cardigan St IP IP1 ...16 F1
Cardinal Cl CHESW EN7 ...229 L5
COLN CO4 ...128 G8
Cardinal Dr BARK/HLT IG6 ...296 D5
Cardinal Rd CDW/CHF RM16 ...349 H1
Cardinal St IP IP1 ...16 F1
Cardinal Wy HVHL CB9 ...41 J2
RAIN RM13 ...337 J2
Card's Rd CHLM/GWD CM2 ...241 H4
Carey Rd DAGW RM9 ...317 M6
Carfax Rd HCH RM12 ...318 G6
Carisbrook Cl EN EN1 ...251 L9
Carisbrooke Av WOS/PRIT SS0 ...182 B6
Carisbrooke Av COS CO15 ...182 B6
PIT SS13 ...304 G9
Carisbrooke Dr RCHLM CM3 ...286 F1
SLH/COR SS17 ...341 P1
Carisbrooke Rd BRWN CM15 ...258 D3
WALTH E17 ...294 B8
WOS/PRIT SS0 ...18 B1
Carleton Rd CHESW EN7 ...230 A6
Carlford Cl WOS/PRIT SS0 ...26 A7
Carlile Cl BOW E3 ...332 C2
Carlina Gdns WFD IG8 ...295 L2
Carlingford Dr WOS/PRIT SS0 ...328 D3
Carlisle Cl COL CO1 ...9 F3
Carlisle Gdns IL IG1 ...315 P1
Carlisle Rd LEY E10 ...314 D3
ROM RM1 ...298 F3
SOSN SS2 ...329 M3
WALTH E17 ...294 B5
WICKE SS11 ...315 J3
Carlton Cl HSTD CO9 ...57 P8
HVHL CB9 ...41 J1
UPMR RM14 ...320 C6
Carlton Dr BARK/HLT IG6 ...296 F7
LOS SS9 ...328 A5
SBF/HAD SS7 ...326 G3
Carlton Rd CDW/CHF RM16 ...340 A9
COS CO15 ...182 F8
LEY E10 ...314 F2
SUD CO10 ...46 F9
Carlton Sq WCHPL E1 ...332 A4
Carlton Ter WAN E11 ...295 L9
Carlton Vis SOSN SS2 * ...19 C2
Carlton Wy IPNE IP4 ...25 M3
Carlyle Cl IP IP1 ...22 C8
Carlyle Gdns BCAYW CM12 ...282 G5
Carlyle Rd MNPK E12 ...315 N6
THMD SE28 ...335 J7
Carmania Cl SBN/FI SS3 ...330 E5
Carmarthen Cl CHTY IP2 ...30 A1
Carmel St SAFWN CB10 ...36 E9
Carmen St POP/IOD E14 ...332 E6
Carnaby Rd BROX EN10 ...208 B8
Carnach Gn SOCK/AV RM15 ...338 E7
Carnanton Rd WALTH E17 ...294 G5
Carnarvon Av EN EN1 ...273 L1
Carnarvon Rd COS CO15 ...182 B6
SOSN SS2 ...18 E1
SRTFD E15 ...315 J8
SWFD E18 ...295 J5
Carnation Cl CHLM/WR CM1 ...218 D4
ROMW/RG RM7 ...318 D4
Carnation Dr SAFWN CB10 ...51 N8
Carnegie Cl PEND EN3 ...252 E6
Carnforth Gdns HCH RM12 ...318 F7
Carnival Cl BSDN SS14 ...304 A7
Carnoustie Ct THMD SE28 ...335 L6
Carol Av WDBR IP12 ...27 M2
Carolbrook Rd CHTY IP2 ...29 N1
Carol Cl FX IP11 ...35 M6
LAIN SS15 ...303 L8
Carolina Cl SRTFD E15 ...315 H7
Carolina Wy K/T/MI CO5 ...174 A8

Caroline Cl RCOLE CO7 ...153 K3
Caroline Ct COLS CO2 * ...151 K3
Caroline Cl SOSN SS2 * ...328 F1
Caroline St WCHPL E1 ...332 A6
Caro Rd CVI SS8 ...344 F2
Carpenter Cl BCAYW CM12 ...282 G4
Carpenter Gdns WCHMH N21 ...272 G8
Carpenter Pth
RBRW/HUT CM13 ...281 N4
Carpenters SBN/FI SS3 ...310 C9
Carpenters Arms La
EPP CM16 ...233 J4
Carpenters Dr BRTR CM77 ...144 E7
Carpenters Rd EN EN1 ...251 P6
SRTFD E15 ...314 E9
The Carpenters BSF CM23 ...136 G9
Carraways WIT CM8 ...197 L4
Carriage Cl FX IP11 ...34 E1
Carriage Dr DART DA1 ...218 D5
Carriage Ms IL IG1 ...316 D4
Carrick Dr BARK/HLT IG6 ...296 D5
Carriers Cl K/T/MI CO5 ...202 D5
Carriers Ct RCOLE CO7 ...80 C6
Carrington Av FOS CO15 ...137 K6
Carrington Ct K/T/MI CO5 ...202 C5
Carrington Gdns FSTGT E7 ...315 K6
Carringtons Rd RCOLE CO7 ...130 A3
Carrington Wy BRTR CM7 ...121 J7
Carroll Cl SRTFD E15 ...315 J7
Carroll Hl LOU IG10 ...276 A2
Carron Cl POP/IOD E14 ...332 E6
Carron Md RCHLM CM3 ...287 J2
Carron Rd DAGW RM9 ...317 J9
Carrs Av WLTH E11 ...111 L2
Carrs La WCHMH N21 ...273 J4
Carrs Ct FOS CO15 ...6 B3
Carr St IPNE IP4 ...17 F4
POP/IOD E14 ...332 B6
Carruthers Dr WICKE SS15 ...285 J7
Carsey Cl BCAYE CM11 ...284 B4
Carsey Hl CBE/LIN CB1 ...39 N5
Carshalton End COLW CO5 ...151 J2
Carsington Gdns DART DA1 ...233 L5
CAN/RD E16 ...333 L5
Carsons Dr SUD CO10 ...61 M5
Carswell Gdns WICKW SS12 ...305 J2
Cartbridge Cl WOTN CO14 ...159 J6
Cartel Cl CRW RM5 ...298 A4
Carter Dr CRW RM5 ...298 A1
Carter Rd PLSTW E13 ...333 L1
Carterhatch La EN EN1 ...251 L9
EN EN1 ...273 M1
Carters Cl CHES/WCR EN8 ...230 C6
Carters Ct CT SAFWN CB10 ...52 C1
Cartersfield Rd WAB EN9 ...252 F4
Carters Hl BSF CM23 ...113 M6
COLN CO4 ...103 K2
Carters La EPP CM16 ...252 C5
RBSF CM22 ...115 J2
WIT CM8 ...198 A6
Carters Leys BSF CM23 ...137 J6
Carters Md HLWE CM17 ...211 J4
Cart La CHING E4 ...275 H7
GRAYS RM17 ...349 L3
Cartlodge Av WICKE SS11 ...285 K8
Cartwright Rd SBF/HAD SS7 ...306 A8
Cartwright Wk
CHLM/GWD CM2 ...218 D3
Carvers Wd BCAYE CM11 ...283 K9
Cary Rd WAN E11 ...315 H6
Cascade Rd BKHH IG9 ...275 N8
Case La RIPS/CAP IP9 ...81 N3
Casey La BOC CM0 ...248 B6
Cashiobury Ter SOS SS1 ...18 E5
Cashmere Wy VGE SS16 ...324 C3
Caspian Wk CAN/RD E16 ...333 N6
Cassandra Ga CHES/WCR EN8 ...230 C5
Cassel Av CVI SS8 ...326 F9
Cassino Rd CHLM/WR CM1 ...217 M5
COLS CO2 ...152 A1
Cassiobury Rd WALTH E17 ...294 A9
Cassland Rd HOM E9 ...314 B8
Castelian Av GPK RM2 ...299 J8
Casteli Rd LOU IG10 ...254 D9
Castle Av CHING E4 ...294 G3
EN EN1 ...251 H1
RAIN RM13 ...318 D9
Castle Cl ENC/FH EN2 ...272 G7
Castle Meadow HSTD CO9 ...72 C7
Castle Rd COL CO1 ...8 E4
COS CO15 ...6 D4
DAGW RM9 ...335 J4
GRAYS RM17 ...349 H4
HOD EN11 ...208 F2
IP IP1 ...22 F2
PEND EN3 ...252 B9
RAYL SS6 ...306 F6
WDBR IP12 ...27 H4
Castle St BSF CM23 ...137 L8
CHONG CM5 ...235 M8

STHGT/OAK N14..............272 B4
STHGT/OAK N14..............272 B4
Chase Rd East RCOLE CO7....131 H8
Chase Rd West RCOLE CO7....130 F9
Chase Side STHC/FH EN2.....273 H1
Chaseside RAYL SS6.........307 H7
Chase Side STHGT/OAK N14...272 A6
Chase Side Av ENC/FH EN2...273 H1
Chaseside Cl ROM RM1 *.....298 D5
Chase Side Crs ENC/FH EN2..251 J9
The Chase BCAYE CM11.......283 K6
BOC CM0....................269 J5
BRTR CM7...................121 K8
BRTR CM7...................144 F9
BRW CM14...................300 E1
BSF CM23...................137 L8
BXLYHN DA7.................346 A8
CHESW EN7..................228 C7
CHIG IG7...................296 C5
CHLM/GWD CM2...............127 H9
COLW CO5 *.................182 C8
DAGE RM10..................318 C5
GTDUN CM6..................166 C1
HLWE CM17..................211 K2
HVHL CB9...................55 L3
K/T/MI CO5.................173 H5
K/T/MI CO5.................202 F6
KESC IP5...................27 M4
LAIN SS15..................303 G5
LOU IG10...................275 M6
MAL CM9....................200 A8
MAL CM9....................223 N9
MAL CM9....................225 J2
MGTR CO11..................106 C5
MINPR E12..................315 N6
RAYL SS6...................307 J6
RBRW/HUT CM13..............301 M2
RBSF CM22..................288 D9
RCFD SS4...................105 M6
RCHLM CM5..................264 F9
RCOLE CO7..................105 H4
RCOLW CO6..................130 A9
RCOLW CO6..................125 H7
RCOLW CO6..................125 N7
ROM RM1....................298 D7
SBF/HAD SS7................326 C1
SBN/FI SS3.................293 J9
SOSN SS1...................19 J5
SUD CO10...................45 P5
UPMR RM14..................320 B5
VGE SS16...................323 M5
WARE SG12..................184 D6
WICKW SS12.................23 F4
WICKW SS12.................305 K3
WTHK RM20..................348 G4
Chaseville Pde WCHMH N21 *..272 E4
Chaseville Park Rd
WCHMH N21.................272 D4
Chase Wy STHGT/OAK N14.....272 A7
Chaseway VGE SS16..........324 E2
Chaseways SBW CM21.........187 J4
The Chaseway BRTR CM7......145 M4
The Chase Wy COLW CO5......127 M6
Chasewood Av ENC/FH EN2....272 E7
Chaters Hl SAFWN CB10......191 M9
Chatham Hall La RCHLM CM3..193 P2
WALTH E17..................294 B7
Chatham Wy BRW CM14........280 F8
Chatley Rd RCHLM CM3.......196 C6
Chatsworth SBF/HAD SS7.....306 C9
Chatsworth Av BRTR CM7.....144 F2
Chatsworth Crs CHTY IP2....157 H7
FX IP11....................34 F4
Chatsworth Dr EN EN1.......273 M6
IPNE IP4...................26 D6
Chatsworth Gdns COS CO15....6 B6
HOC/HUL SS5................307 N1
Chatsworth Rd DART DA1.....347 H9
K/T/MI CO5.................202 F5
SRTFD E15..................315 J7
Chatterford End BSDN SS14..299 H5
Chatteris Av WALTH E17.....299 H1
Chattisham Rd RIPW IP8.....28 D2
Chatton Cl WICKW SS12......305 K2
Chaucer Cl COS CO15........206 F5
MAL CM9....................244 B2
TIL RM18...................350 C7
Chaucer Crs BRTR CM7.......145 K6
Chaucer Rd CHLM/GWD CM2....240 C1
FSTGT E7...................315 K8
FX IP11....................11 G3
HARH RM3...................298 C4
IP IP1.....................22 C9
WALTH E17..................46 C9
WALTH E17..................294 C7
WAN E11....................315 K1
Chaucer Wk WICKW SS12......305 H2
Chaucer Wy COLW CO3........347
DART DA1...................347 M9
HOD EN11...................208 D1
Chauntcey Cl ED N9.........273 M9
Chaunter Rd CAN/RD E16.....333 L6
Chauntry Rd HVHL CB9.......41 H4
Cheapside East RAYL SS6....306 F3
Cheapside West RAYL SS6....306 E8
Cheddar Av WOS/PRIT SS0....328 B2
Chedington SBN/FI SS3......307 K6
Cheeleon Rd SOCK/AV RM15..338 F2
Cheffins Rd HOD EN11.......208 C2
Cheldon Barton SBN/FI SS3..330 B6
Chelmer Av RAYL SS6........306 F4
DART DA1...................194 A7
Chelmer Cl FOS CO13........158 F7
HARH RM3...................199 J8
Chelmer Crs BARK IG11......200 C9
Chelmer Dr GTDUN CM6.......141 M6
RBRW/HUT CM13..............281 P5
SOCK/AV RM15...............338 F7
Chelmer Lea CHLM/GWD CM2...240 D3

Chelmer Pl CHLM/WR CM1......5 J2
Chelmer Rd BRTR CM7......145 M5
CDW/CHF RM16..............350 B5
CHLM/GWD CM2..............218 D9
HOM G9....................314 A7
HVHL CB9..................41 L3
UPMR RM14.................320 A1
WIT CM8...................197 H2
Chelmerton Av
CHLM/GWD CM2.............240 D3
Chelmer Valley Rd
CHLM/WR CM1..............218 B5
Chelmer Village Wy
CHLM/GWD CM2.............218 E9
Chelmer Wy BOC CM0........290 F2
SBN/FI SS3................330 C7
Chelmsford Av CRW RM5.....298 C4
SOSN SS2..................18 D1
Chelmsford Cl EHAM E6.....334 A6
Chelmsford Dr UPMR RM14...319 L5
Chelmsford Gdns IL IG1....315 P2
CDW/CHF RM16..............281 K4
CHLM/WR CM1...............239 K1
CHONG CM5.................182 D7
COS CO15..................182 D7
GTDUN CM6.................141 M7
GTDUN CM6.................166 G1
GTDUN CM6.................167 N1
ING CM4...................190 G6
ING CM4...................237 H6
MAL CM9...................188 G2
RBSF CM22.................193 P5
RCHLM CM5.................243 L7
STHGT/OAK N14.............272 B6
SWFD E18..................295 J5
WALTH E17.................314 D1
Chelmsford Gdns EHAM E6...333 P7
LOU IG10..................275 P5
Chelsea Av RAYL SS6.......306 E5
Chelsea Cl IP IP1.........24 C2
Chelsea Ct SUD CO10.......21 F5
Chelsea Flds WARE SG12....208 L1
Chelsea Gdns HLWE CM17....211 M4
Chelsea Rd SUD CO10.......21 F5
Chelsfield Av ED N9.......274 A6
Chelsworth Av IPNE IP4....25 L2
SUD CO10..................21 K7
Chelsworth Cl SOS SS1.....329 N6
Chelsworth Crs SOS SS1....329 M6
Chelsworth Dr HARH RM3....299 K5
Chelsworth Rd FX IP11.....10 C3
Cheltenham Av IP IP1......25 J2
Cheltenham Dr LOS SS9.....328 A4
SBF/HAD SS7...............306 E8
Cheltenham Gdns EHAM E6...333 P7
LOU IG10..................275 P5
Chelwater CHLM/GWD CM2....240 C2
Chelwood Cl CHING E4......274 E5
Chelmsford Rd WICKE SS11..286 B7
Chenappa Cl PLSTW E13.....333 K3
Cheney Rw WALTH E17.......294 C5
Cheneys Rd WAN E11........315 H5
Chenies Dr LAIN SS15......303 J6
Chepstow Av HCH RM12......319 K5
Chepstow Cl BCAYE CM11....283 L3
Chepstow Rd FX IP11.......316 F1
IP IP1....................23 J8
Chequers BKHH IG9.........275 L7
BSF CM23..................137 H6
Chequers Ct RCFD SS4 *....289 L6
Chequers La DAGW RM9......355 N4
GTDUN CM6.................141 L6
MAL CM9...................222 B9
Chequers Ri NHMKT IP6.....22 A2
Chequers Rd ABR/ST RM4....279 K8
BSF CM23..................28 D2
COS CO15..................206 C5
FOS CO13..................158 D8
LOU IG10..................130 C1
MGTR CO11.................130 C1
The Chequers ING CM4 *....260 D5
RCOLE CO7.................153 P7
Cherbury Cl THMD SE28.....335 L6
Cheriton Av CLAY IG5......296 B6
Cheriton Rd BRTR CM7......145 M5
The Cherries CVI SS8......344 E3
Cherry Av RBRW/HUT CM13...281 J9
Cherry Blossom Cl RIPW IP8..24 C9
Cherry Blossom La
RCHLM CM5................266 A4
Cherrybrook SOS SS1......330 B5
Cherry Cha K/T/MI CO5....174 A9
Cherry Cl CVI SS8........344 B1
HOC/HUL SS5..............307 N2
Cherrydene Cl HOC/HUL SS5..287 H6
Cherrydown CDW/CHF RM16...339 N4
RAYL SS6..................306 G3
Cherrydown Av CHING E4....274 C4
Cherrydown Cl CHING E4....274 C9
Cherrydown East VGE SS16...2 E7
Cherrydown Wk
ROMW/RG RM7..............298 A6
Cherrydown West VGE SS16...2 D7
Cherrygarden La
CHLM/GWD CM2.............4 D7
Cherry Garden La
RCHLM CM5................242 D3
SAFWS CB11................64 C9
Cherry Garden Rd MAL CM9..221 P9
Cherry Gdns BCAYW CM12....282 E4
BRTR CM7..................137 L4
BSF CM23..................144 G6
DAGW RM9..................137 N5
SBW CM21..................162 B9
Cherry Gardens La IPNE IP4..26 A4
Cherry La HSTD CO9........71 P1
WICKE SS11................285 L9
Cherrymeade SBF/HAD SS7...326 D2
Cherry Orch BOC CM0.......269 K5
Cherry Orchard La RCFD SS4..308 C7

Cherry Orchard Wy RCFD SS4..308 C7
Cherry Rd PEND EN3........251 P8
Cherry Rw COLW CO5........151 J1
Cherry St ROMW/RG RM7.....298 C9
Cherrytree Cha SBN/FI SS3..331 H5
Cherry Tree Cl HAR CO12...109 L9
HSTD CO9..................98 B6
RAIN RM13.................336 F2
Cherry Tree Dr
SOCK/AV RM15..............358 G4
Cherry Tree La COLS CO2...152 B8
RAIN RM13.................336 E5
Cherry Tree Ri BKHH IG9...295 M1
Cherrytree Ri WIT CM8.....171 P8
Cherry Tree Rd ERITH DA8..347 H5
HOD EN11..................208 D4
Cherrytree Rd SUD CO10....21 J6
Cherrytrees BCAYW CM12....282 G8
Cherry Trees ING CM4 *....260 C5
Cherry Wk CDW/CHF RM16....350 B1
RAIN RM13.................336 E2
Cherry Wd RIPW IP8 *......29 H5
Cherrywood Cl BOW E3......332 E3
Cherrywood Dr COLW CO3....151 J1
Cherrywoods RCOLE CO7.....155 J6
Cherston Gdns LOU IG10....276 B5
Cherston Rd LOU IG10......276 B5
Chertsey Cl SBN/FI SS3....330 C5
Chertsey Rd IL IG1........316 E6
WAN E11...................314 C4
Chervil Cl K/T/MI CO5.....173 P9
Chervil Ms THMD SE28......335 J8
Cherwell Dr CHLM/WR CM1...217 K6
Cherwell Gv SOCK/AV RM15..338 C7
Chesapeake Rd IPSE IP5....35 N2
Chesfield Cl BSF CM23.....137 L9
Chesham Ct ROMW/RG RM7....298 C8
Chesham Dr LAIN SS15......303 J6
Chesham Rd CHTY IP2.......157 H7
Cheshire Cl EMPK RM11.....299 M9
WALTH E17.................294 E5
Chesnut Dr RAYL SS6.......306 E1
Chesnunt Rd FSTGT E7......315 L8
Chesnunts PIT SS13........304 F9
Chesnut Wash
CHES/WCR EN8..............230 B6
Chesley Gdns EHAM E6......333 N2
Chesnut Av North WALTH E17.294 F8
Chessington Gdns IP IP1...24 G3
Chess La WIT CM8..........197 K2
Chester Av SOS SS1........329 L8
SOS SS1...................320 B4
Chester Cl CHLM/GWD CM2...217 L4
Chester Crs CLPT E5.......332 A6
Chesterfield Av SBF/HAD SS7..306 A9
Chesterfield Crs LOS SS9..307 N9
Chesterfield Dr IP IP1....24 C1
Chesterfield Rd LEY E10...314 F1
PEND EN3..................252 B7
Chesterford Gdns BSDN SS14..304 E7
Chesterford Rd MNPK E12...316 A7
Chester Gdns ED N9........273 N5
Chester Hall La BRW CM14..305 P6
Chester Path CHLM/WR CM1..217 P6
Chester Rd CAN/RD E16.....333 H4
CHIG IG7..................276 B9
ED N9.....................273 N7
FSTGT E7..................315 J6
FX IP11...................35 J6
GDMY/SEVK IG5.............316 C5
LOU IG10..................254 D9
WALTH E17.................294 A9
WAN E11...................315 H1
Chesterton Cl CHTY IP2....29 P1
Chesterton Rd PLSTW E13...333 K3
Chesterton Ter PLSTW E13..333 K3
Chestnut Av BCAYW CM12....282 G6
BKHH IG9..................275 N9
CDW/CHF RM16..............339 N6
COS CO15..................207 H2
FOS CO13..................158 D8
FSTGT E7..................315 L6
HCH RM12..................319 H6
RCHLM CM5.................196 D9
SAFWS CB11................50 D9
WARE SG12.................184 C1
Chestnut Av South WALTH E17..294 F9
Chestnut Cl BKHH IG9......275 N9
BOC CM0...................290 F3
HCH RM12..................319 H6
HOC/HUL SS5...............308 A1
HVHL CB9..................26 D2
KESC IP5..................26 D2
STHGT/OAK N14.............272 B4
SUD CO10..................47 P8
WARE SG12.................185 H3
Chestnut Ct SAFWS CB11....57 H9
VGE SS16..................324 F2
Chestnut Dr NHMKT IP6.....22 D4
RBSF CM22.................188 E1
SAFWN CB11................315 K1
Chestnut Farm Dr
RCHLM CM5.................267 M7
Chestnut Gln HCH RM12.....318 E4
Chestnut Gv BARK/HLT IG6..296 F5
BRTR CM7..................145 H4
BRW CM14..................280 F8
SBF/HAD SS7...............306 C1
SOSN SS2..................329 H4
Chestnut Ms SUD CO10 *....20 C6
WFD IG8...................295 K2
Chestnut Rd PEND EN3......252 B6
RCOLE CO7 *...............130 A9
VGE SS16..................324 F2
Chestnuts RBRW/HUT CM13...281 J9
The Chestnuts CHTY IP2....24 D9
RAYL SS6..................307 H3
Chestnut Ter CHLM/WR CM1..217 P6
Chestnut Wk CHLM/GWD CM2..240 B2
EPP CM16..................232 C4

GTDUN CM6.................143 H8
RCHLM CM3.................242 B1
RCOLE CO7.................179 K6
Chestwood Cl BCAYW CM12...283 L1
Cheswick Cl DART DA1......346 E9
Chetwood Cl ERITH DA8.....346 D6
Chevalier Rd FX IP11......35 L7
Chevallier St IP IP1......25 H4
Cheveling Rd COLS CO2.....152 E4
Chevely Cl EPP CM16.......233 L8
Chevening Gdns
HOC/HUL SS5...............307 M1
Chevers Pawen PIT SS13....324 F1
Chevet St HOM E9..........314 B7
Chevington Wy HCH RM12....319 J6
Cheviot Cl BXLYHN DA7.....346 D7
ENC/FH EN2................273 J1
Cheviot Rd CHLM/WR CM1....217 L6
EMPK RM11.................318 F2
Chevron Cl CAN/RD E16.....333 K6
Chevy Ct HAR CO12.........109 M6
Chewton Rd WALTH E17......294 B8
Cheyne Av SWFD E18........184 A1
Cheyne Ct SUD CO10........20 C6
WICKW SS12................305 J3
Cheyne Wk WCHMH N21.......272 F4
Chichester Av RCHLM CM5...243 L7
Chichester Cl BSDN SS14...304 E7
CDW/CHF RM16..............348 G2
CVI SS8...................344 D3
EHAM E6...................333 P6
SOCK/AV RM15..............337 P8
Chichester Dr CHLM/WR CM1..218 B7
Chichester Gdns IL IG1....315 P2
Chichester Rd ED N9.......273 L7
SAFWS CB11................65 M1
SOSN SS2..................19 G3
WAN E11...................315 H5
Chichester Whf ERITH DA8..346 D5
Chickney Rd BSF CM23......115 M1
Chieftan Dr PUR RM19......347 M2
Chieveley Pde BXLYHN DA7 *..346 A8
Chieveley Rd BXLYHN DA7...346 A9
Chigborough Rd MAL CM9....222 G5
Chignall Rd CHLM/WR CM1...217 L4
The Chignalls LAIN SS15...303 H9
Chigwell La LOU IG10......276 D9
Chigwell Park Dr CHIG IG7..276 B1
Chigwell Ri CHIG IG7......276 B8
Chigwell Rd WFD IG8.......295 P5
Chilburn Rd COS CO15......182 A6
Childerditch Hall Dr
RBRW/HUT CM13.............301 J6
Childerditch La
RBRW/HUT CM13.............301 H4
Childerditch St
RBRW/HUT CM13.............301 K7
Childers Cl RIPS/CAP IP9..35 M8
Childers Fld FX IP11......34 G6
The Childers WFD IG8......295 J1
Childs Cl EMPK RM11.......319 H1
Childwell Aly COL CO1.....8 E7
Chilham Cl FX IP11........325 H1
Chiltern Cl BXLYHN DA7....346 D6
COL CO1...................8 F7
RAYL SS6..................306 G4
WARE SG12.................184 A1
Chiltern Dene ENC/FH EN2..272 E5
Chiltern Gdns HCH RM12....319 H5
Chiltern Rd BOW E3........332 D4
GNTH/NBYPK IG2............296 F8
The Chilterns WFD IG8.....275 K9
Chiltern Wy WFD IG8.......275 K9
Chilton Cl CHLM/GWD CM2...102 E9
Chilton Cnr SUD CO10......47 P8
Chilton Ct SUD CO10.......21 L6
Chilton Gv SUD CO10.......47 L8
Chilton Lodge Rd SUD CO10..21 J6
Chilton Rd CDW/CHF RM16...350 B1
IPSE IP5..................26 B7
Chilworth Ga BROX EN10....230 C1
The Chimes SBF/HAD SS7....326 B2
Chimney Pot La RCHLM CM3..246 D3
Chimsway Wk HVHL CB9......40 C3
China La UPMR RM14........321 N6
Chinchilla Rd SOS SS1.....329 L5
Chindit Cl BROX EN10......208 A8
Chindits La RBRW/HUT CM13..300 F2
The Chine WCHMH N21.......272 C6
Chingford Av CHING E4.....274 B9
Chingford Cl CHING E4.....274 E4
Chingford La WFD IG8......274 E4
Chingford Mount Rd
CHING E4..................294 D4
Chingford Rd CHING E4.....294 D4
Ching Wy CHING E4.........274 A9
Chinnel La SAFWS CB11.....64 E4
Chinnery Cl EN EN1........251 J8
Chinnery La WOS/PRIT SS0..327 L4
Chinook COLN CO4..........128 C5
Chipka St POP/IOD E14.....332 F9
Chippendale St CLPT E5....314 A5
Chippenham Gdns HARH RM3..299 J2
Chippenham Rd HARH RM3....299 J2
Chipperfield Cl UPMR RM14..320 B5
Chippetts La COLW CO5.....125 P6
Chippingdell WIT CM8......171 N9
Chippingfield HLWE CM17...187 K9
Chipping Hl HSTD CO9......98 C5
WIT CM8...................197 J1
Chipstead Rd ERITH DA8....346 D1
Chipstead Wk RCOS CO16....181 M7
Chisenhale Rd BOW E3......332 B2
Chishill Rd ROY SG8.......48 A2
Chislett Cl WICKW SS12....305 K2
Chislett Rw CHLM/GWD CM2..240 B2
Chiswick Rd ED N9.........273 L8
Chittenden Cl HOD EN11....208 E2

Chittock Cl RCOS CO16.....206 G1
Chittock Ga BSDN SS14.....304 C9
Chittock Md BSDN SS14.....304 D9
Chitts Hl COLW CO3........126 C6
Chitty's La BCTR RM8......53 L1
Chivers Rd BRW CM15.......258 C5
CHING E4..................274 E9
Choats Rd BARK IG11.......335 K4
Choats Wd COLW CO5........126 C6
Chobham Rd SRTFD E15......314 G9
Chopwell Cl SRTFD E15 *...314 G9
Chorley Cl VGE SS16.......322 C1
Chrisanthy Wy RCOLW CO6...125 H6
Chrisp St POP/IOD E14.....332 E6
Christ Church Av ERITH DA8..346 G3
Christchurch Av RAIN RM13..336 E2
WICKW SS12................284 F8
Christchurch Cl ENC/FH EN2..273 H1
Christ Church Cl COLC CO1..151 N1
Christchurch Ct IPNE IP4 *..19 K3
SOS SS1 *.................208 G9
Christchurch Rd IL IG1....316 C3
SOSN SS2..................19 K2
TIL RM18..................350 D6
Christchurch St IPNE IP4..208 G9
Christie Cl BROX EN10.....208 A8
Christie Rd HOM E9........314 B8
WAB EN9...................252 E5
Christina Rd WIT CM8......196 G4
Christina Cha COLW CO5....151 J1
Christine Worsley Cl
WCHMH N21.................272 G7
Christmas Fld HSTD CO9....72 G7
Christopher Cl HCH RM12...319 J6
Christopher Dr SUD CO10 *..20 C6
WARE SG12 *...............19 A3
Christopher Dr RCOS CO16..181 N4
Christopher Gdns DAGW RM9..317 L2
Christopher La SUD CO10...20 C6
Christopher Martin Rd
BSDN SS14.................304 D5
Christy Av CHLM/WR CM1....217 N7
Christy Cl LAIN SS15......302 F8
Christy Ter WFD IG8.......295 P4
Christy Wy LAIN SS15......302 F8
Chudleigh Crs
GDMY/SEVK IG5.............316 F6
Chudleigh Rd HARH RM3.....299 K1
Chudleigh St WCHPL E1.....332 A4
Chudleigh Wy LAIN CM9 *...225 J2
Church Av CHING E4........294 C5
CHLM/WR CM1...............217 P1
Churchbury Cl EN EN1......273 K1
Churchbury La EN EN1......273 K2
Churchbury Rd EN EN1......273 K1
Church Cha RCHLM CM5......285 P5
WIT CM8...................198 A1
Church Cl BRWN CM15.......259 P9
CVI SS8...................344 C2
KESC IP5..................26 G3
RCOLW CO6.................127 H3
SBN/FI SS3................330 C8
SLH/COR SS17..............33 G1
SUD CO10..................45 J1
WIT CM8...................197 H7
Church Cnr RCOLE CO7 *....130 D6
RCOLW CO6.................125 N7
SBF/HAD SS7 *.............326 A5
Church Ct BROX EN10 *.....208 D8
Church Crs BRWN CM15......259 P9
COS CO15..................7 G5
HOM E9....................314 A9
RIPW IP8..................24 B5
SOCK/AV RM15..............338 A8
Church Elm La DAGE RM10...317 P6
Church End BRTR CM7.......120 E8
GTDUN CM6.................141 L4
HLWW/ROY CM19.............210 A7
WALTH E17.................294 E8
Church End La WICKE SS11..285 K6
Church End La WICKE SS11..285 K6
Church Farm Wy COLN CO4...127 P3
Church Fld EPP CM16.......233 H8
SBW CM21..................52 E2
Churchfield HLWW CM20.....211 J3
Church Field Pth
CHES/WCR EN8..............229 P8
Church Field Rd SUD CO10..211 P3
Churchfield Rd RCOLW CO6..159 K6
WOTN CO14.................137 N8
Churchfields BROX EN10....208 D8
K/T/MI CO5................202 G6
LOU IG10..................275 P3
STSD CM24.................114 C9
SWFD E18..................295 K5
Churchfields Av COLW CO5..150 F2
Churchfields Dr HVHL CB9..55 L6
Church Gdns La BROX EN10..208 D8
Church Gdns GTDUN CM6.....141 L4
Churchgate CHES/WCR EN8...229 N8
Churchgate St HLWE CM17...187 M8
Church Gn CHCH CM17.......216 C6
HSTD CO9..................58 C6
RCFD SS4..................289 L7
RCOLW CO6.................147 N4
RIPW IP8..................36 C4
Church Gv RCOLW CO6.......125 N7
Church Hl BRTR CM7........94 C2
DART DA1..................346 D9
EPP CM16..................232 C5
HVHL CB9..................54 F2
K/T/MI CO5................152 G6
LAIN SS15.................303 L8
LOU IG10..................276 A2

MAL CM9 220 G9
MGTR CO11 105 N5
RCHLM CM3 194 B6
RCHLM CM3 243 N9
RCOLW CO6 124 B1
SAFWN CB10 52 F2
SLH/COR SS17 341 K4
WALTH E17 294 D8
WCHMH N21 272 E6
WIT CM8 170 G5
Church Hill Rd WALTH E17 294 E8
Church Hollow PUR RM19 347 M3
Churchill Av HSTD CO9 98 B5
HVHL CB9 41 L2
IPNE IP4 26 A6
Churchill Cl CHONG CM5 235 M6
RCOLE CO7 179 L5
SUD CO10 * 44 A3
Churchill Crs SLH/COR SS17 341 M1
Churchill Dr SUD CO10 47 H9
Churchill Pl POP/IOD E14 332 E8
Churchill Ri CHLM/WR CM1 218 D4
Churchill Rd BRTR CM7 121 H9
CAN/RD E16 333 M6
GRAYS RM17 349 N4
K/T/MI CO5 174 C8
Churchill South SOS SS1 * 19 F3
Churchill Sq SOSN SS2 * 19 F3
Churchill Ter CHING E4 294 D1
Churchill Wy COLS CO2 152 C2
Church La ABR/ST RM4 277 L3
ABR/ST RM4 278 B3
BCAYE CM11 304 A1
BROX EN10 229 N1
BRTR CM7 121 J8
BRWN CM15 258 E7
BSF CM23 162 A3
CBE/LIN CB1 38 B1
CBE/LIN CB1 40 A8
CHES/WCR EN8 229 P8
CHLM/WR CM1 218 C7
CHLM/WR CM1 239 J1
CHONG CM5 235 M3
COLW CO3 127 J9
COLW CO3 150 E2
DAGE RM10 318 B9
ED N9 273 M8
ENC/FH EN2 273 J2
EPP CM16 233 P4
FOS CO13 183 J2
FX IP11 34 E2
FX IP11 35 H5
GTDUN CM6 140 C7
GTDUN CM6 189 P5
HAR CO12 15 G2
HSTD CO9 57 J4
HSTD CO9 71 J2
HSTD CO9 72 D5
ING CM4 260 F3
K/T/MI CO5 201 L1
K/T/MI CO5 203 N3
KIR/NAC IP10 32 C7
KIR/NAC IP10 32 E1
KIR/NAC IP10 33 N7
LOU IG10 276 A2
MAL CM9 222 G3
MGTR CO11 81 P8
MGTR CO11 106 D4
MHAD SG10 160 E2
NHMKT IP6 22 D2
NHMKT IP6 22 E4
NHMKT IP6 23 K1
NHMKT IP6 23 N8
PIT SS13 304 F5
PUR RM19 347 M3
RAIN RM13 337 J7
RBRW/HUT CM13 282 A7
RBRW/HUT CM13 320 F1
RBSF CM22 115 H7
RBSF CM22 139 L7
RBSF CM22 188 C4
RCHLM CM3 167 N7
RCHLM CM3 168 F5
RCHLM CM3 262 F5
RCHLM CM3 263 J9
RCHLM CM3 265 M6
RCOLW CO6 78 A8
RCOLW CO6 149 H3
RCOLW CO6 149 M2
RCOS CO16 133 K9
RCOS CO16 156 D7
RIPS/CAP IP9 84 A6
RIPS/CAP IP9 85 H7
RIPW IP8 24 C6
RIPW IP8 28 F2
RIPW IP8 29 J3
ROM RM1 298 D8
SAFWS CB11 90 D1
SUD CO10 74 G1
UPMR RM14 320 E7
UPMR RM14 322 A7
WALTH E17 294 F8
WAN E11 315 H3
WDBR IP12 33 P1
Church Langley Wy
HLWE CM17 211 K3
Church Leys HLWS CM18 210 G4
Church Manorway ERITH DA8 346 C1
Church Md HLWW/ROY CM19 209 L2
Churchmead WAB EN9 * 230 F1
Church Md WIT CM8 170 G4
Church Mdw BRTR CM7 121 J9
NHMKT IP6 23 J1
Church Ms LAIN SS15 303 J8
Church Pde CVI SS8 326 B9
Church Pk SUD CO10 43 K8
Church Park Rd PIT SS13 324 G1
Church Pth CBE/LIN CB1 38 A5
WAN E11 295 K9
Churchponds HSTD CO9 72 D5
Church Rd ABR/ST RM4 257 J9
ABR/ST RM4 279 J7
BARK IG11 316 D8
BCAYE CM11 284 B4
BKHH IG9 275 L7
BOC CM0 290 G2
BRTR CM77 145 J8
BRTR CM77 146 B8
BRTR CM77 146 E4
BRTR CM77 146 G1
BRW CM14 257 P7
BSDN SS14 3 J2
BSDN SS14 3 K6
BSDN SS14 304 B7
CBE/LIN CB1 39 P6
CHLM/GWD CM2 262 E5
CHONG CM5 213 H9
CHONG CM5 257 J3
COLN CO4 103 H2
COLS CO2 176 A1
COS CO15 7 H5
ERITH DA8 346 B3
FX IP11 35 M1
GNTH/NBYPK IG2 316 F1
HARH RM3 299 M5
HLWE CM17 211 K6
HOC/HUL SS5 287 L9
HSTD CO9 56 E8
HSTD CO9 57 N8
HSTD CO9 73 N2
HSTD CO9 96 G9
HSTD CO9 123 H2
K/T/MI CO5 173 H3
K/T/MI CO5 173 P8
K/T/MI CO5 176 E8
K/T/MI CO5 202 E6
KIR/NAC IP10 31 P6
LAIN SS15 303 M7
LEY E10 314 D3
LOU IG10 275 K2
MAL CM9 220 F5
MAL CM9 222 E1
MAL CM9 223 N1
MGTR CO11 108 B4
MGTR CO11 130 G3
MNPK E12 316 B7
NHMKT IP6 23 L1
PEND EN3 273 P5
PIT SS13 325 K1
RAYL SS6 307 H5
RBRW/HUT CM13 259 P9
RBRW/HUT CM13 322 D1
RBSF CM22 138 D9
RBSF CM22 162 F3
RCFD SS4 288 D9
RCHLM CM3 195 N2
RCHLM CM3 196 D9
RCHLM CM3 219 K3
RCHLM CM3 288 A1
RCOLE CO7 129 P9
RCOLE CO7 131 L8
RCOLE CO7 154 A7
RCOLE CO7 154 C4
RCOLE CO7 154 F9
RCOLE CO7 179 J3
RCOLE CO7 179 K5
RCOLW CO6 101 K4
RCOLW CO6 126 A2
RCOLW CO6 150 B4
RIPS/CAP IP9 81 P3
RIPS/CAP IP9 82 C3
RIPS/CAP IP9 83 H7
RIPS/CAP IP9 83 M5
ROY SG8 48 G7
SAFWN CB10 68 C1
SBF/HAD SS7 305 P9
SBF/HAD SS7 327 H3
SBN/FI SS3 310 D8
SBN/FI SS3 330 B8
SLH/COR SS17 342 A2
SOS SS1 19 G5
STSD CM24 138 C1
SUD CO10 60 B5
SUD CO10 61 K5
SUD CO10 74 D3
TIL RM18 349 P6
TIL RM18 351 N8
UPMR RM14 322 B6
VGE SS16 325 K3
WALTH E17 294 B6
WICKE SS11 286 A9
WIT CM8 172 A4
WIT CM8 197 N7
WOTN CO14 159 K1
Church Rw CDW/CHF RM16 * 340 B4
Church Sq BURES CO8 76 A8
RCOS CO16 180 D9
Church St BCAYE CM11 303 K2
BRTR CM7 121 K6
BSF CM23 137 L7
CHLM/GWD CM2 240 F4
CHLM/WR CM1 5 G2
COL CO1 8 B6
COLN CO4 103 K1
DAGE RM10 318 A9
ED N9 273 K7
ENC/FH EN2 273 H2
GRAYS RM17 349 M4
GTDUN CM6 141 L4
HAR CO12 15 F2
HSTD CO9 72 C8
HSTD CO9 73 J8
HSTD CO9 73 K1
HVHL CB9 55 L3
ING CM4 259 H1
K/T/MI CO5 152 G6
K/T/MI CO5 172 G3
MAL CM9 200 C8
MAL CM9 222 C9
MAL CM9 223 M5
MAL CM9 225 J2
RBSF CM22 115 H1
RCOLW CO6 78 C4
RCOLW CO6 99 H7
RCOLW CO6 147 P4
RIPS/CAP IP9 84 D2
SAFWN CB10 36 B7
SAFWN CB10 36 E9
SAFWN CB10 51 L8
SAFWS CB11 64 F4
SAFWS CB11 65 H8
SAFWS CB11 90 A4
SBW CM21 187 M2
SRTFD E15 333 H1
SUD CO10 20 B7
SUD CO10 44 A3
SUD CO10 44 G9
WAB EN9 252 F3
WARE SG12 184 A3
WIT CM8 171 N9
Church St North SRTFD E15 333 H1
Church Vw BROX EN10 208 C8
RCOLE CO7 104 F9
RCOLW CO6 98 G7
SOCK/AV RM15 337 P9
UPMR RM14 319 N4
Church View Rd SBF/HAD SS7 306 B9
Church Wk COL CO1 8 B6
HVHL CB9 41 P7
SAFWS CB11 50 G6
SBW CM21 187 N2
SUD CO10 20 C5
SUD CO10 46 G1
Churchway SBF/HAD SS7 327 J4
Churchwell Av K/T/MI CO5 149 M7
Churnwood Rd COLN CO4 128 E6
Churston Av PLSTW E13 333 L1
Chuzzlewit Dr CHLM/WR CM1 217 M4
Cillocks Cl HOD EN11 208 D4
Cimarron Cl RCHLM CM3 286 G1
Cinnabar Cl RIPW IP8 29 N2
Cinque Port Rd RCOLE CO7 179 L6
Circular Rd East COLS CO2 152 A1
Circular Rd North COLS CO2 151 P1
Circular Rd South COLS CO2 151 P2
Circular Rd West COLS CO2 151 P1
City Rd K/T/MI CO5 202 D5
Civic Dr IP IP1 16 C4
Civic Sq TIL RM18 350 B7
Civic Wy BARK/HLT IG6 296 D8
Clachar Cl CHLM/GWD CM2 218 F8
Clacton Rd FOS CO13 183 H4
HAR CO12 109 L9
HAR CO12 132 G6
MGTR CO11 106 F8
RCOLE CO7 153 K1
RCOLE CO7 154 A1
RCOLE CO7 154 F9
RCOLE CO7 179 P1
RCOS CO16 156 D8
RCOS CO16 180 E9
WALTH E17 314 B1
Claire Cswy GRH DA9 * 348 B9
Claire Cl RBRW/HUT CM13 301 K1
Claire Rd FOS CO13 158 C8
Clairmont Cl BRTR CM7 145 J4
Clairmont Rd COLW CO3 151 H1
Clairvale EMPK RM11 319 K2
Clandon Rd GDMY/SEVK IG3 316 F4
Clapgate Dr RCOS CO16 181 M3
Clapgate La IPSE IP3 25 P8
Claps Gate La EHAM E6 334 C4
Clapton Hall La GTDUN CM6 141 L9
Clara Reeve Cl COLW CO3 151 J2
Clare Av WICKE SS11 285 J6
Clare Cswy GRH DA9 348 B9
Clare Cl HSTD CO9 97 P9
Clare Ct GTDUN CM6 92 A5
Clare Gdns BARK IG11 316 G8
FSTGT E7 315 K6
Clare Ms CHONG CM5 235 M5
Claremont CHESW EN7 229 L8
Claremont Cl CAN/RD E16 334 B8
CDW/CHF RM16 349 M1
WOS/PRIT SS0 18 B2
Claremont Crs DART DA1 346 D9
Claremont Dr VGE SS16 324 E2
Claremont Gdns
GDMY/SEVK IG3 316 F4
UPMR RM14 320 A3
Claremont Gv WFD IG8 295 M3
Claremont Hts COL CO1 8 A1
Claremont Rd FSTGT E7 315 L7
LAIN SS15 303 K8
RCOLE CO7 153 K6
ROM RM1 318 F1
WALTH E17 294 B6
WAN E11 314 G5
WOS/PRIT SS0 18 A2
Clarence Av IL IG1 316 A1
UPMR RM14 319 M4
Clarence Cl CHLM/GWD CM2 218 F7
SBF/HAD SS7 326 A2
Clarence Ga WFD IG8 296 B3
Clarence Rd BRWN CM15 280 E5
CAN/RD E16 333 H4
FSTGT E7 315 M6
GRAYS RM17 349 L4
IPSE IP3 31 H1
PEND EN3 273 P4
PIT SS13 305 L8
RAYL SS6 307 K6
SBF/HAD SS7 326 A2
SLH/COR SS17 342 B1
SOS SS1 19 F5
STSD CM24 114 B8
SUD CO10 20 C3
SUD CO10 44 A3
WALTH E17 294 A6
Clarence Rd North
SBF/HAD SS7 326 A2
Clarence St SOS SS1 19 F5
Clarendon Gdns IL IG1 316 A3
Clarendon Pk COS CO15 182 C8
Clarendon Rd CHES/WCR EN8 230 A8
CVI SS8 344 F1
HVHL CB9 41 J4
PIT SS13 305 H8
RBSF CM22 139 P7
SWFD E18 295 K7
WALTH E17 314 E1
Clarendon Wy COL CO1 8 B2
WCHMH N21 273 H6
Clare Rd BRTR CM7 144 G4
IPNE IP4 25 N3
SBF/HAD SS7 305 M9
SUD CO10 44 A1
WAN E11 314 G1
Clare Vls MGTR CO11 * 108 D5
Clare Wy RCOS CO16 181 L8
Claridge Rd BCTR RM8 317 L3
Clarissa Rd CHDH RM6 317 L1
Clarkbourne Dr GRAYS RM17 349 N4
Clark Cl ERITH DA8 346 F6
Clarke Ms ED N9 273 N9
Clarke Ri RCHLM CM3 266 A4
Clarkesmead K/T/MI CO5 173 P9
Clarke's Rd HAR CO12 110 A5
Clarkhill HLWS CM18 210 F6
Clarkia Wk COLN CO4 128 E8
Clarks Cl WARE SG12 184 A1
Clarks Farm Rd RCHLM CM3 242 C2
Clarks La EPP CM16 254 G1
Clarkson Rd CAN/RD E16 333 J6
Clarkson St IP IP1 16 B3
Clark's Rd IL IG1 316 E4
Clarks Wood Dr BRTR CM77 145 N3
Clark Wy CHLM/WR CM1 217 P2
Claston Cl DART DA1 346 D9
Claters Cl SOSN SS2 329 N4
Clatterbury La SAFWS CB11 88 C3
Clatterfield Gdns
WOS/PRIT SS0 328 B4
Claude Oliver Cl MGTR CO11 105 P6
Claude Rd LEY E10 314 F3
PLSTW E13 333 L1
Claude St IP IP1 16 D3
Claudian Cl HVHL CB9 41 N4
Claudian Wy CDW/CHF RM16 350 C1
Claud Ince Av BRTR CM77 145 N8
Claudius Rd COLS CO2 152 B1
Claudius Wy WIT CM8 197 H4
Claughton Rd PLSTW E13 333 M2
Claughton Wy
RBRW/HUT CM13 281 N5
Claverhambury Rd WAB EN9 231 K7
Clavering Ct RAYL SS6 306 E4
Clavering Gdns
RBRW/HUT CM13 321 N1
Clavering Rd BRTR CM7 121 J9
MNPK E12 315 N3
Clavering Wy
RBRW/HUT CM13 281 M5
Claverton Wy IPNE IP4 26 D7
Claybrick Av HOC/HUL SS5 307 N2
Clayburn Cir BSDN SS14 3 K5
Clayburn End BSDN SS14 3 K5
Clayburn Gdns
SOCK/AV RM15 338 E8
Claybury Rd WFD IG8 295 P4
Claydon Cl CBE/LIN CB1 40 B7
Claydon Crs BSDN SS14 3 J3
Claydons La SBF/HAD SS7 306 F7
Claygate Cl HCH RM12 318 F6
Clayhall Av CLAY IG5 295 P6
Clayhall La SUD CO10 47 P5
Clayhall Pl SUD CO10 47 N5
Clayhall Rd COS CO15 182 B8
Clay Hl ENC/FH EN2 251 H7
SUD CO10 74 F1
Clay Hill Rd VGE SS16 3 F7
Clayhive Dr HVHL CB9 41 J4
Clay La GTDUN CM6 118 C8
RCOS CO16 180 F5
Clay Lane Gv COLN CO4 128 E3
Claypit Hl RBSF CM22 139 H1
WAB EN9 253 M6
Clay Pit Piece SAFWS CB11 65 M3
Clay Pits BRTR CM7 145 N3
Claypits Av BURES CO8 76 A9
Claypits La SUD CO10 46 A5
Claypits Rd RCHLM CM3 219 L2
Clay Pits Wy BRTR CM77 145 N3
Claypole Rd SRTFD E15 * 332 F2
Claypounds BSF CM23 137 M7
Clayshotts Dr WIT CM8 197 L4
Clayside CHIG IG7 296 E3
Clay's La LOU IG10 254 C9
SRTFD E15 314 E7
Clays Lane Cl SRTFD E15 314 E7
Clayspring Cl HOC/HUL SS5 287 N9
Clays Rd WOTN CO14 159 H6
Clayton Av UPMR RM14 319 N7
Clayton Cl EHAM E6 334 A6
Clayton Pde CHES/WCR EN8 * 230 A9
Clayton Rd HAR CO12 109 M6
ROMW/RG RM7 318 B3
Claytonville Ter BELV DA17 * 336 B9
Clayton Wy MAL CM9 244 B2
Clay Tye Rd UPMR RM14 320 F5
Claywall Br HVHL CB9 55 L3
Cleall Av WAB EN9 252 F4
Clearwater COLS CO2 152 C2
Clearwing Cl RIPW IP8 29 N2
Clegg St PLSTW E13 333 K2
Cleland Pth LOU IG10 254 C9
Clematis Cl HARH RM3 299 H4
Clematis Gdns WFD IG8 295 K2
Clematis Wy COLN CO4 128 F8
Clemence Rd DAGE RM10 336 B1
Clemence St POP/IOD E14 332 C5
Clementhorpe Rd DAGW RM9 317 K8
Clementina Rd LEY E10 314 C3
Clement Rd CHES/WCR EN8 230 B6
Clements Av CAN/RD E16 333 K7
Clements Cl CHLM/GWD CM2 218 G8
HVHL CB9 41 J4
Clements Dr HVHL CB9 41 J4
Clements Gdns HOC/HUL SS5 308 B2
Clements Green La
RCHLM CM3 264 G9
Clements Hall La
HOC/HUL SS5 308 B2
Clements Hall Wy
HOC/HUL SS5 308 B3
Clements La HVHL CB9 41 J4
IL IG1 316 C5
Clements Ms RCFD SS4 * 308 F5
Clements Pl RCHLM CM3 264 G9
Clements Rd EHAM E6 316 A9
IL IG1 316 C5
Clements St WARE SG12 184 B3
Clement Wy HCH RM12 319 L5
Clench Cl IPNE IP4 17 G4
Clench Rd RIPS/CAP IP9 83 L2
Clerks Piece LOU IG10 276 A2
Clermont Av SUD CO10 47 H9
Clevedon Cl BRTR CM77 144 F7
Cleveland Cl COLN CO4 128 D3
Cleveland Dr WOS/PRIT SS0 328 E3
Cleveland Park Av
WALTH E17 294 D8
Cleveland Park Crs
WALTH E17 294 D8
Cleveland Rd BSDN SS14 3 J5
CVI SS8 344 E3
ED N9 * 273 N6
IL IG1 316 C5
SWFD E18 295 K7
Cleves Av BRW CM14 280 E7
Cleves Cl LOU IG10 275 P5
Cleves Ct RCHLM CM3 219 K2
Cleves Rd EHAM E6 333 N1
HVHL CB9 40 G4
Cleves Wk BARK/HLT IG6 296 D4
Clevis Dr RCHLM CM3 287 J3
Clicket Hl BURES CO8 76 C9
Clickett End BSDN SS14 3 J5
Clickett Hl BSDN SS14 3 H5
Clickett Side BSDN SS14 3 J5
Clieveden Rd SOS SS1 329 N8
Cliff Av WOS/PRIT SS0 18 C2
Cliff Crs BRTR CM7 95 K9
Cliff Gdns LOS SS9 328 B6
Cliffield BRTR CM7 95 K9
Cliff La IPSE IP3 25 N8
Clifford Av CLAY IG5 296 C5
Clifford Cl LAIN SS15 323 L1
PLSTW E13 * 333 L3
Clifford Rd CAN/RD E16 333 J4
CDW/CHF RM16 339 J9
ED N9 273 P5
IPNE IP4 17 K5
WALTH E17 294 F6
Cliff Pde LOS SS9 327 P6
WOTN CO14 159 M4
Cliff Pl SOCK/AV RM15 338 F3
Cliff Rd COS CO15 182 F8
FX IP11 35 N6
HAR CO12 14 D7
IPSE IP3 25 M8
LOS SS9 328 B6
Cliffsea Gv LOS SS9 328 A5
Clifftown Pde SOS SS1 18 D6
Clifftown Rd SOS SS1 19 F5
Cliff Wk CAN/RD E16 333 J5
Cliff Wy FOS CO13 159 H9
Clifton Av SBF/HAD SS7 325 P2
WALTH E17 294 A8
Clifton Cl CHES/WCR EN8 230 B8
SBF/HAD SS7 326 A2
Clifton Dr WOS/PRIT SS0 328 E7
Clifton Gdns ENC/FH EN2 272 D3
Clifton Hatch HLWS CM18 211 H6
Clifton Ms SOS SS1 19 F6
Clifton Rd CAN/RD E16 333 H5
CVI SS8 344 E2
EMPK RM11 318 F1
FSTGT E7 315 N8
GNTH/NBYPK IG2 316 E1
LOU IG10 275 P3
PIT SS13 305 L8
RCFD SS4 288 D9
Clifton Ter RCOLE CO7 153 J6
SOS SS1 19 F6
Clifton Wy CHTY IP2 24 E9
RBRW/HUT CM13 281 N7
SBF/HAD SS7 325 P2
WARE SG12 184 A1
Clifton Wd RIPS/CAP IP9 83 L3
Climmen Rd CVI SS8 326 E9
Clinton Cl RCHLM CM3 263 N2
Clinton Crs BARK/HLT IG6 296 F3
Clinton Rd BOW E3 332 B3
CVI SS8 344 A2
FSTGT E7 315 K6
Clipped Hedge RBSF CM22 188 F1
Clipper Bvd GRH DA9 348 B9
Clipper Bvd West GRH DA9 348 A8
Clipper Cl BERM/RHTH SE16 332 A9
Clitheroe Rd CRW RM5 298 B2
Clive Av IP IP1 25 J1
Cliveden Cl BRWN CM15 281 J6
CHLM/WR CM1 217 M8
Clivedon Rd CHING E4 295 H2
Clive Rd COLS CO2 152 A1
EN EN1 273 M3
GPK RM2 298 G9
RBRW/HUT CM13 300 F4
Clive Wy EN EN1 273 M3
Clockhouse Av BARK IG11 334 D1
Clockhouse La
CDW/CHF RM16 338 G8
CRW RM5 298 B4
Clock House Rd BCAYW CM12 302 F2
Clockhouse Wy BRTR CM7 145 L4
Clock Pde EN EN1 * 273 J4
Clock Tower Ms THMD SE28 335 J7
Cloes La RCOS CO16 181 L9
Cloister Cl RAIN RM13 336 G4
Cloisters SLH/COR SS17 341 M3
The Cloisters BRTR CM7 145 K1
K/T/MI CO5 172 G4
LAIN SS15 303 K9
Cloncurry Gdns FX IP11 10 C4
Clopton Dr SUD CO10 46 F5
Clopton Gn BSDN SS14 3 G2
The Close BRTR CM77 145 P8
BRW CM14 280 G9
CDW/CHF RM16 339 L9
CHDH RM6 317 M1
CHING E4 294 F4
COS CO15 206 F5
FOS CO13 158 F9
FOS CO13 183 H2

GNTH/NBYPK IG2..................316 F1
HAR CO12..............................110 B5
RBSF CM22............................188 F1
RIPS/CAP IP9..........................82 E2
SAFWS SS11............................90 E1
SBF/HAD SS7 *........................306 E7
STHGT/OAK N14......................272 C8
SUD CO10..................................21 J5
WARE SG12...........................184 B5
Cloudberry Rd HARH RM3.........299 J3
Clouded Yellow Cl
BRTR CM7..............................145 H6
Cloudesley Rd ERITH DA8.........346 E6
Clough Rd COLN CO4...............128 D1
Clova Rd FSTGT E7..................315 K8
LOS SS9..................................328 A4
Clove Cls CVI SS8....................332 F7
Clovelly Cl IPNE IP4....................26 E7
Clovelly Gdns EN EN1..............273 K6
ROMW/RG RM7....................298 A5
WICKE SS11............................285 H8
Clover Av BSF CM23................136 G8
Clover Cl CHTY IP2 *...............324 D3
VGE SS16 *............................324 D3
WAN E11 *..............................314 G4
Clover Ct CBE/LIN CB1...............38 C1
SUD CO10................................61 M4
Clover Dr RCOLE CO7..............154 F9
Clover Fld HLWS CM18............211 H6
HVHL CB9................................40 G5
Cloverlands COLN CO4.................9 K1
Clover Leas EPP CM16..............252 G8
Cloverley Rd CHONG CM5.........235 M9
Clovers HSTD CO9.....................75 J7
Clover Vls SOS SS1 *..................19 J6
LOS SS9..................................328 A4
Clove St PLSTW E13................333 K4
Clunas Gdns GPK RM2..............299 J7
Clunford Pl CHLM/WR CM1.......218 E4
Cluny Sq SOS SS1.....................19 K4
Clutton St POP/IOD E14............332 E5
Clydach Rd EN EN1..................273 L3
Clyde TIL RM18.......................351 K2
Clyde Crs CHLM/WR CM1.........217 L7
RAYL SS6................................306 F6
UPMR RM14............................320 B1
Clyde Pl LEY E10.....................314 E2
Clyde Rd HOM E9....................208 G7
Clydesdale PEND EN5..............274 A3
Clydesdale Rd BRTR CM7........145 L8
EMPK RM11............................318 E2
Clyde Wy ROM RM1.................298 D5
Clydon Cl ERITH DA8...............346 D4
Clyfton Cl BROX EN10.............230 C2
Coach House Wy WIT CM8........197 J2
Coachmans Cl IPNE IP4 *...........222 A8
Coachman's Paddock
RIPS/CAP IP9..........................83 L3
Coach Ms BCAYE CM11............283 L3
Coach Rd RCOS CO16................54 B8
Coalport Cl HLWE CM17...........211 K4
Coan Av COS CO15...................207 J3
Coast Rd K/T/MI CO5................202 C6
Coates Cl MAL CM9..................209 L7
Coates Quay CHLM/GWD CM2......5 J4
Coats Hutton Rd COLS CO3.......151 L3
Cobbett Cl PEND EN5...............251 P6
Cobbetts Av REDBR IG4...........295 N9
Cobbinsbank WAB EN9 *..........252 C8
Cobbin's Br EPP CM16.............232 E6
Cobbins Cha BOC CM0.............268 G9
Cobbins Cl BOC CM0...............290 C1
Cobbinsend Rd WAB EN9.........231 N8
Cobbins Gv WAB EN9..............231 M8
The Cobbins BOC CM0.............268 G9
WAB EN9................................253 H2
Cobbins Wy HLWE CM17.........187 M8
The Cobbles BRWN CM15.........281 H8
UPMR RM14............................320 C2
Cobbold Cl IPNE IP4..................17 G5
Cobbold Rd FX IP11.................315 J5
WAN E11................................315 J5
Cobbs La RBSF CM22...............140 A3
Cobbs Pl CHLM/WR CM1..........17 G4
Cobden Pl IPNE IP4...................17 G4
Cobden Rd WAN E11...............315 H6
Cobham CDW/CHF RM16.........339 L9
Cobham Cl EN EN1..................273 M2
Cobham Rd GDMY/SEVK IG3...316 F4
COS SS9.................................328 B9
WALTH E17.............................294 F5
WARE SG12............................184 C2
WOS/PRIT SS0........................328 D7
Cobill Cl EMPK RM11..............299 H8
Coblers Wy SUD CO10.............44 A5
Coborn Rd BOW E3.................332 C5
Coborn St BOW E3..................332 C5
Coburg Gdns CLAY IG5............295 N6
Coburg La VGE SS16...............322 G2
Coburg Pl RCHLM CM5............286 G2
Cochrane La RCOLE CO7 *.......153 P5
Cock & Bell La SUD CO10..........46 F3
Cockerell Cl PIT SS13..............304 G6
Cocker Rd EN EN1..................251 N6
Cockethurst Cl WOS/PRIT SS0..328 B2
Cockett Wick La BOC CM0........206 B3
Cockfield Hall La NHMKT IP6....23 M5
Cock Gn HLWW/ROY CM19......210 C5
Cock Inn Cnr HSTD CO9 *..........73 P7
Cock La CHLM/WR CM1............238 A8
SAFWS CB11...........................87 N5
Cockrell's Rd RCOLC CO6.........101 N4
Cock Rd HSTD CO9....................75 M8
Cock St RCOLW CO6................77 M3
Codenham Gn VGE SS16.........324 A2

Codenham Straight VGE SS16...324 A2
Codham Hall La
RBRW/HUT CM13...................300 E9
Codham Little Park Dr
BRTR CM7..............................120 E1
Cody Rd CAN/RD E16..............332 G4
Coe Cle Lion COLN CO4...........128 A5
Cogan Av WALTH E17..............294 B5
Coggeshall Rd BRTR CM7.........146 K3
BRTR CM7..............................146 A3
RCOLE CO7............................104 G6
RCOLW CO6............................124 E8
RCOLW CO6............................124 E8
RCOLW CO6............................147 J4
RCOLW CO6............................148 F3
Coggeshall Rd Feering
K/T/MI CO5.............................148 A5
Coggeshall Wy HSTD CO9.........98 B6
Cogmore SAFWS CB11..............63 C2
Cohen Cl CHES/WCR EN8.........252 B2
Cohort Dr COLS CO2.................151 K4
Cokefield Av SOSN SS2............329 K5
Coker Rd CVI SS8....................344 A3
Coke St HAR CO12......................15 F3
Colam La RCHLM CM5.............219 P7
Colbert Av SOS SS1.................329 M7
Colbourne Cl SLH/COR SS17....341 N2
Colchester Rd BURES CO8........100 E1
CHLM/GWD CM2....................218 G5
COLN CO4...............................153 H1
COS CO15..............................182 D8
HAR CO12..............................132 D4
HARH RM3.............................299 K4
HSTD CO9................................98 A7
IPNE IP4...................................25 N2
K/T/MI CO5.............................174 A6
K/T/MI CO5.............................177 J7
MAL CM9...............................198 E7
MAL CM9...............................200 F6
MGTR CO11............................106 B5
MGTR CO11............................132 A5
RCOLE CO7............................104 F3
RCOLE CO7............................129 K1
RCOLE CO7............................129 J9
RCOLE CO7............................153 J2
RCOLE CO7............................155 K3
RCOLW CO6............................99 M9
RCOLW CO6............................101 N7
RCOLW CO6............................125 J8
RCOLW CO6............................148 A4
RCOS CO16.............................156 A5
RCOS CO16.............................180 C7
SOSN SS2..............................328 G4
WALTH E17............................314 D1
WRT L17.................................197 L1
Cold Hall Cha RCOLE CO7........130 D9
Coldham Gv PEND EN3.............252 B7
Coldharbour POP/IOD E14........332 F8
Coldharbour La
HLW/ROY CM19.......................210 B4
Coldnailhurst Av BRTR CM7......145 J1
Cold Norton Rd RCHLM CM3.....266 E4
Cold Store Rd FX IP11................34 E9
Cole Av CDW/CHF RM16..........350 D2
Colebrooke Dr WAN E11...........315 L2
Colebrook Gdns LOU IG10........276 C1
Colebrook La LOU IG10.............276 C1
Colebrook St ERITH DA8...........346 E4
Cole Cl THMD SE28..................335 J8
Cole End La SAFWN CB10..........66 C5
Colegrave Rd SRTFD E15..........314 G7
Colehill RCHLM CM5.................169 L9
Colehills Cl SAFWS CB11...........88 B4
Colemans Av WOS/PRIT SS0....328 E2
Colemans La RCHLM CM5.........242 A5
WAB EN9................................230 G5
Coleman St SOSN SS2.................19 G2
Cole Ness Rd IPSE IP3...............30 C2
Coleridge Av CHESW EN7.........228 D9
Coleridge Cl CHESW EN7..........254 C9
Colet Hatch HLW CM20.............12 D4
Coleridge Rd DART DA1...........347 M9
BARH RM3..............................298 C4
IP IP1......................................22 G9
MAL CM9................................244 B1
TIL RM18................................350 D7
WALTH E17.............................294 C8
Coleridge Wk
RBRW/HUT CM13...................281 M6
Coles Cl CHONG CM5...............235 M5
Colesdale POTB/CUF EN6..........228 D9
Coles Gn LOU IG10.................254 C9
Coles La CBE/LIN CB1...............38 B1
Coles Oak La RCOLE CO7..........104 D2
Colet Rd RBRW/HUT CM13........281 M4
Colgate PI PEND EN5 *.............252 D7
Colham Av ED N9.....................317 J4
Colard Av LOU IG10.................276 D1
College Av GRAYS RM17..........349 L2
College Cl BSF CM23................137 J7
WARE SG12............................184 A4
College Ct CHES/WCR EN8........229 P9
College Gdns CHING E4............274 E6
ENC/FH EN2............................251 J9
REDBR IG4.............................295 P9
College Ga HLW CM20..............13 G6
College Pk HLW CM20...............13 G6
College PI CHY DA9..................348 F9
WALTH E17............................295 H8
College Rd BRTR CM7..............145 H5
CHES/WCR EN8......................229 N9
COS CO15..............................229 P9
ENC/FH EN2............................273 J1
GRAYS RM17..........................349 M2
HERT/BAY SG13.....................208 A1
WALTH E17.............................294 F9
WCHMH N21...........................272 F5
College Sq HLW CM20................13 G6

College St IPSE IP3......................16 E6
College Wy SOS SS1..................19 F5
Coller Rd HAR CO12.................110 A5
Colles Brook Rd RCOLE CO7.....155 L9
Colless Cha RCOLW CO6...........101 L4
Collett Rd CHES/WCR EN8.........230 A7
Collett Rd SMG12....................184 A2
Colletts Cha RCOLW CO6.........101 L4
Colley Rd CHLM/GWD CM2.......218 B8
Collier EHAM E6......................334 C7
Collier Cl EHAM E6..................26 A9
Collier Row La CRW RM5.........294 F9
Collier Row Rd
ROMW/RG RM7......................297 N5
The Colliers MAL CM9..............222 F8
Collier Rd RIPS/CAP IP9...........84 D1
Collindale Av BRTR CM7..........145 H5
Collindale Cl CVI SS8...............344 C1
Collindale Gdns COLS CO3.......182 D8
Collingwood BSF CM23............137 H9
Collingwood Av IPSE IP5............26 A9
Collingwood Cl BRTR CM7........145 M1
Collingwood Flds RCOLE CO7....80 E5
Collingwood Rd COLW CO3......127 H9
COS CO15..............................207 J3
RAIN RM13............................336 E2
RCHLM CM5..........................287 J2
VGE SS16..............................324 C2
WIT CM8................................197 J4
Collingwood Ter VGE SS16.......324 C1
Collingwood Wy SBN/FI SS3....330 D5
Collins Cl BRTR CM7................145 J4
SLH/COR SS17.......................341 M5
Collins Cross BSF CM23............157 N5
Collins La WIT CM8 *................197 K2
Collins Meadow
HLWW/ROY CM19...................12 D7
Collinson's CHTY IP2..................24 D6
Collins Rd HSTD CO9................308 B9
RBRW/HUT CM13...................281 P4
Collinwood Av PEND EN3.........273 P2
Collinwood Gdns
GNTH/NBYPK IG2....................296 A9
Colman Cl SLH/COR SS17.........341 L2
Colman Pde EN EN1 *...............273 K2
Colman Rd CAN/RD E16...........333 M5
Colmar Cl WCHPL E1................332 A4
Colmore Rd PEND EN3.............273 P3
Coln Dr RM18...........................351 K1
Colne Bank Av CVI SS8.............332 F7
Colne Cswy COLS CO2..............152 C1
Colne Cha WIT CM8.................197 H2
Colne Valley CI K/T/MI CO5.......286 C1
SOCK/AV RM15......................338 F7
Colne Dr HARH RM3................299 L3
SBN/FI SS3............................330 D5
Colneford Hl RCOLW CO6.........124 C1
Colneis Rd FX IP11....................15 K5
Colne Park Rd RCOLW CO6.......99 M9
Colne Pl VGE SS16.....................3 H7
Colne Ri K/T/MI CO5................152 C6
CLPT E5.................................314 A6
COS CO15..................................7 F5
HSTD CO9................................72 D9
HSTD CO9................................98 A6
RCOLE CO7............................129 K7
RCOLW CO6............................125 P8
WCHMH N21..........................273 J6
Colne Springs HSTD CO9...........57 J3
Colne St PLSTW E13................333 K3
Colne Va UPMR RM14.............320 B1
Colne Valley Pd HVHL CB9........97 N6
Colne Valley Rd HVHL CB9.........41 K4
Colne Vw RCOS CO16.............205 H2
Colne Wy RCOS CO16.............179 L9
Colneys Cl SUD CO10...............20 B1
Colombo Rd IL IG1...................316 D3
Colonels Wk ENC/FH EN2.........272 C1
The Colonnade
CHES/WCR EN8......................230 A7
Colson Pth LOU IG10...............276 B3
Colson Rd LOU IG10................276 C3
Colston Crs CHESW EN7...........228 G6
Colston Rd FSTGT E7...............315 N6
Colthurst Dr ED N9..................273 N9
Colthurst Gdns HOD EN11.......208 F4
Coltishall Cl WICKE SS11..........305 N1
Coltishall Rd HCH RM12...........319 H8
Colts Cft ROY SG8......................48 E8
Coltsfield STSD CM24..............114 B8
Coltsfoot Cl COLN CO4.............157 N4
GRAYS RM17..........................349 N4
Coltsfoot Pth HARH RM3..........299 K4
Coltsfoot Rd CHTY IP2...............24 F7
WARE SG12............................184 B1
The Colts BSF CM23................162 B2
Coits Yd WAN E11 *................315 J3
Columbia Cl KESG IP5................26 F4
Columbia Rd RCOLW CO6........182 C1
Columbia Whf PEND EN3 *........274 B4
Columbia Wharf Rd
GRAYS RM17..........................349 K4
Columbine Av EHAM E6............333 P5
Columbine Gdns CHTY IP2.........24 F6
WOTN CO14..........................159 J7
Columbine Ms SOLW CO10.......126 F8
Columbine Wy HARH RM5........299 K5
Colvers HLWE CM17................211 H5
Colville Cl BRTR CM7 *.............144 F7
SLH/COR SS17.......................323 N9
Colville Ms ED N9....................273 N7
Colville Rd COLW CO3.............314 F5
WALTH E17............................314 F5
Colvin Cha CHLM/GWD CM2....240 A9
Colvin Gdns BARK/HLT IG6......296 D4
Colvin Rd EHAM E6.................315 P9

Colwall Gdns WFD IG8.............295 K2
Colworth Cl SBF/HAD SS7........326 C2
Colworth Rd WAN E11.............315 H1
Colyers Cl ERITH DA8..............346 C6
Colyers La ERITH DA8.............346 B6
Colyers Reach
CHLM/GWD CM2....................218 F9
Colyn Pl SAFWN CB10...............51 M7
Combes Rd DAGW RM9...........317 N9
Comely Bank Rd WALTH E17....294 F9
Comet Cl MNPK E12.................315 N6
Comet Rd SLH/COR SS17.........347 M2
Comet Wy SOSN SS2...............308 C9
Comfrey Cl GRAYS RM17.........349 N4
Commerce Wy LAIN SS15.........302 R8
Commodore St WCHPL E1.........332 B4
Common Ap SBF/HAD SS7.......306 D9
Commonfields MAL CM9...........210 F2
Commonhall La SBF/HAD SS7...326 G5
Common Hl SAFWN CB10..........51 L8
Common Md CM4....................220 B9
ROY SG8...................................62 E2
SBF/HAD SS7........................306 D8
Common Quay IPSE IP5 *..........17 F6
Common Rd MG CM4..............261 M6
RBRW/HUT CM13..................301 M2
SBN/FI SS3............................330 C2
WAB EN9...............................209 P9
Commonside Rd HLWS CM18...210 G7
The Commons COLS CO3.........151 L2
Common St SUD CO10...............44 A3
The Common RCHLM CM3.......242 B4
RCHLM CM5..........................263 N1
SBF/HAD SS7........................306 D8
SRTFD E15............................314 F7
Common Whf WARE SG12........184 B5
Community Rd SRTFD E15........314 G7
Como Rd ROMW/RG RM7........298 C9
Como St ROMW/RG RM7.........298 C9
Compass Rd BRTR CM7............146 G1
Compasses Rd BRTR CM7.........146 K1
Compton Av EHAM E6.............334 A2
GPK RM2...............................298 G2
RBRW/HUT CM13..................281 M7
Compton Ct CVI SS8................344 G3
Compton Ms CVI SS8 *.............9 J3
Compton Pl ERITH DA8............346 E4
Compton Rd COLN CO4..............9 J4
WCHMH N21..........................272 F7
WICKE SS11...........................285 K9
Comreddy Cl ENC/FH EN2.......250 G9
Comyns Cl CAN/RD E16...........333 J5
Comyns Rd CHLM/WR CM1......239 J1
Comyns Rd DAGW RM9............317 N9
Conan Doyle Cl BRTR CM7......145 K6
Concorde Dr EHAM E6.............334 A5
Concord Rd CVI SS8................326 C9
PEND EN3..............................273 P4
Conder St POP/IOD E14............332 B6
Conder Wy COLS CO2.............152 D3
Conduit La BUNT SG9................86 D7
Conduit La East HOD EN11.......208 E5
Coney Burrows CHING E4.........275 H8
Coney Gn SBW CM21..............187 L1
Conference Cl CHING E4...........274 F8
Congreve Rd IP IP1....................25 H9
WAB EN9...............................253 H3
Conical Cnr ENC/FH EN2..........273 H1
Conies Rd HLWS CM18.............179 N9
Conifer Av CRW RM5..............298 A2
Conifer Cl CHESW EN7.............229 L8
Conifer Dr BRW CM14..............300 C2
Conifer Gdns EN EN1...............273 J5
Conifers SBF/HAD SS7.............327 H5
Coningsby Gdns CHING E4.......294 E5
Conisbee Ct STHGT/OAK N14...272 B4
Coniscliffe Rd PLMGR N13.......273 H9
Coniston SOSN SS2.................308 B8
Coniston Av BARK IG11............316 F9
UPMR RM14...........................319 P6
Coniston CI CRW RM5..............298 B5
HSTD CO9................................98 A8
KESG IP5..................................27 K3
Coniston Ct CHESW EN7 *........229 L8
COLN CO4..............................153 N7
RCOLE CO7............................126 F4
Coniston Gdns ED N9...............295 P8
REDBR IG4.............................295 P8
Coniston Rd BXLYHN DA7.......346 A4
CVI SS8.................................344 D2
IPSE IP5.................................26 A9
SBF/HAD SS7........................306 B8
Coniston Wy HCH RM12...........318 F7
Connaught Av
CDW/CHF RM16....................339 L9
CHING E4...............................274 C6
EN EN1.................................273 K1
FOS CO15..............................183 N1
LOU IG10...............................276 D1
Connaught Br CAN/RD E16.......333 N8
Connaught Cl EN EN1 *............273 K1
COS CO15.................................7 K3
LEY E10.................................314 B4
Connaught Dr RBSF CM22.......138 F1
Connaught Gdns BRTR CM7.....145 L2
SBN/FI SS3............................330 B8
Connaught Gdns East
COS CO15................................7 K3
Connaught Gdns West
COS CO15................................7 K2
Connaught Hl LOU IG10...........275 N5
Connaught La IL IG1................316 D4
Connaught Rd CAN/RD E16......333 N8
CHING E4...............................275 H6
HCH RM12.............................319 J5

HVHL CB9................................41 H4
IL IG1....................................316 E4
IP IP1......................................24 E1
RAYL SS6...............................307 L7
RCOS CO16............................156 E9
WALTH E17 *..........................294 D9
Connaught Wy BCAYW CM12...218 H5
Connington Crs CHING E4.........274 C5
Connop Rd PEND EN3..............252 A8
Connor St BARK/HLT IG6..........296 D5
WAN E11...............................315 H5
Connor Rd DAGW RM9............317 N6
Connor St HOM E9...................332 A1
Conquerors Cl RCHLM CM5......196 E9
Conrad Cl CDW/CHF RM16.......339 L9
Conrad Gdns CRAYS RM17......349 K9
Conrad Rd SLH/COR SS17........341 M5
WIT CM8................................171 N8
Consort Cl MAN CM4...............300 F2
Constable Av CAN/RD E16........333 L8
Constable Cl COLN CO4............181 M7
K/T/MI CO5...........................177 P5
MGTR CO11...........................106 A4
Constable Ct COLS CO3...........202 C5
Constable Dr FX IP11.................40 G2
HVHL CB9................................97 G1
IPNE IP4...................................17 C1
SUD CO10................................20 B1
Constable Rw RCOLE CO7 *.....105 H2
Constable Vw CHLM/WR CM1...214 E5
Constable Wy BRTR CM77.......145 L9
SBN/FI SS3............................330 E6
Constance Rd CHLM/WR CM1...197 K4
Constance St CAN/RD E16........333 P8
Constantine Rd COLW CO3......151 N1
IP IP1......................................16 B6
WIT CM8................................197 H4
Constitution Hl IP IP1................25 J5
SBF/HAD SS7.......................326 A5
SUD CO10................................20 E4
Convalescent Hl FX IP11............11 J4
Convent La LAIN SS15.............303 K9
Convent HI BRTR CM7.............145 K1
Convent La BRTR CM7.............145 K1
Convent Rd CVI SS8................344 E2
Con Wy SBF/HAD SS7.............326 A3
Conway Cl CHTY IP2..................25 J9
Conway Av CHTY IP2 *..............25 J4
HSTD CO9................................97 N8
RAIN RM13............................318 F9
RCOLE CO7............................153 K6
Conway Crs CHDH RM6...........317 K2
Conway Gdns ENC/FH EN2......251 K8
GRAYS RM17.........................349 L5
Conway's Rd STHGT/OAK N14..272 D1
Conway Rd CDW/CHF RM16....340 B1
Conybury Cl WAB EN9.............253 K2
Conyer St BOW E3...................229 K6
Conyer Cl MAL CM9................244 A2
Conyers St BOW E3.................332 B2
Conyers Wy LOU IG10.............276 C2
Cook Cl COLS CO4...................128 F8
Cooke Cl CAN/RD E16.............333 J4
Cookes Cl WAN E11.................315 J4
Cookham Ct SBN/FI SS3............330 C4
Cookhill Rd ARLY SE2..............248 E8
Cooke's CI CRW RM5...............298 B5
HSTD CO9................................98 A8
KESG IP5..................................27 K3
Cook's Ferry Rbt UED N18........273 N7
Cooks Gn PIT SS13.................305 H6
Cook's Hall Rd RCOLW CO6.....126 F4
Cooks HI COLN CO4................153 N7
Cook's Hole Rd ENC/FH EN2...250 G8
Cooks Spinney HLW CM20......211 H1
Coolfin Rd CAN/RD E16...........333 K6
Coogaralie Av CHIG IG7...........294 G2
CHING E4...............................294 G2
Coolyne Wy COS CO15...........182 C6
Coombe Cnr WCHMH N21.......272 G7
Coombe Dr VGE SS16..............323 K5
Coombe Ri BRWN CM15...........281 J7
CHLM/WR CM1......................218 A4
SLH/COR SS17.......................341 M8
Coombe Rd BOC CM0..............269 J5
HARH RM3.............................299 J2
Coombers RIPS/CAP IP9...........29 B9
Coombes Cl BCAYW CM12.......282 C4
Coombes Gv RCFD SS4............309 H5
Coombewood Dr CHDH RM6....317 N1
SBF/HAD SS7........................306 B1
Cooper Av WALTH E17.............294 A5
Cooper Cl WFD IG8.................295 M4
Cooper Dr BRTR CM7..............144 G2
Coopersale Common
EPP CM16.............................233 L7
Coopersale La EPP CM16.........255 H7
Coopersale Rd HOM E9............314 A7
Coopersales LAIN SS15...........302 G9
Coopers Av MAL CM9.............222 D6
Coopers Cl BSF CM23..............161 N1
CHIG IG7................................277 J8
DAGE RM10...........................318 A8
Coopers Crs RCOLW CO6.........127 J3
Coopers Dr BCAYE CM11.........303 K1
Coopers End Rd RBSF CM22....139 K3
Coopers End Rd HOM E9 *........314 A7
Cooper Shaw Rd TIL RM18.......350 E5
Coopers Hi CHONG CM5..........235 M8
Coopers La COS CO15.............207 H1
LEY E10.................................314 E3

RCHLM CM3 ....169 J6
RCOLE CO7 ....104 C3
Coopers Pk BRTR CM7 * 144 C2
Coopers Rd KESG IP5 ......27 N4
  NHMKT IP6 ....72 F1
Cooper St CAN/RD E16 .....333 J3
Coopers Vls RBSF CM22 ....139 L4
Coopers Wy NHMKT IP6 .....22 C5
  SOCK/AV COL CO4 ......329 H1
Cooper Wk COLN CO4 ....128 E7
Coote Rd BCTR RM8 ....317 N5
Copdook BSDN SS14 ....3 H3
Copeland Rd WALTH E17 ....294 E9
Copeland RCFD SS4 ....308 D1
Copelis CI HVHL CB9 ......41 K1
Copeman Rd
  RBRW/HUT CM13 ....281 N6
Copenhagen PI POP/IOD E14 .332 C6
Copford Av RAYL SS6 ......307 J3
Copford Rd BCAYE CM11 ....283 K6
Copland CI CHLM/GWD CM2 ..240 E2
  CHLM/WR CM1 ....217 P2
Copland Rd SLH/COR SS17 ..341 L4
Copleston Rd BRW 26 B6
Coploe Rd SAFWN CB10 .....56 B8
Coppen Rd BCTR RM8 ....317 N2
Coppens Gn WICKW SS12 ....305 J1
Copperas Rd RCOLE CO7 ....179 L8
Copper Beech CI CLAY IG5 .296 B5
Copper Beeches COLW CO5 ..150 C1
  SBF/HAD SS7 ....306 E8
Copper Beech Rd
  SOCK/AV 338 F5
Copperfield BCAYE CM11 ...303 L1
  CHIG IG7 ....
Copperfield Gdns BRW CM14 .280 E7
Copperfield Rd BOW E3 ....332 B4
  CHLM/WR CM1 ....217 L4
  CHTY IP2 ....24 F6
  THMD SE28 ....137 M8
Copperfields LAIN SS15 ...305 K8
  SAFWS CB11 ....65 K1
Copper Gv RIPS/CAP IP9 ...29 N2
Coppice CI GTDUN CM6 .....141 L5
Coppice End COLN CO4 .....128 A4
Coppice Hatch HLWS CM18 ..210 E5
Coppice La GTDUN CM6 .....167 K5
  SAFWS CB11 ....303 N6
Coppice Pth CHIC IG7 .....296 A6
Coppice Rd RCOLE CO7 .....154 A6
Coppice Rw EPP CM16 ......254 E6
The Coppice COS CO15 .....207 J3
  ENC/FH EN2 ....272 C3
Coppice Wy WBFD E18 ......295 J8
Coppingdown Farm
  HSTD CO9 * ....
Coppingford End RCOLW CO6 .150 A1
The Coppings HOD EN11 ....208 D2
Coppins CI CHLM/WR CM1 ...218 D7
Coppins Rd COS CO15 ......207 J4
Coprolite St IPSE IP3 ....17 H6
Copse HI HLWW/ROY CM19 ...210 C6
The Copse BCAYW CM12 .....283 H4
  BSF CM23 ....137 P6
  CHING E4 ....275 J7
  COLN CO4 ....128 A4
  GTDUN CM6 ....143 L8
Copshall CI CHLM CM18 ....210 F7
Copswood CI KESG IP5 .....27 L4
Copthall CI COS SS15 .....329 H1
Copthall Rd BRW CM14 .....280 F8
Copthall La GTDUN CM6 ....92 C5
Copt Hall K/T/MI CO5 .....201 N1
Copt HI RCHLM CM3 ....242 B4
Copthorne Av BARK/HLT IG6 .296 C2
  BROX EN10 ....208 C8
Copthorne Gdns EMPK RM11 .299 M9
Copton CI BOW E3 ....332 D5
Copy HI HVHL CB9 ....41 H8
Coral CI RCHLM CM3 * 297 K7
  RCHLM CM5 ....
Coral Dr IP IP1 ....24 E2
Coralin Wk COLW CO5 ......126 F9
Coralline Wk ABYW SE2 ....335 K9
Caran Gn RBRW/HUT CM13 ...281 N5
Coram CI ED N9 ....306 F4
Caraseway SBF/HAD SS7 ....326 E1
Corbets Av UPMR RM14 .....319 N7
Corbets Tey Rd UPMR RM14 .319 N5
Corbett Rd WALTH E17 .....294 C6
  WAN E11 ....
Corbicum WAN E11 ....315 H2
Corbridge Ms ROM RM1 .....298 E9
Corby Crs ENC/FH EN2 .....272 C5
Corcorans BRWN CM15 ......280 E5
Cordelia Crs RAYL SS6 ....306 F4
Cordelia St POP/IOD E14 ..332 E6
Cordell CI CHES/WCR EN8 ..230 B7
Cordell PI SUD CO10 ......46 C3
Cordell Rd SUD CO10 ......46 F3
Corder Rd IPNE IP4 ....25 L3
Corioling St POP/IOD E14 .332 C6
Cordova Rd BOW E3 ....332 B5
The Cordwainers SOSN SS2 .329 H1
Cordwinders RCOLE CO7 ....81 H8
Cordy's La FX IP11 ....34 E5
Corfe CI PIT SS13 ....304 C9
Corfield Rd WCHMH N21 ....272 E4
Coriander Av POP/IOD E14 .332 G6
Coriander Rd K/T/MI CO5 ..173 P9
Cories CI BCTR RM8 ....317 L4
Corinthian Manorway
  ERITH DA8 ....346 C2
Cork Tree Wy CHING E4 ....294 B2
Cormorant CI WALTH E17 ...294 A5
Cormorant Rd FSTGT E7 ....315 J7
Cornard Rd SUD CO10 ....26 C6
Cornec Av LOS SS9 ....307 L9
Cornec Cha LOS SS9 ....307 M9
Cornel CI WIT CM8 ....171 L9
Cornelius V CHLM/GWD CM2 .218 G7
Cornelis La SAFWS CB11 ...90 B5
Cornell Wy CRW RM5 ....298 A2

Corner Meadow HLWS CM18 ..211 H7
Corner Pk SAFWN CB10 .....51 M7
Corner Rd BCAYE CM11 .....304 C1
Cornerth Crs SUD CO10 ....61 L4
Cornfields RCHLM CM5 .....264 F9
Cornflower CI CHTY IP2 ...24 F7
  COLW CO3 ....126 F8
Cornflower Dr
  CHLM/WR CM1 ....218 E6
Cornflower Gdns
  BCAYW CM12 ....282 G3
Cornflower Rd COS CO15 ...206 F5
Cornflower Wy HARH RM3 ...299 K5
Cornford Wy MGTR CO11 ....106 A4
Corn HI CHLM/WR CM1 ......217 L4
Cornhill IP IP1 * 16 D4
Cornhill Dr PEND EN3 .....252 B7
Cornish Cv RCHLM CM5 .....287 H2
Cornish Hall End Rd BRTR CM7 .69 N2
  HSTD CO9 ....56 B9
Cornshaw Rd BCTR RM8 .....317 L3
Cornsland BRW CM14 ....280 C9
Cornwall CI BARK IG11 ....316 C8
  CHES/WCR EN8 ....252 C3
  EMPK RM11 ....299 M8
  MGTR CO11 ....106 A5
Cornwallis Av ED N9 ......273 N8
Cornwallis CI ERITH DA8 ..346 E4
  RCOLW CO6 ....149 K3
Cornwallis Gv ED N9 ......273 N8
Cornwallis Rd SAFWN CB10 .51 M7
Cornwallis Rd DAGW RM9 ...317 N6
  ED N9 ....273 N8
  HVHL CB9 ....41 J4
  WALTH E17 ....294 A8
Cornwall Rd BRWN CM15 ....280 E4
  DART DA1 ....347 L8
  FX IP11 ....35 H6
  PIT SS13 ....305 L8
Corn Wy WAN E11 ....314 C5
Cornwall Crs SLH/COR SS17 .341 M2
Cornworthy SBN/FI SS3 ....330 B6
Cornworthy Rd BCTR RM8 ...317 K7
Corona Rd CVI SS8 ....326 F9
  VGE SS16 ....323 J3
Coronation Av BRTR CM7 ...145 J4
  COLS CO2 ....152 B5
  TIL RM18 ....351 K2
Coronation CI BARK/HLT IG6 .296 D8
  SBN/FI SS3 ....330 E2
Coronation Dr FX IP11 ....
  HCH RM12 ....318 C2
Coronation HI EPP CM16 ...232 C9
Coronation Rd BOC CM0 ....290 G4
  BSF CM23 ....137 K9
  COS CO15 ....157 N9
  IPNE IP4 ....26 A6
  PLSTW E13 ....333 M3
  WARE SG12 ....184 A2
Corporation Av
  CHLM/WR CM1 ....217 P7
Corporation St SRTFD E15 .333 H2
Corporation Yd COLN CO4 * .9 J5
Corran Wy SOCK/AV RM15 ...338 E7
Corringham Rd
  SLH/COR SS17 ....341 L4
Corsel Rd CVI SS8 * 345 H2
Cortina Dr DAGW RM9 ......336 B3
Cortoncroft CI FOS CO13 ..158 C7
Corton Rd IPSE IP3 ....31 H1
Corve La SOCK/AV RM15 ....338 E7
Cory Dr RBRW/HUT CM13 ....281 L6
Cosgrove Av LOS SS9 ......327 L3
Cosgrove Rd WCHMH N21 ....272 G8
Cossington Rd WOS/PRIT SS0 .18 B5
Costead Manor Rd
  BRW CM14 ....280 E7
Cotall St POP/IOD E14 ....332 D6
Coteford CI LOU IG10 .....276 C1
Cotelands VGE SS16 ....324 E3
Cotesmore Gdns BCTR RM8 ..316 G2
Cotleigh Rd ROMW/RG RM7 ..318 C1
Cotman Av MGTR CO11 ......106 A3
Cotman Ms BRTR RM8 ....317 J7
Cotman Rd COLW CO3 ....151 K1
  IPSE IP3 ....30 C1
  RCOS CO16 ....181 N7
Cotswold Av IP IP1 ....25 J2
  RAYL SS6 ....306 C4
Cotswold CI BXLYHN DA7 ...346 D6
Cotswold CI COLN CO4 .....128 D3
Cotswold Ct CHLM/WR CM1 ..177 L5
Cotswold Dr SUD CO10 .....46 F5
Cotswold Gdns EHAM E6 ....333 N5
  GNTH/NBYPK IG2 ....316 E2
  RBRW/HUT CM13 ....281 P6
Cotswold PI ENC/FH EN2 ...252 C7
Cotswold Rd COS CO15 .....182 A8
  HARH RM3 ....299 L6
  WOS/PRIT SS0 ....328 E6
Cotswold Wy ENC/FH EN2 ...272 C2
Cottage Dr COLS CO2 ......152 D3
Cottage Gdns CHES/WCR EN8 .229 P6
Cottage Gn RCOS CO16 .....181 M7
Cottage Gv RCOS CO16 .....181 M7
Cottage PI CHLM/WR CM1 ...5 C2
  MGTR CO11 * 107 J8
Cottage St POP/IOD E14 ...332 E7
Cottage Wk RCOS CO16 .....181 L7
Cottenham Rd WALTH E17 ...294 C8
Cottesmore Av CLAY IG5 ...296 A6
Cottesmore CI CVI SS8 ....344 D5
Cottesmore Gdns LOS SS9 ..327 K5
Cottingham Rd BRW CM14 ...281 J5
Cottis CI VGE SS16 ....323 H3
Cotton CI DAGW RM9 ....317 K9
  WAN E11 ....315 H4
Cottons Ap ROMW/RG RM7 ...298 C9
Cotton St POP/IOD E14 ....332 F7

Cottonwood CI COLS CO2 ...151 N4
Couchmore Av CLAY IG5 ....296 A6
Coulde Dennis RCHLM CM3 ..263 N2
Coulston CI RCOS CO16 ....181 M7
Coulson CI BCTR RM8 ......317 K3
Coulter CI POTB/CUF EN6 ..228 C6
Coulter Ms BCAYE CM11 ....285 J5
Counting House La
  GTDUN CM6 ....141 L5
Countisbury Av EN EN1 ....273 L6
County PI CHLM/GWD CM2 ...5 F5
County Rd EHAM E6 ....334 C5
Coupals CI HVHL CB9 ......41 M5
Coupals Ct HVHL CB9 ......41 M5
Coupals Rd HVHL CB9 ......41 M5
Courage CI EMPK RM11 .....319 H1
Courier Rd DAGW RM9 ......336 B4
Courtauld CI HSTD CO9 ....98 A7
Courtauld Rd BRTR CM7 ....145 J2
Courtaulds CI THMD SE28 ..335 H8
Court Av HARH RM3 ....299 M4
Courtenay CI SUD CO10 ....46 C9
Courtenay Dr CDW/CHF RM16 .349 J1
Courtenay Gdns UPMR RM14 .319 H4
Courtenay Ms WALTH E17 ...294 B9
Courtenay Rd WALTH E17 ...294 A9
  WAN E11 ....315 J5
Courtfield CI BROX EN10 ..208 D8
Courtland Av CHING E4 ....304 C5
  IL IG1 ....316 A4
Courtland Dr CHIG IG7 ....276 D9
Courtland Gv THMD SE28 ...335 L7
Courtland Ms MAL CM9 .....244 A2
Courtland Rd EHAM E6 .....333 P1
Courtlands BCAYW CM12 ....282 F6
Courtlands CHLM/WR CM1 ...217 P5
Courtleet Dr BXLYHN DA7 ..346 A6
Courtney Park Rd VGE SS16 .323 J1
Courtney Rd CDW/CHF RM16 .340 D9
Court Rd CHLM/WR CM1 .....193 P9
The Courts FX IP11 ....35 L7
  RAYL SS6 ....307 H4
Court St RCOLW CO6 ....77 P6
Court Vw ING CM4 ....262 M6
Court Wy BARK/HLT IG6 ....296 D7
  HARH RM3 ....299 K6
The Courtyards COLN CO4 * .128 C2
The Courtyard BRTR CM7 * .145 K2
Coval Av CHLM/WR CM1 .....4 D3
Coval La CHLM/WR CM1 .....4 D3
Coval Wls CHLM/WR CM1 ....4 D3
Covelees Wall EHAM E6 ....334 F6
Covenbrook
  RBRW/HUT CM13 ....281 L9
Coventry CI COL CO1 ......8 E4
  EHAM E6 ....334 A6
  HOC/HUL SS5 ....287 J7
Coventry Cross Est BOW E3 .332 F4
Coventry Hill Lower Rd
  HOC/HUL SS5 ....287 H7
Coventry Rd IL IG1 ....316 C3
Coverack CI STHGT/OAK N14 .272 B5
Coverdale WIT CM8 ....171 M9
The Coverdales BARK IG11 .316 C9
Coverley CI RBRW/HUT CM13 .300 F5
Covert CI HVHL CB9 ....41 K2
Covert Rd BARK/HLT IG6 ...296 C3
The Coverts CHLM/WR CM1 ..239 J1
  K/T/MI CO5 ....202 C6
  RBRW/HUT CM13 ....281 K7
Cowbridge La BARK IG11 ...316 C9
Cowdray Av COL CO1 ....8 C2
Cowdray Crs COL CO1 ......8 D6
Cowdray Wy HCH RM12 ......318 F6
Cowdrie La COL CO1 ....8 E6
Cowdrie Wy CHLM/GWD CM2 ..218 G7
Cowell Av CHLM/WR CM1 ....217 M6
Cowell St CHTY IP2 ....25 K8
Cowels Farm La GTDUN CM6 .117 M2
Cowland Av PEND EN3 ......273 P5
Cow La RCOS CO16 ....205 K1
  SAFWN CB10 ....56 C8
Cow Leaze EHAM E6 ....334 B6
Cowles CHESW EN7 ....229 L2
Cowley St WAN E11 ....315 H5
Cowley Rd FX IP11 ....11 J1
  HARH RM3 ....298 C4
  IL IG1 ....316 A2
  WAN E11 ....315 H4
Cowlins HLWE CM17 ....187 L8
Cowper Av BCAYE CM11 .....283 M2
Cowper Av EHAM E6 ....315 P9
  TIL RM18 ....351 N5
Cowper Gdns
  STHGT/OAK N14 ....272 B5
Cowper Rd RAIN RM13 ......336 F4
  STHGT/OAK N14 ....272 A7
Cowper St IPNE IP4 ....26 A5
Cowslip CI CHTY IP2 ......24 F6
Cowslip Rd COLW CO3 ......126 F8
Cowslip Md BSDN SS14 .....3 F4
Cowslip Rd SWFD E18 ......295 L7
Cow Watering La
  CHLM/WR CM1 ....216 G8
Coxbridge Ct BCAYW CM12 ..283 H6
Cox CI KESG IP5 ....26 G5
Coxes CI SLH/COR SS17 ....342 A1
Coxes Farm Rd BCAYE CM11 .283 M9
Coxhall Rd RIPS/CAP IP9 ..29 M9
Cox La IPNE IP4 ....17 F5
Cox Ley RBSF CM22 ....188 F1
Coxon Dr CDW/CHF RM16 ....349 H1
Coxtes Gdns IP IP1 ....16 A5
Cozens La East BROX EN10 .230 C1
Cozens La West BROX EN10 .230 B1
Cozens Rd WARE SG12 ......184 C2
Crabbe St IPNE IP4 ....25 P5
Crabb's HI RCHLM CM5 .....220 C2

Crabb's La BUNT SG9 ......87 M9
Crabs Cft BRTR CM7 ....145 M3
Crabtree FOS CO15 ....158 D6
Crabtree Av CHDH RM6 .....297 L8
Crabtree La RCHLM CM3 ....101 P6
Crabtree Manorway North
  BELV DA17 ....336 B9
Crabtree Manorway South
  BELV DA17 ....336 B9
Crabtree Wk BROX EN10 ....208 B7
Cracknell CI EN EN1 ......251 N6
  RCOLE CO7 ....153 J4
Craddock Rd EN EN1 ....273 L2
Crafton Gn STSD CM24 .....114 B8
Craftsmans Sq SOSN SS2 ...329 H1
Craig CI FX IP11 ....34 E1
Craigdale Rd ROM RM1 .....318 E1
Craigfield Av COS CO15 ...182 A7
Craig Gdns SWFD E18 ......295 J6
Craig's La BURES CO8 .....100 D2
Craigs Wk CHES/WCR EN8 ...230 A7
Craiston Wy CHLM/GWD CM2 .240 D3
Crammavill St
  CDW/CHF RM16 ....339 K8
Cramswell CI HVHL CB9 ....40 C5
Cranberry La CAN/RD E16 ..333 H4
Cranborne Cha IPNE IP4 ...25 P2
Cranborne CI COLN CO4 ....128 E7
  PIT SS13 ....304 C5
Cranborne Rd BARK IG11 ...334 E1
  CHES/WCR EN8 ....252 E4
Cranbourne Av WAN E11 ....295 L8
Cranbourne Dr HOD EN11 ...208 E1
Cranbourne Gdns
  BARK/HLT IG6 ....296 D7
  SRTFD E15 ....314 F6
Cranbrook CI SBF/HAD SS7 .326 F2
Cranbrook CI WARE SG12 ...184 A1
Cranbrook Dr GPK RM2 .....298 G8
Cranbrook La SUD CO10 ....46 C2
Cranbrook Ms WALTH E17 ...294 C9
Cranbrook Ri IL IG1 ......316 A3
Cranbrook Rd IL IG1 ......316 B2
Cranbrook St BETH E2 .....332 A2
Crane Av COLW CO5 ....100 E7
Crane CI DAGE RM10 ....317 P8
Crane Md WARE SG12 ....184 B6
Cranes CI BSDN SS14 ......304 E6
Cranes Farm Rd BSDN SS14 .2 B1
Cranes La BSDN SS14 ......304 E6
  K/T/MI CO5 ....172 E4
Cranfield Crs POTB/CUF EN6 .228 D8
Cranfield Park Av
  WICKW SS12 ....305 K3
Cranfield Park Rd
  WICKW SS12 ....305 K3
Cranford Ct COS CO15 .....158 F9
Cranford St WAP E1W 332 A7
Cranham Gdns UPMR RM14 ...318 G1
Cranham Rd EMPK RM11 .....318 G1
  GTDUN CM6 ....116 A3
Cranleigh CI CHESW EN7 ...229 M7
  RCOS CO16 ....181 L7
Cranleigh Gv LOS SS9 .....327 P4
Cranleigh Gdns BARK IG11 .316 E9
  HOC/HUL SS5 ....286 C9
  LOU IG10 ....276 F4
  SRTFD E15 ....314 F6
Cranley Av WOS/PRIT SS0 ..328 E5
Cranley Dr GNTH/NBYPK IG2 .316 D9
  SBN/FI SS3 ....330 B8
Cranley Gdns PLMGR N13 ...316 D1
  PLSTW E13 ....333 L5
  WOS/PRIT SS0 ....328 E5
Cranmer CI BCAYW CM12 ....283 J2
Cranmer Gdns DAGE RM10 ...318 B6
Cranmer Rd FSTGT E7 ......315 L6
Cranmore Av CHLM/WR CM1 ..177 L5
Cranmore Ct RBSF CM22 ....116 F4
Cranston Av WOS/PRIT SS0 .328 E1
Cranston Gdns CHING E4 ...294 E3
Cranston Park Av
  UPMR RM14 ....319 P6
Cranwell CI BOW E3 ....332 E4
Cranwell St IPSE IP5 .....31 J1
Cranwell Gdns BSF CM23 ...137 P5
Cranwell Gv KESG IP5 .....27 P5
Cranworth Av WCHMH N21 ...273 J6
Cranworth Crs CHING E4 ...274 C7
Craven Av CVI SS8 ....344 D2
Craven Ct RCFD SS4 ....308 E2
Craven CI DAGW RM9 ....128 C3
Craven Gdns BARK IG11 ....334 F2
  BARK/HLT IG6 ....296 E6
  CRW RM5 ....298 B1
  HARH RM3 ....299 L6
Crawford Av CDW/CHF RM16 .339 L8
Crawford Cha WICKW SS12 ..305 M2
Crawford CI BCAYW CM12 ...283 K3
Crawford Gdns PLMGR N13 ..272 C9
Crawford La KESG IP5 .....27 H4
Crawley Av SLH/COR SS17 ..323 P9
Crawley Dr ENC/FH EN2 ....272 C2
Crawley End ROY SC8 ......48 C6
Crawley Rd EN EN1 ....273 L6
  LEY E10 ....294 E8
Craydene Rd ERITH DA8 ....346 E6
Crayfields GTDUN CM6 .....141 L5
Crayford CI MAL CM9 ......244 D2
Crayford High St DART DA1 .346 D9
Crayford Rd DART DA1 .....346 E9
Crayford Wy DART DA1 .....346 F9
Craylands BSDN SS14 ......304 E8
Crays HI BCAYE CM11 ......304 B3
Crays Hill Rd BCAYE CM11 .304 B3
Crayside WICKW SS12 ......305 J2
Creasbrook Av MAL CM9 ....222 B7
Creasey CI EMPK RM11 .....318 G4
Credon CI COS CO15 ....182 A6
Credon Dr COS CO15 ....182 A6

Credon Rd PLSTW E13 ......333 M2
Credo Wy WTHK RM20 ......348 E4
Creekhurst CI RCOLE CO7 ..179 M7
Creek Rd BARK IG11 ....334 G3
Creek St BARK IG11 ....344 G1
Creeksea Ferry Rd RCFD SS4 .289 N8
Creeksea La BOC CM0 ......290 E2
Creekside RAIN RM13 ......336 E4
Creek Vw VGE SS16 * 324 D3
Creek View Av HOC/HUL SS5 .286 F5
Creekview Rd RCHLM CM3 ...287 J1
Creek Wy RAIN RM13 ....336 A4
Creephedge La RCHLM CM3 ..264 A5
Cree Wy ROM RM1 ....298 D4
Creffield Av EHAM E6 .....127 N9
Creighton Av EHAM E6 .....333 N2
Crepping Hall Br RIPS/CAP IP9 .82 G7
Crescent Av GRAYS RM17 ..349 N5
  HCH RM12 ....318 E4
Crescent Ct GRAYS RM17 * .349 N4
Crescent Dr BRWN CM15 ....281 H7
Crescent Gdns BCAYW CM12 .282 G4
Crescent Gdns BCAYW CM12 .282 G4
  BSF CM23 ....137 M8
  CHING E4 ....275 H6
  CHLM/GWD CM2 ....240 F3
  CVI SS8 ....344 G3
  DAGE RM10 ....318 A6
  ENC/FH EN2 ....272 C3
  ERITH DA8 ....346 E4
  FX IP11 ....11 J2
  IP IP1 ....16 B3
  LEY E10 ....314 E4
  LOS SS9 ....327 L5
  MAL CM9 ....222 A6
  MAL CM9 ....244 A1
  PLSTW E13 ....333 K1
  SBF/HAD SS7 ....326 A4
  SOCK/AV RM15 ....338 E8
  SWFD E18 ....295 M6
  WOTN CO14 ....159 K6
The Crescent COLN CO4 ....103 M9
  COS CO15 ....135 L9
  EPP CM16 ....254 C2
  FOS CO15 ....158 C9
  GNTH/NBYPK IG2 ....316 B1
  HLWE CM17 ....187 K6
  HSTD CO9 * 59 L8
  LOS SS9 ....307 N9
  LOU IG10 ....275 N5
  NHMKT IP6 ....169 H8
  RCHLM CM5 ....169 H8
  RCOLW CO6 ....126 C2
  RCOLW CO6 ....149 M3
  RCOS CO15 ....327 J4
  SBF/HAD SS7 ....327 J4
  SBF/HAD SS7 ....320 B2
  WALTH E17 ....204 B9
Crescent Vw LOU IG10 .....275 N5
Crescent Wk SOCK/AV RM15 .338 E8
Cressages CI CHLM/GWD CM6 .143 K8
Cress CFt BRTR CM7 ....145 N5
Cressells LAIN SS15 ......C 6
Cresset CI WARE SG12 .....184 F9
Cressing Rd BRTR CM7 .....145 L4
Cressing Rd BRTR CM7 .....145 L4
  WIT CM8 ....171 L5
Cresswell Wy WCHMH N21 ...273 H6
Crest Av GRAYS RM17 ......349 L5
  PIT SS13 ....
Crestbrook Av PLMGR N13 ..272 G9
Crestbrook PI PLMGR N13 * .272 F2
Crest Dr PEND EN3 ....251 P8
Cresthill Av GRAYS RM17 ..349 M7
Crestlands RCOLE CO7 .....154 A7
The Crest CHESW EN7 ......228 G6
  SBN/FI SS3 * 187 L2
Crest Vw GRH 348 D9
Creswick Av RAYL SS6 .....306 F4
Crib St WARE SG12 ....184 A2
Cricketers Arms Rd
  ENC/FH EN2 * 273 H1
Cricketers CI CHLM/WR CM1 .218 A1
  ERITH DA8 ....346 D3
  STHGT/OAK N14 ....272 B6
  SUD CO10 ....27 J4
Cricketers La
  RBRW/HUT CM13 ....301 N4
Cricketers Rw
  RBRW/HUT CM13 ....301 N4
Cricketers Wy PIT SS13 ...304 C5
Cricketfield Gv LOS SS9 ..328 A4
Cricketfield La BSF CM23 .137 J6
Cricket Hill Rd FX IP11 ..34 C6
Cricketsea Rd SBN/FI SS3 .286 F5
Cricklade Av HARH RM3 ....299 L6
Cridland St SRTFD E15 ....333 J1
Cringle Lock RCHLM CM3 ...287 H3
Cripplegate BOC CM0 ......269 K4
Cripsey Av CHONG CM5 .....235 L5
Crispe CI CHVHL CB9 ......40 C2
Crittal CI BRTR CM7 ......144 G2
Crittall Dr BRTR CM7 .....144 G2
Crittall Dr BRTR CM7 .....144 C2
Crittall Rd WIT CM8 ......171 M1
Crockenhill Rd STSD CM24 .114 B7
Crocus CI CHTY IP2 ....24 F7
Crocus Flds SAFWN CB10 ...51 M7
Crocus Wy CHLM/WR CM1 ....218 D4
Croft CI BRTR CM7 ....145 K3
Croft CI SBF/HAD SS7 .....325 P1
Croft La HVHL CB9 ....33 K7
  KIR/NAC IP10 ....
  RCHLM CM3 ....192 C1
Croft Lodge CI WFD IG8 ...295 L3

Crofton Av SLH/COR SS17 ....341 N1
Crofton Gv CHING E4 ....294 G1
Crofton Rd CDW/CHF RM16 ....339 P9
IPNE IP4 ....26 A4
PLSTW E13 ....333 L4
Crofton Wy ENC/FH EN2 ....272 F1
Croft Rd COS CO15 ....6 C2
K/T/MI CO5 ....172 G3
PEND EN3 ....252 B9
SBF/HAD SS7 ....325 N1
SUD CO10 ....20 C4
The Crofts SBN/FI SS3 ....330 D2
Croft St CHTY IP2 ....25 K8
The Croft BROX EN10 ....230 B2
BURES CO8 ....76 A8
CHING E4 ....275 H8
HSTD CO9 ....57 P8
LOU IG10 ....276 B1
RAYL SS6 ....307 J7
RBSF CM22 ....114 F6
RCOLW CO6 ....123 P1
SUD CO10 ....20 C4
Croft Wy WIT CM8 ....197 K1
Cromarty Rd IPNE IP4 ....26 A3
Crombie Cl REDBR IG4 ....296 A9
Crome Cl COLW CO3 ....151 K1
Cromer Av LAIN SS15 ....303 J7
Cromer Cl LAIN SS15 ....303 J7
Crome Rd RCOS CO16 ....181 N7
Cromer Rd CHDH RM6 ....317 M1
EMPK RM11 ....319 J2
IP IP1 ....24 G3
LEY E10 ....314 G2
ROMW/RG RM7 ....318 B1
SOS SS1 ....19 J4
Crompton Cl BSDN SS14 ....2 B1
Crompton Pl PEND EN3 ....252 D8
Crompton Rd CHTY IP2 ....24 F4
Crompton St CHLM/WR CM1 ....4 B7
Cromwell Av BCAYW CM12 ....283 H5
CHESW EN7 ....229 N9
Cromwell Cl BSF CM23 ....136 G7
Cromwell Hl MAL CM9 ....222 A8
Cromwell La MAL CM9 ....222 A8
Cromwell Pk GTDUN CM6 ....142 G9
Cromwell Rd BRW CM14 ....300 E1
COL CO1 ....128 A9
FSTGT E7 ....315 M9
GRAYS RM17 ....349 K2
HOC/HUL SS5 ....307 P1
SAFWS CB11 ....65 M2
SOSN SS2 ....329 H3
WALTH E17 ....294 F9
WARE SG12 ....184 C3
Cromwell Sq IP IP1 ....16 D5
Cromwell Wy WIT CM8 ....197 H2
Crondon Park La ING CM4 ....261 M5
Crooked Billet Rbt CHING E4 ....294 E4
Crooked Elms HAR CO12 ....14 B7
Crooked Mile WAB EN9 ....230 F9
Crooked Wy WAB EN9 ....231 H1
Croombs Rd CAN/RD E16 ....333 M5
Cropenburg Wk CVI SS8 ....326 E9
Croppath Rd DAGE RM10 ....317 P6
Croquet Gdns RCOLE CO7 ....153 K5
Crosby Rd DAGE RM10 ....336 A2
FSTGT E7 ....315 K8
WOS/PRIT SS0 ....328 C6
Cross Av WICKW SS12 ....305 H1
Crossbow Rd CHIG IG7 ....296 G2
Crossbrook St
CHES/WCR EN8 ....230 A9
Crossby Cl BRWN CM15 ....259 P9
Cross Cl HVHL CB9 ....41 K2
Cross Cottages COLN CO4 ....103 L2
Crossfell Rd SBF/HAD SS7 ....306 C8
Crossfield Rd COS CO15 ....6 E3
HOD EN11 ....208 E3
SOSN SS2 ....329 L4
Crossfields RCOLW CO6 ....78 B4
Cross Field Wy COLN CO4 ....103 L3
Crossfield Wy FOS CO13 ....158 C8
Crossgate Fld FX IP11 ....35 H6
Cross Gn VGE SS16 ....2 C7
Cross Hl HAR CO12 ....133 M6
Crossing Rd EPP CM16 ....255 H2
Cross Keys Cl ED N9 ....273 M8
Cross La K/T/MI CO5 ....203 J6
Crossley Av COS CO15 ....206 D5
Crossley Gdns IP IP1 ....24 D1
Crossness Rd BARK IG11 ....334 G3
Crosspath HSTD CO9 * 72 C7
Cross Rd CHDH RM6 ....317 K2
CHES/WCR EN8 ....252 B3
CHING E4 ....274 G7
EN EN1 ....273 L3
MAL CM9 ....244 B1
PIT SS13 ....305 L8
ROMW/RG RM7 ....297 P7
SBF/HAD SS7 ....326 E2
WFD IG8 ....296 A3
WIT CM8 ....171 N9
Cross Roads LOU IG10 ....275 L1
Cross St ERITH DA8 ....346 D4
FX IP11 ....35 H5
SAFWN CB10 ....51 L9
SUD CO10 ....20 B7
WARE SG12 ....184 B3
Crosstree Wk COLS CO2 ....152 B3
Cross Wy K/T/MI CO5 ....203 H5
Crossway BCTR RM8 ....317 K5
EN EN1 ....273 K6
THMD SE28 ....335 K7
Crossways BRWN CM15 ....281 K5
CBE/LIN CB1 ....38 C1
CHLM/GWD CM2 ....240 B3
COS CO15 ....206 E4
GPK RM2 ....298 G7
RCOLW CO6 ....98 G7
Crossways Bvd GRH DA9 ....347 P9
The Crossways
WOS/PRIT SS0 ....328 B6
Crotchets Cl RIPS/CAP IP9 ....28 C9
Crothall Cl PLMGR N13 ....272 E9
Crouch Av BARK IG11 ....335 J2
HOC/HUL SS5 ....287 H7
Crouch Beck RCHLM CM3 ....286 G1
Crouch Dr WICKE SS11 ....285 J8
WIT CM8 ....197 H2
Crouch La CHESW EN7 ....229 H6
Crouchman Cl
CDW/CHF RM16 ....339 M9
Crouchmans Av SBN/FI SS3 ....330 F3
Crouchman's Farm Rd
MAL CM9 ....220 F5
Crouch Meadow
HOC/HUL SS5 ....287 H4
Crouch Rd BOC CM0 ....290 G3
GRAYS RM17 ....350 B3
Crouch St COLW CO3 ....8 A7
LAIN SS15 ....303 M6
Crouch Va UPMR RM14 ....320 B2
Crouchview Cl WICKE SS11 ....285 N9
Crouch View Crs
HOC/HUL SS5 ....288 A8
Crouch View Gv
HOC/HUL SS5 ....286 G5
Croutel Rd FX IP11 ....35 L6
Crowborough Rd SOSN SS2 ....328 G4
Crowden Wy THMD SE28 ....335 K7
Crowe Hall La RIPS/CAP IP9 ....83 H7
Crowfoot Cl HOM E9 ....314 C7
THMD SE28 ....334 F8
Crow Gn BRWN CM15 ....280 D3
Crow Green La BRWN CM15 ....280 D4
Crow Green Rd BRWN CM15 ....280 C4
Crowhall La MGTR CO11 ....107 J8
Crowhurst Rd COLW CO3 ....8 A6
Crowland Cl CHTY IP2 ....25 H9
Crowland Gdns
STHGT/OAK N14 ....272 D6
Crowland Rd HVHL CB9 ....41 J3
Crowlands Av
ROMW/RG RM7 ....318 A1
Crow La RCOS CO16 ....156 C4
ROMW/RG RM7 ....317 N2
Crown & Anchor Ms IP IP1 * 16 D3
Crown Av PIT SS13 ....305 H8
Crown Bays Rd COLN CO4 ....9 K3
Crown Buildings CHING E4 * 274 G7
Crown Cl BOW E3 ....332 D1
PIT SS13 ....305 H9
RBSF CM22 ....188 B4
WDBR IP12 ....27 N1
Crown Ct COLN CO4 * 128 D1
Crownfield BROX EN10 ....208 D9
Crownfield Av
GNTH/NBYPK IG2 ....296 F9
Crownfield Rd SRTFD E15 ....314 G7
Crown Gdns RAYL SS6 ....306 F5
Crown Ga COLN CO4 ....128 E1
HLW CM20 ....13 H6
Crown Hl RAYL SS6 ....306 F5
WAB EN9 ....254 A3
Crownhill Rd WFD IG8 ....295 P4
Crown La HAR CO12 ....14 E5
RCOS CO16 ....156 A3
STHGT/OAK N14 ....272 B7
Crown La North RCOLE CO7 ....103 P9
Crown La South RCOLE CO7 ....129 H3
Crown Meadow BRTR CM7 ....145 N2
Crown Pde
STHGT/OAK N14 * 272 B7
Crown Rd BARK/HLT IG6 ....296 E8
BCAYE CM11 ....283 J6
BRW CM14 ....258 A9
COS CO15 ....6 A7
EN EN1 ....273 N3
GRAYS RM17 ....349 K4
HOC/HUL SS5 ....307 L2
RCHLM CM3 ....266 A3
Crown St BRTR CM7 ....94 A6
BRW CM14 ....280 F8
DAGE RM10 ....318 B8
FX IP11 ....35 H6
HSTD CO9 ....72 D5
IP IP1 ....16 D3
RCOLE CO7 ....104 G2
Crown Ter BSF CM23 ....137 M7
STHGT/OAK N14 * 272 C7
Crown Wy BOC CM0 ....268 G5
Crown Yd BCAYW CM12 * 283 H6
Crow Pond Rd RCHLM CM3 ....195 P2
Crowsheath La BCAYE CM11 ....284 D2
Crows La RCHLM CM3 ....264 E3
Crows Rd BARK IG11 ....316 C8
EPP CM16 ....232 G9
SRTFD E15 ....332 G3
Crowstone Av WOS/PRIT SS0 ....328 D7
Crowstone Cl WOS/PRIT SS0 ....328 D5
Crowstone Ct
WOS/PRIT SS0 * 18 A5
Crowstone Rd
CDW/CHF RM16 ....339 M9
WOS/PRIT SS0 ....328 D6
Crow St RBSF CM22 ....115 J2
Crowswell Ct FX IP11 ....34 E1
Croxford Wy
ROMW/RG RM7 ....318 C3
Croxon Wy BOC CM0 ....290 G1
Croxton Cl KIR/NAC IP10 ....33 N7
Croydon Rd PLSTW E13 ....333 J4
Croyland Rd ED N9 ....273 M7
Crozier Av BSF CM23 ....137 H6
Crozier Ter HOM E9 ....314 A7
Cruce Wy RCOS CO16 ....204 G1
Crucible Cl CHDH RM6 ....317 J1
Cruick Av SOCK/AV RM15 ....338 F7
Cruikshank Rd SRTFD E15 ....315 H6
Crummock Cl BRTR CM77 ....144 F8
Crunch Cft HVHL CB9 ....41 P6
Crusader Cl PUR RM19 ....347 M2
Crusader Wy BRTR CM7 ....145 N4
Crushes Cl RBRW/HUT CM13 ....281 P5
Crushton Pl CHLM/WR CM1 ....217 N5
Crusoe Rd ERITH DA8 ....346 C3
Crystal Av HCH RM12 ....319 K6
Crystal Wy BCTR RM8 ....317 K3
Cuba Dr PEND EN3 ....273 P1
Cuba St POP/IOD E14 ....332 D9
Cuckfield Av IPSE IP3 ....26 D8
Cuckoo Hall La ED N9 ....273 P6
Cuckoo Hl BURES CO8 ....76 A8
HSTD CO9 ....72 A9
Cuckoo La CDW/CHF RM16 ....339 J9
Cuckoos La GTDUN CM6 ....164 G3
Cuckoo Wy BRTR CM77 ....144 E8
Cuffley Hl CHESW EN7 ....228 G8
Culford Rd CDW/CHF RM16 ....339 M9
Culford Wk FX IP11 ....10 B3
Culgaith Gdns ENC/FH EN2 ....272 D3
Cullen Sq SOCK/AV RM15 ....338 F7
Cullingham Rd IP IP1 ....25 H5
Cullings Ct WAB EN9 ....253 J3
Culloden Rd ENC/FH EN2 ....272 G1
Culloden St POP/IOD E14 ....332 F6
Culpepper Cl CHIG IG7 ....296 C3
Culverdown BSDN SS14 ....2 E4
Culver Ri RCHLM CM3 ....287 H1
Culver Sq COL CO1 * 8 B6
Culver St East COL CO1 ....8 D6
Culver St West COL CO1 ....8 B6
Culver Wk COL CO1 * 8 C6
Cumberland Av HCH RM12 ....319 K5
MAL CM9 ....243 P1
SBF/HAD SS7 ....325 P3
SOSN SS2 ....329 K4
Cumberland Cl
BARK/HLT IG6 * 296 D5
BRTR CM7 ....145 L2
FX IP11 ....35 N5
Cumberland Crs
CHLM/WR CM1 ....217 P4
Cumberland Dr LAIN SS15 ....303 H9
Cumberland Rd
CDW/CHF RM16 ....339 H9
ED N9 ....273 P7
MNPK E12 ....315 N6
PLSTW E13 ....333 L5
WALTH E17 ....294 B6
Cumberland St IP IP1 ....16 B2
Cumbrae Ms WICKW SS12 ....305 L1
Cumbrian Av BXLYHN DA7 ....346 D7
Cumley Rd CHONG CM5 ....234 D9
Cumming Rd BCAYE CM11 ....284 F6
Cummings Hall La
ABR/ST RM4 ....279 H9
Cunard Crs WCHMH N21 ....273 J5
Cundalls Rd WARE SG12 ....184 B2
Cundy Rd CAN/RD E16 ....333 M6
Cunningham Av PEND EN3 ....252 B6
Cunningham Cl CHDH RM6 ....297 K9
SBN/FI SS3 ....330 E5
Cunningham Dr WICKW SS12 ....305 K2
Cunningham Ri EPP CM16 ....234 B4
Cunningham Rd
CHES/WCR EN8 ....230 B6
Cunnington Rd BRTR CM7 ....145 M3
Cunobelin Wy COLS CO2 ....151 K4
Cupids Cha SBN/FI SS3 ....331 H4
Cuppers Cl WIT CM8 ....197 H3
Curds Rd RCOLW CO6 ....123 P4
Curlew Av RCHLM CM3 ....267 P1
Curlew Cl COS CO15 ....182 A7
K/T/MI CO5 ....173 J3
MAL CM9 ....222 D6
THMD SE28 ....335 L7
Curlew Ct BROX EN10 * 230 C2
Curlew Crs VGE SS16 ....324 A3
Curlew Cft COLN CO4 ....128 G7
Curlew Dr SBF/HAD SS7 ....325 P4
Curlew Rd CHTY IP2 ....24 E8
Curling La GRAYS RM17 ....349 J3
Curling Tye BSDN SS14 ....3 K3
Curling Tye La MAL CM9 ....221 J8
Curling Wk BSDN SS14 ....304 C8
Currants Farm Rd
BRTR CM7 ....145 H1
Currents La HAR CO12 ....15 F2
Curriers' La IP IP1 ....16 C5
Curteys HLWE CM17 ....187 L7
Curthwaite Gdns
ENC/FH EN2 ....272 C3
Curtis Cl RCOS CO16 ....206 G1
RIPW IP8 ....29 L1
Curtis Mill La ABR/ST RM4 ....278 D3
Curtis Rd EMPK RM11 ....319 L3
Curtisway RAYL SS6 ....307 H3
Curwen Av FSTGT E7 ....315 L6
Curzon Av PEND EN3 ....274 A4
Curzon Crs BARK IG11 ....334 G3
Curzon Dr GRAYS RM17 ....349 M5
Curzon Rd SUD CO10 ....21 J4
Curzon Wy CHLM/GWD CM2 ....218 F9
Cusak Rd CHLM/GWD CM2 ....218 E9
Cussons Cl CHESW EN7 ....229 M8
Custerson Dr BRTR CM77 ....145 L9
Cut-a-Thwart La MAL CM9 ....221 L8
Cutforth Rd SBW CM21 ....187 M1
Cuthberga Cl BARK IG11 ....316 D9
Cuthbert Cl CHESW EN7 ....229 L8
Cuthbert Rd WALTH E17 ....294 F7
Cut Hedge BRTR CM77 ....144 F8
Cuthedge La RCOLW CO6 ....147 J7
Cutlers La RCOLE CO7 ....80 G4
Cutlers Rd RCHLM CM3 ....265 H9
Cutler St IP IP1 ....16 D6
Cutmore Pl CHLM/GWD CM2 ....239 N2
Cuton Hall La
CHLM/GWD CM2 ....218 F6
The Cut K/T/MI CO5 ....173 P8
Cut Throat La WIT CM8 ....197 K1
Cutting Dr HSTD CO9 ....97 P7
Cygnet Ct BSF CM23 ....137 L8
HSTD CO9 ....72 D8
Cygnet Vw WTHK RM20 ....348 C1
Cygnet Wk COLW CO3 ....150 E2
Cymbeline Wy (Colchester
By-Pass) COLW CO3 ....127 J8
Cypress Av ENC/FH EN2 ....250 F5
Cypress Cl COS CO15 ....181 P6
WAB EN9 * 252 G4
Cypress Ct GTDUN CM6 ....141 J5
Cypress Dr CHLM/GWD CM2 ....240 B4
Cypress Gv BARK/HLT IG6 ....296 F3
COLN CO4 ....128 F7
Cypress Ms K/T/MI CO5 ....202 E5
Cypress Rd WIT CM8 ....171 P9
Cyprus Pl EHAM E6 ....334 B7
Cyprus Rd ED N9 ....273 L8
Cyril Child Cl COLN CO4 ....128 F8
Czarina Ri LAIN SS15 ....303 M7

D

Daarle Av CVI SS8 ....344 D2
Dabbling Cl ERITH DA8 * 346 G5
Dace Rd BOW E3 ....332 D1
Dacre Av CLAY IG5 ....296 B6
SOCK/AV RM15 ....338 A8
Dacre Cl CHIG IG7 ....296 D1
Dacre Crs SOCK/AV RM15 ....338 A8
Dacre Gdns CHIG IG7 ....296 D1
Dacre Rd PLSTW E13 ....333 L1
WAN E11 ....315 J3
Dads Wd HLWW/ROY CM19 ....13 G7
Daen Ingas RCHLM CM3 ....241 P3
Daffodil Av BRWN CM15 ....280 E4
Daffodil Cl CHTY IP2 ....24 F8
Daffodil Gdns IL IG1 ....316 C7
Daffodil Wy CHLM/WR CM1 ....218 D4
Dagenham Av DAGW RM9 ....317 M9
Dagenham Rd DAGE RM10 ....318 B6
LEY E10 ....314 C3
ROMW/RG RM7 ....318 C2
Dagmar Rd DAGE RM10 ....318 B9
Dagnam Park Cl HARH RM3 ....299 M2
Dagnam Park Dr HARH RM3 ....299 K2
Dagnam Park Gdns
HARH RM3 ....299 M3
Dagnam Park Sq HARH RM3 ....299 M3
Dagnets La BRTR CM77 ....169 M1
Dagwood La BRWN CM15 ....258 E8
Dahlia Cl CHESW EN7 ....229 H4
CHLM/WR CM1 ....218 E6
RCOS CO16 ....181 M9
Dahlia Gdns IL IG1 ....316 C8
Dahlia Wk COLN CO4 ....128 E8
Daiglen Dr SOCK/AV RM15 ....338 D7
Daimler Av COS CO15 ....206 C5
Daimler Rd IP IP1 ....24 D1
Daines Cl MNPK E12 ....316 A5
SOCK/AV RM15 ....338 D4
SOS SS1 ....330 A6
Daines Rd BCAYE CM11 ....283 J6
Daines Wy SOS SS1 ....330 A5
Dains Pl FX IP11 ....34 F4
Daintrees WARE SG12 ....160 D9
Dairy Farm Rd RCHLM CM3 ....268 C6
Dairyglen Av CHES/WCR EN8 ....252 A1
Dairyhouse La MGTR CO11 ....107 K8
Dairy Rd CHLM/GWD CM2 ....218 E7
Daisleys La RCHLM CM3 ....194 F2
Daisy Green Rd COLW CO3 ....126 A7
Daisyley Rd GTDUN CM6 ....117 P4
Daisy Rd SWFD E18 ....295 L6
Dakin Pl WCHPL E1 ....332 B5
Dakota Gdns EHAM E6 ....333 P4
Dakyn Dr ING CM4 ....261 L6
Dale Cl COLW CO3 ....126 E8
SOCK/AV RM15 ....338 D6
Dale Ct HAR CO12 ....110 A5
SBW CM21 ....187 L3
Dale Gdns WFD IG8 ....295 L1
Dale Green Rd
FBAR/BDGN N11 ....272 A9
Dale Hall La IP IP1 ....25 J1
Dalen Av CVI SS8 ....344 D2
Dale Rd LOS SS9 ....327 L5
Daleside Gdns CHIG IG7 ....276 D9
Dales Rd IP IP1 ....25 H2
The Dales HAR CO12 ....110 A7
RCFD SS4 ....308 E4
Dales Vw RIPW IP8 ....28 G2
Dales View Rd IP IP1 ....25 H3
The Dale RCOLE CO7 ....153 K6
SBF/HAD SS7 ....326 D2
WAB EN9 ....253 H4
Dale Vw ERITH DA8 ....346 F7
Dale View Av CHING E4 ....274 F8
Daleview Av MGTR CO11 ....132 F2
Dale View Crs CHING E4 ....274 F9
Dale View Gdns CHING E4 ....274 G9
Dalewood Cl EMPK RM11 ....319 L2
Daley St HOM E9 ....314 A8
Dalkeith Rd IL IG1 ....316 D5
Dallwood Wy BRTR CM7 ....145 L3
Dalmatia Rd SOS SS1 ....329 L5
Dalmeney VGE SS16 ....323 J2
Dalmeny Rd ERITH DA8 ....346 A6
Dalroy Cl SOCK/AV RM15 ....338 D6
Dalrymple Cl CHLM/GWD CM2 ....218 C7
STHGT/OAK N14 ....272 C6
Daltes La RCOS CO16 ....206 A1
Dalton Gdns BSF CM23 ....162 B2
Dalton Rd IP IP1 ....16 B4
Daltons Fen PIT SS13 ....305 H7
Dalwood SBN/FI SS3 ....330 C6
Dalwood Gdns SBF/HAD SS7 ....327 H2
Dalys Rd RCFD SS4 ....308 F5
Damant's Farm La FOS CO13 ....157 N6
Damases La RCHLM CM3 ....219 N1
Damask Crs CAN/RD E16 ....333 H4
Damask Ms BRTR CM7 * 145 K4
Damask Rd COLW CO3 ....126 F8
Dames Rd FSTGT E7 ....315 K6
Dampier Rd RCOLW CO6 ....147 N3
Damselfly Rd IPSE IP3 ....31 J2
Danacre LAIN SS15 ....303 M8
Danbury Cl BRW CM14 ....280 C4
CHDH RM6 ....297 L7
LOS SS9 ....328 A2
Danbury Crs SOCK/AV RM15 ....338 E6
Danbury Down BSDN SS14 ....304 C7
Danbury Rd LOU IG10 ....275 P5
RAIN RM13 ....336 E1
RAYL SS6 ....306 E4
Danbury V RCHLM CM3 ....242 D4
Danbury Wy WFD IG8 ....295 M3
Dancing Dicks La WIT CM8 ....196 D2
Dandalan Cl IP IP1 ....24 F4
Dandelion Cl ROMW/RG RM7 ....318 D4
Dandies Cha LOS SS9 ....307 N8
Dandies Cl LOS SS9 ....307 N8
Dandies Dr LOS SS9 ....307 N8
Dane Acres BSF CM23 ....137 J6
Dane Br MHAD SG10 ....161 H2
Dane Bridge La MHAD SG10 ....160 G3
Danebridge Rd MHAD SG10 ....160 F3
Dane Cl HVHL CB9 ....42 B1
Dane Common HVHL CB9 ....42 B2
Danehurst Gdns REDBR IG4 ....295 P9
Danemead HOD EN11 ....208 D2
Dane O'Coys Rd BSF CM23 ....137 K5
Dane Pk BSF CM23 ....137 J6
Dane Pl BOW E3 ....332 B2
Dane Rd CHLM/WR CM1 ....4 A4
IL IG1 ....316 D7
Dane's Av SBN/FI SS3 ....330 E8
Danes Ct SUD CO10 ....61 L6
Danescroft Cl LOS SS9 ....327 N2
Danescroft Dr LOS SS9 ....327 N2
Danesdale Rd HOM E9 ....314 B8
Danesfield SBF/HAD SS7 ....325 N4
Danesleigh Gdns LOS SS9 ....327 N2
Danes Rd ROMW/RG RM7 ....318 B2
Dane St BSF CM23 ....137 M8
SBN/FI SS3 ....330 F8
Danes Wy BRWN CM15 ....280 D4
Danette Gdns DAGE RM10 ....317 N4
Dangan Rd WAN E11 ....315 K1
Daniel Bolt Cl POP/IOD E14 ....332 E5
Daniel Cl CDW/CHF RM16 ....339 H9
CDW/CHF RM16 ....350 C1
Daniel Cole Rd COLS CO2 ....152 A2
Daniell Cl RCOS CO16 ....181 M7
Daniell Dr COLS CO2 ....151 L4
Daniels Cl SUD CO10 ....47 M5
Daniel Wy WIT CM8 ....171 M1
Danyon Cl RAIN RM13 ....337 H2
Daphne Cl BRTR CM77 ....144 F7
Daphne Gdns CHING E4 ....274 F9
Dapifer Dr BRTR CM7 ....145 N3
Darby Dr WAB EN9 ....252 F3
D'Arcy Av MAL CM9 ....244 C1
D'Arcy Cl BOC CM0 ....291 H2
Darcy Cl CHES/WCR EN8 ....252 B1
D'Arcy Cl FOS CO13 ....158 G8
Darcy Cl RBRW/HUT CM13 ....281 L6
D'Arcy Gdns DAGW RM9 ....335 N1
D'Arcy Hts COLS CO2 ....152 D3
Darcy Ri RCHLM CM3 ....242 B1
D'Arcy Rd COLS CO2 ....152 D3
K/T/MI CO5 ....199 N1
RCOS CO16 ....180 E8
D'Arcy Wy MAL CM9 ....200 D8
RCOLE CO7 ....179 K6
Darell Wy BCAYE CM11 ....283 L7
Darenth La SOCK/AV RM15 ....338 D6
Darenth Rd LOS SS9 ....327 L5
Darent Valley Pth DART DA1 ....347 J6
Darina Ct COLW CO3 * 126 E8
Darkhouse La K/T/MI CO5 ....153 H6
Dark La BRW CM14 ....300 D4
CHESW EN7 ....229 M9
SBF/HAD SS7 ....306 D9
Darley Rd ED N9 ....273 L7
Darlinghurst Gv LOS SS9 ....328 B4
Darlington Ct BRWN CM15 ....280 D5
Darlington Gdns HARH RM3 ....299 J2
Darlton Cl DART DA1 ....346 E8
Darndale Cl WALTH E17 ....294 C6
Darnel Wy COLW CO3 ....126 E8
Darnet Rd MAL CM9 ....225 K2
Darnicle Hl CHESW EN7 ....228 F4
Darnley Rd GRAYS RM17 * 349 L4
WFD IG8 ....295 K5
Darrell Cl CHLM/WR CM1 ....218 A5
Darrell Rd FX IP11 ....111 L1
Darsham Cl FX IP11 ....10 C1
Dart Cl UPMR RM14 ....320 A1
WIT CM8 ....196 G2
Darter Cl IPSE IP3 ....31 J2
Dartfields HARH RM3 ....299 J3
Dartford Av ED N9 ....273 P5
Dart Gn SOCK/AV RM15 ....338 E6
Dartmouth Cl RAYL SS6 ....306 G2
Dartmouth Rd
CHLM/WR CM1 ....218 D5
Dartview Cl GRAYS RM17 ....349 P2
Darwell Cl EHAM E6 ....334 B2
Darwin Cl BRTR CM7 ....145 J5
COLS CO2 ....152 C5
FBAR/BDGN N11 ....272 A9
Darwin Rd IPNE IP4 ....25 N6
TIL RM18 ....350 A6
Dash End HVHL CB9 ....42 C1
Dash End La HVHL CB9 ....42 C1
The Dashes HLW CM20 ....13 K4
Dashwood Cl RIPW IP8 ....29 M1
Datchet Dr SBN/FI SS3 ....330 D4
Daubeney Rd CLPT E5 ....314 B7
Daundy Cl CHTY IP2 ....24 E6
Davall Cl HAR CO12 ....109 M7
Davenants PIT SS13 ....304 G7
Davenport HLWE CM17 ....211 M4
Daventry Av WALTH E17 ....314 D1
Daventry Gdns HARH RM3 ....299 H2
Daventry Rd HARH RM3 ....299 H2
Davey Cl COL CO1 ....9 K7
IPSE IP3 ....30 F1
Davey Rd HOM E9 ....314 D9
David Av WICKE SS11 ....285 J6
David Dr HARH RM3 ....299 M3
David Rd BCTR RM8 ....317 M4
Davidson Cl SUD CO10 ....61 M6
Davidson Gdns WICKW SS12 ....305 K2
Davidson Wy ROMW/RG RM7 ....318 D1
David St SRTFD E15 ....314 G8
David's Wk BCAYE CM11 ....283 K6
Davids Wy BARK/HLT IG6 ....296 F4
Davies Cl RAIN RM13 ....337 H3

Davies La WAN E11 ....315 H4
Davington Gdns BCTR RM8 ....317 J7
Davington Rd BCTR RM8 ....317 J8
Davinia Cl WFD IG8 ....296 A3
Davison Cl CHES/WCR EN8 ....230 A7
Davison Dr CHES/WCR EN8 ....230 A7
Davis Rd CDW/CHF RM16 ....349 J1
  SOCK/AV RM15
Davis St PLSTW E13 ....333 L2
Davy Rd COS CO15 ....182 D5
Dawes Av HCH RM12 ....319 J5
Dawes Cl RIPS/CAP IP9 ....28 B9
Dawes La K/T/MI CO5 ....173 L5
Dawley Gn SOCK/AV RM15 ....338 D6
Dawlish Crs RAYL SS6 ....306 C2
Dawlish Rd GDMY/SEVK IG3 ....316 C6
  LOS SS9 ....327 P5
Dawlish Rd COS CO15 ....327 P5
  LEY E10 ....314 F4
Dawn Cl MAL CM9 ....244 C2
Dawn Crs SRTFD E15 ....332 L1
Danford Cl COLW CO13 ....126 F9
Daws Cl CHLM/WR CM1 ....238 C1
Daws Heath Rd SBF/HAD SS7 ....306 F9
Daws Hl CHING E4 ....274 F2
Dawson Av BARK IG11 ....316 C9
Dawson Ct SAFWN CB10 ....51 N8
Dawson Drift KESG IP5 ....27 H4
Dawson Dr FX IP11 ....54 F5
  RAIN RM13
Dawson Gdns BARK IG11 ....316 C9
Dawson Ms BCTR RM8 ....283 J5
Dawson Ter N9 * 259 J2
Daw St BRTR CM7 ....04 D4
  HSTD CO9 ....56 C5
Daylop Dr CHIG IG7 ....277 J9
Days Cl CHLM/WR CM1 ....218 A3
Days Gn RIPS/CAP IP9 ....28 B9
Days La BRWN CM15 ....280 D5
Days Rd RIPS/CAP IP9 ....28 B9
Dayton Dr ERITH DA8 ....347 J4
Dazeley's La RCOLE CO7 ....81 J9
Deacon Cl FX IP11 ....35 N5
Deacon Dr LAIN SS15 ....303 K8
The Deacon Est CHING E4 * 294 C5
Deacon Wy WFD IG8 ....296 A4
Dead La BURES CO8 ....76 F7
  MGTR CO11
  RCOLE CO7 ....04 D8
  RCOS CO16 ....180 C5
  RCOS CO16 ....181 L4
Deadman's La
  CHLM/GWD CM2 ....240 B6
Deal Cl BRTR CM7 ....121 H9
  COS CO15 ....207 H4
Dealtree Cl BRWN CM15 ....258 E5
Deal Wy RCOLE CO7 ....179 K4
Deanery Gdns BRTR CM7 ....121 J8
Deanery Rd SRTFD E15 ....315 H8
Deane's Cl HAR CO12 ....110 B6
Deanes Ct HAR CO12 ....110 B6
Dean Cotes WALTH E17 ....294 C8
Deanhill Av COS CO15 ....186 G2
Dean Rd CBE/LIN CB1 ....38 C4
  THMD SE28 ....335 H7
Dean Rogers Pl BRTR CM7 ....121 J8
Deans Rd BRW CM14 ....280 E9
Dean St FSTGT E7 ....315 K7
  RCOLE CO7 ....179 K6
Deansway Rd EN9 ....273 K9
Dean Wy CHLM/WR CM1 ....239 L1
Dearsley Rd EN11 ....215 L1
Deason St SRTFD E15 * 332 F1
Debden Cl WFD IG8 ....295 N4
Debden Gn SAFWN CB10 ....66 D7
Debden La LOU IG10 ....254 C9
Debden Rd LOU IG10 ....254 C8
  SAFWS CB11
Debden Wy BOC CMO * 290 F2
De Beauvoir Cha
  BCAYE CM11 ....284 C5
Deben Av KESG IP5 ....27 L3
Deben Dr SUD CO10 ....21 C3
Debenham Rd CHESW EN7 ....229 N6
Deben Rd COLN CO4 ....128 F6
  EN EN1 ....41 L3
  IP IP1
Deben Valley Dr KESG IP5 ....27 H4
Deben Wk RCOS CO16 ....181 M7
Deben Wy FX IP11 ....11 F3
De Bohun Av STHGT/OAK N14 ....272 A5
De Brett Dr SAFWN CB10 ....51 M8
Debrabant Cl ERITH DA8 ....346 C4
De Brink-on-the-Green
  KESG IP5 * 27 M4
De Burgh Pl SUD CO10 ....44 A2
De Burgh Rd COLW CO13 ....127 H9
Deck Cl BERM/RHTH SE16 ....332 H4
Dedham Av RCOS CO16 ....181 L9
Dedham Ct BCAYE CM11 ....283 K6
Dedham Meade RCOLE CO7 ....104 G5
Dedham Mi RCOLE CO7 ....104 G1
Dedham Pl IPNE IP4 ....17 F5
Dedham Rd BCAYE CM11 ....283 K6
  COLN CO4 ....103 L2
  MGTR CO11 ....105 M4
  RCOLE CO7 ....80 C9
  RCOLE CO7 ....104 E7
Dee Cl UPMR RM14 ....320 A1
Deepdale SBF/HAD SS7 ....306 C9
Deepdale Rd HAR CO12 ....110 B4
Deepdene ING CM4 ....260 C6
  LOS SS9 ....3 C7
Deepdene Av RAYL SS6 ....306 F3
Deepdene Cl WAN E11 ....295 K8
Deepdene Ct WCHMH N21 ....272 C3
Deepdene Pth LOU IG10 ....276 C3
Deepdene Rd LOU IG10 ....276 C3
The Deeping SOS SS1 ....19 F3
Deeping Wk RCOS CO16 ....180 E8
Deepwater Rd CVI SS8 ....344 B8
Deerbank Rd CHLM/WR CM11 ....285 K5

Deere Av RAIN RM13 ....318 F8
Deerfield Cl WARE SG12 ....184 A2
Deerhurst Cha RCHLM CM5 ....242 C9
Deerhurst Cl SBF/HAD SS7 ....306 E8
Deerleap Gv CHING E4 ....274 E4
Deerleap Wy BRTR CM7 ....145 N2
Deer Park Wy WAB EN9 ....210 B6
Deer Park Wy WAB EN9 ....252 F4
Dees St POP/IOD E14 ....332 F6
Dee Wy ROM RM1 ....298 D5
Defoe Crs COLN CO4 ....127 P2
Defoe Pde CDW/CHF RM16 ....350 C1
Defoe Rd BERM/RHTH SE16 ....332 C9
Defoe Wy RWM 297 P3
Deford Rd WIT CM8 ....196 G4
De Haviland Ct IL IG1 ....316 E5
Deirdre Av WICKW SS12 ....284 C9
Deirdre Cl WICKW SS12 ....284 C9
Delafield Rd GRAYS RM17 ....333 L1
Delamare Rd CHES/WCR EN8 ....230 C8
Delamere Rd COLN CO4 * ....A 4 A6
  COLN CO4 ....128 E4
Delargy Cl CDW/CHF RM16 ....350 C1
Delaware Crs SBN/FI SS3 ....330 C7
Delaware Rd SBN/FI SS3 ....330 B7
Delder Av CVI SS8 ....338 C9
Delft Rd CVI SS8 ....344 D1
Delfzul Rd CVI SSB 344 D1
Delgada Rd CVI SS8 ....344 G2
Delhi Rd EN EN1 ....273 L6
  PIT SS13 ....305 H9
Delimands LAIN SS15 ....2 B5
Delisle Rd THMD SE28 ....334 F9
Delius Wk COLW CO13 ....128 F9
Della Ct CHING E4 * 127 N9
Dell Ct SRTFD E15 ....332 C1
  WFD IG8 ....275 L9
Dell La BSF CM23 ....137 M7
  RBSF CM22 ....162 D5
Dellow Cl GNTH/NBYPK IG2 ....316 E2
Dellows La RBSF CM22 ....114 D5
Dell Rd GRAYS RM17 ....349 L2
  PEND EN3 ....251 P8
Dells Cl CHING E4 ....274 E6
Dells Wood Cl HOD EN11 ....208 C2
The Dell BRW CM14 ....300 E5
  CHLM/GWD CM2 ....240 E4
  COL CO1 ....8 E7
  GTDUN CM6 ....141 M5
  VGE SS16 ....324 A3
  WAB EN9 ....252 F6
  WFD IG8 ....275 L9
  WICKE SS11 ....285 K9
Dellwood Av FX IP11 ....35 K6
Dellwood Gdns CLAY IG5 ....296 B7
Delmar Gdns WICKW SS12 ....285 H6
Delmores VGE SS16 ....323 L7
Delta Rd RBRW/HUT CM13 ....281 N5
De Luci Rd BRTR DA8 ....346 B3
Delvers Md DAGE RM10 ....318 B6
Delview CVI SS8 ....326 C9
Delvins PIT SS13 ....304 F7
Delvyn's La HSTD CO9 ....75 H5
De Mandeville Ga EN EN1 * 273 M3
De Mandeville Rd RBSF CM22 ....114 F5
De-Marci Ct BRTR CM7 ....145 N5
Demesne Gdns KESG IP5 * 27 M3
Denbigh Cl EMPK RM11 ....298 L8
Denbigh Rd EHAM E6 ....333 N1
  LAIN SS15 ....323 J1
Denby Gra HLWE CM17 ....211 M3
Dencourt Crs BSDN SS14 ....324 E1
Denderidge Ct EN EN1 ....251 N7
Dene Cl RAYL SS6 ....306 G3
Dene Ct CHLM/WR CM1 ....217 L6
Denecroft Gdns GRAYS RM17 ....349 N1
Dene Gdns RAYL SS6 ....306 G3
Denehurst Gdns WFD SG16 ....322 F2
  WFD IG8 ....295 L1
Dene Pth SOCK/AV RM15 ....338 D6
Dene Rd BKHH IG9 ....275 P7
Denesmere SBF/HAD SS7 ....324 C4
Deneway VGE SS16 ....324 C4
Dengayne BSDN SS14 ....304 C9
Dengie Cl WIT CM8 ....197 J4
Denham Cl RCOLE CO7 ....153 K6
Denham Ct GNTH/NBYPK IG2 ....316 D1
Denham Ct COS CO15 ....340 D1
Denham V RAYL SS6 ....306 D4
Denham Wy BARK IG11 ....334 F1
Denholm Ct WIT CM8 ....197 J4
Denholme Wk RAIN RM13 ....318 E8
Denleigh Gdns WCHMH N21 ....272 F6
Denman Gdns RIPS/CAP IP9 ....83 L3
Denmark Rd CVI SS8 ....326 F9
Denmark St PLSTW E13 ....333 L5
  WAN E11 ....333 L5
Denner Rd CHING E4 ....274 D8
Dennises La UPMR RM14 ....320 C9
Dennis Pde STHGT/OAK N14 * 272 C7
Dennis Rd UPMR RM14 ....338 D1
Denny Av WAB EN9 ....252 B1
Denny Rd BSF CM23 ....137 N4
Denny Ga CHES/WCR EN8 ....230 C9
Denny Rd ED N9 ....273 N7
Densham Rd SRTFD E15 ....333 H1
Densworth Gv ED N9 ....273 P8
Dent Cl SOCK/AV RM15 ....338 D6
Denton Ap WOS/PRIT SS0 ....328 D1
Denton Av WOS/PRIT SS0 ....328 D1
Denton Crs BRTR CM7 ....145 L9
Denton Gn CLPT E5 ....314 A5
Denton Wy LAIN SS15 ....323 J1
Denver Dr PIT SS13 ....305 H6
De Quincey Ms CAN/RD E16 ....333 K8
Derby Cl BCAYE CM11 ....283 L3
  IPNE IP4
  RCHLM CM3 ....245 N9
  VGE SS16 ....322 G2

Derbydale RCFD SS4 ....308 D1
Derby Rd FSTGT E7 ....315 N9
  HOD EN11 ....208 D7
  HOM E9 ....332 A1
  IPSE IP5 ....25 P2
  PEND EN3 ....273 N4
  SWFD E18 ....295 J5
Derby Road Br GRAYS RM17 ....349 L3
Dereham Av IPSE IP5 ....25 N8
Dereham Cl COLS CO2 ....152 B1
Dereham Pl CRW RM5 ....298 A3
Dereham Rd BARK IG11 ....316 C8
Derek Gdns SOSN SS2 ....328 F1
Derham Gdns UPMR RM14 ....319 P5
Deri Av RAIN RM13 ....336 A1
Derifall Cl EHAM E6 ....334 A5
Dering Crs LOS SS9 ....307 N8
Derry Av SOCK/AV RM15 ....338 D5
Desford Rd CAN/RD E16 ....333 H4
Dessons Ct SLH/COR SS17 * 341 N1
De Staunton Cl RCOLE CO7 ....154 A7
Detling Cl HCH RM12 ....319 H7
Detling Rd ERITH DA8 ....346 C5
Devalls Cl EHAM E6 ....334 B7
Devas St BOW E3 ....332 E4
Devenay Rd SRTFD E15 ....333 H2
Devenish Rd ABYW SE2 ....335 H9
Devereaux Cl WOTN CO14 ....158 C6
Devereaux Pl COLN CO4 ....127 M4
De Vere Av MAL CM9 ....244 C1
De Vere Cl RCHLM CM5 ....196 E9
  RCOLE CO7 ....153 J6
De Vere Gdns IL IG1 ....316 A3
De Vere La RCOLE CO3 ....153 J6
De Vere Rd COLW CO13 ....151 J1
  RCOLW CO6 ....98 C9
De Veres Rd HSTD CO9 * 97 N7
Devereux Rd BCAYW CM12 ....283 H5
  SOS SS1 ....19 F6
Devereux Wy HAR CO12 ....110 A6
Deverill Cl CHLM/WR CM1 ....218 A1
Deveron Gdns SOCK/AV RM15 ....338 D6
Deveron Wy ROM RM1 ....298 D5
De Vigier Av SAFWN CB10 ....51 P8
Devlin Rd RIPW IP8 ....29 K1
Devon Cl BKHH IG9 ....275 L8
Devon Gdns RCFD SS4 ....308 D2
Devonport Gdns IL IG1 ....316 A1
Devon Rd BARK IG11 ....334 F1
  COS CO15 ....151 L5
  FX IP11 ....35 J6
Devonshire Cl LAIN SS15 ....303 H4
Devonshire Dr BRTR CM7 ....145 J2
  SLH/COR SS17 ....341 H9
  WCHMH N21 ....273 H6
Devonshire Rd BOC CMO 269 H5
  BOC CMO 290 G3
  CAN/RD E16 ....333 L6
  CDW/CHF RM16 ....349 H2
  ED N9 ....273 P7
  GNTH/NBYPK IG2 ....316 D1
  HCH RM12 ....319 J4
  IPSE IP5 ....17 K6
  IPSE IP5 ....25 P5
  LAIN SS15 ....303 H7
  WALTH E17 ....314 D1
Devons Rd BOW E3 ....332 E6
Devon Wy COS CO15 ....182 F6
Dewar La KESG IP5 ....27 H4
Dewberry Cl COLN CO4 ....128 E8
Dewberry Gdns EHAM E6 ....333 P5
Dewberry St POP/IOD E14 ....332 F5
Dewes Green Rd BSF CM23 ....87 N7
Dewgrass Gv CHES/WCR EN8 ....252 A5
Dewhurst Rd CHES/WCR EN8 ....229 P8
Dewlands BRTR CM7 ....145 L9
  GHSM 2 E3
Dewsbury Gdns HARH RM3 ....299 J3
Dewsbury Rd HARH RM3 ....299 J3
Dewsgreen VGE SS16 ....324 D2
Dewyk Rd CVI SS8 ....326 F9
Dexter Cl GRAYS RM17 ....349 K1
Deynencourt Gdns WAN E11 ....295 M8
Deynes Rd SAFWS CB11 ....90 E1
Dhobi Pl IP IP1 ....16 E4
Dial La IP IP1 ....16 E4
Dial Rd RCOLE CO7 ....180 B2
Diamond Cl BCTR RM8 ....317 K3
  CDW/CHF RM16 ....349 J1
  IP IP1
Diana Cl CDW/CHF RM16 ....349 J1
  SWFD E18 ....295 L5
Diana Rd WALTH E17 ....294 C7
Diban Av HCH RM12 ....319 J6
Dibden Cl RCHLM CM3 ....194 D9
Dicken's Av DART DA1 ....347 M9
  TIL RM18
Dickens Cl CHESW EN7 ....229 M6
Dickens Ct BRTR CM7 ....145 K6
  ERITH DA8 ....346 A5
  SOSN SS2 ....329 J4
Dickens Dr LAIN SS15 ....303 K8
Dickenson Cl ED N9 ....273 M7
Dickens Rd EHAM E6 ....333 M1
Dickens Pl CHLM/WR CM1 ....217 L4
Dickens Ri CHIG IG7 ....276 B9
Dickens St CHTY IP2 ....24 F5
Dickens Wy ROM RM1 ....298 D8
Dickins Cl CHESW EN7 ....229 M6

Dickinson Ter KESG IP5 ....27 J4
Dickson CHESW EN7 ....229 L6
Dicky Moors RCHLM CM3 ....193 N5
Didsbury Ct CVI IP2 ....284 A6
  EHAM E6 ....334 A1
Digby Cl KESG IP5 ....27 M5
Digby Gdns DAGE RM10 ....335 P1
Digby Rd BARK IG11 ....316 C9
  HOM E9 ....314 A8
  IPNE IP4 ....25 M9
  SLH/COR SS17 ....324 A9
Dig Dag Hl CHESW EN7 ....229 L6
Diggon St WCHPL E1 ....332 A5
Dilbridge Rd East COLN CO4 ....9 J3
Dilbridge Rd West COLN CO4 ....9 H3
Dillwyn St IP IP1 ....16 A4
Dillwyn St West IP IP1 ....16 A4
Dilston RCHLM CM3 ....242 D4
Dimond Cl FSTGT E7 ....315 K6
Dimsdale Crs BSF CM23 ....137 N9
Dimsdale Dr EN EN1 ....273 M6
Dimson Crs BOW E3 ....332 D4
Dinant Av CVI SS8 ....326 B9
Dinant Link Rd HOD EN11 ....208 D4
Dinants Crs RCOLW CO6 ....149 K3
Dingle Gdns POP/IOD E14 * 332 E7
Dinsdale Cl COLN CO4 ....9 K4
Dirleton Rd SRTFD E15 ....333 J1
Dison Cl PEND EN3 ....252 A9
Disraeli Cl THMD SE28 ....335 J8
Disraeli Rd FSTGT E7 ....315 K8
  RAYL SS6 ....307 L7
Distillery La COLS CO2 ....152 E2
Ditchburn Pl POP/IOD E14 ....332 F7
Ditchfield Rd HOD EN11 ....208 D5
Ditchingham Cl IPNE IP4 ....26 D5
Ditton Court Rd WOS/PRIT SS0 ....328 E6
Dixon Av CDW/CHF RM16 ....217 N7
  RCOS CO16 ....180 G2
Dixon Cl EHAM E6 ....334 A6
  MGTR CO11 ....106 A4
Dixons Cl WARE SG12 ....184 B4
Dixon Wy RCOLE CO7 ....153 H3
Dobbies La RCOLW CO6 ....149 L3
Dobbs Dreft KESG IP5 ....27 L4
Dobbs Rd KIR/NAC IP10 ....27 K6
Dobb's Weir Rd HOD EN11 ....208 G6
Dobsons Cl RAYL SS6 ....307 H6
Dock Approach Rd
  CDW/CHF RM16 ....340 A8
  GRAYS RM17 ....349 P3
Dock Basin FX IP11 ....111 K2
Dockfield Av HAR CO12 ....110 A5
Dock Hill Av
  BERM/RHTH SE16 ....332 A9
Docklands Av ING CM4 ....260 D5
Dockland St CAN/RD E16 ....333 P5
Dock La HAR CO12 ....134 B5
Dock Rd CAN/RD E16 ....333 K8
  GRAYS RM17 ....349 N4
  RCHLM CM5 ....246 A9
Dockside Rd CAN/RD E16 ....333 N7
The Docks FX IP11 ....111 K2
Dock St CHTY IP2 ....16 E7
Dockwra La RCHLM CM5 ....242 C5
Doctor's La SUD CO10 ....43 J3
Doctor Watson's La KESG IP5 ....26 C1
Docwra Rd K/T/MI CO5 ....173 H5
Docwra Rd K/T/MI CO5 ....173 H5
Doddemill Cl SAFWN CB10 ....51 M7
Doddinghurst Rd
  BRWN CM15 ....280 F6
Dodsley Pl ED N9 ....273 P9
Dodson's KESG IP5 ....27 H4
Doe St POP/IOD E14 ....332 D6
Doesgate La UPMR RM14 ....332 C4
Doeshill Dr WICKW SS12 ....285 K9
Dogden La BSF CM23 ....113 K5
Doggetts Cl RCFD SS4 ....308 C4
Doggetts Ct RCFD SS4 ....308 G4
Doggetts La RCOLW CO6 ....149 L4
Doghouse Rd BRTR CM77 ....146 F1
Dog Kennel La ING CM4 ....260 C2
Dogs Head St IPNE IP4 ....16 E5
Doherty Rd PLSTW E13 ....333 K4
Dolby Ri CHLM/GWD CM2 ....218 E9
Dollant Av CVI SS8 ....344 D2
Dolphin Ap ROM RM1 ....298 E8
Dolphin Cl CBE/LIN CB1 ....38 C1
Dolphin Gdns BCAYW CM12 ....282 G5
Dolphin La POP/IOD E14 ....332 E7
Dolphin Wy WOS/PRIT SS0 ....328 E1
Dolphin Wy BSF CM23 ....137 M6
Dolphin Yd WARE SG12 ....184 A3
Domanco Ldg LOS SS9 * 327 L5
Dombey Cl CHLM/WR CM1 ....217 N4
Dombey Rd CHTY IP2 ....24 F6
Dominica Cl PLSTW E13 ....333 N3
Dominic Cl WAB EN9 ....252 E5
Dominion Dr CRW RM5 ....298 A5
Dominion Wy HARH RM3 ....336 B1
Domitian Cl COLN CO4 ....128 C2
Domsey Bank RCOLW CO6 ....149 K3
Domsey Cha BCAYE CM11 ....148 G9
Domsey La RCHLM CM3 ....194 D9
Domsey La RCHLM CM3 ....195 M2
Donald Dr CHDH RM6 ....317 L1
Donald Thorn Cl
  WICKW SS12 ....305 J1
Donald Wy CHLM/GWD CM2 ....240 D8
Donard Dr RCOLW CO6 ....126 G5
Doncaster Wy UPMR RM14 ....319 N5
Dondi Ct CHLM/CHF RM16 ....348 F2
Don Ct WIT CM8 ....196 G2
Donegal Rd IP IP1 ....16 A2
Dongola Rd PLSTW E13 ....333 L3
Dongola Rd West PLSTW E13 ....333 L3

Donington Av BARK/HLT IG6 ....296 D5
Donkey La EN EN1 ....273 M1
Donne Dr COS CO15 ....206 F4
Donnella Cl CDW/CHF RM16 ....348 G1
Donne Rd BCTR RM8 ....317 K4
Donovan's Gn
  RBRW/HUT CM13 ....301 P4
Don Wy ROM RM1 ....298 D4
Donyland Wy K/T/MI CO5 ....152 C7
Dooley Rd FX IP11 ....10 B4
  HSTD CO9 ....57 N7
Dora St POP/IOD E14 ....332 C6
Dorchester Av HOD EN11 ....208 C2
Dorchester Ct
  STHGT/OAK N14 ....272 A6
Dorchester End COLS CO2 ....152 C5
Dorchester Gdns CHING E4 ....294 D1
Dorchester Rd BCAYW CM12 ....283 H5
  IPSE IP5 ....26 C8
Dordells LAIN SS15 ....2 A5
Dore Av MNPK E12 ....316 B7
Dorewards Av BRTR CM7 ....121 J8
Dorian Rd HCH RM12 ....318 F3
Doric Av RCFD SS4 ....308 E2
Doris Av BXLYHN DA7 ....346 B6
Dorking Crs RCOS CO16 ....181 M7
Dorking Ri HARH RM5 ....299 J1
Dorking Rd HARH RM5 ....299 J1
Dorking Wk HARH RM5 ....299 J1
Dorkins Wy UPMR RM14 ....320 B2
Dormer Rd ED N9 ....273 M8
Dormer St SRTFD E15 ....315 J8
Dorothy Curtice Ct
  RCOLW CO6 ....150 B1
Dorothy Evans Cl
  BXLYHN DA7 ....346 A9
Dorothy Farm Rd RAYL SS6 ....317 K6
Dorothy Gdns BCTR RM8 ....317 J2
  SBF/HAD SS7 ....326 C1
Dorothy Sayers Dr WIT CM8 ....178 N8
Dorrington Gdns HCH RM12 ....319 J3
Dorset Av CHLM/GWD CM2 ....240 D4
  ROM RM1 ....298 C7
Dorset Cl CHLM/GWD CM2 ....240 D4
  COS CO15 ....182 F7
  IPNE IP4 ....25 N2
Dorset Gdns RCFD SS4 ....308 D2
Dorset Pl SRTFD E15 ....314 C8
Dorset Rd BOC CMO 291 H4
  FSTGT E7 ....315 M9
  MAL CM9 ....244 A1
Dorset Wy BCAYW CM12 ....283 H5
Dorvis La SAFWN CB10 ....52 C1
Doubleday Dr MAL CM9 ....222 A6
Doubleday Gdns BRTR CM7 ....145 L1
Doublegate La WICKW SS12 ....305 N3
Doublet Ms BCAYE CM11 ....283 L3
Douglas Av HARH RM3 ....299 K6
  WALTH E17 ....294 D5
Douglas Cl CDW/CHF RM16 ....349 H1
  CHLM/GWD CM2 ....240 C7
Douglas Gv WIT CM8 ....196 G2
Douglas Rd CAN/RD E16 ....333 K5
  CHING E4 ....275 H6
  COS CO15 ....6 A2
  GDMY/SEVK IG3 ....317 H2
  HAR CO12 ....14 A6
  ROM RM1 ....318 E1
  SBF/HAD SS7 ....327 J5
Douglas Wk CHLM/GWD CM2 ....239 P2
Doug Siddons Ct
  GRAYS RM17 ....349 M4
Doulton Cl HLWE CM17 ....211 M4
Doulton Wy RCFD SS4 ....308 D1
Douro St BOW E3 ....332 D2
Dove Ap EHAM E6 ....333 P5
Dove Cl BSF CM23 ....162 B2
  CDW/CHF RM16 ....349 H1
  STSD CM24 ....114 B8
Dovecote SBN/FI SS3 ....330 D5
Dovedale Cl BCAYE CM11 ....284 B4
  VGE SS16
Dovedale Gdns COS CO15 ....182 D7
Dovedon Cl STHGT/OAK N14 ....272 D8
Dove Dr SBF/HAD SS7 ....325 N4
Doves Ms LAIN SS15 * 17 H4
Dove St IPNE IP4
Dowches Dr RCVI SS8 ....326 F9
Dowches Gdns K/T/MI CO5 ....173 H2
Dowd Cl BOC CMO 269 H5
Dowding Cl HCH RM12 ....319 H3
Dowland Cl K/T/MI CO5 ....341 K2
Dowling Rd BURES CO8 ....100 E5
Downbank Av BXLYHN DA7 ....346 C6
Downer Rd North
  SBF/HAD SS7 ....326 A2
Downes Ct WCHMH N21 ....272 F7
Downesway SBF/HAD SS7 ....326 A3

E

Edgefield Av BARK IG11 ....316 G9
  MGTR CO11 ....106 A5
Edgehill Gdns DAGE RM10 ......317 P6
Edgeworth Rd CHTY IP2 ....24 F9
Edgware Rd RCOLW CO6 ....181 N8
Edies La RCOLW CO6 ....77 K4
Edinburgh Av LOS SS9 ....327 L4
  SLH/COR SS17 ....341 N1
  WIT CM8 ....197 K4
Edinburgh Dr
  CHES/WCR EN8 ....252 B5
Edinburgh Gdns BRTR CM7 ...145 L2
  NHMKT IP6 ....22 D3
Edinburgh Ms TIL RM18 ....350 C7
Edinburgh PI HLW CM20 ....187 H8
Edinburgh Rd PLSTW E13 .....333 L2
  WALTH E17 ....294 D9
Edinburgh's Dr
  ROMW/RG RM7 ....298 B9
Edinburgh Wy HLW CM20 .....13 H1
  PIT SS13 ....304 G9
Edington Rd PEND EN3 ....273 P1
Edison Av HCH RM12 ....318 E3
  HCH RM12 ....145 J5
Edison Cl BRTR CM7 ....145 J5
  HCH RM12 ....318 E3
Edison Gdns COLN CO4 ....128 F6
Edison Rd COS CO15 ....182 F7
  PEND EN3 ....274 C1
Edith Cavell Wy HVHL CB9 ......55 L4
Edith Cl CVI SS8 ....344 B2
Edith Rd CHDH RM6 ....317 L2
  COS CO15 ....66 E6
  CVI SS8 ....344 A2
  EHAM E6 ....315 N9
  FOS CO13 ....158 E6
  SOSN SS2 ....328 C4
  SRTFD E15 ....314 D7
Edith Wy SLH/COR SS17 ....325 P9
Edison Cl WALTH E17 ....294 D9
Edmeston Cl HOM E9 ....314 B8
Edmonton Cl KESG IP5 ....26 F4
Edmonton Rd KESG IP5 ....26 F5
Edmund Cl HVHL CB9 ....41 J4
Edmund Gn HSTD CO9 ....97 H8
Edmund Halley Wy
  GWKCH SE10 ....
Edmund Hurst Dr EHAM E6 ....334 C5
Edmund Rd CDW/CHF RM16 ..338 C9
  RAIN RM13 ....336 D3
  WIT CM8 ....197 H4
Edridge Cl HCH RM12 ....319 J7
Edward Av CHING E4 ....274 C9
  RCOLE CO7 ....179 L6
Edward Bright Cl MAL CM9 * ..222 B9
Edward Cl BCAYW CM12 ....282 C3
  CDW/CHF RM16 ....338 C9
  ED N9 ....273 H4
  GPK RM2 ....299 H7
  IP IP1 ....24 C3
  RCFD SS4 ....308 D1
  RCOS CO15 ....157 H9
Edward Ct CAN/RD E16 ....333 K5
  WAB EN9 ....253 J5
Edward Dr CHLM/GWD CM2 ...240 B3
Edward Gdns WICKE SS11 ......285 J8
Edward Mann Cl East
  WCHPL E1 * 332 A6
Edward Mann Cl West
  K/T/MI CO5 ....177 J2
Edward Marke Dr
  K/T/MI CO5 ....177 J2
Edward Rd CHDH RM6 ....317 M1
  RCOS CO15 ....157 J7
  WALTH E17 ....294 A8
Edwards Cl
  RBRW/HUT CM13 ....281 P5
Edward St CAN/RD E16 ....333 K4
  HAR CO12 ....109 P5
Edwards Wy
  RBRW/HUT CM13 ....281 P5
Edward Temme Av
  SRTFD E15 ....315 J9
Edwina Gdns REDBR IG4 ....295 P9
Edwin Av EHAM E6 ....334 B2
Edwin Cl RAIN RM13 ....336 E3
Edwin's Hall Rd RCHLM CM3 ..264 F6
Edwin's Hall Vw RCHLM CM3 ..264 F6
Edwin Rd WAN E11 ....314 B6
Edwin St CAN/RD E16 ....333 K5
Egbert Gdns WICKE SS11 ....285 J7
Egerton Dr VGE SS16 ....322 F1
Egerton Gdns
  GDMY/SEVK IG3 ....316 G5
Egerton Green Rd COLS CO2 ..151 K3
Egg Hall EPP CM16 ....253 H8
Egglescote Cl CHTY IP2 ....29 P1
Eggshell La HSTD CO9 ....55 P7
Egham Rd PLSTW E13 ....333 L5
Eglantine Wy RCOLW CO6 ....77 J4
Eglington Rd CHING E4 ....274 D6
Eglinton Dr CHLM/GWD CM2 ..218 G7
Egremont Wy COLW CO3 ....150 F2
Egret Crs COLN CO4 ....129 H7
Ehringshausen Wy HVHL CB9 ..41 K4
Eider Cl FSTGT E7 ....315 J7
Eight Acre La COLS CO2 ....151 M4
Eighth Av MNPK E12 ....316 A6
Eisenhower Dr EHAM E6 ....333 P5
Eisenhower Rd LAIN SS15 ....303 H9
Elan Rd SOCK/AV RM15 ....338 C6
Elbury Dr CAN/RD E16 ....333 K6
Eldbert Cl SOSN SS2 ....329 M4
Eldeland LAIN SS15 ....2 A2
Elder Av WICKW SS12 ....304 C1
Elderberry Cl CHESW EN7 ....252 C1
Elderberry Ct VGE SS16 ....323 J1
  WFD IG8 ....296 C4
Elderberry Gdns WIT CM8 ......172 A9
Elderberry Wy EHAM E6 ....334 A3
Elder Rd BRTR CM7 ....144 E9
Elderfield HLWE CM17 ....187 L8
Elderfield Rd CLPT E5 ....314 A6
Elderfield Wk WAN E11 ....295 L9

Elderflower Wy SRTFD E15 .....315 H9
Elder Rd WARE SG12 ....184 C1
Elderstea Av CVI SS8 ....345 H2
Elderton Rd WOS/PRIT SS0 .....328 E6
Elder Wy RAIN RM13 ....337 J5
  WICKW SS12 ....305 H1
Eld La COL CO1 ....8 C6
Eldon Cl COLN CO4 ....128 F6
Eldon Rd HOD EN11 ....273 P7
  HOD EN11 ....208 C7
  WALTH E17 ....294 C8
Eldon Wy HOC/HUL SS5 ....307 N1
Eldred Av COLS CO2 ....151 L3
Eldred Dr SUD CO10 ....61 M6
Eleanor Cha WICKW SS12 ......285 H9
Eleanor Cl K/T/MI CO5 ....174 A7
Eleanor Cross Rd
  CHES/WCR EN8 ....252 B4
Eleanor Gdns BRTR RM8 ....317 N4
Eleanor Rd CHES/WCR EN8 ....252 B3
  SRTFD E15 ....315 J8
Eleanor St BOW E3 ....332 D5
Eleanor Wy BCW CM14 ....500 G2
  CHES/WCR EN8 ....252 C6
Electric Av PEND EN3 ....252 C6
  WOS/PRIT SS0 ....328 D4
Eleven Acre Ri LOU IG10 ....276 A2
Eleventh Av STSD CM24 ....138 E4
Eley Rd UED N18 ....294 A2
Elgar Cl BKHH IG9 ....275 N8
  LAIN SS15 ....303 L7
  PLSTW E13 ....333 M7
Elgar Wy SOSN SS2 ....305 N9
Elgar Dr WIT CM8 ....197 J4
Elgar Gdns TIL RM18 ....350 B6
Elgar St BERM/RHTH SE16 .....332 B9
Elgin Av CHLM/WR CM1 ....4 D5
  HARH IM3 ....299 N4
Elgin Rd BRCX EN10 ....230 C5
  CHES/WCR EN8 ....230 D5
  GDMY/SEVK IG3 ....316 F3
Elham Dr PIT SS13 ....325 H1
Elianore Rd COLW CO3 ....127 L8
Eliot Wy PLSTW E13 ....333 J5
Eliot Rd DAGW RM9 ....317 L6
Eliot Wy MAL CM9 ....244 B1
Elizabeth Av ENC/FH EN2 ....272 C2
  IL IG1 ....316 E4
  RAYL SS6 ....306 F7
  WIT CM8 ....197 K5
Elizabeth Cl COLN CO4 ....128 D3
  HOC/HUL SS5 ....307 P3
  ROMW/RG RM7 ....298 A5
  SAFWN CB10 ....51 N8
  TIL RM18 ....350 C7
  WAB EN9 ....230 C2
Elizabeth Dr EPP CM16 ....254 F6
  WICKW SS12 ....284 C8
Elizabeth Ride ED N9 ....273 N6
Elizabeth Rd BRWN CM15 ......280 E5
  BSF CM23 ....137 K9
  CDW/CHF RM16 ....349 J1
  EHAM E6 ....333 N1
  HAR CO12 ....110 C5
  RAIN RM13 ....336 G5
Elizabeth Sq POP/IOD E14 ......332 B7
Elizabeth Vls MAL CM9 * 199 P2
Elizabeth Wy FX IP11 ....10 D4
  HLWW/ROY CM19 ....12 A7
  HSTD CO9 ....97 P6
  LAIN SS15 ....323 L1
  MAL CM9 ....222 B6
  RCHLM CM3 ....196 D8
  RCOLE CO7 ....153 K5
  RCOLE CO7 ....179 L7
  SAFWN CB10 ....51 N8
  SBF/HAD SS7 ....326 F2
  SUD CO10 ....60 F5

  K/T/MI CO5 ....173 P6
  MGTR CO11 ....81 N8
  RAYL SS6 ....306 G4
  RBSF CM22 ....114 F5
  RBSF CM22 ....339 J7
  RCOLE CO7 ....154 A6
  ROMW/RG RM7 ....298 A5
  SBN/FI SS3 ....330 D7
  WAB EN9 ....252 G4
  WAN E11 ....315 L1
Elm Cl HVHL CB9 ....49 L6
  SAFWS SS1 ....49 J6
Elmcroft COT RCOLE CO7 ......154 A6
Elmcroft Av ED N9 ....273 K5
Elmcroft La FX IP11 ....35 M4
Elmcroft Rd IP IP1 ....25 H1
Elmdale Dr MGTR CO11 ....106 C4
Elmden Ct COS CO15 ....181 P6
Elmdene Av WCHMH N21 ......299 L9
Elmdon Rd SOCK/AV RM15 ....338 D5
Elm Dr CHES/WCR EN8 ....230 B7
  HAR CO12 ....14 B7
  HSTD CO9 ....98 A7
  RAYL SS6 ....306 G4
  RCOLE CO7 ....179 J6
Elmer Ap SOS SS1 ....19 F4
Elmer Av ABR/ST RM4 ....278 D9
  SOS SS1 ....19 F4
Elmer Cl ENC/FH EN2 ....272 E2
  RAIN RM15 ....318 F9
Elmer Gdns RAIN RM15 ....318 F9
Elmers La KESG IP5 ....27 J4
Elmfield Ct COS CO15 ....182 F6
Elmfield Rd CHING E4 ....274 F8
  WALTH E17 ....314 A1
Elm Gdns ENC/FH EN2 ....251 J8
  RCOLE CO7 ....234 A5
  FX IP11 ....34 F4
Elm Gn PIT SS13 ....304 F6
Elmgreen Cl SRTFD E15 ....333 H1
Elm Green La RCHLM CM3 .....241 P2
Elm Gv BSF CM23 ....157 N7
  COS CO15 ....206 F2
  COS CO15 ....206 F2
  EMPK RM11 ....319 K1
  ERITH DA8 ....346 C5
  FOS CO13 ....158 D8
  HOC/HUL SS5 ....286 G6
  RCOLE CO7 ....153 J5
  RCOLW CO6 ....77 N8
  SOSN SS2 ....329 P6
Elm Hall Gdns WAN E11 ....315 L1
Elmham Dr KIR/MLC IP10 ......317 P2
Elmhurst Av SBF/HAD SS7 .....325 N2
Elmhurst Cl BSF CM23 ....137 K7
  IP IP1 ....41 L4
Elmhurst Dr EMPK RM11 ....319 H2
  IPSE IP5 ....25 N8
  SWFD E18 ....295 K6
Elmhurst Rd FSTGT E7 ....315 L9
  HAR CO12 ....110 D5
  PEND EN3 ....251 P7
Elmore Rd LOU IG10 ....276 A6
Elm La K/T/MI CO5 ....148 F5
  RIPS/CAP IP9 ....28 C9
  RIPW IP8 ....28 C9
Elmore Rd PEND EN3 ....252 A9
  WAN E11 ....314 F5
Elmores LOU IG10 ....276 B2
Elm Park Av HCH RM12 ....318 C6
Elm Park Rd LEY E10 ....314 B3
  WCHMH N21 ....273 H6
Elm Rd BCW CM14 ....298 A5
  CHLM/GWD CM2 ....4 D7
  CVI SS8 ....344 F2
  ERITH DA8 ....346 F6
  FSTGT E7 ....315 J8
  GRAYS RM17 ....349 M4
  KESG IP5 ....26 E4
  LOS SS9 ....327 P5
  PIT SS13 ....305 K6
  RCHLM CM3 ....196 C8
  RCOLE CO7 ....80 E6
  RCOS CO16 ....181 M2
  ROMW/RG RM7 ....298 A6
  SBF/HAD SS7 ....326 G4
  SBN/FI SS3 ....330 E6
  SOCK/AV RM15 ....338 A6
  SUD CO10 ....21 G6
  WALTH E17 ....294 F9
  WAN E11 ....314 G4
  WICKE SS11 ....285 J4

Elm Wk BRTR CM77 ....144 C4
Elm Wy BRW CM14 ....280 D9
  GPK RM2 ....298 F7
Elmway COW/CHF RM16 ....219 K2
Elmwood SBW CM21 ....187 N3
Elmwood Av COLS CO2 ....151 L4
  HOC/HUL SS5 ....307 P5
Elmwood Dr K/T/MI CO5 ....202 G6
  WAB EN9 ....252 G4
Elounda Ct SBF/HAD SS7 ....326 A2
Elphinstone Rd WALTH E17 ....294 C6
Elrick Cl ERITH DA8 ....346 D4
Elrington Rd WFD IG8 ....295 K2
Elronds Rest RCHLM CM3 ....286 F2
Elsa St WCHPL E1 * 332 B5
Elsdene Rd N9 ....269 J5
Elsenham Ct RAYL SS6 ....306 E4
Elsenham Crs BSDN SS14 ....304 E9
Elsenham Ms BSDN SS14 ....304 E9
Elsenham Rd MNPK E12 ....316 A7
Elsham Dr BRTR CM77 ....144 E8
Elsham Rd WAN E11 ....315 H5
Elsiedene Rd WCHMH N21 .....273 H6
Elsinge Rd EN EN1 ....251 N6
Elsinor Av CVI SS8 ....344 E9
Elsmere Rd IP IP1 ....25 K3
Elstow Gdns DAGW RM9 ....335M1
Elstow Rd DAGW RM9 ....317 M9
Elstree Gdns ED N9 ....273 N7
  IL IG1 ....316 D7
Elthorne Pk RCOS CO16 ....316 C6
Eltisley Rd IL IG1 ....316 C6
Elton Pk CHTY IP2 ....24 E5
Elverston Cl LAIN SS15 ....303 L7
Elvet Av EMPK RM11 ....299 H8
Elves Cl COLN CO4 ....128 E6
Elwick Rd K/T/MI CO5 ....338 F6
Elwin Rd K/T/MI CO5 ....174 A8
Elwood HLWE CM17 ....211M4
Ely Cl BOC CM0 ....229 N9
  ERITH DA8 ....346 E7
  RAYL SS6 ....306 F3
Ely Gdns DAGE RM10 ....318 B5
Ely Pl WFD IG8 ....296 B2
Ely Rd DIPNE E4 ....25 N2
  K/T/MI CO5 ....314 F1
  LEY E10 ....295 J8
  NHMKT IP6 ....22 D3
  SOSN SS2 ....329 J4
Elysian Gdns MAL CM9 ....225 H2
Ely Wy RAYL SS6 ....306 F3
Emanuel Rd VGE SS16 ....323 J2
Emberson Ct
  CHLM/GWD CM2 ....218 E7
Emberson Vw EPP CM16 ....234 A5
Emblems CTDUN CM6 ....141 K4
Emerald Cl CAN/RD E16 ....333 M7
  KESG IP5 ....27 H5
Emerald Gdns BCTR RM8 ....317 P2
Emerson Dr EMPK RM11 ....319 J2
Emerson Rd IL IG1 ....316 B2
Emes Rd ERITH DA8 ....346 B5
Emilia Cl PEND EN3 ....273 N4
Emily St CAN/RD E16 ....333 J6
Emlen St IP IP1 ....16 A4
Emmanuel Cl CHTY IP2 ....24 C9
Emma Rd PLSTW E13 ....333 J2
Emma's Crs WARE SG12 ....184 E8
Emmaus Wy CHIG IG7 ....296 B2
Emmott Av BARK/HLT IG6 .....296 D9
Emmott Cl WCHPL E1 ....332 B4
Empire Rd HAR CO12 ....14 E6
Empress Av CHING E4 ....295 J4
  IL IG1 ....316 A2
  MNPK E12 ....315 M4
  WFD IG8 ....295 J4
Empress Dr K/T/MI CO5 ....202 G6
Empress Pde CHING E4 * 295 J4
Empson St BOW E3 ....332 E4
Emson's Cl CBE/LIN CB1 ....38 C1
Emsworth Cl ED N9 ....273 P7
Emsworth Rd BARK/HLT IG6 ...296 D9
Enborne Gn SOCK/AV RM15 ...338 D5
Endean Cl RCOLE CO7 ....153 H4
Endeavour Cl BSDN SS14 ....304 A9
Endeavour Rd
  CHES/WCR EN8 ....230 B6
Endeavour Wy BARK IG11 ......335 H2
Endleburg Rd CHING E4 ....274 E8
Endsleigh Ct COLW CO3 ....127 M8
Endsleigh Gdns IL IG1 ....316 A3
Endway SBF/HAD SS7 ....327 H4
The Endway CTDUN CM6 ....116 C8
  HVHL CB9 ....55 M2
  RCHLM CM3 ....268 C7
Enfield Rd EBAR EN4 ....249 N1
  SEVK IP5 ....285 P9
Endsdale Rd WALTH E17 ....294 C8
Endsdale Av FX IP11 ....285 P9
Engayne Gdns UPMR RM14 ....319 N3
Englands La LOU IG10 ....276 D1
Englefield Cl ENC/FH EN2 ......272 F1
  HOC/HUL SS5 ....308 B3
Englefields BOC CM0 ....248 B7
England Side HAR CO12 ....14 E8
Enid Wy COLN CO4 ....127 N5
Ennerdale Av BRTR CM77 ......318 F7
  HCH RM12 ....318 F7
Ennerdale Cl FX IP11 ....35 N4
Ennismore Gdns SOSN SS2 .....329 H9
Ensign Cl LOS SS9 ....328 B5
Ensign Dr PLMGR N13 ....273 H9
Enstone Rd PEND EN3 ....274 B2
Enterprise Cl CHLM/GWD CM2 .145 L4
  WIT CM8 ....197 H4
Enterprise Wy WICKW SS12 ...305 L1
Enville Wy CVI SS8 ....344 C2
Epping Cl CHLM/WR CM1 ....4 A6
  RCOS CO15 ....182 A5
  LOS SS9 ....307 P8
  ROMW/RG RM7 ....297 P6
Epping Gld CHING E4 ....274 G7
Epping La ABR/ST RM4 ....277 J1
Epping New Rd BKHH IG9 ......275 L7

  LOU IG10 ....253 N8
Epping Rd CHONG CM5 ....234 E5
  EPP CM16 ....252 C5
  EPP CM16 ....233 L7
  EPP CM16 ....234 B9
  HLWW/ROY CM19 ....209 L4
  LOU IG10 ....254 A5
Epping Wy CHING E4 ....274 E5
  WAN E11 ....197 H4
Epsom Cl BXLYHN DA7 ....346 A4
  RCOS CO16 ....181 M7
Epsom Dr IP IP1 ....23 J8
Epsom Rd GDMY/SEVK IG3 ....316 C1
  LEY E10 ....314 F1
Epsom Wy HCH RM12 ....319 L6
Epstein Rd THMD SE28 ....335 N5
Erbury Pl SUD CO10 ....44 A3
Erica Wk COLN CO4 ....128 E8
Eric Clarke La BARK IG11 ....334 C4
Eric Est BOW E3 ....332 C4
Eric Rd CHLM/WR CM1 ....218 A4
Eric Rd CHDH RM6 ....317 L2
  FSTGT E7 ....315 K6
  PIT SS13 ....305 L9
Eric St BOW E3 ....332 C4
Eridge Cl CHLM/WR CM1 ....218 C4
Eriswell Rd HVHL CB9 ....41 L5
Erith Crs CHDH RM6 ....317 M4
Erith Crs CRW RM5 ....298 B5
Erith Rigth St ERITH DA8 ....346 E4
Erith Rd BELV DA17 ....346 A3
  BXLYHN DA7 ....346 A8
Erle Havard Rd RCOLW CO6 ...127 H3
Ermine Cl CHESW EN7 ....251 N1
Ermine Side EN EN1 ....273M4
Ernald Av EHAM E6 ....333 P2
Ernan Cl SOCK/AV RM15 ....338 D5
Ernan Rd SOCK/AV RM15 ....338 D5
Ernest Rd EMPK RM11 ....319 K1
  RCOLE CO7 ....153 K5
Ernest St WCHPL E1 * 332 A4
Erneigh Rd IPNE IP4 ....26 A5
Errington Cl CHLM/WR CM1 ...350 D5
Errington Rd COLW CO3 ....151 N1
Erroll Rd ROM RM1 ....298 E8
Erskine PI WICKW SS12 ....305 J1
Erskine Rd WALTH E17 ....294 C8
Ernest St WCHPL E1 * 294 A4
Erwarton Wk RIPS/CAP IP9 ......85 H6
Esdaile Gdns UPMR RM14 ......320 A2
Esdaile La HOD EN11 ....208 D2
Esher Av ROMW/RG RM7 ....298 E8
Esher Rd GDMY/SEVK IG3 .....316 G1
Eskley Gdns SOCK/AV RM15 ...338 E5
Esk Rd PLSTW E13 ....333 L4
Esmond Rd WAN RM13 * 298 E4
Esmond St PUT ....
Esplanade FOS CO13 ....318 O9
Esplanade Gdns
  WOS/PRIT SS0 ....328 C6
The Esplanade COS CO15 ....183 H7
  HOC/HUL SS5 ....286 F5
  COS CO15 ....245M9
Essex Av CHLM/WR CM1 ....217 P4
  COS CO15 ....47 J9
  SUD CO10 ....47 J9
Essex Cl CVI SS8 ....344 D5
  LAIN SS15 ....303 J6
  RAYL SS6 ....307 J6
  ROMW/RG RM7 ....298 B8
  WALTH E17 ....294 B8
Essex Gdns EMPK RM11 ....299M9
  LOS SS9 ....327 P2
  SLH/COR SS17 ....341 H9
Essex Hl SAFWS CB11 ....49 K7
Essex Rd COL CO1 ....8 A1
Essex Regiment Wy
  RCHLM CM3 ....193 P2
Essex Rd BARK IG11 ....316 D9
  BOC CM0 ....291 H3
  BRTR CM7 ....145 L2
  CHDH RM6 ....317 K3
  CVI SS8 ....275 H7
  DAGE RM10 ....318 D7
  ENC/FH EN2 ....275 J5
  HOD EN11 ....208 E4
  MAL CM9 ....244 A1
  MNPK E12 ....315 P7
  ROMW/RG RM7 ....315 P7
  SWFD E18 ....295 L6
  WALTH E17 ....314 A1
  WTHK RM20 ....348 D4
Essex Rd South LEY E10 ....314 G2
Essex St FSTGT E7 ....315 J3
  SOSN SS2 ....19 G3
Essex Wy BRTR CM77 ....146 B9
  CHLM/WR CM1 ....191 N3
  CHONG CM5 ....215 H8
  COLN CO4 ....128 C6
  EPP CM16 ....234 B8
  HAR CO12 ....255 H2
  IPSE IP5 ....109 H6
  MGTR CO11 ....31 L1
  RBRW/HUT CM13 ....300 F3
  RCHLM CM3 ....192 C1
  RCOLW CO6 ....124 G8
  STSD CM24 ....326 B5
  WIT CM8 ....171 H5
Essex Whf CLPT E5 * 314 A4
Essex Yeomanry Wy
  COLW CO3 ....126 E8
Essian St WCHPL E1 ....332 B5
Estate Rd SBF/HAD SS7 ....327 J3
Estate Wy LEY E10 ....314 F7
The Estate Yd RCHLM CM3 .....195 P2
Estella Md CHLM/WR CM1 .....217 M4
Estfeld Cl HOD EN11 * 208 E2
Esther Rd WAN E11 ....315 H2
Estuary Cl BARK IG11 ....335 H1
  COLN CO4 ....127 P5
Estuary Ct MAL CM9 * 225 J1

F

Ferrymead CVI SS8 — 326 C9
Ferry Rd BOC CM0 — 290 D4
FX IP11 — 351A4
HOC/HUL SS5 — 286 C6
K/T/MI CO5 — 153 J8
RCHLM CM3 — 288 B1
SBF/HAD SS7 — 326 A6
TIL RM18 — 350 B7
Feryby Rd CDW/CHF RM16 — 350 C1
Fesants Cft HLW CM20 — 187 J9
Festival CI ERITH DA8 — 346 E5
Festival Gdns MAL CM9 — 200 C8
Festival Link BSDN SS14 — 304 A5
Festival Wy BSDN SS14 — 304 A5
Festoon Wy LAIN SS15 — 313 N7
Fetherston Rd SLH/COR SS17 — 341 L3
Feverills Rd RCOS CO16 — 181 M1
Flat Av COS CO15 — 206 C6
Fiddlers CI GRH DA9 — 348 E9
Fiddlers Folly COLW CO3 — 126 B6
Fiddlers HI COLW CO3 — 126 B5
Fiddlers La RCOLE CO7 — 80 F6
Field CI ABR/ST RM4 — 277 J2
BKHH IG9 — 255M9
CHING E4 — 294 E5
The Fielders CVI SS8 — 344 C3
Fieldfare BCAYW CM12 — 283 K8
Fieldfare Rd THMD SE28 — 335 K7
Field Fuller's NHMKT IP6 — 25M7
Field Gdns CHONG CM5 — 257 K4
Field Gate La RBSF CM22 — 114 D3
Fieldhouse CI SWFD E18 — 295 L5
Fielding Av TIL RM18 — 350 C6
Fieldings Rd CHES/WCR EN8 — 250 C8
Fielding Wy RBRW/HUT SS13 — 281M5
Field Rd FSTGT E7 — 315 K6
SOCK/AV RM15 — 337 P8
Fields CI RCOS CO16 — 156 C7
Fields Farm Rd COLS CO2 — 176 C1
Fieldside SAFWS CB11 * — 65M2
Fields Park Crs CHDH RM6 — 297 L9
Fields Vw SUD CO10 — 21 F3
Field Vw KIR/NAC IP10 — 32 D2
Fieldview CI COLN CO4 — 128 A5
Field View Mr MAL CM9 — 199 K7
Field Wy HOD EN11 — 208 E1
RCOLE CO7 — 153 K4
Fieldway BCTR RM8 — 317 J6
CDW/CHF RM16 — 350 E2
PIT SS13 — 324 G2
WARE SG12 — 184 E8
WICKW SS12 — 305 J4
Fiennes CI BCTR RM8 — 317 K3
Fiesta Dr DAGW RM9 — 336 E4
Fife Rd CAN/RD E16 — 333 K5
IPNE IP4 — 26 A2
Fifth Av CHLM/WR CM1 — 218 A5
CVI SS8 — 344 B1
FOS CO13 — 158 B4
HLW CM20 — 13 H2
HSTD CO9 — 98 C7
MNPK E12 — 316 A6
WICKE SS11 — 305M1
WTHK RM20 — 348 D4
Fifth Avenue Allende Av
HLW CM20 — 13 H2
Filey Rd BOC CM0 — 268 F7
Fillebrook Av EN EN1 — 273 K1
LOS SS9 — 328 B4
Fillebrook Rd WAN E11 — 314 C8
Finbars Wk IPNE IP4 — 27 K5
Finborough CI KESC IP5 — 26 E5
Fincham's CI CBE/LIN CB1 — 38 C1
Finchdale COS CO15 — 182 A1
Finch Dr BRTR CM7 — 144 D1
RCOLE CO7 — 155 J5
Finches La SLH/COR SS17 — 324 B9
The Finches SBF/HAD SS7 — 306 D8
Finches Rd RAVL SS6 — 306 C6
Finch Gdns CHING E4 — 294 D2
Finch HI SUD CO10 — 30 D3
Finchingfield Av WFD IG8 — 295M4
Finchingfield Rd HSTD CO9 — 70 C3
HVHL CB9 — 55M4
The Finchingfields
BRWN CM15 — 258 B7
Finchingfield Wy COLS CO2 — 152 B6
WICKW SS12 * — 305 H2
Finchland Vw RCHLM CM3 — 286 C2
Finchley Av CHLM/GWD CM2 — 239 P2
Finchley Rd GRAYS RM17 — 349 L4
IPNE IP4 — 17 H3
WOS/PRIT SS0 — 328 D6
Finchmoor HLWS CM18 — 210 E6
Finch's WIT CM8 — 198 A6
Finden Rd FSTGT E7 — 315 N1
Findhorn St POP/IOD E14 — 332 F6
Findley CI RIPS/CAP IP9 — 82 C7
Findon Gdns RAIN RM13 — 336 F5
Findon Rd BOC CM0 — 273 N7
Finer CI RCOS CO16 — 181M8
Fingringhoe Rd K/T/MI CO5 — 177 J2
Fingrith Hall La ING CM4 — 237 H6
Finham CI COLN CO4 — 128 C8
Finney's Drift KIR/NAC IP10 — 32 A5
Finnymore Rd DAGW RM9 — 317 K9
Finsbury Pl HSTD CO9 * — 98 A6
Finucane Gdns RAIN RM13 — 318 F6
Fiona CI ENC/FH EN2 * — 272 C2
Firbank CI CAN/RD E16 — 333 N5
ENC/FH EN2 — 273 H3
Firbank Rd CRW RM5 — 275 J5
Fir Ct LAIN SS15 — 305 K6
Fircroft Rd IP IP1 — 25 H1
Firebronds Rd RIPS/CAP IP9 — 83 L4
Firecrest Rd CHLM/GWD CM2 — 240 B5
Firfield Gdns EHAM E6 — 333 J1
Firefly Wy IPSE IP5 — 31 H1
Firfield Rd SBF/HAD SS7 — 306 F9
Firham Park Av HARH RM3 — 299M4
Firlands BSF CM23 — 137 K8
The Firle SS16 — 323 K3
Firle Wk COLS CO2 — 152 B4
Firmans VGE SS16 — 323 J5

Firmins Ct RCOLW CO6 — 126 C3
Fir Pk HLWW/ROY CM19 — 210 C6
Firs Cha K/T/MI CO5 — 202 D6
Firscroft PLMGR N13 — 273 K9
Firs Dr CHLM/WR CM1 — 239 J1
LOU IG10 — 254 B9
Firsgrove Crs BRW CM14 — 300 E1
Firs Hamlet K/T/MI CO5 — 202 D6
Firs La WCHMH N21 — 273 H6
Firs Park Av WCHMH N21 — 273 H7
Firs Park Gdns WCHMH N21 — 273 J7
Firs Rd K/T/MI CO5 — 174 A9
K/T/MI CO5 — 202 E6
First Av BCAYW CM12 — 282 F9
BRWN CM15 — 258 F4
CHDH RM6 — 297 K9
CHLM/WR CM1 — 218 A6
COS CO15 — 182 C9
CVI SS8 — 344 A2
DAGE RM10 — 336 A2
EN EN1 — 273 L4
FOS CO13 — 183 M1
HAR CO12 — 110 D5
HOC/HUL SS5 — 287 J7
HSTD CO9 — 98 C7
MNPK E12 — 315 P6
PLSTW E13 — 333 K3
RCOS CO16 — 156 C5
RCOS CO16 — 206 B6
SBF/HAD SS7 — 326 A4
SLH/COR SS17 — 341 L2
STSD SM24 — 138 E4
SUD CO10 — 21 G2
WALTH E17 — 294 E9
WICKE SS11 — 305M1
WOS/PRIT SS0 — 328 C6
WOTN CO14 — 159 L3
WTHK RM20 — 348 D4
First Avenue Mandela Av
HLW CM20 — 13 K4
The Firs BRWN CM15 — 280 D5
CDW/CHF RM16 — 339M8
CHESW EN7 — 229 K5
CVI SS8 — 326 C9
Firstore Dr COLW CO3 — 127 H8
Firs Wk WFD IG8 — 295 K2
Fir Tree CI COLN CO4 — 128 C3
ROM RM1 — 298 C7
Fir Tree HI RIPS/CAP IP9 — 83 N5
Fir Tree La RCHLM CM3 — 242 B1
Fir Tree RI CHLM/GWD CM2 — 239 P4
RIPW IP8 — 24 D9
Fir Trees ABR/ST RM4 — 277 J2
Fir Trees CI BERM/RHTH SE16 — 332 B8
Fir Tree Wk EN EN1 — 273 K2
MAL CM9 — 222 D6
Fir Wy COS CO15 — 206 F6
Firwood's Rd HSTD CO9 — 97 P8
Fishbane CI IPSE IP5 — 30 C2
Fisher CI HVHL CB9 — 41 N3
PEND EN3 — 252 D7
Fishermans Dr
BERM/RHTH SE16 — 332 A9
Fishermans Wy HOD EN11 — 208 C3
Fisher's La RCOLE CO7 — 81 M6
Fisher's Wy BELV DA17 — 336 B8
Fishguard Wy CAN/RD E16 — 334 C8
Fishmarket St GTDUN CM6 — 92 A6
Fishponds HI RIPS/CAP IP9 — 84 B6
Fishponds Rd RCOLW CO6 — 102 B3
Fishponds La RIPS/CAP IP9 — 83 M4
Fish St MAL CM9 — 223 M5
Fisin Wk COLW CO3 — 151 H3
Fisons Rd CAN/RD E16 — 333 K8
Fitches Crs MAL CM9 — 244 C1
Fitzgerald CI MAL CM9 — 244 C1
Fitzgerald Rd RIPW IP8 — 24 B2
WAN E11 — 295 J5
Fitzgilbert Rd COLS CO2 — 151M2
Fitzilian Av HARH RM3 — 299 L5
Fitzmaurice Rd IPSE IP3 — 26 A8
Fitzpiers SAFWN CB10 — 51 M8
Fitzroy CI BCAYW CM12 — 283 H4
Fitzroy St IP IP1 — 17 H3
Fitzstephen Rd BCTR RM8 — 317 J7
Fitzwalter La RCHLM CM3 — 242 A4
Fitzwalter Pl CHLM/WR CM1 — 217M8
Fitzwalter Rd COLW CO3 — 127 L9
GTDUN CM6 — 142 D7
RCHLM CM3 — 219 L3
Fitzwarren SBN/FI SS3 — 330 C5
Fitzwilliam CI CHTY IP2 — 24 G9
Fitzwilliam Ms LAIN SS15 * — 333 K8
Fitzwilliam Rd COLW CO3 — 127 L8
Fitzwilliams CI CHLM/WR CM17 — 187M8
Five Acres HLWS CM18 — 210 F6
RCHLM CM3 — 242 C7
RIPS/CAP IP9 — 83 L4
STSD CM24 — 114 B7
WOTN CO14 — 159 K4
Fiveash La BRTR CM77 — 146 F5
Five Elms Rd DAGW RM9 — 317 N5
Fivefields CI COLN CO4 — 128 F8
Five Oaks SBF/HAD SS7 — 326 E2
Five Oaks La CHIG IG7 — 297 M5
Fladgate Rd WAN E11 — 315 H1
Flag HI RCOLE CO7 — 180 C4
Flagstaff CI WAB EN9 — 252 E5
Flagstaff Rd COLS CO2 — 128 A9
WAB EN9 — 251 P5
Flail CI RCOLE CO7 — 129 N9
Flambird's Cha RCHLM CM3 — 265 J2
Flamboro CI LOS SS9 — 307 N9
Flamborough St
POP/IOD E14 — 332 B6
Flamborough Wk
POP/IOD E14 * — 332 B6
Flamingo Wk HCH RM12 — 318 F9
Flamstead End Rd
CHESW EN7 — 229 N7
Flamstead Gdns DAGW RM9 — 317 K9
Flamstead Rd DAGW RM9 — 317 K9

Flanders CI BRTR CM7 — 145 H1
Flanders Fld COLS CO2 — 152 C3
Flanders Rd EHAM E6 — 334 A2
Flanders Wy HOM E9 — 314 A8
Flanders Yd TSTGT E7 — 252 D9
Flash La ENC/FH EN2 — 251 H1
Flatford Dr RCOS CO16 — 181 L9
Flatford Rd HVHL CB9 — 40 F3
RCOLE CO7 — 80 C4
Flavian CI HVHL CB9 — 41 N4
Flaxen CI CHING E4 — 274 E9
Flaxen Rd CHING E4 — 274 E9
Fleeming CI WALTH E17 — 294 C6
Fleeming Rd WALTH E17 — 294 C6
Fleet Av UPMR RM14 — 320 A1
Fleet CI UPMR RM14 — 320 A1
Fleethall Gv SBN/FI SS3 — 339 K8
Fleethall Rd RCFD SS4 — 309 H7
Fleet Rd SBF/HAD SS7 — 326 A4
Fleetwood Av COS CO15 — 182 F6
FX IP11 — 35 K6
WOS/PRIT SS0 — 328 D4
Fleetwood CI CAN/RD E16 — 333 N5
Fleming CI BRTR CM7 — 145 J5
CHESW EN7 — 229M5
Fleming Gdns TIL RM18 — 350 D6
Fleming Rd CDW/CHF RM16 — 348 F2
Flemings RBRW/HUT CM13 — 300 F3
Flemings Farm Rd LOS SS9 — 307 N7
Fleming Wy THMD SE28 — 335 L7
Flemish Ct COL CO1 — 8 C4
Flemming Av LOS SS9 — 327 N3
Flemming Crs LOS SS9 — 327 N3
Flempton Rd WALTH E17 — 314 B3
Fletcher CI EHAM E6 — 334 C7
NHMKT IP6 — 22 C3
Fletcher Dr WICKW SS12 — 305 J1
Fletcher La LEY E10 — 314 F2
Fletcher Rd CHIG IG7 — 296 C2
IPSE IP3 — 30 G2
Fletchers VGE SS16 — 323M2
Fletchers La KESC IP5 — 27 J3
Fletchers Sq SOSN SS2 — 329 H1
Flex Meadow
HLWW/ROY CM19 — 209 P4
Flindell Dr RIPW IP8 — 24 B1
Flint CI CHTY IP2 — 25 J9
SRTFD E15 — 315 J8
VGE SS16 — 322 C1
Flint St WTHK RM20 — 348 E4
Flintwich Mnr CHLM/WR CM1 — 217M4
Flitch La GTDUN CM6 — 141 M7
Flitch Wy BRTR CM77 — 143M6
GTDUN CM6 — 116 F5
RBSF CM22 — 138 C7
Flixton CI RCOS CO16 — 181 K9
Floathaven CI THMD SE28 — 335 H8
Flora CI POP/IOD E14 — 333 M3
Flora Gdns CHDH RM6 — 317 K1
Flora Rd WIT CM8 — 171 L9
Florence Av ENC/FH EN2 — 273 H2
Florence CI HCH RM12 — 319 K4
HVHL CB9 — 41 N4
SBF/HAD SS7 — 326 C5
WTHK RM20 — 349 H4
Florence Gdns CAN/RD E16 — 333 K2
Florence Rd CVI SS8 — 333 K2
WAN E11 — 159 L4
Florence St CAN/RD E16 — 333 K2
Florence Ter SLH/COR SS17 * — 340 C1
Florence Wy MGTR CO11 * — 81 N6
Florence Wy VGE SS16 — 323 J1
Florie's Rd RCOLW CO6 — 124 E7
Flowers Wy COS CO15 — 206 F5
Flowmere Rd ROY SG8 — 48 C1
Flux's La ERP CO11 — 81 L8
Fobbing Farm CI VGE SS16 — 323 P3
Fobbing Rd SLH/COR SS17 — 342 B1
Fodderwick BSDN SS14 — 2 E5
Foden Av IP IP1 — 24 D1
Fogerty CI PEND EN3 — 252 E7
Foksville Rd CVI SS8 — 344 B2
Fold CI CBE/LIN CB1 — 38 A1
Fold Cft HLW CM20 — 12 D5
The Fold BSDN SS14 — 3 G4
Folkards La RCOLE CO7 — 179 L5
Folkes La UPMR RM14 — 300 C9
Folkestone Rd EHAM E6 — 334 B2
WALTH E17 — 294 E8
Follett St POP/IOD E14 — 332 F6
Folly Cha HOC/HUL SS5 — 307 L1
Folly La HOC/HUL SS5 — 307 L1
RIPW IP8 — 28 F6
WALTH E17 — 294 B5
Folly Mill La GTDUN CM6 — 116 C1
The Folly COLS CO2 — 151 K8
K/T/MI CO5 — 199 N2
RCOLE CO7 — 153 J7
Folly Vw WARE SG12 — 184 E7
Folly Wall POP/IOD E14 — 333 H2
Fonnereau Rd IP IP1 — 16 D2
Fontayne Av CHIG IG7 — 296 D1
Fonteyn Ct MAL CM9 — 244 B3
Fonteyne Gdns WFD IG8 — 295 N6
Fontwell Park Gdns
HCH RM12 — 319 K6
Forbes CI EMPK RM11 — 318 G3
Ford CI LAIN SS15 — 305 H8
RAIN RM13 — 318 E9
Ford End WFD IG8 — 295 J3
Fordham CI EMPK RM11 — 319M2
Fordham PI IPNE IP4 — 26 E6
Fordham Rd RCOLW CO6 — 100 E6
RCOLW CO6 — 101 J5
Fordhams Rw
CDW/CHF RM16 — 340 C5
Ford HI STDN SG11 — 136 A6

Ford La COLN CO4 — 127 M2
RAIN RM13 — 318 E9
RCOLE CO7 — 178 F2
Ford Rd BDW E3 — 332 B2
COS CO15 — 6 C4
DAGW RM9 — 317 N9
Ford's Gv WCHMH N21 — 273 H7
Fords La COLN CO4 — 127 N2
Fordson Rd CHLM/GWD CM2 — 218 C5
Fords Park Rd CAN/RD E16 — 333 K6
Ford St BOW E3 — 332 B2
CAN/RD E16 — 333 J6
RCOLW CO6 — 125M3
Fordstreet HI RCOLW CO6 — 125 P5
Fordwater CI HSTD CO9 — 42 C8
Fordwich Rd COLE CO7 — 179 K4
Fordyce CI EMPK RM11 — 319M2
Fordyke Rd BCTR RM8 — 317M4
Forebury Av SBW CM21 — 187 N2
The Forebury SBW CM21 — 187 N2
Fore Fld BRTR CM7 — 145 N3
Forefield Gn CHLM/GWD CM1 — 218 E4
Foremark CI BARK/HLT IG6 — 296 C5
Foresight Rd COLS CO2 — 152 B2
Forest Ap CHING E4 — 275 H6
WFD IG8 — 295 K4
Forest Av CHIG IG7 — 296 B2
CHING E4 — 275 H6
Forest CI WAB EN9 — 251 J3
WAN E11 — 295 J9
WFD IG8 — 295 L1
Forest Ct CHING E4 — 275 J7
WAN E11 — 295 H8
Forest Dr CHLM/WR CM1 — 217 P6
CHING E4 — 235 P1
EPP CM16 — 254 F6
MNPK E12 — 315 N5
WAB EN9 — 294 C4
Forest Dr East WAN E11 — 314 C2
Forest Dr West WAN E11 — 314 F2
Forest Edge WFD IG8 — 295M9
Forester CI RIPW IP8 — 29M2
Foresters CI CHESW EN7 — 229 K6
Foresters Crs RCOLE CO7 * — 153 J5
Foresters Crs BXLYHN DA7 — 346 A9
Foresters Dr WALTH E17 — 294 G8
Forest Gld CHING E4 — 295 H2
HVHL CB9 — 233M6
VGE SS16 — 322 D2
WAN E11 — 315 H1
Foresthall Rd STSD CM24 — 138 G2
Forest La CHIG IG7 — 296 B2
FSTGT E7 — 315 K7
KESC IP5 — 27 K4
Forest Mount Rd WFD IG8 — 294 G4
Forest Park Av COS CO15 — 181 P6
Forest Ri SL HLWE CM17 — 187 K8
IPNE IP4 — 17 G8
LAIN SS15 — 303M5
Forest Ri WALTH E17 — 294 G8
Forest Rd BARK/HLT IG6 — 296 F5
BERM — 230 A8
CHES/WCR EN8 — 230 A8
ED N9 — 273 N7
ERITH DA8 — 346 F6
FSTGT E7 — 315 K6
LOU IG10 — 275 N3
PEND EN3 — 252 B6
ROMW/RG RM7 — 298 A7
WALTH E17 — 294 C6
WAN E11 — 294 G4
WFD IG8 — 275 K9
Forest Side CHING E4 — 275 J6
EPP CM16 — 254 E3
FSTGT E7 — 315 K7
Forest St FSTGT E7 — 315 K7
The Forest WALTH E17 — 295 H8
Forest Vw CHING E4 — 275 J6
WAN E11 — 315 J2
Forest View Av WAN E11 — 294 G3
Forest View Dr WAN E11 — 295 J3
Forest View Rd LOU IG10 — 275 N3
MNPK E12 — 315 P6
WALTH E17 — 294 F1
Forest Wy HLWE CM17 — 211 J7
MNPK E12 — 212 B1
LOU IG10 — 275 N9
RBSF CM22 — 138 F8
WAB EN9 — 163 K6
WFD IG8 — 295 L1
Forfar CI POP/IOD E14 — 333 J4
LOS SS9 — 327 L4
Forge CI KIR/NAC IP10 — 32 E1
Forge Crs BRTR CM77 — 146 D8
Forge St RCOLE CO7 — 104 C2
Formount CI CAN/RD E16 — 333 J5
Forres CI HOD EN11 — 208 D3
Forsgill CI LOS SS9 — 327 L4
Forster CI CHING E4 — 294 G4
Forster Rd WALTH E17 — 314 B1
Forsters CI CHDH RM6 — 298 B1
Forsyth CI CHLM/WR CM1 — 218 D4
Forsythia CI CHLM/WR CM1 — 218 D4
Forsyth Pl EN EN1 — 273 L1
Forterie Gdns
GDMY/SEVK IG3 — 317 H5
Fortescue Cha SKS SS1 — 329 N5
Fortin Wy SOCK/AV RM15 — 321 N1
Fortin CI HVHL CB9 — 41 N3
Fortinbras Wy
CHLM/GWD CM2 — 240 A3
Fortin CI SOCK/AV RM15 — 338 D7
Fortis CI CAN/RD E16 — 333M6
Fort Rd TIL RM18 — 350 D9
Fortrose CI POP/IOD E14 — 332 G6
Fort St CAN/RD E16 — 333 L8
Fortune CI RCHLM CM3 — 169 J6
The Fortunes HLWS CM18 — 210 C5

Fort William Rd
SLH/COR SS17 — 324 A4
Forty Acre La CAN/RD E16 — 333 K5
Forty HI EN EN1 — 251 L7
Forum CI BOW E3 — 332 C1
Fossetts La RCOLW CO6 — 126 A2
Fossetts Wy SOSN SS2 — 329 K3
Fossway BCTR RM8 — 317 K4
Fostal CI LOS SS9 — 327 P5
Foster CI CHES/WCR EN8 — 230 A9
Foster Rd CVI SS8 — 344 F1
HAR CO12 — 109 P3
MAL CM9 — 198 B8
PLSTW E13 — 333 K4
Fosters CI CHLM/WR CM1 — 238 C1
SWFD E18 — 295 L5
Foster St HLWE CM17 — 211 N5
Fothergill CI PLSTW E13 — 333 K1
Fothergill Dr WCHMH N21 — 272 C4
Fotheringham Rd EN EN1 — 273 L5
Foulgar CI RCHLM CM3 — 265 H9
Foundation St IPNE IP4 — 17 F5
Founders Wy HOD EN11 — 208 E2
Foundry CI BERM/RHTH SE16 — 332 C8
Foundry La BOC CM0 — 290 C3
WFD IG8 — 16 E6
RCOLW CO6 — 150 A1
RCOLW CO6 — 150 A1
Fountain Farm HLWS CM18 — 210 C5
Fountain La HOC/HUL SS5 — 150 A6
Fountain PI WAB EN9 — 252 F7
Fountain Rd CHLM/WR CM1 — 191 L9
Fountains Crs
STHGT/OAK N14 — 272 D6
Fountains Rd CHTY IP2 — 29 P1
Fouracres PEND EN3 — 252 B9
Four Acres SAFWN CB10 — 36 E8
SAFWS CB11 — 51M9
The Four Acres SBW CM21 — 187 P2
Four Ash HI HSTD CO9 — 56 F1
Four Oaks BRW CM14 — 281 H9
Four Seasons CI BOW E3 — 332 D2
Four Sisters CI LOS SS9 — 328 A1
Four Sisters Wy LOS SS9 — 328 A1
Fourth Av CHLM/WR CM1 — 217 P6
COS CO15 — 183 N1
FOS CO13 — 183 N1
HLW CM20 — 13 H5
HLWW/ROY CM19 — 12 A7
HSTD CO9 — 98 C7
MNPK E12 — 316 A6
RCOS CO16 — 206 A6
ROMW/RG RM7 — 318 B3
SLH/COR SS17 — 323M9
WICKE SS11 — 305M1
WTHK RM20 — 348 D4
Fourways RBSF CM22 — 114 F6
The Four Wents CHING E4 — 274 C8
Fowey La REDBR IG4 — 295 N9
Fowler CI SOS SS1 — 329 N5
Fowler Rd BARK/HLT IG6 — 297 K2
FSTGT E7 — 315 K6
Fowley CI CHES/WCR EN8 — 252 C4
Fowley Mead Pk
CHES/WCR EN8 — 252 C4
Foxborough Cha ING CM4 — 261 P4
Fox Burrow Rd CHIG IG7 — 297 L1
Fox Burrows La
CHLM/WR CM1 — 217 J9
Fox CI CAN/RD E16 — 333 K5
CRW RM5 — 298 A2
SBF/HAD SS7 — 306 C9
Fox Crs CHLM/WR CM1 — 217 N7
Foxdells La BSF CM23 — 137 L4
Foxdell WIT CM8 — 172 C7
Foxendale Folly COLW CO3 * — 126 F8
Foxes Dr CHESW EN7 — 229 L8
Foxes Gn CDW/CHF RM16 — 340 B9
Foxes Gv RBRW/HUT SS13 — 282 C6
Foxes La POTB/CUF EN6 — 226 A7
RCOLW CO6 — 126 A7
SUD CO10 — 57 L1
Foxes Pde WAB EN9 * — 252 F3
Foxes Rd SUD CO10 — 57 L1
Foxfield CI HOC/HUL SS5 — 308 B1
Foxfield Dr SLH/COR SS17 — 323 H8
Foxglove CI BSF CM23 — 137 H8
COS CO15 — 182 A6
ED N9 — 273 P7
HCH RM11 — 208 F2
WIT CM8 — 196 C1
Foxglove Crs IPSE IP5 — 31 L1
Foxglove Dr WAN E11 — 295M8
Foxglove Rd ROMW/RG RM7 — 318 C4
SOCK/AV RM15 — 338 F6
The Foxgloves BCAYW CM12 — 282 G4
Foxglove Wk COLN CO4 — 128 B8
Foxgrove STHGT/OAK N14 — 272 D9
Foxgrove Av FX IP11 — 35M6
Foxglove La FX IP11 — 35M6
Fox Hall Farm SOSN SS2 * — 329 N2
Foxhall Flds RCOLE CO7 — 80 F5
Fox Hall Rd
IPNE IP4 — 17 K6
UPMR RM14 — 319 P7
Fox Hatch BRWN CM15 — 258 B7
Foxhatch WICKW SS12 — 305 N1
Foxhills Rd CDW/CHF RM16 — 339 N8
Foxholes Rd CHLM/GWD CM2 — 240 C8
Fox House Rd BELV DA17 — 346 A2
Foxlands Crs DAGE RM10 — 318 B7
Foxlands Rd DAGE RM10 — 318 B7
Fox La PLMGR N13 — 272 E8
Foxleigh CI BCAYW CM12 — 283 H8
Foxleigh Cha BCAYW CM12 — 283 H8
Foxley Dr BSF CM23 — 137M6
Fox Manor Wy WTHK RM20 — 348 E4
Foxmead WIT CM8 — 172 C7

Foxmead Cl ENC/FH EN2 * ...272 E2
Foxmeadows SBF/HAD SS7 ...306 C9
Fox Rd CAN/RD E16 ...333 J5
Foxtail Rd IPSE IP5 ...31 L2
Foxton Rd HOD EN11 ...208 C5
  WTHK RM20 ...348 G4
Foxwood Cha WAB WAB ...252 F6
Foxwood Cl MGTR CO11 ...105 J6
Foxwood Crs IPNE IP4 ...86 E6
Foxwood Green Cl EN EN1 * ...275 K5
Foxwood Pl LOS SS9 ...327 N4
Foyle Dr SOCK/AV RM15 ...338 D6
Foys Wk BCAYE CM11 ...285 K9
Frambury La SAFWS CB11 ...64 A9
The Frame LAIN SS15 ...303 L8
Framlingham Wy BRTR CM77 ...144 F8
Frampton Rd BSDN SS14 ...304 F6
  EPP CM16 ...233 H7
  IPSE IP5 ...30 C2
Frances Cl RCOLE CO7 ...153 J4
Frances Gdns SOCK/AV RM15 ...338 C6
Frances Ga CHLM/WR CM1 ...218 F4
Frances Rd CHING E4 ...294 D3
Frances Av IL IG1 ...316 E4
Franciscan Wy * IPSE IP5 ...16 D5
Francis Cl HVHL CB9 ...41 J3
  K/T/MI CO5 ...173 P9
  KESC IP5 ...27 K3
Francis Ct WIT CM8 ...146 D9
Francis Ms MAL CM9 ...244 C2
Francis Rd BRTR CM7 ...144 G4
  LEY E10 ...314 F4
  ROM RM7 ...20 C6
  WARE SG12 ...184 A2
Francis Wk RAYL SS6 ...306 F5
Francis Wy COLN CO4 ...128 E6
  WIT CM8 ...331 K1
Franccombe Gdns ROM RM1 ...318 F1
Frank Clater Cl COLN CO4 ...9 J4
Frankland Cl WFD IG8 ...295 M2
Frankland Rd CHING E4 ...294 D3
Franklin Av CHESW EN7 ...229 M9
Franklin Rd HCH RM12 ...319 H8
  IPSE IP5 ...26 A9
  RCHLM CM5 ...266 C9
Franklin St BOW E3 ...332 E5
Franklin Wy WICKE SS11 ...285 K8
Franklyn Gdns BARK/HLT IG6 ...296 E3
Frank Martin Ct CHESW EN7 ...229 M9
Franmil Rd EMPK RM11 ...318 C2
Fraser Cl CHLM/GWD CM2 ...240 B2
  SBN/FI SS3 ...330 E5
Fraser Rd CHES/WCR EN8 ...230 B7
  ED N9 ...273 N9
  ERITH DA8 ...346 B3
  IPP1 ...22 C9
  WALTH E17 ...294 E9
Frating Abbey Farm Rd
  RCOLE CO7 ...155 H8
Frating Crs WFD IG8 ...295 K3
Frating Hl RCOLE CO7 ...154 C5
Frating Rd RCOLE CO7 ...129 N2
  RCOLE CO7 ...154 F1
Frayes Cha CHONG CM5 ...190 D9
Frazer Rd ROMW/RG RM7 ...318 E2
Frederica Rd CHING E4 ...274 C6
Frederick Crs PEND EN5 ...273 P1
Frederick Rd RAIN RM13 ...336 C2
Frederick Sq WALTH E17 ...332 B7
Fredricks Cl MGTR CO11 * ...132 E2
Freeborne Gdns RAIN RM13 ...197 N4
Freebournes Rd WIT CM8 ...197 L1
Freedom Cl WALTH E17 ...294 A8
Freehold Rd IPNE IP4 ...25 P5
Freeland Rd COS CO15 ...6 D7
Freelands RCOLE CO7 ...179 N7
Freeland Wy ERITH DA8 ...346 F6
Freeman Av NHMKT IP6 ...23 J1
Freeman Dr SLH/COR SS17 ...341 N2
Freemantle Av PEND EN5 ...274 A4
Freeman Wy EMPK RM11 ...319 K1
Freemasons Rd CAN/RD E16 ...333 L6
Freewood La SAFWS CB11 ...49 K7
Freezes Barns HVHL CB9 ...55 L3
Freightmaster Est
  RAIN RM13 * ...346 F2
Fremantle SBN/FI SS3 ...330 C9
Fremantle Rd RCHLM CM5 ...268 C8
Fremantle Rd BARK/HLT IG6 ...296 C6
  COLS CO12 ...152 C5
The Fremnells BSDN SS14 ...304 C8
French Horn Ct WAB SS12 * ...184 A3
French's Ct WARE SG12 ...184 D7
Frensham Cl WICKE SS11 ...229 L6
Frensham Ct COLW CO3 ...126 C8
Frere Wy K/T/MI CO5 ...153 J8
Frerichs Cl WICKW SS12 ...63 K9
Freshfield Dr STHGT/OAK N14 ...272 A7
Freshfields Hall COS CO15 ...110 A7
Freshfields Av WICKW SS12 ...319 N7
Freshfields Rd HAR CO12 ...110 B3
Freshwater Crs MAL CM9 ...222 C7
Freshwater Dr VGE SS16 ...182 A5
Freshwater La COS CO15 ...182 A5
Freshwell Av BCTR RM8 ...317 L3
Freshwell Av CHDH RM6 ...297 K8
Freshwell Gdns
  RBRW/HUT CM13 ...321 N1
  SAFWN SS15 ...51 K8
Fresh Wharf Rd BARK IG11 ...334 C1
Fresian Cl BRTR CM7 ...144 F4
Freston Rd BRTR CM7 ...75 J7
Freston St RIPS/CAP IP9 ...30 D7
Freston St RIPS/CAP IP9 ...324 D1
Friar Cl HVHL CB9 ...41 J2
Friars RIPS/CAP IP9 ...81 L1

Friar's Av BRWN CM15 ...281 K6
Friars Bridge Rd IP IP1 ...16 C5
Friars Cl BRWN CM15 ...281 K6
  CHING E4 ...274 F9
  COLN CO4 ...128 D5
  FX IP11 ...55 N5
  HSTD CO9 ...72 B7
  IL IG1 ...316 E3
  LAIN SS15 ...303 K9
  RCOLE CO7 ...105 J6
  RCOS CO16 ...181 P7
Friars Ct COLS CO2 ...152 D3
Friarscroft BROX EN10 ...208 D8
Friars Gate Cl WFD IG8 ...295 K1
Friars La BRTR CM7 ...145 J2
  MAL CM9 ...222 A9
  RBSF CM22 ...188 G3
Friars Md HVHL CB9 * ...42 A7
Friar's Rd EHAM E6 ...333 N1
Friars St IP IP1 ...16 D5
  SBN/FI SS3 ...330 E7
  SUD CO10 ...21 D7
The Friars CHIG IG7 ...296 F1
  CHIG IG7 ...210 C5
Friars Wk CHLM/GWD CM2 ...5 G5
  STHGT/OAK N14 ...272 A7
Friars Wd BSF CM23 ...137 P6
Friary La WFD IG8 ...222 B9
Friary Flds MAL CM9 ...222 B9
Friary Rd WFD IG8 ...295 K1
The Friary CHES/WCR EN8 * ...252 C5
Friday Hl CHING E4 ...275 H9
Friday Hl East CHING E4 ...275 H9
Friday Hl West CHING E4 ...275 H8
Friday Rd EHAM E6 ...346 C5
Friday Wood Cl COS CO15 ...152 B6
Friedberg Av BSF CM23 ...137 J9
Friends Av CHES/WCR EN8 ...252 A2
Friends Fld BURES CO8 ...76 A8
Friendship Wy SRTFD E15 * ...332 F1
  SAFWS CB11 ...65 L2
Friern Gdns WICKW SS12 ...284 C9
Friern Pl WICKW SS12 ...304 C1
Frietuna Rd FOS CO15 ...158 F8
Frimley Av EMPK RM11 ...319 M3
Frimley Rd GDMY/SEVK IG5 ...316 F5
Frimley Wy WCHPL E1 * ...332 A4
Frinsted Rd ERITH DA8 ...346 C8
Frinton Dr WFD IG8 ...294 C4
Frinton Ms IL IG1 ...316 B1
Frinton Rd COS CO15 ...182 E8
  CRW RM5 ...297 P4
  EHAM E6 ...333 N3
  FOS CO15 ...158 D8
  RCOS CO16 ...157 L5
Frith Rd WAN E11 ...314 F6
Frithwood Cl BCAYW CM12 ...282 C9
Frithwood La BCAYW CM12 ...282 C8
Fritton Cl CHTY IP2 ...30 A1
Fritztancs La DAGE RM10 ...318 A5
Frobisher Dr COS CO15 ...206 E3
Frobisher Gdns LEY E10 * ...314 E1
Frobisher Rd EHAM E6 ...334 A6
  ERITH DA8 ...346 F5
  HAR CO12 ...110 A7
  IPSE IP5 ...30 E1
Frobisher Wy BRTR CM7 ...145 M2
  GRH DA9 ...348 E9
  SBN/FI SS3 ...330 D5
Froden Brook BCAYE CM11 ...283 K9
Froden Ct BCAYE CM11 ...303 K1
Frogge St SAFWN CB10 ...36 B7
Frog Hall Cl K/T/MI CO5 ...153 J8
Frog La DAGW RM9 ...336 C5
Frogs Abbey Rd K/T/MI CO5 ...153 J9
Frogs Hl St BRWN CM15 ...258 B9
Frome TIL RM18 ...351 K2
Fronk's Av HAR CO12 ...110 D6
Fronk's Rd HAR CO12 ...110 C6
Front La UPMR RM14 ...320 B4
Front Rd IPSE IP5 ...31 K2
Frowick La RCOS CO16 ...180 C6
Fryatt Av HAR CO12 ...110 B5
Fry Cl CRW RM5 ...297 P2
Fryerning La ING CM4 ...260 A4
Fry Rd EHAM E6 ...315 N9
Fryth Cl HVHL CB9 ...41 K2
The Fryth BSDN SS14 ...304 D7
Fuchsia La IPNE IP4 ...25 P6
Fuchsia Wy RCOS CO16 ...181 M8
Fulbourne Rd WALTH E17 ...254 C6
Fulbrook La SOCK/AV RM15 ...338 C7
Fulcher Av CHLM/GWD CM2 ...218 E8
Fulfen Wy SAFWS CB11 ...65 L2
Fulford Dr LOS SS9 ...308 B9
Fullarton Crs SOCK/AV RM15 ...338 C6
Fullbridge MAL CM9 ...222 B8
Fuller Cl BSF CM23 ...137 M7
Fuller Rd BCTR RM8 ...317 K5
Fuller's Av WFD IG8 ...295 J4
Fullers Cl CRW RM5 ...298 B4
  WAB EN9 ...253 K5
Fullers Md NHMKT IP6 * ...211 K5
Fullers Rd COLS CO2 ...152 E4
  SWFD E18 ...295 J5
Fullers Yd HVHL CB9 * ...4 F2
Fulmar Cl CLAY IG5 ...296 B5
Fulmar Ct COLN CO4 ...129 H7
Fulmar Rd HCH RM12 ...318 G8
Fulmer Rd CAN/RD E16 ...305 M2
Fulready Rd LEY E10 ...294 D9
Fulton Crs BSF CM23 ...137 P5
Fulton Rd WEM HA9 ...332 A2
Furlongs VGE SS16 ...324 C2
The Furlongs ING CM4 ...260 C6
Furlong Wy WARE SG12 ...184 D5
Furneaux La K/T/MI CO5 ...152 C9
Furner Cl DART DA1 ...346 E3
Furness Cl CDW/CHF RM16 ...350 C3
  CHTY IP2 ...29 P2
Furness Wy HCH RM12 ...318 F7

The Furrelis CBE/LIN CB1 ...38 B1
Furriers Cl BSF CM23 ...137 H9
Furrow Cl COLW CO3 * ...151 H1
Furrowfelde VGE SS16 ...323 P2
Further Meadow
  CHLM/GWD CM2 ...239 H2
Further St RCOLW CO6 ...77 J1
Furrze Cl WD SS8 ...344 E1
Furze Crs RCOLE CO7 ...153 P7
Furze Farm Cl CHDH RM6 ...297 M6
Furzefield CHESW EN7 ...229 N7
Furze Gld VGE SS16 ...323 J1
Furze La ING CM4 ...261 P9
  RCOLE CO7 ...154 F1
Furze St BOW E3 ...332 D5
The Furze MAL CM9 * ...244 F9
Fusedale Wy SOCK/AV RM15 ...338 C7
Fyefields PIT SS13 ...305 H7
Fyfield Av WICKW SS12 ...305 H2
Fyfield Cl RBRW/HUT CM13 ...338 C7
Fyfield Dr SOCK/AV RM15 ...338 C7
Fyfield Rd CHONG CM5 ...213 L8
  CHONG CM5 ...214 F8
  CHONG CM5 ...235 M5
  EN EN1 ...273 K2
  RAIN RM13 ...336 E1
  WALTH E17 ...294 D7
  WFD IG8 ...295 M4

G

Gabion Av PUR RM19 ...348 A2
Gablefields CHLM/GWD CM2 ...241 H4
The Gables GRAYS RM17 * ...349 J2
  HAR CO12 * ...14 E7
  PIT SS13 ...304 C7
  SAFWS CB11 * ...57 K8
  SBF/HAD SS7 ...307 K8
Gabriel Cl CRW RM5 ...298 B4
Gaces Acre SAFWS CB11 ...65 H8
Gad Cl PLSTW E13 ...333 L5
Gadsden Cl UPMR RM14 ...320 B1
Gadwall Cl CAN/RD E16 ...333 L6
Gadwall Reach K/T/MI CO5 ...173 J3
Gafzelie Dr CVI SS8 ...145 H3
Gager Dr K/T/MI CO5 ...178 B6
Gage Rd CAN/RD E16 ...333 H5
Gage's Rd SUD CO10 ...58 D5
Gaiger Cl CHLM/WR CM1 ...218 C4
Gainsborough Av CVI SS8 ...145 H3
  K/T/MI CO5 ...202 J7
  RCOS CO16 ...181 M7
Gainsborough Cl
  CHLM/GWD CM2 ...218 D8
  MGTR CO11 ...106 B4
  WOS/PRIT SS0 ...328 F3
Gainsborough La IPSE IP5 * ...30 F2
Gainsborough Pl
  RBRW/HUT CM13 ...321 N7
Gainsborough Rd BCTR RM8 ...317 J6
  COLW CO3 ...151 L1
  FX IP11 ...11 K1
  IPNE IP4 ...40 C2
  IPNE IP4 ...25 L3
  RAIN RM13 ...336 F1
  SRTFD E15 ...332 F1
  SUD CO10 ...20 C4
  WAN E11 ...315 H2
  WFD IG8 ...295 P3
Gainsborough Sd SUD CO10 ...20 C5
Gainsborough Yd SUD CO10 * ...60 F4
Gains Cl CVI SS8 ...344 C1
Gainsford Av COS CO15 ...182 B9
Gainsford End Rd HSTD CO9 ...71 J3
Gainsford Rd WALTH E17 ...294 C8
Gainsthorpe Rd CHONG CM5 ...235 J2
Galadriel Cl CHLM/GWD CM2 ...286 E2
Galahad Cl BOC CM0 ...290 C3
Galahad Rd ED N9 ...273 N6
Galeborough Av WFD IG8 ...294 C4
Gale St BOW E3 ...332 D5
  DAGW RM9 ...317 L8
Gales Wy WFD IG8 ...295 P4
Galey Cl GDMY/SEVK IG5 ...316 F5
Gall End La STSD SM24 ...114 C8
Galleon Bvd GRH DA9 ...348 A9
Galleon Cl ERITH DA8 ...346 C2
Galleons Dr BARK IG11 ...335 H5
Galleon Vw CHLM/WR CM1 ...216 C6
Galleydene SBF/HAD SS7 ...326 F5
Galley Gn HERT/BAY SG13 ...208 D1
Galleyhill Rd WAB EN9 ...253 H5
Galleys Cnr BRTR CM77 * ...145 N6
Gallewood Crs CRW RM5 ...298 C3
Gallywood Rd
  CHLM/GWD CM2 ...239 P6
Galliard Crs ED N9 ...273 M6
Galliard Rd ED N9 ...273 M6
Galliford Rd MAL CM9 ...222 A7
Gallions Cl BARK IG11 ...335 H3
Gallions Rd CAN/RD E16 ...334 C7
Gallions View Rd THMD SE28 ...334 F9
The Gallops VGE SS16 ...323 J1
Galloway Cl BROX EN10 ...137 L6
Galloway Rd BSF CM23 ...137 L6
Galloway Rd RCOS CO16 ...181 M2
Gallows Green Rd
  GTDUN CM6 ...117 M4
Gallows Hl SAFWS CB11 ...65 K2
Gallus Cl WCHMH N21 ...272 E5
Galsworthy Av CHDH RM6 ...317 J2
  POP/IOD E14 ...332 B6
Galsworthy Cl THMD SE28 ...335 J8
Galsworthy Rd TIL RM18 ...350 D6
Galton Rd WOS/PRIT SS0 ...328 C6

Galway Av IP IP1 ...24 F2
Gambleside VGE SS16 ...303 M1
Gamuel Cl WALTH E17 ...254 A1
Gandalf's Ride RCHLM CM5 ...286 F2
Gandhi Cl WALTH E17 ...314 D1
Gandish Cl RCOLE CO7 ...80 C8
Gandish Rd RCOLE CO7 ...81 H7
Ganels Cl BCAYE CM11 ...283 K9
Ganels Rd BCAYE CM11 ...283 K9
Ganges Rd RIPS/CAP IP9 ...85 M9
Gangies Hl SBW CM21 ...187 H1
Gannet Cl LOS SS9 ...298 A6
Gannet Rd CHTY IP2 ...24 F8
Gant Ct WAB EN9 ...253 J4
Gantshill Crs
  GNTH/NBYPK IG2 ...296 B9
Ganwick Cl HVHL CB9 ...41 J1
Garbutt Rd UPMR RM14 ...319 P4
Garden Cl CHING E4 ...294 D2
  CHLM/WR CM1 ...267 N5
  RIPS/CAP IP9 ...85 K6
Garden Ct FOS CO15 * ...99 H9
  RCOLW CO6 ...99 H9
Garden Dr COLW CO3 ...151 H1
Garden End ING CM4 ...261 N7
Gardeners La RCFD SS4 ...289 M7
Gardeners Rd HSTD CO9 ...98 A7
Gardeners Rw K/T/MI CO5 ...240 C5
Garden Farm K/T/MI CO5 ...173 P9
Garden Fld CVI SS8 ...145 H3
Garden Flds BOC CM0 ...246 E7
  GTDUN CM6 ...118 C9
  RCOLW CO6 ...128 C5
Garden Pl SUD CO10 * ...20 B6
Garden Side SUD CO10 * ...20 C5
The Gardens BRWN CM15 ...258 E6
  SUD CO10 ...58 F6
  WCHPL E1 ...332 A5
Garden Terrace Rd
  HLWE CM17 ...187 K8
Garden Wy LOU IG10 ...254 B8
Garden Yd HSTD CO9 ...98 A1
Gardiner Cl BCTR RM8 ...317 L6
  EPP CM16 ...233 L7
Gardiners La North
  BCAYE CM11 ...304 C2
Gardiners La South
  BCAYE CM11 ...304 D5
Gardiners Link BSDN SS14 ...304 D5
The Gardiners HLWE CM17 ...211 J4
Gardiners Wy BSDN SS14 ...304 C5
Gardner Av SLH/COR SS17 ...323 N9
Gardner Cl WAN E11 ...315 L1
Gardner Rd PLSTW E13 ...333 L4
Garfield Cl FX IP11 ...11 H5
Garfield Rd CHING E4 ...274 C7
  FX IP11 ...11 H3
  PEND EN5 ...273 P3
  PLSTW E13 ...333 J4
Garford St POP/IOD E14 ...332 D7
Garganey Wk THMD SE28 ...335 K7
Garland Cl CHES/WCR EN8 ...252 B1
Garland Rd HAR CO12 ...110 A3
  WARE SG12 ...184 B3
Garlandways EMPK RM11 ...299 K8
Garnault Rd EN EN1 ...251 L8
Garner Cl BCTR RM8 ...317 L3
Garner Dr BROX EN10 ...208 C4
Garner Rd WALTH E17 ...294 F5
Garnetts RBSF CM22 ...136 A3
Garnetts La GTDUN CM6 ...143 H8
Garnon Md EPP CM16 ...233 L7
Garnons Cha RCOLW CO6 ...101 M3
Garretlands CHLM/GWD CM2 ...241 L4
Garrett Cl CHLM/GWD CM2 * ...218 E4
Garrick Wy IP IP1 ...23 H9
Garrison La FX IP11 ...11 G4
  SUD CO10 ...47 P8
Garrison Rd BOW E3 ...332 D1
Garrods RIPS/CAP IP9 ...28 D9
Garron La SOCK/AV RM15 ...338 C6
Garry Cl ROM RM1 ...298 D4
Garry Wy ROM RM1 ...298 D4
Garth Rd SOCK/AV RM15 ...338 F4
Garthwood Cl RCOLW CO6 ...127 H3
Gartmore Rd GDMY/SEVK IG3 ...316 D3
Gartons Cl PEND EN5 ...273 P4
Garvary Rd CAN/RD E16 ...333 L6
Gascoigne Dr NHMKT IP6 ...23 J1
Gascoigne Gdns WFD IG8 ...295 H4
Gascoigne Rd BARK IG11 ...334 D1
  VGE SS16 ...9 J3
Gascoigne Wy BCAYE CM11 ...283 L6
Gascony Cl HARH DA1 * ...299 J5
Gascoyne Dr DART DA1 ...346 E8
Gascoyne Rd HOM E9 ...314 A9
Gaselee St POP/IOD E14 ...332 F7
Gaston Bridge Rd RCOLE CO7 ...80 F6
Gaston St RCOLE CO7 ...80 F7
Gatacre Rd IP IP1 ...25 P6
Gate Farm Rd RIPS/CAP IP9 ...85 H4
Gatefield Cl WOTN CO16 ...128 D7
Gatehope Dr SOCK/AV RM15 ...338 C6
Gatehouse Ms ING CM4 ...260 C6
Gatekeeper Cl BRTR CM7 ...145 J5
Gate Lodge Sq LAIN SS15 ...303 N5
Gate Lodge Wy LAIN SS15 ...303 N5
Gater Dr ENC/FH EN2 ...251 J9
Gates St ENC/FH EN2 * ...237 L8
Gate Street Ms MAL CM9 ...222 A8
Gateway SS14 ...3 G5
The Gateways CHESW EN7 ...229 N7
Gathorne St BETH E2 ...332 A2
Gatscombe Cl HOC/HUL SS5 ...307 N1

The Gattens RAYL SS6 ...307 J3
Gatward Cl WCHMH N21 ...272 C5
Gatward Gn ED N9 ...273 K8
Gatwick Cl BSF CM23 ...157 H5
Gatwick Vw BCAYW CM12 ...283 J8
Gauden Rd BRTR CM7 ...121 J8
Gavenny Pth SOCK/AV RM15 ...338 C6
Gavin Wy COLN CO4 ...128 C2
Gawain Wk ED N9 ...273 M9
Gawsworth Cl SRTFD E15 ...315 J7
Gay Bowers La RCHLM CM5 ...304 C8
  HOC/HUL SS5 ...307 L1
Gay Bowers Ra RCHLM CM5 ...242 B6
Gay Bowers Wy WIT CM8 ...197 K5
Gaye St IP IP1 ...16 B5
Gayfer Av RAYL SS6 ...27 L3
Gaygar Cl RAYL IG5 ...296 L3
Gay Gdns DAGE RM10 ...318 B6
Gayleighs RAYL SS6 ...306 C3
Gay Links SS14 ...3 F5
Gaylor Rd TIL RM18 ...349 P6
Gaynes Ct UPMR RM14 ...319 N6
Gaynes Gdns VGE SS16 ...323 M2
Gaynes Hill Rd WFD IG8 ...295 P4
Gaynes Park Rd UPMR RM14 ...319 N6
Gaynes Rd UPMR RM14 ...319 N4
Gay Rd SRTFD E15 ...332 C2
Gaysham Av
  GNTH/NBYPK IG2 ...296 B9
Gays La RCFD SS4 ...289 M6
Gayton Rd SOSN SS2 ...329 H4
Gaywood LAIN SS15 ...303 L6
Gaywood Cl CHES/WCR EN8 ...230 A9
Gaywood Rd WALTH E17 ...294 D7
Gazelle Cl COLN CO4 ...128 D3
Geariesville Gdns
  BARK/HLT IG6 ...296 C5
Geary Cl BRW CM14 ...280 F7
Geddings Rd HOD EN11 ...208 E5
Geere Rd SRTFD E15 ...333 J1
The Geerings SLH/COR SS17 ...341 P2
Geisthorpe Rd CRW RM5 ...326 F9
Geisthorpe Rd CRW RM5 ...298 A4
Generals La RCHLM CM5 ...243 L1
Generals Ms FX IP1 * ...34 C6
The Generals Wk PEND EN5 ...252 B7
Genesta Cl MAL CM9 ...225 J1
Genesta Rd WOS/PRIT SS0 ...328 D6
Geneva Av WDBR IP12 ...27 P5
Geneva Gdns CHDH RM6 ...297 M9
Geneva Rd IPP1 ...16 C3
Genever Cl CHING E4 ...294 D2
Genk Cl CVI SS8 ...326 E9
Gennep Rd CVI SS8 ...326 E9
Genotin Rd EN EN1 ...273 J2
Gentian Ct COLN CO4 ...127 M5
Gentleman's Rw ENC/FH EN2 ...273 H2
Gentry Cl SLH/COR SS17 ...341 K3
Geoffrey Av HARH RM3 ...299 M5
Geoffrey Gdns EHAM E6 ...333 P2
Geoff Seaden Cl COL CO1 ...9 K7
George Av RCOLE CO7 ...179 L6
George Avey Cft EPP CM16 ...234 A5
George Cardnell Wy
  RCHLM CM5 ...245 M9
George Cl COS CO15 ...6 A5
  CVI SS8 ...326 C8
George Cut RCOLE CO7 ...179 L7
George Frost Cl IPNE IP4 * ...17 F1
George Gent Cl HVHL CB9 ...55 L8
George La SWFD E18 ...295 L7
George Lovell Dr PEND EN5 ...252 D7
George Rd BRTR CM7 ...144 C4
  CHING E4 ...294 C2
Georges Dr BRWN CM15 ...280 C4
George St BARK IG11 ...316 D9
  CAN/RD E16 ...333 J6
  CHLM/GWD CM2 ...5 F6
  COL CO1 ...9 J8
  GRAYS RM17 ...349 K4
  HAR CO12 ...15 G3
  ROM RM1 ...318 E1
  SAFWN CB10 ...51 L8
  SBN/FI SS3 ...330 E8
Georgeville Gdns
  BARK/HLT IG6 ...296 C8
George Williams Wy COL CO1 ...9 F7
Gepp Pl CHLM/GWD CM2 ...191 N2
Gepps Cl CHLM/WR CM1 ...216 C6
Gerald Rd BCTR RM8 ...317 N4
  CAN/RD E16 ...333 J4
Geralds Av IPNE IP4 ...25 P6
Geranium Cl RCOS CO16 ...6 A1
Geranium Wk COLN CO4 ...128 E8
Gerard Av BSF CM23 ...162 B1
Gerard Gdns RAIN RM13 ...336 D2
Gerard Rd RCOS CO16 ...181 M7
Germander Wy SRTFD E15 ...333 H5
Gernon Cl CHLM/WR CM1 ...194 A9
  RAIN RM13 ...336 D3
Gernon Rd BOW E3 ...332 B2
  RCOLE CO7 ...104 F9
Gerons VGE SS16 ...323 N2
Gerpins La UPMR RM14 ...319 M9
Gerrard Crs BRW CM14 ...280 F9
Gerrard Gdns RAYL SS6 ...306 B5
Gestingthorpe Rd SUD CO10 ...59 L5
Gew's Cnr CHES/WCR EN8 ...230 B7
Gezina Gdns SS14 ...344 C1
Ghyligrove BSDN SS14 ...304 A7
Ghyligrove Cl BSDN SS14 ...3 J4
Gibb Cft HLWS CM18 ...210 F7
Gibbfield Cl CHDH RM6 ...297 M7
Gibbins Rd SRTFD E15 ...314 F9
Gibbons Ct GTDUN CM6 ...141 L5
Gibbons St IP IP1 ...16 A3
Gibbs Cl CHES/WCR EN8 ...230 C9
Gibbs Fld BSF CM23 ...137 J9
Gibcracks BSDN SS14 ...304 B9
Gibraltar Rd RBRW/HUT CM13 ...300 F3
Gibson Cl EPP CM16 ...234 B4

SAFWN CB10 ... 51 L9
Gibson Gdns SAFWN CB10 ... 51 L9
Gibson Rd BCTR RM8 ... 317 K3
　HSTD CO9 ... 72 C9
Gibson V CHLM/WR CM1 ... 218 A3
Gidea Av GPK RM2 ... 298 F7
Gidea Cl GPK RM2 ... 298 F7
Gideon Cl BELV DA17 ... 346 A2
Gideons Wy SLH/COR SS17 ... 341 L2
Giffins Cl BRTR CM7 ... 145 H5
Gifford Cl RIPS/CAP IP9 ... 83 L3
Gifford Cl PIT SS13 ... 324 C1
Gifford Rd SBF/HAD SS7 ... 326 A1
Giffords Cross Av
　SLH/COR SS17 ... 341 P1
Giffords Cross Rd
　SLH/COR SS17 ... 341 P2
Giffordside CDW/CHF RM16 ... 350 C3
Giffords Pl IPNE IP4 ... 26 E5
Gifhorn Rd CVI SS8 ... 345 H2
Gift La SRTFD E15 ... 333 H1
Gilberd Ct COLN CO4 ... 128 D1
Gilbert Rd COL CO1 ... 152 C2
Gilbert Cl RAYL SS6 ... 307 J5
Gilbert Dr VGE SS16 ... 323 H4
Gilbert Rd CDW/CHF RM16 ... 348 F1
　ROM RM1 ... 298 E8
　SUD CO10 ... 44 A2
　SRTFD E15 ... 315 H6
Gilbert Wy BRTR CM7 ... 145 M1
Gilbey Av BRTR CM7 ... 137 N8
Gilbey Crs STSD CM24 ... 114 D4
Gilbey Gn SAFWS CB11 ... 64 C8
Gilchrist Wy BRTR CM7 ... 145 H2
Gilda Av PEND EN3 ... 274 B4
Gilda Ter BRTR CM7 * ... 144 F4
Gildbome St SLH/COR SS17 ... 324 C9
Gilden Cl HLWE CM17 * ... 187 M8
Gilderdale Cl COLN CO4 ... 128 E4
Gilders SBW CM21 ... 187 L2
Gilders Wy RCOS CO16 ... 181 M8
Giles Cl RAIN RM13 ... 337 J2
Giles Ct NHMKT IP6 ... 22 D5
Giles Wy NHMKT IP6 ... 23 P5
Gilliam Wy RAIN RM13 ... 318 F8
Gillards Ms WALTH E17 ... 294 D8
Gillards Wy WALTH E17 ... 294 D8
Gill Av CAN/RD E16 ... 333 K6
Gill Cl MAL CM9 ... 222 A5
Gillender St BOW E3 ... 332 F4
Gillett Av EHAM E6 ... 333 P2
Gillian Crs GPK RM2 ... 299 H6
Gillman Dr SRTFD E15 ... 333 H1
Gills Av CVI SS8 ... 344 F1
Gill St POP/IOD E14 ... 332 C6
Gilman Dr SBN/FI SS3 ... 330 B7
Gilmore Wy CHLM/GWD CM2 ... 240 G4
Gilmour Cl ENC/FH EN2 ... 251 M5
Gilmour Ri BCAYW CM12 ... 282 C7
Gilpin Rd CLPT E5 ... 314 B6
　WARE SG12 ... 184 B4
Gilpin's Gallop WARE SG12 ... 184 E8
Gilpin Wy BRTR CM77 ... 144 F7
Gilroy Cl RAIN RM15 ... 253 H5
Gilston Pk HLW CM20 ... 156 F8
Gilwell Cl CHING E4 ... 274 E5
Gilwell La CHING E4 ... 274 G3
Gilwell Park COLW CO3 ... 151 K2
Gimli Watch COLW CM5 ... 286 C2
Gimson Cl WIT CM8 ... 197 H2
Ginns Rd BUNT SG9 ... 112 C1
Gippeswick BSDN SS14 ... 3 H3
Gippeswyk Av CHTY IP2 ... 25 J5
Gippeswyk Rd CHTY IP2 ... 25 J7
Gipping Cl NHMKT IP6 ... 41 H5
Gipping Rd NHMKT IP6 ... 22 B3
Gippingstone Rd RIPW IP8 ... 24 B2
Gipping Valley River Pth
　IPI8 ... 22 B9
Gipping Wy RIPW IP8 ... 24 B1
Gipson Park Cl LOS SS9 ... 307 N9
Gipsy La BSF CM23 ... 137 P2
　GRAYS RM17 ... 349 M4
Giralda Cl CAN/RD E16 ... 333 N5
Giraud St POP/IOD E14 ... 332 E6
Girling St SUD CO10 ... 20 D4
Girton Cl CHES/WCR EN8 ... 230 B9
Girton Rd HVHL CB9 ... 41 L4
Girton Wy CHTY IP2 ... 29 P1
Gladback Wy ENC/FH EN2 ... 273 H1
　WCHMH N21 ... 273 P3
Gladden Ct HLWS CM18 ... 210 F7
Gladden Flds RCHLM CM5 ... 286 F2
Gladding Rd CHESW EN7 ... 228 G4
　MNPK E12 ... 315 N6
Gladeside WCHMH N21 ... 272 E6
The Glade CLAY IC5 ... 204 H4
　COLN CO4 ... 128 F5
　ENC/FH EN2 ... 272 F2
　RBRW/HUT CM13 ... 281 K7
　UPMR RM14 ... 319 P7
　VGE SS16 ... 323 J2
　WCHMH N21 ... 272 E5
　WFD IG8 ... 275 L9
Gladeview COS CO15 ... 182 A6
The Gladeway WAB EN9 ... 252 G3
Gladiator Wy CLAS CO2 ... 151 K4
Gladstone Av MNPK E12 ... 315 P9
Gladstone Ct CHLM/GWD CM2 ... 5 G6
Gladstone Gdns RAYL SS6 ... 306 G4
Gladstone Rd BKHH IG9 ... 275 M7
　COL CO1 ... 152 B1
　HOC/HUL SS5 ... 307 P2
　HOD EN11 ... 208 E4
　IPSE IP3 ... 17 K6
　K/T/MI CO5 ... 174 A9
Gladwin Rd COL CO12 ... 151 M2
Gladwyns LAIN SS15 ... 2 A5
Glamis Cl CHESW EN7 ... 229 M8
Glamis Dr EMPK RM11 ... 319 K3

Glamorgan Rd CHTY IP2 ... 30 B1
Glandford Wy CHDH RM6 ... 297 J9
Glanmead BRWN CM15 ... 281 H7
Glanmire BCAYE CM11 ... 283 L2
Glanthams Rd BRWN CM15 ... 281 J8
Glanville Dr EMPK RM11 ... 319 L3
Glanville Pl KESC IP5 ... 26 C5
Glasseys La RAYL SS6 ... 306 F7
Glasshouse Flds WAP E1W ... 332 A7
Glastonbury Av WFD IG8 ... 295 N4
Glastonbury Cha
　WOS/PRIT SS0 ... 328 C1
Glastonbury Ct CHTY IP2 ... 29 P1
Glastonbury Rd EN N9 ... 273 M7
Glaucus St BOW E3 ... 332 E5
Glebe BSDN SS14 ... 304 B7
Glebe Av BRTR CM7 ... 121 H8
　ENC/FH EN2 ... 272 C2
　WFD IG8 ... 295 K5
Glebe Cl BSF CM23 ... 137 J2
　RAYL SS6 ... 306 F4
　RCOLE CO7 ... 129 P9
Glebe Cl CDW/CHF RM16 * ... 333 L2
Glebe Crs CHLM/WR CM1 ... 218 A2
　WIT CM8 ... 171 M9
Glebe Ct BSF CM23 ... 137 N6
Glebe Crs CHLM/WR CM1 ... 218 A2
　WIT CM8 ... 171 M9
Glebe End RBSF CM22 ... 114 F6
Glebe Fld BSDN SS14 ... 3 H1
Glebefield Rd RCHLM CM5 ... 196 E8
Glebe Gdns K/T/MI CO5 ... 148 D9
　RBRW/HUT CM13 ... 301 P4
Glebelands CHIG IG7 ... 277 J9
　DART DA1 ... 346 E9
　HLW CM20 ... 156 E9
　RCOLW CO6 ... 102 E7
　SBF/HAD SS7 ... 305 N8
Glebelands Av
　GNTH/NBYPK IG2 ... 316 E2
　SWFD E18 ... 295 K6
Glebe La BOC CM0 ... 248 A9
　GTDUN CM6 ... 140 C1
　RIPS/CAP IP9 ... 83 P1
Glebe Meadow RCHLM CM5 ... 193 M5
Glebe Rd BCAYE CM11 ... 284 D8
　CHLM/WR CM1 ... 5 F1
　CHONG CM5 ... 235 L8
　COLS CO2 ... 151 M4
　DAGE RM10 ... 318 A8
　K/T/MI CO5 ... 172 C3
　K/T/MI CO5 ... 173 P6
　MAL CM9 ... 222 D6
　RAIN RM13 ... 336 C5
　WICKS SS11 ... 285 K9
Glebe Ter BOW E3 ... 332 E3
The Glebe HLW CM20 ... 210 F2
　HVHL CB9 ... 41 K2
　RCHLM CM5 ... 243 N9
　SAFWS CB11 ... 65 M2
Glebe Wy BOC CM0 ... 205 C5
　COS CO15 ... 206 F5
　EMPK RM11 ... 319 K2
　ERITH DA8 ... 346 D4
　FOS CO13 ... 158 C9
　NHMKT IP6 ... 22 D2
　SBF/HAD SS7 ... 327 J3
Glebeway WFD IG8 ... 295 M2
Glemham Dr IPNE IP4 ... 26 E7
Glemsford Cl FX IP11 ... 10 C4
Glen Av COLW CO3 ... 127 L8
Glenavon Rd IPNE IP4 ... 26 C4
　SRTFD E15 ... 315 H9
Glenbervie Dr LOS SS9 ... 328 A4
Glenbrook North
　ENC/FH EN2 ... 272 E3
Glenbrook South
　ENC/FH EN2 ... 272 E3
Glencairne Cl CAN/RD E16 ... 333 N5
Glencoe Av GNTH/NBYPK IG2 ... 316 F2
Glencoe Dr WICKE SS11 ... 285 M8
Glencoe Rd DAGE RM10 ... 317 P6
　IPNE IP4 ... 26 E4
Glen Ct SBF/HAD SS7 * ... 326 E2
Glencree BCAYE CM11 ... 283 L2
Glen Crs WFD IG8 ... 295 L3
Glen Ctl HOC/HUL SS5 ... 308 A2
Glendale Av CHDH RM6 ... 265 H8
Glendale Av CHDH RM6 ... 317 K2
Glendale Cl BRWN CM15 ... 281 H7
Glendale Gdns WCHMH N21 ... 327 N5
Glendale Gv COLW CO4 ... 128 D4
Glendale Rd BOC CM0 ... 205 C8
　ERITH DA8 ... 346 B2
Glendale Wy THMD SE28 ... 335 K8
Glendower Rd CHING E4 ... 274 C7
Gleneagles SBF/HAD SS7 ... 325 N1
Gleneagles Cl FX IP11 ... 35 M5
　HARH RM3 ... 299 L4
Gleneagles Dr IPNE IP4 ... 26 C6
Gleneagles Rd LOS SS9 ... 327 M1
Gleneagles Wy RCHLM CM5 ... 196 E8
Glenester Cl HOD EN11 ... 208 D2
Glen Faba Rd
　HLWW/ROY CM19 ... 209 J5
Glenfield Av FX IP11 ... 35 K5
Glenfield Rd SLH/COR SS17 ... 324 A9
Glengall Rd WFD IG8 ... 295 L3
Glen Haven Cl GNTH/NBYPK IG2 ... 296 C9
Glen Maer BRWN CM15 ... 258 G5
Glenhurst Av IPNE IP4 ... 26 A3
Glenhurst Rd SOSN SS2 ... 329 H4
Glenloch Rd PEND EN3 ... 273 P1
Glenmere Park Av
　SBF/HAD SS7 ... 326 E3
Glenmore St SOSN SS2 ... 329 J1
Glenmore Wy BARK IG11 ... 335 H3
Glenny Rd BARK IG11 ... 316 D8
Glenparke Rd FSTCT E7 ... 315 L8

Glen Ri WFD IG8 ... 295 L3
Glen Rd LOS SS9 ... 328 B6
　PLSTW E13 ... 333 M4
　SBF/HAD SS7 ... 326 B9
　WALTH E17 ... 294 C9
Glenside BCAYE CM11 ... 283 L6
　CHIG IG7 ... 296 C3
　SUD CO10 ... 61 K4
Glen Ter POP/IOD E14 ... 332 F9
The Glen ENC/FH EN2 ... 272 C3
　HOC/HUL SS5 * ... 287 H5
　RAIN RM13 ... 337 H4
　RAYL SS6 ... 307 H7
　SLH/COR SS17 ... 341 N2
　VGE SS16 ... 324 F2
Glenthorne Gdns
　BARK/HLT IG6 ... 296 B7
Glenthorne Rd WALTH E17 ... 294 D4
Glenton Cl ROM RM1 ... 298 D4
Glenton Wy ROM RM1 ... 298 C4
Glentress Cl COLN CO4 ... 128 E4
Glenville Av ENC/FH EN2 ... 251 H8
Glenwood BROX EN10 ... 208 C9
Glenwood Av HOC/HUL SS5 ... 308 A2
　LOS SS9 ... 308 A9
　RAIN RM13 ... 336 F4
　WOS/PRIT SS0 ... 328 E4
Glenwood Dr GPK RM2 ... 298 F9
Glenwood Gdns
　GNTH/NBYPK IG2 ... 296 B9
　VGE SS16 ... 322 F2
Gleten Rd CVI SS8 ... 344 G1
Glisson Sq COLS CO15 ... 151 L2
Globe Cl K/T/MI CO5 ... 174 A7
Globe Crs BSF CM23 ... 113 J9
Globe Pond Rd
　BERM/RHTH SE16 ... 332 B8
Globe Rd EMPK RM11 ... 318 F1
　SRTFD E15 ... 315 J7
　WFD IG8 ... 295 M3
Globe Yd SUD CO10 ... 20 D5
Gloster Rd KESC IP5 ... 27 N4
Gloster Ter RCFD SS4 * ... 309 J5
Gloucester Av
　CDW/CHF RM16 ... 339 M9
　CHES/WCR EN8 ... 252 B3
　CHLM/GWD CM2 ... 240 A4
　COLS CO2 ... 151 L3
　EMPK RM11 ... 299 M9
　MAL CM9 ... 244 A2
　RAYL SS6 ... 307 K7
　TIL RM18 ... 351 K3
Gloucester Crs
　CHLM/WR CM1 ... 217 P6
Gloucester Gdns BRTR CM7 ... 145 L3
　IL IG1 ... 315 P2
Gloucester Pl BCAYW CM12 ... 283 H3
Gloucester Rd BRWN CM15 ... 280 E4
　ENC/FH EN2 ... 251 H8
　HVHL CB9 ... 41 H4
　IPSE IP3 ... 25 P9
　LEY E10 ... 314 D2
　MNPK E12 ... 316 A5
　ROM RM1 ... 318 D1
　WALTH E17 ... 294 A6
　WAN E11 ... 295 P6
Gloucester Ter SOS SS1 ... 329 N8
　STHGT/OAK N14 * ... 272 C7
Gloucester Wy SUD CO10 ... 46 G9
Glover Cl CHESW EN7 ... 229 L6
Glovers Rd RCHLM CM5 ... 169 J6
Glovers Rd BRWN CM15 ... 258 C7
Glovers La HLWE CM17 ... 211 M8
Glynde Wy SOSN SS2 ... 329 N5
Glynn Rd BOC CM0 ... 290 C2
Glyn Rd CLPT E5 ... 314 A6
　PEND EN3 ... 273 P5
Goat Hall La
　CHLM/GWD CM2 ... 239 N7
Goat House La RCHLM CM5 ... 243 H7
Goat La EN N1 ... 251 L8
Goat Lodge Rd MAL CM9 ... 198 B7
Goatsmoor La BCAYE CM11 ... 283 M3
Goatswood La ABR/ST RM4 ... 278 C6
Gobions VGE SS16 ... 323 P2
Gobions Av CRW RM5 ... 298 C4
Goda Cl WIT CM8 ... 196 G4
Godalming Rd POP/IOD E14 ... 332 F5
Godbold Cl KESC IP5 ... 27 J4
Godbold Rd SRTFD E15 ... 333 H4
Goddard Rd CDW/CHF RM16 ... 339 K8
　IP IP1 ... 22 D9
Goddard Rd East IP IP1 ... 22 E9
Goddards Wy IL IG1 ... 316 E3
Goddard Wy CHLM/GWD CM2 ... 218 F6
　SAFWN CB10 ... 51 M7
Godfreys Ms CHLM/GWD CM2 ... 5 F6
Godfrey St BSF CM23 ... 137 J2
　SRTFD E15 ... 332 F2
Godfrey Wy CHLM/GWD CM2 ... 141 L4
Godlings Wy BRTR CM7 ... 145 H4
Godman Rd CDW/CHF RM16 ... 350 C1
Godmans La RCOLW CO6 ... 149 K3
Godric Pl BRTR CM7 * ... 145 H5
Godric Rd WIT CM8 ... 197 H4
Godstow Rd ABYW SE2 ... 335 K9
Godwin Cl CHING E4 ... 252 F8
Godwin Rd FSTCT E7 ... 315 L6
Goffs Crs CHESW EN7 ... 229 H8
Goff's La CHESW EN7 ... 229 J8
Goff's Oak Av CHESW EN7 ... 228 G7
Goings La K/T/MI CO5 ... 158 D4
Golconda Rd CVI SS8 ... 344 F1
Goldace GRAYS RM17 ... 349 J4
Gold Cl BROX EN10 ... 208 B8
Goldcrest Cl CAN/RD E16 ... 333 N5
　COLN CO4 ... 128 C4
　THMD SE28 ... 335 K6
Goldcrest Dr BCAYE CM11 ... 285 K7
Goldcrest Rd CHTY IP2 ... 29 H2
Goldenacres CHLM/WR CM1 ... 218 A5
Golden Cross Ms RCFD SS4 ... 308 E2

Golden Cross Pde RCFD SS4 * ... 308 E2
Golden Cross Rd RCFD SS4 ... 308 E1
Golden Dawn Wy COLN CO4 ... 127 P5
Golden La RCOS CO16 ... 157 J3
Golden Lion La HAR CO12 ... 53 L8
Goldenlond RCOLW CO6 ... 78 B4
Golden Manor Dr
　SBF/HAD SS7 ... 326 C1
Golden Noble Hl COL CO1 ... 128 B9
Golden Pde WALTH E17 * ... 294 F7
Golden Plover Cl CAN/RD E16 ... 333 K6
Goldfinch Cl COLN CO4 ... 128 C8
Goldfinch La SBF/HAD SS7 ... 306 D8
Goldhanger Cl RAYL SS6 ... 306 D6
Goldhanger Cross BCAYE CM11 ... 304 D6
Goldhanger Rd MAL CM9 ... 222 D7
Goldhaze Cl WFD IG8 ... 295 N4
Golding Crs SLH/COR SS17 ... 341 M2
Goldington Cl HOD EN11 ... 208 C2
Goldington Crs BCAYW CM12 ... 282 C5
Golding Wy RCOS CO16 ... 180 D8
Goldmer Cl SBN/FI SS3 ... 330 F7
Golday Av CHLM/GWD CM2 ... 5 H7
Golday Gdns CHLM/GWD CM2 ... 5 H6
Golday Rd CHLM/GWD CM2 ... 5 H6
Goldsands Rd MAL CM9 ... 223 N5
Goldsmith Dr RAYL SS6 ... 306 B6
Goldsands Rd BOC CM0 ... 269 K7
Goldsborough Crs CHING E4 ... 274 E8
Goldsdown Cl PEND EN3 ... 274 B1
Goldsdown Rd PEND EN3 ... 274 A1
Goldsmith GRAYS RM17 ... 349 J4
Goldsmith Av MNPK E12 ... 315 P8
　ROMW/RG RM7 ... 317 P2
Goldsmith Dr RAYL SS6 ... 286 F9
Goldsmith Rd IP IP1 ... 22 F8
　LEY E10 ... 314 C5
　WALTH E17 ... 294 A6
Goldsmiths VGE SS16 * ... 323 H5
Goldsmiths Av SLH/COR SS17 ... 341 P2
Goldsmiths Whf
　GRAYS RM17 * ... 349 K5
Goldstone Cl WARE SG12 ... 184 A2
Gold St SAFWN CB10 ... 51 L9
Goldsworthy Dr SBN/FI SS3 ... 331 H4
Goldwing Cl CAN/RD E16 ... 333 K6
Golf Course Rd
　CDW/CHF RM16 ... 340 E7
Golfe Rd IL IG1 ... 316 E5
Golf Green Rd COS CO15 ... 206 F4
Golf Ride ENC/FH EN2 ... 250 F5
Golf Rd BKHH IG9 ... 275 H9
Goodall Rd WAN E11 ... 314 F5
Goodchild Rd WIT CM8 ... 196 G4
Goodey Cl COL CO1 ... 152 B1
Goodey Rd CHLM/WR CM1 ... 217 N7
Goodier Rd CHLM/WR CM1 ... 217 N7
Goodlake Cl HAR CO12 ... 109 P6
Goodliffe Pk BSF CM23 ... 137 N4
Goodman Av RCHLM CM5 ... 169 H8
Goodman Rd LEY E10 ... 314 F2
Goodmans SBF/HAD SS7 * ... 330 C3
Goodmans La RCHLM CM5 ... 169 H8
Goodmayes Av
　GDMY/SEVK IG3 ... 317 H3
Goodmayes La
　GDMY/SEVK IG3 ... 317 H6
Goodmayes Rd
　GDMY/SEVK IG3 ... 317 H3
Goodview Rd LAIN SS15 ... 303 P5
Goodway Gdns POP/IOD E14 ... 332 G6
Goodwin Ct CHES/WCR EN8 ... 230 B7
Goodwins Cl SAFWS CB11 ... 50 F7
Goodwin Stile BSF CM23 ... 157 H9
Goodwood Av HCH RM12 ... 319 K6
　PEND EN3 ... 251 P7
　RBRW/HUT CM13 ... 282 A5
Goodwood Cl HOD EN11 ... 208 C4
　IP IP1 ... 23 J8
　SBF/HAD SS7 ... 305 N8
Goojerat Rd COLS CO2 ... 151 N4
Goose La RBSF CM22 ... 162 C6
Gooseley La EHAM E6 ... 334 B3
Gooshays Dr HARH RM3 ... 299 L3
Gooshays Gdns HARH RM3 ... 299 L4
Gordon Av CHING E4 ... 295 H3
　HCH RM12 ... 318 E4
Gordon Cl BCAYW CM12 ... 283 J5
　HOC/HUL SS5 ... 287 P9
　RBRW/HUT CM13 ... 281 M4
　SLH/COR SS17 ... 341 L1
Gordon Dr COLN CO4 ... 128 C2
Gordon Hl ENC/FH EN2 ... 251 H9
Gordon Pl SUD CO10 ... 18 E4
Gordon Rd BARK IG11 ... 334 F1
　BELV DA17 ... 346 B2
　BRWN CM15 ... 281 K7
　BSDN SS14 ... 324 G1
　CDW RM16 ... 339 P9
　CHES/WCR EN8 ... 230 D7
　CHING E4 ... 275 J6
　CHLM/GWD CM2 ... 239 P4
　ED N9 ... 273 N8
　ENC/FH EN2 ... 251 H9
　HAR CO12 ... 110 D6
　IL IG1 ... 316 E5
　IPNE IP4 ... 26 E5
　LOS SS9 ... 327 J5
　SLH/COR SS17 ... 340 G2
　SLH/COR SS17 ... 341 J3
　SOS SS1 ... 18 E5
　SRTFD E15 ... 314 F6
　SWFD E18 ... 295 L5
　WAN E11 ... 315 K1
Granary Rw SAFWS CB11 * ... 51 M7
The Granary
　HLWW/ROY CM19 ... 209 L2
　SUD CO10 ... 44 A5
　WARE SG12 ... 184 F9
Granby Park Rd CHESW EN7 ... 229 L7
Grand Ct West LOS SS9 * ... 328 C6
Grand Dr LOS SS9 ... 328 A6
Grandview Rd SBF/HAD SS7 ... 306 C8
Grange Av WCHPL E1 ... 332 B4
Grange Av LOS SS9 ... 327 K1
　RCHLM CM5 ... 268 A2
　WFD IG8 ... 295 K3
　WICKW SS12 ... 304 C1
Grange Cl FX IP11 ... 35 H6
　HSTD CO9 ... 97 P9
　KESC IP5 ... 27 P5
　LOS SS9 ... 327 P5
　RBRW/HUT CM13 ... 301 N2
　WFD IG8 ... 295 K4
　WOTN CO14 ... 159 H7
Grange Ct WAB EN9 ... 252 F4
Grange Crs CHIG IG7 ... 277 K3
　THMD SE28 ... 335 K6
Grange Farm Av FX IP11 ... 10 C1
Grange Gdns RAYL SS6 ... 306 E4
　SOS SS1 ... 19 H4
　STHGT/OAK N14 ... 272 C7
　WARE SG12 ... 184 B4
Grange La GTDUN CM6 ... 142 A7

Gordons PIT SS13 ... 324 F1
Gordon St PLSTW E13 ... 333 K3
Gordon Wy HAR CO12 ... 110 C6
Gorefield Rd RBSF CM22 ... 139 L2
Gore La BRTR CM7 ... 144 D4
Gore Rd BRTR CM7 ... 144 C5
　WAN E11 ... 309 M1
Goresbrook Rd DAGW RM9 ... 335 K1
The Gore BSDN SS14 ... 2 E4
Goring Cl CRW RM5 ... 298 B6
Goring Gdns BCTR RM8 ... 317 K6
Goring Rd COLN CO4 ... 9 J2
　DAGE RM10 ... 318 C8
　IPNE IP4 ... 26 A5
Gorse Cl CAN/RD E16 ... 333 K6
Gorse La COS CO15 ... 182 B5
　K/T/MI CO5 ... 174 A9
Gorse Rd IPSE IP3 ... 25 J8
Gorse Wy COLW CO3 ... 150 G2
　COS CO15 ... 206 E5
Gorseway ROMW/RG RM7 ... 318 D4
Gosbecks Rd CLAS CO2 ... 151 L4
Gosbecks Vw COLS CO2 ... 151 K3
Gosfield Cl RAYL SS6 ... 306 D4
Gosfield Rd BCTR RM8 ... 317 P5
　BRTR CM7 ... 121 N4
　COLS CO2 ... 152 B6
Gosford Cl SUD CO10 ... 44 A3
Goshawk Av COLS CO2 ... 296 A9
Gosford Wy FX IP11 ... 35 M5
Goshawk Dr CHLM/GWD CM2 ... 240 A5
The Goslings SBN/FI SS3 ... 330 F7
　WIT CM8 ... 146 D9
Gosport Dr HCH RM12 ... 337 L3
Gosport Rd WALTH E17 ... 294 C9
The Gossetts GTDUN CM6 ... 191 H8
Gostling Pl KESC IP5 ... 27 K3
Gotfield Cl SUD CO10 ... 47 M4
Gould Cl CHONG CM5 ... 213 H9
Gouldings Av WOTN CO14 ... 159 J6
Goulds Rd BURES CO8 ... 75 J7
Goulton Rd CLPT E5 ... 314 A1
Gourney Gv CDW/CHF RM16 ... 217 P2
Government Rw PEND EN3 ... 252 D7
Govier Cl SRTFD E15 ... 315 H9
Cowan Brae SBF/HAD SS7 * ... 325 N1
Cowan Cl SBF/HAD SS7 ... 325 N1
Gowers Av FSTGT E7 ... 315 K8
Gowers Av CHLM/GWD CM2 ... 240 D4
Gowers Cl KESC IP5 ... 27 K4
Gowers Vw CDW/CHF RM16 ... 340 C4
The Gowers HLW CM20 ... 211 H1
Goya Ri SBN/FI SS3 ... 330 F6
Goyfield Av FX IP11 ... 11 C2
Grace Cl BARK/HLT IG6 ... 296 C3
Grace Gdns BSF CM23 ... 162 C1
Grace Pl BOW E3 ... 333 J4
Graces La CHLM/GWD CM2 ... 197 K5
Grace St BOW E3 ... 332 E3
Graces Wk FOS CO13 ... 159 H8
　RCHLM CM5 ... 219 L9
Graeme Rd EN EN1 ... 273 K5
Grafton Gdns BCTR RM8 ... 317 K4
Grafton Pl CHLM/GWD CM2 ... 218 F7
Grafton Rd BCTR RM8 ... 317 M4
　CVI SS8 ... 344 F3
　ENC/FH EN2 ... 272 E2
　HAR CO12 ... 15 F5
Grafton Wy IP IP1 ... 16 D6
Graham Av BROX EN10 ... 208 B8
　IP IP1 ... 25 J3
Graham Cl BCAYW CM12 ... 283 J5
　HOC/HUL SS5 ... 287 P9
　RBRW/HUT CM13 ... 281 M4
　SLH/COR SS17 ... 341 L1
Grahame Rd FX IP11 ... 35 J6
　IP IP1 ... 16 B1
　PLSTW E13 ... 333 K4
Grailands BSF CM23 ... 137 J6
Grainger Cl SOSN SS2 ... 19 G1
Grainger Rd SOSN SS2 ... 19 G1
Grammar Cl WIT CM8 ... 314 G4
Grammar School Pl SUD CO10 ... 20 C6
Grampian Gv CHLM/WR CM1 ... 217 L5
The Granaries WAB EN9 ... 253 H4
Granary Cl HOD EN11 ... 209 N6
　RCHLM CM5 ... 267 J4

HLWW/ROY CM19 ....209 M3
KESG IP5 ....17 J5
Grange Pde BCAYE CM11 * ...283 K9
Grange Pk BSF CM25 ....137 L5
Grange Park Av WCHMH N21 ...272 C5
Grange Park Dr LOS SS9 ....328 A4
Grange Park Rd LEY E10 ....314 E4
Granger Av MAL CM9 ....244 A1
Grange Rd BCAYE CM11 ....283 K9
  BOC CM0 ....248 C7
  BSF CM23 ....137 M7
  FX IP11 ....10 D3
  GRAYS RM17 ....349 L4
  HAR CM12 ....110 B6
  HARH RM3 ....298 G3
  IL IG1 ....316 D6
  IPNE IP4 ....17 J5
  K/T/MI CO5 ....173 M8
  LEY E10 ....314 D3
  LOS SS9 ....327 N5
  MGTR CO11 ....105 N7
  PIT SS15 ....305 K7
  PLSTW E13 ....353 K5
  RCHLM CM3 ....192 F2
  RCOLW CO6 ....102 E9
  SAFWN CB10 ....49 K2
  SBF/HAD SS7 ....306 C8
  SOCK/AV RM15 ....337 P8
  WALTH E17 ....294 B9
  WICKE SS11 ....285 H6
  WIT CM8 ....197 N8
Granger Rw CHLM/WR CM1 ......217 M7
Grantham Wy ROM RM1 ....318 F1
Grangeside BSF CM25 ....137 L4
The Grange HOD EN11 * 208 D6
Grange Wk BSF CM25 ....137 M7
Grange Wy COLS CO2 ....346 G5
  ERITH DA8 ....346 G5
Grangeway SBF/HAD SS7 ....306 D9
  WFD IG8 ....295 M1
Grangeway Gdns REDBR IG4 ...295 P9
The Grangeway WCHMH N21 ...272 C5
Grangewood SBF/HAD SS7 * 326 A1
Grangewood Av
  CDW/CHF RM16 ....349 P1
  RAIN RM13 ....357 H4
Grangewood Cl
Grangewood St THAM E6 ....333 N1
Granham Gdns ED N9 ....273 L8
Granites CM BCAYE CM11 ....303 N1
Granleigh Rd WAN E11 ....315 H4
Granta Cl SAFWN CB10 ....65 M2
Granta V CBE/LIN CB1 ....58 C1
Grantchester Pl KESG IP5 ....26 F4
Grant Cl STHGT/OAK N14 ....272 B6
  WICKX SS12 ....305 K2
Grantham Av BRTR CM77 ....144 E7
Grantham Cl COL CO1 ....25 J1
Grantham Crs CHTY IP2 ....25 H7
Grantham Gdns CHDH RM6 .....317 N1
  WARE SG12 ....184 B2
Grantham Rd MNPK E12 ....316 B5
  RCOLW CO6 ....127 L1
Grantham Wy
  CDW/CHF RM16 ....339 K8
Grantley Cl RCOLW CO6 ....150 A1
Grantley St WCHPL E1 ....332 A3
Grantock Rd WALTH E17 ....294 F6
Granton Av HCH RM12 ....319 L4
Granton Rd GDMY/SEVK IG3 ...317 H5
Grant St PLSTW E13 ....333 K5
Granville Av BCAYW CM12 ......282 C6
  RCOLW CO6 ....127 H4
  SBF/HAD SS7 ....326 B2
Granville Gdns HOD EN11 ......208 D7
Granville Rd COL CO1 ....152 C1
  COS CO15 ....7 G4
  EPP CM16 ....233 J8
  FX IP11 ....11 K3
  IL IG1 ....316 C3
  SWFD E18 ....295 L6
  WALTH E17 ....314 E1
Granville St IP IP1 ....16 B5
Granville Wy RCOLE CO7 ....179 M6
Grapnells VGE SS16 ....324 E2
Grasby Cl RCOLE CO7 ....153 J4
Grasmead Av LOS SS9 ....328 A4
Grasmere Av FX IP11 ....35 N5
  HOC/HUL SS5 ....144 F8
  IPSE IP5 ....31 H2
  LOU IG10 ....276 A1
Grasmere Gdns BRTR CM77 .....144 F8
  IPSE IP5 ....31 H2
  LOU IG10 ....276 A1
Grasmere Gdns FOS CO13 ....158 F7
  PSEND SS4 ....295 P9
Grasmere Rd BXLYHN DA7 ......347 J3
  CVI SS8 ....344 B2
  PLSTW E13 ....333 K2
  SBF/HAD SS7 ....306 B9
  WARE SG12 ....184 B2
Grassfields FOS CO13 ....158 F9
Grasshaven Wy THMD SE28 ....354 G8
Grassmere COLN CO4 ....128 C3
Grassmere Rd EMPK RM11 ......299 L8
Gratmore Gn VGE SS16 ....324 D5
Gravel Cl COL CO1 ....277 H8
Gravel Hd RCOLW CO6 ....106 E9
Gravel Hill Wy HAR CO12 ......109 P7
Gravel La CHIG IG7 ....277 H5
Gravelly La CHLM/WR CM1 .....216 C8
Gravelpit La MGTR CO11 ....81 P7
Gravel Pit La MGTR CO11 ....81 P7
Gravel Rd LOS SS9 ....307 L7
The Gravel RCOLW CO6 ....147 N4
Gray Av BCTR RM8 ....317 N3
Gray Gdns HCH RM12 ....318 F8
Graylands GRAYS RM17 * 149 H5
Grayling Ct BRTR CM7 ....145 H5
  CAN/RD E16 * 333 H4
Grayling Dr COLN CO4 ....128 C6
Gray's Av BCTR RM8 ....127 N9
Grays Cl K/T/MI CO5 ....202 F6
Grays Cl BSF CM25 ....137 K6
Grays End Cl CDW/CHF RM16 ...349 K1
Gray's La BRTR CM7 ....95 K4
Grays Md HSTD CO9 ....72 C7
Graysons Cl RAIN RM13 ....307 H5
Gray's Orch KIR/NAC IP10 ......15 J5
Grays Wk RBRW/HUT CM13 .....281 N6
Great Bentley Rd RCOLE CO7 ...154 F3
Great Berry Farm Cha
  VGE SS16 ....323 H2
Great Berry La VGE SS16 ....323 H2
Great Brays WCHMH E18 ....211 H4
Great Burches Rd
  SBF/HAD SS7 ....306 D8
Great Cambridge Rd
  CHES/WCR EN8 ....251 P1
Great Canfield Rd RBSF CM22 ...139 N7
Great Cob CHLM/WR CM1 ....218 D6
Great Colman St IPNE IP4 ....16 E4
Great Cullings
  ROMW/RG RM7 ....318 D4
Great Eastern Av SOSN SS2 .....19 F1
Great Eastern Cl BSF CM23 .....137 M8
Great Eastern Rd BRW CM14 ...300 F1
  HOC/HUL SS5 ....307 P2
  SRTFD E15 ....314 G9
  SUD CO10 ....80 E3
Great Eastern Sq FX IP11 ....35 K6
Great Fld FX IP11 ....34 F5
Greatfield Av EHAM E6 ....333 K4
Greatfields Rd BARK IG11 ....334 E1
Great Fox Meadow
  BRWN CM15 ....258 C7
Great Galley Cl BARK IG11 ......335 J5
Great Gardens Rd
  EMPK RM11 ....318 G1
Great Gibcracks Cha
  RCHLM CM3 ....241 M8
Great Gipping St IP IP1 ....16 C5
Great Godfreys
  CHLM/WR CM1 ....238 C1
Great Gregorie VGE SS16 ....2 A7
Great Gregories La EPP CM16 ...254 F5
Great Groves CHESW EN7 ....229 K7
Great Hadham Rd BSF CM23 ...136 E9
Great Harlings RIPS/CAP IP9 ....85 M8
Great Harrods WOTN CO14 .....159 H7
Great Hays LOS SS9 ....327 M1
Great Holland Common Rd
  COS CO15 ....182 E5
Greathouse Cha
  SLH/COR SS17 ....324 B8
Great House Farm Rd
  COLS CO2 ....151 K9
Great Knightleys LAIN SS15 .....2 B5
Great Lawn CHONG CM5 ....235 M6
Great Leighs Wy PIT SS13 ......305 H1
Great Leylands HLWS CM18 .....211 H4
Great Meadow BROX EN10 .....230 D1
Great Mistley VGE SS16 ....3 J7
Great Nelmes Cha
  EMPK RM11 ....299 L9
Great Notley Av BRTR CM77 ....144 E9
Great Oak Ck HSTD CO9 ....57 P9
Great Oaks BSDN SS14 ....286 F2
  CHIG IG7 ....296 D1
  RBRW/HUT CM13 ....281 L5
Great Owl Rd CHIG IG7 ....276 B9
Great Plumtree HLWE CM20 ....210 C1
Great Ranton PIT SS13 ....305 H7
Great Ropers La BRW CM14 ....300 D3
Great Saling WICKE SS11 ....305 M1
Great Smials RCHLM CM3 ....286 F2
Great Spenders BSDN SS14 .....3 K1
Great Sq BRTR CM7 ....145 J3
Great Stockwood Rd
  CHESW EN7 ....229 J5
Great Tey Rd RCOLW CO6 ......149 H1
Great Totham Rd WIT CM8 .....198 A7
Great Tufts RIPS/CAP IP9 ....28 D9
Great Warley St
  RBRW/HUT CM13 ....300 D5
Great Wheatley Rd RAYL SS6 ...306 D6
Great Whip St CHTY IP2 ....16 E7
Great Yeldham Rd HSTD CO9 ...71 J5
Greaves Ct BARK IG11 ....335 H4
Grebe Cl BARK IG11 ....24 F9
  CHTY IP2 ....315 J7
  RCHLM CM3 ....267 P1
  WALTH E17 * 294 B4
Grebe Crest WTHK RM20 ....348 D2
Greding Wk RBRW/HUT CM13 ...281 L8
Green Acre SUD CO10 ....47 P8
Greenacre Gdns WALTH E17 ...294 F8
Greenacre La ING CM4 ....261 M9
Greenacre Ms LOS SS9 ....327 P4
Greenacres COLN CO4 ....127 P4
  COS CO15 ....182 B8
  EPP CM16 ....232 C7
  RCOLW CO6 ....147 N5
  SBF/HAD SS7 ....327 H5
Greenacres Cl RAIN RM13 ....357 K5
Greenacre Sq
  BERM/RHTH SE16 * 332 A9
Green Acres Cl COLS CO2 ....151 J9
Greenacre Wk
  STHGT/OAK N14 ....272 C5
Greenall Cl CHES/WCR EN8 ....230 B9
Green Av CVI SS8 ....344 B2
Greenaway Av UED N18 * 294 A2
Greenbank CHESW EN7 ....229 N7
Greenbank Cl CHING E4 ....294 B4
  HARH RM3 ....279 J9
Greenbanks LOS SS9 ....328 B4
  UPMR RM14 ....320 B4
Green Chain Wk THMD SE28 ...355 L8
Green Cl CHES/WCR EN8.........251 P2
  CHLM/WR CM1 ....217 N7
  EPP CM16 ....232 C5
  RCHLM CM3 ....196 P9
Green Cnr GTDUN CM6 * 142 E1
Green Crs KIR/NAC IP10 ....15 J2
Greencroft Gdns EN EN1 ....275 K2
Green Dragon La
  WCHMH N21 ....272 E4
Greendyke CVI SS8 ....326 C9
Green End WCHMH N21 ....272 G8
Green End La FOS CO13 ....158 A9
Greene Vw BRTR CM7 ....145 L6
Green Farm Rd RCOLW CO6 ....99 J6
Greenfield WIT CM8 ....197 K3
Greenfield Dr RCOLW CO6 ......124 C6
Greenfield Gdns DAGW RM9 ...335 M3
Greenfield Rd DAGW RM9 ......335 K1
Greenfields BCAYW CM12 ......283 H8
  HSTD CO9 ....97 H9
  LOU IG10 ....276 B3
  POTB/CUF EN6 * 228 D9
  STSD CM24 ....114 B8
  WOTN CO14 ....158 G7
Greenfields Cl BCAYW CM12 ...282 G8
Greenfields St WAB EN9 ....252 F4
Greenfields Wy HVHL CB9 ....41 H5
Greenfinch Av CHTY IP2 ....24 E8
Greenfinch End COLN CO4 .....128 C7
Greenford Rd COS CO15 ....6 A4
Greengate St PLSTW E13 ....333 L2
Green Gld EPP CM16 ....254 F7
Greenham Crs CHING E4 ....294 C5
Greenhaven Dr THMD SE28 ....335 J6
Greenheys Dr SWFD E18 ....295 J7
Greenhill BKHH IG9 ....275 M7
Greenhill Pk BSF CM25 ....137 J9
  RCHLM CM3 ....13 K6
Greenhills HLW CM20 ....210 D3
Greenhurst Rd RCOLE CO7 .....179 M7
Greenlands RCFD SS4 ....308 E3
Green La BCAYW CM12 ....303 H4
  BCTR RM8 ....317 N4
  BOC CM0 ....290 E1
  BROX EN10 ....230 E2
  BRW CM14 ....258 A9
  BRW CM14 ....280 D7
  BRW CM14 ....300 D4
  CBE/LIN CB1 ....339 M5
  CDW/CHF RM16 ....276 D7
  CHIG IG7 ....275 H2
  CHLM/WR CM1 ....216 C7
  COLU CO2 ....102 G3
  COLN CO4 ....128 F4
  CVI SS8 ....344 C2
  GTDUN CM6 ....141 K5
  HLWE CM17 ....212 A4
  IL IG1 ....316 E4
  K/T/MI CO5 ....205 P1
  K/T/MI CO5 ....199 M3
  LOS SS9 ....307 N8
  MAL CM9 ....199 K8
  RCHLM CM3 ....267 N4
  RCOLE CO7 ....129 K6
  RCOLE CO7 ....129 K6
  RCOLW CO6 ....125 N7
  RCOLW CO6 ....127 M1
  RCOS CO16 ....156 D9
  RIPS/CAP IP9 ....82 D2
  VGE SS16 ....325 L2
  WAB EN9 ....253 N5
  WDBR IP12 ....27 N1
  WIT CM8 ....170 B5
  WOTN CO14 ....159 L4
Green Lanes WCHMH N21 ....272 G7
Greenleafe Dr BARK/HLT IG6 ...296 C7
Greenleaf Rd EHAM E6 ....333 M1
  WALTH E17 ....313 J1
Greenleas SBF/HAD SS7 ....306 E9
Green Man La WIT CM8 ....198 A6
Green Md RCHLM CM3 ....286 F1
Green Moor Link
  WCHMH N21 ....272 C6
Greenmoor Rd PEND EN3 ....275 P1
Green Oak BRW CM14 ....29 M2
Greenoaks SBF/HAD SS7 ....326 B3
Greenock Wy ROM RM1 ....298 D4
Green Pond Cl WALTH E17 .....294 B7
Green Pond Rd WALTH E17 .....294 B7
Green Ride LOU IG10 ....275 K5
Green Rd SBF/HAD SS7 ....326 A5
  STHGT/OAK N14 ....272 A5
The Greens LOU IG10 ....276 B1
Greens Farm La BCAYE CM11 ...283 K7
Greenshank Cl WALTH E17 .....294 B4
Greenshaw BRW CM14 ....280 E7
Greenside BCTR RM8 ....317 K4
Greenslade Rd BARK IG11 ......316 E9
Green Sleeves Dr BRW CM14 ...300 E2
Greensmill MGTR CO11 ....105 N8
Greenspire Gv RHW CM13 ......24 C9
Greenstead SBW CM21 ....187 M3
Greenstead Av WFD IG8 ....295 M3
Greenstead Cl
  RBRW/HUT CM13 ....281 P6
Greensted Gdns WFD IG8 ......295 M5
Greenstead Rd COL CO1 ....9 J5
Greensted Cl BSDN SS14 ....324 E1
Greensted CHONG CM5 ....254 F7
  LOU IG10 ....275 P6
Greensted BSDN SS14 ....324 E1
The Greens IPNE IP4 ....26 E7
Greenstone Ms WAN E11 ....315 K1
Green St FSTGT E7 ....315 L7
  GTDUN CM6 ....164 F2
  HLWE CM17 ....211 J2
  ING CM4 ....259 M3
  PEND EN3 ....274 A2
Greensward La HOC/HUL SS5 ...308 A1
The Green BKHH IG9 ....275 L7
  BSF CM23 * 162 C1
  CDW/CHF RM16 ....340 B5
  CHES/WCR EN8 ....229 P7
  CHLM/WR CM1 ....217 N7
  CHLM/WR CM1 ....239 J1
  COS CO15 ....206 C2
  ED N9 ....273 M8
  EPP CM16 ....254 F7
  FOS CO13 ....183 H1
  HAR CO12 ....110 A6
  ING CM4 ....259 H1
LOS SS9 ....307 P8
MGTR CO11 ....106 E4
RAIN RM13 ....337 K7
RCOS CO16 * 206 A6
SLH/COR SS17 ....341 L4
SRTFD E15 ....315 J8
STHGT/OAK N14 ....272 C9
WAN E11 ....315 L1
WARE SG12 ....184 C1
WCHMH N21 ....272 F6
Green Trees EPP CM16 ....255 H1
Green Trees Av CHING E4 ....266 A4
Greenview Pk COS CO15 ....182 B6
Green Wk CHONG CM5 ....235 L9
  DART DA1 ....348 G9
  WFD IG8 ....295 P3
The Green Wk CHING E4 ....274 F7
Green Wy RCOLW CO6 ....99 H6
Greenway BCAYE CM11 ....283 L7
  BCTR RM8 ....137 P8
  FOS CO13 ....158 G9
  HARH RM3 ....299 N3
  HLWW/ROY CM19 ....209 P5
  RBRW/HUT CM13 ....281 K8
  STHGT/OAK N14 ....272 D6
Greenway Av WALTH E17 ....294 G8
Greenway Ct IL IG1 ....316 B3
  SRTFD E15 ....333 H2
Greenway Gdns BRTR CM77 ...144 C7
  CHESW EN7 ....228 G9
  CHLM/WR CM1 ....218 A5
  CVI SS8 ....326 C9
  HSTD CO9 ....97 J9
  K/T/MI CO5 ....173 J2
  RCFD SS4 ....308 G5
  SAFWS CB11 ....65 M2
  SBF/HAD SS7 ....325 N4
  SOS SS1 ....329 M7
Greenways Cl IP IP1 ....25 J5
Greenwich Crs EHAM E6 ....333 P5
Greenwich Rd IPSE IP5 ....25 L9
Greenwich Wy WAB EN9 ....252 D9
Greenwood Cl CHESW EN7 .....251 N1
  HVHL CB9 ....41 H5
Greenwood Dr WAN E11 ....294 F2
Greenwood Gdns
  BARK/HLT IG6 ....296 D4
  PLMGR N13 ....272 G9
Greenwood Rd WY COLN CO4 ...128 D4
Greenwood Rd CHING E4 ....294 B1
  PLSTW E13 ....333 J2
Greenyard WAB EN9 ....252 F5
Greg Cl LEY E10 ....314 F1
Gregory Cl HOC/HUL SS5 ....308 A3
Gregory Ms WAB EN9 ....252 E2
Gregory Rd CHDH RM6 ....297 L8
Gregory St SUD CO10 ....20 C5
Grenade St POP/IOD E14 ....332 C7
Grenadier Rd HVHL CB9 ....40 F3
Grenadier St CAN/RD E16 ......334 B8
Grenadine Cl CHESW EN7 ......229 L6
Grendel Wy COS CO15 ....182 C7
Grenfell Av COS CO15 ....182 C7
  HCH RM12 ....318 E3
Grenfell Cl COLN CO4 ....9 J2
Grennan Cl RBRW/HUT CM13 ...301 N5
Grenville Av BROX EN10 ....208 F4
Grenville Cl CHES/WCR EN8 ....252 A5
Grenville Gdns WFD IG8 ....295 M4
Grenville Rd BRTR CM7 ....145 H5
  CDW/CHF RM16 ....348 E5
  COS CO15 ....47 J9
Gresham Ct BRW CM14 ....280 F9
Gresham Ct CHDH RM6 ....297 J9
Gresham Dr CHDH RM6 ....297 J9
Gresley Cl COLN CO4 ....128 A5
  WALTH E17 ....314 B1
Grevatt Ldg PIT SS13 ....325 H1
Greville Ct WOTN CO14 ....159 M4
Greville Rd WALTH E17 ....294 F8
Greyfriars IP IP1 ....16 C5
  RBRW/HUT CM13 ....281 L6
Grey Friars Rd IP IP1 ....16 D6
Greygoose Pk
  HLWW/ROY CM19 ....210 B6
Greyhound Hl COLN CO4 ....103 P4
Greyhound La
  CDW/CHF RM16 ....340 B9
Greyhound Wy SOSN SS2 ....19 C1
Grey Lady Pl BCAYE CM11 .....283 J5
Grey Ladys CHLM/GWD CM2 ...240 A7
Greys Cl SUD CO10 ....45 H2
Greys Hollow SAFWS CB11 .....89 J8
Greystoke Gdns ENC/FH EN2 ...273 L5
Greystone Gdns
  BARK/HLT IG6 ....296 D6
Greystones Ct COS CO15 ....151 K3
Greyswood Av UED N18 * 294 A2
Grey Towers Av EMPK RM11 ...319 J5
Grey Towers Gdns
  EMPK RM11 ....319 H5
Gridiron Pl UPMR RM14 ....319 N4
Grieves Ct COLW CO5 ....150 F2
Griffin Av CVI SS8 ....326 F9
  UPMR RM14 ....319 P4
Griffith Cl CHDH RM6 ....317 K2
The Griffins CDW/CHF RM16 ...339 L9
Griffith Cl CDW/CHF RM16 .....348 F1
Grifon Rd CDW/CHF RM16 .....348 F1
Griffon Rd CDW/CHF RM16 ....348 F1
Griggs Ap IL IG1 ....316 D4
Griggs Gdns HCH RM12 ....319 H7
Griggs Rd LEY E10 ....314 F1
Grimsby Gv CAN/RD E16 ....334 C9
Grimshaw Wy ROM RM1 ....298 D9
Grimston Av BRTR CM7 ....124 B9
Grimston Rd BSDN SS14 ....304 E6
  COLS CO2 ....152 B2
Grimwade Cl MGTR CO11 ....106 C1
Grimwade La LEY E10 ....159 J7
Grimwade St IPNE IP4 ....17 G6
The Grindle RIPW IP8 ....24 A1
Grinstead La RBSF CM22 ....162 F7
The Grip CBE/LIN CE1 ....38 A2
Groombridge Rd HOM E9 ....314 A9
Groom Pk COS CO15 ....182 E5
Groom Rd BROX EN10 ....230 C5
Groomside BRTR CM7 ....145 K4
Grooms La WIT CM8 ....171 M1
Grosvenor Cl BSF CM23 ....240 C5
  CHLM/GWD CM2 ....240 C5
  IPNE IP4 ....25 M3
  K/T/MI CO5 ....174 A8
  LOU IG10 ....254 C9
Grosvenor Ct WOS/PRIT SS0 * ...328 D7
Grosvenor Dr EMPK RM11 ......319 H5
  LOU IG10 ....276 C1
Grosvenor Gdns
  BCAYW CM12 ....283 H4
  STHGT/OAK N14 ....272 C5
  WAN E11 ....320 A4
  WFD IG8 ....295 K3
Grosvenor Ms WOS/PRIT SS0 ...328 D7
Grosvenor Park Rd
  WALTH E17 ....294 D9
Grosvenor Ri East WALTH E17 ...294 E9
Grosvenor Rd BCTR RM8 ....317 N3
  BROX EN10 ....208 C8
  CDW/CHF RM16 ....340 E6
  ED N9 ....273 N7
  FSTGT E7 ....315 L8
  IL IG1 ....316 D5
  LEY E10 ....314 F3
  RAYL SS6 ....306 E3
  ROMW/RG RM7 ....318 B2
  SBF/HAD SS7 ....326 B5
  SUD CO10 ....46 C9
  WAN E11 ....295 L9
  WOS/PRIT SS0 ....328 D7
The Grotto WARE SG12 ....184 D8
Grove Av K/T/MI CO5 ....202 F7
  VGE SS16 ....323 J3
  WOTN CO14 ....159 J6
Grovebury Cl ERITH DA8 ....346 C4
Grovebury Ct
  STHGT/OAK N14 ....272 B6
Grovebury Rd THMD SE28 .....335 J9
  STHGT/OAK N14 ....272 A6
Grove Cl RAYL SS6 ....307 K6
  WAB EN9 ....252 E5
  WOS/PRIT SS0 ....328 C3
Grove Crs SWFD E18 ....295 J6
Grove Crescent Rd
  SRTFD E15 ....314 G8
Grove Cl CHESW EN7 ....229 J9
Grove End LOS SS9 ....327 P6
  SWFD E18 ....295 J6
Grove Farm Rd WIT CM8 ....198 G3
Grove Gdns PEND EN3 ....252 A9
Grove Green Rd LEY E10 ....314 F5
Groverherst Rd DART DA1 .....347 L8
Grove Hl COLN CO4 ....104 A4
  LOS SS9 ....307 L8
  RIPW IP8 ....29 J3
  STSD CM24 ....114 B8
  SWFD E18 ....295 J6
Grovelands SOSN SS2 ....329 K4
Grovelands Ct
  STHGT/OAK N14 ....272 C5
Grovelands Rd WICKW SS12 ...305 J1
Grovelands Wy GRAYS RM17 ...349 J3
Grove La CHIG IG7 ....277 M6
  EPP CM16 ....233 H9
  IPNE IP4 ....17 J5
  RIPS/CAP IP9 ....85 N7
Grove Orch BRTR CM7 ....121 M6
Grove Pk WAN E11 ....295 L9
Grove Park Av CHING E4 ....294 B9
Grove Park Rd RAIN RM13 .....336 F1
Grove Rd BCAYW CM12 ....282 G6
  BXLYHN DA7 ....346 B9
  CHDH RM6 ....317 K2
  CHING E4 ....274 F9
  CHLM/GWD CM2 ....240 G5
  CVI SS8 ....344 F1
  GRAYS RM17 ....349 M4
  HOM E9 ....332 A3
  K/T/MI CO5 ....81 N9
  RAYL SS6 ....306 D3
  RCOS CO16 ....156 C9
  RIPS/CAP IP9 ....81 P3
  SBF/HAD SS7 ....326 A4
  SLH/COR SS17 ....341 L5
  SWFD E18 ....295 J6
  WALTH E17 ....314 E1
  WAN E11 ....315 J2
  WARE SG12 ....184 C1
Grove Rd West PEND EN3 ......251 P7
Grover St SOS SS1 ....338 C7
Grove St CAN/AV RM15 ....338 C2
Groveside Rd CHING E4 ....275 H9
The Grove BCAYE CM11 ....283 K3
  BRW CM14 ....300 C1
  CHLM/GWD CM2 ....240 G5
  CHING E4 ....274 F7
  ENC/FH EN2 ....272 F1
  IP IP1 ....25 K1
  KESG IP5 ....27 M5
  RBSF CM22 ....163 J3
  RCHLM CM3 ....242 C9
  SLH/COR SS17 * 341 L5

SOSN SS2 ....329 J4
SRTFD E15 ....315 H9
STON SG11 ....136 D7
UPMR RM14 ....319 M6
WIT CM8 ....197 K2
Grove Wk SBN/FI SS5 ....330 D8
Groveway BCTR RM8 ....317 L6
Grovewood Cl CHES SG8 ....307 L8
Grovewood Ct LOS SS9 ....307 L8
Grovewood Pl WFD IG8 ....296 A3
Grundy St POP/IOD E14 ....332 E6
Grymes Dyke Ct COLW CO5 *...126 C9
Gryme's Dyke Wy COLW CO5 ...150 C3
Guardian Av CLW PLTW RM16 ...338 D9
Guardian Cl EMPK RM11 ....318 C4
Guardsman La BRW CM14 ....300 C2
Gubbins La HARH RM5 ....299 L5
Guelph's La GTDUN CM6 ....92 B5
Guernsey Gdns WICKE SS11 .....285 H7
Guernsey Rd LIT E11 ....144 G4
Guernsey Wy BRTR CM7 ....144 G4
Guildford Rd COL CO1 ....8 E4
EHAM E6 ....333 P6
GDMY/SEVK IG3 ....316 F4
SOSN SS2 ....19 G2
WALTH E17 ....294 F5
Guildhall Wy SAFWB CB10 ....52 F3
Guinea Cl BRTR CM7 ....145 N2
Guinevere Gdns
CHES/WCR EN8 ....230 A9
Guinness Cl HOM E9 ....314 B9
Guinness Trust Est
SRTFD E15 ....333 J1
Guithavon Ri WIT CM8 ....197 J2
Guithavon Rd WIT CM8 ....197 J3
Guithavon St WIT CM8 ....197 J2
Gulls Cft BRTR CM7 ....145 M3
Gull's La RCOLE CO7 ....105 H5
Gulpher Rd FX IP11 ....35 H5
Gumley Rd WTHK KM20 ....548 G4
Gunfleet Cl K/T/MI CO5 ....202 E5
Gun Hl COLN CO4 ....104 C1
TIL RM18 ....350 E4
Gun Hill Pl VGE SS16 ....3 H7
Gunmakers La HOM E9 ....332 D1
Gunner Dr PEND EN3 ....252 D7
Gunners Gv CHING E4 ....274 F9
Gunners Rd SBN/FI SS3 ....330 F7
Gunning Rd GRAYS RM17 ....344 M5
Gunson Ga CHLM/GWD CM2 ......240 C3
Gunwhale Cl BERM/RHTH SE16 .332 A8
Gurdon Rd COLS CO2 ....152 A3
Gurlings Cl HVHL CB9 ....41 K1
Gurney Benham Cl COLS CO2 ...151 L2
Gurney Ct BARK IG11 ....316 C6
SRTFD E15 ....315 H7
WALTH E17 ....294 A5
Gurney Rd SRTFD E15 ....315 H7
Gurton Rd RCOLW CO6 ....147 P3
Gustedhall La HOC/HUL SS5 .....307 P5
Guston Gdns KIR/NAC IP10 ....53 N7
Gutteridge Hall La
RCOS CO16 ....156 B7
Gutteridge La ABR/ST RM4 ....278 B5
Gutters La CHLM/WR CM1 ....218 A4
Guy Cook Cl SUD CO10 ....61 M5
Guys Farm Rd RCHLM CM5 ....286 C1
Guysfield Cl RAIN RM13 ....336 F1
Guysfield Dr RAIN RM13 ....336 F1
Gwendalen Av CVI SS8 ....344 C1
Gwendoline Av PLSTW E13 ....333 L1
Gwendoline Rd IPNE IP4 ....26 D7
Gwyn Cl RCHLM CM5 ....219 K2
Gwynne Park Av WFD IG8 ....296 A3
Gwynne Rd HAR CO12 ....14 E5
Gyllyngdune Gdns
GDMY/SEVK IG3 ....316 G5
Gymnasium St IP IP1 ....16 B3
Gypsy Cl WARE SG12 ....184 C8
Gypsy La K/T/MI CO5 ....148 C7
WARE SG12 ....184 D8

H

Haarlem Rd CVI SS8 ....344 A1
Haarle Rd CVI SS8 ....344 C3
Haase Cl CVI SS8 ....326 D8
Habgood Rd LOU IG10 ....275 P2
Hackamore SBF/HAD SS7 ....326 E1
Hackmans La RCHLM CM5 ....245 H7
Hacton Dr HCH KM12 ....319 K6
Hacton La UPMR RM14 ....319 L7
Haddeston Ga BROX EN10 ....230 C5
Haddon Cl EN EN1 ....273 M5
RAYL SS6 ....306 D4
Haddon Rd RCHLM CM5 ....286 C1
Haddon Pk COL CO1 ....9 K7
Hadfield Dr BRTR CM7 ....145 L9
Hadfield Rd SLH/COR SS17 ....341 L4
Hadham Ct BSF CM23 ....137 J6
Hadham Gv BSF CM23 ....137 H6
Hadham Rd BSF CM23 ....136 E5
Hadleigh Ct BROX EN10 ....230 C1
Hadleigh Park Av
SBF/HAD SS7 ....326 F3
Hadleigh Rd ED N9 ....159 H9
FOS CO15 ....327 M5
LOS SS9 ....306 C5
RCOLE CO7 ....79 M4
RCOLE CO7 ....80 E6
RCOS CO16 ....156 B7
RIPW IP9 ....24 D7
WOS/PRIT SS0 ....18 B5
Hadleigh Cl BRTR CM7 ....121 L6
WCHMH N21 ....272 F5
Hadley Gra HLWE CM17 ....211 K4
Hadley Rd ENC/FH EN2 ....250 D8

Hadley Wy WCHMH N21 ....272 F5
Hadrian Cl BOW E3 ....332 D1
COLN CO4 ....128 C1
HVHL CB9 ....41 M4
Hadrian's Ride EN EN1 ....273 L4
Hadrians Wy MAL CM9 ....222 B7
Hadstock Rd CBE/LIN CB1 ....38 A2
Haggars La RCOLE CO7 ....154 E3
Haggers La BRTR W17 * 294 C7
Hagg Hl RCHLM CM5 ....265 M4
Haig Ct CHLM/GWD CM2 ....4 D6
Haig Rd CDW/CHF RM16 ....550 B1
Haig Rd East PLSTW E13 ....333 M3
Haig Rd West PLSTW E13 ....333 M3
Hailes Wd RBSF CM22 ....114 G5
Hailey Av HOD EN11 ....208 D1
Haileybury Av EN EN1 ....273 L5
Hailey La HOD EN11 ....208 A2
Hailey Rd ERITHM DA18 ....335 P9
Hailsham Cl HARH RM5 ....299 H2
Hailsham Rd RCFD SS4 ....308 C7
Hainault Av RCFD SS4 ....308 G7
WOS/PRIT SS0 ....32 A5
Hainault Buildings LEY E10 * 314 F3
Hainault Cl SBF/HAD SS7 ....327 H2
Hainault Gore CHDH RM6 ....297 M9
Hainault Rd CHDH RM6 ....297 J4
CHIG IG7 ....296 D1
RCHLM CM5 ....266 B8
WAN E11 ....298 C7
Hainault St IL IG1 ....316 C4
Halbutt St DAGW RM9 ....317 N6
Halcyon Wy EMPK RM11 ....319 L3
Haldane Cl PEND EN3 ....252 EB
Haldane Rd EHAM E6 ....333 N3
THMD SE28 ....335 L7
Haldan Rd CHING E4 ....294 F3
Hale Cl CHING E4 ....274 F9
CHTY IP2 ....24 E9
Hale End HARH RM5 ....298 C3
Hale End Rd CHING E4 ....294 G5
Hale Rd HARH RM5 ....333 P4
Halesowen Cl CHTY IP2 ....29 P2
Hale St POP/IOD E14 ....332 E7
Halesworth Cl HARH RM5 ....299 K4
Halesworth Rd HARH RM5 ....299 K3
The Hale CHING E4 ....294 G4
Halfacre La BUNT SG9 ....86 B7
Half Acres BSF CM23 ....137 L6
Halfacres WIT CM8 ....197 K5
Halfhide La CHES/WCR EN8 ....230 B5
Halfhides WAB EN9 ....252 C5
Half Moon La EPP CM16 ....254 C1
Halford Ct RIPW IP9 ....24 D9
Halford Rd WALTH E17 ....294 D9
Halfway Ct RUR RM19 ....347 M2
Halidon Ri HARH RM5 ....299 N3
Halifax Rd CHTY IP2 ....25 J9
ENC/FH EN2 ....273 H1
Hallam Cl BRWN CM15 ....281 M5
Hallam Ct BCAYW CM12 ....282 G4
Hall Av SOCK/AV RM15 ....337 P8
Hall Bridge Rd MAL CM9 ....222 D7
Hall Cha GTDUN CM6 ....167 J5
RCOLW CO6 ....149 N3
Hall Cl CHLM/GWD CM2 ....240 F4
COS CO15 ....182 G7
RBSF CM22 ....115 J2
SLH/COR SS17 ....341 M1
Hall Crs SBF/HAD SS7 ....326 G3
SOCK/AV RM15 ....337 P9
Hallcroft Cha COLN CO4 ....128 D5
Hall Cut RCOLE CO7 ....179 L7
Hall Dr HSTD CO9 ....96 G8
Hallet Rd CVI SS8 ....345 H2
Hallett Rd GTDUN CM6 ....142 D8
Hallett Rd FSTGT E7 ....315 M8
Halley St POP/IOD E14 ....332 B5
Hall Farm Cl K/T/MI CO5 ....173 K1
SBF/HAD SS7 ....326 A5
Hall Farm Gn BRTR CM7 * 119 L7
Hall Farm Rd SBF/HAD SS7 ....326 A4
Hall Fld FX IP11 ....335 J6
Hall Gdns CHING E4 ....294 C1

HOC/HUL SS5 ....308 B5
K/T/MI CO5 ....199 K1
KESG IP5 ....27 K1
KIR/NAC IP10 ....27 N1
MAL CM9 ....198 C9
MAL CM9 ....222 C7
RBSF CM22 ....114 G6
RCFD SS4 ....308 E6
RCOLE CO7 ....150 B5
RCOLW CO6 ....126 A2
RCOLW CO6 ....126 G2
RCOLW CO6 ....150 B2
SOCK/AV RM15 ....337 P9
SUD CO10 ....60 A1
WAN E11 ....314 C6
Hallside Rd EN EN1 ....251 L8
Halls Rw SLH/COR SS17 * 340 G2
Hall St CHLM/GWD CM2 ....46 F4
SUD CO10 ....60 B9
Hallsville Rd CAN/RD E16 ....333 J6
Hall Ter SOCK/AV RM15 ....338 A9
Hall View Rd RCOLE CO7 ....155 K7
Hall Wk RIPW IP9 ....24 A7
Hallwood Crs BRWN CM15 ....281 H6
Halsbury Crs EHAM E6 ....334 A5
Halsham Crs BARK IG11 ....316 C8
Halstead Ct WICKW SS12 ....305 H2
Halstead Gdns WCHMH N21 ......273 P2
Halstead Hl CHESW EN7 ....229 K9
Halstead Rd BRTR CM7 ....121 P4
ERITH DA8 ....346 D6
FOS CO15 ....158 D6
HSTD CO9 ....97 G1
RCOLW CO6 ....98 G9
RCOLW CO6 ....125 M3
RCOLW CO6 ....126 B6
WAN E11 ....295 L9
WCHMH N21 ....273 J7
Halstead Wy
RBRW/HUT CM13 ....281 M5
Halston Ct SLH/COR SS17 * 342 A1
Halston Rd MAL CM9 ....244 A2
Halstow Wy PIT SS13 ....185 M5
Halt Dr TIL RM18 ....351 H2
Halton Crs IPSE IP5 ....31 J1
Halton Rd CDW/CHF RM16 ....350 C1
Halt Robin Rd BELV DA17 ....346 A2
Halwerh terrace ....
Halvenor Crs
Halyard Reach RCHLM CM5 ....286 G5
Hamberts Rd RCHLM CM5 ....264 G8
Hamble Cl WIT CM8 ....197 H2
Hamble La SOCK/AV RM15 ....338 C5
Hamble Wy BOC CM9 ....290 F2
Hamboro Gdns LOS SS9 ....327 L5
Hambro Av RAYL SS6 ....306 C5
Hambro Pde RAYL SS6 * 307 H3
Hambro Rd BRW CM14 ....280 G8
Hamburgh Ct CHES/WCR EN8 ...280 A7
Hamden Cl DAGE RM10 ....318 A5
Hamel Wy SAFWS CB11 ....90 A4
Hameway EHAM E6 ....334 B4
Hamford Cl WOTN CO14 ....159 L4
Hamford Dr HAR CO12 ....133 M4
Hamfrith Rd SRTFD E15 ....315 J8
Hamilton Av BARK/HLT IG6 ....296 C8
ED N9 ....273 M6
ROM RM1 ....208 D3
ROM RM1 ....298 C6
Hamilton Cl
BERM/RHTH SE16 ....332 B9
LOS SS9 ....327 K4
Hamilton Ct RCHLM CM5 * 287 H2
Hamilton Crs BRW CM14 ....300 F2
Hamilton Gdns FX IP11 ....11 K3
HOC/HUL SS5 ....287 P9
Hamilton Ms RAYL SS6 ....307 J4
SAFWS CB11 ....31 N8
Hamilton Rd COLW CO15 ....151 N1
ED N9 ....273 M6
FOS CO15 ....158 B9
FX IP11 ....11 K2
GPK RM2 ....298 C9
IL IG1 ....316 C4
IPSE IP5 ....26 A8
RBSF CM22 ....140 A6
RCOLE CO7 ....153 J6
SRTFD E15 ....333 H5
SUD CO10 ....60 A9
WALTH E17 ....294 B6
Hamilton St FX IP11 ....35 H6
HAR CO12 ....110 A3
Hamlet Cl CRW RM5 ....297 P4
Hamlet Court Ms
WOS/PRIT SS0 ....75 P9
Hamlet Court Rd
WOS/PRIT SS0 ....18 B2
Hamlet Dr COLN CO4 ....128 G8
Hamlet Hl HLWW/ROY CM19 .....209 M7
Hamlet Pk HVHL CB9 * 41 L5
Hamlet Rd CHLM/GWD CM2 ....5 F6
CRW RM5 ....297 P4
HVHL CB9 ....41 K4
WOS/PRIT SS0 ....18 C5
Hamlets Wy BOW E3 ....332 C4
Hamley Cl SBF/HAD SS7 ....305 N9
Hammarskjold Rd HLW CM20 ......13 G4
Hammond Cl CHESW EN7 ....229 L5
Hammond Rd EN EN1 ....273 N2
Hammonds Cl BCTR RM8 ....317 J5
Hammonds La BCAYE CM11 ....283 K9
RBRW/HUT CM13 ....300 C5
Hammonds Rd
CHLM/GWD CM2 ....241 J1
Hammondstreet Rd
CHESW EN7 ....228 G4
Ham Park Rd FSTGT E7 ....315 K9
Hampden Cr EPP CM16 ....253 P6
Hampden Crs BRW CM14 ....300 F2

CHESW EN7 ....251 N1
Hampden Hl WARE SG12 ....184 C5
Hampden Hill Cl WARE SG12 .....184 C2
Hampden Rd GRAYS RM17 ....349 L5
Hampden Wy
STHGT/OAK N14 ....272 A7
Hampit Rd SAFWS CB11 ....63 N7
Hampshire Av EMPK RM11 ....299 M8
Hampshire Dr RCOS CO16 ....181 N8
WFD IG8 ....296 B4
Hampstead Cl THMD SE28 ....335 J8
Hampstead Gdns
HOC/HUL SS5 ....288 A9
Hampton Ct SOSN SS2 ....328 F2
Hampton Ct HOC/HUL SS5 ....307 N1
Hampton Gdns SBW CM21 ....187 J5
SOSN SS2 ....328 F2
Hampton Rd CHING E4 ....294 C2
CHLM/GWD CM2 ....240 D4
FSTGT E7 ....315 K9
IL IG1 ....316 D6
IP IP1 ....24 C4
WAN E11 ....314 C5
Hamstel Ms SOSN SS2 * 329 L4
Hamstel Rd HLW CM20 ....12 E2
SOSN SS2 ....329 L4
Hamsters Cl HSTD CO9 ....74 C9
Hanameel St CAN/RD E16 ....333 L8
Hanbury Cl CHES/WCR EN8 ......230 A9
Hanbury Dr WCHMH N21 ....272 E5
Hanbury Gdns COLN CO4 ....128 C2
Hanbury Rd CHLM/WR CM1 ......239 M2
Hance La BRTR CM77 ....144 C4
Hanchet End HVHL CB9 ....40 E2
Hanchetts Orch GTDUN CM6 .....92 B6
Hancock Rd BOW E3 ....332 F3
Handel Crs TIL RM18 ....350 B5
Handel Rd CVI SS8 ....344 G3
Handel Wk COLN CO4 ....128 F9
Handford Cut JP IP1 ....16 A6
Handford Rd IP IP1 ....16 A4
Handforth Rd IL IG1 ....316 C5
Hand La SBW CM21 ....187 K3
Handleys Cha LAIN SS15 ....303 N5
Handleys La WIT CM8 ....198 A7
Handsworth Av CHING E4 ....294 G5
Handtrough Wy BARK IG11 ....334 C2
Hanford Rd SOCK/AV RM15 ......337 P8
Hanging Hill La
RBRW/HUT CM13 ....281 L9
Haning Hill La
RBRW/HUT CM13 ....281 M5
Hankin Av HAR CO12 ....109 M7
Hanlee Brook
CHLM/GWD CM2 ....240 E5
Hannah Cl CVI SS8 ....326 D8
Hannards Wy CHIG IG7 ....297 J2
Hannett Rd CVI SS8 ....345 H2
Hanningfield Cl RAYL SS6 ....306 D4
Hanningfield Wy COLN CO4 ....128 C2
Hanover Av CAN/RD E16 ....333 K8
Hanover Br K/T/MI CO5 ....148 E9
Hanover Dr BSDN SS14 ....324 D1
Hanover Gdns BSDN SS14 ....324 D1
Hanover Gdns BARK/HLT IG6 ....296 D4
Hanover Ms RAYL SS6 ....307 N1
Hanover Pl BRW CM14 ....300 E2
SAFWN CB10 * 51 K9
Hansart Wy ENC/FH EN2 ....250 F9
Hanselis Md
HLWW/ROY CM19 ....209 K3
Hansen Dr WCHMH N21 ....272 E4
Hanson Dr LOU IG10 ....276 D1
Hanwell Ct RCOS CO16 ....181 N8
Hanyards La POTB/CUF EN6 ......228 C7
Ha'Penny Fld RIPS/CAP IP9 ....83 L4
Harberson Rd SRTFD E15 ....333 J1
Harberts Rd
HLWW/ROY CM19 ....210 C4
Harberts Wy RAYL SS6 ....306 F2
Harbet Rd ED N18 ....294 A2
Harborough Hall Rd
K/T/MI CO5 ....174 A3
Harbour Crs HAR CO12 ....15 H4
Harbourer Rd BARK/HLT IG6 .....297 J2
Harbour Wy RCOLE CO7 ....155 J6
Harcarrallow Wy GTDUN CM6 ....97 P1
RBSF CM22 ....138 F9
RBSF CM22 ....163 L1
ROY SG8 ....68 A9
SAFWN CB10 ....51 P5
SBW CM21 ....185 K7
WARE SG12 ....197 M4
Harcourt Av HAR CO12 ....110 B4
MNPK E12 ....316 A6
SOSN SS2 ....18 D1
Harcourt Ms ROM RM1 ....298 E9
Harcourt Rd SRTFD E15 ....333 J2
Hardie Rd DAGE RM10 ....318 B5
SLH/COR SS17 ....341 L5
Harding Rd CDW/CHF RM16 ......550 B1
Hardings Cl RCOLE CO7 ....125 N7
Harding's Elms Rd
BCAYE CM11 ....304 A3
Hardley's La ING CM4 ....260 A2
Hardley Crs EMPK RM11 ....299 N1
Hardwick Ct BRTR CM77 ....144 E7
IPNE IP4 ....26 D6
RAYL SS6 ....306 C5
Hardwicke Rd BARK IG11 ....354 D1
Hardwicke St BCTR RM8 ....317 N7
Hardy Av CAN/RD E16 ....333 K8
Hardy Cl BERM/RHTH SE16 ....332 A8
BRTR CM7 ....144 E7
MGTR CO11 ....106 B1
Hardy Crs CVI SS8 ....326 D8
Hardy Grs IP IP1 ....22 C8
Hardy Gv DART DA1 ....347 M9
Hardy Rd CHING E4 ....294 C3
Hardy Wy CVI SS8 ....326 D8
Hardy Wy ENC/FH EN2 ....250 F9

Harebell Cl BCAYW CM12 ....282 G4
COLN CO4 ....128 C4
Harebell Cl EHAM E6 ....334 B5
COLN CO4 ....197 H1
Harebell Rd CHTY IP2 ....24 G7
Harebell Wy HARH RM5 ....299 L4
Harefield Cl ENC/FH EN2 ....250 F9
Harefield Rd CBE/LIN CB1 ....58 D1
Hare Hall La GPK RM2 ....298 G8
Hares Cha BCAYW CM12 ....282 G4
Haresfield Rd DAGE RM10 ....317 P8
Hareston Cl SBF/HAD SS7 ....327 J1
Hare St HLWW/ROY CM19 ....12 E7
Hare St Springs
HLWW/ROY CM19 ....12 E7
Hares Wk SUD CO10 ....21 F3
Hare Ter WTHK KM20 * 348 G5
Harewood Av RCFD SS4 ....508 D2
Harewood Dr CLAY IG5 ....296 A6
Harewood Hl EPP CM16 ....254 F3
Harewood Rd BRWN CM15 ....280 E5
CHLM/WR CM1 ....239 M1
Harford Cl CHING E4 ....274 E6
Harford Rd CHING E4 ....274 E6
Harford St WHTFLL E1 ....332 B4
Harfred Av MAL CM9 ....222 F8
Hargrave Cl STSD CM24 ....114 B7
Hargreaves Av CHESW EN7 ......251 N1
Hargreaves Cl CHESW EN7 ....251 N1
Harkilees Wy BRTR CM77 ....144 F7
Harkness CHESW EN7 ....229 N8
Harkness Cl HARH RM5 ....299 L2
Harkstead La RIPS/CAP IP9 ....93 G9
Harkstead Rd RIPS/CAP IP9 ....83 N5
Harlech Rd PIT SS13 ....324 C1
STHGT/OAK N14 ....272 D9
Harlesden Cl HARH RM5 ....299 L3
Harlesden Rd HARH RM5 ....299 L3
Harley Gv BOW E3 ....332 C3
Harley St LOS SS9 ....327 M5
Harlings Gv CHLM/WR CM1 ....5 G2
Harlow Common HLWE CM17 ....211 L6
Harlow Gdns CRW RM5 ....298 B5
Harlow Rd CHONG CM5 ....213 H8
HLWE CM17 ....189 M2
HLWW/ROY CM19 ....209 M2
PLMGR N13 ....273 J9
RAIN RM13 ....336 E1
SBW CM21 ....187 K4
Harman Av WFD IG8 ....295 J4
Harman Cl CHING E4 ....294 G1
Harman Rd EN EN1 ....273 L4
Harman Wk RCOS CO16 ....181 M8
Harmer Cl CHLM/WR CM1 ....218 D4
Harness Rd THMD SE28 ....335 H8
Harnham Dr BRTR CM77 ....144 F7
Harold Cl HLWW/ROY CM19 ......210 A4
HSTD CO9 ....98 A7
Harold Court Rd HARH RM5 ....299 N3
Harold Crs WAB EN9 ....252 F2
Harold Gv FOS CO15 ....183 N1
Harold Rd BRTR CM7 ....145 H1
CHING E4 ....274 F9
COS CO15 ....7 G4
FOS CO15 ....183 N1
PLSTW E13 ....333 L1
WAN E11 ....315 K3
WFD IG8 ....295 K5
Harolds Rd HLWW/ROY CM19 ...210 A4
Haroldstone Rd WALTH E17 ....294 A9
Harold Vw HARH RM5 ....299 N3
Haron Cl CVI SS8 ....344 E2
Harpenden Rd MNPK E12 ....315 M4
Harper Cl CDW/CHF RM16 ....250 F9
STHGT/OAK N14 ....272 B4
Harper's Est RCOLW CO6 ....77 N8
Harper's La BRWN CM15 ....77 M7
Harpers La BRWN CM15 ....258 C7
Harper Wy RAYL SS6 ....306 F4
Harp Meadow La COLS CO2 ....151 N3
Harpour Rd BARK IG11 ....316 C8
Harridge Cl LOS SS9 ....327 P3
Harridge Rd LOS SS9 ....327 P3
Harrier Cl HCH RM12 ....31 H1
IPSE IP5 ....31 H1
Harriescourt WAB EN9 ....253 K2
Harrington Cl K/T/MI CO5 ....173 N8
Harrington Rd WAN E11 ....315 H3
Harrington Rd WAN E11 * 259 G9
HARH RM5 ....299 K4
SLH/COR SS17 ....342 A1
WICKW SS12 ....305 L2
Harrison Cl RBRW/HUT CM13 ...281 N4
Harrison Ct CHLM/WR CM1 ....4 B1
Harrison Dr BRTR CM7 ....145 K5
EPP CM16 ....234 A5
Harrison Gdns HOC/HUL SS5 .....286 G6
Harrison Gv KESC IP5 ....27 H3
Harrison Rd COLS CO2 ....152 A3
DAGE RM10 ....318 A8
WAB EN9 ....253 K6
Harrisons BSF CM25 ....138 A4
Harrisons Whf PUR RM19 ....347 M5
Harrison Wk CHES/WCR EN8 .....230 A9
Harrods Wy LOU IG10 ....317 N7
Harris St WALTH E17 ....314 C2
Harrods Ct BCAYE CM11 ....283 M6
Harrogate Dr HOC/HUL SS5 ....288 A8
Harrogate Rd HOC/HUL SS5 ....288 A9
Harrold Rd BCTR RM8 ....317 J7
Harrow Av EN EN1 ....273 M5
Harrow Cl HOC/HUL SS5 ....308 B2
IPNE IP4 ....25 P6
Harrow Crs HARH RM5 ....298 C4
Harrow Dr ED N9 ....273 L7

EMPK RM11 ...319 H2
Harrow Gdns HOC/HUL SS5 ...308 B2
Harrowgate Rd HOM E9 ...314 B9
Harrow Gn WAN E11 ...315 H5
Harrow Hl HSTD CO9 ...70 C3
Harrow La POP/IOD E14 ...332 F7
Harrow Manor Wy THMD SE28 ...335 K8
Harrow Rd BARK IG11 ...334 F1
  COS CO15 ...7 F2
  CVI SS8 ...326 E9
  HVHL CB9 ...41 H4
  IL IG1 ...316 D6
  UPMR RM14 ...321 M7
  WAN E11 ...315 J5
  WICKW SS12 ...305 M5
Harrow St RCOLW CO6 ...77 L2
Harrow Wy CHLM/GWD CM2 ...240 F4
Harsnett Rd COL CO1 ...152 C1
Harston Dr PEND EN3 ...252 D8
Hart CI HVHL CB9 ...41 J1
  SBF/HAD SS7 ...306 D9
Hart Cnr WTHK RM20 * ...348 G5
Hart Crs CHIG IG7 ...206 C2
Hartest Wy SUD CO10 ...61 L4
Hatfield Ter BOW E5 ...332 D2
Hartford CI RAYL SS6 ...306 D3
Hartford End PIT SS13 ...324 F1
Hartington Rd CAN/RD E16 ...19 J5
  SOS SS1 ...19 J6
  WALTH E17 ...314 B1
Hartlake Rd HOM E9 ...314 A8
Hartland Ct LOS SS9 ...307 N8
  WCHMH N21 ...273 H5
Hartland Rd CHES/WCR EN8 ...230 A9
  EPP CM16 ...255 H1
  HCH RM12 ...318 F4
  SRTFD E15 ...331 M5
Hartley Av EHAM E6 ...333 P1
Hartley CI CHLM/GWD CM2 ...218 F7
Hartley Rd WAN E11 ...315 J5
Hartley St CHTY IP2 ...25 K8
Hartmann Rd CAN/RD E16 ...333 N8
Hartmoor Ms PEND EN3 ...252 D7
Harton Rd ED N9 ...273 N8
Hartree Wy KESG IP5 ...27 K4
Hart Rd HLWE CM17 ...187 K7
  SBF/HAD SS7 ...306 D9
Harts Gv WFD IG8 ...295 K2
Hartshorn Gdns EHAM E6 ...334 B4
Harts La BARK IG11 ...316 C9
  RCOLE CO7 ...104 A7
Hartslock Dr ABYW SE2 ...335 L9
Hart St BRW CM14 ...230 C7
  CHLM/GWD CM2 ...A D5
Hartsway PEND EN3 ...273 N3
Hartswood CI BRW CM14 ...301 H1
Hartswood Rd BRW CM14 ...301 H1
Hartsworth CI PLSTW E13 ...333 J7
Hartwell Dr CHING E4 ...294 F5
Harty Ct CDW/CHF RM16 ...339 L8
Harvard Ct COLN CO4 ...128 C3
Harvest CI RCHLM CM3 ...286 C1
Harvest Ct FX IP11 * ...35 L7
  FX IP11 ...173 K1
Harvest End COLW CO3 ...150 C1
Harvesters Wy KESG IP5 ...27 L5
Harvest Rd CVI SS8 ...326 E9
Harvest Wy MAL CM9 ...222 A6
  RCOLE CO7 ...129 N9
Harvey CDW/CHF RM16 ...339 L9
Harvey Ct COLN CO3 ...150 F1
Harveyfields WAB EN9 ...252 F4
Harvey Gdns IG10 ...276 C2
Harvey Rd COLS CO2 ...151 L4
  IL IG1 ...316 C7
  MAL CM9 ...198 B8
  PIT SS13 ...304 C5
  RCOLE CO7 ...153 J5
  WAN E11 ...315 H5
Harvey's La ROMW/RG RM7 ...318 C4
Harvey St HSTD CO9 ...98 A6
Harvey Wy SAFWN CB10 ...51 N8
  SAFWN CB10 ...54 C9
Harwater Dr LOU IG10 ...276 A1
Harwell CI BRTR CM7 ...145 N2
Harwich Rd COLN CO4 ...9 F5
  HAR CO12 ...109 L9
  HAR CO12 ...133 N5
  MGTR CO11 ...105 M6
  MGTR CO11 ...106 F4
  MGTR CO11 ...107 J1
  MGTR CO11 ...107 P7
  MGTR CO11 ...132 C2
  MGTR CO11 ...133 J1
  RCOLE CO7 ...104 G8
  RCOLE CO7 ...130 E9
  RCOS CO16 ...135 K9
  RCOS CO16 ...157 H9
Harwood Av EMPK RM11 ...299 K7
Harwood CI COLS CO2 * ...152 B2
Harwood Hall La UPMR RM14 ...340 E8
Haselbury Rd ED N9 ...273 K9
Haselfoot Rd RCHLM CM3 ...219 L3
Haselmere Gdns FOS CO15 ...158 G7
Haselwood Dr ENC/FH EN2 ...272 C3
Haskard Rd DAGW RM9 ...317 L8
Haskell Ms BRTR CM7 ...145 K6
Haskins SLH/COR SS17 ...341 N1
Haskins Wk KESG IP5 ...27 K4
Haslemere BSF CM23 ...162 D1
Haslemere Dr IPNE IP4 ...17 J2
Haslemere Rd
  GDMY/SEVK IG3 ...316 G4
  WCHMH N21 ...272 G8
  WICKE SS11 ...285 H6
Hasler Rd MAL CM9 ...225 J1
Haslers La GTDUN CM6 ...141 L6

Haslewood Av HOD EN11 ...208 D4
Hasil Rd CVI SS8 ...344 G2
Hassenbrook Rd
  SLH/COR SS17 ...341 L3
Hassett Rd PIT SS13 ...305 G4
Hastings Av BARK/HLT IG6 ...296 D8
  COS CO15 ...207 J4
Hastings CI WTHK RM20 ...349 H4
Hastings PI RCOLE CO7 ...179 L5
Hastings Rd COLW CO3 ...151 K2
  GPK RM2 ...298 G9
  SOS SS1 ...19 J4
The Hastings WICKE SS11 ...285 J7
Hastingwood Rd HLWE CM17 ...211 M8
Hatchcroft Gdns RCOLE CO7 ...129 P9
Hatcher Crs COL CO1 ...152 D1
Hatches Farm Rd
  BARW CM12 ...302 E2
Hatchfields RCHLM CM5 ...193 N5
Hatch Gn RBSF CM22 ...162 E5
Hatch La CHING E4 ...294 C1
Hatch Rd BRWN CM15 ...292 B2
Hatch Side CHIG IG7 ...296 B2
The Hatch PEND EN3 ...253 J3
Hatchwoods WFD IG8 ...295 J1
Hatfield CI BARK/HLT IG6 ...296 C7
  HCH RM12 ...319 J7
  RBRW/HUT CM13 ...281 N6
Hatfield Dr BCAYE CM11 ...280 A7
Hatfield Gv CHLM/WR CM1 ...239 L1
Hatfield Rd CDW/CHF RM16 ...348 G3
  IPS IP3 ...7 P8
  MAL CM9 ...221 L4
  RAYL SS6 ...306 F4
  RCHLM CM5 ...195 P1
  RCHLM CM5 ...197 J8
  SRTFD E15 ...315 H7
  WIT CM8 ...196 C6
Hatfields LOU IG10 ...276 C2
Hathaway CI CHIG IG7 ...296 C3
Hathaway Crs MNPK E12 ...316 A8
Hathaway Gdns CHDH RM6 ...297 L9
Hathaway Rd GRAYS RM17 ...349 L2
Hatherleigh Wy HARH RM3 ...299 J5
Hatherley Gdns EHAM E6 ...333 N3
Hatherley Rd WALTH E17 ...294 C8
The Hatherley BSDN SS14 ...5 J2
Hatley Av BARK/HLT IG6 ...296 D8
Hatley Gdns SBF/HAD SS7 ...325 P1
Hatterill LAIN SS15 ...323 M1
Hatton CI CDW/CHF RM16 ...348 C1
Hatton Rd CHES/WCR EN8 ...230 A8
Haubourdin CI HSTD CO9 ...98 B6
Haughley Dr HARH RM3 ...299 J5
Hauliers Rd FX IP11 ...10 C6
Havannah St BSDN SS14 ...3 K2
Havana CI ROM RM1 ...298 D9
Havana Dr RAYL SS6 ...306 E1
Havannah St POP/IOD E14 ...332 D9
Havant Rd WALTH E17 ...294 F7
Havelock St IL IG1 ...316 C4
Haven Av COS CO15 ...182 G7
Haven CI CVI SS8 ...344 A2
  FX IP11 ...10 D2
  GPK RM2 ...524 D3
Havengore CHLM/WR CM1 ...218 D6
  PIT SS13 ...305 H7
Havenhurst Ri ENC/FH EN2 ...272 C1
Haven PI CDW/CHF RM16 ...339 M9
Haven RI BCAYE CM11 ...303 L1
Haven Rd COLS CO2 ...152 F5
  CVI SS8 ...344 A3
Havenside SBN/FI SS5 ...332 C5
Havens Ms BOW E3 ...332 C5
The Havens KIR/NAC IP10 ...31 L3
The Haven GRAYS RM17 ...350 A2
  HAR CO12 ...110 A5
Haverfield Rd BOW E3 ...332 A3
Haverhill Rd CBE/LIN CB1 ...40 B6
  CHING E4 ...274 F7
  HVHL CB9 ...41 L1
  HVHL CB9 ...54 F2
Havering CI COLN CO4 ...9 C2
  SBN/FI SS5 ...332 C5
Havering Dr ROM RM1 ...298 D8
Havering Gdns CHDH RM6 ...297 K9
Havering Rd ROM RM1 ...298 D8
Havering St WCHPL E1 ...332 G6
Havering Wy BARK IG11 ...335 J5
Havers La BSF CM23 ...137 L9
Havisham Wy RBRW/HUT CM13 ...281 M1
Havis Rd SLH/COR SS17 ...341 M1
Hawarden Rd WALTH E17 ...294 A8
Haward Rd HOD EN11 ...208 E2
Hawbridge RIPS/CAP IP9 ...28 C8
Hawbridge Rd WAN E11 ...314 C5
Hawes La WAB EN9 ...252 F8
Hawes St CHTY IP2 ...25 L8
Hawfinch Rd COLS CO2 ...151 K9
Hawkcombe SBOW E3 ...332 D5
Hawkbush Gn PIT SS13 ...304 C6
Hawk CI WAB EN9 ...253 K4
Hawk Cnr WTHK RM20 * ...348 G5
Hawkdene CHING E4 ...274 E5
Hawkenbury
  HLWW/ROY CM19 ...210 B5
Hawkendon Rd RCOS CO16 ...181 K9
Hawke PI BERM/RHTH SE16 * ...332 A9
Hawker Dr KESG IP5 ...27 N5
Hawkesbury Bush La
  VGE SS16 ...323 P4
Hawkesbury CI BARK/HLT IG6 ...297 J1
  CVI SS8 ...344 C3
Hawkesbury Rd CVI SS8 ...344 E2
Hawkes CI GRAYS RM17 ...349 L4
Hawkes La FX IP11 ...34 C5
Hawkes Rd RCOLW CO6 ...147 N3
Hawkesway COS CO15 ...182 K7
Hawk HI WICKE SS11 ...285 P5
Hawkhurst CI CHLM/WR CM1 ...217 M9
Hawkhurst Gdns CRW RM5 ...298 C3

Hawkinge Wy HCH RM12 ...319 H8
Hawkins CI WICKE SS11 ...285 L9
Hawkins Ct SUD CO10 ...47 J9
Hawkins Dr CDW/CHF RM16 ...338 C9
Hawkins Rd COL CO1 ...128 E9
  RCOLE CO7 ...154 A6
  RCOLE CO7 ...47 K9
Hawkins Wy BRTR CM7 ...145 M2
Hawk La SUD CO10 * ...20 A7
  WICKE SS11 ...286 A6
Hawkridge SBN/FI SS5 ...330 B6
Hawkridge CI CHDH RM6 ...317 K1
Hawkridge Dr GRAYS RM17 ...349 L6
Hawks CI RCHLM CM5 ...242 D5
Hawks Hl HOC/HUL SS5 ...307 P2
Hawks La HOC/HUL SS5 ...307 P2
Hawksmead CI PEND EN5 ...252 A6
Hawksmoor CI EHAM E6 ...333 P6
Hawksmoor Gn
  RBRW/HUT CM13 ...281 N4
Hawksmouth CHING E4 ...274 E6
Hawksway VGE SS16 ...324 A2
Hawkwell Chase BCAYE CM11 ...284 E1
Hawkwell Cha HOC/HUL SS5 ...307 P3
Hawkwell Park Dr
  HOC/HUL SS5 ...308 A2
Hawkwell Rd HOC/HUL SS5 ...307 P1
Hawkwood CI RCHLM CM5 ...265 H8
Hawkwood Crs CHING E4 ...274 C5
Hawkwood Rd HSTD CO9 ...72 D9
Hawley Rd UED N18 ...294 A2
Hawmark End RCOLW CO6 ...149 K1
Hawsted BKHH IG9 ...275 L6
Hawthorn Av COLN CO4 ...128 F8
  RAIN RM13 ...336 F1
  RBRW/HUT CM13 ...281 J9
Hawthorn CI CHLM/GWD CM2 ...240 B4
  HOC/HUL SS5 ...308 A2
  HSTD CO9 ...98 B6
  RBSF CM22 ...162 C2
Hawthorn Dr CHTY IP2 ...24 E9
Hawthorne Av CHESW EN7 ...229 N9
  HOM E9 ...332 C1
Hawthorne CI CHESW EN7 ...221 N1
Hawthorne Gdns
  HOC/HUL SS5 ...307 L2
  WALTH E17 ...294 B6
Hawthornes RCHLM CM5 ...243 N9
Hawthorne Wy ED N9 ...273 N6
Hawthorn Gv ENC/FH EN2 ...251 J8
Hawthorn PI BRTR CM7 ...348 B3
Hawthorn PI RBSF CM23 ...162 C2
Hawthorn Rd BKHH IG9 ...295 M1
  COS CO15 ...6 E5
  CVI SS8 ...344 F2
  HOD EN11 ...208 E3
  HVHL CB9 ...40 G2
  MAL CM9 ...199 P2
  RCHLM CM5 ...196 D7
  SUD CO10 ...21 J6
Hawthorns HLWS CM18 ...210 C7
  SOS SS1 ...327 P2
  SBF/HAD SS7 ...325 P9
  WFD IG8 ...275 K9
  WOTN CO14 ...174 F3
The Hawthorns BOC CM0 ...290 F1
  RCHLM CM5 ...242 D5
  SLH/COR SS17 ...342 B1
  SUD CO10 * ...47 K9
Hawthorn Wk BRTR CM7 ...145 K8
Hawthorn Wy RAYL SS6 ...307 H8
Hawtree CI SOS SS1 ...19 K6
Hayburn Wy HCH RM12 ...318 E5
Hay CI SRTFD E15 ...315 H9
Haycocks La FX IP11 ...203 J3
Haycocks Rd HVHL CB9 ...40 F2
Haycroft BSF CM23 ...137 P8
Hay Currie St POP/IOD E14 ...332 E8
Haycraft Rd ED N9 ...273 K9
Hayden Rd WAB EN9 ...252 F5
Haydens La HLWW/ROY CM19 ...13 C7
Hayden Wy CRW RM5 ...298 B6
Haydock CI HCH RM12 ...319 L6
Haydon CI ENT EN1 ...273 K5
  HARH RM3 ...299 J6
Haye La FX IP11 ...177 K1
Hayes Barton SOS SS1 ...330 B6
Hayes Cha RCHLM CM5 ...286 C3
Hayes CI CHLM/GWD CM2 ...5 F5
  WTHK RM20 ...348 F4
Hayes Dr RAIN RM13 ...318 G9
Hayes Gn CVI SS8 ...344 C2
Hayes Rd RCOS CO16 ...6 E5
Hay Gn HCH RM12 ...319 L6
Hay La North BRTR CM7 ...145 M3
Hay La South BRTR CM7 ...146 M1
Hayle TIL RM18 ...351 K1
Hayley Bell Gdns BSF CM23 ...162 C2
Hayling CI SBN/FI SS5 ...305 M2
Hayman Rd IPSE IP3 ...30 F1
Haymeads La BSF CM23 ...137 P6
Haynes Dr ED N9 ...273 N9
Haynes Green Rd K/T/MI CO5 ...174 D5
Haynes CI CHLM/WR CM1 ...191 N4
Haysoms CI ROM RM1 ...298 D8
Haytor CI BRTR CM7 ...146 A4
The Haywain COS CO15 ...150 C1
Haywards CI CHDH RM6 ...297 K9
  RBRW/HUT CM13 ...281 P5
Haywards Flds KESG IP5 ...27 J5
Haywood PI
  CDW/CHF RM16 ...340 D9
Haywood Gn ...353 J4
Hazelbrouck Gdns
  BARK/HLT IG6 ...296 E4
Hazelbury Gn ED N9 ...273 K9
Hazelbury La ED N9 ...273 K9
Hazel CI CHESW EN7 ...229 K5

HCH RM12 ...318 C5
  HCH RM12 ...41 H4
  LAIN SS15 ...303 N5
  LOS SS15 ...327 M5
  PLMGR N13 ...273 J9
  RCOLE CO7 ...154 F9
  RCOLE CO7 ...327 J4
  RCOLE CO7 ...47 K9
Hazelcroft Rd IP IP1 ...23 L6
Hazeldene CHES/WCR EN8 ...252 B2
Hazeldene Rd BRTR RM8 ...317 J4
Hazeldon CI RCHLM CM5 ...194 B6
Hazel Dr ERITH DA8 ...346 F6
  IPSE IP5 ...31 L1
  SOCK/AV RM15 ...558 F3
Hazeleigh RBRW/HUT CM13 ...281 L9
Hazeleigh Gdns WFD IG8 ...295 P2
Hazeleigh Hall La MAL CM9 ...243 M5
Hazel Gdns BSF CM23 ...137 L5
  CDW/CHF RM16 ...349 P1
Hazelgreen CI WCHMH N21 ...272 G8
Hazel La SUD CO10 ...61 L5
Hazel Rd IP IP5 ...31 L1
Hazel Wy CHING E4 ...294 C3
Hazel CI COS CO2 ...151 K3
Hazell Crs ROMW/RG RM7 ...298 A5
Hazelmere PIT SS13 ...324 F2
Hazelmere Gdns EMPK RM11 ...299 K8
  SBF/HAD SS7 ...326 A1
Hazel Ms RCOLE CO7 ...179 K6
Hazel Ri EMPK RM11 ...319 H1
  NHMKT IP6 ...22 C4
Hazel Rd ERITH DA8 ...346 F6
  SRTFD E15 ...315 H7
  TIL RM18 ...351 M4
Hazelton Wy HVHL CB9 ...41 H4
Hazelville CI HAR CO12 ...109 P7
Hazel Wy CHING E4 ...294 C3
Hazelwood CI CLPT E5 ...314 B5
Hazelwood Crs RCOS CO16 ...181 M4
Hazelwood Gdns
  BRWN CM15 ...280 D4
Hazelwood Gv LOS SS9 ...327 P5
Hazelwood Rd ED N9 ...273 L5
  ENT EN1 ...61 L5
Hazelwood Rd EN1 ...296 B9
Hazelmere Rd COS CO15 ...182 D9
  SBF/HAD SS7 ...326 A1
Hazlitt Rd IP IP1 ...23 H9
Headcorn CI PIT SS13 ...325 H1
Headingham CI CHTY IP2 ...25 N9
Headingley CI CHESW EN7 ...229 L5
  PIT SS13 ...304 F5
Headland Av HVHL CB9 ...41 H4
Headla La SUD CO10 ...61 L5
Headley Ap IL IG1 ...296 B9
Headley Cha BRW CM14 ...300 F1
Headley Common
  RBRW/HUT CM13 ...300 E4
Headley Dr GNTH/NBYPK IG2 ...316 C1
Headley Rd BCAYE CM11 ...283 K4
Head St COL CO1 ...8 B7
  HSTD CO9 ...98 A6
  K/T/MI CO5 ...152 C6
  MAL CM9 ...223 M5
  WCHPL E1 ...332 A6
Heard's La BRTR CM7 ...69 M4
Hearn Rd ROM RM1 ...318 E1
Hearsall Av CHLM/WR CM1 ...218 A4
  SLH/COR SS17 ...341 M3
Hearth CI BCAYW CM12 ...282 C7
  GPK RM2 ...332 G6
  RCOLE CO7 ...80 C6
Heathcote Av CLAY IG5 ...296 B6
Heathcote Gdns HLWE CM17 ...211 M8
Heathcote Gv CHING E4 ...274 F9
Heath Ct FX IP11 ...34 E1
Heathcroft Gdns WALTH E17 ...294 C5
Heathdene Dr BELV DA17 ...346 A2
Heath Dr CHLM/GWD CM2 ...240 A4
  EPP CM16 ...254 F5
  GPK RM2 ...298 G9
  WARE SG12 ...184 A1
Heather Av IPSE IP3 ...30 F1
  ROM RM1 ...298 C6
Heather Bank BCAYE CM11 ...283 K6
Heather CI BRWN CM15 ...280 E4
  BSF CM23 ...137 J8
  COLS CO2 ...182 C6
  CVI SS8 ...344 C3
  EHAM E6 ...334 C5
  KIR/NAC IP10 ...27 L6
  ROM RM1 ...298 C6
Heather Dr ENC/FH EN2 ...251 J8
  ROM RM1 ...298 C6
  SBF/HAD SS7 ...306 A9
Heather Gdns ROM RM1 ...298 C6
  WAB EN9 ...252 F6
Heather Gln ROM RM1 ...298 C6
Heatherhayes CHTY IP2 ...25 J8
Heatherley Dr CLAY IG5 ...296 A3
Heather Wk BRTR CM7 ...146 C4
Heather Wy ROM RM1 ...298 C5
Heatherwood CI MNPK E12 ...315 L1
Heathfield CHING E4 ...274 F9
  KESG IP5 ...27 M5
  SBF/HAD SS7 ...306 F9
Heathfield CI CAN/RD E16 ...333 N5
Heathfield Ms BSF/NAC IP10 ...27 L6
Heathfield Park Dr
  CHDH RM6 ...297 J9
Heathfield Rd CHLM/WR CM1 ...218 A4
  RIPS/CAP IP9 ...83 L4
Heathfields FX IP11 ...33 L9
  RCOLW CO6 ...126 E7

Heathgate WIT CM8 ...197 N6
Heathgate Piece FX IP11 ...34 C5
Heathlands RCOLE CO7 ...154 F9
Heathlands Pk IPNE IP4 ...26 B6
Heath La LIN RM14 ...26 B6
Heathleigh Dr VGE SS16 ...323 J2
Heath Pk Rd GPK RM2 ...298 F9
Heath Rd BCAYE CM11 ...340 A9
  CDW/CHF RM16 ...340 A9
  CHDH RM6 ...317 L2
  COLW CO3 ...126 C6
  COS CO15 ...150 G2
  IPNE IP4 ...26 B4
  K/T/MI CO5 ...152 G6
  MGTR CO11 ...106 G6
  RCOLE CO7 ...80 G6
  RCOLE CO7 ...153 J4
  RCOLE CO7 ...154 A6
  RCOS CO16 ...132 A6
  RCOS CO16 ...181 H4
Heath Rw BSF CM23 ...137 N5
Heath's CI EN EN1 ...273 J1
Heathside RCOLW CO6 ...127 H5
Heathside CI
  GNTH/NBYPK IG2 ...296 E9
Heath Ter MGTR CO11 ...106 G6
The Heath COLS CO2 ...151 K8
Heathvale Rd RCOLE CO7 ...104 C4
  SUD CO10 ...47 J9
Heath Vw KESG IP5 ...26 F5
Heath View Gdns
  CDW/CHF RM16 ...339 M9
Heath View Rd
  CDW/CHF RM16 ...339 M9
Heath Wy ERITH DA8 ...346 B6
  SUD CO10 ...47 P7
Heathway DAGW RM9 ...317 N6
  WFD IG8 ...295 M1
Heatley Wy COLN CO4 ...126 C6
Heaton Av HARH RM3 ...298 C4
Heaton CI CHING E4 ...274 F9
  HARH RM3 ...299 H4
Heaton Orange Rd GPK RM2 ...298 G5
Heaton Wy HARH RM3 ...299 H4
  K/T/MI CO5 ...174 A7
Hecham CI WALTH E17 ...294 B6
Heckford's Rd RCOLE CO7 ...155 K4
Heckford St WAP E1W ...332 A7
Heckworth Ct COLN CO4 ...128 C3
Hedge Dr COS CO2 ...151 L4
Hedge HI ENC/FH EN2 ...250 C9
Hedgehope Av RAYL SS6 ...306 G3
Hedgelands COLW CO3 ...150 A1
Hedge La PLMGR N13 ...272 C9
  SBF/HAD SS7 ...326 C2
Hedgeley REDBR IG4 ...296 A6
Hedgemans Rd DAGW RM9 ...317 L9
Hedgemans Wy DAGW RM9 ...317 M8
Hedgerows CI COS CO15 ...126 C9
  SBW CM21 ...187 N2
The Hedgerows BSF CM23 ...137 M5
The Hedgerow VGE SS16 * ...324 C2
Hedger's Gv HOM E9 ...314 B8
Hedingham Dr WICKE SS11 ...296 B8
Hedingham PI RCFD SS4 * ...308 C3
Hedingham Rd BCTR RM8 ...317 J7
  CDW/CHF RM16 ...348 G3
  EMPK RM11 ...319 M5
  HSTD CO9 ...73 P9
  HSTD CO9 ...97 H7
  HSTD CO9 ...97 N4
Hedley Av WTHK RM20 ...348 F4
Hedworth Av CHES/WCR EN8 ...252 A3
Heenan CI BARK IG11 ...316 D8
Heeswyk Rd CVI SS8 ...326 E9
Heidelberg Rd CVI SS8 ...326 F9
Heigham Rd EHAM E6 ...333 J8
Heighams HLWW/ROY CM19 ...210 A6
The Heights LOU IG10 ...276 A1
  WAB EN9 ...231 L4
Heilsburg Rd CVI SS8 ...326 E9
Helden Av CVI SS8 ...326 E9
Helena La HOC/HUL SS5 ...308 A2
Helena Rd CHING E4 ...294 A3
  COLS CO2 ...182 C6
  CVI SS8 ...344 C3
  EHAM E6 ...334 C6
  KIR/NAC IP10 ...27 L6
Helena Rd RAYL SS6 ...307 H5
Helen How RCHLM CM5 ...169 A6
Helen Rd EMPK RM11 ...299 J7
Helens Ga CHES/WCR EN8 ...230 C5
Helford CI WIT CM8 ...196 C2
Helford Wy UPMR RM14 ...320 A1
Helions Bumpstead Rd
  HVHL CB9 ...41 K6
Helions Park Av HVHL CB9 ...41 K4
Helions Park Gdns HVHL CB9 ...41 K4
Helions Park Gv HVHL CB9 ...41 K4
Helions Park Rd HLWW/ROY CM19 ...12 D7
  HVHL CB9 ...41 K4
Helions Service Rd HVHL CB9 ...41 K4
Helions Wk HVHL CB9 ...41 K6
Hellebodine GRAYS RM17 ...349 J3
Hellen CI RCOLW CO6 ...102 F9
Helmons La CHLM/GWD CM2 ...262 F5
Helmore Ct LAIN SS15 * ...302 C9
Helmore Rd BARK IG11 ...316 C9
Helmores LAIN SS15 ...302 C9
Helmsdale CI ROM RM1 ...298 D4
Helmsdale Rd ROM RM1 ...298 D4
Helpeston BCAYE CM11 ...324 C1
Helston CI KESG IP5 ...26 C5
Helston Rd RCHLM/WR CM1 ...218 D6
Hemingway Rd WIT CM8 ...171 M8
Hemley Rd CDW/CHF RM16 ...340 E6
Hemmells LAIN SS15 ...303 J7
Hemmings CI MAL CM9 ...223 P4
Hemnall St EPP CM16 ...254 C1
Hempstalls LAIN SS15 ...2 C1

Hempstead Cl *BKHH* IG9	275 K8
Hempstead Rd *HVHL* CB9	40 F2
WALTH E17	294 C7
Hemsted Rd *ERITH* DA8	346 D6
Henderson Av *EMPK* RM11	318 C4
HVHL CB9	40 F2
RIPW IP8	24 B2
Henderson Dr *DART* DA1	347 M9
Henderson Gdns *WICKW* SS12	305 K2
Henderson Rd *ED* N9	273 N7
FSTGT E7	315 M8
Hendon Ct *RCOS* CO15	181 N8
WICKW SS12	305 J1
Hendon Rd *ED* N9	273 M8
Hengist Gdns *WICKE* SS11	285 J7
Hengist Rd *ERITH* DA8	346 B5
Hengrave Cl *CHTY* IP2	25 H9
Henham Ct *WICKW* CM11	283 L6
Henham Rd *RBSF* CM22	115 H6
SAFWS CB11	90 C6
Henley Av *IP1*	23 J9
Henley Ct *COLW* CO3	127 H9
Henley Gv *WOS/PRIT* SS0	328 E2
Henley Gdns *CHDH* RM6	297 M9
Henley Rd *CAN/RD* E16	334 A9
IL IG1	316 D6
NHMKT IP6	23 J3
Hennessy Rd *ED* N9	273 P8
Henney Cl *CHLM* CM3	266 A3
Henniker Gdns *EHAM* E6	333 N3
Henniker Ga	
CHLM/GWD CM2	218 F8
Henniker Rd *IP* IP1	24 E3
SRTFD E15	314 C7
Henny Back Rd *BURES* CO8	75 H5
Henny Rd *BURES* CO8	75 L3
Henny Vw *SUD* CO10 *	61 G1
Henrietta Cl *RCOLE* CO7	153 K3
Henrietta St *SRTFD* E15	314 F7
Henry Addington Cl	
EHAM E6	334 C5
Henry Cl *COS* CO15	6 A6
ENC/FH EN2	251 K8
HVHL CB9	40 D5
Henry Dixon Rd *WIT* CM8	172 C7
Henry Dr *LOS* SS9	327 L4
Henry Laver Ct *COLW* CO3	8 A5
Henry Rd *CHLM/WR* CM1	218 A7
EHAM E6	333 P2
IPSE IP5	41 J1
Henry's Av *WFD* IG8	295 J2
Henry St *GRAYS* RM17	349 M4
Henshawe Rd *BCTR* RM8	317 L5
Henslow Rd *IPNE* IP4	26 A6
Henson Av *CVI* SS8	345 H2
Henstead Gdns *IPSE* IP5	25 P9
Henwood Side *WFD* IG8	296 A3
Hepburn Cl *CDW/CHF* RM16	348 C2
Hepscott Rd *HOM* E9	314 D8
Hepworth Gdns *BARK* IG11	317 H7
Herald Cl *BSF* CM23	137 J8
Herbage Park Rd *MAL* CM9	242 F1
Herbert Cl *SUD* CO10	47 K9
Herbert Gdns *CHDH* RM6	297 L7
Herbert Gv *SOS* SS1	19 H5
Herbert Rd *COS* CO15	6 D3
CVI SS8	344 F1
EMPK RM11	319 K2
GDMY/SEVK IG3	316 F4
KESG IP5	27 K3
MNPK E12	315 P6
SBN/FI SS3	330 B8
WALTH E17	314 C2
Herbert St *PLSTW* E13	333 K2
Herd La *SLH/COR* SS17	342 B1
Hereford Cl *CHLM/GWD* CM2	240 E5
COS CO15	182 F8
Hereford Dr *BRTR* CM7	145 M1
Hereford Gdns *IL* IG1	315 P2
Hereford Rd *COL* CO1	9 P5
COS CO15	182 F7
WAN E11	295 L9
Herent Dr *CLAY* IG5	296 A7
Hereward Cl *RCOLE* CO7	153 K3
WAB EN9	252 F2
Hereward Gdns *WICKE* SS11	285 J7
Hereward Gn *LOU* IG10	254 D9
Hereward Wy *BRTR* CM7	95 H5
Herga Hyll *CDW/CHF* RM16	340 B5
Herington Gv	
RBRW/HUT CM13	281 K6
Heriot Rd *CHING* E4	274 D8
Heriot Wy *MAL* CM9	198 C3
Heritage Wy *RCFD* SS4	308 F5
RCHLM CM3	267 J4
Hermes Av *BOC* CM0	290 E7
Hermes Wy *WIT* SS3	330 E6
Hermitage Av *SBF/HAD* SS7	326 D2
SBF/HAD SS7	326 D2
SWFD E18	295 J8
Hermitage Dr *LAIN* SS15	305 K9
Hermitage Mdw *SUD* CO10	44 B2
Hermitage Rd *WOS/PRIT* SS0	18 B4
Hermitage Wk *SWFD* E18	295 J8
Hermit Rd *CAN/RD* E16	333 J1
Hernen Av *WAN* E11	295 H9
Hernen Rd *CLV* SS8	336 F9
Hernshaw *RBRW/HUT* CM13	301 N4
Heron Av *WICKE* SS11	305 L1
Heron Cha *RBRW/HUT* CM13	301 P4
Heron Cl *BKHH* IG9	275 K7
RAYL SS6	306 E5
SBW CM21	187 L3
WALTH E17	294 C6
Heron Ct *BSF* CM23	137 M4
Heron Di *BSDN* SS14	304 C9
Heron Dr *WARE* SG12	184 E8
Heron Flight Av *HCH* RM12	318 F9
Heron Gdns *RAYL* SS6	306 E5
Herongate *SBF/HAD* SS7	325 D2
SBN/FI SS3	330 D6
Herongate Rd	
CHES/WCR EN8	230 A6

MNPK E12	315 M4
Heron Gld *COS* CO15	182 A6
Heron Md *PEND* EN3	252 D8
Heron Ms *IL* IG1	316 C5
Heron Quays *POP/IOD* E14	332 D8
Heron Rd *CHTY* IP2	24 F8
K/T/MI CO5	173 J2
Herongate *FOS* CO13	158 C8
Herons La *CHONG* CM5	235 J1
Herons Wy *HLW* CM20	12 E3
Heron Wy *FOS* CO13	158 F7
MAL CM9	222 D6
RCHLM CM3	267 P1
UPMR RM14	320 B5
WTHK RM20	348 E5
Heronway *RBRW/HUT* CM13	281 L7
Herrick Cl *COLW* CO3	127 K9
Herring's Wy *RCOLW* CO6	126 A1
Herringgate Cl *EN* EN1	273 K1
Herschell Rd *LOS* SS9	327 M5
Hertford Dr *SLH/COR* SS17	324 B5
Hertford La *ROY* SG8	48 G5
SAFWS CB11	49 J6
Hertford Rd *BARK* IG11	316 D9
CLW SS8	344 C2
ED N9	273 N7
GNTH/NBYPK IG2	316 F1
HOD EN11	208 B3
PEND EN3	251 P9
PEND EN3	273 P2
SUD CO10	44 A2
WARE SG12	184 A4
Hertford Road High St	
SRTFD E15	273 P5
Hertfordshire Wy *BSF* CM23	162 B2
Hertfordshire way *BUNT* SG9	38 B3
Hertfordshire Wy	
MHAD SG10	160 E7
STDN SG11	196 D8
Hertsmere Rd *POP/IOD* E14	332 D8
Hervey Cl *RIPS/CAP* IP9	85 M8
Hervey Park Rd *WALTH* E17	294 B8
Hervey St *IPNE* IP4	17 G2
Hervilly Wy *WOTN* CO14	159 J7
Hesketh Rd *FSTGT* E7	315 K5
Hesper Rd *COL* CO1	152 D1
Hesselyn Dr *RAIN* RM13	318 C9
Hester Pl *BOC* CM0	291 H5
Hetherington Cl *COLS* CO2	152 B6
Hetzand Rd *CVI* SS8	345 J2
Hever Cl *HOC/HUL* SS5	307 N1
Hevingham Dr *CHDH* RM6	317 J1
Hewes Cl *COLN* CO4	128 C8
Hewison St *BOW* E3	332 C2
Hewitt Rd *HAR* CO12	109 M7
Hewlett Rd *BOW* E3	332 B2
Heybridge Ap *MAL* CM9	222 A6
Heybridge Dr *INC* CM4	260 A8
Heybridge Dr *MAL* CM9	222 B6
Heybridge Rd *WALTH* E17	314 B2
Heycroft Dr *BRTR* CM7	145 N8
Heycroft Rd *HOC/HUL* SS5	308 A2
LOS SS9	308 A8
Heycroft Wy *CHLM/GWD* CM2	240 E5
K/T/MI CO5	174 A7
RCOLW CO6	77 N8
Heydon La *ROY* SG8	48 E5
SAFWS CB11	49 J6
Heydon Rd *ROY* SG8	49 H6
Heygate Av *SOS* SS1	19 H5
Heynes Rd *BCTR* RM8	317 K6
The Heythrop *CHLM/WR* CM1	218 C7
ING CM4	260 B6
Heywood Cl *CHTY* IP2	29 M1
Heywood Ct *MAL* CM9	222 C5
Heywood La *GTDUN* CM6	141 L7
Heywood Wy *MAL* CM9	222 C5
Heyworth Rd *SRTFD* E15	315 J7
Hibbard Rd *RIPW* IP8	24 F6
Hibbert Rd *WALTH* E17	314 C2
Hickford Hl *SUD* CO10	44 C5
Hickling Cl *LOS* SS9	307 L9
Hickling Rd *IL* IG1	316 C7
Hickman Av *CHING* E4	290 H8
Hickman Ct *BROX* EN10	208 B8
CAN/RD E16	333 N5
Hickman Rd *CHDH* RM6	317 K2
Hicksters La *BCAYE* CM11	283 K9
Hickory Av *COLN* CO4	128 E8
Hicks Wy *HVHL* CB9	41 P6
Hidcote Wy *BRTR* CM7	144 E7
The Hides *HLW* CM20	13 K5
Higgins Pl *KESG* IP5 *	27 M4
Higgins Rd *CHESW* EN7	229 J6
Higham Hall Rd *WALTH* E17	294 B5
Higham Pl *WALTH* E17	294 B7
Higham Rd *RCOLE* CO7	79 M6
High Ash Cl *TIL* RM18	337 J5
Highbank *HOC/HUL* SS5 *	287 H5
High Bank *VGE* SS16	322 C2
Highbank Cl *LOS* SS9	328 A1
High Beach *FX* IP11	35 M7
High Beeches *SBF/HAD* SS7	325 L1
High Beech Rd *LOU* IG10	275 P5
Highbirch Rd *RCOS* CO16	156 A9
Highbridge Rd *BARK* IG11	334 C1
High Bridge Rd	
CHLM/GWD CM2	5 H5
Highbridge St *WAB* EN9	252 E5
Highbury Av *HOD* EN11	208 D5
Highbury Gdns	
GDMY/SEVK IG3	316 F4
Highbury Wy *SUD* CO10	61 L4
Highclere Rd *BRTR* CM77	144 F6
COLN CO4	128 C5

Highcliff Crs *RCFD* SS4	288 D9
High Cliff Dr *LOS* SS9	328 A6
Highcliff Dr *WICKW* SS12	284 E8
Highcliffe Cl *WICKE* SS11	285 L8
Highcliffe Gdns *REDBR* IG4	295 P9
Highcliffe Rd *WICKE* SS11	285 L9
Highcliffe Wy *WICKE* SS11	285 L9
Highcliff Rd *SBF/HAD* SS7	326 B5
High Cloister *WICKE* SS11	283 J6
High Cl *ROY* SG8	48 D5
Highcross La *GTDUN* CM6	140 D9
High Cross La East	
GTDUN CM6	140 F9
High Easter Rd *GTDUN* CM6	166 E3
GTDUN CM6	191 H6
High Elms *CHIG* IG7	296 F1
UPMR RM14	320 B3
WFD IG8	295 K2
High Elms Rd *HOC/HUL* SS5	287 H7
Highfield *HLWS* CM18	211 H4
HOC/HUL SS5 *	287 H5
SUD CO10	44 B4
Highfield Av *BSF* CM23	137 P8
ERITH DA8	346 B4
HAR CO12	14 A7
SBF/HAD SS7	326 E2
Highfield Cl *BRTR* CM7	121 K9
CRW RM5	298 B3
RCHLM CM3	242 A4
WOS/PRIT SS0	328 E4
Highfield Crs *HCH* RM12	319 L4
RAYL SS6	306 C5
WOS/PRIT SS0	328 E4
Highfield Dr *BROX* EN10	208 B9
COLW CO3	127 M9
NHMKT IP6	22 E3
WOS/PRIT SS0	328 E4
Highfield Gdns	
CDW/CHF RM16	339 N9
EPP CM16	254 F1
Highfield Gv *WOS/PRIT* SS0	328 E5
Highfield Link *CRW* RM5	298 B3
Highfield Pl *EPP* CM16	254 F1
Highfield Ri *RCHLM* CM3	267 P6
Highfield Rd *BCAYE* CM11	141 L6
CHESW EN7	229 K5
CHLM/WR CM1	217 M7
CRW RM5	298 B3
FX IP11	11 K2
HCH RM12	319 L4
IP IP1	24 F1
SUD CO10	21 G2
WCHMH N21	272 C8
WFD IG8	295 P4
High Flds *HSTD* CO9	57 P8
Highfields *HSTD* CO9	97 P8
POTB/CUF EN6	228 D7
RBSF CM22	115 J1
RIPS/CAP IP9	85 L8
SAFWN CB10	67 M2
SAFWS CB11	90 E1
Highgate Av *SBW* CM21	187 L2
Highgate Rd *CHING* E4	290 A2
Highgrove Rd *BCTR* RM8	317 K7
High Hall *FX* IP11	34 D1
High House La	
CDW/CHF RM16	350 E1
Highland Av *BRW* CM14	280 F7
DAGE RM10	318 B5
VGE SS16 *	322 C2
Highland Gv *BCAYE* CM11	283 J5
Highland Rd *BSF* CM23	162 C2
SLH/COR SS17	324 A5
WAB EN9	231 H1
Highlands *HSTD* CO9	97 K4
Highlands Av *VGE* SS16	324 C2
Highlands Bvd *LOS* SS9	327 L4
Highlands Crs *PIT* SS13	305 L9
Highlands Gdns *IL* IG1	316 A3
Highlands Hl *RCHLM* CM3	268 C3
Highlands Rd *PIT* SS13	305 L9
WICKE SS11	286 E6
High La *RBSF* CM22	188 C4
STSD CM24	114 B7
High Md *CHIG* IG7	276 D8
HOC/HUL SS5	307 P2
Highmead *RAYL* SS6	306 F5
STSD CM24	114 B7
High Mdw *CHIG* IG7	296 E2
High Meads Rd *CAN/RD* E16	333 N6
High Oak Rd *WARE* SG12	184 A2
High Oaks *ENC/FH* EN2	251 N5
VGE SS16	323 J3
High Pastures *RBSF* CM22	188 C4
High Rdg *POTB/CUF* EN6	228 D6
WIT CM8 *	198 D4
Highridge Pl *ENC/FH* EN2 *	250 E8
High Rd *BKHH* IG9	275 L8
BROX EN10	208 C8
CDW/CHF RM16	339 H8
CHDH RM6	317 N1
CHIG IG7	276 C9
COLS CO2	151 J9
EPP CM16	233 J3
EPP CM16	233 P6
FX IP11	34 E2
GDMY/SEVK IG3	317 H5

HOC/HUL SS5	307 K2
IL IG1	316 C5
LAIN SS15	303 J7
LEY E10	314 E1
RAYL SS6	306 F7
RCOLW CO6	77 K4
SBF/HAD SS7	325 N2
SLH/COR SS17	324 B5
SLH/COR SS17	340 C2
SLH/COR SS17	341 P4
VGE SS16	323 J5
VGE SS16	324 E2
High Rd Broxbourne	
BROX EN10	208 C9
High Rd East *FX* IP11	35 L6
High Rd Leyton *LEY* E10	314 E4
High Rd Leytonstone	
WAN E11	315 H5
High Rd North *LAIN* SS15	303 K6
High Rd Ongar (Chelmsford Rd)	
CHONG CM5	235 N6
High Rd Turnford *BROX* EN10	230 B5
High Rd West *FX* IP11	35 K6
High Rd Woodford Gn	
WFD IG8	275 K9
High Rd Wormley *BROX* EN10	230 C3
High Row Fld *FX* IP11	35 M6
High Silver *LOU* IG10	275 N3
High St *BARK/HLT* IG6	296 D7
BCAYW CM12	283 H6
BOC CM0	258 A1
BOC CM0	269 J5
BOC CM0	290 C4
BRTR CM7	94 A6
BRTR CM7	95 H5
BRW CM14	280 F8
BSF CM23	137 L7
BURES CO8	76 A3
CBE/LIN CB1	38 A1
CBE/LIN CB1	40 B8
CHES/WCR EN8	230 A8
CHES/WCR EN8	252 A2
CHLM/GWD CM2	240 E3
CHONG CM5	235 M6
COL CO1	8 B4
COLN CO4	103 N4
COS CO15	7 G5
CVI SS8	344 F1
EMPK RM11	319 J3
EPP CM16	254 C1
FX IP11	35 H5
GRAYS RM17	349 N4
GRH DA9	348 E9
GTDUN CM6	141 L6
HAR CO12	14 E6
HAR CO12	14 E6
HLWE CM17	187 K8
HLWW/ROY CM19	209 L2
HOD EN11	208 D5
HSTD CO9	57 P9
HSTD CO9	97 N8
HVHL CB9	41 K4
INC CM4	260 C6
INC CM4	260 D8
INC CM4	261 M7
IP IP1	16 C5
K/T/MI CO5	155 H6
K/T/MI CO5	173 H3
K/T/MI CO5	202 E6
LEY E10	314 E2
LOS SS9	328 A6
MAL CM9	222 A8
MGTR CO11	106 C4
MHAD SG10	160 E2
PLSTW E13	333 K2
PUR RM19	347 L3
RAYL SS6	306 F6
RBSF CM22	188 C4
RBSF CM22	115 J2
SAFWN CB10	67 M2
SAFWN CB10	51 L9
SAFWN CB10	54 C8
SAFWS CB11	88 B4
SAFWS CB11	88 B4
SAFWS CB11	90 A4
SBF/HAD SS7	326 A6
SBW CM21	187 K3
SBN/FI SS3	330 F7
SBN/FI SS3	330 F7
SLH/COR SS17	324 A5
SOCK/AV RM15	337 P8
SOS SS1	19 F4
SRTFD E15	332 F2
STHGT/OAK N14	272 C7
SUD CO10	44 E5
SUD CO10	45 J2
SUD CO10	62 C5
WALTH E17	294 B7
WAN E11	315 L1
WARE SG12	184 F8
WARE SG12	185 N3
WICKW SS12	285 J9
WOTN CO14	159 K6

High St North *K/T/MI* CO5	202 F6
MNPK E12	315 P8
High St South *EHAM* E6	334 A2
The High *HLW* CM20	13 G5
High Tree La *WOTN* CO14	159 L4
Hightrees *ING* CM4	261 L7
High Vw *BOC* CM0	247 H2
BSF CM23	137 P5
MGTR CO11 *	81 M9
Highview *HOC/HUL* SS5 *	287 H5
High View Av *VGE* SS16	181 P7
GRAYS RM17	349 M8
High View Cr *COS* CO15	181 P7
LOU IG10	275 M4
Highview Crs	
RBRW/HUT CM13	281 M5
High View Gdns *GRAYS* RM17	349 M8
Highview Gdns *UPMR* RM14	319 M4
High View Ri *BCAYE* CM11	304 B2
High View Rd *IP* IP1	23 J8
SWFD E18	295 J6
Highwood Cl *SBF/HAD* SS7	306 D8
Highwood Cl *BRW* CM14	280 F3
LOS SS9	328 A2
Highwood Gdns *CLAY* IG5	296 A9
Highwood La *LOU* IG10	276 B5
Highwood Rd *CHLM/WR* CM1	238 A6
High Wood Rd *HOD* EN11	208 C2
Highwoods Ap *COLN* CO4	128 C3
Highwoods Sq *COLN* CO4	128 C4
High Wych La *SBW* CM21	187 H2
High Wych Rd *HLW* CM20	186 F1
Hilary Cl *BXLYHN* DA7	346 A6
HCH RM12	319 J7
RCFD SS4	308 F2
Hilary Crs *RAYL* SS6	307 H5
Hilary Rd *CVI* SS8	344 F2
Hildabrook Cl *CHTY* IP2	29 N1
Hilda Rd *CAN/RD* E16	333 H4
EHAM E6	315 N9
Hildaville Dr *WOS/PRIT* SS0	328 C6
Hilden Dr *ERITH* DA8	346 G5
Hilary Cl *CHLM/WR* CM1	218 C7
IPNE IP4	25 P6
MAL CM9	222 C6
Hillary Mt *BCAYW* CM12	282 G7
Hillary St *WAN* E11	285 L9
Hillborough Rd	
WOS/PRIT SS0	328 E3
Hill Cl *SBF/HAD* SS7	326 B2
SUD CO10	46 G5
Hill Crs *CHLM/GWD* CM2	5 K4
EMPK RM11	319 H1
HVHL CB9	41 K2
Hillcrest *COS* CO15	182 A5
FOS CO13	158 E6
RCHLM CM5	245 P9
WCHMH N21	272 C6
Hillcrest Ap *RIPW* IP8	24 C1
Hillcrest Av *HOC/HUL* SS5	287 H6
BOC CM0	348 D4
Hillcrest Cl *SLH/COR* SS17	340 C1
Hillcrest Ct *HAR* CO12	14 D7
SLH/COR SS17 *	340 F2
SOS SS1	19 H4
SUD CO10	47 H9
Hillcrest Vw *VGE* SS16	324 C6
Hillcrest Wy *EPP* CM16	255 H1
Hillcroft *LOU* IG10	276 B1
Hillcroft Rd *EHAM* E6	334 C5
Hildene Av *HARH* RM3	299 J3
Hildene Cl *HARH* RM3	299 J2
Hill Farm La *RIPS/CAP* IP9	84 E2
Hillfield Pk *WCHMH* N21	272 F8
Hillfoot Av *CRW* RM5	298 B5
Hillfoot Rd *CRW* RM5	298 B5
Hillhouse *WAB* EN9	253 J3
Hillhouse Cl *BCAYW* CM12	283 J4
Hillhouse Ct *BCAYW* CM12 *	283 J4
Hill House Ct *RCOLE* CO7	179 M6
Hillhouse Dr *BCAYW* CM12	283 J4
Hill House Dr *BCAYW* CM12	283 J4
Hill House La *CDW/CHF* RM16	350 C1
Hillhouse Rd *IPNE* IP4	17 J6
Hilliards Rd *RCOLE* CO7	131 H5
Hillie Bunnies *RCOLW* CO6	99 J9
Hillingdon Rd *BXLYHN* DA7	346 B7
Hill La *HOC/HUL* SS5	308 A2
HVHL CB9	42 A7
NHMKT IP6	23 P3
Hill Leys *RCOLE* CO7	228 D7
Hillman Av *COS* CO15	206 D6
Hillman Cl *EMPK* RM11	299 J7
Hillridge *COLN* CO4	128 C4
Hill Ri *ED* N9	273 N5
POTB/CUF EN6	228 D7
UPMR RM14	319 M4
Hillrise Rd *CRW* RM5	298 B3
Hill Rd *BRW* CM14	280 D9
CHLM/GWD CM2	5 K4
COS CO15	181 P7
EPP CM16	254 F7
HAR CO12	14 D6
RCOLW CO6	148 A4
SAFWN CB10	68 A1
SOS SS1	328 G3
Hill Rd South *CHLM/GWD* CM2	5 K5
Hill's Chace *BRW* CM14	300 F1
Hills Cl *BRTR* CM7	145 J2
Hills Crs *COLW* CO3	151 K1
Hillside *HOC/HUL* SS5	183 M1
GRAYS RM17	349 N2

HLWE CM17 ....211 K5
HOD EN11..................................208 C4
LOS SS9 ....327 P6
MAL CM9 ....222 B8
WARE SG12 ....184 A4
Hillside Av BSF CM23.................137 M7
CHES/WCR EN8 ....252 A1
HOC/HUL SS5 ....307 P2
WFD IG8 ....295 M2
Hillside Cl BCAYE CM11...............283 J7
WFD IG8 ....295 M2
Hillside Crs CHES/WCR ENB 252 A1
COS CO15 ....182 D8
ENC/FH EN2 ....251 J8
IPSE IP5 ....26 A8
LOS SS9 ....328 B6
WARE SG12 ....184 E8
Hillside Gdns BRTR CM7 ....145 J5
WALTH E17 ....294 C7
Hillside Gv CHLM/GWD CM2 ....239 P4
STHGT/OAK N14........................272 C6
Hillside La WARE SG12 ....184 D7
Hillside Ms CHLM/GWD CM2........259 P5
Hillside Rd BCAYW CM12.............283 J7
BOC CM06.................................290 C5
DAGE RM10 ....142 E8
GTDUN CM6 ....142 E8
HOC/HUL SS5 ....307 M7
LOS SS9 ....307 M7
SBF/HAD SS7 ....325 K5
SUD CO10 ....21 C5
Hillside Wk RBW CM14 ....280 D9
Hill's Rd BKHH IG9 ....275 L7
HSTD CO9 ....72 C9
Hill St SAFWN CB10 ....51 L9
Hill Ter SLH/COR SS17 ....324 B9
SUD CO10 ....44 B4
Hillview Av EMPK RM11 ....319 H1
Hill View Cl K/T/MI CO5 ....152 C6
Hill View Crs IL IG1......................316 A1
Hill View Dr THMD SE28 ....334 F8
Hillview Gdns CHES/WCR ENB 252 B6
SLH/COR SS17 ....323 N9
Hill View Rd RAYL SS6 ....306 N5
Hillway BCAYE CM11...................283 L6
CBE/LIN CB11 ....38 B1
WOS/PRIT SS0 ....328 B6
The Hillway BRWN CM15 ....259 P9
The Hill Wy BRWN CM15..............260 A9
Hillwood Cl RBRW/HUT CM13.......281 L7
Hillwood Gv
RBRW/HUT CM13 ....281 L7
WICKW SS12 ....285 K9
Hillybroom Gdns K/T/MI CO5.......202 G6
Hillyfield WALTH E17 ....210 C7
Hillyfield HAILH E17....................294 B6
Hillyfield Cl HOM E9 ....314 B7
Hillyfields LOU IG10 ....276 B1
Hilton Cl MGTR CO11..................106 A6
Hilton Rd CVI SS8 ....326 D9
IPSE IP5 ....31 J1
KESG IP5 ....27 P5
Hilton Wk CVI SS8.......................326 D9
Hilversum Wy CVI SS8.................326 E9
Hind Cl CHIG IG7 ....36 D4
Hind Crs ERITH DA8 ....346 B5
Hind Gv POP/IOD E14..................332 D6
Hindles Rd CVI SS8......................344 C1
Hindmans Wy DAGW RM9 ....335 N4
Hind Ter WTHK RM20 *................348 G4
Hines Cl RCOLW CO6 ....125 N7
Hines Rd IPSE IP5 ....25 P7
Hinguar St SBN/FI SS3 ....330 E8
Hintesham Cl PINE M14 ....26 E6
Hintlesham Dr FX IP11 ....34 C6
Hipkins BSF CM23 ....162 B1
Hipkins Pl BROX EN10 ....208 B8
Histon Cl KESG IP5 ....26 E4
Hitcham Rd RCOLW CO6 ....147 N5
WALTH E17 ....314 C2
Hitchcock Rd SUD CO10..............20 D1
Hitch Common Rd
SAFWS 64 G9
Hitches Yd WARE SG12 *.............184 A3
Hitchin Cl HARH RM5 ....249 H1
Hitchin Ms BRTR CM7 ....145 L6
Hither Blakers RCHLM CM5 ....264 C9
Hither Fld WARE SG12 ....184 B1
Hitherfield Rd BCTR RM8.............317 M4
Hitherwood Cl RCHLM RM12 ....319 J6
Hobart Cl CHLM/WR CM1.............217 M6
Hobart Rd BARK/HLT IG6 ....296 D6
DAGW RM9................................317 L6
TIL RM18....................................350 B6
Hobbiton Hl RCHLM CM5 ....286 J7
Hobbs Cl CHES/WCR ENB 230 A8
Hobbs Cross Rd EPP CM16 ....255 K4
HLWE CM17 ....187 N9
Hobbs Dr COLN CO4 ....103 K3
Hobby Horse Cl CHESW EN7 ....229 J5
Hobby St PEND EN3 ....151 J8
Hobday St POP/IOD E14..............332 E6
Hobhouse Rd SLH/COR SS17 ....341 L1
Hobleythick La SOSN SS2 ....328 E3
Hobsons Cl HOD EN11.................208 C2

Hobtoe Rd HLW CM20..................12 C4
Hockerill St BSF CM23.................137 M7
Hockley Av EHAM E6 ....333 P2
Hockley Cl BOC CM0 ....226 F9
BSDN SS14 ....3 K4
CBE/LIN CB1..............................39 N6
Hockley Gv DAGE RM10...............298 G6
Hockley Gn BSDN SS14 ....304 D9
Hockley La BOC CM0 ....226 F8
Hockley Ms BARK IG11 ....334 F2
Hockley Ri HOC/HUL SS5 ....307 P2
RAYL SS6 ....307 H4
Hockley Gdns IPSE IP5 ....30 C2
Hoddesdon Rd WARE SG12 ....184 F8
Hodges Cl CDW/CHF RM16..........348 G3
Hodges Holt WIT CM8..................197 K5
Hodgkins Cl THMD SE28 ....335 L7
Hodgkinson Rd FX IP11 ....10 A3
Hodgson Ct WICKM SS12 ....305 M2
Hodgson Wy WICKW SS12 ....305 L1
Hodings Rd HLW CM20 ....12 D5
Hoecroft WAB EN9 ....231 J1
Hoe Dr COLW CO5 ....151 K1
Hoe La ABR/ST RM4....................277 J2
EN EN1 ....251 N8
RCHLM CM3 ....193 M6
RCHLM CM3 ....251 N8
SUD CO10 ....45 L5
WAB EN9 ....231 J1
WARE SG12 ....184 A6
Hoe Mill Rd MAL CM9..................220 G7
Hoestock Rd SBW CM21 ....187 L2
Hoe St CHLM/WR CM1 ....216 D7
WALTH E17 ....294 D9
The Hoe BCAYW CM12.................303 J5
Hoffmanns Wy
CHLM/WR CM1 ....218 A7
Hogarth Av BRW CM14 ....281 H9
Hogarth Cl CAN/RD E16 ....333 N5
K/T/MI CO5................................202 C6
Hogarth Dr SBN/FI SS3................330 F6
Hogarth End FOS CO13................158 F7
Hogarth Reach LOU IG10 ....276 A4
Hogarth Rd BCTR RM8 ....317 J7
IPSE IP5 ....339 K8
Hogarth Sq IPSE IP5 ....30 F1
Hogarth Wy RCFD SS4.................308 D1
Hogg La CDW/CHF RM16 ....349 K1
Hog Hill Rd CRW RM5 ....297 N4
Hog's La ROY SG8 ....48 C7
Hogwell Cha RCHLM CM3 ....265 L8
Holbech Rd BSDN SS14 ....304 E7
Holbeck La CHESW EN7 ....229 L5
Holbek Rd CVI SS8 ....345 H2
Holborn Rd PLSTW E13 ....333 L5
EN EN1 ....251 L9
RCHLM CM3 ....286 C1
RCOS CO16 ....181 L9
SUD CO10 ....47 P8
Holborough Rd COLN CO4............128 C8
Holbrook Cl BCAYE CM11.............283 L6
EN EN1 ....251 L9
RCHLM CM3 ....286 C1
RCOS CO16 ....181 L9
SUD CO10 ....47 P8
Holbrook Crs FX IP11...................10 D1
Holbrook Rd HVHL CM3...............30 E1
IPSE IP5 ....41 H5
RIPS/CAP IP9 ....83 H7
RIPW IP8 ....83 H7
SRTFD E15 ....333 J2
Holbys Rw RCOS CO16 * 157 J4
Holcombe Crs CHTY IP2 ....24 E9
Holcombe Rd IL IG1 ....316 B2
Holdbrook Wy HARH RM3 ....299 L6
Holden Cl BCTR RM8 ....317 J5
Holden Gdns BRW CM14..............300 C2
BSDN SS14 ....3 K6
Holden Rd BSDN SS14 ....304 D6
COLN CO4 ....128 A5
Holden Wy UPMR RM14 ....320 A3
Holecroft WAB EN9 ....253 H4
Holen Cl WDBR IP12 ....27 P7
Holford Rd CDW/CHF RM16 ....340 G8
TIL RM18....................................350 E2
Holgate Pl SS11 ....305 H7
Holgate Rd DAGE RM10 ....317 P7
Holkham Av RCHLM CM3 ....286 C5
Holkham Cl EHAM E6 ....338 E6
Holland Av CVI SS8 ....326 A9
Holland Cl BSDN SS14.................304 C8
COLN CO4 ....128 A5
Holland Pk COS CO15 ....7 J1
Holland Park Av
GDMY/SEVK IG3 ....316 F1
Holland Rd COS CO15 ....334 A1
EHAM E6...................................334 A1
FOS CO13 ....158 C9
FX IP11 ....25 N5
IPNE IP4 ....25 N5
RCOS CO16 ....182 B5
SRTFD E15 ....333 H3
WOS/PRIT SS0 ....18 A5
Holland's Cft WARE SG12 ....185 N3
Holland's Rd HVHL CB9...............41 K5
Hollands Wk SUD CO10 ....324 C4
Holland Vis FOS CO13 ....183 H2
Holledge Crs FOS CO13 ....158 F8
Holleslay Av HVHL CB9 ....40 F5
Holliday Gdns DAGE RM10...........262 D5
Holliday Wy DAGE RM10 ....318 A9
Hollidge Wy DAGE RM10 ....318 A9
Hollies Rd BRTR CM7 ....747 C4
The Hollies SLH/COR SS17 ....341 K4
Hollies Cft RCOLW CO6 ....125 H7
Hollington Rd EHAM E6................334 A3
Hollingtons Gv COS CO15 ....175 K2
Hollis Lock CHLM/GWD CM2 ....218 F8
Hollis PI GRAYS RM17.................349 K1
Holliwell Cl COLW CO5 ....126 C9
Holloway Crs GTDUN CM6............190 F5
Holloway Rd EHAM E6..................334 A3
MAL CM9 ....222 A5
WAN E11 ....314 C5
Hollowfield Av GRAYS RM17 ....349 K2
Hollow La BURES CO8..................76 A4
CHLM/WR CM1 ....217 L4

RIPS/CAP IP9 ....84 E2
Hollow Rd GTDUN CM6 ....168 D1
K/T/MI CO5................................172 E5
RIPW IP8 ....28 F2
ROY SG8 ....48 G9
SAFWS CB11 ....49 L6
SAFWS CB11 ....89 P5
SUD CO10 ....43 M9
The Hollow WFD IG8 ....295 J1
Hollybank WIT CM8.....................197 J3
Holly Blue Cl RIPW IP8 ....29 N2
Hollybush Cl WAN E11 ....295 K9
Holly Bush Gnr RCOLE CO7 ....79 P4
Hollybush Dr FX IP11 ....35 N4
Hollybush Hl RCOLE CO07 ....180 B2
WAN E11 ....315 J2
Hollybush St PLSTW E13..............333 L3
Hollybush Wy CHESW EN7...........229 M7
Holly Cl BKHH IG9 ....275 N9
BOC CM0 ....290 C3
COLS CO2 ....151 M4
IPSE IP5 ....31 M1
Holly Crs WFD IG8 ....294 G4
Hollycroft Cl IP IP1 ....23 H9
Hollycross Rd WARE SG12 ....184 C4
Hollydown Wy WAN E11 ....314 C5
SOCK/AV RM15..........................358 C4
Holly End KESG IP5 ....27 L5
Holly Fld HLWW/ROY CM19 ....270 E6
Hollyfields BROX EN10 ....230 B5
Hollyford BCAYE CM11.................283 K3
Holly La BXLYHN DA7 ....346 B6
Holly Lodge Gdns RAYL SS6.........306 E7
Holllytree Cl COLS CO2 ....151 M5
Hollytree Gdns RAYL SS6 ....306 E7
Hollyview Cl RCOS CO16 ....156 C1
Holly Wy CHLM/GWD CM2 ....240 B5
K/T/MI CO5................................173 P8
RCOLE CO7 ....129 N9
Hollywood
CHLM/GWD CM2 ....240 C4
Hollywood Rd CHING E4 ....294 B2
Hollywood Wy ERITH DA8............346 C6
WFD IG8 ....294 C4
Holman Cl COLW CO5 ....151 K2
Holman Rd HSTD CO9..................97 P8
Holmans RCHLM CM3..................219 K5
Holmbridge Gdns PEND EN3........274 A3
Holmbrook Wy FOS CO13 ....158 F9
Holm Ct KESG IP5 ....27 J5
Holme Cl CHES/WCR ENB 252 B1
Holmer Cross SAFWN CB10 * 51 M7
Holme Rd EHAM E6 ....333 P1
EMPK RM11 ....319 M5
Holmes Av WALTH E17 ....294 C7
Holmes Cl SLH/COR SS17 ....340 G2
Homestead CHES/WCR ENB 251 P5
Holmestead Meadow EPP CM16 ...210 C9
Holmes Rd HSTD CO9 ....97 P8
Holme Wk WICKW SS12 ....305 L1
Holmhurst Rd BELV DA17 ....346 A3
Holmleigh Av DART DA1...............347 H9
Holmsdale Cl WOS/PRIT SS0 ....328 C3
Holmsdale Gv BXLYHN DA7 ....346 D7
Holmswood CVI SS8 ....327 H9
Holmwood Av BRNW CM15 ....281 K4
Holmwood Cl RCOS CO16.............181 L7
Holmwood Rd
GDMY/SEVK IG3 ....316 F4
PEND EN3 ....252 A6
Holness Rd SRTFD E15 ....315 J3
Hoist Av LAIN SS15 ....305 K7
Hoist Cl SLH/COR SS17 ....341 K2
Holstock Rd IL IG1 ....316 D4
Holt Cl CHIG IG7 ....296 C2
THMD SE28 ....335 K1
Holt Dr COLS CO2 ....152 B7
WIT CM8...................................197 P7
Holt Farm Wy RCFD SS4 ....308 E3
Holton Rd CVI SS8 ....345 J2
RAYL SS6 ....307 K6
Holton St WCHPL E1 ....319 H3
Hold Rd CAN/RD E16 ....333 P8
HARH RM3 ....299 K4
Holt's Rd RCOLW CO6 ....101 N5
The Holt BARK/HLT IG6 ....296 D2
Holt Wy CHIG IG7 ....296 C2
Holtwhite Av ENC/FH EN2 ....273 H1
Holtwhite's Hl ENC/FH EN2 ....250 G9
Holtynge SBF/HAD SS7 ....325 P2
Holybread La RCHLM CM5 ....219 P7
Holyhead Cl BOW E3 ....332 D3
Holyoake Ct
BERM/RHTH SE16 ....332 B9
Holyoak La HOC/HUL SS5 ....307 P5
Holyrood CHLM/WR CM1.............110 A6
Holyrood Cl CHTY IP2 ....29 J9
Holyrood Dr WOS/PRIT SS0 ....328 C4
Holyrood Gdns
CDW/CHF RM16 ....350 D2
Holywells Cl IPSE IP5 ....25 M7
Holy Wells Rd IPSE IP5 ....25 M8
Homebridge SAFWN CB10 ....68 D6
Home Cl BROX EN10....................230 C3
HLW CM20 ....210 G3
PEND EN3 ....55 M3
Homecroft Gdns LOU IG10 ....276 C5
Home Farm La RCOLE CO7...........105 H8

Home Farm Rd
RBRW/HUT CM13 ....301 H5
Homefield BOC CM0 ....269 K4
RIPS/CAP IP9 ....28 D9
RIPW IP8 ....253 K2
Homefield Av
GNTH/NBYPK IG2 ....296 F9
Homefield Cl BCAYE CM11...........303 L1
CHLM/WR CM1 ....217 L6
EPP CM16.................................233 H8
Homefield Rd COLS CO2 ....41 J6
HVHL CB9 ....40 F5
WARE SG12 ....184 E2
WIT CM8...................................171 P9
Homefields Av SBF/HAD SS7 ....325 N1
Homefield Wy BRTR CM7.............145 N8
Home Gdns DART DA1.................99 J9
Home Gdns DAGE RM10 ....318 B5
Homelands Gv BCAYE CM11 ....284 B4
Homeleigh Ct CHES/WCR EN8......229 N9
Homelye Cha GTDUN CM6 ....142 A5
Home Md CHLM/GWD CM2 ....240 B8
Home Mead BCAYE CM11 ....240 B8
Home Mdw BCAYW CM12 ....240 B8
Home Pastures RBSF CM22..........188 E1
Homer Cl BXLYHN DA7 ....346 B6
Homer Rd HOM E9 ....314 B8
Homerton Cl COLS CO15 ....182 A5
Homerton Gv HOM E9 ....314 A7
Homerton High St HOM E9 ....314 A7
Homerton Rd HOM E9 ....314 C7
Homesdale Cl WAN E11................295 K9
Homesdale Vls RIPS/CAP IP9 * 85 K6
Homestead CHLM/WR CM1 ....218 A4
Homestead Dr VGE SS16 ....323 K4
Homestead Gdns
SBF/HAD SS7 ....326 G3
Homestead Paddock
STHGT/OAK N14........................272 A4
Homestead Rd BCAYE CM11 ....284 C8
BCTR RM8 ....317 N4
PIT SS13 ....305 K8
SBF/HAD SS7 ....326 G4
Homestead Wy SBF/HAD SS7 ....326 G4
Homeway HARH RM3 ....299 N5
Homewillow Cl WCHMH N21 ....272 G5
Homewood Av
POTB/CUF EN6 ....228 D6
Homewood La
POTB/CUF EN6 ....228 B6
Homing Rd BSF CM23 ....162 B1
Honeybourne BSF CM23 ....162 B1
Honey Brook WAB EN9 ....253 H3
Honey Cl BRWN CM15 ....258 G5
CHLM/GWD CM2 ....240 C4
DAGE RM10 ....318 B8
Honeycroft LOU IG10 ....276 B5
Honey La CHES/WCR EN8 ....252 C4
RCOLW CO6 ....77 L5
SAFWS CB11 ....90 N5
WAB EN9 ....253 H4
Honeymeade HLW CM20 ....319 M4
Honey Pot La RCHLM CM3 ....265 P6
Honeypot La BRW CM14 ....280 D8
BSDN SS14 ....3 C4
ING UM4 ....200 A4
MAL CM9 ....200 A3
MGTR CO11..............................132 C3
RCOS CO16 ....181 K1
Honeypots CHLM/GWD CM2.........240 B4
Honeysuckle Cl BRWN CM15 ....280 C4
BSF CM23 ....137 H8
HARH RM3 ....299 H5
HVHL CB9 ....41 H2
Honeysuckle Gdns CHTY IP2 ....24 F7
Honeysuckle Wy COLN CO4 ....128 F7
RCOLE CO7 ....154 F9
WIT CM8...................................171 J9
Honeywood Av RCOLW CO6 ....147 P5
Honeywood Rd HSTD CO9 ....98 A5
Honiley Av WICKW SS12 ....305 K5
Honington Cl WICKE SS11 ....305 N1
Honiton Rd ROMW/RG RM7 ....318 C1
SOS SS1....................................19 K4
Honorius Dr COLN CO4 ....128 C2
Honor Link CHLM/WR CM1 ....218 F4
Honywood Cl RCOLW CO6 ....318 G4
Honywood Rd BSDN SS14 ....304 E5
COLW CO5 ....127 N9
Horywood Wy FOS CO13 ....158 G2
Hood Av STHGT/OAK N14 ....272 A5
Hood Cl WICKW SS12 ....305 K1
Hoodcote Gdns WCHMH N21 ....22 C4
Hood Dr NHMKT IP6 ....22 A2
Hood Gdns BRTR CM7 ....145M2
Hood Rd IPSE IP5 ....30 E1
RAIN RM13 ....336 D1
Hood Wk ROMW/RG RM7 ....248 G3
Hooe End La BRWN CM15 ....258 E4
Hook End La BRWN CM15 ....258 E5
Hook End Rd BRWN CM15 ....258 E5
Hooker's Rd WALTH E17 ....294 A7
Hook Fld HLWS CM18 ....210 F5
Hook La AR8/ST RM4 ....277 N5
Hooks Hall Dr DAGE RM10 ....318 B5
Hookstone Wy WFD IG8 ....295 N4
Hooley Dr RAYL SS6 ....306 F1
Hooper Rd CAN/RD E16 ....333 M9
The Hoo HLW CM17.....................187 K7
Hoover Dr LAIN SS15 ....302 C9
Hope Av SLH/COR SS17...............323 M9
Hope Cl BRWN CM15 ....259 P9
Hope Dr RCAYE CM11 ....304 B2
Hope Rd BCAYE CM11 ....304 B2
CVI SS8 ....344 C2
SBF/HAD SS7 ....325 P5
Hope Ter WTHK RM20 * 348 G3
Hopewell Cl CDW/CHF RM16 ....348 G3
Hop Gardens La WAB EN9 ....221 J7
The Hoppgrounds BRTR CM7 ....42 C4
Hopkins Cl CHLM/GWD CM2........218 E9
FOS CO13 ....158 G8

GPK RM2....................................299 H7
Hopkins Md CHLM/GWD CM2 ....218 E9
Hopkins Ms SRTFD E15 ....333 J1
Hopkins Rd LEY E10.....................314 E2
Hopkirk Cl RCHLM CM5 ....242 C2
Hop Meadow RCOLE CO7 ....80 E7
Hoppers Rd WCHMH N21 ....272 F9
The Hoppet ING CM4 ....260 D5
Hoppett Rd CHING E4 ....275 H9
Hopping Jacks La
CHLM/GWD CM2 ....242 C3
Hoppit Md BRTR CM7 ....145 J5
The Hoppitt CHONG CM5 ....213 H8
Hopton Ri HVHL CM6...................40 F5
Horace Av ROMW/RG RM7...........318 C3
Horace Eves Cl HVHL CB9 * 41 J3
Horace Rd BARK/HLT IG6 ....296 D7
BCAYE CM11 ....283 J4
FSTGT E7 ....315 L6
SOS SS1....................................19 H5
Horatio Pl POP/IOD E14...............332 F9
Hordle Pl HAR CO12 ....14 F6
Hordle St HAR CO12 ....14 E6
Horkesley Hl RCOLN CO4.............102 G8
RCOLW CO6 ....77 P9
Horkesley Wy WICKW SS12 ....305 K1
Horksley Gdns
RBRW/HUT CM13 ....281 N5
Horley Cl RCOS CO16 ....181 M7
Hornbeam Av UPMR RM14 ....319 M6
Hornbeam Cha
SOCK/AV RM15..........................338 G3
Hornbeam Cl
CHLM/GWD CM2 ....239 P4
COLS CO2 ....151 N4
ENC/FH EN2 ....254 F7
IL IG1 ....316 E7
RBRW/HUT CM13 ....281 L9
Hornbeam Gv CHING E4...............275 H9
Hornbeam La CHING E4................275 H4
Hornbeam Rd BARK/HLT IG6........295 N9
EPP CM16.................................254 E7
Hornbeams SBF/HAD SS7 ....305 N7
Hornbeams Av EN EN1 ....251 P5
Hornbeam Sq BOW E3 ....332 C1
Hornbeam Wy CHESW EN7 ....229 J3
The Hornbeams HAR CO12 * 12 E2
Hornbeam Wy
HLW CM20 ....303 L6
Horn Book SAFWS CB11 ....51 N9
Hornby Av WOS/PRIT SS0 ....328 D1
Hornby Cl SOSN SS2 ....328 E1
Hornchurch Cl WICKE SS11 ....305M1
Hornchurch Rd EMPK RM11 ....319M4
Horndon Cl CRW RM5 ....298 B5
Horndon Gn CRW RM5 ....298 B5
Horndon Rd CRW RM5 ....298 B5
SLH/COR SS17 ....341 H4
Horne Rw RCHLM CM3 ....242 A5
Horner Pl WIT CM8 ....197 K2
Hornet Wy BOC CM0 ....290 G3
Hornford Wy ROMW/RG RM7 ....318 D2
Horn Hl HSTD CO9......................96 F3
Horn La CBE/LIN CB1...................38 C4
WFD IG8 ....295 K3
Hornminster Gln EMPK RM11 ....319M4
Hornsby La CHLM/GWD CM16......340 B7
Hornsby Sq LAIN SS15.................302 F8
Hornsby Wy LAIN SS15 ....302 G8
Hornsland Rd CVI SS8 ....345 H2
Horns Rd BARK/HLT IG6 ....296 C6
Horrocks Cl COLS CO2 ....152 B2
WARE SG12 ....184 A1
Horsa Rd ERITH DA8 ....346 B5
Horsebridges Rd DAGW RM9 ....335 M1
Horsecroft Rd
HLWW/ROY CM19 ....209 P4
Horsehath Rd CBE/LIN CB1 ....39 C7
Horse Leaze EHAM E6 ....336 C1
Horseman Ct RSIG CM5 ....277 P7
Horseman Side BRW CM14 ....279 J5
Horseshoe Cl BCAYW CM12 ....283 H3
WARE SG12 ....49 L6
Horseshoe Crs SBN/FI SS3 ....330 B8
Horseshoe ml BUNT SG9 ....86 B8
WAB EN9 ....253 M3
Horseshoe La BUNT SG9 ....86 A9
ENC/FH EN2 ....273 H2
HVHL CB9 ....41 H4
Horseshoe Lawns
HOC/HUL SS5 * 287 H5
Horsey Rd FOS CO13 ....158 D6
Horsham Av IPSE IP5 ....26 C8
Horsham Cl HVHL CB9 ....40 F2
Horsley Cross RCHLM CM3 ....258 E6
Horsley Rd CHING E4...................274 F8
Hoskin's Cl CHLM/GWD CM2 ....333 M6
Hospital Ap CHLM/WR CM1 ....194 A9
Hospital Fld BRTR CM77 ....145 L9
Hospital La COLW CO5 ....127 N9
Hospital Rd CHLM/WR CM1 ....127 N9
SBN/FI SS3 ....330 E8
Hossack Rd IPSE IP5 ....30 C2
Hotham St SRTFD E15 ....333 H1
Houblons Hl EPP CM16................214 A9
Houchin Dr CHONG CM5 ....214 A9
Houchin's La RCOLW CO6 ....148 C8
Houghton Pl IPNE IP4 ....26 E6
Houndsden Rd WCHMH N21 ....272 E5
Houndsfield Rd ED N9 ....253 L4
Hove Av WALTH E17 ....294 C9
Hove Cn Cl GRAYS RM17.............349 K4
Hovefields Av WICKW SS12 ....305 J3
Hoveton Rd THMD SE28 ....334 E9
Howard Av WFD IG8 ....296 C5
Howard Av HAR CO12 ....110 A6
Howard Cha BSDN SS14 ....303 N7
Howard Cl BRTR CM7 ....145 L3

HVHL CB9 ...40 G4
LOU IG10 ...275 P5
WAB EN9 ...252 G4
Howard Crs PIT SS13 ...325 H1
Howard Dr CHLM/GWD CM2 ...218 F1
Howard Pl CVI SS8 ...344 E3
Howard Rd BARK IG11 ...334 E1
CDW/CHF RM16 ...348 F1
COS CO15 ...182 D9
EHAM E6 ...334 A2
IL IG1 ...316 C6
SAFWN CB10 ...591M8
UPMR RM14 ...319 D4
WALTH E17 ...294 D7
WAN E11 ...315 H5
Howards Cha SOSN SS2 ...328 F4
Howards Cl CHLM CM5 ...219 K3
Howards Crt COLN CO4 ...127 N2
Howard's La PLSTW E13 ...333 K3
Howard's La CBE/LIN CB12 ...39M1
Howard's Rd PLSTW E13 ...333 K3
Howard St IPNE IP4 ...26 A4
Howard Wy KESG IP5 ...27 K3
Howard Vyse Ct COS CO15 ...181 P8
Howard Wy HLW CM20 ...210 G1
Howbridge Hall Rd WIT CM8 ...197 J4
Howbridge Rd WIT CM8 ...197 J4
Howbridge La ERITH DA8 ...346 F7
Howden Cl THMD SE28 ...335 K7
Howe Av IPSE IP3 ...26 B8
Howe Cha HSTD CO9 ...97 P4
Howe Cl COLN CO4 ...128 E8
ROMW/RG RM7 ...59 P7
SAFWS CB11 * ...50 B7
Howe Green Rd RCHLM CM5 ...265 P5
Howe La SAFWN CB10 ...68 D5
Howell Cl CHDH RM6 ...297 L9
Howell Rd SLH/COR SS17 ...323 N8
Howe Rd HHL CB9 ...41 J1
Howfield Gn HOD EN11 ...208 C2
Howland Wy
BERM/RHTH SE16 ...332 B9
Howlett Cl KESG IP5 ...27 K4
Howse Rd WAB EN9 ...252 F5
Hows Md EPP CM16 ...234 C3
Hoxter Wy SUD CO10 ...47 H9
Hoxton Cl RCOS CO16 ...6 B1
Hoylake Gdns HARH RM3 ...299M5
Hoynors RCHLM CM5 ...265M5
Hoy St CAN/RD E16 ...333 J6
Hoy Ter WTHK RM20 ...348 C3
Hubbards Cha EMPK RM11 ...299M9
WOTN CO14 ...159 J5
Hubbards Cl EMPK RM11 ...299M9
Hubbard St SRTFD E15 ...333 J2
Hubert Rd BRW CM14 ...280 E9
COLW CO3 ...127 L7
EHAM E6 ...333 N5
RAIN RM13 ...336 E5
Hucklesbury Av COS CO15 ...182 F7
Hucknall Cl HARH RM5 ...299 L3
Huddart St BOW E3 ...332 C5
Huddlestone Rd FSTGT E7 ...315 L6
Hudson Cl HAR CO12 ...110 B7
HVHL CB9 ...181M9
Hudson Crs LOS SS9 ...307 P9
Hudson Rd LOS SS9 ...307 N9
Hudsons Cl SLH/COR SS17 * ...341 L2
Hudson's Hl BRTR CM7 ...95 J5
Hudsons La RCOLW CO6 ...78 C4
Hudson Wy CVI SS8 ...326 D8
Hughan Rd SRTFD E15 ...314 G2
Hugh Dickson Rd COLN CO4 ...127 P5
Hughes Rd CDW/CHF RM16 ...350 B1
RCOLE CO7 ...105 P9
Hughes Ter CAN/RD E16 * ...333 J5
Hugo Gdns RAIN RM13 ...318 E8
Hullbridge Rd RAYL SS6 ...286 G8
RCHLM CM5 ...265 K1
Hull Cl BERM/RHTH SE16 * ...332 A8
CHESW EN7 ...229 J5
Hullett's La BRWN CM15 ...280 C3
Hull Gn HLWE CM17 ...213 J1
Hull Gv HLWW/ROY CM19 ...210 B8
Hull La RCHLM CM5 ...195M2
Hull's La CHLM/GWD CM2 ...241 K4
Hulse Av BARK IG11 ...316 E8
ROMW/RG RM7 ...298 A5
Hulton Cl RCHLM CM5 ...219 K3
Humber Av COS CO15 ...206 D6
SOCK/AV RM15 ...338 C6
Humber Cl RAYL SS6 ...306 F6
Humber Doucy La IPNE IP4 ...25 P1
Humber Dr UPMR RM14 ...320 A1
Humber Rd CHLM/WR CM1 ...218 C6
WIT CM8 ...196 F1
Humberstone Rd PLSTW E15 ...333M3
Hume Av TIL RM18 ...350 C8
Hume Cl TIL RM18 ...350 B8
Humphrey Cl CLAY IG5 * ...296 A5
Humphrey's Farm La
RCHLM CM5 ...193 K5
Humphries Cl DAGW RM9 ...317 N6
Humphry Rd COLO CO10 ...20 D3
Hundon Cl HVHL CB9 ...42 D1
Hundred Acres
CHES/WCR EN8 * ...252 D4
Hundred La COLN CO4 ...103 L4
Hungerbourn CHING E4 ...274 F7
Hungerdown La RCOLE CO7 ...105 K9
Hunnable Rd BRTR CM7 ...145 H5
Hunsdon Cl DAGW RM9 ...317M9
Hunsdon Rd WARE SG12 ...160 C9
WARE SG12 ...185 H8
Hunt Av MAL CM9 ...222 C6
CL K/T/MI CO5 ...173 J1
Hunt Dr RCOS CO16 ...181 N8
Hunter Av BRWN CM15 ...281 K5
HCH RM12 ...319 H6
WICKW SS12 ...106 A5
Hunter Rd IPSE IP5 ...31 J2
Hunters Av BCAYW CM12 ...283 J9
Hunters Cha CHONG CM5 ...255M9

RBRW/HUT CM13 ...282 D7
RCOLE CO7 ...104 F6
Hunters Cnr COLW CO5 * ...151 J1
Hunters End FX IP11 ...34 F4
Hunter's Gv CRW RM5 ...298 A2
Hunters Hall Rd DAGE RM10 ...317 P6
Hunters Reach CHESW EN7 ...229 L8
Hunters Ride KESG IP5 ...27 N4
Hunters Rdg COLN CO4 ...128 C3
Hunters Rd IL IG1 ...316 C7
Hunters Sq DAGE RM10 ...317 P6
Hunters Wy CHLM/WR CM1 ...218 E4
ENC/FH EN2 ...250 F9
SAFWS CB11 ...65 L2
Huntingdon Cl BROX EN10 ...230 B3
Huntingdon Rd EI N9 ...273 P7
SOS SS1 ...5 L2
Huntingdon St CAN/RD E16 ...333 J6
Huntingdon Wy COS CO15 ...181 P7
Hunting Ga COL CO1 ...9 K9
Hunting Gate Cl ENC/FH EN2 * ...272 F2
Huntings Rd DAGE RM10 ...317 P8
Huntland Cl RAIN RM13 ...336 G5
Hunt Rd RCOLW CO6 ...129M3
Hunt's Cl CHLM/WR CM1 ...239 J2
Hunt's Ct CHLM/WR CM1 ...239 J2
Hunts Farm Cl MAL CM9 ...225 J1
Hunts La SAFWN CB10 ...56 C4
SRTFD E15 ...332 F2
Huntsman Rd BARK/HLT IG6 ...297 J3
Huntsmans Dr UPMR RM14 ...319 P7
Hunts Md DAGW RM9 ...282 G7
PEND EN3 ...274 A2
Hunt Wy FCOS CO13 ...158 F8
Hunwicke Rd COLN CO4 ...128 F9
Hurlock Rd BCAYE CM11 ...285 H6
Hurnard Dr COLN CO4 ...127 K8
Hurrell Down COLN CO4 ...128 B3
RCHLM CM5 ...219 L2
Hurrells La RCHLM CM5 ...219M8
Hurricane Pl IPSE IP5 ...31 J1
Hurricane Wy FH EPP CM16 ...233 N6
WICKE SS11 ...305M2
Hurry Cl SRTFD E15 ...315 H9
Hursley Rd CHIG IG7 ...296 G2
Hurst Av CHING E4 ...274 D9
Hurstbourne Gdns BARK IG11 ...316 E8
Hurst Cl CHING E4 ...274 D9
RCOLE CO7 ...179M7
Hurst Dr CHES/WCR EN8 ...252 A4
Hurstlands Cl EMPK RM11 ...319 H2
Hurstleigh Gdns CLAY IG5 ...296 A5
Hurst Park Av HCH RM12 ...319 K6
Hurst Rd BKHH IG9 ...275 N7
ERITH DA8 ...346 B5
WALTH E17 ...294 E7
WCHMH N21 ...272 F7
Hurst Wy CHLM/GWD CM2 ...218 G9
LOS SS9 ...328 A2
Hurstwood Av BRWN CM15 ...280 E6
ERITH DA8 ...346 D6
SWFD E18 ...295 L8
Hutchings's St POP/IOD E14 ...332 D9
Hutchins Cl HCH RM12 ...319 K5
SRTFD E15 ...314 F9
Hutchins Rd THMD SE28 ...335 H7
Hutland Rd IPNE IP4 ...25 N4
Hutton Cl WFD IG8 ...295 L3
Hutton Ct RBRW/HUT CM13 * ...282 A6
Hutton Gdns RBRW/HUT CM13 ...281 N6
Hutton La RBRW/HUT CM13 ...281 L6
Hutton Pl RBRW/HUT CM13 ...281 L5
Hutton Rd BRWN CM15 ...281 K6
Hutton Village
RBRW/HUT CM13 ...281 P6
Huxley Dr CHDH RM6 ...317 J2
Huxley Rd LEY E10 ...314 F4
Hyacinth Cl MAL CM9 ...225 K2
RCOS CO16 ...181M9
Hyam's La RIPS/CAP IP9 ...82 G8
RIPS/CAP IP9 ...83 K4
Hycliffe Gdns CHIG IG7 ...296 D1
Hyde Cha RCHLM CM5 ...242 F6
Hyde Cl PLSTW E13 ...333 K2
Hydefield Cl EI N9 ...273 J7
Hydefield Ct EI N9 ...273 K8
Hyde Gn RCHLM CM5 ...242 E5
Hyde La BRTR CM7 ...95 N7
RCHLM CM5 ...242 E6
Hyde Md WAB EN9 ...231 H2
Hyde Park Av WCHMH N21 ...273 H8
Hyde Park Gdns WCHMH N21 ...273 H7
Hyderabad Wy SRTFD E15 ...315 H9
Hyde Rd SUD CO10 ...20 D6
Hyde Gn CDW/CHF RM16 ...350 D1
Hydeside Gdns EI N9 ...273 L8
The Hyde VGE SS16 ...323 K2
Hydethorpe Av EI N9 ...273 L8
Hyde Wy ED N9 ...273 L8
WICKW SS12 ...305 J1
Hydeway SBF/HAD SS7 ...326 F4
Hyde Wood La RCFD SS4 ...288 G9
Hydewood Rd HSTD CO9 ...58 A7
Hyem's La FX IP11 ...35 L4
Hyland Cl EMPK RM11 ...318 G2
Hylands Cl CITDUN CM6 ...166 F1
Hylands Rd WALTH E17 ...294 D3
The Hylands HOC/HUL SS5 ...307 N2
Hyland Wy EMPK RM11 ...318 G2
Hyll Cl SAFWN CB10 ...36 E8
Hyntle Cl CHTY IP2 ...24 F6
Hynton Rd BCTR RM8 ...317 K4
Hythe Cl BRTR CM7 ...121 H9
COS CO15 ...207 J4
Hythe Gv RCOLE CO7 ...179 K4
Hythe Hl COL CO1 ...128 D9
Hythe Quay RCOLE CO7 ...79 D9
Hythe Station Rd COL CO1 ...128 E9
The Hythe MAL CM9 ...222 C9

I

Ian Rd BCAYW CM12 ...282 D3
Ibbetson Pth LOU IG10 ...276 D2
Ibbotson Av CAN/RD E16 ...333 J6
Ibscott Cl DAGE RM10 ...318 B8
I Butts Rd SBN/FI SS3 ...331 H5
Iceland Rd BOW E3 ...332 D1
Iceni Wy COLS CO2 ...151 L3
Ickleton Rd SAFWN CB10 ...36 D9
Icknield Cl SAFWN CB10 ...49 K6
Icknield Dr SAFWN/NBYPK IG2 ...296 C9
Icknield Wy ROY SG8 ...48 C7
Icknield Way Pth SAFWN CB10 ...50 C2
Ickworth Cl BRTR CM77 ...144 F7
Ickworth Ct FX IP11 ...9 P5
Ickworth Crs IPNE IP4 ...26 E6
Ickworth Park Rd WALTH E17 ...294 B8
Iconfield Pk HAR CO12 * ...110 B4
Ida St POP/IOD E14 ...332 F6
Idmiston Rd SRTFD E15 ...315 J7
Ilchester Rd BCTR RM8 ...317 J7
Ilex Cl COLS CO2 ...151 N4
Ilford Hi IL IG1 ...316 B5
Ilford La IL IG1 ...316 C6
Ilfracombe Av PIT SS13 ...325 J1
Ilfracombe Crs HCH RM12 ...319 H6
Ilfracombe Gdns CHDH RM6 ...317 J2
Ilford St SOSN SS2 ...329 K5
Ilgars Rd WICKE SS11 ...305 P3
Ilkley Rd CAN/RD E16 ...333M5
Illingworth Wy EN EN1 ...273 K4
Ilmington Dr PIT SS13 ...304 F6
Imber Cl STHGT/OAK N14 ...272 B6
Imogen Ct COLN CO4 ...128 A3
Imperial Av RCHLM CM5 ...245M9
WOS/PRIT SS0 ...328 C5
Imperial Cl WOS/PRIT SS0 ...18 C5
Imperial Rd RAYL SS6 * ...306 F1
Imperial St BOW E3 ...332 F3
Imphal Cl COLS CO2 ...151M5
Inchbonnie Rd RCHLM CM5 ...286 F3
Indescon Ct POP/IOD E14 ...332 E9
Indigo Ms POP/IOD E14 * ...332 F7
Ingal Rd PLSTW E13 ...333 K4
Ingarfield Rd COS CO15 ...181M9
Ingatestone By-Pass
ING CM4 ...260 C4
Ingatestone Rd
CHLM/WR CM1 ...237 P9
ING CM4 ...259 J2
ING CM4 ...260 G8
MNPK E12 ...315M5
WFD IG8 ...295 L4
Ingaway VGE SS16 ...322 E6
Ingelrica Av RCHLM CM5 ...196 E9
Ingels Md EPP CM16 ...232 G8
Ingersoll Rd PEND EN3 ...251 P8
Ingestre Rd FSTGT E7 ...315 K6
Ingestre St HAR CO12 ...115 J5
Ingham Rd HVHL CB9 ...41 L3
Ingleby Gdns CHIG IG7 ...277 J9
Ingleby Rd CDW/CHF RM16 ...350 C1
DAGE RM10 ...318 A8
IL IG1 ...316 C3
Inglefield Gdns SLH/COR SS17 ...324 D6
Ingleglen EMPK RM11 ...319M2
Inglehurst Gdns REDBR IG4 ...296 A9
Inglenook COS CO15 ...182 C6
Ingleside Ct SAFWS CB11 ...51 L9
Inglewood Cl BARK/HLT IG6 ...296 E6
POP/IOD E14 ...332 D9
Inglewood Rd BXLYHN DA7 ...346 C9
Inglis Rd COLO CO4 ...128 A9
Ingram Ms BRTR CM7 ...145 L6
Ingram Rd GRAYS RM17 ...349M2
Ingram's Piece RCOLE CO7 ...104 F8
Ingram's Well Rd SUD CO10 ...21 F6
Ingrave Cl WICKW SS12 ...305 K1
Ingrave Rd BRW CM14 ...281 H9
ROM RM1 ...298 C8
Ingrebourne Gdns
UPMR RM14 ...319 P3
Ingrebourne Rd RAIN RM13 ...336 G4
Ingreway HARH RM5 ...299 N3
Inkerman Rw SUD CO10 ...20 C4
Inkerpole Pl CHLM/GWD CM2 ...218 F4
Inks Gn CHING E4 ...294 F2
Inmans Rw WFD IG8 ...295 J3
Innes Cl WICKW SS12 ...305 J2
Innhamit HI HSTD CO9 ...96 B5
Inworth Rd PLSTW E13 ...333M2
Innova Wy PEND EN3 ...252 C6
Inskip Cl LEY E10 ...314 E4
Inskip Dr EMPK RM11 ...319 K3
Inskip Rd BCTR RM8 ...317 J1
Institute Rd EPP CM16 ...233 L8
Integer Gdns WAN E11 * ...314 C2
Inverness Av EN EN1 ...251 K9
WOS/PRIT SS0 ...328 E4
Inverness Cl COL CO1 ...8 E4
Inverness Rd BARK/HLT IG6 ...296 F3
Invicta Cl CHING E4 ...294 F1
Invicta Ct K/T/MI CO5 ...172 C3
Inworth La RCOLW CO6 ...100 C6
Inworth Rd K/T/MI CO5 ...172 C3
Inworth Wk COLS CO2 ...152 B5
Iona Wy WICKW SS12 ...305 L2
Ipswich Ms WICKW SS12 ...322 C1
Ipswich Rd COLO CO5 ...6 A5
COLN CO4 ...104 C2
COLN CO4 ...128 E2
COS CO15 ...182 E7
KIR/MAC IP10 ...31M4
MGTR CO11 ...81 N8
RCOLE CO7 ...79 P9
RIPS/CAP IP9 ...83 L2
Ireland Cl EHAM E6 ...334 A5
Ireland Rd IPSE IP3 ...30 F1
Ireton Pl GRAYS RM17 ...349 K2

Ireton Rd COLW CO3 ...151 N1
Ireton St BOW E3 ...332 D4
Iris Cl BRWN CM15 ...280 E4
CHLM/WR CM1 ...218 E6
CHTY IP2 ...24 G9
EHAM E6 ...333 P5
Iris Wy CHING E4 ...294 C3
Irkdale Av EN EN1 ...251 L9
Irlam Rd CHTY IP2 ...24 E9
Iron Latch La COLW CO3 ...126 F1
Iron Mill La DART DA1 ...346 E9
Iron Mill Pl DART DA1 ...346 E9
Ironside Cl BERM/RHTH SE16 ...332 A9
Irons Wy CRW RM5 ...298 B4
Ironwell La HOC/HUL SS5 ...308 B9
Irvine Gdns SOCK/AV RM15 ...338 C6
Irvine Pl WICKW SS12 ...305 L2
Irvine Rd COLW CO5 ...151M1
Irvington Cl LOS SS9 ...327 N2
Irvon Hill Rd WICKW SS12 ...285 H9
Irye Md VGE SS16 ...323 K2
Isaac Sq CHLM/GWD CM2 ...240 G4
Isabel Ga CHES/WCR EN8 ...333 N6
Isabella Cl STHGT/OAK N14 ...272 B6
Isabelle Cl CHESW EN7 ...229 H8
Isbourne Rd COLN CO4 ...128 C8
Ishams Cha WIT CM8 ...197M5
Is Dr UPMR RM14 ...320 B1
Island La EOS CO15 ...158 F5
Island Rd COS CO15 ...158 F5
Island Rw POP/IOD E14 ...332 C6
The Island RCOLE CO7 * ...79 P9
Islay Whf POP/IOD E14 * ...332 F5
Isla Cl RCOLW CO6 ...128 E7
Ismailia Rd FSTGT E7 ...315 L9
Isom Cl PLSTW E13 ...333 L3
Iveagh Cl HOM E9 ...332 A1
Ive Farm Cl LEY E10 ...314 D4
Ive Farm La LEY E10 ...314 D4
Ives Gdns ROM RM1 ...298 E8
Ives Rd CAN/RD E16 ...333 H5
Ivinghoe Cl EN EN1 ...273 K1
Ivinghoe Rd BCTR RM8 ...317 J7
Ivry St IP IP1 ...16 C1
Ivy Barns La ING CM4 ...238 B9
Ivybridge BROX EN10 ...208 D7
Ivy Chimneys Rd EPP CM16 ...254 F2
Ivyhouse Rd DAGW RM9 ...317 L8
Ivy La K/T/MI CO5 ...204 C1
Ivy Lodge La HARH RM3 ...299 P6
Ivy Lodge Rd RCOLW CO6 ...102 F8
Ivy Rd CAN/RD E16 ...333 K6
SBF/HAD SS7 ...305M9
STHGT/OAK N14 ...272 C6
WALTH E17 ...314 D1
Ivy Ter COS CO15 * ...206 G1
HOD EN11 ...208 F3
Ivy Todd Hl SAFWS CB11 ...65 P9
Ivy Vis MGTR CO11 * ...81 N8
Ivy Wk DAGW RM9 ...317M8
Ixworth Pl HVHL CB9 ...41 H5

J

Jacaranda Cl CHLM/WR CM1 ...218 E5
Jack Andrews Dr COLN CO4 ...128 C3
Jack Clow Rd SRTFD E15 ...333 H2
Jack Cornwell St MNPK E12 ...316 B2
Jackdaw Cl BCAYE CM11 ...283 K8
SBN/FI SS3 ...330 D6
Jack Evans St SOCK/AV RM15 ...338 D6
Jack Hatch Wy RCOLE CO7 ...155 H5
Jacks Cl WICKE SS11 ...285 L5
Jack's La RBSF CM22 ...159 J5
Jackson Cl EMPK RM11 ...299 L8
HOM E9 ...314 A9
KESG IP5 ...27 M4
Jackson Ct KESG IP5 * ...27M4
Jackson Pl CHLM/GWD CM2 ...240 C4
Jackson Rd BARK IG11 ...334 E1
COS CO15 ...6 E6
WDBR IP12 ...33 K9
Jacksons Cl CHONG CM5 * ...255M8
Jacksons Dr CHESW EN7 ...229 K2
Jacksons La BRTR CM7 ...283 J5
SAFWN CB10 ...36 E8
Jacksons Ms SAFWN CB10 ...36 E8
Jackson's Sq SAFWN CB10 ...36 E8
Jack Stevens Cl HLWE CM17 * ...211 K5
Jacobs Av HARH RM3 ...299 K6
Jacobs Cl DAGE RM10 ...318 A6
Jacquard Wy BRTR CM7 ...145 K4
Jacqueline Gdns
BCAYW CM12 ...283 J4
Jacqueline Vis WALTH E17 * ...294 F9
Jade Cl BCTR RM8 ...317 K3
CAN/RD E16 ...333 N6
Jaffe Rd IL IG1 ...316 D3
Jaggard's Rd RCOLW CO6 ...147 P5
James Av BCTR RM8 ...317M3
James Boden Ct FX IP11 * ...35 H6
James Carter Rd COLW CO5 ...151 H5
PLSTW E13 ...333 K2
RCOLE CO7 ...153 K5
James Crt CHLM/GWD CM2 ...240 A8
James Gdns RCOS CO16 ...180 E8
James La LEY E10 ...314 F2
James Lee Sq PEND EN3 ...252 D8
Jameson Pl SUD CO10 ...20 D4
James Rd COS CO15 ...6 A5
James St BARK IG11 ...316 D9
COL CO1 ...9 H4
EN EN1 ...273 L4
RAIN RM13 ...318 C9
Jamestown Wy POP/IOD E14 ...332 G7
James Watt Wy ERITH DA8 ...346 E4
James Yd CHING E4 * ...294 G3
Jamuna Cl POP/IOD E14 ...332 B5
Janebrook Rd CHTY IP2 ...24 F9

Janette Av CVI SS8 ...344 B2
Janmead RBRW/HUT CM13 ...281 L6
WIT CM8 ...197 K1
Janson Cl SRTFD E15 ...315 H7
Janson Rd SRTFD E15 ...315 H7
Janus Cl HVHL CB9 ...41 N5
Japan Rd CHDH RM6 ...317 L1
Jardine Rd PIT SS13 ...305 H7
WAP E1W ...332 A7
Jarmin Rd COL CO1 ...8 C5
Jarndyce CHLM/WR CM1 ...217 N5
Jarrow Rd CHDH RM6 ...317 K1
Jarrow Wy HOM E9 ...314 B6
Jarvis Cleys CHESW EN7 ...229 L5
Jarvis Fld RCHLM CM5 ...220 A6
Jarvis Rd CVI SS8 ...326 D6
SBF/HAD SS7 ...326 B2
Jarvis Wy HARH RM5 ...299 K6
Jasmin Cl BSF CM23 ...157 H8
Jasmine Cl CHTY IP2 ...24 G8
COLO CO4 ...128 E7
CVI SS8 ...344 C3
FX IP11 ...34 E1
IL IG1 ...316 C7
VGE SS16 ...322 G2
Jasmine Rd ROMW/RG RM7 ...315 H4
Jasmine Wy COS CO15 ...206 F5
Jason Cl CDW/CHF RM16 ...340 F6
CVI SS8 ...344 C3
Jasons Cl BRW CM14 ...300 C1
Jasper Cl PEND EN3 ...251 P6
Jasper Rd CAN/RD E16 ...333 N6
Jay Cl BRTR CM77 ...144 G6
HVHL CB9 ...41M4
Jaycroft ENC/FH EN2 ...250 F9
Jays La RCOLW CO6 ...149 L3
The Jays COLN CO4 ...128 C4
Jaywick La RCOS CO16 ...206 F2
Jaywick Rd HVHL CB9 ...41 K3
Jeans La BSF CM23 ...137 K7
Jeavons La KESG IP5 ...27 K4
Jebb St BOW E3 ...332 D2
Jedburgh Rd PLSTW E13 ...333M3
Jefferies Rd WARE SG12 ...184 B3
Jekylls La BSF CM23 ...69 N5
Jellicoe Wy BRTR CM7 ...145M2
Jena Cl SBN/FI SS3 ...330 D7
Jenkins Dr RBSF CM22 ...114 F4
Jenkins La BARK IG11 ...334 D5
BSF CM23 ...157 P9
Jenner Cl BRTR CM7 ...145 J5
Jenner Md CHLM/GWD CM2 ...218 F6
Jenningham Dr
CDW/CHF RM16 ...339 K8
Jennings Pl ING CM4 ...259 K2
Jenningtree Rd ERITH DA8 ...346 G5
Jenningtree Wy BELV DA17 ...336 B9
Jenny Hammond Cl WAN E11 ...314 D5
Jephson Rd FSTGT E7 ...315M9
Jepps Cl CHESW EN7 ...229 K2
Jeremiah St POP/IOD E14 ...332 E6
Jericho Pl ING CM4 ...259 H1
Jermayns LAIN SS15 ...303M9
Jermyns Cl RIPS/CAP IP9 ...83 J8
Jerningham Av CLAY IG5 ...296 C6
Jerounds HLWW/ROY CM19 ...210 C5
Jersey Cl HOD EN11 ...208 D4
Jersey Gdns WICKE SS11 ...285 J8
Jersey Rd CAN/RD E16 ...333M5
IL IG1 ...316 C6
LEY E10 ...314 C3
MAL CM9 ...244 C1
RAIN RM13 ...318 C9
Jersey Wy BRTR CM7 ...144 G4
Jervis Cl BRTR CM7 ...144 G4
Jervis Rd GRAYS RM17 ...349 K4 (?)
Jervis Cl RIPS/CAP IP9 ...83 L4
Jesmond Rd CDW/CHF RM16 ...339 N8
CVI SS8 ...344 E5
Jessel Dr LOU IG10 ...276 D1
Jesse Rd LEY E10 ...314 F3
Jessett Cl ERITH DA8 ...346 C2
Jessica Cl COLN CO4 ...128 C8
Jessop Cl COS CO15 ...182 B5
Jessup Wy GRAYS RM17 ...349 K4
Jewell Wy KESG IP5 ...27 J4
Jewel Rd WALTH E17 ...294 D7
Jimmy's La MGTR CO11 ...82 A7
Joan Gdns BCTR RM8 ...317M4
Joan Rd BCTR RM8 ...317M4
Jocelyns HLWE CM17 ...211 K8
Jodrell Rd HOM E9 ...332 C1
Jodrell Wy WTHK RM20 ...348 C5
Joes Rd SUD CO10 ...61 P4
John Ball Wk COL CO1 ...9 H5
John Bradshaw Rd
STHGT/OAK N14 ...272 C7
John Burns Dr BARK IG11 ...334 F1
Johnby Cl PEND EN3 ...252 B7
John Childs Wy RAYL SS6 ...307 H5
John Eliot Cl WAB EN9 ...231 H1
John English Av BRTR CM7 ...144 G2
John Gooch Dr ENC/FH EN2 ...250 G9
John Harper St COL CO1 * ...8 B3
John Kent Av COLS CO2 ...151 L4
John Raven Ct K/T/MI CO5 ...173 J2
John Ray St BRTR CM7 ...145 K3
Johnson Cl BRTR CM7 ...145 J7
CHTY IP2 ...25 K8
RCFD SS4 ...308 C2
WICKW SS12 ...305 J2
Johnson Rd CHLM/GWD CM2 ...240 G5
RCOLS CO16 ...180 E9
Johnson's Dr RCOLE CO7 ...129 P9
Johnsons Whf GRH DA9 * ...348 D9
Johns Rd BSF CM23 ...137M5

The Johns CHONG CM5 235 M6
Johnston Cl COS CO15 182 F8
HSTD CO9 98 A8
Johnstone Rd EHAM E6 334 A3
SOS SS1 329 P7
Johnston Rd WFD IG8 295 K2
Johnston Wy MAL CM9 244 B2
John St EN EN1 273 L4
GRAYS RM17 349 M4
RCOLE CO7 179 L7
SBN/FI SS3 330 F8
SRTFD E15 333 J1
John Tibauld Ct HVHL CB9 55 L4
John William Cl WTHK RM20 348 G3
Joiner's Ct CBE/LIN CB1 38 A1
Joiner's Rd CBE/LIN CB1 38 A1
Jollyboys La North
GTDUN CM6 143 H8
Jollyboys La South
GTDUN CM6 167 P1
Jones Cl SOSN SS2 328 F3
Jones Rd CHESW EN7 228 G9
PLSTW E13 333 L4
Jonquil Wy COLN CO4 127 L5
Jordans Cl DAGE RM10 318 A6
Jordans Wy RAIN RM13 337 J2
Joseph Gdns WIT CM8 171 M1
Joseph Ray Rd WAN E11 315 H4
Joseph St BOW E3 332 C5
Joshua St POP/IOD E14 332 F6
Josling Cl GRAYS RM17 349 J4
Joslin Rd PUR RM19 347 P3
Joslyn Cl PEND EN3 252 D8
Josselin Cl RCOLW CO6 99 J9
Josselin Ct PIT SS13 305 H5
Josselin Rd PIT SS13 305 H5
The Josselyns FX IP11 34 F3
Jotmans La SBF/HAD SS7 325 M3
Journeymans Wy SOSN SS2 329 H1
Jovian Wy COLN CO4 128 C1
Joyce Ct WAB EN9 252 G4
Joyce Green La DART DA1 347 J6
Joyce's Cha MAL CM9 223 P3
Joydon Dr CHDH RM6 317 J1
Joyners Cl DAGW RM9 317 N6
Joyners Fld HLWS CM18 210 D7
Jubilee Av CHING E4 294 F3
CHLM/WR CM1 218 A1
COS CO15 181 P6
ROMW/RG RM7 298 B9
WARE SG12 184 C2
Jubilee Cl COLW CO3 126 G8
FX IP11 34 E1
HAR CO12 109 P6
HOC/HUL SS5 307 P2
NHMKT IP6 22 D3
ROMW/RG RM7 298 A9
Jubilee Ct GTDUN CM6 141 K5
HSTD CO9 72 D9
WIT CM8 * 171 K1
Jubilee Crs ED N9 273 M7
Jubilee Dr WICKW SS12 285 H8
Jubilee End MGTR CO11 106 B3
Jubilee La RCOLE CO7 129 K4
Jubilee Ri RCHLM CM3 242 C4
Jubilee Rd BCAYE CM11 304 B3
RAYL SS6 307 H5
SUD CO10 20 E3
WTHK RM20 348 E4
Jubilee Vls RIPS/CAP IP9 * 85 K6
Jubilee Wy FOS CO13 158 G8
Jude St CAN/RD E16 333 J6
Judge Rd CHLM/GWD CM2 218 G7
Judith Av CRW RM5 298 A3
Jules Thorn Av EN EN1 273 M2
Julia Gdns BARK IG11 335 L2
Julian Av COLN CO4 128 C1
Julian Cl CHLM/WR CM1 218 A2
HVHL CB9 41 N4
Julien Court Rd BRTR CM7 145 K2
Juliers Cl CVI SS8 344 G2
Juliers Rd CVI SS8 344 G2
Juliette Rd PLSTW E13 333 K2
Juliette Wy PUR RM19 337 L9
Junction Rd BRW CM14 300 F1
ED N9 273 M7
PLSTW E13 333 L1
RCHLM CM3 266 B3
ROM RM1 298 E8
VGE SS16 324 G2
Junction Rd East CHDH RM6 317 M2
Junction Rd West CHDH RM6 317 L2
June Av IP IP1 25 J1
Juniper Cl BCAYE CM11 283 K4
BROX EN10 230 C4
HSTD CO9 97 N8
Juniper Ct CHDH RM6 317 J1
GTDUN CM6 141 J5
RBRW/HUT CM13 * 281 J9
Juniper Crs WIT CM8 171 P9
Juniper Dr CHLM/GWD CM2 240 A4
SOCK/AV RM15 339 H3
Juniper La EHAM E6 333 P5
Juniper Rd COLW CO3 150 F1
IL IG1 316 B6
LOS SS9 328 A2
RCHLM CM3 219 K3
Juniper Wy COLN CO4 128 E7
HARH RM3 299 K5
Jupes Hl RCOLE CO7 105 K3
RCOLW CO6 100 C6
Jupiter Cl HVHL CB9 41 M5
Jupiter Rd IPNE IP4 26 A4
Jupp Rd SRTFD E15 314 G9
Jupp Rd West SRTFD E15 332 G1
Jurgens Rd PUR RM19 * 347 P2
Justinian Cl HVHL CB9 41 N4
Justin Rd CHING E4 294 C3
Jute La PEND EN3 274 B1
Jutland Rd PLSTW E13 333 K4
Jutsums Av ROMW/RG RM7 318 A1
Jutsums La ROMW/RG RM7 318 A1
Juvina Cl WIT CM8 197 J5

K

Kale Cft COLW CO3 150 G1
Kale Rd ERITHM DA18 335 L9
SBF/HAD SS7 326 B2
Kamerwyk Av CVI SS8 344 F1
Kandlewood
RBRW/HUT CM13 281 L6
Kane Ms COL CO1 * 8 B5
Kaplan Dr WCHMH N21 272 E4
Karen Cl BRWN CM15 280 F6
IP IP1 25 J2
RAIN RM13 336 D2
SBF/HAD SS7 326 A6
SLH/COR SS17 341 K4
WICKW SS12 305 H1
Kariba Cl ED N9 273 P9
Karina Cl CHIG IG7 296 F2
Kate's La SAFWN CB10 53 H2
Katherine Cl
BERM/RHTH SE16 332 A8
RAYL SS6 307 K6
Katherine Gdns BARK/HLT IG6 296 D4
Katherine Rd EHAM E6 315 N9
PIT SS13 305 K8
Katherine's Wy
HLWW/ROY CM19 210 B6
Kathleen Cl SLH/COR SS17 341 L1
Kathleen Dr LOS SS9 328 A4
Kathleen Ferrier Crs
LAIN SS15 303 K7
Katonia Av RCHLM CM3 245 N9
Kavanaghs Rd BRW CM14 280 D9
Kavanaghs Ter BRW CM14 280 E9
Kay Cl RCHLM CM3 169 K6
Kays Ter SWFD E18 * 295 J6
Kay St SRTFD E15 314 G9
Keable Rd RCOLW CO6 149 K3
Keating Cl MGTR CO11 106 A4
Keatley Gn CHING E4 294 C3
Keats Av BRTR CM7 145 J6
CAN/RD E16 333 L8
HARH RM3 298 G4
Keats Cl CHIG IG7 296 D3
MAL CM9 244 B2
PEND EN3 274 A4
WAN E11 295 L9
Keats Crs IP IP1 22 G9
Keats Gdns TIL RM18 350 C7
Keats Pde ED N9 273 M8
Keats Rd BELV DA17 346 B1
COLW CO3 127 J9
Keats Wk RBRW/HUT CM13 281 N6
Keats Wy WICKW SS12 285 H9
Keble Cl COLW CO3 127 N9
Kecksy's SBW CM21 162 C9
Kedington Hl SUD CO10 61 L8
Keeble Cl K/T/MI CO5 174 B8
Keeble Ct RCOLE CO7 155 K7
Keeble Pk MAL CM9 244 A2
Keeble Wy BRTR CM7 145 K3
Keegan Pl CVI SS8 * 344 F1
Keelars La RCOLE CO7 153 M4
Keel Cl BARK IG11 335 K2
BERM/RHTH SE16 332 A8
Keelers Wy RCOLW CO6 102 E9
Keelings La BOC CM0 270 B1
Keelings Rd BOC CM0 270 A1
Keene Wy CHLM/GWD CM2 240 A7
Keepers Gn COLN CO4 127 L4
Keeper's La FX IP11 34 D4
RCOLW CO6 77 N2
Keer Av CVI SS8 344 G3
Keighley Ms SBN/FI SS3 330 C4
Keir Hardie Wy BARK IG11 317 H9
Keith Av WICKE SS11 285 J7
Keith Cl COS CO15 182 C5
Keith Rd BARK IG11 334 E2
WALTH E17 294 C5
Keith Wy EMPK RM11 319 K2
SOSN SS2 328 F1
Kelburn Wy RAIN RM13 336 F3
Kelland Rd PLSTW E13 333 K4
Keller Crs MNPK E12 315 N6
Kellington Rd CVI SS8 326 F9
Kelly Rd CHTY IP2 24 F6
PIT SS13 305 K9
Kelly Wy CHDH RM6 297 M9
Kelman Cl CHES/WCR EN8 252 A1
Kelmscott Cl WALTH E17 294 C5
Kelsie Wy BARK/HLT IG6 296 F3
Kelso Cl RAYL SS6 306 F1
RCOLW CO6 127 M1
Kelston Rd BARK/HLT IG6 296 C6
Kelvedon Cl CHLM/WR CM1 217 P5
RAYL SS6 306 D4
RBRW/HUT CM13 281 P5
Kelvedon Dr IPNE IP4 26 E6
Kelvedon Gn BRWN CM15 258 C7
Kelvedon Hall La BRW CM14 257 N6
K/T/MI CO5 173 J8
Kelvedon Rd BCAYE CM11 283 K6
K/T/MI CO5 173 N6
MAL CM9 200 B6
WIT CM8 198 A7
Kelvedon Wy WFD IG8 296 A3
Kelvin Ct FOS CO13 * 183 N2
Kelvin Rd IP IP1 24 G2
SBF/HAD SS7 306 A8
TIL RM18 350 B7
Kelvinside SLH/COR SS17 323 M9
Kemball St IPNE IP4 25 P6
Kembles RAYL SS6 307 H2
Kemey's St HOM E9 314 B7
Kempe Rd BRTR CM7 94 C2
EN EN1 251 N6
Kemps Dr POP/IOD E14 332 D7
Kemps Farm COLW CO3 * 126 A9
Kempson Dr SUD CO10 61 M5
The Kempsters FX IP11 34 G4
Kempton Av HCH RM12 319 L6
Kempton Cl ERITH DA8 346 B4
IP IP1 23 H9
SBF/HAD SS7 306 E7
Kempton Pk RCOS CO16 156 E9
Kempton Rd EHAM E6 334 A1
IP IP1 23 H9
Kemsley Rd FX IP11 35 J6
RCOLW CO6 123 P1
Kendal Av BARK IG11 334 F1
EPP CM16 233 H9
Kendal Cl HOC/HUL SS5 287 H7
RAYL SS6 307 H5
WFD IG8 275 J8
Kendal Ct WICKE SS11 305 M2
Kendal Cft HCH RM12 318 F7
Kendale CDW/CHF RM16 350 C1
Kendall Rd COL CO1 128 B9
Kendall Ter COL CO1 * 128 B9
Kendal Rd WAB EN9 252 F5
Kendal Wy LOS SS9 307 P8
Kendon Cl WAN E11 295 L9
Kenholme LOS SS9 327 P2
Kenilworth Av HARH RM3 299 N2
WALTH E17 294 D6
Kenilworth Cl BCAYW CM12 * 282 F7
Kenilworth Crs EN EN1 251 K9
Kenilworth Gdns
GDMY/SEVK IG3 316 G4
HCH RM12 319 H5
LOU IG10 276 A5
RAYL SS6 306 E4
WOS/PRIT SS0 328 B3
Kenilworth Gv RCOS CO16 157 K4
Kenilworth Pl LAIN SS15 * 303 M6
Kenilworth Rd BOW E3 332 B2
COS CO15 182 F7
Kenley Cl WICKE SS11 305 M1
Kenley Gdns HCH RM12 319 L4
Kenmore Cl CVI SS8 345 H3
Kennard Rd SRTFD E15 314 G9
Kennard St CAN/RD E16 334 A8
Kennedy Av HOD EN11 208 C5
LAIN SS15 302 G9
PEND EN3 273 P5
Kennedy Cl CHES/WCR EN8 230 B7
IPNE IP4 25 P5
PLSTW E13 333 K2
RAYL SS6 307 K7
SBF/HAD SS7 305 N8
Kennedy Rd BARK IG11 334 F1
Kennedy Wy COS CO15 182 B7
Kennel La BCAYW CM12 283 J9
Kennels Rd KIR/NAC IP10 27 K9
Kennet Cl UPMR RM14 320 B1
Kenneth Av IL IG1 316 C6
Kenneth Gdns SLH/COR SS17 323 N9
Kenneth Moor Rd IL IG1 * 316 C5
Kenneth Rd CHDH RM6 317 M2
PIT SS13 305 H8
SBF/HAD SS7 326 C1
Kennet Rd DART DA1 346 F8
Kenning Rd HOD EN11 208 D3
Kennington Av SBF/HAD SS7 325 P1
Kennylands Rd BARK/HLT IG6 297 H4
Kensington Av MNPK E12 315 P8
Kensington Ct GRAYS RM17 * 349 M4
Kensington Dr WFD IG8 295 N6
Kensington Gdns
BCAYW CM12 283 H4
IL IG1 316 A3
Kensington Rd BRWN CM15 280 D5
IP IP1 25 H3
ROMW/RG RM7 318 B1
SOS SS1 329 L7
Kent Av CVI SS8 326 E9
DAGW RM9 335 P4
LOS SS9 328 A4
Kent Cl LAIN SS15 303 J9
RCOLE CO7 179 L6
Kent Crs BSF CM23 162 B1
Kent Dr HCH RM12 319 J6
Kent Elms Cl SOSN SS2 328 A1
Kentford Rd FX IP11 10 C2
Kent Gdns BRTR CM7 145 L2
Kent Green Cl HOC/HUL SS5 308 A2
The Kentings BRTR CM7 145 H4
Kentlea Rd THMD SE28 334 F9
Kentmere COLN CO4 128 F4
Kenton Rd HOM E9 314 A8
Kenton Wy VGE SS16 322 G1
Kent Rd DAGE RM10 318 A7
GRAYS RM17 349 M4
WCHMH N21 273 J7
Kent's Av COS CO15 182 F7
Kents Farm La
CHLM/GWD CM2 262 C5
Kents Grass MAL CM9 225 J1
Kents Hill Rd SBF/HAD SS7 326 A3
Kents Hill Rd North
SBF/HAD SS7 326 A1
Kents La EPP CM16 212 C9
Kent St PLSTW E13 333 L3
Kents Yd SAFWS CB11 50 G6
Kent Vw SOCK/AV RM15 337 P9
Kent View Av LOS SS9 328 B6
Kent View Gdns
GDMY/SEVK IG3 316 F4
Kent View Rd VGE SS16 324 E1
Kent Vls SOS SS1 * 18 E4
Kent Wy RAYL SS6 307 K7
Kentwell Cl IPNE IP4 26 E7
Kenway RAIN RM13 337 H3
ROMW/RG RM7 298 B6
SOSN SS2 329 H4
Kenway Cl RAIN RM13 337 H3
Kenway Wk RAIN RM13 337 J3
Kenwood Gdns CBE/LIN CB1 38 D1
CLAY IG5 296 B8
SWFD E18 295 L7
Kenwood Rd ED N9 273 M8
SLH/COR SS17 342 A1
Kenworth Cl CHES/WCR EN8 252 A3
Kenworthy Rd BRTR CM7 145 H4
HOM E9 314 B7
Kenyon Cl RCOLE CO7 80 A8
Keogh Rd SRTFD E15 315 H8
Keppel Rd DAGW RM9 317 M6
EHAM E6 316 A9
Kerbey St POP/IOD E14 332 E6
Kerby Ri CHLM/GWD CM2 218 E9
Kerridge's Cut MGTR CO11 106 F4
Kerril Cft HLW CM20 12 C4
Kerrison Rd SRTFD E15 332 G1
Kerry Av IP IP1 24 E2
PUR RM19 337 L9
Kerry Cl CAN/RD E16 333 L6
PLMGR N13 272 E8
UPMR RM14 320 C2
Kerry Ct COL CO1 9 J5
Kerry Dr UPMR RM14 320 C2
Kerry Rd CDW/CHF RM16 339 N8
Kersbrooke Wy
SLH/COR SS17 324 A9
Kersey Av SUD CO10 21 K7
Kersey Dr RCOS CO16 181 L8
Kersey Gdns HARH RM3 299 K4
Kersey Rd FX IP11 10 C3
Kershaw Cl CDW/CHF RM16 348 F1
EMPK RM11 319 J2
Kershaw Rd DAGE RM10 317 P5
Kershaws Cl WICKW SS12 305 H2
Kessler Av BRTR CM7 95 J1
Kesteven Cl BARK/HLT IG6 296 G3
Kesteven Rd CHTY IP2 25 H7
Keston Cl UED N18 273 J9
Kestrel Av EHAM E6 333 P5
Kestrel Cl BARK/HLT IG6 297 J1
HCH RM12 318 G9
Kestrel Gdns BSF CM23 137 H8
Kestrel Gv RAYL SS6 306 E4
Kestrel Ms MAL CM9 244 C2
Kestrel Pk RBRW/HUT CM13 * 281 P4
Kestrel Ri HSTD CO9 98 A7
Kestrel Rd CHTY IP2 24 E8
HVHL CB9 41 M4
WAB EN9 253 K4
Kestrel Wy COS CO15 182 A7
Keswick Av COS CO15 182 D7
EMPK RM11 319 J3
HOC/HUL SS5 287 H6
Keswick Cl FX IP11 35 M5
RAYL SS6 307 H5
Keswick Dr PEND EN3 251 P6
Keswick Gdns REDBR IG4 295 P9
Keswick Rd SBF/HAD SS7 306 B9
Ketley Cl K/T/MI CO5 174 B7
Ketleys CHLM/GWD CM2 240 B7
Ketleys Vw BRTR CM7 120 D8
Kettering Rd HARH RM3 299 K4
PEND EN3 252 A7
Kettlebaston Rd LEY E10 314 C3
Kettlebaston Wy IP IP1 25 L2
Kettlebury Wy CHONG CM5 235 L9
Kettle Green Rd MHAD SG10 160 D3
Kevin Cl BCAYE CM11 283 L9
Kew La FOS CO13 183 H1
Keyes Cl SBN/FI SS3 330 D5
Keyes Rd DART DA1 347 M9
Keyes Wy BRTR CM7 145 M2
Keymer Wy COLW CO3 151 H2
Keynes Wy HAR CO12 110 A7
Keynsham Av WFD IG8 295 H1
Key Rd COS CO15 6 D3
Keysers Rd BROX EN10 230 D1
Keysland SBF/HAD SS7 306 E8
Key St IPSE IP3 17 F6
Keytes Wy NHMKT IP6 22 A2
Keyworth Cl CLPT E5 314 B6
Khartoum Rd IL IG1 316 C7
IPNE IP4 25 N4
PLSTW E13 333 L3
Kibcaps VGE SS16 * 323 N2
Kibes La WARE SG12 184 A3
Kibler Rd BRTR CM77 144 C5
Kielder Cl BARK/HLT IG6 296 G3
Kilburn Gdns RCOS CO16 181 N8
Kildare Av IP IP1 24 E1
Kildare Rd CAN/RD E16 333 K5
Kildermorie Cl COLN CO4 128 E4
Kildowan Rd
GDMY/SEVK IG3 317 H3
Killip Cl CAN/RD E16 333 J6
Killowen Rd HOM E9 * 314 A8
Kilmaine Rd HAR CO12 110 A7
Kilmarnock Gdns BCTR RM8 317 K5
Kilmartin Rd GDMY/SEVK IG3 317 H4
Kilmartin Wy HCH RM12 318 G7
Kilmington Cl
RBRW/HUT CM13 281 L8
Kiln Barn Av COS CO15 182 A6
Kiln Dr SUD CO10 21 H7
Kilner St POP/IOD E14 332 D5
Kilnfield BRWN CM15 258 G5
CHONG CM5 235 L8
Kiln Fld FX IP11 34 G6
Kiln House Cl WARE SG12 184 B2
Kiln La HLWE CM17 211 L4
MGTR CO11 106 C4
Kiln Rd EPP CM16 233 P6
SBF/HAD SS7 326 D2
Kiln Wy GRAYS RM17 349 J3
Kilnwood Av HOC/HUL SS5 307 N2
Kiln Wood La CRW RM5 298 C2
Kilowan Cl VGE SS16 322 G2
Kilsmore La CHES/WCR EN8 230 A7
Kiltie Rd K/T/MI CO5 174 B8
Kilvinton Dr ENC/FH EN2 251 J8
Kilworth Av BRWN CM15 281 K5
SOS SS1 19 J4
Kimberley Av EHAM E6 333 P2
GNTH/NBYPK IG2 316 E2
ROMW/RG RM7 318 A1
Kimberley Cl BSF CM23 137 M9
Kimberley Gdns EN EN1 273 L2
Kimberley Rd CAN/RD E16 333 J4
CHING E4 275 H7
COL CO1 128 C9
SBF/HAD SS7 325 P3
SBN/FI SS3 310 D9
WALTH E17 294 B5
WAN E11 314 G4
Kimberley Wy CHING E4 275 H7
Kimberly Dr LAIN SS15 303 N5
Kimpton Av BRWN CM15 280 E6
Kimpton's Cl CHONG CM5 235 L5
Kinburn St
BERM/RHTH SE16 * 332 A9
Kincaid Rd RCOS CO16 180 D9
Kinder Cl THMD SE28 335 K7
Kinfauns Av EMPK RM11 319 H1
Kinfauns Rd GDMY/SEVK IG3 317 J3
Kingaby Gdns RAIN RM13 318 F9
King Alfred Rd HARH RM3 299 L6
King Arthur Ct
CHES/WCR EN8 252 B1
King Charles Rd K/T/MI CO5 202 G6
King Coel Rd COLW CO3 126 G8
King Edward Av BOC CM0 290 G2
RAIN RM13 337 J2
King Edward Dr
CDW/CHF RM16 349 P1
King Edward Quay COLS CO2 152 E1
King Edward Rd BRW CM14 280 F9
CHES/WCR EN8 252 B3
GRH DA9 348 D9
IPSE IP3 26 A8
LAIN SS15 303 J7
LEY E10 314 F3
ROM RM1 318 E1
WALTH E17 294 B7
King Edward's Rd BARK IG11 334 E1
ED N9 273 N6
PEND EN3 274 A3
RCHLM CM3 264 G9
SLH/COR SS17 341 L5
WARE SG12 184 B2
King Edward Ter LAIN SS15 * 303 J8
King Edward VII Dr
RIPS/CAP IP9 85 N9
King Edward Wy WIT CM8 197 H4
Kingfisher Av CHTY IP2 24 E8
Kingfisher Cl COLN CO4 128 G7
HVHL CB9 41 M3
MAL CM9 222 D6
RBRW/HUT CM13 281 K6
SBN/FI SS3 330 D5
THMD SE28 335 K7
WARE SG12 184 F9
Kingfisher Crs RAYL SS6 306 E4
Kingfisher Dr HAR CO12 109 P7
NHMKT IP6 22 A2
SBF/HAD SS7 325 P4
Kingfisher Ga BRTR CM7 145 K1
Kingfisher Mdw HSTD CO9 98 A7
Kingfisher Rd UPMR RM14 320 C3
Kingfishers COS CO15 182 A7
VGE SS16 * 324 B2
Kingfisher St EHAM E6 333 P5
Kingfisher Wy BSF CM23 137 M7
K/T/MI CO5 173 H3
King George Av CAN/RD E16 333 N6
GNTH/NBYPK IG2 316 E1
King George Cl
ROMW/RG RM7 298 B7
King George Rd COLS CO2 152 B2
WAB EN9 * 252 F4
WARE SG12 184 B2
King George's Av HAR CO12 14 C6
King George's Cl RAYL SS6 306 G5
King George's Rd
BRWN CM15 280 E5
King George VI Av TIL RM18 351 J2
King Harold Rd COLW CO3 151 K2
King Henry Ct WAB EN9 * 252 F6
King Henry's Dr RCFD SS4 308 G8
King Henry's Ms PEND EN3 252 D7
King James Av POTB/CUF EN6 228 D8
King John St WCHPL E1 332 A5
Kinglet Cl FSTGT E7 315 K8
Kingley Cl WICKW SS12 284 G9
Kingley Dr WICKW SS12 284 G9
King & Queen Whf
BERM/RHTH SE16 * 332 A8
Kings Acre RCOLW CO6 147 N4
Kings Av CHDH RM6 317 N1
COS CO15 182 D8
IPNE IP4 17 H5
WCHMH N21 272 G7
WFD IG8 295 M2
Kingsbridge Cl BRTR CM7 121 J7
Kingsbridge Rd BARK IG11 334 E2
BSF CM23 137 M6
HARH RM3 299 K3
Kingsbury Cl RCOLW CO6 149 L3
Kingsbury Rd FX IP11 34 F4
Kingsbury Wk SUD CO10 61 M5
King's Cha BRW CM14 280 F9
WIT CM8 197 K3
Kingsclere Pl ENC/FH EN2 273 H1
Kings Cl CVI SS8 343 P2
DART DA1 346 D9
LEY E10 314 E2
MGTR CO11 106 B4
RAYL SS6 307 H5
RCOS CO16 205 P1
SUD CO10 47 M5
Kings Ct BSF CM23 137 M6
K/T/MI CO5 * 173 P7
PLSTW E13 333 L1
Kings Court Off The Maltings
GTDUN CM6 141 L5
Kings Crs LAIN SS15 303 J6
Kings Cft BOC CM0 269 H5
Kingsdon La HLWE CM17 211 K4
Kingsdown Cl PIT SS13 305 H9
Kingsdown Rd WAN E11 315 H5
Kings Farm RAYL SS6 307 H2
WALTH E17 * 294 E5
Kingsfield HOD EN11 208 D3
Kingsfield Av IP IP1 25 L2
Kingsfield Dr PEND EN3 252 A5
Kingsfield Wy PEND EN3 252 A5
Kings Fleet Rd FX IP11 10 E3
Kingsford Dr
CHLM/GWD CM2 218 G8
Kingsford Wy EHAM E6 334 A5

Kings Gdns *IL* IG1 ....316 E5
UPMR RM14 ....320 B2
Kingsgate Dr *IPNE* IP4 ....25 N3
King's Gn *LOU* IG10 ....275 P2
Kings Gv *ROM* RM1 ....298 F9
Kings Hvn *CVI* SS8 * 344 A2
Kingshawes *SBF/HAD* SS7 ....306 E9
Kings Head Cl *COL* CO1 ....8 B5
Kings Head Rd *CHING* E4 ....274 E6
King's Head St *HAR* CO12 ....15 F2
Kings Head Wk
CHLM/GWD CM2 ....5 H5
King's Hl *HHL* CB9 ....42 B2
SUD CO10 ....21 C7
Kingshill Av *CRW* RM5 ....298 B5
Kings Keep *WOS/PRIT* SS0 ....328 D6
Kingsland *HLWS* CM18 ....210 D5
RIPS/CAP IP9 ....85 K7
Kingsland Beach *K/T/MI* CO5 ....202 F7
Kingsland Cl *K/T/MI* CO5 ....202 F7
Kingsland Hts *K/T/MI* CO5 ....203 J3
Kingsland La *RCOLW* CO6 ....77 J4
Kingsland Rd *K/T/MI* CO5 ....202 F7
PLSTW E15 ....333 M3
Kings La *BRTR* CM77 ....145 P2
SUD CO10 ....47 J4
Kingsley Av *CHES/WCR* EN8 ....229 N8
Kingsley Cl *DAGE* RM10 ....318 A6
........23 H9
Kingsley Crs *GPK* RM2 ....319 G1
Kingsley Crs *SBF/HAD* SS7 ....306 E7
Kingsley Gdns *CHING* E4 ....294 D2
EMPK RM11 ....299 J8
Kingsley La *SBF/HAD* SS7 ....306 E7
Kingsley Ms *IL* IG1 ....316 C6
Kingsley Rd *BARK/HLT* IG6 ....296 C5
FSTGT E7 ....315 K9
LOU IG10 ....276 E2
RBRW/HUT CM13 ....281 N6
WALTH E17 ....311 J4
Kingsley Wk *CDW/CHF* RM16 ....350 B2
Kings Lynn Dr *HARH* RM3 ....299 J5
Kingsman Dr *CDW/CHF* RM16 ....339 L7
........181 M8
Kingsman Rd *SLH/COR* SS17 ....341 J4
Kingsmead *SBF/HAD* SS7 ....287 J4
Kingsmead Ct *K/T/MI* CO5 ....173 H2
Kingsmead Rd *COL* CO1 ....8 C3
Kingsmead Pk *BRTR* CM7 * 145 M2
Kingsmead Wy *HOM* E9 ....314 B6
Kingsmere Cl *K/T/MI* CO5 ....202 D6
Kingsmere *K/T/MI* CO5 ....202 D6
Kings Ms *CHIG* IG7 ....276 D8
RCOLE CO7 ....153 K2
Kings Ml *SAFWN* CB10 * 36 C5
Kingsmill Gdns *DAGW* RM9 ....317 N2
Kingsmill Rd *DAGW* RM9 ....317 N2
Kingsmoor Rd
HLWW/ROY CM19 ....210 C6
Kings Oak *ROMW/RG* RM7 ....297 P7
Kings Pde *COS* CO15 ....182 F8
SLH/COR SS17 * 341 K4
Kings Pk *CVI* SS8 * 344 C1
SBF/HAD SS7 ....326 C1
Kingspark Ct *SWFD* E18 ....295 K2
Kings Pas *WAN* E11 * 315 H2
Kings Pl *LOU* IG10 ....275 N6
King's Quay St *HAR* CO12 ....15 G2
King's Rd *BARK* IG11 ....316 D9
BOC CM0 ....269 J6
BOC CM0 ....290 C4
BRTR CM7 ....121 H9
BRW CM14 ....280 F9
CHES/WCR EN8 ....252 B4
CHING E4 ....274 C7
CHLM/WR CM1 ....217 N7
COS CO15 ....207 J3
CVI SS8 ....343 P2
EHAM E6 ....333 M1
HAR CO12 ....110 C5
HSTD CO9 ....97 P7
LAIN SS15 ....303 H6
MAL CM9 ....198 E5
RAYL SS6 ....306 F6
ROM RM1 ....298 F9
SBF/HAD SS7 ....326 B4
WAN E11 ....315 H2
WOS/PRIT SS0 ....328 C5
Kingsteignton *SBN/FI* SS3 ....330 D8
Kings Ter *SLH/COR* SS17 ....324 A5
Kingston Av *CHLM/GWD* CM2 ....218 D8
SBN/FI SS3 ....330 D4
Kingston Cha *MAL* CM9 ....222 A5
Kingston Ct *CHDH* RM6 ....297 M7
Kingston Crs *CHLM/GWD* CM2 ....218 D8
Kingston Hl *VGE* SS16 ....323 L4
Kingston Pde *GRAYS* RM17 * 349 L2
Kingston Rd *ED* N9 ....273 M8
ILG IL1 ....316 D6
IP IP1 ....24 C3
ROM RM1 ....298 E8
Kingston Wy *SBF/HAD* SS7 ....326 C1
King St *BCTR* CM25 ....137 L7
CHONG CM5 ....236 E7
FX IP11 ....35 H6
IP IP1 ....16 D4
MAL CM9 ....244 B1
MGTR CO11 ....107 H8
PLSTW E13 ....333 K4
SLH/COR SS17 ....341 K4

SUD CO10 ....20 D5
Kings Wk *MAL* CM9 ....225 K2
Kings Wy *BCAYE* CM11 ....303 L1
IPSE IP5 ....28 A9
RCHLM CM5 ....264 F8
Kingsway *HAR* CO12 ....14 E6
HOC/HUL SS5 ....286 G7
K/T/MI CO5 ....175 P7
PEND EN5 ....25 N4
POTB/CUF EN6 ....228 D9
WARE SG12 ....184 A1
WOS/PRIT SS0 ....328 B4
Kingswell Ms *WOS/PRIT* SS0 ....328 B4
Kingswell Ride
POTB/CUF EN6 ....228 D9
Kingswood Cha *LOS* SS9 ....327 N5
Kingswood Cl *BCAYE* CM11 ....283 K5
EN EN1 ....273 L3
Kingswood Ct *BOC* CM0 ....226 D8
Kingswood Crs *RAIN* RM13 ....306 E6
Kingswood Rd *COLN* CO4 ....128 A5
GDMY/SEVK IG3 ....317 N3
VGE SS16 ....3 H7
WAN E11 * 315 H2
Kings Yd *SRTFD* E15 * 314 D8
Kingwell Av *COS* CO15 ....181 P9
King William Ct *WAB* EN9 * 252 F5
Kinlett Cl *COLN* CO4 ....128 C3
Kinloch Cha *WIT* CM8 ....197 J5
Kinnaird Wy *WFD* IG8 ....296 E1
Kino Rd *WTHK* RM20 ....159 L6
Kinross Rd *IPNE* IP4 ....26 A2
Kinross Ter *WALTH* E17 ....294 C6
Kipling Av *TIL* RM18 ....350 C6
Kipling Cl *CHLM/WR* CM1 ....217 D6
Kipling Ms *SOSN* SS2 ....329 H4
Kipling Rd *IP* IP1 ....24 D9
Kipling Ter *ED* N9 * 273 J9
Kipling Wy *BRTR* CM7 ....145 K6
Kirby Cl *BARK/HLT* IG6 ....296 D3
HARH RM3 ....299 M2
IPNE IP4 ....25 P4
LOU IG10 ....275 P6
Kirby St *IPNE* IP4 ....25 N4
Kirkbaye *FOS* CO15 ....158 F8
Kirkdale Rd *WAN* E11 ....315 H5
Kirkham Av *SLH/COR* SS17 ....322 C7
Kirkham Cl *IPIV* CO2 ....25 H9
Kirkham Rd *EHAM* E6 ....333 P6
Kirkham Shaw *SLH/COR* SS17 ....322 G6
Kirkhurst Cl *RCOLE* CO7 ....179 M7
Kirkland Av *CLAY* IG5 ....296 B6
Kirkland Dr *ENC/FH* EN2 ....251 H9
Kirklees Rd *BCTR* RM8 ....317 K7
Kirkmans Rd *CHLM/GWD* CM2 ....240 C7
Kirkmichael Rd *POP/IOD* E14 ....332 H6
Kirk Pl *CHLM/GWD* CM2 ....218 E8
Kirk Rd *WALTH* E17 ....314 C1
Kirkton Cl *RIPS/CAP* IP9 ....85 M8
Kirton Cl *HCH* RM12 ....319 H8
Kirton Rd *KIR/NAC* IP10 ....35 J3
KIR/NAC IP10 ....35 M8
PLSTW E13 ....333 M2
Kitcat Ter *BOW* E3 ....332 D3
Kitchener Rd *FSTGT* E7 ....315 L8
IP IP1 ....24 C3
RCHLM CM5 ....266 B8
WALTH E17 ....294 E5
Kitchener Wy *RIPS/CAP* IP9 ....85 M9
Kitchen Fld *BRTR* CM77 ....145 N3
Kitchen Hl *SUD* CO10 ....60 E4
Kitkatts Rd *CVI* SS8 ....344 D2
Kitson Wy *HLW* CM20 ....13 G5
Kittiwake Cl *CHTY* IP2 ....35 P4
Kittiwake Dr *MAL* CM9 ....222 D6
Kiwi Ter *EHAM* E6 * 318 B1
Knapp Rd *BOW* E3 ....332 D4
Knapton Cl *CHLM/WR* CM1 ....218 C4
The Knares *VGE* SS16 ....323 M2
Knebworth Av *WALTH* E17 ....294 D5
Knightbridge Wk
BCAYW CM12 ....283 H5
Knight Cl *BCTR* RM8 ....317 K4
Knighthood Point
POP/IOD E14 * 332 D9
Knighton Cl *ROMW/RG* RM7 ....318 C1
WFD IG8 ....295 L1
Knighton Dr *WFD* IG8 ....295 L1
Knighton La *BKHH* IG9 ....275 L8
Knighton Rd *FSTGT* E7 ....315 K5
ROMW/RG RM7 ....318 B1
Knights *LAIN* SS15 ....303 L8
Knight St *RCHLM* CM5 ....287 H1
SBW CM21 ....187 M2
Knights Wk *ABR/ST* RM4 ....277 J2
Knights Wy *BARK/HLT* IG6 ....296 D3
GTDUN CM6 ....141 L8
Knightswick Rd *CVI* SS8 ....344 E1
Knightswood Ct *BOC* CM0 ....268 C4
Knightswood Rd *RAIN* RM13 ....336 J2
Knivet Cl *RAYL* SS6 ....307 H6
Knobs Hill Rd *SRTFD* E15 ....332 H4
Knole La *SAFWS* CB11 ....63 K2
Knollcroft *SBN/FI* SS3 ....330 C9

The Knoll *BCAYW* CM12 ....283 J4
RAYL SS6 ....306 G5
Knottisford St *BETH* E2 ....332 A3
Knotts Green Ms *LEY* E10 ....314 E1
Knotts Green Rd *LEY* E10 ....314 F1
Knowles Cl *HSTD* CO9 ....208 D6
The Knowle *HOD* EN11 ....208 D6
VGE SS16 ....324 B2
Knox Cl *MAL* CM9 ....244 B2
Knox Ct *WICKW* SS12 ....306 G1
Knox Gdns *COS* CO15 ....181 P9
Knox Rd *COS* CO15 ....181 P9
FSTGT E7 ....315 K8
Knutsford Cl *RIPW* IP8 ....29 L1
Kohima Rd *COS* CO2 ....151 L5
Kolburg Rd *CVI* SS8 ....344 C5
Kolburg Rd *CVI* SS8 ....344 C5
Kollum Rd *CVI* SS8 ....345 J2
Koln Cl *CVI* SS8 ....343 P2
Komberg Crs *CVI* SS8 ....326 F9
Konnybrook *SBF/HAD* SS7 ....326 D2
Korndyk Av *CVI* SS8 ....344 F1
Kreswell Gv *HAR* CO12 ....110 C6
Kursaal Wy *SOS* SS1 ....19 K5
Kylemore Cl *EHAM* E6 ....333 N2
Kyme Rd *ROM* RM1 ....318 E1
Kynance Cl *HARH* RM3 ....299 M2
Kynaston Pl *WIT* CM8 ....197 L2
Kynaston Rd *BRTR* CM7 ....120 C7
ENC/FH EN2 ....251 J9
Kynoch Rd *SLH/COR* SS17 ....341 M4
Kynoch Rd *UED* N18 ....294 A1

L

Laars Av *CVI* SS8 ....344 F1
Laburnham Cl *UPMR* RM14 ....320 D2
Laburnham Gdns
UPMR RM14 ....320 C2
Laburnum Av *ED* N9 ....273 K8
HCH RM12 ....318 F4
WICKW SS12 ....305 H1
Laburnum Cl *CHES/WCR* EN8 ....252 A1
CHING E4 ....294 C3
COS CO15 ....207 H1
HOC/HUL SS5 ....307 L1
IPSE IP5 ....29 N8
RCOLE CO7 ....155 K6
RIPW IP8 ....24 D9
WICKW SS12 ....285 H9
Laburnum Crs *FOS* CO15 ....158 E8
Laburnum Dr
CHLM/GWD CM2 ....240 A2
Laburnum Gdns *KESG* IP5 ....26 D2
Laburnum Gv *COLN* CO4 ....128 F7
CVI SS8 ....344 A2
HOC/HUL SS5 ....307 L2
SOCK/AV RM15 ....338 C4
WCHMH N21 ....273 H8
Laburnum Rd *EPP* CM16 ....233 K8
HOD EN11 ....196 D9
Laburnum Wy *HCH* RM12 ....319 H7
Laburnum Wy *RAYL* SS6 ....306 E1
CHLM CM5 ....198 E9
RCOLW CO6 ....77 H7
WIT CM8 ....171 P9
Labworth Rd *CVI* SS8 ....344 F3
Lacewing Cl *PLSTW* E13 ....333 K3
RIPS/CAP IP9 ....85 P3
Lacey Cl *ED* N9 ....273 M8
Lacey Dr *BCTR* RM8 ....317 K5
Lacey St *IPNE* IP4 ....17 H3
Lackmore Rd *EN* EN1 ....251 P5
Lacon Rd *RIPW* IP8 ....24 B1
Ladbroke Rd *EN* EN1 ....273 L5
Ladbrook Dr *COLS* CO2 ....152 C5
Ladbrooke Rd *RCOS* CO16 ....181 N7
Ladell Cl *COLN* CO4 ....151 H5
Ladram Cl *SOS* SS1 ....330 B6
Ladram Rd *SOS* SS1 ....330 A6
Ladyfields *LOU* IG10 ....276 C3
Lady La *CHLM/GWD* CM2 ....7 H7
IP IP1 ....16 C4
Ladysmith Wy *LAIN* SS15 ....303 N6
Ladywell La *CHLM/GWD* CM2 ....240 C5
Ladywell Prospect *SBW* CM21 ....187 H1
Ladywell Rd *IPNE* IP4 ....26 B4
Lagado Ms *BERM/RHTH* SE16 ....332 H2
Lagonda Av *BARK/HLT* IG6 ....296 G1
Lagonda Drive *IP* IP1 ....24 D1
Lagonda Wy *DART* DA1 ....347 N9
Laidlaw Dr *WCHMH* N21 ....272 E4
Laindon Common Rd
BCAYW CM12 ....302 G2
Laindon Link *LAIN* SS15 ....2 A7
Laindon Rd *BCAYW* CM12 ....283 H8
Laindon West *LAIN* SS15 ....302 F9
Laing Cl *CHIG* IG7 ....296 E3
Laing Rd *COLN* CO4 ....128 F9
Laird Av *CDW/CHF* RM16 ....339 N9
Lake Av *BCAYW* CM12 ....283 H5
COS CO15 ....181 P9
Lake Cl *BCTR* RM8 ....317 L5
Lake Dr *SBF/HAD* SS7 ....326 B1
Lakefields *CL* RAIN RM13 ....337 J3
Lake Gdns *DAGE* RM10 ....317 P7
Lake House Rd *WAN* E11 ....315 K5
Lakeland Cl *CHIG* IG7 ....277 J1
Lakenheath *STHGT/OAK* N14 ....272 F1
Lake Ri *ROM* RM1 ....298 E7
WTHK RM20 ....348 D2
Lake Rd *CHDH* RM6 ....297 L8
DAGW RM9 ....336 A3

LEY E10 ....314 E2
WAB EN9 ....209 H9
Lakeside *BCAYW* CM12 ....283 H4
ENC/FH EN2 ....272 C5
RAIN RM13 ....337 J5
RAYL SS6 ....306 D5
Lakeside Av *REDBR* IG4 ....295 N8
THMD SE28 ....335 H8
Lakeside Cl *CHIG* IG7 ....296 G1
Lakeside Crs *BRW* CM14 ....280 G9
CHIG IG7 ....296 G1
Lakeside Rd *CHES/WCR* EN8 ....229 P7
CHTY IP2 ....24 F7
Lakeside Wk *COLW* CO3 ....150 E2
Lakes Meadow *RCOLW* CO6 ....147 P5
Lakeview *CVI* SS8 ....326 D9
Lake Vw *VGE* SS16 ....322 G2
Lake View Est *BOW* E3 ....332 A2
Lake Wk *KESG* IP5 ....26 B1
Lake Wy *COS* CO15 ....207 H1
Lakforth *SUD* CO10 ....46 C3
Lakin Cl *CHLM/GWD* CM2 ....218 F8
Lamarsh Hl *BURES* CO8 ....75 L2
BURES CO8 ....75 P8
Lamarsh Rd *BURES* CO8 ....75 K6
Lambeth Cl *IP* IP1 ....24 D3
Lambeth Ms *WALTH* E17 ....294 F6
Lambeth Rd *LOS* SS9 ....307 P9
SBF/HAD SS7 ....305 P9
Lambkins Ms *WALTH* E17 ....294 F6
Lamb La *HSTD* CO9 ....96 C1
Lambley Rd *DAGW* RM9 ....317 J8
Lambourn Cl *SBN/FI* SS3 ....330 C4
Lambourne Cl *CHIG* IG7 ....277 J9
COLW CO3 ....150 C2
COS CO15 ....181 N8
Lambourne Crs *BSDN* SS14 ....324 E1
CHIG IG7 ....277 J9
Lambourne Dr
RBRW/HUT CM13 ....281 P5
CHING E4 ....274 D8
EN EN1 ....273 L1
HCH RM12 ....319 J4
Lambourne Gv *MAL* CM9 ....244 A2
Lambourne Hall Rd *RCFD* SS4 ....289 N7
Lambourne Rd *BARK* IG11 ....316 F9
CHIG IG7 ....296 G1
GDMY/SEVK IG3 ....316 F4
IP IP1 ....23 J8
WAN E11 ....315 H2
Lambourni Cl *SBN/FI* SS3 ....330 D4
Lambs Cl *ED* N9 ....273 M8
POTB/CUF EN6 ....228 E8
Lambs Gdns *WARE* SG12 ....160 C9
Lamb's La North *RAIN* RM13 ....337 J4
Lamb's La South *RAIN* RM13 ....337 H5
Lambs Meadow *WFD* IG8 ....295 N6
Lambs Ms *BCAYW* CM12 ....283 J2
Lambs Wk *ENC/FH* EN2 ....273 H1
Lambton Av *CHES/WCR* EN8 ....229 N8
Lamerton Rd *BARK/HLT* IG6 ....296 C5
Lammas Dr *BARK* IG11 ....316 F9
Lammas Pk *CHING* E4 ....294 C1
Lammasmead *BROX* EN10 ....230 C2
Lammas Rd *HOM* E9 ....314 A9
LEY E10 ....314 A9
Lammas Wy *RCOLE* CO7 ....153 K3
Lamont Cl *WICKW* SS12 ....305 K2
Lamorna Cl *WALTH* E17 ....294 F6
Lamplighters Cl *WAB* EN9 ....253 K4
Lamson Rd *RAIN* RM13 ....336 E5
Lanark Rd *IPNE* IP4 ....26 A2
Lancaster Av *BARK* IG11 ....316 F9
WAN E11 ....295 L8
Lancaster Crs *COS* SS1 ....19 H4
Lancaster Dr *HCH* RM12 ....318 C7
KESG IP5 ....27 N5
LOU IG10 ....275 N9
POP/IOD E14 ....332 F8
VGE SS16 ....322 C1
Lancaster Gdns *RAYL* SS6 ....307 K7
SOS SS1 ....19 J3
Lancaster Gdns East *COS* CO15 ....7 J2
Lancaster Gdns West *COS* CO15 ....7 J3
Lancaster Rd *ENC/FH* EN2 ....251 M9
EPP CM16 ....233 P5
FSTGT E7 ....315 L8
IPNE IP4 ....17 H4
RAYL SS6 ....307 K6
SUD CO10 ....46 C9
WALTH E17 ....294 A6
WAN E11 ....315 G4
WTHK RM20 ....348 D2
Landau Wy *BROX* EN10 ....230 C2
ERITH DA8 ....347 J3
Land Cl *RCOS* CO16 ....181 M8
Landermere *BSDN* SS14 ....3 F2
Landermere Rd *RCOS* CO16 ....157 K5

Landermere Vw *RCOS* CO16 * 157 K4
Lander Rd *GRAYS* RM17 ....349 N3
Landguard Rd *FX* IP11 ....111 M2
Landisdale *RCHLM* CM5 ....242 D3
Land La *COL* CO1 ....8 E5
Landmann Rd *CHES/WCR* EN8 ....230 B8
Landons Cl *POP/IOD* E14 ....332 F9
Landra Gdns *WCHMH* N21 ....272 G5
Landridge Dr *EN* EN1 ....251 N8
Landsburg Rd *CVI* SS8 ....326 G9
Landscape Rd *WFD* IG8 ....295 J8
Landscape Vw *SAFWS* CB11 ....65 L3
Landsdown Rd *SUD* CO10 ....21 G2
Landseer Av *MNPK* E12 ....316 B7
Landseer Cl *EMPK* RM11 ....318 G3
IPSE IP5 ....30 G1
Landseer Rd *COLW* CO3 ....151 L1
EN EN1 ....273 M4
IPSE IP5 ....25 M9
Landview Gdns *CHONG* CM5 ....235 L9
Landwick La *BOC* CM0 ....270 C2
Lane End *BXLYHN* DA7 ....346 A8
HLWE CM17 ....211 M4
Lanercost Gdns
STHGT/OAK N14 ....272 D5
Lanercost Wy *CHTY* IP2 ....30 A1
Lane Rd *RCOLW* CO6 ....124 G1
Laneside Av *BCTR* RM8 ....317 N2
The Lane *K/T/MI* CO5 ....202 D5
MGTR CO11 ....106 E4
Lanfranc Rd *BOW* E3 ....332 B2
Langdale Dr *BRTR* CM7 ....144 F7
Langdale Gdns *HCH* RM8 ....317 K3
FX IP11 ....35 H5
Langdale Dr *COLN* CO4 ....128 C3
Langdale Gdns *CHLM/GWD* CM2 ....5 J7
HCH RM12 ....318 F5
PEND EN5 ....252 A5
Langdon Crs *EHAM* E6 ....334 D2
Langdon Rd *EHAM* E6 ....334 B1
RAYL SS6 ....306 D4
Langdon Wy *SLH/COR* SS17 ....324 A9
Langenhoe Wy *BCAYE* CM11 ....283 J6
Langenhoe *WICKW* SS12 ....305 K1
Langenhoe Hall La
K/T/MI CO5 ....177 J6
Langenhoe Pk *K/T/MI* CO5 ....177 J3
Langer Rd *FX* IP11 ....111 F6
Langfield Cl *WAB* EN9 ....231 H1
Langford Br *CHONG* CM5 ....257 N2
Langford Crs *SBF/HAD* SS7 ....306 D8
FX IP11 ....35 J4
Langford Gv
RBRW/HUT CM13 ....281 M5
Langford Gv *PIT* SS13 ....305 H7
Langford Rd *MAL* CM9 ....221 P5
WFD IG8 ....295 M3
WIT CM8 ....197 M9
Langfords *BKHH* IG9 ....275 N8
Langham Ct *EMPK* RM11 ....319 J2
Langham Crs *BCAYW* CM12 ....283 J9
Langham Dr *GDMY/SEVK* IG3 ....317 J1
RAYL SS6 ....306 D4
Langham Gdns *WCHMH* N21 ....272 F4
Langham La *COLN* CO4 ....103 K9
Langham Pl *COLN* CO4 ....128 C4
Langham Rd *COLN* CO4 ....103 K8
WFD IG8 ....295 L3
Langham Wy *HVHL* CB9 ....40 E2
Langhorne Rd *DAGE* RM10 ....317 P9
Langland Cl *SLH/COR* SS17 ....341 N1
Langley Av *BRTR* CM7 ....95 J1
........10 E1
Langley Cl *FX* IP11 ....35 H6
HAR CO12 ....110 D5
HARH RM5 ....299 J4
LOS SS9 ....307 L8
SOS SS1 ....19 K3
Langley Crs *CHESW* EN7 ....229 H7
Langley Dr *BRW* CM14 ....280 D9
WAN E11 ....315 L2
Langley Gdns *DAGW* RM9 ....317 L9
Langley Gn *WAB* EN9 * 230 D1
Langley Hl *BURES* CO8 ....75 K8
Langleys *VGE* SS16 ....324 A2
Langport Dr *WOS/PRIT* SS0 ....328 B2
Langside *LAIN* SS15 ....303 J7
Langside Crs *STHGT/OAK* N14 ....272 C9
Langston Rd *LOU* IG10 ....276 E5
Langstons *FX* IP11 ....54 C5
Langthorne Crs *GRAYS* RM17 ....349 M2
Langthorne Rd *WAN* E11 ....314 G5
Langton Av *CHLM/WR* CM1 ....217 M6
Langton Rd *HOD* EN11 ....208 C5
Langton Wy *CDW/CHF* RM16 ....350 D2
Languidic Cl *SUD* CO10 ....61 M4
Langwood *K/T/MI* CO5 ....202 F5
Lanham Farm Rd *BRTR* CM77 ....146 B6
Lanham Green Rd
BRTR CM7 ....146 B7
Lanhams *PIT* SS13 ....304 G7
Lanhams Ct *PIT* SS13 ....304 G1
Lanrick Rd *POP/IOD* E14 ....332 G6
Lansbury Av *BARK* IG11 ....317 H9
CHDH RM6 ....317 H9
Lansbury Gdns *POP/IOD* E14 * 332 G6
Lansbury Rd *PEND* EN5 ....252 A9
Lansdown Av *SBF/HAD* SS7 ....307 J9
Lansdowne Av *LOS* SS9 ....328 B5
Lansdowne Cl *K/T/MI* CO5 ....179 J7
Lansdowne Dr *RAYL* SS6 ....306 F4
Lansdowne Rd *CHING* E4 ....274 D8
........35 L5
GDMY/SEVK IG3 ....316 G3
IPNE IP4 ....25 K4
SWFD E18 ....295 K7
WALTH E17 ....314 D1
WAN E11 ....315 J4
Lansdown Rd *FSTGT* E7 ....315 M9
TIL RM18 ....350 C1
Lantern Ter *SOS* SS1 * 19 K6
Lanthorn Cl *BROX* EN10 ....208 B7

Lanvalley Rd COLW CO3 ....127 H9
La Plata Gv BRW CM14 ....280 E9
Lappmark Rd CVI SS8 ....544 C2
Lapwater Ct LOS SS9 ....327 M4
Lapwing Cl ERITH DA8 * 346 G5
Lapwing Dr K/T/MI SS5 ....173 H3
MAL CM9 ....222 D6
Lapwing Ter FSTGT E7 ....315 N7
Larch Cl CHESW EN7 ....229 K6
COLN CO4 ....128 E7
LAIN SS15 ....303 K6
Larchcroft Cl IP IP1 ....25 J1
Larchcroft Rd IP IP1 ....25 J1
Larches Av EN EN1 ....251 P5
The Larches PLMGR N13 ....273 H9
RCHLM CM5 ....219 K3
SBF/HAD SS7 ....305 N7
Larch Gv CHLM/GWD CM2 ....240 B4
RCOLW CO6 ....77 N8
WIT CM8 ....171 P8
Larch Rd LEY E10 ....314 D4
Larch Wk MAL CM9 ....222 C5
Larch Wy GTDUN CM6 ....141 P8
Larchwood BSF CM23 ....137 J9
Larchwood Av ERH EN1 ....298 A3
Larchwood Cl CHTY IP2 ....24 D6
CRW RM5 ....298 B5
LOS SS9 ....307 L9
Larchwood Gdns
BRWN CM15 ....280 D5
Largent Gv KESG IP5 ....27 K3
Lark Cl BRW CM14 ....300 E1
Larke Ri WOS/PRIT SS0 ....328 E2
Larkfield SLH/COR SS17 ....324 A9
Larkfield Cl RCFD SS4 ....308 E3
Larkfield Rd RCOLE CO7 ....155 J5
Larkhill Av RCFD SS4 ....289 H6
Larkhill Ri IPNE IP4 ....26 B6
Lark Hill Rd RCFD SS4 ....288 C7
Larkhill Wy FX IP11 * 34 C6
Larkin Cl RBRW/HUT CM13 ....281 M6
Lark Ri SUD CO10 ....60 C5
Larks Ct HVHL CB9 ....41 N4
Larksfield WARE SG12 ....184 B1
Larksfield Gn HAR CO12 ....14 A6
Larksfield Gv EN EN1 ....251 N9
Larksfield Rd RIPS/CAP IP9 ....83 H6
Larkshall Crs CHING E4 ....294 F1
Larkshall Rd CHING E4 ....294 D1
Lark's La RCHLM CM5 ....193 N7
Larkspur Cl BSF CM23 ....137 J8
SOCK/AV RM15 ....338 F3
WIT CM8 ....171 N8
Larkspur Rd CHTY IP2 ....24 G9
Larks Ri HSTD CO9 ....98 B7
Larksway BSF CM23 ....137 H8
FX IP11 ....10 D4
Larkswood HLWE CM17 ....211 K5
Larkswood Cl ERITH DA8 ....346 F6
Larkswood Rd CHING E4 ....294 D1
SLH/COR SS17 ....342 A1
Larkway FOS CO13 ....158 F7
Larmans Rd PEND EN3 ....251 P6
Larner Rd ERITH DA8 ....346 B5
The Larneys FOS CO13 ....158 F7
Larsen Dr WAB EN9 ....252 C4
Larup Av CVI SS8 ....326 F9
La Salle Cl CHTY IP2 ....25 J8
Lascelles Cl BRWN CM15 ....280 E4
WAN E11 ....314 D1
Lascelles Gdns RCFD SS4 ....308 D2
Latchett Rd SWFD E18 ....295 L5
Latchetts Shaw VGE SS16 ....324 A2
Latchford Pl CHIG IG7 ....297 J1
Latchingdon Cl RAYL SS6 ....306 D4
Latchingdon Gdns WFD IG8 ....295 P3
Latchingdon Rd RCHLM CM5 ....266 A4
Latchmore Bank RBSF CM22 ....162 E4
Latham Cl EHAM E6 ....333 P6
Lathcoates Crs
CHLM/GWD CM2 ....240 D2
Lathkill Ct EN EN1 ....273 M6
Lathom Rd EHAM E6 ....316 A9
Latimer Av EHAM E6 ....334 A1
Latimer Dr HCH RM12 ....319 J5
LAIN SS15 ....303 L6
Latimer Pl FSTGT E7 ....315 N7
Lattice Av IPNE IP4 ....26 B5
Lattinford Br RIPS/CAP IP9 * 81 H2
Latton Gn HLWS CM18 ....210 G7
Latton Hall Cl HLWW CM20 ....211 H2
Latton House HLWS CM18 ....211 H1
Latton St HLWW CM20 ....211 J3
Latymer Rd ED N9 ....273 L8
Latymer Wy ED N9 ....273 J8
Laud's Cl FX IP11 ....34 E3
Launceston Cl COLS CO2 ....152 C5
Launder's La BARK/HLT IG6 ....299 H5
HARH RM3 ....299 M5
Laundry Gdns SUD CO10 * 20 B7
Laundry La BRWN CM15 ....259 N9
WAB EN9 ....231 J4
Laura Ct EN EN1 ....273 K4
Laura Gdns FSTGT E7 * 315 N6
WAN E11 ....295 M9
Laurel Av HAR CO12 ....110 A6
KESG IP5 ....26 F4
WICKW SS12 ....285 H9
Laurel Bank Rd ENC/FH EN2 ....251 H9
Laurel Ct BARK/HLT IG6 ....296 C3
COS CO15 ....182 C6
HVHL CB9 ....40 G2
LOS SS9 ....327 N6
RBRW/HUT CM13 ....281 J8
Laurel Crs ROMW/RG RM7 ....318 D3
Laureldene MHAD SG10 ....160 E4
Laurel Dr GTDUN CM6 ....141 J3
NHMKT IP6 ....22 D4
SOCK/AV RM15 ....338 G4
SUD CO10 ....46 F4
WCHMH N21 ....272 F7
Laurel Gdns CHING E4 ....274 E6
Laurel Gv CHLM/GWD CM2 ....239 P2

Laurelhayes CHTY IP2 ....25 H8
The Laurels BRTR CM7 * 145 K3
CHESW EN7 ....229 K6
RAYL SS6 ....307 J7
RCHLM CM5 ....264 Q9
Laurel Wy NHMKT IP6 ....22 D4
SWFD E18 ....295 J8
Laurence Av WAB E4 ....197 K4
Laurence Ct RCOLE CO7 ....129 N9
Laurence Cft CHLM/WR CM1 ....239 J1
Lauriston Rd HOM E9 ....314 A9
Lavender Av BSF CM23 ....137 J8
Lavender Cl BSF CM23 ....229 L6
CHESW EN7 ....299 J4
HARH RM3 ....299 M2
HLW CM20 ....210 F2
K/T/MI SS5 ....173 P9
SOCK/AV RM15 ....339 H5
WIT CM8 ....171 M9
Lavender Ct DAGE RM10 * 218 E6
Lavender Dr BOC CM0 ....269 H6
Lavender Fld HVHL CB9 ....40 G3
Lavender Gdns ENC/FH EN2 ....250 G8
Lavender Gv WOS/PRIT SS0 ....328 E3
Lavender Hl CHTY IP2 ....24 G7
ENC/FH EN2 ....251 H9
Lavender Ms WOS/PRIT SS0 ....328 E2
Lavender Pl IL IG1 ....316 C7
Lavender Rd
BERM/RHTH SE16 ....332 B8
ENC/FH EN2 ....251 J9
Lavender St SRTFD E15 ....315 H8
Lavender Wk COS CO15 ....206 F5
Lavender Wy COLN CO4 ....127 M5
WICKW SS12 ....285 H9
Lavenham Ct RCOS CO16 ....181 L9
Lavenham Rd CHTY IP2 ....24 F6
SUD CO10 ....47 K2
The Lavers RAYL SS6 ....307 H4
Lavington Ct HOM E9 ....314 C8
Lawford Cl HCH RM12 ....319 H6
Lawford La CHLM/WR CM1 ....217 L8
Lawless St POP/IOD E14 * 332 E7
Lawley Rd STHGT/OAK N14 ....272 H6
Lawling Av MAL CM9 ....222 D6
Lawlinge Rd RCHLM CM5 ....267 J4
Lawn Av WA SOSN SS2 ....329 J4
Lawn Cha CHSM CM8 ....197 J3
Lawn Cl EN EN1 ....273 L6
Lawn Farm Gv CHRH RM6 ....297 M6
Lawn House Cl POP/IOD E14 ....332 F9
Lawns Cl K/T/MI SS5 ....202 F5
Lawnscourt SBF/HAD SS7 ....305 N8
Lawns Crs GRAYS RM17 ....349 N4
The Lawns Dr BROX EN10 ....230 C1
Lawns Pl GRAYS RM17 * 349 N4
The Lawns BRW CM14 ....301 H2
CHING E4 ....294 D2
CHLM/WR CM1 ....218 C6
IPNE IP4 ....26 B3
SBF/HAD SS7 ....305 P8
Lawns Wy CRW RM5 ....298 B4
Lawn Wy FX IP11 ....35 H6
Lawrance Gdns
CHES/WR EN8 ....230 A7
SBW CM21 ....162 B9
WALTH E17 ....294 A5
WARE SG12 ....184 F9
Lawrence Av MNPK E12 ....316 B6
Lawrence Crs DAGE RM10 ....318 A5
Lawrence Gdns TIL RM18 ....350 C5
Lawrence Hl CHING E4 ....274 D8
Lawrence Moorings
SBW CM21 ....187 N3
Lawrence Rd ERITH DA8 ....346 A5
GPK RM2 ....319 L8
PIT SS15 ....305 L7
PLSTW E13 ....333 L1
Lawrence St CAN/RD E16 ....333 J5
Laws Cl SAFWS CB11 ....65 L2
Law's Drift KIR/NAC IP10 ....33 J6
Lawshall's Hl RCOLW CO6 ....99 L7
Lawson Cl CAN/RD E16 ....333 M6
IL IG1 ....316 E7
Lawson Rd DART DA1 ....347 J9
PEND EN3 ....251 M5
Lawton Rd BOW E3 ....332 B5
LEY E10 ....314 F5
LOU IG10 ....276 C2
Laxton Gv FOS CO13 ....158 B9
Laxton Rd RCOLE CO7 ....154 A6
The Laxtons RCFD SS4 ....308 E2
Layard Av EN EN1 ....251 L9
Layer Breton Hl COLS CO2 ....175 K4
Layer Rd COLS CO2 ....175 J8
COS CO15 ....41 H4
K/T/MI CO5 ....175 N9
K/T/MI SS5 ....176 F1
Layzell Cft SUD CO10 ....61 M6
Leabank Sq HOM E9 ....314 A4
Lea Bridge Rd CLPT E5 ....294 F9
Leach Cl CHLM/GWD CM2 ....240 C3
Lea Cl BRTR CM7 ....145 N5
BSF CM23 ....137 N5
Leacroft Cl WCHMH N21 ....272 G8
Leadale Av CHING E4 ....273 M9
Leaden Cl GTDUN CM6 ....190 F4
Leader Av MNPK E12 ....316 B7
Leaforis Rd CHESW EN7 ....229 M7
Leafy Wy RBRW/HUT CM13 ....281 N7
Lea Gv BSF CM23 ....137 N5
MAL CM9 ....221 J2
Lea Hall Gdns LEY E10 * 314 D3
Lea Hall Rd LEY E10 ....314 D3
Lea La WR CM8 * 198 A3
Leam Cl COLN CO4 ....128 G8
Leamington Av WALTH E17 ....294 D9
Leamington Gdns
GDMY/SEVK IG3 ....316 G4
Leamington Rd HARH RM3 ....299 M2
HOC/HUL SS5 ....288 A9
SOS SS1 ....19 K4

Lea Mt CHESW EN7 ....229 K7
Leamouth Rd EHAM E6 ....333 P6
POP/IOD E14 ....332 G6
Leapingwell Cl
CHLM/GWD CM2 ....218 F8
Lea Rd CDW/CHF RM16 ....350 B5
ENC/FH EN2 ....251 J9
HOD EN11 ....208 F5
SBF/HAD SS7 ....325 P1
WAB EN9 ....252 D4
Learoyd Gdns EHAM E6 ....334 B7
Leas Cl WOS/PRIT SS0 ....328 C6
Leas Gdns WOS/PRIT SS0 ....328 C6
Lea Side K/T/MI CO5 ....220 C6
Leas La COLS CO2 ....150 F8
Leasowes Rd LEY E10 ....314 D5
Leas Rd COLS CO2 ....151 M5
.......6 B6
The Leas BOC CM0 ....291 H2
FOS CO13 ....159 J8
ING CM4 ....260 B7
UPMR RM14 ....320 A2
WOS/PRIT SS0 ....328 C7
The Leasway WOS/PRIT SS0 ....328 C6
Leasway VGE SS16 ....280 G9
CDW/CHF RM16 ....350 A3
RAYL SS6 ....306 F5
WICKW SS12 ....319 P5
WICKW SS12 ....304 C1
Leaview WAB EN9 ....252 E3
Lea Wy RBRW/HUT CM13 ....281 N1
Le Cateau Barracks
COLS CO2 * 128 A9
Le Cateau Rd COLS CO2 ....127 P9
Lechmere Ap WFD IG8 ....295 P5
Leckford Gdns CHIG IG7 ....296 D2
Leda Av PEND EN3 ....252 A9
Lede Rd CVI SS8 ....344 E1
Leech's La COLN CO4 ....128 G3
Lee Chapel La VGE SS16 ....323 L3
Leech's La COLN CO4 ....127 N3
Lee Cl WALTH E17 ....294 A5
WARE SG12 ....184 F9
Leaview WAB EN9 ....252 E3
Lee Conservancy Rd HOM E9 ....314 C7
Leecon Wy RCFD SS4 ....308 E8
Leeds Rd IL IG1 ....316 E5
Leefe Wy POTB/CUF EN6 ....228 C7
Leeford Cl WALTH E17 ....294 A5
Lee Gdns Av EMPK RM11 ....319 M3
Lee Gv CHIG IG7 ....276 C8
Lee Lotts SBN/FI SS3 ....305 J8
Lee Park Wy ED N18 ....294 A2
Lee Rd EN EN1 ....273 M5
HAR CO12 ....110 D5
IPSE IP5 ....25 N8
PIT SS15 ....305 L9
Lee Vw ENC/FH EN2 ....250 C9
Lee Vis SOSN SS2 ....19 J6
Lee Wk VGE SS16 ....2 A7
Leeward Cl FX IP11 * 35 K6
Leeward Rd RCHLM CM5 ....287 H3
The Leeway RCHLM CM5 ....242 C5
Lee Woottens La VGE SS16 ....2 A7
Leez La RCHLM CM5 ....168 A4
Lefevre Wy BOW E3 ....332 C1
Left Side STHGT/OAK N14 * 272 C7
Leggatt Dr RIPW IP8 ....24 B1
Leggatt Rd SRTFD E15 ....332 F2
Legg St CHLM/WR CM1 ....5 J2
Legions Wy BSF CM23 ....137 M6
Legion Ter BOW E3 ....332 D1
Legon Av ROMW/RG RM7 ....318 D5
Leicester Av HOD EN11 ....208 A6
Leicester Av RCFD SS4 ....308 C7
Leicester Cl CHTY IP2 ....29 P1
COL CO1 ....8 E4
COS CO15 ....206 E5
Leicester St WIT CM8 * 171 L2
Leicester Gdns
GDMY/SEVK IG3 ....316 G4
Leicester Rd TIL RM18 ....350 A6
WAN E11 ....295 L9
Leige Av CVI SS8 ....344 B1
Leighams Rd RCHLM CM5 ....264 B4
Leigh Av REDBR IG4 ....295 N8
Leigh Beck La CVI SS8 ....345 K4
Leigh Beck Rd CVI SS8 ....345 J2
Leigh Cliff Rd LOS SS9 ....328 A6
Leighcroft Gdns LOS SS9 ....327 P2
Leigh Dr HARH RM3 ....299 J1
RBSF CM22 ....114 F6
WIT CM8 ....197 N7
Leigh Fells PIT SS15 ....305 N9
Leighfields Av LOS SS9 ....327 M5
Leighfields Rd LOS SS9 ....307 M9
Leigh Gdns LOS SS9 ....327 J5
Leigh Hall Rd LOS SS9 ....327 J5
Leigh Hts SBF/HAD SS7 ....327 J7
Leigh Hill Cl LOS SS9 ....327 P6
Leigh Hunt Dr
STHGT/OAK N14 ....272 C8
Leighlands Rd RCHLM CM5 ....286 C1
Leigh Park Cl LOS SS9 ....327 M5
Leigh Park Rd LOS SS9 ....327 N6
Leigh Rd CVI SS8 ....344 E5
Leigh Rd EHAM E6 ....316 B8
Leigh Rd LEY E10 * 314 D1
LOS SS9 ....328 A5
Leighs Rd RCHLM CM5 ....194 D6

Leighton Av LOS SS9 ....328 A4
MNPK E12 ....316 B7
Leighton Gdns TIL RM18 ....350 B5
Leighton Rd EN EN1 ....273 L4
IPSE IP5 ....30 C2
SBF/HAD SS7 ....305 P8
Leighton Sq IPSE IP5 ....30 C2
Leigh View Dr LOS SS9 ....328 A2
Leighville Gv LOS SS9 ....327 N5
Leighwood Av LAIN SS15 ....303 K8
Leinster Rd LAIN SS15 ....41 H4
Leithrin Av SBN/FI SS3 ....330 B8
Lekoe Rd CVI SS8 ....326 C8
Lely Rd IPSE IP5 ....30 F2
Lemmon Rd GNTH/NBYPK IG2 ....296 F9
The Ley BRTR CM7 ....145 N5
Leyspring Rd WAN E11 ....315 J5
Leys Rd RCOLE CO7 ....153 K3
Leys Rd East PEND EN3 ....252 B9
The Leys CHLM/GWD CM2 ....218 E6
LOS SS9 ....324 B2
Leyswood Dr GNTH/NBYPK IG2 ....296 F9
The Ley BRTR CM7 ....145 N5
Leyton Ct COS CO15 ....182 A5
Leyton Gra LEY E10 ....314 C4
Leyton Green Rd LEY E10 ....314 F1
Leyton Park Rd LEY E10 ....314 F4
Leyton Rd SRTFD E15 ....314 F4
SRTFD E15 ....315 H8
Leytonstone Rd SRTFD E15 ....315 H8
LEYW SS15 ....333 H2
Leywood Cl BRTR CM7 ....145 M4
Libra Rd BOW E3 ....332 C1
PLSTW E13 ....333 J1
Lichfield Cl CHLM/GWD CM2 * 217 M7
COL CO1 ....317 J6
Lichfield Rd BCTR RM8 ....317 J6
BOW E3 ....332 B5
ED N9 ....273 M8
EHAM E6 ....333 N5
WFD IG8 ....295 H1
The Lichfields BSDN SS14 ....304 E8
Lichfield Ter UPMR RM14 ....320 B4
Lichfield Wy BROX EN10 ....230 C1
Liddington Rd SRTFD E15 ....333 J1
Liddon Rd PLSTW E13 ....333 L3
Liden Cl WALTH E17 ....314 C2
Lidgate Ct FX IP11 ....10 E2
Le Field Ct BRTR CM7 * 145 K3
Lieutenant Ellis Wy
CHESW EN7 ....251 L1
Lifchild Cl WIT CM8 ....197 K5
Lifstan Wy SOS SS1 ....329 M7
Lightermans Ms WCHPL E1 ....332 A6
Lighterman's Rd
POP/IOD E14 ....332 D9
Lightswood Cl CHESW EN7 ....229 J6
Lilac Av CVI SS8 ....326 F9
EN EN1 ....251 P6
RCOS CO16 ....206 A6
WALTH E17 ....285 H9
Lilac Cl BRWN CM15 ....280 E4
CHESW EN7 ....231 N1
CHING E4 ....240 C3
CHLM/GWD CM2 ....240 C3
Lilac Ct RCOLE CO7 ....153 H4
Lilac Gdns ROMW/RG RM7 ....318 D5
Lilac Pl SBF/HAD SS7 ....325 P1
The Lilacs SOSN SS2 * 329 H4
Lilford Rd BCAYE CM11 ....283 K4
Lilian Gdns RBRW/HUT CM13 ....295 C3
Lilian Gdns WFD IG8 ....295 L5
Lilian Impey Dr COLN CO4 ....128 C2
Lilian Pl RAYL SS6 ....307 K7
Lilian Rd BOC CM0 ....291 H3
Lillechurch Rd BCTR RM8 ....317 J8
Lilley Cl BRW CM14 ....300 C1
Lilley's La RCOLE CO7 ....130 E5
Lilliard Ct HOD EN11 ....208 E2
The Lillies BRTR CM7 ....121 L6
Lilliput Rd ROMW/RG RM7 ....318 C2
Lilyville Wk RAYL SS6 ....307 K6
Lily Cl CHLM/WR CM1 ....218 E5
Lily Rd LEY E10 ....314 D1
Limbourne Av BCTR RM8 ....317 N2
Limbourne Dr MAL CM9 ....222 D6
Limburg Rd CVI SS8 ....344 A1
Lime Av COLN CO4 ....128 E7
HAR CO12 ....14 E7
LOS SS9 ....327 M4
RBRW/HUT CM15 ....281 M9
UPMR RM14 ....319 M6
Limebrook Wy MAL CM9 ....245 J5
Lime Ct BKHH IG9 ....275 N8
IPSE IP5 ....207 H1
ROMW/RG RM7 ....298 B9
SOCK/AV RM15 ....338 F3
WARE SG12 ....184 C1
WIT CM8 ....171 P6
Limecroft Cl IP IP1 ....23 H9
Limefields SAFWN CB10 ....51 L6
Lime Gv BARK/HLT IG6 ....296 C3
BRWN CM15 ....258 F8
SUD CO10 ....60 F5
Limehouse POP/IOD E14 * 332 D7
Limehouse Cswy
POP/IOD E14 ....332 C7
Limehouse Link
POP/IOD E14 ....332 B7
Limehouse Link (Tunnel)
POP/IOD E14 ....332 C7
Limekiln Cl NHMKT IP6 ....22 D4
Limekiln La STSD SC24 ....113 P9
Lime Pl LAIN SS15 ....305 K6
Limerick Cl IP IP1 ....23 J1
Limerick Gdns UPMR RM14 ....320 C2
Lime Rd SBF/HAD SS7 ....326 C2
Limes Av CHIG IG7 ....296 D2
RIPW IP8 ....24 D1
Limes Ct HOD EN11 * 208 D5
Limes Crs BSF CM23 ....137 M7
Limeslade Cl HOD EN11 * 323 P9
Limes Rd CHES/WCR EN8 ....252 A2
The Limes CHLM/GWD CM2 ....240 A8
COS CO15 ....7 H4
HSTD CO9 ....97 H9
ING CM4 ....260 D5
KESG IP5 ....26 C2
PUR RM19 ....347 M3
RBRW/HUT CM13 ....281 J9
RCOLE CO7 ....104 C9
SUD CO10 ....46 F4
Limestone Wk ABYW SE2 ....332 D9
Lime St IL IG1 ....179 L8
WALTH E17 ....294 B8
Limetree Av SBF/HAD SS7 ....325 N2
Limetree Rd CVI SS8 ....344 C1
Lime Tree Wk ENC/FH EN2 ....251 H6

Lime Wk CHLM/GWD CM2 ....240 B4
SRTFD E15 * 333 H1
Lime Wy BOC CM0 ....290 F2
Limewood Cl WALTH E17 ....294 C8
Limewood Rd ERITH DA8 ....346 B5
Lincefield VGE SS16 ....325 J3
Lincoln Av COS CO15 ....206 C6
ROMW/RG RM7 ....318 D3
STHGT/OAK N14 ....272 B9
Lincoln Cha SOSN SS2 ....529 M3
Lincoln Cl BSF CM23 ....137 J9
EMPK RM11 ....299 M9
ERITH DA8 .... J9
IP IP1 ....23 J9
Lincoln Crs EN EN3 ....273 K3
Lincoln La BOW E3 ....332 D4
Lincoln Gdns IL IG1 ....315 P2
NHMKT IP6 ....22 D3
Lincoln La RCOLW CO6 ....102 F7
Lincoln Rd BSDN SS14 ....304 E8
EN EN1 ....273 K5
ERITH DA8 ....346 E7
FSTGT E7 .... J5
PLSTW E13 ....333 L4
RCFD SS4 ....308 C1
SWFD E18 ....295 J5
Lincoln Rd EPP CM16 ....232 C8
Lincolns La BRW CM14 ....279 P5
Lincoln St WAN E11 ....315 H4
Lincoln Ter FX IP11 ....11 G4
Lincoln Wy COL CO1 ....9 F5
CVI SS8 ....344 B1
EN EN1 ....273 N4
RAYL SS6 ....306 F2
Linda Gdns BCAYW CM12 ....282 F4
Lindal Crs STHGT/OAK N14 ....272 D4
Lindbergh Rd IPSE IP5 ....31 J1
Linden Av EN EN1 ....251M9
CHLM/GWD CM2 ....240 B3
COLN CO6 ....128 F6
MGTR CO11 ....106 A5
PUR RM19 ....347 D4
RAYL SS6 ....307 J6
SBF/HAD SS7 ....305 P9
STHGT/OAK N14 ....272 B5
Linden Crs WFD IG8 ....295 L3
Linden Dr COS CO15 ....181 P7
Linden Gdns EN EN1 ....251M9
Linden Lees SBF/HAD SS7 ....305 P9
Linden Ri BRW CM14 ....300 G2
Linden Rd SBF/HAD SS7 ....305 P9
The Lindens BRTR CM7 ....145 K6
BSF CM23 ....137 L8
COLW CO3 * 127 L8
ING CM4 ....261 N7
LOU IG10 ....276 A4
VGE SS16 .... J3
WAB EN9 * 293 J8
WALTH E17 ....253M5
Linden St ROMW/RG RM7 ....298 C8
Linden Wy CVI SS8 ....344 E1
STHGT/OAK N14 ....272 B5
Linde Rd CVI SS8 ....344 E1
Lindfield Rd HARH RM3 ....299 K2
Lindfield St POP/IOD E14 ....332 D6
Lindhull Cl PEND EN5 ....274 A1
Lindhurst Dr BCAYE CM11 ....284 B4
Lindisfarne Av LOS SS9 ....328 B4
Lindisfarne Cl CHTY IP2 ....30 A1
Lindisfarne Rd WICKW SS12 ....305M2
Lindisfarne Rd RBW EN9 ....314 B6
Lindisfarne Rd BCTR RM8 ....317 K5
Lindley Rd LEY E10 ....314 F4
Lindon Rd WICKW SS12 ....285 H5
Lindsell Gn BSDN SS14 ....324 D1
Lindsell La BSDN SS14 ....324 D1
GTDLN CM6 ....118 A4
Lindsey Av SUD CO10 ....21 J7
Lindsey Cl BRW CM14 ....500 D1
BSF CM23 ....137 L5
Lindsey Rd BCTR RM8 ....317 K5
BSF CM23 ....137 L5
IPNE IP4 ....26 B4
SBN/FI SS3 ....330 C2
Lindsey St EPP CM16 ....232 F7
Lindum Cl LBTR CM7 ....147 N2
Linford Cl HLWW/ROY CM19 ....210 D5
Linford Cres SS14 ....324 D1
Linford End
  HLWW/ROY CM19 ....210 D5
Linford Ms MAL CM9 ....243 P2
Linford Rd CDW/CHF RM16 ....350 D5
  WALTH E17 ....294 F7
Lingcroft VGE SS16 ....323 P8
Lingfield Av UPMR RM14 ....319 L5
Lingfield Cl EN EN1 ....273 K5
Lingfield Dr RCFD SS4 ....309 H4
Lingfield Gdns ED N9 ....273 N6
Lingfield Rd IP IP11 ....35 J5
Lingmere Cl CHIG IG7 ....276 D8
Ling Rd CAN/RD E16 ....333 K5
  ERITH DA8 ....346 B4
Lingside KESC IP5 ....27 L5
Ling's La RIPS/CAP IP9 ....84 B6
Lingwood Rd RCHLM CM5 ....242 B3
Link Cl COLN CO4 ....127 P5
Linkdale BCAYW CM12 ....283 C8
Link La RIPS/CAP IP9 ....81 N5
Link Rd BSF CM23 ....137 L6
  COS CO15 ....6 C6
  CVI SS8 ....544 B1
  DAGW RM9 ....536 A2
  HSTD CO9 ....97 N8
  RAYL SS6 ....306 G4
  RCOLE CO7 ....179M7
  RCOS CO16 ....181 P5
  RIPS/CAP IP9 ....28 C9
  RM19 * 85 M8
  SOCK/AV RM15 ....341 L2
Links Av FX IP11 ....35 K5
  GPK RM2 ....298 D6
Links Dr CHLM/GWD CM2 ....239 N3

Linksfield KESC IP5 ....26 D4
Linksfield Gdns KESC IP5 ....26 D4
Linkside ENC/FH IG7 ....296 D1
Linkside Cl ENC/FH EN2 ....272 E2
Linkside Gdns ENC/FH EN2 ....272 E2
Links Rd BCTR RM8 ....137 P8
  RCOS CO16 ....206 A8
  WFD IG8 ....295 K2
Links Side ENC/FH EN2 ....272 E2
The Links BCAYW CM12 ....282 F4
  CRWS/WCR EN8 ....230 A5
  WALTH E17 ....294 B8
Linksway COS SS9 ....327 M2
Links Wy SBF/HAD SS7 ....327 J3
The Link PEND EN3 ....252 B9
  RIPS/CAP IP9 ....81 N3
Linkway BCTR RM8 ....317 K6
  BSDN SS14 ....5 F4
Link Wy BSF CM23 ....137 K8
  EMPK RM11 ....319 K3
Linkway Rd BRW CM14 ....280 C9
Linley Cl RIPS/CAP IP9 ....81 N5
Linley Crs ROMW/RG RM7 ....351 L5
Linley Gdns COS CO15 ....6 B6
Linnet Cl ED N9 ....274 A7
  SBN/FI SS3 ....330 D5
  THMD SE28 ....335 K7
Linnet Dr CHLM/GWD CM2 ....240 A4
  SBF/HAD SS7 ....325 P4
Linnets COS CO15 ....182 A7
  VGE SS16 ....323 P5
Linnett Cl CHING E4 ....294 F1
Linnetts La HVHL CB9 ....42 B7
Linnet Wy PUR RM19 ....347 N3
  RCOLE CO7 ....155 J6
Linroping Av CVI SS8 ....345 J2
Linsdell Rd BARK IG11 ....334 D1
Linstead Cl RCOS CO16 ....181 K9
Linton Cl SAFWS CB11 ....65 N1
Linton Ct ROM RM1 ....298 D6
Linton Gdns EHAM E6 ....333 P6
Linton Rd BARK IG11 ....316 D9
  CBE/LIN CB1 ....38 A3
  SBN/FI SS3 ....330 D8
The Lintons CHLM/GWD CM2 ....241 J4
Linwood Av CHLM/GWD CM2 ....187M2
Linwood Crs EN EN1 ....251M9
Linwood Rd WARE SG12 ....184 C1
Lionel Hurst Cl SUD CO10 ....61 M5
Lionel Rd CVI SS8 ....344 D2
Lionfield Ter CHLM/WR CM1 ....5 K1
Lion Hl SLH/COR SS17 ....342 C1
Lion La BCAYW CM12 ....283 A6
Lion Meadow HVHL CB9 ....55 L5
Lion Rd ED N9 ....273M8
  EHAM E6 ....334 A4
Lion St IP IP1 ....16 D4
Lion Vik COL CO1 * 9 C6
Liphook Cl HCH RM12 ....318 E6
Lippitts HI VGE SS16 ....323 K3
Lippitts HI LOU IG10 ....275 H1
Lisa Cl BCAYW CM12 ....283 J2
Lisbon Cl WALTH E17 ....294 C6
Lisle Pl GRAYS RM17 ....349 K1
Lisle Rd COLS CO2 ....152 B1
Lister Av HARH RM5 ....299 J6
Lister Rd BRTR CM7 ....145 J6
  IP IP1 ....24 G2
  TIL RM18 ....350 B7
  WAN E11 ....315 H6
Lister Tye CHLM/GWD CM2 ....240 B3
Listonhall Cha HSTD CO9 ....96 E3
Liston La SUD CO10 ....46 E4
Liston Wy WFD IG8 ....295M4
Listowel Rd DAGW RM9 ....295 L4
Litchborough Pk RCHLM CM3 ......242 C2
Litchfield Av RM SRTFD E15 * 315 H8
Litchfield Cl COS CO15 ....181 P9
Littell Tweed
  CHLM/GWD CM2 ....218 F8
Little Acres WARE SG12 ....138 A4
Little Aston Rd HARH RM3 ....299 L4
Little Baddow Rd MAL CM9 ....220 F8
Little Bakers WOTN CO6 ....242 B3
Little Belhus Cl
  SOCK/AV RM15 ....338 D4
Little Bentley BSDN SS14 ....3 G3
Little Bentley Rd RCOLE CO7 ....131 N6
Little Berry La VGE SS16 ....323 H2
Little Braxted La WIT CM8 ....197M1
Little Brays HLWS CM18 ....211 H5
Little Bromley Rd RCOLE CO7 ......105 H9
  RCOLE CO7 * 131 K6
Littlebrook Gdns
  CHES/WCR EN8 ....230 A9
Little Brook Rd
  HLWW/ROY CM19 ....209M3
Littlebury Ct BRWN CM15 ....258 C7
Littlebury Gdns COLS CO2 ....152 D2
Littlebury Gn PIT SS13 ....304 F7
Littlebury Green Rd
  SAFWS CB11 ....50 D7
Little Bury St ED N9 ....273 K6
Little Cattins
  HLWW/ROY CM19 ....210 A7
Little Chariton PIT SS13 ....305 H9
Little Chittock BSDN SS14 ....304 D9
Little Clacton Rd COS CO15 ....182 F5
  RCOS CO16 ....181 L6
Littlecotes COLN CO4 ....127 N5
Littlecroft RCHLM CM5 ....286 C2
Little Croft St CHTY IP2 ....25 K8
Little Dorrit CHLM/WR CM1 ....217M4
Little Dragons LOU IG10 ....275 N3
Littlefield Rd COLS CO2 ....151M5
Little Flds RCHLM CM5 ....242 D3
Little Fretches LOS SS9 ....327 P2
Little Friday Rd CHING E4 ....275 H8
Little Garth PIT SS13 ....324 F1

Little Gaynes Gdns
  UPMR RM14 ....319 N6
  DAGW RM9 ....335 J1
  GPK RM2 ....298 F9
Little Gaynes La UPMR RM14 ......319M6
Little Gearies BARK/HLT IG6 ....296 C8
Little Gerpins Rd UPMR RM14 .....357 L1
Little Gipping St IP IP1 ....16 C4
Little & Great Sir Hughes La
  CHLM/GWD CM2 ....240 F8
Little Gregories La EPP CM16 ....254 E5
Little Gw RIPS/CAP IP9 ....81 K1
Little Grove CHESW EN7 ....229 K6
Little Grove Fld
  HLWW/ROY CM19 ....13 F7
Little Gulls RIPS/CAP IP9 ....28 B9
Little Gypps Cl CVI SS8 ....344 C1
Little Gypps Rd CVI SS8 ....344 C2
Little Harrods WOTN CO4 ....159 H7
Little Hayes Rd RCHLM CM5 ....265M8
Little Hays LOS SS9 ....307 L9
Little Heath CHDH RM6 ....297 J8
  RBSF CM22 ....188 E1
Little Horkesley Rd
  RCOLW CO6 ....101M4
Littlehurst La LAIN SS15 ....303 N5
Little Hyde Ch HSTD CO9 ....57 P8
Little Hyde La ING CM4 ....260 D5
Little Hyde Rd HSTD CO9 ....57 P8
Little Ilford La MNPK E12 ....316 A6
Little Kingston VGE SS16 ....323 L4
Little Larchmount
  SAFWS CB11 ....65 L1
Little Laver Rd CHONG CM5 ....213 L8
  HLWE CM17 ....213 K1
Little London HI BRW CM14 ....69 N9
Little London La MAL CM9 ....220 F6
Little Lullaway LAIN SS15 ....2 A3
Little Meadow
  CHLM/WR CM1 ....239 H1
Little Mdw MAL CM9 ....243 H4
Littlemoor Rd ILI IG1 ....316 E5
Littlemore Rd ABYW SE2 ....335 H9
Little Nell CHLM/WR CM1 ....217 M4
Little Norsey Rd
  BCAYW CM12 ....284 K4
Little Oaks BSDN SS14 ....2 K1
Little Oxcroft LAIN SS15 ....323 J1
Little Paddocks BRTR CM7 * 146 E4
Little Park Gdns ENC/FH EN2 ....273 J2
Little Piper's Cl CHESW EN7 ....228 C8
Little Pluckett's Wy BKHH IG9 ......275 N7
Little Pynchons HLWS CM18 ....210 G6
Little Russets
  RBRW/HUT CM13 ....281 P6
Little St Mary's SUD CO10 ....46 F5
Little's Crs CHTY IP2 ....25 K7
Little Searles PIT SS13 ....304 G8
Little Spenders BSDN SS14 ....3 K1
Little Stambridge Hall Rd
  RCFD SS4 ....309 J5
Little Stile CHLM/WR CM1 ....239 H2
Little Stock Rd CHESW EN7 ....229 K4
Little Stone Ct COS CO15 ....207 H4
Little St WAB EN9 ....252 F6
Little Tey Rd K/T/MI CO5 ....148 E7
Little Thorpe SOS SS1 ....329 P5
Littlethorpe VGE SS16 ....324 E2
Littleton Av CHING E4 ....275 J7
Little Totham Rd MAL CM9 ....223 K2
Little Tufts RIPS/CAP IP9 ....28 D9
Little Wakering La
  SBN/FI SS3 ....330 F1
Little Walden Rd SAFWN CB10 ......51 D8
Little Waltham Rd
  CHLM/WR CM1 ....218 C2
Little Warley Hall La
  RBRW/HUT CM13 ....301 H6
Little Wheatley Cha RAYL SS6 ......306 D4
Little Whip St CHTY IP2 ....16 E7
Little Widbury WARE SG12 ....184 C3
Little Widbury La WARE SG12 ......184 C3
Little Wd FOS CO13 ....158 F8
Little Yeldham Rd HSTD CO9 ....58 A8
Liverpool Rd CAN/RD E16 ....333 H5
  LEY E10 ....314 F1
Livingstone Rd SRTFD E15 ....332 F1
  WALTH E17 ....314 E1
Llewellyn Cl CHLM/GWD CM2 ......218 C7
Llewellyn Dri KESC IP5 ....26 C4
Lloyd Rd PEND EN5 ....252 D6
Lloyd Rd DAGW RM9 ....317 N8
  EHAM E6 ....334 A1
  RIPS/CAP IP9 ....85 M9
  WALTH E17 ....294 A8
Lloyds Av IP IP1 ....294 E1
The Lloyds KESC IP5 ....27 H4
Lloyd-taylor Cl STDN SG11 ....136 A4
Lloyd Wise Cl SOSN SS2 ....329 L3
Loamy Hill Rd WIT CM8 ....198 G3
Lobelia Cl CHLM/WR CM1 ....218 E5
Locarno Av WICKE SS11 ....305 K7
Locarno Rd IPSE IP5 ....26 A8
Lochmere Ct ERITH DA8 ....346 A4
Lochnagar St POP/IOD E14 ....332 F5
Lockcheld Av PEND EN3 ....274 B1
Lockgate Cl HOM E9 ....314 C7
Lockhart Av COLW CO3 ....127M4
Lockhart Cl EN EN3 ....273 J8
Lockhurst St CLPT E5 ....314 A6
Lockram La WIT CM8 ....198 D5
Lock Rd HSTD CO9 ....97 P8
Locks Hl RCFD SS4 ....308 C4
Lock's La RCOLW CO6 ....77 H1
Locksley Cl SOSN SS2 ....329 N4
Locksley Est POP/IOD E14 ....332 D6
Locksley St POP/IOD E14 ....332 C5
Lockwood Pl CHING E4 ....294 D5
Lockwood Wy WALTH E17 ....294 A6
Lockyer Rd PUR RM19 ....347 P5
Locton Gn BOW E3 * 332 C1

Lodge Av CHLM/GWD CM2 ....240 E3
  DAGW RM9 ....335 J1
  GPK RM2 ....298 F9
Little Calcot CVI SS8 ....277 H9
  COS CO15 ....277 H9
  RAYL SS6 ....307 H6
  RBRW/HUT CM13 ....326 D1
  SBF/HAD SS7 ....326 D1
Lodge Cl RCOLW CO6 ....127 J3
Lodge Crs CHES/WCR EN8 ....252 A4
  CRW RM5 ....219 K5
Lodge Farm La EPP CM16 .... E5
Lodge Farm Dr FX IP11 ....55 M6
Lodge Farm La RCOS CO16 ....180 G9
Lodge Hall HLWS CM18 ....210 F7
Lodge La REDBR IG4 ....295 P8
Lodgelands Cl RAYL SS6 ....348 H6
Lodge La CDW/CHF RM16 ....339 K9
  COLN CO4 ....103 N8
  CRW RM5 ....297 P6
  K/T/MI CO5 ....176 E5
  K/T/MI CO5 ....177 K4
  NHMKT IP6 ....22 B4
  RCHLM CM5 ....243 L8
  RCOLE CO7 ....129 K1
  RCOS CO16 ....132 C9
  WAB EN9 ....293 J6
Lodge Vls WFD IG8 ....295 J4
Lodore St POP/IOD E14 ....332 F6
Lodwick SBN/FI SS3 ....330 B9
Loewen Rd CDW/CHF RM16 ....350 B1
Loftin Wy CHLM/GWD CM2 ....240 C5
Logan Cl PEND EN5 ....252 A9
Logan La WICKW SS12 ....305 L2
Logan Ms ROM RM1 ....298 D9
Logan Rd ED N9 ....273 N8
Loman Pth SOCK/AV RM15 ....338 C6
Lombard Av GDMY/SEVK IG5 ....316 F5
  PEND EN5 ....251 N6
Lombards Cha
  RBRW/HUT CM13 ....321 N1
The Lombards EMPK RM11 ....319 L2
Lombardy Pl CHLM/WR CM1 ....5 F1
Lombardy Rd SUD CO10 ....46 C9
Lonbarn Hl MGTR CO11 ....107 M6
London City Airport Link
  CAN/RD E16 ....333 J7
Londonderry Pde
  ERITH DA8 * 346 C5
London HI CHLM/GWD CM2 ....239 P8
  CBE/LIN CB1 ....38 D1
  CDW/CHF RM16 ....339 L9
  HOC/HUL SS5 ....183 K2
  SOS SS1 ....287 J5
London Rd ABR/ST RM4 ....256 C9
  ABR/ST RM4 ....277 H2
  BARK IG11 ....316 C9
  BCAYE CM11 ....304 D1
  BCAYW CM12 ....282 D3
  BRTR CM7 ....144 F9
  BRW CM14 ....280 D9
  BSF CM23 ....137M9
  CHDH RM6 ....317 P1
  CHLM/GWD CM2 ....239 M6
  CHONG CM5 ....257 J4
  CHTY IP2 ....25 J4
  COLW CO3 ....126 E9
  COS CO15 ....181 P8
  EN EN1 ....273 J5
  EPP CM16 ....233 J1
  GRAYS RM17 ....349 K4
  HLWE CM17 ....187 K9
  HLWE CM17 ....211 K3
  IP IP11 ....25 H5
  K/T/MI CO5 ....149 H6
  K/T/MI CO5 ....172 G5
  K/T/MI CO5 ....173 K1
  MAL CM9 ....221 L9
  PIT SS13 ....325 J1
  PLSTW E13 ....333 K2
  RAYL SS6 ....306 G4
  RCHLM CM5 ....169 L5
  RCOLW CO6 ....102 B8
  RCOLW CO6 ....149 N2
  RCOS CO16 ....181 N5
  RIPS/CAP IP9 ....81 J1
  RIPS/CAP IP9 ....81 L1
  ROMW/RG RM7 ....318 B1
  SAFWN CB10 ....36 D9
  SAFWS CB11 ....50 G8
  SAFWS CB11 ....65 L1
  SBF/HAD SS7 ....325M1
  SBF/HAD SS7 ....325 P1
  SBF/HAD SS7 ....327 J4
  SBW CM21 ....187M2
  SLH/COR SS17 ....341 J4
  SOCK/AV RM15 ....337 L8
  SOS SS1 ....287 J5
  TIL RM18 ....350 C7
  VGE SS16 ....324 B5
  WARE SG12 ....184 B5
  WICKE SS11 ....305 P1
  WOS/PRTT SS0 ....328 E5
  WRE SS16 ....348 G4
London Rd Purfleet
  PUR RM19 ....347 N4
London Rd West Thurrock
  WTHK WM20 ....
Londons Cl UPMR RM14 ....319 P7
Lone Barn Ct IP IP1 ....24 E3
Longacre BSDN SS14 ....324 B5
  CHLM/WR CM1 ....239 L2
  COLN CO4 ....127 N5

Long Acre HLWE CM17 ....187 J8
Longacre Rd BRTR CM7 ....145 P6
  WALTH E17 ....294 G5
Longacres BRTR CM7 ....145 K5
Long Acres K/T/MI CO5 ....148 E3
Longafori Wy
  RBRW/HUT CM13 ....281M7
Long Banks HLWS CM18 ....210 G6
Long Border Rd RBSF CM22 ....139 H5
Longbarn Cl PIT SS13 ....304 F6
Long Brandocks
  CHLM/WR CM1 ....238 G1
Longbridge Rd BARK IG11 ....316 E8
  BCTR RM8 ....317 H6
Long Common MAL CM9 ....222 A6
Long Ct PUR RM19 ....347M2
Longcroft FX IP11 ....35 H5
Longcroft Dr CHES/WCR EN8 ....252 C4
Longcroft RI LOU IG10 ....276 C4
Longcroft Rd COLN CO4 ....9 A4
Long Deacon Rd CHING E4 ....294 F2
Longdryve COLS CO2 * 151 N2
Longfellow Dr
  RBRW/HUT CM13 ....281M6
Longfellow Rd BOW E3 * 332 B5
  MAL CM9 ....244 B1
  WALTH E17 ....314 C1
Long Fld FX IP11 ....34 G5
Longfield HLWS CM18 ....211 H5
  LOU IG10 ....275M4
  WIT CM8 ....171M8
Longfield Av EMPK RM11 ....318 E2
  EN EN3 ....251 P7
  WALTH E17 ....294 B8
Longfield Cl WICKE SS11 ....285M9
Longfield La CHESW EN7 ....229 L6
Longfield Rd CHLM/GWD CM2 ......240 D3
  RCHLM CM5 ....264 G9
  RIPS/CAP IP9 ....28 C8
  WICKE SS11 ....285M9
Long Flds CHONG CM5 ....235M9
Longfields RCOS CO16 ....180 E9
Long Gages BSDN SS14 ....3 F5
Long Gn BRTR CM7 ....145 P6
  CHIG IG7 ....296 F1
Long Green La
  RBRW/HUT CM13 ....119 H5
Long Grove Cl BROX EN10 ....208 B7
Longhams Dr RCHLM CM5 ....264 F9
Longhayes Av CHDH RM6 ....297 K8
Longhedges SAFWS CB11 ....145M8
Long Horse Cft SAFWS CB11 ....65M2
Longhouse Rd
  CDW/CHF RM16 ....350 C1
Longlands Cl CHES/WCR EN8 ......252 A2
Long La BRTR CM7 ....144 C6
  CBE/LIN CB1 ....38 D1
  CDW/CHF RM16 ....339 L9
  HOC/HUL SS5 ....183 K2
  SOS SS1 ....287 J5
Longleat Dr BRTR CM7 ....145 J6
Longleat Cl CHLM/WR CM1 ....217 N4
Longleat Rd EN EN1 ....273 K4
Long Ley HLW CM20 ....210 G3
Long Leys CHING E4 ....294 E8
Long Lyndenswood LAIN SS15 ....2 C8
Long Mark Rd CAN/RD E16 ....333 N6
Longmarsh La THMD SE28 ....334 F8
Longmans Av
  CHLM/GWD CM2 ....240 E2
Longmead Cl BRWN CM15 ....281M8
Long Meadow BRTR CM7 ....144 E9
  BSF CM23 ....137 J8
  RBRW/HUT CM13 ....281M8
Long Meadow Dr WICKE SS11 .....285 K8
Long Mdw HAR CO12 * 188 C7
Longmeads WIT CM8 ....197 P7
Long Mead CHLM/WR CM1 ....238 G1
Long Moor CHES/WCR EN8 ....230 B8
Longmore Av
  CHLM/GWD CM2 ....240 G2
Longnor Rd WCHPL E1 ....332 A3
Long Perry RIPS/CAP IP9 ....28 D9
Longport Cl BARK/HLT IG6 ....297 H3
Long Reach Rd BARK IG11 ....334 C4
Longridge Cl COLN CO4 ....128 C7
Long Riding BSDN SS14 ....3 H5
Long Ridings Av
  RBRW/HUT CM13 ....281 L4
Longship Wy MAL CM9 ....243 P2
Longshots Cl CHLM/WR CM1 ....217 P2
Longs La RCHLM CM5 ....194 E3
Longstomps Av
  CHLM/GWD CM2 ....239 P4
Longstraw Cl COLW CO6 ....126 C9
Long St IPNE IP4 ....17 H6
  WAB EN9 ....231 P9
Longtail BCAYE CM11 ....283 K5
Longtown Wy HARH RM3 ....299 H2
Longview Wy CRW RM5 ....235 J8
Longwick VGE SS16 ....323 K2
Long Wd HLWS CM18 ....210 E8
Longwood Cl UPMR RM14 ....319 P7
Longwood Gdns CLAY IG5 ....296 A8
Longworth Cl THMD SE28 ....335 L6
Long Wyre St COL CO1 ....9 D4
The Loning PEND EN3 ....251 P8
Lonsdale CBE/LIN CB1 ....38 C2
Lonsdale Av EHAM E6 ....333 N4
  RBRW/HUT CM13 ....281 N5
  ROMW/RG RM7 ....318 B1
Lonsdale Cl EHAM E6 ....333 P4
  IPNE IP4 ....25 H4

Lonsdale Crs
GNTH/NBYPK IG2 316 C1
Lonsdale Dr ENC/FH EN2 272 C3
Lonsdale Dr North
ENC/FH EN2 272 D4
Lonsdale Rd RCOS CO16 157 K4
SOSN SS2 329 L4
WAN E11 315 J2
Looe Gdns BARK/HLT IG6 296 C7
Looe Rd FX IP11 35 M6
Loompits Wy SAFWS CB11 65 K2
Loop Rd WAB EN9 252 E2
Lophams Cl HVHL CB9 41 J2
Loraine Cl PEND EN3 273 P4
Loraine Wy RIPW IP8 22 A8
Lord Av CLAY IG5 296 A8
Lord Gdns CLAY IG5 295 P8
Lord Holland Rd COLS CO2 152 A3
Lord Roberts Av LOS SS9 328 A5
Lords Av BSF CM23 136 G7
Lordship Cl RBRW/HUT CM13 281 N7
Lordship Rd CHES/WCR EN8 229 N9
CHLM/WR CM1 217 J9
Lordsland La BRTR CM77 122 D6
Lord St CAN/RD E16 333 P8
HOD EN11 208 B5
Lordswood Rd COLS CO2 151 M4
Lordswood Vw GTDUN CM6 190 G5
Lorien Gdns RCHLM CM3 286 F2
Lorkin's La HSTD CO9 74 E6
Lorkin Wy RCOLW CO6 127 J3
Lorne Gdns WAN E11 295 M8
Lorne Rd BRW CM14 300 F1
FSTGT E7 315 L6
WALTH E17 294 D9
Lornes Cl SOSN SS2 329 L3
Lorraine Cl BCAYE CM11 303 L1
Lorrimore Cl BCAYW CM12 282 G3
Loten Rd SBF/HAD SS7 325 N4
Lottem Rd CVI SS8 344 G3
Lott's Rd RCOS CO16 181 L1
Lotus Cl IP IP1 24 D2
Lotus Wy COS CO15 206 D6
Loudoun Av GNTH/NBYPK IG2 296 C9
Loughton La EPP CM16 254 E7
Loughton Wy BKHH IG9 275 N7
Louisa Av SBF/HAD SS7 305 N9
Louisa St WCHPL E1 332 A5
Louis Dr RAYL SS6 306 D3
Louis Dr East RAYL SS6 306 E4
Louis Dr West RAYL SS6 306 D3
Louise Cl WOTN CO14 159 M3
Louise Gdns RAIN RM13 336 D3
Louise Rd RAYL SS6 307 H5
SRTFD E15 315 H8
Louisville Cl WARE SG12 184 F8
Louse La RCOLE CO7 104 F5
Louvain Dr CHLM/WR CM1 218 E4
Louvaine Av WICKW SS12 284 G9
Louvain Rd HAR CO12 110 B7
Lovage Ap EHAM E6 333 P5
Lovegrove Wk POP/IOD E14 332 F8
Lovelace Av SOS SS1 329 L6
Lovelace Gdns BARK IG11 317 H6
SOSN SS2 329 L5
Love La CHONG CM5 235 M7
RAYL SS6 306 F5
RCOLE CO7 179 K5
SOCK/AV RM15 337 P9
TIL RM18 351 K4
WFD IG8 296 A3
Lovell Ri LOS SS9 308 B9
Lovell Rd EN EN1 251 N5
Lovell Wk RAIN RM13 318 F8
Lovens Cl CVI SS8 344 F3
Lovering Rd CHESW EN7 229 H4
Lover's La GRH DA9 348 G9
RCOLE CO7 155 M7
RIPS/CAP IP9 84 B5
Loves Wk CHLM/WR CM1 239 J2
Lovetofts Dr IP IP1 24 E1
Lovet Rd HLWW/ROY CM19 210 B4
Love Wy RCOS CO16 181 M7
Lowbrook Rd IL IG1 316 C6
Lowden Rd ED N9 273 N7
Lowe Av CAN/RD E16 333 K5
Lowe Cha WOTN CO14 159 J5
Lowe Cl CHIG IG7 297 H2
Lowefields RCOLW CO6 124 C2
Lowell St POP/IOD E14 332 B6
Lowen Rd RAIN RM13 336 C2
Lower Anchor St
CHLM/GWD CM2 4 D5
Lower Av PIT SS13 305 K7
Lower Barn Rd RIPW IP8 28 C1
Lower Bedfords Rd
ROM RM1 298 F3
Lower Broad St DAGE RM10 335 P1
Lower Brook St IPNE IP4 16 E5
Lower Burnham Rd
RCHLM CM3 265 P7
Lower Bury La EPP CM16 254 F1
Lower Cha RCHLM CM3 267 N5
Lower Church Rd
SBF/HAD SS7 305 N9
Lower Cladbens WARE SG12 184 C3
Lower Cloister BCAYE CM11 283 J6
Lower Crs NHMKT IP6 22 B1
SLH/COR SS17 351 H1
Lower Dales View Rd IP IP1 25 H3
Lower Downs Slade HVHL CB9 41 K3
Lower Dunton Rd
RBRW/HUT CM13 302 E9
UPMR RM14 322 E3
Lower Farm Rd COLN CO4 78 G9
Lower Gn CHLM/GWD CM2 240 A9
RCOLW CO6 100 B7
Lower Hall La CHING E4 294 B2
Lower Harlings RIPS/CAP IP9 85 M9
Lower Holt St RCOLW CO6 124 B1
Lower Houses Rd
RIPS/CAP IP9 84 C6
Lower Island Wy WAB EN9 252 E5
Lower Kenwood Av
STHGT/OAK N14 272 D4
Lower King BRTR CM7 145 N5
Lower Lambricks RAYL SS6 306 G3
Lower Langley RCOLW CO6 125 H6
Lower Lea Crossing
POP/IOD E14 333 H7
Lower Mardyke Av
RAIN RM13 336 B2
Lower Marine Pde HAR CO12 110 D6
Lower Meadow
CHES/WCR EN8 230 A6
HLWS CM18 210 F7
Lower Ml GTDUN CM6 141 M7
Lower Noke Cl BRW CM14 279 K8
Lower Orwell St IPNE IP4 17 F6
Lower Park Crs BSF CM23 137 L9
Lower Park Rd LOU IG10 275 N4
RCOLE CO7 179 K7
WICKW SS12 305 H3
Lower Queen's Rd BKHH IG9 275 P8
Lower Rd BELV DA17 346 B1
BRWN CM15 281 N2
BURES CO8 100 G3
COLS CO2 150 D9
GVW DA11 349 K9
HOC/HUL SS5 286 G7
IP IP1 23 K7
K/T/MI CO5 175 J4
K/T/MI CO5 176 E8
LOU IG10 254 B9
RBSF CM22 162 F6
SUD CO10 45 N1
SUD CO10 46 E8
TIL RM18 350 B9
WARE SG12 184 C6
Lower Southend Rd
WICKE SS11 285 J8
Lower Stock Rd ING CM4 262 A6
Lower St LAIN SS15 303 M6
RCOLE CO7 79 P8
RIPS/CAP IP9 83 H7
RIPW IP8 24 B4
STSD CM24 114 C8
SUD CO10 45 J1
Lower Swaines EPP CM16 232 F9
The Lowe CHIG IG7 297 H2
Lowfield SBW CM21 187 M3
Lowfield La HOD EN11 208 D5
Low Hall Cl CHING E4 274 D6
Low Hall La WALTH E17 314 B1
Low Hill Rd HLWW/ROY CM19 209 J5
Lowland Gdns
ROMW/RG RM7 318 A1
Lowlands Rd SOCK/AV RM15 337 P8
Low Rd HAR CO12 109 P7
Lowry Cl HVHL CB9 40 G2
SBN/FI SS3 330 E6
Lowry Gdns IPSE IP3 30 G2
Lowry Rd BCTR RM8 317 J7
Lowshoe La ROMW/RG RM7 298 A5
Low Street La TIL RM18 350 G3
Lowther Dr ENC/FH EN2 272 D3
Lowther Rd WALTH E17 294 B6
Loxford PIT SS13 304 F7
Loxford Av EHAM E6 333 N2
Loxford La IL IG1 316 D7
Loxford Rd BARK IG11 316 C8
Loxham Rd CHING E4 294 E4
Loxley Ct WARE SG12 * 184 B3
Luard Wy COLS CO2 175 K2
WIT CM8 197 J3
Lubbards Cl RAYL SS6 306 G2
Lubberhedges La
GTDUN CM6 118 C4
Lucas Av CHLM/GWD CM2 240 B4
PLSTW E13 333 L1
RCOLW CO6 126 A2
Lucas Ct WAB EN9 253 J3
Lucas Rd COLS CO2 128 A9
GRAYS RM17 349 K1
SUD CO10 21 F6
Lucas's La RCOS CO16 132 G9
Lucern Cl CHESW EN7 229 K6
Lucerne Cl PLMGR N13 272 D9
Lucerne Dr WICKE SS11 285 M9
Lucerne Gv WALTH E17 294 G8
Lucerne Rd RCOLE CO7 129 P9
Lucerne Wk WICKE SS11 285 M9
Lucerne Wy CHLM/WR CM1 239 J2
HARH RM3 299 J3
Luces La HSTD CO9 72 E5
Lucius Crs COLN CO4 128 C1
Luck's La RCHLM CM3 193 N2
Luckyn La BSDN SS14 303 N7
Luctons Av BKHH IG9 275 M7
Lucy Cl COLW CO3 126 F9
Lucy La North COLW CO3 126 E8
Lucy La South COLW CO3 126 F8
Lucy Rd SOS SS1 19 H6
Ludgores La RCHLM CM3 242 A5
Ludgrove RCHLM CM3 267 H3
Ludham Cl THMD SE28 335 K6
WFD IG8 296 D5
Ludham Hall La BRTR CM77 144 G7
Ludlow Cl IP IP1 23 J8
Ludlow Pl GRAYS RM17 349 L1
Luff Wy WOTN CO14 158 G7
Lufkin Rd COLN CO4 128 A4
Lugano Av WDBR IP12 27 P3
Lugar Cl COLN CO4 128 F9
Lugg Ap MNPK E12 316 B5
Luker Rd SOS SS1 19 F4
Lukin Crs CHING E4 274 G9
Lukin's Dr GTDUN CM6 141 L7
Lullington Rd DAGW RM9 317 M9
Lulworth Av CHESW EN7 228 G8
IPSE IP3 26 C8
Lulworth Cl COS CO15 207 H4
SLH/COR SS17 341 J5
Lulworth Dr CRW RM5 298 A2
HVHL CB9 41 H3
Lumber Leys WOTN CO14 159 H7
Lummis V KESG IP5 27 H4
Luncies Rd BSDN SS14 324 D1
Lundy Cl HVHL CB9 41 N4
SOSN SS2 308 C8
Lunnish Hl HAR CO12 109 J5
Lupin Cl ROMW/RG RM7 318 C4
Lupin Dr CHLM/WR CM1 218 E5
Lupin Rd CHTY IP2 24 F7
Lupin Wy RCOS CO16 6 A1
Luppits Cl RBRW/HUT CM13 281 K7
Lushes Ct LOU IG10 276 C4
Lushes Rd LOU IG10 276 C4
Lushington Av FOS CO13 158 E8
Lushington Rd MGTR CO11 106 B4
Lutea Cl LAIN SS15 303 L6
Luther Dr K/T/MI CO5 174 B8
Luther King Cl WALTH E17 314 B1
Luther King Rd
HLWW/ROY CM19 13 G7
Luther Rd CHTY IP2 25 J7
Luthers Cl BRWN CM15 258 B7
Luton Rd PLSTW E13 333 K4
WALTH E17 294 B7
Lutus Cl SUD CO10 43 P5
Luxborough La CHIG IG7 296 A1
Luxembourg Ms SRTFD E15 315 H7
Luxford Pl SBW CM21 187 N3
Lyal Rd BOW E3 332 B2
Lych Ga LAIN SS15 303 K9
Lydeard Rd EHAM E6 316 A9
Lydford Rd WOS/PRIT SS0 18 B5
Lydgate Cl MGTR CO11 106 A4
Lydia Dr RCOS CO16 205 H2
Lydia Rd ERITH DA8 346 E4
Lygean Av WARE SG12 184 B3
Lyle Cl KESG IP5 27 K4
Lylt Rd CVI SS8 344 D2
Lyme Rd SOSN SS2 19 K1
Lymington Av COS CO15 182 A5
LOS SS9 327 P4
Lymington Rd BCTR RM8 317 L3
Lympstone Cl WOS/PRIT SS0 328 B1
Lynbrook Cl RAIN RM13 336 C2
Lynceley Gra EPP CM16 233 H8
The Lynch HOD EN11 208 E5
Lyndale BRWN CM15 258 C7
Lyndale Av SOSN SS2 329 J3
Lyndene SBF/HAD SS7 325 N1
Lyndhurst Av IPNE IP4 26 B6
Lyndhurst Cl BXLYHN DA7 346 A8
Lyndhurst Dr EMPK RM11 319 H3
LEY E10 314 F2
RCHLM CM3 242 C9
Lyndhurst Gdns BARK IG11 316 F8
EN EN1 273 K3
GNTH/NBYPK IG2 316 E1
Lyndhurst Ri CHIG IG7 296 B1
Lyndhurst Rd BXLYHN DA7 346 A8
CHING E4 294 F4
COS CO15 182 D9
SLH/COR SS17 341 N1
Lyndhurst Wy
RBRW/HUT CM13 281 M7
Lyndsey Pl CHESW EN7 * 229 N9
Lyne Crs WALTH E17 294 C5
Lyneham Wk CLPT E5 * 314 B7
Lynford Gdns GDMY/SEVK IG3 316 G4
Lynfords Av WICKE SS11 285 L5
Lynfords Dr WICKE SS11 285 L6
Lynford Ter ED N9 * 273 L7
Lynmouth Av CHLM/GWD CM2 5 H7
EN EN1 273 L5
Lynmouth Gdns
CHLM/GWD CM2 5 H6
Lynmouth Rd WALTH E17 314 B1
Lynne Cl FOS CO13 158 E8
Lynnett Rd BCTR RM8 317 L4
Lynn Ms WAN E11 315 H4
Lynn Rd GNTH/NBYPK IG2 316 E2
WAN E11 315 H4
Lynn St ENC/FH EN2 251 J9
Lynn View Cl SBF/HAD SS7 325 P1
Lynross Cl HARH RM3 299 K6
Lynstede BSDN SS14 324 F1
Lynton Av ROMW/RG RM7 298 A5
Lynton Cl HAR CO12 14 A6
Lynton Crs GNTH/NBYPK IG2 316 C1
Lynton Dr CHLM/WR CM1 218 D6
Lynton Gdns EN EN1 273 K6
Lynton Pde CHES/WCR EN8 * 230 A9
Lynton Rd CHING E4 294 E2
SBF/HAD SS7 326 F3
SOS SS1 329 N8
Lynwood Av FX IP11 35 L6
Lynwood Cl CRW RM5 298 A3
SWFD E18 295 M5
Lynwood Dr CRW RM5 298 A3
Lynwood Gn RAYL SS6 307 K7
Lynwood Gv WCHMH N21 272 F7
Lyon Cl CHLM/GWD CM2 240 A7
COS CO15 7 J2
Lyon Rd ROM RM1 318 E2
Lyons Hall Rd BRTR CM7 121 N7
Lysander Dr IPSE IP3 31 J2
Lyster Av CHLM/GWD CM2 240 F3
Lytchet Wy PEND EN3 251 P9
Lytham Cl THMD SE28 335 M6
Lyttelton Rd LEY E10 314 E5
Lytton Av PEND EN3 252 B8
PLMGR N13 272 F8
Lytton Rd CDW/CHF RM16 350 B2
GPK RM2 298 G9
WAN E11 315 H2
Lyttons Wy HOD EN11 208 D2

M

Mabbitt Wy COLN CO4 128 C2
Maberly Ct SAFWN CB10 51 L8
Mabey's Wk SBW CM21 187 J3
Mabley St HOM E9 314 B7
Macarthur Cl FSTGT E7 315 K8
Macaulay Rd EHAM E6 333 N2
IP IP1 22 G8
VGE SS16 323 H1
Macbeth Cl COLN CO4 128 G8
Macdonald Av DAGE RM10 318 A5
EMPK RM11 299 K8
WOS/PRIT SS0 328 F4
Macdonald Rd FSTGT E7 315 K6
WALTH E17 294 F6
Macdonald Wy EMPK RM11 299 K8
Macer's La BROX EN10 230 C3
Mace St BETH E2 332 A2
Mace Wk CHLM/WR CM1 4 C1
Macgregor Dr WICKW SS12 305 K2
Macgregor Rd CAN/RD E16 333 M5
Macintosh Cl CHESW EN7 229 J5
Macintyres Wk RCFD SS4 308 D1
Mackay Ct COLS CO2 152 C5
Mackenzie Cl WICKW SS12 305 K1
Mackenzie Dr KESG IP5 26 G3
Mackintosh La HOM E9 314 A7
Mackley Dr SLH/COR SS17 323 N9
Maclarens WIT CM8 198 B6
Maclaren Wy WICKW SS12 * 305 K2
Maclennan Av RAIN RM13 337 J3
Macleod Cl GRAYS RM17 349 N2
Macleod Rd STHGT/OAK N14 272 D4
Macmurdo Cl LOS SS9 307 N8
Macmurdo Rd LOS SS9 307 N8
Macon Wy UPMR RM14 320 C1
Maddams St BOW E3 332 E4
Maddox Rd HLW CM20 13 K4
Madeira Av LOS SS9 327 P4
Madeira Gv WFD IG8 295 M3
Madeira Rd COS CO15 182 E9
WAN E11 314 G3
Madeline Gv IL IG1 316 E7
Madeline Pl CHLM/WR CM1 217 M5
Madells EPP CM16 254 G1
Madge Gill Wy EHAM E6 333 P1
Madgements Rd BRTR CM77 122 D7
Madgeways Cl WARE SG12 * 184 C7
Madgeways La WARE SG12 184 C7
Madles La ING CM4 261 N8
Madras Rd IL IG1 316 C6
Madrid Av RAYL SS6 286 D9
Mafeking Av EHAM E6 333 N2
GNTH/NBYPK IG2 316 E2
Mafeking Rd CAN/RD E16 333 J4
EN EN1 273 L2
Magazine Farm Wy
COLW CO3 127 K9
Magazine Rd SBN/FI SS3 330 D8
Magdalen Cl COS CO15 6 D2
Magdalene Cl CHTY IP2 24 G9
Magdalene Crs WIT CM8 171 L2
Magdalene Gdns EHAM E6 334 B4
Magdalen Gdns
RBRW/HUT CM13 281 P5
Magdalen Gn COL CO1 9 G7
GTDUN CM6 92 B6
Magdalen Rd COS CO15 6 D2
Magdalen St COL CO1 8 E7
Magenta Cl BCAYW CM12 282 F5
Magingley Crs KESG IP5 26 E5
Magna Md SBN/FI SS3 310 C8
Magnaville Rd BSF CM23 162 B1
Magnet Rd WTHK RM20 348 F4
Magnet Ter SLH/COR SS17 * 341 M1
Magnolia Cl CHLM/GWD CM2 240 A4
CVI SS8 344 D3
LEY E10 314 D4
SOCK/AV RM15 339 H4
WIT CM8 171 P8
Magnolia Dr COLN CO4 128 G7
Magnolia La LAIN SS15 303 K6
Magnolia Rd HOC/HUL SS5 308 C2
Magnolias BCAYE CM11 303 K1
Magnolia Wy BRWN CM15 280 E4
RCFD SS4 309 J7
Magnum Cl RAIN RM13 337 H4
Magnus Dr COLN CO4 128 C1
Magpie Cl EN EN1 251 M9
FSTGT E7 315 J7
HAR CO12 109 P7
RIPW IP8 24 D9
Magpie La RBRW/HUT CM13 300 G6
Magpies EPP CM16 232 B3
Magwitch Cl CHLM/WR CM1 217 N4
Mahogany Cl
BERM/RHTH SE16 332 B8
Mahon Cl EN EN1 251 L9
Mahonia Dr VGE SS16 322 G1
Maida Av CHING E4 274 E6
Maida Wy CHING E4 274 E6
Maidenburgh St COL CO1 8 D5
Maidenhall Ap CHTY IP2 25 J9
Maiden La DART DA1 346 F9
Maiden Rd SRTFD E15 315 H9
Maidens Br EN EN1 * 251 M7
Maidment Crs WIT CM8 197 J4
Maids Head Pde RCOS CO16 * 157 J5
Maidstone Av CRW RM5 298 B6
Maidstone Rd FX IP11 35 H6
Mailers La BSF CM23 113 L5
Main Av EN EN1 273 L4
Main Dr RBRW/HUT CM13 322 F1
Maine Crs RAYL SS6 306 E3
Main Ga TIL RM18 * 350 A7
Main Rd BOC CM0 247 H2
CHLM/WR CM1 218 A3
FOS CO13 183 H2
GPK RM2 298 E8
HAR CO12 14 A7
HAR CO12 109 K7
HOC/HUL SS5 * 287 H5
HOC/HUL SS5 307 N1
IPNE IP4 23 P9
KESG IP5 26 F3
KIR/NAC IP10 32 D1
RCHLM CM3 169 H1
RCHLM CM3 169 J7
RCHLM CM3 219 J3
RCHLM CM3 241 M3
RCHLM CM3 242 C9
RCHLM CM3 263 M8
RCHLM CM3 263 P3
RCHLM CM3 285 N2
RCOLE CO7 154 E3
RCOLW CO6 101 L4
RIPS/CAP IP9 30 G8
RIPS/CAP IP9 84 D2
SBF/HAD SS7 * 306 E9
WDBR IP12 27 N1
Main St CBE/LIN CB1 39 L5
Maitland Pl SBN/FI SS3 330 D5
Maitland Rd SRTFD E15 315 J8
STSD CM24 114 B9
WICKW SS12 305 K2
Maizey Ct BRWN CM15 280 D4
Majendie La HSTD CO9 72 E5
Major Rd SRTFD E15 314 G7
Makemores BRTR CM77 144 C4
Makepeace Rd WAN E11 295 K8
Makins Rd HAR CO12 110 A3
Malabar St POP/IOD E14 332 D9
Malam Gdns POP/IOD E14 332 E7
Malan Sq RAIN RM13 318 G8
Malcolms Wy STHGT/OAK N14 272 B4
Malcolm Wy WAN E11 295 K9
Maldon Ct SUD CO10 21 K5
Maldon Rd BOC CM0 246 D8
BOC CM0 247 P3
BOC CM0 268 D9
CHLM/GWD CM2 240 E3
COLS CO2 150 D8
COLS CO2 175 H2
COLW CO3 151 M1
ED N9 273 L9
ING CM4 261 J1
K/T/MI CO5 173 H4
K/T/MI CO5 201 J2
MAL CM9 198 C8
MAL CM9 221 J3
MAL CM9 223 K6
MAL CM9 224 A2
MAL CM9 243 L3
MAL CM9 266 F1
RCHLM CM3 196 E8
RCHLM CM3 242 C3
RCHLM CM3 268 B1
ROMW/RG RM7 318 B2
SOSN SS2 19 G2
WIT CM8 197 J7
Maldon Wk WFD IG8 295 M3
Maldon Wy RCOS CO16 181 L9
Malford Gv SWFD E18 295 J7
Malgraves PIT SS13 304 G8
Malgraves Pl PIT SS13 304 G8
Malin Cl HVHL CB9 41 N4
Malkin Dr HLWE CM17 211 M5
Mallard Cl BRTR CM77 144 F9
COLS CO2 151 K9
K/T/MI CO5 173 H2
MAL CM9 225 J1
UPMR RM14 320 C2
Mallard Ct SOS SS1 * 19 K3
WALTH E17 * 294 G7
Mallard Rd CHLM/GWD CM2 239 P5
Mallards RCHLM CM3 267 P1
SBN/FI SS3 330 D5
Mallards Ri HLWE CM17 211 K3
Mallards Rd BARK IG11 335 H3
WFD IG8 295 L4
Mallard Wy CHTY IP2 24 F9
RBRW/HUT CM13 281 K6
SUD CO10 61 M5
Mallinson Cl HCH RM12 319 H7
Mallion Ct WAB EN9 253 J3
Mallory Wy BCAYW CM12 * 283 H7
Mallow Ct GRAYS RM17 349 N4
Mallow Gdns BCAYW CM12 282 G3
Mallowhayes Cl CHTY IP2 25 J8
Mallows Fld HSTD CO9 98 A7
Mallows Gn HLWW/ROY CM19 210 B8
Mallows Green Rd BSF CM23 113 H5
Mallows La HSTD CO9 70 G6
Mallow Wk CHESW EN7 * 229 J7
The Mall EMPK RM11 318 G3
SRTFD E15 * 314 G9
STHGT/OAK N14 272 D9
Malmesbury Cl CHTY IP2 25 H9
Malmesbury Rd BOW E3 332 C3
CAN/RD E16 333 H5
SWFD E18 295 J5
Malmesbury Ter CAN/RD E16 333 J5
Malmesbury West Est
BOW E3 332 C3
Malmsmead SBN/FI SS3 330 B6
Malpas Rd CDW/CHF RM16 350 D1
DAGW RM9 317 L8
Malta Rd LEY E10 314 D3
TIL RM18 350 A7
Maltby Dr EN EN1 251 N8
Maltese Rd CHLM/WR CM1 217 P7
Malthouse Rd MGTR CO11 106 C4
Malting Farm La RCOLE CO7 104 D6
Malting Green Rd COLS CO2 151 J9
Malting La CDW/CHF RM16 340 B4
FOS CO13 158 D5
MHAD SG10 160 E3
SUD CO10 44 A4
Malting Rd COLS CO2 151 M5
K/T/MI CO5 176 F6
Maltings Cha ING CM4 260 C6
Maltings Cl BURES CO8 75 P8
Maltings Ct WIT CM8 197 J4
Maltings Hl CHONG CM5 213 J8
Maltings La EPP CM16 233 H8
ROY SG8 48 B8
WIT CM8 197 J4
Maltings Pk RCOLW CO6 * 127 J3
Maltings Rd CHLM/GWD CM2 240 F5
RCOLE CO7 179 K5
WICKE SS11 286 B6
The Maltings BOC CM0 269 K5
BRTR CM77 144 D4
GTDUN CM6 92 B6
GTDUN CM6 141 L5
HAR CO12 109 H8
ROM RM1 318 E2
SAFWS CB11 * 65 H9
WICKE SS11 * 286 B6
Maltings Vw BRTR CM7 145 K3

Maiting Villas Rd RCFD SS4 .....308 C5
Maiting Yd RCOLE CO7 ....153 J6
Maitings Park Rd RCOLW CO6 ...127 J5
Malvern Av CHING E4 ....294 C4
 CVI SS8 ....344 A2
Malvern Cl IPSE IP5 ....26 A7
 KESG IP5 ....26 E4
 RAYL SS6 ....36 A6
Malvern Dr GDMY/SEVK IG3 .....316 G6
 WFD IG8 ....295 M2
Malvern Gdns LOU IG10 ....276 A5
Malvern Rd EHAM E6 ....335 P1
 EMPK RM11 ....318 F1
 GRAYS RM17 ....349 P2
 HOC/HUL SS5 ....288 A8
 WAN E11 ....315 H4
Malvern Ter BOC CM0 ....273 C7
Malvern Wy RCOLW CO6 ....102 E9
Malwood Dr SBF/HAD SS7 ....325 N1
Malwood Rd SBF/HAD SS7 ....325 N1
Malyon Court Cl SBF/HAD SS7 ..326 E2
Malyon Rd WIT CM8 ....197 J4
Malyons Cl PIT SS13 ....304 C4
Malyons Gn PIT SS13 ....304 C7
Malyons La HOC/HUL SS5 ....286 G6
Malyons Ms PIT SS13 ....304 C8
Malyons Rd PIT SS13 ....304 C7
The Malyons SBF/HAD SS7 ......326 E2
Managers St POP/IOD E14 * 332 F8
Manager Dr SY SRTFD E15 ......315 H8
Manbey Park Rd SRTFD E15 .....315 H8
Manbey Rd SRTFD E15 ....315 H8
Manbey St SRTFD E15 ....315 H8
Manbrough Av EHAM E6 ....334 B5
Manchester Dr LOS SS9 ....527 N4
Manchester Rd CHTY IP2 ....24 E9
 COS CO15 ....182 F7
Manchester Wy DAGE RM10 * 318 A6
Mandela Rd LINE E16 ....333 K6
Mandeville Cl BROX EN10 ......208 C8
Mandeville Rd PEND EN5 ....252 B7
 RCOLW CO6 ....169 K3
 SAFWS CB11 ....65 L1
 STHGT/OAK N14 ....272 A8
Mandeville St CLPT E5 ....314 B5
Mandeville Wy
 CHLM/WR CM1 ....194 M9
 FOS CO13 ....158 G7
 SBF/HAD SS7 ....305 P8
 VGE SS16 ....325 H1
Mandrake Wy SRTFD E15 * 315 H9
Mandy Cl IPNE IP4 ....273 C5
Manfield Gdns RCOS CO16 ......180 E8
Manford Cl CHIG IG7 ....297 J1
Manford Cross CHIG IG7 ....297 H2
Manford Wy CHIG IG7 ....297 J4
Mangapp Cha BOC CM0 ....268 F9
Manilla Rd SOS SS1 ....329 K7
Manilla St POP/IOD E14 ....332 D9
Manly Dixon Dr PEND EN3 ......252 B7
Mannall Wk KESG IP5 ....27 K5
Mannering Gdns
 WOS/PRIT SS0 ....328 C3
Manners Cnr SOSN SS2 * 328 C3
Manners Wy SOSN SS2 ....328 F1
Manning Gv VGE SS16 ....323 K2
Manning Rd DAGE RM10 ....317 P9
 FX IP11 ....54 B3
 WALTH E17 ....294 B8
Mannings Cl SAFWS CB11 ....65 M2
Mannings La RIPS/CAP IP9 .....30 C8
Mannings St SOCK/AV RM15 .....337 P6
Mannington Cl IPNE IP4 ....24 A1
Manningtree Rd RCOLE CO7 .....81 J8
 RCOLE CO7 ....105 H2
 RCOLE CO7 ....131 L7
 RIPS/CAP IP9 ....49 J8
Mannin Rd CHDH RM6 ....317 J2
Mannock Dr LOU IG10 ....276 D1
Mannock Rd DART DA1 ....347 L8
Manns Wy RAYL SS6 ....306 F2
Manor Av WCHNG CM5 ....214 G8
Manor Av EMPK RM11 ....299 H9
 PIT SS13 ....305 H9
Manor Cl BCAYE CM11 ....284 B5
 DAGE RM10 ....318 C8
 DART DA1 ....346 C9
 RAYL SS6 ....306 E3
 RCOLW CO6 ....102 F9
 ROM RM1 ....298 F9
 SOCK/AV RM15 ....337 P8
 SUD CO10 ....45 H1
 THMD SE28 ....307 J3
Manor Ct CHES/WCR EN8 * 252 A1
 EN EN1 ....251 N6
 SOS SS1 * 329 K7
Manor Crs EMPK RM11 ....299 H9
 RCHLM CM5 ....194 A7
Manor Croft Pde
 CHES/WCR EN8 * 230 A9
Manordene Rd THMD SE28 ....335 K6
Manor Dr CHLM/GWD CM2 ....240 E3
 STHGT/OAK N14 ....272 A6
Manor Farm Cl HVHL CB9 ....41 L4
Manor Farm Dr CHING E4 ....275 H9
Manor Farm Rd EN EN1 ....251 N5
Manor Gdns COLW CO3 * 127 N8
Manor Hall Gdns LEY E10 ......314 D3
Manor Hatch Cl HLWS CM18 .....211 J4
Manor Hatch Cl HLWS CM18 .....211 J4
Manor House Wy RCOLE CO7 .....179 K6
Manor La HAR CO12 ....110 B6
 RIPS/CAP IP9 ....82 F7
Manor Links BSF CM23 ....137 P7
Manor Park Rd MNPK E12 ....315 N6
Manor Pl BRTR CM7 * 145 K3
Manor Rd ABR/ST RM4 ....277 L7
 BARK IG11 ....316 G8
 BOC CM0 ....248 A9
 BSF CM23 ....137 M7
 CAN/RD E16 ....333 H5
 CHDH RM6 ....317 L1

CHIG IG7 ....296 B5
CHLM/GWD CM2 ....296 C5
COLW CO3 ....8 A6
DAGE RM10 ....318 B8
DART DA1 ....346 D9
ENC/FH EN2 ....273 J1
ERITH DA8 ....346 E4
FOS CO13 ....183 H2
FX IP11 ....54 E3
FX IP11 ....111 M1
GRAYS RM17 ....349 M4
HAR CO12 ....140 G1
HLWE CM17 ....110 B5
HOC/HUL SS5 ....507 M1
HO EN11 ....208 D3
HVHL CB9 ....41 L4
IPNE IP4 ....25 L5
KESG IP5 ....27 M5
LAIN SS15 ....303 J8
LEY E10 ....314 D2
LOU IG10 ....253 L9
LOU IG10 ....253 L9
MAL CM9 ....221 H6
RCHLM CM5 ....220 F2
RCHLM CM5 ....264 F9
RCOLE CO7 ....153 K5
RCOLW CO6 ....127 H2
ROM RM1 ....298 F9
SLH/COR SS17 ....341 L3
STSD CM24 ....138 B1
SUD CO10 ....20 D1
TIL RM18 ....550 B7
WAB EN9 ....252 G3
WALTH E17 ....294 B6
WFD IG8 ....295 M9
WOS/PRIT SS0 ....328 E7
WTHM RM20 ....548 H4
Manor Sq BCTR RM8 ....317 K4
The Manors WIT CM8 * 171 L1
Manor St BRTR CM7 ....145 K4
Manor Ter FX IP11 * 111 M2
Manor Wy BRW CM14 ....280 D9
 BXLYHN DA7 ....346 C8
 CHING E4 ....294 G1
 COS CO15 ....183 H7
 GRAYS RM17 ....349 M5
 RAIN RM13 ....336 D4
 SWCM DA10 ....349 H9
Manorway EN EN1 ....273 K6
 WFD IG8 ....295 M2
The Manorway SLH/COR SS17 ...341 L5
 SLH/COR SS17 ....342 G5
Mansard Cl HCH RM12 ....318 F4
Mansbrook Bvd IPSE IP5 ......31 J2
Manse Cha MAL CM9 ....244 B1
Manse Ct HVHL CB9 ....41 L4
Mansel Gv RAYL SS6 ....307 P9
Mansel Gv WALTH E17 ....294 D5
Manser Rd RAIN RM13 ....336 D3
Mansfield SBW CM21 ....187 H5
Mansfield Av IP IP1 ....24 C1
Mansfield Cl ED N9 ....273 M5
Mansfield Gdns HCH RM12 .....319 J4
Mansfield Hl CHING E4 ....274 E7
Mansfield Rd CHING E4 ....316 B4
 WALTH E17 ....294 C8
 WAN E11 ....315 L1
Mansfields CHLM/WR CM1 ......238 C1
Manstead Gdns CHDH RM6 ......317 K2
 RAIN RM13 ....336 C6
Mansted Gdns RCFD SS4 ....308 E2
Manston Cl CHES/WCR EN8 .....229 P9
Manston Dr BSF CM23 ....137 N5
Manston Rd HLW CM20 ....210 F3
Manton Rd EN EN3 ....251 L8
Mantle Wy SRTFD E15 ....315 H9
Manton Rd CHING E4 ....316 A2
Manwick Rd FX IP11 ....11 F6
Manwood St CAN/RD E16 ....334 A8
Maple Av BRTR CM7 ....144 G4
 BSF CM23 ....137 J6
 CHING E4 ....157 P2
 LOS SS9 ....328 A6
 MAL CM9 ....222 D5
 UPMR RM14 ....319 N5
Maple Cl BARK/HLT IG6 ....296 F5
 BKHH IG9 ....275 N9
 BSF CM23 ....137 J6
 CHTY IP2 ....25 H8
 COS CO15 ....206 G1
 HAR CO12 ....14 B7
 HCH RM12 ....318 G5
 HSTD CO9 ....98 B6
 RBRW/HUT CM13 ....281 J9
Maplecroft Cl EHAM E6 ....333 N6
Maplecroft La WAB EN9 ....209 H9
Mapledene Av HOC/HUL SS5 ....287 H6
Maple Dr CHLM/GWD CM2 ....240 A4
 FOS CO13 ....158 E8
 RAYL SS6 ....286 F9
 SOCK/AV RM15 ....338 G4
 WIT CM8 ....171 J8
Mapleford Sweep VGE SS16 ....324 C2
Maple Ga LOU IG10 ....276 B1
Maple Gv BSF CM23 ....137 J6
 NHMKT IP6 ....22 C1
Maple Hl SUD CO10 ....43 L1
Maple La WALTH CB10 ....67 H5
Maple Leaf K/T/MI CO5 ....173 P6
Mapleleaf Cl HVHL CB9 * 41 L4
Mapleleafe Gdns
 BARK/HLT IG6 ....296 C7
Mapleleaf Gdns WICKW SS12 ...304 G1
Maple Leaf Sq
 BERM/RHTH SE16 * 332 A9
Maple Md BCAYW CM12 ....283 J8
Maple Rd GRAYS RM17 ....349 M4
 SUD CO10 ....43 L1
Maplescroft SBF/HAD SS7 .....326 G2
Maple Spring BSF CM23 ....137 H6
Maple Springs WAB EN9 ......253 K3

Maple Sq SOSN SS2 ....329 J4
Maplestead BSDN SS14 ....304 C7
Maplestead Rd DAGW RM9 ......335 J3
The Maples CHESW EN7 ....229 K7
 HLWW/ROY CM19 ....210 C8
 KESG IP5 ....26 D1
Maplin Av RCOS CO16 ....183 H2
Mapleton Crs PEND EN3 ....251 P8
Mapleton Rd CHING E4 ....274 F9
 EN EN1 ....273 N1
Mapletree La ING CM4 ....260 A2
Maple Tree La VGE SS16 ......322 G1
Maple Wy BOC CM0 ....296 C2
 COLS CO2 ....152 B2
 CVI SS8 ....344 B2
 RCOLW CO6 ....77 K4
Maplin Cl SBF/HAD SS7 ....305 P8
 WCHMM N21 ....273 P1
Maplin Gdns BSDN SS14 ....324 D1
Maplin Rd CAN/RD E16 ....333 K6
Maplin St BOW E3 ....332 C5
Maplin Wy SOS SS1 ....330 B7
Maplin Wy North SBN/FI SS3 ..330 B6
Mapperley Dr WFD IG8 ....295 H4
Marabou Cl MNPK E12 ....315 P7
Marasca End COLS CO2 ....152 B7
Maraschino Crs COLS CO2 .....152 B7
Marathon Wy THMD SE28 ....334 C9
Marauder Wy RCOLW CO6 ....123 N5
Marbled White Dr RIPW IP8 ...29 N2
Marchant Rd WAN E11 ....314 C4
Marchmant Cl HCH RM12 ....319 H5
Marconi Rd CHLM/WR CM1 ......44 A2
 LEY E10 ....314 D3
Marcos Rd CVI SS8 ....344 G2
Marcus Av SOS SS1 ....330 A8
Marcus Cha SOS SS1 ....330 A7
Marcus Cl COLN CO4 ....41 N4
Marcus Gdns SOS SS1 ....330 A7
Marcus Rd FX IP11 ....35 N6
Marcus St SRTFD E15 ....333 H1
Mardyke Cl DAGE RM10 ....336 B2
Mardyke Rd HLW CM20 ....211 H1
Mardyke Vw SOCK/AV RM15 * ...348 B1
Marennes Crs RCOLE CO7 ......179 K6
Mareth Rd COLS CO2 ....151 M4
Margaret Av BRWN CM15 * 281 K6
 CHING E4 ....274 E5
Margaret Bondfield Av
 BARK IG11 ....317 H9
Margaret Cl GPK RM2 ....298 C9
 RCOLE CO7 ....179 L7
 WAB EN9 ....252 G3
Margaret Dr EMPK RM11 ....319 L3
Margaret Rd COL CO1 ....6 B1
 EPP CM16 ....213 H8
 GPK RM2 ....298 C9
Margaret St FX IP11 ....35 H6
 GTDUN CM6 ....92 A5
Margaretting Rd
 CHLM/WR CM1 ....239 H2
 ING CM4 ....239 N9
 MNPK E12 ....315 N7
Margarite Wy WICKW SS12 .....284 C9
Margate Rd IPSE IP5 ....26 A8
Margery Girling House
 FX IP11 * 35 M5
Margery Fld Rd FSTGT E7 .....315 K8
Margery Rd BCTR RM8 ....317 C5
Margeth Rd BCAYW CM12 ....304 K4
Margherita Pl WAB EN9 ....253 J4
Margraten Av CVI SS8 ....344 C3
Marguerite Dr LOS SS9 ....328 A5
Marguerite Wy BSF CM23 .....137 H5
Mariam Gdns HCH RM12 ....319 J4
Marian Cl CDW/CHF RM16 ......339 H9
Maria St HAR CO12 ....15 F3
Maria Ter WCHPL E1 ....332 A5
Maria Cl SLH/COR SS17 ....325 P6
Marigold Av CHTY IP2 ....24 F9
 RCOS CO16 ....181 M8
Marigold Cl CHLM/WR CM1 .....218 E5
 COLN CO4 ....128 F7
Marigold La ING CM4 ....261 M9
Marigold Pl HLWE CM17 * 187 J8
Marina Av RAYL SS6 ....306 F4
Marina Cl SOSN SS2 ....328 F2
Marina Ct CHES/WCR EN8 * 229 P9
 COS CO15 ....182 D8
Marina Dr DART DA1 ....347 L2
 ROMW/RG RM7 ....298 A9
Marina Ms WOTN CO14 ....159 K6
Marina Rd RCHLM CM5 ....196 D8
Marine Ap CVI SS8 ....344 E3
Marine Av CVI SS8 ....345 H2
 SOS SS9 ....327 N5
 WOS/PRIT SS0 ....328 C6
Marine Cl LOS SS9 ....327 K5
Marine Ct DART DA1 * 347 L2
 PUR RM19 ....347 J2
Marine Pde DARK IG11 ....335 J3
 HAR CO12 ....14 E7
 LOS SS9 ....327 K5
 RCHLM CM5 ....195 H6
 SOS SS1 ....349 M6
Marine Pde East COS CO15 ....7 F6
Marine Pde West COS CO15 ....207 G1
Mariner Rd MNPK E12 ....316 B6
Mariners Ct SBN/FI SS3 ......331 H5
Mariners Wy MAL CM9 ....244 B2
Marion Av RCOS CO16 ....181 P7
Marion Cl BARK/HLT IG6 ......296 E4
Marion Gv WFD IG8 ....295 H2
Marisco Cl CDW/CHF RM16 .....350 F2
Mariskals PIT SS15 ....324 F1
Maritime Av MAL CM9 ....222 F8
Maritime St BOW E3 ....332 C4
Marjorams Av LOU IG10 ....276 B1

Mark Av CHING E4 ....274 E5
Market Av WICKW SS12 ....285 H8
Market Chambers
 ENC/FH EN2 * 273 J2
Market Cl COL CO1 ....8 A1
Market End RCOLW CO6 ....147 N4
Market Gv HSTD CO9 ....57 N9
Market Hl HVHL CB9 ....41 K3
 MAL CM9 ....222 B8
 RCOLW CO6 ....147 P4
 SUD CO10 ....20 C5
Market La CBE/LIN CB1 ....38 A1
Market Link ROM RM1 ....298 D8
Market Pde ED N9 * 314 E1
 LEY E10 * 314 E1
 WALTH E17 * 294 C7
Market Pavement BSDN SS14 ...2 E6
Market Pl ABR/ST RM4 ....277 J2
 BRTR CM7 ....145 J3
 GTDUN CM6 ....141 L5
 ING CM4 ....260 C5
 ROM RM1 ....298 D9
 SUD CO10 ....19 G5
 TIL RM18 * 550 B7
Market Rd CHLM/WR CM1 ....5 F5
 IP IP1 ....16 C5
 WICKW SS12 ....285 H9
Market Rw SAFWN CB10 ....51 L9
Market Sq BSDN SS14 ....2 E6
 ED N9 ....273 N8
 HLW CM20 ....13 H5
Market St EHAM E6 ....334 A2
 HAR CO12 ....15 C2
 HLWE CM17 ....187 K8
 SAFWN CB10 ....51 L8
Markfield Gdns RCOLE CO7 ....274 E6
Markham Rd CHESW EN7 ....229 H5
Markhams SLH/COR SS17 ....341 N2
Markhams Cha LAIN SS15 ......505 M8
Markhams Cl HVHL CB9 ....41 K3
Markhouse Av WALTH E17 ......314 C1
Markhouse Rd WALTH E17 ......314 C1
Marking's Fld SAFWN CB10 ....51 N4
Markland Dr MAL CM9 ....243 P1
Marklay Dr RCHLM CM5 ....286 F1
Markmanor Av WALTH E17 ......314 B2
Mark Rd BOC CM0 ....248 B7
Mark's Av CHONG CM5 ....235 L6
Marks Cl BCAYW CM12 ....282 F4
 ING CM4 ....260 A8
Marks Ct SOS SS1 ....19 K6
Marks Gdns BRTR CM7 * 145 M5
Marks Hall La GTDUN CM6 .....123 H9
Marks Hall Rd RCOLW CO6 .....123 M9
Marks La RCHLM CM5 ....286 D1
Marks Rd ROMW/RG RM7 ....298 B9
Mark St SRTFD E15 ....315 H6
Markwells RBSF CM22 ....114 G5
Markwell Wk EPP CM16 ....210 C9
Markyate Rd BCTR RM8 ....317 J7
Marlands Rd CLAY IG5 ....295 P7
Marlborough Av BOC CM0 ......248 B7
 STHGT/OAK N14 ....272 B9
Marlborough Cl BSF CM23 ....137 L9
 CDW/CHF RM16 ....339 H9
 COS CO15 ....6 A4
 SBF/HAD SS7 ....305 P8
 UPMR RM14 ....315 M4
Marlborough Dr CLAY IG5 .....295 P5
 SUD CO10 ....21 F4
Marlborough Gdns
 UPMR RM14 ....319 N5
Marlborough Rd BCTR RM8 .....317 K6
 BRTR CM7 ....145 K2
 BRWN CM15 ....280 D5
 CHING E4 ....294 E7
 ED N9 ....273 M7
 FSTGT E7 ....315 M9
 IPNE IP4 ....25 N6
 ROMW/RG RM7 ....297 P6
 SOS SS1 ....329 K5
 SRTFD E15 ....315 H6
 SWFD E18 ....295 K7
Marlborough Wk
 HOC/HUL SS5 ....507 M1
Marlborough Wy
 BCAYW CM12 ....283 H3
Marle Gdns WAB EN9 ....252 F2
Marlescroft Wy LOU IG10 .....276 C4
Marlin Cl SBF/HAD SS7 ....307 H9
Marlow Av PUR RM19 ....347 M2
Marlowe Rd BARK/HLT IG6 .....296 D5
 BCAYW CM12 ....283 J3
 BRTR CM7 ....145 K6
 MAL CM9 ....243 P1
Marlowe Rd COS CO15 ....206 F5
 WALTH E17 ....294 F8
The Marlowes DART DA1 ....346 C9
Marlowe Wy COLW CO3 ....127 J9
Marlpit Av SOSN SS2 ....328 F2
Marlow Cl SBF/HAD SS7 ....307 H9
 IP IP1 ....24 C2
Marlow Wy BERM/RHTH SE16 ....332 A9
Marlpits Rd MAL CM9 ....243 H6
Marlyon Rd BARK/HLT IG6 .....297 J2
Marmion Ap CHING E4 ....294 D1
Marmion Av CHING E4 ....294 D1
Marmion Cl CHING E4 ....294 D1
Marmion Rd COLS CO2 ....151 P2
Marmion Rd CHLM/GWD CM2 .....240 D2
Marney Dr BSDN SS14 ....324 E1
Marney Wy FOS CO13 ....158 J3
Maroon St POP/IOD E14 ....332 B5
Marquis Cl WALTH E17 ....294 D6
Marram Cl COLN CO4 ....128 C3
Marrington Av RCOS CO16 ....181 M8
Marriott Rd SRTFD E15 ....315 H8
Marryat Rd SOCK/AV RM15 .....338 F4
Marryat Rd EN EN1 ....251 N5
Marsden Rd ED N9 ....273 N6
Marshall Cl K/T/MI CO5 ......173 J1

LOS SS9 ....327 K3
Marshall Rd LEY E10 ....314 E6
Marshalls BCTR RM8 ....508 E5
Marshalls Cl RAYL SS6 ....307 J5
Marshalls Dr BRTR CM7 ....298 D7
Marshalls Piece GTDUN CM6 ...118 C9
Marshalls Rd BRTR CM7 ....145 H5
 ROMW/RG RM7 ....298 C8
Marshbarns BSF CM23 ....137 H6
Marsh Cl CHES/WCR EN8 ....252 C5
Marsh Crs K/T/MI CO5 ....152 G6
Marshcroft Dr
 CHES/WCR EN8 * 230 B7
Marsh Farm La RCOLE CO7 .....180 A5
Marsh Farm Rd RCHLM CM5 .....286 G5
Marshfoot Rd GRAYS RM17 .....350 B5
Marshgate La SRTFD E15 ......332 G1
Marsh Green Rd DAGE RM10 ....335 P1
Marsh Hl HOM E9 ....314 B7
 WAB EN9 ....231 H6
Marsh La FX IP11 ....35 N2
 HLWE CM17 ....187 M7
 LEY E10 ....314 C4
 RBRW/HUT CM13 ....282 B1
 SLH/COR SS17 ....324 C8
 WARE SG12 ....184 B4
 WARE SG12 ....184 G9
Marsh Rd BOC CM0 ....248 D6
 BOC CM0 ....291 H2
 RCOLW CO6 ....152 G6
Marshside Cl ED N9 ....273 P8
Marsh St DART DA1 ....347 M8
Marsh View Ct VGE SS16 * 324 D3
Marsh Wall POP/IOD E14 ......332 D9
Marshy La RCOLE CO7 ....179 K7
Marston Av DAGE RM10 ....317 P5
Marston Beck
 CHLM/GWD CM2 ....218 F9
Marston Cl DAGE RM10 ....317 P5
Marston Rd CLAY IG5 ....295 P6
 HOD EN11 ....208 E4
Martello La FX IP11 ....35 N6
Martello Rd WOTN CO14 ....159 K6
Marten Rd WALTH E17 ....294 D6
Martens Av BXLYHN DA7 ....346 D9
Martens La FX IP11 ....35 N6
Marten's La RCOLE CO7 ....179 K6
Martens Meadow BRTR CM7 .....145 N5
Martham Cl BARK/HLT IG6 .....296 C5
 THMD SE28 ....335 L7
Martha Rd SRTFD E15 ....315 H8
Martin Cl BCAYE CM11 ....284 A7
Martindale Av CAN/RD E16 ...333 K7
 LAIN SS15 ....303 L5
Martin Dr RAIN RM13 ....336 C3
Martin End COLS CO2 ....151 K9
Martin La FX IP11 ....35 H1
Martingale SBF/HAD SS7 .....326 E1
Martingale Cl BCAYE CM11 ...283 L9
Martingale Dr CHLM/WR CM1 ...218 E4
Martingale Rd BCAYE CM11 ....283 L1
Martin Rd BCTR RM8 ....317 K6
Martin Rd PEND EN3 ....252 D7
Martin Rd BCTR RM8 ....317 K6
 CHTY IP2 ....25 K7
 SOCK/AV RM15 ....338 A3
Martins Cl SLH/COR SS17 ....341 L2
Martinsdale COS CO15 ....182 A7
Martins Dr CHES/WCR EN8 ....230 B7
Martins La CBE/LIN CB1 .....38 D1
Martins Ms SBF/HAD SS7 ......325 P2
Martins Ri THMD SE28 ....534 F8
Martin's Rd HSTD CO9 ....97 P7
Martin St THMD SE28 ....534 F8
Martins Wk THMD SE28 ....534 F8
Martinsyde KESG IP5 ....27 N5
Martin Wk HOC/HUL SS5 ....308 A3
Martlesham Cl HCH RM12 .....319 H7
Martley Dr IL IG2 ....296 C9
Martock Av WOS/PRIT SS0 .....328 B1
Martyns Gv WOS/PRIT SS0 .....328 C4
Martyns Ri SUD CO10 ....46 F6
Marvell Cl CHLM/GWD CM2 .....240 C7
Marvell Ct ROM RM1 * 318 F1
Marwgborough Gv COLS CO2 ....152 C4
Maryland Pk SRTFD E15 ....315 H7
Maryland Rd SRTFD E15 ....314 C7
Marylands Av HOC/HUL SS5 ....287 N9
Maryland St SRTFD E15 ....315 H7
Mary La North RCOLE CO7 .....130 E7
Mary La South RCOLE CO7 .....130 E7
Mary McArthur Pl STSD CM24 ..114 B7
Mary Rd IPSE IP5 ....31 H2
Mary Park Gdns BSF CM23 .....142 C1
Mary Rose Cl CDW/CHF RM16 ...348 F2
 DART DA1 ....347 P2
Mary Ruck Wy BRTR CM7 ....145 L9
Mary St CAN/RD E16 ....333 J5
Mary Warner Rd RCOLE CO7 ...104 F9
Mascalls Gdns BRW CM14 .....500 C1
Mascalls La BRW CM14 ....500 C1
Mascalls Wy CHLM/GWD CM2 ....240 D2
Mascot Sq COLN CO4 ....152 E1
Masefield Cl ERITH DA8 .....346 E6
 HARH HA3 ....
Masefield Crs BSF CM23 .....299 H5
 STHGT/OAK N14 ....272 B4
Masefield Dr CHLM/GWD CM2 ...127 J9
 UPMR RM14 ....319 P2
Masefield Gdns EHAM E6 ......334 B5
Masefield Rd DART DA1 ....346 A5
 CDW/CHF RM16 ....339 P9
 MAL CM9 ....244 B1
Mashay Rd SUD CO10 ....58 B4
Mashbury Rd CHLM/WR CM1 .....192 C6
 RCHLM CM5 ....192 E6
Mashey Rd HSTD CO9 ....58 C6
Mashiters Hl ROM RM1 ....298 C5
Mashiters Wk ROM RM1 ....298 D7
Mason Cl BXLYHN DA7 ....346 A8

COLS CO2 ...151 L3
Mason Ct NHMKT IP6 ...22 C5
Mason Dr HARH RM5 ...299 K6
Mason Rd COL CO1 ...4
  RCOS CO16 ...206 C1
  WFD IG8 ...295 H1
Masons Cl IPNE IP4 ...25 N5
Masons Ct BSF CM23 ...137 K7
Masons Pde CHESW EN7 * ...229 H7
Mason Rd EN EN1 ...251 N6
Mason Wy WAB EN9 ...253 H5
Massingham St WCHPL E1 ...332 A4
Masterman Rd EHAM E6 ...333 P5
Master's St WCHPL E1 ...332 A5
Masthead Cl GRH DA9 ...347 P9
Mastmaker Rd POP/IOD E14 ...13 D9
Matcham Rd WAN E11 ...315 H5
Matching Fld BRWN CM15 ...258 C4
Matching Gn BSDN SS14 ...304 C7
Matching La BSF CM23 ...137 J6
  RBSF CM22 ...
Matching Rd HLWE CM17 ...188 A8
  RBSF CM22 ...188 C3
Matfield Cl CHLM/WR CM1 ...218 C4
Mathams Dr BSF CM23 ...137 J9
Mather Wy CHTY IP2 ...25 J7
Mathews Av EHAM E6 ...334 B2
Mathews Cl HSTD CO9 ...98 B5
  RCOLE CO7 ...79 P6
Mathews Md BCAYE CM11 ...304 A2
Mathews Park Av SRTFD E15 ...315 J8
Matlock Cl RIPW IP8 ...24 D9
Matlock Rd CVI SS8 ...544 C2
  LEY E10 ...314 F1
Matlock St WCHPL E1 ...332 D6
Matson Rd IP IP1 ...24 B2
Maude Rd WALTH E17 ...294 B9
Maude Ter WALTH E17 ...294 B8
Maud Gdns BARK IG11 ...334 G2
  PLSTW E13 ...333 J2
Maudlyn Rd COL CO1 ...128 D9
Maud Rd LEY E10 ...314 F5
  PLSTW E13 ...333 J2
Maudslay Rd IP IP1 ...24 D1
Maud St CAN/RD2 E16 ...333 J5
Maugham Cl WICKW SS12 ...305 J2
Maunder Ct CDW/CHF RM16 ...348 G2
Maunds Hatch HLWS CM18 ...210 E7
Maurice Av CVI SS8 ...544 G5
Maverton Rd BOW E3 * ...332 D1
Mavis Gv HCH RM12 ...319 K4
Mawney Rd ROMW/RG RM7 ...298 A7
Mawney Rd ROMW/RG RM7 ...298 A7
Maxey Gdns DAGW RM9 ...317 M6
Maxey Rd DAGW RM9 ...317 M6
Maximfeldt Rd ERITH DA8 ...346 D5
Maxim Rd ERITH DA8 ...346 D3
  WCHMH N21 ...272 F5
Maximus Dr COLN CO4 ...128 B1
Maya Cl SBN/FI SS3 ...330 D7
Mayall Cl CHING E4 ...24 D8
Maya Av CVI SS8 ...344 F2
Maybank Av HCH RM12 ...318 C7
  SWFD E18 ...295 L6
Maybank Rd SWFD E18 ...295 M5
Mayberry Wk COLS CO2 ...152 C8
Maybrick Rd EMPK RM11 ...299 H9
Maybury Av CHES/WCR EN8 ...229 H7
Maybury Cl EN EN1 ...251 M8
  RCOLW CO6 ...149 L3
Maybury Rd BARK IG11 ...335 H1
  IPSE IP5 ...31 H1
  PLSTW E13 ...333 M4
Maybush La EX IP11 ...35 M6
Maybush Rd EMPK RM11 ...319 K2
Maycroft Cl IP IP1 ...23 H8
Maycroft Gdns GRAYS RM17 ...349 N3
Maycroft Rd CHESW EN7 ...229 K5
Mayda Cl PIT SS13 ...97 N7
Maydells Cl PIT SS13 ...324 C1
Maydells Ct PIT SS13 * ...324 C1
Maysebrook Rd BARK IG11 ...334 C1
  CDMY/SEVK IG5 ...317 K5
Mayes Cl BSF CM23 ...138 A6
Mayesford Rd CHDH RM6 ...317 K2
Mayes La CHLM/GWD CM2 ...241 K4
  HAR CO12 ...109 L7
  RCHLM CM5 ...242 B4
Mayes Pl GTDUN CM6 ...117 H1
Mayfair Av CHDH RM6 ...317 L1
  IL IG1 ...316 A4
  PIT SS13 ...305 H7
Mayfair Cl COLS CO2 * ...152 C2
Mayfair Gdns WFD IG8 ...295 K4
Mayfair Ter STHGT/OAK N14 ...272 F2
Mayfield RCOLW CO6 ...77 K4
  HLWE CM17 ...187 N8
Mayfield Av HOC/HUL SS5 ...287 H6
  SOSN SS2 ...328 F2
  STHGT/OAK N14 ...272 B8
  WFD IG8 ...295 K3
Mayfield Cl COLN CO4 ...9 J1
  HLWE CM17 ...187 N8
Mayfield Crs ED N9 ...273 N5
Mayfield Gdns BRW CM14 ...280 F7
Mayfield La KESG IP5 ...27 M5
Mayfield Pk BSF CM23 ...162 A2
Mayfield Rd BCTR RM8 ...317 K3
  BELV DA17 ...346 B2
  CHES/WCR EN8 ...229 P7
  CHLM/WR CM1 ...217 H9
  IPNE IP4 ...26 B4
  PEND EN3 ...274 A1
  PLSTW E13 ...333 J4
  WALTH E17 ...294 B6
Mayfields CDW/CHF RM16 ...339 M9
  KESG IP5 ...27 M5
Mayfields Cl CDW/CHF RM16 ...339 M9
Mayflower Av HAR CO12 ...15 G4
Mayflower Cl COLW CO3 * ...126 D8
  SOCK/AV RM15 ...338 F4
  WAB EN9 ...231 H2
Mayflower Dr MAL CM9 ...244 B3
Mayflower Gdns BSF CM23 ...136 G8

Mayflower Rd BCAYE CM11 ...283 J6
  CDW/CHF RM16 ...348 F5
Mayflowers SBF/HAD SS7 ...305 N8
Mayflower Wy CHONG CM5 ...235 M6
  SUD CO10 ...47 J9
Mayfly Cl RIPW IP8 ...29 N2
Mayford Wy RCOS CO16 ...181 L7
Maygreen Crs EMPK RM11 ...318 F2
Mayhew Cl CHING E4 ...274 D9
Mayland Av CVI SS8 ...344 C3
Mayland Cl MAL CM9 ...222 E7
  RCHLM CM5 ...267 P2
Mayland Gn RCHLM CM5 ...268 A1
Mayland Hl RCHLM CM5 ...268 B5
Mayland Rd BRTR CM77 ...144 C6
Maylands Av HCH RM12 ...318 C6
Maylands Dr BRTR CM77 ...144 C6
Maylands Wy HARH RM3 ...299 P5
Maylins Dr SBW CM21 ...187 L2
Maynard Cl ERITH DA8 ...346 E5
  GTDUN CM6 ...141 L5
Maynard Gn RCHLM CM5 ...268 A1
Maynard Pl POTB/CUF EN6 ...228 D8
Maynard Rd WALTH E17 ...294 F9
Maynards EMPK RM11 ...319 K2
The Maynards SAFWN CB10 * ...51 L8
Mayne Crest CHLM/WR CM1 ...218 D5
Mayo Cl CHES/WCR EN8 ...229 P7
Mayplace Av DART DA1 ...346 F9
Mayplace Cl BXLYHN DA7 ...346 A8
Mayplace Rd BXLYHN DA7 ...346 A8
Mayplace Rd East
  BXLYHN DA7 ...346 B8
Maypole Cl SAFWS CB11 ...65 K2
Maypole Crs BARK/HLT IG6 ...296 E4
  ERITH DA8 ...347 J2
Maypole Dr CHIG IG7 ...277 H9
Maypole Green Rd COLS CO2 ...151 M5
Maypole Rd K/T/MI CO5 ...173 P7
  MAL CM9 ...222 A2
  WIT CM8 ...198 A7
The Maypole CHLM/GWD CM6 ...92 A5
May Rd CHING E4 ...294 D3
  IPSE IP5 ...26 B9
  PLSTW E13 ...333 K2
Maysent Av BRTR CM7 ...145 J1
May's La RCOLE CO7 ...104 F4
May St ROY SS40 ...48 B8
Mayswood Gdns DAGE RM10 ...318 B8
Maytree Cl RAIN RM13 ...336 D2
Mayville Rd IL IG1 ...315 H5
  WAN E11 ...315 H5
May Wk CHLM/GWD CM2 ...240 B3
  STSD CM24 ...114 D6
Maywin Dr EMPK RM11 ...319 L3
Maze Green Rd BSF CM23 ...137 H7
Maze Green Rd BSF CM23 ...137 J7
The Maze LOS SS9 ...307 N8
Mazoe Cl BSF CM23 ...137 L9
Mazoe Rd BSF CM23 ...137 L9
McAdam Cl HOD EN11 ...208 D5
McAdam Dr ENC/FH EN2 ...272 C1
McCalmont Dr RAYL SS6 ...286 F9
McCudden Rd DART DA1 ...347 L8
McCullum Rd BOW E3 ...332 C1
McDivitt Wk LOS SS9 ...308 B9
McDowall Cl CAN/RD2 E16 ...333 K5
McEntee Av WALTH E17 ...294 B5
McEwan Wy SRTFD E15 * ...332 C1
McGrath Rd FSTGT E7 ...315 J8
McIntosh Cl ROM RM1 ...298 D7
McIntosh Rd ROM RM1 ...298 D7
McKenzie Rd BROX EN10 ...208 D8
Mead Barn EPP CM16 ...254 F6
Mead Cl CDW/CHF RM16 ...339 L9
  GPK RM2 ...298 F6
  LOU IG10 ...276 C1
Mead Ct WAB EN9 ...252 E4
Mead Crs CHING E4 ...294 F1
Meade Rd BCAYE CM11 ...283 C1
Meadgate PIT SS13 ...305 H7
Meadgate Av CHLM/GWD CM2 ...5 K7
  WFD IG8 ...295 P2
Meadgate Rd HOD EN11 ...208 A3
Meadgate Ter CHLM/GWD CM2 ...5 K7
Mead Gv CHDH RM6 ...297 L7
Mead Monks RCHLM CM5 ...242 C8
Meadowbank WCHMH N21 ...272 E5
Meadow Clays SAFWS CB11 ...50 C6
Meadowcourt Rd CHLM/GWD CM2 ...120 D8
  CHING E4 ...274 F7
  COS CO15 ...182 C6
  FX IP11 ...34 E1
  HOM E9 ...314 C7
  OOD CO5 ...98 A8
  PEND EN3 ...252 B9
  RCOLE CO7 ...130 F9
  SBF/HAD SS7 ...306 E9
  SLH/COR SS17 ...351 H1
Meadow Cl BCAYE CM11 * ...283 K6
  WICKE SS11 ...285 K8
Meadow Crs IPSE IP3 ...31 M1
Meadowcroft STSD CM24 ...114 B8
Meadowcroft Cl
  PLMGR N13 * ...272 C2
Meadowcroft Rd
  SLH/COR SS17 * ...340 C2
Meadowcroft Rd PLMGR N15 ...272 F8
Meadowcross WAB EN9 ...231 K4
Meadow Dr SOS SS1 ...329 N6
  VGE SS16 ...323 J6
Meadowford SAFWS CB11 ...64 G8
Meadowford Cl THMD SE28 ...114 B8
Meadow Grass Cl COLW CO3 ...126 D8
Meadowland BSF CM23 ...137 M5
Meadowlands BSF CM23 ...137 M5
  EMPK RM11 ...319 K2
  KIR/NAC IP10 ...38 A1
Meadow La CBE/LIN CB1 ...64 G8
  K/T/MI CO5 ...202 F7
  SUD CO10 ...66 C3
  WICKE SS11 ...285 K5
Meadow Ms RCHLM CM3 ...264 E9

Meadow Ri BCAYE CM11 ...283 K6
  ING CM4 ...259 H1
Meadow Rd BARK IG11 ...316 G9
  CHLM/WR CM1 ...339 M8
  COLS CO2 ...151 N8
  DACW RM9 ...317 N8
  EPP CM16 ...254 B5
  HOC/HUL SS5 ...287 H6
  IL IG1 ...316 C3
  RCHLM CM5 ...285 P5
  ROMW/RG RM7 ...318 B3
  SAFWN CB10 ...36 E8
  SBF/HAD SS7 ...327 H4
Meadows Cl LEY E10 ...314 D4
  RBRW/HUT CM13 ...301 M5
  RCOLE CO7 ...129 N9
Meadows Gn RCHLM CM3 ...242 D2
Meadowside BRTR CM7 ...145 H1
  CHLM/GWD CM2 ...5 J2
Meadow Side CHLM/WR CM1 ...5 F1
Meadowside Gdns IPNE IP4 ...26 D3
Meadowside Rd UPMR RM14 ...319 P7
The Meadows BSF CM23 ...137 K9
  RBRW/HUT CM13 ...301 M5
  SBW CM21 ...187 P2
Meadowsweet Cl BSF CM23 ...137 H8
  CAN/RD2 E16 ...333 N5
  HVHL CB9 ...41 H2
The Meadow HERT/BAY SG13 ...208 B1
Meadowvale Cl IPNE IP4 ...25 N4
Meadow Vw EPP CM16 ...253 H8
  K/T/MI CO5 ...173 N8
Meadow View Cl COLW CO5 ...151 H1
Meadow View Pk
  RCOS CO16 ...181 L3
Meadow View Rd SUD CO10 ...60 C4
Meadow Wk DAGW RM9 ...317 N8
  SWFD E18 ...295 K8
Meadow Wy BOC CM7 ...290 F1
  BRTR CM77 ...145 M9
  CHIG IG7 ...276 D8
  COS CO15 ...307 P2
  HOC/HUL SS5 ...307 H2
  K/T/MI CO5 ...177 J3
  RCHLM CM5 ...267 H5
  SBW CM21 ...187 P3
  UPMR RM14 ...319 P5
  WICKW SS12 ...305 J4
Mead Vw BUNT SG9 ...
Mead Wk CHONG CM5 ...235 L9
Meadway CVI SS8 ...344 F3
  CHLM/GWD CM2 ...316 F6
  EPP CM16 ...298 F6
  GPK RM2 ...298 F6
  GRAYS RM17 ...349 N2
  HOD EN11 ...208 A4
  HSTD CO9 ...97 H8
  MAL CM9 ...244 C1
  PEND EN3 ...105 P5
  RAYL SS6 ...252 A6
  SBF/HAD SS7 ...307 K8
  STHGT/OAK N14 ...272 C8
  WFD IG8 ...295 M2
The Meadway BKHH IG9 ...275 N7
  POTB/CUF EN6 ...228 E7
  WOS/PRIT SS0 ...328 C5
Meakins Cl LOS SS9 ...308 A9
Meanley Rd MNPK E12 ...315 P7
Mearns Pl CHLM/GWD CM2 ...218 F1
Meath Rd IL IG1 ...316 D5
  SRTFD E15 ...333 J2
Medcalfe Ter SUD CO10 * ...20 D5
Medcalf Rd PEND EN3 ...252 F1
Medebridge Rd
  CDW/CHF RM16 ...339 H2
Mede Wy RCOLE CO7 ...153 K3
Medhurst Cl BOW E3 ...332 B1
Medick Ct GRAYS RM17 ...349 P4
Medina Rd GRAYS RM17 ...349 N4
Medlar Dr SOCK/AV RM15 ...338 C4
Medlar Rd GRAYS RM17 ...349 N4
Medlars Md RBSF CM22 ...144 C4
Medley Rd BRTR CM7 ...144 C4
Medoc Cl IPS1 ...305 H7
Medora Rd ROMW/RG RM7 ...298 C8
Medusa Ct WCO12 ...110 C6
Medway Av WIT CM8 ...196 C2
Medway Cl CHLM/WR CM1 ...316 D7
  IL IG1 ...316 D7
Medway Crs LOS SS9 ...327 L5
Medway Rd BOW E3 ...332 B2
  DART DA1 ...346 F8
Meekings Rd SUD CO10 ...21 J4
The Meers FOS CO15 ...158 F8
Meeson Mdw MAL CM9 ...243 P2
Meeson Rd SRTFD E15 ...315 J9
Meeson's La GRAYS RM17 ...349 J2
Meesons Md RCOLE CO7 ...308 E4
Meesons Wharf SRTFD E15 * ...332 F2
Meeting Fld SUD CO10 ...46 F4
Meeting La HSTD CO9 ...57 J3
  K/T/MI CO5 ...203 M2

Meggison Wy SBF/HAD SS7 ...325 P3
Megs Wy BRTR CM7 ...145 L5
Meister Cl IL IG1 ...316 C3
Melba Ct CHLM/WR CM1 ...239 K1
Melba Gdns TIL RM18 ...350 B4
Melbourne Av CHLM/WR CM1 ...217 L6
Melbourne Cha COLS CO2 ...152 C5
Melbourne Gdns CHDH RM6 ...297 M9
Melbourne Rd COS CO15 ...6 C2
  EHAM E6 ...334 A1
  IL IG1 ...316 C3
  IPNE IP4 ...26 C4
  LEY E10 ...314 E2
  TIL RM18 ...349 P6
  WALTH E17 ...294 B9
Melbourne Wy EN EN1 ...273 L5
Melcombe Rd GDMY/SEVK IG3 ...317 H4
Melford Av BARK IG11 ...316 F8
Melford Cl COLW CO3 ...126 E6
Melford Gv BRTR CM77 ...144 E7
Melford Rd EHAM E6 ...334 A4
  IL IG1 ...316 E4
  SUD CO10 ...45 K1
  SUD CO10 ...46 F9
  WALTH E17 ...294 B8
  WAN E11 ...315 H4
Melford Wy FX IP11 ...10 B4
Melksham Cl HARH RM5 ...299 L4
Melksham Gdns HARH RM5 ...299 K4
Melksham Sn HARH RM5 ...299 K4
Melling Dr EN EN1 ...251 M9
Mellis Av GDMY/SEVK IG3 ...317 K2
Mellis Ct FX IP11 ...11 J2
Mellish Gdns WFD IG8 ...295 K2
Mellish Wy EMPK RM11 ...299 H6
Mellor Cha COLW CO3 ...127 H6
Mellor Rd EHAM E6 ...315 P8
Mellow Purgess Cl LAIN SS15 ...303 K9
Mellow Purgess End
  LAIN SS15 ...303 K9
Mellows Rd CLAY IG5 ...296 A7
Mell Rd MAL CM9 ...225 K3
Melon Rd WAN E11 ...315 H5
Melplash Cl BSF CM23 ...26 D7
Melplash Rd IPSE IP5 ...26 D7
Melrose Gdns COS CO15 ...182 D8
  IPNE IP4 ...26 A3
Melrose Rd K/T/MI CO5 ...202 E6
Melstock Av UPMR RM14 ...319 P6
Melton Cl RCOS CO16 ...181 K9
Melton Gdns ROM RM1 ...298 E6
Melville Dr WICKW SS12 ...305 J2
Melville Heath RCHLM CM5 ...287 H2
Melville Rd IPNE IP4 ...17 K5
  RAIN RM13 ...336 F4
  ROMW/RG RM7 ...298 A4
  WALTH E17 ...294 C4
Melvyn Cl CHESW EN7 ...228 G7
Memorial Av SRTFD E15 ...333 H5
Memory Cl MAL CM9 ...244 B5
Mendip Cl RAYL SS6 ...306 C4
  WICKE SS11 ...285 K9
Mendip Crs WOS/PRIT SS0 ...328 B1
Mendip Dr KESG IP5 ...26 E5
Mendip Rd BXLYHN DA7 ...346 D6
  CHLM/WR CM1 ...217 L5
  EMPK RM11 ...299 K6
  GNTH/NBYPK IG2 ...296 F9
  LOS SS9 ...328 B2
The Mendips WOS/PRIT SS0 * ...328 A1
Mendlesham Cl RCOS CO16 ...181 L9
Mendoza Cl EMPK RM11 ...299 K9
Menin Rd COLS CO2 ...151 N8
Menon Dr ED N9 ...273 N9
Mentmore VGE SS16 ...323 J2
Menzies Av LAIN SS15 ...302 C9
Meon Cl CHLM/WR CM1 ...218 C5
Meppel Av CVI SS8 ...344 E8
Merbury Rd THMD SE28 ...334 E8
Mercer Av SBN/FI SS3 ...330 F2
Mercer Rd BCAYE CM11 ...283 L3
Mercers HLWW/ROY CM19 ...210 B6
Mercers Av SOS SS1 ...
Mercers Wy COL CO1 ...161 N1
Merchant St BOW E3 * ...332 C5
  RCHLM CM5 ...287 H1
Mercia Cl CHLM/GWD CM2 ...240 F5
Mercury Cl WICKE SS11 ...285 L8
Mercury Gdns ROM RM1 ...298 E6
Meredene BSDN SS14 ...324 E1
Meredith Rd CDW/CHF RM16 ...350 B2
  COS CO15 ...6 D4
  IP IP1 ...24 F1
Meredith St PLSTW E13 ...333 K3
Merefield SBW CM21 ...187 M5
Mere Gdns IPNE IP4 ...26 E7
Meres Cl WIT CM8 ...197 H3
Merewood Rd BXLYHN DA7 ...346 B7
Mereworth Rd RCHLM CM5 ...286 F5
Meriadoc Dr RCHLM CM3 ...286 F5
Meriden Cl BARK/HLT IG6 ...296 D5
  RDWN RM9 ...182 B8
Meridian Sq SRTFD E15 ...314 G9
Meridian Wy ED N9 ...273 P9
  WARE SG12 ...
Merilands Rd WOS/PRIT SS0 ...328 C3
Merino Cl WAN E11 ...295 M8
Merivale Cl BARK/HLT IG6 ...106 A5
Merivale Rd MGTR CO11 ...106 A5
Merlewood CHLM/WR CM1 ...297 J1
Merlin Cl BARK/HLT IG6 ...298 C5
  CRW RM5 ...255 K4
  WAB EN9 ...
Merlin Ct COL CO1 ...344 L1
Merlin End COLN CO4 ...128 C6
Merlin Gdns CRW RM5 ...298 C5
Merlin Ms CHLM/WR CM1 ...217 N6
Merlin PI CHLM/WR CM1 ...298 C3
  CRW RM5 ...298 C3
  MNPK E12 ...315 H4
Merlin Rd CHTY IP2 ...315 N4
  CRW RM5 ...298 C5
Merlin Wy EPP CM16 ...233 P6
  WICKE SS11 ...285 J7

Mermagen Dr RAIN RM13 ...318 C9
Mermaid Wy WAB EN9 ...244 C2
Merriam Av HOM E9 ...314 C8
Merriam Cl CHING E4 ...294 F2
Merrick Ct IP IP1 ...81 N9
Merridene WCHMH N21 ...272 G5
Merrielands Crs DAGW RM9 ...335 N2
Merrilees Crs COS CO15 ...182 E7
Merring Wy WAB EN9 ...210 A9
Merrion Cl RIPW IP8 ...24 D9
Merrivale SBF/HAD SS7 ...325 P4
  STHGT/OAK N14 ...272 C1
Merryfield Av REDBR IG4 ...295 N8
Merryfield Cl SBF/HAD SS7 ...325 P5
Merryfields Av HOC/HUL SS5 ...287 H9
Merryhill Cl CHING E4 ...294 E2
Merryhills Dr ENC/FH EN2 ...272 C5
Merrylands LAIN SS15 ...303 H8
Merrymount Gdns COS CO15 ...182 C8
Mersea Av K/T/MI CO5 ...202 E6
Mersea Crs WICKW SS12 ...305 M2
Mersea Fleet Wy SRTFD E15 * ...145 M5
Mersea Rd COLS CO2 ...152 B5
  K/T/MI CO5 ...176 F8
  K/T/MI CO5 ...177 J2
Mersea Vw RCOS CO16 ...205 H1
Mersey Av UPMR RM14 ...320 A1
Mersey Rd ERITH DA8 ...25 N8
  WIT CM8 ...197 H1
Merstham Dr RCOS CO16 ...181 M7
Merten Cl CHDH RM6 ...317 M2
Merten Rd CHDH RM6 ...152 E7
Merton Gv CDW/CHF RM16 ...350 B2
  RCHLM CM5 ...287 J2
Merton Rd BARK IG11 ...316 G9
  COLS CO2 ...151 L5
  CDMY/SEVK IG3 ...287 K8
  HOC/HUL SS5 ...287 K8
  SBF/HAD SS7 ...325 P2
  WALTH E17 ...294 F9
Messant Cl GPK RM2 ...299 J6
Messines Rd COLS CO2 ...151 N2
Messing Gn K/T/MI CO5 ...174 A3
Mess Rd SBN/FI SS3 ...330 E9
Meteor Rd WOS/PRIT SS0 ...328 D1
Metford Crs PEND EN3 ...252 D6
Mettersgate BSDN SS14 ...3 H5
Methuen Rd BELV DA17 ...346 A2
Metropolitan Cl POP/IOD E14 ...332 D5
Metsons La CHLM/WR CM1 ...257 N8
Meux Av CVI SS8 ...344 C2
Meux Cl CHESW EN7 ...251 M1
Mews Ct CHLM/GWD CM2 ...5 F6
Mews Pi WFD IG8 ...295 K1
The Mews BSF CM23 ...162 D2
  HOC/HUL SS5 ...307 M1
  REDBR IG4 ...295 N8
  ROM RM1 ...298 D8
  SBW CM21 ...187 M1
  SUD CO10 * ...61 K3
Meyer Av CVI SS8 ...55 J3
Meyer Gn EN EN1 ...251 M8
Meyer Rd ERITH DA8 ...346 B4
Meynell Av CVI SS8 ...344 F3
Meynell Crs HOM E9 ...314 A9
Meynell Gdns HOM E9 ...314 A9
Meynell Rd HARH RM3 ...298 C3
  HOM E9 ...314 A9
Meyrick Crs COLS CO2 ...152 A1
Mey Wk HOC/HUL SS5 ...307 M1
Micawber Wy CHLM/GWD CM2 ...217 L4
Michael Gdns EMPK RM11 ...299 J8
Michael Rd WAN E11 ...315 H3
Michaels Rd BSF CM23 ...137 N6
Michaelstowe Cl HAR CO12 ...109 M6
Michaelstowe Dr HAR CO12 ...109 M6
Michigan Av MNPK E12 ...315 P6
Michigan Cl KESG IP5 ...26 C4
Mickfield Ms FX IP11 ...34 C6
Micklegate Rd FX IP11 ...11 F6
Mid Colne VGE SS16 ...324 C2
Middleborough COL CO1 ...8 B4
Middle Boy ABR/ST RM4 ...277 J2
Middle Dr SLH/COR SS17 ...324 A5
Middlefield HSTD CO9 ...98 A7
Middlefield Av HOD EN11 ...208 D5
Middlefield Cl HOD EN11 ...208 D5
Middlefield Rd HOD EN11 ...208 D5
  MGTR CO11 ...106 F5
Middle Gn BRWN CM15 ...258 F7
  RCOLW CO6 ...100 B7
Middle King BRTR CM7 ...145 N5
Middle Md RCFD SS4 ...288 D5
Middlemead CHLM/GWD CM2 ...262 E5
  RCHLM CM5 ...263 H7
Middle Mead Cl
  CHLM/GWD CM2 ...262 E5
Middle Ml COL CO1 ...
Middle Rd PLSTW E13 ...333 K2
  RBRW/HUT CM13 ...301 M1
  WAB EN9 ...252 E2
Middle Rw BSF CM23 ...137 L8
Middlesburg PI COL CO1 ...8 D3
Middlesex Av LOS SS9 ...328 A4
Middle St SAFWS CB11 ...88 B4
  WAB EN9 ...231 K2
Middleton Av CHING E4 ...294 C1
Middleton Cl CHING E4 ...274 C9
  CHTY IP2 ...24 E9
  RCOS CO16 ...181 N7
Middleton Dr
  BERM/RHTH SE16 ...332 A9
Middleton Gdns
  GNTH/NBYPK IG2 ...316 C1
Middleton Hall La
  BRWN CM15 ...281 H8
Middleton Rd BRWN CM15 ...281 H7
  NHMKT IP6 ...22 D3
  SUD CO10 ...
Middleton Rw RCHLM CM3 ...287 H2
Middle Wy SUD CO10 ...46 G3
Middlewick Cl COLS CO2 ...152 B5

Midfield Av BXLYHN DA7 ...346 B8
Midguard Wy MAL CM9 ...243 P2
Midhurst Av WOS/PRIT SS0 ...328 E2
Midhurst CI HCH RM12 ...318 F6
Midland CI COLS CO2 ...152 A2
Midland Rd LEY E10 ...314 F2
Midlothian Rd BOW E3 ...332 C4
Midship CI
 BERM/RHTH SE16 * ...332 A8
Midship Point POP/IOD E14 * ...332 D9
Midsummer Meadow
 SBN/FI SS3 ...330 D5
Midway COS CO15 ...206 C6
Midway Rd COLS CO2 ...151 M4
Mighell Av WDBR IG4 ...295 N9
Milano Av WDBR IP12 ...27 P5
Milbank CHLM/WR CM1 ...218 G7
Milbanke CI SBN/FI SS3 ...330 B5
Milburn Crs CHLM/WR CM1 ...239 L1
Milch La RUNW IP3 ...144 B9
Milden Rd CHTY IP2 ...24 F6
Mildmayes VGE SS16 ...323 K2
Mildmay Rd BOC CM0 ...291 H3
 CHLM/GWD CM2 ...5 G7
 IL IG1 ...316 C5
 IPSE IP3 ...30 C1
 ROMW/RG RM7 ...298 B9
Mildmays RCHLM CM5 ...241 P2
Mildred Rd ERITH DA8 ...346 D3
Mile CI WAB EN9 ...252 F3
Mile End PI WCHPL E1... ...332 A4
Mile End Rd BOW E3 ...332 C3
 COLS CO2 ...127 P5
The Mile End WALTH E17 ...294 A5
Miles CI COLW CO3 ...126 F9
 HLWW/ROY CM19 ...210 C4
Miles Dr THMD SE28 ...334 F8
Miles Gray Rd BSDN SS14 ...303 M7
Milestone CI ED N9 ...273 M9
Milford CI RCOLE CO7 ...155 K5
Milford Rd CDW/CHF RM16 ...339 N8
Military Rd COL CO1 ...152 B1
Military Wy HAR CO12 ...109 M6
Milk St CAN/RD E16 ...333 M3
Milkwell Gdns WFD IG8 ...295 L4
Millacres WARE SG12 * ...184 B5
Millais Av MNPK E12 ...316 B7
Millais PI TIL RM18 ...350 B5
Millais Rd EN EN1 ...275 L4
 WAN E11 ...314 F6
Millars CI RCHLM CM3 ...265 H9
The Millars CHLM/WR CM1 ...193 P9
Millbank Av CHONG CM5 ...235 L8
Millbridge Rd WIT CM8 ...197 J2
Millbrook Gdns CHDH RM6...317 M1
 GPK RM2 ...298 D6
Millbrook Rd ED N9 ...273 N7
Mill Cswy ROY SG8 ...48 F5
Mill Cha HSTD CO9 ...97 P6
 HVHL CB9 ...55 M5
Mill CI BOC CM0 ...248 B6
 BRTR CM7 ...94 A6
 CHLM/WR CM1 ...216 B6
 FX IP11 ...10 D2
 K/T/MI CO5 ...173 P7
 RBSF CM22 ...114 F6
 RIPS/CAP IP9 ...28 A9
 WARE SG12 ...184 A3
Mill Ct GTDUN CM6 ...166 F7
Millcrest Rd CHESW EN7 ...228 G7
Millcroft BSF CM23 ...137 M5
Mill End GTDUN CM6 ...92 B6
Millennium CI CAN/RD E16...333 K6
Millennium Wy CRWCH SE10...333 H9
Miller Av PEND EN3 * ...252 D8
Miller's Barn Rd COS CO15 ...206 F3
Millers CI BRTR CM7 ...121 K7
 BSF CM23 ...137 H9
 CHIG IG7 ...277 J8
 COLW CO3 ...126 F9
 GTDUN CM6 ...166 F1
 RCOLW CO6 ...102 E9
Millers Ct CHLM/GWD CM2 ...240 E4
Millersdale HLWW/ROY CM19 ...210 C7
Millers Green CI ENC/FH EN2 ...272 C2
Millers Green Rd CHONG CM5 ...214 E7
Miller's La CHIG IG7 ...277 J7
 COLW CO3 ...126 D9
 WARE SG12 ...184 F8
Millers Md K/T/MI CO5 ...173 K1
Millers Rw BRTR CM7 ...69M3
Millers Vw IP IP1 ...24 D4
 MHAD SG10 ...160 D4
Mill Fld GTDUN CM6 ...166 F1
 HLWE CM17 ...187 K8
 RIPW IP8 ...24 C1
Millfield CHONG CM5 ...235 P7
 RIPS/CAP IP9 * ...84 D2
Millfield La WALTH E17 ...294 C5
Millfield CI RAYL SS6 ...307 H4
Millfield Gdns IPNE IP4 ...25 P4
Millfield La STDN SG11 ...136 C6
Mill Flds RCHLM CM3 ...242 D4
Millfields BOC CM0 * ...290 G4
 CHLM/WR CM1 ...239 H1
 COLS CO2 * ...151 M9
 K/T/MI CO5 ...173 P7
 SBW CM21 ...187 N1
 STSD CM24 ...114 B9
Millfields Wy HVHL CB9 ...41 L3
Mill Gra BOC CM0 ...290 C1
Mill Gn Rd BOC CM0 ...290 G4
 PIT SS15 ...304 F9
Mill Green Ct PIT SS13 * ...304 G8
Mill Green PI PIT SS13 ...304 F8
Mill Green Rd ING CM4 ...260 A1
Mill Gv CHONG CM5 ...214 B5
Millhaven CI CHDH RM6 ...317 J1
Millheat Wy RCFD SS4 ...309 J6
Mill HI BRTR CM7 ...145 K8
 BRWN CM15 ...281 H6
 BSF CM23 ...137 K1
 CHLM/GWD CM2 ...239 N8

HVHL CB9 ...41 J4
Millhurst Ms HLWE CM17 ...187M8
Millicent Rd LEY E10 * ...314 C3
Milligans Cha
 CHLM/GWD CM2 ...240 A9
Milligan St POP/IOD E14 ...332 C7
Milliners Wy BSF CM23 ...161 P1
Mill La ABR/ST RM4 ...279 H1
 BCAYW CM11 ...284 A6
 BROX EN10 ...208 C9
 BRTR CM7 ...70 A6
 BRTR CM77 ...144 B6
 BRWN CM15 ...145 N8
 BRWN CM15 ...258 B7
 BRWN CM15 ...258 B7
 BUNT SG9 ...87 H5
 CBE/LIN CB1 ...38 B1
 CDW/CHF RM16 ...340 B6
 CHES/WCR EN8 ...230 B7
 CHING E4 ...274 E2
 CHLM/WR CM1 ...218 A2
 CHONG CM5 ...213 H6
 CHONG CM5 ...234 D8
 COLS CO2 ...235 P8
 COLS CO2 ...151 L9
 COLS CO2 ...175 J2
 FOS CO13 ...182 F2
 FX IP11 ...11 F2
 GTDUN CM6 ...141 L6
 GTDUN CM6 ...142 C1
 HAR CO12 ...14 E6
 HLWE CM17 ...187 M8
 HSTD CO9 ...57 P7
 HSTD CO9 ...73 K9
 HSTD CO9 ...99 H1
 ING CM4 ...260 B3
 ING CM4 ...261 N7
 K/T/MI CO5 ...148 L4
 MAL CM9 ...199M9
 MAL CM9 ...200 G4
 MAL CM9 ...222 A8
 MGTR CO11 ...107 J7
 NHMKT IP6 ...22 A2
 NHMKT IP6 ...23 H1
 RBSF CM22 ...163 J9
 RCFD SS4 ...168 A6
 RCHLM CM3 ...168 L6
 RCHLM CM3 ...169 L6
 RCHLM CM3 ...195 M1
 RCHLM CM3 ...220 B8
 RCHLM CM3 ...242 C4
 RCHLM CM3 ...243M9
 RCOLE CO7 ...104 G1
 RCOLE CO7 ...130 A3
 RCOLW CO6 ...78 C1
 RCOLW CO6 ...99 H7
 RCOS CO16 ...156 C8
 RCOS CO15 ...157 J5
 RIPS/CAP IP9 ...84 D2
 RIPW IP8 ...28 J1
 RIPW IP8 ...29 J1
 SAFWN CB10 ...36 B4
 SAFWN CB10 ...51 M8
 SAFWS CB11 ...50 G7
 SBW CM21 ...187 N1
 SLH/COR SS17 ...324 B8
 SLH/COR SS17 ...340 G2
 STDN SG11 ...112 C9
 SUD CO10 ...20 B6
 WIT CM8 ...197 J2
 WOTN CO14 ...159 K5
 WTHK RM20 ...348 G5
Mill Lane CI BROX EN10 ...208 C9
 RCOS CO16 ...156 D8
Millmarsh La PEND EN3 ...274 B1
Mill Park Av HCH RM12 ...319 K4
Mill Park Dr BRTR CM7 ...145 L5
Mill Piece KIR/NAC IP10 ...35 J1
Mill PI DART DA1 ...346 F9
 POP/IOD E14 ...332 B6
Mill Race WARE SG12 ...184 B6
Mill Ri RIPS/CAP IP9 ...83 L4
Mill Rd BCAYE CM11 ...505 L1
 BOC CM0 ...248 B6
 BRTR CM7 ...94 A6
 CAN/RD E16 ...94 C3
 CHLM/WR CM1 ...133 L8
 COLN CO4 ...103 J4
 COLN CO4 ...127 P3
 ERITH DA8 ...346 B5
 GTDUN CM6 ...167 M2
 HSTD CO9 ...42 D9
 HSTD CO9 ...56 D7
 HVHL CB9 ...41 H8
 HVHL CB9 ...43 B1
 IL IG1 ...316 B5
 ING CM4 ...261 M7
 IPSE IP5 ...31 M1
 K/T/MI CO5 ...202 F4
 MAL CM9 ...198 E5
 MAL CM9 ...244 C1
 PUR RM19 ...347 N4
 RBSF CM22 ...115 J4
 RCHLM CM3 ...268 A1
 RCOLE CO7 ...81 H6
 RCOLW CO6 ...126 A3
 RCOLW CO6 ...149 P2

SAFWN CB10 ...66 F7
SAFWS CB11 ...51 H5
SOCK/AV RM15 ...337 P7
SUD CO10 ...44 B4
SUD CO10 ...45 P6
Mills CI PIT SS13 ...305 H6
Mills Gv POP/IOD E14 ...86 B1
Mill Side STSD CM24 ...114 A9
Mills La SUD CO10 ...68 F7
Millsmead Wy LOU IG10 ...276 A1
Millson Bank CHLM/GWD CM2...218 F7
Mills Rd SUD CO10 ...21 H4
The Mills IPNE IP4 ...26 D3
Mill St BSF CM23 ...161 K6
 COL CO1 ...128 B9
 HLWE CM17 ...211 M6
 RCOLE CO7 ...179M7
 RCOLW CO6 ...77 P8
 RCOS CO16 ...78 C1
 RCOS CO15 ...180 C9
Mills Wy RBRW/HUT CM13 ...281M7
Mill Tye SUD CO10 ...61 K6
Millview HSTD CO9 * ...123 H2
Mill Vw SAFWN CB10 ...36 D9
Millview Ct RCFD SS4 ...308 G6
Mill Vue Rd CHLM/GWD CM2 ...218 E9
Mill Wk K/T/MI CO5 ...173 P7
Millway MAL CM9 ...198 C8
Millwell Crs CHIG IG7 ...296 E2
Millwrights K/T/MI CO5 ...173 P7
Milner PI BCAYW CM12 ...282 G3
Milner Rd BCTR RM8 ...317 K4
 SRTFD E15 ...333 H5
 SUD CO10 ...18 E5
Milner St IPNE IP4 ...17 H5
Milnrow RIPW IP8 ...24 D9
Milton Av BRTR CM7 ...145 K6
 EHAM E6 ...315 N9
 HCH RM12 ...318 E4
 VGE SS16 ...322 F2
 WOS/PRIT SS0 ...18 B5
Milton CI COLW CO3 ...127 J9
 RAYL SS6 ...307 J5
 SOSN SS2 ...19 G2
Milton Ct WAB EN9 ...252 F4
Milton Crs CHONG CM5 ...235 L5
 GNTH/NBYPK IG2 ...316 D9
Milton Gdns TIL RM18 ...350 C6
Milton Hall CI SBN/FI SS3 ...330 E3
Milton PI CHLM/WR CM1 ...217 N6
 SOS SS1 ...18 E5
Milton Rd BRW CM14 ...280 E9
 GRAYS RM17 ...349 L2
 HAR CO12 ...14 E6
 MAL CM9 ...244 B2
 MGTR CO11 ...106 A6
 ROM RM1 ...318 F1
 SLH/COR SS17 ...323 N8
 WALTH E17 ...294 D8
 WARE SG12 ...184 A2
 WIT CM8 ...171 N8
 WOS/PRIT SS0 ...18 C4
Milton St IPNE IP4 ...25 P4
 SOSN SS2 ...19 F2
Miltsin Av CVI SS8 ...326 F9
Milverton Gdns
 GDMY/SEVK IG3 ...316 G4
Milwards HLWW/ROY CM19 ...210 C7
Mimosa CI BRWN CM15 ...280 E4
 CHLM/WR CM1 ...218 E5
 HARH RM3 ...299 M4
 VGE SS16 ...322 G2
Minchenden Crs
 STHGT/OAK N14 ...272 C9
Mincher Rd HLWW/ROY CM19...211 H2
Minden Rd SUD CO10 ...20 E5
Minerva CI HAR CO12 ...110 A5
Minerva Rd CHING E4 ...294 E4
Ming St POP/IOD E14 ...332 D7
Minos Wy IP IP1 ...24 E3
Minsmere Dr RCOS CO16 ...181M7
Minsmere Wy SUD CO10 ...61 M4
Minson Rd HOM E9 ...332 A1
Minster Wy EMPK RM11 ...319 L3
 MAL CM9 ...243 P2
Mintern CI PLMGR N13 ...272 C9
Minton Hts RCFD SS4 ...308 D1
Minton La HLWE CM17 ...211 K3
Miramar Av CVI SS8 ...344 B2
Miramar Wy HCH RM12 ...319 J7
Miranda Wk COLN CO4 ...128 F8
Mirosa Dr MAL CM9 ...244 C2
Mirosa Reach MAL CM9 ...244 B2
Mission Gv WALTH E17 ...294 C9
Mission La HSTD CO9 ...81 L6
Mistley End VGE SS16 ...3 J7
Mistley Pth VGE SS16 ...3 J7
Mistley Rd HLW CM20 ...211 H1
Mitcham Rd EHAM E6 ...333 P5
 GDMY/SEVK IG3 ...316 G2
Mitchell Av CVI SS8 ...344 G1
Mitchell Cir BRTR CM7 ...95 H2
Mitchell Dr
 CHES/WCR EN8 ...230 B7
Mitchell Wy RCHLM CM3 ...264 C9
Mitford CI IP IP1 ...23 H8
Mitre Gdns BSF CM23 ...162 A2
Mitre Rd SRTFD E15 ...333 H2
The Mitre POP/IOD E14 ...332 C7
Mitre Wy IPSE IP5 ...17 J7
Mitton V CHLM/GWD CM2 ...218 E9
Moat CI BCAYE CM11 ...284 B5
Moat Edge Gdns
 BCAYW CM12 ...283 H4
Moat End SOS SS1 ...330 A5
Moat Farm Cha WIT CM8 ...197 J1
Moat Farm CI IPNE IP4 ...25 N3
Moat Fld BSDN SS14 ...304 B7
Moat Flds RCOLW CO6 ...126 A1

Moat House Ldg BSDN SS14 * ...3 J3
Moat La BURES CO8 ...75 K5
 ERITH DA8 ...346 F6
Moat Rd RAYL SS6 ...306 G6
Moat Rd HSTD CO9 ...56 D5
 RCOLW CO6 ...126 A1
Moatside BUNT SG9 ...86 B1
Moat Side PEND EN3 ...273 P5
Modlen Rd WOTN CO14 ...159 H7
Moffat Av IPNE IP4 ...26 A2
Mohmmad Khan Rd
 WAN E11 * ...315 J3
Moiety Rd POP/IOD E14 ...332 D9
Mole Hall La SAFWS CB11 ...90 C5
Molehill Green Rbt
 RBSF CM22 ...139M1
Molesworth Rd ENC/FH EN11...208 D1
Mollands VGE SS16 ...324 C2
Mollands Ct SOCK/AV RM15 ...339 H4
Mollands La SOCK/AV RM15 ...338 F4
Mollison Av PEND EN5 ...252 B5
 PEND EN3 ...274 B2
Molrams La CHLM/GWD CM2 ...240 G4
Momples Rd HLW CM20 ...211 H2
Monarch CI HVHL CB9 ...40 F3
 RAIN RM13 ...336 F2
 TIL RM18 ...350 C6
Monarch Dr CAN/RD E16 ...333 N5
Monarch PI BKHH IG9 ...275M8
Monarch Wy
 CHES/WCR EN8 ...252 B3
Monastery Gdns ENC/FH EN2 ...273 J1
Monastery Rd LAIN SS15 ...303 K9
Mona St CAN/RD E16 ...333 J5
Monega Rd FSTGT E7 ...315M8
Moneypiece CI HVHL CB9 ...41 J1
Monier Rd BOW E3 ...314 D9
Monkchester CI LOU IG10 ...254 B9
Monkdowns Rd RCOLW CO6 ...148 A3
Monk Dr CAN/RD E16 ...333 K7
Monkfrith Av STHGT/OAK N14...272 A5
Monkfrith Wy
 STHGT/OAK N14 ...272 A5
 SOSN SS1 ...18 E5
Monks CI WIT CM8 ...197 H1
Monksford Dr HOC/HUL SS5 ...286 B9
Monksgrove LOU IG10 ...276 B4
Monks Hvn SLH/COR SS17 ...341 M2
Monks HI SAFWS CB11 ...65 H5
Monks Lodge Rd RCOLW CO6 ...75 J6
Monks Rd ENC/FH EN2 ...272 C1
 RCOLW CO6 ...99 J9
Monks Wk MAL CM9 ...225 K5
Monkswick Rd HLW CM20 ...210 G1
Monkswood Av WAB EN9 ...252 C5
Monkswood Dr BSF CM23 ...137 J8
Monkwood CI ROM RM1 ...298 F9
Monmouth Av SWFD E18 ...295 L8
Monmouth CI CHTY IP2 ...30 B1
Monmouth Ms DAGE RM10 ...317 N7
Monmouth Rd DAGW RM9 ...317 N7
 ED N9 ...273 N8
 EHAM E6 ...334 A3
Monnow Rd SOCK/AV RM15 ...337 P7
Monoux CI BCAYE CM11 ...283 L7
Monoux Gv WALTH E17 ...294 D5
Monroe Crs EN EN1 ...251 N9
Mons Av BCAYE CM11 ...283 L6
Monson Rd BROX EN10 ...208 C8
Mons Rd COLS CO2 ...151 N2
Montague Av LOS SS9 ...327 L4
Montague PI CVI SS8 ...344 B2
Montague Rd FX IP11 ...11 K2
 WAN E11 ...315 J4
Montague Wy BCAYW CM12 ...283 H3
Montagu Gdns
 CHLM/WR CM1 ...218 D4
 WALTH E17 ...294 D1
Montaigu Rd ED N9 ...273 P9
Montait Rd WFD IG8 ...295 L2
Montana Rd KESG IP5 ...26 F4
Montayne Rd CHES/WCR EN8 ...252 A2
Montbretia CI COLW CO3 ...126 G9
Montefiore Av BARK IG11 ...316 D8
Montefiore Av TAYL SS6 ...286 F8
Montesquieu Ter
 CAN/RD E16 * ...333 J6
Montfort Av SLH/COR SS17 ...341 M2
Montfort Gdns BARK/HLT IG6 ...296 D5
Montgomery CI
 CHLM/WR CM1 ...218 D4
 COLS CO2 ...152 C2
Montgomery Crs SBN/FI SS3 ...330 D5
Montgomery Rd HARH RM3 ...299 J2
Montgomery Dr
 CHES/WCR EN8 ...230 B7
Montgomery Rd CHTY IP2 ...30 B1
Monton CI CHTY IP2 ...24 E9
Montpelier CI BCAYW CM12 ...283 H1
Montpelier Gdns CHDH RM6 ...317 K2
 EHAM E6 ...333 N5
Montreal Rd IL IG1 ...316 D2
 TIL RM18 ...350 B8
Montrose Av GPK RM2 ...299 H6
Montrose CI WFD IG8 ...295 K1
Montrose Rd
 CHLM/GWD CM2 ...218 E7
Montsale PIT SS13 ...305 H7
Montserrat Av WFD IG8 ...294 C4
Monument Farm Rd
 KIR/NAC IP10 ...27 H7
Moody St WCHPL E1 ...332 A3

Moon Hall La HVHL CB9 ...41 J6
Moons CI RCFD SS4 ...288 E9
Moorcroft RCFD SS4 ...308 D1
Moorcroft Av SBF/HAD SS7 ...330 F9
Moore Av TIL RM18 ...349 H3
 WTHK RM20 ...349 H5
Moore CI BCAYE CM11 ...283 L3
Moore PI IP IP1 ...22 G9
Moores Av SLH/COR SS17 ...324 B5
Moorescroft BRWN CM15 ...258 B7
Moorey CI SRTFD E15 ...333 J4
Moorfield CI KESG IP5 ...27 H4
Moorfield Rd PEND EN3 ...251 P9
Moorfields HLWS CM18 ...210 D8
Moorhaven SOCK/AV RM15 ...161 N2
 CHESW EN8 ...242 B7
Moor Hall Rd HLWE CM17 ...187 N8
Moorhen Av BOC CM0 ...247 H2
Moorhouse Gn RCOLE CO7 ...104 F8
Moorhurst Av CHESW EN7 ...228 G8
The Moorings BSF CM23 ...137M8
Moorland La UPMR RM14 ...320 C3
Moor Park CI LOS SS9 ...327M1
Moor Park Gdns LOS SS9 ...327M1
Moor Rd COLN CO4 ...103 N5
Moors CI RCOLE CO7 ...155 K5
Moors Cft BRTR CM7 ...145 N3
Moor's Farm Cha MAL CM9 ...199 H9
Moorsfield SUD CO10 ...61 L6
Moorside COL CO1 ...9 H6
Moors La BRTR CM77 ...144 A3
 GTDUN CM6 ...165 C2
 RCOLE CO7 ...155 K5
Mope La WIT CM8 ...197 N7
Mopsies Rd BSDN SS14 ...304 D9
Moran Av CHLM/WR CM1 ...218 A4
Morant Gdns CRW RM5 ...298 A2
Morant Rd CDH/CHF RM16 ...350 C1
 COL CO1 ...152 C1
Morant St POP/IOD E14 ...332 D7
Moray CI ROM RM1 ...298 D4
Morebarn Rd RCOLE CO7 ...130 D5
Morecambe CI HCH RM12 ...318 G7
 WCHPL E1 * ...332 A5
More CI CAN/RD E16 ...333 J6
Moreland CI SBF/HAD SS7 ...305 P8
 SBF/HAD SS7 ...305 P9
 SOS SS1 ...330 F2
Moreland Rd WICKE SS11 ...285 H6
Morelands Av
 CDW/CHF RM16 ...339M9
Moreland Wy CHING E4 ...274 F9
Morella CI RCOLE CO7 ...155 K7
Morello Ct COLS CO2 ...152 B7
Moremead WAB EN9 ...252 G3
Mores La BRW CM14 ...280 A2
Moreton Br CHONG CM5 ...213 H9
Moreton CI CHESW EN7 ...229 N6
Moreton Ct DART DA1 ...346 D8
Moreton Gdns WFD IG8 ...295 P2
Moreton Rd CHONG CM5 ...213 N9
 CHONG CM5 ...234 F2
Moretons CHLM/GWD CM2 ...240 AB
 PIT SS13 ...304 F9
Moretons PI PIT SS13 ...304 F9
Moretons Ms PIT SS13 ...304 F9
Morgan Av WALTH E17 ...294 G8
Morgan CI DAGE RM10 ...317 P9
Morgan Ct NHMKT IP6 ...22 D4
Morgan Dr EPP CM16 ...254 F6
Morgan Dr IP IP1 ...24 D2
Morgan St BOW E3 ...332 B3
 CAN/RD E16 ...333 K5
Morgan Wy RAIN RM13 ...337 H3
 WFD IG8 ...295 P2
Morice Rd HOD EN11 ...208 C3
Morieux Rd LEY E10 ...314 C3
Morland Rd DAGE RM10 ...317 P9
 IL IG1 ...316 C4
 IPSE IP5 ...30 G2
 WALTH E17 ...293 M9
Morland Wy CHES/WCR EN8 ...230 B7
Morley Av CHING E4 ...294 G4
Morley Gv HLW CM20 ...13 G4
Morley HI ENC/FH EN2 ...251 J8
Morley Link SLH/COR SS17 ...323 N9
Morley Rd BARK IG11 ...334 E1
 CHDH RM6 ...297M9
 LEY E10 ...98 A6
 K/T/MI CO5 ...169 L1
 LEY E10 ...314 F2
 SRTFD E15 ...333 J2
Morley Sq CDW/CHF RM16 ...350 B2
Mornington Av ENC/FH EN2 ...273 J1
 IL IG1 ...316 B2
 WAN E11 ...315 K1
Mornington Gv BOW E3 ...22 G2
Mornington Rd CHING E4 ...274 G6
 RCFD SS4 ...309 H5
Mornington Crs CVI SS8 ...344 F1
 SBF/HAD SS7 ...327 J3
Mornington Gv BOW E3 ...314 F3
Mornington Rd CHING E4 ...274 G6
 CVI SS8 ...326 F9
 WFD IG8 ...295 K1
Mornings
 HLWW/ROY CM19 ...210 D8
Morpeth Gv HOM E9 ...332 A1
Morpeth St BETH E2 ...332 A3
Morrab Gdns GDMY/SEVK IG3 ...316 G5
Morris CI HOD EN11 ...208 D1
Morrin's Cha SBN/FI SS3 ...331 J5
Morris CI SBN/FI SS3 ...331 J5
Morris Av BCAYE CM11 ...283 L7
 COS CO15 ...206 D6
 MNPK E12 ...316 A7

Morris Ct CHING E4 ....274 E9
  LAIN SS15 ....303 J8
  WAB EN9 ....253 J4
Morris Harp SAFWN CB10 ....51 M7
Morrison Av CHING E4 ....294 D8
Morris Rd BARK IG11 ....335 M2
Morris Rd BCTR RM8 ....317 N4
  CHLM/GWD CM2 ....218 C9
  HARH RM5 ....332 E5
  POP/IOD E14 ....332 C5
  WAN E11 ....315 H6
Morrow La RCOLE CO7 ....129 P1
Morse Cl PLSTW E13 ....333 K3
Mors End RCOLE CO7 ....80 A7
Morses La RCOLE CO7 ....179 L5
Morston Rd PEND EN3 ....275 M8
Morston Hall Rd FX IP11 ....33 J9
Morten Cl COL CO1 ....8 A2
Mortham St SRTFD E15 ....333 H1
Mortimer Dr EN EN1 ....273 J4
Mortimer Av CHING E4 ....274 D6
Mortimer Pl SUD CO10 ....44 A2
Mortimer Rd EHAM E6 ....334 A3
  ERITH DA8 ....346 C4
  RAYL SS6 ....306 D2
  SLH/COR SS17 ....106 D8
Mortlake Rd CAN/RD E16 ....335 L6
  IL IG1 ....316 D6
Morton Rd MAL CM9 ....198 B8
  SRTFD E15 ....315 J9
Morville St BOW E3 ....332 D2
Mosbach Gdns
  RBRW/HUT CM13 ....281 L8
Moseley St SOSN SS2 ....329 L5
Moss Bank GRAYS SM17 ....349 J3
Moss Cl VGE SS16 ....324 D5
Moss Dr VGE SS16 ....324 D3
Mossfield Cl COLW CO5 ....127 M9
Mossford Gdn BARK/HLT IG6 ....296 C7
Mossford La BARK/HLT IG6 ....296 D6
Mossford St BOW E3 ....332 C4
Moss La NHMKT IP6 ....23 N8
  ROM RM1 ....318 E1
Moss Rd COL CO1 ....151 H2
  DAGE RM10 ....317 P9
  SOCK/AV RM15 ....338 F5
  WIT CM8 ....197 L1
Moss Wy RCOLW CO6 ....127 H4
Mostyn Gv BOW E3 ....332 C5
Motehill VGE SS16 ....323 K2
Motherwell Wy WTHK RM20 ....348 D3
Mottingham Rd ED N9 ....274 A5
Mottram Cl RIPW RM19 ....24 D9
Motts Cl BRTR CM7 ....145 H2
Mott's La HARLW CM19 ....149 J2
  WIT CM8 ....171 P9
Mott St CHING E4 ....253 H9
Motts Yd GTDUN CM6 ....142 D1
Moules La CBE/LIN CB9 ....38 B5
Moulsham Cha
  CHLM/GWD CM2 ....240 B2
Moulsham Dr
  CHLM/GWD CM2 ....240 A3
Moulsham Hall La
  RCHLM CM3 ....169 H2
Moulsham St CHLM/GWD CM2 ....5 G5
Moulsham Thrift
  CHLM/GWD CM2 ....239 P4
Moultrie Wy UPMR RM14 ....320 B2
Mountain Ash Av LOS SS9 ....308 F2
Mountain Ash Cl COLN CO4 ....128 D5
  SBF/HAD SS7 ....307 L9
Mountain's Farm Rd
  GTDUN CM6 ....166 B1
Mountains Rd MAL CM9 ....198 C6
Mount Av CHING E4 ....299 P5
  HARH RM5 ....307 N1
  HOC/HUL SS5 ....307 N1
  RAYL SS6 ....306 F4
  RBRW/HUT CM13 ....281 L6
  WOS/PRIT SS0 ....328 B6
Mountbatten Ct SUD CO10 ....47 J9
Mountbatten Ct BKHH IG9 ....275 N8
  IP IP1 ....16 A2
Mountbatten Dr COLS CO2 ....152 C3
  SBN/FI SS3 ....330 D5
Mountbatten Rd BRTR CM7 ....145 L2
  SUD CO10 ....47 J9
Mountbatten Wy
  CHLM/WR CM1 ....218 C4
Mount Bovers La
  HOC/HUL SS5 ....307 P4
Mount Cl RAYL SS6 ....306 F5
  WICKE SS11 ....285 K8
Mount Crs BRW CM14 ....300 G1
  HOC/HUL SS5 ....307 P4
Mount Dr IPSE IP5 ....31 M1
  STSD CM24 ....138 B1
Mountdale Gdns LOS SS9 ....328 A2
Mount Dr IPSE IP5 ....31 M1
Mount Echo Av CHING E4 ....274 E7
Mount Echo Dr CHING E4 ....274 F6
Mountfield Cl SLH/COR SS17 ....341 M2
Mountfield Rd EHAM E6 ....334 B2
Mountfields PIT SS13 ....324 B3
Mountfitchet Rd STSD CM24 ....138 B1
Mount Hl HSTD CO9 ....97 N7
Mountain Av CHLM/GWD CM2 .....218 C8
Mountjoy Cl THMD SE28 ....335 J9
Mount Leil Ct East
  WOS/PRIT SS0 ....328 C7
Mount Leil Ct West
  WOS/PRIT SS0 * 328 C7
Mount Lodge Cha MAL CM9 ....198 E6
Mountnessing La
  BRWN CM15 ....259 H8
Mountnessing Rd
  BCAYW CM12 ....282 E1
  BCAYW CM12 ....282 G6
  BRWN CM15 ....259 K6
Mountney Cl ING CM4 ....260 A8

Mount Pleasant HSTD CO9 ....97 P7
  MAL CM9 ....222 A9
  MGTR CO11 * 107 J8
Mount Pleasant Av
  RBRW/HUT CM13 ....281 P5
Mount Pleasant Est MAL CM9 ....198 F6
Mount Pleasant Ms
  HSTD CO9 * 97 P7
Mount Pleasant Rd CHIG IG7 ....296 E1
  CHM RM5 ....298 C3
  RCHLM CM3 ....286 C1
  SAFWS CB11 ....65 L1
  WALTH E17 ....294 B6
Mount Hi HSTD CO9 ....97 N7
Mount Rd BCTR RM8 ....317 N3
  BRTR CM7 ....145 K3
  EPP CM16 ....255 M2
  HVHL CB9 ....41 L4
  IL IG1 ....316 C7
  RCOLW CO6 ....148 A4
  SBF/HAD SS7 ....326 C2
  WICKE SS11 ....285 K8
The Mount BCAYE CM11 ....283 M5
  BRW CM14 ....280 F9
  CHESW EN7 ....229 J5
  COLW CO5 ....127 J9
  HARH RM5 ....279 H9
  MAL CM9 ....225 J2
  SLH/COR SS17 ....341 N2
Mount Vw BCAYE CM11 ....283 M6
  ENC/FH EN2 ....250 E8
Mountview Cl VGE SS16 ....324 D5
Mountview Crs BOC CM0 ....247 H1
Mount View Rd CHING E4 ....274 F6
Mountview Rd CHESW EN7 ....229 K5
  COLS CO2 ....182 B8
Mount Wy WICKE SS11 ....285 K8
Mount Zion SBF/HAD SS7 * 326 C5
Moverons La RCOLE CO7 ....178 G3
Movers La BARK IG11 ....316 A1
Mowbray Rd HLW CM20 ....210 C1
Mowbrays Cl CRW RM5 ....298 B5
Mowbrays Rd CRW RM5 ....298 B6
Mowbray Gdns LOU IG10 ....254 D9
Mowden Hall La RCHLM CM3 ....220 B2
Mowlands RIPS/CAP IP9 ....28 D9
Moxom Av CHES/WCR EN8 ....230 B9
Moxon Cl PLSTW E13 ....333 J2
Moyers Rd LEY E10 ....314 F5
Moynihan Dr STNGT/OAK N14 ....152 F1
Moy Rd COLS CO2 ....152 B5
Muckingford Rd TIL RM18 ....350 C2
Mucking Hall Rd SBN/FI SS3 ....310 B7
Mucking Wharf Rd
  SLH/COR SS17 ....341 K6
Muggeridge Rd DAGE RM10 ....318 A6
Muir Pl WICKW SS12 ....305 J2
Muir St CAN/RD E16 ....334 A8
Muirway SBF/HAD SS7 ....305 N8
Mulberry Av COLS CO2 ....152 B2
Mulberry Cl BROX EN10 ....230 C3
  EHAM E6 ....334 C6
  GPK RM2 ....298 C8
Mulberry Ct BSF CM23 ....137 M9
Mulberry Dr PUR RM19 ....347 L2
Mulberry Gdns NHMKT IP6 ....22 B2
  WIT CM8 ....171 P9
Mulberry Hi HLWE CM17 ....187 L8
Mulberry Hi BRWN CM15 ....281 J6
Mulberry Rd CVI SS8 ....343 P2
Mulberry Ms K/T/MI CO5 * 199 L1
Mulberry Wy BARK/HLT IG6 ....296 D6
  BELV DA17 ....336 B9
  CHLM/WR CM1 ....218 C6
  SWFD E18 ....295 L6
Mulberry Gdns VGE SS16 ....323 J1
Mullein Ct GRAYS RM17 ....349 M4
Mullin Rd BRTR CM7 ....121 J9
The Mullions BCAYW CM12 ....282 C5
Multon Lea CHLM/GWD CM1 ....218 F4
Mumford Cl RCOLW CO6 ....126 C3
Mumford Rd IP IP1 ....24 F5
  RCOLW CO6 ....126 C3
Mumfords La FOS CO13 ....158 B7
Munday Rd CAN/RD E16 ....333 K6
Mundells CHENF EN7 ....229 M6
Mundon Gdns IL IG1 ....316 E3
Mundon Rd BRTR CM7 ....145 N6
  MAL CM9 ....244 C2
Mungo Park Rd RAIN RM13 ....318 F8
Munnings Ct HVHL CB9 ....40 G2
  IPSE IP5 ....31 H2
Munnings Dr RCOS CO16 ....181 N7
Munnings Rd COLW CO5 ....151 K1
Munnings Wy ROM CO11 ....106 A3
Munro Ct WICKW SS12 ....305 K2
Munro Rd WICKW SS12 ....171 N8
Munsons Aby BOC CM0 ....269 J5
Munsterburg Rd CVI SS8 ....326 C9
Munster Ct BCAYW CM12 ....282 C5
Murchison Cl CHLM/WR CM1 ....217 M6
Murchison Rd HOD EN11 ....208 E5
  LEY E10 ....314 F4
Murdock Cl CAN/RD E16 ....333 K6
Murfitt Wy UPMR RM14 ....319 M6
Murray Cl BRTR CM7 ....121 H9
Murray Sq CAN/RD E16 ....333 K6
Murray Wy WICKW SS12 ....305 J2
Murrell Lock CHLM/GWD CM2 ....218 F3
Murrels La HOC/HUL SS5 ....287 K9
Murrills Rd IPSE IP5 ....31 M1
Murthering La BRW CM14 ....278 F3
Murton Slade HVHL CB9 ....41 K7
Murtwell Dr CHIG IG7 ....296 D5
Muscade Cl K/T/MI CO5 ....174 A7
Museum St COL CO1 ....8 D6
  IP IP1 ....16 D4
  SAFWN CB10 ....51 L8
Musgrave Cl CHESW EN7 ....229 K5
  HAR CO12 ....110 A7
Muskals Cl CHESW EN7 ....229 M6
Musk Cl COLW CO5 ....126 C8
Musket Gv SUD SS9 ....307 L8
Muskham Rd HLW CM20 ....187 H9

Musleigh Mnr WARE SG12 ....184 C3
Musley Hl WARE SG12 ....184 B2
Musley La WARE SG12 ....184 B2
Muswell Wk RCOS CO16 ....181 N8
Mutlow Hill London Rd
  SAFWS CB11 ....64 G4
Mutton Rw CHONG CM5 ....235 H9
Mychett Cl RCOS CO16 ....181 L7
Myddelton Av EN EN1 ....251 K8
Myddelton Gdns
  WCHMH N21 ....275 H6
Myddleton Rd WARE SG12 ....184 A4
Mygrove Cl RAIN RM15 ....337 J2
Mygrove Gdns RAIN RM13 ....337 J2
Mygrove Rd RAIN RM13 ....337 J2
Myland Hall Cha COLN CO4 ....128 D4
Myles Ct CHESW EN7 ....229 M6
Mylne Cl CHES/WCR EN8 ....229 P6
Myln Meadow ING CM4 ....261 N7
Myrtle Av K/T/MI CO5 * 174 A9
Myrtle Rd ERITH DA8 ....346 D5
Myrtle Gv COL CO1 ....152 C1
  ENC/FH EN2 ....251 J8
Myrtle Rd BRW CM14 ....300 F1
  EHAM E6 ....333 P1
  HARH RM5 ....299 H5
  IL IG1 ....316 C4
  IPSE IP5 ....25 M7
  PLMGR N13 ....273 H9
  WALTH E17 ....314 B1
Myson Wy BSF CM23 ....137 N7

N

Nabbott Rd CHLM/WR CM1 ....217 M9
Nacton Crs IPSE IP5 ....26 A6
  IPSE IP5 ....17 K7
  IPSE IP5 ....31 K2
Naffenton Ri LOU IG10 ....275 N4
Nagle C WALTH E17 ....294 G6
Nag's Head La UPMR RM14 ....299 P5
Nags Head Rd PEND EN3 ....275 P5
Nails La BSF CM23 ....53 J1
Nairn Ct TIL RM18 * 350 A7
Nairn St POP/IOD E14 ....332 F5
Naila Gdns CHLM/WR CM1 ....217 P5
Namur Rd CVI SS8 ....343 P2
Nancy Smith Cl COLS CO2 ....152 A1
Nankin St POP/IOD E14 ....332 C6
Nansen Av RCFD SS4 ....308 E1
Nansen Rd COS CO15 ....182 E7
  IPSE IP5 ....26 A9
Napier Av COS CO15 ....183 G6
  SOS SS1 ....18 E4
Napier Cl BSDN SS14 ....3 K4
  EMPK RM11 ....318 C3
Napier Crs WICKW SS12 ....305 K2
Napier Gdns IL IG1 ....316 E2
Napier Gdns SBF/HAD SS7 ....128 A9
Napier Rd COLS CO2 ....182 C1
  EHAM E6 ....334 B1
  PEND EN3 ....274 A4
  RAYL SS6 ....307 J4
  SRTFD E15 ....315 H5
  WAN E11 ....315 H5
Narboro Ct ROM RM1 ....318 F1
Nare Rd SOCK/AV RM15 ....337 P7
Narrow Boat Cl THMD SE28 ....334 E9
Narrow St POP/IOD E14 ....332 B7
Narvik Cl MAL CM9 ....243 P2
Naseby Rd CLAY IG5 ....296 A5
  DAGE RM10 ....317 P5
Nash Cl COLW CO5 ....151 L1
  MGTR CO11 ....106 A5
Nash Dr CHLM/WR CM1 ....193 P9
Nash Ms CHDH RM6 ....304 F5
  ED N9 ....274 B8
Nassau Rd RCOS CO16 ....180 B9
Natal Rd IL IG1 ....316 C6
Nathan Cl UPMR RM14 ....520 B3
Nathan Ct COLS CO2 ....152 C6
Nathan's La CHLM/WR CM1 ....258 E5
Nathan Wy THMD SE28 ....335 H9
Nation Wy CHING E4 ....274 F7
Nats La SAFWS CB11 ....64 F5
Naunton Wy HCH RM12 ....319 J3
Naval Rw POP/IOD E14 ....332 F7
Navarre Gdns CRW RM5 ....298 A3
Navarre Rd EHAM E6 ....333 P2
Navarre St IP IP1 ....16 E3
Navestock Cl CHING E4 * 274 F9
  RAYL SS6 ....306 A2
Navestock Crs WFD IG8 ....295 M5
Navestock Gdns SOS SS1 ....329 N5
Navestock Side BRW CM14 ....279 P1
Navestock Ter WFD IG8 ....295 M4
Navigation Rd CHLM/GWD CM2 ......3 L5
Nayland Cl WICKW SS12 ....285 K9
Nayland Dr K/T/MI CO5 ....181 L9
Nayland Rd BURES CO8 ....76 A9
  COLN CO4 ....127 N2
  FX IP11 ....10 E5
  HVHL CB9 ....41 M5
  RCOLW CO6 ....102 C1
  RCOLW CO6 ....126 C1
Nayling Rd BRTR CM7 ....144 F4
Naylor Gv PEND EN3 ....274 A4
Nazeing Cl WOT CO14 ....174 F3
Nazeingbury Cl WAB EN9 ....230 G1
Nazeingbury Pde WAB EN9 * 230 G1
Nazeing Common WAB EN9 ....231 M2
Nazeing New Rd BROX EN10 ....208 E9
The Nazeing BSDN SS14 ....159 L4
Neal Cl WAB EN9 ....253 J5
Neale Rd HSTD CO9 ....97 N7
Neale St IP IP1 ....16 E5
Neasden Av RCOS CO16 ....181 N8
Neasham Rd BCTR RM8 ....317 J7

Neath Dr CHTY IP2 ....30 A1
Neatscourt Rd EHAM E6 ....333 N5
Neave Crs HARH RM5 ....299 H5
Needham Ct CHLM/WR CM1 ....283 J5
Needleman St
  BERM/RHTH SE16 ....332 A9
Neil Armstrong Wy LOS SS9 ....308 B9
Nelmes Cl EMPK RM11 ....299 L9
Nelmes Crs EMPK RM11 ....299 L9
Nelmes Rd EMPK RM11 ....319 K2
Nelmes Wy EMPK RM11 ....299 K8
Nelson Cl BRW CM14 ....300 G2
  RAYL SS6 ....307 J3
  ROMW/RG RM7 ....298 A5
Nelson Crs MAL CM9 ....244 C2
Nelson Dr LOS SS9 ....328 A5
Nelson Gdns BRTR CM7 ....147 M2
  IP IP2 ....31 M2
Nelson Gv CHLM/WR CM1 ....4 C2
Nelson Ms SOS SS1 ....19 F5
Nelson Pl RCHLM CM3 ....287 H2
Nelson Rd BSDN SS14 ....304 C9
  BSF CM23 ....137 M9
  CDW/CHF KM16 ....340 E6
  COLW CO5 ....294 E3
  COS CO15 ....127 H8
  COS CO15 ....6 D7
  ED N9 ....273 N9
  HAR CO12 ....114 D6
  IPNE IP4 ....26 A6
  PEND EN3 ....274 A5
  RAIN RM13 ....336 E2
  RAYL SS6 ....307 J4
  RCFD SS4 ....308 E1
  SOCK/AV RM15 ....338 F2
  SUD CO10 ....21 H1
  WAN E11 ....311 H5
  WOS/PRIT SS0 ....328 B4
Nelson St CAN/RD E16 ....333 J7
  EHAM E6 ....334 D1
  RCOLE CO7 ....179 K8
  SOS SS1 ....19 F5
Nelwyn Av EMPK RM11 ....299 L9
Nene Cl RAIN RM15 ....336 E2
Neptune Ct COL CO1 ....127 G9
Neptune Sq IPSE IP5 ....17 G6
Nesbit Rd ERITH DA8 ....347 J4
Nesbit Rd BSDN SS14 ....84 F8
  SBN/FI SS3 ....330 C1
Ness Wk WIT CM8 ....196 G2
Nesta Rd WFD IG8 ....295 J3
The Nesters SUD CO10 * 43 K7
Nestor Av WCHMH N21 ....251 N1
Nestuda Wy WOS/PRIT SS0 ....308 C9
Nethan Dr SOCK/AV RM15 ....337 P7
Netherby Gdns ENC/FH EN2 ....272 D5
Nethercourt Av ED N9 ....256 B5
Netherfield SBF/HAD SS7 ....242 C9
Netherfield Gdns BARK IG11 ....316 E8
Netherfield La RCOLW CO6 ....78 A8
Nethergate St SUD CO10 ....44 A5
Netherhall Rd
  HLWW/ROY CM19 ....209 J5
Nether Hi HSTD CO9 ....59 J7
Nether Mayne LAIN SS15 ....2 D6
  VGE SS16 ....324 A3
Netherpark Dr GPK RM2 ....298 E6
Nether Priors BSDN SS14 ....3 H5
Nether Rd SUD CO10 ....45 H1
Nether St WARE SG12 ....160 D8
Netley Cl CHTY IP2 ....29 P2
Netley Rd GNTH/NBYPK IG2 ....296 E9
  WALTH E17 ....294 C9
Netteswellbury Farm
  HLWS CM18 ....210 G4
Netteswell Orch HLW CM20 ....13 H4
Netteswell Rd HLW CM20 ....13 K2
Nevada Rd CVI SS8 ....326 F9
Nevendon Ms PIT SS13 ....304 F5
Nevendon Rd PIT SS13 ....304 F5
Nevern Cl RAYL SS6 ....307 H7
Nevern Rd RAYL SS6 ....307 H7
Neville Cl WAN E11 ....315 J5
Neville Gdns BCTR RM8 ....317 L5
Neville Rd BARK/HLT IG6 ....296 D5
  BCTR RM8 ....317 L4
  FSTGT E7 ....315 K9
  IL IG1 ....296 D9
Neville Shaw BSDN SS14 ....51 M8
Nevill Wy LOU IG10 ....275 P5
Nevin Dr CHING E4 ....274 E7
Nevis Rd ROM CM8 ....288 D5
New Acres Rd THMD SE28 ....334 F9
New Av CHTY IP2 ....29 P1
New Av VGE SS16 ....324 A4
Newark Knok CHAM E6 ....334 B6
New Av VGE SS16 ....323 H2
New Barn La RBSF CM22 ....162 F4
Newbarn Rd RCOLW CO6 ....124 G6
New Barns La MHAD SG10 ....160 D5
New Barns St PLSTW E13 ....333 K4
Newbery Rd ERITH DA8 ....346 E6
Newbiggen St GTDUN CM6 ....92 A5
Newbourne Gdns FX IP11 ....10 D4
Newbourne Rd KIR/NAC IP10 ....27 N7
Newbourn Rd KIR/NAC IP10 ....33 K2
New Bowers Wy
  CHLM/WR CM1 ....218 E5
New Br CHLM/GWD CM2 ....126 G5
Newbridge Rd K/T/MI CO5 ....174 C8
Newburgh Rd GRAYS RM17 ....349 N5
Newbury Av PEND EN3 ....252 C7
Newbury Gdns HARH RM5 ....299 J3
  UPMR RM14 ....319 L5
Newbury Rd COS CO15 ....294 F5
  GNTH/NBYPK IG2 ....316 E1
  HARH RM5 ....299 H2
  IPNE IP4 ....26 A6
Newbury Wk HARH RM5 ....299 J2

Newby Cl EN EN1 ....273 K1
Newby Dr IPNE IP4 ....26 B6
Newby Pl POP/IOD E14 ....332 E6
New Captains Rd K/T/MI CO5 ....202 E6
New Cardinal St IP IP1 ....16 B6
Newcastle Av BARK/HLT IG6 ....297 H5
  COLW CO5 .... *
New Century Rd LAIN SS15 ....303 J9
New Church Rd RCOLW CO6 ....126 G3
New City Rd PLSTW E13 ....333 M3
Newcombe Rd WAN E11 ....315 J5
New Coombe Rd WAN COLN CO4 ...128 D1
Newcourt Rd
  CHLM/GWD CM2 ....218 C8
Newcroft SLH/COR SS10 * 51 M9
New Cut BURES CO8 ....75 M9
  COLS CO2 ....151 J9
  COL CO1 ....155 K6
Newdales Cl ED N9 ....273 M8
New Dukes Wy
  CHLM/GWD CM2 ....218 E7
Newell Av SBN/FI SS3 ....330 F6
Newell Ri NHMKT IP6 ....22 D4
Newells St POP/IOD E14 ....332 C7
New England Cl RCHLM CM3 ....242 C9
New England Crs SBN/FI SS5 ....331 H4
New Farm Dr ABR/ST RM4 ....277 K2
New Farm Rd COLW CO5 ....158 C6
New Ford Rd CHES/WCR EN8 ....252 G4
New Forest La CHIG IG7 ....296 B5
Newgate St CHING E4 ....275 H9
  WOTN CO14 ....159 K6
Newgatestreet Rd
  CHESW EN7 * 228 G5
Newgate St Village
  HERT/BAY SG13 ....228 C2
Newhall RCFD SS4 ....308 D1
New Hall Ct WAB EN9 ....253 J5
New Hall Dr HARH RM5 ....299 K5
New Hall La MAL CM9 ....244 F7
Newham Wy CAN/RD E16 ....333 J5
  EHAM E6 ....333 P4
Newhouse La CAN/RD E16 ....333 K5
Newhouse Av CHDH RM6 ....302 A9
  WICKW SS12 ....284 E9
New House La CHLM/GWD CM2 ....52 F7
New Hythe Av RCOLW CO6 ....123 N3
Newington Av SOSN SS2 ....329 M4
Newington Cl SOSN SS2 ....329 M4
Newington Gdns COS CO15 ....182 A5
  SOSN SS2 ....329 M4
New Kiln Rd COLW CO5 ....127 M8
Newland Av CHING E4 ....94 A7
Newland Dr EN EN1 ....251 N9
Newland Pl WIT CM8 ....197 K3
Newlands Cl BCAYW CM12 ....283 J5
  RBRW/HUT CM13 ....281 N6
Newlands Dr WIT CM8 ....197 J2
Newlands End LAIN SS15 ....303 J7
Newlands La RCOLW CO6 ....78 A8
Newlands Rd BCAYW CM12 ....283 J6
  CVI SS8 ....326 G9
  WFD IG8 ....275 J8
  WICKW SS12 ....305 J5
Newland St CAN/RD E16 ....333 P8
  WIT CM8 ....197 K2
New La K/T/MI CO5 ....148 E9
  RIPS/CAP IP9 ....83 N5
Newling Cl EHAM E6 ....334 A8
New Lodge Cha RCHLM CM3 ....219 N8
New London Rd
  CHLM/GWD CM2 ....4 D7
Newman Cl EMPK RM11 ....299 K9
New Moor La PLSTW E13 ....333 L3
  WALTH E17 ....294 A9
Newmans Dr
  RBRW/HUT CM13 ....281 M6
Newmans La LOU IG10 ....276 B2
Newmarket Rd SUD CO10 ....36 D8
Newmarket Wy HCH RM12 ....319 K6
Newmarsh Rd THMD SE28 ....334 C8
Newmill La MGTR CO11 ....110 A7
Newminster Ct ENC/FH EN2 * 272 C1
New Moor Cl BOC CM0 ....269 K5
New Moor Crs BOC CM0 ....269 K5
New Mount St SRTFD E15 ....314 C9
New Nabbotts Wy
  CHLM/WR CM1 ....218 D4
Newnham Ct CHTY IP2 ....29 N1
Newnham Gn MAL CM9 ....221 P8
Newnham Pde
  CHES/WCR EN8 * 230 A9
Newnham Pl CDW/CHF KM16 ....350 B2
New North Rd BARK/HLT IG6 ....296 E2
New Pk HSTD CO9 ....72 E6
New Park Av PLMGR N13 ....273 H9
New Park Rd HERT/BAY SG13 ....228 C3
  HOC/HUL SS5 ....288 B8
  SBF/HAD SS7 ....325 P1
New Park St COL CO1 ....128 C9
Newpasture La GTDUN CM6 ....143 H1
Newpiece LOU IG10 ....276 C2
New Pier St WOTN CO14 ....159 K6
New Place Gdns UPMR RM14 ....320 A4
New Plaistow Rd SRTFD E15 ....333 H1
New Pond La SAFWN CB10 ....51 K8
Newport Av POP/IOD E14 ....332 G7
Newport Cl CHLM/GWD CM2 ....240 C4
  HAR CO12 ....252 B7
  PEND EN3 ....252 B7
Newport Dr COS CO15 ....182 B6
  SAFWS CB11 ....89 L4
Newport Rd LEY E10 ....314 G4
  SAFWS CB11 ....89 J4
  WALTH E17 * 294 B8
Newports SBW CM23 ....187 K3
Newport Wy FOS CO13 ....159 L9
Newpots Cl K/T/MI CO5 ....176 F8
Newpots La K/T/MI CO5 ....176 F8
Newquay Cl KESG IP5 ....26 E5

New Queens Rd SUD CO10 ....20 C2
New River Av WARE SG12 ....184 E8
New River Cl HOD EN11 ....208 E4
New Rd ABR/ST RM4 ....277 L5
  BCAYW CM12 ....303 H4
  BOC CM0 ....291 H3
  BROX EN10 ....209 P2
  BRTR CM7 ....144 C5
  BRW CM14 ....280 G8
  CBE/LIN CB1 ....39 N5
  CHING E4 ....294 E1
  CHLM/GWD CM2 ....240 F4
  CHLM/WR CM1 ....218 A4
  CVI SS8 ....344 B2
  DAGW RM9 ....335 P1
  ED N9 ....273 M9
  FX IP11 ....14 L4
  GDMY/SEVK IG5 ....316 H4
  GRAYS RM17 ....349 L4
  HLWE CM17 ....187 L8
  HSTD CO9 ....121 P2
  ING CM4 ....260 D5
  K/T/MI CO5 ....167 L3
  K/T/MI IG5 ....173 P4
  LOS SS9 ....174 A8
  LOS SS9 ....327 N6
  MAL CM9 ....225 J1
  MGTR CO11 ....106 C4
  RAIN RM13 ....336 F3
  RAIN RM13 ....337 L8
  RBSF CM22 ....114 E5
  RCHLM CM5 ....195 P1
  RCHLM CM5 ....196 D5
  RCOLW CO6 ....125 N5
  ROY SS8 ....48 B6
  SAFWN CB10 ....36 C5
  SAFWN CB10 ....51 M9
  SBF/HAD SS7 ....226 G3
  SBN/FI SS3 ....331 H5
  SUD CO10 ....46 E4
  WARE SG12 ....184 B3
New Rd CBE/LIN CB1 * 40 B7
  RCFD SS4 * 310 F2
Newry Av FX IP11 ....14 L4
Newsholme Dr WCHMH N21 ....272 E4
Newson St IP IP1 ....16 C2
Newstead Rd SBN/FI SS3 ....330 C2
New St BRTR CM7 ....145 J4
  CHLM/WR CM1 ....1 K4
  GTDUN CM6 ....141 L6
  HSTD CO9 ....97 N7
  MAL CM9 ....222 A9
  RCOLE CO7 ....179 L8
  SBW CM21 ....25 J1
  SUD CO10 ....20 C4
New Street Flds GTDUN CM6 ....141 L6
Newsum Gdns RAYL SS6 ....306 D4
Newteswald Dr WAB EN9 ....252 G2
New Thorpe Av RCOS CO16 ....157 K4
Newton Cl BRTR CM7 ....145 J5
  HOD EN11 ....208 E1
  WALTH E17 ....314 B1
Newton Dr SUD CO10 ....21 L5
Newton Dr SBW CM21 ....187 L3
Newton Gdns RCOS CO16 ....181 M8
Newton Hall RCFD SS4 ....308 L1
Newton Park Rd
  SBF/HAD SS7 ....306 E2
Newtons Cl RAIN RM13 ....318 D9
Newton's Ct GRH DA9 ....348 A9
Newtons Ct IPNE IP4 ....17 G4
Newton Vls GTDUN CM6 * 141 J5
Newton Wy RCOS CO16 ....180 D8
Newtown Rd BSF CM23 ....239 J2
New Town Rd COL CO1 ....128 B9
  RCOS CO16 ....157 J4
New Wanstead WAN E11 ....315 K1
New Waverley Rd LAIN SS15 ....303 M6
New Wy CHTY IP2 ....24 G5
  RCOS CO16 ....156 B3
New Way La HLWE CM17 ....212 A4
New Writtle St CHLM/GWD CM2 ....4 E5
New Zealand Wy RAIN RM13 ....336 E3
Niagra Cl CHES/WCR EN8 ....230 A8
Nicholas Cl CHLM/WR CM1 ....239 J3
  SOCK/AV RM15 ....338 F3
Nicholas Ct WIT CO6 ....197 J2
Nicholas Dr BCTR RM8 ....317 N4
  FX IP11 ....10 A1
Nichol Cl STHGT/OAK N14 ....272 A2
Nicholl Rd EPP CM16 ....254 C1
  LAIN SS15 ....303 J8
Nicholls Fld HLWS CM18 ....211 J4
Nichols Cl MGTR CO11 ....106 A5
Nichols Gv BRTR CM7 ....145 L5
Nicholson Crs SBF/HAD SS7 ....326 E5
Nicholson Gv WICKW SS12 ....305 K2
Nicholson Pl RCHLM CM3 ....263 N2
Nicholson Rd SBF/HAD SS7 ....326 E5
Nicholsons Gv COL CO1 ....9 F7
Nickelby Cl THMD SE28 ....335 K6
Nickelby Rd CHLM/WR CM1 ....217 L5
Nicola Ms BARK/HLT IG6 ....296 C4
Nien-Oord RCOS CO16 ....181 L9
Nigel Ms IL IG1 ....316 C6
Nigel Rd FSTGT E7 ....315 M7
Nightingale Av CHING E4 ....295 H2
  UPMR RM14 ....320 C3
Nightingale Cl CHING E4 ....295 H1
  COLN CO4 ....129 H7
  COS CO15 ....182 A8
  HAR CO12 ....110 A7
  RAYL SS6 ....306 E4
  SOSN SS2 ....308 F9
  WIT CM8 ....197 H4
Nightingale Hl COLN CO4 ....104 A2
Nightingale La WAN E11 ....295 L9
Nightingale Ms SAFWN CB10 ....51 N8
Nightingale Pl COLW CO5 ....150 F2
Nightingale Rd CHESW EN7 ....229 H4

CVI SS8 ....344 F2
  ED N9 ....273 P6
  IPSE IP5 ....30 C2
Nightingales VGE SS16 ....322 G1
Nightingale Sq IPSE IP5 ....30 G2
Nightingale Wy COS CO15 ....182 A8
Nile Dr EHAM E6 ....333 P5
Nile Dr ED N9 ....273 M2
Nina Mackay Cl SRTFD E15 * 333 H1
Nineacres BRTR CM7 ....145 K5
Nine Acres CHTY IP2 ....24 E5
Nine Acres Cl MNPK E12 ....315 P7
Nine Ashes Rd BRWN CM15 ....258 E5
  ING CM4 ....236 F8
Ninefields WAB EN9 ....253 K3
Ninth Av STSD CM24 ....138 E5
Nipsells Cha RCHLM CM3 ....245 N8
Nita Rd BRW CM14 ....300 F2
Niven Cl WICKW SS12 ....305 K2
Noakes Av CHLM/GWD CM2 ....240 D5
Noak Hill Cl BCAYW CM12 ....303 K4
Noak Hill Rd HARH RM5 ....298 C2
  LAIN SS15 ....303 K4
Noaks Rd HADL IP7 ....80 A1
Nobel Cl UED N18 ....294 A1
Nobel Sq PIT SS13 ....305 H5
Nobles Green Cl LOS SS9 ....307 P8
Nobles Green Rd LOS SS9 ....307 P8
The Nobles BSF CM23 ....137 J8
Nock Gdns KESC IP5 ....26 G5
Noel Rd EHAM E6 ....333 P4
Nonsuch Cl BARK/HLT IG6 ....296 C5
Nonsuch Meadow SUD CO10 ....20 C7
The Nook RCOLE CO7 ....153 K5
  WARE SG12 ....184 E8
Norbiton Rd POP/IOD E14 ....332 C6
Norbury Cl RCOLW CO6 ....149 L2
Norbury Gdns CHDH RM6 ....297 L2
Norbury Rd CHING E4 ....294 D2
  IPNE IP4 ....26 A4
Nordenfeldt Rd ERITH DA8 ....346 C3
Nordland Rd CVI SS8 ....344 C1
Nordmann Pl SOCK/AV RM15 ....338 C4
Noredale SBN/FI SS3 ....330 C8
Nore Rd LOS SS9 ....307 M7
Nore Vw VGE SS16 ....322 G2
Norfolk Av COS CO15 ....182 F7
  K/T/MI CO5 ....202 C5
  LOS SS9 ....328 A1
  LAIN SS15 ....303 H9
  MAL CM9 ....243 P1
Norfolk Crs COLN CO4 ....9 H1
Norfolk Dr CHLM/WR CM1 ....217 P4
Norfolk Gdns BRTR CM7 ....145 L2
Norfolk Rd BARK IG11 ....316 F9
  DAGE RM10 ....318 C9
  EHAM E6 ....334 A1
  GDMY/SEVK IG3 ....316 F3
  IPNE IP4 ....17 G3
  MAL CM9 ....243 P1
  PEND EN3 ....273 M6
  ROMW/RG RM7 ....318 B1
  UPMR RM14 ....319 M5
  WALTH E17 ....294 B5
Norfolk St FSTGT E7 ....315 K7
Norfolk Wy BSF CM23 ....137 L9
  CVI SS8 ....326 C9
Norlington Rd WAN E11 ....314 F3
Norman Av CI FX IP11 ....35 N5
  RCOLW CO6 ....149 K5
  RCOS CO16 ....180 D9
  ROMW/RG RM7 ....298 A6
  WAB EN9 ....252 G3
Norman Crs IPSE IP5 ....25 P9
  RAYL SS6 ....307 H2
  RBRW/HUT CM13 ....281 K9
Normandie Rd BURES CO8 ....75 P9
  COLS CO2 ....152 B3
Normandy Ter CAN/RD E16 ....333 L6
Normandy Wy ERITH DA8 ....346 D6
  HOD EN11 ....208 G5
Norman Gv BOW E3 ....332 B2
Norman Hl RCHLM CM3 ....195 N2
Normanhurst
  RBRW/HUT CM13 ....281 M5
  LOS SS9 * 327 P6
Norman Rd BELV DA17 ....346 A4
  COS CO15 ....182 E7
  EHAM E6 ....334 A4
  EMPK RM11 ....318 F2
  IL IG1 ....316 C7
  MGTR CO11 ....106 C4
  WAN E11 ....315 H4
Normansfield GTDUN CM6 ....141 M7
Normanshire Dr CHING E4 ....294 D1
Normans Rd CVI SS8 ....344 G1
Norman's Wy STSD CM24 ....114 B8
Norman Ter LOS SS9 ....327 P6
Normanton Pk CHING E4 ....295 H1
Norman Wy COLW CO5 ....127 L9
  COS CO15 ....204 G1
  STHGT/OAK N14 ....272 D8
Norris Cl BRTR CM7 ....145 M1
  BSF CM23 ....137 C5
Norris Gv BROX EN10 ....208 B8
Norris La HOD EN11 ....208 D4
Norris Ms HOD EN11 ....208 C6
Norris Rd HOD EN11 ....208 D5
Norris Wy DART DA1 ....346 A8
Norseman Cl GDMY/SEVK IG3 ....317 J3
Norsey Cl BCAYE CM11 ....283 J5
Norsey Rd BCAYE CM11 ....283 K5
Norsey Rd BCAYE CM11 ....283 J5
Norsey View Dr BCAYW CM12 ....283 J7
North Access Rd WALTH E17 ....314 A1
Northallerton Wy HARH RM5 ....299 J2
Northall Rd BXLYHN DA7 ....346 B7
Northampton Cl BRTR CM7 ....145 N1
Northampton Gv VGE SS16 ....322 G2

Northampton Meadow
  BRTR CM7 ....93 P6
Northampton Rd PEND EN3 ....274 E5
North Av CHLM/WR CM1 ....217 N6
  CVI SS8 ....344 C1
  HVHL CB9 ....41 H3
  SOSN SS2 ....19 H1
Northbank Rd WALTH E17 ....294 F6
North Barn BROX EN10 ....230 E1
North Benfleet Hall Rd
  WICKW SS12 ....305 L6
North Birkbeck Rd WAN E11 ....314 C5
Northbourne Rd COS CO15 ....7 G3
North Br COL CO1 ....8 B4
Northbrook Rd IL IG1 ....316 B4
Northbrooks
  HLWW/ROY CM19 ....13 G7
North Circular WALTH E17 ....294 E5
North Circular Rd BARK IG11 ....316 B9
  CHING E4 * 294 B3
  SWFD E18 ....295 M7
North Cl CHIG IG7 ....297 H2
  DAGE RM10 ....335 P1
  IPNE IP4 ....25 M5
North Colne VGE SS16 ....324 C2
North Colonnade POP/IOD E14 ....332 E8
Northcote Rd WALTH E17 ....294 B8
North Countess Rd
  WALTH E17 ....294 C6
North Crs CHING E4 ....260 D6
North Crs CAN/RD E16 ....332 C4
  HVHL CB9 ....55 L3
  SOSN SS2 ....328 D1
  WICKW SS12 ....285 D9
North Crockerford VGE SS16 ....324 D1
Northcroft SUD CO10 ....20 C5
North Cross Rd BARK/HLT IG6 ....296 D8
North Dell CHLM/WR CM1 ....218 C4
Northdene CHIG IG7 ....296 E2
Northdown Rd
  GNTH/NBYPK IG2 ....296 F9
Northdown Rd EMPK RM11 ....318 G2
North Dr CHLM/GWD CM2 ....240 E5
  GPK RM2 ....299 H7
  RBRW/HUT CM13 ....282 C5
  RCHLM CM5 ....245 N8
North End BKHH IG9 ....275 M6
  BOC CM0 ....269 J4
Northend RBRW/HUT CM13 ....300 F7
Northend Rd ERITH DA8 ....346 E6
North End Rd HSTD CO9 ....58 D7
  SAFWN CB10 ....36 C3
Northern Ap COLN CO4 ....127 N2
Northern Av ED N9 ....273 L8
  SBF/HAD SS7 ....325 P1
Northern Quays IPSE IP5 ....17 G6
Northern Relief Rd BARK IG11 ....316 D9
Northern Rd SUD CO10 ....21 J2
Northey St POP/IOD E14 ....332 B7
Northfalls Rd CVI SS8 ....345 J2
North Farm LGU IG10 ....275 M5
Northfield BRTR CM7 ....145 J4
Northfield Crs SBN/FI SS3 ....330 F2
Northfield Gdns COLN CO4 ....128 B9
Northfield Rd CHES/WCR EN8 ....252 B2
  DAGW RM9 ....317 N6
  EHAM E6 ....316 A8
  PEND EN3 ....273 N5
  SAFWS CB11 ....65 M1
  SBW CM21 ....162 B9
Northfields GRAYS RM17 ....349 M2
North Ga HLW CM20 ....13 G5
Northgate End BSF CM23 ....137 L6
North Gv COS CO15 ....204 G1
  IP IP1 ....16 E4
North Gv WALTH E17 ....211 H4
North Gunnels BSDN SS14 ....3 F5
North Hall Rd SAFWS CB11 ....89 M6
North Hill RCOLE CO7 ....8 B5
  RCHLM CM5 ....220 A5
  SLH/COR SS17 ....340 C1
North Hill Dr HARH RM5 ....299 J1
North Hill Gdns IPNE IP4 ....17 J3
North Hill Rd IPNE IP4 ....17 J3
Northlands Ap VGE SS16 ....323 K5
Northlands Cl SLH/COR SS17 ....323 M9
Northlands Farm Cha
  SLH/COR SS17 ....323 M7
Northlands Pk PIT SS13 ....304 F7
Northlands Pavement
  PIT SS13 * 324 C1
North La RCOLW CO6 ....149 N2
North Lawn IPNE IP4 ....26 A3
Northolme V
  CDW/CHF RM16 ....349 M1
Northolt Av BSF CM23 ....137 N5
Northolt Wy HCH RM12 ....319 H7
North Pl HLW CM20 ....187 H7
  WAB EN9 ....252 E3
North Quay FX IP11 * 111 K1
North Rd ABR/ST RM4 ....278 D8
  BCAYE CM11 ....304 C2
  BELV DA17 ....346 A1
  BRW CM14 ....280 G8
  CHDH RM6 ....297 M9
  CHES/WCR EN8 ....252 B5
  COS CO15 ....181 P7
  ED N9 ....273 N7
  GDMY/SEVK IG3 ....316 F4
  HOD EN11 ....208 D4
  MAL CM9 ....225 H1
  PUR RM19 ....347 P2
  RBSF CM22 ....139 M6
  RCOLE CO7 ....179 L6
  SLH/COR SS17 ....320 G9
  SUD CO10 ....59 L4
  WOS/PRIT SS0 ....18 C2
North Road Av BRW CM14 ....280 F7
Northsea Vw HAR CO12 ....110 A6
North Shoebury Rd
  SBN/FI SS3 ....330 D5
North Side BRTR CM7 * 121 K6

North Sq ED N9 ....273 N8
North Station Rd COL CO1 ....8 B3
North St BARK IG11 ....316 D9
  BOC CM0 ....248 B5
  BOC CM0 ....269 J5
  BSF CM23 ....137 L6
  EMPK RM11 ....319 J2
  GTDUN CM6 ....141 L5
  HVHL CB9 ....55 L5
  LOS SS9 ....327 P6
  MAL CM9 ....200 C7
  MAL CM9 ....222 C9
  MGTR CO11 ....106 C4
  PLSTW E13 ....333 H1
  RCFD SS4 ....308 C5
  ROM RM1 ....298 C8
  SBN/FI SS3 ....330 C2
  SUD CO10 ....20 D4
  WAB EN9 ....251 H1
  WOTN CO14 ....159 K5
North Street Pde SUD CO10 ....20 D4
North Ter BSF CM23 ....137 L6
Northumberland Av
  EMPK RM11 ....299 H9
  EN EN1 ....251 N8
  LAIN SS15 ....323 K1
  MNPK E12 ....315 M3
  SOS SS1 ....329 K7
Northumberland Cl
  BRTR CM7 ....145 L2
  ERITH DA8 ....346 B5
Northumberland Ct
  CHLM/GWD CM2 ....218 E7
Northumberland Crs SOS SS1 ....329 L7
Northumberland Gdns ED N9 ....273 L9
Northumberland Pk
  ERITH DA8 ....346 B5
Northumberland Rd
  EHAM E6 ....333 P6
  SLH/COR SS17 ....340 G9
  WALTH E17 ....314 D2
Northumberland Wy
  ERITH DA8 ....346 B6
Northumbria St POP/IOD E14 ....332 D6
North View Av TIL RM18 ....350 B6
Northview Dr WFD IG8 ....295 N6
  WOS/PRIT SS0 ....328 E4
Northville Dr WOS/PRIT SS0 ....328 D2
North Wall RCOS CO16 ....204 G1
North Wy ED N9 ....273 P6
North Weald Cl WICKE SS11 * 305 N1
Northwick Rd CVI SS8 ....343 M1
Northwood CDW/CHF RM16 ....340 C9
Northwood Av HCH RM12 ....318 F6
Northwood Cl CHESW EN7 ....229 L6
North Woolwich Rd
  CAN/RD E16 ....333 L8
Norton Av CVI SS8 ....345 H2
Norton Cl CHING E4 ....294 D2
  SLH/COR SS17 ....341 N1
Norton Heath Rd
  CHONG CM5 ....236 G2
Norton La CHONG CM5 ....236 A4
Norton Rd CHLM/WR CM1 ....4 C3
  DAGE RM10 ....318 C8
  HVHL CB9 ....55 L5
  ING CM4 ....260 C5
  LEY E10 ....314 C3
Norway Crs HAR CO12 ....110 A5
Norway Dr POP/IOD E14 ....332 C6
Norwich Av CVI SS8 ....329 K5
Norwich Cl COL CO1 ....9 F4
  RCOS CO16 ....181 N7
  SOSN SS2 ....329 K4
Norwich Crs CHDH RM6 ....297 J9
  RAYL SS6 ....306 E3
Norwich Rd FSTGT E7 ....315 K8
  IP IP1 ....16 A1
Norwood Av COS CO15 ....182 C8
  ROMW/RG RM7 ....318 C2
Norwood Dr SBF/HAD SS7 ....326 B5
Norwood End BSDN SS14 ....304 C8
  CHONG CM5 ....213 P5
Norwood Wy WOTN CO14 ....159 H7
Notcutts RCFD SS4 * 307 J5
Notley Dr HVHL CB9 ....40 E2
Notley Gn BRTR CM7 ....144 E8
Notley Rd BRTR CM7 ....145 J5
Nottage Cl SLH/COR SS17 ....341 N1
Nottidge Rd IPNE IP4 ....17 J4
Nottingham Av CAN/RD E16 ....333 M5
Nottingham Rd COS CO15 ....182 E7
  LEY E10 ....314 F1
Nottingham Wy VGE SS16 ....322 G1
Nuneaton Rd DAGW RM9 ....317 L9
Nunn Cl WIDBR IP2 ....16 A4
Nunnery St HSTD CO9 ....72 C5
Nunns Cl RCOLW CO6 ....149 P2
  ENC/FH EN2 ....273 H1
Nunns Wy GRAYS RM17 ....349 N2
Nunsbury Dr BROX EN10 ....230 B4
Nun's Meadow HSTD CO9 ....97 H8
Nunty's La BRTR CM7 ....122 G7
Nursery Cl CHDH RM6 ....317 L1
  COLW CO5 ....150 F1
  PEND EN3 ....252 A9
  RAYL SS6 ....306 G6
  WALTH E17 ....338 F4
  WFD IG8 ....295 L2
Nursery Dr BRTR CM7 ....145 K1
Nursery Flds SBW CM21 ....187 L2
Nursery Gdns CHESW EN7 ....229 J7
  LAIN SS15 ....303 K7
  PEND EN3 ....252 A9
  WARE SG12 ....184 D8
Nursery La FSTGT E7 ....315 K8
  RCHLM CM3 ....242 C2
Nursery Ri GTDUN CM6 ....141 M7
Nursery Rd BROX EN10 * 230 B4
  BRWN CM15 ....258 F4

BSF CM23 ....137 L8
CHLM/GWD CM2 ....5 F7
HOD EN11 ....208 E2
LOU IG10 ....275 N5
SLH/COR SS17 ....341 L2
STHGT/OAK N14 ....272 B6
SUD CO10 ....61 L5
WAB EN9 ....230 G1
The Nursery ERITH DA8 ....346 E5
Nursery Wk FX IP11 ....11 H1
Nutberry Av CDW/CHF RM16 ....339 K9
Nutberry Cl CDW/CHF RM16 ....339 K9
Nutbrowne Rd DAGW RM9 ....335 N1
Nutcombe Crs RCFD SS4 ....308 E3
Nutfield Gdns
  GDMY/SEVK IG3 ....316 G4
Nutfield Rd SRTFD E15 ....314 F6
Nuthatch Cl BCAYE CM11 ....283 K8
Nuthatch Gdns THMD SE28 ....334 E9
Nutmeg Cl CAN/RD E16 ....333 H4
Nutmeg La POP/IOD E14 ....332 G6
Nutter La WAN E11 ....295 M9
Nutwood Gdns CHESW EN7 ....229 K5
Nyssa Cl WFD IG8 ....296 A3
Nyth Cl UPMR RM14 ....320 A1

O

Oakapple Cl COLS CO2 ....151 N5
Oak Av BCAYE CM11 ....304 B3
  COS CO15 ....206 F2
  ENC/FH EN2 ....250 E9
  UPMR RM14 ....319 N5
  WICKE SS11 ....305 H2
Oakbank RBRW/HUT CM13 ....281 P4
Oak Bungalows BRTR CM7 ....145 H3
Oak Cha WICKW SS12 ....284 F9
Oak Cl DART DA1 ....10 C2
  FX IP11 ....10 C2
  MAL CM9 ....244 C2
  RCOLW CO6 ....150 G6
  RCOS CO16 ....157 K5
  STHGT/OAK N14 ....272 A1
  WAB EN9 ....252 G4
Oak Crs CAN/RD E16 ....333 H5
Oakdale STHGT/OAK N14 ....272 A7
Oakdale Cl CHING E4 ....294 F2
Oakdale Rd FSTGT E7 ....295 L6
  SWFD E18 ....295 J5
  WAN E11 ....314 C4
Oakdene CHES/WCR EN8 ....230 B9
  KIR/NAC IP10 ....33 M7
Oakdene Rd PIT SS13 ....304 C7
Oak Dr DART DA1 ....187 K4
Oak Dr SBW CM21 ....187 K4
Oak End HLWS CM18 * 210 G5
Oaken Grange Dr SOSN SS2 ....328 F1
Oak Fall WIT CM8 ....171 P6
Oak Farm Rd MAL CM9 ....220 C9
Oakfield CHING E4 ....294 E2
Oakfield Cl SBF/HAD SS7 ....325 P3
Oakfield La RCHLM CM3 ....195 M2
Oakfield Rd EHAM E6 ....333 P1
  HOC/HUL SS5 ....288 B8
  IL IG1 ....316 C5
  RIPW IP8 ....29 H4
  SBF/HAD SS7 ....325 P5
  STHGT/OAK N14 ....272 D8
  WALTH E17 ....294 B6
Oak Gld EPP CM16 ....233 L8
Oak Gln EMPK RM11 ....299 K7
Oak Gv RIPW IP8 ....24 B5
Oak Hall Rd WAN E11 ....315 L1
Oakham Cl VGE SS16 ....322 C1
Oakhaven Har CO12 * 110 A7
Oak Hl BRTR CM7 ....95 M8
  WFD IG8 ....294 G4
Oak Hill Crs WFD IG8 ....295 H4
Oak Hill Gdns WALTH E17 ....295 H5
Oak Hill La CHTY IP2 ....25 J8
Oak Hill Rd ABR/ST RM4 ....278 C6
Oakhill Rd PUR RM19 ....347 N3
Oak Holm COLS CO2 ....152 B3
Oakhurst Cl BARK/HLT IG6 ....296 D5
  WALTH E17 ....295 H3
  WICKW SS12 ....305 H2
Oakhurst Dr WICKW SS12 ....304 G1
Oakhurst Gdns WALTH E17 ....275 J7
  WALTH E17 ....295 H8
Oakhurst Rd PEND EN3 ....252 A6
  RAYL SS6 ....307 J7
  SOSN SS2 ....329 H4
Oakland Gdns
  RBRW/HUT CM13 ....281 M4
Oakland Dr BKHH IG9 ....275 K8
Oakland Rd HAR CO12 ....110 D7
  SRTFD E15 ....315 H6
  WAB EN9 ....230 G1
Oaklands PLMGR N13 ....272 E8
  RCOLW CO6 ....77 L2
Oaklands Av COLW CO5 ....151 H1
  ED N9 ....273 J4
  ROM RM1 ....298 D7
Oaklands Cl BRTR CM7 ....144 G6
  BSF CM23 ....137 N4
Oaklands Crs
  CHLM/GWD CM2 ....240 A2
Oaklands Dr BSF CM23 ....137 N5
  HLWE CM17 ....211 K4
  SOCK/AV RM15 ....338 F5
Oaklands Gv BROX EN10 ....230 B5
Oaklands Ms SBF/HAD SS7 ....308 D3
Oaklands Park Av IL IG1 ....316 D4
Oaklands Rd CHESW EN7 ....229 K5
Oaklands Wy RCHLM CM5 ....220 B9
Oakleas Av CHLM/GWD CM2 ....218 D7
Oaklea Av CHLM/GWD CM2 ....218 D7
Oakleafe Gdns CLAY IG5 ....296 C7

Oakleigh Av HOC/HUL SS5 287 H6
SOS SS1 329 L6
Oakleigh Park Dr LOS SS9 327 P5
Oakleigh Ri EPP CM16 255 H2
Oakleigh Rd COS CO15 182 A5
Oakleighs SBF/HAD SS7 325 P2
Oakley Av BARK IG11 316 C9
RAYL SS6 306 C4
Oakley Cl CHING E4 274 F9
WTHK RM20 348 F4
Oakley Dr BCAYW CM12 282 C5
HARH RM3 299 M2
Oakley Rd BRTR CM7 121 J8
HAR CO12 109 N7
MGTR CO11 133 J2
Oak Lodge Av CHIG IG7 296 E2
Oak Lodge Tye
CHLM CM1 218 F5
Oakmead Rd RCOS CO16 205 H1
Oakmoor Wy CHIG IG7 296 F2
Oak Piece EPP CM16 234 B4
Oak Rdig HAR CO12 109 L9
Oak Ri BKHH IG9 275 N9
Oak Rd BCAYE CM11 284 C3
BCAYE CM11 304 B5
CVI SS8 344 F2
EPP CM16 232 G9
ERITH DA8 346 B5
ERITH DA8 346 F6
GRAYS RM17 349 M4
HARH RM5 299 L5
HSTD CO9 74 C8
HSTD CO9 97 N8
K/T/MI CO5 173 N6
MAL CM9 222 C5
RCFD SS4 308 E5
RCOLW CO6 124 C3
SUD CO10 61 L4
WIT CM8 172 B6
Oak Rd North SBF/HAD SS7 327 H4
Oak Rd South SBF/HAD SS7 327 H4
Oakroyd Av GTDUN CM6 141 M6
Oaks Av CRW RM5 298 B6
Oaks Dr COLW CO3 127 N8
Oaks Gv COLW CO3 275 H8
Oaks La GNTH/NBYPK IG2 296 F9
Oaksmere Gdns CHTY IP5 127 P4
Oaks Pl COLN CO4 127 P4
Oakstead Cl IPNE IP4 25 N5
The Oaks BCAYE CM11 303 K1
FOS CO13 158 G8
KESC IP5 27 L5
WFD IG8 295 H4
Oak St BSF CM23 137 L8
ROMW/RG RM7 298 B9
Oaktree Av PLMGR N13 272 F9
Oak Tree Cl COLU CO1 254 D9
Oaktree Cl BSF CM23 137 L7
RBRW/HUT CM13 281 J9
Oaktree Gv IL IG1 316 E7
Oak Tree Rd RCOLE CO7 124 C8
Oaktrees MAL CM9 199 J7
Oakview HAR CO12 110 A7
Oakview Cl CHESW EN7 229 N7
Oak Wk HOC/HUL SS5 287 P9
HSTD CO9 72 C7
Oakway CDW/CHF RM16 339 L8
Oakwell Dr POTB/CUF EN6 250 A3
Oakwood Av COS CO15 182 F7
K/T/MI CO5 173 N6
LOS SS9 327 P2
RBRW/HUT CM13 281 P5
STHGT/OAK N14 272 C6
Oakwood Cha EMPK RM11 319 L2
Oakwood Cl FOS CO13 158 F8
SBF/HAD SS7 325 N1
STHGT/OAK N14 272 B5
WFD IG8 295 P3
Oakwood Ct RCHLM CM3 267 P6
Oakwood Crs WCHMH N21 272 D5
Oakwood Dr BCAYW CM12 283 K3
BXLYHN DA7 346 B9
K/T/MI CO5 202 G5
Oakwood Gdns
GDMY/SEVK IG3 316 G4
K/T/MI CO5 202 G5
Oakwood Gv PIT SS13 304 C9
Oakwood Hi LOU IG10 276 B5
Oakwood Hill Industrial Est
LOU IG10 276 C4
Oakwood Pde EBAR EN4 * 272 B4
Oakwood Park Rd
STHGT/OAK N14 272 D5
SLH/COR SS17 342 A1
Oakwood Rd RAYL SS6 306 F3
Oak Yd HSTD CO9 * 97 P6
Oasthouse Ct SAFWN CB10 51 L9
Oasthouse Spinney
BRTR CM7 * 121 J9
Oast Wy RCFD SS4 308 C5
Oates Rd CRW RM5 298 A2
Oatfield Cl COLW CO3 126 C9
Oatland Ri WALTH E17 294 B6
Oatlands RCOLE CO7 129 N9
Oatlands Rd PEND EN3 251 P9
Oban Cl PLSTW E13 333 M4
Oban Ct WICKE SS11 305 N2
Oban Rd PLSTW E13 333 M8
Oban St IP IP1 19 K2
POP/IOD E14 332 G4
Oberon Cl COLN CO4 128 C8
Obrey Wy BSF CM23 162 B2
Observer Wy K/T/MI CO5 172 C1
Ocean Est WCHPL E1 * 332 E1
Ocean St WCHPL E1 332 A5
Ockelford Av CHLM/WR CM1 217 N6
Ockendon Wy WOTN CO14 159 H7
Octavia Dr WIT CM8 197 H5
Oddcroft RCOLW CO6 98 G7
Odeon Rbt CHLM/GWD CM2 5 H5

Odessa Rd CVI SS8 344 F2
FSTGT E7 315 J6
Offa's Md HOM E9 314 B6
Office La MAL CM9 199 H8
Ogard Rd HOD E11 208 F3
Ogilvie Cl WICKW SS12 305 K2
Oglethorpe Rd DAGE RM10 317 N5
Ohio Rd PLSTW E13 333 J4
Okehampton Sq HARH RM3 * 299 H5
Old Barn La RCHLM CM3 263 L8
Old Barn Rd EURES CO18 100 E2
Old Barn La ING CM4 237 L4
Old Barn Wy BXLYHN DA7 346 C9
Old Bell Cl STSD CM24 114 A9
Old Bell La RCHLM CM5 263 N8
Oldbury Av CHLM/GWD CM2 240 E5
Old Buryodge La STSD SM24 138 D2
Old Church Rd EN EN1 273 M1
Old Church La
RBRW/HUT CM13 281 P5
SUD CO10 60 C8
Oldchurch Ri ROMW/RG RM7 318 D1
Old Church Rd CHING E4 274 D9
PIT SS13 325 L1
RBRW/HUT CM13 282 A2
RCHLM CM3 263 N4
WCHPL E1 332 A6
Old Coach Rd COL CO7 9 H5
Old Ct CHLM/WR CM1 5 K1
Old Court Rd CHLM/WR CM1 5 K1
Old Crown La BRW CM14 280 A1
Old Dairy Pl SUD CO10 46 F4
Old Farm Av STHGT/OAK N14 272 B6
Old Farm Ct BCAYW CM12 * 283 H4
Old Ferry Rd RCOLE CO7 153 J6
Oldfield Rd RIPW IP8 29 K1
Old Ford Lock SRTFD E15 * 314 D9
Old Ford Rd BOW E3 352 C1
Old Forge Rd COLS CO2 151 J9
EN EN1 251 L8
Old Foundry Rd IPNE IP4 17 F4
Old Grove Cl CHESW EN7 229 J5
Old Hall Cl NHMKT IP6 23 J1
Old Hall Ct SBN/FI SS3 330 F2
Old Hall La MAL CM9 201 H8
RIPS/CAP IP9 85 L5
WOTN CO14 159 M2
Old Hall Ri HLWE CM17 211 M5
Oldhall Rd RIPS/CAP IP9 85 L5
COLS CO2 152 D2
Old Hwy HOD E11 208 E5
Old Hill Av VGE SS16 323 J6
Oldhouse Cft HLW CM20 210 F1
Old House La COLN CO4 103 K6
HLWW/ROY CM19 209 N6
Old House Rd RCOLW CO6 102 C8
Old Ipswich Rd NHMKT IP6 22 D4
RCOLE CO7 105 P9
Old Jenkins Cl SLH/COR SS17 341 J4
Old Kirton Rd FX IP11 34 D1
Old Leigh Rd LOS SS9 328 B5
Old London Rd MAL CM9 242 G2
RIPS/CAP IP9 81 J2
WICKE SS11 285 P9
The Old Maltings BSF CM23 137 M7
Old Manor Wy BXLYHN DA7 346 C7
Old Market Ct SUD CO10 * 20 D5
Old Market Pl SUD CO10 * 20 C5
Old Md SOSN SS2 308 B8
Old Mead Rd RBSF CM22 114 F3
Old Mill Cl MAL CM9 * 222 B8
Old Mill Ct SWFD E18 295 M7
Old Mill La K/T/MI CO5 148 C7
RBSF CM22 162 E7
Old Mill Rd COLN CO4 103 M3
SAFWS CB11 65 M1
Old Nazeing Rd BROX EN10 208 D9
Old Norwich Rd IP IP1 22 E6
Old Oaks WAB EN9 253 H2
Old Orch HLWS CM18 210 E5
Old Paper Mill La NHMKT IP6 22 D5
Old Park Av ENC/FH EN2 273 H5
Old Park Gv WCHMH N21 273 H5
Oldpark Ride CHESW EN7 251 J2
Old Park Ridings
WCHMH N21 272 G5
Old Park Rd ENC/FH EN2 272 G5
PLMGR N13 272 E9
Old Park South
ENC/FH EN2 272 G3
Old Park Vw ENC/FH EN2 272 F2
Old Parsonage Rd FOS CO13 158 G9
Old Pier St WOTN CO14 159 K6
Old Post Office Rw
47 M5
Old Rectory Cl NHMKT IP6 22 D2
Old Rectory Rd CHONG CM5 256 C3
Old River La BSF CM23 137 L7
Old Rd ABR/ST RM4 279 J1
BRTR CM77 146 F1
COS CO15 6 D5
COS CO15 181 P8
DART DA1 346 C9
FOS CO13 183 N1
HARH CM77 147 K6
HSTD CO9 74 A4
K/T/MI CO5 148 E7
PEND EN3 251 P9
RCOLW CO6 148 C4
The Old Rd RCOLW CO6 77 K2
Old Rope Wk HVHL CB9 41 H4
Old Rose Gdns CHLM/WR CM1 * 127 N5
Old School Cl RCOS CO16 180 D9
Old School St RCHLM CM5 * 196 E9
Old School Fld
CHLM/WR CM1 218 D7
Old School La RCOLW CO7 129 P9
Old School Meadow
SBN/FI SS3 330 D2

Old School Yd SAFWS CB11 * 65 L1
WAB EN9 252 E4
Old Ship La RCFD SS4 308 G5
Old Shire La WAB EN9 253 K4
Old Southend Rd
BOC CM0 241 J9
SOS SS1 19 J5
Old Station Rd LOU IG10 275 P4
The Old Station Yd WALTH E17 294 F8
Old St PLSTW E13 333 L2
Old Street Hi RBSF CM22 163 M8
Old Vicarage Dr
CHLM/WR CM1 191 M2
Old Vicarage Rd HAR CO12 110 C5
Old Wy FOS CO13 183 N1
Old Wickford Rd RCHLM CM5 264 E9
Old Worlds End RCFD SS4 * 290 C9
Oldwyk VGE SS16 324 D2
Olga St BOW E3 332 B2
Olive Av LOS SS9 327 K4
Olive Cv COS CO2 151 N4
Oliver Cl WTHK RM20 348 C5
Oliver Gdns EHAM E6 333 P5
Olive Pl PLSTW E13 333 M3
Oliver Pl WIT CM8 197 L2
Oliver Rd BRW CM15 281 K4
LEY E10 314 E5
RAIN RM13 336 E1
WALTH E17 294 F9
WTHK RM20 348 D5
Olivers Cl COS CO15 6 E2
SUD CO10 46 C4
Olivers Cl COS CO15 6 E1
Olivers Crs SBN/FI SS3 330 F2
Olivers Dr WIT CM8 197 L2
Olivers La COLS CO2 151 J7
Olivers Rd COS CO15 6 E2
Oliver Wy CHLM/WR CM1 217 N4
Olive St ROMW/RG RM7 298 C9
Oliveswood Rd GTDUN CM6 141 L7
Olivia Dr LOS SS9 328 A4
Ollard's Gv LOU IG10 275 N5
Ollerton Gn BOW E3 332 C1
Olley Wk K/T/MI CO5 174 B7
Olympus Cl IP IP1 24 D1
Omega Ct WARE SC12 * 184 A2
Omega Maltings
WARE SC12 184 B3
Omnibus Wy WALTH E17 294 D6
Onehouse La IP IP1 25 J2
One Tree Hi SLH/COR SS17 353 N6
Ongar Cl CHDH RM6 297 K9
RCOS CO16 181 L9
Ongar Rd ABR/ST RM4 264 G9
BRW CM14 280 C8
BRW CM15 281 H3
BRWN CM15 257 N5
BRWN CM15 258 B8
BRWN CM15 280 D5
CHLM/WR CM1 238 A3
CHLM/WR CM1 239 J1
COLN CO4 235 N3
GTDUN CM6 141 M8
RAIN RM13 336 D1
Ongar Wy RAIN RM13 314 D2
Onslow Cl CHLM CM6 274 G8
Onslow Crs COLS CO2 152 B5
Onslow Gdns CHONG CM5 235 M6
SWFD E18 295 L7
WCHMH N21 272 F4
Onslow Pde
STHGT/OAK N14 * 272 A7
Ontario Cl BROX EN10 230 B4
Ontario Wy POP/IOD E14 332 D7
Onyx Ms SRTFD E15 315 H8
Opal Av IP IP1 24 E2
Opal Cl CAN/RD E16 333 N6
Ophir Rd RCOLE CO7 179 L8
Optima Pk DART DA1 * 346 F8
Orange Gv CHIG IG7 296 D5
WAN E11 315 H5
Orange Rd CVI SS8 344 C1
Orange Tree Cl
CHLM/GWD CM2 240 B4
Orange Tree Hi ROM RM1 298 C2
Orchard Av BCAYE CM11 284 C6
CHING E4 294 D1
CHLM/GWD CM2 240 B4
CHLM/WR CM1 217 J9
GTDUN CM6 141 M8
HAR CO12 109 K6
HAR CO12 133 M4
HOC/HUL SS5 288 A7
HSTD CO9 57 J4
MAL CM9 222 A9
MAL CM9 225 K2
PEND EN3 273 P4
RCHLM CM3 245 P9
RCOLE CO7 154 A6
RIPW IP8 29 M1
ROMW/RG RM7 298 A6
SBF/HAD SS7 305 N9
SOCK/AV RM15 338 F5

Orchard Ga CHTY IP2 24 D6
Orchard Gv KESG IP5 26 F4
LOS SS9 308 A9
NHMKT IP6 22 D5
Orchard La BRWN CM15 280 C4
WFD IG8 295 P2
Orchardleigh Av PEND EN3 273 P1
Orchard Ldg K/T/MI CO5 174 A9
Orchard Md COS CO15 327 P1
Orchardmede EN EN1 273 J1
Orchard Ms K/T/MI CO5 173 P9
Orchard Piece ING CM4 237 M5
Orchard Pightle CBE/LIN CB1 38 A4
Orchard Pl CHLM/WR CM1 259 J1
POP/IOD E14 333 H7
SUD CO10 20 B7
Orchard Rd BOC CM0 269 J5
BOC CM0 291 H4
BSF CM23 137 N5
COL CO1 8 A3
DAGE RM10 335 P1
K/T/MI CO5 173 H2
PEND EN3 273 P4
RCHLM CM3 245 P9
RCOLE CO7 154 A6
RIPW IP8 20 B7
SBF/HAD SS7 305 N9
SOCK/AV RM15 338 F5
Orchard Rw FX IP11 * 35 H6
Orchards EN EN1 273 M5
The Orchard BROX EN10 208 D8
GTDUN CM6 143 H9
WCHMH N21 273 J5
WICKW SS12 284 G9
Orchard Vw RBRW/HUT CM13 322 E1
CHIG IG7 277 H9
EN EN1 273 K2
Orchid Av WIT CM8 171 M9
Orchid Cl CHTY IP2 24 F7
Orchid Rd RCHLM CM5 264 G9
Orchid St STHGT/OAK N14 272 B6
Orchis Gv GRAYS RM17 349 J2
Orchis Wy HARH RM3 299 L3
Ordell Rd BOW E3 332 C2
Ordnance Crs GNWCH SE10 333 H5
Ordnance Rd CAN/RD E16 333 J5
PEND EN3 252 A7
Oregon Av MNPK E12 316 A6
Oregon Rd KESG IP5 26 F5
Oreston Rd RAIN RM13 337 J5
Orford Crs CHLM/WR CM1 218 B6
Orford Rd FX IP11 41 J5
HVHL CB9 41 J5
SWFD E18 295 L7
WALTH E17 294 E9
Orford St IP IP1 16 B2
Oriel Cl SUD CO10 * 296 A7
Oriel Gv COLS CO2 151 K7
Oriel Rd HOM E9 314 A8
Oriental Rd CAN/RD E16 333 N8
Orient Wy CLPT E5 314 A5
Oriole Wy BSF CM23 135 J7
Orion Cl BSDN SS14 304 E6
Orion Wy BRTR CM7 145 L2
Orkney Cl HVHL CB9 41 N4
Orkney Rd PBW RM3 315 H5
Orlando Cl WOTN CO14 159 K6
Orlando Dr PIT SS13 305 H6
Ormesby Chine RCHLM CM5 286 C3
Ormonde Av RCFD SS4 308 A4
SBF/HAD SS7 327 K4
Ormonde Cl RCOLW CO6 127 H3
Ormonde Gdns LOS SS9 327 K4
Ormonds Crs RCHLM CM3 344 A3
Ormsby Rd CVI SS8 126 C3
Orpen Cl RCOLW CO6 126 C3
Orpen's Hi COLS CO2 150 D8
Orpington Gdns ED N9 273 K9
Orpington Rd WCHMH N21 272 F7
Orrmo Rd CVI SS8 345 J2
Orsett Av LOS SS9 327 M1
Orsett End SBN/FI SS14 327 M1
Orsett Heath Crs
CDW/CHF RM16 350 B1
Orsett Rd GRAYS RM17 349 L3
Orsett Ter WFD IG8 295 M5
Orton Cl ING CM4 261 H1
Orvis La RCOLE CO7 81 H8
Orwell Br IPSE IP3 30 E5
Orwell Cl WICKE SS11 305 N2
Orwell Gdns CHTY IP2 * 25 H8
Orwell Pl IPNE IP4 17 F5
Orwell Rd IPNE IP4 17 F4
RIPS/CAP IP9 84 E1
RCOS CO15 6 B2
FX IP11 11 H5
HAR CO12 15 F6
IPSE IP3 25 H8
PLSTW E13 333 M2
Orwell View Rd RIPS/CAP IP9 85 J6
Orwell Wy RCOS CO16 181 M8
Osbert Rd WIT CM8 197 H4
Osborne Cl CHES/WCR EN8 230 A9
EMPK RM11 318 C1
GRAYS RM17 * 349 L3
Osborne Rd
BRWN CM15 280 E5
CHES/WCR EN8 230 B6
EMPK RM11 318 C1
FSTGT E7 315 L7
HOM E9 314 C8
IPSE IP3 25 P7
K/T/MI CO5 203 H6
PEND EN3 274 B1
PIT SS13 305 K7
PLMGR N13 272 F9
SOS SS16 22 D1
WOS/PRIT SS0 18 C2
Osbornes Rd RCOLE CO7 179 L7
Osborne Sq DAGW RM9 317 N6
Osborne St COL CO1 8 D7
Osbourne Av HOC/HUL SS5 307 N1
Osea Rd MAL CM9 223 J8
Osea Wy CHLM/WR CM1 218 E6
O'Shea Gv BOW E3 332 C1
Osier Dr LAIN SS15 303 K6
Osier Wy LEY E10 314 E5
Osler Rd EN EN9 273 M9
Osmond Cl BRTR CM77 145 J3
Osprey Cl EHAM E6 333 P5
SBN/FI SS3 330 D5
SWFD E18 295 K8
WALTH E17 294 B4
Osprey Ms PEND EN3 273 N4
Osprey Rd HVHL CB9 41 M4
WAB EN9 253 K4
Ospreys COS CO15 182 A7
Osprey Wy CHLM/GWD CM2 240 B4
Ostell Crs PEND EN3 252 D8
Osterberg Rd DART DA1 347 L9
Osterley Dr VGE SS16 323 G1
Osterley Pl RCHLM CM3 286 G3
Ostler Cl BSF CM23 161 P1
Oswald La SAFWS CB11 63 L4
Oswald's Md CLPT E5 314 B6
Oswald St CLPT E5 314 A5
Osward Pl ED N9 273 M8
Othello Cl COLN CO4 128 G7
Otley Cl SIX BOW E3 332 F5
Otley Dr GNTH/NBYPK IG2 316 C1
Otley Rd CAN/RD E16 333 M6
Ottawa Gdns DAGE RM10 318 C9
Otten Cl SOS SS1 330 F2
Otten Rd SUD CO10 58 G1
Otterbourne Rd CHING E4 274 C9
Ottershaw Wy RCOS CO16 181 L7
Ottley Pl ING CM4 * 261 N8
Oudle La MHAD SG10 160 G2
Ouida Rd CVI SS8 344 G2
Oulton Cl HAR CO12 110 A5
THMD SE28 335 K6
Oulton Crs BARK IG11 316 G8
Oulton Rd IPSE IP3 25 M9
Ousden Cl CHES/WCR EN8 230 B9
Ousden Dr CHES/WCR EN8 230 B9
Ouse Cha WIT CM8 196 C2
Outing Cl SOS SS1 19 K5
Outing's La BRWN CM15 258 B8
Outpart Eastward HAR CO12 * 15 C2
Outram Rd EHAM E6 333 P1
Outwood Common Rd
BCAYE CM11 283 K9
Outwood Farm Cl
BCAYE CM11 283 M6
Outwood Farm Rd
BCAYE CM11 283 M6
Oval Gdns GRAYS RM17 349 M1
Oval Rd North DAGE RM10 336 B1
Oval Rd South DAGE RM10 336 B2
The Oval BROX EN10 230 B4
Overbury St CLPT E5 314 A6
Overcliff WOS/PRIT SS0 328 E7
Overcliff Rd GRAYS RM17 349 N3
Overhall Hi RCOLW CO6 99 J9
Over Hall La SAFWN CB10 39 J9
Overlord Cl BROX EN10 208 B8
Overmead Dr RCHLM CM3 265 H9
Overshot Br RCHLM CM3 242 B6
Overton Cl SBF/HAD SS7 317 K2
Overton Dr CHDH RM6 297 J9
SBF/HAD SS7 305 J2
WAN E11 315 L2
Overton Wy SBF/HAD SS7 305 N9
Ovington Gdns BCAYW CM12 283 H5
Owen Cl CRW RM5 297 P5
THMD SE28 335 K8
Owen Gdns WFD IG8 295 P5
Owen Ms WAN E11 315 H4
Owen Ward Cl COLS CO2 151 K3
Owlets Hall Cl HARH RM3 299 L1
Owl Pk LOU IG10 * 275 J1
Owl's Hi COLS CO2 195 N1
Owls Retreat COLN CO4 128 C7
Oxborrow Cl FOS CO13 158 B8
Oxcroft BSF CM23 162 C2
Oxendon Dr HOD EN11 208 D6
Oxenford Cl HAR CO12 110 A7
Oxford Av CDW/CHF RM16 350 B2
EMPK RM11 299 M8
STHGT/OAK N14 272 B7
Oxford Cl CHES/WCR EN8 229 P8
ED N9 273 N8
VGE SS16 322 G1
Oxford Ct BRW CM14 300 C1
CHLM/GWD CM2 218 D7
COLW CO3 * 127 N9
RCOLW CO6 124 A1
Oxford Gdns WCHMH N21 275 H6
Oxford La HSTD CO9 72 B7
Oxford Meadow HSTD CO9 72 C7
Oxford Pl RCOLW CO6 124 A1
Oxford Rd COLW CO3 127 N9
COS CO15 6 E1
CVI SS8 344 F1

Peakes La CHESW EN7 ...229 L6
Peakes Wy CHESW EN7 ...229 L6
Peaketon Av REDBR IG4 ...295 N9
Pea La UPMR RM14 ...320 D8
Pearce Mnr CHLM/GWD CM2 ...239 N2
Pearce Rd IPSE IP5 ...25 P6
Pearcroft Rd IP IP1 ...23 J9
BRWN E11 ...314 C4
Peacy Cl HARH RM3 ...299 K4
Pearswood Rd ERITH DA8 ...346 E6
Pearl Cl EHAM E6 ...334 B6
Pearl Rd IP IP1 ...24 D3
WALTH E17 ...294 D7
Pearmains Cl WICKE SS11 ...285 J7
Pearmains RCHLM CM5 ...169 J6
Pearmain Wy COLW CO3 ...150 F2
Pear Rd WAN E11 ...314 C5
Pearse Wy IPSE IP5 ...31 L1
Pearson Rd IPNE IP4 ...26 B6
Pearsons Cl CAR SS17 ...341 N2
Pearsons Av RAYL SS6 ...306 E3
Pearsons Wy RIPW IP8 ...29 H1
Pear Tree Cl ERITH DA8 ...346 C6
Peartree Cl BRTR CM7 ...145 K5
BRWN CM15 ...258 C8
MAL CM9 ...223 M5
SOCK/AV RM15 ...338 F3
SOSN SS3 ...329 K3
Peartree Gdns BCTR RM8 ...317 J7
Peartree La BURES CO8 ...100 G4
Peartree La BRWN CM15 ...258 C8
RCHLM CM5 ...242 C7
UPMR RM14 ...322 A5
Pear Tree Md HLWS CM18 ...211 L5
Peartree Rd COLW CO3 ...150 G2
EN EN1 ...273 K2
Peartrees RBRW/HUT CM15 ...301 M5
Pear Tree Wk CHESW EN7 ...229 J5
Peartree Wy RCOS CO16 ...181 M5
Pease Cl HCH RM12 ...318 C9
Pease PI HCH RM12 ...263 N5
Peasey La KESG IP5 ...27 H5
Peaslands Rd SAFWS CB11 ...65 M1
Peasmead Ter ENING E4 * ...294 F1
Pebmarsh Cl COLS CO15 ...152 B6
Pebmarsh Dr WICKW SS12 ...305 K1
Pebmarsh Rd BURES CO8 ...75 H8
HSTD CO9 ...96 C5
RCOLW CO6 ...98 G6
Peck's HI WAB EN9 ...209 H9
Pecockes Cl SUD CO10 ...61 M5
Pedder's Cl COLW CO5 ...151 J5
Pedlars Ct RCHLM CM5 ...242 D4
Pedlars End COING CM5 ...242 D8
Pedlars Pth RCHLM CM5 ...242 D4
Pedley Rd BCTR RM8 ...317 K3
Pedro St CLPT E5 ...314 A5
Peel Av SBN/FI SS3 ...330 F7
Peel Cl CHING E4 ...274 E8
ED N9 ...277 J3
Peel Crs BRTR CM7 ...145 H5
Peel Dr CLAY IG5 ...295 P7
Peel PI CLAY IG5 ...295 P6
Peel Rd CHLM/GWD CM2 ...218 B4
SWFD E18 ...295 J5
Peel St IP IP1 ...16 D5
Peel Wy HARH RM5 ...299 L6
Peel Yd KESG IP5 ...27 M5
Peerage Wy EMPK RM11 ...319 L2
Peerglow Est PEND EN3 * ...273 P4
Peers Sq CHLM/GWD CM2 ...218 F7
Peerswood Rd COLS CO15 ...151 N4
Peewit Ct FX IP11 * ...10 D5
Peewit HI FX IP11 ...10 D5
Pegamoid Rd LIE N18 ...275 P9
Pegasus Wy BRTR CM7 ...145 H1
COLN CO4 ...9 K1
Pegelm Gdns EMPK RM11 ...319 L2
Peggotty Cl CHLM/WR CM1 ...217 N5
Peggy's Wk SAFWS CB11 ...50 F7
Pegmiller's La RCHLM CM5 ...170 D7
Pegrams Rd HLWS CM18 ...210 D6
Pegs La WARE CM20 ...160 C8
Pekin St POP/IOD E14 ...332 D6
Peldon Pavement BSDN SS14 ...304 C7
Peldon Rd HLWW/ROY CM19 ...210 E5
K/T/MI CO5 ...177 H5
K/T/MI CO5 ...201 M1
Pelham Av BARK IG11 ...334 G1
Pelham Cl HAR CO12 ...110 A6
Pelham Ct STLK/CL SO SS17 ...341 M1
Pelham Rd IL IG1 ...316 E4
SAFWS CB11 ...88 A4
SOSN SS3 ...329 M5
SWFD E18 ...295 L7
Pelhams La COL CO1 ...6 C6
Pelican Cl CHTY IP2 ...24 F8
Pelling St POP/IOD E14 ...332 C6
Pellipar Cl PLMGR N13 ...272 F9
Pelly Av WIT CM8 ...197 K4
Pelly Cl EPP CM16 ...254 C1
Pelly Rd PLSTW E13 ...333 K2
Pembar Av WALTH E17 * ...294 B7
Pemberton Av GPK RM2 ...298 G2
ING CM4 ...260 C5
Pemberton Ct ING CM4 * ...260 C5
Pemberton Fld RCFD SS4 ...304 C7
Pemberton Gdns CHDH RM6 ...297 P8
Pembrey Wy HCH RM12 ...319 H8
Pembroke Av EN EN1 ...251 N9
MAL CM9 ...223 M4
SLH/COR SS17 ...341 P1
Pembroke Cl BCAYW CM12 ...283 H3
BROX EN10 ...230 D3
CHTY IP2 ...25 J8
COLS CO2 ...152 D5
EMPK RM11 ...299 M8
ERITH DA8 ...346 B2
Pembroke Dr CHESW EN7 ...229 H7
Pembroke Gdns COS CO15 ...182 F7
DAGE RM10 ...318 A5

Pembroke La CBE/LIN CB1 ...38 D1
Pembroke Ms PIT SS13 ...305 H7
Pembroke Pde ERITH DA8 * ...346 B5
Pembroke PI CHLM/WR CM1 ...217 P4
SUD CO10 ...46 C9
Pembroke Rd EHAM E6 ...334 A5
ERITH DA8 ...346 B3
GDMY/SEVK IG5 ...316 C5
PLMGR N13 ...273 H9
WALTH E17 ...294 E9
Pembury Rd WOS/PRIT SS0 ...328 D7
Penda Rd ERITH DA8 ...346 A5
Pendle Cl BSDN SS14 ...304 F6
Pendle Dr BSDN SS14 ...304 E6
Pendlestone Rd WALTH E17 ...294 E9
Pendleton Rd CHTY IP2 ...29 M1
Pendower RAYL SS6 ...306 E7
Penenley Rd RAIN RM13 ...336 C5
Penfold Rd COS CO15 ...6 E6
ED N9 ...274 A7
FX IP11 ...11 K1
Pengelly Cl CHESW EN7 ...229 N9
Penge Rd PLSTW E13 ...315 M9
Penhurst Av SOSN SS2 ...328 C4
Penhurst Dr RCHLM CM5 ...286 G3
Penhurst Rd BARK/HLT IG6 ...296 C4
Penlan Hall La RCOLW CO6 ...125 N1
Penlow Rd HLWS CM18 ...210 D6
Pennant Ter WALTH E17 ...294 C6
Penn Cl CDW/CHF RM16 ...340 C4
RIPS/CAP IP9 ...28 D8
Penn Gdns CRW RM5 ...297 P4
Pennial Rd CRW RM5 ...344 D1
Pennine Rd CHLM/WR CM1 ...217 L5
Pennine Wy BXLYHN DA7 ...346 D6
Pennington Dr CRW RM5 ...297 P5

Pennington Dr
STHGT/OAK N14 ...272 C4
Pennington La STSD CM24 ...114 A7
Penningtons LE DUT SS13 ...137 H9
Penn Ms BRTR CM7 ...145 K6
Pennsylvania La K/T/MI CO5 ...173 N8
Penny Cl RAIN RM13 ...336 C5
Penny Flds BRW CM14 ...500 F1
Pennyfields POP/IOD E14 ...332 D7
Penny La IPSE IP5 ...31 M1
Pennymead HLW CM20 ...211 H3
Penny Meadow RIPS/CAP IP9 ...28 C9
Pennyroyal Av EHAM E6 ...334 B6
Pennyroyal Cl WANT CM6 ...171 M9
Pennyroyal Gdns CHTY IP2 ...24 F7
Penny Royal Rd RCHLM CM5 ...242 A4
Penny's La ING CM4 ...260 C1
Pennystone Rd SAFWS CB11 ...65 M1
Penrhyn Av WALTH E17 ...294 D5
Penrhyn Crs WALTH E17 ...294 D5
Penrhyn Gv WALTH E17 ...294 D5
Penrice Cl COLN CO4 ...128 F9
Penrith Crs HARH RM5 ...318 F7
Penrith Rd BARK/HLT IG6 ...296 C6
HARH RM5 ...299 M5
Penrose Md CHLM/WR CM1 ...239 J2
Penryn Rd KESG IP5 ...26 E4
Penshurst Cl WALTH E17 ...187 J9
Penshurst PI BRTR CM7 ...144 E8
Penshurst Rd HOM E9 ...314 A9
IPSE IP5 ...26 C7
Penson's La CHONG CM5 ...234 F7
Penticton Rd BRTR CM7 ...144 G4
Pentire Cl UPMR RM14 ...320 B1
Pentland Av ERITH DA8 ...294 C5
Pentland Av CHLM/WR CM1 ...217 P5
SBN/FI SS3 ...330 B3
Pentland Cl ED N9 ...273 P8
Pentlow Dr SUD CO10 ...45 J9
Pentlow Hawke Cl H/VHL CB9 ...41 L4
Pentlow HI SUD CO10 ...45 M5
Pentlow Wy BKHH N19 ...275 P6
Pentney Rd CHES/WCR EN8 ...274 C7
Penton Dr CHES/WCR EN8 ...230 A8
Pentrich Av EN EN1 ...251 M8
Penventon Ct TIL RM18 * ...350 B7
Penwood Cl BCAYE CM11 ...283 L2
Penzance Cl CHLM/WR CM1 ...218 D6
COS CO15 ...207 H4
Penzance Gdns HARH RM3 ...299 M3
Peony Ct HARH RM3 ...299 M3
KESG IP5 ...26 E5
Pepper Cl EHAM E6 ...334 A5
Peppercorn Cl COLN CO4 ...128 A5
Peppercorn Wy CHTY IP2 ...25 K8
Pepper's Rd COLN CO4 ...103 H7
Pepples La SAFWN CB10 ...66 F8
Pepys Cl TIL RM18 ...350 D6
Pepys St HART CO12 ...15 F3
Percival Gdns CHDH RM6 ...317 K1
Percival Rd EMPK RM11 ...319 H1
EN EN1 ...273 L5
FOS CO15 ...158 E5
WOTN CO14 ...159 L4
Percy Cottis Rd RCFD SS4 ...508 F4
Percy Gdns PEND EN3 ...274 A4
Percy Rd CAN/RD E16 ...333 H5
GDMY/SEVK IG5 ...317 H2
LOS SS9 ...327 N4
ROMW/RG RM7 ...298 B7
WAN E11 ...315 H2
WCHMH N21 ...273 H6
Percy Ruse Cl SUD CO10 ...21 J5
Percy St GRAYS RM17 ...349 M4
Peregrine Cl BSF CM23 ...135 J3
SBN/FI SS3 ...330 D5
VGE SS16 ...324 A2
Peregrine Ct COLN CO4 ...128 C7
Peregrine Dr
CHLM/GWD CM2 ...239 P5
BSF CM23 ...325 P4
Peregrine Gdns RAYL SS6 ...306 E4
Peregrine Rd BARK/HLT IG6 ...297 J3
Peregrin Rd WAB EN9 ...253 K4
Peridot St EHAM E6 ...333 P5

Perkins Rd BARK/HLT IG6 ...296 E9
Perkins Wy IPSE IP5 ...30 F1
Perran Cl BROX EN10 ...230 B5
Perriciose CHLM/WR CM1 ...218 C4
Perrin PI CHLM/GWD CM2 ...4 D6
Perriors Cl CHESW EN7 ...229 M6
Perry Cl RAIN RM13 ...336 C2
Perryfield HLWE CM17 ...213 H1
Perry Gdns ED N9 ...273 K9
Perry Gn BSDN SS14 ...303 J2
Perry Gv DART DA1 ...347 M9
Perry HI CHLM/WR CM1 ...5 K1
WAB EN9 ...231 J2
Perry La COLN CO4 ...104 A4
Perrymans Farm Rd
GNTH/NBYPK IG2 ...316 E1
Perry Md ENC/FH EN2 ...272 G1
Perry Rd HLWS CM18 ...217 L5
K/T/MI CO5 ...173 N8
SBF/HAD SS7 ...326 C3
WIT CM8 ...197 L3
Perrysfield Rd
CHES/WCR EN8 ...230 B6
Perry Spring HLWE CM17 ...211 K5
VGE SS16 ...3 K7
Perry St BCAYW CM12 ...282 C5
DART DA1 ...347 L8
Perry Wy SOCK/AV RM15 ...337 P7
WIT CM8 ...197 L3
Persardi Ct COLS CO2 ...152 B7
Pershore Cl GNTH/NBYPK IG2 ...296 C9
Pershore End COLW CO3 ...151 H1
Perth Cl COLS CO2 ...152 B5
Perth Rd BARK IG11 ...334 E2
GNTH/NBYPK IG2 ...316 C1
LEY E10 ...314 B3
PLSTW E13 ...333 L2
Perth Ter GNTH/NBYPK IG2 ...316 D2
Pertwee Cl RCOLE CO7 ...179 K5
Pertwee Dr CHLM/GWD CM2 ...240 E4
RCHLM CM5 ...286 F1
Pertwees Ct COL CO1 ...128 D9
Pertwee Wy K/T/MI CO5 ...177 J5
Pesthouse La HAR CO12 ...133 M4
NHMKT IP6 ...22 B1
Peterborough Av
UPMR RM14 ...320 B3
Peterborough Rd LEY E10 ...294 F9
Peterborough Wy BSDN SS14 ...304 C2
Peter Bruff Av RCOS CO16 ...181 M8
Peterfield's La HSTD CO9 ...121 P2
Peterhouse Cl CHTY IP2 ...24 F9
Peters Cl BCTR RM8 ...317 L3
Petersfield CHLM/WR CM1 ...218 A3
Petersfield Av HARH RM3 ...299 K3
Petersfield Cl HARH RM3 ...299 M3
Peter's Gv RIPS/CAP IP9 ...28 C9
Peterstone Rd ABYW SE2 ...335 J9
Peter St ING CM4 ...261 N8
Petersfield Wy CHLM/WR CM1 ...218 G4
Peters Wood HI WARE SC12 ...184 A5
Peto Av COLN CO4 ...128 A5
Peto St North CAN/RD E16 ...333 H6
Petrebrook CHLM/GWD CM2 ...218 F8
Petre Cl ING CM4 ...260 D7
Petrel Wy CHLM/GWD CM2 ...240 B4
Petresfield Wy
RBRW/HUT CM13 ...321 M1
Petrolea Cl COL CO1 ...128 C2
Petronius Wy COL CO4 ...128 C2
Petro St South CAN/RD E16 ...333 J7
Pett Cl EMPK RM11 ...318 G4
Pettit La BRTR CM7 ...171 H1
Pettits Bvd ROM RM1 ...298 D6
Pettits Cl ROM RM1 ...298 D5
Pettits La ROM RM1 ...298 D7
Pettits La North ROM RM1 ...298 C5
Pettit's PI DAGE RM10 ...317 P7
Pettit's Rd DAGE RM10 ...317 P7
Pettley Gdns ROMW/RG RM7 ...298 C9
Petts La SAFWN CB10 ...51 M1
Pettys Cl CHES/WCR EN8 ...230 A8
Petunia Crs CHLM/WR CM1 ...218 E5
Petworth Cl BRTR CM7 ...144 E7
RCOLE CO7 ...130 G5
Petworth Gdns COLN CO4 ...128 A5
Petworth Wy HCH RM12 ...318 E6
Pevensey Av EN EN1 ...273 J1
Pevensey Dr COS CO15 ...207 H4
Pevensey Gdns HOC/HUL SS5 ...287 J8
Pevensey Rd FSTGT E7 ...315 J1
Pevensey Wy PIT SS13 ...304 G9
Peverel Av RCHLM CM5 ...220 F2
Pewsey Cl CHING E4 ...294 D2
Pewterers Av BSF CM23 ...161 P1
Pharos La K/T/MI CO5 ...202 F6
Pheasant Cl CAN/RD E16 ...333 L6
Pheasant Ri RIPW IP8 ...29 H1
Pheasant Rd CHTY IP2 ...24 F8
Phelips Rd EPP CM16 ...210 B8
Philan Wy CRW RM5 ...297 P1
Philbrick Crs West RAYL SS6 ...306 E4
Philip Av FX IP11 ...10 D4
ROMW/RG RM7 ...298 C6
Philip Cl BRWN CM15 ...280 E5
Philippa Cl HARH RM3 ...299 N5
Philip Rd CHTY IP2 ...24 F8
Philip Rd RAIN RM13 ...336 D3
WIT CM8 ...197 H4
Philip Sydney Rd WTHK RM20 ...348 G3
Phillida Rd HARH RM3 ...299 M6
Phillipps Rd RCOLE CO7 ...153 J6
Phillips Cl BRTR CM7 ...145 K1
Phillips Field Rd SUD CO10 ...45 H5
Philmead Rd SBF/HAD SS7 ...325 N4
Philpot End La GTDUN CM6 ...166 A2
Philpott Av SOSN SS2 ...329 L4
Phipps Hatch La ENC/FH EN2 ...251 H8
Phoenix Cl WALTH E17 ...294 C6

Phoenix Gv CHLM/GWD CM2 ...4 C7
Phoenix Rd WAN E11 ...294 E6
Phoenix Wy SBF/HAD SS7 ...306 F8
Picardy Manorway
BELV DA17 ...336 A9
Picasso Wy SBN/FI SS3 ...330 F5
Piccotts La BRTR CM7 ...119 M7
Pickard Cl STHGT/OAK N14 ...272 C7
Pickering Av EHAM E6 ...334 D2
Pickers Wy COS CO15 ...182 F6
Picketts RCHLM CM5 ...286 G2
Picketts Av CHLM/WR CM1 ...217 L5
Picketts Cl LOS SS9 ...327 P2
Pickett's Lock La ED N9 ...274 A8
Picketts HI WAB EN9 ...253 M6
Pickhill WAB EN9 ...253 A2
Pickpocket La BRTR CM7 ...144 G8
Pickwick Av CHLM/WR CM1 ...217 L5
Pickwick Cl LAIN SS15 ...303 L8
Pickwick Rd CHTY IP2 ...24 F8
Picton Av IP IP1 ...25 L2
Picton Cl RAYL SS6 ...307 H6
Picton Gdns RAYL SS6 ...306 G6
Pier Ap WOTN CO14 ...159 K7
Pier Av COS CO15 ...6 E5
Pierce Gld K/T/MI CO5 ...173 P8
Piercing HI EPP CM16 ...254 E5
Pier Gap COS CO15 ...7 F6
Pier Hill SOS SS1 ...7 G4
Pierrefitte Wy BRTR CM7 ...145 H3
Pier Rd CAN/RD E16 ...334 B9
ERITH DA8 ...346 D4
IP IP1 ...11 K2
GRH DA9 ...348 G5
Pier Whf GRAYS RM17 ...349 K5
Piggotts Wy BSF CM23 ...137 K9
Piggs Cnr GRAYS RM17 ...349 M1
The Pightle BRTR CM7 ...94 C2
HVHL CB9 ...41 K3
RIPS/CAP IP9 ...28 D8
Pightle Wy WOTN CO14 ...159 H7
Pig La BSF CM23 ...162 D2
Pigstye Green Rd
CHONG CM5 ...237 J2
Pike La UPMR RM14 ...320 C7
Pike Wy EPP CM16 ...255 P6
Pilborough Wy COLW CO3 ...151 H5
Pilcox Hall La RCOS CO16 ...131 P8
Pilgrim Cl BRTR CM7 ...145 J1
BRWN CM15 ...280 B3
CDW/CHF RM16 ...338 F8
Pilgrims Ms POP/IOD E14 ...333 H9
Pilgrims' Rd SWCM DA10 ...349 H9
Pilgrims Wy SBF/HAD SS7 ...327 J5
Pilgrim Wy LAIN SS15 ...303 K9
Pilkingtons HLWE CM17 ...211 L3
Pilot Cl WICKE SS11 ...305 M2
Pimblett Rw RBSF CM22 ...115 J2
Pimpernel Rd CHTY IP2 ...24 G8
Pinceybrook Rd HLWS CM18 ...210 D7
Pincey Rd STSD CM24 ...139 J3
Pinchpools Rd BSF CM23 ...113 M4
Pindar Rd HOD EN11 ...208 F4
Pine Av GTDUN CM6 ...141 J3
IP IP1 ...25 J2
SRTFD E15 ...314 G7
Pine Bank KESG IP5 ...27 L5
Pine Cl CHES/WCR EN8 ...229 P7
CVI SS8 ...344 B2
ING CM4 ...260 D8
LEY E10 ...314 D4
LOS SS9 ...327 L1
MGTR CO11 ...81 N9
RCOLE CO7 ...130 B6
STHGT/OAK N14 ...272 B6
The Pines CHDH RM6 ...339 J4
FX IP11 ...35 P5
LAIN SS15 ...303 L8
RCHLM CM5 ...196 D7
STHGT/OAK N14 ...272 B6
WFD IG8 ...275 K9
Pinetree Cl KESG IP5 ...26 E4
Pinetrees SBF/HAD SS7 ...326 F3
Pine View Rd IP IP1 ...23 P2
Pinewood Av COS CO15 ...207 J5
RAIN RM13 ...336 G4
Pinewood Cl COS CO15 ...181 P6
FOS CO15 ...158 E2
HLWE CM17 ...211 K5
HOC/HUL SS5 ...287 M6
TIL RM18 ...351 J2
Pinewood Dr ABR/ST RM4 ...298 B1
Pinewood Wy
RBRW/HUT CM13 ...281 N4
Pinkeneys ROY SG8 ...48 G5
Pinkham Dr WIT CM8 ...197 J4
Pink La WIT CM8 ...170 G6
Pinkney Cl SAFWN CB10 ...66 D7
Pinkuah La SUD CO10 ...45 L5
Pinley Gdns DAGW RM9 ...335 J1
Pin MI BSDN SS14 ...320 C3
Pin Mill Cl RIPW IP8 ...29 L1
Pinmill Rd RIPS/CAP IP9 ...84 C1
Pinnacle HI BXLYHN DA7 ...346 A8
Pinnacle HI North
BXLYHN DA7 ...346 A8
Pinnacles WAB DA7 ...253 H4
Pintail Crs BRTR CM7 ...144 F8
Pintail Rd WFD IG8 ...295 L4
Pintolls RCHLM CM5 ...286 G2
Pioneer PI COL CO1 ...128 B9
Pipchin Rd CHLM/WR CM1 ...217 M5
Piperell Wy HVHL CB9 ...41 K6
Piper Rd COLW CO3 ...127 L8
Pipers Cl HVHL CB9 ...41 K5
Pipers Tye CHLM/GWD CM2 ...240 C7
Pipers Vale Cl IPSE IP5 ...30 E1
Piper Wy IL IG1 ...316 E3
Pippins Rd BOC CM0 ...291 H2
Pippins HSTD CO9 ...97 N6
Pipps Hill Rd North
BSDN SS14 ...304 A4
Pipps Hill Rd South
BSDN SS14 ...304 A7
Pippo's La NHMKT IP6 ...23 M6
Pirie Rd RCOLW CO6 ...127 H5
Pirie St CAN/RD E16 ...333 L8
Pishiobury Dr SBW CM21 ...187 L4
Pitcairn Cl ROMW/RG RM7 ...297 P8
Pitcairn Rd IP IP1 ...7 D8
Pitchford St SRTFD E15 ...314 C9
Pitfield Crs THMD SE28 ...335 H8
Pitfield Cl CHLM/GWD CM2 ...240 C2
Pitfield Wy PEND EN3 ...251 P9
Pitmans Cl SOS SS1 ...19 G4
Pitmire La BURES CO8 ...75 L3
Pitsea Hall La VGE SS16 ...324 C3
Pitsea PI WCHPL E1 ...332 A6
Pitsea Rd PIT SS13 ...304 F9
Pitsea St WCHPL E1 ...332 A6
Pitsea View Rd BCAYE CM11 ...304 C3
Pitseaville Gv VGE SS16 ...324 D1
Pitt Av WIT CM8 ...197 K4
Pitt Cha CHLM/GWD CM2 ...240 D5
Pittfields VGE SS16 ...323 H1
Pittman Cl RBRW/HUT CM13 ...301 M1
Pittman Gdns IL IG1 ...316 D7
Pittman's Fld HLW CM20 ...210 G2
Pitts End RCOLE CO7 ...130 B6
Pixley St POP/IOD E14 ...332 C6
Place Farm La BRWN CM15 ...258 D7
Pladda Ms WICKW SS12 ...305 L2
Plains Farm Cl RCOLE CO7 ...128 E1
Plains Fld BRTR CM7 ...145 N5
Plains Rd MAL CM9 ...198 G6
The Plain EPP CM16 ...253 J8
Plaistow Green Rd HSTD CO9 ...122 D2
Plaistow Gv SRTFD E15 ...333 J1
Plaistow Park Rd PLSTW E13 ...333 L2
Plaistow Rd PLSTW E13 ...333 K2
Plaistow Wy ROY SG8 ...48 B8
Plane Tree Cl BOC CM0 ...290 G2
CHLM/GWD CM2 ...240 A4
Plane Tree Cl COS CO15 ...206 G2
Plantagenet Rd WAB EN9 ...252 E3
Plantagenet Gdns CHDH RM6 ...317 L2
Plantagenet PI WAB EN9 ...252 E3
Plantain Gdns WAN E11 ...314 C5
Plantation Cl SAFWS CB11 ...65 M3
Plantation Rd ERITH DA8 ...346 D6
RCHLM CM5 ...249 G1
Planton Wy RCOLE CO7 ...179 J6
Plashet Gdns
RBRW/HUT CM13 ...301 K1
Plashet Gv EHAM E6 ...333 M1
Plashet Rd PLSTW E13 ...333 K1
Plashets RBSF CM22 ...188 B3
The Plashets RBSF CM22 ...188 B3
Plashetts BSDN SS14 ...304 C8
Plas Newydd SOS SS1 ...329 M8
Platford Gn EMPK RM11 ...299 K8
Platters Cl IPSE IP5 ...30 G3
Platters Rd FX IP11 ...11 F6
Platts Rd PEND EN3 ...251 P9
Plaw Hatch Cl BSF CM23 ...143 H8
Players Ct GTDUN CM6 ...143 H8
Playfield Av CRW RM5 ...298 B5
Playfield Rd RIPS/CAP IP9 ...28 D9
Playford La SAFWS CB11 ...26 D2
Playford Rd IPNE IP4 ...26 D2
Playhouse Sq HLW CM20 ...210 G3
Playle Cha MAL CM9 ...198 B8
Plaza Wy SOS SS1 ...329 L4
Pleasant Dr BCAYW CM12 ...282 F4
Pleasant Ms MGTR CO11 ...19 J6
Pleasant PI MGTR CO11 ...107 H6
Pleasant Rd BCAYW CM23 ...137 K6
SOS SS1 ...19 J5
Pleasant Mw IPNE IP4 ...17 F6
Pleasant Ter SBF/HAD SS9 ...327 P6
Pleasant Vw SAFWS CB11 ...65 L2
Pleshey Cl ERITH DA8 ...346 D3
SOSN SS2 ...329 N5
Pleshey Cl SOS SS1 ...305 K1
Pleshey Rd RCHLM CM5 ...167 M9
Plevna Rd ED N9 ...273 H9
Plimsoll Cl POP/IOD E14 ...332 E6
Plough Dr COLW CO3 ...151 K1
Plough HI RDPB/CUF EN6 ...228 D8
Plough La RCOLW CO6 ...77 L4
COL CO1 ...20 B6
Ploughmans Cl BSF CM23 ...137 H9
Roughmans Headland
COLW CO3 ...150 G1
Plough Ri UPMR RM14 ...320 B2
Plough Rd RCOLE CO7 ...155 K6
RIPS/CAP IP9 ...17 J7
Plough St IPSE IP5 ...25 M3
Plover Cl FOS CO15 ...158 F8
Plover Gdns UPMR RM14 ...320 C3

Plover Rd *CHTY* IP2 ....24 F9
Plovers Md *BRWN* CM15 ....258 C6
The Plovers *BOC* CM0 ....247 J5
Plowmans *RAYL* SS6 ....307 H5
Plowman Wy *BCTR* RM8 ....317 K3
Ployters Rd *HLWW/ROY* CM19 ....210 D7
Plumberow La *HAW* SS5 ....303 L9
Plumberow Av *HOC/HUL* SS5 ....287 P9
Plumberow Mount Av
 HOC/HUL SS5 ....287 P8
Plume Av *COLW* CO3 ....151 K2
Plume Av *MAL* 244 A1
Plummers *PIT* SS13 ....304 D8
Plummers Dell *NHMKT* IP6 ....22 B2
Plummers Rd *ROCFW* CO6 ....126 B1
Plumpton Av *HCH* RM12 ....319 L6
Plumpton Rd *HOD* EN11 ....208 F3
Plump Tree La *RCHLM* CM3 ....242 A5
Plumptre La *BCAYW* CM12 ....242 A5
Plums La *BRTR* CM7 ....119 K3
Plumtree Av
 CHLM/GWD CM2 ....240 E4
Plumtree Cl *DAGE* RM10 ....318 A8
Plymouth Rd *DAGE* RM16 ....335 F5
 CDW/CHF RM16 ....348 F5
 CHLM/WR CM1 ....218 D6
 FX IP11 ....35 J5
Plymtree *SOS* SS1 ....330 B5
Pochard Wy *BRTR* CM77 ....144 F9
Pocklington Ct
 CHLM/GWD CM2 ....218 F7
Pod's Brook Rd *BRTR* CM7 ....144 C5
Pods Cl *BRTR* CM77 ....144 A4
Point Bourne *COLW* CO3 ....150 E8
Point Clear Rd *RCOS* CO16 ....205 L2
Point Cl *CVI* SS8 ....345 J2
Pointer Cl *SDE* SE28 ....335 L6
Point Rd *CVI* SS8 ....345 J2
Pointwell La *RCOLW* CO6 ....147 P7
Pole Barn La *FOS* CO13 ....158 C9
Polecat Rd *BRTR* CM77 ....146 A8
Pole Hill Rd *CHING* E4 ....274 F6
Pole La *WIT* CM8 ....170 D2
Polesworth Rd *DAGW* RM9 ....335 N2
Poley Rd *SLH/COR* SS17 ....341 K5
Pollard Cl *CAN/RD* E16 ....333 K7
 CHIG IG7 ....297 H2
Pollard Hatch
 HLWW/ROY CM19 ....210 C6
Pollards Cl *CHESW* EN7 ....229 H8
 LOU IG10 ....275 M4
 RCFD SS4 ....308 F5
Pollards Gn *CHLM/GWD* CM2 ....218 G9
Pollards Wk *RCOS* CO16 ....181 M8
Polstead Br *RCOLW* CO6 ....78 C2
Polstead Cl *RAYL* SS6 ....306 D4
Polsteads *VGE* SS16 ....324 D3
Polstead St *RCOLW* CO6 ....78 C3
Polsteads Wy *RCOS* CO16 ....181 L9
Pomfret Md *BSDN* SS14 2
Pompadour Cl *BRW* CM14 ....300 F2
Pond Cha *COLW* CO3 ....151 K2
Pond Cl *FX* IP11 ....34 C6
 HOC/HUL SS5 ....287 H5
Pond Cross Farm
 SAFWS CB11 ....65 H9
Pond Cross Wy *SAFWS* CB11 ....64 C9
Ponders Rd *RCOLW* CO6 ....125 P4
Pondfield La
 RBRW/HUT CM13 ....301 K1
Pondfield Rd *COLN* CO6 ....128 E6
 DAGE RM10 ....318 A2
Pond La *RBSF* CM22 ....188 F1
Pond Rd *SRTFD* E15 ....333 G2
Ponds Rd *CHLM/GWD* CM2 ....240 A8
Pond Wk *LANF* RM6 ....320 B4
Poney Cha *WIT* CM8 ....198 A7
Poole Cl *IPSE* IP5 ....26 C8
Poolehurst Wk
 HOC/HUL SS5 ....287 H5
Pooles La *EMPK* RM11 ....319 L2
 HOM E9 ....314 A8
Pooles La *HOC/HUL* SS5 ....287 H5
Poole St *HSTD* CO9 ....71 P2
 SUD CO10 ....45 H2
Poolmans St
 BERM/RHTH SE16 ....332 A9
Pool's La *CHLM/WR* CM1 ....238 A6
Poore St *SAFWS* CB11 ....64 A9
Poors Cl *BSF/HAD* SS7 ....324 G8
Poors La North *SBF/HAD* SS7 ....327 K1
Poperinghe Av *COLS* CO2 ....152 A2
Popes Ct *HVHL* CB9 ....41 P6
Popes La *RCOLW* CO6 ....215 J5
Pope's Rd *RCOLW* CO6 ....8 A6
Popes Wy *WARE* SG12 ....184 A1
Popes Wk *RAYL* SS6 ....307 J5
Popis Gdns *WARE* SG12 ....184 B2
Poplar Av *RCOS* CO16 ....206 F2
Poplar Bath St *POP/IOD* E14 ....332 E7
Poplar Cl *CHLM/GWD* CM2 ....240 A6
 COS CO15 ....206 G2
 HOM E9 ....314 C7
 HSTD CO9 ....98 A8
 HVHL CB9 ....40 C2
 ING CM4 ....194 G2
 ING CM4 ....260 B7
 NHMKT IP6 ....22 D4
 RCHLM CM3 ....264 F9
 SOCK/AP RM15 ....338 C4
 WIT CM8 ....171 P6
Poplar Gv *RBRW/HUT* CM13 ....281 M5
Poplar Grove Cha *MAL* CM9 ....222 C4
Poplar High St *POP/IOD* E14 ....332 F7
Poplar La *BRW* CM14 ....314 E3
Poplar Mt *BELV* DA17 ....346 A2
Poplar Pl *THMD* SE28 ....335 K7
 RAYL SS6 ....307 J7
Poplar Rd *CVI* SS8 ....345 J2
 SUD CO10 ....21 J6
Poplar Rw *EPP* CM16 ....254 F7
Poplars Av *HOC/HUL* SS5 ....307 P3

Poplars Cl *RCOLE* CO7 ....154 A7
Poplar Shaw *WAB* EN9 ....253 J3
Poplars Rd *WALTH* E17 ....314 E1
The Poplars *ABR/ST* RM4 ....277 J2
 CHESW EN7 ....229 K5
 GTDUN CM6 ....141 K4
 MGTR CO11 ....81 N7
 STHGT/OAK N14 ....272 A4
Poplar St *ROMW/RG* RM7 ....298 B8
Poplar Wy *BARK/HLT* IG6 ....296 D8
 FOS CO13 ....158 E8
Poppleton Rd *WAN* E11 ....315 H1
Poppy Cl *BELV* DA17 ....346 A1
 CHTY IP2 ....24 C9
Poppyfield Cl *LOS* SS9 ....307 N9
Poppy Gdns *COLS* CO2 ....152 D5
Poppy Wk *CHESW* EN7 ....229 J7
Porchester Cl *EMPK* RM11 ....319 K1
Porchester Rd *BCAYW* CM12 ....283 H5
Pork La *FOS* CO13 ....157 P9
Porlock Rd *WOS/PRIT* SS0 ....328 B2
Porlock Rd *EN* EN1 ....273 L6
Portal Av *KESG* IP5 ....27 M2
Porticullis Lodge Rd
 ENC/FH EN2 ....273 J2
Portelet Rd *WCHPL* E1 ....332 A3
Porter Cl *WTHK* RM20 ....348 F4
Porter Rd *EHAM* E6 ....334 A6
 IPSE IP5 ....27 P2
Porters *PIT* SS13 ....305 H7
Porters Av *DAGW* RM9 ....317 J8
Porters Brook Wk *COLN* CO6 ....128 D5
Porters Cl *BRW* CM14 ....280 D7
 COLS CO2 ....126 C5
Porter's La *COLW* CO3 ....126 E5
Porters Pk *RCHLM* CM3 ....219 M1
Porter Wy *RCOS* CO16 ....181 L9
Portia Wy *BOW* E3 ....332 C4
Portland Av *HAR* CO12 ....14 D7
 SOS SS1 ....19 H5
Portland Cl *BRTR* CM7 ....145 L5
 CHDH RM6 ....297 M9
Portland Crs *HAR* CO12 ....14 C7
Portland Dr *CHESW* EN7 ....251 M1
 ENC/FH EN2 ....251 K8
Portland Gdns *CHDH* RM6 ....297 L9
Portland Pl *BSF* CM23 ....137 L7
 FX IP11 ....137 L7
 COL CO1 ....8 D7
Port La *COL* CO1 ....8 D7
 RBSF CM22 ....162 E5
Portlight *MGTR* CO11 ....106 F4
Portman Dr *BCAYW* CM12 ....283 J3
Portman Rd *IP* IP1 ....16 C4
Portmeadow Wk *ABYW* SE2 ....335 L9
Portmeers Cl *WALTH* E17 *.......314 C1
Portmore Gdns *CRW* RM5 ....297 P2
Portnol Cl *ROM* RM1 ....298 C6
Port of Felixstowe Rd *FX* IP11 ....11 D6
Portreath Pl *CHLM/WR* CM1 ....217 P4
Portree Rd *POP/IOD* E14 ....332 C6
Portsea Rd *TIL* RM18 ....350 D6
Portsmouth Rd *COS* CO15 ....207 H4
Portway *CHLM/GWD* CM2 ....218 G7
 RAIN RM13 ....336 F1
 SRTFD E15 ....333 K1
Portway Ct *HSTD* CO9 ....98 A5
Posford Ct *COLN* CO4 ....128 A2
Postern Gn *ENC/FH* EN2 ....272 F1
Postman's La *RCHLM* CM3 ....220 B8
Post Meadow *BCAYE* CM11 ....305 L1
Post Mill Cl *IPNE* IP4 ....17 K3
Post Office Ap *FSTGT* E7 ....315 L7
Post Office La *MAL* CM9 ....199 J8
Post Office Rd
 CHLM/WR CM1 ....218 A3
 HLW CM20 ....6 C5
 ING CM4 ....260 C6
 MAL CM9 ....243 H5
Post Office Rw *RCFD* SS4 *.......290 C9
Postway Ms *IL* IG1 ....316 C5
Post Wood Rd *WARE* SG12 ....184 B5
Potash La *RIPS/CAP* IP9 ....81 P7
Potash Rd *BCAYE* CM11 ....283 J3
 HLWE CM17 ....189 J9
Potipher Rd *BRW* CM14 ....300 E1
Pot Kiln Cha *HSTD* CO9 ....59 L8
Pot Kiln Rd *SUD* CO10 ....61 L4
The Pot Kilns *SUD* CO10 ....61 M4
Potters Fld *EN* EN1 *.......273 K3
 HLWE CM17 ....211 L5
Potters La *RCHLM* CM3 ....264 A7
Potter St *BSF* CM23 ....137 L7
 HLWE CM17 ....211 K4
 HSTD CO9 ....97 H1
Potters Wy *SOSN* SS2 ....328 G3
Pottery La *CHLM/WR* CM1 ....217 P6
 HSTD CO9 ....72 E6
Potton Dr *WICKW* SS12 ....305 L2
Pouch Mi *FX* IP11 ....34 E3
Poulett Rd *EHAM* E6 ....334 A2
Poulk Hall La *RCHLM* CM3 ....169 K7
Poulteney Rd *STSD* CM24 ....114 B7
Poulton Cl *MAL* CM9 ....244 B2
Pound Cl *WAB* EN9 ....231 H2
Pound Farm Dr *HAR* CO12 ....14 A5
Poundfield Rd *RCOLE* CO7 *.......154 A7
Poundfield Rd *LOU* IG10 ....275 P4
Pound Flds *CHLM/WR* CM1 ....239 J2
Pound Ga *GTDUN* CM6 ....118 C9
Pound La *CDW/CHF* RM16 ....348 A4
 LAIN SS15 ....303 L7
 RIPS/CAP IP9 ....81 P6
 RIPW IP9 ....39 J3
 WICKW SS12 ....305 L6
Pound La Central *LAIN* SS15 ....303 L6
Pound La North *LAIN* SS15 ....303 L6
Pound Wk *SAFWN* CB10 ....51 L8
Powdermill La *WAB* EN9 ....252 E5
Powdermill Ms *WAB* EN9 ....252 E5

Powdermill Wy *WAB* EN9 ....252 E3
Powell Gdns *DAGE* RM10 ....317 P6
Powell Rd *BKHH* IG9 ....275 M6
 LAIN SS15 ....303 J8
Power Dr *EN* EN3 ....252 C6
Powers Hall End *WIT* CM8 ....196 C1
Powis Rd *BOW* E3 ....332 E3
Powling Rd *IPSE* IP3 ....25 P9
Pownall Crs *COLS* CO2 ....152 A2
Pownsett Ter *IL* IG1 ....316 D7
Poynder Rd *TIL* RM18 ....350 C6
Poynings Av *SOSN* SS2 ....329 M4
Poynings Wy *HARH* RM3 ....299 K5
Poyntens *RAYL* SS6 ....306 G5
Poynter Pl *COS* CO15 ....158 F7
Poynter La *EN* EN1 ....273 L4
Poynters La *SBN/FI* SS3 ....330 C4
Pragel St *PLSTW* E13 ....333 L2
Pratts Farm La *RCHLM* CM3 ....194 C8
Pratt's La *RIPS/CAP* IP9 ....30 G8
Premier Av *CDW/CHF* RM16 ....339 M9
Premiere Pl *POP/IOD* E14 ....332 D7
Prentice Cl *RCFD* SS4 ....308 G5
Prescot La *MAL* CM9 ....224 F3
Prescott Cl *EMPK* RM11 ....318 C8
Prescott Gn *LOU* IG10 ....276 D2
Prescott Rd *CHES/WCR* EN8 ....230 B6
Presdales Dr *WARE* SG12 ....184 B4
President Rd *COS* CO15 ....151 H1
Prestage Wy *POP/IOD* E14 ....332 F7
Prestbury Rd *FSTGT* E7 ....315 M9
Preston Av *CHING* E4 ....294 C5
Preston Dr *IP* IP1 ....24 C1
 WAN E11 ....315 L6
Preston Gdns *IL* IG1 ....315 P1
 PEND EN3 ....252 B7
 RAYL SS6 ....306 C3
Preston Rd *COS* CO15 ....182 E8
 HARH RM3 ....299 M6
 WAN E11 ....315 H1
 WOS/PRIT SS0 ....18 A4
Preston's Rd *POP/IOD* E14 ....332 F8
Prestwick Av *FX* IP11 ....11 P7
Prestwick Dr *BSF* CM23 ....137 N5
Prestwood Cl *SBF/HAD* SS7 ....306 C9
Prestwood Dr *CRW* RM5 ....298 B2
 SBF/HAD SS7 ....306 D8
Pretoria Av *WALTH* E17 ....294 B8
Pretoria Cl *LAIN* SS15 *.......303 N6
Pretoria Crs *CHING* E4 ....274 F7
Pretoria Rd *CAN/RD* E16 ....333 J5
 CHING E4 ....274 F7
 HSTD CO9 ....98 A6
 IL IG1 ....316 A1
 ROMW/RG RM7 ....298 B8
 WAN E11 ....314 G5
Prettygate Rd *COLW* CO3 ....151 J2
Pretyman Rd *FX* IP11 ....11 P7
 IPSE IP3 ....26 A8
Priestley Gdns *CHDH* RM6 ....297 L1
Priestley Wy *WALTH* E17 ....294 A7
Priests Av *ROM* RM1 ....298 C6
Priests Fld *RBRW/HUT* CM13 ....301 M2
Priest's La *BRWN* CM15 ....281 H8
Priest's Rd *RBRW/HUT* CM13 ....281 J8
Primrose Av *ENC/FH* EN2 ....251 J9
 GDMY/SEVK IG3 ....317 K2
Primrose Cl *BOW* E3 ....332 D2
 BSF CM23 ....137 H6
 CVI SS8 ....326 D8
 VGE SS16 ....323 J2
Primrose Fld *HLWS* CM18 ....210 C6
Primrose Gln *EMPK* RM11 ....299 K8
Primrose Hl *BRW* CM14 ....280 F9
 CHLM/WR CM1 ....4 C1
 ING CM4 ....194 C3
 RIPS/CAP IP9 ....83 L5
Primrose La *K/T/MI* CO5 ....173 P7
 MGTR CO11 ....108 E8
Primrose Path *CHESW* EN7 ....251 M1
Primrose Pl *WIT* CM8 ....171 M9
Primrose Rd *COS* CO15 ....182 F7
 LEY E10 ....314 E3
 SWFD E18 ....295 L6
Primrose Wk *BOC* CM0 ....269 H6
 COLN CO4 ....128 A1
Primula Wy *CHLM/WR* CM1 ....218 E5
Prince Albert Rd *K/T/MI* CO5 ....202 F6
Prince Av *WOS/PRIT* SS0 ....328 A1
Prince Charles Av
 CDW/CHF RM16 ....340 C4
 SUD CO10 ....20 E3
Prince Charles Rd *COS* CO15 ....152 A5
Princedale Cl *IP* IP1 ....25 H2
Prince Edward Rd
 BCAYE CM11 ....285 K6
 HOM E9 ....314 C8
Prince George Av
 STHGT/OAK N14 ....272 B4
Princel La *RCOLE* CO7 ....104 C1
Prince of Wales Dr *CHTY* IP2 ....25 H9
Prince of Wales Rd
 CAN/RD E16 ....333 M4
 WIT CM8 ....198 B9
Prince Philip Av
 CDW/CHF RM16 ....339 K8
 COS CO15 ....207 H3
Prince Philip Rd *COLS* CO2 ....152 A5
Prince Regent La *PLSTW* E13 ....333 M4
Princes Av *BOC* CM0 ....268 B5
 RCHLM CM3 ....267 H6
 SBF/HAD SS7 ....306 C9
 SLH/COR SS17 ....341 P2
 WFD IG8 ....295 L1
Princes Cl *BCAYW* CM12 ....283 K2
 EPP CM16 ....234 B4
 LAIN SS15 ....303 M7
Princes's Esp *WOTN* CO14 ....159 L6

Princesfield Rd *WAB* EN9 ....253 L3
Princes Gdns *FX* IP11 ....11 H7
Princes Ga *BOC* CM0 *.......269 J5
Princes Pk *RAIN* RM13 ....318 F9
Princes Riverside Rd
 BERM/RHTH SE16 ....332 A8
Princess Alice Wy *THMD* SE28 ....334 E9
Princess Anne Cl *COS* CO15 ....207 H5
Princess Av *TIL* RM18 ....350 D2
Princess Gdns *RCFD* SS4 ....308 D2
Princess Margaret Rd
 TIL RM18 ....351 J2
Princess Rd *RAYL* SS6 ....307 J4
Princess St *COS* CO15 ....110 A5
Princes St *IP* IP1 ....16 C3
 WARE SG12 ....184 A2
 WOS/PRIT SS0 ....18 E3
Prince's Wy *BKHH* IG9 ....41 H5
 RBRW/HUT CM13 ....281 K8
Prince's Ter *PLSTW* E13 ....333 L1
Prince St *SUD* CO10 ....20 C4
Princes Wy *BKHH* IG9 ....275 M8
 RBRW/HUT CM13 ....281 K8
Princethorpe Rd *IPSE* IP5 ....26 B7
Princeton Ms *COLN* CO4 ....128 C5
Prince William Av *CVI* SS8 ....326 C8
Printers Wy *HLW* CM20 ....187 H7
Prior Cha *GRAYS* RM17 ....349 J2
Prior Cl *HSTD* CO9 ....97 N8
The Priories *HOC/HUL* SS5 ....287 H8
Prior Rd *IL* IG1 ....316 B5
Priors Cl *BSDN* SS14 ....3 H4
Priors Ct *WALTH* E17 ....294 B6
Priors East *BSDN* SS14 ....3 J5
Priors Pk *EN* EN1 ....294 C6
Priors Pk *HCH* RM12 ....319 K8
Prior's Wy *BOC* CM0 ....269 K5
 RCOLW CO6 ....128 C6
Prior Wy *COLN* CO4 ....127 N5
Priory Av *CHING* E4 ....274 C9
 HLWE CM17 ....187 K7
 HVHL CB9 ....41 J4
 SOSN SS2 ....328 C3
 WALTH E17 ....294 D9
Priory Cl *BROX* EN10 ....209 P3
 BRWN CM15 ....280 D4
 CHING E4 ....274 C9
 CHLM/WR CM1 ....4 A4
 HOD EN11 ....208 D6
 RCHLM CM3 ....242 G1
 RCOS CO16 ....205 P6
 SAFWN CB10 ....50 A8
 STHGT/OAK N14 ....272 A4
Priory Ct *BSF* CM23 ....137 L8
 HLWS CM18 ....211 J6
 WALTH E17 ....295 K5
Priory Crs *SOSN* SS2 ....328 C3
Priory Dr *STSD* CM24 ....138 B1
Priory Farm Rd *RCHLM* CM3 ....220 E1
Priory Ga *CHES/WCR* EN8 ....230 C6
Priory Gv *HARH* RM3 ....299 M6
Priory La *RCHLM* CM3 ....242 C9
Priory Md *BRWN* CM15 ....258 F6
Priory Ms *EMPK* RM11 ....318 G3
 WALTH E17 ....220 F1
Priory Pk *RCOS* CO16 ....180 D9
Priory Pth *HARH* RM3 ....279 K9
Priory Rd *BARK* IG11 ....316 E9
 CHING E4 ....6 D4
 DART DA1 ....347 J9
 EHAM E6 ....333 N1
 FX IP11 ....35 N6
 HARH RM3 ....299 M6
 LOU IG10 ....275 P3
 RCHLM CM3 ....242 B9
 RCOLW CO6 ....128 C6
 SLH/COR SS17 ....341 M2
 SUD CO10 ....20 D5
 WIT CM8 ....198 C1
Priory St *BOW* E3 ....332 E3
 COL CO1 ....8 E6
 RCOLW CO6 ....99 J9
The Priory *BCAYW* CM12 ....283 K2
Priory View Rd *LOS* SS9 *.......327 P1
Priory Wk *COL* CO1 ....8 E6
Priory Wd *COLN* CO4 ....128 C5
Priory Wood Crs *LOS* SS9 ....327 P1
Priory Wood Rbt *RBSF* CM22 ....138 A5
Pritchett Cl *PEND* EN3 ....252 D7
Prittle Cl *SBF/HAD* SS7 ....326 F1
Prittlewell Cha *WOS/PRIT* SS0 ....328 A1
Prittlewell Sq *SOS* SS1 ....18 E6
Prittlewell St *SOSN* SS2 ....19 G2
Private Rd *EN* EN1 ....273 J4
Proctor Cl *K/T/MI* CO5 ....173 N9
Proctors Wy *BSF* CM23 ....162 D1
Proctor Wy *RCOLW* CO6 ....149 M9
Professional La *WICKW* SS12 *.......305 M2
Progress Rd *LOS* SS9 ....308 C1
Progress Rd *LOS* SS9 ....308 C1
Progress Wy *EN* EN1 ....273 M4
 RCOS CO16 ....181 M4
Promenade *COS* CO15 ....206 C6
 MAL CM9 ....110 D6
The Promenade *FX* IP11 ....35 J6
Promenade Wy *RCOLE* CO7 ....179 J8
Prospect Av *SLH/COR* SS17 ....341 J4
Prospect Cl *RCHLM* CM3 ....196 D9

Prospect Hl *SUD* CO10 ....61 N7
 WALTH E17 ....294 E8
Prospect Pl *GRAYS* RM17 *.......349 L4
 RAIN RM13 ....298 B6
 SAFWS CB11 ....51 N9
Prospect Rd *CHES/WCR* EN8 ....229 P7
 EMPK RM11 ....299 L7
 IP IP1 ....16 A2
 WALTH E17 ....295 M2
Prospect St *IP* IP1 ....25 H5
Prospect Wy
 RBRW/HUT CM15 ....281 N3
Prospero Cl *CALN* CO4 ....128 G8
Protea Cl *CVI* SS8 ....333 J4
Provence Cl *CVI* SS8 ....344 E1
Provence Cl *CVI* SS8 ....126 F8
Providence Cl *SUD* CO10 ....21 J6
Providence La *IP* IP1 ....16 A1
Providence La *IP* IP1 ....16 A1
Providence St *IP* IP1 ....16 D4
 ROMW/RG RM7 ....297 N5
Provident Sq *CHLM/GWD* CM2 ....5 H4
Prower Cl *BCAYE* CM11 ....283 J7
The Pudgell *ROY* SG8 ....48 B8
Pudsey Hall La *RCFD* SS4 ....289 H6
Puffin Cl *BARK* IG11 ....335 J5
 WICKW SS12 ....305 L2
Puffin Dr *SBN/FI* SS3 ....330 D5
Puffinsdale *COS* CO15 ....182 A8
Pugh Pl *SLH/COR* SS17 ....341 L1
Pulham Av *BROX* EN10 ....208 B9
Pulleyns Av *EHAM* E6 ....333 P5
Pullman Ct *WICKE* SS11 ....285 J8
Pulpitfield Cl *WOTN* CO14 ....159 H6
Pulpits Cl *HOC/HUL* SS5 ....288 A9
Pulteney Cl *BOW* E3 ....332 C1
Pulteney Rd *SWFD* E18 ....295 M5
Pump Hl *BUNT* SG9 ....87 H6
 CHLM/GWD CM2 ....240 E4
 LOU IG10 ....276 A1
 RCOS CO16 ....182 B8
Pump La *CHLM/WR* CM1 ....218 D3
 EPP CM16 ....232 C3
 RAIN RM13 ....338 A1
 RCHLM CM3 ....243 N9
Pump Mead Cl *BOC* CM0 ....269 J5
Pump St *SLH/COR* SS17 ....341 H3
Punchard Wy *FX* IP11 ....34 F5
Purbeck Rd *EMPK* RM11 ....318 F2
Purcell Cl *CHLM/WR* CM1 ....239 H1
 COLN CO4 ....128 D5
 LAIN SS15 ....303 J7
Purdeys Wy *RCFD* SS4 ....309 H7
Purdis Av *IPSE* IP5 ....31 M1
Purdis La *IPSE* IP5 ....26 E9
Purdis Rd *KIR/NAC* IP10 ....27 J9
Purdis St *BOW* E3 ....332 E4
Purfleet By-Pass *PUR* RM19 ....347 P5
Purfleet Deep Whf
 PUR RM19 *.......347 P6
Purfleet Rd *SOCK/AJ* RM15 ....357 N8
Purford Gn *HLWS* CM18 ....211 H4
Purland Rd *THMD* SE28 ....334 D9
Purleigh Av *WFD* IG8 ....295 P5
Purleigh Cl *PIT* SS13 ....305 H6
Purleigh Gv *RCHLM* CM5 ....266 C4
Purleigh Rd *RAYL* SS6 ....306 E4
Purleigh St *RCHLM* CM3 ....244 A9
Purleigh St *RCHLM* CM3 ....244 A9
Purley Cr *BSF* CM23 ....296 B6
Purley Rd *ED* N9 ....273 J9
Purley Wy *RCOS* CO16 ....181 L7
 WOS/PRIT SS0 ....328 D1
Purling Wy *EPP* CM16 ....254 F5
Purplett St *CHTY* IP2 ....25 L7
Purvis Wy *COLN* CO4 ....128 C2
Puttocks La *RCOLE* CO7 ....81 H6
Pyefleet Vw *K/T/MI* CO5 ....153 K8
Pyefleet Vw *K/T/MI* CO5 ....177 J2
Pyenest Rd *HLWW/ROY* CM19 ....210 C6
Pyesand *COS* CO15 ....158 D6
Pygot Pl *BRTR* CM7 ....145 H2
Pymmes Brook Trail
 FBAR/BDGN N11 ....272 A8
Pymmes Gdns South *ED* N9 ....273 J9
Pymmes Gdns South *ED* N9 ....273 J9
Pym Pl *GRAYS* RM17 ....349 K2
Pyms Rd *CHLM/GWD* CM2 ....240 A7
Pynchbek *BSF* CM23 ....162 B2
Pynchon Dr *CHLM/WR* CM1 ....5 K2
Pynchon Paddocks
 RBSF CM22 ....162 G6
Pyne Ga *CHLM/GWD* CM2 ....240 A9
Pynest Green La *WAB* EN9 ....253 K7
Pyrles Gn *LOU* IG10 ....276 C1
Pyrles La *LOU* IG10 ....276 C1
Pytt Fld *HLWE* CM17 ....211 J4

Quadling St *IP* IP1 ....16 C6
The Quadrant *PUR* RM19 ....347 P2
Quaker La *WAB* EN9 ....252 F4
Quaker Rd *WARE* SG12 ....184 A3
Quaker's La *HVHL* CB9 ....41 K4
Quakers Pl *FSTGT* E7 ....315 N7
Quakers Wk *WCHMH* N21 ....273 J5

Quale Rd *CHLM/GWD* CM2 ....218 G7
Quantock Cl *KESG* IP5 ....26 E4
Quantock Rd *BXLYHN* DA7 ....346 D7
Quarles Cl *CRW* RM5 ....297 P4
Quarles Park Rd *CHDH* RM6 ....317 J1
Quarry Ms *PUR* RM19 ....547 M2
Quarry Springs *RLW* CM20 ....211 H8
Quarry Wy *WTHK* KM20 ....348 C4
Quarter Ga *GNTH/NBYPK* IG2 ....287 H5
Quartermile La *LEY* E10 ....314 E6
Quatre Ports *CHING* E4 ....294 G2
Quay House *POP/IOD* E14 * 332 D9
Quay La *FOS* CO15 ....158 E5
    GRH DA9 ....348 E9
    RCOS CO16 ....157 L2
    SUD CO10 ....20 C7
Quay St *MGTR* CO11 ....162 C9
The Quay *BOC* CM0 ....291 H4
    HAR CO12 ....15 F1
    RCOLE CO07 ....153 J7
    RCOS CO16 ....180 B9
Quebec Av *SOS* SS1 ....19 G4
Quebec Cl *SOS* SS1 ....19 H4
Quebec Dr *KESG* IP5 ....26 G5
Quebec Rd *GNTH/NBYPK* IG2 ....288 C5
    TIL RM18 ....350 B7
Queebec Wy *BERM/RHTH* SE16 ......332 A9
Queech La *RIPS/CAP* IP9 ....82 D9
The Queech *RIPS/CAP* IP9 ....28 D8
Queen Anne Dr *K/T/MI* CO5 ....202 C6
Queen Anne Gdns
    WOS/PRIT SS0 ....328 D2
Queen Anne Rd *HOM* E9 ....314 A8
    K/T/MI CO5 ....202 C6
Queen Anne's Dr
    WOS/PRIT SS0 ....328 D2
Queen Anne's Gdns *EN* EN1 ....273 K5
Queen Anne's Gv *EN* EN1 ....273 K5
Queen Anne's Pl *EN* EN1 ....273 K5
Queen Anne's Wy *HOC/HUL* SS5 ....286 G8
Queenborough Gdns
    GNTH/NBYPK IG2 ....296 B8
Queenborough La
    BRTR CM77 ....144 D5
Queenborough Rd *BOC* CM0 ....269 J5
Queenbury Cl *K/T/MI* CO5 ....202 C6
Queen Edith Dr *CHLM* CB9 ....55 L4
Queen Elizabeth Av
    COS CO15 ....207 H3
    TIL RM18 ....351 K2
Queen Elizabeth Cha
    RCFD SS4 ....308 C0
Queen Elizabeth Ct
    WAB EN9 * 252 C5
Queen Elizabeth Dr
    SLH/COR SS17 ....323 N9
Queen Elizabeth II Br
    WTHK KM20 ....348 B7
Queen Elizabeth Rd
    WALTH E17 ....294 B7
Queen Elizabeth's Dr
    STHGT/OAK N14 ....272 C7
Queen Elizabeth Wy
    COLS CO2 ....152 B5
    TIL RM18 ....351 K2
Queen Mary Av *COLS* CO2 ....152 B3
Queen Marys Ct *WAB* EN9 * 252 F5
Queens Av *HOC/HUL* SS5 * 287 H5
    LOS SS9 ....327 P5
    MAL CM9 ....244 B1
    WCHMH N21 ....272 G7
    WFD IG8 ....139 M5
Queen's Cl *SBW* CM21 ....7 M7
Queensdale Cl *IP* IP1 ....25 J2
    STSD CM24 ....114 B7
    SUD CO10 ....20 E4
Queens Crs *BSF* CM23 ....137 K9
Queensdale Cl *IP* IP1 ....25 J2
Queen's Dr *CHES/WCR* EN8 ....252 D4
    LEY E10 ....314 D2
Queen's Gdns *BRTR* CM7 ....120 D8
    RAIN RM13 ....336 C2
    UPMR RM14 ....320 C1
Queensgate Dr *IPNE* IP4 ....25 N5
Queen's Gate Ms
    BCAYW CM12 * 282 G3
Queen's Grove Rd *CHING* E4 ....274 C7
Queen's Head Rd *COLN* CO4 ....102 G6
Queensland Av *RIPS/CAP* IP9 ....85 K7
Queensland Cl *WALTH* E17 ....294 C6
Queensland Crs
    CHLM/WR CM1 ....217 L4
Queensland Dr *COLS* CO2 ....152 B5
Queensmere *SBF/HAD* SS7 ....326 F1
Queens Park Av *BCAYW* CM12 ......283 H5
Queens Park Rd *HARH* RM3 ....299 L5
Queen's Rd *BARK* IG11 ....316 D9
    BCAYE CM11 ....304 A3
    BKHH IG9 ....275 L8
    BOC CM0 ....291 J4
    BRTR CM7 ....145 J1
    BRW CM14 ....280 F9
    CHES/WCR EN8 ....252 B4
    CHLM/GWD CM2 ....5 K4
    COLW CO15 ....127 M9
    COS CO15 ....63 A7
    ED N9 ....273 N8
    EN EN1 ....273 K5
    EPP CM16 ....234 B4
    ERITH DA8 ....346 D4
    FOS CO15 ....11 J5
    HAR CO12 ....110 B9
    LAIN SS15 ....303 K6
    LOS SS9 ....327 P6
    LOU IG10 ....276 A2
    PLSTW E13 ....333 L1
    RAYL SS6 ....306 G6

RCOLE CO07 ....153 J6
RCOLW CO6 ....99 J9
RCOLW CO6 ....346 D4
SBF/HAD SS7 ....326 A4
SUD CO10 ....21 G4
WALTH E17 ....314 C1
WAN E11 ....315 H2
WARE SG12 ....184 C2
WOS/PRIT SS0 ....18 E4
Queen's Rd West PLSTW E13 ....333 K2
Queen's Sq IPSE IP5 ....26 A9
Queens Ter PLSTW E13 ....333 L1
Queens Town Gdns
    RAIN RM13 ....336 E3
Queen St BOC CM0 ....268 G5
    BRW CM14 ....300 F2
    CHONG CM5 ....214 B9
    COL CO1 ....8 D6
    ERITH DA8 * 346 D4
    FX IP11 ....35 H5
    HVHL CB9 ....41 K5
    IP IP1 ....16 D5
    MAL CM9 ....222 B9
    RCOLE CO07 ....179 L7
    RCOLW CO6 ....147 P4
    Queens Ter MGTR CO11 * 318 C1
    Queens Wk CHING E4 ....274 C7
    Queensway CHONG CM5 ....235 L5
    COS CO15 ....182 E8
    HVHL CB9 ....41 H5
    K/T/MI CO5 ....173 P7
    MGTR CO11 ....106 B4
    PEND EN3 ....235 P3
    SOS SS1 ....18 E3
    SUD CO10 ....47 M5
    SUD CO10 ....61 L5
Queenswood Av
    RBRW/HUT CM13 ....281 N4
    WALTH E17 ....294 F5
Queenswood Gdns WAN E11 ....315 L3
Queen Victoria Dr
    RIPS/CAP IP9 ....85 N9
Quendon Dr WAB EN9 ....252 C5
Quendon Rd BSDN SS14 ....304 D7
Quendon Wy FOS CO15 ....159 H8
Quennell Wy
    RBRW/HUT CM13 ....281 M6
Quentin Cl IP IP1 ....24 F3
Quickset Rd SAFWS CB11 ....49 L5
Quilp Dr CHLM/WR CM1 ....217 N4
Quilter Dr RIPW IP8 ....29 L1
Quilter Rd FX IP11 ....35 L7
Quilters Cl BSDN SS14 ....304 C7
    COS CO15 ....182 C7
Quilters Dr BCAYW CM12 ....283 H8
Quilters Straight BSDN SS14 ....304 C7
Quince Cl MGTR CO11 ....81 N8
Quince Tree Cl SOCK/AV RM15 ....338 F4
Quinion Cl CHLM/WR CM1 ....217 L4
Quinions Rd CHLM/WR CM1 * 4 B1
Quinton's La FX IP11 ....35 M6
Quinton's Rd RCOLE CO07 ....80 F6
Quinton Wy WAB EN9 ....252 F5
Quixley St POP/IOD E14 ....332 C7
Quoits Fld NHMKT IP9 ....22 D4
Quorn Gdns LOS SS9 ....327 K5
The Quorn ING CM4 ....260 B7

Railey Rd SAFWS CB11 ....65 M2
Railway Ap FX IP11 ....35 K6
    LAIN SS15 ....303 H9
    SOSN SS2 * 329 H4
Railway Cottages COS CO15 ....7 F5
Railway Cres/WCR ENB 252 C5
Railway Sq CHLM/WR CM1 ....4 B2
Railway Station Whf
    LEY E10 ....314 B3
Railway St BCTR RM8 ....317 K3
    BRTR CM7 ....145 K4
    CHLM/WR CM1 ....4 E2
    MGTR CO11 ....106 C4
Railway Ter MGTR CO11 * 106 C4
    SOSN SS2 ....329 H5
    WALTH E17 ....294 F5
Rainham Rd North
    DAGE RM10 ....318 A4
Rainham Rd South
    DAGE RM10 ....318 B6
Rainham Wy FOS CO13 ....159 J4
Rainhill Wy BOW E3 ....313 K2
Rainsborowe Rd COLS CO2 ....151 M2
Rainsford Av CHLM/WR CM1 ....4 B2
Rainsford La CHLM/WR CM1 ....4 C3
Rainsford Rd CHLM/WR CM1 ....4 B1
    STSD CM24 ....114 A7
Rainsford Wy HCH RM12 ....318 F5
Raith Av STHGT/OAK N14 ....272 C9
Raleana Rd POP/IOD E14 ....332 F8
Raleigh Cl ERITH DA8 ....346 E4
    SUD CO10 ....47 K9
Raleigh Dr LAIN SS15 ....15 J7
    SHTHGT/OAK N14 ....272 C7
Rambler Cl CHLM CO3 ....126 E8
Ramblers Wy BOC CM0 ....291 J4
Ram Gorse HLW CM20 ....12 E5
Ramney Dr PEND EN3 ....252 D6
Ramparts Cl RCOLW CO6 ....102 E9
Ramparts Ct COLN CO04 * 127 L5
The Ramparts RAYL SS6 ....307 H5
Rampart St SBN/FI SS3 ....330 E8
Rampart Ter SBN/FI SS3 ....330 F8
Ramplings Av COS CO15 ....181 P8
Rampton Cl CHING E4 ....274 D9
Ramsay Cl BROX EN10 ....208 B9
Ramsay Dr RAIN RM13 ....336 C2
Ramsay Gdns GPK RM2 ....298 C5
Ramsay Rd FSTGT E7 ....315 K5
Ramscroft Cl ED N9 ....273 K6
Ramsden Dr CRW RM5 ....297 P4
Ramsden Park Rd
    BCAYE CM11 ....284 B7
Ramsden Rd ERITH DA8 ....346 C5
Ramsden View Rd
    WICKW SS12 ....304 E1
Ramsey Cha RCHLM CM3 ....267 H3
Ramsey Cl CHTY IP2 ....30 A1
    MAL CM9 ....222 E7
Ramsey Rd HAR CO12 ....109 N6
    HSTD CO9 ....97 H8
Ramsgate Dr HSTD CO9 * 72 C8
Ramsgate Ap IPSE IP5 ....26 A8
Ramsgill Dr GNTH/NBYPK IG2 ....296 D5
Rams Gv CHDH RM6 ....297 M8
Ramshaw Dr
    CHLM/GWD CM2 ....218 B8
Ramuz Dr WOS/PRIT SS0 ....328 E4
Rana Ct BRTR CM7 ....145 J2
Rana Dr BRTR CM7 ....145 J2
Rancliffe Rd EHAM E6 ....333 P2
Randall Cl ERITH DA8 ....346 E4
    GTDUN CM6 ....141 L5
    KESG IP5 ....27 K4
Randall Rd HCH RM12 ....319 H6
Randalls Dr RBRW/HUT CM13 ....281 P5
Randolph Ap CAN/RD E16 ....333 L8
Randolph Cl BXLYHN DA7 ....346 B8
    COS CO15 ....207 P3
    MAL CM9 ....244 A2
Randolph Rd WALTH E17 * 294 E9
Rands Cl GTDUN CM6 ....165 N5
Randulph Ter CHLM/WR CM1 ....5 K1
Randway RAYL SS6 ....306 C6
Randwell Cl IPNE IP4 ....26 A6
Ranelagh Gdns IL IG1 ....316 B5
    RBRW/HUT CM13 ....281 M5
Ranelagh Rd CHTY IP2 ....24 C6
    EHAM E6 ....334 B1
    FX IP11 ....11 K2
    WAN E11 ....315 H6
Rangers Bd BKHH IG9 ....275 J7
Ranger Wk COLS CO2 ....152 C5
Rangoon Cl COLS CO2 ....151 L5
Ransome Cl RIPW IP8 ....24 B5
Ransome Rd IPSE IP5 ....26 A9
Ransomes Wy CHLM/WR CM1 ....218 A7
    IPSE IP5 ....31 K2
Ransom Rd K/T/MI CO5 ....173 P8
Rantree Fold VGE SS16 ....323 N2
Ranulf Cl HLWE CM17 ....57 N2
Ranulph Wy RCHLM CM3 ....196 E9
Ranwell Cl BOW E3 * 332 C1
Ranworth Av HOD EN11 ....208 E1
Ranworth Cl ERITH DA8 ....346 D7

Ranworth Rd ED N9 ....273 P8
Raphael Av ROM RM1 ....298 E7
    TIL RM18 ....350 B6
Raphael Dr CHLM/WR CM1 ....218 E4
    LOS SS9 ....330 F6
Rapier Cl PUR RM19 ....347 L2
Ratcliffe Ct K/T/MI CO5 ....173 L3
Ratcliffe Cross St WCHPL E1 * 332 A6
Ratcliffe La POP/IOD E14 ....332 A6
Ratcliffe Rd FOS CO15 ....151 H1
Ratcliff Rd FSTGT E7 ....315 M7
Rathbone St CAN/RD E16 ....333 J5
Rat HI RIPS/CAP IP9 ....84 D8
Rat La SBF/HAD SS7 ....306 F7
Ratsborough Cha BOC CM0 ....269 H7
Rat's La COLN CO04 ....253 L8
Rattwick Dr CVI SS8 ....345 J2
Ratty's La HOD EN11 ....208 G5
Ravel Gdns SOCK/AV RM15 ....337 P6
Ravel Rd SOCK/AV RM15 ....338 A6
Raven Cl BCAYW CM12 ....282 G4
Raven Crs BCAYW CM12 ....282 G4
Ravencroft CDW/CHF RM16 ....340 C9
Ravendale Wy SBN/FI SS3 ....330 C4
Raven Dr SBF/HAD SS7 ....325 N4
Ravenhill Rd PLSTW E13 ....333 H1
Raven La BCAYW CM12 ....282 G4
Ravenoak Wy CHIG IG7 ....296 F2
Raven Rd SWFD E18 ....295 M6
Ravenscar Cl COS CO15 * 98 B3
Ravensbourne Crs HARH RM3 ....299 L7
Ravensbourne Dr
    CHLM/WR CM1 ....4 A4
Ravensbourne Gdns CLAY IG5 ....296 B5
Ravensbrook Rd RT DART IG3 ....346 F8
Ravens Ct EN EN1 ....273 K1
Ravens Ct CVI SS8 ....18 D5
Ravenscourt Cl HCH RM12 ....319 K5
Ravenscourt Cl HCH RM12 ....319 K5
    VGE SS16 ....324 O1
Ravenscourt Av HCH RM12 ....319 K4
Ravenscroft BROX EN10 ....208 C8
Ravenscroft Cl CAN/RD E16 ....333 K5
Ravenscroft Rd CAN/RD E16 ....333 K5
Ravensdale COS CO15 ....182 A7
    VGE SS16 ....324 A7
Ravensfield BSDN SS14 ....304 E9
    DAGW RM9 ....317 L6
Ravensfield Rd IP IP1 ....24 F1
Ravenside Cl UED N18 * 294 A2
Ravens La RIPW IP8 ....24 B1
Ravensmere EPP CM16 ....233 H9
Ravens Wy WDBR IP12 ....31 H2
Ravenswood Av FSTGT E7 ....315 K7
Ravenswood Cl CRW RM5 ....298 A2
Ravenswood Rd WALTH E17 ....294 F5
Raven Wy COLN CO04 ....127 P5
Rawden Cl HAR CO12 ....110 B4
Rawdon Dr HOD EN11 ....208 D6
Rawlings Crs COLN CO04 ....128 C2
Rawlyn Cl CDW/CHF RM16 ....348 F3
Rawreth Gdns WICKE SS11 * 286 B7
Rawreth La WICKE SS11 ....306 A3
Rawsthorne Ct CAN/RD E16 ....334 A8
Rawstorn Rd COLW CO15 ....8 A6
Ray Av HAR CO12 ....110 B4
Rayburn Rd EMPK RM11 ....319 M2
Raycliff Av RCOS CO16 ....181 P6
Ray Cl CVI SS8 ....344 D5
    LOS SS9 ....327 L5
Raydons Gdns DAGW RM9 ....317 M6
Raydons Rd DAGW RM9 ....317 M7
Ray Fld CAN/RD E16 ....232 C9
Rayfield Cl GTDUN CM6 ....166 F1
Rayfield EPP CM16 ....25 K5
Ray Gdns BARK IG11 ....335 H2
Rayhaven HAR CO12 ....109 M6
Ray Lamb Wy ERITH DA8 ....346 C4
Rayleigh Av LOS SS9 ....307 L7
    WOS/PRIT SS0 ....18 B1
Rayleigh Cl BRTR CM7 ....145 M2
    COLN CO4 ....9 C2
    PLMGR N13 ....281 M6
Rayleigh Downs Rd RAYL SS6 ....307 K8
Rayleigh Dr LOS SS9 ....327 N5
Rayleigh Pde
    RBRW/HUT CM13 * 281 M5
Rayleigh Rd CAN/RD E16 ....333 L8
    HCH RM12 * 24 F2
    LOS SS9 ....307 M8
    PLMGR N13 ....273 H9
    RBRW/HUT CM13 ....281 M5
    SBF/HAD SS7 ....326 D1
    SLH/COR SS17 ....341 L4
    SWFD E18 ....295 M4
    WFD IG8 ....295 M4
The Rayleighs COLW CO3 * 151 M1
Rayley La EPP CM16 ....233 P5
Ray Lodge Rd WFD IG8 ....295 K3
Ray Md RCOLM CM3 ....195 N5
Rayment Av CVI SS8 ....344 C2
Rayment Drift KESG IP5 ....27 H4
Raymond Av SWFD E18 ....295 J7
Raymond Gdns CHIG IG7 ....277 J9
Raymond Rd
    GNTH/NBYPK IG2 ....316 E2
    PLSTW E13 ....315 M9
Raymonds Cl RCHLM CM3 ....286 F1
Raymonds Dr SBF/HAD SS7 ....306 C9
Rayne Rd BRTR CM7 ....144 D4
Rayne Rd BRTR CM7 ....151 L2
Rayner Rd RCOLM CM3 ....97 P7
Rayner Wy HSTD CO9 ....97 P7
Raynes Av WAN E11 ....315 M2
Raynham Rd BSF CM23 ....137 L6
Raynhams SAFWN CB10 * 49 L8
Raynsford Rd WARE SG12 ....184 B3
Raynton Rd PEND EN3 ....252 A7
Ray Rd CRW RM5 ....298 A2
Rayside BSDN SS14 ....3 J6

The Ray CHLM/WR CM1 ....218 D6
Ray Wk LOS SS9 ....327 L5
Read Cl HOC/HUL SS5 ....308 B3
Read Rd RIPS/CAP IP9 ....253 K3
Reade Rd RIPS/CAP IP9 ....85 L3
Reader Cl CHLM/GWD CM2 ....240 D4
Reading Cl VGE SS16 ....322 G1
Reading Rd IPNE IP4 ....26 A4
The Readings HLWS CM18 ....210 C6
Reads Cl IL IG1 ....316 C5
Reaper Rd COS CO15 ....151 K2
Rebecca Gdns WIT CM8 ....171 M1
Rebecca Meade GTDUN CM6 ....166 E7
Rebels La SBN/FI SS3 ....329 N2
Rebow Rd HAR CO12 ....110 B6
    RCOLE CO07 ....153 J6
Rebow St COL CO1 ....128 C9
Reckitts Cl COS CO15 ....7 K2
Recreation Av HARH RM3 ....299 L6
    LOS SS9 ....327 N6
    ROMW/RG RM7 ....298 B9
    SLH/COR SS17 ....324 A9
Recreation Cl FX IP11 ....35 J5
Recreation Gnd STSD CM24 ....114 A9
Recreation La FX IP11 ....35 J5
Recreation Rd COL CO1 ....152 C1
    COS CO15 ....7 G3
    HSTD CO9 ....72 C8
    HVHL CB9 ....41 J4
Recreation Wk BCAYE CM11 ....284 B5
    SUD CO10 ....61 L5
Recreation Wy IPSE IP5 ....26 A9
    RCOLE CO07 ....179 L6
Rectory Av RCFD SS4 ....308 D1
Rectory Cha BRWN CM15 ....258 F1
    RBRW/HUT CM13 ....301 H8
    SOS SS1 ....329 M5
Rectory Cl CHING E4 ....274 D9
    COLN CO04 ....3 J5
    DART CM1 ....346 D9
    ING CM4 ....260 C5
    ING CM4 ....261 L7
    RCHLM CM3 ....194 B6
    SAFWS CB11 ....50 G6
    WARE SG12 ....185 N4
Rectory Ct PIT SS13 ....305 L1
Rectory Fld HLWW/ROY CM19 ....210 C5
    RIPS/CAP IP9 ....84 D2
Rectory Gdns PIT SS13 ....325 H1
    UPMR RM14 ....320 A4
Rectory Garth RAYL SS6 ....306 C4
Rectory Gv LOS SS9 ....327 N6
    WICKE SS11 ....285 L9
Rectory HI RCOLE CO07 ....80 F8
    RCOLE CO07 ....153 K5
Rectory La BSF CM23 ....113 H9
    CHLM/WR CM1 ....218 A7
    HAR CO12 ....109 K7
    HLWW/ROY CM19 ....210 C5
    HSTD CO9 ....72 P3
    K/T/MI CO5 ....155 M6
    KIR/NAC IP10 ....33 M6
    LOU IG10 ....276 B1
    MAL CM9 ....243 J4
    MGTR CO11 ....81 P6
    RBRW/HUT CM13 ....301 P4
    RCHLM CM3 ....168 G5
    RCHLM CM3 ....267 J5
    SAFWN CB10 * 52 F1
Rectory Meadow BRTR CM77 ....146 D3
    HSTD CO9 ....72 C8
Rectory Mdw HSTD CO9 ....72 C8
Rectory Park Dr PIT SS13 ....324 G1
Rectory Rd BCAYW CM12 ....122 C8
    BRTR CM77 ....146 D1
    CDW/CHF RM16 ....340 C5
    CHLM/WR CM1 ....25 K8
    COLU CO4 ....102 A3
    DAGE RM10 ....317 P8
    FOS CO13 ....183 H2
    GRAYS RM17 ....109 J9
    HAR CO12 ....109 J9
    HOC/HUL SS5 ....308 B4
    HSTD CO9 ....72 C8
    HVHL CB9 ....42 C1
    K/T/MI CO5 ....173 P7
    K/T/MI CO5 ....175 P7
    MAL CM9 ....220 G8
    MGTR CO11 ....106 C5
    MNPK E12 ....316 A7
    PIT SS13 ....305 H8
    RCOLE CO07 ....153 K4
    RCOLW CO6 ....154 C5
    RCOLW CO6 ....125 L7
    RCOS CO16 ....149 P5
    RCOS CO16 ....181 J2
    SBF/HAD SS7 ....84 B6
    SLH/COR SS17 ....341 K4
    SUD CO10 ....50 F4
    WALTH E17 ....294 E8
Rectory Sq WCHPL E1 * 332 A5
Rectory Ter SLH/COR SS17 * 341 L4
Rectory Wd HARE SG12 ....13 F4
Redan Rd WARE SG12 ....184 B3
Redan St IP IP1 ....16 B2
Red Barn Dr RCOLW CO6 ....77 J4
Red Barn La HAR CO12 ....133 L4
Red Barn Rd RCOLE CO07 ....179 L5
Redbourne Dr THMD SE28 ....335 L4
Redbridge La East REDBR IG4 ....315 N1
Redbridge La West WAN E11 ....315 L1
Redbridge Rd COS CO15 ....182 A5
Redbury Cl RAIN RM13 ....336 C4
Redcar Rd HARH RM3 ....299 L2
Red Rd CRW RM5 ....298 A2
Redcliff Dr LOS SS9 ....328 A6

Redcliffe Gdns *IL* IG1.....316 B3
Redcliffe Rd *CHLM/GWD* CM2.....A E6
Redclyffe Rd *EHAM* E6.....333 M1
Reddells Cl *SUD* CO10.....21 F5
Redden Court Rd *HARH* RM3.....299 K7
Reddings La *BOC* CM0.....247 P7
Reddings La *SAFWS* CB11.....65 M2
Reddy Rd *ERITH* DA8.....346 E4
Rede La *NHMKT* IP6.....22 G4
Rede Wy *SOS* CO10.....61 M4
Redfern Gdns *GPK* RM2.....299 J6
Redgate St *WICKE* SS11.....285 M8
Redgate La *RIPS/CAP* IP9.....50 C5
Redgates La *SAFWS* CB10.....52 C6
Redgates Pl *CHLM/WR* CM1.....218 C7
Redgrave Rd *VGE* SS16.....324 D2
Redhills Rd *RCHLM* CM3.....265 H9
Red House Cl *FX* IP11.....34 D1
  WARE SG12.....184 B5
Red House La *SUD* CO10.....61 K6
Red House Wk *KIR/NAC* IP10.....32 C6
The Redinge *BCAYE* CM11.....283 L9
Redlands Rd *PEND* EN3.....252 B9
Red La *RIPS/CAP* IP9.....81 K1
Redlie Cl *SLH/COR* SS17.....341 L2
Red Lion Crs *HLWE* CM17.....211 K5
Red Lion La *HLWE* CM17.....211 K5
Red Lion Yd *COL* CO1 *.....8 C6
Redmayne Dr
  CHLM/GWD CM2.....239 N3
Redmill *COLW* CO3.....151 K3
Redricks La *HLW* CM20.....186 G6
Redriffe Rd *PLSTW* E13.....333 J2
Redriff Rd *ROMW/RG* RM7.....298 A6
Red Rd *BRW* CM14.....300 E1
Redrose La *HHS/HCT*.....237 H9
Redrose Wk *RCOS* CO10.....61 M4
Redruth Cl *CHLM/WR* CM1.....218 D6
Redruth Rd *HARH* RM3.....299 L2
Redshank Crs *RCHLM* CM3.....264 G8
Redshank Dr *MAL* CM9.....222 D6
Red Sleeve *RIPS/CAP* IP9.....28 B9
Redstart Cl *EHAM* E6.....333 P5
Redstock Rd *SOSN* SS2.....329 H4
Redvers Cl *BSF* CM23.....137 M4
Redwald Rd *CLPT* E5.....314 A6
Red White & Blue Rd
  BSF CM23.....137 N4
Red Willow *HLWW/ROY* CM19.....210 A4
Redwing Cl *CHTY* IP2.....24 E8
Redwing Dr *BCAYE* CM11.....285 K8
Redwood Cl *SOCK/AV* RM15.....338 F4
Redwood Cl
  BERM/RHTH SE16.....332 B8
  BOW E3.....332 D2
  COLN CO4.....128 C7
  STHGT/OAK N14.....272 C6
  WIT CM8.....171 P8
Redwood Dr *CHLM/WR* CM1.....238 C1
  LAIN SS15.....303 L6
Redwood Gdns *CHING* E4 *.....274 A8
The Redwoods *CVI* SS8.....344 B2
Reed Cl *CAN/RD* E16.....333 K5
  RCOS CO10.....181 M8
Reede Rd *DAGE* RM10.....317 P8
Reede Wy *DAGE* RM10.....318 A8
Reed Hall Av *COLS* CO2.....151 N3
Reedings Wy *SBW* CM21.....162 C9
  VGE SS16.....323 J2
Reeds La *HVHL* CB9.....41 K5
Reeds Wy *WICKW* SS12.....285 H8
Reesland Cl *MNPK* E12.....316 B8
Reeve Cl *HVHL* CB9.....41 M4
Reeve Ldg *FX* IP11 *.....34 E2
Reeves Cl *BRWN* CM15.....258 G4
  VGE SS16.....322 G2
Reeves La *HLWW/ROY* CM19.....209 M7
Reeves Pightle *ROY* SG8.....48 C7
Reeves Rd *BOW* E3.....332 E4
Reeves Wy *RCHLM* CM3.....287 H1
Refinery Rd *HAR* CO12.....109 N3
Reform Ter *MGTR* CO11.....106 C4
Regal Cl *CHLM/WR* CM1.....240 C2
Regan Cl *SLH/COR* SS17.....341 M1
Regarder Rd *CHIG* IG7.....297 J2
Regarth Av *ROM* RM1.....318 D1
Regency Cl *BSF* CM23.....137 K7
  CHIG IG7.....296 D2
  RCFD SS4.....308 F5
  WICKE SS11.....285 J6
Regency Ct *BRW* CM14.....280 F8
  COLS CO2.....152 D2
  EN EN1.....273 J4
  HLWS CM18.....211 H6
  MAL CM9.....222 B6
Regency Gdns *EMPK* RM11.....319 H2
Regency Gn *SLH/COR* SS17.....37 L2
  SOSN SS2.....328 G4
Regent Cl *CDW/CHF* RM16.....339 M9
  RAYL SS6.....306 C3
  RCOLE CO7.....179 L6
Regent Dr *BCAYE* CM11.....282 C8
Regent Gdns *GDMY/SEVK* IG3.....317 H1
Regent Rd *EPP* CM16.....204 C7
  RCOLE CO7.....179 L6
Regents Cl *BOC* CM0.....269 J5
  COLN CO4.....128 D2
Regents Dr *WFD* IG8.....296 B3
Regents Pl *LOU* IG10.....275 N6
Regent Sq *BELV* DA17.....346 A4
  BOW E3.....332 E3
Regent St *IPNE* IP4.....17 H4
  K/T/MI CO5.....152 C6
  MGTR CO11.....106 C4
Regimental Wy *HAR* CO12.....109 M7
Regina Pl *IPNE* IP4.....26 A5
Reginald Ms *HLWE* CM17.....211 K2
Reginald Rd *FSTGT* E7.....315 K9
  HARH RM3.....299 M5

Regina Rd *CHLM/WR* CM1.....5 H1
Reigate Av *RCOS* CO16.....181 N7
Reigate Cl *IPSE* IP5.....26 A8
Reigate Rd *GDMY/SEVK* IG3.....316 G4
Rembrandt Cl *CVI* SS8.....344 D2
Rembrandt Gv
  CHLM/WR CM1.....218 D5
Rembrandt Wy *COLW* CO3.....151 L1
Rembrow Rd *RIPS/CAP* IP9.....28 C9
Remembrance Av *BOC* CM0.....290 G4
  RCHLM CM3.....196 D9
Remercie Rd *MGTR* CO11.....106 C2
Remington Rd *EHAM* E6.....333 P6
Remus Rd *BOW* E3.....314 D9
Renacres *VGE* SS16.....323 N2
Rendlesham Rd *ENC/FH* EN2.....250 G9
  FX IP11.....34 G6
  IP IP1.....16 A3
Renfrew Cl *EHAM* E6.....334 B7
Renfrew Rd *IPNE* IP4.....26 A2
Renness Rd *WALTH* E17.....294 B7
Rennie Pl *CHLM/GWD* CM2.....218 G8
Rennison Cl *CHESW* EN7.....250 C1
Renoir Pl *CHLM/WR* CM1.....218 E4
Renown Cl *ROMW/RG* RM7.....297 P5
Rensburg Rd *WALTH* E17.....294 A9
Renshaw Cl *WALTH* E17 *.....294 A9
Renwick Rd *BARK* IG11.....335 J4
Repton Av *GPK* RM2.....298 F7
Repton Cl *PIT* SS13.....304 F6
Repton Ct *PIT* SS13 *.....304 F6
Repton Dr *GPK* RM2.....298 F8
Repton Gdns *GPK* RM2.....298 F7
Repton Gv *CLAY* IG5.....296 A5
  SOSN SS2.....308 B8
Repton St *POP/IOD* E14.....332 B6
Repulse Cl *ROMW/RG* RM7.....298 A5
Reservoir Rd *STHGT/OAK* N14.....272 B4
Reston Wy *CAN/RD* E16.....333 N7
Retford Cl *HARH* RM3.....299 M3
Retford Pth *HARH* RM3.....299 M3
Retford Rd *HARH* RM3.....299 M4
Retingham Wy *CHING* E4.....274 E8
Retreat Rd *HOC/HUL* SS5.....307 P1
  WOS/PRIT SS0.....18 B5
The Retreat *BRTR* CM7 *.....145 K2
  BRW CM14.....280 E7
  GRAYS RM17.....349 L4
  RBRW/HUT CM13.....281 L5
  RCOLW CO6.....127 H4
  WIT CM8.....197 K5
Retreat Wy *CHIG* IG7.....277 J9
Rettendon Cl *RAYL* SS6.....306 D4
Rettendon Gdns *WICKE* SS11.....285 K7
Rettendon Vw *WICKE* SS11.....285 L8
Reubens Rd *RBRW/HUT* CM13.....281 L5
Reveley Sq *BERM/RHTH* SE16.....332 B9
Review Rd *DAGE* RM10.....336 A2
Reydon Av *WAN* E11.....315 M1
Reymead Cl *K/T/MI* CO5.....202 F5
Reynard Copse *BSF* CM23.....137 L5
Reynards Cl *COLS* CO2.....151 N3
Reynards Copse *COLN* CO4.....128 B4
Reynards Ct *SUD* CO10 *.....45 P5
Reynolds Av *CHDH* RM6.....317 K2
  COLW CO3.....151 L1
  IPSE IP5.....30 C2
  MNPK E12.....316 B7
Reynold's Cl *HVHL* CB9.....40 C2
Reynolds Ct *FX* IP11.....34 G6
Reynolds Gdns *RCFD* SS4.....308 D2
Reynolds Ga *RCHLM* CM3.....287 H2
Reynolds Pl *IPSE* IP5.....30 C2
Reynolds Wy *SUD* CO10.....45 P5
Rhapsody Crs *BRW* CM14.....300 E2
Rhoda Rd North
  SBF/HAD SS7.....326 B1
Rhodes Av *BSF* CM23.....137 L9
Rhodesia Rd *WAN* E11.....314 G4
Rhodeswell Rd *BOW* E3.....332 B5
Rhondda Gv *BOW* E3.....332 B3
Rhugarve Gdns *CBE/LIN* CB1.....38 C1
Rhum Ms *WICKW* SS12.....305 M2
Ribble Cl *WFD* IG8.....295 M5
Riby Rd *FX* IP11.....11 G3
Ricardo St *POP/IOD* E14.....332 E6
Richard Av *RCOLE* CO7.....179 L7
Richard Burn Wy *SUD* CO10.....47 H9
Richard House Dr
  CAN/RD E16.....333 N6
Richards Av *ROMW/RG* RM7.....298 B9
Richardson Crs *CHESW* EN7.....228 G4
Richardson Pl *CHLM/WR* CM1.....4 C1
Richardson Rd *RCOLE* CO7.....300 B6
  SRTFD E15 *.....333 H2
Richardsons La *RIPS/CAP* IP9.....84 C2
Richardson Wk *COLW* CO3.....151 J1
Richards Pl *WALTH* E17.....294 D1
Richards Wk *RCOS* CO16.....181 P7
Rich Cl *RCHLM* CM3.....169 J6
Riche Cl *GTDUN* CM6.....142 G9
Riches Rd *IL* IG1.....316 D4
Richford Rd *SRTFD* E15.....333 J1
Richmer Rd *ERITH* DA8.....346 F5
Richmond Av *CHING* E4.....294 G2
  SBF/HAD SS7.....325 P4
  SBN/FI SS3.....330 C8
  WOS/PRIT SS0.....18 E1
Richmond Cl *BSF* CM23.....137 H7
  WALTH E17.....314 C1
Richmond Crs *BROX* EN10.....208 C8
Richmond Crs *CHING* E4.....294 G2
  ED N9.....273 M1
  HAR CO12.....110 C6
Richmond Dr *COS* CO15.....185 J6
  RAYL SS6.....306 C2
  WFD IG8.....296 B4
  WOS/PRIT SS0.....328 D2
Richmond Rd *CHING* E4 *.....274 G7
  CHLM/GWD CM2.....218 F7
  FSTGT E7.....315 L7
  GRAYS RM17.....349 M4

IL IG1.....316 D5
IP IP1.....24 G4
K/T/MI CO5.....202 G6
ROM RM1.....318 E1
WAN E11.....314 G4
WICKE SS11.....285 H6
Richmond St *PLSTW* E13.....333 K2
  SOSN SS2.....329 L5
Richmond Vis *WALTH* E17 *.....294 E5
Richmond Wv *WAN* E11.....315 K4
Rich St *POP/IOD* E14.....332 C7
Ricketts Dr *BCAYW* CM12.....282 G5
Ricklins *VGE* SS16.....324 E2
Rickling Green Rd *SAFWS* CB11.....89 K7
Rickling Rd *SAFWS* CB11.....88 G2
Rick Roberts Wy *SRTFD* E15.....332 G1
Rickstones Rd *WIT* CM8.....171 P6
Riddiford Dr *CHLM/WR* CM1.....217 N7
Riddings La *HLWS* CM18.....211 H7
Riddies Dr *COLN* CO4.....128 A5
The Ride *PEND* EN3.....273 P2
Ridgdale St *BOW* E3.....332 D2
Ridge Av *WCHMH* N21.....273 H6
Ridge Cl *THMD* SE28.....334 E9
Ridge Crest *ENC/FH* EN2.....250 E9
Ridgemead Cl
  STHGT/OAK N14.....272 D8
Ridgemount *SBF/HAD* SS7.....326 B2
Ridgemount Gdns
  ENC/FH EN2.....272 G2
Ridge Rd *WCHMH* N21.....273 J7
Ridge Ter *WCHMH* N21 *.....273 H6
The Ridge *RCHLM* CM3.....220 B9
Ridgeway *BCAYW* CM12.....283 H8
  COLN CO4.....128 B3
  GRAYS RM17.....349 P2
  HOC/HUL SS5 *.....287 H5
  ING CM4.....260 B8
  MAL CM9.....244 B2
  RAYL SS6.....306 F6
  RBRW/HUT CM13.....281 L7
  STDN SC11.....136 A5
  WFD IG8.....295 M1
Ridgeway Gdns *REDBR* IG4.....295 P9
  WOS/PRIT SS0.....328 C6
Ridgeways *HLWE* CM17.....211 M5
The Ridgeway *BRTR* CM7.....145 K5
  CBE/LIN CB1.....38 D1
  CHING E4.....274 F7
  ENC/FH EN2.....250 B6
  GPK RM2.....298 F8
  HAR RM3.....145 K2
  HARH RM3.....299 K5
  LOS SS9.....328 D6
  STHGT/OAK N14.....272 D8
Ridgewell Av *CHLM/WR* CM1.....217 N7
Ridgewell Cl *DAGE* RM10.....336 A1
Ridgewell Rd *CAN/RD* E16.....333 M5
Ridings Av *WCHMH* N21 *.....273 H4
  WCHMH N21.....272 G3
The Ridings *BSF* CM23.....162 A1
  CHLM/GWD CM2.....238 D2
  CVI SS8.....326 D9
  RCFD SS4.....308 G6
  RCOLW CO6.....77 L2
Ridlands Cl *BRTR* CM77.....145 P8
Ridler Rd *EN* EN1.....251 K8
Ridley Cl *HARH* RM3.....298 G5
Ridley Gdns *RBSF* CM22.....114 F5
Ridley Rd *CHLM/WR* CM1.....218 A5
  FSTGT E7.....315 L6
  PIT SS13.....305 H6
Riffams Ct *PIT* SS13.....305 H7
Riffams Dr *PIT* SS13.....305 H7
Riffams *RBRW/HUT* CM13.....281 L9
Riffams Cha *RCHLM* CM3.....242 A1
Riffams Dr *CHLM/GWD* CM2.....240 E3
Ridings Av *BRTR* CM7.....241 P7
Rifle Hl *BRTR* CM7.....145 J5
Rifle St *POP/IOD* E14.....332 E5
Rigby Av *MGTR* CO11.....106 B3
Rigby Gdns *CDW/CHF* RM16.....350 C2
Rigby Ms *IL* IG1.....316 B4
Rigby Rd *POP/IOD* E14.....332 E6
Rigden St *POP/IOD* E14.....332 E6
Rigg Ap *LEY* E10.....314 A3
Right Side *STHGT/OAK* N14 *.....272 C7
Rignals La *CHLM/GWD* CM2.....240 C7
Riley Cl *IP* IP1.....24 D2
Riley Rd *PEND* EN3.....251 P8
Rimmer Cl *SUD* CO10.....47 K9
Ringham St *SUD* CO10.....47 K9
Ringlet Cl *CAN/RD* E16.....333 L5
Ringmer Pl *WCHMH* N21.....273 J4
Ringwood Av *HCH* RM12.....319 J4
Ringwood Dr *LOS* SS9.....307 L8
Ringwood Rd *WALTH* E17.....314 C1
Ringwood Wy *WCHMH* N21.....272 G6
Ripley Cl *RCOS* CO16.....181 L7
Ripley Ms *WAN* E11.....315 H1
Ripley Rd *CAN/RD* E16.....333 M6
  ENC/FH EN2.....251 K9
  GDMY/SEVK IG3.....316 G4
Ripley Vw *LOU* IG10.....254 C8
Ripley Wy *CHESW* EN7.....229 N9
Ripon Gdns *IL* IG1.....315 P1
Ripon Rd *ED* N9.....273 M1
Ripple Rd *BARK* IG11.....316 D9
  DAGW RM9.....335 M2
Rippleside *BSDN* SS14.....324 E1
Ripple Vw *BSDN* SS14.....324 D1
Ripston Rd *ASHF* TW15.....19 H4
Risbridge Dr *HVHL* CB9.....9 H7
Risby Cl *IPNE* IP4.....26 A5
  RCOS CO16.....181 K9
Risdens *HLWS* CM18.....210 D7
Risebridge Cha *ROM* RM1.....298 E4
Risebridge Rd *GPK* RM2.....298 E6
Risebia Cl *BARK/HLT* IG6.....296 F5

Risedale Rd *BXLYHN* DA7.....346 A8
Rise Pk *LAIN* SS15.....2 B5
Rise Park Bvd *ROM* RM1.....298 E5
Rise Park Pde *ROM* RM1.....298 D6
The Rise *BKHH* IG9.....275 N7
  DART DA1.....346 E9
  RCOLW CO6.....126 D7
  ROM RM1.....295 K9
  WAN E11.....295 K9
Riseway *BRWN* CM15.....281 H9
The Risings *WALTH* E17.....294 G8
The Rising *BCAYW* CM12.....283 K7
Ritabrook Rd *CHTY* IP2.....29 N1
Ritchings Av *WALTH* E17.....294 B8
Rivenell V *RCHLM* CM3.....286 F2
Rivenhall *SBF/HAD* SS7.....306 E7
Rivenhall Sbw
  WICKE SS11.....305 M1
Rivenhall Flds *WIT* CM8 *.....171 N7
Rivenhall Gdns *SWFD* E18.....295 J8
River Av *HOD* EN11.....208 E4
River Bank *BSF* CM23 *.....137 K6
  PLMGR N13.....273 Q9
River Bank *WCHMH* N21.....273 H6
River Barge Cl *POP/IOD* E14.....332 F9
River Cl *CHES/WCR* EN8.....252 D4
  HSTD CO9.....98 A7
  RAIN RM13.....336 C5
  WAN E11.....315 M1
Riverdale *LOS* SS9.....307 N8
Riverdale Rd *ERITH* DA8.....346 A3
Riverdene Rd *IL* IG1.....316 B5
River Dr *UPMR* RM14.....319 P6
Riverfield La *SBW* CM21.....187 M1
River Front *EN* EN1.....273 J2
Riverhead Cl *WALTH* E17.....294 A6
River Hl *WICKW* SS12.....195 N1
River Md *BRTR* CM7.....145 K2
Rivermead Rd *UED* N18 *.....294 A2
River Meads *WARE* SG12.....184 F7
Rivermill *HLW* CM20.....13 F3
River Rd *BARK* IG11.....335 G3
  BKHH IG9.....275 P7
  BRW CM14.....300 B1
Riversdale Rd *CRW* RM5.....278 G2
Riversfield Rd *EN* EN1.....273 K2
Riverside *BRTR* CM77.....146 E3
  BSF CM23 *.....137 L7
  CHLM/WR CM1.....5 J2
  GTDUN CM6.....141 M5
Riverside Av *BROX* EN10.....230 D1
Riverside Av East *MGTR* CO11.....106 B8
Riverside Av West
  MGTR CO11.....106 B3
Riverside Cl *CHING* E4 *.....106 B3
  HLW CM20.....187 K6
Riverside Gdns *ENC/FH* EN2.....273 H1
Riverside Ms
  BROX EN10 *.....230 B2
  WARE SG12 *.....184 A1
Riverside Pl
  FBAR/BDGN N11 *.....272 B9
Riverside Rd *BOC* CM0.....291 H4
  IL IG1.....316 C5
  IP IP1.....24 C4
  SRTFD E15.....332 F2
Riverside Wk *K/T/MI* CO5.....173 H4
Riversmead *HOD* EN11.....208 D6
Rivers St *IPNE* IP4.....17 K2
River St *WARE* SG12.....184 B1
Riverton Dr *BOC* CM0.....246 C1
River Vw *CDW/CHF* RM16.....350 B5
  WIT CM8.....197 K4
Riverview *VGE* SS16.....324 F2
River View Cl *LAIN* SS15.....303 K6
Riverview Gdns *HOC/HUL* SS5.....286 F5
River View Rd *RIPS/CAP* IP9.....84 C7
  SBF/HAD SS7.....326 A4
Riverview Ter *POP* RM19 *.....347 N3
River View Ter *RCHLM* CM3.....267 M7
River Wy *HLW* CM20.....187 H7
  LOU IG10.....276 B5
River Whf *BELV* DA17 *.....336 C9
Riviera Dr *SOS* SS1.....329 K6
Rivington Av *WFD* IG8.....295 N6
Rivish La *SUD* CO10.....46 F4
Rixsen Rd *MNPK* E12.....315 P2
Roach Av *RAYL* SS6.....306 F6
Roach Rd *BOW* E3.....314 D9
Roach Valley Wy
  HOC/HUL SS5.....307 M4
  RCFD SS4.....308 B7
  RCFD SS4.....308 B7
Robeck Rd *IPSE* IP5.....30 E1
Robert Cl *BCAYW* CM12.....282 G6
  CHIG IG7.....297 J2
  CHLM/GWD CM2.....218 E7
Roberts Cl *CHES/WCR* EN8.....230 B9
  HARH RM3.....298 G5
Robert's Hl *BURES* CO8.....100 E5
Robertson Cl *BROX* EN10.....230 B5
Robertson Rd *SRTFD* E15.....332 F1
Roberts Rd *COLS* CO2.....152 A1
  LOU IG10.....303 J8
  RCHLM CM3.....287 H2
  WALTH E17.....294 E5
Robert Wallace Cl *BSF* CM23.....137 L5
Robertson St *SOS* SS1.....332 C5
Robin Cl *BCAYW* CM12.....283 K2
  CRW RM5.....278 C4
  RCOLE CO7.....179 J3
  WARE SG12.....184 F9
Robin Crs *COLW* CO3.....150 E2
Robin Dr *CHTY* IP2.....24 E8
Robin Hood Gdns
  POP/IOD E14 *.....332 F7
Robin Hood La *POP/IOD* E14.....332 F7
Robin Hood Rd *BRWN* CM15.....280 E6
Robina Cl *BARK/HLT* IG6.....296 F5

LAIN SS15.....303 L1
Robinia Crs *LEY* E10.....314 E4
Robinsbridge Rd *RCOLW* CO6.....147 N4
Robinsdale *COS* CO15.....182 A7
Robinson Av *CHESW* EN7.....228 G7
Robinson Cl *BSF* CM23.....157 L9
  HCH RM12.....318 G9
  IPNE IP4.....31 H5
  WAN E11.....295 K9
Robinson Rd *CDW/CHF* RM16.....340 E1
  DAGE RM10.....317 P6
  ROCLE CO7.....179 M6
Robinsons Cl *BOC* CM0.....269 H6
The Robins *BRWN* CM15.....258 C5
Robin Wy *CHLM/GWD* CM2.....240 C3
  POTB/CUF EN6.....228 D7
  SUD CO10.....60 F5
Robjohns Rd *CHLM/WR* CM1.....239 M2
Robletts Wy *RCOLW* CO6.....101 K4
Robson Cl *EHAM* E6.....333 P6
  ENC/FH EN2.....272 G9
Robsons Cl *CHES/WCR* EN8.....229 P8
Rochdale Rd *WALTH* E17.....314 D2
Rochdale Wy *COLN* CO4.....128 F9
Roche Av *RCFD* SS4.....308 F5
Rochehall Dr *RCFD* SS4.....308 G7
Rochehall Wy *RCFD* SS4.....309 J7
Rochelle Cl *GTDUN* CM6.....92 B5
Rochester Av *PLSTW* E13.....333 M1
  EN EN1.....251 K9
Rochester Dr *WOS/PRIT* SS0.....328 D2
Rochester Gdns *IL* IG1.....316 A2
Rochester Ms *WOS/PRIT* SS0.....328 D2
Rocheway *RCFD* SS4.....309 H5
Rochford Av *BRWN* CM15.....281 K4
  CHDH RM6.....297 K9
  WAB EN9.....252 G4
  WOS/PRIT SS0.....18 B1
Rochford Cl *BROX* EN10.....230 B5
  EHAM E6.....333 N2
  WICKE SS11.....305 L1
Rochford Garden Wy
  RCFD SS4.....308 F4
Rochford Gn *LOU* IG10.....276 D2
Rochford Hall Cl *RCFD* SS4.....308 C6
Rochford Rd *BRTR* CM7.....157 N5
  CHLM/GWD CM2.....5 H5
  CVI SS8.....344 G2
  RCOS CO16.....180 E9
  SOSN SS2.....328 F1
Rochford Wy *WOTN* CO14.....158 G7
Rockall *SOSN* SS2.....308 B8
Rockall Cl *HVHL* CB9.....41 N4
Rockchase Gdns *EMPK* RM11.....319 K6
Rockfield Av *REDBR* IG4.....296 A1
Rockingham Av *EMPK* RM11.....318 G1
Rockingham Cl *COLN* CO4.....128 E4
Rockleigh Av *LOS* SS9.....328 B5
Rockleigh Ct *BRWN* CM15.....281 K6
Rockwell Rd *DAGE* RM10.....318 A7
Rockwood Gdns *LOU* IG10.....276 D2
Rodbridge Dr *SOS* SS1.....329 N6
Rodbridge Hl *SUD* CO10.....46 E7
Roddam Cl *HLWE* CM17.....127 M9
Roden Cl *HLWE* CM17.....187 N8
Roden St *IL* IG1.....316 B5
Roding Cl *ERITH* DA8.....346 G6
Roding La *SLH/COR* SS17.....341 L1
The Rodings *LOS* SS9.....307 N8
  UPMR RM14.....320 A1
Roding Vw *BKHH* IG9.....276 D3
  CHONG CM5.....235 N6
Roding Wy *RAIN* RM13.....337 J2
  WICKW SS12.....285 K9
Roding Ms *WAP* E1W *.....332 C6
Roebuck Cl *HOD* EN11.....208 D3
  WALTH E17.....294 D4
Roebuck La *BKHH* IG9.....276 C1
Roebuck Rd *BARK/HLT* IG6.....297 J3
Roedean Av *PEND* EN3.....251 P9
Roedean Cl *PEND* EN3.....251 P9
  SOSN SS2.....329 N5
Roedean Gdns *SOSN* SS2.....329 N5
Roffey St *POP/IOD* E14.....332 F9
Rogation Cl *COLS* CO2.....150 G1
Rogers Cl *CHESW* EN7.....229 J6
  FX IP11.....35 J5
Rogers Gdns *DAGE* RM10.....317 P7
  DAGE RM10.....317 P7
  GRAYS RM17.....349 M2
Roggel Rd *CVI* SS8.....344 G3
Rokeby Rd *WALTH* E17.....295 K5
Rokeby St *SRTFD* E15.....333 H1
Rokells *BSDN* SS14.....303 P1
Rokell Wy *FOS* CO15.....158 G3
Rokescroft *PIT* SS13.....324 F1
Roland La *CVI* SS8.....328 F1
Roland Ms *WICKE* SS11 *.....352 A5
Roland Rd *WALTH* E17.....294 G8
Roles Gv *CHDH* RM6.....297 M8
Rollesby Wy *THMD* SE28.....335 K7
Rolley La *BRTR* CM7.....173 H5
Roll Gdns *GNTH/NBYPK* IG2.....296 B9
Rolls Park Av *CHING* E4.....294 D3
Rolls Park Rd *CHING* E4.....294 E2

Rolph La RCOS CO16 ....157 K4
Roma Av WDBR IP12 ....27 P3
Romagne Cl SLH/COR SS17 ......340 G2
Romainville Wy CVI SS8 ....259 N9
Roman Cl BRWN CM15 ....222 A7
RAIN RM13 ....336 C2
Roman Ct BRTR CM7 ....145 M5
Romanhurst MAL CM9 ....187 L2
Roman Ri SBW CM21 ....187 L2
Roman Rd BRTH E2 ....332 A2
BRWN CM15 ....281 M2
COL CO1 ....8 E4
EHAM E6 ....533 P4
IL IG1 ....316 C8
ING CM4 ....260 B7
RCHLM CM3 ....194 A6
Romans CI CHLM/WR CM1 ....239 J1
Roman Sq THMD SE28 ....335 H8
Roman St HOD EN11 ....208 D4
Romans Wy CHLM/WR CM1 ......239 J1
Roman V HLWE CM17 ....187 K7
Roman Wy BCAYW CM12 ....283 H8
BOC CM0 ....290 C1
EN EN1 ....273 L4
FX IP11 ....35 N5
HVHL CB9 ....41 N5
RCOS CO16 ....205 H1
SAFWS CB11 ....50 C6
SUD CO10 ....46 F5
WAB EN9 ....252 E5
Roma Rd WALTH E17 ....294 E7
Rom Crs ROMW/RG RM7 ....318 D2
Romeland WAB EN9 ....252 F5
Romford Cl COLN CO4 ....9 L8
Romford Rd CHIG IG7 ....297 J1
CHONG CM5 ....257 K3
MNPK E12 ....316 B5
SOCK/AV RM15 ....337 P7
SRTFD E15 ....315 J8
Romney Cha EMPK RM11 ....319 L1
Romney Cl BRTR CM7 ....121 H9
FOS CO15 ....158 F7
RCOLE CO7 ....179 K4
RCOS CO16 ....181 N7
Romney Rd BCAYW CM12 ....392 G2
IPSE IP5 ....30 C2
Romsey Cl HOC/HUL SS5 ....307 N1
SBF/HAD SS7 ....325 N1
SLH/COR SS17 ....341 J4
Romsey Crs SBF/HAD SS7 ....325 M1
Romsey Dr SBF/HAD SS7 ....325 M1
Romsey Rd DAGW RM9 ....335 L1
SBF/HAD SS7 ....325 M1
Romsey Wy SLH/COR SS17 ......325 N1
Romulus Cl COLN CO4 ....128 A2
Rom Valley Wy
    ROMW/RG RM7 ....318 D1
Ronald Av SRTFD E15 ....333 H3
Ronald Dr RAYL SS6 ....306 D3
Ronald Hill Gv LOS SS9 ....327 N5
Ronald Park Av
    WOS/PRIT SS0 ....328 D4
Ronald Rd HARH RM3 ....299 M5
    HSTD CO9 ....97 P8
Roneo Cnr ROMW/RG RM7 .....318 E3
Roneo Link HOT RM12 ....318 E3
Ron Green Ct ERITH DA8 ....346 C5
Ron Leighton Wy EHAM E6 ......333 P1
Ronnie La BCTR RM8 ....317 K4
Roodegate BSDN SS14 ....2 D4
Rookby Ct WCHMH N21 ....272 C8
Rook End La SAFWS CB11 ....90 E2
The Rookeries RCOLW CO6 ......149 N2
Rookery Cha RCOLE CO7 ....104 F6
Rookery Cl RAYL SS6 ....306 F5
    RCHLM CM3 ....196 D7
    SAFWS CB10 ....30 C8
Rookery Ct WTHK RM20 ....348 D4
Rookery Hl SLH/COR SS17 ....342 B2
Rookery La K/T/MI CO5 ....173 P6
    MAL CM9 ....198 F5
    RCHLM CM3 ....265 P9
    SAFWS CB11 ....44 B6
Rookery Md RCHLM CM3 ....264 G9
Rookery Rd ING CM4 ....236 F8
The Rookery MGTR CO11 ....106 B4
    STSD CM24 ....114 B7
    WTHK RM20 ....348 D4
Rookery Vw GRAYS RM17 ....349 N3
Rookes BSDN SS14 ....51 L6
Rookes Crs CHLM/WR CM1 ....4 C7
Rookwood Av LOU IG10 ....276 D2
Rookwood Cl GRAYS RM17 ......349 N2
    RCOS CO16 ....181 P6
Rookwood Gdns EHAM E4 * 275 P2
Rookyards VGE SS16 ....324 D1
Roosevelt Rd LAIN SS15 ....303 H9
Roosevelt Wy COLS CO2 ....152 C2
    DAGE RM10 ....318 C8
Roos Hill Debden Rd
    SAFWS CB11 ....65 M4
Roots Hall Av SOSN SS2 ....328 C4
Roots Hall Dr SOSN SS2 ....328 F4
Roots La WIT CM8 ....197 P8
Ropemaker Rd
    BERM/RHTH SE16 ....332 B9
Ropemaker's Flds
    POP/IOD E14 * 332 C7
Ropers Av CHING E4 ....294 F2
Ropers La SUD CO10 ....46 E7
Ropery St BOW E3 ....26 C5
Ropes Dr KESG IP5 ....26 C3
Rose Wk IPNE IP4 ....17 C5
    MAL CM9 ....244 B1
Rosabelle Av RCOLE CO7 ....153 J5
Rosalind Cl COLN CO4 ....128 G8
Rosalind Gdns WOS/PRIT SS0 ..328 C2
Rosbach Rd CVI SS8 ....344 D2
Rosberg Rd CVI SS8 ....345 H2
Roscommon Wy CVI SS8 ....343 P1
Rose Acre BSDN SS14 ....304 E9

RCOLE CO7 ....80 C3
Roseacre Cl EMPK RM11 ....319 L3
Roseacres RBSF CM22 ....139 M7
SBW CM21 ....187 L1
Rose Av COLW CO5 ....150 F2
SWFD E18 ....295 L6
Rose Bank BRW CM14 ....280 G9
Rosebank HAR CO12 ....110 B5
    WAB EN9 ....253 H6
Rosebank Av HCH RM12 ....319 H7
Rosebank Est BOW E3 ....332 C2
Rosebank Gdns BOW E3 * 332 B2
Rosebank Gv K/T/MI CO5 ....250 F9
Rosebank Rd K/T/MI CO5 ....202 D6
    WALTH E17 ....314 D1
Rosebay Av BRTR CM12 ....282 C3
Rosebay Cl WIT CM8 ....196 C1
Roseberry Cl SBF/HAD SS7 ......305 P9
    VGE SS16 ....323 J2
Roseberry Cl UPMR RM14 ....320 C1
Roseberry Gdns UPMR RM14 ...320 C2
Rosebery BSF CM23 ....137 P8
Rosebery Av COL CO1 ....152 E6
    MNPK E12 ....315 P9
Rosebery Rd CHLM/GWD CM2 ....5 G7
    ROM RM1 ....273 M9
    GRAYS RM17 ....349 H4
    IPNE IP4 ....17 K5
Rosedale Av CHESW EN7 ....229 L8
Rosedale Gdns DAGW RM9 ......317 J9
Rosedale Rd DAGW RM9 ....317 J9
    FSTGT E7 ....315 M7
    GRAYS RM17 ....349 N3
    ROM RM1 ....298 B7
Rosedale Wy CHESW EN7 ....229 M6
Rosedene Gdns
    GNTH/NBYPK IG2 ....296 B8
Rosedene Ter LEY E10 ....314 E4
Rose Dr BOC CM0 ....269 J6
Rosefield POP/IOD E14 * 332 D7
Rosefield Gdns POP/IOD E14 ...332 D7
Rosefinch Cl HVHL CB9 ....41 M4
    RCOS CO16 ....206 A6
Rose Gln CHLM/GWD CM2 ......240 G3
    ROMW/RG RM7 ....318 D5
Rose Gn SUD CO10 ....76 F2
Rosehatch Av CHDH RM6 ....297 L7
Rose Hl BRTR CM7 ....145 K4
Rosehill Cl HOD EN11 ....208 C5
Rosehill Crs IPSE IP5 ....17 K7
Rosehill Rd IPSE IP5 ....25 N7
Roselaine BSDN SS14 ....3 F5
Roselands Av HOD EN11 ....208 C3
Rose La BCAYW CM12 ....283 H6
    CHDH RM6 ....297 M8
    IPNE IP4 ....18 E1
    MAL CM9 ....200 C4
    RCOLE CO7 ....153 J7
    SAFWN SB10 ....36 F9
Roselawn Flds
    CHLM/WR CM1 ....218 A3
Rosemary Av BRTR CM7 ....145 J2
    ED N9 ....273 N7
    ENC/FH EN2 ....251 J9
    FX IP11 ....35 L5
    ROM RM1 ....298 E7
Rosemary Cl GTDUN CM6 ....141 K5
    K/T/MI CO5 ....173 P8
    SOCK/AV RM15 ....338 F3
Rosemary Dr POP/IOD E14 ......332 C6
    REDBR IG4 ....295 N9
Rosemary Gdns BCTR RM8 ......317 N3
    SUD CO10 ....47 J9
Rosemary La GTDUN CM6 ....141 K6
    HSTD CO9 ....72 E4
    HSTD CO9 ....97 P6
    RCOLE CO7 ....154 G9
Rosemead Gdns
    RBRW/HUT CM13 ....281 N3
Rosemount
    HLWW/ROY CM19 ....210 C6
Rosenath Av WCHMH N21 ....272 C7
Rosenath Wk EN EN1 ....273 K5
Roserna Rd CVI SS8 ....344 D2
Rose Rd CVI SS8 ....344 D2
Roserton St POP/IOD E14 ....332 F9
Rosery Ms FOS CO15 ....183 H1
The Roses WFD IG8 * 295 J4
Rose V HOD EN11 ....208 A6
Rose Va SRW CM14 ....280 F9
Rose Valley Crs SLH/COR SS17 .341 L1
Rose Vls MGTR CO11 * 81 N9
Rose Wy RCFD SS4 ....309 H7
Rosewood Av HVHL CB9 ....41 K1
Rosewood Cl COLN CO4 ....128 B3
    SOCK/AV RM15 ....339 H5
Rosewood Dr ENC/FH EN2 ....250 F5
Rosewood La SBN/FI SS13 ....330 E8
Rose Yd HSTD CO9 * 98 A6
Rosher Cl SRTFD E15 ....315 H8
Roslian Dr HOC/HUL SS5 ....340 C7
Rosina St HOM E9 ....314 A8
Roslings CI CHLM/WR CM1 ......217 L1
Roslyn Cl BROX EN10 ....208 B9
Roslyn Gdns GPK RM2 ....298 E6

Rossall Cl EMPK RM11 ....318 F1
Ross Av BCTR RM8 ....317 N4
Ross Cl HVHL CB9 ....41 M4
Rossdale Dr ED N9 ....275 P5
Rossdene Gdns GTDUN CM6 ....190 G5
Rossell Rd TIL RM18 ....350 A4
Rossendale CHLM/WR CM1 ....4 A6
Rossendale Ct COLN CO4 ....128 D4
    ENC/FH EN2 ....250 C7
Rosetta Cl RCOLE CO7 ....153 J4
Rossington Cl EN EN1 ....251 N8
Rossiter Rd SBN/FI SS13 ....330 C6
Rossiyn Av BCTR RM8 ....317 N2
    CHING E4 ....275 J8
    HARH RM3 ....299 K6
Rosslyn Cl HOC/HUL SS5 ....307 P1
Rosslyn Rd BARK IG11 ....316 E9
    DART DA1 ....282 G6
    HOC/HUL SS5 ....307 P1
    WALTH E17 ....294 F8
Ross Rd IPNE IP4 ....26 A2
Ross Wy VGE SS16 ....16 A2
Roswell Ct CHLM/WCR EN8 ......230 B9
Rothbury Av RAIN RM13 ....336 G5
Rothbury Rd CHLM/WR CM1 ...219 H1
    HOM E9 ....314 C9
Roth Dr RBRW/HUT CM13 ....281 L8
Rotherfield Rd PEND EN3 ....252 A7
Rotherhithe St
    BERM/RHTH SE16 ....332 A8
Rothesay Av CHLM/GWD CM2 ....4 E7
Rothmans Av
    CHLM/GWD CM2 ....240 D7
Rothsay Rd FSTGT E7 ....315 M9
Rothwell Cl LOS SS9 ....307 M9
Rothwell Gdns DAGW RM9 ....317 K9
Rothwell Rd DAGW RM9 ....335 K1
Roughtalys EPP CM16 ....315 N5
Roughtons CHLM/GWD CM2 ....240 G7
Roundacre HSTD CO9 ....97 P8
Roundaway Rd CLAY IG5 ....296 A6
Roundbush Rd K/T/MI CO5 ......174 G4
    WITHC CM8 ....266 B1
Round Cl COLN CO4 ....127 L8
Round Coppice Rd
    STSD CM24 ....138 D6
Roundcroft CHESW EN7 ....229 L5
Roundhedge Wy ENC/FH EN2 ..250 F6
Roundhill Dr ENC/FH EN2 ....272 E3
Round Hill Rd SBF/HAD SS7 .....326 D4
Roundhills WAB EN9 ....253 H4
Roundmead Av LOU IG10 ....276 B2
Roundmead Cl LOU IG10 ....276 B2
Roundmoor Dr
    CHES/WCR EN8 ....230 B8
Roundridge Rd
    RIPS/CAP IP9 ....28 D8
Roundwood Av
    RBRW/HUT CM13 ....281 K7
Roundwood Gv
    RBRW/HUT CM13 ....281 L6
Roundwood Rd IPNE IP4 ....25 P4
Rounton Rd BOW E3 ....332 D4
Rous Cha CHLM/GWD CM2 ......240 A9
Rous Rd BKHH IG9 ....275 P7
Routemaster Cl PLSTW E13 .....333 L3
Routh Av IPSE IP5 ....31 M1
Routh St EHAM E6 ....334 A1
Rover Av BARK/HLT IG6 ....296 C5
    COS CO15 ....206 D5
Rowallan Cl COLW CO5 ....151 K3
Rowan Av CHLM/WCR EN8 ......294 C3
Rowan Cl COLW CO5 ....150 C2
    COS CO15 ....207 H1
    HAR CO12 ....14 B7
    IL IG1 ....316 E7
    RAYL SS6 ....306 E1
    RCOLE CO7 ....155 L6
Rowan Dr BROX EN10 ....230 C3
Rowan Gn East
    RBRW/HUT CM13 ....301 J1
Rowan Gn West
    RBRW/HUT CM13 ....301 J1
Rowan Gv SOCK/AV RM15 ......337 P7
Rowanhayes Cl CHTY IP2 ....25 J8
Rowan Pl COL CO1 ....8 B2
The Rowans BCAYE CM11 ....283 L8
    BROX EN10 ....208 B7
    PLMGR N13 ....272 A8
    SOCK/AV RM15 ....337 P8
Rowans Waw RCOLW CO6 ....77 J3
Rowans Wy LOU IG10 ....276 A3
    WICKE SS11 ....285 K8
Rowantree Cl WCHMH N21 .....299 J8
Rowantree Ms ENC/FH EN2 .....272 C1
Rowantree Rd ENC/FH EN2 .....272 C1
    WCHMH N21 ....273 J7
Rowan Wk EMPK RM11 ....299 J8
    LOS SS9 ....307 M9
    SBW CM21 ....187 M2
Rowan Wy CHDH RM6 ....297 K7
    RCFD SS4 ....289 M7
    SBN/FI SS13 ....196 D9
    SOCK/AV RM15 ....171 P9
Rowarth Av KESG IP5 ....27 H4
Rowden Pde CHING E4 * 294 D3
Rowden Rd CHING E4 ....294 E3
Rowdowns Rd DAGW RM9 ....335 N1
Rowe Gdns BARK IG11 ....334 C2
Rowell Cl HVHL CB9 ....41 K1
Rowenhall LAIN SS15 ....302 C9
Rowheath Rd CHLM/WR CM1 ..281 K9
Rowhedge Cl PIT SS13 ....305 J3
Rowhedge Rd RCOLE CO7 ....155 L2
Rowland Crs CHIG IG7 ....296 F1
Rowland Rd CHES/WCR EN8 ....230 A9

Rowlandsfields
    CHES/WCR EN8 * 230 A9

Rowlands Rd BCTR RM8 ....317 N4
The Rowlands SBF/HAD SS7 .....326 B2
Rowland's Yd HAR CO12 ....109 P6
Rowland Vs MGTR CO11 * 81 N9
Rowley Ct CHLM/WR CM1 ....41 P6
Rowley Hi HVHL CB9 ....41 L4
Rowley Md EPP CM16 ....233 K4
Rowley Rd CDW/CHF RM16 .....340 B5
Rowney Av SAFWN CB10 ....66 D7
Rowney Gdns DAGW RM9 ....317 K8
    SBW CM21 ....187 K3
Rowney Rd DAGW RM9 ....317 J8
Rowney Wd SBW CM21 ....187 K3
Rowntree Cl PLSTW E13 ....333 L4
Rowntree Wy SAFWS CB11 ....51 M2
Rowse Cl SRTFD E15 ....332 F1
Rowsley Rd CLAY IG5 ....130 E5
Roxborough Gdns WICKE SS11 ...3 K6
Roxburgh Av UPMR RM14 ....319 P5
Roxburghe Rd RCOS CO16 ......156 C8
Roxburgh Rd IPNE IP4 ....26 A2
Roxwell Av WCR RM16 ....217 L8
Roxwell Gdns
    RBRW/HUT CM13 ....281 M4
Roxwell Rd BARK IG11 ....335 H2
    CHLM/WR CM1 ....216 A3
    CHLM/WR CM1 ....216 C7
    RBRW/HUT CM13 ....281 M4
Roxy Av CHDH RM6 ....317 K2
Royal Albert Rd EHAM E6 ....317 K2
Royal Albert Wy CAN/RD E16 ...533 N7
Royal Artillery Wy SOSN SS2 ...329 M5
Royal Av CHES/WCR EN8 ....252 B3
Royal Cl GDMY/SEVK IG3 ....317 H2
    RCFD SS4 ....308 E2
Royal Ct COLN CO4 ....128 F6
    EN EN1 * 273 K5
    MAL CM9 ....244 B1
Royal Crescent Monarch Wy
    GNTH/NBYPK IG2 ....316 E1
Royal Ms SOSN SS2 ....19 F6
Royal Oak Cha LAIN SS15 ....303 M7
Royal Oak Gdns BSF CM23 ......137 K8
Royal Rd CDW/CHF RM16 ....333 N6
The Royals SOS SS1 * 19 G5
Royal Ter SOS SS1 ....19 F6
Royal Victor Pl BOW E3 ....332 A2
Roy Av IPNE IP4 ....26 A6
Royce Cl BROX EN10 ....208 C9
Roy Cl KESG IP5 ....26 C4
Roycraft Av BARK IG11 ....334 C2
Roycroft Cl SWFD E18 ....295 L3
Roydon Br BSDN SS14 ....304 C2
Roydon Cl LOU IG10 ....295 P2
Roydon Rd HLWW/ROY CM19 ...209 P6
    WARE SG12 ....184 G8
Roydon Wy FOS CO15 ....158 G3
Royer Cl HOC/HUL SS5 ....340 B6
Roy Gdns CHLM/WR CM1 ....219 H1
Royle Cl GPK RM2 ....298 G8
Roy Sq POP/IOD E14 ....332 C7
Royston Av CHING E4 ....294 D2
    LAIN SS15 ....303 L6
    SOSN SS2 ....329 J5
Royston Dr CHTY IP2 * 28 C6
Royston Gdns IL IG1 ....315 N1
Royston La SAFWN CB10 ....49 K2
Royston Rd HARH RM3 ....299 M5
    SAFWS CB11 ....64 B4
Ruaton Dr RCOS CO16 ....155 J8
Rubens Av WICKE SS11 ....285 L8
Rubens Ct CHLM/WR CM1 ....218 E4
Rubens Rd IPSE IP3 ....30 C1
Rubens Wk SUD CO10 ....47 K9
Rubicon Av WICKE SS11 ....285 L8
Ruby Ms WALTH E17 ....294 D7
Ruckholt Cl LEY E10 ....314 E5
Ruckholt Rd LEY E10 ....314 F5
Ruddington Cl CLPT E5 ....314 B6
Rudkin Rd COLN CO4 ....128 A2
Rudland Rd BCTR RM8 ....348 A8
Rudlands RIPW IP9 ....29 L1
Rudolph Rd PLSTW E13 ....333 K2
Rudsdale Wy COLW CO5 ....151 J8
Rue De St Lawrence
    WAB EN9 ....252 F4
Rue's La FX IP11 ....35 M3
Ruffels Fld GTDUN CM6 ....142 D2
Ruffles Cl RAYL SS6 ....307 H4
Ruffles Rd HVHL CB9 ....41 L4
Rugby Av ED N9 ....273 L7
Rugby Gdns DAGW RM9 ....317 K8
Rugby Rd DAGW RM9 ....317 J9
    SUD CO10 ....61 L6
Rugg Cl POP/IOD E14 ....332 D7
Rugosa Cl COLN CO4 ....126 F6
Rumballs Cl BSF CM23 ....161 P1
Rumbold Rd HOD EN11 ....208 F3
Rumbullion Dr BCAYW CM12 ...282 G5
Rumsey Flds RCHLM CM3 ....242 C3
Rumsley CHESW EN7 ....229 M4
Rundells HLWE CM18 ....211 H7
Rundells Wk BSDN SS14 ....304 D8
The Rundels SBF/HAD SS7 ....326 D1
Runacles St WIT CM8 ....146 D9
Runacles Wy FX IP11 ....34 G6
Runnemede WOS/PRIT SS0 ......328 D7
Running Mare La
    CHLM/GWD CM2 ....239 P7
Running Waters
    RBRW/HUT CM13 ....301 K1
Runnymede Cha
    SLH/COR SS17 ....326 D2
Runnymede Rd CVI SS8 ....344 E2
    SLH/COR SS17 ....341 K4
Runsell Cl RCHLM CM5 ....242 C3
Runsell La RCHLM CM5 ....242 C2
Runsell Vw RCHLM CM5 ....242 C2
Runwell Cha WICKE SS11 ....285 M6

Runwell Gdns WICKE SS11 ....285 J6
Runwell Rd WICKE SS11 ....285 K7
    WICKE SS11 ....285 N5
Runwell Ter SOS SS1 ....18 E5
Runwood Rd CVI SS8 ....343 P2
Rupert Rd BOC CM0 ....269 H5
Rural Cl EMPK RM11 ....318 C3
Rurik Ct MAL CM9 ....187 L2
Ruscoe Rd CAN/RD E16 ....333 J6
Rushbottom La SBF/HAD SS7 ..305 N9
Rushbrook Crs WALTH E17 ......294 C5
Rushbury Cl IPNE IP4 ....26 A3
Rush Cl SBF/HAD SS7 ....305 N9
    WARE SG12 ....184 F8
Rushcroft Rd CHING E4 ....294 E4
Rushdene Rd BCAYW CM12 ......282 G8
    BRWN CM15 ....280 F6
Rushden Gdns CLAY IG5 ....296 B7
Rushdon Cl CDW/CHF RM16 ...349 K1
    ROM RM1 ....298 F9
Rushes Dr WAB EN9 ....252 F6
Rushes La RCOS CO16 ....247 M9
Rushey Hl HLWS CM18 ....210 C5
Rushey Hl ENC/FH EN2 ....272 E5
Rushfield SBW CM21 ....187 M2
Rush Green Gdns
    ROMW/RG RM7 ....318 B5
Rush Green Rd RCOS CO16 ......206 G1
    ROMW/RG RM7 ....318 B3
Rush La RBSF CM22 ....114 F7
Rushleigh Av CHES/WCR EN8 ...230 A9
Rushleigh Gn BSF CM23 ....162 A2
Rushmead Cl IPSE IP5 ....305 J7
Rushley Pl SS13 ....330 F2
Rushley Cl CDW/CHF RM16 ......339 N8
    SBN/FI SS13 ....330 F2
Rushleydale CHLM/WR CM1 ....218 D6
Rushmeadow Wy FX IP11 ....35 N4
Rushmere Av UPMR RM14 ....319 P5
Rushmere Cl K/T/MI CO5 ....202 F6
Rushmere Rd IPNE IP4 ....25 P4
Rushmere St KESG IP5 ....26 D2
Rusholine Av DAGE RM10 ....317 P5
Rushton Cv HLWE CM17 ....187 K8
Ruskin Av MNPK E12 ....315 P8
    SOSN SS2 ....329 H4
    UPMR RM14 ....319 P2
    WAB EN9 ....225 H5
Ruskin Cl CHESW EN7 ....229 L5
    FOS CO15 ....158 F7
    HVHL CB9 ....40 G2
Ruskin Dene BCAYW CM12 ......283 H5
Ruskin Gdns HARH RM5 ....298 G5
Ruskin Rd CDW/CHF RM16 ......350 B2
    CHLM/GWD CM2 ....218 D3
    IPNE IP4 ....23 N6
    SLH/COR SS17 ....341 K4
The Ruskins BRTR CM77 ....144 C5
Ruskin Wk ED N9 ....273 M8
Rusper Rd BCAYW CM12 ....317 K8
Russell Cl BRWN CM15 ....280 E6
    DART DA1 ....346 F8
    LAIN SS15 ....303 J9
Russell Gdns CHLM/GWD CM2 .239 P6
    WICKE SS11 ....285 K9
Russell Gv RCFD SS4 ....309 H5
Russell Rd BKHH IG9 ....333 K6
    CAN/RD E16 ....294 C1
    COS CO15 ....175 P8
    EN EN1 ....251 L8
    FX IP11 ....16 B5
    IP IP1 ....314 E1
    RCHLM CM5 ....349 P6
    TIL RM18 ....294 C7
Russell Rw RCFD SS4 * 289 M6
Russell's Dr CHES/WCR EN8 ....230 B9
Russell's Ride
    CHES/WCR EN8 ....252 A1
Russell's Rd HSTD CO9 ....97 K7
Russell Wy CHLM/WR CM1 ......239 N3
Russel Rd GRAYS RM17 ....349 K2
    CHESW EN7 * 229 K5
    SLH/COR SS17 ....341 L2
Russets Cl CHING E4 ....294 G1
The Russets RCFD SS4 ....308 E2
Russets Cl HVHL CB9 ....40 F3
Russetts EMPK RM11 ....299 K8
    VGE SS16 ....323 H1
Russet Wy BOC CM0 ....291 N7
    HOC/HUL SS5 ....340 A3
Russia Dock Rd
    BERM/RHTH SE16 ....332 B8
Rustic Cl UPMR RM14 ....319 P3
Ruston St BOW E3 ....332 C1
Rutherford Cl UPMR RM12 ....283 H3
    LOS SS9 ....307 M9
Rutherfords CHLM/WR CM1 .....218 A2
Ruthven Av CHES/WCR EN8 .....252 A3
Ruthven Cl WICKW SS12 ....305 J1
Ruthven St HOM E9 ....314 A8
Rutland Ap EMPK RM11 ....299 M9
Rutland Av COLS CO2 ....151 L3
    SOS SS1 ....329 N6
Rutland Cl LAIN SS15 ....303 H9
Rutland Dr EMPK RM11 ....299 M9
    RAYL SS6 ....286 E9
Rutland Gdns BCTR RM8 ....317 K7
    BRTR CM7 ....145 K2
    RCFD SS4 ....308 D2
Rutland Ga BCTR RM8 ....346 A3
Rutland Pl BRTR CM7 * 94 A5
Rutland Rd CHLM/WR CM1 ......217 P5
    HARH RM3 ....299 N9
    HOM E9 ....332 A1
    IL IG1 ....314 D1
    WALTH E17 ....314 D1
    WAN E11 ....295 L9
Rydal Av FX IP11 ....35 N4
Rydal Cl HOC/HUL SS5 ....286 G6
    RAYL SS6 ....307 H5

Rydal Dr *MAL* CM9 ....244 C2
Rydal Wk *IPSE* IP5 ....26 B9
Rydal Wy *BRTR* CM77 ....144 F8
   PEND EN15 ....273 P5
Ryde Av *COS* CO15 ....182 B6
Ryde Cl *LOS* SS9 ....327 L1
   THMD SE28 ....341 K5
Ryder Gdns *RAIN* RM13 ....318 E8
Ryder Wy *PIT* SS13 ....305 J5
The Ryde *LOS* SS9 ....327 L1
Rye Cl *COLW* CO3 ....150 G1
   IPSE IP5 ....26 C7
   RCHLM CM5 ....196 D9
   RCOLE CO7 ....179 K4
Ryecroft *HLWW/ROY* CM19 ....12 E7
Ryecroft Av *CLAY* IG5 ....296 C6
Ryedene *VGE* SS16 ....324 D3
Ryedene Cl *VGE* SS16 ....324 D5
Ryedene Pl *VGE* SS16 ....324 D5
Ryefield Cl *HOD* EN11 ....208 E1
The Rye Fld *RCHLM* CM5 ....220 A8
Ryegate Rd *COL* CO1 ....8 D4
Rye Grass Wy *BRTR* CM7 ....145 L5
Rye Hill Rd *HLWS* CM18 ....210 E8
Rye Hills *HSTD* CO9 ....98 A8
Rye La *COLS* CO2 ....176 B1
Rye Mill La *K/T/MI* CO5 ....173 J1
Rye Rd *HOD* EN11 ....208 E4
Ryes La *RBSF* CM22 ....163 L6
   SUD CO10 ....60 D8
Rye St *BSF* CM23 ....137 L5
The Rye *STHGT/OAK* N14 ....272 B6
Rye Wk *ING* CM4 ....260 B7
Rykhill *CLHM* RM16 ....350 C1
Rylands *RIPS/CAP* IP9 ....28 C8
Rylands Rd *SOSN* SS2 ....329 K4
The Ryle *CHLM/WR* CM1 ....239 H2
Rylstone Wy *SAFWS* CB11 ....65 N1
Ryiston Rd *PLMGR* N13 ....273 J9
Rymill St *CAN/RD* E16 ....334 B8
Rysley *RCHLM* CM5 ....220 A7

S

Sabbarton St *CAN/RD* E16 ....333 J6
Sabina Rd *CDW/CHF* RM16 ....350 D2
Sabines Rd *ABR/ST* RM4 ....279 L2
Sackville Cl *CHLM/WR* CM1 ....217 M8
Sackville Crs *HARH* RM3 ....299 K5
Sackville Gdns *IL* IG1 ....316 A3
Sackville Rd *SOSN* SS2 ....329 M5
Sackville Wy *RCOLW* CO6 ....126 G3
Sacombs Ash La *SBW* CM21 ....161 K6
Saddle Ri *CHLM/WR* CM1 ....218 D3
Saddlers Cl *BRTR* CM77 ....144 E7
Saddlers Pl *KESC* IP5 ....27 M4
Sadler Cl *CHESW* EN7 ....229 H4
   COL CO1 ....152 C2
Sadlers *SBF/HAD* SS7 ....305 N9
Sadlers Ct *BCAYE* CM11 ....283 C3
   FOS CO15 ....158 D8
Sadlers Md *HLWS* CM18 ....211 H4
Saffory Cl *LOS* SS9 ....307 M8
Saffron Cl *BRTR* CM7 ....95 H5
   HOD EN11 ....208 C4
   RBRW/HUT CM15 ....321 N1
   SLH/COR SS17 ....341 H2
Saffron Gdns *BRTR* CM7 ....94 G5
   SLH/COR SS17 ....340 G4
Saffron Rd *CDW/CHF* RM16 ....348 F2
   CRW RM5 ....298 C6
   BRTR CM7 ....94 G5
Saffron Wy *K/T/MI* CO5 ....173 P9
Sage Cl *EHAM* E6 ....334 A5
Sagehayes *CHTY* IP2 ....25 J8
Sage Rd *COLS* CO2 ....152 B4
Sages End Rd *HVHL* CB9 ....54 D2
Saigasso Cl *CAN/RD* E16 ....333 N6
St Agnes Dr *CVI* SS8 ....344 A2
St Agnes Rd *BCAYW* CM12 ....303 K4
St Agnes Wy *KESC* IP5 ....26 E4
St Alban's Rd *COLW* CO3 ....127 N8
   EPP CM16 ....233 L8
   GDMY/SEVK IG3 ....316 C3
   WFD IG8 ....295 K4
St Alphege Rd *ED* N9 ....273 H6
St Andrew's Av *COLN* CO4 ....9 J5
   HCH RM12 ....318 E7
St Andrews Cl *CVI* SS8 ....344 A1
   EPP CM16 ....234 B3
   IPNE IP4 ....26 C6
   RCOLE CO7 ....154 A7
   THMD SE28 ....335 L6
St Andrews Dr *BCAYW* CM12 ....283 J5
   RIPS/CAP IP9 ....84 D2
St Andrews Gdns *COLN* CO4 ....9 H4
St Andrews La *LAIN* SS15 ....303 K8
St Andrews Meadow
   HLWS CM18 ....210 G4
St Andrews Pl *BRWN* CM15 ....281 J8
   RCOLE CO7 ....179 K4
St Andrew's Ri *COS* CO15 ....6 D5
St Andrew's Rd *SUD* CO10 ....40 D8
   ED N9 ....273 P6
   EN EN1 ....273 J2
   FX IP11 ....35 K6
   HSTD CO9 ....98 C5
   IL IG1 ....316 A2
   PLSTW E13 ....333 L3
   RCFD SS4 ....308 F5
   RCHLM CM5 ....196 D8
   RCHLM CM5 ....196 D3
   RCOS CO16 ....156 C5
   ROMW/RG RM7 ....318 C1
   SBN/FI SS3 ....330 B8

SUD CO10 ....61 K4
TIL RM18 ....349 P7
WALTH E17 ....143 J6
WAN E11 ....315 H1
St Andrews Wy *BOW* E3 ....332 E4
St Annes Ct *CDW/CHF* RM16 * 339 L8
   CHENV EN7 * 229 M7
   RCOLW CO6 ....148 A4
St Annes Ct *CHLM/WR* CM1 * 5 J2
St Anne's Pk *BROX* EN10 ....208 D8
St Anne's Pas *POP/IOD* E14 * 332 C6
St Anne's Rd *BRWN* CM15 ....259 M9
   CVI SS8 ....344 G2
   LEY E10 ....314 G4
St Anne's Rw *POP/IOD* E14 ....332 C6
St Anne St *POP/IOD* E14 ....332 C6
St Ann's Bark *IG11 ....334 D1
   COS CO15 ....6 D1
   ED N9 ....273 L8
   SOSN SS2 ....19 G2
St Anthony's Av *WFD* IG8 ....295 M3
St Anthony's Dr
   CHLM/GWD CM2 ....240 B4
St Antony's Ra *FSTGT* E7 ....315 L9
St Aubyns Rd *IPNE* IP4 ....25 P6
St Augustine Ms *COL* CO1 * 8 E6
St Augustine Rd
   CDW/CHF RM16 ....350 C2
   IPSE IP5 ....26 C7
St Augustine's Av *SOS* SS1 ....330 A8
St Augustines Cl *BROX* EN10 ....208 C8
St Augustines Ct *HAR* CO12 * 14 D6
St Augustines Dr *BROX* EN10 ....208 C8
St Augustine's Gdn *IPSE* IP5 ....26 B8
St Augustines Wy
   CHLM/WR CM1 ....218 D5
St Austell Cl *KESC* IP5 ....26 F3
St Austell Rd *COLW* CO3 ....128 E5
St Austin's La *HAR* CO12 * 15 G2
St Awdry's Rd *BARK* IG11 ....316 E9
St Barbara's La *COLS* CO2 ....151 N2
St Barnabas Rd *SWFD* E18 ....295 L5
   WALTH E17 ....314 D1
St Barnabas Ter *HOM* E9 ....314 A7
St Bartholomew Cl *COLN* CO4 ....128 D4
St Bartholomews La
   SUD CO10 ....20 B1
St Bartholomew's Rd
   EHAM E6 ....333 P1
St Benet's Rd *SOSN* SS2 ....328 G3
St Bernard Rd *COLN* CO4 ....128 E5
St Barnabas Rd *COLN* CO4 ....333 N1
St Botolph's Church Wk
   COL CO1 * 8 D7
St Botolph's St *COL* CO1 ....8 D7
St Botolph's Ter
   WOTN CO14 * 159 K6
St Botolph's Wy *HVHL* CB9 ....41 J3
St Bride Cl *COLN* CO4 ....128 E5
St Brides Cl *ERITHM* DA18 ....335 L9
St Catharine's Rd *BROX* EN10 ....208 D7
St Catherines Cl *COLS* CO2 ....151 N5
   WICKE SS11 * 285 L8
St Catherine's La *CHTY* IP2 ....29 N1
St Catherines Rd *CHING* E4 ....274 D8
   CHLM/WR CM1 ....217 M9
   SUD CO10 ....46 F4
St Cecilia Rd *CDW/CHF* RM16 ....350 C2
St Chads Cl *LAIN* SS15 ....303 K8
St Chad's Gdns *CHDH* RM6 ....317 M2
St Chad's Rd *CHDH* RM6 ....317 M1
   TIL RM18 ....350 B6
St Charles Dr *WICKE* SS11 ....285 K9
St Charles Rd *BRW* CM14 ....280 E8
St Christopher Rd *COLN* CO4 ....128 E5
St Christophers Cl *CVI* SS8 ....344 A1
St Christophers Wy *COS* CO15 ....206 E5
St Clair Cl *CLAY* IG5 ....296 B2
   COS CO15 ....182 A5
St Clair Rd *PLSTW* E13 ....333 L2
St Clair's Dr *RCOS* CO16 ....180 E8
St Clair's Rd *RCOS* CO16 ....180 E8
St Clare Dr *COLW* CO3 ....127 K8
St Clare Meadow *RCFD* SS4 ....308 G4
St Clare Rd *COLW* CO3 ....127 K9
St Clement Rd *COLN* CO4 ....128 E5
St Clements *GTDUN* CM6 ....92 B6
St Clement's Av *LOS* SS9 ....327 P4
   WTHK RM20 ....348 D4
St Clements Church La
   IPNE IP4 * 17 G6
St Clements Cl *HOC/HUL* SS5 ....308 B3
   SBF/HAD SS7 ....325 P1
St Clement's Ct *PUR* RM19 ....347 M2
St Clement's Crs
   SBF/HAD SS7 ....326 A1
St Clement's Dr *LOS* SS9 ....327 P3
St Clement's Rd *SBF/HAD* SS7 ....325 P1
St Cleres Cl *WICKE* SS11 ....285 J8
St Cleres Hall La *RCOS* CO16 ....206 A2
St Cleres Wy *RCHLM* CM5 ....242 A4
St Columb Ct *COLN* CO4 ....128 D5
St Cross Ct *HOD* EN11 ....208 D7
St Cuthberts Rd *HOD* EN11 ....208 F2
St Cyrus Rd *COLN* CO4 ....128 D5
St Davids Cl *COLN* CO4 ....128 E5
St David's Dr *BROX* EN10 ....208 C7
St David's Rd *BOW* E5 ....332 B5
   VGE SS16 ....323 J2
St Davids Ter *LOS* SS9 ....327 K3
St David's Wy *WICKE* SS11 ....285 K9
St Denis Cl *HAR* CO12 ....110 B7
St Dominic Rd *COLN* CO4 * 128 E5
St Dunstans Rd *FSTGT* E7 ....315 L8
   WARE SG12 ....185 N4
St Edith's Cl *BCAYW* CM12 ....283 H7
St Ediths La *BCAYW* CM12 ....283 H7
St Edmunds Cl *ABYW* SE2 ....336 C1
   HAR CO12 ....110 B7
   SOSN SS2 ....329 K3

St Edmund's Ct *COLN* CO4 ....9 J4
St Edmunds Flds *GTDUN* CM6 ....141 M4
St Edmund's Rd *SUD* CO10 ....75 N5
St Edmunds La *BURES* CO8 ....96 F1
   GTDUN CM6 ....141 M4
St Edmund's Pl *IP* IP1 ....25 K3
St Edmunds Rd *DART* DA1 ....347 L9
   ED N9 ....273 M6
   FX IP11 ....35 H1
   IL IG1 ....316 A1
   IP IP1 ....25 J3
St Edmund's Wy *HLWE* CM17 ....187 K8
St Edmund Wy *BURES* CO8 ....96 F2
   RCOLE CO7 ....105 L1
St Edwards Wy *ROM* RM1 ....298 D8
St Egberts Wy *CHING* E4 ....274 F7
St Elmos Rd
   BERM/RHTH SE16 ....332 B9
St Erkenwald Ms *BARK* IG11 ....334 E1
St Erkenwald Rd *BARK* IG11 ....334 E1
St Evroul Ct *WARE* SG12 ....184 A2
St Fabian's Dr *CHLM/WR* CM1 ....217 M7
St Faith Rd *COLN* CO4 ....128 E5
St Faith's Cl *ENC/FH* EN2 ....251 H9
St Fidelis' Rd *ERITH* DA8 ....346 C2
St Fillan Rd *COLN* CO4 ....128 E6
St Francis Cl *IP* IP1 * 16 D5
St Francis Wy
   CHLM/WR CM16 ....350 D2
   IL IG1 ....316 E6
St Gabriel's Cl *WAN* E11 ....315 L3
St Gabriels Ct *PIT* SS13 ....324 C1
Saint George's Av
   EMPK RM11 ....319 L2
St George's Av *FSTGT* E7 ....315 L9
   GRAYS RM17 ....349 M2
   HAR CO12 ....110 D6
St Georges Cl *BRWN* CM15 ....258 E5
   MAL CM9 ....222 F8
   RCOLE CO7 ....130 D6
   THMD SE28 ....335 L6
St George's Dr *WOS/PRIT* SS0 ....328 F3
St George's La *SBN/FI* SS3 ....330 E8
St George's Park Av
   WOS/PRIT SS0 ....328 C4
St Georges Rd *DAGW* RM9 ....317 N6
   ED N9 ....273 M9
   FSTGT E7 ....251 L8
   FX IP11 ....35 M5
   IL IG1 ....316 A2
   LEY E10 ....314 F5
   PLMGR N13 ....272 E9
St George's Sq *FSTGT* E7 ....315 L9
St George's St *IP* IP1 ....16 D3
St George's Wy *KESC* IP5 ....26 E4
St Georges Wk *SBF/HAD* SS7 * 305 N9
St Giles Av *DAGE* RM10 ....318 A9
   DAGE RM10 ....318 A9
   HSTD CO9 ....73 J7
   MAL CM9 ....221 P9
St Giles Crs *MAL* CM9 ....221 P9
St Giles Cl *CDW/CHF* RM16 ....340 B5
St Gotthards Av *KESC* IP5 ....27 P5
St Gregory's Ct *SUD* CO10 ....20 C4
St Guiberts Rd *CVI* SS8 ....326 B9
St Helena Ms *COLW* CO3 ....151 N1
St Helena Rd *COLW* CO3 ....151 N1
St Helens Av *COS* CO15 ....182 B6
St Helen's Gn *HAR* CO12 ....15 G2
St Helen's La *ENC/FH* EN2 ....8 C5
St Helens Rd *ERITH* DA18 ....335 L9
   IL IG1 ....316 A1
   WOS/PRIT SS0 ....328 A1
St Helen's St *IPNE* IP4 ....17 H4
St Helens Wk *BCAYW* CM12 ....282 D4
St Helier's Rd *LEY* E10 ....314 E1
St Isidores Rd *KESC* IP5 ....27 K4
St Ives Cl *HARH* RM3 ....299 L4
   KESC IP5 ....26 F5
   RCOS CO16 ....206 O1
St Ives Rd *K/T/MI* CO5 ....176 F7
St Ivians Dr *GPK* RM2 ....298 F7
St James' Av *CHONG* CM5 ....235 L9
   SOS SS1 ....330 A8
St James Av East
   SLH/COR SS17 ....341 M2
St James Av West
   SLH/COR SS17 ....341 M2
St James Cl *CVI* SS8 ....344 A1
   SOS SS1 ....330 A8
St James Gdns
   GNTH/NBYPK IG2 ....297 J8
   WOS/PRIT SS0 ....328 D1
St James Ms *BCAYW* CM12 ....283 H6
St James Pk *CHLM/WR* CM1 ....217 L7
St James Rd *BRTR* CM7 ....146 C1
   ED N9 ....273 N8
   FSTGT E7 ....251 L9
   VGE SS16 ....324 D1
St James's Ms *WALTH* E17 ....294 B9
St James's Rd *BRW* CM14 ....280 F9
   CHESW EN7 ....229 H7
   HSTD CO9 ....72 E5
   WALTH E17 ....294 B9
St James's Wk *HOC/HUL* SS5 * 307 M1
St James Wy *BSF* CM23 ....136 G9
St Joans Rd *ED* N9 ....273 L8
St John Gdns *COS* CO15 ....181 P7
St Johns Av *BRTR* CM7 ....145 J4
   BRW CM14 ....300 G1
   CHLM/GWD CM2 ....240 A2
   FX IP11 ....35 H1
   HLWE CM17 ....187 K8
St John's Cl *COLN* CO4 ....128 E5
   LAIN SS15 * 303 K8
   RAIN RM13 ....318 F9
   SAFWS CB11 * 65 J2
   STHGT/OAK N14 ....272 A1
St John's Ct *BKHH* IG9 ....275 L7
   FX IP11 ....11 H2
   MAL CM9 ....225 H2
   RCHLM CM5 ....267 P1
   WOS/PRIT SS0 * 18 D6
St Marys Ctyd *WARE* SG12 * 18 A3
St Mary's Crs *FX* IP11 ....35 H1
   PIT SS13 ....305 H8

STSD CM24 ....114 B8
St Johns Dr *RAYL* SS6 ....306 C5
St John's Gn *CHLM/WR* CM1 ....239 J1
   COLS CO2 ....8 B7
St John's La *STSD* CM24 ....114 B8
   WARE SG12 ....184 D6
St Johns Ms *SLH/COR* SS17 ....341 N1
St Johns Pl *BCAYE* CM11 ....284 A4
St John's Rd *BARK* IG11 ....334 F1
   BCAYE CM11 ....283 J5
   CAN/RD E16 ....333 K6
   CDW/CHF RM16 ....350 C3
   CHING E4 ....274 E9
   CHLM/GWD CM2 ....239 J1
   CHLM/WR CM1 ....239 J1
   COLN CO4 ....128 E4
   COS CO15 ....181 P8
   CRW RM5 ....298 B2
   EHAM E6 ....333 P1
   EPP CM16 ....232 G9
   ERITH DA8 ....346 C3
   GNTH/NBYPK IG2 ....316 F2
   IPNE IP4 ....25 N5
   LOU IG10 ....216 A1
   RCOLE CO7 ....153 K7
   RCOS CO16 ....180 G9
   RCOS CO16 ....181 L8
   SBF/HAD SS7 ....326 F5
   SBN/FI SS3 ....330 C5
   SUD CO10 ....47 L9
St John's St *COL* CO1 ....8 B7
   MAL CM9 ....225 H2
   ENC/FH EN2 ....251 J7
   FSTGT E7 ....315 L8
St Johns Wk *HLWE* CM17 ....187 K8
St John's Wy *SLH/COR* SS17 ....341 N1
St Joseph Rd *COLN* CO4 ....128 E5
St Joseph's Rd *ED* N9 ....273 N6
St Jude Gdns *COLN* CO4 ....128 E5
St Judes Cl *COLN* CO4 ....128 E5
St Julian Gv *COL* CO1 ....8 E7
St Katherines Rd
   ERITHM DA18 ....335 L9
St Kilda's Rd *BRWN* CM15 ....280 E6
St Laurence Dr *BROX* EN10 ....230 B2
St Lawrence Dr *BOC* CM0 ....246 G2
St Lawrence Gdns *ING* CM4 ....259 H1
   LOS SS9 ....307 P9
St Lawrence Hl *BOC* CM0 ....247 K5
St Lawrence Rd *BOC* CM0 ....247 N5
   COLN CO4 ....128 D4
   UPMR RM14 ....319 P4
St Lawrence St *POP/IOD* E14 ....332 F8
St Lawrence Wy *KESC* IP5 ....26 D2
St Leonard's Av *CHING* E4 ....294 G3
St Leonards Cl *GRAYS* RM17 ....349 K4
   SAFWS CB11 ....65 H6
St Leonards Gdns *IL* IG1 ....316 D7
St Leonard's Rd *COL* CO1 ....128 D9
   IPSE IP5 ....26 A8
   POP/IOD E14 ....332 F6
   SOS SS1 ....329 M9
   WAB EN9 ....230 C3
St Leonard's St *BOW* E3 ....332 E5
St Leonards Ter *COL* CO1 * 128 D9
St Leonards Wy *EMPK* RM11 ....318 G3
St Lucia Dr *SRTFD* E15 ....333 J1
St Luke's Av *ENC/FH* EN2 ....316 C7
   IL IG1 ....316 C7
St Luke's Cha *K/T/MI* CO5 ....174 A9
St Luke's Cl *COLN* CO4 ....128 D9
   CVI SS8 ....344 A1
   LAIN SS15 ....303 K8
St Luke's Rd *SOSN* SS2 ....329 K3
St Malo Av *ED* N9 ....273 P4
St Margarets *BARK* IG11 ....334 E1
St Margaret's Av
   SLH/COR SS17 ....341 K5
St Margaret's Gv *WAN* E11 ....315 J3
St Margarets Pin *IP* IP1 ....16 E3
St Margaret's Rd
   CHLM/GWD CM2 ....218 D8
   MNPK E12 ....315 M4
   WARE SG12 ....208 D1
St Margaret's St *IPNE* IP4 ....17 F3
St Mark Dr *COLN* CO4 ....128 E5
St Mark's Fld *RCFD* SS4 ....308 G5
St Marks Rd *COS* CO15 ....6 D1
   CVI SS8 ....344 A1
   EN EN1 ....273 L5
   SBF/HAD SS7 ....326 A1
St Martin's Av *EHAM* E6 ....333 N2
St Martins Cl *COS* CO15 ....6 D1
   EN EN1 ....273 L4
   ERITHM DA18 ....335 L9
   GTDUN CM6 ....189 P5
   RAYL SS6 ....306 F7
   RBRW/HUT CM13 * 281 M7
   SBF/HAD SS7 ....305 N8
St Martins Ct *KESC* IP5 ....27 K4
St Martins Gn *FX* IP11 ....34 B1
St Martin's Rd *ED* N9 ....273 N8
St Martins Sq *BSDN* SS14 ....2 D5
St Martins Wy *CHLM/WR* CM1 ....218 B8
St Mary's Av *BCAYW* CM12 ....283 H6
   BRWN CM15 ....281 K4
St Mary's Cl *BRTR* CM7 ....120 E8
   CHLM/GWD CM2 ....240 E4
   FX IP11 ....34 G1
   GRAYS RM17 ....349 N4
   SBF/HAD SS7 * 326 A5
   SBN/FI SS3 ....330 C5
   SUD CO10 ....47 L9

St Mary's Dr *SBF/HAD* SS7 ....326 B5
   STSD CM24 ....114 C9
St Mary's Flds *COLW* CO3 ....8 A5
St Mary's La *MAL* CM9 ....222 C9
   UPMR RM14 ....319 M4
   UPMR RM14 ....320 D4
   UPMR RM14 ....321 J2
St Marys Md *CHLM/WR* CM1 * 217 P2
St Mary's Ms *MAL* CM9 ....225 J1
St Marys Pk *KIR/NAC* IP10 ....32 E2
St Mary's Pl *GTDUN* CM6 ....142 C7
St Mary's Rd *BOC* CM0 ....290 G2
   BRTR CM7 ....145 L3
   BRTR CM7 ....350 C2
   CHES/WCR EN8 ....229 P8
   COS CO15 ....6 D2
   ED N9 ....273 P7
   FOS CO13 ....159 H9
   IL IG1 ....316 D4
   IP IP1 ....17 K3
   K/T/MI CO5 ....173 H5
   LEY E10 ....314 F5
   PLSTW E13 ....333 L2
   RCOLE CO7 ....155 L9
   SBF/HAD SS7 ....326 A6
   SOSN SS2 ....328 G4
   WICKW SS12 ....304 G2
   WIT CM8 ....172 A6
St Marys Vw *SAFWN* CB10 ....51 M6
St Mary's Wk *HVHL* CB9 ....55 L4
St Marys Wy *CHIG* IG7 ....296 B2
   NHMKT IP6 ....23 N8
St Matthew's La *RAIN* RM13 ....318 F9
St Matthews Ct *SRTFD* E15 ....315 J9
St Matthew's St *IP* IP1 ....16 C3
St Mellion Cl *THMD* SE28 ....335 L6
St Michaels Av *ED* N9 ....273 P6
   PIT SS13 ....324 C2
St Michael's Cha
   RCOLW CO6 ....150 A4
St Michaels Cl *CAN/RD* E16 ....335 L9
   ERITHM DA18 * 335 L9
   HLW CM20 ....210 F2
   KESC IP5 ....26 F5
   RCHLM CM5 ....267 H4
   SOCK/AV RM15 ....337 P7
St Michaels Ct *BRTR* CM7 * 145 J4
   MGTR CO11 ....106 C4
St Michael's Dr
   CHLM/WR CM1 ....216 B6
St Michael's La *BRTR* CM7 ....145 J4
St Michael's Rd *BROX* EN10 ....208 C8
   BRTR CM7 ....145 J4
   CDW/CHF RM16 ....350 C3
   CHLM/GWD CM2 ....240 A2
   COS CO15 ....151 M5
   CVI SS8 ....344 A2
   HAR CO12 ....110 C6
   RCOS CO16 ....157 J4
   SBF/HAD SS7 ....307 J9
St Mildreds Rd
   CHLM/GWD CM2 ....240 A2
St Monance Wy *COLN* CO4 ....128 E5
St Nazaire Rd *CHLM/WR* CM1 ....217 M5
St Neots Cl *COLN* CO4 ....128 E5
St Neot's Rd *HARH* RM3 ....299 L4
St Nicholas Av *HCH* RM12 ....318 E5
St Nicholas Cl *WIT* CM8 ....171 N9
St Nicholas Rd *BOC* CM0 ....248 B6
   WIT CM8 ....171 N9
St Nicholas Rbt *HAR* CO12 ....110 B4
St Nicholas St *COL* CO1 ....8 D6
   IP IP1 ....16 D5
St Nicholas Wy *RCOLW* CO6 ....147 P5
St Olave's Rd *EHAM* E6 ....334 B1
   KESC IP5 ....27 H3
St Omer Cl *WKSW* SS12 ....305 J1
St Osyth Cl *CHTY* IP2 ....29 P2
St Osyth Rd *RCOLE* CO7 ....154 C7
   RCOS CO16 ....181 L5
St Osyth Rd East *RCOS* CO16 ....181 M4
St Osyth Rd West *RCOS* CO16 ....181 L4
St Patrick's Pl
   CDW/CHF RM16 ....350 C2
St Paul's Av
   BERM/RHTH SE16 * 332 A8
St Paul's Cl *SOCK/AV* RM15 ....337 P7
St Paul's Dr *SRTFD* E15 ....314 G7
St Pauls Gdns *BCAYW* CM12 ....283 H4
St Paul's Pl *SOCK/AV* RM15 ....337 P7
St Pauls Rd *BARK* IG11 ....334 D1
   COL CO1 ....8 A3
   COS CO15 ....6 D1
   CVI SS8 ....344 A1
   ERITH DA8 ....346 B5
St Paul's Wy *POP/IOD* E14 ....332 C5
   WAB EN9 ....252 G3
St Peter's Av *CHONG* CM5 ....235 L5
   MAL CM9 ....222 A9
   NHMKT IP6 ....22 D5
   WALTH E17 ....295 H4
St Peter's Cl *BRTR* CM7 ....145 J5
   GNTH/NBYPK IG2 ....296 F8
   MAL CM9 ....223 M5
   NHMKT IP6 ....22 C5
   NHMKT IP6 ....23 J1
St Peter's Ct *BOC* CM0 ....248 B2
   COL CO1 ....8 B4
   NHMKT IP6 ....22 D5
   SUD CO10 ....20 C6
St Peters Fld *BOC* CM0 ....290 F1
St Peter's Pavement
   BSDN SS14 ....304 E6
St Peter's Rd *BRTR* CM7 ....145 J2
   BRW CM14 ....300 E1
   CDW/CHF RM16 ....350 C2
   CHLM/WR CM1 ....217 M9

CVI SS8 .... 344 A1
ED N9 .... 273 N7
HOC/HUL SS5 .... 287 L9
K/T/MI CO5 .... 202 E6
RCOLW CO6 .... 148 A3
St Peters St COL CO1 .... 8 B4
IPNE IP4 .... 16 E5
St Peters Ter WICKW SS12 .... 285 M9
St Peters Vw HSTD CO9 .... 72 C8
St Peters Wk BCAYW CM12 .... 142 B1
BRTR CM7 .... 145 J5
St Peter's Wy BOC CM0 .... 248 D5
CHLM/GWD CM2 .... 262 F4
CHONG CM5 .... 235 N7
ING CM4 .... 259 H1
ING CM4 .... 261 K5
RCHLM CM5 .... 243 H9
RCHLM CM5 .... 245 P6
St Quintin Rd PLSTW E13 .... 333 L3
St Ronans Crs WFD IG8 .... 295 K4
St Runwald St COL CO1 .... 8 C5
St Saviour Cl COLN CO4 .... 128 E5
Saints Dr FSTGT E7 .... 315 N7
St Stephen's Av WALTH E17 .... 294 F9
St Stephen's Wk WALTH E17 .... 294 E9
St Stephens Crs
RBRW/HUT CM13 .... 301 K1
St Stephen's Rd BOW E3 .... 332 C2
EHAM E6 .... 315 M9
PEND EN3 .... 252 A7
RCHLM CM5 .... 243 H9
WALTH E17 .... 294 E9
St Teresa's Wk CDW/CHF RM16 .... 350 D2
St Teresa Wk CDW/CHF RM16 .... 350 C2
St Thomas Cl CHESN CO4 .... 128 F2
St Thomas Gdns IL IG1 .... 316 D8
St Thomas Rd BELV DA17 .... 336 B9
BRW CM14 .... 280 C8
CAN/RD E16 .... 333 K6
RCFD SS4 .... 288 B4
STNGT/OAK N14 .... 272 C6
St Thomas's Cl WAB EN9 .... 253 L3
St Thomas's Rd GRAYS RM17 .... 349 M4
St Valery RBSF CM22 .... 139 M7
St Vincent Cha BRTR CM7 .... 145 L1
St Vincent Rd COS CO15 .... 207 J3
St Vincents Rd
CHLM/GWD CM2 .... 240 A2
WOS/PRIT SS0 .... 18 C5
St Winefride's Av MNPK E12 .... 316 N7
St Winifred's Cl CHIG IG7 .... 206 G3
Sainty Cl RCOLE CO7 * 155 K6
Sairard Cl LOS SS9 .... 307 N8
Sairard Gdns LOS SS9 .... 307 N8
Sakins Cft HLWS CM18 .... 210 C6
Saladin Dr PUR RM19 .... 347 N2
Salamons Wy RAIN RM13 .... 356 D6
Salary Cl COLN CO4 .... 128 F6
Salcombe Dr CHDH RM6 .... 317 N1
Salcombe Rd BRTR CM7 .... 145 M5
WALTH E17 .... 314 C2
Salcott Crs WICKW SS12 .... 285 K9
Salcott St MAL CM9 .... 200 C4
Salehurst Rd IPSE IP3 .... 26 D8
Salerno Crs COLS CO2 .... 151 M4
Salerno Wy CHLM/WR CM1 .... 217 M5
Salesbury Dr BCAYE CM11 .... 283 L6
Salforal Cl RCHLM CM5 .... 263 N8
Salhouse Cl THMD SE28 .... 335 N6
Saling Gn LAIN SS15 .... 303 N5
Salisbury Av BARK IG11 .... 316 E9
COLW CO3 .... 127 N9
SLH/COR SS17 .... 341 L4
WOS/PRIT SS0 .... 18 C2
Salisbury Cl BSF CM23 .... 137 L9
Salisbury Crs CHES/WCR EN8 .... 252 A2
Salisbury Rd CHING E4 .... 274 D9
COS CO15 .... 182 E8
DAGE RM10 .... 318 A8
ED N9 .... 273 M9
FSTGT E7 .... 315 K8
GDMY/SEVK IG3 .... 316 F4
GPK RM2 .... 298 C9
GRAYS RM17 .... 349 M4
HOD EN11 .... 208 F4
IPSE IP3 .... 25 P8
LEY E10 .... 314 F4
LOS SS9 .... 307 M2
MNPK E12 .... 315 N7
PEND EN3 .... 252 C7
WALTH E17 .... 294 F9
Salisbury Vls RIPS/CAP IP9 * 85 K6
Salix Rd GRAYS RM17 .... 349 N4
Sallows Cl IP IP1 .... 24 C4
Sally Murray Cl WARE SG12 .... 316 B6
Salmen Rd PLSTW E13 .... 333 J2
Salmon Cl COLN CO3 .... 151 J2
Salmond's Gv
RBRW/HUT CM13 .... 301 M2
Salmon La POP/IOD E14 .... 332 B6
Salmon Rd DART DA1 .... 347 L8
Salmons Cl WARE SG12 .... 184 A1
Salmon St POP/IOD E14 * 332 C6
Salmons Rd PLSTW E13 .... 333 M5
Salop Rd WALTH E17 .... 314 A1
Saltash Rd BARK/HLT IG6 .... 296 E4
Saltcoats RCHLM CM5 .... 263 L9
Saltcote Maltings MAL CM9 .... 222 F7
Salter Hall Ms SUD CO10 .... 20 B6
Salter Pl CHLM/GWD CM2 .... 218 F5
Salter Rd BERM/RHTH SE16 .... 332 F5
Salters BSF CM23 .... 161 P1
Salter's Meadow MAL CM9 .... 200 C8
Salthouse La WALTH E17 * 17 F6
The Saltings SBF/HAD SS7 .... 326 G3
Saltings La LAIN SS15 .... 333 H6
Salt's Gn CHLM/WR CM1 .... 215 N1
Saltwell St POP/IOD E14 .... 332 D7
Salvia Cl RCOS CO16 .... 6 A1

Salway Cl WFD IG8 .... 295 K4
Salway Cl SRTFD E15 .... 314 G8
Salway Rd SRTFD E15 .... 314 G8
Salwey Crs BROX SS10 .... 208 C8
Samantha Cl WALTH E17 .... 314 C2
Samford Cl RIPS/CAP IP9 .... 83 L2
Samford Pl RIPW IP8 .... 24 C5
Samian Cl MAL CM9 .... 222 A6
Samphire Cl WIT CM8 .... 196 C1
Samphire Ct GRAYS RM17 .... 349 P4
Sampson Dr SUD CO10 .... 46 C3
Sampson's La K/T/MI CO5 .... 176 F9
Samsons Cl RCOLE CO7 .... 179 K5
Samson's Rd RCOLE CO7 .... 179 K4
Samson St PLSTW E13 .... 333 M2
Samuel Cl IPNE IP4 .... 17 G4
Samuel Mnr CHLM/GWD CM2 .... 218 E8
Samuel Rd VGE SS16 .... 323 J2
Samuels Dr SOS SS1 .... 330 A6
Sanctuary Gdn SLH/COR SS17 .... 341 M5
Sanctuary Rd LOS SS9 .... 327 K5
Sandal St SRTFD E15 .... 333 H1
Sandalwood La WCHPL E1 .... 332 B4
Sandbanks SBF/HAD SS7 .... 326 C4
Sandcliff Rd ERITH DA8 .... 346 C2
Sandeman Gdns WARE SG12 .... 184 B2
Sanderling Gdns MAL CM9 .... 222 D6
Sanderlings SBF/HAD SS7 .... 325 P4
Sanders Cnr ENC/FH EN2 * 250 C5
Sanders Dr COLW CO3 .... 127 L8
Sanderson Cl
RBRW/HUT CM13 * 321 M1
Sanderson Ms COL CO1 * 8 C5
Sanders Rd CVI SS8 .... 326 D6
Sanderstead Rd LEY E10 .... 314 B5
Sandford Av LOU IG10 .... 276 D2
Sandford Rd RCOLE CO7 .... 153 K6
Sandford Mill Rd
CHLM/GWD CM2 .... 218 F9
Sandford Rd CHLM/GWD CM2 .... 218 C8
EHAM E6 .... 334 A3
Sandgate Cl ROMW/RG RM7 .... 318 B2
Sandhill Rd LOS SS9 .... 307 L7
Sandhurst CVI SS8 .... 343 P2
Sandhurst La WIGE IP5 * 25 N7
Sandhurst Cl LOS SS9 .... 328 A2
Sandhurst Crs LOS SS9 .... 328 A2
Sandhurst Dr GDMY/SEVK IG3 .... 316 G6
Sandhurst Rd ED N9 .... 273 P5
TIL RM18 .... 350 D7
Sandleigh Rd LOS SS9 .... 328 B5
Sandle Rd BSF CM23 .... 137 M7
Sandling Crs IPNE IP4 .... 26 D6
Sandmartin La COLW CO3 .... 150 F2
Sandon Br CHLM/GWD CM2 .... 241 L3
Sandon Brook Pl
CHLM/GWD CM2 .... 241 K3
Sandon Cl BSDN SS14 .... 324 E1
RCFD SS4 .... 308 E4
RCOLW CO6 .... 102 F9
Sandon Ct BSDN SS14 * 324 E1
Sandon Hall Bridleway
CHLM/GWD CM2 .... 241 J7
Sandon Hl RCHLM CM5 .... 167 M6
Sandon Pl CHONG CM5 .... 235 M9
Sandon Rd BSDN SS14 .... 324 E1
CHES/WCR EN8 .... 229 P9
Sandown Av DAGE RM10 .... 318 B6
HCH RM12 .... 319 J4
WOS/PRIT SS0 .... 328 C4
Sandown Cl COS CO15 .... 182 B5
WICKE SS11 .... 285 M9
Sandown Dr DAGE RM10 .... 318 C9
Sandown Rd CDW/CHF RM16 .... 340 F5
IP IP1 .... 23 H9
SBF/HAD SS7 .... 306 E8
WICKE SS11 .... 285 M9
Sandpiper Cl
BERM/RHTH SE16 .... 332 C9
COLN CO4 .... 129 H8
HVHL CB9 .... 9 J2
MAL CM9 .... 222 D6
SBN/FI SS3 .... 330 D6
WALTH E17 .... 294 A4
Sandpiper Dr ERITH DA8 .... 346 G5
Sandpiper Rd CHTY IP2 .... 24 F9
Sandpiper Ter CLAY IG5 * 296 C7
Sandpit La BOC CM0 .... 26 E6
Sandpit La BOC CM0 .... 291 H9
BRW CM14 .... 280 C5
Sandpit Rd DART DA1 .... 347 H9
Sandpits Rd SOS SS1 .... 330 C6
Sandringham Av
HLWW/ROY CM19 .... 209 P5
HOC/HUL SS5 .... 307 M1
EN EN1 .... 273 K1
SLH/COR SS17 .... 341 M2
Sandringham Gdns
BARK/HLT IG6 .... 296 D7
Sandringham Pl
CHLM/GWD CM2 .... 218 D6
Sandringham Rd BARK IG11 .... 316 G8
BRWN CM15 .... 280 E4
FSTGT E7 .... 315 M7
LAIN SS15 .... 303 M7
LEY E10 .... 314 C2
SOS SS1 .... 329 L6
Sandringham Wy
CHES/WCR EN8 .... 251 P4
Sandstone La CAN/RD E16 .... 333 M7
Sands Wy WFD IG8 .... 296 A5
Sandwich Cl BRTR CM7 .... 121 H9
Sandwich Rd COS CO15 .... 207 H4
RCOLE CO7 .... 179 L5
Sandy Cl FX IP11 .... 34 E1
Sandy Hl RCOLW CO6 .... 101 J4
Sandyhill La IPNE IP4 * 18 B6
Sandyhill Rd IL IG1 .... 316 C6
Sandy La CDW/CHF RM16 .... 350 C4
NHMKT IP9 * 23 J7
SOCK/AV RM15 .... 337 M2
SUD CO10 .... 60 C1

WTHK RM20 .... 348 E4
San Juan Dr CDW/CHF RM16 .... 348 G2
San Marcos Dr
CDW/CHF RM16 .... 348 F3
San Remo Pde WOS/PRIT SS0 .... 18 B6
San Remo Rd CVI SS8 .... 344 C2
Sansom Rd WAN E11 * 315 J4
Santiago Wy WTHK RM20 .... 348 G5
Sapling Pl IPNE IP4 .... 26 C6
Sappers Cl SBW CM21 .... 187 N2
Sapphire Cl BCTR RM8 .... 317 K5
Saracen St POP/IOD E14 .... 332 D6
Sara Crs GRH DA9 .... 348 B5
Saran Ct RCOLE CO7 .... 153 H4
Sarcel BRTR CM77 .... 122 C9
Sargeant Cl COS CO2 .... 152 C3
Sark Cv WICKW SS12 .... 305 L2
Sarnesfield Rd ENC/FH EN2 * 273 J5
Sarre Av HCH RM12 .... 319 H5
Sarre Wy RCOLE CO7 .... 180 A1
Sarum Ter BOW E3 .... 332 C4
Sassoon Wy MAL CM9 .... 244 B1
Satanita Cl CAN/RD E16 .... 333 N6
Satanita Rd WOS/PRIT SS0 .... 330 D6
Saul's Av WIT CM8 .... 197 K4
Sauls Bridge Cl WIT CM8 .... 197 K4
Sauls Gn WIT CM8 .... 315 H5
Saunders Av BRTR CM7 .... 144 G2
Saunders Cl CHES/WCR EN8 .... 229 P7
IL IG1 .... 316 C7
POP/IOD E14 * 332 C7
Saunders Wy THMD SE28 .... 335 J7
Saunton Rd HCH RM12 .... 318 F4
Savage Gdns EHAM E6 .... 334 A6
Savernake Rd CHLM/WR CM1 .... 4 A6
ED N9 .... 273 M5
Savill Cl CHESW EN7 * 229 H4
Saville Cl SAFWS CB11 .... 88 A4
Saville Rd CAN/RD E16 .... 333 P6
CHDH RM6 .... 317 N1
The Savilles SUD CO10 * 58 F1
Saville St WOTN CO14 .... 159 K5
Savill Rd COLS CO2 .... 152 D4
Savill Rw WFD IG8 .... 295 J5
Savoy Cl SRTFD E15 .... 333 H1
VGE SS16 .... 323 H1
Savoy Pde EN EN1 * 273 K2
Savoy Wd EPP CM16 .... 210 B9
Sawbridgeworth Rd
RBSF CM22 .... 162 B6
SBW CM21 .... 188 B1
Sawells BROX SS10 .... 208 C9
Sawkins Cl CHLM/GWD CM2 .... 240 C4
Sawkins Cl CHLM/GWD CM2 .... 240 C4
Sawkins Gdns
CHLM/GWD CM2 .... 240 C4
Sawmill La KIR/NAC IP10 .... 31 P4
Sawney Brook
CHLM/WR CM1 .... 239 H1
Sawpit La BSF CM23 .... 88 C9
Sawston Cl CHTY IP2 .... 25 H9
Sawyer Cl ED N9 .... 273 M8
Sawyers Cl RIPS/CAP IP9 .... 28 C9
Sawyers Gv BRWN CM15 .... 280 C7
Sawyer's Hall La BRWN CM15 .... 280 F6
Sawyer's Rd MAL CM9 .... 199 K3
Saxham Rd BARK IG11 .... 334 F1
Saxlingham Rd CHING E4 .... 274 D9
Saxmundham Wy RCOS CO16 .... 206 F1
Saxon Bank BRTR CM7 .... 145 L4
Saxon Cl COLW CO3 .... 151 J2
FX IP11 .... 35 N5
HARH RM3 .... 299 L6
HSTD CO9 .... 98 A6
RAYL SS6 .... 307 H2
RBRW/HUT CM13 .... 281 K9
WALTH E17 .... 314 D2
WICKE SS11 .... 285 K7
Saxon Dr MAL CM9 * 222 B8
Saxon Gdns SBN/FI SS3 .... 330 B7
Saxon La RIPW IP8 .... 28 F2
Saxon Rd BOW E3 .... 332 C2
EHAM E6 .... 334 A4
IL IG1 .... 316 C8
Saxon Shore Wy
HOC/HM ME3 .... 351 P9
Saxonville SBF/HAD SS7 .... 325 N2
Saxon Wy CHLM/WR CM1 .... 218 A4
COS CO15 .... 182 G7
MAL CM9 .... 244 C1
SAFWN CB10 .... 58 F7
SOS SS1 .... 325 P4
STHGT/OAK N14 .... 272 C5
Sayers SBF/HAD SS7 .... 306 D9
Sayesbury Av SBW CM21 .... 187 M2
Sayesbury Rd SBW CM21 .... 187 M2
Sayes Gdns SBW CM21 * 187 N2
Saywell Brook
CHLM/GWD CM2 .... 218 D4
Scalby Rd BOC CM0 .... 268 F7
Scaidhurst PIT SS13 .... 305 H9
Scarborough Rd BOC CM0 .... 268 F7
ED N9 .... 273 P6
LOS SS9 .... 327 P4
WAN E11 .... 314 G3
Scarfe Wy COLN CO4 .... 128 F9
Scarletts BSDN SS14 .... 3 H1
Scarletts Cl WIT CM8 .... 197 K5
Scarletts Rd COL CO1 .... 152 D1
Sceptre Cl MAL CM9 .... 225 J1
Schneider Cl FX IP11 .... 111 L2
Scholars Rd CHING E4 .... 274 F7
School Cha HSTD CO9 .... 98 D6
School Cl DART DA1 .... 346 E9
RIPS/CAP IP9 .... 28 C9
School Ct RCOLE CO7 .... 42 B1
Schoolfield Rd WTHK RM20 .... 348 D4
School Green La EPP CM16 .... 234 F4
School Hl RCOLW CO6 .... 75 K4
RIPW IP8 .... 30 A1
Schoolhouse La WAP E1W * 332 A7
School Houses
CDW/CHF RM16 * 340 B5
School La CDW/CHF RM16 .... 340 B5

CHIG IG7 .... 296 G1
CHLM/WR CM1 .... 191 L1
CHLM/WR CM1 .... 217 N5
CHONG CM5 .... 190 B9
CHONG CM5 .... 212 C5
CHONG CM5 .... 214 C2
COLS CO2 .... 175 K2
COLS CO2 .... 175 H5
HLW CM20 .... 13 K1
HVHL CB9 .... 40 G3
ING CM4 .... 261 L7
K/T/MI CO5 .... 175 P9
MGTR CO11 .... 81 N8
MGTR CO11 .... 105 P6
MGTR CO11 .... 106 E4
RBRW/HUT CM13 .... 301 M3
RBSF CM22 .... 115 J2
RCHLM CM5 .... 169 H5
RCOLE CO7 .... 80 A7
RCOLE CO7 .... 68 G1
RCOLE CO7 .... 104 G1
RCOLW CO6 .... 102 A5
RCOLW CO6 .... 102 D6
RCOLW CO6 .... 127 H5
SAFWS CB11 .... 63 J2
SAFWS CB11 .... 64 G8
SBF/HAD SS7 .... 326 A6
SUD CO10 .... 46 F2
WICKW SS12 .... 305 M5
School Rd BCAYE CM11 .... 284 D5
BCAYW CM12 .... 283 J8
BRTR CM7 .... 144 B7
BRWN CM15 .... 258 B7
CHLM/WR CM1 .... 191 M7
CHONG CM5 .... 234 E9
COLN CO4 .... 103 P4
COLS CO2 .... 152 B4
DAGE RM10 .... 335 P1
FOS CO15 .... 158 F9
HAR CO12 .... 133 M4
HSTD CO9 .... 58 C7
HSTD CO9 .... 73 N4
HSTD CO9 .... 73 N9
HSTD CO9 .... 96 F1
HVHL CB9 .... 10 C3
K/T/MI CO5 .... 173 P4
MAL CM9 .... 198 G9
MAL CM9 .... 223 J1
MNPK E12 .... 316 A6
RCOLE CO7 .... 80 G8
RIPS/CAP IP9 .... 29 M9
RIPS/CAP IP9 .... 85 N9
SUD CO10 .... 48 A3
WIT CM8 .... 197 M2
WIT CM8 .... 198 A7
School St RCOLW CO6 .... 78 C4
SAFWN CB10 .... 36 E9
SUD CO10 .... 20 C6
School Vw BRTR CM7 .... 145 H4
School View Rd CHLM/WR CM1 .... 4 C1
School Wk BRTR CM7 .... 145 K6
School Wk BCTR RM8 .... 317 J5
LOS SS9 .... 307 J3
Schooner Cl BARK IG11 .... 335 J5
Schooner Ct GRH DA9 .... 347 P9
Schreiber Rd IPNE IP4 .... 26 A4
Scimitar Pk PIT SS13 .... 305 J3
Scofield Cl SUD CO10 .... 21 H7
Scopes Rd KESG CO5 .... 27 H3
Scotland Green Rd PEND EN3 .... 274 A4
Scotland Green St
North PEND EN3 .... 274 A3
Scotland Rd BKHH IG9 .... 275 M7
Scotland St RCOLW CO6 .... 95 H5
Scott Av BRTR CM7 .... 145 H4
WARE SG12 .... 184 B8
Scott Cl BRTR CM7 .... 145 K6
Scott Crs ERITH DA8 .... 346 E6
Scott Dr COLW CO3 .... 127 J9
Scottes La BRTR CM7 .... 317 L3
Scott Rd BSF CM23 .... 137 K8
CDW/CHF RM16 .... 350 B2
IPSE IP5 .... 31 H1
Scotts Cl HCH RM12 .... 319 H7
WARE SG12 .... 184 A4
Scotts Hall Rd RCFD SS4 .... 289 L8
Scott's Rd LEY E10 .... 314 F5
WARE SG12 .... 184 A4
Scoulding Rd CAN/RD E16 .... 333 J6
Scouler St POP/IOD E14 .... 332 G7
Scraley Rd MAL CM9 .... 222 E5
Scratton Rd SLH/COR SS17 .... 341 L3
SOS SS1 .... 18 E5
Scrattons Ter BARK IG11 .... 335 J3
Scrip's Rd RCOLE CO7 .... 147 P7
Scrivener Dr RIPW IP8 .... 24 D9
Scrub La SBF/HAD SS7 .... 327 H3
Scurvy Hall La RCHLM CM5 .... 194 A3
Scylla Cl MAL CM9 .... 222 D5
Scythe Wy COLC CO5 * 151 J2
Seabourough Rd
CDW/CHF RM16 .... 350 D1
Seabrooke Ri GRAYS RM17 .... 349 L4
Seabrooke Gdns RCHLM CM5 .... 219 P2
Seabrook Rd BCTR RM8 .... 317 J5
CHLM/GWD CM2 .... 240 F4
Seaburn Cl RAIN RM13 .... 336 D5
Sea Cornflower Wy
COS CO15 .... 206 F5
Seacourt Rd ABYW SE2 .... 335 N6
Sea Crs COS CO15 .... 206 E6
Seafield Av CDMY/SEVK IG3 .... 316 H6
Seafield Rd HAR CO12 .... 110 C6
Seafields Gdns COS CO15 .... 206 F6
Seafields Rds COS CO15 .... 182 D6
Sea Flowers Wy COS CO15 .... 206 F5

Seaford Rd EN EN1 .... 273 K3
WALTH E17 .... 294 E7
Seaforth Av SOSN SS2 .... 329 K4
Seaforth Cl ROM SN07 .... 298 D4
Seaforth Dr CHES/WCR EN8 .... 252 A4
Seaforth Gdns WCHMH N21 .... 272 E6
WFD IG8 .... 295 M2
Seaforth Rd WOS/PRIT SS0 .... 328 E7
Seager Pl BOW E3 .... 332 C5
Seagers MAL CM9 .... 198 C8
Sea Glebe Wy COS CO15 .... 206 F5
Seagrave Cl WCHPL E1 * 332 A5
Seagry Rd WAN E11 .... 315 K1
Seagull La CAN/RD E16 .... 333 K7
Sea Holly Wy COS CO15 .... 206 F6
Sea King Crs COS CO15 .... 206 F5
Sea Lavender Wy COS CO15 .... 206 F6
Seally Rd GRAYS RM17 .... 349 K5
Seaman La MAL CM9 .... 262 A7
Seamer Rd BOC CM0 .... 268 F7
Sea Pink Wy COS CO15 .... 206 F6
Sea Reach LOS SS9 .... 327 P6
Searles Dr EHAM E6 .... 334 C5
Searle Wy COLW CO3 .... 126 F6
Sea Rd FX IP11 .... 111 F7
Sea Rosemary Wy COS CO15 .... 206 F5
Sea Shell Wy COS CO15 .... 206 F5
Sea Thistle Wy COS CO15 .... 206 F5
Seaton Av GDMY/SEVK IG3 .... 316 F7
Seaton Cl MGTR CO11 .... 333 K4
PLSTW E13 .... 333 K3
Seaton Rd FX IP11 .... 35 H6
Seaview Av HAR CO12 .... 109 M9
K/T/MI CO5 .... 203 H5
VGE SS16 .... 324 C3
Seaview Dr SBN/FI SS3 .... 331 H4
Seaview Gdns RCOLE CO7 .... 179 L6
Seaview Hts WOTN CO14 .... 159 K7
Sea View Pde BOC CM0 .... 245 N8
Sea View Prom BOC CM0 .... 246 G1
Seaview Rd CVI SS8 .... 345 H5
LOS SS9 .... 327 P6
RCOLE CO7 .... 179 L6
Seaview Ter RCOS CO16 .... 205 H1
SBF/HAD SS7 * 326 C4
Seaway BOC CM0 .... 247 H2
Sea Wy COS CO15 .... 206 E5
Seaway CVI SS8 .... 344 C3
SOS SS1 .... 19 H6
Seax Ct LAIN SS15 .... 302 A6
Seax Wy LAIN SS15 .... 302 C8
Sebastian Av BRWN CM15 .... 281 K5
Sebastian Cl COLN CO4 .... 128 F8
Sebert Cl BCAYE CM11 * 283 L9
Sebert Rd FSTGT E7 .... 315 M6
Seckford Cl IPNE IP4 .... 26 A2
Second Av BCAYW CM12 .... 283 J8
BRWN CM15 .... 258 F4
CHDH RM6 .... 299 K9
CHLM/WR CM1 .... 217 P5
COS CO15 .... 182 C9
CVI SS8 .... 344 A1
DAGE RM10 .... 336 A2
EN EN1 .... 273 L4
FOS CO15 .... 183 M1
FX IP11 .... 34 E4
HAR CO12 .... 110 D5
HLWE CM17 .... 211 J4
HLWS CM18 .... 13 K7
HOC/HUL SS5 .... 287 J8
HSTD CO9 .... 315 P6
MNPK E12 .... 315 P6
PLSTW E13 .... 333 K3
RCOS CO16 .... 156 C6
RCOS CO16 .... 206 A6
SBF/HAD SS7 * 306 E9
SLH/COR SS17 .... 341 L2
STSD CM24 .... 138 E4
SUD CO10 .... 21 H7
WALTH E17 .... 294 D9
WICKE SS11 .... 305 M1
WOS/PRIT SS0 .... 328 C1
WOTN CO14 .... 159 M3
WTHK RM20 .... 348 D6
Seddons Rd PEND EN3 .... 273 P4
Seddons Wk HOC/HUL SS5 .... 307 P1
Sedgefield Cl HARH RM5 .... 299 L2
Sedgefield Crs HARH RM5 .... 299 L2
Sedgefield Wy BRTR CM7 .... 145 L5
Sedgemoor HLWW/ROY CM19 .... 209 J7
Sedgemoor Dr DAGE RM10 .... 317 P6
Sedgwick Rd LEY E10 .... 314 F4
Sedgwick St HOM E9 .... 314 F1
Sedley Cl IPNE IP4 .... 26 B2
Sedley Rd LOU IG10 .... 276 A1
Sedop Cl SAFWS CB11 .... 65 L2
The Seedbed Centre
HLWW/ROY CM19 .... 210 B4
The Seedfield K/T/MI CO5 .... 202 E6
Seeleys HLWE CM17 .... 187 K8
Sefton Ct ENC/FH EN2 * 272 C1
Selborne Av MNPK E12 .... 316 B6
Selborne Rd IL IG1 .... 316 B4
STHGT/OAK N14 .... 272 D9
WALTH E17 .... 294 C9
Selbourne Rd HOC/HUL SS5 .... 307 P1
SBF/HAD SS7 .... 326 A1
SOSN SS2 .... 329 J3
Selby Cl COLS CO2 .... 151 N5
Selby Rd PLSTW E13 .... 333 L5
WALTH E17 .... 315 H5
Seldon Cl WOS/PRIT SS0 .... 328 C3
Seldon Rd K/T/MI CO5 .... 174 A8
Selhurst Rd ED N9 .... 273 J9
Selinas La BRTR CM8 .... 198 A8
Selkirk Dr ERITH DA8 .... 346 D6
Selkirk Rd IPNE IP4 .... 26 B3
Sell Cl CHESW EN7 .... 228 G4

Sells Rd WARE SG12 ....184 C2
Selsdon Cl CRW RM5 ....298 B5
Selsdon Rd PLSTW E13 ....333 M1
WAN E11 ....315 K2
Selsey Av COS CO15 ....207 H4
Selsey St POP/IOD E14 ....332 D5
Selvale Wy FX IP11 ....10 E2
Selwood Rd BRW CM14 ....280 C9
Selworthy Cl BCAYE CM11 ....283 K9
WAN E11 ....295 K9
Selwyn Av CHING E4 ....294 F3
GDMY/SEVK IG3 ....316 C1
Selwyn La CHTY IP2 ....25 K7
Selwyn Rd BOW E3 ....332 C2
PLSTW E13 ....333 L1
SOSN SS2 ....329 K4
TIL RM18 ....350 A7
Semper Rd CDW/CHF RM16 ....340 D9
Semples CDW COS SS17 ....341 N5
Sennen Rd EN EN1 ....273 L6
Senrab St WCHPL E1 ....332 A6
Serbin Cl LEY E10 ....314 F2
Serpentine Gd IPSE IP3 ....26 A9
Serpentine Wk COL CO1 ....8 B5
Service Route No 1
SRTFD E15 ....314 C9
Service Route No 2
SRTFD E15 ....314 C9
Service Route No 3
SRTFD E15 ....314 C8
Seton Gdns DAGW RM9 ....317 K9
Settle Rd HARH RM5 ....299 M1
Seven Acres WICKE SS11 ....285 K8
Seven Arches Rd BRW CM14 ....248 C9
Seven Ash Gn CHLM/WR CM1 ....218 B6
Seven Cottages La KESC IP5 ....26 B2
Seven Devils La SAFWS CB11 ....65 L3
Seven Hills KIR/NAC IP10 * 32 B3
Seven Kings Rd
GDMY/SEVK IG3 ....316 F3
Sevenoaks Cl HARH RM5 ....299 H1
Seventh Av CHLM/WR CM1 ....218 A5
CVI SS8 ....344 B1
MNPK E12 ....316 A6
STSD CM24 ....138 E4
Severalls La COLN CO4 ....105 K9
Severn Rd CRW RM5 ....298 C7
Severn Av GPK RM2 ....298 C7
Severn Dr EN EN1 ....251 M8
UPMR RM14 ....320 A1
Severn Rd COS CO15 ....182 A8
IPSE IP3 ....25 N8
Severns Fld EPP CM16 ....233 H6
Sewards End WICKW SS12 ....305 K1
Sewardstone Rd CHING E4 ....274 E3
WAB EN9 ....252 F4
Sewardstone St WAB EN9 ....252 F4
Sewardstone Wy WAB EN9 ....252 F6
Sewdley St CLPT E5 ....314 A5
Sewell Cl CDW/CHF RM16 ....348 F3
Sewell Harris Cl HLW CM20 ....210 C2
Sewell Rd ABYW SE2 ....335 H9
Sewell's La SUD CO10 ....58 F1
Sewell St PLSTW E13 ....333 K3
Sewell Wontner Cl KESC IP5 ......26 C3
Sexton Cl CHESW EN7 ....228 C4
COLS CO2 ....152 C6
RAIN RM13 ....5 J5
Sexton Rd TIL RM18 ....350 A6
Sextons La WIT CM8 ....198 C2
Seymer Rd ROM RM1 ....298 C7
Seymour Dr HVHL CB9 ....40 C4
Seymour Cl LOU IG10 ....215 J2
Seymour Gdns IL IG1 ....316 A3
Seymour Rd CDW/CHF RM16 ....348 F1
CHING E4 ....274 E7
CHTY IP2 ....25 K7
COS CO15 ....206 C8
ED N9 ....273 N8
EHAM E6 ....333 N1
LEY E10 ....314 C3
SBF/HAD SS7 ....327 J3
TIL RM18 ....350 A6
WOS/PRIT SS0 ....506 D6
Seymours MAL CDW/CWD CM19 ......210 B6
Seymour St CHLM/GWD CM2 ....4 D4
Shackleton Cl HAR CO12 ....110 A7
Shackleton Rd IPSE IP3 ....26 A8
Shadbolt Av CHING E4 ....294 B2
Shadowbush Cl HVHL CB9 ....41 J2
Shafter Rd DAGE RM10 ....318 B8
Shaftesbury LOU IG10 ....275 N2
Shaftesbury Av HAR CO12 ....14 A6
PEND EN3 ....274 A1
SOS SS1 ....329 M8
Shaftesbury Ct HVHL CB9 ....41 H4
PIT SS13 ....305 H8
Shaftesbury La DART DA1 ....347 N9
Shaftesbury Rd CHING E4 ....274 C7
EPP CM16 ....252 E8
FSTGT E7 ....315 M9
LEY E10 ....314 D3
ROM RM1 ....318 E1
WALTH E17 ....294 E9
Shaftesbury Sq IPNE IP4 * 17 J7
The Shaftesburys BARK IG11 ......334 D2
Shafton Ms HOM E9 * 332 A1
Shafton Rd HOM E9 * 332 A1
Shafto Rd IP IP1 ....24 F3
Shair La RCOLE CO7 ....155 N4
Shakespeare Av BCAYE CM11 ....283 K6
RAYL SS6 ....307 J5
TIL RM18 ....350 C7
VGE SS16 ....323 H1
WOS/PRIT SS0 ....328 E4
Shakespeare Ct BRTR CM7 ....145 J2
Shakespeare Dr MAL CM9 ....244 B2
WOS/PRIT SS0 ....328 F4
Shakespeare Rd COLW CO3 ....127 J9
DART DA1 ....347 M9
IP IP1 ....25 H1
ROM RM1 ....318 E1
WALTH E17 ....294 A6

Shakespeare Sq
BARK/HLT IG6 ....296 C3
Shakeston Cl CHLM/WR CM1 ....239 J2
Shakletons CHONG CM5 ....235 M7
Shalbourne Sq HOM E9 ....314 C8
Shalcross Dr CHES/WCR EN8 ....230 C9
Shalford Rd BCAYE CM11 ....283 L6
BRTR CM7 ....144 A2
Shambrook Rd CHESW EN7 ....228 G4
Shamrock Av CHTY IP2 ....24 F7
Shamrock Cl MAL CM9 ....225 J1
Shamrock Wy
STHGT/OAK N14 ....272 A7
Shandy St WCHPL E1 ....332 A5
Shangani Rd BSF CM23 ....137 L9
Shanklin Av BCAYW CM12 ....283 H6
Shanklin Cl CHESW EN7 ....229 L8
COS CO15 ....182 B5
Shanklin Dr WOS/PRIT SS0 ....328 B4
Shannon Av RAYL SS6 ....306 F6
Shannon Cl HVHL CB9 ....41 N4
LOS SS9 ....327 P2
Shannon Rd IPSE IP3 ....30 D3
Shannon Wy CVI SS8 ....344 A2
SOCK/AV RM15 ....337 P7
Shardelow Av CHLM/WR CM1 ....218 C3
Shardlow Cl HVHL CB9 ....40 F2
Shardlows La WICKE SS11 ....285 L8
Sharlands Rw MAL CM9 ....200 F4
Sharnbrook SBN/FI SS5 ....330 C4
Sharon Rd PEND EN3 ....274 B1
Sharpecroft HLWW/ROY CM19 ....13 C7
Sharpington Cl
CHLM/GWD CM2 ....240 B7
Sharp Wy DART DA1 ....347 L8
Shatters Rd COLS CO2 ....175 K4
Shaw Av BARK IG11 ....335 M2
Shawbridge
HLWW/ROY CM19 ....210 D6
Shaw Cl CHES/WCR EN8 ....229 P8
EMPK RM11 ....318 C3
FOS CO15 ....158 C7
THMD SE28 ....335 J8
WICKW SS12 ....305 J2
Shaw Crs POP/IOD E14 ....332 B6
RBRW/HUT CM15 ....281 N4
TIL RM18 ....350 C6
Shaw Dr BRTR CM7 ....145 J1
Shaw Gdns BARK IG11 ....335 M2
Shawlands Av SUD CO10 ....21 K5
Shaw Rd PEND EN3 ....252 A9
SUD CO10 ....46 G3
WIT CM8 ....171 N8
Shaw Sq WALTH E17 ....294 B5
The Shaw RBSF CM22 ....188 F1
Shaw Valley Rd WDBR IP21 ....27 N1
The Shearers BSF CM23 ....161 P1
Shearman Ct HVHL CB9 * 41 K4
Shears Crs K/T/MI CO5 ....202 C7
Shearwater Cl BARK IG11 ....335 H5
Sherwood Crs DART DA1 ....346 E8
Sheds La SAFWN CB10 ....83 M8
Sheene Dr BRTR CM7 ....145 N1
Sheepcoates La MAL CM29 ....222 G2
Sheepcote La BSF CM23 ....113 K4
Sheepcotes CHLM/GWD CM2 ....218 G5
Sheepcotes La BOC CM0 ....90 D9
RCHLM CM3 ....194 B5
WIT CM8 ....146 F9
Sheepcotes Rd CHDH RM6 ....297 L8
Sheepcot Rd HSTD CO9 ....72 D6
Sheepen Pl COLW CO3 ....8 A4
Sheepen Rd COLW CO3 ....127 N7
Sheepshead Hl SUD CO10 ....61 M4
Sheering Ct RAYL SS6 ....306 D4
Sheering Dr HLWE CM17 ....187 M9
Sheering Lower Rd
HLWE CM17 ....187 N5
Sheering Mill La SBW CM21 ....187 N2
Sheering Rd HLWE CM17 ....187 N7
Sheering Wk COLS CO2 ....152 A4
Sheerwater Cl BOC CM0 ....290 C3
Sheerwater Ms COLN CO4 ....159 J7
Sheerwater Rd CAN/RD E16 ....333 N5
Sheffield Dr HARH RM5 ....299 M2
Sheila Rd CRW RM5 ....298 A4
The Sheilings EMPK RM11 ....299 L9
Shelbourn Br BRTR CM7 ....146 D2
Shelbourne Cl KESG IP5 ....27 J4
Sheldon Av CLAY IG5 ....296 C6
Sheldon Cl CHESW EN7 ....229 J5
HLWE CM17 ....211 M3
Shampton Rd CAN/RD E16 ....333 L6
Sheldon Rd CVI SS8 ....345 H2
DAGW RM9 ....317 M9
Sheldrake Cl CAN/RD E16 ....334 A8
Sheldrake Dr CHTY IP2 ....24 F9
Shelduck Cl FSTGT E7 ....315 J7
Shellbeach Rd CVI SS8 ....344 G3
Shellcroft RCOLW CO6 ....98 C7
Shellduck Crs BRTR CM7 ....144 F9
Shelley Av HCH RM12 ....318 E4
K/T/MI CO5 ....174 B8
MNPK E12 ....315 P8
SUD CO10 ....21 K7
Shelley Cl CHONG CM5 ....235 L5
MAL CM9 ....244 B2
Shelley La LOU IG10 ....276 A3
Shelley Pl WALTH E17 ....315 H3
TIL RM18 ....350 C6
Shelley Rd CHLM/GWD CM2 ....218 C9
COLW CO3 ....8 C3
RBRW/HUT CM15 ....281 N6
TIL RM18 ....350 C6
Shelley Sq SOSN SS2 ....329 J4
Shellow Rd CHONG CM5 ....214 G7
Shelly Av VGE SS16 ....323 H1
Shelmerdine Cl BOW E3 ....332 D5
Shelsley Dr VGE SS16 ....305 H7
Shenfield Cl HLWS CM18 ....210 D6
Shenfield Crs BRWN CM15 ....281 H8

Shenfield Gdns
RBRW/HUT CM13 ....281 L5
Shenfield Gn BRWN CM15 ....281 K6
Shenfield Pl BRWN CM15 ....281 H6
Shenfield Rd BRWN CM15 ....281 H7
WFD IG8 ....295 L4
Shenley Rd IPSE IP3 ....31 H1
Shenstone Dr IP IP1 ....23 H9
Shenstone Gdns HARH RM5 ....299 H5
Shepard Cl LOS SS9 ....308 B9
Shepeshall LAIN SS15 ....303 M9
Shepherd Dr RIPW IP8 ....24 D9
Shepherds Cl BSF CM23 ....137 L6
CHDH RM6 ....297 L9
SBF/HAD SS7 ....327 H2
Shepherds Cft COLW CO3 ....150 C1
Shepherds Hl HARH RM5 ....299M6
Shepherd's La ROM E18 ....314 A7
THMD SE28 ....334 F8
Shepherds Wk SBF/HAD SS7 ......327 H2
Shepherds Wy SAFWN CB10 ....51 N8
Shepley Cl HCH RM12 ....319 J7
Shepley Ms PEND EN3 ....252 D8
Shepperd Cl EN EN1 ....251 N8
RCOS CO16 ....181 N7
Sheppard Dr
CHLM/GWD CM2 ....218 F7
Sheppards HLWW/ROY CM19 ....210 A6
Sheppard St CAN/RD E16 ....333 J4
Sheppards Wy KESG IP5 ....27 J4
Sheppey Cl ERITH DA8 ....346 C5
Sheppey Gdns DAGW RM9 ....317 K9
Sheppey Rd DAGW RM9 ....317 J9
Sherards Orch
HLWW/ROY CM19 ....210 C5
Sherborne Av IPNE IP4 ....25 P1
PEND EN3 ....273 P1
Sherborne Rd CHLM/WR CM1 ....218 C6
Sherbourne Cl FOS CO13 ....158 B8
SOSN SS2 ....308 F9
Sherbourne Dr PIT SS13 ....304 F6
Sherbourne Gdns SOSN SS2 ....308 G9
Sherbourne Rd COLN CO4 ....128 G8
Sherbrook Gdns WCHMH N21 ....272 C6
Sheredan Rd CHING E4 ....294 G2
Sheredes Dr HOD EN11 ....208 C7
Shere Rd GNTH/NBYPK IG2 ....296 B9
Sherfield Rd GRAYS RM17 ....349 L4
Sheridan Av SBF/HAD SS7 ....326 A5
Sheridan Cl HARH RM5 ....298 C4
RAYL SS6 ....307 J5
Sheridan Ct DART DA1 ....347 M9
Sheridan Rd FSTGT E7 ....315 J5
MNPK E12 ....316 C6
Sheriden Wk BROX EN10 ....208 B8
Sheriffs Wy RCOS CO16 ....181 P6
Sheringham Av CHLM/WR CM1 .....316 A6
ROMW/RG RM7 ....318 B1
STHGT/OAK N14 ....272 C5
Sheringham Dr SLH/COR SS17 .....341 M2
Sheringham Dr BARK IG11 ....316 C7
BRTR CM7 ....144 F7
Sheriton Sq RAYL SS6 ....306 C5
Sherman Gdns CHDH RM6 ....317 K1
Shernbroke Rd WAB EN9 ....253 J4
Shernhall St WALTH E17 ....294 F7
Sherrard Rd FSTGT E7 ....315 M8
Sherrington Rd IP IP1 ....25 H3
Sherry Ms BARK IG11 ....316 E9
Sherwood Av CHDH RM6 ....317 N8
Sherwood CDW/CHF RM16 ....339 H8
Sherwood Av SWFD E18 ....295 L7
VGE SS16 ....323 H2
WALTH E17 ....294 D9
Sherwood Crs SBF/HAD SS7 ......327 H2
Sherwood Dr CHLM/WR CM1 ....239 L1
COS CO15 ....181 P7
Sherwood Flds KESC IP5 ....27 H4
Sherwood Gdns BARK IG11 ....316 D9
Sherwood Rd BARK/HLT IG6 ......296 E8
Sherwood Wy K/T/MI CO5 ....173 J1
SOSN SS2 ....329M4
Shetland Cl IPNE IP4 ....25 P3
Shetland Rd BOW E3 ....332 C2
HVHL CB9 ....41 K4
Shevon Wy BRW CM14 ....300 C1
Shewell Wk COL CO1 ....8 B6
Shillibeer Wk CHIG IG7 ....276 G9
Shillingstone SBN/FI SS3 ....330 C5
Shillito Cl COLW CO3 ....151 J2
Shingle Cl WAB EN9 ....253 K5
Ship La MGTR CO11 ....107 K5
RIPW IP8 ....24 C2
SOCK/AV RM15 ....338 A9
Shire Hall Tard IPNE IP4 ....17 F6
Shire Hl SAFWS CB11 ....51 N9
Shire Hill La SAFWN CB10 ....65 P1
Shires Cl BRTR CM7 ....144 E7
Shirley Cl BROX EN10 ....208 B8
CHES/WCR EN8 ....229 P8
DART DA1 ....347 H9
WALTH E17 * 294 B9
Shirley Gdns BARK IG11 ....316 F8
HCH RM12 ....319 H4
PIT SS13 ....305 H7
Shirley Gv ED N9 ....273 P6
Shirley Rd ENC/FH EN2 ....251 K1
LOS SS9 ....327 P1

SRTFD E15 ....315 H9
Shirley St CAN/RD E16 ....333 J6
Shoebridge's Hl RCOLE CO7 ......104 F2
Shoebury Av SBN/FI SS3 ....330 E7
Shoebury Common Rd
SBN/FI SS3 ....330 B9
Shoebury Rd EHAM E6 ....316 A9
SBN/FI SS3 ....330 C3
SOS SS1 ....329 P5
Shonks Mill Rd ABR/ST RM4 ......256 C8
Shooters Dr WAB EN9 ....231 H1
Shooters Rd ENC/FH EN2 ....250 F6
Shopland Hall Rd RCFD SS4 ......309 J9
Shopland Rd RCFD SS4 ....309 J8
Shop La K/T/MI CO5 ....204 A1
Shoprife Pde FOS CO13 ....158 C8
RCFD SS4 ....289M7
Shop Rd MGTR CO11 ....130 C1
Shop Rw RCFD SS4 * 310 F2
Shorefield SBF/HAD SS7 ....525 N5
Shorefield Gdns WOS/PRIT SS0 ...18 A6
Shorefield Rd WOS/PRIT SS0 .....18 A5
Shoreham Rd COS CO15 ....207 H4
Shore La KIR/NAC IP10 ....31 F7
MGTR CO11 ....107 K5
RIPS/CAP IP9 ....83 P7
Shore Rd BOC CM0 ....291 H4
Shortacre BSDN SS14 ....3 H4
Short Cft BRWN CM15 ....281 K6
Shortcroft BSF CM23 ....138 A6
Shortcrofts Rd DAGW RM9 ....317 N8
Short Cut Rd COL CO1 ....8 B5
Shorter Av BRWN CM15 ....281 J5
Shortlands BSDN SS14 ....3 H4
CHTY IP2 ....29M1
Shortlands Av CHONG CM5 ....235 L5
Shortlands Cl UED N18 ....273 J9
Shortlands Pl BSF CM23 ....137 L6
Shortlands Rd LEY E10 ....314 E2
Short La BCAYE CM11 ....284 B5
Shortmead Dr
CHES/WCR EN8 ....252 B1
Shortridge Ct WIT CM8 ....344 E1
Short La SOSN SS2 ....322 G1
SBF/HAD SS7 ....344 E1
WAN E11 ....315 H4
Short St SOSN SS2 ....19 F1
Shotley Cl FX IP11 ....10 D1
RCOS CO16 ....206 F1
WICKE SS11 ....285 H8
Shotley Wk RIPS/CAP IP9 ....85 K4
Shott Lower CHESW EN7 ....229 L5
Shoulder of Mutton Aly
POP/IOD E14 ....332 B7
Shrewsbury Cl VGE SS16 ....322 C1
Shrewsbury Dr SBF/HAD SS7 .....306 A8
Shrewsbury Rd MNPK E12 ....315 N8
Shropshire Cl
CHLM/GWD CM2 ....240 E5
The Shrubberies CHIG IG7 ......276 D8
CHLM/WR CM1 ....238 G2
SWFD E18 ....295 K6
Shrubbery Cl FX IP11 ....11 G1
LAIN SS15 ....303 C1
Shrubbery Gdns WCHMH N21 ......272 C6
Shrubbery Rd ED N9 ....273 M9
The Shrubbery UPMR RM14 ....319 P5
Shrub End Rd COLW CO3 ....151 K3
Shrubland Ct COS CO15 ....128 A9
Shrubland Gv IPNE IP4 ....26 E6
Shrubland Rd COLC CO1 * 128 A9
MGTR CO11 ....106 C5
WALTH E17 ....294 D9
Shrublands SAFWN CB10 ....51 M7
Shrublands Cl CHIG IG7 ....296 D2
CHLM/GWD CM2 ....5 J5
Shums Hl FOS CO13 ....158 D6
Shuttle Rd DART DA1 ....346 F8
Siam Pl SUD CO10 ....20 D5
Sibley Gv MNPK E12 ....315 P9
Sibneys Gn HLWS CM18 ....210 F8
Sicklefield Cl CHESW EN7 ......229 L5
Sidegate Av IPNE IP4 ....25 P3
Sidegate La IPNE IP4 ....25 P5
Sidegate La West IPNE IP4 .....25 N2
Sidmouth Av SOSN SS2 ....328 E1
Sidmouth Rd CHLM/WR CM1 ....239 J2
LEY E10 ....314 F5
Sidney Elson Wy EHAM E6 ....334 D2
Sidney Pl CHLM/WR CM1 ....218 E6
Sidney Rd EPP CM16 ....254 E6
SRTFD E15 ....315 K1
Sidney Ter BSF CM23 ....137 L8
Sidwell Av SBF/HAD SS7 ....326 B5
Sidwell Cha SBF/HAD SS7 ....326 B5
Sidwell La SBF/HAD SS7 ....326 B5
Sidwell Pk SBF/HAD SS7 ....326 B5
Siena Ms COLS CO2 ....152 C2
Sierra Dr DAGW RM9 ....336 B2
Siggin's La CBE/LIN CB1 ....38 C5
Silcock Cl COLN CO4 ....128 D5
Silcott St RCOLE CO7 ....104 E6
Silent St IPNE IP4 ....25 J1
Silifield Pl CHLM/WR CM1 ......218 C6
Silk Ms COL CO1 * 145 J4
Sillett Cl RCOS CO16 ....181 N7
Silvadene SBF/HAD SS7 * 525 P7
Silva Island Wy WICKW SS12 ....305 L2
Silvanus Cl COLW CO3 ....127 N9
Silver Birch Av CHING E4 ......293 M6
EPP CM16 ....233 M6
Silver Birch Cl THMD SE28 .....335 H8
Silver Birches
RBRW/HUT CM13 ....281 K7
Silver Birch Ms BARK/HLT IG6 ..296 D5
Silverdale ENC/FH EN2 ....250 C6
RAYL SS6 ....307 H7
SBF/HAD SS7 ....326 E5
SLH/COR SS17 ....341 L1
Silverdale Av WOS/PRIT SS0 ....328 E4
Silverdale Dr HCH RM12 ....318 C2

Silverdale East SLH/COR SS17 ...341 L1
Silverdale Rd BXLYHN DA7 ......346 A1
CVI SS8 ....294 G3
Silverfield BROX EN10 ....230 C1
Silver La CHONG CM5 ....215 K9
Silver Leys RIPS/CAP IP9 ......81 P3
Silvermead CHING E4 ....350 C5
Silvermere VGE SS16 ....323 H1
Silvermere Av CRW RM5 ....298 A3
Silvermere Dr UED N18 ....273 N3
Silverpoint Marine CVI SS8 ....345 K2
Silver Rd BOC CM0 ....291 H4
Silversea Dr WOS/PRIT SS0 .....328 B4
Silver Spring G ERITH DA8 .....346 A4
Silver St ABR/ST RM4 ....277 J2
BRTR CM7 ....94 G5
CHESW EN7 ....229 J9
EN EN1 ....273 J2
HVHL CB9 ....42 C1
MAL CM9 ....222 A8
STSD CM24 ....114 A9
WAB EN9 ....252 F4
WAN E11 ....17 L1
Silverthorn Cl RCFD SS4 ....308 E3
Silverthorne CVI SS8 ....344 C2
Silverthorn Gdns CHING E4 .....274 D8
Silvertown Wy CAN/RD E16 ......333 L3
Silvertree La SLH/COR SS17 ....341 L3
Silvertree Cl HCH/HGL SS5 .....307 L1
Silver Wk BERM/RHTH SE16 .....332 C8
Silver Wy ROMW/RG RM7 ....298 A7
WICKE SS11 ....285 H8
Silvester Rd
CDW/CHF RM16 ....339 K7
Silvesters HLWW/ROY CM19 .....210 A5
Simmonds La MAL CM9 ....244 B9
Simmonds Rd COLS CO2 ....242 C2
Simmons Dr BCTR RM8 ....317 M5
Simmons La CHING E4 ....274 G8
Simmons Pl CDW/CHF RM16 ......339 K8
Simonds Rd LEY E10 ....314 D4
Simons La COL CO1 ....1 G7
Simons Wk SRTFD E15 ....314 G7
Simpson Cl WCHMH N21 ....272 E4
Simpson Rd RAIN RM13 ....318 E8
Simpsons La K/T/MI CO5 ....199 H1
Simpson's Rd POP/IOD E14 .....332 E7
Sims CI RCOLW CO6 ....99 J9
ROM RM1 ....298 E9
Sim's La HVHL CB9 ....42 E2
Sinclair Cl COLN CO4 ....128 A5
Sinclair Dr CHTY IP2 ....25 K8
Sinclair La COLC CO4 ....294 C2
Sinclair Wk WICKW SS12 ....505 J2
Sinclare Cl EN EN1 ....251 J9
Singer Av COS CO15 ....158 C8
Singleton Cl HCH RM12 ....318 E6
Singleton Ct COL CO10 ....61 K5
Singleton Rd DAGW RM9 ....317 N7
Sinnington End COLN CO4 ......128 D3
Sinnott Rd WALTH E17 ....294 A5
Sioux Cl COLN CO4 ....128 D3
Sir Alf Ramsey Wy IP IP1 .....16 A5
Sirdar Rd IP IP1 ....25 H5
RAYL SS6 ....306 C7
Sir Francis Wy BRW CM14 ......280 E8
Sir Isaac's Wk COL CO1 ....8 B6
Sir Walter Raleigh Dr
RAYL SS6 ....306 F3
Siskin Cl COLN CO4 ....128 C7
Sisley Rd BARK IG11 ....316 D9
Sittang Cl COLS CO2 ....151 M5
Sittingbourne Av EN EN1 ......273 J5
Sitwell Ct MGTR CO11 ....106 A4
Siward Rd DAGE RM10 ....196 C4
Six Bells Ct BRTR CM7 ....145 J1
Sixth Av CHLM/WR CM1 ....218 A5
CVI SS8 ....344 B1
MNPK E12 ....316 A6
STSD CM24 ....138 E4
Skarnings Ct WAB EN9 ....253 K5
Skate's Hl SUD CO10 ....45 N1
Skeffington Rd EHAM E6 ....334 A1
Skelmersdale Wy SAFWS CB11 ....88 B4
Skelley Rd SRTFD E15 ....315 J9
Skelmersdale Rd COS CO15 .....7 F3
Skelton Cl MGTR CO11 ....162 F4
Skelton Rd FSTGT E7 ....315 K8
Skelton's La LEY E10 ....314 E2
Skerry Rd CHLM/WR CM1 ....218 A4
Sketty Rd EN EN1 ....273 L2
Skiddaw Ct BRTR CM7 ....144 C7
Skiers St SRTFD E15 ....333 H1
Skinner's La CHLM/GWD CM2 ....240 A7
Skinners St BSF CM23 ....161 P1
Skippers Cl RIPW IP8 ....29 N2
Skipper Ct BRTR CM7 ....145 J6
Skipper Rd RIPW IP8 ....29 N2
The Skippers MAL CM9 * 225 J2
Skipsea Av EHAM E6 ....334 A3
Skirmett Cl BRTR CM7 ....145 K5
Skreens Ct CHLM/WR CM1 ......217 L7
Sky Hall Hl COLN CO4 ....103 M1
Skylark Cl BCAYE CM11 ....283 K7
Skylark La RIPW IP8 ....24 D9
Sky Peals Rd WFD IG8 ....294 D5
Skyrmans Fee COS CO15 ....158 D8
Slacksbury Hatch
HLWW/ROY CM19 ....12 E7
Sladburys La COS CO15 ....182 G6
Slade End EPP CM16 ....254 F6
Slade Gdns ERITH DA8 ....346 A6
Slade Green Rd ERITH DA8 .....346 B6
Slade Rd COS CO15 ....182 D7
Slades Cl ENC/FH EN2 ....272 F2
Slades Gdns ENC/FH EN2 ......272 F2
Slades Hl ENC/FH EN2 ....272 F2
Slades Rd ENC/FH EN2 ....272 F2
Slade's La CHLM/GWD CM2 .....239 G7
The Slades VGE SS16 ....324 D4
Slade St IPNE IP4 ....17 F6
The Slade NHMKT IP6 ....22 E3

SAFWN CB10 .....51 N3
Slaney Rd ROM RM1 .....298 D9
Slate HSTD CO9 .....98 A7
Slated Rw RCFD SS4 * 308 G6
Slaters CI FOS CO13 .....158 C8
Sleaford CI CHTY IP2 .....25 J8
Sleepers Farm Rd
  CDW/CHF RM16 .....340 C9
Slewins CI EMPK RM11 .....299 H9
Slewins La EMPK RM11 .....299 H9
Slipe La BRCW EN10 .....230 C3
Slocum CI THMD SE28 .....335 K7
Sloe HI HSTD CO9 .....97 N6
Slough Farm Rd HSTD CO9 .....97 N6
Slough Rd CI BRTR CM7 .....145 N5
Slough La RCOLE CO7 .....129 J9
  SUD CO10 .....47 N5
Slough Rd CHLM/WR CM1 .....191 L2
  MGTR CO11 .....81 M7
  RCHLM CM3 .....242 F8
Slushy La RPLS/CAP IP9 .....84 A6
Smaley La SUD CO10 .....46 F5
Smallbridge Entry BURES CO8 .....76 E3
Smallgains Av CVI SS8 .....344 G1
Small Gains La ING CM4 .....261 M9
Smallgains La ING CM4 .....261 M9
Smallholdings K/T/MI CO5 * 173 H4
Smallwood Rd COLS CO2 .....151 L3
Smart CI HARH RM5 .....298 C5
Smarts Gn CHESW EN7 .....229 L5
Smart La RCOLE CO7 .....275 P5
Smart St BETH E2 .....332 A3
  IPNE IP4 .....17 F6
Smartt Av CVI SS8 .....344 D1
Smeaton CI COLN CO4 .....152 B8
  WAB EN9 .....253 H8
Smeaton Rd PEND EN3 .....252 D7
  RCHLM CM3 .....296 A2
Smeed Rd BOW E3 .....314 D9
Smeetham Hall La SUD CO10 .....60 B4
Smith CI BERM/RHTH SE16 .....332 A8
Smither's Cha SOSN SS2 .....329 J1
Smithers CI RIPS/CAP IP9 .....28 C9
Smithers Dr CHLM/GWD CM2 .....240 F4
Smiths Av RCHLM CM3 .....296 A2
Smiths Fld BRTR CM77 .....144 C4
  COLS CO2 .....152 D1
Smiths La CHESW EN7 .....229 J5
Smiths PI KESG IP5 .....27 J4
Smith St SBN/FI SS3 .....330 E8
The Smithy STDN SG11 .....136 A4
Smyarts CI BOC CM0 .....269 J6
Smythe CI RCOS CO16 .....181 M7
Smythe Rd POP/IOD E14 .....332 E7
Smythies Av CCLE CO1 .....152 B3
Snakes HI BRW CM14 .....279 P2
Snakes La EBAR EN4 .....272 A2
  RBSF CM22 .....114 D5
  SOSN SS2 .....328 B1
Snakes La East WFD IG8 .....295 M5
Snakes La West WFD IG8 .....295 K5
Snape CI RCOS CO16 .....181 K9
Snape Wy FOS CO13 * 158 C7
Snaresbrook Rd WAN E11 .....295 J8
Sneating Hall La FOS CO15 .....157 P6
Snelling Gv CHLM/GWD CM2 .....240 E4
Snipe CI ERITH DA8 .....346 G5
Sniveller's La K/T/MI CO5 * 172 C2
Snoreham Gdns RCHLM CM3 .....267 H4
Snowberry Ct BRTR CM7 .....145 N2
Snowberry Gv COLS CO2 .....152 E3
Snowcroft RIPS/CAP IP9 .....28 C9
Snowdonia La CI PIT SS13 .....305 H7
Snowdon Rd CHTY IP2 .....25 J9
Snowdrop CI BSF CM23 .....137 H8
  CHLM/WR CM1 .....218 D4
  RAIN RM13 .....171 M9
Snow HI SUD CO10 .....44 A2
Snow Hill La RCOLW CO6 .....79 J4
Snowshill Rd MNPK E12 .....315 P7
Soames Md BRWN CM15 .....258 F3
Soane St IPNE IP4 .....17 F5
  PIT SS13 .....304 G7
Soft Rd SUD CO10 .....59 L5
Softwater La SBF/HAD SS7 .....326 C3
Soham Rd PEND EN3 .....252 C7
The Soils HAR CO2 .....133 P2
Solar Wy PEND EN3 .....252 C6
Solebay St WCHPL E1 .....332 B4
Solent Ri PLSTW E13 .....333 K3
Solid La BRWN CM15 .....258 C9
Solna Rd WCHMH N21 .....273 J7
Solway Rd TIL RM18 .....351 K1
Somerby CI BRWN CM15 .....208 D9
Somerby Rd BARK IG11 .....316 E9
Somerford Wy
  BERM/RHTH SE16 .....332 B9
Somersby Gdns REDBR IG4 .....296 A9
Somerset Av RCFD SS4 .....308 F4
  WOS/PRIT SS0 .....328 C2
Somerset CI COLS CO2 .....151 L3
  WFD IG8 .....295 K5
Somerset Crs WOS/PRIT SS0 .....328 C3
Somerset Gdns EMPK RM11 .....319 M3
  PIT SS13 .....304 G9
Somerset PI CHLM/WR CM1 .....217 P4
  RCHLM CM3 .....25 N3
  LAIN SS15 .....303 J9
  SLH/COR SS17 .....341 H9
  WALTH E17 .....294 D9
Somerset Wy COS CO15 .....206 E3
Somers Rd COLS CO2 .....151 K2
  WALTH E17 .....294 C8
Somerton Av WOS/PRIT SS0 .....328 B2
Somerville Gdns LOS SS9 .....328 A6
Somerville Rd CHDH RM6 .....297 K9
Somme Rd COLS CO2 .....151 N2
Sommers Ct WARE SG12 * 184 B4
Sonning Wy SBN/FI SS3 .....330 C5
Sonters Down RCHLM CM3 .....285 P3
Soper CI CHING E4 .....294 C2
Soper Ms PEND EN3 .....252 D8

Sopers Rd POTB/CUF EN6 .....228 E8
Sophia CI CAN/RD E16 .....333 L6
  LEY E10 .....314 E3
Sophia Sq POP/IOD E14 .....332 B7
Sopwith Crs WICKE SS11 .....305 N2
Sorrel CI CHTY IP2 .....25 H8
  COLN CO4 .....127 M5
  THMD SE28 .....335 H8
Sorrel Gdns EHAM E6 .....333 P5
Sorrel Gv BRTR CM77 .....144 E7
Sorrel La POP/IOD E14 .....332 C6
Sorrel CI MAL CM9 .....223 M4
  RCHLM CM3 .....194 A6
The Sorrells SLH/COR SS17 .....341 N5
The Sorrels SBF/HAD SS7 .....306 A8
Sorrel Wk ROM RM1 .....298 E7
South Access Rd LEY E10 .....314 A2
Southall CI WARE SG12 .....184 A2
Southall Wy BRW CM14 .....300 C1
Southampton Ms
  CAN/RD E16 * 333 L8
South Av CHING E4 .....274 E6
  HOC/HUL SS5 .....287 H7
  SOSN SS2 .....19 H1
  VGE SS16 .....323 J7
South Beech Av WICKE SS11 .....285 J9
South Birkbeck Rd WAN E11 .....314 C5
Southborough Rd
  CHLM/GWD CM2 .....4 D7
Southborough Rd
  WOS/PRIT SS0 .....328 C4
  WOS/PRIT SS0 .....328 C2
Southbourne Gdns IL IG1 .....316 D7
  WOS/PRIT SS0 .....328 C2
Southbourne Gv
  HOC/HUL SS5 .....308 A1
  WICKW SS12 .....284 F8
  WOS/PRIT SS0 .....328 C3
Southbrook SBW CM21 .....187 M3
Southbrook Dr
  CHES/WCR EN8 .....230 A7
Southbury Av EN EN1 .....273 M5
Southbury CI HCH RM12 .....319 J7
Southbury Rd EN EN1 .....273 L5
South Charlton Mead La
  HOD EN11 .....208 P6
Southchurch Av SBN/FI SS3 .....330 F7
  SOS SS1 * 19 J4
Southchurch Hall CI SOS SS1 .....329 M5
Southchurch Hall CI SOS SS1 .....329 K6
Southchurch Rd EHAM E6 .....334 A2
  SOS SS1 .....19 G3
Southcliff SBF/HAD SS7 .....325 P2
  WOTN CO14 .....159 K7
Southcliff Prom WOTN CO14 .....159 K7
South CI DAGE RM10 .....335 P1
  HSTD CO9 .....97 P8
  IPNE IP4 .....25 M3
  RCOS CO16 .....180 D9
Southcombe VGE SS16 .....324 C2
The South Colonnade
  POP/IOD E14 .....332 D8
Southcote Crs BSDN SS14 .....304 D7
Southcote Rd WALTH E17 .....294 A9
  SOSN SS2 .....171 N9
Southcroft Rd BSDN SS14 .....304 E7
South Countess Rd
  WALTH E17 .....294 C7
South Ct ING CM4 * 260 D6
South Crs CAN/RD E16 .....332 G5
  SOSN SS2 .....328 A7
South Crockerford VGE SS16 .....324 D2
Southcroft CI FOS CO15 .....158 D9
South Cross BARK/HLT IG6 .....296 D9
Southdale CHIG IG7 .....296 E5
Southdown Crs
  GNTH/NBYPK IG2 .....296 F9
Southdown Rd EMPK RM11 .....318 C2
South Dr BRW CM14 .....300 C1
  GPK RM2 .....299 H7
  POTB/CUF EN6 .....228 D7
South Eastern Av ED N9 .....273 L9
Southend Arterial Rd
  EMPK RM11 .....299 K7
  LAIN SS15 .....302 G6
  RAYL SS6 .....306 A1
  ROM RM3 .....300 D9
  WICKW SS12 .....305 P5
Southend La WAB EN9 .....253 L4
Southend Rd BCAYW CM12 .....283 J7
  CHLM/GWD CM2 .....4 E7
  EHAM E6 .....316 A9
  GRAYS RM17 .....349 M2
  MAL CM9 .....242 F5
South End Rd RAIN RM13 .....336 F1
Southend Rd RCFD SS4 .....308 G8
  RCHLM CM3 .....263 J5
  REDBR IG4 .....295 P7
  SBN/FI SS3 .....330 B3
  WICKE SS11 .....285 L8
Southend Road Main Rd
  HOC/HUL SS5 .....307 N2
Southend Rd (North Circular)
  WALTH E17 .....294 G5
Souther Cross Rd
  CHLM/WR CM1 .....191 N7
Southern Dr LOU IG10 .....276 A5
  RCHLM CM3 .....332 C3
Southern Gv BOW E3 .....332 C3
Southernhay BSDN SS14 .....323 J7
  LOS SS9 .....327 N1
  LOU IG10 .....275 N4
Southern Rd PLSTW E13 .....333 L2
Southern Ter HOD EN11 * 208 E2
Southern Wy CHDH RM6 .....317 P1
  HLWW/ROY CM19 .....210 C6
South Esk Rd FSTGT E7 .....315 M8
South CI MAL CM9 .....222 D7
Southey Wk TIL RM18 .....350 C6
Southfalls Rd CVI SS8 .....345 J2
Southfield SAFWN CB10 .....36 B8
Southfield Cha RCHLM CM3 .....302 F6
Southfield CI SBF/HAD SS7 .....327 H1
Southfield Dr WEN11 * 327 H1
Southfield Gn CHES/WCR EN8 .....252 B2

HOD EN11 .....208 D3
  SOSN SS2 .....273 N5
Southfields RCOLE CO7 .....104 G2
Southfield Wy BOC CM0 .....268 G5
South Ga HLW CM20 .....13 H6
  PUR RM19 .....347 P2
Southgate Crs SLH/COR SS17 * 174 B8
Southgate Gdns SUD CO10 .....46 F5
Southgate St SUD CO10 .....46 F5
South Green Rd K/T/MI CO5 .....177 N2
South Gv WALTH E17 .....294 C9
South Gunnels BSDN SS14 .....3 F5
South Hall Dr RAIN RM13 .....336 C5
South Hanningfield Rd
  RCHLM CM3 .....263 H5
South Hanningfield Wy
  WICKE SS11 .....285 J5
South Heath Rd RCOLE CO7 .....180 C2
South HI FX IP11 .....11 H4
  SLH/COR SS17 .....323 H7
South Hill Crs SLH/COR SS17 .....341 H2
South House Cha MAL CM9 .....244 C5
South Hill St POP/IOD E14 .....332 E6
Southland CI COLN CO4 .....9 K1
Southlands Cha
  CHLM/GWD CM2 .....241 K8
Southlands Rd BCAYE CM11 .....304 C1
Southland Ter PUR RM19 * 347 N3
South Lodge Crs ENC/FH EN2 .....272 C3
South Lodge Dr
  STHGT/OAK N14 .....272 D4
South Mayne PIT SS13 .....304 F9
Southmead Crs
  CHES/WCR EN8 .....230 B9
Southmill Rd BSF CM23 .....137 M8
Southminster Rd BOC CM0 .....247 L7
  RCHLM CM3 .....290 C1
Southminster Road Button's HI
  RCHLM CM3 .....267 P5
Southminster Road Scotts HI
  BOC CM0 .....288 G5
South Molton Rd
  CAN/RD E16 .....333 K6
Southmoor Wy HOM E9 .....314 C8
South Ordnance Rd
  PEND EN3 .....252 D7
South Pde CVI SS8 .....345 H3
South Park Crs IL IG1 .....316 E5
South Park Dr IL IG1 .....316 E5
South Park Dr IL IG1 .....316 E5
South Park Ter IL IG1 .....316 E5
South Pk IG1 .....316 E5
South Rd LOU IG10 .....187 H9
  PEND EN3 .....273 P4
South Primrose HI
  CHLM/WR CM1 .....4 C1
South Rdg BCAYW CM11 .....283 K7
South Riding BSDN SS14 .....304 D2
South Rd BCAYE CM11 .....304 C2
  BSF CM23 .....137 M9
  BRW CM14 .....279 J1
  ED N9 .....273 M7
  HLW CM20 .....202 B5
  RBSF CM22 .....139 M6
  SAFWS CB11 .....51 M9
  SOCK/AV RM15 .....338 F7
Southsea Av CVI SS8 .....327 N4
South Strd MGTR CO11 .....81 M9
South St BOC CM0 .....226 D9
  BOC CM0 .....248 B7
  BRTR CM7 .....145 H2
  BRW CM14 .....280 F8
  BSF CM23 .....137 L8
  COLS CO2 .....127 P9
  IP11 .....11 H1
  MAL CM9 .....200 C8
  MGTR CO11 .....106 C4
  PEND EN3 .....274 A4
  RAIN RM13 .....336 C3
  RCFD SS4 .....308 G6
  RCHLM CM3 .....193 M5
  ROM RM1 .....298 D9
  SAFWN CB10 .....36 E8
  SBF/HAD SS7 .....306 A9
  WALTH E17 .....294 B9
South Vw COW/CHF RM16 .....340 C5
  GTDUN CM6 * 92 B5
  GTDUN CM6 .....141 K6
  RCOLE CO7 .....104 G2
South View Av TIL RM18 .....350 B6
South View CI BARK IG11 .....307 J7
Southview CI CHESW EN7 .....229 K5
  RCHLM CM3 .....264 C9
South View Crs
  GNTH/NBYPK IG2 .....316 C1
Southview Dr UPMR RM14 .....319 M5
Southview Dr COS CO15 .....182 G7
South View Rd LOU IG10 .....276 A5
  RCHLM CM3 .....285 P5
  SBF/HAD SS7 .....348 F6
Southview Rd HOC/HUL SS5 .....288 A9
  RCHLM CM3 .....242 A4
  VGE SS16 .....316 C1
South Wk BSDN SS14 .....2 E6
Southwalters CVI SS8 .....344 C1
South Wash Rd LAIN SS15 .....303 M5
Southway COL CO1 .....8 C7
South Wy HOM E9 * 348 B1
  WAB EN9 .....252 E7
South Weald Dr WAB EN9 .....252 G5
South Weald Rd BRW CM14 .....280 A2
Southwell CI CDW/CHF RM16 .....348 F5
Southwell Grove Rd WAN E11 .....315 H4
Southwell Rd SBF/HAD SS7 .....326 B2
Southwest Rd WAN E11 .....314 B3
South Wharf Rd GRAYS RM17 .....349 J4
Southwick Gdns CVI SS8 .....344 G4
Southfield Dr CHES/WCR EN8 .....252 B2

Southwold Crs SBF/HAD SS7 .....325 P1
Southwold Dr BARK IG11 .....317 H7
Southwold Wy RCOS CO16 .....181 K9
Southwood Cha RCHLM CM5 .....242 D6
Southwood Gdns
  BARK/HLT IG6 .....296 C8
  RAYL SS6 .....307 J7
Southwood Rd THMD SE28 .....335 J7
Southy Ms CAN/RD E16 .....145 N2
Sovereign CI BRTR CM7 .....145 N2
  RCFD SS4 .....308 F5
Sovereign Ct
  HLWW/ROY CM19 .....210 C6
Sovereign Crs COLS CO2 * 127 M9
  POP/IOD E14 .....332 D7
Sovereign Rd BARK IG11 .....335 K5
Sowberry CI
  CHLM/WR CM1 .....217 N4
Sowrey Av RAIN RM13 .....318 E8
Spa CI HOC/HUL SS5 .....307 P1
Spa Dr BOC CM0 .....288 G1
Spains Hall Av VGE SS16 .....324 B2
Spains Hall Rd CHONG CM5 .....214 G8
Spalding Av CHLM/WR CM1 .....145 H2
Spalding Wy CHLM/GWD CM2 .....240 F4
Spait CI RBRW/HUT CM13 .....281 K8
Spanbeek Rd CVI SS8 * 326 E9
Spanbies Rd RCOLE CO7 * 80 A8
Spanby Rd BOW E3 .....332 D4
Spareleaze HI LOU IG10 .....276 A3
Sparepenny La North
  SAFWN CB10 .....88 D5
Sparepenny La South
  SAFWN CB10 .....68 E5
Spar-hawks MAL CM9 * 220 C8
Sparkbridge LAIN SS15 .....303 H9
Sparke Ter CAN/RD E16 * 333 J6
Sparkey CI WIT CM8 .....197 K5
Sparks CI BCTR RM8 .....317 L4
Sparks La HSTD CO9 .....72 C9
Spar La RCHLM CM3 .....243 M7
Sparling CI COLS CO2 .....151 L4
The Sparlings FOS CO15 .....158 D6
Spar Rd HOC/HUL SS5 .....307 N1
  K/T/MI CO5 .....173 K1
  PEND EN3 .....197 H1
Sparrow CI HSTD CO9 .....72 C9
Sparrow Gn DAGE RM10 .....318 A5
Sparrow La MAL CM9 .....61 L4
Sparrows CI ING CM4 .....238 B5
Sparrows Herne CO5 CO15 .....182 A7
  VGE SS16 .....323 P3
Sparrow's La RBSF CM22 .....189 K5
Sparsholt Rd BARK IG11 .....334 F1
Speckled Wood Ct BRTR CM7 .....145 H6
Speedwell CI WIT CM8 .....196 C1
Speedwell Rd CHTY IP2 .....24 C7
  COLS CO2 .....152 E4
Speldhurst Rd HOM E9 .....314 A9
Spellbrook CI WICKW SS12 .....305 K1
Spellbrook La East
  BSF CM23 .....162 B6
Spellbrook La West
  BSF CM23 .....162 C5
Spells CI BOC CM0 .....269 J5
Spence CI
  BERM/RHTH SE16 .....332 C9
Spencer Av CHESW EN7 .....229 K5
Spencer CI BCAYW CM12 .....282 G5
  MAL CM9 .....244 B2
  RBSF CM22 .....114 F4
  STSD CM24 .....114 B9
  WFD IG8 .....295 M2
Spencer Ct RCHLM CM5 .....287 H2
Spencer Gdns EHAM E6 .....333 N1
  RAIN RM13 .....336 C5
  RCOS CO16 .....157 K4
Spenser Crs UPMR RM14 .....319 P2
Spencer Rd IP IP1 .....22 G9
Spenser Wy COS CO15 .....206 E3
Spert St POP/IOD E14 .....332 B7
Speyside STHGT/OAK N14 .....272 B5
Spey Wy ROM RM1 .....298 D4
Spey Wy ROM RM1 .....298 D4
Spicersfield CHESW EN7 .....229 M6
Spicers La SUD CO10 .....59 L5
Spielman Rd DART DA1 .....347 L9
The Spike SAFWS CB11 .....51 N8
Spillbutters BRWN CM15 .....258 E6
Spilsby Rd HARH RM3 .....299 K4
Spindle Beams RCFD SS4 .....308 G6
Spindle Rd HVHL CB9 .....40 C8
Spindles TIL RM18 .....350 B5
Spindle Wd COLN CO4 .....128 B3
Spingate CI HCH RM12 .....319 H7
Spinks La WIT CM8 .....197 H5
Spinnaker CI BARK IG11 .....335 J5
The Spinnaker SBF/HAD SS7 .....325 N2
The Spinnaker RCHLM CM5 .....287 H5
Spinnel's HI MGTR CO11 .....132 F1
Spinnel's La MGTR CO11 * 24 E5
Spinney CI RAIN RM15 .....336 D2
Spinneyfields K/T/MI CO5 .....174 A7
Spinney Gdns DAGW RM9 .....317 N7
The Spinneys HOC/HUL SS5 .....307 N2
  LOS SS9 .....308 A3
  RAYL SS6 .....307 K6

The Spinney BCAYW CM12 .....283 J4
  BRTR CM7 .....145 M5
  CDW/CHF RM16 .....340 B4
  CHONG CM5 .....235 L9
  HOD EN11 .....211 H2
  HOD EN11 .....208 C7
  IPNE IP4 .....26 E7
  RBRW/HUT CM13 .....281 M5
  SAFWS CB11 .....89 M1
  STSD CM24 .....138 B1
Spinneywood LAIN SS15 * 303 H7
Spinning Wheel Md
  WALTH E17 * 211 H6
Spire Cha SUD CO10 .....47 K9
Spire Green Centre
  HLWW/ROY CM19 .....209 P4
Spire CI LAIN SS15 .....303 K8
The Spires CHLM/GWD CM2 .....240 E4
Spital Av BRW CM14 .....280 C9
Spital Rd MAL CM9 .....243 H3
Spitfire CI IPNE IP3 .....31 H1
Sporehams La
  CHLM/GWD CM2 .....241 L6
Sporhams VGE SS16 .....323 N2
Sportsmans CI BOC CM0 .....220 D1
Sportsway COL CO1 .....8 D3
Spout La SUD CO10 .....75 N2
Spratt Hall Rd WAN E11 .....315 K1
Spratts La MGTR CO11 .....260 D5
Spreadeagle PI IPNE IP4 * 25 J6
Spriggs La ING CM4 .....257 J7
Springbank PI RAIN RM15 .....272 E5
Springbank Av HCH RM12 .....319 H7
  MGTR CO11 .....106 A5
Spring Gv RCOLE CO7 .....153 J4
  RCOLE CO7 .....219 P9
Spring CI BCTR RM8 .....317 L3
  COLN CO4 .....128 D4
  RCHLM CM3 .....220 A6
  RCOS CO16 .....181 M8
Spring Court Rd ENC/FH EN2 .....250 F8
Spring Elms La RCHLM CM5 .....220 C8
Springett's HI BURES CO8 .....75 N7
Springfarm La RAIN RM15 .....337 J5
Spring Gdns EPP CM16 .....254 G2
  SBF/HAD SS7 .....326 C2
Springfield Av FX IP11 .....35 K5
  RBRW/HUT CM13 .....281 P6
Springfield CI CHONG CM5 .....235 L5
Springfield Gn
  CHLM/WR CM1 .....218 D7
Springfield La IP IP1 .....24 G3
Springfield Lyons Ap
  CHLM/GWD CM2 .....218 F5
Springfield Park Av
  CHLM/GWD CM2 .....218 C9
Springfield Park HI
  CHLM/GWD CM2 .....5 K3
Springfield Park La
  CHLM/GWD CM2 .....218 D8
Springfield Park Pde
  CHLM/GWD CM2 .....218 D8
Springfield Park Rd
  CHLM/GWD CM2 .....218 C9
Springfield PI CHLM/WR CM1 .....218 D5
Springfield Rd BCAYW CM12 .....283 J5
  BOC CM0 .....290 F2
  BXLYHN DA7 .....346 A8
  CDW/CHF RM16 .....339 P9
  CHES/WCR EN8 .....252 B2
  CHING E4 .....251 J5
  CVI SS8 .....345 J2
  EHAM E6 .....316 A9
  SRTFD E15 * 333 H3
  SUD CO10 .....20 C1
  WALTH E17 .....294 C8
  WICKE SS11 .....285 L8
Springfields BROX EN10 .....208 C7
  BRTR CM7 .....144 F4
  GTDUN CM6 .....141 K6
  RCOLE CO7 * 153 C2
  WICKE SS11 .....324 E3
Springfield Ter SUD CO10 * 20 C4
Spring Gdns HCH RM12 .....318 D6
  RAYL SS6 .....306 F5
  ROMW/RG RM7 .....298 B9
  SUD CO10 * 46 F5
  WFD IG8 .....295 M4
Springhead Rd
  SLH/COR SS17 .....341 J7
Springhouse Rd
  SLH/COR SS17 .....341 N1
Springhurst CI IPNE IP4 .....25 N1
Springland CI IPNE IP4 .....25 P5
Springlands Wy SUD CO10 .....47 J9
Spring La COLW CO3 .....127 K8
  MAL CM9 .....198 E5
  MAL CM9 .....221 J7
  RCHLM CM3 .....221 J4
  RCOLE CO7 .....153 J4
  RCOLW CO6 .....126 D7
  RCOLW CO6 .....127 H4
  WIT CM8 .....197 K5
Springville CI HERT/BAY SG13 .....184 C9
Springmeed BRTR CM77 .....144 C7
Spring Pond CI
  CHLM/GWD CM2 .....240 D2

Spring Pond Meadow
BRWN CM15...........................258 F4
Springpond Rd DAGW RM9 ...317 M7
Spring Rd IPNE IP6 ....17 J4
K/T/MI CO5 ....173 P9
RCOLE CO7 ....179 L6
RCOS CO16 ....D0 D9
Spring Sedge Cl COLW CO5 ..126 F8
The Springs BROX EN10 ....230 C5
Springtail Rd RIPW IP8 ....29 N2
Spring V BXLYHN DA7 ....346 A9
Springvalley La RCOLE CO7 ...129 K4
Springwater Cl COS SS9 ....307 M8
Springwater Gv LOS SS9 ....307 M8
Springwater Rd LOS SS9 ....307 M8
Spring Wy HSTD CO9 ....72 D9
Springwell Ct WARE SG12 * ...184 F8
Springwell Rd SAFWN CB10 ...51 H5
Springwood CHESW EN7 ....229 M5
Springwood Dr BRTR CM7 ....144 F2
Springwood Wy ROM RM1 ....298 F9
Sprites End FX IP11 * 34 G4
Spriteshall La FX IP11 ....34 G4
Sprites La FX IP11 ....24 D9
Sproughton Rd RIPW IP8 ....24 E4
Sprowston Ms FSTGT E7 ....315 K8
Sprowston Rd FSTGT E7 ....315 K7
Spruce Av COLN CO4 ....128 F7
GTDUN CM6 ....141 J5
Spruce Cl K/T/MI CO5 ....202 E5
LAIN SS15 ....305 K6
WIT CM8 ....171 P9
Spruce Hl HLWS CM18 ....210 F8
Spruce Hills Rd WALTH E17 ....294 F6
Sprundel Av CVI SS8 ....344 G3
Spur Cl ABR/ST RM4 ....277 J2
Spurgate RBRW/HUT CM13 ....281 K8
Spurgeon Rd COLN CO1 ....72 D8
Spurgeon St COL CO1 ....9 K7
Spurling Rd DAGW RM9 ....317 N8
Spur Rd BARK IG11 ....334 D5
The Spur CHES/WCR E4 * 230 A7
Squadrons Ap HCH RM12 ....319 H8
The Square BOC CM0 ....248 B6
BROX EN10 ....230 B2
BRTR CM77 * 144 E8
ILL IG5 ....151 L3
ING CM4 ....261 M7
K/T/MI CO5 * 202 E6
MAL CM9 * 222 B6
SBW CM21 ....187 M2
SLH/COR SS17 * 540 G2
WFD IG8 ....295 K2
Squires Ct BSF CM23 ....137 H6
Squire La RCHLM CM3 ....D4 D1
Squire St RCHLM CM3 ....287 H1
Squirrells Ct CHLM/WR CM1 ...217 N6
Squirrels VGE SS16 ....323 J5
Squirrel's Cha
CDW/CHF RM16 ....340 B9
Squirrels Cl BSF CM23 ....137 L6
Squirrels Fld COLN CO4 ....128 A2
Squirrel's Heath Av GPK RM2 ...298 C7
Squirrels Heath La
HARH RM5 ....299 K6
Squirrels Heath Rd
EMPK RM11 ....299 H8
The Squirrels RIPS/CAP IP9 ...28 C4
Stable Cl COLW CO3 ....126 C9
K/T/MI CO5 ....203 H5
Stable Ct KESC IP5 ....27 M3
Stablecroft CHLM/WR CM1 ....218 D3
Stablefield Rd WOTN CO14 .....159 H7
Stable Ms K/T/MI CO5 ....203 H4
Stacey La LEY E10 ....294 C9
Stacey Dr VGE SS16 ....323 K4
Stacey's Mt BCAYE CM11 ....304 B2
The Stackyard Cl MALD CM20 ...187 J9
The Stackyard SAFWN CB10 ...36 B8
Staddles RBSF CM22 ....162 E4
Stadium Rd SOSN SS2 ....329 H4
Stadium Wy
HLWW/ROY CM19 ....210 A2
SBF/HAD SS7 ....304 D9
Staffa Cl WICKW SS12 ....305 L2
Staffa Rd LEY E10 ....314 B5
Staffhouse Rd WICKE SS11 * ..285 M5
Stafford Av EMPK RM11 ....299 J7
Stafford Cl CDW/CHF RM16 ...348 F2
CHES/WCR EN8 ....230 B7
FOS CO13 ....158 F8
LOS SS9 ....308 B9
SLH/COR SS17 ....351 H1
STHGT/OAK N14 ....272 B4
WALTH E17 ....314 B6
Stafford Crs BRTR CM7 ....145 N2
Stafford Dr BROX EN10 ....208 D8
Stafford Gn VGE SS16 ....322 G2
Stafford Rd BOW E3 ....532 C2
FSTGT E7 ....315 M9
Staffords HLWE CM17 ....187 M8
Stagden Cross BSDN SS14 ......324 E1
Staggart Gn BARK/HLT IG6 .....296 G2
Stag La BKHH IG9 ....275 L8
Stags Cl BSF CM23 ....137 H9
Staines Rd IL IG1 ....316 E6
Stainforth Rd
GNTH/NBYPK IG2 ....316 E2
WALTH E17 ....294 D8
Stainsby Pl POP/IOD E14 * 332 D6
Stainsby Rd POP/IOD E14 ......332 D6
Stains Cl CHES/WCR EN8 ....230 B7
Stainton Rd PEND EN3 ....251 P9
Stairs Rd SBN/FI SS3 ....331 K2
Staith Wy WFD IG8 ....296 C5
Staithe Rd COLS CO2 ....100 G9
Stalbridge Rd COS CO15 ....158 F8
Stambourne Rd HSTD CO9 ....56 C5
Stambridge Rd COS CO15 ....6 A1
Stamford Cl CHTY IP2 ....29 P2
Stamford Gdns DAGW RM9 ....317 K9
Stamford Rd DAGW RM9 ....335 H1
EHAM E6 ....333 P1

Stammers Pl KESC IP5 ....27 K4
Stamvers Rd COLN CO4 ....128 A3
Stanbridge Rd WCHMH N21 ...272 G8
Stanbrook Rd ABYW SE2 ....335 J9
Standard Av CVI SS8 ....206 C5
Standard Rd COL CO1 ....128 D9
PEND EN3 ....252 B8
Standen Av HCH RM12 ....319 J5
RCHLM CM3 ....286 C5
Standfield Rd DAGE RM10 ......317 P7
Standingford EPP CM16 ....210 C8
Standley Rd WOTN CO14 ....159 L5
Standrums GTDUN CM6 ....141 L5
Stane Cl BSF CM23 ....137 L6
Stane Fld RCOLW CO6 ....149 K5
Stanes Rd BRTR CM7 ....121 H9
Staneway VGE SS16 ....323 L3
Stanfield Cl COLW CO3 ....151 H5
Stanfield Rd BOW E3 ....332 B2
SOSN SS2 ....329 H4
Stanfields Ct HLW CM20 ....13 K5
Stanford Cl ROMW/RG RM7 ...318 A1
WFD IG8 ....295 P2
Stanford Ct WAB EN9 ....253 K3
Stanford Gdns
SOCK/AV RM15 ....338 B9
Stanford Hall
SLH/COR SS17 * 341 N2
Stanford-le-Hope By-Pass
CDW/CHF RM16 ....340 D6
SLH/COR SS17 ....323 P6
Stanford Rivers Rd
CHONG CM5 ....257 M1
Stanford Rd CDW/CHF RM16 ..339 P9
CDW/CHF RM16 ....340 C8
CVI SS8 ....344 D2
Stanham Pl DART DA1 ....346 P9
Stanhope Cl
BERM/RHTH SE16 * 332 A9
Stanhope Gdns
BCTR RM8 ....317 N5
IL IG1 ....316 A3
Stanhope Rd BCTR RM8 ....317 N4
CHES/WCR EN8 ....252 B5
RAIN RM13 ....336 F2
WALTH E17 ....295 L3
Stanier Cl SOS SS1 ....19 K3
Stanley Av BARK IG11 ....334 C3
RCHLM CM3 ....317 N3
Stanley Cl GPK RM2 ....298 F8
IPSE IP5 ....25 P7
RCOLE CO7 ....179 M6
Stanley Cl GPK RM2 ....298 F8
HCH RM12 ....319 H4
Stanley Pl CHONG CM5 ....235 M8
Stanley Ri CHLM/GWD CM2 ...218 E8
Stanley Rd CHING E4 ....274 C7
COS CO15 ....207 H2
CVI SS8 ....344 F4
ED N9 ....275 K2
EN EN1 ....275 K2
FX IP11 ....11 K3
GRAYS RM17 ....349 L4
HCH RM12 ....319 H4
HSTD CO9 ....98 A9
IL IG1 ....316 E4
MNPK E12 ....315 P7
RCFD SS4 ....288 D9
SAFWN CB10 ....36 F8
SBF/HAD SS7 ....326 A1
SOS SS1 ....19 J5
SRTFD E15 ....332 C1
SUD CO10 ....20 D3
SWFD E18 ....295 J5
UPMR RM14 ....322 A6
WALTH E17 ....314 E1
Stanley Rd North RAIN RM13 ...336 D1
Stanley Rd South RAIN RM13 ...336 E2
Stanley Farm Rd SAFWS CB11...65 N1
Stanley Ter BCAYW CM12 ....283 H7
Stanley Vls SLH/COR SS17 * ...341 K4
Stanley Wood Av SUD CO10 ...21 H7
Stanley Wooster Wy
COLN CO4 ....128 F9
Stanmore Ct RCOS CO16 ....181 N8
Stanmore Rd BELV DA17 ....346 B2
WAN E11 ....315 J3
WICKE SS11 ....305 N1
Stanmore Wy LOU IG10 ....254 B9
RCOS CO16 ....180 E9
Stannard Wy SUD CO10 ....61 K4
Stannetts LAIN SS15 ....305 J7
Stansfield Rd CAN/RD E16 .....333 N6
Stansfield Rd SBF/HAD SS7 ...305 N4
Stansgate Rd BOC CM0 ....246 E5
DAGE RM10 ....317 P4
Stanstead Dr HOD EN11 ....208 E5
Stanstead Rd HSTD CO9 ....98 A8
WAN E11 ....295 L2
WARE SG12 ....184 A7
Stansted Cl BCAYE CM11 * 283 J7
CHLM/WR CM1 ....240 M1
HCH RM12 ....318 G8
Stansted Hl MHAD SG10 ....160 F4
Stansted Rd BSF CM23 ....137 M6
COLS CO2 ....152 B5
RBSF CM22 ....114 F6
Stansted Wy FOS SS11 ....159 H8
Stanstreta Fld BRTR CM77 .....144 E9
Stanton Hughes Wy
MGTR CO11 ....106 A4
Stanton Cl CHIG IG7 ....296 F2
Stanway Rd SBF/HAD SS7 ......325 P1
WAB EN9 ....253 K3
Stanwell St COL CO1 ....8 C7
Stanwyck Gdns HARH RM3 .....298 G2
Stanway Av COS CO15 ....6 E3
Stapleford Av
GNTH/NBYPK IG2 ....296 F9
Stapleford Cl CHING E4 ....274 F9
CHLM/GWD CM2 ....4 E5
Stapleford End WICKE SS11 ...305 M1
Stapleford Gdns CRW RM5 .....297 P3
Stapleford Rd ABR/ST RM4 ....278 A5

Stapleford Wy BARK IG11 ......335 J3
Staplegrove SBN/FI SS3 ....330 B6
Staplers Cl MAL CM9 ....198 C5
Staplers Heath MAL CM9 ....198 C8
Staplers Wk MAL CM9 ....198 C8
Staples Cl BERM/RHTH SE16 ..332 B8
Staples Rd LOU IG10 ....275 P2
Stapleton Crs RAIN RM13 ....318 F9
Starboard Vw RCHLM CM3 ....287 H3
Starch House La
BARK/HLT IG6 ....296 E6
Starfield Cl IPNE IP4 ....26 A5
Star Holme Ct WARE SG12 .....184 B5
Starkey Cl CHESW EN7 ....229 H4
Star La CAN/RD E16 ....333 H4
EPP CM16 ....333 H9
GTDUN CM6 ....141 L5
INE CM4 ....260 D5
IPNE IP4 ....16 E6
SBN/FI SS3 ....330 D3
Starling Cl BKHH IG9 ....275 K7
Starling La POTB/CUF EN6 .....228 E7
Starmans Ct DAGW RM9 ....335 M1
Starr Md GTDUN CM6 ....92 B6
Starr Rd RBSF CM22 ....115 J2
Star St WARE SG12 ....184 B5
Station Ap BKHH IG9 * 295 N1
BOC CM0 ....290 C3
BRTR CM7 ....145 K4
BXLYHN DA7 ....346 B7
CHES/WCR EN8 * 252 B4
CHING E4 * 275 H6
CLAY IG5 ....294 C3
COS SS16 ....326 C8
FOS CO13 ....158 C9
FSTGT E7 * 315 L5
HOC/HUL SS5 ....307 P1
LAIN SS15 ....323 K1
RCHLM CM3 ....264 F9
RCHLM CM3 ....286 C5
SOS SS1 ....19 F4
SWFD E18 ....328 C3
VGE SS16 ....295 L6
WALTH E17 ....294 D9
WAN E11 ....315 J1
WAN E11 ....315 H6
WFD IG8 * 295 M3
WICKW SS12 * 285 J8
Station Av RAYL SS6 ....306 E4
SOSN SS2 ....329 J5
WICKE SS11 ....285 H7
Station Crs RAYL SS6 ....306 G4
RCHLM CM3 ....266 A4
Station Goods Yd
SBF/HAD SS7 * 326 A6
Station HI BURES CO8 ....75 P9
Station HI HAR CO12 ....14 D6
HCH RM12 ....319 K4
IL IG1 ....260 C6
PIT SS13 ....295 L6
Station Pde BARK IG11 ....316 D9
EHAM E6 * 315 P9
EHAM E6 * 333 M1
HCH RM12 ....318 C6
ROM RM1 ....318 C6
STHGT/OAK N14 * 272 C7
Station Pas SWFD E18 ....295 L6
Station Rd BARK/HLT IG6 ....296 E7
BCAYW CM12 ....282 C6
BCTR RM8 ....317 L3
BOC CM0 ....269 J5
BROX EN10 ....208 C8
BRTR CM77 ....144 C5
BSF CM23 ....137 M8
CBE/LIN CB1 ....113 P5
CHES/WCR EN8 ....252 D4
CHESW EN7 ....228 G8
CHIG IG7 ....276 C9
CHING E4 ....274 C7
COS CO15 ....6 B2
CVI SS8 ....345 H3
EHAM E6 ....315 N9
EPP CM16 ....255 H1
FOS CO13 ....158 C8
FX IP11 ....11 N4
GPK RM2 ....298 G8
GTDUN CM6 ....141 M6
HAR CO12 ....24 E6
HAR CO12 ....15 F3
HARH RM3 ....110 A3
HARH RM5 ....299 L5
HLWE CM17 ....187 K8
HOC/HUL SS5 ....307 P1
HOD EN11 ....56 E2
HSTD CO9 ....72 C7
HVHL CB9 ....41 K3
IL IG1 ....316 C5
K/T/MI CO5 ....173 P9
LOS SS9 ....307 P4
LOU IG10 ....275 P4
MAL CM9 ....200 E6
MAL CM9 ....222 B8
MGTR CO11 ....225 J1
MGTR CO11 ....106 A3
MGTR CO11 ....107 K6
MGTR CO11 ....108 C5
MHAD SG10 ....160 D4
MNPK E12 ....315 N6
NHMKT IP6 ....22 C3
RAYL SS6 ....306 F4
RBRW/HUT CM13 ....321 P1
RBSF CM22 ....114 F5
RBSF CM22 ....139 M7
RCHLM CM3 ....196 C7
RCHLM CM3 ....266 B4
RCHLM CM3 ....267 N8
RCOLE CO7 ....153 J6
RCOLE CO7 ....155 H5
RCOLE CO7 ....153 H6
RCOLE CO7 ....154 F5
RCOLE CO7 ....154 F6
RCOLE CO7 ....155 K7

RCOLE CO7 ....179 K7
RCOLW CO6 ....98 G7
RCOLW CO6 ....99 M9
RCOLW CO6 ....125 J1
RCOLW CO6 ....149 M2
RCOS CO16 ....157 J6
RIPS/CAP IP9 ....81 N5
SAFWS CB11 ....64 F4
SAFWS CB11 ....65 H9
SAFWS CB11 ....65 K9
SBF/HAD SS7 ....326 A6
SBW CM21 ....187 N1
SOS SS1 ....330 A6
STSD CM24 ....114 B9
SUD CO10 ....20 E6
SUD CO10 ....40 F6
TIL RM18 ....351 F3
UPMR RM14 ....319 P4
WALTH E17 ....231 H6
WARE SG12 ....184 B5
WARE SG12 ....184 F8
WCHMH N21 ....272 C7
WICKE SS11 ....285 H6
WICKW SS12 ....285 J8
WIT CM8 ....170 G3
WIT CM8 ....197 K1
WIT CM8 ....197 M1
WOS/PRIT SS0 ....18 B5
Station Rd North BELV DA17 ...346 A1
Station Sq CHTY IP2 ....25 K8
SAFWS CB11 ....51 L9
SRTFD E15 ....314 C9
WOTN CO14 ....159 K7
Station Wy BKHH IG9 ....295 N1
VGE SS16 ....323 J2
Staverton Rd EMPK RM11 ......319 J1
Stave Yard Rd
BERM/RHTH SE16 ....332 B8
Stayner's Rd WCHPL E1 ....332 A4
Stays La CHONG CM5 ....215 K8
Steamer Ter CHLM/WR CM1 ...4 E1
Steam Mill Rd MGTR CO11 .....107 H8
Stebbing Rd GTDUN CM6 ......142 G7
Stebbings VGE SS16 ....323 K2
Stebbing Wy BARK IG11 ....335 H2
Steed Cl EMPK RM11 ....318 C4
Steeds Meadow SUD CO10 .....46 F3
Steeds Wy LOU IG10 ....275 P2
Steel Ap BARK IG11 ....335 J2
Steele Cl RCOLW CO6 ....149 L3
Steele Rd WAN E11 ....315 H6
Steen Cl ING CM4 ....260 C5
Steeple Bumpstead Rd
HVHL CB9 ....54 G2
Steeple Cl MAL CM9 ....198 C5
RCFD SS4 ....308 E4
Steeplefield LOS SS9 ....307 P3
Steeplehall PIT SS13 ....324 F1
Steeple Hts SBF/HAD SS7 ......305 M9
Steeple McIw BOC CM0 ....268 G5
Steeple Rd BOC CM0 ....268 C8
RCHLM CM3 ....267 J3
Steeple Vw BSF CM23 ....137 L5
Steeple Wy BRWN CM15 ....258 E6
Steerforth Cl CHLM/WR CM1 ...217 L4
Steering Cl ED N9 ....275 P7
Steers Wy BERM/RHTH SE16 ..332 B9
Stela Av CVI SS8 ....326 C9
Stella Maris Cl CVI SS8 ....345 J2
Stella Maris Cl CVI SS8 ....345 J2
Stelling Rd ERITH DA8 ....346 C5
Sten Cl PEND EN3 ....252 D7
Stennetts Cl FX IP11 ....34 E3
Stenning Av TIL RM18 ....351 J2
Stepfield WIT CM8 ....197 N2
Stephen Av RAIN RM13 ....318 F8
Stephen Cl HVHL CB9 ....41 J3
Stephen Cranfield Cl
K/T/MI CO5 ....153 H7
Stephen Marshall Av
BRTR CM7 ....94 B2
Stephens Cl BXLYHN DA7 ......346 B8
KESC IP5 ....27 K3
Stephens Cl HARH RM5 ....299 H2
Stephen's Cl IPNE IP4 ....11 N5
Stephens Crs SLH/COR SS17 ...340 G2
Stephenson Av TIL RM18 ....145 N5
Stephenson Rd BRTR CM7 .....145 K5
COLN CO4 ....128 E1
COS CO15 ....182 C5
LOS SS9 ....307 M9
RCHLM CM3 ....287 N9
WALTH E17 ....294 B9
Stephenson West
COS CO15 ....182 B4
Stephenson St CAN/RD E16 ...333 H5
Stephen's Rd SRTFD E15 ....332 A1
Stepney Gn WCHPL E1 ....332 A5
Stepney High St WCHPL E1 ....332 A5
Sterling Av CHES/WCR EN8 ...252 A4
Sterling Cl COLW CO5 ....151 H1
Sterling Rd ENC/FH EN2 ....251 J9
Stern Cl BARK IG11 ....334 G7
Sterry Crs DAGE RM10 ....317 P9
Sterry Rd BARK IG11 ....334 G7
DAGE RM10 ....317 P6
Stevenage Rd EHAM E6 ....316 C2
Stevens Cl CVI SS8 ....344 G1
Stevens La CDTUN CM6 ....143 L8
Stevenson Cl ERITH DA8 ....346 G5
Stevenson Rd IP IP7 ....16 B5
Stevenson Wy WICKW SS12 ...305 H2
Stevens Rd BCTR RM8 ....317 J4
WALTH E17 ....197 H5
Stevens Wy CHIG IG7 ....296 F4
Steward Cl CHES/WCR EN8 ...230 E9
Stewards Cl EPP CM16 ....255 H5
FOS CO13 ....155 K7

Stewards Elm Farm La
RCFD SS4 ....309 L3
Stewards Green Rd
RCOLE CO6 ....255 J5
Stewart Av UPMR RM14 ....319 N5
Stewart Pl WICKW SS12 ....305 L2
Stewart Rd CHLM/GWD CM2 ...239 P4
WAN E11 ....314 G6
The Stewarts BSF CM23 ....137 K7
Stewart Wy BSF CM23 ....113 L5
Stewarts Young Gv KESC IP5 ...27 J4
Steyning Av SOSN SS2 ....329 M4
Stifford Clays Rd
CDW/CHF RM16 ....339 J8
Stifford HI CDW/CHF RM16 ....358 G8
Stifford Rd CDW/CHF RM15 ...358 C7
Stile Cft HLWS CM18 ....211 H5
Stile La RAYL SS6 ....306 G5
Stilemans WICKE SS11 ....285 J8
Stilemans Wd BRTR CM77 .....145 N6
Stiles Ct ERITH DA8 ....346 A3
The Stiles MAL CM9 ....199 H6
Stirling Av LOS SS9 ....327 L4
Stirling La RAIN RM13 ....336 C5
RAYL SS6 ....306 E2
Stirling Dr HVHL CB9 ....41 H5
Stirling Pl PIT SS13 ....324 A3
Stirling Rd PLSTW E13 ....333 L2
WALTH E17 ....294 B7
Stirrup Cl CHLM/WR CM1 ......218 D4
Stivvy's End MAL CM9 ....198 D5
Stock Cha MAL CM9 ....222 C6
Stock Cl SOSN SS2 ....328 G2
Stockdale Rd BCTR RM8 ....317 N4
Stockfield Gdns DAGW RM9 ...317 K9
Stockfield Av HOD EN11 ....208 D8
Stockhouse Cl MAL CM9 ....199 P2
Stockhouse Rd K/T/MI CO5 ....174 E6
Stockingswater La PEND EN3 ..268 D4
Stockland Rd ROMW/RG RM7 ...318 C1
Stock La ING CM4 ....260 F6
Stockley Cl HVHL CB9 ....41 J4
Stockmen Fld BSF CM23 ....137 H9
Stockmers End RIPS/CAP IP9 ...28 C9
Stock Rd BCAYW CM12 ....283 J6
CHLM/GWD CM2 ....240 C7
ING CM4 ....261 L8
SOSN SS2 ....329 H2
Stocksfield Rd WALTH E17 * ...294 F7
Stocks Hl BSF CM23 ....138 C4
Stocks PI POP/IOD E14 ....332 C7
Stock St PLSTW E13 ....333 K2
Stocks Yd SAFWN CB10 * 51 L9
Stockwell COL CO1 ....8 B5
Stockwell Cl BCAYE CM11 .....283 J6
CHESW EN7 ....229 M7
Stockwood Rd BSF CM23 ....306 D8
Stokeash Cl RCOS CO16 ....206 F1
Stoke Av BARK/HLT IG6 ....297 H5
Stoke Br IP IP7 ....16 E7
Stokebridge Maltings
IPSE IP5 * 16 E7
Stokefelde PIT SS13 ....304 G8
Stoke Hall Rd CHTY IP2 ....26 D7
Stoke Park Dr CHTY IP2 ....29 N2
Stoke Quay IPSE IP5 ....16 F7
Stoke Rd RAIN RM13 ....337 J2
RCOLW CO6 ....77 M1
RCOLW CO6 ....78 A8
SUD CO10 ....43 P5
Stoke St EHAM E6 ....353 P4
The Stokes WOTN CO14 ....159 J5
Stoke St CHTY IP2 ....16 E7
Stollery Cl KESC IP5 ....27 H4
Stonard Rd BCTR RM8 ....317 J7
PLMGR N13 ....272 F9
Stonards Hl EPP CM16 ....255 K2
LOU IG10 ....276 A5
Stondon Rd CHONG CM5 ....235 K8
Stonebridge HI RCOLW CO6 ...98 E9
Stonechat Rd BCAYW CM12 ...283 K8
Stonechat Sq EHAM E6 ....333 P5
Stone Cl BCTR RM8 ....317 J4
BRTR CM7 ....145 J4
Stonecrofot Gdns CHTY IP2 * ...25 H7
Stonecroft Rd ERITH DA8 ....346 B5
Stonecrop COLN CO4 ....127 M5
Stonegrove Rd FX IP11 ....11 L1
Stonehall Av IL IG1 ....315 P1
Stonehall Dr RCOS CO16 ....132 E6
Stonehall La RCOS CO16 ....181 N4
Stone Hall Rd WCHMH N21 ....272 E6
Stoneham Av RCOS CO16 ......181 N4
Stoneham St RCOLW CO6 ......147 N4
Stonehill Cl LOS SS9 ....328 A2
Stonehill Rd CHLM/WR CM1 ...216 B6
Stonehill Wy CHTY IP2 ....327 P2
Stonehill Wy K/T/MI CO5 ....202 D5
Stonehorse Rd PEND EN3 ......273 H4
Stonehouse La PUR RM19 ......348 B3
Stone La K/T/MI CO5 ....198 G2
Stone St COL CO1 ....108 C4
Stoneleigh SBW CM21 ....187 L1
Stoneleigh Av EN EN1 ....251 N8
Stoneleigh Cl CHES/WCR EN8 ...252 A4
Stoneleigh Dr HOD EN11 ....208 E2
Stoneleigh Pk COLW CO3 ......151 J3
Stoneleigh Rd CLAY IG5 ....295 P7
Stoneleighs SBF/HAD SS7 .....306 C9
Stone Lodge La CHTY IP2 ....26 A7
Stone Lodge La West CHTY IP2 ...24 C8
Stone Lodge Wk CHTY IP2 ......26 A7
Stoneness Rd WTHK RM20 ....348 E4
Stone Path Dr RCHLM CM3 ....196 C8
Stones End K/T/MI CO5 ....174 D8
Stones Green Rd HAR CO12 ...132 G5
Stonewall EHAM E6 ....334 B5
Stonewood Rd ERITH DA8 ......346 D3
Stoneyard La POP/IOD E14 ....332 E7
Stoney Common STSD CM24 ...138 D1
Stoney Common Rd
STSD CM24 ....138 A1

Stoneycroft Rd WFD IG8 ....295 P3
Stoneydown WALTH E17 ....294 B8
Stoneydown Av WALTH E17 ....294 B8
Stoney Hills BCAYE CM11 ......284 A3
  BOC CM5
Stony La RCOLE CO7 ....179 M5
Stonycroft Cl PEND EN5 ....274 B1
Stonyfield Dr STSD CM24 ....138 B1
Stony La CHONG CM5 ....234 G2
  GTDUN CM6 ....92 B6
Stony Pth LOU IG10 ....234 A2
Stonyshotts WAB EN9 ....253 H4
Stony Wd HLWS CM18 ....210 E4
Stopford Ct IP1 ....16 A3
Stopford Rd PLSTW E13 ....333 K1
Storey Rd CAN/RD E16 ....334 B9
Stores Rd K/T/MI CO5 ....173 P7
Store St SRTFD E15 ....314 C2
Storey Rd WALTH E17 ....294 C8
Stork Rd FSTGT E7 ....315 J8
Stormonts Wy SOSN SS2 ....323 L4
Stornoway Rd SOSN SS2 ....329 K5
Storr Gdns RBRW/HUT CM13 ...281 N4
Stortford Hall Pk BSF CM23 ....137 N6
Stortford Hall Rd BSF CM23 ....137 N6
Stortford Rd GTDUN CM6 ....140 F7
  HOD EN11 ....190 D6
  HOD EN11 ....208 E4
  RBSF CM22 ....139 J7
  RBSF CM22 ....163 H9
  SAFWS CB11 ....88 B4
  STDN SG11 ....136 B4
Stort Ldg BSF CM23 ....137 J6
Stort MI HLW CM20 ....187 J6
Stort Rd BSF CM23 ....137 L8
Stort Valley Pk HLW CM20 ....187 L5
  HLWE CM17 ....212 D1
  HLWE CM17 ....234 B1
  HLWW/ROY CM19 ....209 K2
  SBW CM21 ....187 M3
Stour Av FX IP11 ....11 E5
Stour Cl HAR CO12 ....109 N6
  SBN/FI SS3 ....330 D7
  SUD CO10 ....45 P1
Stourdale Cl MGTR CO11 ....105 P1
Stour Gdns SUD CO10 ....61 K6
Stourmead Cl HVHL CB9 ....42 B8
Stour Rd BOW E3 ....314 D9
  CDW/CHF RM16 ....350 B3
  DAGE RM10 ....317 P4
  DART DA1 ....346 F8
  HAR CO12 ....15 F4
Stourside RIPS/CAP IP9 ....85 M9
Stour St MGTR CO11 ....106 C4
  SUD CO10 ....20 B6
  SUD CO10 ....45 H3
Stour Ter MGTR CO11 * 19 N5
Stourton Rd WIT CM8 ....197 H1
Stour V HSTD CO9 ....42 E8
  SUD CO10 * 44 A5
Stour Valley Pth BURES CO8 ....75 P7
  RCOLW CO6 ....77 J7
  RCOLW CO6 ....77 J4
  SUD CO10 ....43 M7
  SUD CO10 ....44 F1
  SUD CO10 ....75 J2
Stour Valley Rd HVHL CB9 ....41 L4
Stour Valley Wk SUD CO10 ....60 G4
Stour Vw MGTR CO11 * 82 A7
  MGTR CO11 * 108 D3
Stourview Av MGTR CO11 ....106 F4
Stourview Cl MGTR CO11 ....106 G4
Stour Vls MGTR CO11 * 107 J8
Stour Wk COLN CO4 ....20 F1
Stour Wy UPMR RM14 ....320 B1
Stow Crs WALTH E17 ....294 B5
Stowe Gdns ED N9 ....273 L7
Stowe's La BOC CM5 ....247 P6
Stowmarket Rd NHMKT IP6 ......25 A2
Stow Rd RCHLM CM3 ....265 N5
The Stow HLW CM20 ....210 G1
Stow Vls RCHLM CM3 * 265 M6
Stradbroke Dr CHIG IG7 ....296 C3
Stradbroke Gv BKHH IG9 ....295 P7
  CLAY IG5
Stradbroke Pk CHIG IG7 ....296 C3
Stradbroke Rd IPNE IP4 ....25 P4
Strafford Av CLAY IG5 ....296 B6
Strafford Rd POP/IOD E14 ....332 D9
Strahan Rd BOW E3 ....332 B5
Straight Rd COLN CO4 ....103 H8
  COLW CO3 ....127 H9
  HARH RM3 ....298 C2
  KIR/NAC IP10 ....32 A2
  MGTR CO11 ....107 H7
  RCOLE CO7 ....180 D2
Straight Wy COLS CO2 ....175 K3
Strait Rd EHAM E6 ....333 P7
The Straits WAB EN9 ....252 E2
The Strand CHTY IP2 ....30 A4
Strangman Av SBF/HAD SS7 .....326 D9
Strasbourg Rd CVI SS8 ....326 D9
Stratfield Dr BROX EN10 ....208 B7
Stratfield Park Cl
  WCHMH N21 ....272 G6
Stratford Cl BARK IG11 ....317 H9
  DAGE RM10 ....318 B9
Stratford Gdns SLH/COR SS17 ..341 L3
Stratford Rd COS CO15 ....182 E7
  IP IP1 ....24 C1
  PLSTW E13 ....333 K1
  RCOLE CO7 ....104 D7
Stratfield Gdns BARK IG11 ....316 E8
Strathmore TIL RM18 ....351 K2
Strathmore Gdns HCH RM12 ....318 E3
Strathmore Rd RCHLM CM3 ......266 C9
  SDEN ESS EN2 ....251 J7
Stratton Dr BARK IG11 ....316 D3
Strattonhall Drift
  KIR/NAC IP10 ....32 D8
Stratton Rd HARH RM3 ....299 M2
  SOSN SS2 ....329 H2
Strawberry Cl BRTR CM7 ....145 L4
Strawberry Flds HVHL CB9 ....40 G4
Strawberry La K/T/MI CO5 ....199 M1

Strawbrook HI RCHLM CM3 ....169 H9
Straw La SUD CO10 ....20 B6
Strayfield Rd ENC/FH EN2 ....250 F6
Streamside Cl ED N9 ....273 L7
Streatfeild Av EHAM E6 ....334 A1
The Street BOC CM5 ....246 D8
  BRTR CM7 ....122 C9
  BRTR CM7 ....144 B5
  BRTR CM7 ....146 B8
  BRTR CM7 ....146 E4
  BSF CM23 ....88 A9
  BSF CM23 ....113 L5
  CHLM/GWD CM2 ....240 A8
  CHLM/WR CM1 ....191 N2
  CHLM/WR CM1 ....216 B5
  CHONG CM5 ....214 G8
  CHONG CM5 ....236 C6
  FOS CO13 ....158 D5
  GTDUN CM6 ....142 C6
  GTDUN CM6 ....165 M6
  HAR CO12 ....109 K7
  HSTD CO9 ....56 C4
  HSTD CO9 ....71 J2
  HSTD CO9 ....97 H8
  HSTD CO9 ....99 H1
  K/T/MI CO5 ....148 D9
  K/T/MI CO5 ....174 A3
  KIR/NAC IP10 ....32 A5
  MAL CM9 ....199 J7
  MAL CM9 ....200 F4
  MAL CM9 ....220 G9
  MGTR CO11 ....82 B8
  MGTR CO11 ....107 K7
  NHMKT IP6 ....25 P4
  RBSF CM22 ....188 C4
  RBSF CM22 ....192 B2
  RCHLM CM3 ....194 A6
  RCHLM CM3 ....195 P1
  RCHLM CM3 ....196 C8
  RCHLM CM3 ....264 E6
  RCHLM CM3 ....265 M5
  RCHLM CM3 ....265 P1
  RCHLM CM3 ....266 G4
  RCOLE CO7 ....80 E7
  RCOLE CO7 ....104 F8
  RCOLW CO6 ....124 G7
  RCOS CO16 ....125 H2
  RCOS CO16 ....156 D1
  RCOS CO16 ....181 M1
  RIPS/CAP IP9 ....28 B9
  RIPS/CAP IP9 ....29 P3
  RIPS/CAP IP9 ....30 A4
  RIPS/CAP IP9 ....63 L5
  RIPS/CAP IP9 ....84 A7
  RIPS/CAP IP9 ....84 C7
  RIPS/CAP IP9 ....85 J6
  RIPW IP8 ....24 B1
  RIPW IP8 ....28 B2
  RIPW IP8 ....29 L4
  RIPW IP8 ....43 J8
  SUD CO10 ....45 M3
  SUD CO10 ....45 P5
  SUD CO10 ....57 L1
  SUD CO10 ....59 H2
  SUD CO10 ....60 B5
  SUD CO10 ....60 G7
  WIT CM8 ....170 F4
  WIT CM8 ....197 P7
Streimer Rd SRTFD E15 ....332 F2
Stretford Ct WIT CM8 * 171 L2
Strethall Rd SAFWS CB11 ....50 C5
Strickland Av DART DA1 ....347 L9
Strickmere RCOLE CO7 ....79 P7
Stridy Rd PLSTW E13 ....333 J2
Strimon Cl ED N9 ....273 P6
Strode Rd FSTGT E7 ....315 K6
Stroma Gdns SBN/FI SS3 ....330 C8
Stromburg Rd CVI SS8 ....326 B9
Stromness PI EDSW N22 ....19 K3
Stromness Rd SOSN SS2 ....329 K5
Strone Rd FSTGT E7 ....315 M8
Strood Av ROMW/RG RM7 ....318 C3
Strood Cl K/T/MI CO5 ....202 E5
The Strood K/T/MI CO5 ....177 J9
Strouds Cl CHDH RM6 ....297 J9
Struan Av SLH/COR SS17 ....323M9
Strudwick Cl BRTR CM7 ....145 J4
Struggler's La 23 P4
Strutt Cl RCHLM CM3 ....196 D8
Stuart Cl BRWN CM15 ....240 G4
  CHLM/GWD CM2 ....341 E1
  FX IP11 ....35 N4
  IPNE IP4 ....17 K2
  SBN/FI SS3 ....330 E2
Stuart Mantle Wy ERITH DA8 ...346 C5
Stuart Pawsey Ct
  RCOLE CO7 * 153 K5
Stuart Rd BARK IG11 ....334 G1
  GRAYS RM17 ....349 L5
  SOSN SS2 ....329 H4
Stuarts St SOSN SS2 ....329 H5
Stuarts Wy BRTR CM7 ....145 L4
Stuart Wy BCAYE CM11 ....283 M7
  CHESW EN7
Stubbers La UPMR RM14 ....320 B8
Stubbs Cl COS CO15 ....158 F7
  HVHL CB9 ....40 G2
  IPSE IP3 ....30 C1
Stubbs St BRTR CM7 ....145 M4
Stublands BSDN SS14 ....304 E9
Studd's La COLN CO4 ....127 N3
Studland Av WICKW SS12 ....284 E8
Studley Av CHING E4 ....294 C4
Studley Cl CLPT E5 ....314 B7
Studley Dr REDBR IG4 ....315 N1
Studley Rd DAGW RM9 ....317 L9
  FSTGT E7 ....315 L8
Stukeley Rd FSTGT E7 ....315 L9

Stump La CHLM/WR CM1 ....218 C7
Sturdee Av IPSE IP5 ....26 A8
Sturge Av WALTH E17 ....294 E5
Sturlas Wy CHES/WCR EN8 ....252 A3
Sturmer Rd HVHL CB9 ....42 B5
Sturrick La RCOLE CO7 ....155 J5
Sturrocks VGE SS16 ....324 D3
Sturry St POP/IOD E14 ....332 E6
Stutton Cl RIPS/CAP IP9 ....83 H7
Stutton Gn RIPS/CAP IP9 ....83 K8
Stutton La RIPS/CAP IP9 ....82 D4
Stutton Rd MGTR CO11 ....82 F7
Styles BRTR CM7 ....95 L6
Sub-Station Rd FX IP11 ....10 D6
Sudbourne Av RCOS CO16 ....181 K9
Sudbourne Rd FX IP11 ....34 C6
Sudbrook Cl WICKW SS12 ....334 B6
Sudbury EHAM E6 ....334 B6
Sudbury Cl HOC/HUL SS5 ....308 A3
Sudbury Rd BARK IG11 ....316 C7
  BCAYE CM11 ....284 F3
  BURES CO8 ....76 A8
  FX IP11 ....10 B2
  HSTD CO9 ....59 L8
  HSTD CO9 ....72 F5
  HSTD CO9 ....98 A5
  SUD CO10 ....46 E7
  SUD CO10 ....47 M5
  SUD CO10 ....60 C4
Sudburys Farm Rd
  BCAYE CM11 ....302 D1
Sudeley Gdns HOC/HUL SS5 .....307 N1
Sudicamps Ct WAB EN9 ....253 K3
Suez Rd PEND EN3 ....274 B3
Suffield Rd CHING E4 ....274 E9
Suffolk Av K/T/MI CO5 ....202 C5
  LOS SS9 ....328 A3
Suffolk Cl COLN CO4 ....9 H2
  COS CO15 ....182 F6
Suffolk Coast & Heaths Pth
  FX IP11 * 35 L8
  IPSE IP5 ....30 C4
  KIR/NAC IP10 ....31 K3
  RIPS/CAP IP9 ....31 L9
  RIPS/CAP IP9 ....83 K7
Suffolk Crs MAL CM9 ....243 P1
Suffolk Dr CHLM/GWD CM2 .....218 F7
Suffolk Rd BARK IG11 ....316 C7
  DAGE RM10 ....318 A7
  GDMY/SEVK IG3 ....316 F1
  IPNE IP4 ....17 H2
  MAL CM9 ....243 P1
  PEND EN3 ....273 N4
  SOSN SS2 ....333 J3
  SUD CO10 ....20 D4
Suffolk Sq SUD CO10 ....20 D3
Suffolk St FSTGT E7 ....315 K7
  WOTN CO14 ....159 K6
Suffolk Wy CVI SS8 ....326 A9
  EMPK RM11 ....299M8
Sugar House La SRTFD E15 ....332 F2
Sugar La HSTD CO9 ....96 A1
Sugden Av WICKW SS12 ....284 F9
Sugden Wy BARK IG11 ....334 C2
Sulleys Hi HADL IP7 ....79 N1
Sullivan Av CAN/RD E16 ....333 N5
Sullivan Cl COLN CO4 ....128 F9
Sullivan Rd TIL RM18 ....350 B6
Sullivan Wy VGE SS16 ....323 H1
Sultan Rd WAN E11 ....295 L8
Summercourt Rd
  WOS/PRIT SS0 ....18 C3
Summerdale BCAYW CM12 ......283 H6
Summerfield LOU IG10 ....267 P6
Summerfield Cl IPNE IP4 ....266 C3
Summerfield Rd LOU IG10 ....275 N5
Summerfields HSTD CO9 ....72 D8
  ING CM4 ....260 D6
Summerhill RCHLM CM3 ....267 N6
Summerhill Gv EN EN1 ....273 J2
Summer Hill Rd SAFWS CB11 .....65 L1
Summerlands CVI SS8 ....326 C9
Summer PI WOTN CO14 * 159 L4
Summerskille Cl PEND EN3 ....273 N8
Summerton Wy THMD SE28 .....335 L7
Summerwood Cl
  SBF/HAD SS7 ....326 F5
Summit Cl STHGT/OAK N14 .....272 B8
Summit Dr WFD IG8 ....295 N6
Summit Rd WALTH E17 ....294 E8
The Summit LOU IG10 ....268 A3
Summit Wy STHGT/OAK N14 ....272 A8
Sumners Farm Cl EPP CM16 ......210 B8
Sumpters Wy SOSN SS2 ....308 C9
Sunbank GTDUN CM6 ....141 M6
Sunbeam Av COS CO15 ....206 D6
Sunbeam Cl K/T/MI CO5 ....153 H6
Sunbury Ct SBN/FI SS3 ....350 D4
Sunbury Wy MAL CM9 ....244 A2
Sun Ct ERITH DA8 ....346 E7
Sundale Cl COS CO15 ....182 G7
Sundal PI RCOLE CO7 * 104 E9
Sunderland Rd FX IP11 ....111 L2
Sunderland Wy MNPK E12 ....315 N4
Sunfield Cl IPNE IP4 ....26 A5
Sunflower Wy HARH RM3 ....299 J5
Sun Lido Square Gdns
  BRTR CM7 * 144 F4
Sunnedon VGE SS16 ....324 C1
Sunningdale BSF CM23 ....137 K8
  CVI SS8 ....344 F1
Sunningdale Av BARK IG11 ....316 F3
  IPNE IP4 ....26 C6
  LOS SS9 ....328 B5
  RAIN RM13 ....336 G4
Sunningdale Cl THMD SE28 .....335 M6
Sunningdale St SOS SS1 * 19 F4
Sunningdale Dr FX IP11 ....95 L5
Sunningdale Fall RCHLM CM3 ..196 B8
Sunningdale Rd
  CHLM/WR CM1 ....217 M7
  RAIN RM13 ....318 F9
  RCHLM CM3 ....267 M7

Sunningdale Wy FOS CO13 ....158 F7
Sunnybank LA SUD CO10 ....320 A8
Sunnybank Cl LOS SS9 ....308 A9
Sunny Cft HLWS CM18 ....210 C6
Sunnycroft Gdns
  UPMR RM14 ....320 C2
Sunnyfield Gdns CHING E4 ....294 C2
Sunnydene Cl HARH RM3 ....299 L4
Sunnyfield Gdns
  HOC/HUL SS5 ....307 L1
Sunnyfields Rd BRTR CM7 ....121 N5
Sunnyhill Cl CLPT E5 ....314 B1
Sunnymede CHIG IG7 ....277 J9
Sunnymede Cl SBF/HAD SS7 ....306 D9
Sunnymede Dr BARK/HLT IG6 ..296 C8
Sunny Ms CRW RM5 ....298 B4
Sunny Point WOTN CO14 ....159 M3
Sun Ray Av RBRW/HUT CM13 ...281 P5
Sunrise Av CHLM/WR CM1 ....217 P6
  HCH RM12 ....319 H5
Sunset Av CHING E4 ....274 E7
  WFD IG8 ....295 K2
Sunset Ct ERITH DA8 ....346 G5
Sunnyside Cl CHING E4 ....274 F6
Sunnyside Gdns UPMR RM14 ...319 P7
Sunnyside Av EPP CM16 ....254 C2
  IL IG1 ....316 D5
  LEY E10 ....314 D3
  RCOLW CO6 ....126 A2
Sunnyside Rd East ED N9 ....273 M9
Sunnyside Rd North ED N9 ....273 L9
Sunnyside Rd South ED N9 ....273 L9
Sunnyside Wy RCOS CO16 ....181 M4
Sunny Wy BOC CM3 ....247 H2
Sunnyvale FX IP11 ....55 L5
Sun St SBCAYW CM12 ....187 N5
  WAB EN9 ....252 F3
Surbiton Av SOS SS1 ....329 L6
Surbiton Rd IP IP1 ....24 G4
  SOSN SS2 ....329 L5
Surig Rd CVI SS8 ....326 C9
Surlingham Cl THMD SE28 ....335 L7
Surman Crs RBRW/HUT CM13 ..281 M6
Surmans Cl DAGW RM9 ....335 K1
Surrey Av LOS SS9 ....328 A3
Surrey Cl BRTR CM7 ....144 E5
Surrey La K/T/MI CO5 ....173 P9
Surrey Rd BARK IG11 ....316 F9
  DAGE RM10 ....318 B7
  FX IP11 ....11 J7
  IP IP1 ....25 H5
Surrey St PLSTW E13 ....333 L3
Surrey Water Rd
  BERM/RHTH SE16 ....332 A8
Surrey Wy LAIN SS15 ....305 H9
Surridge Cl RAIN RM13 ....337 H5
Susan Cl ROMW/RG RM7 ....298 B7
Susannah St POP/IOD E14 ....332 E6
Sussex Av HARH RM3 ....299 H9
Sussex Cl CVI SS8 ....326 D9
  HOD EN11 ....208 D4
  LAIN SS15 ....303 J9
  RCHLM CM3 ....219 L3
  REDBR IG4 ....316 A1
Sussex Gdns COS CO15 ....182 F7
Sussex Rd BRW CM14 ....300 E1
  COLW CO3 ....127 M8
  EHAM E6 ....334 B2
  ERITH DA8 ....346 A5
Sussex St PLSTW E13 ....333 L3
Sussex Ter PUR RM19 * 347 N5
Sussex Wy BCAYW CM12 ....283 J2
  CVI SS8 ....326 D9
  EBAR EN4 ....272 A4
Sutcliffe Cl WICKW SS12 ....305 J1
Sutherland Av POTB/CUF EN6 ..228 C7
Sutherland Bvd LOS SS9 ....327 L4
Sutherland House
  WALTH E17 * 294 E7
Sutherland PI WICKW SS12 ....305 J2
Sutherland Rd BOW E3 ....332 C2
  ED N9 ....273 M7
  PEND EN3 ....274 A5
  WALTH E17 ....294 B7
Sutherland
  POTB/CUF EN6 ....228 C7
Sutton Acres SBF/HAD SS7 ......162 G6
Sutton Cl BROX EN10 ....208 G8
  LOS SS9 ....275 P6
Sutton Ct WARE SG12 * 184 B4
Sutton Court Dr RCFD SS4 ....308 G8
Sutton Court Rd PLSTW E13 .....333 M3
Sutton Md CHLM/GWD CM2 ....218 F7
Sutton Park Av COLW CO3 ....145 L1
Sutton Rd BARK IG11 ....334 F2
  PLSTW E13 ....333 J4
  RCFD SS4 ....309 H7
  SOSN SS2 ....19 H5
Suttons Av HCH RM12 ....319 H5
Suttons Gdns HCH RM12 ....319 J5
Suttons La HCH RM12 ....319 J7
Suttons La SBN/FI SS3 ....330 G6
Swale Cl SOSN SS2 ....329 M4
Swale Rd DART DA1 ....346 F8
  SBF/HAD SS7 ....326 E1
Swallowcliffe SBN/FI SS3 ....330 C5
Swallow Cl BXLYHN DA7 ....346 D6
  CDW/CHF RM16 ....348 F2
  COS CO15 ....151 K9
  FX IP11 ....35 M4
  RAYL SS6 ....306 E4
Swallowdale COLS CO2 ....152 D5
  COS CO15 ....182 A7
Swallow Dl VGE SS16 ....324 A2
Swallow Dr SBF/HAD SS7 ....325 N4

Swallow Fld RCOLW CO6 ....124 A1
Swallow Rd CHTY IP2 ....24 D8
  WICKE SS11 ....285 H6
Swallows HLWE CM17 ....187 K6
Swallow's Rw RCOLE CO7 ....155 N5
The Swallows BCAYE CM11 ......283 K6
Swallow St EHAM E6 ....333 P5
Swallowtail Cl RIPW IP8 ....29 N2
Swallow Wk HSTD CO9 ....38 A7
Swanage Rd EHAM E6 ....294 F4
  SOSN SS2 ....19 H2
Swan And Pike Rd PEND EN5 ....253 P8
Swan Ap EHAM E6 ....335 P5
Swan Av UPMR RM14 ....320 C5
Swanbourne Dr HCH RM12 ......319 J6
Swan Cha HSTD CO9 ....72 D9
Swan Cl COLN CO4 ....128 F9
  KESG IP5 ....27 M4
  LAIN SS15 ....2 A1
  RCHLM CM3 ....196 C8
  WALTH E17 ....294 C8
Swan Ct BSF CM23 ....137 L8
  HSTD CO9 ....72 D9
  IP IP1 ....222 C7
  OUL CO10 ....106 F5
Swan Dl COS CO15 ....182 A7
Swanfield Rd CHES/WCR EN8 ...252 B3
Swanfield Rd RCOLE CO6 ....125 H2
Swan La BRWN CM15 ....258 B7
  HVHL CB9 ....41 K3
  ING CM4 ....261 L1
  MGTR CO11 ....215M6
  NHMKT IP6 ....25 M6
  SUD CO10 ....46 F4
  WICKE SS11 ....285 J7
Swan Md VGE SS16 ....324 C2
Swan Meadow RCOLE CO7 ....79 P8
Swan Pas COL CO1 * 8 D5
Swan Rd RCOS CO16 ....156 C1
Swanscombe
  RCOLW CO6 ....124 E3
Swans Av SBF/HAD SS7 ....30 B1
Swansea Rd PEND EN5 ....273 P5
Swans Green Cl
  SBF/HAD SS7 ....306 D9
Swanshope LOU IG10 ....276 C1
Swan Side BRTR CM7 ....145 J5
Swans Pasture
  CHLM/WR CM1 ....218 C5
Swans Rd CHES/WCR EN8 ....252 A4
Swanstead VGE SS16 ....324 D2
Swan St HSTD CO9 ....72 D8
  K/T/MI CO5 ....173 J2
  RCOLW CO6 ....125 H4
Swan Wy PEND EN3 ....274 A1
Swan Yd RCOLW CO6 ....147 P4
Swanwick CI PUT/ROE SW15 ......31 H2
Swaton Rd BOW E3 ....332 D4
Swaynes RCOLE CO7 ....79 P7
Sweden Cl HAR CO12 ....110 A4
Sweet Briar BSF CM23 ....136 G8
Sweet Briar Av SBF/HAD SS7 ....326 A4
Sweet Briar Cl RCOLW CO6 ....77 J4
Sweet Briar Dr LAIN SS15 ....303 L8
Sweet Briar Gn ED N9 ....273 L9
Sweet Briar Gv ED N9 ....273 L9
Sweet Md SAFWN CB10 ....51 H7
Sweete St PLSTW E13 ....211 K6
Sweyne Av HOC/HUL SS5 ....308 B3
  SOSN SS2 ....18 D2
Sweyne Cl CV RAYL SS6 ....306 E3
Swift Av COLW CO3 ....150 F2
  COS CO15 ....206 E6
Swift Cl BRTR CM7 ....145 K6
  THMD SE28 ....335 J6
  UPMR RM14 ....320 B5
  WALTH E17 ....294 B4
  WARE SG12 ....184 F9
Swiftsure Rd
  CDW/CHF RM16 ....348 F2
Swinborne Cl PIT SS13 * 304 G6
Swinborne Rd PIT SS13 ....305 H6
Swinbourne Dr BRTR CM7 ....144 D3
Swinbornes Cft
  RCOLW CO6 * 149 K3
Swinburne Gdns TIL RM18 ....350 C7
Swinburne Rd IP IP1 ....22 F9
Swindon Cl GDMY/SEVK IG3 ....316 F4
Swindon Gdns HARH RM3 ....299 L2
Swindon La HARH RM3 ....299 L2
Swinnerton St HOM E9 ....314 B7
Swiss Av CHLM/WR CM1 ....217 N7
Sworders Yd BSF CM23 * 137 L7
Sybourn St WALTH E17 ....314 C2
Sycamore Av BOW E3 ....332 D5
  UPMR RM14 ....319 M5
Sycamore Cl CAN/RD E16 ....333 H4
  CHESW EN7 ....229 L6
  CVI SS8 ....344 C2
  RAYL SS6 ....306 E1
  RBSF CM22 ....139 M7
  RIPW IP8 ....29 L1
  TIL RM18 ....171 P8
  WIT CM8 ....171 P8
Sycamore Dr BRW CM14 ....240 B4
Sycamore Fld
  HLWW/ROY CM19 ....210 B7
Sycamore Gv BRTR CM7 ....144 G4
  SOSN SS2 ....329 J4
Sycamore Ms ERITH DA8 * 346 C3
Sycamore PI RCOLE CO7 ....155 K6
Sycamore Rd COLN CO4 ....222 C5
  SUD CO10 ....21 J6
The Sycamores BSF CM23 ....137 L8
Sycamore Wy
  CHLM/GWD CM2 ....240 B4
  COS CO15 ....207 H1
  FOS CO13 ....158 D5

MGTR CO11 .81 N9
RCFD SS4 .289 L7
SOCK/AV RM15 .538 C4
Sydenham La BARK/HLT N21 .272 E4
Sydenham Cl ROM RM1 .298 E8
Sydervelt Rd CVI SS8 .344 D1
Sydner Cl CHLM/GWD CM2 .240 F5
Sydney Rd BARK/HLT IG6 .296 D6
ENC/FH EN2 .273 J5
LOS SS9 .327 L4
SBF/HAD SS7 .325 P2
TIL RM18 .350 B7
WAN E11 .295 K2
WFD IG8 .295 K2
Sydney St COLS CO2 .152 C5
RCOLE CO7 .179 L8
Sykes Md RAYL SS6 .306 G6
Sylvan Cl CDW/CHF RM16 .349 H2
CHLM/GWD CM2 .240 A4
CVI SS8 .344 E3
LAIN SS15 .303 J9
Sylvan Ct LAIN SS15 * .302 G8
Sylvan Ms GRH DA9 .548 E9
Sylvan Rd FSTGT E7 .315 K8
IL IG1 .316 D4
WAN E11 .295 K9
Sylvan Tryst BCAYW CM12 .283 J4
Sylvan Wy BCTR RM8 .317 J5
CHIG IG7 .277 J9
LAIN SS15 .302 G8
Sylvester Rd WALTH E17 * .314 C2
Sylvesters HLWW/ROY CM19 .210 A5
Sylvia Av RBRW/HUT CM15 .281 M8
Symington Ms HOM E9 * .314 A7
Symmons Cl BRTR CM77 .144 C1
Symonds Ct CHES/WCR EN8 .230 A7
Symons Av LOS SS9 .307 P9
Syracuse Av RAIN RM13 .337 J5

T

Tabernacle Av PLSTW E13 .333 K4
Taber Pl WIT CM8 * .197 L1
Tabora Av CVI SS8 .326 C9
Tabor Av BRTR CM7 .145 H3
Tabor Cl RCOLE CO7 .179 K5
Tabors Av CHLM/GWD CM2 .240 E3
Tabrum's La RCHLM CM3 .286 E1
Tabrums Wy UPMR RM14 .320 B2
Tacket St IPNE IP4 * .23 N3
Tacon Rd FX IP11 * .11 F7
Tadlows Cl UPMR RM14 .319 N7
Tadworth Pde HCH RM12 .318 C6
Taffrail Gdns RCHLM CM5 .287 H3
Tailors BSF CM23 .136 C4
Tailors Ct SOSN SS2 .328 C1
Tailors Wy SOSN SS2 .328 C1
Tait Ms MAL CM9 .222 B9
Taits SLH/COR SS17 .341 N3
Takeley Cl CRW RM5 .298 C6
WAB EN9 .252 C3
Takely Ride VGE SS16 .324 C8
Talbot Av COLS CO15 .206 E6
RAYL SS6 .306 F4
Talbot Gdns GDMY/SEVK IG3 .317 N9
Talbot Rd DAGW RM9 .317 J7
EHAM E6 .334 A2
FSTGT E7 .315 K6
RCOS CO16 .181 M1
SUD CO10 .21 F1
Talbot St HAR CO12 .14 B6
Talbrook BRW CM14 .280 C9
Talcott Rd COLS CO2 .152 B4
Talisman Cl GDMY/SEVK IG3 .317 J3
K/T/MI CO5 .174 A7
Tallack Rd LEY E10 .314 C3
Talliboys Cl KESC IP5 .2 A4
Tallis Cl CAN/RD E16 .333 L6
SLH/COR SS17 .341 K2
Talliss Wy BRW CM14 .300 E2
Tallow Rd RBRW/HUT CM13 .281 H4
Tallow Ga RCHLM CM5 .287 H1
Tall Trees COLN CO4 .127 P4
Tall Trees Cl EMPK RM11 .319 J1
Tallyho Cnr RCOLE CO7 .80 A8
Tally-Ho Dr RBRW/HUT CM13 .282 C7
Talus Cl PUR RM19 .348 B3
Talwin St BOW E3 .332 E3
Talza Wy SOSN SS2 .328 C1
Tamage Rd SUD CO10 .47 M5
Tamar Cl BOW E3 * .332 C1
UPMR RM14 .
Tamar Dr SOCK/AV RM15 .337 P6
Tamarisk SBF/HAD SS7 .325 P2
Tamarisk Rd SOCK/AV RM15 .338 F4
Tamarisk Wy COLN CO4 .128 F8
Tamar Rd CHLM/WR CM1 .218 B5
Tamdown Wy BRTR CM7 .144 F2
Tamworth Av WFD IG8 .295 H3
Tamworth Cha COLS CO12 .152 B4
Tanfield Cl CHESW EN7 .229 L9
Tanfield Dr BCAYW CM12 .283 H6
Tangent Link HARH RM3 .299 J5
Tangent Rd HARH RM3 .299 J5
Tangerine Cl COLN CO4 .128 E9
Tangham Wy BSDN SS14 .3 G2
Tangmere Cl WALTH SS11 .305 N1
Tangmere Crs HCH RM12 .318 C8
Tan House La BRW CM14 .279 M2
Tankerville Dr LOS SS9 .327 N3
Tank Hill Rd PUR RM19 .347 M2
Tank La PUR RM19 .347 M2
Tan La RCOS CO16 .157 H9

Tanner Cl RCOS CO16 .206 G1
Tanners La BARK/HLT IG6 .296 D7
Tanners Meadow BRTR CM7 .145 N4
Tanners Sq RCHLM CM3 .316 D8
Tanners Vw IP IP1 .24 G4
Tanners Wy RCHLM CM5 .264 F9
SAFWN CB10 .51 M9
WARE SG11 .15 P4
Tannery Cl DAGE RM10 .318 A5
Tanswell Rd PIT SS13 .304 C8
Tanswell Cl PIT SS13 .304 G9
Tansy Cl EHAM E6 .334 B6
HARH RM3 .299 K1
Tant Av CAN/RD E16 .333 J6
Tantony Gv CHDH RM6 .297 L7
The Tanyard GTDUN CM6 .92 B6
Tanys Dell HLW CM20 .187 H9
Tapestry Ct RCOLW CO6 * .124 A1
Tapley Rd CHLM/WR CM1 .217 N5
Tapsworth Cl RCOS CO16 .181 N8
Tapwoods COLS CO15 .127 K8
Tara Cl COLN CO4 .128 E6
Taranto Rd CVI SS8 .344 C2
Tarling Rd CAN/RD E16 .333 H4
Tarnbank STHGT/OAK N14 .272 D4
Tarn Hows Cl FX IP11 .35 N5
Tarnwood Rd HARH RM3 .299M2
Tarpan Wy BROX EN10 .230 C5
Tarragona Ms COLS CO2 .152 C2
Tarragon Ct K/T/MI CO5 .173 P8
Tasker Rd CDW/CHF RM16 .350 C1
Tasman Cl SLH/COR SS17 .341 N1
Tasmania Rd IPNE IP4 .26 C5
Tasman Rd HWL CM9 .411 M4
Tattersall Gdns LOS SS9 .327 J8
Tattersalls Cha BOC CM0 .269 K5
Tattersall Wy CHLM/WR CM1 .239M5
Tatton St HLWE CM17 .211 K2
Taunton Cl BARK/HLT IG6 .296 C3
BXLYHN DA7 .346 C8
IP IP1 .23 J8
Taunton Dr ENC/FH EN2 .272 C2
WOS/PRIT SS0 .328 C2
Taunton Rd CHLM/WR CM1 .218 D6
FX IP11 .35 J6
HARH RM3 .299 H2
Taverners Green Cl
WICKW SS12 .305 K1
Taverners Wk WIT CM8 .171 N9
Taverners Wy CHING E4 .275 H7
HOD EN11 .208 D5
Tavern St IP IP1 .24 D4
Tavistock Av WALTH E17 .294 A7
Tavistock Cl HARH RM3 .299 J2
Tavistock Dr BCAYW CM12 .282 G3
Tavistock Gdns
GDMY/SEVK IG3 .316 F6
Tavistock Rd PIT STHGT/OAK N14 * .272 A5
CHLM/WR CM1 .218 D6
LAIN SS15 .303 K8
SWFD E18 .295 K7
WAN E11 .315 J6
Tavy Br ABYW SE2 .335 K9
Tawell Ms K/T/MI CO5 .174 A8
Tawney Cl HLWS/ROY CM19 .28 C9
Tawney Common EPP CM16 .255 P2
Tawney La ABR/ST RM4 .256 B2
EPP CM16 .256 B2
Tawney Rd THMD SE28 .335 J7
Tawneys Ride BURES CO8 .76 B8
Tawneys Rd HLWS CM18 .210 C5
Tawny Av UPMR RM14 .319 N7
Tayburn Cl POP/IOD E14 .332 F6
Taylifers HLWW/ROY CM19 .210 B8
Taylor Av CHLM/WR CM1 .217 M6
Taylor Cl CRW RM5 .297 P4
Taylor Ct COL CO1 .8 C5
Taylor Dr MGTR CO11 .106 B4
Taylors Av HOD EN11 .208 D6
Taylors End Rd RBSF CM22 .139 H5
Taylor's Rd K/T/MI CO5 .152 C6
Tay Wy ROM RM1 .298 E5
Teagles LAIN SS15 .2 A4
Teak Cl BERM/RHTH SE16 .332 B8
Teal Av RCHLM CM5 .267 P1
Teal Cl BRTR CM77 .144 E9
CAN/RD E16 .333 N5
CHTY IP2 .24 E8
RCOLE CO7 .129 H7
Teal Wy K/T/MI CO5 .173 J5
Teasel Crs THMD SE28 .334 F8
Teasel Wy SRTFD E15 .333 H5
Tedder Cl COLS CO2 * .152 B2
Teddington Vls SOSN SS2 * .328 C1
Tees Cl UPMR RM14 .320 A2
Teesdale Rd WAN E11 .315 J1
Tees Dr HARH RM5 .279 J9
Tees Rd CHLM/WR CM1 .218 B5
Teign Dr WIT CM8 .196 D2
Teigngrace SBN/FI SS3 .330 C6
Teignmouth Dr RAYL SS6 .306 G2
Telegraph Ms GDMY/SEVK IG3 .316 G3
Telese Av CVI SS8 .344 C2
Telford Cl WALTH E17 .314 B2
Telford PL CHLM/GWD CM2 .218 C7
Telford Rd BRTR CM7 .145 K5
COS CO15 .182 C5
Telham Rd EHAM E6 .334 B2
Tempest Md EPP CM16 .254 B2
Tempest Wy RAIN RM13 .318 F8
Templar Dr THMD SE28 .335 L6
Templar Ct WIT CM8 .171 N9
Temple Bank HLW CM20 .187 H8
Temple Cl CHESW EN7 .251 M1
FOS CO13 .159 H8
LAIN SS15 .303 K8
SBF/HAD SS7 .327 J3
WALTH E17 .315 H2
Temple Ct COLN CO4 .128 E5

Temple Gdns BCTR RM8 .317 L5
WCHMH N21 * .272 G8
Temple Md ENC/FH EN2 .272 G2
Temple La BARK/HLT .171 K2
Templemead WIT CM8 .197 J1
Temple Mills La LEY E10 .314 E6
Temple Pattle MGTR CO11 .106 B1
Temple Av CDW/CHF RM16 .350 B2
Temple Rd COLS CO2 .151 K4
EHAM E6 .333 P1
IPSE IP3 .26 B7
Templeton Av CHING E4 .294 D1
Temple Wy MAL CM9 .222 C8
Templewood Ct SBF/HAD SS7 .326 C5
Templewood Rd COLN CO4 .128 F6
PIT SS15 .304 C9
SBF/HAD SS7 .326 C5
Tempsford Cl ENC/FH EN2 .272 C2
Tempton Av CVI SS8 .345 H2
Ten Acre Ap MAL CM9 .222 A6
Tenbury Cl FSTGT E7 .315 N1
Tenby Cl CHDH RM6 .317M1
Tenby Rd CHDH RM6 .317M1
CHTY IP2 .26 B1
PEND EN3 .273 P2
WALTH E17 .294 D9
Tendring Av RAYL SS6 .306 D4
Tendring Rd HLWS CM18 .210 C4
RCOLE CO7 .131 M7
RCOS CO16 .132 C5
RCOS CO16 .156 C2
Tenner Av CHDH RM6 .297 K9
Tennand Cl CHESW EN7 .229 L5
Tennants Rw TIL RM18 .349 P7
Tenniswood Rd EN EN1 .251 L9
Tennyson Av HCH RM12 .318 E3
MNPK E12 .315 P9
SOSN SS2 .327 K4
WAB EN9 .253 H4
WAN E11 .315 K2
Tennyson Cl BRTR CM7 .145 J6
LOS SS9 .327 K4
PEND EN3 .274 A4
Tennyson Rd CHLM/WR CM1 .217 N6
HARH RM5 .299 H4
IPNE IP4 .25 N6
MAL CM9 .244 B1
RBRW/HUT CM13 .281M6
SRTFD E15 .315 H9
WALTH E17 .314 C1
Tennyson Wk TIL RM18 .350 C7
Tenpenny Hi RCOLE CO7 .154 D8
Tensing Gdns BCAYW CM12 .282 C7
Tenterden Rd RCHLM CM5 .317 N4
Tenterfield GTDUN CM6 .141 M5
Tenterfield Rd MAL CM9 .222 C8
Tenterfields PIT SS13 .305 H7
SAFWS CB11 .64 G8
Tenth Av HI STSD CM24 .138 F4
Tenth Rd KIR/NAC IP10 .32 F4
Teramo Rd CVI SS8 .344 G2
Tercel Pth CHIG IG7 .297 J1
Terence Webster Rd
WICKW SS12 .305 J1
Teresa Gdns CHES/WCR EN8 .251 P4
Terling SS13 .3 G7
Terling Cl COLS CO2 .152 B5
WAN E11 .315 J5
Terling Hall Rd RCHLM CM5 .195 L3
Terling Rd BCTR RM8 .317 P4
RCHLM CM3 .196 D5
WIT CM8 .196 D2
The Terlings BRW CM14 .280 D9
Terminal Cl CAN/RD E16 .333 L6
Terminal Rd North
RBSF CM22 .139 L3
Terminal Rd South
RBSF CM22 .139 L3
Terminus Dr VGE SS16 .324 C2
Terminus Rd SUD CO10 .13 H5
Termitts Cha RCHLM CM5 .196 D5
Terms Av CVI SS8 .326 D9
Tern Cl HVHL CO9 .41 M4
K/T/MI CO5 .173 J2
RCHLM CM5 .267 P1
Terndale COS CO15 .182 A7
Tern Gdns UPMR RM14 .320 B3
Tern Rd CVI SS8 .344 G2
Tern Ms RCOLE CO7 .153 J6
Tern Rd CHTY IP2 .24 E7
Tern Wy BRW CM14 .300 B1
Terrace Hall Cha RCOLW CO6 .127M7
Terrace Rd HOM E9 .314 A9
PLSTW E13 .333 K1
The Terrace EHAM E4 * .275 H9
GTDUN CM6 * .142 G9
K/T/MI CO5 * .177 H2
LOS SS9 * .327 N9
RAYL SS6 * .286 F9
RCOLE CO7 * .104 F9
SBN/FI SS3 .330 B4
Terrace Wk DAGW RM9 .317M7
Terry Gdns KESC IP5 .27 K4
Teviot Av SOCK/AV RM15 .337 N6
Teviot St POP/IOD E14 .332 F5
Tew Cl K/T/MI CO5 .174 A7
Tewkesbury Cl LOU IG10 .275 P5
Tewkesbury Pde COS CO15 * .181 P8
Tewkesbury Rd COS CO15 .181 P8
Tewkes Rd CVI SS8 .326 G9
Teynham Av EN EN1 .273 J5
Tey Rd RCOLW CO6 .125 J6
RCOLW CO6 .148 A3
Tey Road Cl RCOLW CO6 .148 B3
Thackeray Av TIL RM18 .350 C6
Thackeray Cl BRTR CM7 .145 K6
Thackeray Dr CHDH RM6 .316 F4
Thackeray Rw WICKW SS12 .305 J1

Thai Massing Cl
RBRW/HUT CM13 .281 L8
Thame Rd BERM/RHTH SE16 .332 A9
Thames Av CHLM/WR CM1 .217 L6
DAGW RM9 .336 B5
Thames Cha WOT CM14 .145 N1
Thames St RCOLE CO7 .129 L3
RAIN RM13 .337 K5
RAYL SS6 .306 F6
SLH/COR SS17 .341 P2
Thames Crs SLH/COR SS17 .324 A9
Thames Dr CDW/CHF RM16 .350 B3
SLH/COR SS17 .327 K5
Thames Haven Rd
SLH/COR SS17 .341 P2
Thameside Crs CVI SS8 .344 C2
Thamesmere Dr THMD SE28 .335 H7
Thames Rd BARK IG11 .335 H5
CVI SS8 .344 C3
DART DA1 .346 F8
Thames Vw GRAYS RM17 .350 B3
VGE SS16 .325 K5
Thames Wy BOC CM0 .290 F2
Thamley PUR RM19 .347 M2
Thanet Gra WOS/PRIT SS0 .328 D2
Thanet Rd ERITH DA8 .346 D5
IPNE IP4 .26 A5
Thant Cl LEY E10 .314 E6
Thatchers Cl HOD IG10 .276 D1
Thatchers Crt RCHLM CM5 .266 F5
Thatchers Dr RCOLE CO7 .129 H9
Thatchers Gv CHDH RM6 .297M8
The Thatchers BSF CM25 .137 H9
The Thatches CHDH RM6 .297M8
Thaxted Gn RBRW/HUT CM13 .281 M4
Thaxted Rd BKHH IG9 .275 P6
CHLM/WR CM1 .218 A7
COLN N18 .273 P9
SAFWS CB11 .65 N1
Thaxted Wk WAB EN9 .252 C3
Thear Cl WOS/PRIT SS0 .328 D2
Theberton Rd EPP IG8 .31 H1
Thele Av WARE SG12 .184 C8
Theleway Cl HOD EN11 .208 E2
Thelma Av CVI SS8 .344 D1
Theobald Rd WALTH E17 .314 C2
Theobalds Av GRAYS RM17 .349M5
Theobalds Cl POTB/CUF EN6 .228 E3
Theobald's Dr
CHES/WCR EN8 * .252 A2
Theobald's La CHES/WCR EN8 .251 N2
Theobalds Park Rd
ENC/FH EN2 .250 G5
POTB/CUF EN6 .228 E9
Thetford Rd LAIN SS15 .327 M5
Thetford Rd DAGW RM9 .317 L9
IP IP1 .24 C4
Theydon Ct WAB EN9 .253 L3
Theydon Crs BSDN SS14 .304 E6
Theydon Ga EPP CM16 .254 F6
Theydon Gro EPP CM16 .254 F6
EPP CM16 .233 H9
Theydon Park Rd EPP CM16 .254 F9
Theydon Pl EPP CM16 .254 G1
Theydon Rd EPP CM16 .254 G1
SE WALTH E17 .314 C2
Thicket Gv DAGW RM9 .317 K8
Thielen Rd CVI SS8 .326 D9
Thieves Cnr CHLM/WR CM1 .216 G7
Third Av CHDH RM6 .317 N4
CHLM/WR CM1 .218 A6
COS CO15 .182 C9
CVI SS8 .344 B1
DAGE RM10 .336 B2
EN EN1 .273 L4
FOS CO13 .183M1
HAR CO12 .110 D5
HLWS CM18 .13 H7
HLWW/ROY CM19 .210 C4
HSTD CO9 .98 C7
MNPK E12 .315 P6
PLSTW E13 .333 K3
RCOS CO16 .206 A6
SBF/HAD SS7 .341 M1
SLH/COR SS17 .341 M1
Thirimere Cl CHLM/WR CM7 .144 C7
Thirlmere Rd BXLYHN DA7 .346 B7
SBF/HAD SS7 .306 B8
Thirslet Dr MAL CM9 .222 D7
Thirtieth St STSD CM24 .139 J3
Thirtle Ct RCOS CO16 .181 N7
Thistle Cl CHTY IP2 .24 C8
LAIN SS15 .303 H6
Thistledene Av CRW RM5 .298 A2
Thistledown BRTR CM7 .120 D8
BSDN SS14 .3 J4
Thistledown Cl BSDN SS14 .3 J4
Thistley Cl LOS SS9 .276 B2
MAL CM9 .223M5
Thistley Crs SAFWS CB11 .89 K7
Thistley Green Rd BRTR CM7 .126 E4
Thoby La BRWN CM15 .259 K7
Thomas Av FX IP11 .34 F3
Thomas Bata Av TIL RM18 .351 H2
Thomas Cribb Ms EHAM E6 .334 B3
Thomas Dr CVI SS8 .326 B9
Thomasin Rd PIT SS13 .305 H6

Thomas North Ter
CAN/RD E16 * .333 J5
Thomas Rd COS CO15 .6 C2
PIT SS13 .305 K8
POP/IOD E14 .332 E3
Thomas Rochford Wy
CHES/WCR EN8 .230 C6
Thomas St RCOLE CO7 .179 L7
Thomas Wakley Cl COLN CO4 .128 A2
Thomas Wk SAFWS CB11 .50 A9
Thompson Av COLW CO3 .127 J9
CVI SS8 .345 J2
Thompson Cl IL IG1 .316 D4
Thompson Rd DAGW RM9 .317 N5
IP IP1 .24 C4
Thompsons Cl CHESW EN7 .229 L8
Thorington Av
SBF/HAD SS7 .306 C9
Thorington Cl BRTR CM77 .144 F8
Thorington Rd RAYL SS6 .307 K6
Thorin's Ga RCHLM CM5 .286 F2
Thorley Cl BSF CM25 .137 J9
Thorley La BSF CM25 .161 N1
BSF CM25 .161 P1
Thorley Park Rd BSF CM25 .162 C1
Thorley Rd CDW/CHF RM16 .339 F8
Thornbera Cl BSF CM25 .162 C1
Thornbera Gdns BSF CM25 .162 C1
Thornbera Rd BSF CM25 .162 C1
Thornborough Av
RCHLM CM5 .287 H1
Thornbury Cl HOD EN11 .208 E1
Thornbury Rd COS CO15 .7 F1
LAIN SS15 .155 H5
Thornbush La RIPW IP8 .24 A3
Thorncroft EMPK RM11 .318 C1
SAFWN CB10 .51 N8
Thorndale SBF/HAD SS7 .306 E8
Thorndales BRW CM14 .300 C1
Thorndon Ap
RBRW/HUT CM13 .301 N4
Thorndon Av
RBRW/HUT CM13 .301 M9
Thorndon Ga
RBRW/HUT CM13 .301 N4
Thorndon Park Cl LOS SS9 .327 N1
Thorndon Park Crs LOS SS9 .327 L1
Thorndon Rd CVI SS8 .344 D1
Thorne Cl CAN/RD E16 .333 K6
ERITH DA8 .346 A4
WAN E11 .315 H6
Thorne Rd K/T/MI CO5 .172 G3
Thorney Bay Rd CVI SS8 .344 C5
Thorneycroft Dr PEND EN3 .252 D9
Thorney Rd RIPS/CAP IP9 .28 C8
Thornfield Rd BSF CM25 .137 K6
Thornford Gdns SOSN SS2 .328 C1
Thorn Gv BSF CM25 .137 N8
Thorngrove Rd PLSTW E13 .333 K2
Thornham Gv SRTFD E15 .314 G7
Thornhayes Cl CHTY IP2 .24 C8
Thornhill EPP CM16 .234 B5
RCHLM CM3 .306 C6
Thornhill Cl FOS CO13 .158 C7
Thornhill Gdns BARK IG11 .316 F9
LEY E10 .314 E4
Thornhill Rd LEY E10 .314 E4
NHMKT IP6 .22 D2
Thorn La RAIN RM13 .337 J2
Thornley Dr IPNE IP4 .26 B3
Thornley Rd FX IP11 .35M7
Thornridge BRW CM14 .280 E6
Thorns Wy WOTN CM14 .159 H7
Thornton Dr RCOLW CO6 .128 A5
Thornton Pl HNC CM6 .261M7
Thornton Rd BELV DA17 * .348 A2
IL IG1 .316 C6
RBSF CM22 .140 A6
UCND N18 .273 P9
WAN E11 .314 G2
Thorntons Farm Av
ROMW/RG RM7 .318 B4
Thornton Wy LAIN SS15 .323 H1
Thorn Wy FX IP11 .11 F2
Thornwood Cl K/T/MI CO5 .202 C6
Thornwood Rd EPP CM16 .233 J7
Thorogood Gdns SRTFD E15 .315 H7
Thorogood Wy RAIN RM13 .336 D1
Thorold Rd IL IG1 .316 C4
Thorolds VGE SS16 .324 G4
Thoroughfare IP IP1 * .16 D4
Thoroughgood Rd COS CO15 .7 H4
Thorpe Bay Gdns SOS SS1 .329 P8
Thorpe Cl HOC/HUL SS5 .308 A3
Thorpe Crs WALTH E17 .294 C6
Thorpedale Gdns
GNTH/NBYPK IG2 .296 B8
Thorpedene Av HOC/HUL SS5 .287 H6
Thorpedene Gdns SBN/FI SS3 .330 C7
Thorpe Esp SOS SS1 .329 P8
Thorpe Gn SBN/FI SS3 .330 E7
Thorpe Hall Av SOS SS1 .329 P6
Thorpe Hall Cl SOS SS1 .329 P6
Thorpe La RCOS CO16 .206 C5
Thorpe Park Rd RCOS CO16 .157 K7
Thorpe Rd BARK IG11 .316 E9
EHAM E6 .334 A1
FOS CO13 .158 A7
FSTGT E7 .315 J1
HOC/HUL SS5 .308 A4
RCOS CO16 .156 D1
RCOS CO16 .182 A3
WALTH E17 .294 F6
Thorp Leas CVI SS8 .344 E3
Thorrington Cross BSDN SS14 .3 H1
Thorrington Rd RCOLE CO7 .155 H6
RCOS CO16 .181M1
Thors Oak SLH/COR SS17 .341 N1
Thoydon Rd BOW E3 .332 B2

Thracian Cl COLS CO2 ......151 K3
Threadneedle St
  RCOLE CO7 ......104 C1
Three Acres RCOS CO16 ......180 D9
Three Colt St POP/IOD E14 * 332 C7
Three Corners BXLYHN DA7 ......346 A7
Three Crowns Rd COLN CO4 ......127 P5
Three Forests Wy
  ABR/ST RM4 ......256 C7
  CHONG CM5 ......214 A3
Three Forests Wy
  CHONG CM5 ......214 A7
Three Forests Wy LOU IG10 ......253 N9
  SBF/HAD SS7 ......163 H1
  SBW CM21 ......187 N4
  WAB EN9 ......209 N9
  WAB EN9 ......253 M6
Three Gates Cl HSTD CO9 ......97 N8
Three Horseshoes Rd
  HLWW/ROY CM19 ......210 C5
Three Mile Hl ING CM4 ......239 K8
Three Mill La BOW E3 ......332 F5
Thremhall Av RBSF CM22 ......138 C6
  RBSF CM22 ......139 J5
Thresherford VGE SS16 ......323 N2
Thresher Cl BSF CM23 ......137 H9
Threshers End COLW CO3 ......150 C1
Thrifts Md EPP CM16 ......254 F7
Thrift Wd RCHLM CM5 ......242 B9
Throckmorten Rd CAN/RD E16 ......333 L6
Through Jollys KESG IP5 ......27 J5
Throwley Cl PIT SS13 ......325 H1
Thrushdale COS CO15 ......182 A7
Thrush La POTB/CUF EN6 ......228 D7
Thundercourt WARE SG12 ......184 A2
Thunderer Rd DAGW RM9 ......335 M4
Thundersley Church Rd
  SBF/HAD SS7 ......326 A1
Thundersley Gv SBF/HAD SS7 ......326 C1
Thundersley Park Rd
  SBF/HAD SS7 ......326 A3
Thurgood Rd HOD EN11 ......208 D3
Thurlby Cl WFD IG8 ......296 A3
Thurlestone Av
  GDMY/SEVK IG3 ......316 C6
Thurleston La IP IP1 ......22 G7
Thurlow Gdns ROM RM1 ......318 D1
Thurlow Wk GRAYS RM17 ......349 K1
Thurlow Dr SOS SS1 ......329 N6
Thurlow Gdns CHIG IG7 ......296 E5
Thurlton Cl COLN CO4 ......128 E6
Thurstone SBF/HAD SS7 ......326 F1
Thurmans La FX IP11 ......34 E3
Thurrock Park Wy
  GRAYS RM17 ......349 N5
Thurso Cl HARH RM3 ......299 N3
Thurstable Cl MAL CM9 ......225 K1
Thurstable Rd MAL CM9 ......225 J1
Thurstable Wy MAL CM9 ......225 K1
Thurstans HLWW/ROY CM19 ......210 C8
Thurston Ct FX IP11 ......12 D8
Thwaite Rd ERITH DA8 ......346 B4
Thyme Rd K/T/MI CO5 ......173 P8
Thynne Rd BCAYE CM11 ......283 K6
Tibbatt's Rd BOW E3 ......333 L1
Tiberius Cl COLN CO4 ......128 C2
  HVHL CB9 ......41 N4
Tiberius Gdns WIT CM8 ......197 H4
Tickenhall Dr HLWE CM17 ......211 L3
Tickfield Av SOSN SS2 ......329 M5
Tickford Cl ABYW SE2 ......335 K9
Tidal Basin Rd CAN/RD E16 ......333 J7
Tideswell Cl BRTR CM7 ......145 N2
Tideway MAL CM9 ......244 C2
Tidey St BOW E3 ......332 D5
Tidings Hl HSTD CO9 ......97 N7
Tidworth Av WICKE SS11 ......285 K6
Tidworth Rd BOW E3 ......332 D4
Tidy's La EPP CM16 ......233 H8
Tiffin Dr K/T/MI CO5 ......174 D8
Tigfield Wk RCHLM CM5 ......287 P8
Tigres Cl ED N9 ......273 P8
Tilburg Rd CVI SS8 ......344 D1
Tilbury Md HLWS CM18 ......211 H5
Tilbury Rd EHAM E6 ......334 A2
  HSTD CO9 ......57 K3
  HSTD CO9 ......97 H2
  LEY E10 ......314 F2
  RBRW/HUT CM13 ......301 P8
Tildesley FOS CO13 ......158 B8
Tile Barn La MGTR CO11 ......105 H8
Tilegate Rd CHONG CM5 ......212 B7
  HLWS CM18 ......210 G5
Tile House Rd CHESW EN7 ......102 E8
Tilekiln Cl CHESW EN7 ......229 L8
Tilkey Rd RCOLW CO6 ......147 N2
Tillingham Ct LAIN SS15 ......303 H9
Tillingham Gn LAIN SS15 ......303 H9
Tillingham Rd BOC CM0 ......269 L4
Tillingham Wy RAYL SS6 ......306 D4
Tillotson Rd ED N9 ......273 L8
  IL IG1 ......315 N8
Tillwicks Rd HLWS CM18 ......210 G4
Tilney Rd DAGW RM9 ......317 N8
Tilney Turn VGE SS16 ......324 E2
Tilsit Pl RCOLE CO7 * 104 E9
Tilston Cl WANT E11 ......315 J5
Timberdene Av BARK/HLT IG6 ......296 D5
Timber Hl COL CO1 ......128 D9
Timberlog Cl BSDN SS14 ......303 J8
Timberlog La BSDN SS14 ......304 D9
Timbermans Vw VGE SS16 ......324 E5
Timber Pond Rd
  BERM/RHTH SE16 ......332 A9
Timbers Cl BRTR CM7 ......144 E7
Timothy Rd POP/IOD E14 ......332 C5
Timsons La CHLM/GWD CM2 ......218 F7
Tinabrook Cl CHMF E4 ......295 N5
Tindall Cl HARH RM3 ......299 L6
Tindal St CHLM/PLC CM1 ......6 C4
Tindon End Rd SAFWN CB10 ......68 A7
Tine Rd CHIG IG7 ......296 F2
Tinker Av DAGW RM9 ......95 H2

Tinker La RCFD SS4 ......308 G6
Tinker St HAR CO12 ......108 F8
Tinkler Side BSDN SS14 ......3 G4
Tinnocks La BOC CM0 ......246 G1
Tintagel Wy MAL CM9 ......243 P2
Tintern Av WOS/PRIT SS0 ......328 D4
Tintern Cl CHTY IP2 ......25 H9
Tintern Gdns WCHMH N21 ......272 D6
Tintern Rd CAN/RD E16 ......333 K5
Tipers Br BCAYE CM11 ......284 A3
Tippersfield SBF/HAD SS7 ......326 B2
Tippett Cl COLN CO4 ......128 F9
Tippetts Cl ENC/FH EN2 ......251 H9
Tipps Cross La BRWN CM15 ......258 E4
Tips Cross Md BRWN CM15 ......258 E5
Tiptree Cl CHLM CM1 ......274 F9
  EMPK RM11 ......319 M3
  LOS SS9 ......328 A2
Tiptree Crs RBRW/HUT CM13 ......281 N4
Tiptree Ct CLAY IG5 ......296 B7
Tiptree Dr ENC/FH EN2 ......273 J5
Tiptree Gv WICKW SS12 ......285 J9
Tiptree Hall La K/T/MI CO5 ......199 J1
Tiptree Rd WIT CM8 ......198 A7
Tiptree Cha WICKW SS12 ......305 L2
Titania Cl COLN CO4 ......128 G8
Titan Rd GRAYS RM17 ......349 K3
Titchfield Rd PEND EN3 ......252 B7
Titchwell Dr CHTY IP2 ......31 K2
Tithe Cl WIT CM8 ......197 H1
Titlelands HLWW/ROY CM19 ......210 A6
The Tithe WICKW SS12 ......304 C1
Titley Cl CHING E4 ......313 J8
Titmuss Av THMD SE28 ......335 J7
Titus Wy COLN CO4 ......128 C1
Tiverton Av CLAY IG5 ......296 B7
Tiverton Gv HARH RM3 ......299 M2
Tiverton Rd WFD IG8 ......296 C7
Tobago St POP/IOD E14 ......332 D9
Tobruk Rd CHLM/WR CM1 ......217 K6
  COLS CO2 ......151 N5
Toddbrook HLWW/ROY CM19 ......210 C4
Todd Cl RAIN RM13 ......337 J4
Toft Av GRAYS RM17 ......349 N2
Tofts Cha RCHLM CM3 ......170 D8
Tofts Wk BRTR CM7 ......145 J5
Toga Cl COLS CO2 ......151 K4
Tog La RCOLW CO6 ......102 D5
Tokely Rd RCOLE CO7 ......154 F5
Tokio Rd IPNE IP4 ......25 P5
Toledo Cl SOS SS1 ......19 H4
Toledo Rd SOS SS1 ......19 H4
Toller Rd IPSE IP5 ......25 M8
Tollesbury Cl WICKW SS12 ......305 K1
Tollesbury Gdns
  BARK/HLT IG6 ......296 E7
Tollesbury Rd MAL CM9 ......200 D8
Tolleshunt D'Arcy Rd
  MAL CM9 ......199 N9
Tollet St WCHPL E1 ......332 A4
Tollgate Dr COLW CO3 ......306 F9
Tollgate Dr COLW CO5 ......126 E9
Tollgate East COLW CO5 ......126 F9
Tollgate Rd CHES/WCR EN8 ......252 A5
  COLW CO5 ......126 F9
  EHAM E6 ......333 P5
Toll Gate Rd RIPS/CAP IP9 ......28 C9
Tollgate West COLW CO5 ......150 F1
Tolliday Cl RCOLE CO7 ......153 H4
Tolmers Av POTB/CUF EN6 ......228 B9
Tolmers Crs POTB/CUF EN6 ......228 D8
Tolmers Rd POTB/CUF EN6 ......228 C6
Toljuddle Av PLSTW E13 ......333 M1
Tolworth Gdns CHDH RM6 ......297 L9
Tolworth Rd IPNE IP4 ......25 P5
Tom Jenkinson Rd
  CAN/RD E16 ......333 K8
Tomkins Ct SLH/COR SS17 ......341 K5
Tomkyns La UPMR RM14 ......300 A7
Tomline Rd FX IP11 ......11 J3
  IPSE IP5 ......25 M6
Tomlin's Gv BOW E3 ......332 D5
Tomlins Orch BARK IG11 ......334 D1
Tomlin's Ter POP/IOD E14 ......332 B6
Tomlyns Cl RBRW/HUT CM13 ......281 P5
Tom Mann Cl BARK IG11 ......334 F1
Tom Nolan Cl SRTFD E15 ......333 H2
Tom's La BRTR CM7 ......93 P2
Tomswood Hl BARK/HLT IG6 ......296 D5
Tomswood Rd CHIG IG7 ......296 B5
Tom Tit La MAL CM9 ......243 N2
Tonbridge Rd HARH RM3 ......299 J4
  HOC/HUL SS5 ......288 A9
Tongres Rd CVI SS8 ......344 D1
Tony Webb Cl COLN CO4 ......128 C3
Took Dr RCHLM CM3 ......286 F2
Toot Hill Rd CHONG CM5 ......234 E9
Top House Rd CHING E4 ......274 F6
Toplands Av SOCK/AV RM15 ......337 N8
Topmast Point
  POP/IOD E14 * 332 D9
Toppesfield Av HSTD CO9 ......305 H2
Toppesfield Rd HSTD CO9 ......73 H1
Top Rd WIT CM8 ......199 P7
  MAL CM9 ......220 D9
  SAFWN CB10 ......67 K6
Tor Bryan ING CM4 ......260 C7
Tor Gv THMD SE28 ......334 F8
Torney Cl VGE SS16 ......324 F5
Toronto Av EHAM E6 ......334 A6
Toronto Rd IL IG1 ......316 C3
  TIL RM18 ......350 B7
Torquay Cl RAYL SS6 ......306 G2
Torquay Gv LOS SS9 ......327 M5
Torquay Gdns REDBR IG4 ......295 N8
Torquay Rd CHLM/WR CM1 ......218 C6
Torrance Cl EMPK RM11 ......319 H5
Torrens Cl SRTFD E15 ......315 J8
Torrens Rd SRTFD E15 ......315 J8
Torrington Cl CHLM/WR CM1 ......218 D6
Torrington Rd BCTR RM8 ......317 N5
Torrington Gdns LOU IG10 ......276 D5
Torsi Rd CVI SS8 ......344 G2

Tortoiseshell Cl CHTY IP2 ......29 N2
Tortoiseshell Wy BRTR CM7 ......145 H5
Tortosa Cl COLS CO2 ......152 C2
Torver Cl BRTR CM7 ......144 F8
Totham Hill Gn MAL CM9 ......198 F6
Totlands Dr COS CO15 ......182 A6
Tot La BSF CM23 ......138 A3
Totman Cl RAYL SS6 ......306 C7
Totman Crs RAYL SS6 ......306 C7
Totnes Wk CHLM/WR CM1 ......218 D5
Tottan Ter WCHPL E1 * 332 G4
Totteridge Cl RCOS CO16 ......181 N8
Totteridge Rd PEND EN3 ......252 A7
Toucan Cl SBN/FI SS3 ......350 C5
Toucan Wy COS CO15 ......182 A7
  VGE SS16 ......323 P3
Toulmin Rd RCHLM CM3 ......196 D8
Tovell's Rd IPNE IP4 ......25 N5
Tovey Av HOD EN11 ......208 D3
Tovey Cl WAB EN9 ......231 H2
Towcester Rd BOW E3 ......344 E1
Tower Av CHLM/WR CM1 ......4 E1
  LAIN SS15 ......303 K8
Tower Cl CHIG IG7 ......296 C6
  EPP CM16 ......234 C3
Tower Ct BRW CM14 ......281 M5
  WOS/PRIT SS0 ......18 C5
Tower Court Ms WOS/PRIT SS0 ......18 C5
Tower Cut RCOLE CO7 ......179 L7
Towerfield Cl SBN/FI SS3 ......350 D7
Towerfield Rd SBN/FI SS3 ......350 D7
Tower Hamlets Rd FSTGT E7 ......315 J6
  WALTH E17 ......290 D7
Tower Hl BRW CM14 ......281 M5
  MHAD SG10 ......160 E5
Tower Ms CLPT E5 * 314 B7
Tower Mill Rd IP IP1 ......24 G4
Tower Ramparts IP IP1 ......16 E5
Tower Rd BELV DA17 ......346 B2
  BXLYHN DA7 ......346 A5
  CHLM/WR CM1 ......238 C1
  COS CO15 ......6 E7
  EPP CM16 ......232 F9
  FX IP11 ......11 H5
  RCOLE CO7 ......153 J4
  WARE SG12 ......184 C5
Tower Side HOC/HUL SS5 * 287 H5
Towers Rd GRAYS RM17 ......349 M5
Tower St IP IP1 ......16 E4
  RCOLE CO7 ......179 L8
Tower Wharf GVW DA11 * 349 N4
Town Cft CHLM/WR CM1 ......217 P6
Town End Rd WIT CM8 ......197 H1
Townfield GTQUN CM6 * 92 C6
Townfield Rd RCFD SS4 ......308 G6
Townfield St CHLM/WR CM1 ......4 E2
Townfield Wk SBN/FI SS3 ......330 D2
Towngate BSDN SS14 ......3 J2
Town Ga Cl SRTFD E15 ......315 J8
Town Mead Rd WAB EN9 ......252 F4
Town Quay BARK IG11 ......334 D1
Town Rd ED N9 ......273 N8
Townsend Rd K/T/MI CO5 ......175 P7
Town Sq SLH/COR SS17 ......341 J5
Town St GTDUN CM6 ......92 B6
Towpath Rd UED N18 * 294 A2
Towse Cl RCOS CO16 ......181 M8
Tracyes Rd HLWS CM18 ......211 J5
Traddles Ct CHLM/WR CM1 * 137 J5
Trader Rd EHAM E6 ......334 C6
Trafalgar Av BROX EN10 ......208 C9
Trafalgar Cl IPNE IP4 ......25 N5
Trafalgar Gdns WCHPL E1 * 332 G4
Trafalgar Pl WANT E11 ......295 K8
Trafalgar Rd COLW CO3 ......127 H9
  ......6 D7
  RAIN RM13 ......336 E2
  SBN/FI SS3 ......330 C7
Trafalgar Sq BCAYW CM12 ......283 J5
  BRTR CM7 ......145 L2
  POP/IOD E14 ......332 F8
Trafalgar Yd HAR CO12 * 110 A5
Trafford Cl SRTFD E15 ......314 E7
Trajan Cl COLN CO4 ......128 C6
Tramway Av ED N9 ......273 N6
  SRTFD E15 ......314 G9
Tranmere Gv IP IP1 ......24 C1
Tranmere Rd ED N9 ......294 A2
Tranquil Hl ERITH DA8 ......346 D3
Trap's Hl LOU IG10 ......253 K6
Travers Cl WALTH E17 ......294 A5
Travers Wy PIT SS13 ......304 F9
Treby St BOW E3 ......332 C4
Tredegar Rd BOW E3 ......332 D2
Tredegar Sq BOW E3 ......332 C3
Treebeard Coppse
  RCHLM CM5 * 286 C2
Tree Cl ABR/ST RM4 ......277 J2
  COS CO15 ......182 A6
Treecot Dr LOS SS9 ......328 A2
Treelawn Cl LOS SS9 ......328 A2
Treelawn Gdns LOS SS9 ......328 A2
Tree Rd CAN/RD E16 ......333 M6
Tree Tops BRWN CM15 ......280 C7
Treetops FX IP11 ......35 H4
Treetops Vw LOU IG10 ......252 D7
Trefgarne Rd DAGE RM10 ......317 P4
Trefoil Cl CHTY IP2 ......24 C7
Tregelles Rd HOD EN11 ......208 D5
Tregenna Cl CHLM/WR CM1 ......274 F9
Trego Rd HOM E9 ......314 F3
Trehearn Rd BARK/HLT IG6 ......296 E4
Trelawney Cl WAN E11 ......314 F5
Trelawny Cl WALTH E17 ......294 E8
Terrance Gdns
  GDMY/SEVK IG3 ......317 H5
Trenchard Crs CHLM/WR CM1 ......218 C4
Trenders Av RAYL SS6 ......306 E1
Trenham Av THMD SE28 ......335 J8
Trent TIL RM18 ......351 K2
Trent Gdns CHLM/WR CM1 ......320 A1

Trentbridge Cl BARK/HLT IG6 ......296 G3
Trent Cl BOC CM0 ......
  WICKW SS12 ......305 J1
Trent Ct WAN E11 ......295 P8
Trent Gdns STHGT/OAK N14 ......272 A5
Trent Pk EBAR EN4 * 272 B1
Trent Rd BKHH IG9 ......275 L7
  CHLM/WR CM1 ......217 K6
  IPSE IP5 ......26 N9
  WIT CM8 ......197 H2
Trentwood Side
  ENC/FH EN2 ......272 E2
Tresco Gdns CRW RM5 ......298 B2
Tresco Gns GDMY/SEVK IG3 ......316 C4
Tresham Rd BARK IG11 ......316 C9
Tresillian Av WICKW SS12 ......305 M2
Treslian Av DAGW RM9 ......335 M1
Trevelyan Av HARLE 316 A6
Trevelyan Cl DART DA1 ......347 L9
Trevelyan Rd SRTFD E15 ......315 H5
Trevera Ct CHES/WCR EN8 * 252 B5
Trevereux Hill OXTED ......208 C...
Treves Cl WCHMH N21 ......272 E4
Trevithick Dr DART DA1 ......347 L9
Trevor Rd WFD IG8 ......295 K4
Trevose Rd DAGW RM9 ......282 C9
Trews Gdns K/T/MI CO5 ......173 H2
Triangle Ct CAN/RD E16 ......333 N5
Trimble Cl ING CM4 ......260 C5
Trimley Cl BSDN SS14 ......3 J2
  RCOS CO16 ......181 L9
Trimley Rd KIR/NAC IP10 ......33 H7
Trindehay LAIN SS15 ......323 M1
Trinder Wy WICKW SS12 ......304 F1
Tring Cl BARK/HLT IG6 ......296 D9
  HARH RM3 ......299 L1
Tring Gdns HARH RM3 ......299 L1
Trinidad Gdns DAGE RM10 ......318 C9
Trinidad St POP/IOD E14 ......332 C7
Trinity Av EN EN1 ......273 L5
  FX IP11 ......11 H3
  WOS/PRIT SS0 ......18 C5
Trinity Buoy Whf
  POP/IOD E14 * 332 G5
Trinity Cl BCAYE CM11 ......284 B4
  BSF CM23 ......137 L8
  K/T/MI CO5 ......202 F5
  KESG IP5 ......26 E4
  LAIN SS15 ......303 K9
  MGTR CO11 ......106 C5
  RAYL SS6 ......307 H6
  RCOLE CO7 ......153 K6
  WAN E11 ......315 H4
Trinity Gdns CAN/RD E16 ......333 J5
Trinity La CHES/WCR EN8 ......252 B2
Trinity Link HVHL CB9 ......41 K2
Trinity Ms HSTD CO9 * 97 N7
  K/T/MI CO5 ......202 F5
Trinity Pk CHING E4 ......294 C3
Trinity Rd BARK/HLT IG6 ......296 D7
  BCAYE CM11 ......303 K1
  CHLM/GWD CM2 ......97 N7
  HSTD CO9 ......106 C5
  MGTR CO11 ......184 B2
  WARE SG12 ......294 C3
Trinity Sq COL CO1 * 8 C6
  CAN/RD E16 ......333 J5
  COL CO1 ......
  ENC/FH EN2 ......273 H1
Trinity St COLW CO3 ......127 H9
  RAIN RM13 ......336 E2
  SBN/FI SS3 ......330 C7
  CHING E4 ......294 C3
Trinity Wood Rd
  HOC/HUL SS5 ......288 B8
Trinovantian Wy BRTR CM7 ......145 K4
Tripat Cl SLH/COR SS17 ......324 C9
Tripton Rd HLWS CM18 ......210 F4
Tristram Cl WALTH E17 ......314 E7
Tristram Dr ED N9 ......273 M9
Triton Wy SBF/HAD SS7 ......306 E9
Triumph Av COS CO15 ......206 D5
Triumph Cl CDW/CHF RM16 ......348 F2
Triumph Rd EHAM E6 ......334 A6
Troon Gdns IPNE IP4 ......26 A3
Troon St WCHPL E1 ......332 E6
Troopers Dr HARH RM3 ......299 J1
Trotters Fld BRTR CM7 ......145 L3
Trotter's Gap WARE SG12 ......185 H8
Trotters Rd HLWS CM18 ......211 J6
Trotwood CHIG IG7 ......296 E5
Trotwood Cl CHLM/WR CM1 ......217 M4
Troubridge Cl RCHLM CM5 ......287 J1
Trowbridge Rd HARH RM3 ......299 J3
  HOM E9 ......314 G2
Troys Cha RCHLM CM3 ......170 D7
Trueloves La ING CM4 ......259 P7
Truman Cl LAIN SS15 ......303 H9
Trumpington Rd FSTGT E7 ......315 J6
Trunette Rd COS CO15 ......6 A4
The Trunnions RCFD SS4 ......308 G6
Truro Crs KESG IP5 ......26 F5
  RAYL SS6 ......306 F2
Truro Gdns IL IG1 ......315 P2
Truro Rd WALTH E17 ......294 C8
Trusedale Rd EHAM E6 ......334 A6
Trusses Rd BOC CM0 ......226 C8
Trustons Gdns EMPK RM11 ......318 F2
Trust Rd CHES/WCR EN8 ......252 B4
Tryfan Cl REDBR IG4 ......295 N9
Tucker Dr WIT CM8 ......197 J1
Tucker's Rw BSF CM23 ......137 L8
Tuck Rd HARH RM3 ......318 F8
Tudder Gn BARK/HLT IG6 ......314 C2
Tuddenham Av IPNE IP4 ......17 H2
Tuddenham La KESG IP5 ......26 A1
Tuddenham Rd IPNE IP4 ......17 H2
  CHLM/WR CM1 ......4 D2
  GPK RM2 ......298 F7

SLH/COR SS17 ......341 M1
Tudor Chambers PIT SS13 * 324 G1
Tudor Cl BRWN CM15 ......281 J5
  CHESW EN7 ......251 N1
  CHIG IG7 ......296 B1
  COS CO15 ......206 F3
  ING CM4 ......292 B4
  LOS SS9 ......307 M7
  RAYL SS6 ......307 J5
  RCOLE CO7 ......179 K5
  RIPS/CAP IP9 ......85 M8
  SBF/HAD SS7 ......326 C3
  WARE SG12 ......185 N4
  WFD IG8 ......295 L2
  WOTN CO14 ......159 L4
Tudor Ct K/T/MI CO5 * 202 F5
  LAIN SS15 ......303 N5
  WALTH E17 ......314 C2
Tudor Crs BARK/HLT IG6 ......296 D5
  ENC/FH EN2 ......251 H9
Tudor Dr GPK RM2 ......298 F8
Tudor Gdns GPK RM2 ......298 F8
  LOS SS9 ......327 N5
  SBN/FI SS3 ......330 C8
  UPMR RM14 ......319 P4
Tudor Gn COS CO15 ......206 F3
Tudor Man PIT SS13 * 324 G1
Tudor Ms LOS SS9 ......307 M7
Tudor Ri BROX EN10 ......208 B9
Tudor Rd BARK IG11 ......316 C9
  CHING E4 ......294 A2
  CVI SS8 ......344 A2
  ED N9 ......273 N6
  EHAM E6 ......333 M1
  LOS SS9 ......307 M7
  SUD CO10 ......20 C1
  WOS/PRIT SS0 ......328 E4
Tudor Rose Cl COLW CO3 ......126 F8
Tudor Sq WARE SG12 * 184 A3
Tudor Vls CHESW EN7 * 229 K8
Tudor Wk WARE SG12 * 184 A3
Tudor Wy HOC/HUL SS5 ......308 A3
  STHGT/OAK N14 ......272 C7
  WAB EN9 ......252 C3
Tudor Wy COLS CO2 ......151 J4
Tudwick Rd MAL CM9 ......199 M7
Tufnell Wy COLN CO4 ......127 M5
Tufted Cl BRTR CM77 ......144 F9
Turfer Rd CHIG IG7 ......296 G2
Tufton Rd RAYL SS6 ......307 H6
Tugboat St THMD SE28 ......334 F9
Tugby Pl CHLM/WR CM1 ......217 M5
Tukes Wy SAFWS CB11 ......65 N1
Tulip Cl BRWN CM15 ......280 E4
  EHAM E6 ......218 D4
  EHAM E6 ......333 P5
  HARH RM3 ......299 J5
Tulip Gdns CHING E4 ......274 C9
  IL IG1 ......316 C9
Tulip Wk COLW CO4 ......128 E8
Tulip Wy RCOS CO16 ......181 H4
Tumbler Rd HLWS CM18 ......211 H4
Tumbling Bay Weir
  WARE SG12 ......184 C2
Tumulus Wy COLS CO2 ......151 J4
Tunbridge Rd SOSN SS2 ......328 C4
Tunfield Rd HOD EN11 ......208 E2
Tunley Gn POP/IOD E14 ......333 M5
Tunmarsh La PLSTW E13 ......333 M3
Tunnan Leys EHAM E6 ......334 B6
Tunnel Av GNWCH SE10 ......332 C9
Tunnmeade HLW CM20 ......211 H2
Tunstall Av BARK/HLT IG6 ......297 L3
Tunstall Cl PIT SS13 ......325 H1
  RCOS CO16 ......180 E8
Tupelo Rd LEY E10 ......314 E4
Turin Rd ED N9 ......273 P6
Turin St CHTY IP2 ......25 K7
Turkentine Cl SUD CO10 ......61 N5
Turkey Cock La COLW CO3 ......149 M4
Turkey Oaks CHLM/WR CM1 ......5 J2
Turkey St EN EN1 ......251 N5
Turley Cl SRTFD E15 ......333 H1
Turnage Rd BCTR RM8 ......317 M3
Turnberry Cl EHAM E6 ......106 A3
Turner Ct BRTR CM77 ......170 C1
  HVHL CB9 ......40 G2
  RCOLE CO7 ......153 K5
  SBN/FI SS3 ......330 E6
  SUD CO10 ......20 C1
Turner Rd COLN CO4 ......127 P5
  COLN CO4 ......128 A5
  IPSE IP5 ......30 C2
  WALTH E17 ......294 F8
Turners Cl CHONG CM5 ......235 L8
Turners Crs BSF CM23 ......161 P1
Turner's HI CHES/WCR EN8 ......230 A9
Turner St CAN/RD E16 ......333 M6
  WCHPL E1 ......332 F4
Turnfield Vls BROX EN10 ......230 C5
Turnors HLWW/ROY CM19 ......11 P8
Turnpike Cl RCOLE CO7 ......103 P8
Turnpike La CDW/CHF RM16 ......350 E3
Turnpike Pl BRW CM14 ......333 K5
Turnstone End COLN CO4 ......128 G7
Turold Rd SLH/COR SS17 ......341 M1
Turp Av CDW/CHF RM16 ......339 M9
Turpin Av CRW RM5 ......298 A9
Turpington Cl 257 D7
Turpin La ERITH DA8 ......346 F4
Turpins Av COS CO15 ......182 D8
Turpins Cl COS CO15 ......182 D8
  WFD IG8 ......296 A2
The Turpins BSDN SS14 ......3 J2
Turret La IPNE IP4 ......16 E6

Turstan Rd WIT CM8 ....197 H4
Tusser Ct WIT CM8 ....172 A6
Tusser Ct CHLM/GWD CM2 ....240 C2
Tutors Wy CCOW CO5 ....127 H8
Tutors Wy RCHLM CM3 ....287 H1
Tweed TIL RM18 ....351 K2
Tweed Cl HSTD CO9 ....97 N8
Tweedmouth Rd PLSTW E13 ....333 L2
Twelve Acre ROM RM1 ....298 C4
Twelve Acre Ap KESC IP5 ....26 C4
Twelve Ayres BRTR CM7 ....145 N5
Twelvetrees Crs BOW E3 ....332 F4
Twentyfirst St STSD CM24 ....139 J4
Twentyman Ct WFD IG8 ....295 K2
Twickenham Rd WAN E11 ....314 C4
Twig Folly Cl BOW E3 ....332 A2
Twig Folly Whf BETH E2 * 332 A2
Twigg Cl ERITH DA8 ....346 D5
Twine Cl BARK IG11 ....335 J3
Twine Ter BOW E3 * 332 A2
Twining Rd COLW CO5 ....151 H2
Twin Oaks CHLM/GWD CM2 ....218 F7
Twin Turnps Wy THMD SE28 ....335 H7
Twitten La CHLM/GWD CM2 ....240 A6
Twitty Fee RCHLM CM3 ....242 D1
Twizzlefoot Br BOCMO 291 N1
Two Acres RIPS/CAP IP9 ....28 D8
Twyford Av SBN/FI SS3 ....330 F2
Twyford Bury La BSF CM23 ....162 D1
Twyford Ct BSF CM23 ....137 L2
Twyford Gdns BSF CM23 ....162 C1
Twyford Rd BSF CM23 ....137 M9
   IL IG1 ....316 D7
Twyzel Rd CVI SS8 ....344 F1
Tyas Rd CAN/RD E16 ....333 J4
Tyberry Rd PEND EN3 ....273 N2
Tyburn Hl RCOLW CO6 ....124 F1
The Tyburns
   BRHW/HUT CM13 ....281 M8
Tycehurst Hl LOU IG10 ....276 A3
Tydeman Cl COLW CO3 ....150 F2
Tye Common Rd
   BCAYW CM12 ....302 F2
Tyefields PIT SS13 ....305 H8
Tye Green Rd RBSF CM22 ....114 F8
Tye Green Village
   HLWS IP4 * 210 G6
Tyehurst Crs COLN CO4 ....128 D5
Tyelands BCAYW CM12 ....282 G8
Tye La RCOLE CO7 ....155 M1
Tye Rd RCOLE CO7 ....129 M8
Tyfield Cl CHEX/WCR EN8 ....209 N8
Tyle Gn EMPK RM11 ....299 K9
Tylehurst Gdns IL IG1 ....316 D7
Tyler Av LAIN SS15 ....303 K9
   RCOS CO16 ....206 C1
Tylers SAFWN CB10 ....52 D9
Tylers Av BCAYW CM12 ....283 J5
   SOS SS1 ....19 G4
Tylers Cswy HERT/BAY SG13 ....228 B1
Tylers Cl CHLM/GWD CM2 ....240 A4
Tylers Crs HCH RM12 ....319 H7
Tylers Gn FX IP11 ....54 F4
Tylers Ride RCHLM CM3 ....287 H1
Tylers St WLWW/ROY CM19 ....209 N8
Tyler St CHTY IP2 ....25 L7
   HAR CO12 ....110 A3
Tyler Wy BRW CM14 ....298 C4
Tylewood BSF/HAD SS7 ....326 F4
Tylney Av RCFD SS4 ....308 F4
Tylney Cft HLWW/ROY CM19 ....210 C5
Tylney Rd FSTGT E7 ....315 M6
Tylneys Rd HSTD CO9 ....98 B8
Tyms Wy RAYL SS6 ....307 H3
Tyndale Cl HOC/HUL SS5 ....286 G5
Tyndale Dr COS CO15 ....206 F3
Tyndales La RCHLM CM3 ....242 E5
Tyndall Rd LEY E10 ....314 F4
Tyne Cl UPMR RM14 ....320 A1
Tynedale Sq COLN CO4 ....128 C3
Tyne Gdns SOCK/AV RM15 ....337 P7
Tynemouth Cl EHAM E6 ....334 C6
Tynemouth Dr EN EN1 ....251 M8
Tyne Sq BETH E2 ....332 F2
Tyrell Pl BRWN CM15 * 281 J7
Tyrell Ri RBRW/HUT CM13 ....300 F2
Tyrells HOC/HUL SS5 ....307 N3
Tyrells Cl RCHLM CM1 ....218 D7
   UPMR RM14 ....319 N4
Tyrells Wy CHLM/GWD CM2 ....240 E5
Tyrone Cl BCAYE CM11 ....303 K1
   IP IP1 ....24 E1
Tyrone Rd BCAYE CM11 ....303 K1
   EHAM E6 ....334 A2
   SOS SS1 ....329 P8
Tyrrel Dr SOS SS1 ....6 B2
Tyrrell Rd SBF/HAD SS7 ....325 N4
Tyrrells Hall Cl GRAYS RM17 ....349 N4
Tyrrells Rd BCAYE CM11 ....303 L1
Tyrwhitt La CHLM/GWD CM2 ....210 G6
Tysea Hl ABR/ST RM4 ....278 E3
Tysea Rd HLWS CM18 ....210 G6
Tysoe Av PEND EN3 ....252 C6
Tyssen Md RCHLM CM5 ....219 K3
Tyssen Pl SOCK/AV RM15 ....338 F2
Tythe Barn Wy RCHLM CM5 * 264 F9
Tythe Cl CHLM/GWD CM2 ....240 C7
The Tythings HSTD CO9 ....97 N8

U

Uamvar St POP/IOD E14 ....332 E1
Uckfield Rd PEND EN3 ....252 A7
Udall Gdns CRW RM5 ....253 P5
Ullin St POP/IOD E14 ....332 F5
Ullswater Av FX IP11 ....35 N4
Ullswater Cl BRWN CM15 ....144 F8
Ullswater Rd SBF/HAD SS7 ....306 B8
Ullswater Wy HCH RM12 ....318 F7

Ulster Av IP IP1 ....24 E2
   SBN/FI SS3 ....330 B8
Ulting Hall Rd MAL CM9 ....221 H4
Ulting La MAL CM9 ....220 C5
Ulting Rd RCHLM CM3 ....196 F9
Ulting Wy WICKE SS11 ....285 M8
Ulverston Rd WALTH E17 ....294 C6
Una Rd HAR CO12 ....109 P4
   PIT SS13 ....305 L9
Undercliffe Gdns LOS SS9 ....328 A6
Undercliff Rd East FX IP11 ....35 M7
Undercliff Rd West FX IP11 ....11 L4
Underhill Rd SBF/HAD SS7 ....326 B3
Underne Av STHGT/OAK N14 ....272 A8
Underwood Rd CHING E4 ....294 E2
   WFD IG8 ....295 N4
Underwood Sq LOS SS9 ....327 M4
Union Cl WAN E11 ....314 C6
Union Dr WCHPL E1 * 332 B4
Union La RCFD SS4 ....308 D5
Union Rd COS CO15 ....206 F4
Union St IPNE IP4 * 17 F4
   SRTFD E15 ....332 C1
Unity Cl COLS CO2 ....152 C2
Unity Rd PEND EN3 ....251 P7
Unity St IPSE IP5 ....25 M7
University Wy DART DA1 ....347 J8
   EHAM E6 ....334 B7
Uphall Rd IL IG1 ....316 C7
Upland Cl BCAYW CM12 ....282 G4
Upland Court Rd HARH RM3 ....299 L6
Upland Crs K/T/MI CO5 ....202 F5
Upland Dr BCAYW CM12 ....282 G4
   COLN CO4 ....128 D5
Upland Rd BCAYW CM12 ....282 G4
   EPP CM16 ....232 E4
   IPNE IP4 ....25 P5
   K/T/MI CO5 ....202 F5
   LOS SS9 ....328 B6
   PLSTW E13 ....333 K4
Uplands WARE SG12 ....184 C2
Uplands Av WALTH E17 ....294 A7
Uplands Cl HOC/HUL SS5 ....308 A2
   SBF/HAD SS7 ....325 N2
Uplands Crs SUD CO10 ....6 C7
Uplands Dr CHLM/GWD CM2 ....20 D1
Uplands Dr CHLM/WR CM1 ....218 C4
Uplands Park Rd ENC/FH EN2 ....272 F1
   RAYL SS6 ....306 G3
Uplands Rd CHDH RM6 ....297 L2
   COS CO15 ....6 C7
   HOC/HUL SS5 ....308 A2
   SBF/HAD SS7 ....325 N2
   SUD CO10 ....20 D1
   WFD IG8 ....295 P4
The Uplands LOU IG10 * 276 A2
Uplands Wy WCHMH N21 ....272 F4
Upminster Rd North
   RAIN RM13 ....337 H3
Upminster Rd South
   RAIN RM13 ....336 F4
Upney Cl HCH RM12 ....319 H7
Upney La BARK IG11 ....316 G9
Uppark Dr GNTH/NBYPK IG2 ....316 D1
Upper Acres WIT CM8 ....171 N8
Upper Av PIT SS13 ....305 K7
Upper Bank St POP/IOD E14 ....332 E8
Upper Barclay St IPNE IP4 * 17 F5
Upper Branston Rd COS CO15 ....6 D7
Upper Brentwood Rd
   GPK RM2 ....299 H8
Upper Bridge Rd
   CHLM/GWD CM2 ....4 D5
Upper Brook St IPNE IP4 ....16 E5
Upper Chapel St HSTD CO9 ....97 P6
Upper Cha CHLM/GWD CM2 ....4 D7
   RCHLM CM5 ....267 N7
Upper Clabdens WARE SG12 ....184 C3
Upper Cornsland BRW CM14 ....280 G9
Upper East St SUD CO10 ....20 E4
Upper Farm Rd SUD CO10 ....57 L2
Upper Fenn Rd HSTD CO9 ....98 B8
Upperfield Dr FX IP11 ....35 L5
Upper Fourth Av FOS CO13 ....158 G9
Upper High St IP IP1 ....16 D2
Upper Holly Hill Rd
   BELV DA17 ....346 A3
Upper Holt St RCOLW CO6 ....124 B1
Upper Hook HLWS CM18 ....210 C5
Upper Lambricks RAYL SS6 ....307 H3
Upper Market Rd
   WICKW SS12 ....285 J8
Upper Mayne La HOD EN11 ....208 D6
Upper Mayne LAIN SS15 ....2 B3
Upper Mealines HLWS CM18 ....211 H6
Upper Mill Fld GTDUN CM6 ....141 M7
Upper Moors RCHLM CM3 ....193 N5
Upper North St POP/IOD E14 ....332 E6
Upper Orwell St IPNE IP4 ....17 F5
Upper Pk HLW CM20 ....12 D5
   LOU IG10 ....275 N4
Upper Park Rd BELV DA17 ....346 A2
   COS CO15 ....6 E6
   RCOLE CO7 ....179 K6
   WICKW SS12 ....305 J3
Upper Rainham Rd
   HCH RM12 ....318 C3
Upper Raypits RCFD SS4 * 289 K6
Upper Rd BCAYE CM11 ....304 C2
   PLSTW E13 ....333 K3
   SUD CO10 ....75 N1
Upper Roman Rd
   CHLM/GWD CM2 ....5 G6
Upper Ryle BRW CM14 ....280 E6
Upper Second Av FOS CO13 ....158 F9
Upper Shott CHESW EN7 ....229 L5
Upper Stonefield
   HLWW/ROY CM19 ....12 E6
Upper Swaines EPP CM16 ....232 C9
Upper Third Av FOS CO13 ....158 F9
Upperton Rd East PLSTW E13 ....333 M3
Upperton Rd West
   PLSTW E13 ....333 M3

Upper Trinity Rd HSTD CO9 ....97 P7
Upper Walthamstow Rd
   WALTH E17 ....294 G8
Upshers SAFWS CB11 ....65 N3
Upshire Rd WAB IG9 ....253 K5
Upsons Wy KESC IP5 ....27 K3
Upton Av FSTGT E7 ....315 K9
   SLH/COR SS17 ....341 L8
Upton Cl IPNE IP4 ....17 J4
Upton La FSTGT E7 ....315 L8
Upton Park Rd FSTGT E7 ....315 L9
Upway RAYL SS6 ....306 G4
The Upway BSDN SS14 ....3 G1
Urban Av HCH RM12 ....319 H5
Urban Rd BSF CM23 ....137 N7
Urmond Rd CVI SS8 ....344 D1
Urswick Rd DAGW RM9 ....317 M9
Usher Rd BOW E3 ....332 C2
Usk Rd SOCK/AV RM15 ....337 P6
Usk St BETH E2 ....332 F2
Usterdale Rd SAFWN CB10 ....51 M7
Uttons Av LOS SS9 ....327 N6
Uvedale Rd DAGE RM10 ....317 P5
   ENC/FH EN2 ....273 J4
Uxbridge Cl WICKE SS11 ....305 L1
Uxbridge Crs IPSE IP5 ....31 J1

V

Vaagen Rd CVI SS8 ....344 F1
Vadsoe Rd CVI SS8 ....344 E1
Valance Av CHING E4 ....275 J7
Valance Rd SAFWS CB11 ....87 P1
Valance Wy VGE SS16 ....323 K2
Vale Av SOSN SS2 ....329 H4
Vale Cl BRWN CM15 ....280 C4
   COLN CO4 ....128 C3
Vale Ct ING CM4 * 261 N8
Vale End CHLM/GWD CM2 ....240 B7
Vale La RIPS/CAP IP9 ....82 C5
Valence Av BCTR RM8 ....317 L3
Valence Cir BCTR RM8 ....317 L3
Valence Dr CHESW EN7 ....229 M7
Valence Rd ERITH DA8 ....346 C5
Valence Wood Rd BCTR RM8 ....317 L5
Valenta Cl COL CO1 ....128 D9
Valentine Rd HOM E9 * 314 A5
Valentines ING CM4 ....261 N7
Valentines Dr IL IG1 ....316 C3
Valentines Wy DAGE RM10 ....318 D4
Valerian Cl WIT CM8 ....171 L1
Valerian Wy SRTFD E15 ....333 H5
Vale Rd FSTGT E7 ....315 L8
The Vale BRW CM14 ....280 F7
   ING CM4 ....283 L1
   STHGT/OAK N14 ....272 A8
   VGE SS16 ....324 C5
   WFD IG8 ....295 K4
Valetta Gv PLSTW E13 ....333 K2
Valfreda Wy RCOLE CO7 ....153 J5
Valiant Cl ROMW/RG RM7 ....277 J8
Valiant Rd KESG IP5 ....27 M4
Valiant Wy EHAM E6 ....334 A5
Valkyrie Cl MAL CM9 ....225 J1
Valkyrie Rd WOS/PRIT SS0 ....328 E6
Vallance Cl SOSN SS2 ....329 M3
Vallance Cl WARE SG12 ....184 E5
Vallentin Rd WALTH E17 ....294 F8
Valletta Cl CHLM/WR CM1 ....4 D1
Valley Br CHLM/WR CM1 ....218 A5
Valleybridge Rd COS CO15 ....182 B8
Valley Cl COLW CO5 ....151 H5
   IP IP1 ....16 A2
   LOU IG10 ....276 A5
   MGTR CO11 ....81 N8
   WAB EN9 ....252 F2
Valley Crs RCOLW CO6 ....127 H4
Valley Fields Crs ENC/FH EN2 ....272 F1
Valley Hi LOU IG10 ....275 P6
Valley La RIPS/CAP IP9 ....29 P6
Valley Rd BCAYE CM11 ....283 J6
   BRTR CM7 ....145 K2
   COS CO15 ....182 B8
   ERITH DA8 ....346 B2
   HAR CO12 ....109 N6
   IP IP1 ....16 A2
   RCOLE CO7 ....153 K6
   SOCK/AV RM15 ....337 P6
   SUD CO10 ....61 P1
Valley Side CHING E4 ....274 D7
Valley Vw BRTR CM7 ....94 C2
   CHESW EN7 ....229 H7
   RCOLW CO6 ....127 H4
Valley Vw Cl COLN CO4 ....128 B4
Valleyview Dr IPNE IP4 ....26 C7
Valley Walk FX IP11 ....35 J6
Valmar Av SLH/COR SS17 ....341 J4
Valognes Av WALTH E17 ....294 B5
Vanburgh Cl CAN/RD E16 ....333 N5
Vancouver Rd BROX EN10 ....230 D4
Vandenburg Cir BRTR CM7 ....95 J3
Vanderbilt Av RAYL SS6 ....286 F8
Vanderwalt Av CVI SS8 ....344 G2
Van Dieman's La
   CHLM/GWD CM2 ....5 J7
Van Dieman's Rd
   CHLM/GWD CM2 ....5 J7
Van Diemans Pass CVI SS8 ....345 J2
Vandome Cl CAN/RD E16 ....333 L4
Van Dyck Rd COLW CO3 ....151 K1
Vange Corner Dr
   SLH/COR SS17 ....324 A5
Vange Hill Dr VGE SS16 ....324 A5
Vange Park Rd SLH/COR SS17 ....324 A5
Vanguard Cl CAN/RD E16 ....333 K5
   ROMW/RG RM7 ....277 J9
The Vanguards SBN/FI SS3 ....330 E7
Vanguard Wy BRTR CM7 ....145 L2

Vanners Rd HVHL CB9 ....41 K4
Vansittart Rd FSTGT E7 ....315 K6
Vansittart St HAR CO12 ....15 F4
Vantorts Cl SBW CM21 ....157 M3
Vantorts Rd SBW CM21 ....187 M3
Vaughan Av CHLM/GWD CM2 ....217 N5
Vardon Dr LOS SS9 ....327 L3
Varley Rd CAN/RD E16 ....333 L6
Varney Cl CHESW EN7 ....229 L6
Vaughan Av HCH RM12 ....319 J6
Vaughan Cl BRTR CM77 ....144 C4
   RCFD SS4 ....308 F2
Vaughan Gdns IL IG1 ....316 A2
Vaughan Rd SRTFD E15 ....315 J8
Vaughan St
   BERM/RHTH SE16 ....332 C9
   CHTY IP2 ....25 K7
Vaughan Williams Rd
   LAIN SS15 ....303 K7
Vaughan Williams Wy
   BRW CM14 ....300 G2
Vaulx Rd CVI SS8 ....344 E1
Vaux Av HAR CO12 ....110 A7
Vauxhall Av COS CO15 ....206 D6
Vauxhall Dr BCAYW CM12 ....144 G4
Veerman Pk SAFWN CB10 * 65 P2
Vega Cl COL CO1 ....128 D9
Velizy Av HLW CM20 ....13 H4
Vellacotts CHLM/WR CM1 ....218 A4
Venables Cl SS9 ....344 F2
   DAGE RM10 ....318 A6
Venette Cl RAIN RM13 ....336 C5
Venlo Rd CVI SS8 * 326 E9
Venmore Dr GTDUN CM6 ....141 M6
Venners Cl BRW CM14 ....246 D7
Venta Wy MAL CM9 ....244 C2
Ventnor Dr COS CO15 ....182 B5
Ventnor Gdns BARK IG11 ....316 F8
Ventris Cl CHY IP2 ....222 C5
Ventura Dr COL CO1 ....128 D9
Venue St POP/IOD E14 ....332 E5
Veny Crs HCH RM12 ....319 J7
Vera Av WCHMH N21 ....272 F4
Vera Cl LYNN G FSTGT E7 ....315 K7
Vera Rd BCAYE CM11 ....284 F6
Verbena Cl CAN/RD E16 ....333 J4
   SOCK/AV RM15 ....338 F6
Verderers Rd CHIG IG7 ....297 H2
Vere Gdns IP IP1 ....25 L3
Vere Rd LOU IG10 ....276 D3
Vermeer Crs SBN/FI SS3 ....330 F6
Vermeer Ride CHLM/WR CM1 ....218 E4
Vermont Cl COS CO15 ....7 J1
   ENC/FH EN2 ....272 G5
   PIT SS13 ....305 H7
Vermont Crs IPNE IP4 ....17 C2
Vermont Rd IPNE IP4 ....17 C2
Verney Gdns DAGW RM9 ....317 M6
Vernon Av CHING E4 ....274 E5
Vernon Gdns DAGW RM9 ....317 M7
Vernon Av MNPK E12 ....316 A6
   PEND EN5 ....252 B6
   RAYL SS6 ....306 E3
   WFD IG8 ....295 L3
Vernon Cnr ING CM4 ....261 L7
Vernon Crs RBRW/HUT CM13 ....281 M7
Vernon Rd BOW E3 ....332 C2
   CRW RM5 ....298 B2
   GDMY/SEVK IG3 ....316 C3
   LOS SS9 ....327 M5
   SRTFD E15 ....315 H8
   WALTH E17 ....294 C8
   WAN E11 ....315 H3
Vernon's Cl RBSF CM22 ....115 J2
Vernons Rd RCOLW CO6 ....125 K2
Vernon St CHTY IP2 ....25 K7
Vernon Wy BRTR CM7 ....145 M1
Veronica Cl HARH KN3 ....299 H4
Veronica Wk COLN CO4 ....128 B4
Veronique Gdns
   GNTH/NBYPK IG2 ....296 D9
Verulam Av WALTH E17 ....314 C2
Vesta Cl RCOLW CO6 ....147 N4
Vestry Cl LAIN SS15 ....303 K8
Vestry Rd WALTH E17 ....294 E9
Vexil Cl PUR RM19 ....348 A2
Veyses End RCOLE CO7 ....80 A7
Viaduct Rd CHLM/WR CM1 ....4 E3
   WARE SG12 ....184 B4
The Viaduct SWFD E18 * 295 H4
Vian Av PEND EN5 ....252 B5
Viborg Gdns MAL CM9 ....243 P2
Vicarage Cl BRTR CM7 ....170 G4
   BRW CM14 ....119 M8
   CVI SS8 ....344 A2
   ERITH DA8 ....346 B4
   LAIN SS15 ....303 K9
   MAL CM9 ....200 C8
   RIPW IP8 ....44 C2
Vicarage Crs RCHLM CM3 ....196 E8
Vicarage Dr BARK IG11 ....316 D9
   COS CO15 ....6 D5
Vicarage Fld SUD CO10 ....61 L5
Vicarage Hill SLH/COR SS17 ....326 A5
Vicarage La BOC CMO 248 B6
   BSF CM23 ....137 K5
   CHIG IG7 ....276 F2
   EHAM E6 ....334 A3
   EPP CM16 ....234 B5
   GTDUN CM6 ....141 M5
   IL IG1 ....316 E3
   LAIN SS15 ....303 L8
   RBSF CM22 ....114 C2
   RCOS CO16 ....157 J4
   RIPS/CAP IP9 ....28 C2
   RIPW IP8 ....47 L2
   SUD CO10 ....47 L2
   WOTN CO14 ....159 K6
Vicarage Meadow BOC CMO 269 J6
   HSTD CO9 ....97 P7
Vicarage Ms CHLM/GWD CM2 ....240 E4

   SBN/FI SS3 ....330 E6
Vicarage Rd BRTR CM7 ....94 C2
   CHLM/GWD CM2 ....239 P2
   CHLM/WR CM1 ....216 D6
   DAGE RM10 ....318 A9
   EMPK RM11 ....318 F3
   FX IP11 ....233 K8
   FX IP11 ....10 D2
   LEY E10 ....314 E2
   RCHLM CM3 ....192 F2
   SUD CO10 ....58 F1
   WARE SG12 ....184 B3
   WFD IG8 ....295 P4
Vicarage Sq GRAYS RM17 ....349 K4
Vicarage Wd HLW CM20 ....210 G2
Vicar's Cl EN EN1 ....273 K1
   SRTFD E15 ....333 K1
Vicar's Moor La WCHMH N21 ....272 F6
Vicars Orch SUD CO10 ....60 B5
Vicerons Pl BSF CM23 ....162 A1
Viceroy Ct COLS CO2 ....152 C5
Viceroy Crs SLH/COR SS17 * 340 C2
Vickers Rd ERITH DA8 ....346 C3
   SOSN SS2 ....8 A5
Victor Ap HCH RM12 ....319 J3
Victor Av PIT SS13 ....305 J5
Victoria Av CHELM CM3 ....319 J5
   HOC/HUL SS5 ....308 A6
Victor Dr LOS SS9 ....328 A6
Victor Gdns HCH RM12 ....319 J3
   HOC/HUL SS5 ....308 A2
Victoria Av CDW/CHF RM16 ....359 M9
   LAIN SS15 ....305 J8
   RCOLE CO7 ....153 J4
Victoria Ct MAL CM9 * 222 C9
   WICKE SS11 * 305 M2
   WOS/PRIT SS0 * 18 C5
Victoria Crs CHLM/WR CM1 ....4 E1
   LAIN SS15 ....303 J7
   MGTR CO11 ....106 B4
   WICKW SS12 ....284 G9
Victoria Dock Rd CAN/RD E16 ....333 P5
   SBN/FI SS3 ....331 H4
Victoria Esp K/T/MI CO5 ....202 G7
Victoria Gdns CO15 ....128 C4
   SAFWS CB11 ....51 M9
Victoria Ga HLWE CM17 ....211 J3
Victoria Park Rd HOM E9 ....332 H1
   RCOLE CO7 ....179 L7
Victoria Plaza SOSN SS2 * 19 F3
Victoria Rd BARK IG11 ....316 C8
   BKHH IG9 ....275 N8
   BRW CM14 ....275 H7
   CHLM/WR CM1 ....5 H2
   COLW CO5 ....151 M1
   COS CO15 ....7 J3
   DAGE RM10 ....318 D7
   ED N9 ....273 L9
   ERITH DA8 ....346 D4
   FX IP11 ....11 H5
   HVHL CB9 ....9 K2
   LAIN SS15 ....303 H8
   LOS SS9 ....327 P6
   MAL CM9 ....222 B9
   PLSTW E13 ....333 K2
   RAYL SS6 ....307 H4
   RCHLM CM5 ....266 A5
   RCHLM CM3 ....286 G2
   RCOS CO16 ....192 E9
   ROM RM1 ....298 E9
   SLH/COR SS17 ....340 C2
   SOS SS1 ....329 L7
   SWFD E18 ....295 J1
   UPMR RM14 ....322 A6
   VGE SS16 ....324 C4
   WAB EN9 ....252 F4
   WALTH E17 ....294 C8
   WAN E11 ....314 G6
   WOTN CO14 ....159 K6
Victoria Rd South
   CHLM/WR CM1 ....5 J4
Victoria St BRTR CM7 ....115 J3
   FX IP11 ....11 J2
   HAR CO12 ....14 E5
   IP IP1 ....16 A3
   SRTFD E15 ....333 H9
Victor Mew Cl WICKW SS12 ....305 J2
Victor Rd WALTH E17 ....294 G8
Victor's Crs RBRW/HUT CM13 ....281 L8
Victor Vls MGTR CO11 * 81 K9
   UED N18 * 273 J9
Victory Cl CDW/CHF RM16 ....348 F2
Victory La RCFD SS4 ....308 E1
Victory Rd COS CO15 ....6 C3
   IPNE IP4 ....25 P4
   K/T/MI CO5 ....202 D6
   RAIN RM13 ....336 F2
   WAN E11 ....295 K8
Victory Wy BERM/RHTH SE16 ....332 B9
   GRH DA9 ....348 B2
   ROMW/RG RM7 ....317 P2
Vienna Cl CLAY IG5 ....295 N4
Viennese Rd SUD CO10 ....110 B7
Viewpoint BSF CM23 ....296 E2
View Point Rd FX IP11 ....111 L3
Viga Rd WCHMH N21 ....272 F4
Vigerons Wy CDW/CHF RM16 ....350 C2
Vignoles Rd ROMW/RG RM7 ....317 P2
Viking Cl WDBR IP12 ....35 J9
Viking Gdns EHAM E6 ....333 P5
Viking Hts WDBR IP12 ....17 F1
Viking Pl LEY E10 ....314 C3
Viking Rd MAL CM9 ....243 P2

Vikings Wy CVI SS8 ....344 A2
Viking Wy BELV DA17 ....280 E6
BROW CM15.........................280 E6
COS CO15............................182 C7
WICKE SS11 ....285 A6
Village Ar CHING E4 * 274 C2
Village Cl CHING E4 ....294 F2
FOS CO15.............................158 E7
HOD EN11............................208 C3
Village Dr CVI SS8.................344 B2
Village Ga CHLM/GWD CM2 ...218 F8
Village Green Rd DART DA1 .....346 F9
Village Hall Cl CVI SS8 * 344 A2
Village Park Cl EN ENT1 ....273 K5
Village Rd EN EN1..................273 K5
Village Wy BARK/HLT IG6........296 D7
FOS CO15.............................158 E8
Villa Rd COLW CO3................150 F1
Villas Wy SBF/HAD SS7 ....325 P2
Villiers Pl RCHLM CM3............219 K2

Villiers-sur-Marne Av
BSF CM23 ....137 J9
Villiers Wy SBF/HAD SS7 ....326 C1
Vince Cl K/T/MI CO5...............202 F6
Vincent Av SLH/COR SS17 ....340 G2
Vincent Cl BARK/HLT IG6 ....296 E5
CHES/WCR EN8 ....230 B7
IP IP1 ....24 F5
SLH/COR SS17 ....542 A2
Vincent Rd CHING E4..............294 C3
DAGW RM9 ....317 M9
RAIN RM13 ....337 H4
Vincents Cl BERM/RHTH SE16 ..352 B9
Vincent St CAN/RD E16..........335 K5
Vincent Wy MAL CM9..............282 C5
Vine Cl BSDN SS14 ....304 D9
Vine Dr RCOLE CO7 ....153 K3
Vine Farm Rd RCOLE CO7 ....153 K3
Vine Gdns IL IG1 ....316 D7
Vine Gv HLW CM20 ....186 E7
Vine Rd K/T/MI CO5 ....173 N7
STHGT/OAK N14 ....272 B5
SRTFD E15 ....315 J9
Vinesse Rd RCOLW CO6 ....102 A7
Vine St BRTR CM7...................94 A6
ROMW/RG RM7 ....298 B9
Vineway BRW CM14 ....280 F7
The Vineway HAR CO12 ....110 B4
Vineyard Ga COL CO1 ....8 C6
Vineyards Rd POTB/CUF EN6 ...228 A8
Vineyard St COL CO1...............8 D7
The Vineyard WARE SG12 ....184 C2
Vint Crs COLW CO5 ....153 K7
The Vintners SOSN SS2 ....328 C1
Vintry Ms WALTH E17 ....294 D8
Viola Cl SOCK/AV RM15 ....338 F5
Violet Av CHLM/FN EN2...........251 J8
Violet Cl CAN/RD E16 ....333 H4
CHLM/WR CM1 ....218 D4
CHTY IP2 ....24 E3
Violet Rd BOW E3 ....332 E4
SWFD E18 ....295 L6
WALTH E17 ....294 E6
Violets La BUNT SG9 ....112 A5
Virgil Dr BRXX EN10 ....230 C2
Virgil Rd WIT CM8 ....171 N8
Virginia Cl COS CO15 ....206 F3
CRW RM5 ....298 B4
SBF/HAD SS7 ....305 N8
Virginia Gdns BARK/HLT IG6....296 E6
Virley Cl MAL CM9.................222 E7
Viscount Dr COLN CO4 ....128 D2
EHAM E6..............................334 A5
Vista Av FOS CO15.................158 E5
PEND EN3................................
Vista Dr REDBR IG4 ....295 N9
Vista Rd COS CO15.................285 L9
WICKE SS11 ....285 L9
The Vista CHING E4................274 C6
Vittius Cl COLN CO4 ....128 C1
Vivian Cl WOTN CO14 ....159 K6
Vivian Rd BOW E3..................332 B2
Voluntary Pl WAN E11............315 K1
Volwycke Av MAL CM9 ....244 A2
Voorburg Rd CVI SS8 ....344 A6
Vowler Rd VGE SS16 ....323 J2
Voyagers Cl THMD SE28 ....335 K6
Voysey Gdns PIT SS13 ....304 C6
Vulcan Cl EHAM E6 ....334 B6
Vulcan Ga ENC/FH EN2 ....272 F1
The Vyne BXLYHN DA7 ....346 A8

W

Waalwyk Dr CVI SS8 ....344 A4
Waarden Rd CVI SS8 ....344 D1
Waarem Av CVI SS8 ....344 D1
Wacketts CHESW EN7.............229 M6
Waddesdon Rd HAR CO12 ....14 E5
Waddington Cl EN EN1 ....273 K5
Waddington Rd SRTFD E15 .....314 C7
Waddington St SRTFD E15 ......314 C8
Wade Reach WOTN CO14 ....159 H6
Wade Rd CAN/RD E16 ....335 K4
COS CO15.............................182 C5
Wades Gv KESC IP5 ....27 K4
WCHMH N21 ....272 F6
Wade's Hl WCHMH N21 ....272 F5
Wade's La RIPS/CAP IP9 ....85 J3
Wade's Pl POP/IOD E14..........332 E7
Wadeville Av CHDH RM6 ....317 M1
Wadgate Rd FX FX1 ....10 E1
Wadham Av WALTH E17...........294 E4
Wadham Cl ING CM4 ....260 C5
Wadham Park Av
HOC/HUL SS5 ....287 K8
Wadham Rd CHING E4 ....294 E4
Wadhurst Rd IPSE IP3 ....26 C8
Wadley Cl K/T/MI CO5 ....174 B8
Wadley Rd WAN E11...............315 H2

Wadsworth Cl PEND EN3.........274 A4
Wager St BOW E3 ....332 C4
Waggoners Yd WARE SG12 ......184 A2
Waghorn Rd PLSTW E13..........333 M1
Wagon Md RBSF CM22 ....188 F1
Wagstaff Gdns DAGW RM9......317 K9
Wagtail Cl EN EN1 ....251 N9
Wagtail Dr MAL CM9 ....222 D6
Wagtail Pl K/T/MI CO5 * 173 H5
Wainfleet Av CRW RM5 ....298 A4
Wainwright Av BRTR CM77 ......144 F6
RBRW/HUT CM13 ....281 N6
Wainwright Gdns NHMKT IP6...22 A2
Wainwright Wy KESC IP5.........27 J5
Wakefield Cl EN EN1...............273 K5
Wakefield Gdns IL IG1............315 P1
Wakefield Rd BCAYW CM12 .....283 H6
Wakefield Cl COL CO1 ....8 E4
Wakefield Gdns IL IG1.............315 P1
Wakefield St EHAM E6 ....333 P1
Wakefields Wk
CHES/WCR EN8 * 252 B1
Wakelin Cha ING CM4 ....260 B6
Wakeling St WCHPL E1 * 332 D6
Wakeling Rd SRTFD E15 ....333 H2
Wakelin Wy WIT CM8 ....197 K2
Wakerfield Cl EMPK RM11........299 L9
Wakering Av SBN/FI SS3 ....330 E7
Wakering Rd BARK IG11 ....315 N5
SBN/FI SS3 ....329 P4
SBN/FI SS3 ....330 F6
Wakerly Cl EHAM E6 ....334 A6
Wakescolne WICKE SS11 ....305 M1
Wakeshall La SUD CO10 ....58 B5
Wakes St RCOLW CO6 ....124 C1
Walcot Rd PEND EN3 ....274 C1
Waldegrave Cl
UPMR RM14 ....319 N4
Waldegrave Rd BCTR RM8 ....317 K4
MGTR CO11 * 106 B5
Waldegraves La K/T/MI CO5 .....203 K5
The Waldegraves BURES CO8...76 A9
Waldegrave Wy MGTR CO11 .....106 B5
Walden Cl RAIN RM13 ....336 C2
SAFWN CB10 ....66 D7
Walden Cl MAL CM9 ....198 B8
Walden House Rd WALTH E17 * .198 B7
Walden Rd CBE/LIN CB1 ....38 A5
EMPK RM11 ....159 M1
GTDUN CM6 ....92 A3
SAFWN CB10 ....36 G9
SAFWN CB10 ....52 C5
SAFWN CB10 ....67 H1
SAFWN CB11 ....92 A6
Walden Wy BARK/HLT IG6 ....296 F4
EMPK RM11 ....319 J1
FOS CO15.............................159 H8
Waldgrooms GTDUN CM6.........141 K5
Waldingfield Rd SUD CO10 .....21 F5
Waldon Til YM18.....................351 J2
Waldringfield BSDN SS14 ....3 C2
Waldrist Wy ERITHM DA18.......335 N9
Waldstock Rd THMD SE28 ....335 H7
Waleys St WCHPL E1 * 452 A5
Walford Pl CHLM/GWD CM2 .....218 E9
Walfords Cl HLWE CM17 ....187 K9
Walford Wy RCOLW CO6 ....147 P4
Walfrey Gdns DAGW RM9 ....317 M9
Walker Av CHONG CM5 ....214 A9
Walker Cl DART DA1 ....346 E8
IPNE IP4 ....26 B6
Walker Dr LOS SS9 ....327 K4
Walkers Cl CHLM/WR CM1 ....218 C4
Walkers Sq SLH/COR SS17 ......341 L4
Walkey Wy SBN/FI SS3 ....330 C6
The Walk BCAYW CM12 * 283 H7
EMPK RM11 ....319 L4
HOC/HUL SS5 ....35 H6
IL IG1 ....16 E4
KESC IP5 ....26 C5
PLMGR N13 * 272 F9
RCOLW CO6 ....126 D7
Wallace Binder Cl MAL CM9 .....244 A1
Wallace Binder Gnd
MAL CM9 ....244 D2
Wallace Cl HOC/HUL SS5 ....286 C5
THMD SE28 ....335 L7
Wallace Crs CHLM/GWD CM2 ...240 B2
Wallace Dr WICKW SS12 ....305 K2
Wallace La RCHLM CM3 ....167 N6
Wallace Rd GRAYS RM17 ....349 K2
IP IP1 ....24 F3
Wallace's La RCHLM CM3 ....195 H8
Wallace St SBN/FI SS3 ....330 E7
Wallace Wy ROM CM1 ....298 C5
Wallasea Gdns
CHLM/WR CM1 ....218 A6
Wall Cha RCHLM CM3 ....167 L6
Wall End Rd EHAM E6..............316 B9
Wallenger Av GPK RM2 ....298 C7
Wallers St DAGW RM9 ....317 P8
Waller's Gv CHTY IP2 ....24 C7
Waller's Hoppet LOU IG10 ....276 A1
Wallers Wy HOD EN11 ....208 E2
Wallflower Ct CHLM/WR CM1 ...218 E5
Wallington Rd
GDMY/SEVK IG3 ....316 G2
Wallis Av SOSN SS2 ....328 G4
Wallis Cl EMPK RM11 ....308 G5
Wallis Ct SL COLW CO5 ....151 H5
Wallis Rd HOM E9 ....314 C8
Wallis Wy HOM E9..................314 C8
The Walls MGTR CO11 ....106 D4
Wall St RCOS CO16 ....205 K6
Wallwood Rd WAN E11 ....314 C2
Wallwood St POP/IOD E14........332 C5
Walmer Cl CHING E4 ....274 E8
ROMW/RG RM7 ....298 A6
Walnut Cl BARK/HLT IG6 ....296 D6
FX IP11 ....35 N4

MHAD SG10 ....160 E3
WALTH E17 ....47 M4
Walnut Cl HOC/HUL SS5 ....287 P9
Walnut Ct BSF CM23 ....162 A2
WIT CM8 ....171 P9
Walnut Gdns SRTFD E15..........145 H4
Walnut Gv BRTR CM7 ....145 H4
EN EN1 ....275 J4
Walnut Rd LEY E10 ....314 D4
Walnut Tree Av SBW CM21 ......184 A6
Walnut Tree Cl
RBRW/WCR E6 * 252 A1
HOD EN11............................208 D5
Walnut Tree Crs
SBW CM21 * 187 M1
Walnut Tree La RIPS/CAP IP9 ...88 A7
SUD CO10 ....20 B5
Walnut Tree Rd BCTR RM8.......346 D3
ERITH DA8 ....346 D3
Walnut Tree Wk WARE SG12 ....184 A6
Walnut Tree Wy COLS CO5 ......151 L3
K/T/MI CO5 ....173 P6
Walnut Wy BXHH IC9 ....275 N9
COS CO15.............................207 H1
RCOLE CO7 ....179 K6
Walpole Cl CHLM/GWD CM2 ....280 B7
Walpole Rd EHAM E6 ....315 M9
SWFD E18 ....295 J5
WALTH E17 ....294 B8
Walsham Cl THMD SE28 ....335 L7
Walsingham Cl LAIN SS15........303 K8
SUD CO10 ....61 M5
Walsingham Rd COLS CO2 ....280 E6
ENC/FH EN2 ....273 J5
SOSN SS2 ....329 J3
Walsingham Wy
CBAY IK17 ....283 J1
Walter Radcliffe Wy
RCOLE CO7 ....155 K7
Walters Cl CHLM/GWD CM2 .....280 B7
LOS SS9 ....307 P9
Walters Rd PEND EN3 ....273 P4
Walter St BETH E2 ....332 A5
Walters Yd COL CO1 ....8 C5
Walter Ter WCHPL E1 * 332 D6
Walter Wy CHLM/WR CM8 ....146 D9
Waltham Cl CHTY IP2 ....25 H9
RBRW/HUT CM13 ....281 M5
Waltham Crs SOSN SS2 ....329 J3
Waltham Gdns PEND EN3 ....251 P6
Waltham Ga CHES/WCR EN8 ....230 B5
Waltham Gln
CHLM/GWD CM2 ....240 B3
Waltham Pk WALTH E17 ....294 D4
Waltham Rd RAYL SS6 ....306 E4
RCHLM CM3 ....105 L8
WAB EN9 ....231 H5
WFD IG8 ....105 L8
Walthams PIT SS13 ....304 G8
Walthams Pl PIT SS13 ....304 G8
Walthamstow Av CHING E4.......294 D4
Walthamstow Av (North
Circular) CHING E4 ....294 B2
Waltham Wy CHING E4 ....274 C9
FOS CO15.............................159 H9
Walton Av FX FX11 ....10 A4
Walton Ct LAIN SS15...............303 K7
Walton Gdns
RBRW/HUT CM13 ....281 M4
WAB EN9 ....252 E5
Walton Rd COS CO15...............7 C3
FOS CO13.............................157 P4
FOS CO13.............................158 F6
HOD EN11............................208 E5
MNPK E12............................316 B6
PLSTW E13 ....333 M2
RCOS CO16 ....157 L3
SOS SS1 ....329 N8
WALTH E17 ....184 A4
Walton's Hall Rd
SLH/COR SS17 ....341 J8
Walton St ENC/FH EN2 ....251 J9
Wambrook SBN/FI SS3 ....330 C5
Wambrook Cl
RBRW/HUT CM13 ....281 M8
Wamburg Rd CVI SS8..............344 C1
Wanderer Dr BARK IG11 ....335 J3
Wandford Rd RM6..................317 L2
Wanlip Rd PLSTW E13.............333 N3
Wannock Gdns BARK/HLT IG6...296 C4
Wansbeck Rd HOM E9 ....314 C9
Wansfell Gdns SOS SS1 ....329 N5
Wansford Rd WFD IG8.............295M5
Wanstead La IL IG1.................315 P2
Wanstead Park Av MNPK E12 ...315 N4
Wanstead Pl WAN E11 ....315 P5
Wanstead Rd IL IG1 ....315 K1
Wantz Cha MAL CM9 ....222 B9
Wantz Hvn MAL CM9 * 222 B9
Wantz La RAIN RM13 ....336 C4
Wantz Rd DAGE RM10 ....318 A6
ING CM4 ....238 C9
MAL CM9 ....222 B9
Wapping La POP/IOD E14........178 C3
Warboys Crs CHING E4 ....294 F2
Warburton Av HSTD CO9 ....72 C9
Warburtons SLH/COR SS17 .....341 N2
Warburton Ter WALTH E17 ....294 E6
Ward Av GRAYS RM17 ....349 L2
Ward Cl CHESW EN7 ....229 M8
ERITH DA8 ....346 C4
Warde Cha WOTN CO14 ....159 J6
Warden Av CRW RM5 ....298 B2
Ward Hatch HLW CM20 ....187 J9
Wardle St HOM E9..................314 A7
Wardley Cl LAIN SS15..............303 K9
Wardley Cl CHTY IP2 ....29 M1
Ward Pth CHLM/GWD CM2 ......218 D9
Ward Rd RIPW IP8 ....24 C9
SRTFD E15 ....332 L1
Wards Cft SAFWS CB11 ....68 C2
Wards End MAL CM9 * 222 B9
Wards Rd GNTH/NBYPK IG2 ....316 D2
Wards Wharf Ap CAN/RD E16...333 N8

Wareham Av IPSE IP3 ....26 C8
Warehouse Rd GTDUN CM6 .....142 F2
Waremead Rd
GNTH/NBYPK IG2 ....296 C9
Warepoint Dr THMD SE28 ....334 E9
Ware Rd HOD EN11 ....208 D3
WARE SG12 ....160 B9
WARE SG12 ....184 D9
Warescot Cl BRWN CM15.........280 E6
Warescot Rd BRWN CM15 ....280 E6
Wares Rd CHLM/WR CM1 ....192 A7
Wargrave Rd COS CO15 ....6 B2
Warham Rd HAR CO12 ....109 P6
Warley Av ROMW/RG RM7 ....317 N2
Warley Cl BRTR CM7 ....145 M3
Warley Gap RBRW/HUT CM13 ..300 E4
Warley Hl RBRW/HUT CM13 ....300 E4
Warley Mt BRTR CM7 ....300 F1
Warley Rd CLAY IG5 ....296 B5
ED N9 ....273 P8
RBRW/HUT CM13 ....300 B8
WFD IG8 ....295 L4
Warley St BETH E2 ....332 A5
UPMR RM14 ....320 C2
Warley Wy FOS CO13 ....159 J8
Warlow Cl PEND EN3...............252 D7
Warming Cl FOS CO15 * 314 A5
Warmington St PLSTW E13 ......333 L4
Warner Cl BCAYE CM11 ....283 C7
BRTR CM7 ....144 C5
SRTFD E15 ....315 H7
Warner Dr BRTR CM7 ....144 B8
WARE SG12 ....184 A1
Warner Rd CHLM/WR CM1 ....198 A9
ED N9 ....274 A6
RAYL SS6 ....306 F7
RBSF CM22 ....139 N7
Warren Cl CHLM/WR CM1 ....198 C6
COLW CO5 ....150 E5
KESC IP5 ....27 M4
RIPS/CAP IP9 ....85 H5
Warren Cha CHIG IG7 ....296 E1
Warren Crs ED N9 ....273 L6
Warren Dr BSDN SS14 ....304 D9
HCH RM12 ....318 F5
WICKE SS11 ....285 M8
The Warren Dr WAN E11...........315 P2
Warrene Cl SLH/COR SS17 ......341 L4
Warren Fld EPP CM16 ....255 H2
Warren Heath Av IPSE IP3 ....26 C9
Warren Heath Rd IPSE IP3 ....275 M4
Warren Hl LOU IG10 ....275 M4
Warren La BRWN CM15 ....258 C9
COLW CO6 ....127 M6
GTDUN CM6 ....116 D8
HLWW/ROY CM19 ....209 P7
STDN/SEVK IG3 ....316 G3
Warren Lingley Wy
K/T/MI CO5 ....174 B8
Warren Pond Rd CHING E4 ......275 J6
Warren Rd BARK/HLT IG6 ....296 E9
BRTR CM7 ....145 M4
CHING E4 ....274 F8
HSTD CO9 ....97 N7
LEY E10 ....314 F5
LOS SS9 ....327 J8
RCHLM CM5 ....284 G2
WAN E11 ....315 P3
Warrenside BRTR CM7 ....145 L6
The Warrens FOS CO15 ....158 F8
WIT CM8 ....198 A7
Warren Ter CDW/CHF RM16 * ...338 C9
The Warren BCAYW CM12 ....282 F4
MNPK E12............................315 P6
SLH/COR SS17 ....341 M6
Warrier Av HCH RM12..............319 J4
Warriner Dr ED N9 ....273 M9
Warrington Gdns
EMPK RM11 ....319 H1
Warrington Pl POP/IOD E14 * ...332 F8
Warrington Rd BCTR RM8 ....317 L4
Warrington Sq
BCAYW CM12 * 282 F5
BCTR RM8 ....317 L4
Warrior Sq MNPK E12..............315 P6
Warrior Sq East SOS SS1 ....19 G4
Warrior Sq North SOS SS1 ....19 G5
Warrior Square Rd
SBN/FI SS3 ....330 E9
SOS SS1 ....332 F1
Warwall EHAM E6 ....334 C6
Warwick Av POTB/CUF EN6 .....228 C5
Warwick Bailey Cl COLN CO4...127 N5
Warwick Cl BRTR CM7 ....144 C5
COS CO15.............................326 D9
MAL CM9 ....244 B1
POTB/CUF EN6 ....228 C6
RAYL SS6 ....307 J6
SBF/HAD SS7 ....306 A8
Warwick Ct COS CO15 * 152 D2
MAL CM9 ....244 B1
Warwick Dr CHES/WCR EN8 ....230 A7
MAL CM9 ....244 A1
RCFD SS4 ....306 A6
Warwick Gdns GPK RM2 ....299 H7
RAYL SS6 ....307 J6
Warwick Gn RAYL SS6 ....307 K6
Warwick La RAIN RM13 ....336 C4
VGE SS16.............................322 G2
Warwick Rd BSF CM23 ....137 ND5
CHING E4 ....294 D2

COS CO15.............................6 D2
FSTGT E7 ....315 J8
IPNE IP4 ....17 J3
MNPK E12............................315 P7
PEND EN5.............................252 D7
RAIN RM13 ....337 H4
RAYL SS6 ....307 J6
RBSF CM22 ....139 P6
SOS SS1 ....329 N8
WAN E11 ....295 J9
Warwick Sq CHLM/WR CM1 .....217 N7
Warwick Ter WALTH E17 * 294 C9
Washall Dr BRTR CM7 ....144 C6
Washford Gdns COS CO15 ....6 C6
Washingham Av LAIN SS15.......503 H9
MNPK E12............................315 P6
Washington Cl BOW E3 ....332 E5
MAL CM9 ....243 P1
Washington Rd EHAM E6 ....315 M9
HAR CO12 ....110 D6
MAL CM9 ....244 A1
SWFD E18 ....295 J6
Wash La
COS CO15.............................207 J5
MAL CM9 ....223 J2
SLH/COR SS15 ....305 L6
RBRW/HUT CM13 ....281 P4
The Wash BUNT SG9 ....112 C2
Watchfield La RAYL SS6 ....306 F6
Watch House Rd GTDUN CM6 ...142 D1
Watchouse Gn CTDUN CM6 * ...143 L3
Watchouse Rd
CHLM/GWD CM2 ....240 A8
Waterbeach Rd DAGW RM9......317 K8
Watercrest Rw SAFWS CB11 * ...89 K1
Waterdene CVI SS8 ....326 B9
Waterden Rd SRTFD E15 ....314 D7
Waterfall Rd CHLM/WR CM14 ..272 B9
The Waterfalls VGE SS16 ....323 J3
Waterfield Cl THMD SE28 ....335 J8
Waterford Rd IP IP1 ....24 E1
SBN/FI SS3 ....330 C8
Waterfront WTHK WM20 * 348 D1
Waterhall Av WALTH E17 ....294 F6
Watergate WALTH E17 ....294 A5
Waterhale SOS SS1 ....329 P5
Waterhall Av CHING E4 ....295 H1
Waterhall Cl WALTH E17 ....294 A5
Water Hall La BRTR CM7 ....120 C1
Waterhead Cl ERITH DA8 ....346 D5
Waterhouse La CHLM/WR CM1..A A6
RCOLE CO7 ....130 D2
Waterhouse Moor
HLWS CM18 ....210 F4
Waterhouse St CHLM/WR CM1..210 D4
BRTR CM7 ....120 C4
BSF CM23 ....137 L6
BURES CO8 ....75 P8
COLW CO5 ....127 M7
ED N9 ....273 N7
GTDUN CM6 ....116 D8
HLWW/ROY CM19 ....209 P7
HSTD CO9 ....99 H1
HVHL CB9 ....143 M2
HVHL CB9 ....145 M2
PGR RM19 ....347 M2
RCOLW CO6 ....67 N9
SAFWN CB10 ....67 K1
SAFWS CB11 ....65 H8
SRTFD E15 ....315 H8
STSD CM24 ....114 B9
SUD CO10 ....45 J1
Waterloo Gdns
ROMW/RG RM7 ....318 C1
Waterloo La CHLM/WR CM1 .....5 G3
Waterloo Rd BARK/HLT IG6 .....296 D6
BRW CM14 ....280 F7
EHAM E6..............................315 M9
FSTGT E7 ....315 J7
IP IP1 ....25 H4
LEY E10 ....314 D2
ROMW/RG RM7 ....298 C9
SBN/FI SS3 ....330 C7
Watermans Wy EPP CM16........253 P6
GRH DA9 ....347 J2
Watermeadow Cl ERITH DA8....346 C5
Water Mdw K/T/MI CO5 ....173 K1
Watermill Rd K/T/MI CO5 ....173 K1
WDBR IP12 ....29 J3
Water Rw WARE SG12 ....184 A3
Waterside RCOLE CO7 ....114 B9
STSD CM24 ....114 B9
Waterside Cl BARK IG11 ....317 H6
HARH RM3 ....299 N4
HOM E9 ....332 C1
Waterside Rd BOC CM0 ....226 C8
RCFD SS4 ....506 E2
Watermeet
HLWW/ROY CM19 ....210 C7
Watersmeet Wy THMD SE28 ....335 L6
Waterson Rd CDW/CHF RM16 ..350 C2
Waterson St CHLM/GWD CM2 ..240 B3
Waterville Dr VGE SS16 ....324 F2
Waterville Ms COLS CO2 ....152 C3
Waterwick Hl SAFWS CB11 ......62 E8
Waterworks Cl RCOS CO16 ......181 L8
Waterworks Dr RCOLS CO16 ....314 A4
SLH/COR SS15 ....328 B8
Waterworks La CLPT E5 ....314 A4
Waterworks St IPNE IP4 ....17 G5
Waterworks Yd
CHONG CM5 ....213 J5
GTDUN CM6 ....116 D8
RCOLW CO6 ....147 H5
WICKE SS11 ....286 F7
Watery Stones SAFWS CB11 * ...88 A4
Watery Wy BRWN CM15 ....280 E6
Watford Rd CAN/RD E16 ....333 K5
Watkins Cl PIT SS13 ....305 J6
Watkins Wy SBN/FI SS3 ....330 C5
Watling La GTDUN CM6 ....92 A4

BRW CM14 ....280 F9
BSF CM23 ....137 L8
CHLM/GWD CM2 ....5 J4
GRAYS RM17 ....149 J4
MAL CM9 ....222 C7
PEND EN5 ....274 B5
SLH/COR SS17 ....341 M6
SLH/COR SS17 ....342 C1
SRTFD E15 ....332 C1
The Wharf GRH DA9 * 348 E9
Wharley Hook HLWS CM18 ....210 C6
Wharton Dr CHLM/WR CM1 ....218 F4
Wheat Cft BSF CM23 * 162 B1
Wheatear Pl BCAYE CM11 ....283 K7
Wheatfield Rd COLW CO3 ....126 C9
Wheatfields HLWE CM17 ....187 L6
PEND EN5 ....252 B9
RCFD SS4 ....309 L3
Wheatfield Wy CHLM/WR CM1 ....4 C2
VGE SS16 ....323 H2
Wheatlands ED N9 ....275 K8
Wheatley Av BRTR CM7 ....145 M5
Wheatley Cl EMPK RM11 ....299 J9
RCFD SS4 ....308 E3
SBW CM23 ....187 K5
Wheatley Gdns ED N9 ....275 K8
Wheatley Rd SLH/COR SS17 ....324 A9
Wheatley Terrace Rd
ERITH DA8 ....346 E4
Wheaton Rd HLW CM1 ....197 L2
Wheatsheaf Cl CHLM/WR CM1 ....108 A5
Wheatsheaf La MGTR CO11 ....108 A5
Wheatsheaf Rd ROM RM1 ....318 E1
WARE SG12 ....185 N2
Wheeler Cl COLN CO4 ....128 F9
Wheelers EPP CM16 ....232 G8
Wheelers Cl WAB EN9 ....231 H1
Wheelers Cross BARK IG11 ....334 E2
Wheelers Farm Gdns
EPP CM16 ....234 A5
Wheelers Hi RCHLM CM5 ....169 J4
Wheelers La BRW CM14 ....279 N5
SLH/COR SS17 ....324 C9
Wheel Farm Dr DAGE RM10 ....318 D5
Wheelock Cl ERITH DA8 ....346 A5
Wheelwrights FX IP11 ....34 F5
SOSN SS2 ....329 H1
The Wheelwrights FX IP11 ....34 F5
Whernside Av CHLM/WR CM1 ....326 F9
Wherry La IPSE IP3 * 17 F6
Wherstead Rd CHTY IP2 ....25 K9
Whights' Cnr RIPW IP8 ....29 J1
Whinbanks Cl CHTY IP2 ....24 E8
Whinfield KESG IP5 ....27 M4
Whinfield Av HAR CO12 ....110 A7
Whinfield Ct KESG IP5 ....27 M5
Whinhams Wy BCAYE CM12 ....282 G5
The Whinneys KESG IP5 ....27 J3
Whinyard Wy FX IP11 ....35 N4
Whipps Cross Rd WAN E11 ....295 H9
Whist Av WICKE SS11 ....285 L7
Whistler Ri SBN/FI SS3 ....330 F6
Whitakers Wy LOU IG10 ....254 A9
Whitbreads Farm La
RCHLM CM5 ....168 G2
Whitby Av RBRW/HUT CM13 ....301 N3
Whitby Rd BOC CM0 ....268 C7
IPNE IP4 ....25 H5
Whitchurch Rd HARH RM3 ....299 K1
Whitcroft VGE SS16 ....323 K3
Whitear Wk SRTFD E15 ....314 G8
Whitebarn La DAGE RM10 ....335 P2
White Barns RCHLM CM5 ....167 N7
Whitebeam La BUNT SG9 ....87 H9
Whitebeam Ct CHESW EN7 ....229 K5
CHLM/GWD CM2 ....239 N3
Whitebeam Dr
SOCK/AV RM15 ....338 F7
White Bear STSD CM24 ....114 B7
Whiteditch La SAFWS CB11 ....66 D7
White Elm Rd RCHLM CM5 ....242 D8
White Elm St IPSE IP3 ....17 J7
Whitefields Rd
CHES/WCR EN8 ....229 P7
Whitefriars Crs WOS/PRIT SS0 ....328 D7
Whitefriars Wy COLW CO3 ....151 K1
White Gdns DAGE RM10 ....317 P8
Whitegate Rd RCOLE CO7 ....179 M7
SOS SS1 ....19 G4
White Gates HCR RM12 ....319 H4
Whitegates Cl BRTR CM77 ....144 F8
White Hall Cl SUD CO10 ....47 P8
Whitehall Cl CHIG IG7 ....277 H9
COLS CO12 ....152 D2
WAB EN9 ....231 H1
Whitehall Ct WIT CM8 ....97 L7
Whitehall Gdns CHING E4 ....274 C7
Whitehall La BKHH IG9 ....275 K8
BSF CM23 ....137 L5
ERITH DA8 ....346 E7
GRAYS RM17 ....156 F5
RCOS CO16 ....156 F5
SLH/COR SS17 ....324 B7
Whitehall Rd BSF CM23 ....137 K5
CHING E4 ....275 H8
COLS CO12 ....152 D3
GRAYS RM17 ....349 M2
White Hall Rd SBN/FI SS3 ....330 C2
Whitehands Cl HOD EN11 ....208 C5
White Hart La
CHLM/WR CM1 ....218 F5
HLW CM20 ....15 F2
HOC/HUL SS5 ....307 P2
RCOLW CO6 ....127 H2
ROMW/RG RM7 ....297 P5
Whitehaven CHESW EN7 * 229 K7
White Hern Ct
CHES/WCR EN8 ....229 P9
White Horse Av HSTD CO9 ....97 N8
White Horse Rd FX IP11 ....35 M5

White Horse Hi RIPS/CAP IP9 ....29 M9
White Horse La MAL CM9 ....222 A9
SAFWS CB11 ....65 H8
WCHPL E1 ....13 M8
WIT CM8 ....197 J1
White Horse Rd EHAM E6 ....334 A3
HVHL CB9 ....42 B1
RCOLE CO7 ....200 A8
RIPS/CAP IP9 ....28 D9
Whitehorse Rd WCHPL E1 ....332 B5
White Horse Rd WCHPL E1 ....332 B5
White House Cha RAYL SS6 ....307 H7
Whitehouse Crs
CHLM/GWD CM2 ....240 C2
Whitehouse La MAL CM9 ....200 F5
White House La ENC/FH EN2 ....251 H9
Whitehouse La RCOLW CO6 ....126 G4
SUD CO10 ....58 C1
Whitehouse Mdw LOS SS9 ....308 B9
Whitehouse Rd GTDUN CM6 ....142 E1
White House Rd IP IP1 ....308 A9
LOS SS9 ....308 A9
Whitehouse Rd RCHLM CM5 ....264 H9
Whitehouse Wy
STHGT/OAK N14 ....272 A8
Whitehurst Dr UED N18 * 274 A1
Whitelands BRWN CM15 ....258 G5
Whitelands Cl WICKE SS11 ....285 K7
Whitelands Wy HARH RM3 ....299 J5
Whitelegg Rd PLSTW E13 ....333 J2
White Lodge Crs RCOS CO16 ....157 M5
White Lyons Rd BRW CM14 ....280 F9
White Md CHLM/WR CM1 ....218 A1
White Post Fld SBW CM21 ....187 C2
White Post La HOM E9 ....314 D9
White Rd SRTFD E15 ....315 H9
Whites Av GNTH/NBYPK IG2 ....316 F1
Whitesbridge La ING CM4 ....239 L9
Whites Fld RCOLE CO7 ....80 E6
Whites Hi HKI CM4 ....261 N7
Whiteshott VGE SS16 ....323 P2
Whiteshot Wy SAFWN CB10 ....51 N8
Whites La RCHLM CM5 ....169 J7
Whitesmith Dr BCAYW CM12 ....282 F5
Whitethorn Cl ST GTDUN CM6 ....141 L6
Whitethorn Cl COLN CO4 ....128 E8
Whitethorn Gdns
CHLM/GWD CM2 ....240 B5
EMPK RM11 ....319 H1
ENC/FH EN2 ....273 J4
Whitethorn St BOW E3 ....332 D4
White Tree Ct RCHLM CM5 ....286 E2
Whitewaits HLW CM20 ....210 G3
Whiteways BCAYE CM11 ....283 L6
CVI SS8 ....344 G5
LOS SS9 ....308 A9
Whiteways Ct WIT CM8 ....197 H1
Whitewebbs La ENC/FH EN2 ....251 L5
Whitewebbs Pk
ENC/FH EN2 * 251 K5
Whitewebbs Rd ENC/FH EN2 ....250 C5
Whitewell Rd COL CO1 ....8 C7
Whitfield Link
CHLM/GWD CM2 ....240 C3
Whitfield Rd EHAM E6 ....315 M9
Whitfields SLH/COR SS17 ....341 N3
Whit Hern Ct
CHES/WCR EN8 * 229 N7
Whitings Wy EHAM E6 ....334 B5
Whitland Ct CHTY IP2 ....30 A2
Whitley Rd HOD EN11 ....208 E5
Whitlock Dr HSTD CO9 ....57 N9
Whitman Rd BOW E3 ....332 B4
Whitmore Av CDW/CHF RM16 ....339 L7
HARH RM3 ....299 K6
Whitmore Crs
CHLM/GWD CM2 ....218 G8
Whitney Av REDBR IG4 ....295 N8
Whitney Rd LEY E10 ....314 D2
Whittaker Rd EHAM E6 ....315 M9
Whitta Rd MNPK E12 ....315 N6
Whittingham Av WALTH E17 ....294 G3
Whittingstall Rd HOD EN11 ....208 E3
Whittington Rd
RBRW/HUT CM13 ....281 N5
Whittington Wy BSF CM23 ....162 B2
Whittle Cl WALTH E17 ....314 B1
Whittle Rd CHTY IP2 ....24 C5
Whitton Church La IP IP1 ....24 C1
Whitton Leyer RIPW IP8 ....24 D1
Whitton Pk IP IP1 * 23 H7
Whitwell Rd PLSTW E13 ....333 K3
Whitworth Ct CHTY IP2 ....24 E8
Whydrews SLH/COR SS17 ....341 N5
Whybridge Cl RAIN RM13 ....336 D1
Whyteville Rd FSTGT E7 ....315 L8
Whytewaters VGE SS16 ....324 E3
Whyverne Cl CHLM/WR CM1 ....218 D5
Wick Beech Av WICKE SS11 ....285 K9
Wick Cha SOSN SS2 ....329 M5
Wick Crs WICKW SS2 ....305 K2
Wick Dr WICKW SS12 ....285 J9
Wicken Rd SAFWS CB11 ....64 A8
Wick Farm Rd BOC CM0 ....247 H2
Wickfield Ash
CHLM/WR CM1 ....217 L5
Wickford Dr PIT SS13 ....304 F9
Wickford Dr HARH RM3 ....299 L2
Wickford Ms PIT SS13 ....304 F9
Wickford Pl PIT SS13 ....324 F1
Wickford Rd RCHLM CM5 ....264 D9
WOS/PRIT SS0 ....18 B5
Wickford Wy WALTH E17 ....294 A8
Wick Gln BCAYW CM12 ....282 C4
Wickham Bishop Rd
RCHLM CM5 ....196 G8
Wickhambrook Ct FX IP11 ....10 B2
Wickham Cl PEND EN5 ....273 N2
Wickham Crs CHLM/WR CM1 ....217 N5

Wickham Hall La WIT CM8 ....197 M9
Wickham Pl VGE SS16 ....3 H7
Wickham Rd CDW/CHF RM16 ....340 D9
CHING E4 ....294 F4
COLW CO5 ....151 N1
WIT CM8 ....197 J1
Wickham's Cha RCHLM CM5 ....242 F8
Wickhams WH WARE SG12 * 180 B3
Wickhay LAIN SS15 ....2 B6
Wicklands Rd WARE SG12 ....185 N5
Wick La BOW E3 ....332 D2
HAR CO12 ....110 C7
K/T/MI CO5 ....178 C2
Wicklow Av CHLM/WR CM1 ....217 L5
Wicklow Rd IP IP1 ....24 E1
Wicklow Wy SBN/FI SS3 ....330 B7
Wickmead Cl SOSN SS2 ....329 M4
Wick Rd BOC CM0 ....291 J4
COLN CO4 ....79 H7
COLN CO4 ....104 A5
COLS CO12 ....152 E4
HOM E9 ....314 B8
RCOLE CO7 ....155 N9
Wick Ter COLN CO4 * 104 A5
Widbrook BRWN CM15 ....258 F6
Widbury Gdns WARE SG12 ....184 C5
Widbury Hi WARE SG12 ....184 D3
Wid Cl RBRW/HUT CM13 ....281 N4
Widdin St SRTFD E15 ....315 H9
Widecombe Cl HARH RM3 ....299 J5
Widecombe Gdns
REDBR IG4 ....295 P8
Widford Cha CHLM/WR CM1 ....239 N3
Widford Cl CHLM/GWD CM2 ....239 N3
Widford Gv CHLM/GWD CM2 ....239 N3
Widford Park Pl
CHLM/GWD CM2 ....239 N3
Widford Rd CHLM/GWD CM2 ....239 N3
MHAD SG10 ....160 D7
WARE SG12 ....185 N2
Widgeon Cl CAN/RD E16 ....333 L6
CHTY IP2 ....24 C8
Widgeon Rd CHLM/WR CM1 ....173 H3
Widgeons PIT SS13 ....305 H9
Widleybrook La BRTR CM7 ....95 L5
Widworthy Hayes
RBRW/HUT CM13 ....281 L7
Wigborough Rd COLS CO16 ....175 P4
K/T/MI CO5 ....176 D9
Wigboro Wick La RCOS CO16 ....205 M2
Wiggins La BRW CM14 * 280 D8
Wiggin's La BRTR CM77 ....282 F9
Wiggins Vw CHLM/GWD CM2 ....218 G7
Wigley Bush La BRW CM14 ....280 B8
Wigmore Ct CHTY IP2 ....29 P1
Wigmore Rd CHTY CO11 ....105 N5
Wigram Rd WAN E11 ....315 M1
Wigram Sq WALTH E17 ....294 F7
Wigston Rd CAN/RD E16 ....333 L4
Wigton Rd HARH RM3 ....299 K1
Wilberforce St IP IP1 ....16 A3
Wilbye Cl COLS CO12 ....151 L2
Wilde Cl TIL RM18 ....350 D7
Wilde Rd ERITH DA8 ....346 A5
Wildern Gv BCAYE CM11 ....258 F6
Wilding Rd RIPW IP8 ....29 L1
Wilford Cl ENC/FH EN2 * 273 J2
Wilfred Rd RAIN RM13 ....336 F5
Wilkes Rd RBRW/HUT CM13 ....281 N4
Wilkin Ct COLW CO5 ....151 G8
Wilkin Dr K/T/MI CO5 ....174 B8
Wilkinson Cl CHESW EN7 ....229 H5
Wilkinson Dr KESG IP5 ....27 H5
Wilkinson Gv BRTR CM7 ....145 L9
Wilkinson Rd CAN/RD E16 ....333 M6
Wilkinsons Md
CHLM/GWD CM2 ....218 F7
Willan Wall CAN/RD E16 ....333 J7
Willett Rd COLS CO12 ....151 L3
Willetts Fld SAFWN CB10 ....68 D6
Willett Ms SRTFD E15 ....313 H9
William Booth Wy FX IP11 ....54 C6
William Boys Cl COLN CO4 ....128 E7
William Cl CRW RM5 ....298 B5
William Covell Cl
ENC/FH EN2 * 250 E8
William Dr COLS CO12 ....6 B5
William Gdns HOC/HUL SS5 * 287 H5
William Groom Av HAR CO12 ....110 B6
William Guy Gdns BOW E3 ....332 E5
William Hunter Wy
BRW CM14 ....280 F8
William Morley Cl EHAM E6 ....333 N1
William Morris Cl WALTH E17 ....294 C7
William Rd PIT SS13 ....305 K9
Williams Av WALTH E17 ....294 C5
Williamsons Wy
SLH/COR SS17 ....323 N9
William Sparrow Ct
RCOLE CO7 * 153 K4
William Sq BERM/RHTH SE16 ....332 B8
Williams Rd CHLM/WR CM1 ....218 D3
William St BARK IG11 ....349 M4
GRAYS RM17 ....349 M4
IP IP1 ....16 E5
LEY E10 ....314 F1
William's Wk COL CO1 ....8 C5
Williamville Rd RAYL SS6 ....306 D4
Willingale Cl
RBRW/HUT CM13 ....281 P5
Willingale Rd BRTR CM7 ....145 N2
CHONG CM5 ....214 B9
CHONG CM5 ....214 D9
LOU IG10 ....254 D9
The Willingales LAIN SS15 ....303 H9
Willingale Wy SOS SS1 ....329 P5
Willinghall Cl WAB EN9 ....252 C2
Willingham Wy CLPT E5 ....314 G1
Willis Rd ERITH DA8 ....346 B2

SRTFD E15 ....333 J2
Willis St POP/IOD E14 ....332 E6
Wilmott Rd SOSN SS2 ....308 E9
Willoughby Av K/T/MI CO5 ....202 D6
Willoughby Cl BROX EN10 ....208 B9
Willoughby Dr
CHLM/GWD CM2 ....218 G9
BARN RM13 ....318 D9
Willoughby Rd CHTY IP2 ....16 C7
Willoughby's La BRTR CM7 ....121 M7
Willow Av FOS CO13 ....158 E8
RCOS CO16 ....206 A6
Willowbank CHM CM2 ....240 A7
Willow Cl BKHH IG9 ....275 N9
BOC CM0 ....290 G2
BRWN CM15 ....258 G8
BSF CM23 ....137 K6
BUNT SG9 ....86 B3
CHESW EN7 ....229 K5
CHLM/WR CM1 ....218 A2
CVI SS8 ....344 C2
HCH RM12 ....318 C5
HOC/HUL SS5 ....308 A1
HVHL CB9 ....40 C2
LOS SS9 ....307 P9
NHMKT IP6 ....29 C2
RBRW/HUT CM13 ....281 L5
RCOLE CO7 ....179 J7
RCOLE CO7 ....179 J7
SUD CO10 ....20 D7
Willow Crs RCHLM CM5 ....196 D9
Willowcroft Rd IP IP1 ....25 H1
Willowdene BRWN CM15 ....280 C6
CHES/WCR EN8 ....230 B6
HSTD CO9 ....72 C7
Willowdene Ct BRW CM14 ....300 F1
Willow Dr RAYL SS6 ....306 F3
Willowfield HLWS CM18 ....210 E4
LAIN SS15 ....303 K7
Willow Gn ING CM4 ....260 C5
Willow Gv RCHLM CM5 ....264 D8
RCOLW CO6 ....77 N7
Willow Hall La BARK IG11 ....108 A8
Willowhill SLH/COR SS17 ....323 M9
Willowmead BCAYW CM11 ....284 B4
CHIG IG7 ....277 H9
Willow Md SBW CM21 ....187 M3
Willow Mdw HSTD CO9 ....72 D9
Willow Pk RCHLM CM5 ....150 B1
Willow Pl HLWE CM17 ....211 N7
Willow Ri WIT CM8 ....171 P8
Willow Rd CHDH RM6 ....317 M1
EN EN1 ....273 K8
ERITH DA8 ....346 F6
Willow Springs BSF CM23 ....137 J6
The Willows BCAYE CM11 ....283 L9
COLS CO2 ....152 B5
GRAYS RM17 ....349 N4
HARH RM3 ....299 N3
KESG IP5 ....219 K3
SAFWN CB10 ....68 E8
SBF/HAD SS7 ....325 N2
SOS SS1 ....329 P5
WARE SG12 ....184 E8
Willow St CHING E4 ....274 C6
ROMW/RG RM7 ....298 B8
Willow Tree Cl HOM E9 ....332 B1
Willow Tree Wy RCOLW CO6 ....124 A1
Willow Vw WARE SG12 * 184 B4
Willow Wk HOC/HUL SS5 ....308 A1
K/T/MI CO5 ....173 N6
RCFD SS4 ....289 L7
SBF/HAD SS7 ....326 C3
UPMR RM14 ....320 B3
WALTH E17 ....294 C9
WCHMH N21 ....272 E5
Willow Wy COS CO15 ....206 F5
HAR CO12 ....110 A2
HARH RM3 ....299 N3
HSTD CO9 ....72 C9
Will's Ayley La SAFWN CB10 ....52 D8
Wills Hi SLH/COR SS17 ....341 L2
Wilmer Lea Cl SRTFD E15 ....314 F9
Wilmington Gdns BARK IG11 ....316 E9
Wilmington Rd COLN CO4 ....128 E7
Wilmot Gn RBRW/HUT CM13 ....300 F3
Wilmot Rd LEY E10 ....314 D6
Wilmslow Dr RIPW IP8 ....29 J7
Wilmslowe CVI SS8 ....326 C9
Wilrich Av CVI SS8 ....344 C2
Wilshire Av CHLM/GWD CM2 ....218 E8
Wilsman Rd SOCK/AV RM15 ....338 F2
Wilsner PIT SS13 ....305 H8
Wilson Cl BSF CM23 ....137 L9
RCOLE CO7 ....153 L7
SLH/COR SS17 ....341 K5
Wilson Marriage Rd COLN CO4 ....128 E7
Wilson Rd IL IG1 ....316 A2
PLSTW E13 ....333 H1
RIPW IP8 ....29 K1
Wilsons La RCOLW CO6 ....149 K5
Wilson's Cnr CHLM/GWD CM2 * 6 E3
Wilson's Pl POP/IOD E14 ....332 C5
Wilson St WALTH E17 ....294 F9
WCHMH N21 ....272 F6
Withorne Gdns DAGE RM10 ....318 A9
Wilton Cl BSF CM23 ....137 N7
Wilton Dr CRW RM5 ....298 B4
Wiltshire Av EMPK RM11 ....299 L8
Wimarc Crs RAYL SS6 ....306 E3
Wimbish End PIT SS13 ....304 G9
Wimbish Ms PIT SS13 ....305 H9
Wimbish Wk SAFWN CB10 ....66 D7
Wimborne Av IPSE IP3 ....26 E5
Wimborne Cl BKHH IG9 ....275 M8
SBW CM21 ....187 L2
Wimborne Rd ED N9 ....273 M8
SOSN SS2 ....19 H2
Wimbourne LAIN SS15 ....303 H8
Wimhurst Cl HOC/HUL SS5 ....287 P9
Wimpole Cl KESG IP5 ....26 E5
Wimpole Rd COL CO1 ....128 C9
Winbrook Cl RAYL SS6 ....307 H7

Winbrook Rd RAYL SS6 ....307 H7
Wincanton Cl IPNE IP4 ....25 P2
Wincanton Gdns
BARK/HLT IG6 ....296 C7
Wincanton Rd HARH RM3 ....279 J9
Wincelow Hall Rd SAFWN CB10 ....54 A4
Winchcombe Cl LOS SS9 ....327 P5
Winchelsea Dr
CHLM/GWD CM2 ....240 C3
Winchelsea Pl RCOLE CO7 ....179 L5
Winchelsea Rd FSTGT E7 ....315 K6
Winchester Av UPMR RM14 ....320 C3
Winchester Cl BSF CM23 ....162 A1
EN EN1 * 273 K4
LOS SS9 ....308 A8
Winchester Gdns LAIN SS15 ....303 K6
NHMKT IP6 ....22 E2
Winchester Rd CHING E4 ....274 B8
COL CO1 ....152 B1
ED N9 ....273 L7
FOS CO15 ....159 H9
IL IG1 ....316 E5
Winchester Wy CHTY IP2 ....29 P2
Winchmore Hill Rd
STHGT/OAK N14 ....272 D6
Winchmore Vls
WCHMH N21 * 272 E6
Winch Vw EPP CM16 ....233 J8
Winckford Cl CHLM/GWD CM2 ....194 A6
Wincoat Cl SBF/HAD SS7 ....325 P3
Wincoat Dr SBF/HAD SS7 ....325 N5
Windermere Av HCH RM12 ....318 F7
WLSDN NW10 ....286 C6
Windermere Ct BRTR CM77 ....144 F8
Windermere Gdns REDBR IG4 ....295 P9
Windermere Rd BRTR CM77 ....144 F8
BXLYHN DA7 ....346 B7
COS CO15 ....182 D7
FX IP11 ....35 M4
SBF/HAD SS7 ....306 B8
SOS SS1 ....19 K3
Windham Rd SUD CO10 ....21 J4
Windhill BSF CM23 ....137 K8
Windhill Old Rd BSF CM23 ....137 K7
Winding Rd HLW CM20 ....160 F1
Winding Piece RIPS/CAP IP9 ....28 C9
Winding Wy BCTR RM8 ....317 K5
Windley Tye CHLM/WR CM1 ....217 M8
Windmill Cl COLN CO4 ....103 J4
GTDUN CM6 ....141 M5
HLWE CM17 ....211 J8
HAR CO12 ....109 J7
UPMR RM14 ....319 M4
WAB EN9 ....253 H4
Windmill Ct COLN CO4 * 127 P5
RCOLW CO6 ....150 A2
Windmill Fld WARE SG12 ....184 A4
Windmill Flds HLWE CM17 ....147 N5
RCOLW CO6 ....147 N5
Windmill Gdns BRTR CM7 ....121 K7
ENC/FH EN2 ....272 F1
Windmill Hts BCAYE CM11 ....283 J8
Windmill Hi ENC/FH EN2 ....272 G2
RIPS/CAP IP9 ....28 D8
SAFWN CB10 ....51 J7
SUD CO10 ....21 H5
Windmill La CHES/WCR EN8 ....230 B9
SRTFD E15 ....314 G8
Windmill Mdw GTDUN CM6 ....190 F1
Windmill Pk COS CO15 ....182 M8
Windmill Rd HSTD CO9 ....97 N7
MGTR CO11 ....107 H7
Windmills RCOLW CO6 ....125 H7
The Windmills CHLM/WR CM1 ....159 P9
Windmill Vw RBRW/HUT CM13 ....173 P7
Windmill Wy BRWN CM15 ....258 B7
MHAD SG10 ....160 D4
Windrush Dr CHLM/WR CM1 ....218 A5
Windrush Rd KESG IP5 ....27 H3
Windsor Av CDW/CHF RM16 ....339 L9
COS CO15 ....5 B4
SLH/COR SS17 ....323 P9
WALTH E17 ....294 B6
Windsor Cl CHESW EN7 ....229 M9
COLS CO12 ....152 B4
CVI SS8 ....344 E2
LOS SS9 ....327 P3
Windsor Ct RCOLE CO7 ....179 L7
STHGT/OAK N14 ....272 B6
Windsor Gdns BRTR CM7 ....145 L2
BSF CM23 ....137 H7
HOC/HUL SS5 ....308 C3
SBF/HAD SS7 ....326 F2
WICKE SS11 ....285 J7
Windsor Ms RAYL SS6 ....306 F6
Windsor Pl SUD CO10 ....21 H5
Windsor Rd BCAYE CM11 ....284 C3
BCTR RM8 ....317 K5
BRWN CM15 ....258 G8
CHING E4 ....294 E1
COS CO15 ....6 B5
EMPK RM11 ....319 H2
FSTGT E7 ....315 L7
FX IP11 ....11 G3
IL IG1 ....316 D6
IP IP1 ....24 G4
K/T/MI CO5 ....174 B8
LEY E10 ....314 E2
PEND EN5 ....305 K7
PIT SS13 ....305 K7
PLMGR N13 ....315 K3
WAN E11 ....295 K5
WOS/PRIT SS0 ....18 B2
The Windsors BKHH IG9 ....275 P8
Windsor Wd WAB EN9 ....253 H5
Windward Cl PEND EN5 ....253 H5
Windy Hi RBRW/HUT CM13 ....281 N7
Winfields PIT SS13 ....305 H4

Winford Dr BROX EN10.....230 C1
Winfrith Rd IPSE IP5.....26 C7
Wingate Cl BRTR CM7.....145 H2
Wingate Rd IL IG1.....316 C7
Wingfield GRAYS RM17.....349 J3
Wingfield Cl RBRW/HUT CM13.....281 K9
Wingfield Gdns UPMR RM14.....320 B7
Wingfield Rd SRTFD E15.....315 H7
  WALTH E17.....294 E9
Wingfield St IP4.....17 F5
Wingletye La EMPK RM11.....319 L3
Wingrave Crs BRW CM14.....300 B1
Wingway BRW CM14.....280 F7
Winifred Av BRW CM14.....319 J6
Winifred Rd BCTR RM8.....317 M4
  ERITH DA8.....346 C8
  PIT SS13.....304 C9
Winifred St CAN/RD E16.....334 A8
Winifred Ter EN EN1.....273 L6
Winn Bridge Cl WFD IG8.....295 N5
Winnington Rd PEND SN18.....251 P6
Winnock Rd COL CO1.....128 B9
Winns Av WALTH E17.....294 C7
Winns Ter WALTH E17.....294 D6
Winsbeach WALTH E17.....294 G9
Winsey Cha BRW CM14.....280 F7
Winsford Gdns WOS/PRIT SS0.....328 B2
Winsford Wy CHLM/GWD CM2.....218 C3
Winsley Rd COL CO1.....128 B9
Winsley SG COL CO1.....152 C1
Winslow Gv CHING E4.....275 H8
Winsor Ter EHAM E6.....334 C5
Winstanley Rd SAFWS CB11.....65 N2
Winstanley Wy BSDN SS14.....308 P7
Winstead Gdns DAGE RM10.....318 F7
Winston Av COLW CO5.....151 L2
  IPNE IP4.....26 B3
  K/T/MI CO5.....174 B8
Winston Churchill Wy CHES/WCR EN8.....251 P5
Winston Cl BRTR CM7.....121 H9
  FX IP11.....34 C6
  ROMW/RG RM7.....298 A8
Winston Wy HSTD CO9.....98 B5
  IL IG1.....316 C5
Winstree PIT SS13.....304 C7
Winstree Rd BOC CM0.....290 C3
  COLW CO3.....126 C9
Winstreet Cl COLS CO2.....151 J9
Winter Av EHAM E6.....333 P7
Winterbourne Rd BCTR RM8.....317 K4
Winterbournes WOTN CO14.....159 H7
Winter Folly LAIN SS15.....323 M1
Winter Gardens Ptn CVI SS8.....326 B7
Winterscroft Rd HOD EN11.....208 C5
Winter's Rd K/T/MI CO5.....175 J4
Winters Wy WAB EN9.....253 K3
Winterswyk Av CVI SS8.....345 N2
Winton Av WICKW SS12.....284 F8
  WOS/PRIT SS0.....18 B5
Winton Cl ED N9.....274 H6
Winton Dr CHES/WCR EN8.....230 B8
Winton Rd RCOLW CO6.....147 P5
Wisdoms Ct DAGE RM10.....318 A5
Wiseman Rd LEY E10 *.....314 D4
Wisemans Gdns SBW CM21.....187 K3
Wise Rd SRTFD E15.....332 F1
Wissington Uplands RCOLW CO6.....77 J8
Wistaria Cl BRWN CM15.....280 E4
Wistaria Pl RCOS CO16.....181 M8
Wisteria Cl IL IG1.....316 C7
Wiston Rd RCOLW CO6.....77 J7
Witchards VGE SS16.....3 C7
Witch Elm HAR CO12.....110 A6
Witchtree La SAFWN CB10.....54 C7
Witcham Cl LOU IG10.....275 P5
Witham Gdns RBRW/HUT CM13 *.....321 N1
Witham Ldg WIT CM8.....196 C4
Witham Rd BRTR CM77.....145 L9
  BRTR CM77.....171 H2
  DAGE RM10.....318 A7
  GPK RM2.....298 G9
  MAL CM9.....199 K7
  MAL CM9.....221 N4
  RCHLM CM3.....196 B3
  WIT CM8.....170 D1
  WIT CM8.....197 N6
The Witherings EMPK RM11.....299 K9
Withersfield Rd HVHL CB9.....41 H2
Withipol St IP IP1.....17 F3
Withrick Wk RCOS CO16.....180 D8
Withy Me CHING E4.....274 G9
Withypool SBN/FI SS3.....330 C5
The Withywindle RCHLM CM3.....286 F2
Witnesham Church La NHMKT IP6.....23 N2
Witney Rd BOC CM0.....291 H4
Wittem Rd CVI SS8.....345 N3
Wittenham Wy CHING E4.....274 G9
The Witterings CVI SS8.....326 D9
Witting Cl RCOS CO16.....181 N8
Witton Wood Rd FOS CO13.....158 F9
Wivenhoe Cross RCOLE CO7.....153 K4
Wivenhoe Rd BARK IG11.....335 H2
  RCOLE CO7.....129 K6
  RCOLE CO7.....153 P7
Wix By-pass MGTR CO11.....132 E2
Wix Rd DAGW RM9.....335 L1
  HAR CO12.....109 J7
  HAR CO12.....133 L4
  MGTR CO11.....107 L8
  MGTR CO11.....132 F4
  RCOLE CO7.....132 G7
Woburn Av BSF CM25.....157 L9
  EPP CM16.....254 F7
  FOS CO13.....158 E7
  HCH RM12.....318 F6

Woburn Pl BCAYW CM12.....282 G3
Wodehouse Rd DART DA1.....347 M9
Wokindon Rd CDW/CHF RM16.....350 C1
Wolferton Rd MNPK E12.....316 A6
Wollaston Crs PIT SS13.....305 J5
Wollaston Wy PIT SS13.....305 J4
Wolmers Hey RCHLM SM5.....195 N5
Wolseley Rd CHLM/GWD CM2.....4 E4
  ROMW/RG RM7.....318 C2
Wolsey Av CHESW EN7.....229 L8
  EHAM E6.....334 B3
  WALTH E17.....294 C7
Wolsey Gdns BARK/HLT IG6.....296 D3
  FX IP11.....11 J3
Wolsey Rd EN EN1.....273 N1
Wolsey St IP1.....16 D6
Wolton Rd COLS CO2.....151 L3
Wolvercote Rd ABYW SE2.....335 L9
Wolverton Wy STHGT/OAK N14.....272 B4
Wolves Hall La RCOS CO16.....132 B6
Wonston Rd BOC CM0.....269 H5
Woodale La
Woodall Rd PEND SN5.....5 B5
Wood Av HOC/HUL SS5.....287 P8
  PUR RM19.....347 P2
Wood Barn La MGTR CO11.....105 L7
Woodberry Av WCHMH N21.....272 F8
Woodberry Cl CVI SS8.....326 D8
  LOS SS9.....327 M1
Woodberry Down EPP CM16.....233 H8
Woodberry Rd WICKE SS11.....305 M1
Woodberry Wy CHING E4.....274 F6
  WOTN CO14.....159 J7
Woodbine Cl HLWW/ROY CM19.....210 D5
Woodbine Pl WAN E11.....315 K1
Woodbridge Cl HARH RM3.....279 J9
Woodbridge Gv RCOS CO16.....181 K9
Woodbridge La HARH RM3.....279 J9
  IPNE IP4.....17 H4
Woodbridge Rd East IPNE IP4.....26 B4
Woodbridge Rd Crs BCAYW CM12.....282 C5
Woodbrooke Wy SLH/COR SS17.....324 A9
Woodbrook Gdns WAB EN9.....253 H3
Woodburn Crl BSF CM23.....326 E2
Woodbury Cl WAN E11.....295 L8
Woodbury Hl LOU IG10.....275 P1
Woodbury Rd WALTH E17.....294 E8
Woodcock La COLN CO4.....128 F9
  HVHL CB9.....41 M4
Woodcocks CAN/RD E16.....333 M5
Woodcot Cl ED N9.....273 P5
Woodcote Ap SBF/HAD SS7.....305 N8
Woodcote Av HCH RM12.....318 F6
Woodcote Crs CHES/WCR EN8.....251 J8
Woodcote Crs PIT SS13.....305 J9
Woodcote Ms LOU IG10.....275 N6
Woodcote Rd LOS SS9.....328 B4
  WAN E11.....315 K2
Woodcotes SBN/FI SS3.....330 D5
Woodcote Wy SBF/HAD SS7.....305 N8
Woodcroft HLWS SM18.....210 E5
  WCHMH N21.....272 E7
Woodcroft Cl SBF/HAD SS7.....326 F2
Woodcutters Av CDW/CHF RM16.....339 M9
  LOS SS9.....327 M1
Wood Dl CHLM/GWD CM2.....240 D4
Woodedge Cl CHING E4.....275 J7
Wood End SAFWS CB11.....90 A5
Wood End Av HOC/HUL SS5.....307 N2
Woodend Cl SBF/HAD SS7.....326 F2
Wooden Gdns FSTGT E7.....272 D3
Woodend Rd WALTH E17.....294 F6
Wooder Gdns FSTGT E7.....315 J6
Woodfall Dr DART DA1.....346 E9
Wood Farm Cl LOS SS9.....327 N2
Woodfield Cl EN EN1.....273 K3
  STSD CM24.....114 A9
  WOTN CO14.....159 H7
Woodfield Dr GPK RM2.....298 F8
  K/T/MI CO5.....202 E5
Woodfield End COLS CO2.....151 K9
Woodfield Gdns LOS SS9.....328 A6
Woodfield Park Dr LOS SS9.....328 B5
Woodfield Rd BRTR CM7.....145 K5
  LOS SS9.....328 B5
  SBF/HAD SS7.....327 K3
Woodfields STSD CM24.....114 B9
Woodfield Ter STSD CM24.....114 B9
  RCHLM CM5.....196 D6
The Woodfines EMPK RM11.....319 J1
Woodford Av GNTH/NBYPK IG2.....296 A9
Woodford Bridge Rd REDBR IG4.....295 N7
Woodford Cl COS CO15.....182 A5
Woodford Ct WAB EN9.....253 K3
Woodford New Rd WALTH E17.....295 H8
Woodford Rd FSTGT E7.....315 L6
  SWFD E18.....295 K8
Woodgate Av POTB/CUF EN6.....250 A3
Woodgates Rd RCOLE CO7.....80 C4
Woodget Cl EHAM E6.....333 P6
Woodgrange Av EN EN1.....273 M5
  SOS SS1.....329 M6
Woodgrange Dr SOS SS1.....19 K5
Woodgrange Ter EN EN1 *.....273 M5
Wood Gn PIT SS13.....304 C6
Woodgreen Est RCOLE CO7.....155 L9
Woodgreen Rd WAB EN9.....253 M3

THMD SE28.....335 K7
Woodhall Cl SUD CO10.....20 D2
Woodhall Crs EMPK RM11.....319 L2
Woodhall Gv BSF CM23.....137 J8
Woodhall Hl CHLM/WR CM1.....193 J9
Woodhall Rd CHLM/WR CM1.....217 P4
  SUD CO10.....20 C2
Woodham Ct SWFD E18.....295 J8
Woodham Dr BRTR CM7.....145 J9
Woodham Rd RCHLM CM3.....196 E8
Woodham Halt RCHLM CM3.....264 F9
Woodham Mortimer Rd MAL CM9.....243 H2
Woodham Park Dr SBF/HAD SS7.....325 N4
Woodham Rd RCHLM CM3.....265 J9
  RCHLM CM3.....286 A5
  SBF/HAD SS7.....325 N4
Woodham Wy WARE SG12.....184 F8
Woodhatch Cl EHAM E6.....333 P5
Woodhaven Gdns BARK/HLT IG6.....296 D8
Woodhill HLWS SM18.....210 F6
Woodhill Common Rd RCHLM SM5.....241 N5
Woodhill CHLM/GWD CM2.....241 H4
  RCHLM SM5.....241 N4
Woodhouse La KIR/NAC IP10.....193 P8
  KIR/NAC IP10.....27 H9
Woodhouse Rd WAN E11.....315 J5
Woodhouse Sq IPNE IP4 *.....17 G5
Woodhurst Rd CVI SS8.....344 B2
Woodison St BOW E3.....332 B4
Woodland Av RBRW/HUT CM13.....281 M4
Woodland Cha COLW CO3.....126 C6
Woodland Cl ING CM4.....260 D5
  RBRW/HUT CM13.....281 M4
  SBF/HAD SS7.....327 J3
  WFD IG8.....275 L9
Woodland Dr COLW CO3.....151 J1
Woodland Gv EPP CM16.....255 H1
Woodland Park Cha RCHLM.....267 P2
Woodland Rd CHING E4.....274 F7
  CHLM/WR CM1.....193 J9
  LOU IG10.....275 P2
Woodlands BRTR CM7.....145 L3
  BSF CM23.....157 P6
  COLN CO4.....128 C6
  HAR CO12.....133 L5
  RCHLM SM5.....267 P6
  RIPS/CAP IP9.....84 D2
Woodlands Av CHDH RM6.....317 M1
  EMPK RM11.....299 J9
  RAYL SS6.....306 D7
  WAN E11.....315 L3
Woodlands Cl CDW/CHF RM16.....349 P1
  COS CO15.....182 B5
  HOC/HUL SS5.....307 N2
  HOD EN11 *.....208 D6
  RAYL SS6.....306 C7
  SLH/COR SS17.....324 E2
Woodlands Dr HOD EN11.....208 D7
Woodlands Gdns WALTH E17.....295 H8
Woodlands Pde HOC/HUL SS5.....307 N2
Woodlands Pk LOS SS9.....327 K3
Woodlands Park Dr GTDUN CM6.....141 J5
Woodlands Ri RCOS CO16.....156 B5
Woodlands Rd ED N9.....273 P7
  ENC/FH EN2.....90 A5
  ENF E17.....299 M5
  HOC/HUL SS5.....307 N2
  IL IG1.....316 D5
  RIPS/CAP IP9.....83 K2
  WALTH E17.....294 F7
  WAN E11.....315 H4
  WICKW SS12.....285 J9
The Woodlands RCOLE CO7.....179 K5
  SBN/FI SS3.....330 E6
  STHGT/OAK N14.....272 A7
Woodlands Wy RIPW IP8.....22 C8
Woodland Wy CHESW EN7.....228 C7
  CHONG CM5.....235 L9
  EPP CM16.....254 F5
  HSTD CO9.....99 J9
  RCOLE CO7 *.....153 J5
  WCHMH N21.....272 F8
  WFD IG8.....275 L9
Wood La BSF CM23.....138 B4
  BUNT SG9.....87 H2
  CHONG CM5.....235 M9
  COLW CO5.....126 C6
  DAGE RM10.....317 P4
  GTDUN CM6.....190 C3
  HCH RM12.....318 F7
  HOC/HUL SS5.....307 N2
  MAL CM9.....222 B6
  MAL CM9.....244 F9
  WFD IG8.....295 J2
Woodleigh Av SS SS9.....327 N5
Woodley Rd WARE SG12.....184 C2
Woodley Wk SBN/FI SS3.....330 DL
Woodlow SBF/HAD SS7.....326 F2
Woodmanhurst Rd SLH/COR SS17.....323 N9
Woodman La CHING E4.....274 C4
Woodman Pth BARK/HLT IG6.....296 F7
Woodman Rd BRW CM14.....300 F2
Woodman St CAN/RD E16.....334 B8
Wood Meads EPP CM16.....233 H8
Woodmill Ms HOD EN11 *.....208 E5
Woodpecker Cl BSF CM23.....157 L9
  ED N9.....273 N5
Woodpecker Rd CHTY IP2.....24 E8

GRH DA9.....348 E9
RCHLM CM3.....245 P9
SLH/COR SS17.....341 L2
VGE SS16.....322 C1
Worcester Ct CHLM/GWD CM2.....240 E5
Worcester Crs RCOLE CO7.....154 A6
  WFD IG8.....295 M1
Worcester Dr RAYL SS6.....307 J6
Worcester Gdns IL IG1.....315 P2
Worcester Rd BOC CM0.....291 H2
  COL CO1.....6 E4
  IL IG1.....6 E4
  IPSE IP5.....30 C2
  MNPK E12.....316 A5
  WALTH E17.....294 A6
Worcesters Av EN EN1.....251 M8
Wordsworth Av MAL CM9.....244 B2
  MNPK E12.....315 P9
  SWFD E18.....295 J7
Wordsworth Cl HARH RM3.....299 H5
  SOSN SS2.....329 J4
  TIL RM18.....337 H5
Wordsworth Crs IP IP1.....22 D7
Wordsworth Rd BRTR CM7.....121 J8
  COLW CO3.....127 M3
Wordsworth Wy DART DA1.....347 M9
Workhouse Hl COLN CO4.....103 H4
Workhouse La COLN CO4.....128 F9
Workhouse Rd RCOLW CO6.....101 P5
Workshop La KIR/NAC IP10.....27 H9
Worland Rd SRTFD E15.....315 H9
Worlds End La K/T/MI CO5.....173 J2
  WCHMH N21.....272 E4
Wormley Ct WAB EN9.....253 K3
Wormley Lodge Cl BROX EN10.....230 C2
Wormyngford Ct WAB EN9.....253 K3
Worrin Cl BRWN CM15.....281 J7
Worrin Rd BRWN CM15.....281 J8
Worsdell Wy COLN CO4.....128 A5
Worsley Cl CHTY IP2.....24 E9
Worsley Rd WAN E11.....315 H6
Wortham Pl HVHL CB9.....41 K4
Worthing Cl SRTFD E15.....333 H1
  WTHK RM20.....349 H4
Worthing Ms COS CO15.....207 H4
Worthing Rd LAIN SS15.....303 H9
Worthington Wy COLW CO5.....151 J1
Wortley Rd EHAM E6.....315 N9
Wouldham Rd CAN/RD E16.....333 J4
  WTHK RM20.....349 H4
Wrabness Rd HAR CO12.....108 F5
Wraghy Rd WAN E11.....315 L2
The Wraglins BSF CM23.....137 N9
Wrampling Pl ED N9.....273 N7
Wrangley Ct WAB EN9.....253 K3
Wratting Rd HVHL CB9.....41 K3
Wray Av CLAY IG5.....296 B7
Wray Cl EMPK RM11.....319 J2
Wraysbury Dr LAIN SS15.....303 L6
Wren Av CHTY IP2.....24 E8
  LOS SS9.....307 M8
Wrenbrook Rd BSF CM23.....157 L9
Wren Cl BCAYE CM11.....283 K6
  CAN/RD E16.....333 J6
  COLW CO3.....150 F2
  ED N9.....274 A7
Wren Ct COLW CO7 *.....155 J5
  SBF/HAD SS7.....305 N9
Wrendale COS CO15.....182 A7
Wren Dr WAB EN9.....253 K3
Wren Gdns DAGW RM9.....317 L7
Wren Rd DAGW RM9.....317 L8
  EHAM E6.....280 C9
Wren Pl BRW CM14.....280 C9
Wren Rd DAGW RM9.....317 L7
Wrens Pk FX IP11.....35 N4
The Wrens HLWW/ROY CM19.....12 E7
Wren Ter LOU IG10.....254 C9
Wren Tr MAL CM9.....350 C5
Wrexham Rd BOW E3.....332 D2
  HARH RM3.....323 J1
  LAIN SS15.....323 J1
Wright La KESG IP5.....27 J3
Wright Md CHLM/GWD CM2.....218 P7
Wright Rd IPSE IP5.....26 B9
Wright's Av BRTR CM7.....145 P7
Wrights Cl DAGE RM10.....318 A6
Wright's Green La RBSF CM22.....162 F6
Wrights Cl DAGE RM10.....318 A6
Wright's Piece RBSF CM22.....115 K1
Wright's Rd BOW E3.....332 C2
Wrights Wy RCOLW CO6.....77 J4
Wrigley Cl CHING E4 *.....294 C2
Writtle Cl RCOS CO16.....181 L9
Writtle Rd CHLM/WR CM1.....4 C7
  ING CM4.....238 C7
Wroths Pth LOU IG10.....254 A9
Wroxall Rd DAGW RM9.....317 K8
Wroxham Cl COLW CO5.....127 L9
Wroxham Rd IPSE IP5.....25 N8
  THMD SE28.....335 J7
Wryneck Cl COLN CO4.....128 A4
Wyatt Rd DART DA1.....348 E8
  FSTGT E7.....315 K8
Wyatts Dr SS SS1.....329 N7
Wyatts Green La BRWN CM15.....258 G6
Wyatt's Green Rd BRWN CM15.....258 G6
Wychbury Cl SUD CO10.....75 N1
  WALTH E17.....294 F7
Wyburn Rd IPSE IP5.....306 G9
Wyburns Av RAYL SS6.....307 H7
Wyburns Av East RAYL SS6.....307 H7
Wych Elm HLW CM20.....13 G5
Wych Elm Rd EMPK RM11.....319 H1
Wychford Dr SBW CM21.....187 K3
Wychwood Gdns CLAY IG5.....296 A9
Wycke Hl MAL CM9.....243 N2
Wycke La MAL CM9.....243 N2
Wyclife Gv CO COL CO1.....8 A2
Wycombe Av SBF/HAD SS7.....305 M9

Wycombe Rd
 GNTH/NBYPK IG2 ......296 A9
Wyemead Crs CHING E4 ...275 H8
Wye Rd IPSE IP3 ......25 P8
Wyfields CLAY IC5 ......296 C5
Wykeham Av DAGW RM9 ...317 K8
 EMPK RN11 ......319 J1
Wykeham Gn DAGW RM9 ...289 J1
Wykeham Rd CHLM/WR CM1 ...289 J1
Wyke Rd BOW E3 ......314 D9
Wykes Bishop St IPSE IP3 * ...25 M7
Wykes Gn BSDN SS14 ...3 K3
Wyldfield Gdns ED N9 ...273 L8
Wyldwood Cl HLWE CM17 ...187 K6
Wymark Cl RAIN RM13 ...336 E2
Wynchgate STHGT/OAK N14 ...272 D6
Wyncolls Rd COLN CO4 ...128 D2
Wyndam Cl COLS CO2 ...152 C6
Wyndcroft Cl ENC/FH EN2 ...272 C2
Wyndham Crs COS CO15 ...7 H1
Wyndham Rd EHAM E6 ...315 N9
Wynndale Rd SWFD E18 ...295 L5
Wynters VGE SS16 ...324 A2
Wynterton Cl IPSE IP3 ...31 H1
Wynyard Rd SAFWN CB10 ...51 M7
Wyse's Rd ING IG4 ...238 A4
Wythefield PIT SS13 ...304 F9
Wythenshawe Rd
 DAGE RM10 ......317 P5
Wythes Rd CAN/RD E16 ...333 P8
Wyvern Rd IPSE IP5 ...31 J1
Wyvis St POP/IOD E14 ...332 E5

Y

Yabsley St POP/IOD E14 ...332 F8
Yale Ms COLN CO4 ...128 C3
Yale Wy HCH RM12 ...318 F6
Yamburg Rd CVI SS8 ...344 G2
Yardley Cl CHING E4 ...305 M9
Yardley Cl CHING E4 ...274 E4
Yardley Hall La GTDUN CM6 ...91 N2
Yardley La CHING E4 ...274 E4
Yare Av WIT CM8 ...145 K4
Yarmouth Cl RCOS CO16 * ...181 P7
Yarmouth Rd IP IP1 ...22 G5
Yarnacott CHLM/GWD CM2 ...
Yarncott Cl IPSE IP3 ...31 H1
Yarnton Wy ABYW SE2 ...335 K9
Yarrow Crs EHAM E6 ...335 P5
Yarwood Rd CHLM/GWD CM2 ...218 D9
Yearling Cl WARE CM20 ...184 C6
Yeldham Lock
 CHLM/GWD CM2 ......218 F9
Yeldham Pl HVHL CB9 ...41 K3
Yeldham Rd HSTD CO9 ...72 B5
Yellowpine Wy CHIG IG7 ...297 J1
Yelverton Cl HARH RM3 ...299 H5
Yeoman Cl EHAM E6 ...316 A9
Yeoman Rd FX IP11 ...10 D3
Yeomans Cl BSF CM23 ...137 J9
Yeomans Wy PEND EN3 * ...273 N1
Yeomen Wy BARK/HLT IG6 ...296 D3
Yeo St BOW E3 ...332 E5

Yeovil Cha WOS/PRIT SS0 ...328 C2
Yerril Gdn HVHL CB9 ...41 H4
Yevele Wy EMPK RM11 ...319 K2
Yew Cl BKHH IG9 ...275 N8
 CHESW EN7 * ...229 K6
 LAIN SS15 ...303 L6
 WIT CM8 ...172 A8
Yewlands Rd EN11 ...208 D6
 SBW CM21 ...187 M3
Yewlands Dr HOD EN11 ...208 D6
Yews Av EN EN1 ...251 N6
Yew Tree Cl LOU IG10 ...128 F7
 RBRW/HUT CM13 ...281 L5
 RCHLM CM5 ...196 D7
 WCHMH N21 ...272 F6
Yew Tree Gdns CHDH RM6 ...297 M9
 CHLM/GWD CM2 ...240 B4
 ROMW/RG RM7 ...298 C9
Yewtree Cv KESC IP5 ...26 E4
Yew Tree Pl BSF CM23 ...137 L6
Yewtree Ri RIPW IP8 ...29 L1
Yew Wy HOD EN11 ...208 D6
Yew Wy COS CO15 ...206 E6
Yonge Cl RCHLM CM5 ...219 K2
Yorick Av K/T/MI CO5 ...202 F6
Yorick Rd K/T/MI CO5 ...202 F6
York Av SLH/COR SS17 ...323 P9
York Cl BRWN CM15 ...281 J6
 EHAM E6 ...334 A6
 RAYL SS6 ...307 K7
 SUD CO10 ...20 D2
York Crs LOU IG10 ...275 P2

NHMKT IP6 ...22 D3
Yorkes HLWS CM18 ...210 G5
York Gdns BRTR CM7 ...145 L2
York Ga STHGT/OAK N14 ...272 D6
York Hi LOU IG10 ...275 P2
York Ms IL IG1 ...316 B4
York Pl COL CO1 * ...9 F4
 IL IG1 ...316 B4
York Ri RAYL SS6 ...307 K7
York Rd BCAYW CM12 ...283 H5
 BOC CM0 ...291 H4
 BRWN CM15 ...281 J6
 CHES/WCR EN8 ...252 B4
 CHING E4 ...294 D2
 CHLM/GWD CM2 ...4 E7
 COS CO15 ...182 E8
 EPP CM16 ...233 P6
 FSTGT E7 ...315 K8
 FX IP11 ...11 K1
 HLWB CB9 ...41 H4
 IL IG1 ...316 B5
 IPSE IP3 ...25 P7
 KESC IP5 ...27 M5
 LEY E10 ...314 F5
 RAIN RM13 ...318 C9
 RAYL SS6 ...307 K7
 RCFD SS4 ...288 D9
 RCOLE CO7 ...179 K7
 RCOLW CO6 ...124 A1
 SLH/COR SS17 ...340 G1
 SOS SS1 ...19 H5
 SUD CO10 ...20 D3
 WALTH E17 ...294 D9

WCHMH N21 ...273 J6
York Road Ar SOS SS1 * ...19 G5
Yorkshire Rd POP/IOD E14 ...332 B6
York Sq POP/IOD E14 * ...332 B6
York St BARK IG11 ...334 C1
 MGTR CO11 ...106 C4
York Ter ENC/FH EN2 ...251 H8
 ERITH DA8 ...346 B6
Young Cl LOS SS9 ...308 B9
 RCOS CO16 ...181 M8
Youngmans Cl ENC/FH EN2 ...251 H9
Young Rd CAN/RD E16 ...333 M6
Youngs Rd GNTH/NBYPK IG2 ...296 E9
Yoxley Ap GNTH/NBYPK IG2 ...316 D1
Yoxley Dr GNTH/NBYPK IG2 ...316 D1
Ypres Rd COLS CO2 ...151 P5
Yunus Khan Cl WALTH E17 ...294 D9

Z

Zambesi Rd BSF CM23 ...137 L9
Zambezie Dr ED N9 ...275 P9
Zandi Rd CVI SS8 ...344 G5
Zealand Dr CVI SS8 ...345 H2
Zealand Rd BOW E3 ...332 B2
Zelham Dr CVI SS8 ...345 J2
Zenith BSDN SS14 ...304 D5
Zetland St POP/IOD E14 ...332 F5
Zider Pass CVI SS8 ...345 J2

Index - featured places

Aaron House Clinic of Physiotherapy
 WOS/PRIT SS0 ...328 C3
Abbey Lane Commercial Estate
 SRTFD E15 ...332 G2
Abbey Mead Industrial Estate
 WAB EN9 ...252 E4
Abbey Park Industrial Estate
 BARK IG11 ...334 C2
Abbey Road Health Centre
 SRTFD E15 ...333 H1
Abbey Sports Centre
 BARK IG11 ...334 D1
Abbey Wharf Industrial Estate
 BARK IG11 ...334 E5
Abbotswell Primary School
 WCHMH CM18 ...210 E5
Abbotts Hall Primary School
 SLH/COR SS17 ...341 M2
ABC Cinema
 BRW CM14 ...280 F8
Abridge Golf & Country Club
 EPP CM16 ...255 N7
Acacia Business Centre
 WAN E11 ...315 H5
Acorn Trading Centre
 WTHK RM20 ...349 H4
Acton CE Primary School
 SUD CO10 ...47 M5
Acton Place Industrial Estate
 SUD CO10 ...47 L3
Adams Business Centre
 BSDN SS14 ...304 D6
Adath Yisroel Cemetery
 EN EN1 ...251 L9
The Adult College of Barking & Dagenham BARK IG11 ...316 F8
Adult Community College
 ...8 E5
Adult Community College Chelmsford
 CHLM/WR CM1 ...4 A3
Adventure Island
 SOS SS1 ...19 H6
Ainslie Wood Primary School
 CHING E4 ...294 E2
Airborne Business Park
 LOS SS9 ...327 P1
Airport Business Park
 SOSN SS2 ...308 F9
Albany School (Grant Maintained) PEND EN3 ...252 A8
The Albany School
 HCH RM12 ...318 G4
Albright Industrial Estate
 RAIN RM13 ...336 E5
Alderman Blaxill School
 COLS CO2 ...151 L3
Alderbrook County Secondary School
 MNPK E12 ...315 M3
Aldersbrook Primary School
 WAN E11 ...315 L3
The Alderton Primary School
 LOU IG10 ...276 B4
The Alec Hunter High School
 BRTR CM7 ...145 M4
Alexandra Business Centre
 PEND EN3 ...274 A3
Alfred Salter Primary School
 BERM/RHTH SE16 ...332 A9
Alfreds Way Industrial Estate
 BARK IG11 ...335 H1
Alleyn Court Preparatory School SBN/FI SS5 ...529 P5
Alleyn Court Pre-Preparatory School WOS/PRIT SS0 ...328 D5
All Nations Christian College
 WARE ...184 L5
All Saints Catholic School
 BRTR RM8 ...317 P5
All Saints CE Middle School
 SUD CO10 ...47 K9

All Saints CE Primary School
 HAR CO12 ...110 B5
 MAL CM9 ...221 P9
All Saints Primary School
 BSF CM23 ...137 N6
Allum Medical Centre
 WAN E11 ...314 G2
Alma Primary School
 PEND EN3 ...274 B4
Alnesbourne Priory Golf Club
 KIR/NAC IP10 ...31 J5
Al-Noor Primary School
 GDMY/SEVK IG3 ...317 J5
Alpha Business Centre
 WALTH E17 ...294 C9
Alpha Business Park
 EHAM E6 ...22 F9
Alpine Business Centre
 EHAM E6 ...334 B5
Alresford Business Centre
 RCOLE CO7 ...154 A6
Alresford Primary School
 RCOLE CO7 ...154 A7
Alsa Business Park
 STSD CM24 ...114 C6
Altmore Infant School
 EHAM E6 ...316 A9
Alton Park Junior School
 COS CO15 ...6 B5
Alton Water Sports Centre
 RIPS/CAP IP9 ...83 J6
Amberfield School
 KIR/NAC IP10 ...32 A4
Ambresbury Banks Fort
 EPP CM16 ...254 C4
Amwell View Special School
 WARE SG12 ...184 E8
Anchor Bay Industrial Estate
 ERITH DA8 ...346 E5
Anchor Press Social & Sports Club K/T/MI CO5 ...174 A8
Ancient House
 IP IP1 ...16 E4
Andrewsfield (Saling) Aerodrome GTDUN CM6 ...119 J9
Andrews Lane J & I School
 CHESW EN7 ...229 N7
Anglian Industrial Estate
 BARK IG11 ...334 G4
Anglia Polytechnic University
 BRWN CM15 ...280 G7
 CHLM/WR CM1 ...193 P9
Anglia Polytechnic University (Central Campus)
 ...4 E5
Anglia Polytechnic University (Rivermead Campus)
 CHLM/WR CM1 ...218 A7
Anglia Trading Estate
 COL CO1 ...8 B2
Anglo European School
 ING CM4 ...260 D5
Animal Cemetery
 REDBR IG4 ...295 N7
Annandale Clinic
 WOS/PRIT SS0 ...328 C3
Annwood Lodge Business Park
 WICKW SS12 ...306 A5
Anstey First School
 BUNT SG9 ...86 B2
Antonys RC Primary School
 WFD IG8 ...295 K1
Appleton School
 SBF/HAD SS7 ...325 P1
Ardleigh Green Primary School
 HARH RM11 ...299 J7
Ardleigh St Marys CE Primary School RCOLE CO7 ...104 E8
Arena Essex
 WTHK RM20 ...338 D9
Arena Sports & Leisure Club
 COLS CO2 ...151 P1

Arthur Bugler J & I School
 SLH/COR SS17 ...341 M2
The Arthur Findlay College
 STSD CM24 ...138 D1
Arts Centre
 COL CO1 ...8 B6
Arts Centre Cinema
 HVHL CB9 ...41 K4
Ashdon Primary School
 SAFWN CB10 ...52 G1
Ashgrove College
 WALTH E17 ...294 D7
Ash Industrial Estate
 HLWW/ROY CM19 ...210 A4
Ashingdon Primary School
 RCFD SS4 ...288 C7
Ashmole Centre
 STHGT/OAK N14 ...272 B7
Ashmole School
 STHGT/OAK N14 ...272 B7
Ashton Playing Fields Track
 WFD IG8 ...295 P3
Asquith School
 PEND EN3 ...275 P3
Atherton Leisure Centre
 FSTGT E7 ...315 J8
Atlantic Hotel
 CHLM/WR CM1 ...5 H1
Audley End House & Gardens
 SAFWN CB11 ...51 J9
Aveley FC
 SOCK/AV RM15 ...337 P7
Aveley Medical Centre
 SOCK/AV RM15 ...338 F4
Aveley Primary School
 SOCK/AV RM15 ...338 B8
Aveley School (School House)
 SOCK/AV RM15 ...338 B8
The Aveley School
 SOCK/AV RM15 ...338 A7
Aveling Park School
 WALTH E17 ...294 D6
Avenue Industrial Estate
 CHING E4 ...294 C3
 GPK RM2 ...299 J6
Avenue Primary School
 MNPK E12 ...315 P6
Avon House School
 WFD IG8 ...295 K1
Axis Business Centre
 SRTFD E15 ...332 E1
Aylands School
 PEND EN3 ...251 P6
Ayloff Primary School
 HCH RM12 ...318 G6
Bacon's College
 BERM/RHTH SE16 ...332 B8
Baddow Hall J & I School
 CHLM/GWD CM2 ...240 F4
Balam Leisure Centre
 PLSTW E15 ...333 K4
Balfour Medical Centre
 GRAYS RM17 ...349 M2
Ballards Gore Golf Club
 RCFD SS4 ...309 M1
Ballingdon Hill Industrial Estate
 SUD CO10 ...60 F4
Ballingdon Trading Estate
 SUD CO10 ...60 F4
Balmoral Hotel
 WOS/PRIT SS0 ...328 E6
Balmoral Trading Estate
 BARK IG11 ...334 G5
Bancrofts School
 WFD IG8 ...295 P7
Bankside Park Industrial Estate
 BARK IG11 ...335 H3
Barbara Castle Health Centre
 HLWW/ROY CM19 ...210 B7
Barclay J & I School
 CHLM E10 ...314 G1
Barkantine Clinic
 POP/IOD E14 ...332 D9

Barking Abbey Comprehensive School (Lower) BARK IG11 ...316 E7
Barking Abbey Comprehensive School (Upper)
 BARK IG11 ...316 D8
Barking Abbey Industrial Estate
 BARK IG11 ...334 C1
Barking Abbey Leisure Centre
 BARK IG11 ...317 H8
Barking College
 ROMW/RG RM7 ...318 C4
Barking FC
 BCTR RM8 ...317 J7
Barking Hospital
 BARK IG11 ...316 G9
Barking Industrial Park
 BARK IG11 ...334 G1
Barking RUFC
 DAGW RM9 ...335 L1
Barkingside Cemetery
 BARK/HLT IG6 ...296 C7
Barkingside FC
 BARK/HLT IG6 ...296 E8
Barley Lane Primary School
 GDMY/SEVK IG3 ...317 H2
Barling Magna Primary School
 SBN/FI SS5 ...310 C8
Barn Croft Primary School
 WALTH E17 ...314 D1
Barnehurst Primary School
 BXLYHN DA7 ...346 D6
Barnehurst Public Pay & Play Golf Club BXLYHN DA7 ...346 C8
Barnes Cray Primary School
 DART DA1 ...346 F9
Barnes Farm J & I School
 CHLM/GWD CM2 ...218 F8
Barons Court County Infant School WOS/PRIT SS0 ...18 C4
Barratt Industrial Park
 BOW E3 ...332 F4
Barstable School
 BSDN SS14 ...304 E9
Bartlet Hospital
 FX IP11 ...35 L7
The Basildon Centre
 BSDN SS14 ...2 D5
Basildon & District Crematorium PIT SS13 ...325 K2
Basildon Golf Club
 VGE SS16 ...324 A3
Basildon Hospital
 VGE SS16 ...323 N3
Basildon RFC
 BSDN SS14 ...304 C6
Basildon United FC
 BSDN SS14 ...304 C6
Bata Business Park
 TIL RM18 ...351 K2
Bates Industrial Estate
 HARH RM5 ...299 M4
Battlesbridge Motorcycle Museum WICKE SS11 ...286 A6
Baynards Primary School
 K/T/MI CO5 ...173 N6
BBC Radio Suffolk
 IP IP1 ...16 C3
Beacon Hill Industrial Estate
 PUR RM19 ...347 N2
Beacon Hill Special School
 CHTY IP2 ...28 G8
Beal High School
 REDBR IG4 ...295 P7
Beam Primary School
 DAGE RM10 ...336 B2
Bearwalden Business Park
 SAFWS CB11 ...64 F4
Beauchamps GM School
 WICKE SS11 ...285 M8
Beaumont Primary School
 LEY E10 ...314 E2

Beckers Green CP School
 BRTR CM7 ...145 N4
Beckenham Business Park
 MAL CM9 ...223 L1
Beckton Ski Centre
 EHAM E6 ...334 B4
Beckton Special School
 CAN/RD E16 ...333 N5
Beckton Triangle Retail Park
 EHAM E6 ...334 C3
Becontree Day Hospital
 BCTR RM8 ...317 M4
Becontree Primary School
 BCTR RM8 ...317 J5
Beehive Preparatory School
 REDBR IG4 ...296 A8
Belchamp St Paul CE Primary School CO10 ...58 F1
Belcon Industrial Estate
 HOD EN11 ...208 F5
Belfairs Golf Club
 LOS SS9 ...327 M2
Belfairs High School
 LOS SS9 ...327 N1
Belfairs Sports Ground
 LOS SS9 ...327 N2
Belfairs Swimming Pool
 LOS SS9 ...327 N1
Belhus Golf Club & Leisure Centre SOCK/AV RM15 ...338 B8
Belhus Woods Country Park
 SOCK/AV RM15 ...338 A3
Belsheys Wharf
 BERM/RHTH SE16 ...332 A8
Belmont Park School
 LEY E10 ...314 F1
Belstead School
 RCOW CO6 ...24 D9
Belvedere Industrial Estate
 BELV DA17 ...336 C8
Belvedere Link Business Park
 BELV DA17 ...346 B1
Belvedere Primary School
 BELV DA17 ...346 A2
Benbridge Industrial Estate
 MAL CM9 ...222 B6
Benfleet Business Centre
 SBF/HAD SS7 ...326 A4
Benhurst JMI School
 HCH RM12 ...318 G5
Ben Jonson Primary School
 WCHPL E1 ...332 B4
Bentalls Industrial Estate
 MAL CM9 ...222 B6
Bentalls Shopping Centre
 MAL CM9 ...222 C6
Bentfield Primary School
 STSD CM24 ...114 A7
Bentley Car Club
 BRWN CM15 ...258 B9
Bentley Primary School
 RIPS/CAP IP9 ...82 A2
Benton Hall Golf Club
 WIT CM8 ...197 L6
Benyon Primary School
 SOCK/AV RM15 ...338 F2
Berger Primary School
 HOM E9 ...314 A8
The Beth Chatto Gardens
 RCOLE CO7 ...153 P1
Bexley College
 ERITH DA8 ...346 B2
Bexleyheath Marriott Hotel
 BXLYHS DA6 ...346 A9
Billericay IT Learning Centre
 BCAYW CM12 ...283 H7
The Billericay School
 BCAYW CM12 ...283 H8
Billericay Swimming Pool
 BCAYW CM12 ...283 H5
Billericay Town FC
 BCAYW CM12 ...282 F7
Billingsgate Fish Market
 POP/IOD E14 ...332 E8

Birchanger CE Primary School
 BSF CM23 ....138 A3
Birchanger Industrial Estate
 BSF CM23 ....137 M4
Birch Business Centre
 COLS CO2 ....150 D7
Birch CE Primary School
 COLS CO2 ....175 K1
Birch Grove Golf Club
 COLS CO2 ....151 L6
Birchmere Business Park
 THMD SE28 ....334 C9
Birchwood CP School
 KESG IP5 ....27 M4
Birchwood High School
 BSF CM23 ....137 P6
The Bishop CE & RC Primary
 School CHLM/WR CM1 ......218 E5
Bishop John Robinson CE
 Primary School
 THMD SE28 ....335 N7
Bishops Park College
 RCOS CO16 ....206 F1
Bishop's Park Health Centre
 BSF CM25 ....137 L6
Bishop's Stortford
 Business Centre
 BSF CM23 ....137 M8
Bishop's Stortford College
 BSF CM25 ....137 K7
Bishop's Stortford Golf Club
 BSF CM23 ....138 A7
The Bishop's Stortford
 High School BSF CM23 ......162 C1
Bishop's Stortford RFC
 BSF CM25 ....137 J5
Bishop Stopford's School
 EN EN1 ....273 M1
Bishop William Ward
 CE Primary School
 RCOLW CO6 ....102 E9
Blackall Industrial Estate
 RCHLM CM5 ....265 J8
Blackfriars Priory Hall
 IPNE IP4 ....17 F5
The Black Lion Hotel
 SUD CO10 ....46 F1
Blackmore CP School
 ING CM4 ....259 H1
Black Notley Hospital
 BRTR CM77 ....146 E4
Blackshots Leisure Centre
 CDW/CHF RM16 ....339 N9
Blackwall Trading Estate
 POP/IOD E14 ....332 C5
Blackwater Leisure Centre
 MAL CM9 ....244 C1
Blackwater Sailing Club
 MAL CM9 ....222 G8
Blackwater Trading Estate
 MAL CM9 ....222 B7
Blenheim Primary School
 LOS SS9 ....328 A3
Blessed John Roche Catholic
 School POP/IOD E14 ....332 D6
Blois Meadow Business Centre
 HVHL CB9 ....55 M2
Bluebridge Industrial Estate
 HSTD CO9 ....98 C7
Blyth's Wharf
 POP/IOD E14 ....332 B7
Bocking Church Street Primary
 School BRTR CM7 ....121 J7
Boleyn Cinema
 EHAM E6 ....333 N2
Bonner Primary School
 BETH E2 ....332 A2
Bonner's Sailings Nature
 Reserve K/T/MI CO5 ....202 E1
Bonney Grove SPLD Base
 CHESW EN7 ....229 M9
Bonnygate Primary School
 SOCK/AV RM15 ....338 E5
Boomes Industrial Estate
 RAIN RM13 ....336 E4
Boreham Airfield
 RCHLM CM3 ....194 G8
Boreham Industrial Estate
 RCHLM CM5 ....219 L1
Boreham Primary School
 RCHLM CM3 ....219 L3
The Boswells School
 CHLM/WR CM1 ....218 C5
Botany Bay CC
 ENC/FH EN2 ....250 C6
Bournemouth Park
 Primary School SOSN SS2 ..329 J4
Bournes Green
 Primary School SOS SS1 ....330 A6
Bourneside Sports Club
 STHGT/OAK N14 ....272 C7
Bow County Court
 SRTFD E15 ....315 H8
Bower Hill Industrial Estate
 EPP CM16 ....255 H2
Bower Park School
 ROM RM1 ....298 D3
Bow Industrial Park
 SRTFD E15 ....314 D9
Bow Secondary School
 BOW E3 ....332 D2
Bow Triangle Business Centre
 BOW E3 ....332 D4
Boxted CE Primary School
 COLN CO4 ....103 J1
Boyce Hill Golf Club
 SBF/HAD SS7 ....326 B4
Boyd CC
 UPMR RM14 ....320 B4
Boynton Vineyard
 SUD CO10 ....43 K7
The Brackenbury Sports Centre
 FX IP11 ....35 M6
Bracken Industrial Estate
 BARK/HLT IG6 ....296 G4

Bradfield Primary School
 MGTR CO11 ....107 K7
Bradwell Quay Yacht Club
 BOC CM0 ....226 B7
Brady Primary School
 RAIN RM13 ....337 H5
Braeside Senior School
 BKHH IG9 ....275 L7
Braintree Athletics Track
 BRTR CM7 ....144 G2
Braintree College
 BRTR CM7 ....145 K1
Braintree Golf Club
 BRTR CM77 ....122 B9
Braintree RFC
 BRTR CM7 ....145 N4
Braintree Town FC
 BRTR CM7 ....145 M4
Bramford CE Primary School
 BRTR CM7 ....24 B2
Brampton Manor School
 PLSTW E15 ....333 N4
Brampton Primary School
 EHAM E6 ....333 P5
Bramston Sports Centre
 WIT CM8 ....197 J3
Brandy Hole Yacht Club
 HOC/HUL SS5 ....287 K4
Bramfi J & I School
 UPMR RM14 ....319 M6
Branollys Health Centre
 PLSTW E13 ....333 K4
Brantham Athletic &
 Social Club MGTR CO11 ....106 B1
Braxted Park Golf Club
 WIT CM8 ....172 F8
Brays Grove School
 HLWS CM18 ....211 J5
Brentwood Chiropody Surgery
 BRW CM14 ....280 G8
The Brentwood Clinic
 BRWN CM15 ....280 G7
Brentwood Community
 Hospital BRWN CM15 ....281 H7
Brentwood County
 High School BRW CM14 ....280 G9
Brentwood IT Learning Centre
 BRW CM14 ....280 F8
Brentwood Pre-Preparatory
 School BRWN CM15 ....281 H7
Brentwood RFC
 BRW CM14 ....301 H1
Brentwood School
 BRWN CM15 ....280 G8
Brentwood Sports Ground
 BRWN CM15 ....280 G7
Brentwood Theatre
 BRW CM14 ....280 G7
Brentwood Ursuline Convent
 High School BRW CM14 ....280 G9
Brett Vale Golf Club
 HADL IP7 ....80 A1
Brewery Museum
 IPSE IP3 ....25 M8
Briarswood Clinic
 CVI SS8 ....326 C9
Brick Lane Music Hall
 CAN/RD E16 ....333 N8
Bridge Hospital
 WIT CM8 ....197 J4
Bridge Trading Estate
 NHMKT IP6 ....22 C3
Bridge View Industrial Estate
 WTHK RM20 ....348 D4
Bridgewick Arts Centre
 BOC CM0 ....270 C5
Briggens House Hotel
 WARE SG12 ....185 M9
Brightlingsea J & I School
 RCOLE CO7 ....179 K7
Brightlingsea Sailing Club
 RCOLE CO7 ....179 K8
Brightlingsea United FC
 RCOLE CO7 ....179 L6
Brightside Primary School
 BCAYW CM12 ....282 F3
Brimsdown Industrial Estate
 PEND EN3 ....275 P1
Brimsdown Primary School
 PEND EN3 ....274 A2
Brinkley Grove Primary School
 COLN CO4 ....128 C2
Briscoe Primary School
 PIT SS13 ....304 C7
Britannia Business Centre
 CHES/WCR EN8 ....252 C4
Britannia Primary School
 IPNE IP4 ....26 A6
Britannia Sports Ground
 WALTH E17 ....294 D4
Britannia Village Primary
 School CAN/RD E16 ....333 L8
Brittania Business Park
 CHES/WCR EN8 ....252 C4
Brittons School
 Technology College
 RAIN RM15 ....318 E9
Broadfields Primary School
 HLW CM20 ....210 F2
Broadford Primary School
 HARH RM3 ....299 J3
Brocks Business Park
 WICKE SS11 ....305 L1
Broke Hall Primary School
 IPNE IP4 ....26 D6
Bromfords School
 WICKW SS12 ....304 C1
Bromfords Sports Centre
 WICKW SS12 ....304 C2
Brook Craft Market
 IP IP1 ....16 E4
Brooke Trading Estate
 ROM RM1 ....318 E2
Brook Farm Industrial Estate
 ABR/ST RM4 ....278 C6

Brookfield Retail Park
 CHES/WCR EN8 ....230 A6
Brookhouse Business Park
 CHTY IP2 ....24 G5
Brookland J & I School
 CHES/WCR EN8 ....230 B7
Brooklands Primary School
 MGTR CO11 ....81 N9
Brook Natural Health Centre
 SUD CO10 ....344 B2
Brook Road Industrial Estate
 RAYL SS6 ....306 C7
Brookside Business Centre
 BRTR CM22 ....162 C4
Brookside Primary School
 RM5 ....299 K2
Brook Street Business Centre
 COL CO1 ....9 G7
Brookweald CC
 CHLM/WR CM1 ....280 B7
Broomfield FC
 CHLM/WR CM1 ....218 A3
Broomfield Hospital
 CHLM/WR CM1 ....193 P9
Broomfield Primary School
 CHLM/WR CM1 ....218 A2
Broomgrove County
 J & I School
 RCOLE CO7 ....153 J3
Broomhills Industrial Estate
 BRTR CM7 ....144 C4
Broom Hill Swimming Pool
 IP IP1 ....25 H3
Broomvale Business Centre
 RIPW IP6 ....22 B5
Broxbourne Business Centre
 CHES/WCR EN8 ....230 A5
Broxbourne Primary School
 BROX EN10 ....208 D9
Broxbourne Sailing Club
 HOD EN11 ....208 G8
The Broxbourne School
 BROX EN10 ....250 B1
Broxbourne Sports Club
 BROX EN10 ....208 C9
Brunel Court Industrial Centre
 COLN CO4 ....128 D2
Buckhurst Hill FC
 BKHH IG9 ....275 P7
Buckhurst Hill Primary School
 BKHH IG9 ....275 P8
Buckingham Road Cemetery
 IL IG1 ....316 E4
Bucklesham Primary School
 KIR/NAC IP10 ....32 F2
Building Crafts College
 SRTFD E15 ....314 F9
Bull Hill Industrial Estate
 COS CO15 ....182 A8
The Bull Hotel
 SUD CO10 ....46 F3
Bull Lane Industrial Estate
 SUD CO10 ....47 K3
Bulmer Road Industrial Estate
 SUD CO10 ....60 F7
Bulmer St Andrews CE
 Primary School SUD CO10 ..60 B7
Bulphan CE Primary School
 UPMR RM14 ....322 A5
Bunsay Downs Golf Club
 MAL CM9 ....220 F9
BUPA Roding Hospital
 REDBR IG4 ....295 N7
Bures Primary School
 BURES CO8 ....76 A8
Burleigh Primary School
 CHES/WCR EN8 ....230 A9
Burnham Business Park
 BOC CM0 ....290 C2
Burnham Clinic
 BOC CM0 ....291 H3
Burnham Museum
 BOC CM0 ....290 G4
Burnham-on-Crouch Golf Club
 BOC CM0 ....290 D2
Burnham-on-Crouch
 Primary School BOC CM0 ..291 J3
Burnham Road Clinic
 LOS SS9 ....327 M5
Burnham Trading Estate
 DART DA1 ....347 J9
Burnside Industrial Estate
 BARK/HLT IG6 ....297 J2
Burnt Mill Industrial Estate
 HLW CM20 ....13 F1
Burnt Mill School
 HLW CM20 ....210 F1
Burnt Mills Industrial Estate
 PIT SS13 ....304 G6
Burrsville County J & I School
 COS CO15 ....182 B7
The Burstead Golf Club
 BCAYW CM12 ....302 F2
Bursted Wood Primary School
 BXLYHN DA7 ....346 A7
Burton End Community
 Primary School HVHL CB9 ..40 G4
Burwell Industrial Estate
 LEY E10 ....314 B3
Bush Hill Park Golf Club
 WCHMH N21 ....273 H4
Bush Hill Park Medical Centre
 EN EN1 ....273 L5
Bush Hill Park Primary School
 EN EN1 ....273 M4
The Business Academy Bexley
 ERITHM DA18 ....335 M9
Business Aviation Terminal
 STSD CM24 ....138 C4
Bustermarket Shopping Centre
 IP IP1 ....16 E5
Buttsbury Infant School
 BCAYW CM12 ....283 J5
Buttsbury Junior School
 BCAYW CM12 ....283 J5

Buzzard Creek Industrial
 Estate BARK IG11 ....334 G3
Bygrove JMI School
 POP/IOD E14 ....332 E6
Cabot Place
 POP/IOD E14 ....332 D8
Calverton Primary School
 CAN/RD E16 ....333 N6
Cambell Primary School
 DAGW RM9 ....317 L9
Camelia Hotel
 SOS SS1 ....329 M8
Campanile Hotel
 BSDN SS14 ....303 M6
 GRH DA9 ....348 A8
Campion School
 EMPK RM11 ....299 L8
Canada Place
 POP/IOD E14 ....332 E8
Canada Square
 POP/IOD E14 ....332 E8
Canada Wharf Museum
 POP/IOD E14 ....332 C8
Canary Riverside
 POP/IOD E14 ....332 C8
Canary Wharf Pier
 POP/IOD E14 ....332 C8
Canary Wharf Tower
 POP/IOD E14 ....332 C8
Canewdon Endowed
 Primary School
 RCFD SS4 ....289 M7
Canfield CC
 GTDUN CM6 ....165 H4
Cann Hall Primary School
 RCOS CO16 ....181 M7
 WAN E11 ....315 J5
Cannon Hill Clinic
 STHGT/OAK N14 ....272 D9
Canon Palmer RC High School
 IL IG1 ....316 F5
Canons Brook Golf Club
 HLW CM20 ....12 B4
Canvey Island FC
 CVI SS8 ....345 J3
Canvey Primary School
 CVI SS8 ....344 C2
Capel Manor College
 EN EN1 ....251 N6
Capel St Mary CE Primary
 School RIPS/CAP IP9 ....28 C9
Capital Industrial Estate
 BELV DA17 ....336 B8
 BELV DA17 ....346 A2
Capitol Industrial Centre
 WICKE SS11 ....305 M2
Cardinal Park
 IP IP1 ....16 D6
Cardinal Pole RC School
 HOM E9 ....314 B8
Cardinal Pole RC Secondary
 Lower School HOM E9 ......314 A9
Car Ferry Terminal
 HAR CO12 ....109 P3
Carnarvon Medical Centre
 SOSN SS2 ....328 G4
Carpenters Business Park
 HOM E9 ....314 D8
Carpenters Primary School
 SRTFD E15 ....332 F1
Carterhatch Primary School
 EN EN1 ....251 N9
Castillion Primary School
 THMD SE28 ....335 K6
Castle Camps CE VC Primary
 School CBE/LIN CB1 ....80 B8
The Castledon Special School
 WICKW SS12 ....304 G2
Castle Garden Medical Centre
 COL CO1 ....9 F5
Castle Hill J & I School
 IP IP1 ....23 H9
Castle Hill Middle School
 HVHL CB9 ....40 G3
Castle House
 RCOLE CO7 ....105 H3
Castle Manor Upper School
 HVHL CB9 ....41 H3
Castle Point Athletics Track
 CVI SS8 ....326 A8
Castle Point Golf Club
 CVI SS8 ....326 C8
Castlepoint Museum
 CVI SS8 ....345 J2
Castle View Secondary School
 CVI SS8 ....326 E8
Caterham High School
 CLAY IG5 ....296 A6
Cathall Leisure Centre
 WAN E11 ....314 G5
Cathedral CE Primary School
 CHLM/WR CM1 ....5 H2
Cathedral of St Mary &
 St Helen BRWN CM15 ......280 G8
The Causeway Business Centre
 BSF CM23 ....137 L7
Causeway Industrial Estate
 MGTR CO11 ....106 A3
Causton Junior School
 FX IP11 ....35 H5
Cavalry Barracks
 COLS CO2 ....151 P1
Cavendish CE Primary School
 SUD CO10 ....45 H1
Cayley Primary School
 POP/IOD E14 ....332 B5
Cecil Jones High School
 SOSN SS2 ....329 L3
Cedar Hall Special School
 SBF/HAD SS7 ....306 E9
The Cedar School
 FSYCT E7 ....315M8
Cedarwood Primary School
 KESG IP5 ....27 H5
Central Foundation
 Girls School BOW E3 ....332 B3

Central Park Pool
 HARH RM3 ....299 K2
Central Park Primary School
 EHAM E6 ....333 N2
Chace Community School
 EN EN1 ....251 K9
Chadwell Heath
 Industrial Park BCTR RM8 ..317 M3
Chadwell Heath Leisure Centre
 CHDH RM6 ....317 L1
Chadwell Heath School
 CHDH RM6 ....317 J1
Chadwell Infant &
 Primary School CHDH RM6 ..317 K2
Chadwell St Mary Primary
 School CDW/CHF CM16 ....350 B2
Chafford School
 RAIN RM13 ....337 H5
Chaffords Sports Complex
 RAIN RM13 ....337 H5
Chalkstone Middle School
 HVHL CB9 ....41 K3
Chalkwell Hall Primary School
 LOS SS9 ....328 B5
Chalvedon School & Sixth
 Form College PIT SS13 ....304 G9
Chancellor Park Primary School
 CHLM/GWD CM2 ....218 G8
Channelsea Business Centre
 SRTFD E15 ....332 G2
Channels Golf Club
 RCHLM CM3 ....194 D9
Chantry Clinic
 CHTY IP2 ....24 F8
Chantry High School
 CHTY IP2 ....24 G8
Chantry J & I School
 CHTY IP2 ....24 F7
Chapel End Infant School
 WALTH E17 ....294 E5
Chapel End Junior School
 WALTH E17 ....294 E5
Chapel High Shopping Centre
 BRW CM14 ....280 G8
Chapel Mill Business &
 Retail Park BRTR CM77 ....145 M6
Chappel Primary School
 RCOLW CO6 ....125 J2
Charfleet Industrial Estate
 CVI SS8 ....343 P2
Charfleets Farm
 Industrial Estate CVI SS8 ..344 A2
Charter Hall
 COL CO1 ....8 E3
Charterhouse Trading Estate
 HVHL CB9 ....41 M5
Chase Farm Hospital
 ENC/FH EN2 ....250 F8
Chase Lane Infant & Junior
 School CHING E4 ....294 C1
 HAR CO12 ....109 P6
Chase Side Primary School
 ENC/FH EN2 ....273 H1
Chaseville Clinic
 WCHMH N21 ....272 C1
Chelmer Valley High School
 CHLM/WR CM1 ....217 P1
Chelmer Village Retail Park
 CHLM/GWD CM2 ....218 D9
Chelmondiston CP School
 RIPS/CAP IP9 ....84 D2
Chelmsford Athletics Club
 CHLM/WR CM1 ....217M5
Chelmsford Cathedral
 CHLM/WR CM1 ....5 G3
Chelmsford College
 CHLM/GWD CM2 ....4 E7
 CHLM/GWD CM2 ....240 B3
Chelmsford County High
 School CHLM/WR CM1 ....217 P7
Chelmsford Crematorium
 CHLM/WR CM1 ....239M2
Chelmsford & Essex Centre
 (Hospital) CHLM/GWD CM2 ..5 F5
Chelmsford & Essex Museum
 CHLM/GWD CM2 ....239 F2
Chelmsford Golf Club
 CHLM/GWD CM2 ....239 N4
Chelmsford RFC
 CHLM/GWD CM2 ....218 D7
Chelmsford Road Industrial
 Estate GTDUN CM6 ....141 N7
Chelmsford Squash Club
 CHLM/GWD CM2 ....240 A3
Cherry Tree Primary School
 COLS CO2 ....152 B6
 VGE SS16 ....3 K6
Cheshunt Community Hospital
 CHES/WCR EN8 ....252 B1
Cheshunt FC
 CHES/WCR EN8 ....251 P2
Cheshunt Field
 COLS CO2 ....151 J3
Cheshunt Golf Club
 CHESW EN7 ....229 N6
Cheshunt School
 CHES/WCR EN8 ....229 P7
Chesterfield Primary School
 PEND EN3 ....252 B7
Chetwood Primary School
 ROM RM1 ....286 C2
Chichester Hotel
 WICKE SS11 ....306 C4
Chigwell Golf Club
 CHIG IG7 ....296 B2
Chigwell Junior School
 CHIG IG7 ....276 D8
Chigwell Primary School
 CHIG IG7 ....276 D8
Chigwell Row Infants School
 CHIG IG7 ....277 K8
Childerditch Industrial Park
 RBRW/HUT CM13 ....301 D3
Childs Welfare Clinic
 DAGW RM9 ....317 K7

Chilton Industrial Estate
 SUD CO10 ....21 H1
 SUD CO10 ....21 H4
 SUD CO10 ....21 J5
 SUD CO10 ....21 K2
Chimnocks Wharf
 POP/IOD E14 ....332 B7
Chinese Herbal Medical Centre
 CHLM/GWD CM2 ....5 C5
Chingford CE Infant School
 CHING E4 ....274 G7
Chingford CE Junior School
 CHING E4 ....274 G7
Chingford Foundation School
 CHING E4 ....274 E7
Chingford Hall Primary School
 CHING E4 ....294 C3
Chingford Health Centre
 CHING E4 ....294 C1
Chingford Industrial Centre
 CHING E4 ....294 B2
Chingford RFC
 CHING E4 ....274 D7
Chipping Hill School
 WIT CM8 ....197 J1
Chipping Ongar
 Primary School
 CHONG CM5 ....235 L9
Christchurch Mansion
 IP IP1 ....16 E3
Chisenhale Primary School
 BOW E3 ....332 B2
Chrisp Street Health Centre
 POP/IOD E14 ....332 E6
Christ Church Cemetery
 BRW CM14 ....300 F1
Christ Church Primary School
 ERITH DA8 ....346 C4
 WARE SG12 ....184 B5
The Christian School
 RBSF CM22 ....139 L7
Chudleigh Hotel
 COS CO15 ....6 E6
Churchfield Primary School
 ED N9 ....273 L7
Churchfields J & I School
 SWFD E18 ....295 K5
Churchgate CE Primary
 School *HLWE* CM17 ....187 M9
Church Lane School
 UPMR RM14 ....320 E7
Church Langley Primary
 School *HLWE* CM17 ....211 K3
Church Mead Infant School
 LEY E10 ....314 D3
Church Mead Junior School
 LEY E10 ....314 D3
Church Street Industrial Estate
 WARE SG12 ....184 A2
Church Trading Estate
 ERITH DA8 ....346 F5
Cineplex Movie Starr Cinema
 CVI SS8 ....344 F4
Cineworld Cinema
 BRTR CM77 ....145 M6
 BSF CM23 ....137 L8
 BXLYHS DA6 ....346 A9
City of London Cemetery
 MNPK E12 ....315 P4
City of London Crematorium
 MNPK E12 ....315 N5
Civic Hall Cinema
 HOD EN11 ....208 C6
Civic Industrial Estate
 HVHL CB9 ....41 J6
Civic Theatre
 CHLM/WR CM1 ....4 D2
Civil Service Sports Club
 KIR/NAC IP10 ....32 A1
Clacton Airfield
 COS CO15 ....206 C3
Clacton Covered Market
 COS CO15 ....7 F5
Clacton & District Hospital
 COS CO15 ....6 D7
Clacton Factory
 Shopping Village *COS* CO15 ...182 B4
Clacton High School
 Performing Arts College
 COS CO15 ....7 H2
Clacton Leisure Centre
 COS CO15 ....7 H1
Clacton-on-Sea Golf Club
 COS CO15 ....207 H4
Clacton Pier
 COS CO15 ....7 G7
Clacton RFC
 COS CO15 ....182 B8
Clara Grant Primary School
 BOW E3 ....332 D4
Clare Castle Country Park
 SUD CO10 ....44 B4
Clare CP School
 SUD CO10 ....44 A3
Clare Middle School
 SUD CO10 ....44 C3
Claremont Clinic
 FSTGT E7 ....315 L7
Clarklands Industrial Estate
 SBW CM21 ....162 A8
Clavering Primary School
 SAFWS CB11 ....88 B4
Claverings Industrial Estate
 ED N9 ....273 P8
Claydon Business Park
 NHMKT IP6 ....22 B2
Claydon Country House Hotel
 NHMKT IP6 ....22 C4
Claydon High School
 NHMKT IP6 ....22 D4
Claydon Primary School
 NHMKT IP6 ....22 D3
Clayhall Clinic
 CLAY IG5 ....295 P7
Clement Primary School
 HVHL CB9 ....41 J4

Clements Hall Leisure Centre
 HOC/HUL SS5 ....308 B5
Cleveland Primary School
 IL IG1 ....316 C6
Cleves Primary School
 EHAM E6 ....333 N1
Cliff Hotel
 HAR CO12 ....14 D7
Cliff Lane Primary School
 IP IP3 ....25 M8
Clifford Road Primary School
 IP IP4 ....25 N5
Cliffs Bandstand
 SOS SS1 ....18 E6
Cliffs Pavilion
 WOS/PRIT SS0 ....18 B6
Clockhouse Primary School
 CRW RM5 ....298 A3
Clock Museum
 COS CO1 ....8 C6
Clore Tikva School
 BARK/HLT IG6 ....296 D6
Coalhouse Fort
 TIL RM18 ....351 M6
Coastal Business Centre
 COS CO15 ....6 B4
Cockridden Farm Industrial
 Estate *RBRW/HUT* CM13 .....302 A6
Coggeshall Town FC
 RCOLW CO6 ....147 L5
Colbayns High School
 RCOS CO16 ....6 B1
Colchester Business Park
 COL CO1 ....128 D1
Colchester Camping
 Caravan Park *COLW* CO3 ...127 J7
Colchester Castle
 COL CO1 ....8 C5
Colchester Cemetery
 COLS CO2 ....152 B3
Colchester County Court
 COL CO1 ....8 B7
Colchester County High School
 COLW CO3 ....127 L9
Colchester Crematorium
 COLS CO2 ....152 A3
Colchester & Essex Museum
 COL CO1 ....8 D5
Colchester Garrison Athletics
 Stadium
 COLS CO2 ....152 A1
Colchester General Hospital
 COLN CO4 ....127 P4
Colchester Golf Club
 COLN CO4 ....127 M4
Colchester High School
 COLW CO3 ....8 A7
Colchester Institute
 COLW CO3 ....127 N7
 COS CO15 ....7 H5
Colchester Leisure Centre
 COL CO1 ....8 E2
Colchester Mercury Theatre
 COL CO1 ....8 B6
Colchester Retail Park
 COLW CO3 ....127 N8
Colchester RFC
 COLN CO4 ....128 B1
Colchester Royal
 Grammar School
 COLW CO3 ....127 N9
Colchester United FC
 (Layer Road) *COLS* CO2 ...151 M2
Colchester Zoo
 COLW CO3 ....150 F6
Cold Norton CP School
 RCHLM CM3 ....265 P4
Colegrave School
 SRTFD E15 ....314 G7
College of Teachers
 EPP CM16 ....254 E6
College St Pierre
 LOS SS9 ....328 B5
Collier Row Clinic
 ROMW/RG RM7 ....298 A5
Collier Row FC
 ROMW/RG RM7 ....297 N5
Collingwood Primary School
 RCHLM CM3 ....287 H2
The Colne Community School
 RCOLE CO7 ....179 K5
Colne Engaine CE
 Primary School *RCOLW* CO6 ...99 H6
Colneis Junior School
 FXN IP11 ....35 L5
Coine Medical Centre
 RCOLE CO7 ....179 K7
Coine Valley Golf Club
 RCOLW CO6 ....99 H9
Coine Valley Railway
 HSTD CO9 ....72 B4
Coine View Retail Park
 COL CO1 ....8 E1
Coine Yacht Club
 RCOLE CO7 ....179 L8
Colyers Lane Medical Centre
 ERITH DA8 ....346 C6
Colyers Primary School
 ERITH DA8 ....346 C6
Commonside School
 HLWS CM18 ....210 G7
Community Care Centre
 ENC/FH EN2 ....251 J9
Connaught Girls School
 Language College
 LEY E10 ....315 H3
Convent School
 CHLM/WR CM1 ....218 F5
Coopersale Hall School
 EPP CM16 ....255 J4
Coopersale & Theydon Garnon
 CE School *EPP* CM16 ....233 L8
Coopers Company & Coborn
 School *UPMR* RM14 ....320 A5
Co-ordinated Industrial Estate
 SBF/HAD SS7 ....306 G8

Copdock CC
 RIPW IP8 ....29 H3
Copdock Primary School
 IPNE IP4 ....29 H2
Copford CE Primary School
 RCOLW CO6 ....149 P4
Copleston High School
 IPNE IP4 ....26 B6
Coppermill Primary School
 WALTH E17 ....294 A9
Coppice Primary School
 CLAY IG5 ....297 H2
Coppins Tey School
 COS CO15 ....181 N8
Corbets Tey School
 UPMR RM14 ....319 N7
The Cornelius Vermuyden
 School *CVI* SS8 ....326 B9
Cornell Estate
 CHLM/GWD CM2 ....5 K4
Corn Exchange & Film Theatre
 IP IP1 ....16 D4
Cornwallis Business Centre
 BSDN SS14 ....303 P7
Corringham Cemetery
 SLH/COR SS17 ....342 A1
Corringham Health Centre
 SLH/COR SS17 ....342 A2
The Corringham Leisure Centre
 SLH/COR SS17 ....341 N1
Corringham Primary School
 SLH/COR SS17 ....342 B1
Corton Trading Estate
 BRTR CM77 ....306 A8
The Cottage Museum
 BRTR CM77 ....93 P7
County Hotel
 CHLM/WR CM1 ....4 D2
 RIPW IP8 ....28 G3
The County Hotel
 WFD IG8 ....295 H4
County Junior School
 CHLM/WR CM1 ....239 H2
Coupals Primary School
 HVHL CB9 ....41 N4
Court Industrial Estate
 CHLM/GWD CM2 ....5 J4
Courtyard by Marriott Hotel
 KIR/NAC IP10 ....31 L3
Coward Industrial Estate
 CDW/CHF RM16 ....350 C3
Cramphorn Theatre
 CHLM/WR CM1 ....4 D2
Cranbourne JMI School
 HOD EN11 ....208 E2
Cranbrook College
 IL IG1 ....316 B4
Cranes Industrial Centre
 BSDN SS14 ....304 E5
Cranham Health Centre
 UPMR RM14 ....320 B2
Craylands Clinic
 BSDN SS14 ....304 D8
Crays Hill Primary School
 BCAYE CM11 ....304 C1
Crayside Industrial Estate
 DART DA1 ....346 F8
Creekmouth Industrial Estate
 BARK IG11 ....334 G4
Cressing Primary School
 BRTR CM77 ....145 P8
Crews Hill Golf Club
 ENC/FH EN2 ....250 E4
Cricketers Retail Park
 PIT SS13 ....304 F4
Cricklefield Stadium
 IL IG1 ....316 F4
Criton Industrial Centre
 CDW/CHF RM16 ....340 F6
Cromwell Business Centre
 BARK IG11 ....334 F3
Crouch Yacht Club
 BOC CM0 ....290 G4
Crowlands Primary School
 ROMW/RG RM7 ....318 B1
Crown Close Business Centre
 BOW E3 ....332 D1
Crown College
 WOS/PRIT SS0 ....18 C2
Crownfield Primary School
 ROMW/RG RM7 ....297 P6
Crown Hall
 RAYL SS6 ....306 F5
The Crown House Hotel
 SAFWN CB10 ....36 D9
Crown Lane Clinic
 STHGT/OAK N14 ....272 B7
Crown Pools
 IP IP1 ....16 D3
Crowstone Preparatory School
 RCFD SS4 ....309 J7
 WOS/PRIT SS0 ....328 C6
Crusader Business Park
 COS CO15 ....182 B5
Cudmore Grove Country Park
 K/T/MI CO5 ....204 C2
Cuffley Primary School
 POTB/CUF EN6 ....228 E9
Culloden Primary School
 POP/IOD E14 ....332 G6
Culver Shopping Centre
 COL CO1 ....8 B6
Cumberland Comprehensive
 School *CAN/RD* E16 ....333 J5
Curwen Primary School
 PLSTW E13 ....333 K2
Cygnet Clinic Beckton
 EHAM E6 ....334 C5
Cyril Jackson Primary School
 POP/IOD E14 ....332 C7
Dabchicks Sailing Club
 K/T/MI CO5 ....202 D5
Dacre Industrial Estate
 CHES/WCR EN8 ....230 C8
Dagenham Chest Clinic
 BCTR RM8 ....317 N5

Dagenham Civic Centre
 DAGE RM10 ....318 A4
Dagenham Priory
 Comprehensive School &
 Performing Arts College
 DAGE RM10 ....318 A9
Dagenham & Redbridge FC
 DAGE RM10 ....318 A7
Dagenham Superbowl
 DAGE RM10 ....336 A2
Dagenham Swimming Pool
 BCTR RM8 ....317 N4
Daiglen School
 BKHH IG9 ....275 M7
Dale Hall Primary School
 IP IP1 ....25 J1
Dame Johane Bradburys
 School *SAFWN* CB10 ....51 N8
Dame Tipping CE
 Primary School
 ABR/ST RM4 ....278 C9
Danbury Clinic
 RCHLM CM3 ....242 C3
Danbury Country Park
 RCHLM CM3 ....241 N3
Danbury Park Primary School
 RCHLM CM3 ....241 P3
Darent Industrial Park
 ERITH DA8 ....347 J3
Darlinghurst Primary School
 LOS SS9 ....328 A4
Dartford Tunnel
 DART DA1 ....348 A6
Datapoint Business Centre
 CAN/RD E16 ....332 C4
Daubeney Primary School
 CLPT E5 ....314 B6
Davenant Foundation School
 LOU IG10 ....254 D8
David Lloyd Sports Centre
 EN EN1 ....273 M1
Davies Lane Infant School
 WAN E11 ....315 J4
Dawlish Primary School
 LEY E10 ....314 F4
Days Inn
 RBSF CM22 ....138 B6
The Deanes School
 SBF/HAD SS7 ....306 F9
Deans Trading Estate
 RAIN RM13 ....337 J4
Debden CE Primary School
 SAFWS CB11 ....90 D1
Debden Park High School
 LOU IG10 ....276 E2
Debden Sports Club
 LOU IG10 ....276 D4
Deben High School
 FX IP11 ....11 G1
De Bohun Primary School
 STHGT/OAK N14 ....272 A4
Dedham CE Primary School
 RCOLE CO7 ....105 H3
Dedham Sports Club
 RCOLE CO7 ....104 C2
De la Salle School
 BSDN SS14 ....3 G1
Delta Wharf
 GNWCH SE10 ....332 G9
Deneholm Primary School
 CDW/CHF RM16 ....339 M9
Dengie Hundred Sports Centre
 BOC CM0 ....290 F4
Denver Industrial Estate
 RAIN RM13 ....336 E5
Dersingham Infant School
 MNPK E12 ....316 A7
De Vere Arms Hotel
 RCOLW CO6 ....99 H9
De Vere CP School
 HSTD CO9 ....72 D5
Dewhurst St Mary JMI School
 CHES/WCR EN8 ....229 N8
Diane Matthews Clinic
 ROMW/RG RM7 ....298 C8
Dilkes Primary School
 SOCK/AV RM15 ....338 C6
Dipple Medical Centre
 PIT SS13 ....324 G1
Dockmaster's House
 POP/IOD E14 ....332 D7
Doddinghurst Infant School
 BRWN CM15 ....258 E7
Doddinghurst Junior School
 BRWN CM15 ....258 E7
Doggetts Primary School
 RCFD SS4 ....308 G4
The Dolphin Leisure Centre
 ROM RM1 ....298 E8
Dome
 GNWCH SE10 ....333 H8
Dominion Business Park
 ED N9 ....274 A8
Dominoes Health Centre
 GRAYS RM17 ....349 K4
Dorma Trading Park
 LEY E10 ....314 A3
Dorothy Barley Primary School
 BCTR RM8 ....317 J7
Doucecroft School
 K/T/MI CO5 ....173 H2
Dovercourt Swimming Pool
 HAR CO12 ....110 C7
Dovers Corner Industrial Estate
 RAIN RM13 ....336 E3
Downfield Primary School
 CHES/WCR EN8 ....252 B1
Down Hall Country
 House Hotel *RBSF* CM22 ...188 F5
Down Hall Primary School
 RAYL SS6 ....306 F2
Downham CE Primary School
 BCAYE CM11 ....284 B4
Downing Primary School
 CHTY IP2 ....24 G9

Downsell Primary School
 WAN E11 ....314 G6
Downshall Primary School
 GNTH/NBYPK IG2 ....316 F2
The Downs Primary School
 HLW CM20 ....13 J6
Drakes Lane Industrial Estate
 RCHLM CM3 ....194 G5
Drapers Sports Club
 MAL CM9 ....222 E6
Drapers Sports Ground
 SRTFD E15 ....314 F6
Drew Primary School
 RD E16 ....333 P8
Dr Walkers CE Primary School
 CHONG CM5 ....214 A9
Dry Ski Slope
 RBRW/HUT CM13 ....300 F4
Dukes Park Industrial Estate
 CHLM/GWD CM2 ....218 G6
The Dukes Priory Hospital
 CHLM/WR CM1 ....218 C7
Dunbar Wharf
 POP/IOD E14 ....332 C7
Duncan's Gate
 COL CO1 ....8 D4
Dundee Wharf
 POP/IOD E14 ....332 C7
Dunmore St Marys
 Primary School
 GTDUN CM6 ....141 K6
Dunmow Sports Centre
 GTDUN CM6 ....141 K3
Dunningford Primary School
 HCH RM12 ....318 E7
Durands Wharf
 POP/IOD E14 ....332 C9
Durants School
 PEND EN3 ....251 P9
Dycourts School
 HARH RM3 ....299 M1
Earlham Primary School
 FSTGT E7 ....315 J7
Earls Colne Primary School
 RCOLW CO6 ....124 A1
Earls Hall Primary School
 WOS/PRIT SS0 ....328 E2
East Anglian Railway Museum
 RCOLW CO6 ....125 J1
East Barking Centre
 BCTR RM8 ....317 K7
East Beckton District Centre
 EHAM E6 ....334 A6
East Bergholt CE Primary
 School *RCOLE* CO7 ....80 E6
East Bergholt High School
 RCOLE CO7 ....80 G5
Eastbrook Comprehensive
 School *DAGE* RM10 ....318 B6
Eastbrook End Cemetery
 DAGE RM10 ....318 D5
 LOU IG10 ....275 N3
Eastbrookend Country Park
 DAGE RM10 ....318 C6
Eastbury Comprehensive
 School *BARK* IG11 ....334 G1
Eastbury Infant School
 BARK IG11 ....316 C9
Eastcourt Independent School
 GDMY/SEVK IG3 ....317 H3
East Essex Adult Community
 College *MAL* CM9 ....222 A9
East Essex Aviation Society
 & Museum *RCOLE* CO7 ...179 K9
Eastfield Primary School
 PEND EN3 ....252 A8
Eastgate Business Park
 LEY E10 ....314 B3
Eastgate Centre
 BSDN SS14 ....3 F5
Eastgate Shopping Centre
 IPNE IP4 ....17 F4
East Gates Industrial Estate
 COL CO1 ....9 H6
East Ham Industrial Estate
 CAN/RD E16 ....333 N4
East Ham Jewish Cemetery
 EHAM E6 ....333 P3
East Ham Leisure Centre
 EHAM E6 ....334 A1
East Ham Memorial Hospital
 FSTGT E7 ....315 N9
East Ham Nature Reserve
 EHAM E6 ....334 A4
East Hanningfield CE Primary
 School *RCHLM* CM3 ....263 N2
East Hanningfield Industrial
 Estate *RCHLM* CM3 ....263 N3
Eastlea Community Centre
 CAN/RD E16 ....333 J3
Eastlea Community School
 CAN/RD E16 ....333 H4
East London Business College
 PLSTW E13 ....315 H3
East London Cemetery
 PLSTW E13 ....333 J5
East London Crematorium
 PLSTW E13 ....333 J3
East London RFC
 EHAM E6 ....334 C1
East London RUFC
 PLSTW E13 ....333 J2
East Thamesmead Business
 Park *ERITHM* DA18 ....335 N9
East Thurrock FC
 SLH/COR SS17 ....342 A1
East Tilbury J & I Schools
 TIL RM18 ....351 K3
Eastwood GM Infant School
 LOS SS9 ....328 A1
Eastwood High School
 LOS SS9 ....328 A1
Eastwood Industrial Estate
 LOS SS9 ....307 M9
Eastwood Primary School
 LOS SS9 ....308 A1

The Eastwood School
  LOS SS9 ....327 P1
Eaton Manor RFC
  WAN E11 ....295 M9
Edinburgh Primary School
  WALTH E17 ....294 C9
Edith Borthwick School
  BRTR CM7 ....121 J7
Edmonton Cemetery
  ED N9 ....273 J8
Edmonton Green
  Shopping Centre *ED* N9 ....273 N8
Edmonton Leisure Centre
  ED N9 ....273 N9
Edmonton Upper School
  EN EN1 ....273 L6
Edward Francis Junior School
  RAYL SS6 ....306 C4
Edwards Hall Primary School
  LOS SS9 ....307 M8
Edwin Lambert School
  EMPK RM11 ....318 F1
Eight Ash Green CE
  Primary School *COLW* CO3 ...126 C6
Elbourne Trading Estate
  BELV DA17 ....346 A1
Eldenwall Industrial Estate
  BCTR RM8 ....317 M3
Eldon JMI School
  ED N9 ....273 N7
Eldon Way Industrial Estate
  HOC/HUL SS5 ....307 P1
Eleanor Estate
  CHES/WCR EN8 ....252 C4
Eleanor Smith Special School
  PLSTW E15 ....333 K2
Electric Palace Cinema
  HAR CO12 ....15 G2
Elizabeth Orwell Hotel
  FX IP11 ....35 L6
Ellen Wilkinson Primary School
  EHAM E6 ....333 N5
Elm Green Preparatory School
  RCHLM CM3 ....220 A8
Elm Hall CP School
  WIT CM8 ....171 N7
Elmhurst Primary School
  FSTGT E7 ....315 L9
Elms Business Park
  WICKW SS12 ....305 K3
Elms Industrial Estate
  HARH RM5 ....299 N4
Elmstead CP School
  RCOLE CO7 ....129 P9
Elmwood Primary School
  RCHLM CM5 ....286 C1
Elsenham Primary School
  RBSF CM22 ....114 C6
Elton Park Business Centre
  CHTY IP2 ....24 F5
Elton Park Industrial Estate
  CHTY IP2 ....24 F5
Embroidery World
  Business Centre *WFD* IG8 ....295 N6
EMD Walthamstow Cinema
  WALTH E17 ....294 D8
Emerson Park School
  EMPK RM11 ....319 N2
Emery Theatre
  POP/IOD E14 ....332 E6
Empire Cinema
  HSTD CO9 ....97 N6
The Endeavour School
  BRWN CM15 ....281 J8
Enfield Business Centre
  PEND EN3 ....273 P1
Enfield Chace Lower School
  ENC/FH EN2 ....251 K8
Enfield College
  PEND EN3 ....273 P2
Enfield County Upper School
  EN EN1 ....273 J2
Enfield Crematorium
  EN EN1 ....251 N7
Enfield CC
  EN EN1 ....273 K3
Enfield FC
  ED N9 ....273 P8
Enfield Golf Club
  ENC/FH EN2 ....272 C3
Enfield Grammar School
  (Upper) *ENC/FH* EN2 ....273 J2
Enfield Hotel
  ENC/FH EN2 ....272 C1
Enfield Lower Grammar School
  ENC/FH EN2 ....273 J1
Engaines Primary School
  RCOS CO16 ....181 M3
Engayne Primary School
  UPMR RM14 ....320 B1
Enterprise Business Park
  POP/IOD E14 ....332 E9
Enterprise Trading Estate
  BRTR CM7 ....144 C5
Epping CE Primary School
  EPP CM16 ....232 B5
Epping County Infant School
  EPP CM16 ....232 F8
Epping Forest Conservation
  Centre *LOU* IG10 ....253 M8
Epping Forest District Museum
  WAB EN9 ....252 F3
Epping Forest Tertiary College
  LOU IG10 ....276 C2
The Epping Golf Course
  EPP CM16 ....255 J5
Epping Junior School
  EPP CM16 ....232 C9
Epping Ongar Railway
  CHONG CM5 ....235 K6
Epping Sports Centre
  EPP CM16 ....233 J9
Erith Cemetery
  ERITH DA8 ....254 G1

Erith & District Hospital
  ERITH DA8 ....346 C4
Erith Health Centre
  ERITH DA8 ....346 D4
Erith Library & Museum
  ERITH DA8 ....346 D3
Erith Playhouse
  ERITH DA8 ....346 E3
Erith School
  ERITH DA8 ....346 B5
Erith School Community
  Sports Centre
  ERITH DA8 ....346 B5
Erith Small Business Centre
  ERITH DA8 ....346 E4
Erith Sports Centre
  ERITH DA8 ....346 E4
Erith Stadium
  ERITH DA8 ....346 D4
Erismere Hotel
  WOS/PRIT SS0 ....328 E7
Esplanade Hotel
  COS CO15 ....7 G6
Essex Agricultural Showground
  RCHLM CM3 ....169 K3
Essex County Council Youth
  Camp *K/T/MI* CO5 ....203 M5
Essex CCC (County Ground)
  CHLM/GWD CM2 ....5 F4
Essex County Hospital
  COLW CO3 ....127 N9
Essex Cricket School
  CHLM/GWD CM2 ....4 E4
The Essex Golf & Country Club
  RCOLW CO6 ....125 N5
The Essex Nuffield Hospital
  BRWN CM15 ....281 H7
Essex Primary School
  MNPK E12 ....315 P8
Ethel Davis School
  CHDH RM6 ....297 J9
Euro Business Centre
  SRTFD E15 ....333 J1
Europa Trading Estate
  ERITH DA8 ....346 C3
  WTHK RM20 ....348 G3
Euro Retail Park
  IPSE IP5 ....31 K1
Everest Sports Club
  CHES/WCR EN8 ....229 N8
Everik Business Centre
  RBRW/HUT CM13 ....281 P4
Eversley College
  SBW CM21 ....187 L2
Eversley Primary School
  PIT SS13 ....305 J9
  WCHMN N21 ....272 D4
ExCel Exhibition Centre
  CAN/RD E16 ....333 L7
The Exchange
  IL IG1 ....316 C4
Express by Holiday Inn
  BKHH IG9 ....275 L8
  CAN/RD E16 ....333 H6
  CHING E4 ....294 D4
  DART DA1 ....347 N9
  RAYL SS6 ....306 F7
  RIPW IP6 ....24 B7
  SRTFD E15 ....333 H7
The Faircross Complementary
  Medical Centre *BARK* IG11 ...316 F8
Fairfield Clinic
  BKHH IG9 ....275 L7
Fairfield Infant School
  FX IP11 ....35 K6
Fairfields Primary School
  CHESW EN7 ....229 M6
Fairhouse J & I School
  BSDN SS14 ....3 K5
Fairlop Primary School
  BARK/HLT IG6 ....296 D5
Fairview Industrial Centre
  DAGW RM9 ....336 C6
Fairway Medical Centre
  LOS SS9 ....327 N2
Fairways Business Park
  LEY E10 ....314 B4
Fairways Primary School
  LOS SS9 ....327 M2
Farnham CE Primary School
  BSF CM23 ....113 J9
Farnham Green Primary
  School *GDMY/SEVK* IG3 ....317 H1
Farthing Road Industrial Estate
  IP IP1 ....24 E4
Fawbert & Barnards Primary
  School *HLWE* CM17 ....187 K9
Feering Primary School
  K/T/MI CO5 ....173 K1
Felixstowe Cemetery
  FX IP11 ....11 F1
Felixstowe College
  FX IP11 ....35 M7
Felixstowe Ferry Golf Club
  FX IP11 ....35 P4
Felixstowe General Hospital
  FX IP11 ....35 L7
Felixstowe International College
  FX IP11 ....35 M6
Felixstowe Leisure Centre
  FX IP11 ....11 H4
Felixstowe Pier
  FX IP11 ....11 J4
Felixstowe RFC
  FX IP11 ....10 D3
Felixstowe & Walton FC
  FX IP11 ....35 K5
Felstead Vineyard
  RCHLM CM3 ....148 A8
Felsted CP School
  GTDUN CM6 ....143 J7
Felsted Preparatory School
  GTDUN CM6 ....142 G9
Ferry Lane Industrial Estate
  RAIN RM13 ....336 F5

Festival Leisure Park
  BSDN SS14 ....304 C4
Financial Times
  POP/IOD E14 ....332 F6
Finchingfield CE Primary School
  BRTR CM7 ....94 C2
Finchingfield Guildhall
  & Museum *BRTR* CM7 ....94 C2
Fingringhoe CE Primary
  School *K/T/MI* CO5 ....152 G9
Firs Farm Primary School
  PLMGR N13 ....273 J9
The Firs Junior School
  BSF CM23 ....137 K8
Fisher Athletic FC
  BERM/RHTH SE16 ....332 A8
Fitness Unlimited Leisure
  Centre *BOW* E3 ....332 D2
The Fitzwilliam School
  RAYL SS6 ....307 H4
Five Elms Primary School
  DAGW RM9 ....317 N5
Five Lakes Hotel, Golf, Country
  Club & Spa *MAL* CM9 ....200 E4
Flamstead End Primary School
  CHESW EN7 ....229 M6
Flatford Bridge Cottage (NT)
  RCOLE CO7 ....105 L1
Flitch Industrial Estate
  GTDUN CM6 ....141 L7
Flix Cinema
  RCHLM CM3 ....287 H1
Florence Nightingale
  Health Centre *HLWE* CM17 ...211 K3
Fondu Sports Club
  PUR RM19 ....347 P2
Ford End CE Primary School
  RCHLM CM3 ....167 N7
Fordgate Business Park
  BELV DA17 ....336 B9
Fordham All Saints CE
  Primary School
  RCOLW CO6 ....126 A3
Ford Industrial Park
  DAGW RM9 ....336 A5
Ford Road Industrial Estate
  COS CO15 ....6 C4
Fordview Industrial Estate
  RAIN RM13 ....336 C3
Forest Business Park
  WALTH E17 ....314 A2
Forest Gate Community
  School *FSTGT* E7 ....315 K7
Forest House Business Centre
  WAN E11 ....315 J2
Forest Industrial Park
  BARK/HLT IG6 ....296 F4
Forest Medical Centre
  LOU IG10 ....275 P4
Forest Park Cemetery &
  Crematorium
  BARK/HLT IG6 ....297 K2
Fore Street Pool
  IP IP4 ....17 G6
Forest Road Medical Centre
  WALTH E17 ....294 C7
Forest School
  WALTH E17 ....295 H8
Forest Trading Estate
  WALTH E17 ....294 A7
Forres CP School
  HOD EN11 ....208 E2
Forrester Park Golf &
  Tennis Club *MAL* CM9 ....198 D7
Forty Hall
  ENC/FH EN2 ....251 L7
Forty Hill CE Primary School
  EN EN1 ....251 M7
Four Seasons Hotel
  POP/IOD E14 ....332 C8
Four Swannes Primary School
  CHES/WCR EN8 ....252 B3
Foxhall Heath Stadium
  IPNE IP4 ....26 F6
Frances Bardsley School
  for Girls *ROM* RM1 ....298 F9
Freeport Retail Village
  BRTR CM77 ....145 L5
Free Trade Wharf
  WAP E1W 332 A7
Freight Services Office
  HAR CO12 ....110 B3
Freshwell Health Centre
  BRTR CM7 ....94 C2
Fresh Wharf Estate
  BARK IG11 ....334 C1
Friars Clinic
  SUD CO10 ....20 C6
Friars Grove Infant School
  COLN CO4 ....128 D5
Friars Grove Junior School
  COLN CO4 ....128 D5
Friars Primary School
  SBN/FI SS3 ....330 E6
Friends School
  SAFWS CB11 ....65 M1
Frinton Golf Club
  FOS CO13 ....183 M3
Frinton-on-Sea Lawn
  Tennis Club *FOS* CO13 ....183 M2
Frinton-on-Sea
  Primary School *FOS* CO13 .....158 F9
Frinton Road Medical Centre
  COS CO15 ....182 E7
Frinton Summer Theatre
  FOS CO13 ....158 G9
The Frinton & Walton Heritage
  Museum *WOTN* CO14 ....159 L4
Frinton & Walton Swimming
  Pool *WOTN* CO14 ....159 L5
Frobisher Primary School
  COS CO15 ....206 E3
Frost Business Centre
  BRTR CM77 ....146 D5
The Fryerns Medical Centre
  BSDN SS14 ....304 D7

Fullmen Industrial Park
  CVI SS8 ....343 P2
Fullwell Cross Health Centre
  BARK/HLT IG6 ....296 D6
Fullwell Cross Swimming
  Pool & Recreation Centre
  BARK/HLT IG6 ....296 D6
Fullwood Primary School
  BARK/HLT IG6 ....296 D8
Funland
  SOS SS1 ....19 J6
Furze Infant School
  CHDH RM6 ....317 M1
Fynn Valley Golf Club
  NHMKT IP6 ....23 P5
Gable Hall School
  SLH/COR SS17 ....323 N9
Gainsborough Primary School
  HOM E9 ....314 C8
  SRTFD E15 ....333 H5
Gainsborough's House
  SUD CO10 ....20 C5
Gainsborough Sports Centre
  IPSE IP5 ....31 H2
Galleywood County Infant
  School *CHLM/GWD* CM2 ....240 A8
Galliard Primary School
  ED N9 ....273 M5
Galliford Road Industrial
  Estate *MAL* CM9 ....222 B7
Gallions Primary School
  EHAM E6 ....334 C6
Gallions Reach Shopping Park
  EHAM E6 ....334 C5
Ganges Museum
  RIPS/CAP IP9 ....85 P9
Gants Hill Medical Centre
  GNTH/NBYPK IG2 ....316 B1
Garon Park Track
  SOSN SS2 ....329 L2
Gascoigne Primary School
  BARK IG11 ....334 D1
Gatehouse School
  BETH E2 ....332 A2
Gateway Community College
  North *CDW/CHF* RM16 ....340 A9
Gaynes School
  UPMR RM14 ....319 P7
Gearies Infant School
  GNTH/NBYPK IG2 ....296 B9
Gearies Junior School
  GNTH/NBYPK IG2 ....296 C9
The Geoffrey Lloyd Foulkes
  Clinic *IL* IG1 ....316 B4
Geoffrey Whitworth Theatre
  DART DA1 ....346 F9
George Hotel
  COLN CO4 ....8 C5
George Mitchell School
  LEY E10 ....314 E3
George Spicer Primary School
  EN EN1 ....273 L2
George Tomlinson
  Primary School *WAN* E11 ....315 H3
George Yard Shopping Centre
  BRTR CM7 ....145 H3
Ghyllgrove Primary School
  BSDN SS14 ....2 E3
Gidea Park College
  GPK RM2 ....298 F7
Gidea Park Primary School
  GPK RM2 ....298 E8
Gidea Park Sports Ground
  GPK RM2 ....299 H6
Giffards Primary School
  SLH/COR SS17 ....341 N1
The Gilberd School
  COLN CO4 ....128 C2
Gilbert Colvin Primary School
  CLAY IG5 ....296 B5
The Glade Business Centre
  WTHK RM20 ....348 C3
Glade Primary School
  CLAY IG5 ....296 A5
Glebe Infant School
  RAYL SS6 ....306 F4
Glebe Junior School
  RAYL SS6 ....306 F4
Glenham College
  IL IG1 ....316 C4
Glenwood Special School
  SBF/HAD SS7 ....305 M8
Globe Industrial Estate
  GRAYS RM17 ....349 M4
Globe Wharf
  BERM/RHTH SE16 ....332 A4
Globe Works Industrial Estate
  GRAYS RM17 ....349 M5
Gloucester Park Athletic
  Stadium *BSDN* SS14 ....2 C1
Gloucester Park
  Swimming Pool *LAIN* SS15 ....2 C4
Godwin Junior School
  FSTGT E7 ....315 L6
Goffs Oak JMI School
  CHESW EN7 ....229 M8
Goffs School
  CHESW EN7 ....229 M8
Goldings Hill Clinic
  LOU IG10 ....276 B1
Golds Nurseries Business Park
  RBSF CM22 ....114 F4
Goodmayes Retail Park
  GDMY/SEVK IG3 ....317 J2
Gordon Infant School
  IL IG1 ....316 E5
Goresbrook Leisure Centre
  DAGW RM9 ....335 L1
Goresbrook Sports Centre
  DAGW RM9 ....335 L1
Gorseland Primary School
  KESG IP5 ....27 L3
Gorse Lane Industrial Estate
  COS CO15 ....182 C5
Gosbecks Primary School
  COLS CO2 ....151 K3

Gosfield Community
  Primary School *HSTD* CO9 ....97 H8
Gosfield Lake Golf Club
  HSTD CO9 ....96 F8
Gosfield School
  HSTD CO9 ....97 J6
Gosford Primary School
  REDBR IG4 ....296 A9
Gove Farm Retail Park
  CHDH RM6 ....317 K2
Grafton Primary School
  BCTR RM8 ....317 M4
Grainger Road Industrial Estate
  SOSN SS2 ....19 F1
Grange Barn (NT)
  RCOLW CO6 ....147 N5
Grange Infant School
  CAN/RD E16 ....333 J4
Grange Paddocks Pool & Gym
  BSF CM23 ....137 L5
Grange Park Industrial Estate
  COLS CO2 ....152 E3
Grange Park Preparatory
  School *WCHMH* N21 ....272 G5
Grange Park Primary School
  ENC/FH EN2 ....272 F3
Grange Primary School
  FX IP11 ....10 D1
  WICKW SS12 ....304 C1
Grange Way Business Park
  COLS CO2 ....152 E3
Grangewood Independent
  School *FSTGT* E7 ....315 N9
Grays Athletic FC
  GRAYS RM17 ....349 L4
Grays Business Centre
  GRAYS RM17 ....349 M1
Grays Convent School
  GRAYS RM17 ....349 L4
Grays Country Court
  GRAYS RM17 ....349 K4
Grays Health Centre
  GRAYS RM17 ....349 K3
The Grays School
  GRAYS RM17 ....349 L1
Great Baddow High School
  CHLM/GWD CM2 ....240 C4
Great Bardfield Primary School
  BRTR CM7 ....94 A6
Great Bentley Primary School
  RCOLE CO7 ....155 J7
Great Berry Primary School
  VGE SS16 ....322 C2
Great Bradfords
  Primary School *BRTR* CM7 .....145 J3
Great Cambridge
  Industrial Estate *EN* EN1 ....273 N4
Great Chesterford Primary
  School *SAFWN* CB10 ....36 G9
Great Cornard Upper School
  SUD CO10 ....61 L6
The Great Dunmow Maltings
  Museum
  GTDUN CM6 ....141 L6
Great Dunmow Primary
  School *GTDUN* CM6 ....141 K5
Great Easton CE Primary
  School *GTDUN* CM6 ....116 G7
Great Hadham Golf &
  Country Club *MHAD* SG10 ......161 J1
Great Leighs Primary School
  RCHLM CM3 ....169 K6
Great Leighs Racecourse
  (open 2006) *RCHLM* CM3 ......169 J2
Great Oakley CE Primary School
  HAR CO12 ....133 L4
Great Oaks Clinic
  BSDN SS14 ....2 D5
Great Sampford CP School
  SAFWN CB10 ....68 D5
Great Stony School
  CHONG CM5 ....235 M6
Great Tey CE Primary School
  RCOLW CO6 ....126 H6
Great Totham CP School
  MAL CM9 ....198 B7
The Great Wakering
  Health Centre *SBN/FI* SS3 ......330 E2
Great Wakering Primary
  School *SBN/FI* SS3 ....330 F3
Great Wakering Sports Centre
  SBN/FI SS3 ....330 E2
Great Waltham Primary School
  RCHLM CM3 ....193 M5
Greengate Medical Centre
  PLSTW E13 ....333 L3
Greengrove College
  STHGT/OAK N14 ....272 D8
Greenleaf Primary School
  WALTH E17 ....294 C7
The Green Man Hotel
  HLWE CM17 ....187 L8
Greenshields Industrial Estate
  CAN/RD E16 ....333 K8
Greenstead Clinic
  COLN CO4 ....128 F7
Greenstead St Andrews
  Primary School *COLN* CO4 .....128 F8
Greensted Primary School
  COS CO15 ....304 E9
Greensward College
  HOC/HUL SS5 ....287 P9
Greenwich Business Park
  IPSE IP5 ....31 J3
Greenwood School
  HSTD CO9 ....98 A5
Greenwoods Estate Health
  Spa & Retreat *ING* CM4 ....261 M6
Greyhound Trading Park
  SOSN SS2 ....19 G1
The Grove Centre
  WIT CM8 ....197 K2
Grovelands Priory Hospital
  STHGT/OAK N14 ....272 D7
Grove Primary School
  CHDH RM6 ....297 J9

RAYL SS6 ....307 K6
Grove Tennis Club
 CHLM/GWD CM2 ....240 A3
Grundy Park Leisure Centre
 CHES/WCR EN8 ....230 B9
Gt Bromley St Georges CE
 Primary School RCOLE CO7 ...130 D6
Gt Waldingfield Vcp
 Primary School SUD CO10 ....47 P8
Guardian Angels RC
 Primary School BOW E3 ....332 B4
Guardian Business Centre
 HARH RM5 ....299 J4
Guardian Newspapers
 POP/IOD E14 ....332 E9
Gulpher Business Park
 FX IP11 ....35 J3
Guru Gobind Singh Khalsa
 College CHIG IG7 ....276 A7
Gusford Primary School
 IP2 ....29 M1
Gwyn Jones Primary School
 WAN E11 ....314 G2
GX Superbowl
 EHAM E6 ....334 B5
Hackney Sports Centre
 HOM E9 ....314 D6
Hacton Primary School
 HCH RM12 ....319 K6
Hadleigh Business Centre
 SBF/HAD SS7 ....327 H4
Hadleigh Castle
 SBF/HAD SS7 ....326 C5
Hadleigh Castle Country Park
 SBF/HAD SS7 ....326 E5
Hadleigh Clinic
 SBF/HAD SS7 ....326 F3
Hadleigh Junior School
 SBF/HAD SS7 ....327 H3
Hadleigh Road Industrial Estate
 CHTY IP2 ....24 F5
Haileybury College
 HERT/BAY SG13 ....208 A1
Haileybury College Track
 HERT/BAY SG13 ....208 A1
Hailey Hall Special School
 HOD EN11 ....208 C1
Hailey Road Business Park
 ERITHM DA18 ....335 P9
Hainault Business Park
 BARK/HLT IG6 ....297 K2
Hainault Forest Country Park
 CHIG IG7 ....277 L9
Hainault Forest Golf Club
 CHIG IG7 ....297 L3
Hainault Forest High School &
 the Learning Centre
 BARK/HLT IG6 ....297 H2
Half Moon Theatre
 WCHPL E1 ....332 A4
Halifax Primary School
 CHTY IP2 ....25 J9
Halley Primary School
 POP/IOD E14 ....332 B5
Hallmark Industrial Estate
 BOC CM0 ....269 K5
Hall Mead School
 UPMR RM14 ....320 A2
Hallsford Bridge Industrial Estate
 CHONG CM5 ....257 P1
Hallsford Business Centre
 CAN/RD E16 ....333 K6
Halstead Business Centre
 HSTD CO9 ....97 P6
Halstead Hospital
 HSTD CO9 ....97 P5
Halstead Town FC
 HSTD CO9 ....97 P6
Hamer Indoor Market
 BOW E3 ....332 C2
Hamford CP School
 FOS CO13 ....158 G7
Hamilton Primary School
 COLW CO5 ....151 N1
Hamlet International
 Industrial Estate
 ERITH DA8 ....346 C3
Hamstel Primary School
 SOSN SS2 ....329 L4
Handford Hall Primary School
 IP IP1 ....25 H5
Handsworth Health Clinic
 CHING E4 ....294 G3
Handsworth Primary School
 CHING E4 ....294 G3
Hare Street Primary School
 HLWW/ROY CM19 ....13 F7
Harlowbury Primary School
 HLWE CM17 ....187 L8
Harlow Business Park
 HLWW/ROY CM19 ....209 P3
Harlow College
 HLW CM20 ....13 H7
Harlow Museum (Passmores
 House) HLWS CM18 ....210 D4
Harlow RFC
 HLW CM20 ....12 E2
Harlow Sailing Club
 RCHLM CM5 ....245 N8
Harlow Sports Centre
 HLW CM20 ....13 G3
Harlow Swimming Pool
 HLW CM20 ....13 K3
Harold Court Primary School
 HARH RM3 ....299 M4
Harold Wood Clinic
 HARH RM3 ....299 L6
Harold Wood JMI School
 HARH RM3 ....299 M7
Hartley Primary School
 EHAM E6 ....333 P1

The Hartswood Clinic
 RBRW/HUT CM13 ....300 E3
Hartswood Golf Club
 BRW CM14 ....301 H1
Harvey Centre
 HLW CM20 ....13 H6
Harwich Community Primary
 School HAR CO12 ....15 G5
Harwich & District Hospital
 HAR CO12 ....110 B5
Harwich & Dovercourt
 Golf Club HAR CO12 ....110 A4
Harwich Industrial Estate
 HAR CO12 ....110 A3
Harwich & Parkeston FC
 HAR CO12 ....14 C7
Harwich Primary School
 HAR CO12 ....15 G4
Harwich Redoubt Fort
 HAR CO12 ....15 G4
Harwich School
 HAR CO12 ....110 B6
Harwich Sports Centre
 HAR CO12 ....110 B6
Harwich Town Sailing Club
 HAR CO12 ....15 G2
Harwood Equestrian Centre
 UPMR RM14 ....319 N8
Haselbury Infant School
 ED N9 ....273 K9
Haslemere Business Centre
 EN EN1 ....273 N3
Haslemere Industrial Estate
 BSF CM23 ....162 D1
 HLWW/ROY CM19 ....12 B7
Hassenbrook School
 SLH/COR SS17 ....341 M3
Hassengate Medical Centre
 SLH/COR SS17 ....341 K3
Hastingwood Business Centre
 HLWE CM17 ....211 K5
Hastingwood Trading Estate
 UED N18 ....294 B5
Hatfield Forest (NT)
 RBSF CM22 ....139 H9
Hatfield Heath Primary School
 RBSF CM22 ....188 F1
Hatfield Peverel Infant School
 RCHLM CM3 ....196 E9
Hatton School
 REDBR IG4 ....295 N7
Haverhill Golf Club
 HVHL CB9 ....41 P5
Haverhill Leisure Centre
 HVHL CB9 ....41 L4
Haverhill Rovers FC
 HVHL CB9 ....41 K5
Havering College
 HARH RM5 ....299 L1
Havering College of FE & HE
 EMPK RM11 ....299 K8
 EMPK RM11 ....318 C2
Havering Country Park
 ABR/ST RM4 ....298 C1
Havering CC
 ABR/ST RM4 ....278 E1
Havering Hospitals
 HARH RM5 ....299 K5
Havering Magistrates Court
 ROM RM1 ....298 D8
Havering Sixth Form College
 EMPK RM11 ....319 L3
The Havers School
 BSF CM23 ....137 K9
Hawksmoor Primary School
 THMD SE28 ....335 J7
Hawkswood School & Centre
 CHING E4 ....274 F4
The Hayward Special School
 CHLM/WR CM1 ....217 P7
Hazelmere Infant School
 CHING E4 ....128 F7
Heathcote School
 RCHLM CM5 ....242 B5
Heathcote Secondary School
 RCHLM CM5 ....275 H8
Heathlands CE Primary School
 RCOLW CO6 ....127 H2
Heath Primary School
 KESG IP5 ....26 G4
The Heath School
 COLW CO5 ....150 G1
Heathside Special School
 IPNE IP4 ....26 B5
Heathway Industrial Estate
 DAGE RM10 ....318 A6
Heathway Medical Centre
 DAGW RM3 ....317 N6
Heckford Street
 Business Centre WAP E1W ...332 A7
Hedgerows Business Park
 CHLM/WR CM1 ....218 F5
Hedges & Butler Estate
 SRTFD E15 ....332 F2
Hedingham Castle
 HSTD CO9 ....72 E5
Hedingham School
 HSTD CO9 ....72 C6
Helena Romanes School
 GTDUN CM6 ....141 M4
Henham & Ugley
 Primary School RBSF CM22 ...115 J2
Henry Green Primary School
 BCTR RM8 ....317 L3
Henry Maynard Junior School
 WALTH E17 ....294 F9
The Hereward County School
 LOU IG10 ....254 D9
Herington House School
 RBRW/HUT CM13 ....281 L5
Heron Industrial Estate
 SRTFD E15 ....332 E2
Herons Gate Trading Estate
 BSDN SS14 ....304 F5
Herringham Primary School
 CDW/CHF RM16 ....350 C1

Hertford Regional College
 WARE SG12 ....184 A4
Hertford Regional College
 (Northgate Centre)
 BSF CM23 ....137 L6
Hertfordshire & Essex
 Community Hospital
 BSF CM23 ....137 P8
Hertfordshire & Essex
 High School BSF CM23 ....137 N7
Hester House
 HLW CM20 ....13 F3
Heybridge CP School
 MAL CM9 ....222 D6
Heybridge House
 Industrial Estate MAL CM9 ...222 C7
Heybridge Swifts FC
 MAL CM9 ....222 E5
Heydon Grange Golf &
 Country Club ROY SG8 ....48 A1
Highams Lodge Business
 Centre WALTH E17 ....294 H7
Highams Park School
 CHING E4 ....294 G3
High Beech CE Primary School
 LOU IG10 ....253 K9
High Beech Golf Club
 LOU IG10 ....253 L7
Highbridge Retail Park
 WAB EN9 ....252 E4
High Chelmer Shopping Centre
 CHLM/WR CM1 ....5 F5
Highfield Primary School
 WCHMH N21 ....272 C7
Highlands Primary School
 MGTR CO11 ....106 B4
Highlands J & I School
 IL IG1 ....316 A3
Highlands Primary School
 IL IG1 ....316 A3
High Ongar Primary School
 CHONG CM5 ....235 P6
High Street Business Park
 CHES/WCR EN8 ....252 B2
The Highway Trading Centre
 WCHPL E1 ....332 A7
High Wood Hospital
 BRWN CM15 ....280 E7
Highwood Primary School
 BRWN CM15 ....238 B6
Highwoods Community
 Primary School COLN CO4 .....128 C3
High Woods Country Park
 COLN CO4 ....128 B4
Hilldene Primary School
 HARH RM3 ....299 H3
Hill Farm Industrial Estate
 COLN CO4 ....103 K2
Hillgrove Business Park
 WAB EN9 ....230 F1
Hillmead JMI School
 BSF CM23 ....137 P5
Hillmead Primary School
 BSF CM23 ....137 H7
Hillside Community
 Primary School
 CHTY IP2 ....25 K8
Hillside Special School
 SUD CO10 ....20 E1
Hilltop Primary School
 WICKE SS11 ....285 M8
Hill View Business Park
 NHMKT IP6 ....22 E6
Hillyfield Primary School
 WALTH E17 ....294 B7
Hilton Docklands Pier
 POP/IOD E14 ....332 C8
The Hiltongrove Business
 Hingham Primary School
 SBN/FI SS3 ....330 E7
HM Prison
 CHLM/GWD CM2 ....218 C8
Hoblongs Industrial Estate
 GTDUN CM6 ....141 M8
Hockerill Anglo European
 College BSF CM23 ....137 M7
Hockerill Sports Club
 BSF CM23 ....137 N9
Hockley Primary School
 HOC/HUL SS5 ....307 M1
Hoddesdon Health Centre
 HOD EN11 ....208 D6
Hoddesdon Industrial Estate
 HOD EN11 ....208 F4
Hoddesdon Lawn Tennis Club
 HOD EN11 ....208 C5
Hogarth Primary School
 BRWN CM15 ....281 H8
Holbrook CP School
 RIPS/CAP IP9 ....83 L3
Holbrook High School
 RIPS/CAP IP9 ....83 L3
Holbury Centre
 ERITH DA8 ....346 F5
Holdbrook Primary School
 CHES/WCR EN8 ....252 C4
Holiday Inn
 BRW CM14 ....300 B1
 COLW CO5 ....126 E8
 ROY SG8 ....24 C8
Holiday Park
 RCOS CO16 ....206 B5
Holland Haven Primary School
 COS CO15 ....182 F7
Holland Park Primary School
 COS CO15 ....182 C8
Holly House Private Hospital
 BKHH IG9 ....275 L8
Hollytrees Junior School
 IL IG1 ....300 E1
Hollytrees Museum
 COL CO1 ....8 D5
Holly Trees Primary School
 BRW CM14 ....300 F1

Hollywood Bowl
 BSDN SS14 ....304 D4
Holmwood House School
 COLW CO3 ....126 C7
Holt Farm Infant School
 RCFD SS4 ....308 E4
Holy Cross Catholic Primary
 School HLWS CM18 ....211 H5
Holy Cross RC Primary School
 SOCK/AV RM15 ....338 C7
Holy Family RC Primary School
 POP/IOD E14 ....332 D7
 SBF/HAD SS7 ....326 A2
Holy Family Technology College
 WALTH E17 ....294 E8
Holy Trinity CE Primary School
 HSTD CO9 ....97 N6
Holy Trinity Museum of Social
 History
 COL CO1 ....8 C6
Holy Trinity Primary School
 CHES/WCR EN8 ....252 A2
Holywells High School
 IPSE IP3 ....31 H1
Home Farm CP School
 COLW CO5 ....103 P4
Home Farm Industrial Estate
 WARE SG12 ....185 J7
Homeopathic Health Centre
 PLSTW E13 ....333 K4
The Honeywood School
 RCOLW CO6 ....147 P5
Honilands Primary School
 EN EN1 ....251 N6
Horizon Business Centre
 ED N9 ....274 A8
Hormead Primary School
 BUNT SG9 ....86 A8
Hornchurch Clinic
 EMPK RM11 ....319 K3
Hornchurch Country Park
 HCH RM12 ....319 K6
Hornchurch Sports Centre
 EMPK RM11 ....319 H4
Hornchurch Stadium
 UPMR RM14 ....319 M4
Horndon Industrial Park
 RBRW/HUT CM15 ....321 L1
Horndon on the Hill CE
 Primary School
 SLH/COR SS17 ....340 G1
Horn Stairs
 POP/IOD E14 ....332 C8
Hotel Continental
 HAR CO12 ....110 D5
Hotel Ibis
 BARK IG11 ....334 C1
 POP/IOD E14 ....332 F7
 SRTFD E15 ....315 H8
 WTHK RM20 ....348 C4
Houndsfield Primary School
 ED N9 ....273 M6
House on the Hill Museum
 Adventure
 STSD CM24 ....114 C8
Howard Business Park
 WAB EN9 ....252 G4
Howard Hall
 BRTR CM7 ....145 J2
Howbridge CE Junior School
 WIT CM8 ....197 J4
Howe Green House School
 RBSF CM22 ....162 G3
HSBC Tower
 POP/IOD E14 ....332 E8
Hubbinet Industrial Estate
 ROMW/RG RM7 ....298 B7
Hullbridge Clinic
 HOC/HUL SS5 ....286 G6
Hullbridge Sports Club
 HOC/HUL SS5 ....287 H7
Hunters Hall Primary School
 DAGE RM10 ....318 A7
Hurst Drive Primary School
 CHES/WCR EN8 ....251 P4
Hutton All Saints CE
 Primary School
 RBRW/HUT CM13 ....281 N5
Hutton Clinic
 RBRW/HUT CM13 ....281 N4
Hyderaad Barracks
 COLS CO2 ....152 B1
Hyland House School
 WALTH E17 ....294 C6
Hylands Golf Club
 ING CM4 ....239 J8
Hylands House & Park
 CHLM/WR CM1 ....239 K5
Hylands School
 CHLM/WR CM1 ....239 L1
Hyleford Leavers
 Unit School
 BARK/HLT IG6 ....296 E6
Hyleford School
 IL IG1 ....316 F7
Ian Mikardo High School
 BOW E3 ....332 E5
IKEA Store Lakeside
 WTHK RM20 ....348 E3
Ilford County Court
 IL IG1 ....316 E4
Ilford County High School
 BARK/HLT IG6 ....296 D6
Ilford Golf Club
 IL IG1 ....316 A3
Ilford Jewish Primary School
 BARK/HLT IG6 ....296 E7
Ilford Medical Centre
 IL IG1 ....316 C5
Ilford Preparatory School
 GDMY/SEVK IG3 ....316 G3

Ilford Retail Park
 IL IG1 ....316 D4
Ilford Swimming Pool
 IL IG1 ....316 E4
Ilford Trading Estate
 BSDN SS14 ....304 D5
Immanuel School
 ROM RM1 ....298 D3
Imperial Trading Estate
 RAIN RM13 ....337 H4
Infant College
 IL IG1 ....316 B4
Ingatestone & Fryerning CE
 Junior School
 ING CM4 ....260 B5
Ingatestone Infant School
 ING CM4 ....260 B5
Ingrave Johnstone CE
 Primary School
 RBRW/HUT CM13 ....301 M3
Ingrebourne Primary School
 HARH RM3 ....299 H1
Innkeeper's Lodge
 STHGT/OAK N14 ....272 D8
 WICKE SS11 ....285 N5
Innova Business Centre
 PEND EN3 ....252 C6
International Business Centre
 CVI SS8 ....344 A3
International Business Park
 CVI SS8 ....343 P2
Invicta Industrial Estate
 SRTFD E15 ....332 F3
Ipswich Airport (disused)
 IPSE IP3 ....31 J5
Ipswich Crematorium
 IPNE IP4 ....25 N3
Ipswich Golf Club
 IPSE IP5 ....26 C9
Ipswich High School GDST
 RIPS/CAP IP9 ....31 J8
Ipswich Hospital
 IPNE IP4 ....26 B5
Ipswich Museums & Galleries
 IP IP1 ....16 D3
Ipswich Regent Theatre
 IP IP1 ....17 G4
Ipswich RUFC
 KESG IP5 ....26 A1
Ipswich School
 IP IP1 ....16 D1
Ipswich School Pre-Preparatory
 Department IP IP1 ....16 C2
Ipswich Sports Club
 IP IP1 ....16 C1
Ipswich Town FC
 (Portman Road) IP IP1 ....16 B5
Ipswich Transport Museum
 IPSE IP3 ....26 B9
Island Clinic
 POP/IOD E14 ....332 F9
Ivanhurst Industrial Estate
 HARH RM3 ....286 A4
Ivry Street Medical Practice
 IP IP1 ....16 C1
Ivy Chimneys Primary School
 EPP CM16 ....254 C2
Jack Hatch Way
 MGTR CO11 ....107 M5
The James Hornsby School
 LAIN SS15 ....303 L8
James Oglethorpe Primary
 School UPMR RM14 ....320 C4
Janet Duke Primary School
 LAIN SS15 ....303 L9
Jenny Hammond Primary
 School WAN E11 ....315 H6
Jerounds J & I School
 HLWW/ROY CM19 ....210 C6
The Joe Richardson
 Community School
 DAGW RM9 ....335 L1
John Bramston Primary School
 BARK/HLT IG6 ....297 H3
John Bunyan J & I School
 BRTR CM7 ....145 H2
John F Kennedy Special School
 SRTFD E15 ....332 C1
John Perry Primary School
 DAGE RM10 ....318 C8
John Ray Junior School
 BRTR CM7 ....145 J4
The John Warner School
 HOD EN11 ....208 E2
Joseph Clarke Special School
 CHING E4 ....294 G3
Jotmans Hall Primary School
 SBF/HAD SS7 ....325 N2
Jubilee Primary School
 THMD SE28 ....335 K7
Jubilee Sports Ground
 CHING E4 ....294 G1
The Junior School
 BSF CM23 ....137 J7
Kaizen Primary School
 PLSTW E13 ....333 L4
Katella Trading Estate
 BARK IG11 ....334 F3
Keble Medical Centre
 FSTGT E7 ....315 M8
Katherine Semar Infant School
 SAFWS CB11 ....65 M3
Katherine Semar Junior School
 SAFWS CB11 ....65 M3
Katherines Primary School
 HLWW/ROY CM19 ....210 A5
Keble Preparatory School
 WCHMH N21 ....272 F6
Keir Hardie Primary School
 CAN/RD E16 ....333 K6
Keith Davis Cue Sports Club
 DAGW RM9 ....317 L9
Kelmscott Community Centre
 WALTH E17 ....314 C1
Kelmscott Leisure Centre
 WALTH E17 ....314 C1

Kelmscott School
WALTH E17 ....**314** C1
Kelrose Swimming Pool Centre
RBRW/HUT CM13 ....**301** H9
Kelvedon Hatch Primary
School *BRWN* CM15 ....**258** B6
Kelvedon St Marys CE
Cont School
K/T/MI CO5 ....**173** H3
Kendall CE Primary School
COLS CO2 ....**152** D2
Kenneth More Theatre
IL IG1 ....**316** D5
Kennington Primary School
SOCK/AV RM15 ....**337** P6
Kensington Primary School
MNPK E12 ....**316** A8
Kent Kraft Industrial Estate
GVW DA11 ....**349** J9
Kents Hill Primary School
SBF/HAD SS7 ....**326** A2
Kesgrave High School
KESG IP5 ....**27** J5
Kestner Industrial Estate
GRH DA9 ....**348** D9
Keys Meadow Primary School
PEND EN3 ....**252** C6
Kimberley Industrial Estate
WALTH E17 ....**294** C4
The King Edmund School
RCFD SS4 ....**308** F2
King Edward Industrial Park
COLS CO2 ....**152** E1
King Edward VI Grammar
School *CHLM/WR* CM1 ....**4** E1
King Edward VI Grammar
Sports Ground
CHLM/WR CM1 ....**193** N8
Kingfisher Leisure Park
SUD CO10 ....**20** E6
King George Hospital
GDMY/SEVK IG3 ....**297** H9
King Harold GM School
WAB EN9 ....**253** H5
The King John School
SBF/HAD SS7 ....**326** E3
King & Queen Wharf
WAP E1W **332** A7
Kingsdale Industrial Estate
CHLM/WR CM1 ....**5** H1
The Kingsdale
CHLM/WR CM1 ....**5** H1
Kingsdown Special School
LOS SS9 ....**308** B9
Kings Estate
HCH RM12 ....**318** F6
Kings Fleet Primary School
FXN IP11 ....**35** M5
Kingsford Community School
PLSTW E13 ....**333** M4
Kings Ford Infant School
COLS CO2 ....**151** M3
Kingshill Primary School
WARE SG12 ....**184** A1
Kingsland College of Business
Studies
SRTFD E15 ....**332** C2
Kingsmead Primary School
CLPT E5 ....**314** B6
Kingsmead School
ENF EN1 ....**273** M3
Kingsmoor Infant School
HLWW/ROY CM19 ....**210** D7
Kingsmoor Recreation Centre
HLWW/ROY CM19 ....**210** C7
The Kings Oak Private Hospital
ENC/FH EN2 ....**250** F8
King Solomon High School
BARK/HLT IG6 ....**296** E6
Kings Private Clinic
GDMY/SEVK IG3 ....**316** G5
Kings Road Primary School
CHLM/WR CM1 ....**217** N7
Kingston Primary School
SBF/HAD SS7 ....**306** B9
Kingsway Hall
HAR CO12 ....**14** E6
Kingswode Hoe School
COLW CO3 ....**127** M8
Kingswood Medical Centre
VGE SS16 ....**324** A2
Kingswood Primary School
VGE SS16 ....**3** G7
Kingswood School
HARH RM5 ....**299** M1
Kirby Primary School
FOS CO15 ....**89** J3
Knightsmead Special School
SOCK/AV RM15 ....**338** C7
Knightswick Centre
CVI SS8 ....**344** E1
KP Estate
RAIN RM13 ....**336** D7
Kubrick Business Estate
FSTGT E7 ....**315** L6
The Kursaal Entertainment
Centre *SOS* SS1 ....**19** K6
Laburnum Health Centre
DAGE RM10 ....**317** P4
Laindon Health Centre
LAIN SS15 ....**303** J9
Laindon Park Primary School
LAIN SS15 ....**303** M7
Laindon Road Clinic
BCAYW CM12 ....**283** H8
Lakeside Retail Park
WTHK RM20 ....**348** D2
Lakeside Shopping Centre
WTHK RM20 ....**348** E1
Lakes Industrial Estate
BRTR CM7 ....**145** K4
Lambourne Primary School
ABR/ST RM4 ....**277** J3
Lambs Court
POP/IOD E14 ....**332** B7

Lancaster Ipswich Athletics
Track & Stadium
IPNE IP2 ....**25** N1
Lancaster Special School
WOS/PRIT SS0 ....**328** D3
Landguard Fort
FX IP11 ....**111** K4
Lanford Obesity Clinic
ED N9 ....**273** N6
Langdon Hills Country Park
VGE SS16 ....**323** J5
Langdon Hills Golf Club
SLH/COR SS17 ....**322** F6
Langdon Park School
POP/IOD E14 ....**332** E6
Langdon School
EHAM E6 ....**334** C2
Langenhoe Community
Primary School
K/T/MI CO5 ....**177** H3
Langer Park Industrial Estate
FX IP11 ....**11** F4
Langer Primary School
FX IP11 ....**11** F6
Langham Primary School
COLN CO4 ....**104** A4
Langthorne Health Centre
WAN E11 ....**314** G5
Langthorne Hospital
WAN E11 ....**314** G6
Langtons J & I School
EHAM E6 ....**315** P9
Lansbury Lawrence Primary
School *POP/IOD* E14 ....**332** E6
Lansdowne Primary School
TIL RM18 ....**350** A7
La Salette RC Primary School
CHING E4 ....**274** G8
Laser Clinic
CHESW EN7 ....**229** N9
Latchingdon Primary School
RCHLM CM5 ....**267** J3
Lathom Junior School
EHAM E6 ....**315** P9
Latton Bush Business Centre
HLWS CM18 ....**210** C6
Latton Bush Recreation Centre
HLWS CM18 ....**210** F6
Latymer All Saints CE
Primary School *ED* N9 ....**273** L8
The Latymer School
ED N9 ....**273** K8
Laurence Industrial Estate
SOSN SS2 ....**308** C9
Lauriston Primary School
HOM E9 ....**332** A1
Lavender Primary School
ENC/FH EN2 ....**251** J8
Lawford CE Primary School
MGTR CO11 ....**105** P6
Lawford Mead Primary School
CHLM/WR CM1 ....**217** L6
Lawn Cemetery
CHLM/GWD CM2 ....**240** E6
Lawrence Trading Estate
GRAYS RM17 ....**349** M2
Lawrence Wharf
POP/IOD E14 ....**332** C8
Layer Marney Tower
K/T/MI CO5 ....**174** C5
Leah Manning Centre
HLW CM20 ....**13** J3
Lea Park Trading Estate
LEY E10 ....**314** C2
Lea Road Industrial Park
CHES/WCR EN8 ....**252** D4
Leaside Business Centre
PEND EN3 ....**274** C1
The Leas Special School
CGS CO15 ....**6** B5
Lea Valley High School
PEND EN3 ....**251** P5
Lea Valley Trading Estate
UED N18 ....**294** A3
Lee Chapel Primary School
VGE SS16 ....**323** N1
Leeside Court
BERM/RHTH SE16 ....**332** A8
Lee Valley Campsite
CHING E4 ....**274** E1
Lee Valley Caravan Park
HOD EN11 ....**208** F7
Lee Valley Leisure Centre
Camping & Caravan *ED* N9 ...**274** A7
Lee Valley Leisure Golf Club
ED N9 ....**274** B6
Lee Valley Park
WAB EN9 ....**230** E7
Lee Valley Park Farms
WAB EN9 ....**230** F7
Lee Valley Watersports Centre
CHING E4 ....**294** B3
Leigh Beck Primary School
CVI SS8 ....**345** H2
Leigh Cemetery
LOS SS9 ....**327** N4
Leigh North Street
Primary School *LOS* SS9 .....**327** P6
Leopold Street Clinic
BOW E3 ....**332** C5
The Leventhorpe School
SBW CM21 ....**162** B9
The Leverton Infant School
WAB EN9 ....**253** J4
Lexden Primary School
COLW CO3 ....**127** H9
Lexden Springs Special School
COLW CO3 ....**127** H8
Lexden Squash Club
COLW CO3 ....**126** G8
Lexden Wood Golf Club
COLW CO3 ....**127** K7
Ley Park CP School
BROX EN10 ....**230** C1

The Leys Primary School
DAGE RM10 ....**318** B9
Leyton Business Centre
LEY E10 ....**314** C4
Leyton FC
LEY E10 ....**314** C3
Leyton Industrial Village
LEY E10 ....**314** A2
Leyton Leisure Centre
LEY E10 ....**314** E2
Leyton Orient FC
(Matchroom Stadium)
LEY E10 ....**314** E5
Leytonstone School
WAN E11 ....**315** H1
Leyton VI Form College
LEY E10 ....**314** C1
Leyton Youth Sports Ground
LEY E10 ....**314** E3
Liberty II Centre
ROM RM1 ....**298** D8
The Liberty
ROM RM1 ....**298** D9
Lime Grove Estate
HVHL CB9 ....**41** M6
Limehouse Hole Stairs
POP/IOD E14 ....**332** C8
Limes Farm Primary School
CHIG IG7 ....**296** E3
The Limes Medical Centre
EPP CM16 ....**233** J8
EPP CM16 ....**234** A5
Lincewood Primary School
VGE SS16 ....**323** J3
Lincoln Road Clinic
EN EN1 ....**273** M4
Lingwood Clinic
WAN E11 ....**314** G6
Links Business Centre
BSF CM23 ....**137** P7
Linton CE (Aided) Infant School
CBE/LIN CB1 ....**38** B1
Linton Health Centre
CBE/LIN CB1 ....**38** B1
Linton Heights Junior School
CBE/LIN CB1 ....**38** C1
Linton Mead Primary School
THMD SE28 ....**335** J7
Linton Village College
CBE/LIN CB1 ....**38** A1
Linton Zoological Gardens
CBE/LIN CB1 ....**38** A2
Lionmede Bowling Club &
Tennis Courts
CHLM/GWD CM2 ....**218** C8
Lion Walk Shopping Centre
COL CO1 ....**8** C6
Lister Community School
Performing Arts College
PLSTW E13 ....**333** L2
Lister Medical Centre
HLWS CM18 ....**210** D6
Littlebrook Business Centre
DART DA1 ....**347** P6
Littlegarth School
RCOLW CO6 ....**102** E1
Little Hadham Primary School
STDN SG11 ....**136** B4
Little Hallingbury CE Primary
School *RBSF* CM22 ....**162** F5
Little Heath School
CRH RM6 ....**297** J8
Little Ilford School
MNPK E12 ....**316** A7
Little Malgraves Industrial
Estate *UPMR* RM14 ....**322** G5
Little Oakley CE School
HAR CO12 ....**109** L9
Little Thurrock Primary School
GRAYS RM17 ....**349** N1
Little Waltham CE Primary
School *RCHLM* CM3 ....**194** A5
Lloyd Park Centre
WALTH E17 ....**294** D6
Locks View Court
POP/IOD E14 ....**332** B7
Log Church
CHONG CM5 ....**235** J7
London City Airport
CAN/RD E16 ....**333** P8
London Industrial Estate
EHAM E6 ....**334** B5
London Industrial Park
EHAM E6 ....**334** C5
London International
Cruise Terminal *TIL* RM18 ..**350** B9
London, Leyton-Lee Valley
Ice Centre *LEY* E10 ....**314** A4
London Road Retail Park
WOS/PRIT SS0 ....**18** D3
London Stansted Airport
RBSF CM22 ....**139** K3
London Transport Bus Depot
BXLYHN DA7 ....**346** A8
Longfield Medical Centre
MAL CM9 ....**222** C6
Longlands Primary School
BROX EN10 ....**230** C4
Long Melford CE Primary
School *SUD* CO10 ....**46** F4
The Long Melford Practice
SUD CO10 ....**46** F3
Long Ridings J & I School
RBRW/HUT CM13 ....**281** L4
Longshaw Primary School
CHING E4 ....**274** G9
Longview Adolescent Unit
COLN CO4 ....**128** A4
Lord Butler Leisure Centre
SAFWS CB11 ....**65** N2
Lord Lister Health Centre
FSTGT E7 ....**315** K6
Lorimar Business Centre
RAIN RM13 ....**336** D6
Loughton CC
LOU IG10 ....**276** A2

Loughton Golf Club
LOU IG10 ....**254** C9
Loughton Hall Clinic
LOU IG10 ....**276** C2
Loughton Health Centre
LOU IG10 ....**275** P2
Loughton Mental
Health Centre *LOU* IG10 .....**275** P4
Lowewood Museum
HOD EN11 ....**208** D6
Lowfield Sports Ground
HOD EN11 ....**208** C5
Low Hall Sports Ground
WALTH E17 ....**314** A1
Low House Touring Caravan
Centre *KIR/NAC* IP10 ....**32** A1
Loxford School of Science
& Technology *IL* IG1 ....**316** E7
Loyola Preparatory School
BKHH IG9 ....**275** M7
LPR Sports Club
BARK/HLT IG6 ....**296** G5
Lubbins Park Primary School
CVI SS8 ....**344** F3
Lutomer House
Business Centre
POP/IOD E14 ....**332** E8
Lychgate Industrial Estate
SBF/HAD SS7 ....**306** B6
Lyon Business Park
BARK IG11 ....**334** F2
Lyons Hall CP School
BRTR CM7 ....**145** M2
Mabwin Supplementary School
ED N9 ....**273** N8
Madeira Grove Clinic
WFD IG8 ....**295** L2
Magnet Estate
CDW/CHF RM16 ....**348** F3
Maidenhall Sports Centre
CHTY IP2 ....**25** K9
Maidstone County Infant School
FX IP11 ....**35** H6
Maison Talbooth Hotel
RCOLE CO7 ....**104** E2
Maldon Agricultural Museum
MAL CM9 ....**223** M4
Maldon Court Preparatory
School *MAL* CM9 ....**222** A8
Maldon Golf Club
MAL CM9 ....**221** P6
Maldon Museum
MAL CM9 ....**222** C9
Maldon Primary School
MAL CM9 ....**222** B9
The Maltings Industrial Estate
BOC CM0 ....**269** K5
SWF CM3 ....**187** N2
WARE SG12 ....**184** G8
Mandeville Primary School
CLPT E5 ....**314** B5
Manford Industrial Estate
ERITH DA8 ....**346** G4
Manford Way Health Centre
BARK/HLT IG6 ....**296** C3
Mangapps Farm Railway
Museum *BOC* CM0 ....**268** F9
Manifest Theatre
MGTR CO11 ....**106** A5
Manningtree High School
MGTR CO11 ....**106** A5
Manningtree Sports Centre
MGTR CO11 ....**106** A4
Manorfield Primary School
POP/IOD E14 ....**332** E5
Manor Fields Primary School
BSF CM23 ....**137** J9
Manor Infant School
BARK IG11 ....**316** G8
The Manor of Groves Golf Club
SBW CM21 ....**186** G2
Manor Park Cemetery
FSTGT E7 ....**315** N6
Manor Park Crematorium
FSTGT E7 ....**315** M6
Manor Park Methodist School
MNPK E12 ....**315** P6
Manor Primary School
BSDN SS14 ....**3** H1
SRTFD E15 ....**333** H2
The Manor Primary School
ROM RM1 ....**298** E9
Manor Trading Estate
SBF/HAD SS7 ....**306** A8
Manor Way Business Centre
DAGW RM9 ....**336** C5
Manor Way Industrial Estate
GRAYS RM17 ....**349** M5
Manuden Primary School
BSF CM23 ....**113** M6
Maple River Industrial Estate
HLW CM20 ....**187** J6
Margaretting CE
Primary School *ING* CM4 ....**260** F1
Marillac Hospital
RBRW/HUT CM13 ....**300** C3
Marion Richardson
Primary School *WCHPL* E1 ..**332** A6
Market Field School
RCOLE CO7 ....**153** P1
Mark Hall Comprehensive
School *HLWE* CM17 ....**211** K1
Mark Hall Cycle Museum
HLWE CM17 ....**187** J3
Markhams Chase
Leisure Centre *LAIN* SS15 ...**303** L9
Marks Gate Junior School
CDH RM6 ....**297** M7
Marks Hall Arboretum
RCOLW CO6 ....**123** N8
Marks Hill (Nature Reserve)
VGE SS16 ....**323** K2
Marlborough Hotel
FX IP11 ....**11** G1
Marner Primary School
BOW E3 ....**332** E4

Marshalls Park School
ROM RM1 ....**298** D6
Marsh Farm Country Park
RCHLM CM5 ....**287** J3
Marsh Gate Business Centre
SRTFD E15 ....**332** F2
Marshgate Trading Estate
SRTFD E15 ....**314** E9
Marsh Green School
RAIN RM13 ....**335** P2
Marsh View Industrial Estate
RAIN RM13 ....**337** L3
Martells Industrial Estate
RCOLE CO7 ....**129** L2
Martinbridge Industrial Estate
EN EN1 ....**273** M4
Martindale Industrial Estate
EN EN1 ....**273** K4
Martlesham Beacon Hill
Primary School *WDBR* IP12 ...**27** M1
Marvgreen Manor Hotel
BRW CM14 ....**300** C1
Maryland Industrial Estate
SRTFD E15 ....**315** H7
Maryland Primary School
SRTFD E15 ....**315** H7
Matching Green CE Primary
School *HLWE* CM17 ....**213** J1
Maunds Wood CP School
HLWS CM18 ....**210** E7
The Mawney School
ROMW/RG RM7 ....**298** C9
Mayesbrook Park Arena
BCTR RM8 ....**317** H7
Mayespark Primary School
GDMY/SEVK IG3 ....**317** H5
Mayfair Industrial Estate
RCHLM CM5 ....**266** G3
Mayfield Infant School
CHES/WCR EN8 ....**230** B6
Mayfield School & College
BCTR RM8 ....**317** K3
Mayflower High School
RAIN RM13 ....**283** K3
Mayflower Primary School
HAR CO12 ....**14** B6
POP/IOD E14 ....**332** D6
Mayflower Retail Park
BSDN SS14 ....**304** C5
Maylandsea CP School
RCHLM CM5 ....**267** N1
Maylandsea Medical Centre
RCHLM CM5 ....**245** M9
Maylands Golf Club &
Country Club *HARH* RM3 .....**299** N2
Mayplace Primary School
BXLYHN DA7 ....**346** C9
Maytime School
IL IG1 ....**316** B5
Mayville J & P School
WAN E11 ....**315** H5
McEntee School
WALTH E17 ....**294** C5
Meadgate Primary School
CHLM/GWD CM2 ....**240** C7
Mead Industrial Park
HLW CM20 ....**186** G8
Mead JMI School
HARH RM3 ....**299** L3
The Meadows Shopping Centre
CHLM/GWD CM2 ....**5** H4
The Mead School
HLWS CM18 ....**210** F5
Meadow Barracks
COL CO1 ....**152** B1
Megabowl
CHLM/WR CM1 ....**239** M3
Melbourne Park Athletics
Centre *CHLM/WR* CM1 ....**217** M5
Melbourne Park Primary
School *CHLM/WR* CM1 ....**217** N5
Melford Hall (NT)
SUD CO10 ....**46** G2
Memorial Grounds
SOSN SS2 ....**329** J1
Menzies Prince Regent Hotel
WFD IG8 ....**296** A3
Mercers College
WARE SG12 ....**184** A2
Merrielands Retail Park
DAGW RM9 ....**335** N1
Merryhills Clinic
ENC/FH EN2 ....**272** E2
Merryhills Primary School
ENC/FH EN2 ....**272** E3
Merylands Primary School
LAIN SS15 ....**303** H9
Mersea Community &
Sports Centre *K/T/MI* CO5 ....**202** F6
Mersea Island School
K/T/MI CO5 ....**202** F6
Mersea Island Vineyard
K/T/MI CO5 ....**203** L2
Messing cum Inworth
Community Primary School
K/T/MI CO5 ....**173** P3
Midas Business Centre
DAGE RM10 ....**317** P6
Midas Industrial Estate
DAGE RM10 ....**317** P6
Middle School Team
ROM RM1 ....**318** L2
Middlesex University (Enfield
Campus)
PEND EN4 ....**273** N4
Middlesex University (Trent
Park Campus)
EBAR EN4 ....**272** E1
Middleton Special School
WARE SG12 ....**184** A5
Mid Essex Adult
Community College
RBRW/HUT CM13 ....**281** L5
Mid Essex Magistrates Courts
CHLM/WR CM1 ....**5** G1

Mildmay Industrial Estate
BOC CM0 ....290 G3
Mildmay Infant School
CHLM/GWD CM2 ....240 A5
Mile End Hospital
WCHPL E1 ....332 A3
Mile End Stadium
BOW E3 ....332 B5
Milehams Industrial Estate
HOD EN11 ....347 M1
Milbrook School
CHES/WCR EN8 ....230 B8
Mildene Primary School
K/T/MI CO5 ....174 A7
Millennium Harbour
Development *POP/IOD* E14 ....332 C9
Millfields Primary School
RCOLE CO7 ....153 L5
Mill Hall
RAYL SS6 ....306 G5
The Mill Hotel
SUD CO10 ....20 B5
Millhouse Primary School
LAIN SS15 ....303 K7
Mill River Trading Estate
PEND EN3 ....274 B3
Millside Industrial Estate
DART DA1 ....347 J9
Mill Studio Business Centre
WARE SG12 ....184 B3
Milson's Hotel
RCOLE CO7 ....104 D1
Milton Hall Primary School
WOS/PRIT SS0 ....18 C3
Mint Business Park
CAN/RD E16 ....333 K5
Mirravale Trading Estate
BCTR RM8 ....317 M2
Mission Grove Primary School
WALTH E17 ....294 C9
Mistley Norman CE Primary
School *MGTR* CO11 ....106 F4
Mistley Towers
MGTR CO11 ....106 E3
Mole Hall Wildlife Park
SAFWS CB11 ....90 C5
Monega Primary School
MNPK E12 ....315 N7
Monkwick Primary &
Infant School *COLS* CO2 ....152 A4
Monkwick Sports Centre
COLS CO2 ....152 A4
Monro Industrial Estate
CHES/WCR EN8 ....252 B4
Montagle Primary School
DAGW RM9 ....335 J1
Montessori School
RBSF CM22 ....139 L3
The Montgomerie Primary
School *SBF/HAD* SS7 ....305 N8
Montgomery Infant School
COLS CO2 ....151 M4
Moonhall Business Park
HVHL CB9 ....41 K6
Moot Hall
MAL CM9 ....222 A8
Moreton Bay Industrial Estate
GPK RM2 ....299 D3
Moreton CE Primary School
ONG CM5 ....213 H8
Morland Primary School
IPSE IP5 ....30 C2
Mossford Green Primary
School *BARK/HLT* IG6 ....296 D6
Moulsham High School
CHLM/GWD CM2 ....240 A3
Moulsham Lodge Clinic
CHLM/GWD CM2 ....240 A4
Moulsham Primary School
CHLM/GWD CM2 ....240 A3
Mountfitchet Castle &
Norman Village *STSD* CM24 ....114 C9
The Mountfitchet High School
STSD CM24 ....138 C2
Mountnessing CE Primary
School *BRWN* CM15 ....259 N9
MSF Whitehall College
BSF CM23 ....137 K5
Mudlands Estate
RAIN RM13 ....336 D3
Mulberry Business Centre
BERM/RHTH SE16 ....332 A9
Murrayfield Pavillion
BSDN SS14 ....2 B1
Murrayfield Primary School
IPSE IP5 ....25 P8
Museum in Docklands
POP/IOD E14 ....332 D7
Myland Primary School
COLN CO4 ....127 N3
Nabbotts County Junior School
CHLM/WR CM1 ....218 D4
Nacton CE VC Primary School
KIR/NAC IP10 ....31 P5
Natural History Museum
COL CO1 ....8 D6
Nayland CP School
RCOLW CO6 ....77 P8
Nazeing CP School
WAB EN9 ....231 H2
Nazeing Golf Club
WAB EN9 ....231 M3
Nazeing Park School
WAB EN9 ....231 M1
Nelmes Primary School
EMPK RM11 ....299 L8
Nelson Dock Museum
POP/IOD E14 ....332 C8
Nelson Primary School
EHAM E6 ....334 B2
Nether Hall
SUD CO10 ....45 H1
Nevendon Trading Estate
PIT SS13 ....304 C6
Newbury Park Health Centre
GNTH/NBYPK IG2 ....316 E1

New Cangle Primary School
HVHL CB9 ....41 J2
New Cemetery
IPNE IP4 ....25 M3
New City Primary School
PLSTW E13 ....333 M3
New England Industrial Estate
BARK IG11 ....334 D2
HOD EN11 ....208 F4
New Hall Preparatory School
RCHLM CM5 ....218 F2
New Hall Vineyard
RCHLM CM5 ....243 N8
Newham College of Further
Education
EHAM E6 ....334 A2
SRTFD E15 ....315 H9
Newham Community College
CAN/RD E16 ....333 H4
Newham General Hospital
PLSTW E13 ....333 M4
Newham Leisure Centre
PLSTW E13 ....333 M5
Newham Medical Centre
PLSTW E13 ....333 M2
Newham Sixth Form College
PLSTW E13 ....333 L4
New Industrial Site
RIPW IP8 ....22 B4
Newlands Shopping Centre
WIT CM8 ....197 K2
Newlands Spring
Primary School
CHLM/WR CM1 ....217 L4
Newmans Estate
COS CO15 ....6 B4
Newport Free Grammar School
SAFWS CB11 ....64 G8
Newport J & I School
LEY E10 ....314 F4
Newport Primary School
SAFWS CB11 ....64 G9
New River Trading Estate
CHES/WCR EN8 ....230 A5
New Rush Hall School
IL IG1 ....316 D4
New Southgate Cemetery
FBAR/BDGN N11 ....272 A9
New Southgate Crematorium
FBAR/BDGN N11 ....272 A9
New Spitalfields Market
LEY E10 ....314 D5
Newton Industrial Estate
CHDH RM6 ....297 L8
Newtons Primary School
RAIN RM13 ....336 C2
Nightingale Clinic
PLSTW E13 ....333 M2
Nightingale Primary School
SWFD E18 ....295 M8
Noak Bridge Medical Centre
LAIN SS15 ....303 N6
Noak Bridge Primary School
LAIN SS15 ....303 N6
Noak Hill School
HARH RM3 ....279 K8
Noor Ul Islam School
LEY E10 ....314 E4
Norlington School
WAN E11 ....314 G3
Norman Booth Leisure Centre
HLWE CM17 ....187 L9
Normandy Primary School
ERITH DA8 ....346 C6
Normanhurst School
CHING E4 ....274 C6
Norsey Wood (Nature Reserve)
BCAYE CM11 ....283 L4
North Beckton Primary School
EHAM E6 ....334 A4
Northbury Primary School
BARK IG11 ....316 C8
North Crescent Primary School
WICKW SS12 ....285 J9
Northend Primary School
ERITH DA8 ....346 E6
North End Trading Estate
ERITH DA8 ....346 D5
North Fambridge Yacht Club
RCHLM CM5 ....288 A1
Northfleet Industrial Estate
GVW DA11 ....349 J9
Northgate Business Centre
EN EN1 ....273 N2
Northgate County High School
IPNE IP4 ....25 N2
Northgate Industrial Park
ROMW/RG RM7 ....297 N6
Northgate Primary School
BSF CM23 ....137 K5
Northgate Sports Centre
IPNE IP4 ....25 N2
North Havering College of
Adult Education *ROM* RM1 ....298 D3
North Hill Business Park
SLH/COR SS17 ....340 C2
North Primary School
COL CO1 ....8 A3
Northumberland Heath
Medical Centre *ERITH* DA8 ....346 C5
Northumberland Heath
Primary School
ERITH DA8 ....346 A5
North Weald Airfield
EPP CM16 ....233 N5
North Weald Golf Club
EPP CM16 ....233 P2
North & West Essex Adult
Community College
GTDUN CM6 ....92 A5
HLW CM20 ....13 G3
Northwick Park J & I School
CVI SS8 ....344 A1
Notley Green Primary School
BRTR CM77 ....144 F7

Notley High School
BRTR CM77 ....145 J6
Novotel
CAN/RD E16 ....333 L7
IP IP1 ....16 D6
NTGB Sports Ground
EHAM E6 ....316 B8
Nuclear Bunker
BRW CM14 ....257 P6
Nuffield Hospital
ENC/FH EN2 ....272 F1
Number 10 Bowling
BRW CM14 ....298 D9
Number Ten Bowling Centre
BRTR CM7 ....145 L5
Oakdale Infant School
SWFD E18 ....295 L6
Oakdale Junior School
SWFD E18 ....295 M6
Oakhill Primary School
WFD IG8 ....295 H3
Oak Industrial Park
GTDUN CM6 ....141 N7
Oaklands Farm Industrial Estate
BCAYE CM11 ....283 M2
Oaklands Infant School
CHLM/GWD CM2 ....5 F7
Oaklands School
LOU IG10 ....275 N4
Oak Lodge Hotel
EN EN1 ....273 K5
Oaks Hospital
COLN CO4 ....127 P5
The Oaks Industrial Estate
HLW CM20 ....186 G9
Oak Tree Medical Centre
GDMY/SEVK IG3 ....316 F4
Oakwood Business Park
COS CO15 ....182 B4
Oakwood County Infant School
COS CO15 ....6 B5
Oakwood Estate
LOU IG10 ....187 H8
Oakwood Hill Industrial Estate
LOU IG10 ....276 C4
Oakwood Medical Centre
STHGT/OAK N14 ....272 B4
Occupational Health Centre
HAR CO12 ....109 P5
Ockendon School
SOCK/AV RM15 ....338 D5
Odeon Cinema
CHLM/GWD CM2 ....5 H4
COL CO1 ....8 B6
GNTH/NBYPK IG2 ....316 B1
HLW CM20 ....13 G5
ROM RM1 ....298 E9
SOS SS1 ....19 F3
SWFD E18 ....295 K6
Odessa Infant School
FSTGT E7 ....315 K7
Old Bancroftians FC
BKHH IG9 ....295 N1
The Old Brickworks Business
Centre *HARH* RM3 ....299 M4
Old Cemetery
IPSE IP5 ....25 M3
Old Chigwellians Sports Club
CHIG IG7 ....276 C7
Oldchurch Hospital
ROMW/RG RM7 ....318 C1
Old Court Theatre
CHLM/WR CM1 ....5 K2
Old Ford Primary School
BOW E3 ....332 C2
Old Grammar School
RCOLE CO7 ....104 C1
Old Harlow Health Centre
HLWE CM17 ....187 K8
Old Heath Primary School
COLS CO2 ....152 D3
Old Market Retail Park
PIT SS13 ....324 C1
Old Palace Primary School
BOW E3 ....332 E3
Old Station Museum
CAN/RD E16 ....334 B9
Old Sun Wharf
POP/IOD E14 ....332 B7
Old Westcliffians RFC
RCFD SS4 ....308 D7
Olga Primary School
BOW E3 ....332 B2
The Olive Branch Hotel
RCOS CO16 ....157 J5
Olympic Business Park
SRTFD E15 ....304 E5
One Tree Hill Country Park
SLH/COR SS17 ....323 M6
Ongar & District Sports Club
CHONG CM5 ....235 M7
Ongar Health Centre
CHONG CM5 ....235 M7
Ongar Leisure Centre
CHONG CM5 ....235 M5
Ongar Road Trading Estate
GTDUN CM6 ....141 M7
Ongar War Memorial Hospital
CHONG CM5 ....235 M5
Optima Business Park
HOD EN11 ....208 F4
The Orchard Health Centre
BARK IG11 ....334 D2
Orient Industrial Park
LEY E10 ....314 D4
Orsett CE Primary School
CDW/CHF RM16 ....340 B5
Orsett Golf Club
CDW/CHF RM16 ....340 F7
Orsett Hospital
CDW/CHF RM16 ....340 B5
Orsett Industrial Estate
CDW/CHF RM16 ....340 G5
Orwell Business Centre
IPSE IP3 ....25 M9

Orwell Country Park
IPSE IP3 ....30 F2
Orwell High School
FX IP11 ....35 H6
Orwell Park School
KIR/NAC IP10 ....31 P7
Orwell Retail Park
CHTY IP2 ....24 G6
Orwell Yacht Club
CHTY IP2 ....30 C1
Osidge JMI School
STHGT/OAK N14 ....272 B7
Our Lady Immaculate RC
Primary School
CHLM/GWD CM2 ....4 E5
Our Lady of Lourdes Catholic
Primary School
LOS SS9 ....328 B4
Our Lady of Lourdes RC
Primary School *WAN* E11 ....315 L1
Our Lady RC Primary School
POP/IOD E14 ....332 C6
Oxford House School
COLW CO3 ....127 N8
Oyster Business Centre
MAL CM9 ....225 L1
Palace Cinema
FX IP11 ....11 K1
Palace Gardens Shopping
Centre *ENC/FH* EN2 ....273 J2
Palace Theatre
WOS/PRIT SS0 ....18 A2
Palmer's College
GRAYS RM17 ....350 A2
Palmers Green High School
WCHMH N21 ....272 F8
Paringdon Primary School
HLWS CM18 ....210 E7
Parkhill Primary School
CLAY IG5 ....296 A7
Park Infants School
SRTFD E15 ....315 J9
Parklands Primary School
ROM RM1 ....298 C9
Park School
RAYL SS6 ....306 E1
Park School for Girls
IL IG1 ....316 B4
Parkway Middle School
HVHL CB9 ....40 G3
Parndon Wood
HLWS CM18 ....210 E9
Parndon Wood Cemetery
HLWW/ROY CM19 ....210 D9
Parndon Wood Crematorium
HLWW/ROY CM19 ....210 D9
Parsloes Primary School
DAGW RM9 ....317 N8
Parsonage Farm Industrial
Estate *STSD* CM24 ....138 C3
Parsonage Farm Primary
School *RAIN* RM13 ....337 H3
Parsons Heath Primary School
COLN CO4 ....128 F5
Passenger Ferry Terminal
COLN CO4 ....110 A2
Passmores School
HLWS CM18 ....210 E5
Pauls Theatre School
EMPK RM11 ....319 J2
Paycocke's House (NT)
RCOLW CO6 ....147 N5
PDSA Hospital
REDBR IG4 ....295 N7
Peartree Business Centre
COLW CO3 ....151 H2
Peewit Caravan Park
FX IP11 ....10 E5
Pembroke Business Centre
BSDN SS14 ....304 D5
The Peninsula Business Centre
RIPS/CAP IP9 ....30 B5
Perry Fields Primary School
CHLM/WR CM1 ....218 C5
Peter Hills School
BERM/RHTH SE16 ....332 A8
Phoenix Business Centre
COLW CO3 ....151 L1
The Phoenix Primary School
LAIN SS15 ....303 K9
Phoenix Secondary &
Primary School *BOW* E3 ....332 C3
Picture House Cinema
SRTFD E15 ....314 G8
The Pier at Harwich Hotel
HAR CO12 ....15 F1
Pier Avenue Cinema
COS CO15 ....6 D4
Pilgrims Hatch CP School
BRWN CM15 ....280 D5
Pinewood Primary School
CRW RM5 ....298 A2
Pinewood Special School
WARE SG12 ....184 A5
Pioneer School
BSDN SS14 ....3 K2
Piper's Vale CP School
IPSE IP3 ....30 F1
Pipps Hill Retail Park
BSDN SS14 ....2 A1
Pitsea Health Clinic
PIT SS13 ....324 C1
Pitsea Leisure Centre
PIT SS13 ....324 D1
Pitsea Primary School
PIT SS13 ....324 C1
Pitsea Swimming Pool
PIT SS13 ....324 C1
Place Farm Community
Primary School *HVHL* CB9 ....41 J3
Plaistow Hospital
PLSTW E13 ....333 L2
Plaistow Primary School
PLSTW E13 ....333 M1

Plashet Jewish Cemetery
MNPK E12 ....315 N8
Plashet Road Medical Centre
FSTGT E7 ....315 L9
Plashet School
EHAM E6 ....315 P9
Playhouse Theatre
HLW CM20 ....13 H6
Plaza Business Centre
PEND EN3 ....274 C1
Plume School
MAL CM9 ....222 A9
Police Cadet School
WAN E11 ....315 K3
Ponders End Industrial Estate
PEND EN3 ....274 C3
Ponsbourne St Marys Primary
School *HERT/BAY* SG13 ....228 D3
Ponsbourne Tunnel
HERT/BAY SG13 ....228 E3
Pontlands Park Country Hotel
CHLM/GWD CM2 ....240 F5
Poplar Business Park
POP/IOD E14 ....332 F7
Porters Grange Primary School
SOS SS1 ....19 J3
Portmans Walk
Industrial Centre *IP* IP1 ....16 A5
Portway Primary School
SRTFD E15 ....333 K1
Pot Kiln Primary School
SUD CO10 ....21 H7
Potter Street Primary School
HLWE CM17 ....211 J5
Power Industrial Estate
ERITH DA8 ....346 E6
Powers Hall Junior School,
Speech & Language Unit
WIT CM8 ....196 G1
Premier Travel Inn
BARK IG11 ....334 C1
BRTR CM77 ....145 N5
BSDN SS14 ....303 P6
CAN/RD E16 ....333 N7
CDW/CHF RM16 ....348 F1
CHDH RM6 ....297 M9
CHLM/GWD CM2 ....218 G4
CHTY IP2 ....30 C2
COLN CO4 ....128 E1
EHAM E6 ....334 B5
HLW CM20 ....187 J6
LOU IG10 ....252 G8
NHMKT IP6 ....22 C5
PEND EN3 ....252 C6
PIT SS15 ....304 F7
PUR RM19 ....347 L3
PUR RM19 ....348 B2
RAIN RM13 ....337 L6
RCHLM CM5 ....219 H5
REDBR IG4 ....295 N9
ROM RM1 ....298 E9
SLH/COR SS17 ....324 B5
WOS/PRIT SS0 ....328 C1
Presdales School
WARE SG12 ....184 A4
Prettygate Primary School
COLW CO3 ....151 K2
Prince Avenue Primary School
WOS/PRIT SS0 ....328 E1
Prince of Wales Primary School
PEND EN3 ....252 C7
Princess Alexandra Hospital
HLW CM20 ....13 F5
Priors Wood JMI School
WARE SG12 ....184 D1
Priory Park
KIR/NAC IP10 ....31 J4
Priory Park Industrial Estate
SOSN SS2 ....329 H2
Priory School
SOSN SS2 ....328 F3
Pritllebrook Industrial Estate
SOSN SS2 ....328 G2
Prittlewell Centre
SOSN SS2 ....18 D2
Prittlewell Priory Museum
SOSN SS2 ....328 D3
The Prittlewell Technology
College *WOS/PRIT* SS0 ....328 D3
Prospect Business Park
HLW CM20 ....276 E3
Prout Industrial Estate
CVI SS8 ....345 J2
Pump House
BERM/RHTH SE16 ....332 B8
Purdeys Industrial Estate
RCFD SS4 ....309 H6
Purfleet Industrial Park
PUR RM19 ....337 L8
Purfleet Primary School
PUR RM19 ....347 M2
Purford Green Primary School
HLWS CM18 ....211 H5
Purleigh CP School
RCHLM CM5 ....243 N9
Pylon Trading Estate
CAN/RD E16 ....332 G4
Quarry Hill Infant School
GRAYS RM17 ....349 L3
Quarry Hill Junior School
GRAYS RM17 ....349 L3
Quatro Business Park
BSDN SS14 ....304 F5
Quayside Industrial Estate
MAL CM9 ....222 B7
The Quay Theatre
SUD CO10 ....20 C7
Quebec Industrial Estate
BERM/RHTH SE16 ....332 B9
Queen Elizabeth Museum
CHING E4 ....275 J6
Queen Elizabeth Stadium
EN EN1 ....273 L1
Queen Mary & Westfield College
SWFD E18 ....295 K5
WCHPL E1 ....332 A4

Queensgate Centre
HLW CM20 ....186 F8
Queensland Preparatory
School *WOS/PRIT* SS0 ....328 D6
Queens Theatre
EMPK RM11 ....319 J2
Queensway Business Centre
PEND EN5 ....273 P5
Quest End Industrial Estate
RAYL SS6 ....306 F1
Quilters J & I School
BCAYW CM12 ....283 H7
Qurwwat Ul Islam Girl's School
FSTGT E7 ....315 K8
RA Butler J & I School
SAFWS CB11 ....51 M9
Radford Business Centre
BCAYW CM12 ....282 C5
Radwinter CE Primary School
SAFWN CB10 ....67 L2
Raglan Infant School
EN EN1 ....273 K5
Raglan Junior School
EN EN1 ....273 K6
Rainham Cemetery
RAIN RM13 ....337 H5
Rainham Hall (NT)
RAIN RM13 ....336 F4
Rainham Trading Estate
RAIN RM13 ....336 F4
Rainham Village
RAIN RM13 ....336 F4
The Ramsden Hall Special
School *BCAYE* CM11 ....285 N5
The Ramsey School
HSTD C09 ....98 B6
Ranelagh Primary School
SRTFC E15 ....333 H2
Ransomes Industrial Park
IPSE IP5 ....31 K3
Raphael Independent School
EMPK RM11 ....318 F1
Ravensbourne School
HARH RM5 ....299 J5
Ravenscroft Primary School
PLSTW E13 ....333 K4
RCOS CO16 ....181 L9
Ravenside Retail Park
UED N18 ....294 A2
Ravenswood Community
Primary School *IPSE* IP5 ....31 J2
Ravenswood Industrial Estate
WALTH E17 ....294 F8
Rawreth Industrial Estate
RAYL SS6 ....306 D2
Ray Island Nature Reserve
K/T/MI CO5 ....202 E2
Rayleigh Lanes Indoor Market
RAYL SS6 ....306 G5
Rayleigh Primary School
RAYL SS6 ....306 F5
Ray Lodge Primary School
WFD IG8 ....295 N3
Rayne Primary School
BRTR CM77 ....144 B4
Raynham Road Industrial
Estate *BSF* CM23 ....137 N6
Redbridge College
CHDH RM6 ....297 J9
Redbridge Drama Centre
SWFD E18 ....295 K5
Redbridge Museum
IL IG1 ....316 C5
Redbridge Primary School
REDBR IG4 ....295 P9
Redbridge Sports Centre
BARK/HLT IG6 ....296 E5
Redbridge Tuition Service
GNTH/NBYPK IG2 ....316 D1
Redburn Industrial Estate
PEND EN3 ....274 A5
Redden Court School
HARH RM3 ....299 L7
Redford Lodge Psychiatric
Hospital *ED* N9 ....273 M8
Redriff Primary School
BERM/RHTH SE16 ....332 B9
Regent Leisure Centre
SLH/COR SS17 ....341 L4
Regional Sports Centre
TIL RM18 ....350 C7
Renwick Industrial Estate
BARK IG11 ....335 J2
Research & Engineering
Centre *LAIN* SS15 ....302 G7
Rettendon Primary School
RCHLM CM3 ....285 P3
RHS Garden Hyde Hall
RCHLM CM3 ....264 B5
Rice Bridge Industrial Estate
RCOS CO16 ....157 K7
Richard Alibon Primary School
DAGE RM10 ....317 P7
The Richard De Clare
Primary School *HSTD* C09 ....98 A7
Richard Whittington Primary
School *BSF* CM23 ....162 B1
Richmond Avenue Primary
School
SBN/FI SS3 ....330 C7
Rickling CE Primary School
SAFWS CB11 ....89 K8
Rickstones School
WIT CM8 ....171 N7
Ridge House Clinic
WCHMH N21 ....273 J6
Ridgewell Primary School
HSTD C09 ....57 J3
Ridleys Brewery
RCHLM CM5 ....168 A6
Rio Cinema
BOC CM0 ....291 H4
Ripple J & I School
BARK IG11 ....334 E1

Risebridge Golf Club
ROM RM1 ....298 E4
Rise Park Primary School
ROM RM1 ....298 C5
Rivenhall CE Primary School
WIT CM8 ....172 A5
Rivenhall Oaks Golf Club
WIT CM8 ....172 A8
River Lee Country Park
CHES/WCR EN8 ....230 E8
WAB EN9 ....230 E3
Rivermead Industrial Estate
CHLM/WR CM1 ....218 A7
River Road Business Park
BARK IG11 ....334 F3
Riverside Business Park
STSD CM24 ....114 B9
Riverside Golf Club
THMD SE28 ....335 M6
Riverside Health Centre
MGTR CO11 ....106 B4
Riverside Ice & Leisure Centre
CHLM/WR CM1 ....5 H3
Riverside Industrial Estate
BARK IG11 ....335 H3
ED N9 ....274 B5
MAL CM9 ....222 A7
RCFD SS4 ....308 G6
Riverside Industrial Park
CHTY IP2 ....25 L8
Riverside Primary School
HOC/HUL SS5 ....287 H5
Riverside Retail Park
CHLM/WR CM1 ....5 J1
Riverside Swimming Centre
ERITH DA8 ....346 D3
The RJ Mitchell Primary School
RCH RM12 ....318 G8
Roach Vale Primary School
COLN CO4 ....128 F6
Robert Clack School
BCTR RM8 ....317 N3
Robert Drake Primary School
SBF/HAD SS7 ....306 A8
The Robert Frew Medical
Centre *WICKW* SS12 ....305 L2
Robert Leonard Industrial
Estate *SOSN* SS2 ....308 D8
Robert Leonard Industrial Site
SOSN SS2 ....328 G1
Rochford Adult Community
College *RCFD* SS4 ....309 H6
Rochford Hundred Golf Club
RCFD SS4 ....308 E6
Rochford Primary School
RCFD SS4 ....308 F5
Rochford Swimming Pool
RCFD SS4 ....309 H5
Roding Primary School
BCTR RM8 ....317 K6
WFD IG8 ....295 P4
Rodings Primary School
GTDUN CM6 ....190 F4
Roding Valley High School
LOU IG10 ....275 P4
LOU IG10 ....276 C3
The Roebuck Hotel
BKHH IG9 ....275 M6
Roebuck Road Trading Estate
BARK/HLT IG6 ....297 J3
Roger Ascham Primary School
WALTH E17 ....294 C5
Rokeby School
SRTFC E15 ....314 G9
Rolph CE Primary School
RCOS CO16 ....157 J5
Roman Road Primary School
EHAM E6 ....333 N4
Romford Cemetery
ROMW/RG RM7 ....318 B2
Romford Clinic
ROM RM1 ....298 E8
Romford County Court
GPK RM2 ....298 E7
Romford Golf Club
GPK RM2 ....298 F7
Romford Ice Rink
ROMW/RG RM7 ....318 D2
Romford IT Learning Centre
ROM RM1 ....298 D9
Romford Shopping Hall
ROM RM1 ....298 D8
The Rose & Crown Hotel
COLN CO4 ....9 H5
Rosedale Clinic
CHESW EN7 ....229 M7
Rose Hill Primary School
IPSE IP3 ....25 P7
Roseland JMI School
HOD EN11 ....208 C2
Rosetta Primary School
CAN/RD E16 ....333 L5
Rosewood Medical Centre
HCH RM12 ....318 G7
Roslin Hotel
SOS SS1 ....329 N8
Rosshill Industrial Park
SOSN SS2 ....329 J2
Roxwell CE Primary School
CHLM/WR CM1 ....216 B5
Roxwell Trading Park
WALTH E17 ....314 B2
Royal Burnham Yacht Club
BOC CM0 ....291 H4
Royal Chace Hotel
ENC/FH EN2 ....250 E8
Royal Corinthian Yacht Club
BOC CM0 ....291 H5
The Royal Dock
Community School
CAN/RD E16 ....333 M6
Royal Docks Medical Centre
EHAM E6 ....334 B6
Royal Epping Forest Golf Club
CHING E4 ....275 H6

Royal Hospital School
RIPS/CAP IP9 ....83 L6
Royal Liberty School
GPK RM2 ....299 H7
Royal London Sports Centre
COLN CO4 ....128 C1
The Royals Shopping Centre
SOS SS1 ....19 G5
Royal Victoria Docks
Watersports Centre
CAN/RD E16 ....333 K7
Roydonbury Industrial Estate
HLWW/ROY CM19 ....210 A3
Roydon CP School
HLWW/ROY CM19 ....209 L3
Roydon Mill Leisure Park
HLWW/ROY CM19 ....209 K2
RSPB Reserve
HOD EN11 ....208 G2
Runwell Community
Primary School
WICKE SS11 ....285 J6
Runwell Hospital
RCHLM CM3 ....285 L3
Rush Croft School
CHING E4 ....294 E4
Rush Green Junior School
IL IG1 ....316 A4
Rush Green Primary School
ROMW/RG RM7 ....318 C3
Rush Green Sports Centre
RCOS CO16 ....206 G1
Rushmere Golf Club
IPNE IP4 ....26 C5
Rushmere Hall Primary School
IPNE IP4 ....25 P2
Rushmere Sports Club
KESG IP5 ....26 D2
Russet House School
EN EN1 ....251 N9
Ryedene Community School
VGE SS16 ....324 E3
Rye House Stadium
HOD EN11 ....208 G3
Ryelands JMI School
HOD EN11 ....208 E4
Rye Park Industrial Estate
HOD EN11 ....208 F3
The Ryes School
SUD CO10 ....60 F8
The Sacred Heart of Mary
RC School *UPMR* RM14 ....319 N4
Sacred Heart RC
Primary School *SOS* SS1 ....19 K3
Saffron Business Centre
SAFWN CB10 ....51 P8
Saffron Hotel
SAFWN CB10 ....51 L8
Saffron Walden County
High School *SAFWS* CB11 ....65 K1
Saffron Walden Golf Club
SAFWN CB10 ....51 K8
Saffron Walden Hospital
SAFWS CB11 ....51 P8
Saffron Walden Museum
SAFWN CB10 ....51 L8
Saffron Walden Town FC
SAFWN CB10 ....51 L7
Sai Medical Centre
POP/IOD E14 ....332 F8
St Agnes RC Primary School
BOW E3 ....332 D3
St Aidans RC Primary School
IL IG1 ....316 E3
St Alban's Catholic High School
IPNE IP4 ....26 B4
St Albans Primary School
HLW CM20 ....210 G1
St Albans RC Church & School
Presbytery
HCH RM12 ....318 F7
St Albans RC JMI School
HCH RM12 ....318 G9
St Andrews BA CE Primary
School *RCOS* CO16 ....156 C6
St Andrews CE Junior School
RCHLM CM5 ....196 E9
St Andrews CE Primary School
EN EN1 ....273 J1
EPP CM16 ....234 B4
HSTD C09 ....57 N8
MHAD SG10 ....160 E3
RCGW CO6 ....101 K3
RCOLW CO6 ....149 K5
STHGT/OAK N14 ....272 B6
St Andrews Hospital
BOW E3 ....332 E4
St Andrews Primary School
WARE SG12 ....184 G8
St Angelas Ursuline Convent
School *FSTGT* E7 ....315 L8
St Anne Line RC Infant School
WICKE SS11 ....2 B5
St Annes Convent School
EN EN1 ....273 J3
St Annes Preparatory School
CHLM/GWD CM2 ....4 E6
St Annes Primary School
COLN CO4 ....9 J2
St Anne's Trading Estate
POP/IOD E14 ....332 C6
St Antonys RC Primary School
FSTGT E7 ....315 K9
St Aubyns School
WFD IG8 ....295 J4
St Augustines RC Infant School
GNTH/NBYPK IG2 ....296 C9
St Augustines RC Primary
School *GNTH/NBYPK* IG2 ....296 C9
HOD EN11 ....208 E6
St Bedes RC Primary School
CHDH RM6 ....297 K9
St Benedicts College
COLW CO5 ....127 L9
St Bernards High School
WOS/PRIT SS0 ....18 B4

St Bonaventures School
FSTGT E7 ....315 K9
St Botolph's Priory Ruin
COL CO1 ....8 E7
St Catherines Hoddesdon CE
Primary School *HOD* EN11 ....208 E5
St Cedds CE VA Primary School
BOC CM0 ....226 E9
St Cedds School
CHLM/WR CM1 ....4 C1
St Christopher Special School
LOS SS9 ....328 A2
St Clares RC Primary School
RCOS CO16 ....181 L9
St Clements Hospital
BOW E3 ....332 C5
IPSE IP5 ....26 A7
St Clements Junior School
CHES/WCR EN8 ....230 B6
St Cleres Hall Golf Club
SLH/COR SS17 ....341 J5
St Cleres School
SLH/COR SS17 ....341 K5
St Cross RC Primary School
HOD EN11 ....208 D7
St Edmunds RC Primary School
ROM RM1 ....273 N7
St Edwards CE Comprehensive
School *CHDH* RM6 ....317 P1
St Edwards CE Primary School
ROM RM1 ....298 C8
St Elizabeths School & Home
MHAD SG10 ....160 C7
St Felix RC Primary School
HVHL CB9 ....40 G4
St Fidelis Catholic
Primary School *ERITH* DA8 ....346 B4
St Francis RC Primary School
BRTR CM7 ....145 J2
MAL CM9 ....222 A8
SRTFC E15 ....315 H7
St Georges Hospital
HCH RM12 ....319 K6
St Georges New Town
Junior School *COLS* CO2 ....152 B1
St Georges Primary School
COLS CO2 ....152 B2
St Georges RC Primary School
ENC/FH EN2 ....273 J1
SBN/FI SS3 ....330 D6
St Giles CE Primary School
HSTD C09 ....73 J7
St Gregorys CEVC
Primary School *SUD* CO10 ....20 B6
St Helena School
COLW CO3 ....127 N7
St Helens Catholic
Infant School *WALTH* E17 ....294 F9
St Helens Primary School
IPNE IP4 ....17 G4
St Helens RC Junior School
BRWN CM15 ....280 G6
St Helens RC Primary School
PLSTW E13 ....333 J4
St Hildas School
WOS/PRIT SS0 ....328 D5
St Ignatius College
EN EN1 ....251 M7
St James CE Primary School
HLWS CM18 ....210 C7
PEND EN5 ....273 P1
St James CE VA Primary School
COL CO1 ....9 F5
St James CE Junior School
FSTGT E7 ....315 J7
St James's Health Centre
WALTH E17 ....294 B9
St Joachims RC Primary School
CAN/RD E16 ....333 M6
St John Baptist CE Primary
School *HSTD* C09 ....74 D9
St John Fisher RC Primary
School *LOU* IG10 ....276 D1
St John Payne RC School
CHLM/WR CM1 ....217 N5
St John's Abbey Gateway
COLS CO2 ....128 A9
St Johns Green Primary School
COLS CO2 ....8 C7
St John's Hospital
CHLM/GWD CM2 ....239 N4
St Johns Industrial Estate
RBSF CM23 ....139 P7
St Johns RC Primary School
BERM/RHTH SE16 ....332 B9
St Johns RC Special School
WFD IG8 ....296 B2
St Johns School
BCAYW CM12 ....283 J4
ENC/FH EN2 ....272 F1
EPP CM16 ....232 F9
St John's Walk Shopping
Centre *COL* CO1 ....8 C7
St John the Baptist Primary
School *WARE* SG12 ....184 D7
St Josephs Catholic
Infant School *LEY* E10 ....314 C3
St Josephs College
CHTY IP2 ....25 H8
St Josephs Convent School
WAN E11 ....311 K9
St Josephs RC Aided
Primary School *HAR* CO12 ....110 C6
St Josephs RC JMI School
CHES/WCR EN8 ....252 B5
St Josephs RC Junior School
LEY E10 ....314 C3
St Josephs RC Primary School
BARK IG11 ....334 D1
BSF CM23 ....137 J8

CVI SS8 ....344 E1
DAGW RM9 ....317 N6
DART DA1 ....346 C9
SLH/COR SS17 ....341 L3
SUD CO10 ....20 B4
St Josephs School
UPMR RM14 ....319 N4
St Joseph the Worker RC
Primary School
RBRW/HUT CM13 ....281 M5
St Katherine School
CVI SS8 ....326 D9
St Lawrence CE Primary
School *K/T/MI* CO5 ....152 G6
St Lawrence CE School
WAB EN9 ....253 J3
St Leonards CE Junior School
BOC CM0 ....269 J5
St Leonards Hospital
SUD CO10 ....21 F5
St Lukes Catholic Primary
School *HLWW/ROY* CM19 ....210 D5
St Lukes CE Primary School
CAN/RD E16 ....333 J6
St Lukes Church Primary
School *K/T/MI* CO5 ....174 A8
St Luke's Health Centre
CAN/RD E16 ....333 J6
St Lukes Special School
LOU IG10 ....276 B3
St Margaret Clitherow RC
Primary School
THMD SE28 ....335 J8
St Margarets CE Primary School
HSTD C09 ....71 K2
IP IP1 ....17 F3
PIT SS13 ....325 K1
St Margarets Hospital
EPP CM16 ....233 J8
St Margarets Preparatory
School *HSTD* C09 ....96 G8
St Marks Industrial Estate
CAN/RD E16 ....334 C1
St Marks RC Primary School
CHTY IP2 ....25 J6
St Marks West Essex Catholic
School *HLWS* CM18 ....210 F4
St Martins School
RBRW/HUT CM13 ....281 M7
St Mary's Business Centre
COLW CO5 ....8 A7
St Marys Catholic
Primary School *CHING* E4 ....274 G7
HCH RM12 ....318 F3
St Mary's Catholic School
BSF CM23 ....137 K7
St Marys CE Primary School
BOC CM0 ....291 H2
BRWN CM15 ....281 J5
RBSF CM22 ....264 E5
RCHLM CM3 ....264 E5
SAFWN CB10 ....51 L8
STSD CM24 ....114 B8
WALTH E17 ....294 E8
St Marys Hare Park School
GPK RM2 ....299 J7
St Marys High School
CHESW EN7 ....229 N9
St Marys Junior School
WARE SG12 ....184 A1
St Marys Lower School
COLW CO5 ....150 C1
St Marys RC Junior School
WALTH E17 ....294 F7
St Marys RC Primary School
PEND EN5 ....273 P4
TIL RM18 ....350 A7
St Marys Upper School
COLW CO5 ....127 M8
St Matthew's CE
Primary School *IP* IP1 ....16 B7
St Matthews CE
Primary School *PEND* EN3 ....273 P3
St Michaels CE Junior School
CHLM/GWD CM2 ....240 B8
St Michaels CE Primary School
BRTR CM7 ....144 G3
BSF CM23 ....137 K7
ENC/FH EN2 ....251 H9
St Michaels Hospital
BRTR CM7 ....145 H3
St Michaels Preparatory School
LOS SS9 ....327 M5
St Michaels Primary School
COLS CO2 ....151 M5
St Michaels RC Primary School
EHAM E6 ....334 A2
St Monicas RC Primary School
STHGT/OAK N14 ....272 C9
St Nicholas CE Primary School
WICKE SS11 ....248 A6
WICKE SS11 ....286 B9
St Nicholas School
HLWE CM17 ....187 N9
St Nicholas Special School
HLWE CM17 ....329 M4
St Osyth CE Primary School
RCOS CO16 ....180 E9
St Pancras Catholic
Primary School *IP* IP1 ....
St Patricks JMI School
ROMW/RG RM7 ....298 A—
St Patricks RC Primary School
WALTH E17 ....294 B8
St Paulinus CE Primary School
DART DA1 ....346 D9
St Pauls CE Primary School
BRWN CM15 ....280 A1
WCHMH N21 ....272 G6
St Pauls RC Primary School
CHESW EN7 ....229 N6

St Pauls Way School
BOW E3 ....332 D4
St Pauls with St Lukes CE
Primary School *BOW* E3 .....332 C5
St Peters Catholic
Primary School *ROM* RM1 ....298 C7
St Peters CE Primary School
BRW CM14 ....280 A8
CHLM/GWD CM2 ....262 E5
HSTD CO9 ....72 B9
RCOLW CO6 ....147 P4
St Peters College
CHLM/WR CM1 ....217 M7
St Peters High School
BOC CM0 ....290 G2
St Peters Hospital
MAL CM9 ....222 A9
St Peters RC Primary School
BCAYE CM11 ....303 M1
DAGW RM9 ....335 N1
St Philomena School
FOS CO15 ....158 G9
St Pius X RC Primary School
CHLM/WR CM1 ....217 N5
St Saviours CE Primary School
POP/IOD E14 ....332 E5
WALTH E17 ....314 C2
St Stephens Primary School
EHAM E6 ....315 M9
St Teresa RC Primary School
BCTR RM8 ....317 K6
St Teresas Primary School
COLW CO5 ....151 H1
St Teresas RC Primary School
RCFD SS4 ....308 F4
St Thomas More High School
for Boys *WOS/PRIT* SS0 ......328 B3
St Thomas More RC
Primary School *SAFWS* CB11 ....65 M1
St Thomas Mores Catholic
Primary School *COL* CO1 ....9 F6
St Thomas of Canterbury
CE J & I School *BRWN* CM15 ....280 C6
St Thomas of Canterbury RC
Primary School
GRAYS RM17 ....349 L4
St Ursulas RC Infant School
HARH RM5 ....298 G3
St Ursulas RC Junior School
HARH RM5 ....298 G3
St Vincents RC Primary School
BCTR RM8 ....317 K4
St Winefrides Catholic
Primary School *MNPK* E12 ....316 A7
Salcombe Preparatory School
(Infants) *STHGT/OAK* N14 ....272 A4
Salcombe Preparatory School
(Juniors) *STHGT/OAK* N14 ....272 A6
Salisbury Primary School
MNPK E12 ....315 N7
Salisbury School
ED N9 ....273 P7
Salisbury Upper School
ED N9 ....273 P6
Saithouse Harbour Hotel
IPSE IP5 ....17 G6
Samuel Ward Upper School &
Technology College
HVHL CB9 ....41 L2
Sanders Draper School
HCH RM12 ....319 J6
Sandon School
CHLM/GWD CM2 ....240 G4
Sandringham Primary School
FSTGT E7 ....315 M8
Saracens House
Business Centre *IP* IP1 ....16 E3
Sarah Bonnell School
SRTFD E15 ....315 H8
Sarbir Industrial Park
HLW CM20 ....187 K7
Sawbridge Health Clinic
SBW CM21 ....187 M2
Sawyers Hall College of
Science & Technology
BRWN CM15 ....280 F6
Schooling Licensed
Conveyancers *GRAYS* RM17 ..349 L3
Scimitar Park Industrial Estate
PIT SS13 ....305 J5
Scott's Grotto
WARE SG12 ....184 A4
Scotts Primary School
HCH RM12 ....319 H7
Scott Wilkie Primary School
CAN/RD E16 ....333 M6
Sealife Adventure
SOS SS1 ....19 K7
Seedbed Business Centre
SBN/FI SS3 ....330 E7
Seevic College
SBF/HAD SS7 ....326 D1
Selwyn Primary School
CHING E4 ....294 F5
Seven Kings Health Centre
GDMY/SEVK IG3 ....316 F3
Seven Kings High School
Technology College
GNTH/NBYPK IG2 ....316 E2
Seven Mills Primary School
POP/IOD E14 ....332 D9
Seymour Gardens
Medical Centre *IL* IG1 ....316 A3
Shadwell Dock Stairs
WAP E1W 332 A7
Shaftesbury Primary School
FSTGT E7 ....315 M9
Shaw Primary School
SOCK/AV RM15 ....338 E6
Sheepen Road Retail Park
COLW CO3 ....127 N7

Sheering CE Primary School
RBSF CM22 ....188 C3
Shelley Primary School
CHONG CM5 ....235 L5
Shenfield CC
BRWN CM15 ....281 J5
Shenfield High School
BRWN CM15 ....281 K4
Shenfield Sports Centre
BRWN CM15 ....281 K4
Shenval Industrial Estate
HLW CM20 ....187 H8
Sheredes School
HOD EN11 ....208 C6
Sheringham Junior School
MNPK E12 ....316 A6
Shire Hill Industrial Estate
SAFWS CB11 ....51 N9
Shoeburyness High School
SBN/FI SS3 ....330 C7
Shotley Primary School
RIPS/CAP IP9 ....85 L6
Shotley Sailing Club
RIPS/CAP IP9 ....85 N9
Showcase Newham Cinema
BARK IG11 ....334 D3
Shrewsbury Road
Health Centre *FSTGT* E7 ....315 N9
Shrub End Clinic
COLS CO2 ....151 L3
Sidegate Primary School
IPNE IP4 ....25 P3
Sidney Russell School
DAGW RM9 ....317 M6
Silver End Primary School
WIT CM8 ....171 M2
Sir Charles Lucas Art College
COLN CO4 ....128 F7
Sir Charles Lucas School
COLN CO4 ....128 G8
Sir George Monoux College
WALTH E17 ....294 E6
Sir John Cass Foundation/
Redcoat School *WCHPL* E1 ..332 A5
Sir Thomas Lipton
Memorial Hospital
STHGT/OAK N14 ....272 A6
Sir William Burrough Primary
School *POP/IOD* E14 ....332 B6
Ski Centre
CHTY IP2 ....30 B3
Skillion Business Centre
BSDN SS14 ....303 P7
Skillion Business Park
BARK IG11 ....334 G3
Skitts Hill Industrial Estate
BRTR CM7 ....145 L5
Slade Green FC
ERITH DA8 ....346 G6
Slade Green Primary School
ERITH DA8 ....346 F5
SMA Medical Centre
LEY E10 ....314 E2
Smilers Industrial Estate
PIT SS13 ....305 L7
Snap Theatre
BSF CM23 ....137 L7
Snaresbrook College
SWFD E18 ....295 K6
Snaresbrook Crown Court
WAN E11 ....295 J9
Snaresbrook Primary School
SWFD E18 ....295 K8
Somers Heath Primary School
SOCK/AV RM15 ....338 D7
Sorsby Health Centre
CLPT E5 ....314 A6
South Benfleet Primary School
SBF/HAD SS7 ....325 P4
Southbury Primary School
PEND EN3 ....275 N5
Southchurch Hall Museum
SOS SS1 ....329 K6
South East Essex College
SOS SS1 ....18 E3
SOSN SS2 ....18 E1
SOSN SS2 ....328 G4
Southend Adult Community
College *SOS* SS1 ....329 K6
Southend Airport
SOSN SS2 ....308 E8
Southend Borough FC
WOS/PRIT SS0 ....308 C9
Southend County Court
SOS SS1 ....19 G4
Southend High School for Boys
SOSN SS2 ....328 F3
Southend Hospital
WOS/PRIT SS0 ....328 D3
Southend Museum, Planetarium
& Discovery Centre
SOSN SS2 ....18 E2
Southend-on-Sea Crematorium
SOSN SS2 ....329 J2
Southend Pier
SOS SS1 ....19 H7
Southend Pier Railway
SOS SS1 ....19 H7
Southend RFC
SOSN SS2 ....308 G9
Southend United FC
(Roots Hall) *SOSN* SS2 ....328 F4
Southern Road Primary School
PLSTW E13 ....333 L2
South Essex Clinical
Trials Centre *LOS* SS9 ....327 L4
South Essex Crematorium
UPMR RM14 ....320 A7
Southfields Business Park
LAIN SS15 ....302 G8
Southgate Cemetery
STHGT/OAK N14 ....272 B8
Southgate College
STHGT/OAK N14 ....272 B8

Southgate Leisure Centre
STHGT/OAK N14 ....272 C6
Southgate School
EBAR EN4 ....271 N4
South Green Primary School
BCAYW CM12 ....283 J9
South Grove Primary School
WALTH E17 ....314 B1
Southlake Primary School
WLY SE2 ....335 L9
Southmill Trading Centre
BSF CM23 ....137 M8
Southminster Infant School
BOC CM0 ....269 J6
Southminster Medical Centre
BOC CM0 ....269 J5
South Park Business Centre
IL IG1 ....316 F4
South Park Clinic
IL IG1 ....316 F6
South Park Primary School
GDMY/SEVK IG3 ....316 F5
South Quay Plaza
POP/IOD E14 ....332 E9
South Suffolk Business Centre
SUD CO10 ....21 G5
Southview School
WIT CM8 ....171 N7
South West Essex Magistrates
Court *BSDN* SS14 ....2 D4
South Woodford Health Centre
SWFD E18 ....295 K5
South Woodham Ferrers
Leisure Centre *RCHLM* CM3 ..287 H1
Southwood Primary School
DAGW RM9 ....317 M6
Sovereign Business Centre
PEND EN3 ....274 C2
Spa Pavillion Theatre
FXI IP11 ....35 L8
Spellbrook Primary School
BSF CM23 ....162 C6
The Spinney J & I School
HLWG CM20 ....211 H2
Springfield CC
CHLM/GWD CM2 ....218 D7
Springfield Industrial Estate
BOC CM0 ....290 E3
Springfield Junior School
IP IP1 ....24 C3
Springfield Medical Centre
CHLM/WR CM1 ....218 B5
Springfield School
CHONG CM5 ....235 P9
Spring Meadow Primary School
HAR CO12 ....110 A5
Springwood Industrial Estate
HLW CM20 ....144 G2
Sprites Junior School
CHTY IP2 ....24 D9
Sproughton Business Park
IP IP1 ....24 D4
Sproughton CE Primary School
RIPW IP8 ....24 C5
Squirrels Heath Junior School
GPK RM2 ....298 C9
Ss Angelas & Bonaventures
Sixth Form *FSTGT* E7 ....315 L8
Ss Peter & Pauls RC
Primary School *IL* IG1 ....316 E5
Stadium Trading Estate
SBF/HAD SS7 ....306 F8
Stafford Industrial Estate
EMPK RM11 ....299 J7
Stambridge Primary School
RCFD SS4 ....309 L5
Standard Industrial Estate
CAN/RD E16 ....333 N9
Stanford Industrial Estate
SLH/COR SS17 ....341 K4
Stanford-le-Hope Infant School
SLH/COR SS17 ....341 L4
Stanhope Industrial Park
SLH/COR SS17 ....341 N6
Stansted Clinic
STSD CM24 ....114 B8
Stansted Manor Hotel
BSF CM23 ....138 A5
Stanway Fiveways
Primary School *COLW* CO3 ..150 G1
Stanway Primary School
COLW CO3 ....126 F9
Stanway School
COLW CO3 ....150 F1
Stanway Swimming Centre
COLW CO3 ....150 C1
Stapleford Abbotts Golf Club
ABR/ST RM4 ....278 F6
Stapleford Abbotts Primary
School *ABR/ST* RM4 ....278 A4
Staples Road J & I School
LOU IG10 ....275 P2
Staple Tye Shopping Centre
HLWS CM18 ....210 E6
Star Business Centre
DAGW RM9 ....336 C5
Star Lane Industrial Estate
SBN/FI SS3 ....330 E3
Starr Primary School
CAN/RD E16 ....333 H4
Starr Hotel & Restaurant
GTDUN CM6 ....141 L5
Station Industrial Estate
BOC CM0 ....290 F3
Station Road Industrial Estate
MAL CM9 ....200 D7
Station Yard Industrial Park
GTDUN CM6 ....141 M7
Stebbing Primary School
GTDUN CM6 ....118 D9
Stebon Primary School
POP/IOD E14 ....332 C5
Steeple Bumpstead Primary
School *HVHL* CB9 ....55 L4

Stephen Hawking Primary
School *POP/IOD* E14 ....332 B6
Stepney Greencoat CE Primary
School *POP/IOD* E14 ....332 C6
Stepney Green School
WCHPL E1 ....332 N3
Sterling Industrial Estate
DAGE RM10 ....318 A4
Stewards School
HLWS CM18 ....210 D7
Stifford Clays Health Centre
CDW/CHF RM16 ....339 L8
Stifford Clays Primary School
CDW/CHF RM16 ....339 L8
Stifford Primary School
GRAYS RM17 ....349 H5
Stisted CE Primary School
BRTR CM77 ....122 C8
Stock Brook Golf &
Country Club *BCAYW* CM12 ..283 J1
Stock CE Primary School
ING CM4 ....261 L6
Stock Industrial Park
SOSN SS2 ....329 H2
Stockwell Lodge Medical
Centre *CHESW* EN7 ....229 M6
Stoke-by-Nayland School
Primary School *RCOLW* CO6 ..78 B4
Stoke-by-Nayland Golf Club
& Hotel *RCOLW* CO6 ....77 N2
Stoke-by-Nayland
Middle School *RCOLW* CO6 ..78 B3
Stoke College
SUD CO10 ....43 K8
Stoke Country High School
CHTY IP2 ....25 K8
Stonehill Business Centre
UED N18 ....294 A3
Stonehill Business Park
UED N18 ....294 A2
Stoneydown Park
Primary School *WALTH* E17 ..294 B8
Storey Primary School
CAN/RD E16 ....334 B8
Stortford Hall Industrial Park
BSF CM23 ....137 N7
Stort Valley Industrial Estate
BSF CM23 ....137 N4
Stour Sailing Club
MGTR CO11 ....106 C4
St Paul & All Hallows
Junior School *ED* N9 ....273 N6
Stratford College
SRTFD E15 ....315 H9
Stratford Magistrates Court
SRTFD E15 ....314 G9
Stratford St Mary
Primary School *RCOLE* CO7 ..79 P8
Stratford School
FSTGT E7 ....315 K9
Stratford Shopping Centre
SRTFD E15 ....315 H9
The Street Industrial Estate
MAL CM9 ....222 C6
Strumer End Industrial Estate
HVHL CB9 ....41 L5
Stuarts Industrial Estate
CHLM/GWD CM2 ....5 K5
Stubbers (Outdoor Pursuits
Centre) *UPMR* RM14 ....320 C8
Stump Cross
SAFWN CB10 ....36 E6
Stutton CE Primary School
RIPS/CAP IP9 ....83 H7
Sudbury Bowl
SUD CO10 ....21 H2
Sudbury Health Centre
SUD CO10 ....20 E3
Sudbury RUFC
SUD CO10 ....61 L6
Sudbury Town FC
SUD CO10 ....20 C7
Sudbury Upper School
SUD CO10 ....20 E1
Sue Ryder Foundation
SUD CO10 ....45 J2
Suffolk College
IPNE IP4 ....17 H5
The Suffolk Nuffield Hospital
at Christchurch Park
IP IP1 ....16 D2
Suffolk Retail Park
IP IP1 ....25 H5
Suffolk Showground
EN EN1 ....31 N1
Suffolks Primary School
EN EN1 ....273 N1
Suffolk Water Park
RIPW IP8 ....22 B7
Summercroft Infant School
BSF CM23 ....137 P6
Summercroft Junior School
BSF CM23 ....137 P6
Sumners Community
Recreation Centre
HLWW/ROY CM19 ....210 D7
Sunnymede Primary School
BCAYE CM11 ....283 L7
Surrey Docks Farm
BERM/RHTH SE16 ....332 C9
Surrey Docks Health Centre
BERM/RHTH SE16 ....332 B9
Sutton Road Cemetery
SOSN SS2 ....329 H2
Suttons Business Park
RAIN RM13 ....336 C3
Suttons JMI School
HCH RM12 ....319 J6
Suttons Manor Clinic
ABR/ST RM4 ....256 D9
Swaines Industrial Estate
RCFD SS4 ....308 F4
Swan Business Park
DART DA1 ....347 J9
The Sweyne Park School
RAYL SS6 ....306 F3

Sybourn Infant School
WALTH E17 ....314 C2
Sybourn Junior School
WALTH E17 ....314 C2
Sydney Russell
Comprehensive School
DAGW RM9 ....317 L7
Tabor High School
BRTR CM7 ....144 C2
Tabor Middle School
BRTR CM7 ....145 H3
Takeley Business Centre
RBSF CM22 ....139 M7
Takeley Primary School
RBSF CM22 ....139 M6
Tanys Dell Primary School
HLW CM20 ....187 H9
Tattingstone CE Primary School
RIPS/CAP IP9 ....82 E2
Tavy Clinic
ABYW SE2 ....335 K9
TCA Leisure Centre
TIL RM18 ....350 B7
Templars County J & I School
WIT CM8 ....171 N8
Temple Farm Trading Estate
CHLM/GWD CM2 ....262 B2
Temple Sutton Primary School
SOSN SS2 ....329 K3
Tendring Adult Community
College *COS* CO15 ....6 E3
Tendring Primary School
RCOS CO16 ....132 B9
Tendring Technology College
FOS CO15 ....159 H8
RCOS CO16 ....157 J4
Terence McMillan Stadium
PLSTW E13 ....333 M4
Terling CE Primary School
RCHLM CM5 ....195 P1
Thames Barrier
CAN/RD E16 ....335 J5
Thameside Community
Health Care *WLY* SE16 ....324 C1
Thameside Industrial Estate
CAN/RD E16 ....333 N8
Thameside Primary School
GRAYS RM17 ....349 M4
Thameside Theatre
GRAYS RM17 ....349 K3
Thames Industrial Park
TIL RM18 ....351 K2
Thames Magistrates Court
BOW E3 ....332 D5
Thamesmead Leisure Centre
THMD SE28 ....335 H7
Thamesmead Shopping Centre
THMD SE28 ....335 H7
Thamesview Business Centre
RAIN RM13 ....336 D5
Thames View Clinic
BARK IG11 ....334 C2
Thames View J & I School
BARK IG11 ....335 H2
Thaxted Hall Hotel
GTDUN CM6 ....92 B4
Thaxted Primary School
GTDUN CM6 ....92 B6
Theatre Royal
SRTFD E15 ....314 G8
Theydon Bois Golf Club
EPP CM16 ....254 E4
Theydon Bois Primary School
EPP CM16 ....254 F6
Thomas Arnold Primary
School *DAGW* RM9 ....317 N9
Thomas Gamuel Primary
School *WALTH* E17 ....314 D1
Thomas Lord Audley School
Language College
COLS CO2 ....152 A4
Thomas Rivers Medical
Centre *SBW* CM21 ....187 K3
Thomas Road Industrial Estate
POP/IOD E14 ....332 D5
Thomas Tallis School
WAB EN9 ....253 J3
Thomas Willingale Primary
School *LOU* IG10 ....276 D2
Thomas Wolsey Special School
IP IP1 ....22 F9
Thorley Hill Primary School
BSF CM23 ....162 C1
Thorndon Country Park
RBRW/HUT CM13 ....301 K4
Thorndon Park Golf Club
RBRW/HUT CM13 ....301 L3
Thorn Grove Primary School
BSF CM23 ....137 N8
Thorpe Bay School
SOS SS1 ....329 N5
Thorpe Cross
FOS CO15 ....157 N6
Thorpedene Primary School
SBN/FI SS3 ....330 B7
Thorpe Hall Golf Club
SOS SS1 ....329 P7
Thorpe Hall Primary School
SBN/FI SS3 ....329 P4
Three Mills Heritage Centre
SRTFD E15 ....332 F3
Three Rivers Golf &
Country Club
RCHLM CM3 ....265 P4
Thresheltofts Business Centre
K/T/MI CO5 ....173 K2
Thriftwood School
CHLM/GWD CM2 ....239 P7
Thundersley J & I School
SBF/HAD SS7 ....306 D9
Thurleston County High School
IP IP1 ....23 H8
Thurrock Athletics Stadium
CDW/CHF RM16 ....359 H4

Thurrock & Basildon College
CDW/CHF RM16 .....350 A2
Thurrock & Basildon College
(Nethermayne Campus)
VGE SS16 .....323 N2
Thurrock Business Centre
WTHK RM20 .....348 C4
Thurstable School
K/T/MI CO5 .....174 A7
Tilbury Fort
TIL RM18 .....350 D9
Tilbury/Gravesend
Passenger Ferry TIL RM18 .....350 C9
Tilbury Manor Infant School
TIL RM18 .....350 C5
Tilbury Manor Junior School
TIL RM18 .....350 C5
Tillingham Medical Centre
BOC CM0 .....248 B7
Tiptree Heath Primary School
K/T/MI CO5 .....199 J1
Tiptree Museum
K/T/MI CO5 .....174 A9
Tiptree Sports Centre
K/T/MI CO5 .....174 A6
Titan Industrial Estate
GRAYS RM17 .....349 K2
Tithe Barn Museum
UPMR RM14 .....319 P2
Tollesbury Primary School
MAL CM9 .....225 J2
Tollesbury Sailing Club
MAL CM9 .....225 L1
Tolleshunt D'Arcy CE
Primary School MAL CM9 .....200 C8
Tollgate Primary School
PLSTW E13 .....333 M4
Tom Hood School
WAN E11 .....315 J5
Toot Hill Golf Club
CHONG CM5 .....256 E1
Top Meadow Golf Club
UPMR RM14 .....320 G8
Tottenham Park Cemetery
ED N9 .....273 N9
Tower Business Park
K/T/MI CO5 .....173 N6
Tower Hamlets College
POP/IOD E14 .....332 E7
Towerlands Golf Club
BRTR CM7 .....120 G8
Tower Ramparts
Shopping Centre IP IP1 .....16 E4
Towers Infant School
EMPK RM11 .....319 H2
Towers Junior School
EMPK RM11 .....319 H2
Towngate Theatre
BSDN SS14 .....2 D1
Trafalgar Business Centre
BARK IG11 .....334 C4
Trafalgar Trading Estate
PEND EN3 .....274 C3
Travelodge
BSDN SS14 .....304 A6
EPP CM16 .....234 C3
HLW CM20 .....13 H1
K/T/MI CO5 .....148 F8
POP/IOD E14 .....332 C6
RBRW/HUT CM13 .....301 P8
REDBR IG4 .....316 A1
RIPS/CAP IP9 .....28 F6
ROM RM1 .....298 D9
WTHK RM20 .....348 C1
Treetops Special School
GRAYS RM17 .....349 L2
Trent Park Golf Club
EBAR EN4 .....272 B3
Triangle Shopping Centre
WOTN CO14 .....158 G7
Tricor Business Park
CHES/WCR EN8 .....252 B4
Tricor Trading Estate
CHES/WCR EN8 .....252 B4
Trident Industrial Estate
HOD EN11 .....208 F4
Trimley St Martin
Primary School FX IP11 .....33 M8
Trimley St Mary Primary School
FX IP11 .....34 F3
Trinity Business Centre
BERM/RHTH SE16 .....332 C9
Trinity Catholic Lower
High School WFD IG8 .....295 K1
Trinity RC High School (Upper)
WFD IG8 .....295 K1
Trinity Road Primary School
CHLM/GWD CM2 .....5 K3
Trinity School
DAGE RM10 .....317 P5
Trinity School Belvedere
BELV DA17 .....346 B2
Trocoll Point Development
Site THMD SE28 .....334 G7
Tudor CE Primary School
SUD CO10 .....20 E2
Tudor Court Primary School
CDW/CHF RM16 .....339 J4
Tunnel Avenue Trading Estate
GNWCH SE10 .....332 G9
Tunnel Industrial Estate
WTHK RM20 .....348 C2
Turner Rise Retail Park
COLN CO4 .....128 A6
Turnford School
CHES/WCR EN8 .....230 B7
Two Village Primary School
HAR CO12 .....109 J7
Twyford Business Centre
BSF CM25 .....162 D1
The Tyrrells Primary School
CHLM/WR CM1 .....218 D6
UCI Cinema
BSDN SS14 .....304 A6
ED N9 .....274 A6
WTHK RM20 .....348 C2

UGC Cinema
EN EN1 .....273 M3
HLW CM20 .....186 G8
IP IP1 .....16 D6
Unity Health Centre
SUD CO10 .....20 D5
Unity Trading Estate
WFD IG8 .....295 N7
University of East London
BCTR RM8 .....317 H7
EHAM E6 .....334 B7
PLSTW E13 .....333 L3
SRTFD E15 .....314 F9
University of Essex
COLN CO4 .....152 G2
University of London
ENC/FH EN2 .....251 M6
University Yacht Club
RCOLE CO7 .....179 L8
Uphall Primary School
IL IG1 .....316 C7
Uplands Business Park
WALTH E17 .....294 A6
Uplands Middle School
SUD CO10 .....20 E2
Upminster Cemetery
UPMR RM14 .....320 A7
Upminster Golf Club
UPMR RM14 .....319 P2
Upminster Primary School
UPMR RM14 .....319 P5
Upminster Trading Park
UPMR RM14 .....320 G2
Upper Clapton RFC
EPP CM16 .....233 J3
Upshire Primary School
WAB EN9 .....253 L3
Upton Cross Primary School
PLSTW E13 .....333 L1
Upton Lane Medical Centre
FSTGT E7 .....315 L8
Ursuline High School
IL IG1 .....316 C4
Valence House Museum &
Library BCTR RM8 .....317 L4
Valence Junior School
BCTR RM8 .....317 L4
Valentine High School
IL IG1 .....316 B1
Valentines High Lower School
GNTH/NBYPK IG2 .....296 C9
Valley Farm Holiday Park
COS CO15 .....182 C7
Vange Primary School
VGE SS16 .....324 B3
Vanguard Trading Estate
SRTFD E15 .....332 F1
Vestry House Museum
WALTH E17 .....294 E8
Vicarage Fields Health Clinic
BARK IG11 .....316 D9
The Vicarage Field
Shopping Centre
BARK IG11 .....316 D9
Vicarage Primary School
EHAM E6 .....334 A3
VI Components Industrial Park
ERITH DA8 .....346 D3
Victoria Park Industrial Estate
HOM E9 .....314 C9
Victoria Plaza Shopping Centre
SOSN SS2 .....19 F5
Victoria Wharf
POP/IOD E14 .....332 B7
Viking Business Centre
ROMW/RG RM7 .....318 B2
Village Infant School
DAGE RM10 .....317 P9
VUE Cinema
DAGW RM9 .....335 M1
ROM RM1 .....298 D9
WTHK RM20 .....348 D1
Wadham Lodge Sports Centre
WALTH E17 .....294 E5
Waldegraves Holiday Park
K/T/MI CO5 .....205 K6
Walker Primary School
STHGT/OAK N14 .....272 C8
Walnut Tree Hospital
SUD CO10 .....20 B5
Waltham Abbey Gatehouse
WAB EN9 .....252 F5
Waltham Abbey Marriott Hotel
WAB EN9 .....253 J4
Waltham Abbey
Swimming Pool WAB EN9 .....252 G5
Waltham Forest College
WALTH E17 .....294 A6
WALTH E17 .....294 E7
Waltham Forest Magistrates
Court WALTH E17 .....294 C7
Waltham Forest Pool & Track
WALTH E17 .....294 E6
Waltham Forest Theatre
WALTH E17 .....294 C7
Waltham Holy Cross
Junior School WAB EN9 .....252 G3
Walthamstow Business Centre
WALTH E17 .....294 F6
Walthamstow Greyhound
Stadium CHING E4 .....294 E4
Walthamstow School for Girls
WALTH E17 .....294 E8
Walton & Frinton Yacht Club
WOTN CO14 .....159 K5
Walton Pier
WOTN CO14 .....159 L7
Walton Primary School
WOTN CO14 .....159 L5
Wansfell College
EPP CM16 .....254 E5
Wanstead CC
WAN E11 .....315 L2
Wanstead CE Primary School
WAN E11 .....295 K9

Wanstead Golf Club
WAN E11 .....315 L2
Wanstead High School
WAN E11 .....315 M1
Wanstead Hospital
WAN E11 .....295 L8
Wanstead Leisure Centre
WAN E11 .....315 M1
Wardmaster Infirmary
RIPS/CAP IP9 .....83 L6
Wareside Primary School
WARE SG12 .....185 H1
Warley Hill Business Park
RBRW/HUT CM13 .....300 F3
Warley Hospital
BRW CM14 .....300 E2
Warley Lodge Hospital
RBRW/HUT CM13 .....300 C5
Warley Park Golf Club
RBRW/HUT CM13 .....300 G6
Warley Primary School
BRW CM14 .....300 F2
Warner Industrial Park
CHDH RM6 .....21 G4
Warren Comprehensive School
CHDH RM6 .....297 N9
Warren Golf Club
MAL CM9 .....242 F1
Warren Junior School
CHDH RM6 .....297 N9
Warren Primary School
CDW/CHF RM16 .....348 F1
Warren Sports Centre
CHDH RM6 .....297 N9
Warriors Swim Centre
SOS SS1 .....19 G4
Warwick School for Boys
WALTH E17 .....294 F8
Water Gardens Shopping
Centre HLW CM20 .....13 H6
Waterglade Retail Park
COS CO15 .....6 D5
Watermill Business Centre
PEND EN3 .....274 C1
Waterside Business Park
WIT CM8 .....172 A9
Waterside Farm Sports Centre
CVI SS8 .....326 B8
Waterside Industrial Estate
HOD EN11 .....208 G6
Waterside School
BSF CM25 .....113 K8
Waterways Business Centre
PEND EN3 .....252 C8
Wat Tyler Country Park
VGE SS16 .....324 C5
Waverley School
PEND EN3 .....273 P5
Weald Park (Country Park)
BRW CM14 .....280 B6
Weald Park Hotel (Golf &
Country Club) BRW CM14 .....279 M3
Wellesley Hospital
SOSN SS2 .....329 K3
Wellington Primary School
BOW E3 .....332 D3
Well Lane Industrial Estate
RCHLM CM5 .....241 P3
Wells Hall Community
Primary School SUD CO10 .....61 M6
Wells Hall Primary School
SUD CO10 .....61 L6
Wells Park School
CHIG IG7 .....296 C1
Wells Primary School
WFD IG8 .....295 L1
Wennington Hall Farm
Business Centre RAIN RM13 .....337 K6
Wentworth Primary School
MAL CM9 .....244 A2
West Beckton Health Centre
CAN/RD E16 .....333 M5
The Westborough Primary
School WOS/PRIT SS0 .....328 F4
Westbourne High School
IP IP1 .....24 F2
Westcliff High School for Boys
WOS/PRIT SS0 .....328 B3
Westcliff High School for Girls
LOS SS9 .....328 B3
Westcliff Hotel
WOS/PRIT SS0 .....18 C5
Westcliff Leisure Centre
WOS/PRIT SS0 .....18 C6
West Cliff Theatre
COS CO15 .....6 D7
Westerfield Business Centre
NHMKT IP6 .....23 M9
Westerings Primary School
HOC/HUL SS5 .....307 N3
Western House Hospital
WARE SG12 .....184 A2
West Essex Golf Club
LOU IG10 .....275 H3
Westfield Community Primary
School HOD EN11 .....208 C4
HVHL CB9 .....41 L4
Westfleet Trading Estate
WICKE SS11 .....305 L1
Westgate Park
BSDN SS14 .....2 D6
West Grove Primary School
STHGT/OAK N14 .....272 C6
West Ham Church
Primary School SRTFD E15 .....333 J1
West Ham Lane Clinic
SRTFD E15 .....333 H1
West Ham United FC
(Upton Park) EHAM E6 .....333 N2
West Hatch High School
CHIG IG7 .....296 A2
West Horndon Primary School
RBRW/HUT CM13 .....301 N9
West India Pier
POP/IOD E14 .....332 C9

West India Shopping Centre
POP/IOD E14 .....332 D8
Westlands Community Primary
School CHLM/WR CM1 .....4 A3
Westlands County Secondary
School CHLM/WR CM1 .....239 L1
West Lea School
ED N9 .....273 K9
West Leigh Primary School
LOS SS9 .....327 N4
Westley Heights Country Park
VGE SS16 .....323 J4
Westmayne Industrial Park
LAIN SS15 .....302 F9
West Mersea Museum
K/T/MI CO5 .....202 E7
West Station Industrial Estate
MAL CM9 .....243 P1
West Station Yard
MAL CM9 .....243 P1
West Thurrock Primary School
WTHK RM20 .....348 D4
Westwood Primary School
BSDN SS14 .....326 G2
Wetherfield Airfield
BRTR CM7 .....95 K1
Wethersfield CE Primary School
BRTR CM7 .....95 H5
Wheatear Industrial Estate
WIT CM8 .....197 L3
Whipps Cross Hospital
LEY E10 .....314 C1
White Bridge Primary School
LOU IG10 .....275 P6
White Court CP School
BRTR CM77 .....144 F8
Whitefield School & Leisure
Centre WALTH E17 .....294 G5
Whitehall Road School
HLWW/ROY CM19 .....209 P4
Whitehall Hotel
GTDUN CM6 .....116 A4
Whitehall Industrial Estate
COLS CO2 .....152 E2
Whitehall Primary School
CHING E4 .....275 H8
White Hart Hotel
BRTR CM7 .....145 J5
RCOLW CO6 .....147 N4
Whitehouse Industrial Estate
IP IP1 .....22 D9
White House J & I School
IP IP1 .....24 F2
White Notley CE
Primary School WIT CM8 .....170 G4
The Whitewebbs Museum of
Transport & Industry
ENC/FH EN2 .....250 C5
Whitewebbs Park Golf Club
ENC/FH EN2 .....251 J7
Whitmore Primary School
BSDN SS14 .....304 D7
Whittingham Community
Primary School WALTH E17 .....294 B5
Whitton CE
Primary School IP IP1 .....22 F9
Whybridge Infant School
RAIN RM13 .....336 F1
Whybridge Junior School
RAIN RM13 .....336 E1
Wickford Business Park
WICKW SS12 .....305 L1
Wickford Junior School
WICKW SS12 .....285 H9
Wickford Swimming Pool
WICKW SS12 .....285 H8
Widford Industrial Estate
CHLM/WR CM1 .....239 M3
Widford J & I School
WARE SG12 .....160 C9
Widford Lodge
Preparatory School
CHLM/GWD CM2 .....239 N3
William Bellamy J & I School
DAGE RM10 .....317 P4
William Davies Primary School
FSTGT E7 .....315 N8
William de Ferrers School
RCHLM CM5 .....287 H1
William Edwards School
CDW/CHF RM16 .....339 M7
William Ford CE Junior School
DAGE RM10 .....317 P9
William Julien Courtauld
Hospital BRTR CM7 .....145 H4
William Morris Gallery
WALTH E17 .....294 D7
William Morris School
WALTH E17 .....294 B5
William Read Primary School
CVI SS8 .....344 C2
William Torbitt J & I School
GNTH/NBYPK IG2 .....296 F9
Willis Corroon Building
IP IP1 .....16 D5
Willowbrook Adult Education
Centre WALTH E17 .....294 A7
Willowfield School
WALTH E17 .....294 B7
Willowmere Caravan Park
SUD CO10 .....61 L7
Wimbish Primary School
SAFWN CB10 .....67 H5
Winchmore Hill Clinic
WCHMH N21 .....272 G2
Winchmore Hill CC
WCHMH N21 .....273 H7
Winchmore School
WCHMH N21 .....273 H5
Windrush Primary School
THMD SE28 .....335 J8
Windsor School Clacton
COS CO15 .....182 C9
Windsor Trading Estate
BCAYE CM11 .....284 C4

Winns Primary School
WALTH E17 .....294 C6
Winsor Primary School
EHAM E6 .....334 B6
Winter Gardens Junior School
CVI SS8 .....326 C9
Witham Cemetery
WIT CM8 .....171 P9
The Witham Health Centre
WIT CM8 .....197 K2
Witham RUFC
WIT CM8 .....197 H3
Witham Town Football &
Social Club WIT CM8 .....197 K2
Wivenhoe Business Centre
RCOLE CO7 .....153 K6
Wivenhoe Family
Health Centre RCOLE CO7 .....153 J4
Wivenhoe Sailing Club
RCOLE CO7 .....153 K7
Wivenhoe Town CC
RCOLE CO7 .....153 K4
Wix & Wrabness Primary School
MGTR CO11 .....132 F2
Wolfson Hillel Primary School
STHGT/OAK N14 .....272 C5
Wolsey Art Gallery
IP IP1 .....16 E3
Wolsey Theatre
IP IP1 .....16 C3
Woodacre Special School
SOCK/AV RM15 .....338 C5
Woodbridge High School &
Language College
WFD IG8 .....295 L4
Woodcroft School
LOU IG10 .....254 A9
Woodford County High School
WFD IG8 .....295 J3
Woodford Golf Club
WFD IG8 .....295 J2
Woodford Green Preparatory
School WFD IG8 .....295 K3
Woodford Green Primary
School WFD IG8 .....295 J2
Woodford Medical Clinic
RCHLM CM5 .....241 P3
Woodford Trading Estate
WFD IG8 .....295 M6
Woodgrange Infant School
FSTGT E7 .....315 L6
Woodgrange Park Cemetery
FSTGT E7 .....315 N7
Woodgreen Animal Shelter
ROY SG8 .....48 D7
Woodhall Business Park
SUD CO10 .....47 J9
Woodhall CP School
SUD CO10 .....47 J9
Woodham Ley Primary
School SBF/HAD SS7 .....305 N9
Woodham Walter CE
Primary School MAL CM9 .....220 G8
Woodlands J & I School
IL IG1 .....316 E6
Woodlands Preparatory
School RBRW/HUT CM13 .....300 G8
Woodlands School
VGE SS16 .....323 P2
Wood Lane Sports Centre
BCTR RM8 .....318 A3
Woodman Road Cemetery
BRW CM14 .....300 G2
Woodside Junior School
WALTH E17 .....294 F7
Woodside Primary School
CDW/CHF RM16 .....350 A1
CHESW EN7 .....229 H8
Woodside Road School
BELV DA17 .....346 A2
Wood Street Health Centre
WALTH E17 .....294 F7
Woodville Primary School
WALTH E17 .....264 F8
Wood Wharf
POP/IOD E14 .....332 E8
Wood Wharf Business Park
POP/IOD E14 .....332 F9
Woolwich Crown Court
THMD SE28 .....334 F9
Woolwich Polytechnic School
THMD SE28 .....335 H8
Worcester Primary School
EN EN1 .....251 L8
The Working Silk Museum
BRTR CM7 .....145 J4
World End
TIL RM18 .....350 C9
Wormley Primary School
BROX EN10 .....230 B2
Writtle College
CHLM/WR CM1 .....217 J8
Writtle Primary School
CHLM/WR CM1 .....239 H2
Wyburns Primary School
RAYL SS6 .....307 J7
Wycke Hill Business Park
MAL CM9 .....243 P2
Wykeham Primary School
HCH RM12 .....318 F3
Yale Business Centre
IPSE IP5 .....31 M2
Yardley Business Park
BSDN SS14 .....303 N6
BSDN SS14 .....304 C5
Yardley Primary School
CHING E4 .....274 E4
Yellow Dot Sports Club
SUD CO10 .....21 G4

The Post Office is a registered trademark of Post Office Ltd. in the UK and other countries.

Schools address data provided by Education Direct.

Petrol station information supplied by Johnsons

One-way street data provided by © Tele Atlas N.V.

Garden centre information provided by

Garden Centre Association Britains best garden centres

Wyevale Garden Centres

The statement on the front cover of this atlas is sourced, selected and quoted from a reader comment and feedback form received in 2004

Notes

AA **Street by Street** QUESTIONNAIRE

Dear Atlas User
Your comments, opinions and recommendations are very important to us.
So please help us to improve our street atlases by taking a few minutes
to complete this simple questionnaire.

You do not need a stamp (unless posted outside the UK). If you do not want to remove this page from your street atlas, then photocopy it or write your answers on a plain sheet of paper.

Send to: The Editor, AA Street by Street, FREEPOST SCE 4598,
Basingstoke RG21 4GY

ABOUT THE ATLAS...

Which city/town/county did you buy?

Are there any features of the atlas or mapping that you find particularly useful?

Is there anything we could have done better?

Why did you choose an AA Street by Street atlas?

Did it meet your expectations?

Exceeded ☐ **Met all** ☐ **Met most** ☐ **Fell below** ☐

Please give your reasons

Where did you buy it?

For what purpose? (please tick all applicable)

To use in your own local area ☐ **To use on business or at work** ☐

Visiting a strange place ☐ **In the car** ☐ **On foot** ☐

Other (please state)

LOCAL KNOWLEDGE...

Local knowledge is invaluable. Whilst every attempt has been made to make the information contained in this atlas as accurate as possible, should you notice any inaccuracies, please detail them below (if necessary, use a blank piece of paper) or e-mail us at *streetbystreet@theAA.com*

ABOUT YOU...

Name (Mr/Mrs/Ms)

Address

Postcode

Daytime tel no　　　　　　　　　　　**Mobile tel no**

E-mail address

Please only give us your e-mail address and mobile phone number if you wish to hear from us about other products and services from the AA and partners by e-mail or text or mms.

Which age group are you in?

Under 25 ☐　**25-34** ☐　**35-44** ☐　**45-54** ☐　**55-64** ☐　**65+** ☐

Are you an AA member? **YES** ☐　**NO** ☐

Do you have Internet access? **YES** ☐　**NO** ☐

The information we hold about you will be used to provide the product(s) and service(s) requested and for identification, account administration, analysis, and fraud/loss prevention purposes. More details about how that information is used is in our Privacy Statement, which you will find under the heading "Personal information" in our Terms and Conditions and on our website. Copies are available from us by post, by contacting our Data Protection Manager at AA, Fanum House, Basing View, Hampshire, Basingstoke RG21 4EA.

We may want to contact you about other products and services provided by us or our partners but please tick the box if you DO NOT wish to hear about such products and services from us by mail or telephone. ☐

Thank you for taking the time to complete this questionnaire. Please send it to us as soon as possible, and remember, you do not need a stamp (unless posted outside the UK).　　ML031z